S0-BKR-512

THE WORLD COUNCIL OF CHURCHES

Almost incidentally the great world fellowship has arisen; it is the great new fact of our era.

—*William Temple*

THE WORLD COUNCIL OF CHURCHES

***

A Study of Its Background and History

by

David P. Gaines

RICHARD • R • SMITH
NOONE HOUSE
PETERBOROUGH • NEW HAMPSHIRE

PUBLISHED BY THE RICHARD R. SMITH CO. INC.
PETERBOROUGH, NEW HAMPSHIRE
LIBRARY OF CONGRESS CATALOG CARD NO. 63-17177

FIRST EDITION
TEXT AND TITLES IN TIMES ROMAN
MANUFACTURED IN THE UNITED STATES OF AMERICA
BY THE COLONIAL PRESS, INC., CLINTON, MASS.

This book is dedicated to Lena Alma Gaines, without whose understanding encouragement it could not have been written.

PREFACE

My aim in these pages has been to describe the origin and growth of the World Council of Churches.

What was intended to be a small book has grown, as is plain to be seen, into a large one. It could have been shortened by excluding such subject matter as consisted of passages from program addresses, reports of committees, pronouncements, constitutions and other official documents, and the findings of study conferences, some of which have been given considerable space. But much of this material is essential to the story which was to be told. One cannot understand the World Council of Churches without a knowledge of the opinions and purposes of those who speak for it and of the attitude of the denominations they represent, which are reflected most fully in records of this kind. It has seemed best to print most of those chosen in the body of the book, where they stand in logical and generally chronological relation to the context.

If it is suggested that the introductory chapters in Part I[1] are too long, I can see that this may indeed be a warrantable criticism. But the World Council of Churches gathered up the ideals and hopes of the movement toward unity in the Church over many centuries, and history holds the key to its genius and potentialities and to its triumphs and failures as an organ of the Christian faith. It is not explained alone by what happened at Amsterdam on an August day in 1948 when it was formally constituted.

My purpose had been originally to write only a simple factual account of the World Council's formation and early years, with a brief sketch of the ecumenical landscape, for which parts of two summers were spent in study in Europe. The interpretative pages were unpremeditated and were written because, as it seemed, they demanded to be. They were thrown out and put back a number of times before the final decision to retain them

[1] Part I is concerned with the ecumenical background of the World Council of Churches.

was reached. The aspects of the World Council of Churches with which they deal should be discussed with complete frankness, I am persuaded, by those who are in any way responsible for its program or hope for its fulfillment.

An unofficial association with the ecumenical movement through forty years became the unplanned preparation for the undertaking here ended, for which I know with even greater certainty now than at the beginning one could never have really sufficient knowledge or wisdom. I have, of course, read much of what others have written. The titles consulted have been too numerous to be listed outside a bibliography. Acknowledgment of help derived from books must be made, with a few exceptions, in general terms and without the satisfaction of naming each author.

I will say, however, that I have found especially helpful in its survey of the growth of Christian unity in the modern missionary movement William Richey Hogg's *Ecumenical Foundations,* published by Harper & Row. *Toward a United Church,* by William Adams Brown, from the press of Charles Scribner's Sons, has been most useful in verifying my notes on a number of important events and correcting them on others, as well as in supplying fresh information and illuminating insights out of what was a unique experience in interchurch work. My indebtedness to these two historians, and to their publishers for permission to quote from their books, I would gratefully acknowledge here. And I would express my appreciation also of the kindness of Dr. Willem Adolf Visser 't Hooft who granted me, on behalf of the World Council of Churches, the privilege of using freely matter in its publications, including *The Ecumenical Review.*

My original manuscript had been finished in 1954, but I returned to it after reading relevant chapters of *A History of the Ecumenical Movement* (published by the Westminster Press in that year), to revise in its light certain parts of what I had written on ecumenical background. I will at least begin paying my debt to those who produced this valuable work by expressing the hope that it may be translated and otherwise made available for wider reading in the churches. It gathers into comparatively limited compass a wealth of information indispensable to a study of the ecumenical history of the Church, which can be got elsewhere only by more extensive research than most readers are in a position to undertake.

The writing of this book has occupied spare hours for upwards of twelve years. The attention it deserved had at times to be sacrificed to prior commitments which were of such a nature that they could not be put off. But I have recognized the responsibility implicit in this self-imposed extra assignment and have left undone nothing I could do reasonably to insure accuracy and thoroughness in reporting the facts which seemed to me to fall within its purview.

All such efforts notwithstanding, errors will undoubtedly have been made and have escaped detection; and I can only conclude this final word by expressing regret because of them and offering earnest apologies.

I shall hope, let me add, that those who may not agree with my judgments concerning the World Council of Churches will nevertheless believe that I have endeavored to write in goodwill and the charity which rejoices in the truth.

DAVID P. GAINES

Waterbury, Connecticut
September 1, 1964

CONTENTS

PART ONE: THE ECUMENICAL BACKGROUND

II. Assembly Addresses

III. Sections at Study

IV. Other Reports

PART FOUR: THE WORLD COUNCIL, THE ECUMENICAL MOVEMENT, AND THE CHURCHES

PART FIVE: THE FIRST SIX YEARS OF THE WORLD COUNCIL OF CHURCHES

I. The Central Committee

II. Pronouncements of the Central Committee

III. Evaluation of the Pronouncements

IV. New Structures and Past Performances

V. The Council's Membership

PART SEVEN: AFTER EVANSTON

I. The Central Committee

II. Major Areas of Tension

III. The Post-Evanston Study Program

IV. Progress and Problems

APPENDIXES

Part One
THE ECUMENICAL BACKGROUND

INTRODUCTION

In the World Council of Churches were brought together the Universal Christian Council for Life and Work and the Continuation Committee of the World Conference on Faith and Order (Edinburgh, 1937), and the histories of these two bodies and the causes they served should be consulted for essential information about its antecedents.

The study of background should be extended to include other ecumenical [1] organizations which, though not incorporated in the World Council of Churches, had by their work helped bring to fullness its time, chart the course it would take, and prepare many of its leaders.

Where to commence such a survey is something of a problem. The principles of ecumenism appear in the New Testament and are traceable in the life of the Church in subsequent ages, and it would seem logical to start at the beginning. But those who make books must take account of technical limitations, as well as of available time, and in this instance these are such that even the most cursory review of the whole of Christian history from this standpoint may not be attempted.

[1] "Ecumenical" derives from the Greek word *oikoumenikos,* meaning "the whole inhabited earth," and describes, according to *Webster's New Standard Dictionary,* "that which belongs to all the world, or is world-wide in its breadth or inclusiveness." *Oikoumene* occurs a number of times in the New Testament, where it may properly be rendered, after Hellenic usage, as "the whole civilized world" or "empire." As it increased in extent and power, the Roman Empire became for those within its bounds the world, and its edicts and actions were designated "ecumenical." In time, the Church appropriated the description for its acts which concerned the whole of Christendom. Hence the term "ecumenical council." Explained the Conference on Church, Community and State, which was held at Oxford, England, in 1937: "The term 'ecumenical' refers to the expression within history of the given unity of the Church. The thought and action of the Church are ecumenical, in so far as they attempt to realize the *Una Sancta,* the fellowship of all Christians who acknowledge the one Lord." (*The Churches Survey Their Task,* pp. 168 ff.) The present currency of the word "ecumenical" has resulted from a consensus in interchurch circles that it expresses better than any other word (e.g., "international," "universal," "catholic") "the nature of the modern movement for co-operation and unity which seeks to manifest the fundamental oneness and universality of the Church of Christ." (See *A History of the Ecumenical Movement,* pp. 735 ff.)

As a starting point, the eighteenth century may be considered as perhaps the least arbitrary of possible choices short of the first century, since it was in this general period that the idea of Christian unity, until then a concern mainly of a few prophetic souls and church authorities who had been obliged to deal with it in ecclesiastical and political programs, first began to interest the larger body of Christians to a significant degree.

The Church remembers the eighteenth century particularly for the Evangelical Awakening, which was a major influence in bringing to life this wider consciousness of the spiritual unity of Christians. Arising in part from a natural reaction to the rationalism of the Enlightenment and quickened by an intercontinental prayer movement, this ocean-spanning revival restored the earlier emphasis of Spiritualism[2] and Pietism on personal religion, and those who came under its power were affected by a lively sense of fellowship with one another by reason of their common experience. Many felt the urge to expressive action, and this soon emphasized their need to work together. They realized that Christ's commission to his followers—to share their own blessings of redemption with all peoples—called for cooperation by those who were one in him, whatever their divisions as members of his Church. From these revelations arose the impetus which would carry the ecumenical movement forward to its later phenomenal developments—and to the vision which assumed form and substance eventually in the World Council of Churches.

[2] In Europe a much-used term for those forms of religion which stressed Christianity as an inner experience, sometimes to the point of depreciation of outward organization, including the visible church.

I

THE MISSIONARY MOVEMENT

1. The Revival of Missions

The effect of the Evangelical Awakening was felt first in the reviving missionary movement. Work in the mission fields and the circumstances under which it had to be done accentuated the interdependence of the churches and the advantages to be gained through collaboration.

Thomas Coke, whom John Wesley sent to be the first superintendent of the Methodist Church in the United States, advocated the establishment of an all-inclusive missionary board as early as 1784, the year he sailed for America.

William Carey considered founding his mission to India on an interdenominational basis and apparently would have done so but for the fear that this would provoke disruptive sectarian dissension. He appealed to the missionary societies which were being formed to maintain friendly communication with one another and to organize on the fields, where they would often find themselves working side by side, for conference and mutual assistance. He and his associates, upon reaching Bengal, sought out the German missionaries of the Danish-Halle Mission in South India for their counsel.[1] He wrote home of the cordial relations that existed between the missionaries. "The utmost harmony prevails," he said, "and a union of hearts unknown between persons of different denominations in England."[2] In 1805 he proposed calling a conference "of Christians of all denominations" in 1810 at Capetown, South Africa, and decennially thereafter similar gatherings in which experiences might be shared and common problems discussed. Writing to Andrew Fuller, the Baptist divine of England, he opined that Christians meeting together in this way could "more entirely enter into one another's views by two hours' conversation than by two or three years' epistolary correspondence."

A century before Coke and Carey, John Eliot, busy with his mission

[1] The Danish-Halle Mission had been established for ninety-odd years.

[2] To Dr. Ryland, January 20, 1806. Quoted by George Smith in *William Carey*, p. 190. For correspondence, see also Eustace Carey, *Memoir of William Carey*.

to North American Indians, had written to Richard Baxter, probably the most influential apostle of unity at that time, sketching a design for cooperation among Christians in evangelizing the world. His proposal evoked favorable comment from Cotton Mather of Boston but met with no general response. Now the spiritual climate was changing, if only slowly. Certain of the mission boards which were being organized around the end of the eighteenth century were adopting plans of inclusive membership.

The announced aim of the London Missionary Society (1795) was to encourage "an increase of union and friendly intercourse among Christians of different denominations at home." Its organization was hailed as "the funeral of bigotry." It enrolled as members Congregationalists, Presbyterians, Methodists, and Anglicans. A clergyman of the Church of England who preached the founding sermon declared that, with the world the field, church orders should in the united endeavor "lose their identity and win a right to the greater name of Christian." A resolution defined the purpose of the Society as "not to send Presbyterianism, Independency, Episcopacy or any other form of Church Order and Government . . . but the Glorious Gospel of the blessed God to the heathen."[3]

The American Board of Commissioners for Foreign Missions began (1810) as an independent interdenominational agency. As in the case of the older British society, a majority of the members were Congregationalists. But the General Assembly of the Presbyterian Church, having no foreign mission agency, adopted the American Board in 1812, as did the United Foreign Mission Society (1826), which had been organized in 1817 "to spread the Gospel among Indians of North America, the inhabitants of Mexico and South America, and in other portions of the heathen and anti-Christian world."[4]

The Religious Tract Society (1799) and the British and Foreign Bible Society (1804), essentially auxiliaries of the missionary movement, were interdenominational. Each had a board of directors, of whom half were Anglicans and half Nonconformists, and three secretaries—one chosen from the Church of England, another representing Dissent, and the other having ecclesiastical connections qualifying him especially for work on the Continent. Through its branches in Europe, the Bible Society supplied Bibles to Lutheran and Reformed churches in France, Germany, Hungary, Holland, Switzerland, and the Scandinavian countries, and to Orthodox churches in Russia and Greece; also to Coptic, Armenian, Abyssinian, Jacobite, and Syrian churches of the Middle East and India. In some places it served the Church of Rome, employ-

[3] The Society retained its inclusive membership basis after the organization of denominational boards reduced the roll largely to Congregationalists. See Richard Lovett, *History of the London Missionary Society*.

[4] Arthur Judson Brown, *One Hundred Years: A History of the Foreign Missionary Work of the Presbyterian Church, U.S.A.*, pp. 19-20.

ing Roman Catholic agents and circulating the Catholic version of the Scriptures.

The Tract Society cooperated with the Bible Society. C. F. A. Steinkopf (1773-1859), a Lutheran, who as Secretary of the German Christian Fellowship in Basle had made friends in all the churches, including the Roman Catholic, served both agencies, traveling widely in Europe and, with his regular duties, recruiting candidates for all the missionary societies.

The Awakening[5] spread from country to country, and wherever its power was felt Christians of different nations and denominations recognized their spiritual kinship in Christ and in growing numbers joined efforts in his service.

The American Bible Society (1816) and the American Tract Society (1825) were likewise founded on an interdenominational basis, their memberships embracing Baptists, Congregationalists, Episcopalians, Methodists, Presbyterians, Friends, members of the Dutch Reformed Church, and representatives of a few other religious groups.

The American Education Society (1815), the American Sunday School Union (1824), and the American Home Missionary Society (1826), all missionary in their objectives, invited the cooperation of all Christians.

Interchurch organization on the mission fields seems to have appeared with the formation in 1825 of the Bombay Missionary Union "to foster Christian fellowship and to provide a forum for the exchange of ideas on ways to extend Christianity in India." Within a few years similar local endeavors were reported from Calcutta and Madras. The interest led eventually to regional and national conferences.

The programs of all these meetings afforded opportunity to discuss, among many other timely subjects, the need for practicing comity and the possibilities of collaboration.

A steady increase in attendance indicated not only that the missions were growing but that the missionaries were finding the fellowship helpful. Each gathering registered some movement of thought in the direction of full acceptance of each other as one in the more essential matters of faith and life and of the missionary task as belonging to all and impossible of accomplishment under the conditions of their separate approaches.

Those who went to Lahore (1862) for the Third North India Conference rejoiced for "the united action of Christian men who prayed,

[5] In America it may be said to have centered in the personality and work of Jonathan Edwards (1703-58), whose writings on prayer as a condition of revival continued to bear fruit long after his death. The resurgent evangelistic and missionary activity of the nineteenth century, which extended to Britain and Europe as well, has been called the Second Awakening, although obviously linked with the earlier Evangelical Awakening. It undoubtedly owed its deeper impulses to the earlier movement.

conferred and worked together, in order to advance the interests of their Master's Kingdom." They observed the Lord's Supper, Baptist deacons receiving the elements from Presbyterian celebrants and passing them to the others.

The delegates at Ootacamund for the First South India Conference (1858) had been encouraged, according to the minutes, to see the manifestation of "practical Christian union" which they believed characteristic of "evangelical Protestant missionaries in India."

Supporting this judgment, the South India Missionary Association had by the end of the century gone beyond discussion to cooperation in actual work projects. And the same pattern of progress was discernible in the decennial all-India conferences—Allahabad, 1872; Calcutta, 1882; Bombay, 1892; and Madras, 1902.

These developments in India were in a general way paralleled in other mission countries. A series of conferences in Japan, which began in 1872, ended with the gathering at Tokyo in 1900 of nearly two thousand nationals, missionaries and mission board members, who voted to call upon all Christians to pray for "corporate oneness" and elected "a standing committee of the missions" to promote unity, which would lead, as it happened, in organizing two years later the important Conference of Federated Missions.

In the general missionary conferences of China likewise (Shanghai, 1877, 1890, and 1907), Christian unity and its problems in a variety of presentations occupied the attention of the delegates. At one of them the time-worn metaphor of the Church as an army of many regiments under one banner was criticized as inept and misleading, because of the practice of the denominations of developing their strategy and deploying their forces independently of one another. The speaker, who came from the China Inland Mission, urged that foreign missionaries ought to unite to change "this blind and absurd" policy. In 1907, at the gathering marking the centenary of Protestant missions in China, the delegates affirmed their unity in Christ and recommended "a Christian Federation for China." The unification of churches of the same ecclesiastical orders would be, they resolved, a practical step to be taken immediately.

In other countries in the missionary orbit Protestant missions took counsel thus with one another, realizing that they had one Master and that their disunity must be healed if they were not only to meet together, but beyond the conference hall to go together, as he commanded, "into all the world."

It is not to be supposed that the subject of Christian unity always dominated the discussions or that all those present shared the mounting interest in it. There was frank questioning of the wisdom of striving for corporate union of the churches abroad or elsewhere by those wishing only that information might be shared at the meetings and practical plans considered for such work as could be done together effectively without administrative complications or any dismantling of organizations. Some attended whose belief in closer collaboration was inhibited by the adverse position of the boards sending them out, so that they could not speak freely as they felt. Whatever the motives bringing them together, by meeting they exposed themselves to influences that would inevitably affect their thinking. Fellowship with one another in worship and deliberation in the presence always of the formidable work for which all were responsible was an experience which all would remember and many desire to have repeated. Friendships formed under such circumstances would strengthen the religious bonds between them, holding together the far-flung Christian movement. They were not likely to return to their places the persons they had been.

Carey, who had seen that theological and other differences made common action by the denominations under a single sponsoring board impossible in the case of his own mission, suggested that Christians of all names could nevertheless unite in praying for the evangelization of the world; and those who responded to his entreaty, as many did over the years, undoubtedly found themselves lifted into new perspectives they could never have gained by a solitary way.[6]

Cooperation on the mission fields was part of a wider movement. The founding denominations organized concurrently for consultation on missionary promotion and management.

The earliest action of this kind appears to have been the formation in 1819 of the London Secretaries' Association by the four executive secretaries of the Baptist, London, Church, and Wesleyan Missionary Societies, which welcomed into membership the corresponding officers of other church boards with headquarters in London, among them the China Inland Mission, the Society for the Propagation of the Gospel, the Society for the Promotion of Christian Knowledge, and the British and Foreign Bible Society. It was a body without a constitution or delegated authority but successful as an instrument of cooperation.

The Northern Lutheran Conferences dated from 1863; the Continental Missions Conferences, with their base and most of their operations in Germany, from 1866; and the General Dutch Missionary Conferences from 1887. All these were loosely constituted but useful, the Scandinavian and Netherlands series especially so in the education and enlistment of pastors and laymen through their well-attended popular

[6] Not all the missions joined in the conferences or the activities originating in them. The Society for the Propagation of the Gospel (Anglican) usually stood aloof, as did the so-called "faith" missions and those under denominations not given to cooperating at home.

It is to be noted also that, while there was often strong sentiment for unity among them, the native Christians were sometimes as divided in their theological beliefs and church loyalties as were their teachers from the parent denominations; and they occasionally came up with new causes for schism to add to the ancient ones. As the twentieth century advanced through its early decades, the demand for union became insistent in many of the younger churches.

programs, and the Continental with their more restricted sessions in the development of intensive study of missionary policy and strategy.

In Germany cooperation had a most effective agency in the Standing Committee of the German Protestant Missionary Societies (*Der Ausschuss der deutschen evangelischen Missionsgellschaften*), which from its organization in 1885 served as an intermediary between the mission boards of the four major confessions and the government, particularly during the momentous era of German expansion and colonization under Bismarck. It handled also the complicated problems of comity in the relations of the German missions with those of churches of other countries, which were extraordinarily difficult in this period of political change and intense nationalistic spirit, characteristically expressed, in the case of Germany, by the popular slogan, "Only German missionaries for German colonies!" The Standing Committee bore in many ways the stamp of the genius of Gustav Warneck, the eminent missionary authority who was the chief architect of its administration; and its influence reached far beyond the bounds of Germany.

Twenty-three missionary organizations in Canada and the United States founded the Foreign Missions Conference of North America in 1893. A subsidiary Committee of Reference and Counsel, which in its functions and its relation to the larger body resembled the Standing Committee of the German Protestant Missionary Societies (*Der Ausschuss*), was created in 1907. The rapid growth of the Conference in membership proved its general acceptance by the denominations as their agent in missionary cooperation. One hundred seven societies were to join it by 1948, and it was to become in 1950 the Division of Foreign Missions of the National Council of Churches in the United States of America.[7]

International interdenominational gatherings for the furtherance of missions were conspicuous events in the second half of the nineteenth century. In a certain sense, the meetings under the Continental Missions Conferences from 1866 onward—six or more—fitted this description, in that they represented several different confessions and were attended by delegates from churches outside Germany—in France, Holland, Denmark, Sweden, Norway. Of a different order were others which were held in England and the United States: the General Missionary Conference in London (1854), the Liverpool Conference in Liverpool, England (1860), the General Conference on Foreign Missions in London (1878), the Centenary Conference on Foreign Missions in London (1888), and the Ecumenical Missionary Conference in New York City (1900). Whereas the Continental conferences were an established routine of a continuing organization, these latter grew spontaneously out of popular missionary interest, with a minimum of planning and promotion.

[7] With organizational adjustments in relation to the Canadian societies.

The British Organization of the Evangelical Alliance was responsible for the first in 1854. Early that year Alexander Duff, the famed missionary and a member of the committee on arrangements, went to the United States, where persons who had known him, with others moved by the reports of his work in India, sponsored a meeting in New York City in May, which they called the Union Missionary Convention. The venture was a marked success, interest being so keen that the Broadway Tabernacle would not accommodate all who came for the final session.

Duff's able addresses guaranteed programs of high inspirational and educational quality, and the impression was lasting. Fifty years afterwards, John R. Mott in *The Evangelization of the World in This Generation* quoted in its entirety what Duff had said in answer to the question "What are the divinely appointed and most efficient means of extending the gospel of salvation to all men?" as having left nothing to be added after the passage of time.

There is no way of knowing whether or not this meeting had an adverse effect upon the London Conference later in the same year, the attendance at which appears to have fallen below expectations.

Persons identified with the mid-century revival activity in Great Britain, with help from the London Secretaries' Association, took the lead in organizing and conducting the Liverpool Conference in 1860, "that all Christians of the United Kingdom might be stirred up to greater zeal . . . in this work of the Lord." The "work of the Lord" was evangelism of world dimensions. Of the members of the Conference, fifty-two were executives or directors of missionary boards, and under their leadership it advanced in the deliberations on such subjects as the development of indigenous churches and Christian education on the field well beyond general views at the time. Its recommendations influenced missionary policy in years to come. Anthony Ashley Cooper, Lord Shaftesbury, who presided at some of the sessions, thought that the gathering might properly be regarded as "an ecumenical council of the dominions."

In 1878, 160 representatives of 34 missionary societies, including 6 American and 5 Continental, went to the General Conference on Foreign Missions in London. American Baptists had with them a Burmese pastor, the only Oriental present. Speakers who told of their work, country by country, spoke of growing unity but agreed that denominational diversities were not in themselves evil. On the program were James Stewart of Lovedale and Donald Fraser and Hudson Taylor of China. Comity and cooperation had a central place in the discussions.

There were more Americans at the Centenary Conference in London in 1888, and the European delegation, although comparatively small, was larger than usual. Interest in organic union for mission churches was manifested by the missionaries themselves but kindled little response in the assembly. Gustav Warneck of Germany spoke prophetically of a "general missionary conference meeting each decade, to bring about gradually . . . a certain amount of unity in Protestant missionary labors," with a standing committee to act between assemblies. "We must learn to look upon missions as a common cause," he said, "to kindle a missionary *esprit de corps,* to accustom ourselves to a solidarity of missionary interests, and to place in the foreground the vital truths of the gospel common to all."

The Ecumenical Missionary Conference of 1900, marking the end of the old century and the beginning of the new, achieved the distinction of being the largest such gathering up to that time, and probably none after it—under missionary auspices alone—was to equal its record in this respect. More than four thousand persons crowded Carnegie Hall daily for nearly two weeks, and overflow meetings were conducted for the many turned away. It was estimated that the total attendance at all sessions came close to 200,000. One hundred sixty-two mission boards —sixty-four North American, fifty Continental, thirty-five British, and thirteen from other countries—responded to the invitation. Their representatives, numbering about 2,500, constituted the deliberative body within the Conference. The program comprehended all phases of missionary work. At the opening session President William McKinley spoke and former President Benjamin Harrison presided. The Foreign Missions Conference of North America looked after the arrangements.

The purpose of those who sponsored these conventions was to popularize the work of foreign missions and so to increase financial support. In this they undoubtedly succeeded, although the results could not be tabulated. It is significant, however, that income in contributions for British affiliated missions was approximately 40 percent greater in 1890 than in 1888, the year of the Centenary Conference in London. Incidentally, these conferences may have advanced the cause of Christian unity more—in which many of their promoters also believed. They brought together Christians of different nations, confessions, and denominations, who got acquainted and discovered the educational and religious stimulation of such fellowship. They focused attention on the world's need and made clearer the insufficiency of human resources, even when employed together, for the task of evangelization. They created thus a situation in which imponderable influences worked with the more palpable to shape the course of Christian history toward ecumenical developments which, although just over the horizon, could not in the closing decades of the nineteenth century have been predicted or, indeed, believed possible.

2. The Evangelical Alliance

The sense of spiritual kinship and common responsibility for the work of the Kingdom of God, quickened in many Christians by the Evangelical Awakening, had further fruitful embodiment in an association formed in Great Britain in 1846 and given the name "Evangelical Alliance."

For the meeting in London to found this organization there were some eight hundred representatives of not fewer than fifty-two denominations in Canada, England, France, Germany, Holland, Ireland, Sweden, Switzerland, the United States, and Wales. The founding resolution read:

> That members of this Conference are deeply convinced of the desirability of forming a Confederation, on the basis of great evangelical principles held in common by them, which may afford opportunity to members of the Church of Christ of cultivating brotherly love, enjoying Christian intercourse, and promoting such other objects as they may hereafter agree to prosecute together; and they hereby proceed to form such a Confederation, under the name of "The Evangelical Alliance." [8]

The first and foremost of the "objects" the members chose "to prosecute together" was missions, and on its behalf they performed an effective service.

The plans for the first of the interdenominational missionary conferences (London, 1854) originated, as stated, with the Alliance, which supported also the rest of that great series, at least through the energetic unofficial action of many of its members. Its special concern in that connection was reflected by the program of the first meeting, which with the topical slogan "A Plea for Mutual Sympathy and Practical Cooperation" primed the delegates for a discussion of "the essential unity of evangelical missions."

The branches of the Alliance in the different countries joined in holding international conventions of their own, not fewer than eight from 1846 to the end of the century—Paris, 1855; Berlin, 1857; Geneva, 1861; Amsterdam, 1867; New York, 1873; Basle, 1879; Copenhagen, 1884; Florence, 1896—and at these at least one session would be given over to missions. A regular feature was a world-wide survey of missionary work, and some of these studies were of more than passing worth. The programs presented such important questions as the self-support of mission churches, indigenous leadership, and missionary comity generally with insight and understanding.

[8] J. W. Massie, *The Evangelical Alliance: Its Origin and Development,* p. 416.

It would appear that the Alliance did not succeed in gaining the formal cooperation of the missionary boards to the extent it contemplated. The fact that it consisted only of individuals without representative authority from the churches stood in the way of this. The "basis," which restricted membership to those of a particular theological outlook and, in effect, prevented discussion of doctrinal differences, interfered perhaps even more. And, notwithstanding its declared purpose to "cultivate brotherly love," the Alliance manifested hostility to certain other Protestant groups and was outspokenly anti-Roman Catholic. But at that time the missionary societies also had their peculiar ideas and attitudes which stood in the way of more extensive collaboration.

The Alliance journals, *Evangelical Christendom* of the British organization in particular, were for many years most effective instruments of education in international and interdenominational thinking, providing, according to one historian, "more and wider information about the churches and religious conditions in different countries than can be found in any ecumenical journal today." [9]

Perhaps the most telling accomplishment of the Alliance on behalf of Christian unity was the establishment of the Universal Week of Prayer, which after a hundred years is still observed.

3. Student Christian Movement

During the middle decades of the nineteenth century, the unitive impulse, which had been set in motion by the Evangelical Awakening, gathered renewed force in fusion with the idealism and enthusiasm of youth in the Student Christian Movement. The missionary cause early became a beneficiary of this service.

The Student Christian Movement comprised the interrelated organizations promoting religious activity among young men and women of the colleges and universities from about the 1850's onward: the Young Men's Christian Association, the Young Women's Christian Association, the American Intercollegiate Young Men's Christian Association, the Interseminary Missionary Alliance, the Student Volunteer Movement, and other agencies in many countries with different names but similar programs. Eventually the formation of the World's Student Christian Federation brought them together in many activities.

In its early stages the movement centered in the Young Men's Christian Association (Y.M.C.A.), which was organized in Great Britain (London) in 1844 and in the United States (Boston) in 1851 and began soon to work with students, as did the Young Women's Christian Association (Y.W.C.A.), which was founded in 1854—the two cooperating in this field after a time.

[9] Ruth Rouse, in *A History of the Ecumenical Movement,* p. 321.

Within seven years of its institution in 1877, the Intercollegiate Y.M.C.A. numbered as constituents 181 Y.M.C.A.'s which had for their object study of the Bible, personal evangelism, and the encouragement of prayer and worship.

The Y.M.C.A. and the Y.W.C.A. were, of course, interdenominational in their membership and programs, but in this early period they were not interested in the question of *rapprochement* between the churches as such, though some individuals in them were. Henri Dunant, one of the founders of the Y.M.C.A. (and founder of the Red Cross), felt its aim should be: "to spread abroad that ecumenical spirit which transcended nationalities, languages, denominations, ecclesiastical problems, ranks and occupations: to realize, in a word, and as far as possible, that article in the Creed which we all adhere to—'I believe in the Communion of Saints and in the Holy Catholic Church.'" This sentiment was to grow and in time to influence strongly both Associations.

From the colleges, the Student Movement spread to the theological seminaries, through the initiative at first of Robert Mateer of Princeton University, who, with his colleagues, saw an opportunity to win recruits for missionary service. Their work led to the founding of the Interseminary Missionary Alliance.

All evangelical Christian work in these decades had been reinvigorated in some degree by the revival movements rooted in the earlier "Second Awakening." Dwight Lyman Moody, the evangelist, who had been an enthusiastic worker in the Y.M.C.A., stepped into a position of influence in the Student Christian Movements. During a series of meetings in Edinburgh, Scotland, in 1873, students flocked to hear him; and Henry Drummond became his eloquent co-worker. Another campaign, in Cambridge, England, in 1882, led to the organization of a team of undergraduates to speak in the colleges. Two of these students —C. T. Shedd and Stanley Smith—volunteered for work on the mission fields. J. E. K. Shedd in 1885 visited the United States and spoke in many of the universities there, and through his influence John R. Mott, of Cornell, became a recruit.

Upon an invitation from Moody, Luther Wishard and C. K. Ober, secretaries of the Intercollegiate Young Men's Christian Association, 251 students in 1886 gathered at the evangelist's school for boys at Mount Hermon, Massachusetts, for a month of conference. When interest in the prepared program began to flag midway, Robert Wilder, who, with his sister Grace Wilder of Mount Holyoke College, had enlisted for missionary work, turned the deliberations to world evangelization. The outcome was that at the end of the assembly 100 of those present signed what came to be known as "the Princeton declaration": "We, the undersigned, declare ourselves willing and desirous, God permitting, to go to the unevangelized portions of the world."

Following the Mount Hermon meeting, Robert Wilder and John N.

Forman toured the educational institutions of the United States and enrolled, within two years, 2,100 volunteers, among them Robert E. Speer and Samuel Zwemer.

So began the Student Volunteer Movement, "the missionary wing" of the Student Christian Movement, which spreading through North America, Great Britain and its Dominions, and the universities of Europe, with its watchword "The Evangelization of the World in This Generation," would record during the next fifty years more than 20,000 enlistments for missionary service.

Those volunteering at Mount Hermon included John R. Mott. When indicating the field where he desired to serve, he wrote "The world." He was to become the foremost leader of the Student Christian Movements. Their international scope is shown by the list of meeting places of the World's Student Christian Federation which he led in organizing in 1895: 1895, Vadstena Castle, Sweden; 1897, Williamstown, Massachusetts; 1898, Eisenach Castle, Germany; 1900, Versailles, France; 1902, Sorö, Denmark; 1905, Zeist, Holland; 1907, Tokyo, Japan; 1909, Oxford, England; 1911, Constantinople, Turkey; 1912, Lake Mohonk, United States; 1920, Beatenberg, Switzerland; 1922, Peking, China; 1924, High Leigh, England; 1926, Mysore, India.

The reasons for the strength and influence of the Student Christian Movement are quite evident. It was composed of young people of ability, education, and adventurous spirit, who were committed to Christ and believed in cooperation. Its meetings were of a cosmopolitan character and surmounted sectarian barriers. Its programs took an intellectual, as well as a spiritual, approach to the problems of faith. It had talented and wise leaders and succeeded in gaining the support of theological and ecclesiastical groups which other interdenominational causes had not enlisted. It is credited, for example, with having brought into the ecumenical movement the influential Anglo-Catholic element of the Church of England. The Constantinople conference of the World's Student Christian Federation in 1911 was significant chiefly for the fact that it helped to bring about participation by the ancient Eastern Orthodox Churches, long isolated from Western Christendom.

The Movement took young men and women of the churches and prepared them through study and experience for responsibility anywhere they would be needed in the ecumenical movement as its successive stages unfolded. "The thoughts of youth are long, long thoughts." Miss Ruth Rouse, early a member of the Movement, was reported[10] to have said that there were few leaders in the Conference on Church, Community and State at Oxford, England, in 1937 whom she did not recognize as associates in the World's Student Christian Federation. Those who rose through this organization to eminence in the interchurch movement included, besides John R. Mott, Robert Wilder, Nathan

[10] William Adams Brown, *Toward a United Church,* p. 34.

Söderblom, W. A. Visser 't Hooft, Valdemar Ammundsen, J. H. Oldham, Tissington Tatlow, Zoë Fairfield, Ruth Rouse, William Temple, William Paton, Henry Louis Henroid, Marc Boegner, Suzanne Diètrich, Friedrich Wilhelm Siegmund-Schultze, Hannes Lilje, V. S. Azariah, David Yui, T. Z. Koo, Michi Kawai, Germanos Strenopoulos, and Stefan Zankov. These names—excepting her own, which is here added—have been listed by Miss Rouse, who comments: "All these and hundreds more began their ecumenical careers as members or officers in some Student Christian Movement, or were won for ecumenism by some contact with the movement."

4. First World Missionary Conference

The World Missionary Conference at Edinburgh in 1910 carried into the twentieth century the series of international meetings[11] in Great Britain and the United States which had begun with the General Missionary Conference in London and the Union Missionary Convention in New York in 1854; but it was more than just another conference. It brought to the series a degree of progression which is seen in retrospect to have made it epochal.

The preceding conferences had been organized chiefly as demonstrations of interest on behalf of the cause of foreign missions. The aim at Edinburgh was concerned more with the development of missionary policy and administration consonantly with the growing spirit of unity. It called expressly for study and discussion. The planning committee had been favorably impressed by the Madras Conferences of 1900 and 1902 and the Centennial of Foreign Missions in China at Shanghai in 1907—all of which had employed successfully the consultative method in their programs—and had recommended much the same procedure for Edinburgh. By this scheme, which was to become routine in ecumenical meetings, committees appointed in advance prepared and presented the subjects chosen for consideration, whereupon initiative passed to the delegates, whose conclusions and actions became the will of the body.

The eight themes set before the Edinburgh Conference were: (1) Carrying the Gospel to All the Non-Christian World; (2) The Church in the Mission Field; (3) Education in Relation to the Christianization of National Life; (4) The Missionary Message in Relation to Non-Christian Religions; (5) The Preparation of Missionaries; (6) The Home Base of Missions; (7) Missions and Governments; (8) Cooperation and the Promotion of Unity. The members of the several commis-

[11] They are sometimes characterized as "Anglo-American" because the British and American delegates greatly outnumbered the others and there were few representatives from mission churches.

sions which developed these topics had been drawn from many countries, confessions, and denominations, and the reports submitted covered well-nigh the whole mission field. The name "World Missionary Conference" was thus justified before the Conference convened.

Dr. Kenneth Scott Latourette has written concerning the bearing of three of the subjects "upon the growth of the ecumenical movement":[12]

> The first report emphasized the world-wide mission of the Church. The second stressed the development of what later were called the younger churches, and made abundantly clear that a leading purpose of the missionary enterprise was, as indeed it had long been, to bring into being self-governing, self-supporting and self-propagating Churches in every field. The eighth was ecumenical in both title and intention. . . . The issue of co-operation and unity was given exhaustive attention. It was reported without evident disagreement that "the ideal which is present to the minds of the great majority of missionaries is" that it is "the aim of all missionary work to plant in each non-Christian nation one undivided Church of Christ." It was also declared that in some mission fields, at any rate, the problem of unity may, before long, be settled, or at any rate taken in hand, by the indigenous churches independently of the views and wishes of western missionaries.[13]

The membership of the Conference consisted of officially appointed delegates from 159 missionary societies. Some of the earlier gatherings had been composed, in part, of representatives from the various mission organizations; but they had opened their sessions to anyone choosing to attend and planned their programs with the larger public and the church constituencies in mind. The Ecumenical Missionary Conference of 1900 in New York was regarded as a particularly notable success because of the thousands who crowded and overflowed its meetings.

The 1910 Conference attained a greater measure of internationality than its predecessors, the membership of which had been almost wholly British and North American. Forty-one Continental missionary boards sent 170 delegates to Edinburgh; and there were 17 representatives from the younger churches,[14] who had been appointed by the societies with which their missions were affiliated.

Although the delegation from the missions was not large in proportion to the total enrollment of the Conference, it assumed an importance in comparison with the smaller representations from the mission fields on previous occasions. There is apparently no discoverable record that anybody from a mission church attended the great

[12] Dr. Latourette calls the World Missionary Conference, Edinburgh, 1910, "the birthplace of the modern ecumenical movement." "It cannot be said too often or too emphatically," he declares, "that the ecumenical movement arose from the missionary movement." (*A History of the Ecumenical Movement*, p. 362.)

[13] *World Missionary Conference, 1910, Minutes and Reports*, Vol. VIII, pp. 83, 86.

[14] Mission churches.

Centenary Conference of the Protestant Missions of the World in London in 1888. One Indian had spoken before the Liverpool Conference in 1860, and several representatives of the younger churches had addressed the Ecumenical Missionary Conference of 1900. But at the Centenary Conference of Chinese Missions in 1907 there had been only a half-dozen or so natives among the nearly twelve hundred persons attending, and these had come as visitors. The decennial all-India conferences had likewise made little room for delegates from the missions.

Moreover, Edinburgh had reserved prominent places in the program and discussions for the nationals who came from mission lands—Burma, India, China, Korea, and Japan. Chêng Ching-yi of China spoke on "The Contribution of Non-Christian Races to the Body of Christ," declaring that Chinese Christians looked forward to "a united Christian Church without any denominational distinctions." The address of V. S. Azariah of India on "The Problem of Co-operation between Foreign and Native Workers" made a lasting impression. Explaining with great frankness the barriers separating missionaries and Indian leaders, he concluded: "Through all the ages to come the Indian Church will rise up in gratitude to attest the heroism and self-denying labour of the missionary body. You have given your goods to feed the poor. You have given your bodies to be burned. We also ask for love. Give us friends!" [15]

The presence of Anglo-Catholics at the Conference gave it an ecclesiastical comprehensiveness none before it had achieved—or perhaps desired; for their disinclination to cooperate outside the Church of England's Society for the Propagation of the Gospel had been scarcely less pronounced than that of the main body of supporters of the interdenominational missionary movement to associate themselves with Christians of the Catholic tradition. Their participation had an immediate importance, and it also proved to be the beginning of a new policy of collaboration on their part which influenced profoundly the whole course of ecumenism.

The qualifying subtitle of the Conference, "To Consider Missionary Problems in Relation to the Non-Christian World," pointed to serious limitations of the program. It implied the exclusion from discussion of those missions in European, Near Eastern, and Latin American countries, conducted mainly by American denominations, which the older churches of these areas looked upon as aimed chiefly at proselytizing their adherents. No other way could be found to handle this problem and gain the cooperation of the Anglo-Catholics and the Continental missionary societies, particularly the German. Its adoption met with vigorous objection. Representatives of the denominational boards maintaining the missions not included met in specially called

[15] *World Missionary Conference, 1910,* Vol. IX, p. 315.

conferences of their own while in Edinburgh to discuss their common complaint. These consultations led to the Conference on Missions in Latin America two years later in New York and, through the Committee on Cooperation in Latin America appointed by it, to the Congress on Christian Work in Latin America at Panama in 1916. Despite all attempts to dismiss it, this issue was to remain an acute one in the interchurch fellowship.

Through this eventful Conference the world had an introduction to a number of persons whose names would be linked inseparably with the ecumenical movement in the new era it was ushering in. Foremost were John R. Mott, the Chairman, and Joseph Houldsworth Oldham, the Executive Secretary, whose work in the preparatory commissions and in the Conference itself exerted a determinative influence. Charles H. Brent, at the time Missionary Bishop for the Philippines of the Protestant Episcopal Church, was to lead in founding the Faith and Order Movement. V. S. Azariah would bring to the cause of Christian cooperation the power of his office as the first native Anglican Bishop of India, to which he was soon to be elevated; and Chêng Ching-yi would grow into an outstanding figure in the International Missionary Council, the National Christian Council of China, and the Church of Christ in China.

Among the younger men who served the Conference as stewards, or ushers, most of them members of the Student Christian Movements in Great Britain and Ireland, were John Baillie, John McLeod Campbell, Kenneth Escott Kirk, Walter Moberly, Neville Stuart Talbot, and Herbert George Wood, all of whom would advance into larger stewardship in the ecumenical movement. And in the company also was William Temple, "without whom it would be impossible to think of the ecumenical movement in its contemporary form."[16]

The Conference was to be remembered chiefly perhaps for its demonstration of the fact that Christians of different denominational allegiances could meet and discuss matters pertaining to practical cooperation without feeling that they were compromising their convictions, or that they had to wait until they could agree theologically to begin working together. The delegates, moved by the experience they had shared, voted apparently unanimously to appoint a Continuation Committee to translate the vision of Edinburgh into deed.

For Chairman of the Committee hardly anybody but John R. Mott could have been chosen, and for Secretary only Joseph H. Oldham, who had, as noted, served the Conference in the corresponding positions.

The returning delegates and the reports of the Conference stimulated the organization in Great Britain and Continental countries of missionary councils, after the pattern of the Foreign Missions Conference of North America, to serve the mission boards as organs of cooperation.

[16] Kenneth Scott Latourette, in *A History of the Ecumenical Movement,* p. 360.

Meetings on the foreign fields were convened to consider the problems and policies of work in the missions in the light of what had transpired at Edinburgh.

The first of these developments came about more or less spontaneously. For the other Dr. Mott was chiefly responsible. As Chairman of the Continuation Committee, he visited the Far East during the winter of 1912-13 and there attended eighteen regional and three national conferences—in Ceylon, India, Burma, Malaya, China, Korea, and Japan—called for consultation on organization.

The Continuation Committee had been instructed to set up a larger substitute body to be a permanent agency of missionary cooperation. At a meeting at Lake Mohonk, New York, in 1912, representatives of the mission boards decided to defer this step and to ask the original Committee to continue for the time and to assume, so far as it could, "broader responsibilities."

With its members living in different parts of the world, the Continuation Committee, upon the outbreak of war in 1914, ceased to function, except through the labors of the Chairman and the Secretary. As colleagues they were ideally suited to each other and fully equipped by their complementing talents to serve the Christian cause in this momentous period. The Committee itself did not meet again. The duties implicit in its mandate, and others even heavier, which arose out of the war and the resulting social upheaval, they bore with a creative wisdom that went far toward saving the foundations of world Christian cooperation.

Important events and significant labors, to which volumes could be devoted, must in this review be given but a line or passed without mention.

During the years from 1914 to 1918, Mott divided his time between the Committee and the demands of war work. He felt obliged to accept the chairmanship of the International Committee of the Young Men's Christian Association, with its far-flung ministry to the growing masses of prisoners in war camps, and to the men of the armed forces at home and overseas. At the same time, he led in drives for money for these and other causes, while traveling almost continuously and counseling those with public interests who sought him out because of his wide contacts. The first weeks of the war saw him on a hurried trip to Germany and neighboring countries to confer with church officials and to return to the United States by way of London for talks with Sir Edward Grey, British Foreign Secretary, Lord Balfour of Burleigh, and various missionary executives about the issues at stake for the churches.

In 1916 he took time to preside over the business sessions of the Congress on Christian Work in Latin America, which had been organized to supplement the World Missionary Conference of Edinburgh. Although having declined appointment as ambassador to China by

President Woodrow Wilson in 1912, he allowed himself to be drafted in 1917 for a diplomatic mission to Russia in company with Elihu Root, with the stipulation that he be permitted to confine himself to "religious, educational and humanitarian contacts."

In 1918 he was again in Great Britain, helping to set up the Emergency Committee of Cooperating Missions to take the place of the now long inactive Continuation Committee. Mention of all these services does not exhaust the list. Not included are the secretaryship of the World's Christian Student Federation, which he had long borne, and the chairmanship of the Continental Missions Relief Fund of the Foreign Missions Conference of North America.

This sketch of his wartime activities shows something of Mott's unique position in the ecumenical movement, as also of his character and ability as a leader. Of him Dr. Kenneth Scott Latourette writes:

> In an unusual degree he combined a dignified, commanding presence, deep religious faith, evangelistic zeal, the capacity to discern ability and promise in youth and to inspire it, wide-ranging vision, courage, tact, administrative ability, power over public assemblies as a presiding officer, and compelling and convincing speech. A layman, not theologically trained, not using for conversation or public address any other language than his native English, he won the respect and co-operation of thousands of men and women of many races, nations, tongues and ecclesiastical connections. A prodigious and seemingly indefatigable worker, he found time for an enormous amount of solid and diversified reading. An incessant traveller, there were few phases of the ecumenical movement in which he did not play an outstanding part. . . .He dreamed and acted in terms both of individuals and of movements which would influence nations and mankind as a whole.[17]

Through him and Christians of all races whose loyalty he inspired, more than by the operations of boards and councils, the structure of Christian cooperation was preserved during years in which the forces of disintegration unleashed by war threatened to tear it apart.

Joseph H. Oldham was a man of quite a different type but also extraordinarily competent and able to win the confidence of others. With his superior associate working from a base in America, he remained at the office in Edinburgh, where he edited *The International Review of Missions,* which he had founded in 1912, and handled the interviews and voluminous correspondence in reference to the wartime problems of the mission fields.

All missions had been affected. Travel and the transmission of money and supplies had been interrupted. German missions, located mostly in lands under Allied control, had been closed and their missionaries repatriated or interned. With their families, they numbered some two thousand. Churches in Europe and America organized to provide relief for them personally and for the work from which they had been separ-

[17] *A History of the Ecumenical Movement,* p. 356.

ated. Because of the extensive colonial involvements of Great Britain, London became the focal point of these operations and the Emergency Committee of Cooperating Missions the agent. Having wider contacts with the churches and a more comprehensive knowledge of missionary affairs than anyone else on the scene, the Secretary became liaison executive of the Emergency Committee in its almost continuous dealings with the British government and, through it, with the other Allied nations. He brought to this duty an ability quickly recognized. Policies which he helped to shape proved of such practical effect that they were remembered and revived by governments twenty years afterwards when confronted by essentially the same situation in World War II.

War brought to the churches in all lands incalculable losses. Among the greatest of these was the rupture of fellowship and of collaboration in missionary work, which extended throughout the ecumenical movement and was long in healing. That the disaster was not more serious must be attributed to the service of those leaders who with godly wisdom and invincible goodwill stood in the breach, steadfast in hope when the tides of darkness were sweeping around them.

5. The International Missionary Council

The larger and more widely representative body to supplant the Continuation Committee was finally organized in 1921 at Lake Mohonk, New York. It had taken the events of a revolutionary decade to make unmistakably clear the need for this action. The name given the new agency was the International Missionary Council.

The preamble of its constitution read:

> The Council is established on the basis that the only bodies entitled to determine missionary policy are the churches and the missionary societies and boards, representing the churches. It is recognized that the successful working of the International Missionary Council is entirely dependent on the gift from God of the spirit of fellowship, mutual understanding, and desire to co-operate.

The section on functions was as follows:

> (1) To stimulate thinking and investigation on questions related to the mission and expansion of Christianity in all the world, to enlist in the solution of these questions the best knowledge and experience to be found in all countries, and to make the results available for all who share in the missionary work of the churches;
>
> (2) To help to co-ordinate the activities of the national missionary organizations and Christian councils of the different countries, and to bring about united action where necessary in missionary matters;
>
> (3) Through consultation to help unite Christian public opinion in support of freedom of conscience and religion and of missionary liberty;

(4) To help to unite the Christian forces of the world in seeking justice in international and inter-racial relations;

(5) To be responsible for the publication of *The International Review of Missions* and such other publications as in the judgment of the Council may contribute to the study of missionary questions;

(6) To call a world missionary conference if and when this should be deemed advisable.

The roster of member organizations reflected the international character of the Council:

The Foreign Missions Conference of North America
The Conference of Missionary Societies in Great Britain and Ireland
The German Protestant Missions Committee (*Ausschuss*)
The United Missionary Council of Australia
The Committee of Advice of the Netherlands
The General Swedish Missionary Conference
The Norwegian General Missions Committee
The Danish Missions Council
The National Joint Missions Committee of Finland
The Japan Continuation Committee
The China Continuation Committee
The National Missionary Council of India, Burma and Ceylon
The Belgian Society of Protestant Missions of the Congo
The Paris Evangelical Missionary Society
A group of Swiss churches (without corporate status)
A group of churches in South Africa (without corporate status)
A group of churches in New Zealand (without corporate status)

During the next two decades other national councils of churches, which were organized in various countries, including a number in the mission fields, became members. By the time of the Third World Missionary Conference at Madras in 1938, the total of the constituents was twenty-six, and by 1948 it had increased to thirty. Sixteen were councils of younger churches and missions representing Brazil, Ceylon, China, the Congo, India, Japan, Korea, Latin America (Committee on Cooperation in Latin America), Malaya, Mexico, the Near East, the Netherlands Indies, the Philippine Islands, Puerto Rico, the River Plata Confederation (Argentina, Uruguay, and Paraguay), and Thailand. The fourteen national or regional missionary agencies were in Australia, Belgium, Denmark, Finland, France, Germany, Great Britain, the Netherlands, New Zealand, North America (Canada and the United States), Norway, South Africa (representing the younger churches), Sweden, and Switzerland.

Non-member councils which had a relationship with the Council through correspondence, consultation, or occasional representation were: in Africa—Angola, French Equatorial Africa, Ethiopia, the Gold Coast, Kenya, Madagascar, Nigeria, Northern Rhodesia, Nyasaland, Mozambique (Portuguese East Africa), Sierra Leone, Southern Rhodesia, and Tanganyika; in Latin America—Honduras, Chile, and Peru; and in the Caribbean area—Antigua, Barbados, Cuba, Jamaica, Trinidad, and Tobago.

The preceding three paragraphs cannot be dismissed as mere dry gazetteerish lists. They make graphic the universality of Christianity in the first quarter of the twentieth century. Etymologically, the word "ecumenical" describes that which is coextensive with the inhabited world. The Church and its historic councils in the early centuries could be called ecumenical only in the sense that their authority extended throughout Christendom, which then was a comparatively small spot on the map of the world. Not until modern times had the gospel been preached in all nations and the Christian faith become, at least by report, global.

The enthusiastic young men who in the early days of the Student Volunteer Movement set as their goal the evangelization of the world in their lifetime (if they meant carrying the evangel to all nations, rather than converting all mankind, as it is asserted they did) now are seen not to have been excessively optimistic.

Credit for the increasing participation of the mission churches in the ecumenical movement belongs largely to the International Missionary Council. Scarcely a score of nationals were at the World Missionary Conference at Edinburgh in 1910—fewer than 2 percent of the enrollment—and they came as appointees of Western missionary societies. At the Second World Missionary Conference, in Jerusalem in 1928, representatives of the younger churches numbered nearly one hundred—about 25 percent of the registration. Their delegation of 250 at the Third World Missionary Conference, at Madras (India) in 1938, constituted approximately one-half of the membership.

The new churches brought with them into the councils of world fellowship manifold problems. They were beset by ideological conflicts, dictatorships, revolutions. They spoke for peoples who were beneficiaries and at the same time victims of Western influences. They represented youth that reached out for the opportunities of education beyond its limited facilities. They were overshadowed in their work by the old indigenous ethnic faiths and assaulted by a militant secularism which the program of the Jerusalem Conference listed for study as one of the religions competing with Christianity. They were restive under the denominational systems inherited from the West, with their divisions, competitions, and confusions. They felt that they needed and must have unity in faith and work. "If there is one God and one Christ, one gospel of love and one hope," they asked, "why should there be more than one church?"

The statement on unity presented by a committee of their delegates at Madras in 1938 reflected their thinking on this difficult issue and the competence they had attained in forming and expressing their own convictions:[18]

> During the discussion it became abundantly clear that the divisions of Christendom were seen in their worst light in the mission field. Instances were cited by the representatives of the younger churches of disgraceful competition, wasteful over-lapping, and of groups of individuals turned away from the Church because of the divisions within.
>
> Disunion is both a stumbling-block to the faithful and a mockery to those without. We confess with shame that we ourselves have often been the cause of thus bringing dishonor to the religion of our Master.
>
> The representatives of the younger churches in this section, one and all, give expression to the passionate longing that exists in all countries for visible union of the churches. They are aware of the fact of spiritual unity; they record with great thankfulness all the signs of co-operation and understanding that are increasingly seen in various directions; but they realize that this is not enough. Visible and organic union must be our goal.
>
> This, however, will require an honest study of those things in which the churches have differences, a widespread teaching of the common church membership in things that make for union and venturesome sacrifice on the part of all.
>
> Such unions alone will remove the evils arising out of our divisions. Union proposals have been put forward in different parts of the world. Loyalty, however, will forbid the younger churches going forward to consummate any union unless it receives the whole-hearted support and blessing of those through whom these churches have been planted. We are thus torn between loyalty to our mother churches and loyalty to our ideal of union.
>
> We, therefore, appeal with all the fervor we possess, to the missionary societies and boards and the responsible authorities of the older churches, to take this matter seriously to heart, to labor with the churches in the mission field to achieve union, to support and encourage us in all our efforts to put an end to the scandalous effects of our divisions and to lead us in the path of union—the union for which our Lord prayed, through which the world would indeed believe in the Divine Mission of the Son, our Lord Jesus Christ.

The election of John R. Mott as Chairman and J. H. Oldham as Secretary assured the success of the Council. Headquarters were in Edinburgh House in London, and an office was opened in New York, with A. L. Warnshuis in charge. William Paton became Oldham's associate in England. The Council "extended its activities in many directions as a coordinating and central planning agency for the large majority of the Protestant missions."[19]

The conferences at Jerusalem (1928), Madras, India (1938), and Whitby, Ontario (1947) were augmented gatherings of the International Missionary Council, which included official representatives of cooperating missionary organizations. The records of their deliberations

[18] *Madras Conference Series,* Vol. IV, pp. 376 ff.
[19] *History of the Ecumenical Movement,* pp. 368 ff.

constitute a significant part of the history of the missionary movement in the second quarter of the century.

This period closed with a remarkable demonstration of the ecumenical spirit in practical service. The world-wide economic depression of the 1930's reduced the financial support of foreign missions, at its European sources particularly. World War II closed German work, which was located mainly in territory under British mandate.[20] The war also seriously affected the missions of other Continental churches, as well as those of the British societies. Roughly one-fifth of Protestant missionary work was cut off from its base, and 168 missions with their 3,500 missionaries were "orphaned." With the International Missionary Council leading and the churches outside the stricken areas helping, notably the Lutheran, more than eight million dollars was raised between 1940 and 1949 for Continental and British missions, six and one-half millions of which came from the United States.

Of this extraordinary accomplishment William Richey Hogg writes:

> For hundreds of stranded missionaries it kept soul and body together. For members of younger churches it maintained necessary institutions . . . and . . . bore constant testimony to the fellowship of which they [were] a part. . . . In conception and achievement the project was unique in the history of the Christian Church. The reality of the world Christian community in action, the manner in which it operated, indeed, the very fact of giving under the circumstances of the times had a significance that far outweighed the sums involved. . . . The majority of the orphaned missions were sustained by Christians from countries at war with the lands of those who normally supported them. Across warring lines Christians were praying for one another, working for one another . . . because they were unitedly involved in a humanly overwhelming task, the evangelization of mankind. Here was actual proof of a Christian world fellowship transcending nation and denomination and uniting its members in faith and love.[21]

Through the missionary movement, by the middle of the twentieth century, the gospel had been preached to all nations and the expansion of Christianity organizationally carried to global bounds. In its manifold cooperative phases it had become the most extensive expression of the growing spirit of Christian unity. It had been throughout an experimental laboratory for the development of ecumenical techniques and strategies and the most fruitful training ground for leaders in all fields of interchurch work. Apart from it, the World Council of Churches and other international Christian bodies of interdenominational character would not have been possible.

[20] As had World War I. See earlier reference.

[21] W. R. Hogg, *Ecumenical Foundations,* p. 316.

II

THE LIFE AND WORK MOVEMENT

The revivalism that followed upon the Evangelical Awakening, although at times divisive, succeeded often, as we have seen, in overpassing denominational lines; but cooperation, whether at home or overseas, did not stop with evangelism of the conventional kind.

1. The Social Emphasis

Foreign missions were set in the midst of conditions which called for a social ministry, and the answer is common knowledge—material relief, promotion of health programs, medical and hospital care for the sick, education, counseling on the problems of family life, vocational guidance in agriculture, industry, and business, and measures for the improvement of racial and international relations.

These services became the studied practical response of Christian compassion to human need. Many persons in the sponsoring churches had reservations about some of them at first, but they were accepted in time as a part of evangelism inseparable from what had been thought of as its more characteristic spiritual functions. Through them many avenues for interdenominational work were opened. Home missions were likewise informed by a serious social concern.

The *Innere Mission*[1] in Germany, which served as the organ of the major three confessions, owed its foundation (1847) to Johann Hinrich Wichern (1807-81), and its policy and administration took their shape from his varied experiences in social welfare work in the cities and his strong conviction that "the regeneration of fundamental conditions in State . . . and community" ought to be an aim of the churches.

Wichern spoke for others besides himself, not only in his own country, but in Europe outside Germany. It was not uncommon for pastoral evangelism to be linked closely with social reform.

[1] The German term *Innere Mission* comprehended a broader range of activities than "home missions" as used originally in Great Britain and the United States.

One example of this was the ministry of Jean Frédéric Oberlin (1740-1826) as Protestant (Lutheran) pastor of Waldbach, a remote and poverty-stricken region in the Steinthal (Ban de la Roche) in Alsace. By constructing roads and bridges, helping the peasantry to build themselves new cottages, introducing various industrial arts and improved methods of agriculture, and founding a system of schools he transformed his parish into a prosperous and growing community, winning at the same time the goodwill and cooperation of many of the inhabitants not of his church, including Roman Catholics.

In their early period, home missions in the United States were confined largely to building churches and providing what might have been considered a minimum spiritual ministry for the westward-moving population, and the denominations went about this task, for the most part, in a highly individualistic way. What they found time to do for the Negroes, the Indians, and the scattered immigrant groups proceeded by the same independent, and often competitive, methods. Not until the land had been possessed did they begin to give special attention to more unyielding moral frontiers which had already engaged the churches of the older nations, and so to learn their need of one another and the imperativeness of working together.

Attempts to apply Christian teaching to social problems antedated, of course, the modern missionary movement, and many such efforts continued independently of it. In Great Britain the Quakers and other Nonconformists had begun the attack on the slave trade during the seventeenth century, a cause to which William Wilberforce (1759-1833) was later to rally influential Evangelicals of the Church of England. The American Anti-Slavery Society, which drew its members from all faiths, was founded in 1833. The Evangelical Alliance, organized in 1846, took its place among these crusading groups but had to abandon its plan to establish a branch in the United States, because of its determined denial of membership to slaveholders.[2]

The work of John Howard (1726-90) and his followers for prison reform in the eighteenth century gathered support outside England from Protestants on the Continent—Lutherans and Reformed—and from many representatives of the Eastern Orthodox and Roman Catholic Churches, who helped Elizabeth Fry (1780-1845) likewise in her espousal of this cause.

Other social evils, particularly war and intemperance, early became targets of organized resistance. The American Society for the Promotion of Temperance was founded in 1826, and the American Peace Society in 1828. The latter was only one of the first of several such bodies. The campaign for temperance (or abstinence and prohibition) was carried by the Independent Order of Good Templars (1851), the Woman's

[2] The Evangelical Alliance in the United States was not formed until 1873—after the issue of slavery had been settled by the Civil War.

Christian Temperance Union (1874), the Anti-Saloon League (1895), the International Prohibition Confederation (1909), the World League against Alcoholism (1919) and other such organizations into many countries of the world, including—besides the United States, Great Britain and most of Europe—East and West Africa, India and Australasia.

The middle decades of the nineteenth century saw in many nations the burgeoning of socio-religious agencies, among them the institute of Theodor Fliedner (1800-64) at Kaiserswerth for the training of deaconesses and nurses, Johann Hinrich Wichern's center for work with juvenile delinquents (*Das Rauhes Haus*) in Hamburg, Dr. Bernardo's Homes in England, Sir Wilfred Grenfell's Mission to Labrador, the Salvation Army, Ragged Schools, social settlements (Toynbee Hall in Whitechapel, Oxford House in Bethnal Green, Cambridge House in Camberwell, Mansfield House in West Ham, Neighborhood House on the Lower East Side, New York, Hull House in Chicago, South End House in Boston, and many others), and institutional churches.

During this period, important reforms through governmental action both stimulated and expressed the awakening conscience of the churches.

From 1802 to 1878 the British Parliament was engaged by the long series of legislative proposals, styled at their passage as Factory Acts, which asserted and defined the right of the state to control, for its physical and moral well-being, industrial and other establishments depending upon the labor of women and children. A leading exponent of these laws after about 1830 was Lord Shaftesbury (Anthony Ashley Cooper, 1801-85), an earnest and able Evangelical churchman who received wide Nonconformist support.

At the same time, John Bright and Richard Cobden were waging their political battles for repeal of the Corn Laws and extension of the voting franchise, while maintaining vigorous opposition against large military establishments and the annexation of more territory by war.

All these political causes—and there were others—enlisted support, if not from the churches as such, from Christians of nearly all connections, and the effects of their progress were felt in other countries.[3]

2. Christian Socialism

This was the era also of Christian Socialism. Frederick Denison Maurice (1805-72), Charles Kingsley (1819-75), and other churchmen, lay and clerical, who were associated with the launching of the movement in England around 1830, were apparently influenced little by current socialistic philosophies—the speculative idealism of Comte Claude Henri de Saint-Simon and François Maríe Charles Fourier, the utopian

[3] During this period slavery was, of course, both a religious and a political issue in the United States until its abolition in 1863. The churches were divided.

collectivist schemes of Robert Owen, or, later, the "scientific socialism" of Karl Marx. They were socialists only in that they stressed, in opposition to individualism, the corporate nature of society and the need for economic, as well as political, solidarity based on the fatherhood of God and the brotherhood of man. With others who were called socialists, they were seeking a solution to the problems of industrialism, especially those involving the condition of the working classes, but their approach was from the standpoint of the Church. They were concerned with rescuing religion from its "social apostasy" and making its principles effective in the common life. They identified themselves with many of the activities intended to promote the well-being of the laboring classes, such as the Workingmen's College and producers' cooperatives. As could only have been expected, in view of the inexperienced and untrained leadership and the strong resistance with which they had to contend, not all their ventures proved successful. But in the large the movement succeeded; it gave religious direction to the thinking of the churches on social questions, against the day, not far distant, when the Marxist doctrines of materialistic determinism and class revolution would rise to challenge the Christian concept of society.

Two disciples of Frederick Denison Maurice—Brooke Foss Westcott (1825-91) and Fenton John Anthony Hort (1828-92), the famous New Testament scholars of Trinity College, Cambridge—became co-founders, with Canon Charles Gore (afterwards Bishop of Birmingham and then of Oxford), Canon Henry Scott-Holland, and other prominent Anglo-Catholics, of the Christian Social Union and the Industrial Christian Fellowship. These were Anglican organizations, but they acted with the Social Service Unions of the Free Churches of England in forming the Interdenominational Social Service Council, membership in which was opened to "all the religious bodies which name the name of Christ," including the Roman Catholic Church. Wrote Dr. Gore of this move: "Some of us . . . felt that, while denominational societies must convert their own bodies, there was needed a fellowship of all. . . . The Christian Social Crusade seeks to form and affiliate to one another interdenominational agencies, whereby the sundered portion of the Christian Church may learn to act as one body in the task of public social and moral witness."

From the series of annual gatherings at Swanwick under the auspices of the Interdenominational Social Service Council came inspiration for the historic Conference on Christian Politics, Economics and Citizenship (COPEC) at Birmingham, England, in 1924. "The basis" of the Conference formulated conclusions reached by the churches concerning the application of the Christian religion to social problems:

> The basis of this Conference is the conviction that the Christian faith, rightly interpreted and consistently followed, gives the vision and the power

essential for solving the problems of today, that the social ethics of Christianity have been greatly neglected by Christians with disastrous consequences to the individual and to society, and that it is of the first importance that these should be given a clearer and more persistent emphasis.

In the teaching and work of Jesus Christ are certain fundamental principles—such as the universal Fatherhood of God with its corollary that mankind is God's family, and the law "that whoso loseth his life findeth it"—which, if accepted, not only condemn much in the present organization of society, but show the way of regeneration.

Christianity has proved itself to possess also a motive power for the transformation of the individual, without which no change of policy or method can succeed. In the light of its principles the constitution of society, the conduct of industry, the upbringing of children, national and international politics, the personal relations of men and women, in fact, all human relationships, must be tested.

It is hoped that through this Conference the Church may win a fuller understanding of its Gospel, and hearing a clear call to practical action, may find courage to obey.[4]

The program of the Conference showed how broad and thoroughgoing had been the search of the churches for the will of God in the everyday life of the individual and society. An introductory theological statement on "The Nature of God and His Purpose for the World" was followed by reports on the themes set for discussion: "Education," "The Home," "The Relation of the Sexes," "Leisure," "The Treatment of Crime," "International Relations," "Christianity and War," "Industry and Property," "Politics and Citizenship," and "The Social Function of the Church." A final study presented examples of the social effects of Christianity.

Socialist parties of the 1870's and 1880's generally were conceived in Marxian terms. The *Christlich-sozialer Arbeiter Partei* in Germany was organized by Adolf Stoecker in 1878. During the chancellorship of Bismarck socialism was under proscription. In 1890, Stoecker, with Ludwig Weber and Adolf Harnack, formed the *Evangelischer-Soziale Kongress,* which in its religious principles corresponded somewhat to the Christian Social Union in Great Britain. The appearance in its membership of theological and sociological radicalism soon led to Stoecker's withdrawal, and in 1896 he founded the *Freie Kirchlich-Soziale Konferenz* for the promotion of more conservative policies, while Friedrich Naumann, who belonged to the liberal wing, started the *National-Sozialer Verein,* a purely political party "dedicated to the building of national strength through social reform." These bodies laid the foundations for the extraordinary socialistic developments in Germany following the First World War.

The *Volksverein für das katholische Deutschland,* founded by Franz Brandts, became a power in German politics.

The encyclical *Rerum Novarum* of Pope Leo XIII in 1891 had a

[4] H. G. Wood, ed., COPEC Reports, Vol. I, London, 1924, p. iv.

quickening influence upon all Christian social efforts. "The worker," the Pontiff declared, "must have a subsidiary source of security, based on possession of property."

In France, the adjustment of Roman Catholic theory and practice to the changed social conditions after the Revolution of 1848 was accelerated by the work of those responsible for the organization of *Action Libérale Populaire*. The Christian Socialist program of Protestants centered in the *Association Protestante pour l'Étude Pratique des Questions Sociales,* which managed to accommodate both the conservatives and the liberals, on the principle that where there was unity in the will to do good dogmatic differences had little significance. This body was organized in 1887 and had for its interpreter the influential review which later was called *Le Christianisme Social.*

According to the historians of the Christian Socialists in France, Tommy Fallot (1844-1904) was the founder of their movement. His interest in social Christianity had resulted partly from his connections, through his grandfather, Daniel Le Grand, with Jean Frédéric Oberlin and his work in Alsace. Two of his disciples, Élie Gounelle and Wilfred Monod, and his nephew, Marc Boegner, were to become leaders in the Life and Work Movement.

Christian social movements in Switzerland sought to form alliances with the Socialist party, their leaders holding that the plans of labor for the reconstruction of the economic system were essentially Christian. The churches were criticized for their slowness in recognizing the social teaching of the gospel and in cooperating with those who were endeavoring to give them regnancy in the life of the nation.

As socialism spread through Europe, some people of the churches supported its political parties. Others, while recognizing the justice of many of the efforts to right social wrongs, thought that their own duty was to work for solutions under religious auspices, and found their opportunity, as they believed, in the Christian Socialist movements. In nearly all countries there were outstanding churchmen who in one or the other sphere, or in both, gained experience and training for leadership in the Christian action program which was later to be undertaken through ecumenical cooperation. Prominent among them were Valdemar Ammundsen of Denmark, Nathan Söderblom of Sweden, and Friedrich Wilhelm Siegmund-Schultze of Germany, in addition to churchmen in England, France, and Germany already named in preceding pages, and many others.

The Christian Socialist movement appeared in the United States in the late 1880's. There had been, however, earlier semi-utopian experiments in collective living, such as that of Hopedale, which Adin Ballou had described as "practical Christian socialism." The Church Association for the Advance of the Interests of Labor was organized in 1887, and the Society of Christian Socialists in 1889. These bodies followed closely the plans of Christian Socialists in England, and the Christian Social Union, founded in America in 1891, affiliated with the English organization of the same name. During the 1890's a number of small, obscure societies, denominational and interdenominational, worked for the reform of the economic order, most of them, in the end, allying themselves with political socialism. The Christian Socialist Fellowship (1906) and the Church Socialist League (1911-19) furnished leaders for various reform movements and nuclei for socially minded church groups.

IN AMERICA

3. The Federal Council of the Churches of Christ

The Federal Council of the Churches of Christ in America, founded in 1908, became almost immediately the main focus of interest in what was coming to be called the social gospel or social Christianity. The fourth of its five announced objectives was "to secure a larger combined influence for the Churches of Christ in all matters affecting the moral and social condition of the people, so as to promote the application of the law of Christ in every relation of human life." At its first meeting a survey on "The Church and Modern Industry," prepared by a committee headed by Frank Mason North, was prophetic of the course the implementation of this program would take.

A survey of the social and industrial conditions of our American people reveals certain indisputable facts which should be candidly stated.

1. There is an estrangement between the Church and the industrial workers. . . .

2. There is a separation between the rich and the cultured and the churches. . . .

3. Industrial progress has . . . taken the Church unawares. Christianity has created a civilization which it is now its first task to inspire and direct. It has produced a social crisis in which its visions must concrete themselves into principles of action. . . .

4. There are many phases of the present industrial conditions in the United States which cry aloud for immediate remedy. Multitudes are deprived, by what are called economic laws, of that opportunity to which every man has a right. That to these impersonal causes are added the cruelties of greed, the heartlessness of ambition and the cold indifference of corporate selfishness, every friend of his fellow must with grief and shame admit. The "homes" of the wage earners of our great cities are an indictment of our civilization. The meager income, which is easily reckoned sufficient by the fortunate who are not forced to live upon it, is without warrant of reason. The helplessness of the individual worker, the swift changes in location of industrial centers, the constant introduction of labor-saving appliances, the exactions of landlords, add uncertainty to privation.

That workingmen should organize for social and industrial betterment belongs to the natural order. The effort of the world's toilers to secure better conditions of work and larger possession of themselves is welcome evidence of a Divine call within them to share in the higher experiences of the intellectual and spiritual life. . . . Trades unionism should be accepted not as the Church's enemy, but as the Church's ally.

The Committee . . . makes earnest appeal that this Federal Council . . . give utterance, by appropriate resolution, to its convictions touching the industrial conditions which concern the multitudes to whom the churches are appointed to present . . . our Lord: and . . . that without ignoring points of sharp divergence in opinion, without endorsement of proceedings at times strongly condemned, without commitment to a specific program, this . . . Council extend to all the toilers of our country and to those who seek to organize the workers of the land for the furtherance of industrial justice, social betterment and the brotherhood of man, the greetings of sympathy and confidence and the assurance of goodwill and co-operation in the name of Him who was known as the Son of the Carpenter, . . . the Son of God.

Statement and Resolution

1. This Federal Council places upon record its profound belief that the complex problems of modern industry can be interpreted and solved only by the teachings of the New Testament, and that Jesus Christ is final authority in the social as in the individual life.

2. Christian practice has not always harmonized with Christian principle . . . , and the organized church has not always spoken when it should have borne witness, and its plea for righteousness has not always been uttered with boldness.

3. The Church now confronts the most significant crisis and the greatest opportunity of its long career. In part its ideals and principles have become the working basis of organizations for social and industrial betterment which do not accept its spiritual leadership and which have been estranged from its fellowship. We believe, not for its own sake but in the interest of the kingdom of God, the Church must not merely acquiesce in the movements outside . . . which make for human welfare, but must demonstrate, not by proclamation but by deeds, its primacy among all the forces which seek to lift the plane and better the conditions of human life.

4. We recognize the complex nature of industrial obligations affecting employer and employee, society and government, rich and poor, and most earnestly counsel tolerance, patience and mutual confidence; we do not defend or excuse wrongdoing in high places or low, nor purpose to adapt the ethical standards of the Gospel to the exigencies of commerce or the codes of a confused industrial system.

5. While we assert the natural right of men—capitalist and workingmen alike—to organize for common ends, we hold that the organization of capital or the organization of labor cannot make wrong right or right wrong; that essential righteousness is not determined by numbers either of dollars or of men; that the Church must meet social bewilderment by ethical lucidity, and by gentle and resolute testimony to the truth must assert for the whole Gospel its prerogative as the test of the rightness of both individual and collective conduct everywhere.

6. We regard with the greatest satisfaction the efforts of those employers, individual and corporate, who have shown in the conduct of their business a fraternal spirit and a disposition to deal humanely and justly with their employees as to wages, profit-sharing, welfare work, protection against accidents, sanitary conditions of toil, and readiness to submit differences to arbitration. We record our admiration for such labor organizations as have under wise leadership throughout many years, by patient cultivation of just feelings and

temperate views among their members, raised the efficiency of service, set the example of calmness and self-restraint in conference with employers, and promoted the welfare not only of men or their own craft but of the entire body of workingmen.

7. In such organization is the proof that the fundamental purposes of the labor movement are ethical. . . .

8. We note as omens of industrial peace and goodwill the growth of a spirit of conciliation and of the practice of conference and arbitration in settling trade disputes.

9. We deem it the duty of all Christian people to concern themselves directly with certain industrial problems. To us it seems that the churches must stand:

For equal rights and complete justice for all men in all stations of life.

For the right of all men to the opportunity for self-maintenance, a right ever to be wisely and strongly safeguarded against encroachments of every kind.

For the right of workers to some protection against the hardships often resulting from the swift crises of industrial change.

For the principle of conciliation and arbitration in industrial dissensions.

For the protection of the workers from dangerous machinery, occupational disease, injuries and mortality.

For the abolition of child labor.

For such regulation of the conditions of toil for women as shall safeguard the physical and moral health of the community.

For the suppression of the "sweating system."

For the gradual and reasonable reduction of the hours of labor to the lowest practicable point, and for that degree of leisure for all which is a condition to the highest human life.

For a release from employment one day in seven.

For a living wage as a minimum in every industry and for the highest wage that each industry can afford.

For the most equitable division of the products of industry that can ultimately be devised.

For suitable provision for the old age of the workers and for those incapacitated by injury.

For the abatement and prevention of poverty.

For the protection of the family, by the single standard of purity, uniform divorce laws, proper regulation of marriage, and proper housing. [This and the following paragraphs added in 1912.]

For the fullest possible development of every child, especially by the provision of proper education and recreation.

For the protection of the individual and society from the social, economic, and moral waste of the liquor traffic.

For the conservation of health.[5]

These aims came to be known as the Social Creed of the Churches. They had been adopted, in substance, by the General Conference of the Methodist Episcopal Church earlier in the same year (1908). In them

[5] See C. S. MacFarland, *Christian Unity in the Making: The Federal Council of Churches, 1905-1930*. The second paragraph (Section 9) was amended in 1912 to read, "For the right of all men to the opportunity for self-maintenance, for safeguarding this right against encroachment of every kind, and for the protection of workers from the hardships of enforced unemployment."

was reflected the influence of such writers as Josiah Strong,[6] Shailer Mathews, Washington Gladden, Francis G. Peabody, Frank Mason North,[7] Walter Rauschenbusch,[8] Charles Stelzle, and Harry F. Ward,[9] who had been directing attention to social evils in the United States—the slums of the cities, widespread unemployment, the malnutrition of children, class divisions, and racial prejudice—and insisting that if Christ was to be followed, all areas of society must be brought under his control.

The Federal Council of the Churches of Christ in America was eventually to gather into its program all phases of interchurch work, but social reform would remain prominent, if not predominant, among its interests. While the original "Social Creed" was revised from time to time, it was always with the purpose of strengthening, and not of weakening, the position to which the Council had committed itself at the beginning.

Within two years of its organization, the Federal Council launched a crusade for a shorter working day and week in industry and better pay, with more favorable physical conditions for labor in factories, bringing it into notorious and dangerous conflict with the powerful steel companies for more than a decade.

An example of the Federal Council's activities may be seen in the record of its transactions for 1923. The minutes of the Council for that year record a crowded schedule of actions on social issues, with scarcely any mention of other matters, aside from the usual more or less conventional report of the Commission on Evangelism. It will be remembered as the year in which the American Iron and Steel Institute yielded to the appeal of President Warren G. Harding to abolish the "long shift"; thus—in the words of the Council's secretary, Dr. Charles S. MacFarland—"concluded an effort of the . . . Council which began as early as 1910."

In the records of 1923 are resolutions against mob violence and lynching and against the Italian ultimatum to Greece and Albania (" so nearly identical with similar provocative acts of war in the past"); approval of appeals for material aid for sufferers from famine in Russia, Japanese earthquake victims, children of the Near East, and the war-impoverished people of Germany; and approval of plans for raising money toward the rebuilding and temporary support of demolished churches in the European war zones.

That same year the government of the United States was called upon "to do all in its power to cultivate amity and friendship with the Latin-American nations, and so to prevent the development on our continent of

[6] *Our Country: Its Possible Future and Present Crisis* (1885).
[7] "Where Cross the Crowded Ways of Life."
[8] *Christianity and Social Crisis* (1907).
[9] *The Social Creed of the Churches* (1914).

a spirit of distrust and suspicion that has led the European continent into its present morass." And it was resolved that the United States "should take the initiative in calling an international conference to consider the whole economic and political situation in Europe, including reparations, debts and armaments, in the endeavor to accomplish in Europe a result comparable to that which was achieved by the Four-Power Pact in the Far East." "Our Government will not be true to its ideals," the resolution asserted, "unless it records a definite protest against any settlement of the Near Eastern question on a basis of expediency or commercial advantage, and without some amends for tragic wrongs which have resulted in the persecution and practical destruction of the Armenian people and the confiscation of their property."

The Commission on International Justice and Goodwill was charged to take practical steps for promoting goodwill between Jews and Christians and to combat anti-Semitism.

The senior secretary, MacFarland, reported on his conference with Senator Borah on the economic situation in Europe, in which the Chairman of the Senate Committee on Foreign Relations had said he did not consider that the foreign relations of the United States included any concern for Europe's economy. "Let them put their own house in order," he had concluded, "or else get their League of Nations to take care of them."

There was a telegram to Russia to be authorized: "The Federal Council of the Churches of Christ in America, including constituency twenty million Protestant Christians who have shown friendship for Russian people by generous contributions for famine relief, respectfully urges Russian Government that in the interest of humanity and religious liberty it reconsider reported decision to execute Roman Catholic and Eastern Catholic church officials."

Support of the Permanent Court of International Justice was voted.

In 1923 it was further reported that the Chairman of the Commission on International Justice and Goodwill, Dr. John H. Finley, had visited Europe "from Sweden to Russia, Greece, Italy and France"; attended the Turkish National Assembly; come by important information on Germany through the Rhineland Commission; heard Lord Robert Cecil on the League of Nations; received from the Bankers' Trust Company of New York an up-to-date survey on the economic conditions of Europe; sent a message of goodwill to President Obregón of Mexico upon the resumption of diplomatic relations by his government and the United States; maintained contact with the situation in Haiti and Santo Domingo "through conferences with representatives of the State Department"; taken cognizance of the mission of Dr. Sidney L. Gulick to the Orient and of his book, *The Winning of the Far East*; and studied decisions of the Supreme Court in cases having to do with the rights and privileges of Japanese nationals in the United States.

During the same year a conference on International Relations from the Christian Point of View was held. Copies of the Council's declaration urging membership for the United States in the World Court were sent to all senators, and a World Court Week, culminating in World Court Sunday, was designated. A document entitled *The Churches of America and the World Court of Justice* was prepared, "with the help of such experts as George W. Wickersham and Elihu Root," and sent to 70,000 pastors. A delegation from the Council waited upon President Calvin Coolidge and Secretary of State Charles Evans Hughes and expressed "what was believed to be the mind of the churches in regard to membership in the Court."

The Commission on the Church and Social Service endeavored, according to the minutes, to interest communities in the jails and their "inhabitants" and made a study of the work of penitentiary chaplains.

There were twenty-two conferences on industry during the twelve months. Addresses before ministers' meetings, chambers of commerce, luncheon and women's clubs, councils of social agencies, labor temples, colleges, universities, and other organizations dealt with Christian principles in industrial relations, the seven-day church and its social program, housing and administration, relations between the churches and social movements, and religion and labor.

The Council sponsored interracial conferences in Chicago, Toledo, Johnstown, Boston, Kansas City, Atlanta, and other cities.

At a session of the Executive Committee in Columbus, Ohio, which was opened to the public, Senator Woodbridge N. Ferris spoke on "Law Enforcement." The Committee issued an appeal to the churches "to uphold, by precept and practice, obedience to and enforcement of all the laws of the land," which included those prohibiting the manufacture and sale of intoxicating liquors for beverage purposes.

At another session in 1923 William Adams Brown spoke on the question "How Can the Churches Promote a More Adequate Movement for the United Study of the Meaning of Christianity for Our Contemporary Life?" and "a survey of some of the international relations of the United States was presented from the standpoint of Christian ideals."

In its "message" the Executive Committee said, among other things:

> We believe that the United States should accept its full share of responsibility for bringing about an effective settlement of international problems. . . .
>
> We believe that the United States should take the initiative in calling an international conference to consider the whole economic and political situation in Europe. . . . In calling such a conference we believe that the United States should make it known, as it did at the opening session of the Conference on the Limitation of Armaments, that we are ready to make, in common with other nations, whatever concessions, financial or otherwise, may be necessary to bring about an ordered international life. We are convinced that a sacrificial spirit on our part would evoke a willingness in other nations also

to make the adjustments that may be needed. Our plans for reconstruction should include not only our allies, but our former enemies. . . . The well-being of our country is inseparably bound up with an unselfish consideration of the well-being of the other nations of the world.[10]

This partial recapitulation of a year's transactions of the Federal Council will suggest how, in part, the churches of the United States came by their reputation for activism. Certainly, the Council was outdistancing all religious agencies in the number and range of works in the field of social Christianity; and it was significantly an organization of denominations, and not of church boards or individuals acting independently.

4. World War I and the Churches

The last decade before World War I was marked by a growing sense of the need for international cooperation by the churches in the search for solutions of social problems.

Reference has already been made to the organizations which carried the cause of temperance into most of the world.

At the invitation of French Christian Socialists, representatives from England, Belgium, Germany, Italy, and Switzerland met at Besançon, France, in 1910 for a general conference on social questions, at which was organized *La Fédération Internationale des Chrétiens Sociaux*. A second meeting scheduled for August of 1914 at Basle, Switzerland had to be canceled on account of the war and was never held.

Interest in the churches turned in these years more specifically to world peace. Concern was felt because of the mounting tension between Great Britain and Germany and of the amassing of arms by these and other European nations. The Balkan states were seething with political strife, and this added to the foreboding. Notwithstanding the optimistic outlook induced by the prevalent belief in the inevitability of human progress, there were Christian leaders who saw danger in the situation which was building up and sought to bring about some effective concert by the churches to ease it.

A meeting of J. Allen Baker of England with Baron Eduard de Neufville of Germany at the World Peace Conference at Lucerne, Switzerland, in 1905 led to the launching of a plan to arrange an exchange of visits by churchmen of their two nations to promote better understanding. With the help of other interested persons, they got together committees—or "councils"—to promote the project; and in the summer of 1908 a delegation of 130 representatives of the principal confessions of Ger-

[10] MacFarland, *Christian Unity in the Making*, p. 244.

many, including the Roman Catholic Church, spent some days in Britain as guests of the churches. The following year more than a hundred British clergy and laymen were welcomed similarly by Christians of Germany.

This neighborly interchange was followed by the organization in 1910 of the Associated Councils of Churches in the British and German Empires for Fostering Friendly Relations between the Two Peoples, with Mr. Baker and Sir Willoughby Dickinson Chairman and Secretary, respectively, of the English council, and Direktor F. A. Spiecker and Professor Friedrich Siegmund-Schultze accepting responsibility for the corresponding offices in Germany. Steps were taken immediately to form affiliated councils in other countries.

5. The World Alliance for Promoting International Friendship through the Churches

There had been discussion of a proposal to organize a church world peace conference, and Mr. Baker, while in the United States in 1909, got promises of support for such an undertaking from influential persons in the Federal Council of the Churches of Christ in America. One of the latter, Dr. Charles S. MacFarland, while on a mission to Europe in 1911, consulted both the British and the German officials of the Associated Councils, and from that time the American organization assumed an active role in the movement.

The chain of events here being assembled had many links, and an important one was forged by Andrew Carnegie, the steel magnate. While attending Kaiser Wilhelm's jubilee in Berlin in 1913, he had been favorably impressed by what he heard of the work of the Associated Councils of the Churches in the British and German Empires, and in February, 1914, he offered to establish an endowment of two million dollars to finance a peace program of the churches, on the condition that the Federal Council of the Churches of Christ in America should share in the income and cooperate in the promotion of an international peace conference. To administer the fund, the Church Peace Union was founded in New York.

No time was lost in preparing for a conference. The date appointed for it was August 3-4, 1914, and the place Konstanz, Germany. *La Ligue Internationale des Catholiques pour la Paix,* a Roman Catholic organization which had been formed in 1911, also decided to meet, August 10 and 11 at Liége, under the chairmanship of Cardinal Mercier. The Church Peace Union agreed to underwrite the expense of both gatherings.

Because of the outbreak of war, only 85 of the 153 delegates expected at Konstanz arrived, and these, at the end of their first day together, were escorted to the German border by government authorities through swarming masses of mobilizing troops. It was August 3, the date of Germany's declaration of war on France. Of the experience, Bishop Eivind Josef Berggrav, afterwards Primate of Norway, remarked: "A peace conference athwart a war-front on the very day . . . war broke out . . . is, in truth, something unique!" The Roman Catholic conference, which had been scheduled to convene the next week at Liége, could not, of course, be held.

The delegates who succeeded in reaching Konstanz met long enough to initiate the organization of an international peace society. After adopting resolutions to the effect that the churches had a responsibility for persuading the governments to do all in their power to preserve friendly relations, that national committees should be created to encourage and direct such action, and that these should be gathered into a world body for effective cooperation, they chose a provisional committee of fifteen members and gave it the power to co-opt others. On August 5 this group met in London and organized, electing J. Allen Baker of England Chairman, William Pierson Merrill of the United States Vice-Chairman, and Sir Willoughby Dickinson of England, Louis Emery of Switzerland, Frederick Lynch of the United States, Friedrich Siegmund-Schultze of Germany, and Jacques Dumas of France Co-ordinate Secretaries. Dickinson and Lynch were appointed also General Executive Secretaries. It was voted to increase the membership of the committee to sixty and to name the new body the World Alliance of Churches for Promoting International Friendship. However, it later was seen that, inasmuch as those associated in the movement were, for the most part, individuals acting only on their own initiative, they could not properly constitute themselves an agency of the churches, and the title was changed to the World Alliance for Promoting International Friendship through the Churches.

The war made communication between the churches difficult, when it was possible at all, and nearly destroyed the will and the desire of Christians on opposing sides to communicate. Manifestoes issued by prominent churchmen of the belligerent powers revealed distrust toward one another which seemed to threaten the extinction of the fellowship they had cherished in time of peace. Yet the organization of national committees of the World Alliance proceeded with considerable success, even in the countries at war. Delegates from eleven nations were at Berne, Switzerland, in August of 1915 for the first annual meeting of the Alliance—Great Britain, Germany, the United States, France, Italy, Holland, Switzerland, Denmark, Norway, Sweden, and Finland.

Some journals of international affairs in Europe maintained publication, including *The Peacemaker* in Great Britain, which in 1915 changed its name to *Goodwill* but retained Dr. J. H. Rushbrooke as editor; *Die Eiche,* which under the continuing editorship of Siegmund-Schultze was devoted largely to matters relating to mutual understanding through the churches; and Professor Adolf Deissmann's *Evangelische Wochenbriefe,* the aim of which was to keep its readers, in the neutral countries particularly, informed concerning German views on current questions.

6. Wartime Movements

Soon after the war started—in November, 1914—Nathan Söderblom of Sweden, who had the preceding May been made Archbishop of Uppsala, addressed "an appeal for peace and Christian fellowship" to all churches, calling upon them earnestly to "make manifest the supranational unity of Christians against the disruptive forces of war." He had invited the corresponding authorities of other communions to associate themselves with him in this action, and some of those in the neutral nations complied. The Federal Council of the Churches of Christ in America gave its endorsement. The message spoke for those who felt that the churches must not keep silent, who hoped that something might be done to preserve the spirit of Christian cooperation, against the day when the bloodletting would end and the churches would have in the rebuilding of civilization such a task as they had never faced, and one which they could hope to accomplish only if undertaking it together.

During the war years there were numerous proposals for a convention of the churches. It was hoped that such a meeting, with both neutrals and belligerents present, might hasten the end of hostilities. If this proved impossible, there still would be opportunity to discuss in advance the common problems peace would raise. Meanwhile, representatives of labor groups in some of the countries at war and certain of the neutral states conferred at Stockholm (1917) and announced their agreement that a peace of conciliation should be sought, with no reparations, no annexations, and the right of self-determination for all peoples. This conference seemed to make it all the more important for the churches to act.

"The socialists are already at Stockholm: when shall we get as far?" asked a writer in *Die Christliche Welt.*[11] In *The Challenge* William Temple, then rector of St. James's Church in Piccadilly, London, declared that the time had come for "a Christian Stockholm." Reasonable opinion in all countries, he felt, had reached a consensus on the principles for a peace settlement, and he added, "The churches ought at once to take steps to encourage the growth into all areas of the sentiment for conciliation." But obvious obstacles stood in the way of an international gathering of churchmen. Political authorities had something to say on the matter, and the governments of some of the principal contending nations made it clear to church officials that they would not risk weaken-

[11] *A History of the Ecumenical Movement,* p. 522.

ing their positions militarily by consenting to a public consultation of the kind proposed.[12]

"Practical reasons" also blocked the suggestion of a church conference immediately upon the ending of the war (or simultaneously with the meeting of the nations at the peace table). The prevailing view was voiced by Randall Davidson, Archbishop of Canterbury: "A conference held during the diplomatic and international negotiations would undoubtedly be regarded, however mistakenly, as an attempt to intervene in the negotiations themselves. . . . Christian churches and communities will be able to speak both more freely and with greater weight after the conclusion of peace, when the process of reconstruction under new conditions is going on."

The Archbishop of Uppsala persisted in his advocacy of a wartime world convocation of Christians. The small Neutral Church Conference, which he succeeded in organizing at Stockholm late in 1917 (with the help of the Primates of Denmark and Norway) was significant mainly for its formulation of his thoughts on ecumenical social action.[13] It defined the unity of Christians as an inward spiritual gift of God through the cross of Christ, in which was a power to unite men, whatever their natural differences, not by compelling them to seek uniformity, but by calling them to cooperate in love. It insisted that the Church had a duty to bring the whole of life under the light of the gospel for judgment, challenging all doctrines of the autonomy of social and political activity. It declared the development of international law to be essential to lasting peace, with the churches working "to evoke and foster a spirit of Christian brotherhood and love, self-discipline and mutual justice."

Another movement of ecumenical importance centered in the Fellowship of Reconciliation, which was founded in Great Britain in 1914 by those who believed that the solution of—or the right way of dealing with—the problems posed for Christians by war lay in pacifism. Gaining rapidly in membership and influence, it extended its scope in 1919 by organizing the International Fellowship of Reconciliation, which, within a few years, numbered a score of branches in as many countries. Circumstances favored its growth. In the First World War the churches divided on national lines and with patriotic fervor supported the military operations of their respective nations. After the conflict, many Christians experienced a strong reaction from wartime frenzy, especially when they saw peace eluding all efforts for its establishment and the nations re-

[12] The Reichstag's resolution of July, 1917, favoring peace by conciliation was regarded by the Allies as evidence of realization by the Central Powers that they could not win the war.

[13] Söderblom's ideas were widely shared, but his energetic leadership in Life and Work made him their most outstanding exponent and interpreter.

forming their forces for another war. Considerable numbers of them were ready in frustration to lend an ear to the pacifist philosophy.

7. Postwar Developments

Within less than a year after the signing of the armistice the International Committee of the World Alliance for Promoting International Friendship through the Churches met (September 30-October 3, 1919) at Oud Wassenaar, Holland, for "the first Christian conference after the war,"[14] about sixty delegates attending. It fell to Archbishop Söderblom to introduce the proposal of a world gathering of Christians which would be as fully representative of the churches as possible and competent to speak on their behalf on religious and social issues. He was supported by the officials of the Swiss Protestant Federation and the Federal Council of the Churches of Christ in America in the delegations, and the entire body gave its endorsement.

However, the World Alliance not having authority from the churches to organize a conference, it was voted to refer the matter to the national committees of the Alliance for presentation to the proper ecclesiastical officials. Archbishop Söderblom, Dr. Charles S. MacFarland, and Dr. Otto Herold were requested to direct the necessary steps from that point. They appointed forthwith a meeting for November 17 in Paris for such representatives from the various countries as could be assembled; out of the Paris meeting came the decision to hold a preliminary conference at Geneva, Switzerland, from August 9 to 12 of the next year (1920). The Federal Council of the Churches of Christ in America was made responsible for its organization.

Representatives from churches in fourteen countries came to Geneva for the "preparatory conference," as it was called: Austria, Belgium, Denmark, France, Germany, Great Britain, Hungary, Italy, Yugoslavia, the Netherlands, Norway, Spain, Sweden, and the United States. The American delegation, which was the largest, had been chosen by the Federal Council of the Churches, "in consultation with its member denominations." The Swedish group, next in size, had been appointed officially, with Archbishop Söderblom as Chairman. Adolf Keller was among those representing the Swiss Federation of Protestant Churches. The invitation for Germany had gone to Professor Julius Richter, who had been at the Oud Wassenaar meeting; but, at the personal bidding of Archbishop Söderblom, Professor Friedrich Siegmund-Schultze also attended and persuaded Professor A. Lang and Missiondirektor A. W. Schreiber to come with him. The German Free Church Joint Committee named Pastor A. Melle.

[14] *A History of the Ecumenical Movement*, p. 530.

The Conference had first to dispose of two controversial questions, either of which might have wrecked it. One of these divisive issues was war guilt. The German delegates at Oud Wassenaar had on their personal responsibility admitted and deplored the moral wrong of their country in its violation of Belgium's neutrality, but their churches had not officially supported this action, and widespread disapproval of it was known to exist in Germany. A statement from the Federation of French Protestant Churches expressed the conviction that satisfactory cooperation was impossible so long as this "unresolved moral problem" stood in the way. It admitted that all the churches shared in the guilt of the war, because of their failure to teach the nations the way of peace, but held that those of the Central Powers—the German and the Austro-Hungarian—especially rested under condemnation for not having spoken out against the manifest crimes of their governments in such acts as the invasion of Belgium. The Conference disposed of the subject by sustaining the ruling that it did not belong in the agenda, since no mention of it had been made in the invitation to the churches.

The other major difference in opinion arose over the proposal to invite the Roman Catholic Church to the intended conference. Opposition was voiced by the Swiss Federation of Protestant Churches and by individual members of the delegation from the United States. On the other hand, it was understood that the Anglican Church would not participate unless both the Roman Catholic and the Eastern Orthodox Churches were included in the invitation.[15] Archbishop Söderblom insisted that all Christian churches should be invited. An ecumenical conference of Protestant churches, he declared, involved a contradiction in terms. It was not likely that the Roman Catholic Church would agree to take part, he said, but the decision should be left to Rome. The exclusion of any communion would brand the conference as sectarian from the start. The inclusive policy prevailed.

Some representatives of the Eastern Orthodox Churches, who were at Geneva for another meeting,[16] had been invited by Archbishop Söderblom to attend the preparatory conference as visitors. Given opportunity to speak, Dr.Germanos Strenopoulos, Archbishop of Thyateira and Exarch of the Ecumenical Patriarchate in the West, who was of the company, expressed satisfaction upon learning of the plans for an international Christian assembly. He explained that these agreed broadly with an encyclical sent out by the Ecumenical Patriarchate in January, 1920, which had recommended the organization of a "league of churches" to promote "co-operation in certain areas."

The Committee on Arrangements for the forthcoming conference consisted of twenty-five persons. It organized immediately by electing

[15] The Anglican Church was not represented at Geneva, because of its policy of not supporting ecumenical movements excluding the Roman Catholic Church.

[16] A preparatory conference of Faith and Order.

the Archbishop of Uppsala Chairman and Dr. Charles S. MacFarland and Dr. Frederick Lynch General Secretaries, and dividing into sections for America, Great Britain, and Europe. At Peterborough, England, the next year it created a fourth division for representatives of Eastern Orthodox Churches. The name of the conference to be held was changed from Universal Conference of the Church of Christ on Life and Work[17] to Universal Christian Conference on Life and Work.

At a meeting in Hälsingborg, Sweden, in 1922, the original provisional committee was replaced by a larger and more widely representative body, which was thenceforward to carry the responsibility for arrangements. An invitation from the Church of Sweden and the Swedish Royal Family to hold the Conference in Stockholm was accepted, and the date was changed to 1925. The Archbishop of Canterbury (Randall Davidson), the Archbishop of Uppsala, the Patriarch of Constantinople, and Dr. Arthur J. Brown, Vice-President of the World Alliance for Promoting International Friendship through the Churches, were elected to preside at Stockholm. Dr. Henry A. Atkinson, Secretary of the Church Peace Union, which had agreed to bear part of the expenses of the meeting, became Organizing Secretary. The program projected in outline at this time was left for development by the International Committee, the new executive group, in sessions held later at Zürich, Switzerland, and Birmingham and Farnham Castle (Winchester), England.

"No Christian can doubt that the world's greatest need is the Christian way of Life not merely in personal and social behaviour but in public opinion and its outcome in public action," declared the invitation which in 1924 went from the Committee to the churches. "In short, we hope under the guidance of the Spirit of God, through the counsel of all, to be able to formulate programmes and devise means for making them effective, whereby the fatherhood of God and the brotherhood of all peoples will become more completely realized through the Church of Christ. . . . We depend for success from first to last upon the guidance of the Holy Spirit." [18]

8. The Universal Christian Conference on Life and Work

The Universal Christian Conference on Life and Work met at Stockholm August 19-30, 1925. The 600 delegates represented 91 denominations in 37 countries.[19] From the opening service in the Storkyrken cathedral, they repaired to the palace where they were received by the King and Queen. The Crown Prince acted as Honorary Chairman of the Conference. The people of Stockholm left nothing undone in bestow-

[17] Chosen tentatively at Geneva in 1920.

[18] G. K. A. Bell, *The Stockholm Conference on Life and Work,* 1925, p. 17.

[19] Figures varied somewhat in the several reports. These are approximate.

ing hospitality. Many of the members of the Conference were provided with quarters in private homes. The city's official welcome was expressed at a banquet in the new Town Hall. For the closing session the assembly went to the historic cathedral at Uppsala, the former capital of Sweden.

"It is doubtful," wrote William Adams Brown, "whether up to that time a more representative gathering of church leaders had come together in one place." Among them—to mention but a few—were Dr. Walter Simon, Chief Justice of the Reich, Anton Lang of Oberammergau, and Professor Adolf Deissmann, New Testament scholar, of Germany; Dr. Theodore Wood, Bishop of Winchester, Principal Alfred E. Garvie, New College, London, and Sir Henry Lunn of England; Dr. Adolf Keller and Professor Eugene Choisy of Switzerland; Dr. Nathan Söderblom, Archbishop of Uppsala, and Dr. Yngve Brilioth of Sweden; Bishops H. Ostenfeld and Valdemar Ammundsen of Denmark; Bishop S. Motoda of Tokyo; Gideon Cheng of the National Christian Council of China; and Bishop Charles H. Brent, Dean Shailer Mathews, Dr. Charles S. MacFarland, Dr. S. Parkes Cadman, Dr. Peter Ainslee, Dr. William Adams Brown, Dr. Arthur J. Brown, Dr. Theodore A. Greene, Dr. Henry A. Atkinson, Dr. Samuel McCrea Cavert, and Dr. Henry Smith Leiper of the United States. In the Dutch delegation was Dr. Willem Adolf Visser 't Hooft, reported to have been "the youngest delegate," who would later become General Secretary of the World Council of Churches.

The presence of a number of representatives of Eastern Orthodox Churches[20] had a special significance as marking a change in the rela-

[20] There were nineteen of these churches, each ecclesiastically autonomous under its own metropolitan or patriarch but recognizing the Ecumenical Patriarch of Istanbul as their "senior in dignity"—*primus inter pares*. They included the Ecumenical Patriarchate of Constantinople, the Patriarchate of Alexandria, the Patriarchate of Antioch, the Patriarchate of Jerusalem, the Patriarchate of Russia, the Patriarchate of Serbia, the Patriarchate of Rumania, the Church of Cyprus, the Church of Sinai, the Church of Greece, the Church of Bulgaria, the Church of Poland, the Church of Georgia, the Church of Albania, the Church of Finland, the Church of Estonia, the Church of Latvia, the Church of Lithuania, and the Church of Czechoslovakia. (Since 1945, the Churches of Estonia, Latvia, and Lithuania have been under the Patriarchate of Russia, and since 1948 also the Church of Czechoslovakia.) All in their doctrinal faith recognize the authority of the seven historical ecumenical councils—Nicaea, Constantinople, Ephesus, Chalcedon, Second Constantinople, Third Constantinople, and Second Nicaea.

Some five million Orthodox Christians in the United States are members of the following bodies: Albanian Orthodox Church, Bulgarian Orthodox Church, Carpatho-Russian Orthodox Diocese (sometimes called Ruthenian), Greek Archdiocese of North and South America (representing the Ecumenical Patriarchate), Rumanian Orthodox Church, Russian Orthodox Church, Serbian Orthodox Church, Syrian Antiochian Orthodox Archdiocese, and Ukrainian Orthodox Church.

The Orthodox Churches trace their history back to the earliest days of Christianity. In addition to those named above, there are five of equal antiquity which are regarded by the others as heretical—the Abyssinian Church, the Armenian Apostolic Church, the Assyrian (Nestorian) Church, the Coptic Church, and the Syrian (Jacobite) Church. Some of each group have affiliated themselves with the ecumenical movement from Stockholm onward.

tion of these ancient communions with the churches of the West. The way for their cooperation had been opened by the encyclical of the Ecumenical Patriarchate in 1920, already mentioned in connection with the Geneva preparatory conference, which stated that, notwithstanding doctrinal differences, there was no reason why the Orthodox should not join with Protestants in many Christian services, and recommended the convening of a "pan-Christian conference to examine questions of common interest to all Churches."

The program at Stockholm was built around six topics reflecting the purpose of the Conference to emphasize the responsibility of the churches to cooperate with "all men of goodwill in working for a better social order": "The Church's Obligation in View of God's Purpose for the World," "The Church and Economic and Industrial Problems," "The Church and Social and Moral Problems," "The Church and International Affairs," "The Church and Christian Education," "Methods of Cooperation and Federative Efforts of the Churches."

All these themes except the first had been studied in advance of the Conference by committees which brought to the sessions written statements of their conclusions for discussion. Seven theologians had been asked to prepare half-hour papers on the first theme, to be received without comment for printing.

The committees' reports on certain of the subjects aroused spirited discussion, notably the one concerning social and moral questions. In this connection Dr. James G. Cannon, Jr., expressed his well-known views in favor of the legal prohibition of alcoholic beverages, in opposition to several speakers who advocated principles of moderation and temperance.

Hardly less sharply conflicting were opinions on economic and industrial problems. The British delegation favored a stronger declaration of the churches' responsibility in this area than was proposed, and this evoked resistance from the German members, "who felt less optimistic about the improvability of human relations." The argument finally came to rest on the common premise that it was the admitted duty of Christians, even if it was not the purpose of God that Christ's prayer for the coming of his kingdom should be fulfilled on earth, to work to make the corporate life, of which they were a part, conform as fully as possible with the teaching of the gospel.

Because of the fear that the unity of the gathering might not be strong enough to survive action on controversial matters, it had been decided beforehand that no formal vote should be taken on any question. An exception was made, however, of the message to be sent to the churches, which the delegates adopted with but three or four dissenting voices.

Following the precedent established at Edinburgh,[21] the Conference approved the recommendation of the Committee on Methods of Coop-

[21] See earlier section on "First World Missionary Conference," p. 17 ff.

eration and Federative Effort of the Churches that a continuation committee be created "to carry on the work of the Conference and to consider how far and in what ways its practical suggestions may be made operative." The Continuation Committee was to consist of sixty-seven members. Archbishop Nathan Söderblom was chosen Chairman and the Bishop of Winchester (England), Dr. Theodore Wood, head of the Administrative Committee. The appointment of Dr. Henry A. Atkinson as the General Secretary and Dr. Adolf Keller as Co-ordinate General Secretary followed.[22]

The message to the churches set forth the principles which had guided the Conference in its deliberations:

> The Conference has deepened and purified our devotion to the Captain of our salvation. Responding to his call, "Follow me," we have in the presence of the Cross accepted the urgent duty of applying his gospel to all the realms of human life—industrial, social, political and international.
>
> Thus, in the sphere of economics we have declared that the soul is of supreme value, that it must not be subordinated to the rights of property or to the mechanism of industry, and that it may claim as its first right . . . salvation.
>
> Therefore, we contend for the free and full development of the human personality. In the name of the gospel, we have affirmed that industry should not be based solely on the desire for individual profit, but that it should be conducted for the service of the community.
>
> Property should be regarded as a stewardship for which an account must be given to God.
>
> Co-operation between capital and labor should take the place of conflict, so that employers and employed alike may be enabled to regard their part in industry as the fulfillment of a vocation. Thus alone can we obey our Lord's command to do unto others even as we would they should do unto us.
>
> In the realm of social morality we considered the problem presented by overcrowding, unemployment, laxity of morals, drink and its evils, crime and the criminal. Here we were led to recognize that these problems are so grave that they cannot be solved by individual effort alone, but that the community must accept responsibility for them, and must exercise such social control over individual action as in each instance may be necessary for the common good.
>
> We have not neglected the more intimate questions which a high appreciation of personality raises in the domain of education, the family and the vocation—questions which affect women, the child and the worker.
>
> The Church must contend not for the rights of the individual as such, but for the rights of the moral personality, since all mankind is enriched by the full unfolding of even a single soul.
>
> We have set forth the guiding principle of a Christian internationalism. We

[22] The proposal that Dr. Atkinson, who was Director of the Church Peace Union, be elected the sole Secretary of the Continuation Committee met with rejection on the part of representatives of the Continental churches, which disapproved of "the non-theological and activist emphasis of British and American churches." On nomination by Dr. Adolf Deissmann, Dr. Keller was appointed to have charge of the International Christian Social Institute and, later, of "ecumenical education and extension."

have affirmed the universal character of the Church and its duty to preach and practise the love of the brethren. We have considered the relation of the individual conscience to the state. We have examined the race problem, the subject of law and arbitration, and the constitution of an international order which would provide peaceable methods for removing the causes of war—questions which in the tragic conditions of today make so deep an appeal to our hearts. We summon the churches to share with us our sense of the horror of war, and of its futility as a means of settling international disputes, and to pray and work for the fulfillment of the promise that under the sceptre of the Prince of Peace, "mercy and truth shall meet together, righteousness and peace shall kiss each other."

We have not attempted to offer precise solutions, nor have we confirmed by a vote the results of our friendly discussions. This was due not only to our respect for the convictions of individuals and groups, but still more to the feeling that the mission of the Church is, above all, to state principles and to assert the ideal, while leaving to individual consciences and to communities the duty of applying them with charity, wisdom and courage. . . .

We have said that this Conference is only a beginning. We cannot part without making some provision for the carrying on of our work. We have, therefore, decided to form a Continuation Committee to follow up what has been begun, to consider how effect can be given to the suggestions which have been made, to examine the practicability of calling another such conference at a future date, and in particular to take steps for that further study of difficult problems and that further education of ourselves and our Churches, on which all wise judgment and action must be based.

May we not hope that through the work of this body, and through the increasing fellowship and co-operation of the Christians of all nations in the one Spirit, our oneness in Christ may be more and more revealed to the world in Life and Work.[23]

Appraisals of the Conference varied, as could only have been expected. "The most important ecclesiastical event of the century," some reporters described it, while in the eyes of others it was a failure. There were those also who assailed it as "misleading and evil." In certain quarters, in Germany particularly, it was looked upon with suspicion as possibly "a move of Allied imperialism under the guise of religion." It was unacceptable to Pietists, orthodox Lutherans, and dialectical theologians who saw in its social idealism and in its vigorous attack upon the ills of society "exhibitions of Anglo-Saxon naïveté and American activism."

In Great Britain it was regarded as "an international indorsement" of social principles at which the churches there had arrived through a century of study and experiment, and formulated the year before (1924) in the findings of their Conference on Christian Politics, Economics and Citizenship.[24] Church leaders in the United States took much

[23] G. K. A. Bell, *The Stockholm Conference,* pp. 711 ff.

[24] The churches of England considered the Conference on Christian Politics, Economics and Citizenship their preparation for Stockholm, and made the series of printed reports issued by it available to the program committee of the Universal Christian Conference on Life and Work. (See section on "Christian Socialism," p. 30 ff.)

the same view of it, in relation to the so-called Social Creed of the Churches which their Federal Council of the Churches of Christ had adopted in 1908. In neither England nor the United States was it credited with having marked any real advance in Christian social thought. Lack of a proper theological basis condemned it in the eyes of Roman Catholic critics; but some unofficial comment from that source was favorable to the extent of confessing regret that the Church had not been able to join in so serious and well-meaning an attempt to "unite Christian forces for practical social tasks." The Eastern Orthodox, although feeling it their duty to express dissatisfaction on account of its doctrinal deficiencies, were grateful for the opportunity it had afforded for them to come together, not only with other communions, but with one another.[25]

As those familiar with its aims and limitations understood, any success which the Conference might attain was to be looked for, not in new progress in social philosophy, but in the broadening of mutual trust and the will to cooperate, which would give foundation for a beginning of Christian social education and action on a world pattern; and from this viewpoint the results were generally satisfactory. In fact, there was agreement among those who knew its inherent difficulties that the pioneering venture accomplished more than anyone could reasonably have expected.

For one thing, the Conference had been beset during the period of preparation and finally at Stockholm by persisting war tensions, particularly between the Germans and the French. The former still smarted under the verdict of Versailles that their country alone bore the guilt for starting World War I, and French Christians manifested no disposition after seven years to modify this charge. Because of this feeling, some German church leaders refused to attend, and those who had come to Stockholm declared themselves unable to understand how anyone professing to be a Christian could uphold so unjust a position. But through private personal contacts and irenic discussion in the atmosphere of friendliness and prayer the Conference eased somewhat the strain of international antagonisms.

Another difficulty arose from the fact that, while the Conference had been convened to study how Christians might cooperate in helping "to build a better social order," some of the delegates belonged to churches of pietistic traditions not recognizing any such responsibility in this sphere. Whatever could be done rested, they held, with Christians individually, whose duty it was to live according to the principles in which their churches instructed them. However, some observers felt that

[25] The Orthodox Churches were organized generally on national lines, so that differences between their respective countries often disturbed their own relationships, e.g., the Greek- and Arabic-speaking branches and those in Slavonic countries. A pan-Orthodox conference could not have been assembled in the period under review.

a beginning had been made toward helping delegates with this outlook to see that Christian duty extended at times to corporate action.

The organization of the Conference had left it with only a tenuous official relationship with the denominations. No uniform procedure had been followed in constituting the membership. In some instances, delegates had been appointed by their churches. Others had come under designation by interchurch bodies or by voluntary societies of individuals. Some had been co-opted by the committee which organized the Conference. Few had authority to speak or to act for their churches, and the Conference understood and acknowledged that its actions were not binding upon the denominations, however represented, unless accepted by their own decision. But this was hardly to be regarded as a disadvantage, inasmuch as the venture proceeded by an unmarked trail with uncertain destination. Had it failed, as it might well have, the denominations would, under the circumstances, have borne little blame. When its success became apparent, they willingly owned it.

An unfortunate weakness of the Conference was the inadequate representation of the younger churches. Six nationals from countries of the Far East—India, China, and Japan—were present. The distance and the cost of travel accounted, in part, for this. Moreover, the year was 1925, when the ecumenical movement still was "an essentially Western phenomenon."

With all its limitations, the Conference was declared by so discerning an observer as Bishop Charles H. Brent to have "justified its ambitious title of . . . universal in motive and operation. It envisaged the whole Church."[26]

9. The Continuation Committee

The duties of the Continuation Committee, as prescribed, were

To perpetuate and strengthen the spirit of fellowship which this Conference so happily exemplifies. . . .

To carry on the work of the Conference and to consider how far and in what ways its practical suggestions may be made operative.

To gather information regarding the methods of co-operation among the churches in the various countries for the objects which are the concern of the Conference, to take counsel with them as to the methods of closer international co-operation, to do what may be found wise to facilitate the formation of such agencies in countries where they do not exist. . . .

To consider the practicability of holding another Universal Conference on Life and Work at some future date.[27]

[26] Charles H. Brent, in *Understanding,* p. 7.
[27] Bell, *The Stockholm Conference,* pp. 707 ff.

Provisions for the promotion of this program in the different countries were left in each instance largely to the denominations and followed no uniform pattern.

In the United States, the Federal Council of the Churches of Christ in America, which had a direct official relationship with the major communions and an efficient and experienced social service department, and which had been associated with the launching of the Life and Work movement, was asked to be the organ of the Continuation Committee. While in some respects providential, this arrangement was found to have serious disadvantages, because of the Federal Council's disfavor with large conservative elements in the churches who objected to its supposed "theological liberalism and sociological radicalism."

Fraternities of "Companions of Stockholm" were organized in Europe to educate and work for social reforms "in conformity with the ideals of Stockholm."

Life and Work headquarters were established in 1928 at Geneva, Switzerland, where the Continuation Committee would have ready contact through its secretariat with other world Christian organizations, the League of Nations and the International Labor Office, which had their offices there.

To the sections for Great Britain, Continental Europe, America, and the Eastern Orthodox Churches, into which the Committee had organized its membership for promotional purposes, a fifth was added for the younger churches of mission countries; but it never became operative. The International Missionary Council was found to be a more natural and acceptable channel of action for this constituency in the areas of Life and Work. The Committee and the Council established an effective relationship through the latter's Department of Social and Economic Research, which had been set up in Geneva after the Second World Missionary Conference (Jerusalem, 1928).

In 1930, the Continuation Committee was reconstituted the Universal Christian Council for Life and Work, and, simultaneously, there was formed in the United States the American Section of The Universal Christian Council for Life and Work, with headquarters in New York City. Dr. Henry Smith Leiper was named Secretary of the American Section.

The death of Nathan Söderblom in 1931 was a severe loss to the ecumenical movement. The Bishop of Chichester, Dr. George Kennedy Allen Bell, whose acquaintance with him had dated from a time prior to the Universal Christian Conference on Life and Work, wrote that during the first half of the twentieth century Söderblom stood out as "the man who did more than any other Christian leader or teacher to unite Orthodox and Evangelical Churches of all nations and communions in a common fellowship, for the sake of Christ and his truth and justice and peace." [28] Dr. Nils Ehrenström, a fellow countryman, said: "His efforts opened . . . to the churches new fields and new possibilities of common action: if there had been no Söderblom there would have been no Stockholm 1925; if there had been no Stockholm 1925, the World Council of Churches, at least in its present form, would not exist." [29]

The Life and Work Movement became a prolific source of ideas and projects. One of the earliest and most characteristic acts of the Continuation Committee—characteristic, that is, of the general attitude and purpose of the Life and Work Movement—was the founding at Geneva of the International Christian Social Institute, "to be a center for mutual knowledge, correlation and co-operation of all socially active Christian organizations in the different communions and countries"; to "study in the light of Christian ethics by strictly scientific methods the social and industrial facts and problems in the widest sense"; and "to be a center of information, by which the exchange will be facilitated of knowledge, experience and methods which can be serviceable to the Church in its social-ethical tasks." [30] The proposal to establish such an institute apparently originated with Bishop Einar Billing of Västerås, Sweden, and Pastor Élie Gounelle of France.[31] Dr. Adolf Keller and Dr. Worth M. Tippy, an American Methodist, prepared the charter in 1927.

Under the editorial direction of Dr. Keller, and with the assistance of Dr. Alfred A. Garvie, Pastor Élie Gounelle, Professor D. A. Titius, and Dr. Worth M. Tippy, the Institute published from 1929 until 1931 a trilingual quarterly bearing the name *Stockholm,* which had soon to be discontinued because of a lack of funds. Addressing itself to the task of "explaining the churches to one another," the Institute developed what it called "the science of ecclesiology," and it was successful to a marked degree in bringing about a reorientation to the ecumenical movement of the teaching of church history in theological seminaries. In the course of this work, Dr. Keller visited more than a hundred schools of theology in Europe and America, giving lectures and conferring with the faculties.

Steps to organize a graduate school of ecumenical studies in cooperation with the theological faculty of the University of Geneva could not be carried to completion at the time. But annual seminars at Geneva were begun in 1933 and continued until interrupted by World War II. Over a number of years, before and during that conflict, similar conferences for study were conducted at various centers in the United

[28] In his introduction to *Nathan Söderblom: A Prophet of Christian Unity* by P. Katz, p. 10.
[29] *A History of the Ecumenical Movement,* p. 546.
[30] Minutes of the Continuation Committee on Life and Work, Winchester, 1927, pp. 10-13.
[31] *A History of the Ecumenical Movement,* p. 555.

States. It was not until 1952 that a graduate school of ecumenics came into being at Geneva.

Upon the reorganization of the Institute in 1931, a Department of Research was added, and Dr. Hans Schönfeld became its Director. Dr. Nils Ehrenström also joined the staff. Study of the problem of unemployment was begun immediately, for at that time there were, it was estimated, between twenty and twenty-five millions of unemployed in the Western nations. The following year (1932), the Department conducted at Basle, Switzerland, an international conference of economists, industrialists, and clergymen, from which was issued a report entitled "The Churches and the World Economic Crisis."

In 1933 the Department of Research organized at Rengsdorf, Germany, a conference on "The Church and Contemporary Social Systems," at which socialism and capitalism and their variants under communism and fascism were examined. Here the Life and Work Movement ran head-on into conflict with totalitarianism. The German Reichstag had just yielded to the demands of the Nazis. In their findings the representatives of the churches, disregarding possible interruption by the local Gestapo, declared: "The State must not arbitrarily violate the legal rights of the individual, nor of associations in society, nor may it destroy the institutions of the family nor of the Church, which exist alongside of it, but . . . should respect them in their own right and also for the sake of its own well-being. Consequently the Christian must reject the all-inclusive and completely authoritarian state."

The Universal Christian Council for Life and Work early adopted the plan of promoting its activities through commissions. Among these was one on Church and Labor, whose assignment was to seek ways of breaking down the barriers between the laboring classes and the churches, and so to free the latter from what was described by some students as "middle-class isolationism."

A Theological Commission was created by the Council to lead in rethinking the biblical foundations for Christian social work, and it was successful in enlisting the services of such scholars as Adolf Deissmann and Martin Dibelius in a study (from this standpoint) of "The Kingdom of God," *"Mysterium Christi,"* "The Gospel," and "The Church."

The Council set up a Youth Commission, whose aim was to answer the missionary appeal of secular movements with the challenge of the gospel and to prepare leaders for the future. For practical reasons, it was united, after a short time, with the corresponding department of the World Alliance to form the Ecumenical Youth Commission, which in 1939 was one of the sponsoring agencies of the First World Conference of Christian Youth at Amsterdam, Holland.

The International Press Commission had responsibility for disseminating information about the Life and Work Movement through the press and other media. It originated in 1933 an information sheet called *International Christian Press and Information Service.*

During World War I the Federal Council of the Churches of Christ in America, the Swiss Federation of Protestant Churches, and certain other consociations of churches cooperated in a European relief project, the need for which continued after the signing of the armistice. At a meeting in Copenhagen, Denmark, in 1922 these bodies organized the European Central Bureau of Inter-Church Aid, with offices in Geneva and New York City, and appointed Dr. Adolf Keller General Director of its activities. In 1933 it joined with the World Alliance in forming the International Christian Commission for Refugees, primarily to aid exiles from Nazi Germany. The Bishop of Chichester, Dr. G. K. A. Bell, became Chairman of this body.

The Life and Work Movement encountered from its beginning many hindrances. There was the problem of keeping alive the interest of a widely scattered following, which was rendered more difficult by the inevitable waning of early enthusiasm and by the untimely death of some of those who had led in the launching of the Movement and had been its ablest promoters and interpreters.

Moreover, it never had adequate financial support for its entire program, and there were times, particularly during the great depression, when the state of its resources was such that the leaders feared it would be necessary to close the offices of the Universal Christian Council for Life and Work. By contrast the World Alliance, with its subsidy from the Church Peace Union, suffered no crippling lack of means. Its financial detachment from the denominations, however, was to work eventually to its disadvantage.

More serious were persistent internal tensions. Two opposing points of view existed among those who supported the Movement, one welcoming it as a vehicle for Christian cooperation, the other seeing in it an opportunity for the inward renewal of the churches. These differences in emphasis often tended to obscure wide areas of agreement. For example, those who stressed collaboration were no less concerned about spiritual growth in the churches, but they felt that there was more hope of achieving it by working together than by occupying themselves altogether with the ultimate problems of unity. The division was, in part, theological. The idea of "building the kingdom of God" was, according to the exegesis of some, "unbiblical and presumptuous." Others, while allowing for the scriptural warning that "except the Lord build the house, they labor in vain that build it," believed themselves "laborers together with God" with a duty to help toward the task as they could. (This, for their own sakes, at least.) The words of Jesus concerning himself, "I must work the works of him that sent me, while it is day: the night cometh when no man can work," seemed to them to describe, in a sense, their own case: they saw night descending—the dark, fast-approaching shadow of renewed world conflict which threatened to snuff out the lamps of civilization. Only God, indeed, could stay that doom; but what those who put their trust in him could do must, they felt, be done.

10. Life and Work and the World Alliance

In 1932, Dr. Henry A. Atkinson resigned from the general secretaryship of the World Alliance, and the following year this organization and the Universal Christian Council for Life and Work engaged Dr. H. L. Henroid to serve them jointly as Executive Director. Their cooperation was extended on other lines. As previously noted, they merged their youth commissions. They also collaborated in issuing periodic bulletins, *The Churches in Action* and *International Christian Press and Information Service*. A "consultative group," which consisted of representatives of both bodies, was so acceptable in its counsel that the Executive Secretary at the annual meeting in 1934 said it "could, without revolution, become the joint administrative committee of both movements, pending their full amalgamation." [32]

Some persons close to the ecumenical movement thought that steps should be taken to bring together in one body the World Alliance and the Universal Christian Council for Life and Work, their courses lying, to a great extent, parallel and often overlapping;[33] but there was never any general assent to this proposal. Opposition arose from both sides. While enjoying the favor of many of the denominations in its work and looking to them for its leaders, the older organization, with its substantial subsidy from the Church Peace Union, occupied a position independent of formal ecclesiastical authority. And there were those in its constituency who maintained that it should remain so, because its autonomy enabled it to act with a freedom and celerity impossible to denominationally controlled organizations, a definite advantage in the kind of program it existed to promote. On the other hand, the judgment grew steadily stronger among those associated more closely with the Universal Christian Council for Life and Work that, if they were to continue and expand their activities in the sphere of social Christianity, the churches should be served by an agency belonging definitely and fully to them. Even influential churchmen who held the World Alliance in warm appreciation and were among its officials shared this view. Said Bishop Valdemar Ammundsen of Copenhagen, Denmark, in his presidential address before the International Council of the World Alliance in 1936: "Our social and international work shall neither be isolated from the regular activity of the Church, nor try to

[32] World Alliance: *Minutes and Reports*, 1933-34, pp. 42 ff.

[33] Cf. Record of Proceedings of the Ninth International Conference of the World Alliance, Chamby, Switzerland, 1935.

replace it. . . . Our endeavors must be rooted in personal faith and in the whole doctrinal, educational and sacramental life of the Church. . . . [In co-operating with workers for peace holding other beliefs, we must] accentuate our definite Christian motive and message, which will also determine the methods." [34] When the discussion of plans for a comprehensive integration of the ecumenical movement matured in the decision to organize a World Council of Churches (in which Life and Work and Faith and Order would be united) many Christian leaders—in Great Britain, Holland, and Scandinavia particularly—wished the World Alliance included; but the Commission on Faith and Order was unwilling for theological reasons, and resistance to the suggestion asserted itself in some quarters of the World Alliance, where it was feared that "ecclesiasticism would stifle the spirit and voice of prophecy." The result was a reaffirmation by the World Alliance of its traditional policy of being "a free organization working primarily in and through the Churches for the cause of peace, and in association with the other branches of the ecumenical movement," [35] and the issuance, after consultations, of a joint statement with the World Council of Churches (at the time—1938—in process of formation) that "the two movements are distinct, in that the World Council of Churches desires to represent the Churches direct, and the World Alliance desires to remain an autonomous and independent movement which serves the Churches."

The incompatibility arose thus from causes which made reconciliation impossible beyond existing cooperation which, so far as it went, was generally cordial and not without good effect. It is to be remembered that the World Alliance helped to organize the Universal Christian Conference on Life and Work.

One hindrance to the uniting of the two bodies was a provision in the charter of the Church Peace Union that the trusteeship of the financial foundation established by Mr. Carnegie should be divided among Protestants, Roman Catholics, and Jews. The feeling was widely shared that peace movements promoted with the help of this fund should, by the letter of this stipulation, be under the auspices of these three religious groups. In that case the World Alliance had no logical place in the contemplated World Council of Churches, which represented but one of them.

At its inception, the Universal Christian Council for Life and Work emphasized "the responsibility of the churches to co-operate with all men of goodwill in working for a better social order." This proved an obstacle to the union of the Life and Work and Faith and Order Move-

[34] Address reprinted in *In Memoriam, Bishop Valdemar Ammundsen,* 1937, pp. 35 ff.

[35] Minutes of business sessions of the International Council of the World Alliance, Larvik, Norway, 1938, p. 23.

ments, many supporters of the latter considering that it opened the way to the exclusion of due theological and ecclesiastical control. The merger was finally effected through a constitution that did not specifically forbid collaboration by commissions of the department for Life and Work with outside persons or groups, but provided that only members of those churches which accepted "Christ as God and Saviour" —the so-called doctrinal basis of the World Council of Churches— might be appointed to offices responsible for matters relating to Faith and Order. Intense preoccupation with the Church followed in most phases of the ecumenical movement, and the principle of inclusiveness which characterized the policies of Life and Work in its early years received less and less emphasis.

In its independent and autonomous capacity, the World Alliance served an important mission, the many-sidedness of which was suggested by a statement of objectives adopted by the conference of the constituent national councils at Prague in 1928:

> The work of the World Alliance for International Friendship through the Churches rests upon the readiness of its National Councils and of the Churches working together in them to use their influence with the peoples, parliaments and governments of their own countries to bring about good and friendly relations between the nations. . . .
>
> Among the international questions which affect moral-religious or Church interests, the following are the most important:
>
> (a) The securing of religious freedom and of the rights of Churches, groups or sections of people in any country.
> (b) The prevention of every oppression, injury or obstruction of any Churches, congregations, schools, institutes and other works in any sphere of religious activity.
> (c) The elucidation of other political or church events which are calculated to endanger good relations between the Churches.
> (d) The promotion of positive relations between Christians, congregations and Churches of the different lands.
> (e) Endeavours towards the conciliation of class and race antagonisms which become of international importance.
> (f) Support of proposals and measures calculated to promote justice in the relations between the peoples.[36]

The deterioration of the international situation gave emphasis and direction to the work of the World Alliance within the general scope of these aims. It raised in many countries the issue of just treatment of religious and national minorities, the problem of the care of growing numbers of political refugees, and the threat to peace from rising tensions between certain nations. The question of disarmament called for study and action. Measures were needed for strengthening the League of Nations. The World Alliance worked tirelessly at all these points.

[36] *World Alliance Handbook,* 1938, pp. 24 f.

Its Prague meeting in 1928 coincided with the signing of the Kellogg-Briand Pact outlawing war, and it urged the churches in all countries to call upon their respective governments and the League of Nations to "complete with all despatch international arrangements . . . for a universal system of settling disputes by peaceful judicial methods." At a meeting in Avignon, France, in 1929, it approved and commended to the churches for "most effective possible action" a resolution transmitted to it from a meeting of the Universal Christian Council for Life and Work at Eisenach, Germany, the previous year, declaring:

> We believe that war considered as an institution for the settlement of international disputes is incompatible with the mind and method of Christ, and therefore . . . with the mind and method of his Church.
>
> While convinced that the time must come for the revision of existing treaties in the interest of peace, we maintain that all disputes and conflicts between nations, for which no solution can be found through diplomacy or conciliation, ought to be settled or solved through arbitration, whether by the World Court or by some other tribunal mutually agreed on. . . .
>
> We earnestly appeal to the respective authorities of all Christian communions to declare in unmistakable terms that they will not countenance, nor assist in any way in, any war with regard to which the government of their country has refused a bona fide offer to submit the dispute to arbitration.[37]

The worsening of international relations in the 1930's and eventually the outbreak of World War II made it increasingly difficult for the World Alliance to continue its work. During this period it had, unlike the World Council of Churches ("in process of formation"), no adequate staff strategically located in different countries and therefore able to function despite the cleavages of battle lines. Owing to its waning activity its financial support from the Church Peace Union had been withdrawn. In March of 1944 its office in Geneva was closed. When the war ended, attempts were made to re-establish the Alliance on an international basis. Under the leadership of Dr. Robert Dexter, of the United States, a Unitarian, it was proposed to reorganize more definitely on an interfaith basis, "bringing together in each country groups of religious-minded individuals," and not involving "questions of faith, order and other ecclesiastical or creedal issues." This was in 1944. Two years later the Management Committee of the Alliance, in a meeting at Tring, England, took the position that if the work was to be continued at all, it must be on the original unmistakably Christian basis. The Church Peace Union favored the establishment of a proposed World Alliance for International Friendship through Religion. In August, 1946, the World Council of Churches and the International Missionary Council set up the Commission of the Churches on International Affairs and charged it, so far as they were concerned, with most of the work for which the World

[37] *Ibid.*, p. 52.

Alliance had been responsible. Two years later—on June 30, 1948—the World Alliance, unable to continue longer with the adequate staff and the cooperation of the churches which it had once enjoyed, voted to dissolve.

One who had been associated with it in many cooperative endeavors with the Universal Christian Council for Life and Work and knew from experience the worth of its service paid the Alliance this tribute:

> It had lived and done its work through a period of intense and growing strain. Now its concerns were to be in the hands of others, and it was to live on, not as itself, but through those who had breathed deeply of its spirit, and were able to carry forward something of its achievements into an ecumenical movement which was developing new forms to meet new needs in a world radically changed by the upheavals of the Second World War.[38]

11. Life and Work Finds its Mission

Current events were to have, as it proved, a determinative influence upon the course of the Life and Work Movement. According to its constitution, the Universal Christian Council had been organized "to perpetuate and strengthen the fellowship between the churches in the application of Christian ethics to the social problems of modern life";[39] but seven years after the Stockholm Conference (1925) this purpose had not been focalized in any concrete or unifying way. Opinions on its implementation differed, and the actions of the ablest leaders often revealed them hesitant and uncertain.

The Bishop of Chichester, Dr. Bell, in his presidential address at the annual meeting in Geneva in 1932 spoke of the urgent need for "a deeper spiritual experience" and an effort to bring together "the keen minds in the different churches . . . to interpret to the present generation in terms it will understand the necessity of God in Christ" and to formulate "the fundamental principles for which the Christian religion stands in a material or secular age." [40] At the same time, Professor Arvid Runestan, the late Archbishop Söderblom's son-in-law, called for a re-examination of the aims of Life and Work, suggesting that there might have been "a subtle reversal of values" in which sight had been lost of the true "first things" envisaged by the founders.

At a meeting of the Executive Committee of the Council in Novi Sad, Yugoslavia, a year later (1933), Dr. William Adams Brown, then Chairman of the Administrative Committee, stressed "the need of fixing some

[38] Dr. Nils Ehrenström, in *A History of the Ecumenical Movement,* p. 568.

[39] Minutes of the Continuation Committee of Life and Work, Chexbres, Switzerland, September, 1930, pp. 16 ff.

[40] Minutes of the Universal Christian Council for Life and Work, Geneva, Switzerland, 1932, pp. 1 ff.

comprehensive goal which the ecumenical movement as a whole [might] take as its ultimate objective, and the need for reinforcing the motives which furnished the movement with its driving power."[41]

It was in the darkness descending upon Europe in those days that the destined way began to appear. The Novi Sad conference had opened with the reading of the Stockholm "Message" by the secretary, to which the delegates had been invited to listen in a spirit of rededication; but one among them, a member from Nazi Germany, spoke against this historic pronouncement, calling it "obsolete . . . the offspring of the humanitarian ideals of the Enlightenment and the French Revolution," and asserting that "the rising Reformation theology today would put a critical question-mark at almost every sentence in it."

The newly elected Reichstag early in 1933 had capitulated to Adolf Hitler. In March the Conference on the Church and Contemporary Social Systems, which had been organized by the Research Department of the Universal Christian Council for Life and Work at Rengsdorf, Germany, had been moved to issue the warning that "the State must not arbitrarily violate the legal rights of the individual, nor of associations in society, nor may it destroy the institutions of the family nor of the Church, which exist alongside of it. . . . The Christian must reject the all-inclusive and completely authoritarian State."

During the summer, the Department conducted in the churches a study of the function and authority of the state "in its relation to the individual, the Church, the community and the international order." The interest awakened led to the appointment of a conference on "The Church and the State of Today" in Paris in April, 1934, which was attended by officials of other ecumenical bodies—the World Alliance, the Commission on Faith and Order, the International Missionary Council, and the World's Christian Student Federation—and representatives of a score of countries, among whom were such eminent thinkers and scholars as Nicholas Berdyaev, Emil Brunner, Max Huber, and Joseph H. Oldham. The program, chaired by Dr. Marc Boegner, President of the Protestant Federation of France, was of extraordinary significance for the quality of the deliberations and their effects in the councils of Life and Work in the months that followed.

Consideration of the theme of the Paris conference was resumed at the annual meeting of the Universal Christian Council for Life and Work in August, 1934, at Fanø, Denmark. After hearing a speech by a delegate representing Reichsbischof Müller of the Nazi administration, the Council declared in a resolution "its conviction that autocratic Church rule, especially when imposed upon the conscience in solemn oath; the use of methods of force; and the suppression of free discussion are in-

[41] Minutes of the Executive Committee of the Universal Christian Council, Novi Sad, Yugoslavia, 1933, p. 6.

compatible with the true nature of the Christian Church." It further resolved that it would support as it could the cause of the "Confessing Church" in Germany against the so-called "German Christians" and the Nazi regime. This action evoked a vehement protest from Bishop Heckel, on behalf of the German delegates, in which he said:

> The German Delegation rejects the one-sided stress on a particular group in the German Church and the approval given by the Council to the special theological view of that group. The Delegation find in this an attitude to the internal situation of the German Church which transgresses the limits of the task of the Universal Christian Council in a very questionable way.[42]

So had swift and incredible events set the Church at the focus of ecumenical action. Rengsdorf, Paris, and Fanø had made it clear that the Life and Work Movement belonged to the Church. The Church was the true center of social renewal. Apart from it and the values it upheld, what were called human rights had no chance. Civilization stood or fell with it. The real nature of the Church must be understood, its unity repaired, and its mission to bring to all mankind the salvation of the living and victorious Christ given pre-eminence. Before adjournment at Fanø, the Universal Christian Council had found a name for the world conference which it had voted to hold three years thence: the Conference on Church, Community and State. If this title sounded academic and unpromising in quarters well removed from the European political storm center, its relevance and the discernment which dictated its choice were soon to be recognized. In announcing the conference, the Council issued a statement explaining the conditions which had led to the adoption of the theme:

> The great extension of the function of the State everywhere in recent times and the emergence in some countries of the authoritarian or totalitarian State raise in a new and often an acute form the age-long question of the relation between the Church and the State. The gravity of the modern problem lies in the fact that the increasing organization of the life of the community, which is made possible by modern science and technique and which is required for the control and direction of economic forces, coincides with a growing secularization of the thought and life of mankind. . . . No question, therefore, more urgently demands the grave and earnest consideration of Christian people than the relation between the Church, the State and the Community, since on these practical issues is focused the great and critical debate between the Christian faith and the secular tendencies of our time. In this struggle the very existence of the Christian Church is at stake.[43]

[42] Dr. Nils Ehrenström in *A History of the Ecumenical Movement,* p. 583.
[43] Minutes of the Meeting of the Universal Christian Council for Life and Work, Fanø, Denmark, 1934, pp. 47 ff.

12. The Conference on Church, Community and State

Soon after the Paris Conference of 1934 on "The Church and the State of Today," in which he had participated, Dr. Joseph H. Oldham went from the secretaryship of the International Missionary Council to the Universal Christian Council for Life and Work to become Chairman of the important Commission on Research. He was charged with special responsibility for developing the program of the forthcoming world convention, to be held at Oxford, England, in July, 1937. The preparatory study under his supervision touched upon nine interrelated subjects embodied or implicit in the name chosen for the gathering, on which over 300 persons collaborated in writing some 250 papers for exchange and criticism among themselves before releasing them to the churches. These manuscripts in their final form became helpful briefing material for the members of the Conference, parts of them having been made available in advance; and some of them were eventually printed in a series of volumes, which would be a permanent record of the thinking of the Life and Work Movement in the period between Stockholm and Oxford.

The list of topics covered included: "The Church and Its Function in Society," "Church and Community,"[44] "Church and State," "Church, Community, and State in Relation to Education," "Church, Community, and State in Relation to the Economic Order," "The Christian Understanding of Man," "The Kingdom of God in History," "Christian Faith and the Common Life," "The Universal Church and the World of Nations."

This "venture in ecumenical thinking," which centered in Geneva, Switzerland, where the research staff had its office, extended afar and enlisted large numbers of interested persons in many other parts of the world. In the United States it proceeded under the auspices of the American Section of the Universal Christian Council for Life and Work, with supervision by the Secretary, Dr. Henry Smith Leiper, and a special advisory committee, of which Dr. John R. Mott was Chairman and Dr. Henry Pitney Van Dusen and Dr. John Coleman Bennett were Secretaries. Sir Walter Moberly, a distinguished figure in educational circles, presided over a similar commission sponsoring the study in the churches of Great Britain. Christian leaders on the Continent with a close-up view of the political revolution in progress in Germany realized that the issues confronted by the churches were of the utmost gravity and joined eagerly in their exploration. In Paris a group of exiled Russian churchmen pre-

[44] The word "Community" presented a problem in definition. As the closest equivalents, the German, French, and American phrasings of the title used, respectively, were *"Volk," "Nation,"* and "Society."

pared for publication a volume on *Church, State and Man.* Roman Catholic scholars of Europe published their interpretation of the general theme in a book entitled *Die Kirche Christi: Grundfragen der Menschenbildung und Weltgestaltung,* which evidenced their realization that the totalitarian state had become a menace to Catholicism and Protestantism alike and forced the churches to take counsel of each other in an effort to combat it.

"Catholic and Protestant are separated by many important matters of dogma," declared Cardinal Michael Faulhaber, Archbishop of Munich, while the preparation for the Oxford Conference was in progress, "but there are great central convictions common to both and now subject to the sharpest attack. What we face today is a conflict, not between two halves of Christianity, but between Christianity and the world." [45]

The preparatory study achieved two important practical results. It enabled the representatives of the churches to come to Oxford in 1937 with a knowledge of the subjects which would engage them and experience in group thinking which did much to enhance the effectiveness of the consultations. And it was also a means of winning new adherents to the ecumenical movement.

The 300 delegates to the Conference on Church, Community and State at Oxford during the latter half of July, 1937, came from 120 denominations in 40 countries. In addition to them, the Universal Christian Council for Life and Work had co-opted for membership 100 persons, laymen as well as clergymen—scientists, economists, statesmen, jurists, educators, authors, journalists, sociologists—with special competence for serving as counselors and resource leaders. Fraternal delegates and representatives from other ecumenical bodies brought the total number of official members to 425. Approximately three-fourths of these were from the United States and nations of the British Commonwealth, an unfortunate disproportion accentuated somewhat by the absence of the delegation appointed by the German Evangelical Church. Although their leaders had taken part in the preparations for the Conference, the German delegation had at the last moment been refused passports by the Nazi government. The Orthodox and Lesser Eastern Churches were represented by forty-odd dignitaries and scholars.[46] There were thirty members from the younger (mission) churches. Three Germans—one Methodist and two Baptists—had been permitted by their governmental authorities to attend. Besides the official membership, there was altogether about an equal number of alternates, visitors, and youth repre-

[45] Dr. Samuel McCrea Cavert, in an article in *The Christian Century,* October 25, 1935.

[46] The Orthodox delegation represented the Ecumenical Patriarchate, the Patriarchate of Alexandria and Antioch, the Churches of Cyprus, Greece, Rumania, Yugoslavia, Bulgaria, Poland, the Russian Church in Exile, the Coptic Orthodox Church, the Armenian Church, and the Church of the Assyrians.

sentatives. Several Roman Catholics, by invitation, attended the sessions throughout, and one served as a co-opted delegate.[47]

The city of Oxford and its churches joined with the University in providing accommodations for the Conference, the colleges making available, as needed, their dormitories and refectories. Historic Town Hall was opened for the plenary programs. Dr. John R. Mott presided at the opening service, and the Archbishop of Canterbury, Dr. Cosmo Gordon Lang, came from Lambeth to address the delegates.

The Conference met within about a year and a half of the outbreak of World War II and could hardly have escaped becoming, as one reporter wrote, "a presentation in miniature of the human pandemonium." [48] Cloister doors could not bar the strife out of which—and through which—the conferees had come. Many Americans had crossed the Atlantic on the great new German steamships *Bremen* and *Europa,* whose construction for quick conversion into troop transports was a matter of common report. Bulletin boards in the vestibule of Town Hall displayed daily notices of meetings of classes for the training of local civilians for various home-defense services, against the possibility of enemy invasion by air. While everybody hoped for peace, the feeling in the streets and the Conference alike was that war had to be considered a probability.[49]

The delegates prayed for "their brethren in the Evangelical Church in Germany" and at the opening session sent a message of sympathy to Dr. Martin Niemöller and other members of the Evangelical delegation, who, it was reported, had been seized and placed under guard or imprisoned. Dissenting, the German Methodist member publicly declared "the Federation of Evangelical Free Churches in Germany grateful for the full liberty of proclaiming the Gospel of Jesus Christ," and for the fact "that God in his providence had sent a leader who was able to banish the danger of Bolshevism in Germany . . . and to give the nation a new faith in its mission and future." [50]

The subjects to which the delegates gave their attention at once threw open the windows of the Conference upon the world, and the preparatory addresses during a week of plenary meetings interpreted the universal scene from the perspective of the churches. During the second week the study proceeded in five sections, with chairmen and subjects as follows: "Church and State"—Sir Walter Moberly; "Church and Community"—Dr. Max Huber; "The Church and the Economic Order"—Hon. J. R. P. Maud; "The Church and Education"—Dr. Henry Sloane Coffin; "The

[47] *A History of the Ecumenical Movement,* p. 588. (Ehrenström).

[48] The Presidents of the Conference were the Archbishop of Canterbury, Archbishop Eidem of Sweden, Archbishop Germanos of Thyateira, Dr. William Adams Brown, Dr. Marc Boegner of France, and Bishop Azariah of India.

[49] Indeed, newspapers displayed the headline "Japanese planes bomb Chinese villages," while delegates to the Conference from these countries sat side by side at Oxford.

[50] From the stenographic report of the Conference proceedings.

Universal Church and the World of Nations"—Dr. John Alexander Mackay. The several divisions had been asked to submit written reports of the conclusions reached in their deliberations. Lack of time prevented casting these in their final form, and the Conference returned them to the sections for further revision, and for release, on completion, to the churches "for serious and favorable consideration."

While the studies occupied the minds of the delegates, a committee under the chairmanship of Dr. William Temple, Archbishop of York, was drafting the Conference message, which upon its presentation was adopted unanimously.

Worship had a central place. One observer thought "the most abiding impression retained by the delegates was neither [the Conference's] world-embracing company of communions and nations, nor the quality of its thought, but its interweaving of devotion and deliberation." [51]

Wrote Dr. Joseph H. Oldham: "In the periods of silence, there was often an overpowering sense that things were happening in the spiritual world, and that in the coming years one might expect to see in the breaking out of new life in countless directions an answer to the prayers that were being offered together to God." [52]

Observance of the Lord's Supper had no part in the official program, but on the last Sunday baptized members of the Conference who were regular communicants of churches were invited by the Church of England to receive Communion[53] at a service in St. Mary's Church, at which the Archbishop of Canterbury was the celebrant and Bishop V. S. Azariah of Dornakal, India, and Bishop Bell of Chichester assisted.

At a service in St. Paul's Cathedral, London, the following month, which had been arranged for the delegates of both the Conference on Church, Community and State and the Second World Conference on Faith and Order (held in Edinburgh during the first half of August), the Archbishop of Canterbury preached on the text from Joshua "Speak to the children of Israel, that they go forward," and distinguished representatives of the Eastern Orthodox and Protestant communions read the Scripture lessons and prayers.[54]

The Conference members in their clericals formed an impressive processional. On going to their places before the chancel, they witnessed an amusing incident which recalled that civil and religious liberties (the abrogation of which in many countries the conferees had taken occasion to condemn) still were inviolable in the nation where they had been meeting. Seated among them in the reserved section was an elderly citizen

[51] Dr. Nils Ehrenström, in *A History of the Ecumenical Movement,* p. 589.

[52] J. H. Oldham, in *The Churches Survey Their Task,* pp. 18 ff.

[53] There was another Communion service with similar appointments at St. Aldate's.

[54] A number of the delegates to the Conference on Church, Community, and State had stayed over to represent their churches also at the Conference on Faith and Order.

determined to see and hear what transpired. The ushers tried to dislodge him, but he insisted that it was his privilege as a member of the parish to attend any public service, and remained throughout the solemn proceedings, an interested and appreciative spectator.

The Oxford Conference is one of the greater landmarks of the ecumenical movement. Its essential theme was "the life-and-death struggle between Christian faith and the secular and pagan tendencies of our time." [55] It brought to the grave questions this raised authentic religious insight and rare scientific and technical understanding, thanks to the broad basis and thoroughness of the preparatory study. How seriously the Research Commission had undertaken and carried through the educational task assigned it was seen in the Chairman's description of the methods employed:

More important than the Conference itself is the continuing process, in which the Conference was not more than an incident, of an attempt on the part of Christian churches collectively . . . to understand the true nature of the vital conflict between the Christian faith and the secular and pagan tendencies of our time, and to see more clearly the responsibilities of the church in relation to the struggle. What is at stake is the future of Christianity. The Christian foundations of western civilization have in some places been swept away and are everywhere being undermined. The struggle today concerns those common assumptions regarding the meaning of life without which, in some form, no society can cohere. These vast issues are focused in the relation of the church to the state and to the community, because the non-Christian forces of today are tending more and more to find embodiment in an all-powerful state, committed to a particular philosophy of life and seeking to organize the whole of life in accordance with a particular doctrine of the end of man's existence, and in an all-embracing community life which claims to be at once the source and goal of all human activities: a state, that is to say, which aims at being a church.

To aid in the understanding of these issues, the attempt was made in preparation for the Conference . . . to enlist as many as possible of the ablest minds in different countries in a common effort to think out some of the major questions connected with the theme of the Conference. During the three years preceding . . . studies were undertaken wider in range and more thorough in their methods than any previous effort of similar kind on the part of the Christian churches. This was made possible by the fact that the Universal Christian Council for Life and Work . . . possessed a department of research at Geneva with two full-time directors and was able . . . to establish an office in London with two full-time workers, and to set up an effective agency for the work of research in America. There was thus provided the means of circulating a large number of papers for comment, and of maintaining close personal touch with many of the leading thinkers and scholars. . . . The results . . . [were] embodied in six volumes. . . . The plan and contents of each . . . were discussed in at least two or three . . . international conferences or groups. The contributions were circulated in first draft to . . . critics in different countries, and comments were received often from as many as thirty or forty persons. Nearly all the papers were revised, and in some instances entirely rewritten, in the light of these criti-

[55] *The Churches Survey Their Task,* pp. 9 ff.

cisms. . . . They thus provided an opportunity such as hardly existed before for the study in ecumenical context . . . of grave and pressing problems which . . . concern the Christian church throughout the world.[56]

With the advantage of this background of study, the published findings of the Conference carried a weight beyond that of usual pronouncements of the kind. Of them Dr. J. H. Nichols wrote, in *Democracy and the Churches:* "The authority of the Oxford reports was unprecedented, at least in Protestant social ethics, and their competence enabled them to rank with the best of secular thought, a phenomenon scarcely seen since the seventeenth century." [57]

The Conference spoke also with theological authority. It approached so-called secular issues as in fact—without exception—religious issues, and under the guidance of scholarship as competent in its field as that consulted in the exploration of economic, social, and political questions.

All the subjects on the program were presented and discussed in their relation to the Church: "Church and State," "Church and Community," "The Church and the Economic Order," "The Church and Education," and "The Universal Church and the World of Nations." Perhaps the emphasis would be better placed if it were said that the Church was in each instance studied in relation to the subject. Many delegates thought that too much was said about the Church. Some criticized the Conference for its "introversive ecclesiasticism."

Because of the different conceptions of the Church, it was at this point undoubtedly confusing. The slogan "Let the Church be the Church!" which was dropped by a speaker and soon was echoing through the corridors, owed its popularity partly to its ambiguities.[58] Like other catchwords, it was all things to all people. What it meant depended on what the speaker happened to believe about the Church. What should it mean? Was it a challenge to the Church to concern itself more with direct action in secular affairs? Did it call the Church to renewed faithfulness in its spiritual ministry on traditional lines? Oxford could not be expected to give a definitive answer. The reports underscored the duty of the Church to preserve, at all costs, its independence in the face of rising statism, and in this they perhaps came nearest to a consensus:

The primary duty of the Church to the State is to be the Church, namely, to witness for God, to preach his Word, to confess the faith before men, to teach both young and old to observe the divine commandments, and to serve

[56] From the preface to the Official Reports of Oxford Conference, ed. by J. H. Oldham.

[57] *Democracy and the Churches,* p. 235.

[58] The words "Let the Church be the Church!" did not appear in printed matter relating to the Conference. The first draft of the report on "The Universal Church and the World of Nations," which was written by the Chairman of the section, Dr. John A. Mackay, contained these words: "The first duty of the Church, and its greatest service to the world, is that it be in very deed the Church."

the nation and the State by proclaiming the Will of God as the supreme standard to which all human wills must be subject and all human conduct must conform. . . . These functions of worship, preaching, teaching and ministry the Church cannot renounce, whether the State consent or not.[59]

Stressed also with apparent unanimity was the obligation resting on the Church to act according to the implications of its declared universality and its international fellowship, as, for example, in wartime:

If war breaks out, then pre-eminently the Church must manifestly be the Church, still united as one body of Christ, though the nations wherein it is planted fight one another, consciously offering the same prayers that God's name may be hallowed, his kingdom come, and his will be done in both, or all, warring nations.[60]

If the Church was to be the Church, there had to be room in it, the Conference agreed, for both those who, while condemning war as sinful, might feel it their duty to support their nations when attacked and the conscientious objector who refused to cooperate.

This fellowship of prayer must hold together in one spiritual fellowship those of its members who take different views concerning their duty as Christian citizens in time of war. . . .

The nature and mission of the Church would have to be studied further in the days ahead. For the time, the important thing was the decompartmentalizing of theology resulting from the search of Life and Work for guidance in the effort "to perpetuate and strengthen the fellowship between the churches in the application of Christian ethics to the social problems of modern life." It was becoming plain—if it had not been so—that "the human predicament" could be dealt with hopefully only in the light of Christian doctrine; and when thus approached it proved a spectrum bringing out the deeper glories of that heavenly light. Life and Work and Faith and Order were seen to be, not two causes, but one. Their objectives were so complementary that they marched or halted together. This had become clear.

The way had been prepared for the presentation of a resolution calling for the merging of the Universal Christian Council for Life and Work and the Commission on Faith and Order in one organization. On the motion to adopt only two dissenting voices were recorded.[61]

[59] *The Churches Survey Their Task*, p. 82.

[60] See the Conference "message," next page.

[61] The delegates had been given the resolution early in the Conference and so had had ample opportunity to discuss its proposals and to arrive at a conclusion concerning it. The churches, however, were not given information concerning it before the Oxford Conference, so that they could instruct their delegates and give them power to act. The result was that another conference was held the following year at Utrecht to give the churches a chance to approve the Oxford—and Edinburgh—action.

The "message of the Conference," a summation of the conclusions reached in study and discussion, was to become a most influential document in the churches. It was especially significant as showing how Life and Work had set the Church at the center of the ecumenical process.

The first duty of the Church, and its greatest service to the world, is that it be in very deed the Church—confessing the true faith, committed to the fulfillment of the will of Christ . . . and united in him in a fellowship of love and service. . . .

The Christian sees distinctions of race as part of God's purpose to enrich mankind with a diversity of gifts. Against racial pride and race antagonism the Church must set its face implacably as rebellion against God. Especially in its own life and worship there can be no barriers because of race and color. Similarly, the Christian accepts national communities as part of God's purpose to enrich and diversify human life. Every man is called of God to serve his fellows in the community to which he belongs. But national egotism tending to the suppression of other nationalities or of minorities is, no less than individual egotism, a sin against the Creator of all peoples and races. The deification of nation, race or class, or of political or cultural ideals, is idolatry, and can lead only to increasing division and disaster.

On every side we see men seeking for a life of fellowship in which they experience their dependence on one another. . . . In such a world the Church is called to be in its own life that fellowship which binds men together in their common dependence on God and overlaps all barriers of social status, race or nationality.

In consonance with its nature as a true community, the Church will call the nations to order their lives as members of the one family of God. The universal Church . . . must pronounce a condemnation of war unqualified. . . . War can occur only as a fruit and manifestation of sin. This truth is unaffected by any question of what may be the duty of a nation which has to choose between entry upon war and a course which it believes to be the betrayal of right, or what may be the duty of a Christian citizen whose country is involved in war. The condemnation of war stands. . . If war breaks out, then pre-eminently the Church must manifestly be the Church, still united as one body of Christ, though the nations wherein it is planted fight one another, consciously offering the same prayers that God's name may be hallowed, his kingdom come, and his will be done in both, or all, warring nations. This fellowship of prayer must hold together in one spiritual fellowship those of its members who take different views concerning their duty as Christian citizens in time of war. . . .

We recognize the State as being in its own sphere the highest authority. . . . But as all authority is from God, the State stands under his judgment. . . . The Christian can acknowledge no ultimate authority but God; his loyalty to the State is part of his loyalty to God and must never usurp the place of that primary and only absolute loyalty. . . .

In the economic sphere, the first duty of the Church is to insist that economic activities . . . stand under the judgment of Christ. The existence of economic classes presents a barrier to human fellowship which cannot be tolerated by the Christian conscience. . . . The ordering of economic life has tended to enhance acquisitiveness and to set up a false standard of economic and social success. . . . Christians have a double duty—both to bear witness to their faith within the existing economic order and also to test all economic institutions in the light of their understanding of God's will.

. . . The responsibility of the Church is to insist on the true relationship of spiritual and economic goods. Man cannot live without bread, and man cannot live by bread alone. . . .

In . . . education . . . the Church has a twofold task. . . . It must be eager to secure for every citizen the fullest possible opportunity for the development of the gifts that God has bestowed on him. . . . The Church must condemn inequality of educational opportunity as a main obstacle to fulness of fellowship in the life of the community. . . .

In education . . . , if God is not recognized, he is ignored. The Church must claim the liberty to give a Christian education to its own children. It is in the field of education that the conflict between Christian faith and non-Christian conceptions of the ends of life, between the Church and an all-embracing community life which claims to be the source and goal of every human activity, is in many parts of the world most acute. In this conflict, all is at stake, and the Church must gird itself for the struggle.

III

THE FAITH AND ORDER MOVEMENT[1]

The Evangelical Awakening of the eighteenth century quickened in many Christians the sense of their spiritual oneness in Christ and set them working together in the missionary movement and in cognate causes for the amelioration of social conditions; but it did little toward healing theological disunity in the churches. It tended in fact to accentuate—or to create—division. Persons most affected by the Awakening were disposed to connect their experience with its particular doctrinal emphases, which made the keeping of a creedal balance difficult and encouraged the formation of groups outside the churches, and even new denomina-

[1] On the meaning of "faith and order," Dr. Angus Dun, Chairman of the North American Faith and Order Study Conference at Oberlin, Ohio, September 3-10, 1957, spoke as follows:

"That word, faith, is familiar and meaningful. . . . We can all agree that faith, in some sense of the word, is constitutive of the Church. . . .

"The same cannot be said for the term 'order.' . . . The word refers to visible, identifiable structures within a community of Christians, which are held to belong to its being as a Church, or its well-being, or fullness, or wholeness as a Church. Most familiarly . . . , [it] refers to the ordering of the ministry in one of three, or more, 'orders of ministers' and to the basic polity or structure of government which determines where authority is centered in the matters most sensitively related to the Church's faith and worship. Order in this sense is clearly to be distinguished from what is often spoken of as 'mere organization,' the changing practical arrangements for getting things done. This is true, even though 'order' and 'organization' inevitably interpenetrate each other.

"Certain Churches clearly hold that a particular, visible ordering of the ministry belongs to the essential order of the Church. Some Christian communions hold that the 'congregation' has an identifiable structure, is the visible locus of the Church, and the seat of authority. That is a view of Church order. Many of the traditions . . . do not hold that any particular form of ministry or of government belongs to the essential order of the Church. Those standing within such traditions may be helped to appreciate the force of the term, if they recall that the major Churches of the Reformation inheritance have held that a faithful preaching of the Word and a right use of the two sacraments of the Gospel are visible marks of the Church. These, then, belong to order. Even the place given to an identifiable book, the Holy Bible, and the use made of it, may be seen as a visible structure by which the Church is, in part, known to be present."

tions,[2] in which their peculiar convictions could be given full play. Their ecumenism has been described as "of the heart," and for all that it wrought much good, it could not avoid in the long run the hurt which follows upon divorcement of heart and head.

Illustrating this last problem, the Bible societies, which were among the earliest and most broadly cooperative Christian organizations, suffered from division over theories of scriptural interpretation and had to adopt the policy of printing the Bible without explanatory comment. Violent controversy arose over the decision to include or exclude the Old Testament Apocrypha. To "avoid all interference with the various opinions of members regarding the forms of religious worship," they felt obliged to dispense with the ordinary formal conventions—prayers, devotional remarks, and sermons—at their meetings.

It appears to have been the general expectation that the denominations could not meet together without falling into contentious disputation, loyalty to truth demanding declaration and defense of one's own beliefs and denunciation of "heretical" views of others on any and all occasions. Because of this attitude, in part, Andrew Fuller dismissed William Carey's proposal of a world missionary conference with the observation that "in a meeting of all denominations, there would be no unity . . . without which, we had better stay at home"; and Carey himself had already put aside his early interest in organizing an interdenominationally supported mission. "Their [the denominations'] private discords might . . . much retard their public usefulness," he had decided.

The Evangelical Alliance—"the one and only definitely ecumenical organization . . . which arose out of the . . . Awakening in the nineteenth century" [3]—had been founded in 1846. Dr. Edward Steane, its first Secretary, wrote: "It has required incessant thoughtfulness and the most watchful care, lest an indiscreet word spoken or a sentence written should . . . wound the sensitiveness or offend the prejudices of the curiously mixed and balanced ideas of which our association is composed—Churchmen and Dissenters, Presbyterians and Methodists, Establishmentarians and Voluntaries." [4]

"Ecumenism of the heart" was not always characterized by manifestations of Christian love. The Evangelical Alliance, although founded "to afford opportunity to members of the Church of Christ of cultivating brotherly love," was harshly critical of some groups and denominations of fellow Christians. Its castigations of the Roman Catholic Church called

[2] The Methodist denomination was a notable example. In Scotland, Congregationalists and Baptists arose from the evangelistic activity of the Haldane brothers. The Plymouth Brethren and the Catholic Apostolic Church emerged in England. Brethrenism and Irvingism spread to the Continent, and beyond, the latter winning in Bavaria even Roman Catholics, including priests influenced by the Evangelical Awakening.

[3] *A History of the Ecumenical Movement,* p. 320.

[4] *Ibid.* p. 320

forth protest from some of its own members, who pleaded that "even Roman Catholics should be addressed in a spirit of kindness."

1. The Evangelical Alliance—Its Theological Basis

The Evangelical Alliance adopted a doctrinal "basis" with the explanation that: "First . . . this brief summary is not to be regarded, in any formal or ecclesiastical sense, as a creed or a confession, nor the adoption of it as involving any assumption of the right authoritatively to define the limits of Christian brotherhood, but simply as an indication of the class of persons whom it is desirable to embrace within the Alliance; and, second, that the selection of certain tenets, with the omission of others, is not to be held as implying that the former constitute the whole body of important truth, or that the latter are unimportant."

The parties composing the Alliance shall be such persons only as hold and maintain what are usually understood to be Evangelical views, in regard to the matters of Doctrine understated, namely:

(1) The Divine Inspiration, Authority and Sufficiency of the Holy Scriptures;
(2) The Right and Duty of Private Judgment in the Interpretation of the Holy Scriptures;
(3) The Unity of the Godhead, and the Trinity of the Persons therein;
(4) The utter Depravity of Human Nature, in consequence of the Fall;
(5) The Incarnation of the Son of God, His Work of Atonement for sinners of mankind, and His Mediatorial Intercession and Reign;
(6) The Justification of the sinner by Faith alone;
(7) The Work of the Holy Spirit in the Conversion and Sanctification of the sinner;
(8) The Immortality of the Soul, the Resurrection of the Body, the Judgment of the World by our Lord Jesus Christ, with the Eternal Blessedness of the Righteous, and the Eternal Punishment of the Wicked;
(9) The Divine Institution of the Christian Ministry, and the obligation and perpetuity of the Ordinances of Baptism and the Lord's Supper.

The Evangelical Alliance in adopting the foregoing "basis" gave implicit recognition to the need of at least some meeting of minds, as well as of hearts, in the Christian cause; but no provision was made to extend through study and discussion the grounds of doctrinal agreement. The opinion that steps in that direction were impracticable, if not dangerous, prevailed. Revival movements, Bible conferences, and the interdenominational missionary gatherings of the nineteenth century, which owed much to the influence of the Evangelical Alliance, shunned controversial beliefs, confining their programs to those areas of faith on which the more conservative evangelicals could manage to stand together. As late as 1910 it was considered necessary, in order to preserve unity in the first World Missionary Conference (Edinburgh), to exclude from the discussions all questions relating to faith and order.

There were attempts to broaden the theological basis of Christian co-operation. By the time the Evangelical Alliance was organized in the United States,[5] dissatisfaction with its policy had markedly increased among liberal evangelicals, who were convinced that doctrinal disagreements ought to be faced with searching inquiry and Christian love, in hopes that a more comprehensive fellowship might with better understanding become possible.

2. The American Congress of Churches

The American Congress of Churches represented this view. Organized by a group of New England ministers at Pittsfield, Massachusetts, in 1884, it proposed to deal frankly with those things which divided the churches. The Congress drew inspiration from "the quiet convergence of the churches toward one another in doctrine and Christian work," and especially from the experience of the Anglican and Episcopal Churches with their congresses which had "proved conclusively that a full and free discussion of burning questions in theology and social life (for which there was not time in their conventions) was practicable and safe."

At meetings in different parts of the nation, the programs introduced subjects from social Christianity which would not receive the serious attention of interchurch conferences until many years later. The Congress undoubtedly made a worthy contribution toward the preparation of the churches for facing such matters in the fullness of time.

The address of Dr. Joseph Anderson of Waterbury, Connecticut, who was Chairman of the governing council of the body, at its first meeting (in New Haven, Connecticut) is significant still for its reflection of the thinking of able leaders of the churches on ecumenical problems in the last quarter of the nineteenth century:

From an early period, the followers of Christ have been compelled to witness the spectacle of a divided Christendom. For many centuries, the Eastern Church and the Western have stood apart in very positive antagonism; and when the Reformation took place, not only was one of these great divisions broken in two, but a process of sub-division began to which there has seemed to be no limit. As a result . . . the Church has resolved itself into a multitude of "churches." In some quarters, this division . . . has been looked upon with favor . . . as a thing likely to occur under the sway of Protestantism . . . an advantage rather than a disadvantage to the cause of true religion. . . . Others have mourned over the disruptions of the Church and prayed earnestly for the restoration of its lost unity. Meanwhile, the conviction has been growing that serious evils, of a very practical sort, are connected with the division of the Church into sects, and that something ought to be done, for the sake of our common Christianity, to mitigate the sectarian

[5] Because of the controversy over slavery, the Evangelical Alliance could not be organized in the United States until after the Civil War (1867).

spirit, and to bring the various denominations of Christians into closer fraternal relations with one another. Even as long ago as the time of Calvin and Cranmer, the institution of a league was seriously considered, "in which all varieties of evangelical Protestantism should be allied in defense of common interests and in furtherance of the common faith"; and in our own country, as early as 1742, the good Count Zinzendorf brought together six or eight different denominations, in a synod at Germantown, Pennsylvania, for union in Christian work.

The most noteworthy enterprise of this kind was the establishment, forty years ago, of the Evangelical Alliance. The movement was entered into with great fervor by representatives of many branches of the Church in Europe and America, and it seemed full of promise. But it proceeded, unfortunately, upon the unwise and unsafe plan of sinking all differences out of sight, and uniting by specific agreement upon a common theological platform. A basis of belief was adopted upon which some could stand, but from which many felt themselves excluded; and among those who came together a feeling of uncertainty and discomfort was developed, for which no relief could be provided. The Evangelical Alliance is still in existence, but it exerts no very marked influence upon the religious thought and life of the times.

An effort of a very different kind was that made by Dr. Muhlenberg . . . an excellent and devout clergyman of the Protestant Episcopal Church. . . . It was a project to establish a council or congress of churches, with a view to healing the divisions of the Christian world. The last years of his life were spent in persistent and fruitless efforts to secure a commission on Christian unity, by which to reach forth to the scattered bodies of Protestantism from the basis of the Anglican communion. Muhlenberg's effort was perhaps no more significant than others which might be mentioned, but it was put forth in the Episcopal Church and left its impress there.

While men have been making definite attempts of this kind, a widespread but undefined movement has been going forward throughout the Christian world. There has been a quiet convergence of the churches toward one another in doctrine and Christian work. The old theological issues have ceased to interest the mass of Christians—have become almost obsolete; and earnest men of all communions have come to see the necessity of uniting their forces against a common foe. The process of denominational organization has indeed gone forward; the denominational life of most of the churches has been intensified rather than diminished; but at the same time Christians everywhere have come to recognize the inferior importance of those beliefs and practices which separate churches from one another, and the transcendent value of the few essentials upon which all are agreed.

In this process of convergence the Episcopal Church has shared to a less extent than the others, because of its views concerning the Church and the ministry, and because of the different type of Christian life developed in it. But there has been, all along, a reaching out in this direction, of which the effort of Muhlenberg was only a single instance. In the meantime, both in England and in America, the Episcopal Church has been undergoing a special education through the development within its bounds of a new institution—namely, the Church Congress. The "conventions" of that Church are largely devoted to routine business, so that they afford but little opportunity for the discussion of great questions. To secure such opportunity, the Church Congress was established, first in England and then in this country. The first gathering of this kind in America took place ten or eleven years ago, and was small and inconspicuous. But the Congress has grown from year to year; it has become widely popular and is now educating both old and young in new methods and habits of thought. It has already proved conclusively that a full and free discussion of burning questions in theology and in social life is practicable and safe.

It has seemed necessary to refer to these various facts, in order to explain the origin of the enterprise which we are launching. . . . "A Call for an Inter-ecclesiastical Church Congress" . . . spoke of the possibility of organizing a movement which would be to the different religious bodies of Protestant Christendom very much what the Episcopal Church Congress has been to the Episcopal Church in uniting the different schools of thought contained in it. "All attempts in the past," it said, "such as that represented by the Evangelical Alliance, have failed because they have endeavored to ignore differences, instead of affirming positive convictions." It was something very different that was now proposed. . . .[6]

Moving in the latitude of "free and full discussion of the great subjects in which all Christians are interested," staked out by the Congress, those who appeared from time to time on the programs ranged afar, presenting the usual variety of views on Christian unity. The evils of disunity were described and deplored, and suggestions were offered for their cure or mitigation. Heard also was the paradoxical optimism of those who confessed themselves pessimists about all efforts "to restore the unity of the Church," as in an address by Dr. George F. Pentecost, the evangelist, at the annual meeting in Hartford, Connecticut, in 1885:

So far as abolishing the sects is concerned, it is too late to attempt that. Pandora's box has been opened, and the furies are out, and in my judgment they will never be caught and imprisoned again; but they may be converted, and that will be better. . . . It is delightful to be present in such a meeting and listen to the papers from these brethren, representing as they do the extremes in church organization and polity, all uniting to denounce sectarianism, and all praising the beauties of union. But who expects to see any of them other than he is? . . . But I am . . . a cheerful and even hopeful pessimist. We have heard how the sects are destroying Christianity. . . . Fearful pictures of "a house divided against itself" have been limned before our eyes. The dreadful spectacle of a score of sects (I wish there were two score) being at work in Japan and China trying to convert the heathen. Well, what of it? Why, the beautiful thing is that they are doing it. . . . For a divided Christianity, I think we are doing fairly well. There are more sects today than ever in the history of the Church, and yet there never was an age in which Christianity made such progress. . . . Sectarianism does not represent "a house divided against itself," for our Lord says such a house "cannot stand." But Christianity has stood for nineteen centuries, and it is still standing, . . . its walls and palaces . . . lifting their lofty and beautiful heights toward the skies. Standing! yea, more, Christianity is marching and conquering. . . . Unity in the real body of Christ is daily manifesting itself, more and more. Why! fifty or a hundred years ago such a meeting as this could not have been held. The brethren would have been at each others' throats in no time. Then sectarianism would have been uppermost; now it is nethermost, and Christ is uppermost. We all recognize the Christianity of each other

[6] *The American Congress of Churches, Proceedings of the Annual Meeting*, Hartford, Connecticut, 1885, pp. 20 ff.

who have believed on and are united by the Spirit to Christ. . . . That is the only real unity—the only unity . . . worth having or working for. . . Already the unity among us is taking whatever of poison there ever was in sectarianism out of it. . . . Let us magnify the unity that exists, minimize our diversities, stand together in Christ; and God by the Spirit will work out a unity of faith which is far more important than unity of form or polity.[7]

Contrary to its name, the American Congress of Churches was an organization only of individual churchmen without official appointment or authority, which, with the fact that it limited its program to discussion, accounted, for the most part, for the rather short-lived interest in it. The Evangelical Alliance, whose membership was constituted similarly, attained more enduring strength and popularity by avoiding theological discussion and concentrating on Christian service, but Dr. Anderson's statement in 1885, "it exerts no very marked influence upon the religious thought and life of the times," showed that these were already waning.

During this period sentiment was increasing that approaches to a more comprehensive theological basis of fellowship and cooperation should be related immediately and realistically to denominational situations. In retrospect, efforts on behalf of Christian unity meeting this practical condition had, on the whole, a significance from the standpoint of faith and order lacking in the voluntary movements of individuals. There were several of them during the nineteenth century.

3. Presbyterians and Congregationalists

Presbyterians of the Middle Atlantic States and Congregationalists of Connecticut, Massachusetts, Vermont, and New Hampshire worked together from 1801 to 1852 under the so-called Plan of Union, by which the ministers of each communion were eligible for pastorates in the other and the local congregations of both might unite, if they chose to do so, for worship and parish activities. During the early decades of the nineteenth century all the denominations were adapting their extension programs to the conditions created by the rapid westward movement of the population. The churches founded by these two, when they united, could affiliate with either the presbyteries of the one or the consociations of the other. This procedure, which Timothy Dwight, grandson of Jonathan Edwards and a foremost figure in New England of the Second Awakening, helped to chart, met with general acceptance in New York State and through Ohio, Indiana, Illinois, Michigan, and Wisconsin.

Presbyterians and Congregationalists were nearer in respect of polity than their ecclesiastical nomenclatures would imply, and cooperation in the colonial period had prepared them psychologically for closer union. Their rapprochement extended to foreign missions, the Presbyterian

[7] *Ibid.*, pp. 51 ff.

Church carrying on its work for some time through the American Board of Commissioners for Foreign Missions, which Congregationalists had founded.

A contemporary historian wrote of the Plan of Union and the results achieved under it:

> Never was an article framed in more catholic spirit, or more perfectly adapted to promote Christian charity, and union, between the people of God who happen to be thrown together in a forming society, and yet differ in their views of what is the best method of conducting church order and discipline. . . . [The Plan] met with the approbation of the missionaries and of the people, and soon went into practical and successful operation. Under it all antagonisms seemed to be harmonized; Presbyterian and Congregationalist, each found the essentials of his favourite polity combined with some of the better features of the other; and they two becoming one, united heart, hand, and resources, in building up Christ's Kingdom.[8]

But the Plan of Union was not without disappointments for either party. The revivals inspired by the Second Awakening during the first half of the nineteenth century fastened upon the churches generally the pattern of evangelical orthodoxy, but their effect in this respect was less pronounced in New England than in other parts. Liberal theology there had come to stay, and Presbyterianism through intercourse with Congregationalism was affected by it. "The New England element, which came into the service of the Presbyterian Church . . . where the Plan of Union was in operation, liberalized it to an extent unknown in areas where no Congregational influence penetrated. The historic position of Union Theological Seminary in New York City, as over against conservative Princeton, is a good case in point. There are still churches in the Middle States which express written preference for a Princeton graduate." The unfortunate schism in the Presbyterian General Assembly (1837-38) between the Old and New Schools, which took a generation to heal, was an outgrowth partly of this doctrinal conflict.

The Congregationalists voted to terminate the Plan of Union in 1852. The main reason for this action was the too rapid absorption of their consociations by the presbyteries. Congregational procedures were favored, on the whole, by the churches of the two communions, when they united, for their local governance; but when it came to denominational affiliation, they preferred the more tightly organized Presbyterian system, particularly in New York State where by 1822 amalgamation had become practically complete. Under an "Accommodation Plan" adopted in 1808, Congregational Churches and ministers could join presbyteries and retain their distinctive Congregational "rights," but the latter privilege had no meaning apart from the denomination, and, the drift of the population being westward, there was no compensating accession of

[8] William S. Kennedy, *The Plan of Union,* pp. 151 ff.

Presbyterians to Congregational churches in New England. At best, Congregationalism by the exodus of its mission churches to the neighboring presbyteries would be shut within its native regional confines east of the Hudson River.

There were, of course, other factors in the abrogation of the Plan of Union. Competition and proselytism on the frontier had hardened denominational lines, and Presbyterians and Congregationalists were not immune to the effects of this. Their rapprochement in the preceding century had been strengthened by joint sectarian aims. For one thing, they had made common cause of resistance to the appointment by the British Parliament of bishops for the Anglican Church in the American Colonies, holding between 1766 and 1775 a series of conferences to protest the proposed action and to give encouragement to committees of dissenters in England who sided with them.

Ecclesiastical rivalries and antagonisms are unsure foundations for a unity which finds in them even part of its *raison d'être*. Some occasion is likely to arise to turn those harboring them against each other. The homely saying popular at the time that "Presbyterians milked Congregationalist cows, only to make Presbyterian butter and cheese," suggested that this may have happened under the Plan of Union in 1852.

In the century since their separation, these two denominations have looked away from each other for opportunities to unite with other Christians. With episcopacy no longer anathema, the Presbyterian Church in the United States of America from 1937 to 1946 considered a proposed merger with the Protestant Episcopal Church, which was dropped only upon the unfavorable action of the latter body. It had in 1920 received into membership the Welsh Calvinistic Methodist Church, and from 1925 to 1930 carried on negotiations at different times with the Methodist Episcopal Church (North), the Reformed Church in America, and the Associate Reformed Presbyterian Synod, with a view to union.

Congregationalists in 1917 began explorations with the Disciples of Christ of common grounds on which it was hoped they might unite, in 1925 took into their National Conference the Evangelical Protestant Churches of North America, and in 1931 voted to form with certain of the so-called "Christian" churches the denomination bearing the name "Congregational Christian Churches," which in turn joined with the Evangelical and Reformed Church in founding in 1958 the United Church of Christ.

While pursuing thus their aim of acting in practical ways to heal ecclesiastical divisions, Presbyterians and Congregationalists[9] have not chosen to try again anything resembling their own early Plan of Union.

[9] Their respective denominations took part also in the Conference on Organic Union in Philadelphia in 1918 and the Greenwich (Connecticut) Convention in 1949. In 1958-59 the Presbyterian Church in the United States of America united with the United Presbyterian Church, to form the United Presbyterian Church in the United States of America.

4. Disciples of Christ

A movement very different from the Plan of Union of Presbyterians and Congregationalists was started by Thomas Campbell (1763-1854), a Presbyterian preacher with Scotch-Irish antecedents. Before migrating to the United States in the early years of the nineteenth century, he had felt deep concern because of the divisions of Christians, particularly those rending the fellowship of Presbyterians in Ulster, who were organized in several small bodies, all sprung from the Secession Church (1733), itself an outgrowth of schism in the Church of Scotland.

Campbell's attempts to do something about disunity had been of little avail in Ireland, and again on the frontiers of the United States, where sectarianism thrived unchecked, they met with swift rebuff. "Rebuked and admonished" by his Presbyterian Church for overstepping in his zeal its laws,[10] he withdrew in 1808 and a year later organized his following into the Christian Association of Washington (Pennsylvania). As set forth in a statement by him entitled "Declaration and Address," Campbell's hope was to further Christian unity through individual action. He bade members of the creed-ridden and divided denominations to be done with speculative theologies and ecclesiastical warrings and join those who in the Association worked to "restore the Church to its primitive unity, purity and prosperity." There was already agreement, he declared, on the basic beliefs, "and our differences, at most, are about things in which the kingdom of God does not consist—that is, about matters of private opinion or human invention." He insisted that as articles of faith "nothing but what the Bible expressly taught, but what Christ and the apostles enjoined" was required. "Where the Scriptures speak, we speak; where they are silent, we are silent"—as runs the now familiar motto. In keeping with their rule of using "Biblical terms for Biblical things," Campbell and his followers called themselves "Disciples of Christ." They adopted a congregational polity, rejected "overhead organizations," drew only slight distinctions between the clergy and the laity, and observed the Lord's Supper each Lord's Day; they practiced informality in their worship and attended to what they considered biblical preaching.

The mantle of leadership descended to Alexander Campbell (1788-1866), the son of Thomas, who in *Christianity Restored* and *The Christian System* developed the principles of the "current reformation," as the movement came to be called. In his exposition, the object was the conversion of the world, in which—on the human side—only the union and cooperation of Christians were essential, if based solely upon "the Apostles' teaching and testimony." "Neither truth nor union alone is

[10] The rebuke was apparently for admitting non-Seceder Presbyterians to Communion.

sufficient to subdue the unbelieving nations, but truth and union combined are omnipotent." The "material principle" of the "new reformation" was the union of all believers, and the "formal principle" the restoration of primitive Christianity.

The Campbells contributed nothing original to Christian thought. They were influenced by Glassites and the Haldane brothers of Scotland, who called for the restoration of apostolic teaching and practice. Others also urged a return to primitive Christianity as the only road to unity. Elias Smith (1769-1840) of New England, James O'Kelly (1735-1826) of Virginia and North Carolina, Barton W. Stone (1772-1844) of Kentucky, John Winebrenner (1797-1870) of Pennsylvania—these all made the Bible alone their creed, called themselves simply "Christians" and offered their way as the heavenly condition to a united Protestantism. Some of the churches they organized merged with the Disciples of the Campbells. Others of them, as noted previously, in 1931 joined with Congregational churches in forming the denomination bearing the name "Congregational Christian Churches." The rest are loosely "Churches of Christ."

Paradoxically, all these movements which were aimed at restoring the unity of Christendom ended in new divisions. The denomination of Thomas and Alexander Campbell through its emphasis on the Bible and its simple democratic practices won wide acceptance in the pioneer society with which it moved westward, and outdistanced others among the smaller group in numerical growth. Remaining loyal to its early passion for the union of Christians, it has bred able leaders of the ecumenical movement and in manifold other ways made significant contributions to both national and international church life.

5. The Congregation of God in the Spirit

The promise of religious liberty had drawn to Pennsylvania a strangely mixed immigration. Besides the English and Welsh Quakers, who were mentioned in William Penn's patent of toleration, there were Anglicans, Roman Catholics, Baptists and other separatists of Britain, Scotch-Irish Presbyterians of Ulster, and (after a tour of the Rhineland and Switzerland by the founder in 1677) many German-speaking Lutherans, Reformed, Brethren, Mennonites, Amish, and Moravians. The colony presented a problem in religious unification of manifest difficulty, albeit a problem whose solution found hopeful approaches in the pietistic inheritance of a majority of the groups involved and in the common cultural background, particularly of the Continental element.

The situation challenged Count Nikolaus Ludwig von Zinzendorf when he went from Herrnhut, Germany, to Pennsylvania in 1741 to take charge of the Moravian mission to the Indians, and he responded with characteristic ecumenical boldness. The Count began by conferring with the Associated Brethren of the Skippack, a group of Pietists from the Perkiomen Valley who had been meeting regularly for some years for worship and "mutual edification." Agreeable with von Zinzendorf's purpose, Henrich Antes, one of their leaders, sent out a "Call" to the pastors and such of their people as might be interested to join "The Pennsylvania Congregation of God in the Spirit," to help "remedy the frightful evil wrought in the church of Christ . . . through mistrust and suspicion."

The invitation asked "whether it would not be possible to appoint a general assembly, not to wrangle about opinions, but to treat with each other in love on the most important articles of faith, in order to ascertain how closely we can approach each other fundamentally, and, as for the rest, bear with each other in love on opinions which do not subvert the ground of salvation."

This was in 1741, the year of the Count's arrival; and, beginning the following year, a series of "Pennsylvania Synods" was held, which drew wide attention for their unitive purpose. They were attended by Presbyterians, Episcopalians, Quakers, Lutherans, Reformed, Sabbatarians, Mennonites, Brethren, Separatists, and members of other churches.

The Congregation of God in the Spirit was formed according to the *Trope* principle of Count Zinzendorf, by which those joining retained membership in their respective denominations but cooperated in Christian work—in this instance, evangelism among the Indians. They were asked also to practice intercommunion and to take part in a plan for an interchange of ministers.

This movement had the unfortunate effect of drawing the lines of denominational division only more rigidly. In 1742, the year of the first synod, Heinrich Melchior Muhlenberg (1711-87) arrived in America with a commission to gather the German Lutheran Churches into a synod of their own; and Michael Schlatter (1716-90) followed to perform a like service for the Reformed congregations in Pennsylvania. One after another the churches in the new fellowship withdrew, and only the Moravians were left. By 1748 the experiment had reached an end.

The churches had apparently not been sure of Count Zinzendorf's purpose. They were hazy about the meaning of the "Congregation of God in the Spirit." For the founder, it meant a body of Christian believers who, while retaining their membership in their own denominations, sought by Moravian pietistic methods to attain a deeper religious experience; but the other denominations feared that he was trying to make Moravians of their people.

6. Lutheran and Reformed Churches

In the succeeding century, men of ecumenical spirit who tried to unite the German Lutheran and the Reformed Churches of Pennsylvania and nearby states failed, as had Zinzendorf with his more inclusive federative scheme; but their experience is part of the distant background of the Faith and Order Movement in its modern phase.

In connection with the Lutheran Tercentenary of 1817, Gottlieb Schober (1756-1836), an ex-Moravian Lutheran pastor in North Carolina, voiced in a sermon the hope that "the spirit of love and union" might be rekindled "among all who believe the divinity of Jesus Christ, the sole Mediator between God and man, so that we might come to the blessed time foretold of old when we shall live in peace as one flock under one shepherd." He expressed the belief that Christians should look forward to the constitution of "a general assembly" in which "all the denominations might come together." At about this time, Schober sent a letter to the Ministerium of Pennsylvania, urging the Lutheran and the Reformed Churches to take immediate steps to unite, "after the European example."[11]

Johann Augustus Probst (1792-1844), a later advocate of union, published in 1826 an influential tract entitled *Die Wiedervereinigung der Lutheraner und Reformirten,* in which he suggested the forming of an "Evangelical Church" accommodated in its creedal requirements to the broad leveling of doctrine which had already taken place.

The church papers opened their pages for discussion of the question, and it was debated in the synods from time to time, until 1837, when it was dropped, apparently because the preservation of the distinctive heritages of their denominations seemed to the official clergy to be more important than union.

For once, at least, conditions at the "grass roots" were more favorable to union than in the higher echelons of leadership.

> So companionable were the spiritual descendants of Luther, Calvin, and Zwingli in early America on the local and lay level that thoughts of a wedding were seriously entertained. The common German cultural background of both groups, and their common pietistic heritage, led . . . to the development of a peculiarly Pennsylvania German religious institution, the "union church." By the term "union church" was meant a co-operative affiliation in the local community between the Lutheran and the Reformed congregations, who owned and used a common church property and building, where they

[11] "The European example" referred to was the union of Lutheran and Reformed Churches in Germany under Frederick William III in 1817. This action was brought about by political pressure and was resisted by many churches. Hailed at first by some religious leaders as a forward step, its results did not fulfill the promise they saw in it.

worshipped on alternate Sundays. The degree of co-operation ranged from joint ownership of the property, with separate services, consistories, and Sunday Schools, to churches with a common consistory, Sunday School, treasury, and even union services. Hundreds of these union or community churches were founded until about 1900, when the respective synods began to discourage any new unions. There are still in eastern Pennsylvania over 175 of these historic churches in operation.

In some cases the Lutheran and Reformed country parishes were so constituted that both of them embraced the same five or six union churches, each served in circuit by a Lutheran and a Reformed pastor. Intercommunion and intermarriage further strengthened the bond. For the union church a whole literature issued from the German presses of eastern Pennsylvania, including religious periodicals, prayer-books, liturgies, catechisms, and the ever-present *Gemeinschaftliches Gesangbuch* of 1817, which reached its twenty-second edition in 1884. So close and congenial was the relation among the laymen of a union church that it used to be proverbial among the farmers of German Pennsylvania that the only difference between the Lutherans and Reformed was that the Reformed began the Lord's Prayer with *Unser Vater,* the Lutherans with *Vater Unser.*[12]

To be remembered for his ecumenical activity during the next generation is Samuel Simon Schmucker (1799-1873), for some forty years head of the Lutheran Theological Seminary at Gettysburg, Pennsylvania, and an influential leader in the Lutheran General Synod. He advocated founding an "Apostolic Protestant Church," in which all denominations might unite and at the same time retain their respective disciplines and ways of worshiping. For the "basis" of his federation he prepared a confession of faith embodying in brief compass the doctrines of the older creeds which he considered essential. The churches adopting it would be expected to give up their "party" names. The plan envisaged general recognition of the validity of the ministry of each, an interchange of pastors, intercommunion, meetings together for prayer for missions, and cooperation in such work in the local parishes as might be found practicable. His proposal, while never adopted, helped to open the way for the organization later of the Evangelical Alliance and the Federal Council of the Churches of Christ in America. His *Fraternal Appeal to the American Churches, with a Plan for Catholic Union on Apostolic Principles,* published in 1839, ran to several editions, and his *True Unity of Christ's Church: Being a Renewed Appeal to the Friends of the Redeemer on Primitive Christian Union and the History of Its Corruption* also had an extensive circulation.

Paradoxically, the elements of experience which made for strength in Schmucker's leadership also hindered his success. Born and educated in the United States, and familiar—through travel and wide contacts with the churches—with the peculiar religious problems of the new country, he strove to get his own Church to "Americanize" itself in the interest of a more effective ministry under frontier conditions.

[12] Donald Herbert Yoder, in *A History of the Ecumenical Movement,* p. 242.

He advised the adoption of the English language for its services and the employment of adaptable prevailing revivalistic methods in its evangelistic work. He was able to convince his own synod, which ventured into cooperation with the American Home Mission Society and other interdenominational organizations. But other Lutheran groups withheld support, the General Lutheran Synod in 1872 enacting the so-called Galesburg Rule reserving "Lutheran pulpits for Lutheran ministers only, Lutheran altars for Lutheran communicants."

A broadening influence in Schmucker's life was the friendship of Robert Baird, a Presbyterian, which had begun at Princeton Theological Seminary, where they were roommates. Baird distinguished himself as a historian by assessing the achievements of the various denominations from an ecumenical standpoint—a new approach in the study of church history, which had been written generally in sectarian terms. Between 1847 and 1850 he edited *The Christian Union and Religious Memorial,* "the pioneer unionist periodical in America," which owed its appearance to the movement centering at the time in the organization of the Evangelical Alliance.

In 1844 the theological seminary of the German Reformed Church at Mercersburg, Pennsylvania, called from Switzerland to its faculty Philip Schaff (1819-93), a young theologian and historian, who became, mainly through his writings, one of the most earnest apostles of Christian unity of the century. Holding the broadest views on the subject, he began in his inaugural address, entitled "The Principle of Protestantism," the exposition of his theory that Protestantism and Romanism were stages in the divinely appointed development of the Christian Church, which would bring them eventually into union in an "Evangelical Catholicism." [13] His book on the Apostolic Church (*Geschichte der Apostolichen Kirche*) appeared in 1851, and the publication of his *History of the Christian Church* followed during the period from 1852 to 1892. Both became standard works, as did the Schaff-Herzog *Encyclopaedia of Religious Knowledge,* which was edited by him after his transfer in 1870 to a professorship at Union Theological Seminary in New York City, and his *Bibliotheca Symbolica Ecclesiae Universalis: the Creeds of Christendom,* which was published in 1877.

While Schaff elaborated in these and companion volumes the ecumenical meaning of Christian history, his colleague at Mercersburg, John Williamson Nevin (1803-86), a Presbyterian of Scotch-Irish antecedents, developed his version of the scriptural basis of church unity. Their work was of a complementary nature. Their combined influence strongly supported the Reformed Church in the United States in its unsuccessful negotiations toward union with various denomina-

[13] During a stay of six months in England en route to the United States, Schaff had met with Edward Bouverie Pusey and other Tractarians.

tions—Lutherans (1817-37), Dutch Reformed (1838-1920), and Presbyterians (1908-12).

George Warren Richards, who became the head of the Lancaster Theological Seminary—Mercersburg's successor—inherited their passion for Christian unity. Under his lead the move to merge the Reformed Church in the United States and the Evangelical Synod of North America (the counterpart in the New World of the Prussian Evangelical Union of 1817) was brought to success with the formation in 1934 of the Evangelical and Reformed Church.[14]

7. The Episcopal Church and Unity

During the middle decades of the nineteenth century many Episcopalians came to share the belief that their Church, by reason of its history and theological views, occupied a position which, with some modifications of doctrines and practices, could be offered hopefully to all Christians as a practicable ground of reunion. Certain of their prominent churchmen, on their own initiative and responsibility, brought forward overtures conceived in these general terms.

Among them was the Rev. Thomas Hubbard Vail (1812-89) of Hartford, Connecticut. In a book published in 1841 he presented the claims of his Church as follows:

> Instead of endeavoring to strike out an entirely new system of ecclesiastical unity, the proper and only feasible course is to select, for the purpose of uniting within it, some system already established, and which realizes most nearly the idea of a Comprehensive Church, and if it be not in every respect perfect, to improve it, if it will allow improvement, into perfection. . . .
>
> It may be that there is such a system amongst us—a system whose structure is capable of modification, and in whose organization are instrumentalities by which it may be shaped into any form which the majority of the Christians in our country may desire. . . .
>
> We believe there is such a system among us.

If those who thought the Protestant Episcopal Church was such a system were right, it became the "bounden duty of all Christians," he urged, "to unite themselves with it at once."

> We call for a true Christian unity, which shall expand itself through the land; which shall go into all the little villages, and all the private dwellings, over the whole length and breadth of our long and our broad country, and unite hearts, and unite voices, and unite labour, and strength, and wealth,

[14] Merged in 1958 with the Congregational and Christian denomination to form the United Church of Christ in U.S.A. See above, p. 82.

that have always before been separated—which shall bring into one Comprehensive Church all the disciples of Christ.[15]

If this plan should necessitate "some personal sacrifice" by those coming from the other communions, they might be reminded that it could cause greater trouble for the parishes and the diocesan and general conventions of the Church, over which, by reason of their numerical preponderance, they would inevitably gain control. So far as he was concerned, however, he would be willing, if it came to that, for them to "revise and re-arrange" the laws of the Church. Said he: "We are willing to be melted down with you, in our own crucible, into one mass of Christian love and fellowship."

The Episcopal General Convention of 1853 was signalized by the presentation to the House of Bishops of a memorial by Dr. William Augustus Muhlenberg[16] (1796-1877), Rector of the Church of the Holy Communion in New York City, and a group of presbyters, who petitioned that "some ecclesiastical system" be set up, "surrounding and including the Protestant Episcopal Church" as it was, "leaving that Church untouched, identical with that Church in all its great principles, yet providing for as much freedom in opinion, discipline, and worship as would be compatible with the essential Faith and Order of the Gospel." Into it might be brought by episcopal ordination "able ministers of the New Testament . . . among the other bodies of Christians," with the understanding that they would not have "to conform in all particulars to . . . prescriptions and customs" of the Protestant Episcopal Church, so long as they accepted the Holy Scriptures as the Word of God, the Apostles' and Nicene creeds, the two sacraments, and the "doctrines of grace" as taught in the Thirty-nine Articles, celebrated the Eucharist according to the rubric of the Prayer Book, and agreed to report periodically, as required, to the ordaining bishops.

While the Church took no action on it, the Muhlenberg Memorial,[17] as it came to be called, thrust his irenic Broad Church point of view and spirit into the consideration of Christian unity. It did much to confirm Episcopalians in their feeling that their Church could logically be made the center and rallying ground for the reunion of the widely varying forms of Protestant Christianity in the United States.

In a book entitled *The Church Idea—An Essay Toward Unity,* which appeared in 1870, William Reed Huntington (1838-1918), at the time Rector of Grace Episcopal Church in New York City, suggested the "essentials" of Anglican faith, on which he believed it possible for

[15] Thomas Hubbard Vail, *The Comprehensive Church: or Christian Unity and Ecclesiastical Union in the Protestant Episcopal Church.*

[16] Grandson of Heinrich Melchior Muhlenberg, founder of American Lutheranism.

[17] See Charles C. Tiffany, *A History of the Protestant Episcopal Church in the United States of America,* Appendix D.

all Christians to join with the Protestant Episcopal Church in forming the "Catholic Church of America."[18] The formulation included:

> The Holy Scriptures as the Word of God.
> The primitive Creeds as the rule of faith.
> The two Sacraments ordained by Christ.
> The historic episcopate as the keystone of governmental unity.

Huntington's scheme aroused considerable discussion and criticism. "Should the invitation be heeded," wrote one friendly critic, "the little consolidating body, with all its conservative vigour, would soon be resisting the intrusion of so much foreign and uncongenial material, or find it not very easy of assimilation."[19]

Other persons were moved to nominate their own denominations as more promising candidates for the role which it had been proposed the Protestant Episcopal Church undertake. "She has more affinity with all diverse elements of our ecclesiastical life than any other Church," wrote a Presbyterian of his church, whether seriously or in veiled jest. "She has been a Puritan church in a Puritan age, and a Methodist church in the age of the Awakening; and she is returning to what she was before the Puritan influence touched her, in adapting herself to the churchly tendencies of the present age."[20]

Abandoning the notion of his church as a nucleus, Huntington in 1898 put out another book, under the title *A National Church* (see footnote 18), in which he advocated discarding all denominational superstructures and having the local churches retain or adopt the forms of worship they preferred and organize themselves into presbyteries, synods, and conferences, by the established geographical divisions of the country—county, state, and national.

Huntington's statement of the four "essentials of Anglicanism" was incorporated, with some elaboration, in the historic declaration of the House of Bishops at the General Convention of the Protestant Episcopal Church in Chicago in 1886:

> We do hereby affirm that the Christian unity now so earnestly desired . . . can be restored only by the return of all Christian Communions to the principles of unity exemplified by the undivided Catholic Church during the first ages of its existence; which principles we believe to be the substantial deposit of Christian Faith and Order committed by Christ and His Apostles to the Church unto the end of the world, and therefore incapable of compromise or

[18] See *The Church Idea—An Essay Toward Unity,* and *A National Church,* The Bedell Lectures for 1897.

[19] Charles W. Shields, *The Church of the United States,* pp. 95-98, cited by D. H. Yoder in *A History of the Ecumenical Movement,* p. 251.

[20] Robert Ellis Thompson, *A History of the Presbyterian Churches in the United States,* p. 313, cited by D. H. Yoder in *A History of the Ecumenical Movement,* p. 251.

surrender by those who have been ordained to be its stewards and trustees for the common and equal benefit of all men.

As inherent parts of this sacred deposit, and therefore as essential to the restoration of unity among the divided branches of Christendom, we account the following, to wit:

(1) The Holy Scriptures of the Old and New Testament as the revealed Word of God.
(2) The Nicene Creed as the sufficient statement of the Christian Faith.
(3) The two Sacraments—Baptism and the Supper of the Lord—ministered with unfailing use of Christ's words of institution and of the elements ordained by Him.
(4) The Historic Episcopate, locally adapted in the methods of its administration to the varying needs of the nations and peoples called of God into the unity of His Church.[21]

With its acceptance in 1888 by the Lambeth Conference Committee on Home Reunion, as supplying "a basis on which approach [might] be, under God's blessing, made towards Home Reunion," this "declaration" came to be known as the Chicago-Lambeth Quadrilateral. In adopting it, the Committee changed the first three points to read as follows:

(a) The Holy Scriptures of the Old and New Testaments, as "containing all things necessary to salvation," and as being the rule and ultimate standard of faith.
(b) The Apostles' Creed, as the Baptismal Symbol; and the Nicene Creed, as the sufficient statement of the Christian Faith.
(c) The two Sacraments ordained by Christ Himself—Baptism and the Supper of the Lord—ministered, etc.

The form of the whole instrument was recast by the Lambeth Conference of 1920 in its "Appeal to All Christian People":

We believe that visible unity of the Church will be found to involve the whole-hearted acceptance of:

The Holy Scriptures, as the record of God's revelation of Himself to men, and as being the rule and ultimate standard of faith; and the Creed commonly called Nicene, as the sufficient statement of Christian Faith, and either it or the Apostles' Creed as the Baptismal Confession of belief.

The divinely instituted Sacraments of Baptism and the Holy Communion, as expressing for all the corporate life of the whole fellowship in and with Christ.

A ministry acknowledged by every part of the Church as possessing not only the inward call of the Spirit, but also the Commission of Christ and the authority of the whole body.

The Episcopate is the one means of providing such a ministry.[22]

[21] *Journal of the General Convention,* 1886, p. 80.
[22] G. K. A. Bell, *Documents on Christian Unity,* pp. 3-4.

The General Convention of 1862 appointed a committee "to consider the expediency of communication" with the Russo-Greek Church on the qualifications of the Protestant Episcopal Church, "as a part of the Church Catholic," to assume care of the Orthodox in the Pacific area of North America.

This action was occasioned by the purchase of Alaska and the Aleutian Islands by the United States from Russia and the transfer of the Orthodox episcopal see from Sitka to San Francisco.

On their way to Russia, the members of the Episcopal mission conferred with representatives of the Church of England on the problem of intercommunion between the Anglican and Eastern Churches and of recognition by the latter of Anglican orders. Through Father Joseph Vassiliev, the Russian chaplain at Paris, and Father Eugene J. Popov of the London Russian Church, they were given to understand that there could be no intercommunion until changes were made in the Anglican formularies. The English were unwilling to consider such revisions but hoped the Americans, who were less bound by tradition, would proceed independently and possibly create a precedent.

The Moscow Synod took no formal action but recommended further study. The great Russian theologian V. M. Philaret[23] was favorable and suggested five points for exploration: the Thirty-nine Articles of Religion, the *filioque* clause and its place in the Creed, apostolic succession, holy tradition, the doctrine of the seven sacraments—especially of the Eucharist.

The Episcopal committee expressed the hope that the Russian Church would establish a bishopric in San Francisco and a parish in New York City.

Bishop Samuel Wilberforce of Oxford moved in the Convocation of Canterbury in 1863 that "His Grace the President be requested to direct the Lower House to appoint a Committee to communicate with the Committee appointed at a recent Synod of the Bishops and clergy of the United States of America as to Intercommunion with the Russo-Greek Church, and to communicate the result to Convocation at a future Session."

The General Convention continued the committee on the Russo-Greek Church, upon receiving its report in 1865, and authorized further correspondence with the Eastern Orthodox Churches for information.

8. Movements Relating to Faith and Order in Europe

With this reference to a common action of the Protestant Episcopal Church in the United States and the Church of England on matters

[23] Vasili Mihailovich Philaret—see pp. 134 ff.

involving Russian Orthodoxy, this review of faith and order in the eighteenth and nineteenth centuries shifts to the Old World. In England and on the Continent certain movements, whose influence was also apparent in American church life, come more closely into view. Four of them—Pietism, the Counter Reformation, the Enlightenment, and the system of political alliances—arose prior to 1700 and were to affect, directly and indirectly, the churches' concern with faith and order.

Pietism had its origins in Germany in the seventeenth century. The faith of the Pietists held as central spiritual regeneration and holy living. These experiences and the fellowship of those sharing them were considered essentials of the true Church. For them, holy living was not withdrawal from the world, nor did it mean moral uprightness alone; it meant adding works to faith, works which were the fruit of an inwardly renewed life making visible before the eyes of men the Church Invisible, which was to be found in all the churches but in none of them in its wholeness. They depreciated ecclesiastical organization and the institutional incorporation of the Church in liturgy, sacrament, and polity, and likewise any form of union which might concern itself with them. The Pietists were indebted in many ways to German Protestant Spiritualism and to the Latin mysticism of Spanish and French Roman Catholicism, of the preceding century, . . . even owed something to the quietism of Miguel de Molinos and Madame Jeanne Marie Bouvier de la Motte Guyon. The ecumenical significance of their activity lay in their emphasis on the spiritual unity of all true believers beneath the forms and superstructure of organized religion and in their extensive and extraordinarily successful missionary work, which cut across all confessional divisions.

Another of these movements was the Roman Catholic Counter Reformation, which extended into the seventeenth century. With its direction in the capable hands of the Jesuits, it presented both a political and a theological challenge which compelled the establishment by the Protestant Churches of a common front of resistance running through France, Germany, the Netherlands, England, and Switzerland. This led to closer acquaintance and a fresh study and comparison of fundamentals in their doctrinal positions. They discovered unsuspected areas of agreement and began to realize the potential strength of Christian fellowship when the inhibitions of dogmatic assumptions were temporarily removed. The churches principally involved were the Reformed and Lutheran, the latter mainly in Germany and the Scandinavian countries. Such agreement, however, did not extend to separatist groups, generally called "Anabaptists," who were not interested in defending the Reformation but, as they said, in "completing" it. Those churches which had taken leave of Rome, whether Lutheran,

Reformed, or Anglican, had not, in their opinion, made a clean enough break nor gone far enough.

The intellectual awakening of the eighteenth century, known as the Enlightenment, also had profound effects for the churches. Gathering impetus from the skepticism of Pierre Bayle, the new physical doctrines of Sir Isaac Newton, and the epistemological theories of John Locke, it evolved philosophical and political concepts which permeated Western thought for a century or more. Chief among its tenets were supreme faith in human reason and belief in the perfectibility of man on *earth*. Everywhere it was marked by a questioning of authority, an avid interest in the pursuit of knowledge and culture, and the employment of empirical method in science.

Perhaps its most notable spokesman was Voltaire, and in France its ideas found expression as well in the naturalism of Rousseau and the publication (1751-80) of the *Encyclopédie, ou Dictionnaire raisonné des Sciences, des Arts et des Métiers* by d'Alembert and Denis Diderot. In Germany, exponents of the *Aufklärung,* as it was called, included such thinkers as Leibniz, Lessing, von Herder, and Hermann Samuel Reimarus. The writings of Reimarus[24] and Franz Volkmar Reinhard,[25] a later rationalist thinker, were significant for their application of scientific historical criticism to the Bible and the study of the life of Jesus. The force of the Enlightenment reached across the Atlantic through the political ideas of such leaders of the American Revolution as Franklin, Jefferson, and Thomas Paine.

The rationalism of the Enlightenment and its rejection of Christian dogma was a further reason for the churches to make common cause of defending the faith and seeking to arrive at some consensus on its essentials. Moreover, antithetical as the Enlightenment may have been to supernatural religion, its spokesmen spread the principle of religious toleration, helping in the long run to weaken sectarian barriers and create a more favorable ecumenical climate.

Plans for uniting the churches during the eighteenth century and the early part of the nineteenth were often only ancillary to larger schemes of political alliances. The principle set forth in the Latin phrase *cuius regio eius religio,*[26] established under the Peace of Augsburg in 1555 and reaffirmed in the Treaty of Westphalia, 1648, was still valid. According to it, princes of the Empire might force their subjects to adopt the forms of the Christian faith they themselves professed. These politically motivated unitive moves were often vehicles for the personal ambitions of monarchs who sought only to improve their own fortunes; but in other instances they had the disinterested support of responsible

[24] *The Aims of Jesus and His Disciples,* etc.
[25] *Essay upon the Plan which the Founder of the Christian Religion Adopted for the Benefit of Mankind,* etc.
[26] Literally translated: "Whose realm, his religion."

citizens—statesmen, educators, philosophers, clergymen, writers, and others—who hoped that through them something might be done to repair and strengthen the cultural unity of Europe. With the Holy Roman Empire little more than a name and the European system becoming more and more disordered, many thoughtful persons were willing to support proposals to insure the survival of orderly Christian civilization. Separation of church and state was advocated by Pietists and in separatist circles, but such a reversal of tradition and custom was far ahead of its time.

Whatever their motive, the periodic attempts at unification were always occasion for renewed study and comparison by the churches of their doctrines and practices—in preparation for adjustments which would have to be made, if the proposed new schemes were successful, or for effective resistance, if it developed that they called for opposition.

The foregoing has touched briefly upon some of the principal reasons why concerns of faith and order engaged the clergy and scholars of the churches more or less continuously during this period.

9. Reasonable Orthodoxy

The temper of the time was reflected particularly in a movement of the early eighteenth century known as "reasonable orthodoxy," which arose initially in opposition to the extreme Calvinism of the Helvetic Consensus Formula enacted by the Swiss Reformed Churches in 1675 against the "heresies of Saumur." [27] Among its exponents was Jean Alphonse Turretini (1671-1737), Professor of Ecclesiastical History at Geneva,[28] whose close associates were Samuel Werenfels (1657-1740), Professor of theology at Basle, and Jean Frédérick Ostervald, pastor at Neuchatel. Aside from theological reform, their common interest was the promotion of union between the Reformed and Lutheran Churches, and on this subject they wrote many treatises examining and comparing the creeds of the two confessions.[29] Their views revealed the trend away from "pure doctrine" and the growing influence of Pietism. They were in substantial accord on the kind of union they wanted. It should not mean, they

[27] The teaching of Moses Amyraut (1596-1664), known as Amyraldism—a liberal version of Calvinism. In *Traité de la Prédestination* (1634), he suggested a modification of the strong predestinarian theory of the Synod of Dort by the *universalismus hypotheticus,* i.e., the theory that God offers salvation to all under the conditions of faith.

[28] Turretini's father, François (1623-87), had been a signer of the Helvetic Consensus. See E. de Bude, *The Lives of the Elder and the Younger Turretini.*

[29] Turretini: *Oration on the Reconciliation of the Differences between Protestants* and *The Cloud of Witnesses on behalf of Moderate and Peaceful Judgment in Theological Affairs and Reconciliation among Protestants.* Werenfels: *General Discussion as to Means of Uniting the Protestant Churches Commonly Distinguished by the Names Lutheran and Reformed.*

were agreed, uniformity. There should be liberty in the less essential matters, and in all things brotherly love. Whatever should be held fundamental must have been revealed clearly. It must also be free of differences of interpretation and useful in developing piety. The sole aim of the Christian faith was sanctification. Theology should strive for simplicity. Learned doctrinal debates were as nothing, as compared with the plain proclamation of the Scriptures of Jesus Christ as Son of God and Redeemer and their call to a life of true belief and virtue.

Reformed and Lutheran Churches had confessional differences, the "Swiss Triumvirate" said, but emphasis should be upon what they held in common. Both agreed that Christ was truly present in the Lord's Supper. Their disagreement concerned only the nature of his presence. Their acceptance of him as omnipotent and everlasting God and Saviour outweighed their conflicting views on his Person. As for the doctrine of predestination, their Churches ought to bear in mind the inscrutability of God's judgments recognized by the Apostle Paul in his Epistle to the Romans and discipline their speculations accordingly.

Werenfels, in his travels, and Ostervald, mainly through his books, introduced "reasonable orthodoxy" in Roman Catholic circles, meeting with an especially friendly reception in Paris.

Turretini conducted negotiations with the Lutheran representatives of Frederick I of Prussia when they came to Geneva in 1707 to discuss the possibility of union with the Reformed Church, taking the position that both communions were "in agreement on every important and essential point" and that such differences as they had ought not hinder their uniting. But no union came of the conference. The only result was permission for the establishment in Geneva of an independent Lutheran congregation.

Many liberal Reformed churchmen looked with favor at this time upon a union of the Protestants of Europe with the Church of England. The latter, in its polity and worship, its doctrinal latitude, and its widely accepted continuity with Apostolic Christianity, seemed to them to achieve a comprehensiveness meeting the essential conditions for such a move.

Turretini had been in England and knew many of its prominent churchmen. Werenfels and Ostervald were known there through their books. The last had studied Anglican liturgies and made use of them in revising the worship of his church at Neuchâtel. All three belonged to the Society for Promoting Christian Knowledge and the Society for the Propagation of the Gospel in Foreign Parts, corresponding membership in which had been opened by the Church of England to leading divines of the Lutheran and the Reformed Churches of Europe.

Cognizance of the advances of the Swiss theologians was taken by William Wake, Archbishop of Canterbury from 1716 to 1737, who informed them that arrangements might be made for episcopal ordination of their ministers by Anglican bishops and sought to impress upon them the Church of England's tradition of inclusiveness:

> The moderation of the Church . . . in this respect has been very exemplary; and we have felt the good effect of it in that peace we enjoy among our ministers, notwithstanding their known difference of opinion in many considerable articles of Christian doctrine. The XXXIX Articles . . . have been subscribed more than once in our public synods, indifferently, by bishops and clergy of different persuasions. We have left everyone to interpret them in his own sense; and they are indeed so generally framed that they may, without any equivocation, have more senses than one fairly put upon them.

The exchange, however, never reached the stage of actual negotiations. In addition to insurmountable political complications, the Swiss Reformed Churches could not resolve their prolonged controversy over the Helvetic Consensus Formula, and this in turn affected their relations with the Lutheran Churches—now also being wooed by the Archbishop of Canterbury.

10. The Churches of the Reformation and Anglicanism

A foremost Continental figure in the unity movement during the early part of the eighteenth century was Daniel Ernst Jablonski (1660-1747), whose family connections, religious inheritance, education, and fields of professional employment combined to prepare him in an exceptional degree for an ecumenical mission. A grandson of the famous Czech educator and bishop, Johann Amos Komensky (Comenius), he was born in Nassenhuben, on the border of Poland and Germany, and, although mainly of Polish descent, spent his youth in German environments and spoke German as his mother tongue. He attended the University of Frankfort-on-Oder and studied three years at Oxford University. He was reared in the Church of the Brethren, which from 1540 had maintained confessional relations with the Reformed Churches, and entered its ministry. In England Jablonski gained a favorable impression of the Anglican Church and formed an acquaintance with a number of its clergy, including William Wake, who became a close friend. He early conceived the plan of bringing together the evangelical churches on the basis of the scriptural orthodoxy of the Brethren and the episcopal tradition which his church held in common with the Church of England, and to the promotion of this plan he devoted his life.

His strategy was, first, to get the churches of the Reformation on the Continent to unite and to adopt episcopacy, then to turn them in the direction of the Anglican Church. On the problems and prospects of union, Jablonski studied carefully Lutheran and Reformed doctrines and concluded that they could not be reconciled sufficiently to be made to serve as the basis of a merger. So far as he was concerned, this was no actual obstacle. Consciously or not, he took the Pietistic view that the churches should seek accord in the Christian way of living, rather than on doctrinal grounds. Like many churchmen of the Enlightenment, he was influenced by the tendency to treat theological and confessional disagreements as of minor significance. He declared, in fact, that the Reformed and the Lutherans did not in their differences touch the essentials of Christian faith, and pleaded for acceptance by each of the other in a spirit of broad tolerance, under which there would be good reason to hope, he said, that they might grow into the unity God willed, which would surely be found to allow room for diversity.

In the early years of the eighteenth century it appeared that the English crown itself might bring about a measure of Church unity. After the Revolution of 1688, William of Orange had come to the throne, to be followed in rather quick succession by Queen Anne and the House of Hanover. William and his Dutch entourage entered into communion with the Church of England. Always an earnest Anglican, Anne was joined at the altar by a Lutheran consort, Prince George of Denmark. The Hanoverians, George I and George II, adhered to the Act of Settlement of 1701, which required future sovereigns to "join in communion with the Church of England." Thus the way appeared to be open for union between the Reformed and Lutheran Churches and the Anglican Church.

The principal Protestant power of the Holy Roman Empire was Prussia, and its king, Frederick I, was more than willing to fall in with the plan for ecclesiastical unification, if not for other reasons for the political prestige it promised. The practical effect of England's example of royal supremacy in affairs of the Church was probably not lost on him. There were exchanges of diplomatic approval. From Queen Anne came assurance of Her Majesty's readiness "to give all possible encouragement." Jablonski was able to make a fair beginning toward popularizing the Anglican liturgy, Frederick giving him permission to use the Book of Common Prayer, which had been printed in German, in the palace church and the cathedral.

In the end, however, union eluded all efforts. The unyielding opposition of conservative Protestant theologians, the deep hurts inflicted by the War of the Spanish Succession and the Treaty of Utrecht, and the alternating indifference and self-seeking opportunism of rulers made clear that its time was not yet. (In the *Corpus Evangelicorum* at Ratisbon were not fewer than thirty-nine princes whose approval had to be won for any policy before it could be accepted.) The cause suffered even greater setbacks by the deaths of its friends in high position, among them Queen Anne and John Sharp, Archbishop of York, in England,

and Frederick I of Prussia. Jablonski had the full favor of William Wake, both before and after the latter became Archbishop of Canterbury (1716), but the auspicious conjunction of conditions favorable to unity in the churches and in the various states involved was not destined to be repeated. Moreover, whether Jablonski sensed it or not, he and those who shared his hopes had been overtaken by the new age, in which their ideas already had little relevance.

The best result of their labors was perhaps Jablonski's renewal of the emphasis of Thomas Cranmer (1489-1566) and other sixteenth-century Anglican theologians on unity in adoration and prayer. He was dissatisfied with the services in Reformed Churches because of their barrenness and dullness. He held a low opinion of the preaching heard in them and suggested that the sermon need not be regarded as among the essential elements of worship, which in his view, consisted of confession of sin, adoration on bended knees, praise and thanksgiving, self-dedication to God, intercession, the reading of the Scriptures, administration of the sacrament, the giving of alms, and fasting. From this it would appear that his interest in the liturgy of the Church of England as a practical means of union had not been without a lively appreciation of its devotional quality and its greater usefulness in the cultivation of spiritually enriching worship.

The theologians of "reasonable orthodoxy," seeking to soften the harsh dogmas of an earlier day and to reconcile their confessions, which beneath divisions were one in faith; Jablonski working to bring about union of the Continental churches of the Reformation with the Church of England and thus restore their continuity with the traditions of early Christianity and lay a foundation for consolidation of Protestantism; William Wake, while giving encouragement to this aim, consulting with the scholars and clergy of Paris in the hope of repairing the broken fellowship of Canterbury and Rome; Christoph Matthäus Pfaff, Chancellor of the University of Tübingen, proposing at the bicentenary of the Reformation (1717), with the backing of King Frederick William I of Prussia and the princes of the *Corpus Evangelicorum,* that Lutherans and Reformed unite to resist the efforts of the Roman Catholic Church to undo the work of the Reformers—all these and others who toiled for the same ends, were affected by a nostalgic devotion to an order of life which had passed away and at the same time by the nascent universalism of the age which compelled its exist. They are to be understood and judged accordingly.

All of these men were influenced by the ideas of Gottfried Wilhelm von Leibniz (1646-1716), whose massive genius had been dedicated to the re-establishment of the cultural and political unity of Europe. It was significant that Leibniz, who perhaps stood first among intellectuals, having attained eminence in nearly all branches of learning—

history, literature, philosophy, divinity, politics, natural science, mathematics, engineering—saw the Church as assuming a major role in his grandiose plan. He conceived of the Church as comprising all the churches. He sought to win the cooperation of Rome; and, for a time, he hoped that through the good offices of Peter the Great, with whom he enjoyed friendly personal and professional relations, he might be able to enlist the Russian Orthodox Church. He even went so far as to develop and reduce to writing "a system of theology," under which he thought all the churches could live and work together—and would, if they faced levelly their interdependence and the urgent need of united action for the preservation of Christian culture. He believed that experience should have taught both the nations and the churches that, instead of keeping on in their destructive warrings among themselves, "they must join hands in defending their common heritage against the barbarians."

But, in the eyes of most churchmen, what Leibniz envisaged in his sweeping syncretism bore little resemblance to the true Church and its mission; and the end of it could not have been other than it was. He made a large contribution toward the growth of knowledge and helped profoundly to give shape to the institutions of the modern world, but his schemes for the immediate reconstruction of society along semi-utopian lines failed, as did those of lesser minds.

11. The Influence of Pietism

In contrast to the impotence of unitive efforts which depended for their success upon skill in diplomacy, theological accommodation, and realignments in political and ecclesiastical structures was the recurring quiet power of Pietism, which arose in divers manners and places as from unseen spiritual sources and brought unity by creation rather than manipulation.

The German Christian Fellowship (*Deutsche Christentums Gesellschaft*) was founded by Johann August Urlsperger (1728-1806) at Basle, Switzerland, in 1780. It revived and broadened the work of the Fellowship of Good Friends (*Gesellschaft guter Freunde*), which had been organized in 1765 by Hieronymus Annoni (1697-1770) while pastor at nearby Wallenburg and Muttenz, to "promote the honour of God and the salvation of men." Emphasizing "pure doctrine" expressed in "active piety," the new Fellowship spread rapidly through Germany into Holland and England, gathering members wherever the idea of the "spiritual society" had been sown. Its appeal was interconfessional, as well as international.

Urlsperger, a Lutheran, took the position that doctrinal differences between the churches, especially his and the Reformed, should not hinder the unity of those who were true believers. Members of the Fellowship came from many churches, including the Anglican and Roman Catholic. They joined in organizing and working at many activities, out of which grew the Basle Mission House and the Basle Missionary Society, as well as Bible and tract societies in various places. The first secretary of the Fellowship was C. F. A. Steinkopf (1773-1859). The Pietist spirit so evident in the movement was traceable to a number of sources, but to none more certainly than August Hermann Francke (1663-1727), the Pietist leader of Halle and a close friend of Samuel Urlsperger (1685-1772), father of Johann August Urlsperger.[30]

12. The Rise of Nationalism

The Holy Roman Empire came to an end in 1806, and with it the *Corpus Evangelicorum,* which from 1653 had held together the Protestant princes. During the decade that followed, Protestantism fell apart, so to speak, and there was chaos in the churches, as in the states. After Waterloo, the resurgence of nationalism revived interest in church union. King Frederick William III of Prussia was persuaded by his advisers to undertake a merger of the Lutheran and Reformed Churches of his domains. The *cuius regio eius religio* prerogative granted at the Peace of Augsburg in 1555, under which a ruler had the right to require his subjects to adopt his religious faith, had ended with the collapse of the Holy Roman Empire; and the King, unable to gain voluntary cooperation for his plan, resorted to compulsive measures. His autocracy can be understood when allowance is made for the long-time alliance which had existed between the churches and the government and the problems encountered in unlearning traditional ways when the authority for them had been withdrawn.

As a matter of fact, a considerable degree of civil control still was exercised over the churches in Prussia through a ministry of spiritual affairs, and these officials were strongly in favor of union.

Moreover, prominent Lutheran and Reformed churchmen had for more than a century agreed that the differences between their confessions were not such as to justify their separateness and had attempted many plans for bringing them together. So great an authority as Friedrich Daniel Ernst Schleiermacher (1768-1834), the foremost theologian of the time, had said that under conditions existing in the German

[30] It was the elder Urlsperger who, in assuming the responsibility of providing pastoral care for German emigrants to North America, from the settlement of refugees from Salzburg in 1734, prepared the way for the founding in 1742 of the Lutheran Church in Pennsylvania.

states only rulers could successfully initiate movements for a union of the churches.[31]

Frederick William III acted in 1817, the Reformation tercentenary. He issued a proclamation uniting the churches and directing that differences of doctrine were thenceforth to be disregarded in pastoral assignments and admission to Holy Communion. Necessary steps were to be taken in other matters relating to the full consummation of union. There was only partial compliance. When in 1822 he tried to have the churches adopt a new liturgy which the clergy had not approved, resistance rose into actual rebellion and was followed by the suspension of the pastors involved. In Breslau the dissenters founded in 1841, the year after Frederick William III's death, the Evangelical Church in Prussia. Meantime, many orthodox Lutherans had emigrated to America. Chiefly because of an influential center party which believed strongly in its policy, the Prussian Union was able to maintain itself against all opposition and to survive for well over a century.

Upon his accession in 1840, Frederick William IV revived Jablonski's plan to introduce episcopacy into the Reformed and Lutheran Churches—now united—as a first step toward union with the Church of England. English churchmen were receptive. The procedure called for establishing a joint Anglican and Prussian bishopric in Jerusalem and ordaining candidates to the priesthood who subscribed to either the Augsburg Confession or the Thirty-nine Articles. England and Prussia would alternate in the appointment of bishops.

The ready concurrence of the British Parliament, which in 1841 passed an act authorizing the consecration of bishops for territories not under the crown, suggested that there were perhaps political motives in the proposal. Henry Renaud Turner Brandreth describes it as "an attempt, by an Anglo-German protectorate over Protestants in the Levant, to balance the traditional protectorate over Latin Christians, which had so long given France a dominant political influence in that area." [32] In any case, the unique undertaking involved many questions of faith and order.

England chose Michael Alexander, a converted Jewish rabbi, to be

[31] Schleiermacher did not contemplate that such action would be carried to the point of coercion. Union gained at violation of the liberty of the individual he considered worse than division, and he did not endorse the policy of Frederick William III.

Schleiermacher has been called "the father of modern theology." He belonged to the Reformed Church. In his education he came under the pietistic influences of a Moravian school. Beneath the doctrinal formulations there had to be an inner piety, he thought or religion had no reason or power. He stood for the position of ecumenism in its modern emphasis: "The Protestant Church is not well adapted to present a complete agreement throughout the whole range of doctrine and practice—an agreement which has not as a matter of fact been realized in either of the great Confessions—but rather a variety in doctrine and practice, which yet is not allowed to break up the fellowship of the Church," he declared.

[32] *A History of the Ecumenical Movement,* Chapter 6, p. 288.

the first bishop but he died after a short tenure. Prussia then named as his successor Samuel Gobat (1799-1879), a Swiss, who had prepared for missionary work at the Basle Mission House and received a commission from the Church Missionary Society of London to Abyssinia and the Near East. He was able and well qualified from the standpoint of both education and experience, and he did notable work, particularly in his orphanages and hospitals. But he met with problems no ingenuity could resolve. The spirit he brought to them is revealed in his own account of his handling of the applications of excommunicated members of Eastern Orthodox Churches for admission to the Anglican Church:[33]

> What am I to do? I have never wished to make converts from the old Churches, but only to lead to the Lord and to the knowledge of his truth as many as possible. From henceforth I shall be obliged to receive into our communion such as are excluded for Bible-truth's sake from other Churches, and I trust that in doing so, even though men should blame me for it, the Lord will grant his blessing.[34]

The Jerusalem bishopric did not prove to be an effective means of "restoring the historic episcopate" to the Protestant Churches. Gobat ordained only two German pastors, and their communions refused to recognize them as ministers. The plan was not continued beyond his incumbency. The agreement was terminated formally in 1886.

From the middle of the nineteenth century onward, there were recurring attempts to bring the churches of Germany together in orderly and mutually agreeable relationship.

The League of German Evangelical Churches, which was organized at Wittenberg in 1848, held regular meetings during the next twenty-five years. Like other church councils during this period, it had no synodal status; but the Central Committee of the Home Missions of the German Evangelical Churches (*Centralausschus für die Innere Mission der deutschen evangelischen Kirchen*), set up at the first meeting, achieved permanence through its extraordinary work. It is still functioning.

The Eisenach Conference of German Evangelical Church Governments (*Eisenacher Konferenz deutscher evangelischer Kirchenregierungen*), a more inclusive body, was formed in 1852. Without authority over the churches, it became a needed symbol of the desire for unity and greater freedom from governmental interference. It undertook successfully various useful services, such as the revision of the lectionary and of Luther's translation of the Bible.

The Committee of the German Evangelical Churches, appointed by

[33] Gobat was charged with trying to make proselytes from the Eastern Churches, which, if true, was contrary to the policy of the Anglican Church. The High Church party was especially sensitive on this point, because it strove for recognition by Orthodoxy of the Church of England as a branch of the Catholic Church.

[34] Consult Madame Roerich's biography of Gobat (English translation, with preface by Lord Shaftesbury, London, 1884).

the Eisenach Conference in 1903, prepared the way for the formation in 1922 of the Federation of German Evangelical Churches, in which were brought together twenty-eight autonomous regional churches.

The Evangelical Church in Germany, consisting of twenty-seven regional churches, was founded in 1948; likewise the United Evangelical Lutheran Church in Germany, comprising ten regional units.

13. The Anglican and Gallican Churches

To return to England and the eighteenth century: William Wake, after his elevation to the archbishopric in 1716, corresponded with Roman Catholic scholars at the Sorbonne and certain of the Paris clergy with whom he was acquainted. These discussions continued for a decade or longer and touched upon most of the phases of unity from the standpoint of the Anglican and Roman Churches.

Wake's position was that in both "matters of doctrine" and "matters of order and discipline" there should be differentiation between "fundamentals, in which all ought to agree" and non-fundamentals, "in which error or difference could be tolerated," and that those working for union would find that they "must at the last come to the Creeds of the first four General Councils" if they would "restore peace to the Church."

There were exhaustive examinations of Roman and Anglican teachings and practices. The French submitted eventually a statement laying down six conditions of reunion, substantially as follows:

In non-essentials differences of usage should not be regarded as a barrier;
Worship could be without the use of images;
The invocation of saints should not be required, every Christian being left free to pray directly to God;
Communion of the laity in both kinds should be permitted;
The authority of bishops proceeded from God alone, but subordination within the episcopate was allowable;
The Eucharist could be celebrated without elevation.

This statement the Archbishop found acceptable; but the most difficult problem, the papacy, remained unsolved. He apparently hoped that the Gallican Church would be led to renounce the authority of the Pope and become a national church, like the Anglican, conceding him "only a primacy of place and honour . . . as once bishop of the imperial city."

The whole correspondence must be described as unrealistic. Wake is believed to have carried it on not only without the approval of the English bishops but without their knowledge. And he was dealing with a small group of French Catholic dissentients who could have held no serious expectations of the slightest consideration from their Church or from Philippe, Duke of Orleans, Regent of France.

All the participants appear from the record to have had a good time, but nothing else came of it. The leaders on the French side drew severe censure for their part. The interest of this study in their exchange is their handling of questions of faith and order which still remain unanswered.

The *Commonitorium*[35] on the Thirty-nine Articles of Religion by Louis Ellies Du Pin, a Jansenist theologian and a professor at the Sorbonne, who joined in the symposium, is a comprehensive although perhaps not an entirely original treatise on the differences of the two churches in faith and polity. Along with the author's more important writings, it was placed on the *Index Expurgatorius.*[36]

14. The Non-jurors and Eastern Orthodoxy

The case of the Non-jurors of the Church of England introduces some of the characteristic obstacles to rapprochement between the Western and Orthodox Churches.

William Sancroft (1616-93), Archbishop of Canterbury, in 1688 concurred with the Lords in declaring James II incapable of ruling and appointing the Prince of Orange *custos regni,* but withheld consent when William and his consort were given the throne, on the grounds that he had already taken the oath of allegiance to the exiled monarch as king *divino jure.* Whereupon he was deposed. Parliament also deprived seven bishops and several hundred priests who supported Sancroft of their church offices.

These Non-jurors, as they were called, nevertheless continued to exercise their spiritual ministry as opportunity afforded, and attracted a considerable following of the laity. They charged the Established Church with being schismatic. There were circumstances which encouraged them to seek recognition by the Orthodox Churches.

In the first place, the Non-jurors stood upon the tradition of the influential Caroline theologians who appreciated Orthodoxy. One of their number, Bishop Frampton, had spent some time in the East, and his favorable impression had been shared by Archbishop Sancroft. Moreover, Peter the Great was inclined to their cause, for political reasons. When Charles I was executed, Russia had in protest canceled the concessions of British merchants. The Czar personally received the appeal of the Non-jurors and passed it to the hierarchs.

But the reply, which had been drafted by Chrysanthos, the Patriarch of Jerusalem, dashed their hopes. It declared "the Oriental Faith . . .

[35] J. L. Mosheim, *An Ecclesiastical History,* edited by Archibald Maclaine, Vol. V, Appendix III. Cf. *A History of the Ecumenical Movement,* pp. 139 f., on Christopher Davenport's *Deus, Natura, Gratia,* and p. 156 f. on Du Pin's *Commonitorium.*

[36] Du Pin's *Bibliothèque universelle des auteurs ecclésiastiques* (58 vols., 1686-1704), a complete history of the theological literature of the Church, etc.

the only true Faith." Complete agreement with the Church was necessary for recognition and intercommunion. This meant acceptance of the canons of the seven ecumenical councils, no less than of the Holy Scriptures.

The correspondents had suggested that actions of the councils were not to be regarded as of the same authority as "the Sacred Text" and therefore might be dispensed with, if need be. It was their position that in the Eucharist no certain interpretation of the Mystery should be required, the communicants being left free to receive the sacrament in faith and to commune with Christ in spirit, "without being obliged to worship the sacred Symbols of His presence." This was rejected as "blasphemy." They were admonished that it was not enough to believe that some "grace" was united with the sacrament; otherwise, there would be no communion "in the Body of Christ." The elements were "changed," they were informed, "to become one with Christ's Body in heaven."

The Non-jurors had ventured to believe that their Communion rite, compiled from the ancient services and the 1549 Book of Common Prayer, would be found acceptable. They prayed that, an agreement having been reached, a church might be built in which worship would be conducted by the new rite as well as by the Eastern ritual. But they were given to understand that, rather than agreeing to strange improvised liturgies, the Russian churchmen looked forward to the day when the Liturgy of St. John Chrysostom would be sung in St. Paul's Cathedral.[37]

After five years the hopes of the Non-jurors had revived, and in 1723 they addressed the Eastern Churches again. The newly established Russian Synod proposed that two British delegates be sent for "a friendly conference in the name and spirit of Christ" with representatives of the Church. The invitation was accepted and the delegation appointed; but before the consultation could be arranged, Peter the Great died and William Wake had written to the Orthodox authorities emphasizing the schismatic status of the Non-juring Church.

15. The Church of England and Dissent

Relations between the Church of England and dissenters were marked in the eighteenth century by much show of goodwill. There were repeated conversations between their leaders about "comprehension"—a concept of unity which could hardly be defined precisely but implied a recasting or reinterpretation by the Church of its order and doctrine to make room for receiving Nonconformists, with complementary accommodation on their part.[38] In high places on both sides were men of irenic natures; the

[37] See comment by Father Georges Florovsky in *A History of the Ecumenical Movement,* Chapter 3, p. 192.

[38] See the Muhlenberg plan, in section 7 above, "The Episcopal Church and Unity."

broadening influences of the age of learning had not been without effect on the minds of such men in the Established Church as Joseph Butler, bishop and author,[39] and Thomas Secker, Archbishop of Canterbury; and, of the separatists, such figures as Isaac Watts, Independent minister and hymn-writer; John Leland, trenchant apologist; and, most notably, Philip Doddridge. The last was a theologian, educator, and composer of hymns who in his literary work and ecumenical activities resembled Richard Baxter. These men were agreed that an acceptable scheme might be devised for bringing their communions together, but their talking came to no action. Secker sized up the circumstances in a letter to Doddridge, as follows:

> I agree with you heartily in wishing that such things as we think indifferent and you cannot be brought to think lawful, were altered or left free, in such a manner as that we might all unite. . . . I have no reason to believe that any one of the bishops wishes otherwise; and I know some who wish it strongly. . . . Nor were the body of the clergy ever so well disposed to it as now. But still I see not the least prospect of it.[40]

There was the familiar and obstinate problem of orders. Could the non-Anglicans receive ordination at the hands of the bishops without repudiating their previous setting apart for the ministry? Or could episcopal ordination be understood as the bishops' commending them for their known and accepted qualifications "to public service in their society or constitution"? By the latter version, the act might not be too unpalatable.

With reference to a conversation with Archbishop Herring, Doddridge wrote:

> When I mentioned to him . . . a sort of medium between the present state and that of a perfect coalition, which was that of acknowledging our churches as unschismatical, by permitting the clergy to officiate among us, if desired, which he must see had a counterpart of permitting Dissenting ministers occasionally to officiate in churches, it struck him much, as a new and very important thought; and he told me more than once, I had suggested what he should lay up in his mind for further consideration.[41]

How deeply the sentiments expressed penetrated into the ranks of the constituencies in either direction is undetermined. Perhaps the clergy and the ministers doubted that they were widely enough understood to justify an attempt to translate them into union; or the natural inertia of a period of comparative rest after revolution may have been a sufficient explanation of failure to act.

[39] *On Human Nature* (sermons in Rolls Chapel); *The Analogy of Religion, Natural and Revealed, to the Constitution and Course of Nature.*

[40] *The Correspondence and Diary of Philip Doddridge,* edited by J. D. Humphreys, Vol. IV, cited by Norman Sykes in *A History of the Ecumenical Movement,* p. 163.

[41] *The Correspondence and Diary of Philip Doddridge,* Vol. V, pp. 75 f.

During the Enlightenment religious dogmas lost much of their authority and importance for many churchmen; it is a paradox that, when beliefs are felt not to be of consequence, unity, which thus is made easier, suffers depreciation. In this kind of situation there are always non-theological arguments for maintaining the *status quo*. For one thing, easy doctrinal agreement makes fellowship of the sort experienced in discussions too pleasant to be exposed to the hazards of merger. They who worshiped in the Church and they who gathered in the conventicle would better stay in their defined preserves, where they could differ as they must and still keep on friendly terms, rather than try to crowd into one place and so risk losing their joy in each other. If there were some to suggest that, loving God, they could hope to dwell together in peace, the reply might have been that in his will separateness did not mean separation, which could not really exist where love was.

"Art is long, and time is fleeting," and men must find a goal and satisfaction day by day in the momentary and the incomplete, fragments of the eternal. Did the prelate who would "lay up in his mind for further consideration" the "new and very important thought" concerning "comprehension" reflect that the pursuit of Christian unity, greatest of the arts, was perhaps better than its possession?

16. The Society for Promoting Christian Knowledge

The Society for Promoting Christian Knowledge, founded in 1698, brought to its work during the eighteenth century a spirit of catholicity and cooperation which in unexampled ways surmounted sectarian bias in the area of faith and order. This was seen in its admission of non-Anglicans to membership, particularly Lutheran and Reformed clergy of Europe; also in its liberal use of books by Protestant authors. Among the works printed and circulated at home and in the colonies were John Arndt's *True Christianity,* August Hermann Francke's *Introduction to the Practice of the Christian Religion,* and Hugo Grotius' *The Truth about the Christian Religion.*

The wish to encourage favor for the plan to introduce episcopacy in the Protestant Churches on the Continent as a step toward union with the Church of England may have had something to do with shaping this policy. Jean Frédéric Ostervald, whose *Grounds and Principles of the Christian Religion* was published by the Society, was one of the leaders of this movement, as was Daniel Ernst Jablonski, whose translation of Josiah Woodward's *Account of the Rise of the Religious Societies in London* appeared in the list of books chosen. But, this aside, the history of the Society leaves no doubt that it was actuated, on the whole, by the spirit of catholicity.

Early evidence of this was its response to an appeal for help from the

Danish-Halle Mission in Tanquebar, India. The Society gave substantial financial aid and later contributed a printing press and provided for its operation. The Mission had been founded in 1705 by Frederick IV of Denmark, with the assistance of August Hermann Francke, the Pietist educator, who recruited the missionaries for it at the University of Halle.

Some years afterwards, the Society, unable to man its missions with British volunteers, got its missionaries through Francke at Halle. Those employed at various times numbered altogether close to sixty. Most were German Lutherans who served without being reordained. They ministered to the scattered congregations of Anglicans in the colonies and to the native churches, officiating at Communion and giving catechetical instruction. On occasion, they ordained Indian candidates for the ministry according to the order of the Church of England.

The Church Missionary Society, founded in 1799, followed the precedent established by the Society for Promoting Christian Knowledge, employing Lutheran missionaries trained at the Basle Mission House. Some 150 were engaged over the years. However, after 1825, "episcopal ordination became the rule for all ministers serving under Anglican auspices in India." [42]

The Society for Promoting Christian Knowledge and the Society for the Propagation of the Gospel in Foreign Parts, which had been organized in 1701, owed much of their eventual success to the support of the Evangelical element in the Church of England, who stressed salvation through personal faith in Christ and believed in cooperating with Christians of like mind in other denominations in proclaiming to all the world the gospel of redemption from sin.

These Evangelicals associated themselves with various evangelistic, missionary, and social movements which did their part in creating among the churches a sense of fellowship transcending ecclesiastical and even national boundaries. They constituted, for example, about half of the membership of the London Missionary Society formed by the Congregationalists in 1795.

In *The Unity of the Church: Another Tract for the Times, Addressed Respectfully to the Members of the Establishment,* the Hon. Baptist Noel in 1836 described the Evangelical's point of view, as follows:

> He would hold brotherly communion with those who after examination of the Scriptures, with prayer and reflection, believe that it is the will of the great Head of the Church that they should, on various particulars, dissent from us, allowing us, at the same time, the liberty which they claim for themselves. . . . To deny them to be members of the Body of Christ, to be alienated from them and to treat them with coldness or with jealousy, while they bear in their character and conduct all the great scriptural marks which

[42] An Anglican bishopric had been established at Calcutta. This brought the authority of the Church closer; and with the rise of Tractarianism in England emphasis on episcopacy and apostolic succession was increased. See *A History of the Ecumenical Movement,* p. 161.

prove them to be the children of God, is to do them wrong, and to manifest a spiritual blindness, a want of power to discern Christian character, affording a fearful sign that we have never been taught of God ourselves.[43]

17. Dissent and Tractarianism

The earlier tide of mutual goodwill in the churches had ebbed by 1836. This was apparent in Baptist Noel's tract, published that year, in which he wrote of the cold and jealous treatment of the Evangelicals and of the denial to them, on occasion, of membership in the Church.

That the harmonious relations between the denominations should have given way to unfriendliness or, at best, become less ready and free than they had been can be explained only by the peculiar shaping of events at the time.

Baptist Noel was drawing attention to one of the contributory conditions: the severe resentment of High Churchmen of the Establishment toward Evangelicals. In addition, a major thrust of the rising Tractarian Movement was aimed at dissent. John Henry Newman, who would soon initiate the movement for reconciliation with Rome, led the assault, and his writings reflect the acerbity of the feeling that existed. "There is not a dissenter living," he declared on one occasion, "but inasmuch, and so far as he dissents, he is in sin." [44]

Dissent provoked attack. Its very existence was provocation, destroying, as it did, the unity of the Church.

The Evangelical Awakening aggravated disunity. The majority of those who came under its influence belonged to—or, if not, joined—the separatist or Nonconformist denominations, which in many instances experienced phenomenal growth. Congregations affiliated with them appeared even in places where none had existed, as in Scotland, where Baptist and Independent groups emerged from the evangelistic missions conducted by Robert Haldane and his associates. In France and Switzerland these same elements and Methodists withdrew from the Reformation churches and formed themselves into separate communions. The followers of John Wesley in England and America had already settled into a denominational status. Soon there were Baptists and Methodists in Germany, Scandinavia, and other parts of Europe.[45]

[43] *The Unity of the Church: Another Tract for the Times, Addressed Respectfully to the Members of the Establishment,"* by Baptist Noel, cited in *A History of the Ecumenical Movement*, p. 272, with the comment: "This pronouncement, though written by one who twelve years later became a Baptist, is an accurate picture of the general Evangelical attitude."

[44] *Parochial and Plain Sermons*, Vol. III, p. 220.

[45] "The unpalatable conclusion must be accepted that one feature of the Evangelical Awakening, as of other dynamic spiritual awakenings, was a tendency to create divisions or new denominations. . . . Methodism, the earliest form of the Evangelical Awakening, produced a mighty division in Protestant Christendom. The *Réveil* in Switzerland and France played its part in leading to the formation of

This was not the whole picture. Dissent advocated disestablishment, which in the eyes of all parties of the Church was tantamount to destruction. The conflict became acrimonious almost beyond belief. "Black and infernal hag" was the street's epithet for the Church, but a prominent Congregational minister (Thomas Binney—1798-1874) could say from his pulpit: "It is with me . . . a matter of deep, serious religious conviction, that the Established Church is a great national evil; that it is an obstacle to the progress of truth and godliness in the land; that it destroys more souls than it saves; and that therefore its end is to be devoutly wished by every lover of God and man."

The activities of the British Anti-Church Association, whose first leader was Edward Miall, editor of *The Nonconformist,* were such as to create distrust of evangelicals even among Anglicans desiring to be friendly and cooperative.

The controversy was not alone between the Established Church and the dissenting denominations. The latter had their own sundering dissensions. It is true that many of their members as individuals realized the unity they shared in Christ and looked for (and found) opportunities to cooperate with one another;[46] but their churches as such, because of differences of doctrine and practice, generally stood rigidly apart.

In America, where the state churches, never strong, had by now been disestablished, the denominational cleavages persisted. As in Europe, most unitive measures failed. The resurgence of the spirit of the Awakening in the revivals of the first half of the nineteenth century brought no healing to disunion.

Latitudinarians added, in their way, to the agitation in England, but to the discomfort quite as much of their fellow Anglicans of other parties as of the Nonconformists.

The proposal of Thomas Arnold (1795-1842) of Rugby in 1833 that, to save the nation from moral collapse, Parliament reshape the structure of the Church of England so as to bring within it the dissenting denominations could not have pleased the latter, with either its plan of "constitutional episcopacy" or its announced intentions of "modifying their fanaticism and dissociating them from the utter coarseness and deformity of their chapels." [47] But the almost unanimous opposition within the Church itself made resistance from without unnecessary.

Free Churches in several Swiss cantons and in France. It was the Evangelical ministers of the Church of Scotland whose conscience in the matter of spiritual freedom in the Church drove them to the Disruption in 1843 and to the foundation of the Free Church of Scotland." (Ruth Rouse, in *A History of the Ecumenical Movement,* p. 316.)

[46] In the united missionary and social reform efforts which were the fruit of the Evangelical Awakening, there were abundant signs in many lands that the active co-operation between the members of Protestant Churches had led to the development of an ecumenical spirit." (Ruth Rouse, in *A History of the Ecumenical Movement,* p. 316.)

[47] *Principles of Church Reform* (4th ed.), pp. 75 and 90.

The religio-philosophical ideas of Frederick Denison Maurice were rather too vague and unrealistic to be seriously disturbing. Interesting questions of faith and order were raised by his theory that, since the whole human race had been created in Christ and redeemed by his death, all men were in some sense in the Universal Church, whether they recognized themselves to be or not. In his book *The Kingdom of Christ,* he elaborated his conception of the position of the Church of England and its relation with the non-Anglican churches within the Universal Church—which was universal, actually, with the limitations that Romanists and Unitarians could not be included.

At a later date, Arthur Penrhyn Stanley, after 1864 Dean of Westminster, was the recognized leader of the Broad Church party. A student for five years at Rugby, he had been influenced by Thomas Arnold, who had, as noted, liberal views on church union. A biographer wrote of Stanley: "Our need for some larger framework for the Church of Christ haunted him in youth and was to his last consciousness the cherished and dominating idea of his life." [48] He cultivated acquaintance with Nonconformists and, on occasion, had ministers of the Free Churches preach in the Abbey pulpit. This course gave offense to many of his colleagues. Their exasperation rose to high pitch when he invited the committee created by the Lambeth Convocation in 1870 to revise the New Testament, before commencing their labors, to receive Holy Communion in Henry VII's Chapel. He believed that there was in the Church of England "a ground of antiquity, of freedom, and of common sense," on which it could "calmly and humbly confront" not only "both of the great divisions of Christendom" but the Protestant and the dissenting denominations as well, with a bid for reunion, without laying itself open to the "charge of ignorant presumption, or of learned trifling, or of visions that [could] never be realized." [49] The foundation of unity would have to be laid, he thought, in better knowledge, mutual appreciation, and frank recognition of the different vocations of the churches.

Broad Churchmen, more than Evangelicals and those who made up the High Church party, were intellectually children of the age, although most of them probably would not have admitted sympathy with humanism.

Maurice was careful to explain that his concept of a Universal Church rested upon "the very nature of God" and his union with his creatures, rather than upon "human inventions and human thoughts." Yet his philosophy betrayed the influence of Leibnizianism, particularly in its allowance for social, political, and ecclesiastical manipulations in the quest of unity. It was his and his colleagues' depreciation of orthodox interpretations and of ancient forms, always a mark of liberalism, that made them Broad Churchmen.

[48] R. E. Prothero, *Life and Letters of Dean Stanley,* Vol. II, p. 114.
[49] *A History of the Ecumenical Movement,* p. 276.

The history of the second half of the eighteenth century and of the first three-quarters of the nineteenth shows that Christianity had to pay dearly for what it gained from the Enlightenment and from the Awakening as well. The one had not been an unmixed evil, nor the other an unalloyed blessing. Both movements had to establish the bounds of their spiritual conquests within the Church, and the intermingling of their respective rationalism and romanticism could only have resulted in turbulence.

18. Tractarianism and Rome

Beginning with John Henry Newman's first tract in 1833 the original mission of Tractarianism was "to combat Popery and Dissent," but within a few years some of its leaders were drawn toward reunion with Rome. It was not so much a case of deciding to join an enemy who could not be conquered, perhaps, as of attempting marriage with the view of reforming an erring but desired partner. The hope of many on the Anglican side was that as the two churches drew closer together the other would abandon practices they could not bring themselves to accept.

Newman and other Tractarians studied to establish the Catholic character of the Church of England and by reinterpretation to reconcile the Articles of Religion with the decrees of Trent.

So competent an authority as the Roman Catholic Archbishop Nicholas Patrick Stephen Wiseman (1802-65) admitted that the second of these aims was measurably accomplished. "That the feelings that have been expressed in favour of a return to unity by the Anglican Church are every day widely spreading and deeply sinking," he wrote to the Earl of Shrewsbury, "no one who has means of judging, I think, can doubt. . . . Such interpretations can be given to the most difficult articles as will strip them of all contradiction to the decrees of the Tridentine Synod." [50]

The main problem, however, was not the Roman Catholic Church of official definition, which could be shown to be "not too remote from . . . Anglicanism," [51] but "that vast practical system which lay beyond the letter of the Council of Trent—things which were taught with quasi-authority in the Roman Church." [52] And in respect of these last there was no sign that Rome considered mending her ways. She had not, of course, recognized the claim of the Church of England to true Catholicity.

The definition of papal infallibility by the Vatican Council in 1870,

[50] *A Letter on Catholic Unity*, pp. 21 and 38.
[51] *A History of the Ecumenical Movement,* p. 279.
[52] E. B. Pusey, *Eirenicon,* 1st ed., p. 98. Pusey was regarded as the theologian of the Oxford Movement.

favored strongly by Archbishop Henry Edward Manning,[53] brought an end to the long effort of the Tractarians to find a way to reunion. "I have done what I could," wrote Edward Bouverie Pusey to Cardinal John Henry Newman, upon the conclusion of the third, and last, *Eirenicon,* "and now have done with controversy and *Eirenica.*" [54]

The Holy See had in 1864 condemned "in principle" the Association for the Promotion of the Unity of Christendom and forbidden Roman Catholics to take part in its program, which sought only to enlist Anglican, Latin, and Greek Christians "for united prayer that visible unity might be restored to Christendom." This condemnation was believed to have been contrived by Cardinal Manning. The Association had been formed in 1857 upon the initiative of Ambrose Phillipps De Lisle, formerly an Anglican layman who had joined the Church of Rome before the beginning of the Oxford Movement. It had the support of various prominent Anglicans and Romanists, but Dr. Manning had not shared his Archbishop's[55] friendliness toward it. By the end of seven years, the Association had succeeded in enrolling for prayer for the unity of Christendom five thousand Anglicans, one thousand Roman Catholics, and three hundred communicants of the Eastern Orthodox Churches.[56] These were pledged to offer daily the following petition, with the Lord's Prayer:

> O Lord Jesus Christ, who saidst unto Thine Apostles, Peace I leave with you; My Peace I give unto you: regard not my sins, but the faith of Thy Church; and grant her that Peace and Unity which is agreeable to Thy Will, who livest and reignest for ever and ever. Amen.[57]

It may be said that Rome could have justified her disapproval on the ground that the Association for the Promotion of the Unity of Christendom tended to encourage the presumption that she recognized the

[53] Manning left the Church of England for Rome in 1851. He was ordained to the priesthood within a few months and advanced rapidly, until in 1865 he succeeded Archbishop Wiseman. His intense loyalty to the Roman Church left in his heart little room for kindly sentiments for the Church of England, which he came to regard as "the mother of all the intellectual and spiritual aberrations which covered the face of England."

[54] H. P. Liddon, *Life of E. B. Pusey,* Vol. IV, p. 193.

[55] The Archbishop was Wiseman, who was to be succeeded by Manning in 1865.

[56] These figures are approximate. See *A History of the Ecumenical Movement,* p. 347.

[57] It is interesting to note that the Lambeth Conference, influenced by the Association for the Promotion of the Unity of Christendom, urged that prayer be offered in the Church of England for the reunion of Christendom. Its action in 1878 was: "Believing that intercession ever tends to deepen and strengthen that unity of His Church for which our Lord earnestly pleaded . . . your Committee trusts that this Conference will recommend the observance throughout the Churches of the Communion of a season of prayer for the unity of Christendom. . . . They venture to suggest that . . . the time should be the Tuesday before Ascension Day, or any of the seven days thereafter." (*The Lambeth Conferences,* pp. 53, 86 and 205.)

Church of England and the Eastern Orthodox Churches as her Catholic equals—which they claimed to be and she denied.

19. The Free Churches and Unity

Nineteenth-century records show few instances of inquiry by Nonconformists into questions of doctrine in their bearing upon denominational relations. Such actions of this kind as occurred were undertaken, for the most part, by individuals, rather than by the churches, in response to approaches from Anglicans.

Some of the Free Church leaders took an interest in the Home Reunion Society, founded in 1873 by A. T. Mowbray, a layman of the Anglican Church, with encouragement by representatives of all parties, "to present the Church of England in a conciliatory attitude towards those who [regarded] themselves as outside her pale, so as to lead them to the corporate reunion of all Chritsians holding the doctrines of the Ever-Blessed Trinity and the Incarnation and Atonement of our Lord Jesus Christ."[58] This organization had for its chairman Horatio, third Earl Nelson (1823-1913), a man of quiet and irenic spirit, who devoted the last forty years of his life to it. He gave himself to it and assumed its responsibilities so completely that it expired with him, not having developed any program beyond meetings for the hearing and discussing of papers on subjects within the scope of its concern.

In 1888 the Archbishop of Canterbury, Edward White Benson (1829-96), forwarded to the heads of the Free Churches the Chicago-Lambeth Quadrilateral resolutions. He received acknowledgments from the Baptist Union, Congregational Union, Wesleyan Methodist Conference, and Presbyterian Synod.

Comments from these sources dealt mainly with the clause proposing adoption of the historic episcopate as a condition of reunion. Discussion of the document was not confined to official communications. Henry Robert Reynolds, co-editor of the *British Quarterly Review,* wrote that it signified "obviously a very strong and Godly feeling arising in favour of some close union with all Christians."

The sentiments of many outside the Church of England were more frankly expressed by Robert Forman Horton, at the time minister of Lyndhurst Road Church (Congregational), Hampstead:

> To come forward and invite Nonconformists to reunion on the bland terms that they should incontinently surrender the very point for which they had striven, the very point in which their conviction had been established in their

[58] Second article of the constitution, which continued: "The Society, though it cannot support any scheme of comprehension compromising the three Creeds, or the Episcopal constitution of the Church, will be prepared to advocate all reasonable liberty in matters not contravening the Church's Faith, Order, or Discipline."

favour, first by experience, and latterly by impartial scholarship, was not, when one comes to reflect, a probable way of securing the object. Confusion of thought could hardly go further; it raised a previous question, whether Episcopal intelligence could justify the surrender, which Episcopal charity demanded.[59]

20. The Ecumenical Influence of Books

If books should be included with other means, revealing and shaping Christian faith and organization, the two volumes of essays by Free Church scholars, most of them Congregationalists, which were published around 1870 under the title *Ecclesia* are worthy of a place in the ecumenical record of this period. In them were ably treated subjects touching the relations between the churches and questions involved in a constructive approach to reunion, with especial attention to the nature and functions of the Church. Henry Robert Reynolds of the *British Quarterly Review* was editor.

At the same time a committee of Anglicans, under the chairmanship of William Dalrymple Maclagan (1826-1910), later Archbishop of York, was preparing a work of similar character on *The Church and the Age, Essays on the Principles and Present Position of the Anglican Church,* and there is a legend to the effect that the two groups dined together and toasted each other on the success of their respective enterprises.

John Stoughton's (1807-97) *A History of Religion in England*[60] was of special value because of its attention to relations between the denominations and its careful record of unitive movements. The author and Dean Stanley were close friends and much alike in their liberal-mindedness and in their interest in the cause of Christian unity. H. R. T. Brandreth calls Stoughton "the ecumenical peacemaker amongst British Church historians."[61]

The century in its middle and later periods saw the production of various theological reference works which demonstrated the overpassing of sectarian lines by scholarship, among them *The Expositor's Bible, The International Critical Commentary, The International Theological Library* and the several *Dictionaries* of James Hastings.[62]

No complete listing of books which chronicled or otherwise contributed to the advances of thought in the churches on doctrinal and ecclesiological questions bearing upon unity can be undertaken here. Some of special significance may be found in the Bibliography.

[59] *The Reunion of English Christendom,* pp. 143 f.
[60] *A History of Religion in England,* 8 vols. Note particularly Vols. III and IV.
[61] *A History of the Ecumenical Movement,* p. 284.
[62] *Dictionary of the Bible,* 1898; *Dictionary of Christ and the Gospels,* 1906; *Dictionary of the Apostolic Church,* 1914 *et seq.; Encyclopaedia of Religion and Ethics,* 1908 *et seq.* All these works were projected before the turn of the century.

21. The Grindelwald Conferences

During the last decade of the century, Henry S. Lunn, through his *Review of the Churches* and Grindelwald Conferences, helped the churches in their growth toward the "better knowledge" which such ecumenically minded persons as Dean Stanley and John Stoughton—and before them Philip Doddridge and Archbishop Secker—knew to be a primary condition of reunion.

Like many Christian leaders at that time, Lunn believed the churches should be brought together to discuss with full frankness the things which divided them. Within some of them, too, there were parties at odds with one another on theological or other questions, and he thought that they should face their disagreements in the same way. There was little likelihood, however, that such a meeting of minds could be arranged through official action on the part of the ecclesiastical authorities. He turned to the launching of a journal as the only practical alternative. Published monthly from 1891 to 1895 under an editorial board of churchmen drawn from various communions and schools of thought, it opened its pages to influential spokesmen of all connections and points of view, including Unitarians, Old Catholics, and Roman Catholics, and gave them freedom to write as they would on any subject, controversial or not. Under this policy the journal became in successive issues a series of symposia on the widest variety of themes: disestablishment, the teaching of religion in the elementary schools, biblical criticism, the nature of the Church, episcopacy and other polities, apostolic succession, and many more. Besides being a forum for discussion, it specialized in reporting movements of general interest in the churches. In addition, it covered the news, by way of informing the churches of one another's activities, and introduced from time to time persons who were distinguishing themselves in some phase of religious or social work. "The conditions prevailing in Christendom in the five years during which . . . *The Review* appeared," wrote Miss Ruth Rouse, "live again for the student as during no other lustrum between 1800 and 1910."[63]

A Methodist minister, physician, missionary, journalist, and travel agent, Lunn had a genius, as his success in this instance proved, for bringing diverse persons together and helping them discover for themselves that their ideas were often more complementary than contradictory. The assisting board of editors consisted of John Clifford, minister of the Melbourne Terrace Church (Baptist), London; Sir Percy William Bunting (Methodist), editor of *The Contemporary Review*; Canon Frederick William Farrar (Anglican), Dean of Canterbury;[64] Donald

[63] *A History of the Ecumenical Movement,* p. 339.
[64] Author of the popular *Life of Christ.*

Fraser (Presbyterian), minister of Marylebone Presbyterian Church, London; and Alexander Mackennal (Congregationalist), pastor at Bowdoin, Cheshire, and "prime organizer of the International Congregational Council in 1891."

These same men and others whom they persuaded to join them cooperated with Lunn when he set about supplementing the journalistic program with holidays in Switzerland combining the attractions of recreation in the Alps with conferences in which ecumenical conversations could be carried on vis-à-vis with the same freedom afforded by the columns of *The Review*.

The addresses and reports of the discussions at Grindelwald were printed in *The Review* and picked up by the press. New interest in Christian reunion was aroused "all over the world and in many churches." [65] The meetings were a means of broader and more accurate knowledge, as well as of better acquaintance and closer fellowship, and for this reason did much to soften the feeling over theological and ecclesiastical differences.[66]

Prayer for reunion was emphasized in the promotion of the movement. The churches generally responded to an appeal of prominent churchmen in *The Times* of London to set aside for this purpose certain Sundays preceding the opening of the conferences. In 1894, the Archbishop of Canterbury[67] approved the suggestion that Whitsunday be observed as a day of prayer for the drawing together of all Christians, asking the bishops and clergy to use the Prayer for Unity from the Accession Service in the Book of Common Prayer. He expressed the hope that the Free Churches would join in the observance in such ways as they considered suitable. The following year Pope Leo XIII directed that special prayers for unity be offered in the Roman Catholic Church in England on Whitsunday.

There were six Home Reunion Conferences, five at Grindelwald and one at Lucerne.[68] The Free Church representatives at them were mainly responsible for the founding in England of the Free Church Congress in 1892 and of the National Council of Evangelical Free Churches in 1896.

22. The Church of England and the Church of Sweden

The relations of the Anglican communion and the Church of Sweden had over the years been such as to encourage the belief that differences between them on matters of faith and order could be fully resolved.

[65] Ruth Rouse, in *A History of the Ecumenical Movement*, p. 339.
[66] *Chapters of My Life, with Special Reference to Reunion,* by Sir Henry S. Lunn, published in 1918, helped to sustain the interest the movement created in "Home Reunion."
[67] Edward White Benson.
[68] There were both summer and winter conferences. The period during which they were held covered the years from 1892 to 1895.

No question had been raised as to the adequacy of the ordination of either Peter Fjellstedt,[69] a Swedish minister trained at the Mission House in Basle, whom the Church Missionary Society appointed in 1829 to its service, or the bishops of Sweden requested by the Anglican Church[70] in 1837 to confirm the children of British families residing in Sweden.

When they encountered each other in the United States, the Church of Sweden and the Protestant Episcopal Church practiced a policy of reciprocity, communicants of each accepting, when without pastors, the ministry of the other. When Swedish immigrants in 1841 chose Gustaf Unonius to be their minister, their Church at home instructed them to have him seek ordination by Episcopal bishops; and after 1866 the Swedish Church for many years commended its members in the United States to the Episcopal Church for shepherding, if they had no access to churches of their own confession.[71]

Experience seemed to lend reasonableness, therefore, to the conclusion of a committee of the Lambeth Conference of 1888 with reference to the Church of Sweden: "As its standards of doctrine are to a great extent in accord with our own and its continuity as a national Church has never been broken, any approaches on its part should be most gladly welcomed with a view to mutual explanation of differences, and the ultimate adjustment, if possible, of permanent intercommunion on sound principles of ecclesiastical polity." [72]

But for more than twenty years the mutual interest between the Churches did not proceed beyond discussion.

An Anglican commission on relations with the Church of Sweden was appointed by the Archbishop of Canterbury, Randall Thomas Davidson, in 1909. Two years later it reported that "the succession of bishops" had been "maintained unbroken by the Church of Sweden," and that it had "a true conception of the episcopal office"—and further that the office of priest was "rightly conceived as a divinely instituted instrument for the ministry of Word and Sacraments" and had been "in intention handed on throughout the whole history of the Church of Sweden." [73]

The Lambeth Conference recommended in 1920 "that members of that Church, qualified to receive the Sacraments in their own Church, should be admitted to Holy Communion in ours . . . also that on suitable occasions permission should be given to Swedish ecclesiastics to give addresses in our Church . . . further, that in the event of an invitation being extended to an Anglican Bishop or Bishops to take part in the consecration of a Swedish Bishop, the invitation should, if possible, be accepted, subject to the approval of the Metropolitan."

Uppsala in 1922 accepted the Lambeth proposals, and they have

[69] See Carl Anshelm, *Peter Fjellstedt,* Vol. I, pp. 80-83, 139-49.

[70] The request was made by C. J. Bromfield, Bishop of London, through the King of Sweden.

[71] *Documents on Christian Unity,* edited by G. K. A. Bell, Vol. I, pp. 186 f.

[72] *Lambeth Conference,* Report, 1888, p. 67.

[73] *Lambeth Conference,* Report, 1918, p. 109.

proved a practicable basis of rapprochement. They were never adopted, however, by any Anglican convocation, and the practice of intercommunion, the interchange of pulpits, and fellowship in the consecration of bishops to which they have led has been, from the Church of England's side, only semi-official.

The leisurely way in which the two Churches proceeded indicated that neither was moved by great enthusiasm. Their communications with each other brought out important differences in emphasis. Insofar as the bishops expressed its mind, the Church of England was concerned especially with historic succession in the ministry and ecclesiastical order.[74] The Swedish Church stressed doctrine. The reason for the slow progress of their negotiations may have lain here. So long as they could be assured that the conditions of episcopacy had been met, the English were disposed to allow the widest latitude in the definition of dogma. The Lutherans wanted to know, before acting, that the Anglican Church set the Scriptures above all other sources of divine revelation and believed in salvation by grace and justification through faith alone.

For some Anglicans an obstacle to closer ties with the Church of Sweden was the fact that it stood in full communion with the Churches of Norway, Denmark, and Iceland, which, according to the views of the Church of England, had "lost the continuity of their episcopal succession." The Lambeth Conference, however, took the position that churches might enter into "a measure of fellowship" without involving one another in other ecclesiastical relationships which they had contracted. At the same time, the Conference agreed that "abnormalities" in the practice of a church need not prevent all intercourse with it, though delaying the establishment of intercommunion. With an eye upon the foreign mission field, where churches might be without proper episcopal supervision, as the Church of England knew from its own early missionary experience, the Lambeth Conference of 1920 added to its resolution on relations with the Church of Sweden this qualification:

> If the authorities of any province of the Anglican Communion find local irregularities in the order or practice of the Church of Sweden outside that country, they may legitimately, within their own region, postpone any such action as is recommended in this resolution[75] until they are satisfied that these irregularities have been removed.

[74] "The Swedes made it clear that they did not consider any system of Church order as having exclusive divine authority, though they were glad to 'regard the peculiar forms and traditions of their Church with the reverence due a venerable legacy from the past.'" (Stephen Charles Neill, in *A History of the Ecumenical Movement,* p. 471.)

[75] The resolution of 1920: "The Conference recommends that members of that Church [Swedish], qualified to receive the Sacraments in their own Church, should be admitted to Holy Communion in ours . . . also that on suitable occasions permission should be given to Swedish ecclesiastics to give addresses in our Church . . . and further, that in the event of an invitation being extended to an Anglican Bishop or Bishops to take part in the consecration of a Swedish Bishop, the invitation should, if possible, be accepted, subject to approval of the Metropolitan."

23. The Anglican and Moravian Churches

The Anglican communion lacked sufficient unity in matters of faith and order to pursue successfully its ecumenical concerns. Another instance was its action with reference to *Unitas Fratrum*.[76]

Holding to the Zinzendorfian principle that confessional formulations of doctrine were divinely ordained means (*Tropen*) of Christian edification, whereby each denomination had a distinctive contribution to make to the Church Universal, the Moravian Church was not forward in seeking union as one ecclesiastical body with another, though its members looked for opportunity to share "spiritual gifts" individually through fellowship and cooperation with other Christians. However, it manifested interest in a discussion by the Lambeth Conference of 1878 of problems which stood in the way of closer relations between Anglicans and Moravians. But the Conference took thirty years (until 1908) to decide that doctrinal agreement presented no great difficulty. It rejected at the same time the validity of Moravian orders but suggested that these could be set right through fraternal officiation by Anglican bishops at Moravian consecrations.

Recognition by Archbishop William Wake of the episcopal succession of *Unitas Fratrum* was apparently regarded as a precedent too far removed or too much influenced by considerations of expediency to have any authority; but the Archbishop of Canterbury, Randall Davidson, sent a letter of good will to the Moravian Synod meeting in 1908 in Dukinfield, England.

The bearer of this message was Bishop Ethelbert Talbot of Pennsylvania, who attended the synod and spoke during its course of the rather general practice of intercommunion by the Protestant Episcopal and Moravian Churches in the United States. He said further:

> Your bishops have come down in historical continuity through the first of the bishops, through Christ and the holy Apostles down to the present time. That is what we call the historical succession or historic episcopacy, and something which you hold as precious and very sacred. We recognize that, and that is a very strong point of kinship and alliance already between you and us.[77]

The General Synod of the Moravian Church considered the Lambeth proposals for several years[78] and concluded that acceptance of them

[76] The Moravian Church.

[77] "Verbatim Report of a Closed Session of the Synod of the Moravian Church" Dukinfield, England, p. 7.

[78] The letters exchanged on this issue are printed in Vol. II, pp. 117-142, of *Documents on Christian Unity*, edited by G. K. A. Bell.

would be tantamount to "absorption." Fuller relations with the Anglican Church were not desirable, it agreed, on the condition of giving up intercommunion with other churches.

24. Lord Halifax and the Churches of England and Rome

The Tractarians thought of their later mission in terms primarily of reunion with Rome and Eastern Orthodoxy. For them the basic reality was the Catholic Church, which, however divided outwardly, was inwardly one through the sharing of a common sacramental life. Said John Henry Newman,[79] "We are the English Catholics; abroad are the Roman Catholics, some of whom are also among ourselves; elsewhere are the Greek Catholics." But neither they nor their successors were able to gain, East or West, acceptance of their thesis concerning the Church of England's equal Catholic estate. Rome closed the door upon them in 1896, with the issuance of the papal bull *Apostolicae Curae,* which declared Anglican orders invalid.

This action was precipitated by the activity of Hon. Charles Wood, Second Viscount Halifax, a devout Roman Catholic, who believed in the aims of Tractarianism. He and Ferdinand Portal, a French priest, whom he persuaded to examine the history and faith of Anglicanism, conceived the idea of a direct approach to Rome. The response was an apostolic letter in 1895 by Pope Leo XIII appealing to the English people to return to the Church of Rome. The following year he convened the commission of inquiry which pronounced the adverse judgment against Anglican orders.

Discussion through the press evoked some support of Anglican claims even from Roman Catholics.[80] Ferdinand Portal had concluded from his study of Anglicanism that they were probably of uncertain validity. Herbert Cardinal Vaughan, Archbishop of Westminster, manifested an unfavorable, not to say hostile, attitude. Copies of the answer to the papal bull, which appeared over the names of Frederick Temple and William Dalrymple Maclagan, Archbishops, respectively, of Canterbury and York,[81] were sent to the bishops of the Eastern Orthodox Churches, who later received also Cardinal Vaughan's reply to this Anglican *Responsio.* Professor V. A. Sokolov of Moscow Theological Academy published *An Enquiry into the Hierarchy of the Anglican Episcopal Church,* in which he analyzed *Apostolicae Curae* and expressed the opinion that

[79] In a sermon on "Submission to Church Authority" (November 29, 1829, included in *Parochial and Plain Sermons,* Vol. III, edition of 1885, pp. 191 ff.

[80] Abbé L. M. O. Duchesne favored validity.

[81] The *Responsio* was reported to have been written, for the most part, by Christopher Wordsworth, Bishop of Lincoln; Mandell Creighton, Bishop of Oxford; and William Stubbs, Bishop of Peterborough (later of London). Archbishop Temple was credited with revision.

Anglican orders could be recognized by the Orthodox Churches. In a similar monograph, Professor Athanasius Bulgakov of Kiev Theological Academy came to the same conclusion. Their studies were printed in English by the Church Historical Society.[82]

Lord Halifax did not lose faith in the cause of reunion between Canterbury and Rome, and when, a quarter of a century later (1920), Cardinal Désiré Joseph Mercier, Archbishop of Malines (Mechlin, Belgium), replied in friendly vein to Lambeth's "Appeal to All Christian People," [83] he was easily persuaded that the way had been opened for a renewal of effort on its behalf, which he undertook forthwith, in association again with Ferdinand Portal. The Cardinal received their proposal of informal conferences under his presidency favorably, and Cardinal Enrico Gasparri, who had been a member of the commission of inquiry in 1896, conveyed to him by letter the Pontiff's (Benedict XV) approval. "The Holy See approves and encourages your conversation," he wrote.

The conversations took place in the Palace at Malines, with Dr. Armitage Robinson, Dean of Wells, and Dr. W. H. Frere, Bishop of Truro, in attendance as representatives of the Anglican Church, and, besides Halifax and Portal, Abbe Hippolyte Hemmer and Monseigneur Pierre Batiffol for Rome. The Cardinal had his Vicar-General, Monseigneur Joseph Ernest van Roey, present also; and Bishop Charles Gore of Oxford and Dr. B. J. Kidd, the patristic scholar, were added to the Anglican delegation.[84]

The death of Cardinal Mercier occurred after the fourth conversation of 1925, and Ferdinand Portal died the following year. The new Archbishop, Cardinal Joseph Ernest van Roey,[85] presided over the fifth conversation, which was the last.[86] The papal encyclical *Mortalium Animos,* issued in 1928, condemned the Malines conferences by implication, a verdict made explicit soon thereafter by a statement in *Osservatore Romano*. By that time Lord Halifax had almost reached the age of ninety.

Of the results of the venture, H. R. T. Brandreth says:

> It is not easy to assess the value of the Malines Conversations. To-day, both on the Anglican and the Roman side, there is a clear conviction that they must not be repeated. But that is not necessarily to label them a failure, for, indeed, the spirit of Malines has informed many small and informal

[82] See *A History of the Ecumenical Movement*, pp. 210, 211, in a chapter by Dr. Georges Florovsky. The English titles of the tracts referred to are: "One Chapter from an Enquiry into the Hierarchy of the Anglican Episcopal Church" (Sokolov) and "The Question of Anglican Orders, in Respect of the 'Vindication' of the Papal Decision" (Bulgakov), London, 1899.

[83] Issued in an encyclical letter from the Conference of 252 Anglican bishops, proposing the consideration of a union of all Christians on the basis of episcopacy.

[84] Monseigneur van Roey succeeded Cardinal Mercier in 1926.

[85] Died 1961.

[86] See *The Conversations at Malines: Original Documents,* by Halifax.

meetings between members of the Roman and other Churches, and has shown itself as a torch whose light has waxed rather than waned.[87]

It will be remembered, of course, that the Tractarian Movement represented the aspirations of the High Church party, and that many Anglicans were not in sympathy with its purpose to bring about a union of the Church of England with the Church of Rome. Some of the bishops objected even to the guarded recognition given the Malines conversations by Archbishop Randall Davidson, as they—or their predecessors—had read with disapproval, because of its Anglo-Catholic overtones, the response of Archbishops Frederick Temple and William Dalrymple Maclagan to the papal bull, *Apostolicae Curae,* rejecting the validity of Anglican orders.

Here is seen the disunity, already referred to, which beset the Anglican Church in all its negotiations with the Catholic communions looking to union or closer rapprochement. The question of its character as a church was always near the surface. The Russian Orthodox Synod, responding to the invitation of Ecumenical Patriarch Joachim III in 1902 to all autocephalous Orthodox Churches to give their opinion of relations with other denominations, said concerning the Anglican Church: "It was indispensable that the desire for union with the Eastern Orthodox Church should become the sincere desire, not only of a certain section of Anglicanism, but of the whole Anglican community, and that the other . . . Calvinistic current . . . should be absorbed in the above-mentioned pure current, and should lose its perceptible, if we may not say exclusive, influence . . . upon the whole Church life of this Confession." [88]

25. The Old Catholic Churches

The Old Catholic Movement originated in the refusal of groups of Roman priests and laymen in scattered communities of Central Europe to accept the dogma of papal infallibility proclaimed by the Vatican Council in 1870. The movement was interpreted by its leaders as "not simply a protest against the new dogmatic definitions . . . , but a return to the true catholicism of the one undivided Church, and a challenge to all Christian confessions to unite on the basis of the original Christian Faith." [89] The announced purpose of the churches associating themselves

[87] *A History of the Ecumenical Movement*, p. 299.

[88] Quoted by Georges Florovsky in *A History of the Ecumenical Movement,* p. 211.

[89] From a paper by Monseigneur E. Lagerwey, Bishop of Deventer, in the archives of the World Council of Churches, Geneva.

The German school of Catholic theologians who had been opposed to the promulgation of the dogma of infallibility took a position between the Gallican theory of the competence of a council to define the faith and the ultramontane

with it to seek union with certain communions and friendly intercourse with others raised serious questions of faith and order—particularly of order. "We hope," resolved the first Old Catholic Congress, at Munich in 1871, "for union with the Greek-Oriental and Russian Churches, the separation of which was not brought about by any decisive causes, and which is not based on any irreconcilable doctrinal differences. We hope for a gradual *rapprochement* with the Protestant and with the Episcopal Churches." [90]

The phrasing of this resolution suggested that its framers felt they could approach the Eastern Orthodox Churches as Catholic equals, the equality extending, as it would appear, to Orthodoxy's uncertainty concerning the episcopal succession of the Anglican churches, which were mentioned in a category apart. However, in the end their bid to the East was rejected, and they eventually adopted intercommunion with the Church of England.

Both the Anglican and the Orthodox Churches had interested themselves in the problems and aspirations of the Old Catholic cause, the one through its Anglican and Continental Churches Society, and the other through its Society of the Friends of Religious Instruction. Representatives from these boards attended the so-called Conferences on Reunion at Bonn, Germany, in 1874 and 1875. On these occasions, which were little more than informal discussions by theologians, some progress was made toward agreement in matters of doctrine. The main problem was reconciling Eastern and Western views on the *Filioque* clause in the Niceno-Constantinopolitan Creed, but a statement summa-

---

view, holding that the concurrence of Pope and Council—the voice of the united episcopate—was requisite. The bishops gave assent to the Vatican decree, many reluctantly, in dread of schism and isolation. Even Karl Josef Hefele, the author of a learned work on the history of councils which exposed the groundlessness of the doctrine of papal infallibility, yielded after delay, though he had declared that he would lay down his office before he would renounce his convictions. "I believed that I was serving the Catholic Church," he later said, "and I was serving the caricature which Romanism and Jesuitism had made out of it. Not until I was in Rome was it perfectly clear to me that what they pursue and practise (*treibt und übt*) there has only the false semblance (*Schein*) and name of Christianity—only the shell; the kernel is gone: everything is utterly externalized." A considerable number of theologians, headed by Ignatius von Döllinger, "the ablest and most learned of the German Catholic divines," refused to submit, claiming that the Council had not been united, and that the decision had been obtained by unfair tactics. The movement attained to some strength in Switzerland. Père Hyacinthe Loyson, an eloquent preacher, gathered a congregation in Paris in affiliation with it. There were other Old Catholic churches in Austria and Holland. It had not been the intention of the dissentients to found a separate church. Their hope was in the reformation of Rome. When this proved vain and a new church had been organized, its first bishop was ordained by the Jansenist Churches of Holland, in which the episcopal succession had been preserved.

"The Old Catholic movement commanded the approval of a highly respectable body of cultivated men. But it had no deep root among the common people." (George P. Fisher, *History of the Christian Church.*)

[90] See *Minutes of the Old Catholic Congress at Munich, 1871,* English edition, London, 1872.

rizing the doctrines of the Holy Spirit[91] in the age of the Ecumenical Councils met with acceptance. The Orthodox delegates would not commit themselves in any opinion on Anglican orders. In official sessions, the Conferences voted to abolish compulsory fasting and confession, to use the vernacular in public worship, to permit the marriage of priests, and to give Communion in both kinds to "members of the English Episcopal Church."

The report of a special committee of the Russian Synod on Orthodox and Old Catholic relations was communicated in 1892 to the Eastern Patriarchs, and their responses were, on the whole, favorable to recognition; but at this juncture the doctrine of the Church was raised, and it proved an insurmountable hurdle. The continuity of the episcopal orders of the Old Catholic Churches had been preserved through the ordination of their first bishop by Hermann Heykamp, Bishop of Deventer.[92] But there remained their involvement in the schism of Rome. As members of the Church of Rome, they had never been of the "true undivided Church," and their renunciation of the Pope could not atone for this. They could be received into communion with the Orthodox Church only on the basis of a formal acceptance in full of its theological system.[93] Conversations continued, notwithstanding, until interrupted by World War I, and Orthodox visitors and observers attended the congresses of the Old Catholic Churches.

The Society of Saint Willibrod[94] was founded in 1908 to promote union between the Anglican and the Old Catholic Churches, with a chairman and a secretary in each. The fruits of its labors appeared twenty-three years later in the establishment of intercommunion between the two Churches. At the meeting on July 2, 1931 in Bonn, where this transaction took place, the commissions of the Churches embodied their conclusions in what has come to be known as the Bonn Agreement, as follows:

1. Each Communion recognizes the catholicity and independence of the other, and maintains its own.
2. Each Communion agrees to permit members of the other Communion to participate in the Sacraments.

[91] *Filioque* is the Latin for "and from the Son," equivalent to *et filio,* inserted by the third Council of Toledo (A.D. 589) in the clause *qui ex Patre procedit* ("who proceedeth from the Father") of the Niceno-Constantinopolitan Creed (A.D. 381), which makes the creed state that the Holy Ghost proceeds from the Son, as well as from the Father. Hence the doctrine itself, which is not admitted by the Eastern Churches. Some hold it heretical, and all object to it on the ground that no part of the Church has a right to make an addition to a creed which has behind it the authority of an Ecumenical Council.

[92] Of the Jansenist Church, which originated in the seventeenth century through the teachings of the Roman Catholic Bishop Cornelis Jansen (1585-1638) and was declared heretical. Its doctrines resembled in some points Calvinism. It was strongly evangelical and opposed to Jesuitism.

[93] Georges Florovsky, in *A History of the Ecumenical Movement,* p. 209.

[94] Apostle of the Frisians, and first Archbishop of Utrecht (657-738?).

3. Intercommunion does not require from either Communion the acceptance of all doctrinal opinion, sacramental devotion, or liturgical practice characteristic of the other, but implies that each believes the other to hold the essentials of the Christian Faith.[95]

26. The Eastern Orthodox Churches and the Ecumenical Movement

The Eastern Orthodox Churches carried an important ecumenical role. There was no extended period from the fifteenth century onward in which they were not engaged in negotiations of some kind with one religious group or another.

Those who came for conference with them often found the procedure baffling and irritating and the practical results disappointing. But from the standpoint of the Church they did not necessarily go away empty-handed. Christian duty was to give those seeking desired ends what was good for them, and not what they asked if it was not good; those approached had to be the judges of what should be granted.

Negotiators were often actuated by mixed motives. They sometimes looked to gain advantage for their cause, as in the case of the Nonjuring Anglicans. However convinced these prelates may have been of the rightness of their action in refusing to pledge allegiance to the House of Orange, they had been adjudged schismatics and deposed by the Church of England, and it would have strengthened their position politically, as well as ecclesiastically, had they succeeded in winning recognition by the Orthodox Churches.

The Hussites were in the way of being excommunicated by Rome when they decided to seek an alliance with the Eastern Churches. Though the Orthodox tradition had been established at one time in Moravia through the ministry of St. Cyril and St. Methodius, it is doubtful that Hus himself had been influenced directly by it.

> We may with confidence go so far as to say that some of the Hussites were interested in the Greek Church chiefly as an example of what might be termed non-Roman Catholicism, but also because in the teaching and practice of the Eastern Church they could find an extra argument in favor of Communion in both kinds which to them was the Ark of the Covenant. At a later stage of development . . . there was a specially strong reason for an appeal to the East, in the hope of securing recognition from the Patriarchs, and so of dealing with the problem of a regular succession in the ordained ministry.[96]

The Old Catholics were likewise detached and adrift when they sought "union with the Greek-Oriental and Russian Churches." And

[95] *A History of the Ecumenical Movement,* p. 470.
[96] Georges Florovsky, in *Ibid.*, p. 173.

the bishops and doctors of the Gallican Church in their overtures to the Orthodox prelates through Peter the Great in 1717 were trying to find allies in their struggle against the papacy.

The Reformers on the Continent had similar reasons to interest the Orthodox Churches in their cause. Protestants held that the Reformation was a return to the doctrine and practice of the primitive Church. Both they and Roman Catholics regarded the Eastern Church as a faithful guardian of the ancient tradition. Roman apologists insisted that there had been an unbroken unity of doctrine through the ages between the two Catholic communions, and that otherwise they were in accord under the Union of Florence.[97] Protestant spokesmen denied this, declaring Roman Catholicism with its innovations and accretions irreconcilable with the Greek.

Lutherans were forward in their attempts to establish theological agreement with Orthodoxy. In 1557 Laurentius Petri, the first Archbishop of Uppsala, accompanied by the Finnish Reformer Michael Agricola, journeyed to Moscow for a discussion of doctrine with the authorities of the Church, in the course of which special consideration was given to the veneration of icons and to fasting.

At about the same time, representatives of German Lutherans connected with Tübingen University, acting through diplomatic channels, placed a Greek translation of the Augsburg Confession in the hands of Patriarch Jeremiah II of Constantinople, with the suggestion that he might see that Lutheranism and Orthodoxy, despite their differences in ritualistic practices, were basically in doctrinal agreement.

There were even more elaborate attempts to arrive at a theological accommodation between Calvinism and Orthodoxy. Gottfried Wilhelm von Leibniz early in his career regarded Russians as barbarians; but later, doubting that Rome could be enlisted in support of his scheme for the cultural and political unification of Europe, he began cultivating the Russian Orthodox Church, and incidentally Peter the Great, who gave him a commission to assist with the founding of the Academy of Science in St. Petersburg and made him a pensioner of the crown.

These are some examples of typical approaches to the Eastern Orthodox Churches. The negotiations were not all one-sided, however. The universal involvement of organized religion in politics made impossible action of any kind by the Church without regard to the secular situation. How an alliance might be formed with Western powers which would help them in their struggle for liberation from Turkish rule was an ever-present and pressing question with the Eastern Churches; and their plight was at times so desperate that almost any means of escape could have been justified. But, aside from preoccupation in that direction, they were perhaps not less ready than other churches to identify

[97] 1439. Repudiated by most Orthodox.

with the Christian cause any political venture seeming to promise some temporal ecclesiastical gain.

Orthodox support of the Holy Alliance in 1815 fell into the international pattern of the day. This organization had the romantic aim of restoring "the unity of Christendom under the sovereignty of Jesus Christ." The initiative lay with Russia's Czar Alexander I, who had the cooperation of Frederick William III of Prussia and Francis II of Austria. Acting in the name of religion, justice, and peace, these rulers were out to thwart popular tendencies toward constitutional government; and all the sovereigns of Europe, except the King of England and the Pope, joined them. Although officially Orthodox, Alexander was known to be an ardent believer in the teachings of Franz Xaver Baader (1765-1841) and Johann Heinrich Stilling (1740-1817) and a personal friend of Madame Barbara Juliane von Krüdener (1764-1824). Even German Pietism and mysticism were thus ranged with the Eastern, Roman,[98] and Protestant confessions on the side of the Alliance.

This mingling of the temporal and the spiritual should not discount altogether achievements in the religious realm. Under such circumstances, conflicts in faith and order could be faced together without unworthy compromise, and some of the fruits of any reconciliation would remain when the transitory had passed. In no age is it possible to detach ecumenical endeavor from non-ecclesiastical interests, because churches do not exist in a vacuum. Their representatives cannot check their worldly concerns at the door, when they meet to confer.

The method of the Orthodox Churches followed a simple pattern. They were the Holy Orthodox Catholic Apostolic Eastern Church. If those who had come to deliberate were in search of the truth, they had found its seat and were in communication with it. Good faith dictated accepting it as the gift of God, which meant joining the Church, as well as agreeing to its doctrine. When this had been done, more mundane matters could be considered with hope of finding their solution.

So, in effect, ended the Patriarch's reply to the Lutherans from Tübingen, after their discussion of the Scriptures, tradition, original sin, human freedom, the grace of God, faith, good works, the sacraments, the invocation of saints, mariology, veneration of icons, monastic vows, fasting, the Church, holy orders, creeds. If they were prepared wholeheartedly to adhere to the doctrine as expounded, he was willing to receive them into communion, and in this way the two Churches could be made one. The incidental purpose of their coming could then be considered.

A letter of Archbishop Anthony Khrapovitski of Kharkov, a member of the synod of the Russian Orthodox Church, in reply to the invitation to the first Conference on Faith and Order was quite characteristic of offi-

[98] Through Roman Catholic monarchs.

cial orthodoxy. There was no divine grace outside the Orthodox Church, he wrote. Talk of validity was sophistry. "This world, foreign to Christ's redemption and possessed by the devil," was outside the Orthodox Church. That many non-Orthodox Christians held Orthodox beliefs was not enough. Actual membership in the Orthodox Church was necessary. Then he added that he would attend the Conference.[99]

Why, if the end was known from the beginning, should there have been negotiations? The Orthodox and those on the other side of the conference table had their respective answers to this question. It would have been said by the Orthodox, no doubt, that a Church believing itself to be in possession of the truth had a responsibility to talk with other religious groups interested enough to seek an interview. Truth was given for the salvation of the souls of men, and Christian love left no choice but to share it. Truth exerted its power through personal encounter. What traditions and books preserved for the ages must be made incarnate in living contacts.

Its exclusive claims did not mean that the Orthodox Church had perfect understanding of the truth and looked for no new insights beyond the ponderings of its own theologians. Discussion with others could be a vital process with justifying rewards, if only because it saved dogma from petrifaction and inquiring minds from the wounds of bitterness which pride of opinion inflicted. "We are not going to concelebrate there," wrote Archbishop Khrapovitski of the Conference on Faith and Order, "but shall have to search together for a true teaching on the controversial points of faith."[100]

From the standpoint of the other side also, a case for conferring could be made out, apart from opportunistic motives. Those approaching the Orthodox Churches believed they themselves had the truth. William Palmer (1811-79) of Magdalen College, Oxford, in 1840 took his interpretation of the Thirty-nine Articles to lay before Archpriest Basil Koutnevich, his Orthodox interlocutor; two years afterwards Palmer presented his *A Harmony of Anglican Doctrine with the Doctrine of the Catholic and Apostolic Church of the East,* just as the Lutherans from Tübingen—Martin Crusius, Jakob Andreae, and the others—went with their Greek version of the Augsburg Confession to a consultation with Patriarch Jeremiah II of Constantinople. All these felt themselves under compulsion also to speak. And where more eagerly than in the presence of the ancient Church of the East?

And who but the utterly ignorant could think Orthodoxy had nothing to share in return, besides its repetitious claim to be the one true undivided Church? There were theological divisions in the Orthodox Church which might have appeared to outsiders of sufficient depth to

[99] Correspondence of Archbishop Anthony Khrapovitski with representatives of the Protestant Episcopal Church in the United States, 1915 and 1916.

[100] By "concelebrate" the Archbishop had reference to joining in the Eucharist.

crack the rigid façade of unity on its traditional policy in relations with other churches. Because of this, the churches of the West could have believed that negotiations toward rapprochement might proceed with reasonable hope that conditions more conducive to reciprocal adjustments in faith and practice would develop.

There was evidence that some Orthodox themselves may have had like anticipations. During a long period after the fall of Constantinople in 1453, the Eastern Churches, particularly in countries conquered by the Turks, had to depend largely upon Western universities for the education of their clergy, a course resulting inevitably in a leavening by foreign ideas and consequent theological confusion. Some of those studying abroad returned convinced that the doctrinal isolationism of the Orthodox Church was unnecessary and unjustifiable, and a costly disadvantage politically and culturally which should be ended.

Cyril Loukaris,[101] Patriarch of Constantinople from 1621 until his death in 1638, who had traveled extensively in Europe and become widely acquainted with prominent churchmen of other confessions, made bold to try to do something about this. With the help of one Antoine Leger, a Protestant, who had been sent to Constantinople by the Church at Geneva, he wrote an interpretation of the Orthodox faith in terms of the doctrines of Calvinism, published in 1629 under the title, *The Confession of Faith of the Most Reverend Lord Cyril, Patriarch of Constantinople, Set forth in the Name and with the Consent of the Patriarchs of Alexandria and Jerusalem and Other Heads of the Eastern Churches*. Just what he expected to accomplish was not clear. The result was violent controversy and a division it took a century to repair. Did he act as one impelled to give expression to his faith and hoping to win the Church to his position? Or was he taking the way which seemed most likely at the moment to lead to an alignment of Protestant nations with the Eastern countries in their fight for liberation from Turkish despotism? There is no question as to the intensity of his desire to free his people, but it seems doubtful that he would have gone about the undertaking in this manner. Certainly he had been influenced strongly by his contacts with the West and had become interested in the possibility of a synthesis of Orthodox and Protestant theologies. Was his *Confession* the outcome of this study? Or was it "an ecumenical gesture"? Perhaps it was both. Whatever it was, the fact that the names of other Orthodox hierarchs appeared with his in its title, and

[101] A Cretan, he studied in Italy and became Patriarch of Alexandria at thirty. As Patriarch of Constantinople he resisted the attempts of the Roman Catholic Church to make its position dominant in the Turkish Empire, which probably cost him his life, since it involved him in political intrigue. He was executed July 7, 1638, by the order of Sultan Murad, and his body was thrown into the Sea of Marmora. He was known to be deeply interested in rapprochement between the Eastern and the Protestant Churches. He knew many prominent Protestant scholars and was a student of theology.

that he was not unseated because of it, showed that he received support as well as condemnation.

Georges Florovsky writes of him, "He stands out as the most remarkable figure in the history of the Orthodox Churches since the capture of Constantinople by the Turks . . . and he is still widely venerated in Greece, and in Crete, his native island, as a great national leader and martyr." [102]

The theological schools founded by the Orthodox Churches themselves in the sixteenth and seventeenth centuries long were centers of Western influence. They were organized mainly by the clergy educated abroad and drew their faculties, for the most part, from the same source. Patterned after the seminaries of Italy, their instruction was in Latin, and they sometimes used Roman Catholic textbooks.

These circumstances signified less a deliberate purpose to Romanize, perhaps, than to bring about a theological leveling. The system remained unchanged when a Protestant vogue had replaced the Roman. The use of Latin in Classes was continued into the eighteenth century.

"Lutheranizing" was popular during the time of Peter the Great, whose new Academy of Science in St. Petersburg became a gathering place of scholars from Germany. "Lutheran Orthodoxy" was listed in the seminary courses.

A chief exponent among the clergy of this Protestantizing was Theophanes Prokopovich (1681-1736), who in his own experience exemplified the strong synthesizing tendency. He had gone to Rome an Orthodox student to study at the Jesuit College, and there had joined the Roman Catholic Church. Returning to Kiev to become Rector and Professor of Theology in the seminary[103] organized by Peter Moglia (1597-1647), he had readopted his early faith but soon had introduced Protestant textbooks in his courses, in which he offered a Reformed version of Christian doctrine, said to have been adapted from the *Syntagma* of Armand Polanus of Basle.[104] Meantime, he had become ecclesiastical adviser to the Czar (Peter the Great) who had appointed him Bishop of Pskov.

The Pietist Movement in the seventeenth century and the Evangelical Awakening in the eighteenth extended into Russia and southeastern Europe.

August Hermann Francke (1663-1727) had the Bible translated into Russian, Czech, and Polish, and also Johann Arndt's (1555-1621) *True Christianity* into Russian, for circulation in those parts. His agents worked among the German prisoners of war[105] in Siberia, and with German Lutheran groups in various communities of Russia. Among his

[102] *A History of the Ecumenical Movement,* p. 184.
[103] The first of the theological schools founded in this period.
[104] Georges Florovsky, in *A History of the Ecumenical Movement,* p. 186.
[105] The war between Russia and Sweden.

"missionaries" were persons of many different walks of life—diplomats, military officers, merchants, scholars, teachers, tourists, letter-writers; which last included Francke himself, who with extraordinary skill and effect directed operations from the University and the Mission House in Halle.

Madame Barbara Juliane von Krüdener, who enjoyed the royal favor of Alexander I, and her Spiritualist followers in Russia[106] helped further the activities inspired by the Awakening. By 1812 the Russian Bible Society had been organized and within a decade it had printed and distributed close to three-quarters of a million copies of the Scriptures in forty-three of the languages and dialects of the Russian Empire.

The leaders in this work carried on with it a type of successful personal evangelism, to which the Church objected as tending to create a demand for a new denomination. Largely for this reason, the Society was disbanded by order of the government in 1826, the year following the death of Alexander I. Madame von Krüdener had died in 1824.

The ready hospitality toward new teachings, which characterized the policy of the theological schools, and the response outside them to popular religious movements could only have encouraged those churches which sought rapprochement with the Eastern Churches, and, in particular, with the Russian Orthodox Church. Catherine the Great must have expressed the mind of many beyond the borders of her country, as well as of multitudes of her own subjects, when she admitted that she could see no difference between the Protestant and the Orthodox doctrines. But the Church, detached from public sentiment and with a better historical perspective, was not so inclined to theological accommodation.

The nineteenth century brought official resistance in Orthodoxy, particularly in Russia, to the doctrinal laxity in the seminaries and the court, and to the popular enthusiasm for mystical expressions of faith.

The promise in the transitional theology of Vasili Mihailovich Drosor Philaret (1782-1867) of the evolution of a broad doctrine in the Church was not destined to be realized. By education and experience—leaving aside his genius as "probably the greatest theologian of the Russian Church in modern times"[107]—Philaret was especially qualified to develop the "dynamic theory of tradition," which claimed the attention of the Church in the second quarter of the century. But the conservatives had reasons for looking to other scholars for this.[108]

[106] By "Spiritualists" was meant those who stressed "inner Christianity" and depreciated the organizations and forms of religion.

[107] Georges Florovsky, in *A History of the Ecumenical Movement,* p. 195.

[108] Philaret had been a student while Protestant theology still exerted its influence in the seminaries and continued in his reading and travels to keep his contacts with other confessions. He was especially interested in mystical literature. He was

By the dynamic theory,[109] tradition was conceived as a power for growth, rather than a formal pattern of belief and practice—a power perpetually renewed in the experience of the Church as the past alive in and giving depth to the present. As interpreted by Alexis S. Khomiakov (1804-60)[110] and other theologians,[111] it had the effect actually of fortifying further the static conception of the Orthodox Church as "the one true Church," with which other churches could be in communion only on the condition of accepting its teaching *in toto* and joining it. They were all, it held, in schism. The division could be healed by their return to Orthodoxy. Unity was nothing, "if not inward harmony of creed and outward harmony of expression." The Church could not be "a harmony of discords . . . a numerical sum of Orthodox, Latins, and Protestants." The sacraments could be performed "only in the bosom of the true Church." They could not be separated from that unity in faith and grace which was the very being of the Church, created by the Spirit of God and not by organization.

This was essentially the doctrine of the Church and of its unity the Orthodox Church desired, at least officially, and was prepared to maintain. Against it all advances of other churches with proposals of union have ended. It has withstood the dissent of able and loyal Orthodox churchmen in every generation.

In *An Enquiry into the Hierarchy of the Anglican Episcopal Church* (written after the promulgation of the papal bull of 1896 against the validity of Anglican orders) Professor V. A. Sokolov of the Moscow Theological School expressed the belief that Anglican orders could be recognized by the Orthodox Church; and Professor Athanasius Bulgakov of Kiev Theological Academy concurred in this opinion.

On the occasion of a trip to England in 1870 to officiate at the consecration of the new Greek Church in Liverpool, Alexander Lykurgos, the Archbishop of the Cyclades, after a conference with Anglican representatives at Ely, in which there had been a thorough discussion

---

a man of liberal spirit. His sermons were read abroad. His book, *The Doctrine of the Russian Church*, was published in London in 1845. He held the idea that the Orthodox Church had preserved the original deposit of faith in its purity and was, in that sense, the true Church. He was persuaded, however, that the Church, as the Body of Christ, had "weak members"; and he would not "presume to call false any Church which believed Jesus was the Christ." Only those were separated from the Church spiritually who did not confess Christ Son of God, God Incarnate, and Redeemer. The true composition of the Church, visible and invisible, was known only to Christ the Head. The destiny of Christendom was one, he said; and he would not judge or condemn other Christian bodies.

[109] The dynamic theory of interpretation apparently originated with the teaching of Johann Adam Möhler of the Catholic Theological Faculty of Tübingen University. See his *Unity in the Church, or the Principle of Catholicism.*

[110] Khomiakov's dogmatism was tempered somewhat by his indorsement of the "principle of economy" followed by the Greek Church, which allowed, on occasion, as a pastoral dispensation, *ad hoc* modifications of policies theologically binding.

[111] Professor V. V. Bolotov, Dr. Crestos Androustos, Archbishop Khrapovitski, Professor Zikos Rhosis, *et al.*

of theological differences between the two communions, said the Church of England was "a sound Catholic Church, very like our own," and added that "by friendly discussion, union between the two Churches might be brought about."

As for the Old Catholic Churches, the Orthodox bishops were generally favorable to recognition, in response to the report of a committee appointed by the Russian Synod in 1892. Professor V. Kerensky of the Theological Academy of Kazan agreed with this view in his book on *Old Catholicism,* published in 1894. Archbishop Nicephorus of Patras and Professor Diomedes Kyriakos of the University of Athens likewise approved. Replying to the reunion encyclical of Leo XIII, *Preclare Gratulationis,* in 1895, Patriarch Anthimos of Constantinople declared the Old Catholics defenders of the "true faith in the West." Dr. Paul Svetlov, Professor of Religion in the University of Kiev, said the Orthodox Church could regard itself "only as a part of the Church Universal," of which "the Old Catholic Church was, in its own right, another part."

The Greek Church adopted, in time, the so-called principle of economy, which admitted of departures, as a pastoral dispensation from policies theologically binding, when dictated by considerations of Christian charity or circumstances of practical urgency. For example, the Church has waived, on occasion, repetition of baptism and confirmation in the case of persons from other churches joining the Orthodox without implying recognition of such non-Orthodox ministrations.

In the Russian Church the same end was attained on the basis of the theory that other churches could be related existentially to the Orthodox, as many authorities of the Church believed they were, which would invest their sacraments with some charismatic virtue.[112]

27. Faith and Order in Holland

Questions relating to faith and order were emphasized in nineteenth-century Holland more by division in the churches than by successful unitive endeavor.

The Remonstrant Church in 1796 began an effort to obtain the cooperation of all Protestant denominations in plans it put forward on behalf of union. The concrete results were small, but the movement created greater interest in the problems of unity and led to exchanges of pulpits by pastors and of visits by synods.

Christo Sacrum, a society to promote union among Protestants, was organized at Delft in 1797. It worked with some effectiveness in bring-

[112] Chapter 4 of *A History of the Ecumenical Movement,* on "The Orthodox Churches and the Ecumenical Movement," by Georges Florovsky, will invite study by those interested in Orthodoxy's part in the ecumenical movement. The author of these pages gratefully acknowledges its helpfulness as one of a number of books consulted as references.

ing together members of the different denominations. Those belonging to it were expelled by the Netherlands Reformed Church for heresy and formed an independent church.

The national Church in 1817 adopted the practice of admitting members of other Protestant bodies to Communion.

The organization in 1834 of the Christian Reformed Church was a result of the conflict between rationalism and orthodoxy which agitated all Protestant lands. The new denomination was composed of dissentient members of the Netherlands Reformed Church. This controversy produced in the latter body three parties: strict Calvinists, the more liberal Calvinists, and the rationalist school.

Doctrinal instruction in the Dutch schools was forbidden by law after 1856; and in 1876 the old theological chairs in the universities were displaced by professorships of the history of religion. The national Church synod became responsible for providing doctrinal instruction, with funds granted by the government. When it engaged for teachers those with the reputation of being rationalists, the Calvinists founded the Free Reformed University at Amsterdam, which opened in 1880.

Because of the reputed liberalism of the synod, the Netherlands Reformed Church suffered another and more serious defection in 1886. The separatists this time were led by Abraham Kuyper in organizing *Gereformeerde Kerken,* a strict Calvinistic denomination, which in 1892 was joined by about half of the members of the Christian Reformed Church.

28. The Movement Toward Unity in Austria and Hungary

The Evangelical Church of the Augsburg and Helvetic Confessions, in which were brought together in 1891 the Lutheran and the Reformed Churches of Austria, was a very successful partial union. The constituent bodies acted through it as a unit in many matters of common concern, such as necessary dealings with the state or other ecclesiastical organizations, but reserved to themselves the liberty of individual action with reference to doctrine, worship, and confessional polity. It was agreed that the Augsburg Confession should be the authority of the Lutheran Church, and the Heidelberg Catechism and the Second Helvetic Confession of the Reformed Church. The children of both studied their respective catechisms in the same classes at school.

In Hungary, a movement in 1840 to unite the Lutheran and the Reformed Churches led to the appointment by their official courts of a committee of sixty members to prepare a plan. Because of revolutionary social unrest and political confusion, the effort failed to achieve any permanent results. However, the ecumenical relationships which were formed bore fruit at a later period.

29. World Denominational Fellowships

The international denominational federations[113] which made their appearance around the end of the nineteenth century are not easily characterized ecumenically. They were sectarian, of course, in that they each consisted of "churches of like faith and order" and were concerned mainly with furthering the confessional interests of their constituents. But they were generally not organized or staffed to engage successfully in Christian work, aside from activities incidental to self-maintenance. They drew criticism at times for—in the critics' opinion—diverting their member churches from the ecumenical movement, by satisfying their sense of participation in the world Christian fellowship with only a limited experience of it. But they must, more often, have helped them discover the inadequacy of the fragmented forces of Christianity for its global mission. The Lambeth Conference, the earliest of these bodies, interested itself seriously in the promotion of plans for a reunion of the churches, with the important results noted previously. If it did not find its *raison d'être* in this phase of its work, it derived therefrom a quickening and unifying power which was imparted to the whole.

The Friends' World Committee for Consultation (1937) represented forty-five independent Quaker groups in twenty-four countries, which were distinguished particularly for relief and reconstruction work in areas of need and for their efforts on behalf of peace and international reconciliation on a religious basis.

The International Association for Liberal Christianity and Religious Freedom, founded in 1930, comprised so-called "liberal" religious groups, such as the Magyar Unitarian Churches of Hungary and Rumania, the Remonstrant Church in Holland, and the Unitarian and the Universalist Churches of the United States. Their purpose was:

> To maintain communications with free Christian groups in all lands, who are striving to unite religion and liberty and to increase fellowship and cooperation among them.
>
> To bring into closer union the historic liberal Churches, the liberal elements in all churches and isolated congregations, and workers for religious freedom.
>
> To draw into the same fellowship other religious groups throughout the world which are in essential agreement with our ways of thinking.[114]

[113] The Lambeth Conference, 1867; the Alliance of Reformed Churches throughout the World Holding the Presbyterian System, 1875; the Methodist Ecumenical Conference, 1881; the International Congregational Conference, 1891; the Union of Utrecht (Old Catholic Churches), 1889; the Baptist World Alliance, 1905; the Lutheran World Convention, 1923 (after 1947, the Lutheran World Federation). World Convention of the Churches of Christ, 1930.

[114] Statement of the Secretariat of the International Association, 1938.

30. The Modern Faith and Order Movement

In October, 1910, the General Convention of the Protestant Episcopal Church in the United States passed a resolution providing for the appointment of "a Joint Commission"[115] "to bring about a Conference for the consideration of questions touching Faith and Order," and directing "that all Christian Communions throughout the world which confess Our Lord Jesus Christ as God and Saviour be asked to unite with us in arranging for and conducting such a Conference."

This action was attributable directly to the initiative of Charles H. Brent, Protestant Episcopal Bishop of the Philippine Islands. In an interpretative report of the World Missionary Conference of 1910, Bishop Brent had spoken of the need for Christian unity, made especially manifest by that gathering, and of his own conviction that the time had come for the churches of the world to meet in "a conference on faith and order" given over altogether to frank and full examination and discussion of their differences. He had associated himself with those delegates at Edinburgh who believed it next to futile to continue holding conventions which excluded from their programs all references to doctrinal subjects outside the restricted limits of evangelical agreement.[116] In an address there, he had said: "We are sons of God, and being sons of God, it is not fitting that we should have anything less than a task which will bring out all the capacity of God's children. During these past days a new vision has been unfolded to us. But whenever God gives a vision He also points to some new responsibility, and you and I, when we leave this assembly, will go away with some fresh duties to perform."[117] Privately, he had made known to friends his purpose to ask his own Church to take the lead in preparing the way for another conference, in which Christians should face together their theological disagreements. This he had now done successfully, with the help of others. The resolution had been presented by Dr. William T. Manning, Rector of Trinity Episcopal Church in New York City (later Bishop of New York).

As events showed, he had acted at the full tide of a resurgent interest

[115] The Convention was being held in Cincinnati, Ohio. The resolution was passed first by the House of Deputies and then by the House of Bishops.

[116] The World Missionary Conference of 1910 was the last of the series of decennial meetings which had begun in 1854. As a condition of the participation in it of the Society for the Propagation of the Gospel of the Church of England, the organizers had "pledged . . . that questions affecting the differences of Doctrine and Order between the Christian bodies" should not be brought before the sessions for discussion or resolution. (See "Minutes of the Society for the Propagation of the Gospel," 1908.)

[117] *World Missionary Conference, 1910,* Vol. IX, p. 330.

in Christian unity. On the same day, the National Council of Congregational Churches in the United States had appointed a commission to consider what steps should be taken "in view of the possibility of fraternal discussion of Church unity suggested by the Lambeth Conference of . . . 1908"; and on the day before, the Annual Convention of the Disciples of Christ in the United States, led by its President, Dr. Peter Ainslie, had moved to form the Commission on Christian Union.[118]

The Joint Commission, as finally constituted by the General Convention, consisted of twenty-one members—seven bishops, seven priests, and seven laymen. Electing Bishop C. P. Anderson of Chicago President and Robert Hallowell Gardiner, one of its lay members, Secretary, it set to work immediately. Information was sent to the Protestant denominations in the United States, and within six months reports of favorable action by eighteen of them had been received. Each had been asked, according to the enabling resolution by the Houses of Deputies and Bishops, to appoint a commission to assist with "arranging and conducting" the proposed conference on faith and order.

"The conference is for the definite purpose of considering those things in which we differ," explained the letters and the printed matter which had gone out to the churches, "in the hope that a better understanding of divergent views of faith and order will result in a deepened desire for reunion and in official action on the part of the separate Communions. . . ." "It is the business of the conference," they emphasized, "not to take such official action, but to inspire it and to prepare the way for it." [119]

Moved by the promise of world-wide endeavor on these lines, J. Pierpont Morgan, a layman on the Commission, volunteered to contribute $100,000 toward the expense of organizing and holding the conference.

In June of 1912, the Commission sent a deputation to the Anglican Churches of Great Britain and Ireland, consisting of Bishop C. P. Anderson of Chicago, Bishop Boyd Vincent of Southern Ohio, Bishop A. C. A. Hall of Vermont, and Dr. William T. Manning. A meeting with representatives[120] of the Church of England at Lambeth Palace resulted in the appointment of a committee "to watch the progress of arrangements for the . . . conference, organize support and help in England . . . and especially to stimulate general interest and regular and widespread prayer." In Scotland the Primus of the Episcopal

[118] Later the Association for the Promotion of Christian Unity. Dr. Ainslie became President of this body, founding in 1911 *The Christian Union Quarterly,* which he edited until his death in 1934.

[119] *Report of the Committee on Plan and Scope,* adopted April 20, 1911; No. 1 in the Series of Faith and Order Pamphlets.

[120] Archbishop Randall Davidson of Canterbury, Archbishop Cosmo Gordon Lang of York, Bishop Winnington Ingram of London, Bishop G. W. Kennion of Bath and Wells, Bishop E. C. S. Gibson of Gloucester, Bishop A. R. Tucker of Uganda, Bishop William Walsham How of Wakefield and the Deans of Westminster, St. Paul's, Wells, and Ely.

Church and his associates[121] gave assurances of their purpose to cooperate. The Primate of the Church of Ireland likewise promised to name a commission in due time.[122]

By May, 1913, it could be announced that in the United States, Canada, and England twenty-two denominational commissions had been appointed. Many more churches were represented among the nearly eight thousand persons who had requested that their names be put upon the mailing list of the Joint Commission's publications.

A second deputation, of which Dr. Peter Ainslie of Baltimore, Dr. Newman Smyth of New Haven, and Dr. H. W. Roberts of Philadelphia were members, was successful in the spring of 1914 in obtaining promises of the Free Churches of Great Britain and the Presbyterian Churches of Scotland to form commissions, or cooperating committees.

The outbreak of World War I in the summer of 1914 made necessary the suspension of all international plans. However, the work which had been done continued to produce results; and the number of denominations expressing their intention to participate in the forthcoming conference on faith and order grew, until in 1920 it stood at sixty-nine.

During the war years, the Joint Commission evinced its hope for the future by organizing an American preparatory conference, which brought together at Garden City, New York, from January 4 to 6, 1916, sixty-three representatives of fifteen denominations for study and deliberation. The subjects to which they addressed themselves, after some briefing in advance of the meeting—"The Church, Its Nature and Functions"; "The Catholic Creeds, as the Safeguards of the Faith of the Church"; "Grace and the Sacraments in General"; "The Ministry, Its Nature and Functions"; and "Practical Questions Connected with the Missionary and Other Administrative Functions of the Church"—were to become in the years ahead a familiar part of ecumenical agenda.

In Great Britain, a joint committee of the Anglican and the Free Churches on matters of faith and order of mutual interest, including a conference for which arrangements had been begun, held several meetings. In February, 1916, and in March, 1918, it published reports of its proceedings under the title *Towards Christian Unity,* which became of special importance for their influence upon later actions of the churches.[123]

The Episcopal Joint Commission's plan to send a deputation to "the Churches of the Continent of Europe and of the Near East, and also the

[121] Bishop W. J. F. Robberds of Brechin; advisers—Bishop Archibald Ean Campbell of Glasgow, Bishop Arthur John Maclean of Moray, and Bishop Charles Edward Plumb of St. Andrews.

[122] Bishop J. B. Crozier; advisers—Bishop J. B. Keene of Meath, Bishop Charles Frederick D'Arcy of Down, Connor, and Dromore.

[123] E.g., Lambeth's *An Appeal to All Christian People* in 1920 was recognized as having been inspired by these two reports. See Chapter 9, p. 412 (by Tatlow), in *A History of the Ecumenical Movement.*

Roman Catholic Church," which had been interrupted by the War, was resumed immediately upon the signing of the armistice. Its members, Bishop C. P. Anderson of Chicago, Bishop Boyd Vincent of Southern Ohio, Bishop R. H. Weller of Fond du Lac, Dr. E. L. Parsons (later Bishop of San Francisco), and Dr. B. T. Rogers, sailed from New York City on March 6, 1919. At Athens, Constantinople, Smyrna, Sofia, Bucharest, Belgrade, and other ecclesiastical capitals of Southeastern Europe and the Near East, they were received cordially and informed that the Eastern Orthodox Churches would cooperate. A letter placed in their hands by the Church authorities of Greece expressed the common sentiment:

> We are very well disposed toward the proposal for the summoning of a world-wide Ecclesiastical Conference, which the American Episcopal Church is addressing to the Churches through you and your fellow bishops. From the letter which you have placed in our hands, and from the oral explanation which you have added to it, we are convinced that the purpose of the Conference is indeed holy, in accordance with the prayer of our Lord "That all" those who believe on Him "may be one." We heartily congratulate the Episcopal Church in America which has undertaken this noble effort, from which we rightfully expect progress for the better in the relations between the Churches "until we all come together into the unity of the faith and of the knowledge of the Son of God."
>
> Accepting with readiness the invitation addressed to us, and embracing your Holiness [the Chairman of the deputation, Bishop Anderson] and your companions with much love, we pray our Saviour Jesus Christ to direct your steps unto every good work.[124]

In Constantinople they talked also with representatives of the Armenian Church, who agreed to refer the invitation to the Catholicos and his synod at Etchmiadzin and expressed confidence that it would be accepted.

On the island of Halki, in the Sea of Marmora, they conferred with Dr. Germanos Strenopoulos,[125] President of the Orthodox Theological College, and had an interview with Archbishop Platon, Metropolitan of Odessa, then in exile, who said, "The Church of Russia is now sick in body, mind and soul; but when she gets well again she will be represented at the conference." [126] They were unable to enter Russia or to see any of the hierarchs of the Church then in authority.

The invitation of the Joint Commission in Latin and a statement in English concerning the world conference on faith and order had been presented to Pope Benedict XV in advance of their arrival. The decision

[124] Faith and Order Pamphlet No. 32, *Report of the Deputation to Europe and the Near East.*

[125] Afterwards Archbishop of Thyateira and a President of the World Council of Churches.

[126] Platon had been head of the Russian Orthodox Church in the United States, and the Commission had had some contact with him during that time.

had been reached also in advance of their coming. Reported the deputation:

> The contrast between the Pope's personal attitude towards us and his official attitude towards the Conference was very sharp. One was irresistibly benevolent, the other irresistibly rigid. The genuineness of the Pope's personal friendliness towards us was as outstanding as the positiveness of his official declination of our invitation.

The following statement was handed to them as they took their departure:

> The Holy Father, after having thanked them for their visit, stated that as successor of St. Peter and Vicar of Christ he had no greater desire than that there should be one fold and one shepherd. His Holiness added that the teaching and practice of the Roman Catholic Church regarding the unity of the visible Church of Christ was well known to everybody and therefore it would not be possible for the Catholic Church to take part in such a Congress as the one proposed. His Holiness, however, by no means wishes to disapprove of the Congress in question for those who are not in union with the Chair of Peter, on the contrary, he earnestly desires and prays that, if the Congress is practicable, those who take part in it may, by the Grace of God, see the light and become reunited to the visible Head of the Church, by whom they will be received with open arms.[127]

From Rome, Bishop Weller and Dr. Rogers went to the Near East for further visits with Orthodox prelates. There they met with good success, the Patriarchs of Alexandria, Jerusalem, and Antioch accepting their invitation to cooperate. They saw also the Coptic Patriarch in Cairo, who responded favorably.

The other members of the deputation made their way to France, Norway, and Sweden. They were able to accomplish their mission in these countries and to continue homeward with the assurance of unanimous cooperation by their main Protestant Churches.

Unforeseen circumstances prevented the emissaries from going to Holland, Denmark, and Finland as they had planned; and "the German Churches at this stage refused all bids to take part in the World Conference," [128] looking upon the Faith and Order Movement as a veiled Anglican imperialistic plot—a misgiving shared, to some extent, in certain other Continental nations.

The next step by the Joint Commission was the issuance of an invitation to all the denominations which had made known their intention to cooperate to send three delegates each to a preparatory conference, which would be held in Geneva August 12-20, 1920. Seventy "autono-

[127] See Faith and Order Pamphlet No. 32, *Report of the Deputation to Europe and the Near East.*

[128] Tissington Tatlow, in *A History of the Ecumenical Movement,* p. 417.

mous Churches" in about forty different countries were represented at this meeting.

There were eighteen Orthodox in attendance, whose leaders explained that the invitation to join in promoting a world conference had come when the Ecumenical Patriarchate at Constantinople had itself decided to prepare an encyclical letter to "all the Churches of Christ," stressing their need to foster understanding and collaboration; and they, the representatives of Orthodoxy, had accepted it "with great joy." They had not come, however, without hesitation on account of the proselytizing of their members by non-Orthodox missionaries. If they took part in the movement, they said, they would have to be given assurance that this practice would be stopped.

A few leaders of the German churches were present. They came unofficially, through the influence largely of Professor Friedrich Siegmund-Schultze, who in the pages of his quarterly *Die Eiche* reported regularly the activities of the Faith and Order Movement. Among them were Missiondirektor A. W. Schreiber of the United Church, Professor A. Lang, a member of the Reformed Church, and Dr. Ihmels of the Lutheran Church.

The Geneva Conference appointed a Continuation Committee to be in charge of preparations for the World Conference on Faith and Order—arranging the program, choosing a meeting place, and deciding on a date. Fifty-odd members were appointed to it—Anglicans, Armenians, Baptists, Congregationalists, Czech Brethren, Disciples, Eastern Orthodox, members of the Society of Friends and of the German Evangelical Church, Lutherans, Methodists, Old Catholics, Presbyterians, and Reformed. Bishop Charles H. Brent was elected Chairman, Dr. George Zabriskie Treasurer, and Robert Hallowell Gardiner Secretary. With this action, responsibility for the Movement, which had been borne by the Protestant Episcopal Church in the United States, devolved upon all the cooperating denominations.

Bishop Brent said of the Geneva Conference:

> The Spirit of God was the strength of the pilgrims. He made us one in our fellowship. The Conference was a living body. Life touched life, nation touched nation, the spirit of the East held communion with the spirit of the West as perhaps never before. By invitation on the last day . . . we gathered . . . in the Russian Orthodox Church in Geneva for the solemn worship of the Divine Liturgy. Anglican, Baptist, Old Catholic, Presbyterian, Wesleyan, Lutheran, Quaker were all there, and there to worship. The Metropolitan of Seleukia [Germanos] . . . in a spiritual address spoke to the pilgrims of his own joy in the vision of unity, and told how, out of the transfigured troubles and pains of the present, would rise the glory of the future.[129]

The Continuation Committee met at Geneva before the end of the Conference, at Stockholm in 1925 during the Universal Christian Con-

[129] Faith and Order Pamphlet No. 33, *Report of the Preliminary Meeting at Geneva, Switzerland, August 12-20, 1920*, p. 92.

ference on Life and Work, and in 1926 at Berne, Switzerland. On all these occasions the reports of the Subjects Committee, which had the work of preparing an agenda for the World Conference, occupied much of the time.

The following topics were finally chosen:[130]

(1) The Call to Unity.
(2) The Church's Message to the World—the Gospel.
(3) The Nature of the Church.
(4) The Church's Common Confession of Faith.
(5) The Church's Ministry.
(6) The Sacraments.
(7) The Unity of Christendom and the Places of the Different Churches in It.

At Stockholm, August 3-21, 1927, was chosen for the date of the World Conference on Faith and Order, and Lausanne, Switzerland, the place of meeting.

Robert Hallowell Gardiner died on June 15, 1924. All who had observed his work as Secretary of the Episcopal Commission and of the Geneva Continuation Committee realized that in his passing the Faith and Order Movement had sustained a serious loss. He had carried the burden of his office together with his professional responsibilities as a busy attorney, receiving no remuneration for his services. He was a quiet man of sound judgment and deeply religious spirit. An Episcopalian, he proved himself a friend of all the churches. No American ecumenical leader was regarded with greater trust by the churches of Europe. "The profound impression made upon the Christian world by what he was and did baffles description," wrote Bishop Brent. "It is not too much to say that there is not a Church in Christendom, great or little, ancient or new, that does not know his name and feel kinship with his lofty soul."

31. The First World Conference on Faith and Order—Lausanne

Four hundred six persons registered for the first World Conference on Faith and Order, which was held, according to plan, at Lausanne, August 3-21, 1927. Most of them were clergymen. Attendance reports mentioned the presence of nine women and "a few laymen." There were twelve staff members. Together, they represented 108 denominations.

The committee on place had chosen a city impressive for situation. For some of the conferees, the slopes of Jorat were an ordeal. "It took

[130] *Faith and Order: Proceedings of the World Conference, Lausanne, August 3-21, 1927,* edited by H. N. Bate, pp. 36-40; Faith and Order Pamphlets Nos. 46 and 52.

a stout spirit to negotiate the hill," remembered one.[131] But there was compensation in the tempered summer of the upper elevations, the vista there afforded of the Lake of Geneva and the snowy skyline of the Savoy Alps beyond, the cloistered peacefulness of the University and Cathedral precincts in which the meetings were held, the unostentatious but open-handed hospitality of the Swiss government, of which they were guests, and the symbolism of the mountains, which reminded them of the steep ascent they had undertaken into those spiritual heights where divisions are left behind for the time and those who have walked apart discover "how good and how pleasant it is for brethren to dwell together in unity" (Psalm cxxx, 1).

The Conference opened with worship in the Cathedral and proceeded forthwith to business by electing Bishop Charles H. Brent Chairman, and Principal Alfred E. Garvie of Hackney and New College, London, Vice-Chairman. Ralph W. Brown, who as the assistant of Robert Hallowell Gardiner had become, upon the death of the latter, Secretary of the Episcopal Commission and the Geneva Continuation Committee, was appointed Secretary of the Conference.

Because of misunderstanding which became manifest at the meeting of the Continuation Committee the year before, the Subjects Committee, of which Edwin James Palmer, Bishop of Bombay, India, and Canon H. N. Bate, Dean of Carlisle (afterwards Dean of York), were, respectively, Chairman and Secretary, had not been permitted to finish its work on the program for Lausanne. It had set out to gather the conclusions of study groups on the four themes, "The Faith of the Reunited Church," "The Nature of the Church," "The Ministry," and "The Sacraments," with the view of helping to determine in advance of the World Conference the range of the agreements and disagreements between the churches. But it had been charged at Berne in 1926 that decisions were being shaped which would have the effect of restricting the freedom of the Conference when it met, and the Continuation Committee had thereupon declared null previous actions on the agenda for Lausanne.

The printed report of the Subjects Committee[132] was not accepted officially by the Conference, but Canon Bate, at the request of Chairman Brent, made a statement at the first session relative to the work which had been done. The results of the study of the topics, all of which were chosen finally for consideration by the Conference, were thus made available to the delegates for use in their discussion.

That plans had miscarried and preparations been incomplete is not to be wondered at; something never done before was being attempted, and this at a time when war had added to the old disharmony and distrust

[131] William Adams Brown in *Toward a United Church,* p. 98.

[132] *Statements by the Subjects Committee of the World Conference on Faith and Order,* Boston, Massachusetts, 1926. See also *Faith and Order: Proceedings of the World Conference,* pp. 36-40, and Faith and Order Pamphlets 46 and 52.

between the churches international rancors and suspicions too strong and insidious to be resisted altogether, even by Christians.

The Conference listened four days to expositions of the subjects in the first half of the agenda by speakers representing various confessional or denominational points of view. Then the delegates withdrew in sections to which they had been assigned for simultaneous discussion and the drafting of reports of their findings for presentation to a plenary session. Three days were allowed for this. During the second week, the same procedure was followed with the remainder of the program. The chairmen of the groups were: Charles H. Brent for "The Unity of the Church"; Adolf Deissmann, "The Church's Message to the World—the Gospel"; William Adams Brown, "The Nature of the Church"; Tissington Tatlow, "The Church's Common Confession of Faith"; A. C. Headlam, "The Church's Ministry"; James Cannon, Jr., "The Sacraments"; and Nathan Söderblom, "The Unity of Christendom and the Places of the Different Churches in It."

The first six reports were accepted for transmission to the churches. The one on "The Unity of Christendom and the Places of the Different Churches in It" was referred to the Continuation Committee of the Conference for revision. This report commended the statement of the Ecumenical Patriarch of the Orthodox Churches in 1920 that world Christian conferences might well be called to examine questions of interest to all Christian churches; it suggested that a council might be formed of existing organizations, such as the Continuation Committee of the Universal Christian Conference on Life and Work, which consisted of representatives appointed officially by a large number of the denominations, and the World Alliance for Promoting International Friendship through the Churches. There were those who thought its adoption would commit the Conference to a policy under which federation for the purposes of cooperation would be emphasized at the expense of unity in faith and order.[133] A majority of the members would have voted to adopt, but there were enough in the comparatively small opposition to block the passage of a resolution, under the rules of the Conference. The report contained nothing inimical to the true objectives of the Faith and Order Movement, as the Continuation Committee of the Conference found, and the theological conditions of collaboration in Christian work which it laid down met the strictest requirements.[134] But Lausanne was too

[133] Consult *A History of the Ecumenical Movement*, p. 422.

[134] The report said that there must be, as a basis for cooperation, "a common Faith, a common message to the world; Baptism as the rite of incorporation into the one Church; Holy Communion as expressing the corporate life of the Church and as its signal act of corporate worship; a ministry in all parts of the Church recognized by the whole Body; for all the uniting Communions, liberty in regard to interpretations about sacramental grace and ministerial order and authority; and due provision for the exercise of the prophetic gift." See *Faith and Order: Proceedings of the World Conference*, p. 398.

close to Stockholm to escape the toll in fellowship of the rivalries between the causes they symbolized.

Bishop Charles H. Brent's statement on the first of the subjects, "The Call to Unity," was accepted by the Conference without discussion.[135]

The report on "The Church's Message to the World—the Gospel," which had been drafted by Professor Adolf Deissmann and submitted to his section for criticism and amendment, was accepted in the plenary session after a few minor changes. It became an important ecumenical document. Major parts of it were incorporated in the message of the International Missionary Conference at Jerusalem in 1928, and it was adopted by the Church of Christ in China as its statement of faith.

The message of the Church to the world is and must always remain the Gospel of Jesus Christ.

The Gospel is the joyful message of redemption, both here and hereafter, the gift of God to sinful man in Jesus Christ.

The World was prepared for the coming of Christ through the activities of God's Spirit in all humanity, but especially in His revelation as given in the Old Testament; and in the fulness of time the eternal Word of God became incarnate, and was made man, Jesus Christ, the Son of God and the Son of Man, full of grace and truth.

Through His life and teaching, His call to repentance, His proclamation of the coming of the Kingdom of God and of judgment, His suffering and death, His resurrection and exaltation to the right hand of the Father, and by the mission of the Holy Spirit, He has brought to us forgiveness of sins, and has revealed the fulness of the living God, and His boundless love toward us. By the appeal of that love, shown in its completeness on the Cross, He summons us to the new life of faith, self-sacrifice, and devotion to His service and the service of men.

Jesus Christ, as the crucified and the living One, as Saviour and Lord, is also the centre of the world-wide Gospel of the Apostles and the Church. Because He Himself is the Gospel, the Gospel is the message of the Church to the world. It is more than a philosophical theory; more than a theological system; more than a programme for material betterment. The Gospel is rather the gift of a new word from God to this old world of sin and death; still more, it is the victory over sin and death, the revelation of eternal life in Him who has knit together the whole family in heaven and on earth in the communion of saints, united in the fellowship of service, of prayer, and of praise.

The Gospel is the prophetic call to sinful man to turn to God, the joyful tidings of justification and of sanctification to those who believe in Christ. It is the comfort of those who suffer; to those who are bound, it is the assurance of the glorious liberty of the sons of God. The Gospel brings peace and joy to the heart, and produces in men self-denial, readiness for brotherly service, and compassionate love. It offers the supreme goal for the aspirations of youth, strength to the toiler, rest to the weary, and the crown of life to the martyr.

The Gospel is the sure source of power for social regeneration. It proclaims the only way by which humanity can escape from those class and race hatreds

[135] Brent's statement had been prepared by the officers of the Conference and the chairmen and secretaries of the six sections.

which devastate society at present into the enjoyment of national well-being and international friendship and peace. It is also a gracious invitation to the non-Christian world, East and West, to enter into the joy of the living Lord.

Sympathising with the anguish of our generation, with its longing for intellectual sincerity, social justice and spiritual inspiration, the Church in the eternal Gospel meets the needs and fulfills the God-given aspirations of the modern world. Consequently, as in the past, so also in the present, the Gospel is the only way to salvation. Thus, through His Church, the living Christ still says to men, "Come unto me! . . . He that followeth me shall not walk in darkness, but shall have the light of life."[136]

The section on "The Nature of the Church" could do little more than report the common obstacles to agreement it had encountered. Some of the members believed that the order of the visible church had been divinely predetermined and revealed and was therefore unchangeable. Others held that as an organism already infused by the Holy Spirit the Church was free to evolve whatever structures seemed to make for its fullness and well-being under given necessities. The former saw as a condition of reunion general acceptance of their conception of the prescribed constitution of the Church, while the latter thought it could be achieved only through modification and readjustment of present ecclesiastical forms and procedures. Some did not believe in union at all, beyond the natural drawing together of churches with the same faith and order where this would have practical advantages. These regarded existing denominational cleavages as the inevitable result of peculiar endowments of the Spirit and insurmountable non-theological barriers, which, however, need not prevent cooperation in areas of agreement or the mutual expression of the love of Christ under all circumstances.

Those who had dealt with "The Church's Ministry" found themselves in much the same predicament. The old divergencies on such issues as ordination and apostolic succession had lost none of their traditional rigidity. It was agreed, however, that in the "Reunited Church," if it ever materialized, place would have to be made for all the characteristic elements of the episcopal, presbyterial, and congregational orders of the ministry.

When the commission on the sacraments reported without suggesting any steps by which at least a beginning might be made of resolving the impasse in which the churches found themselves at the Communion table, William Adams Brown offered the following amendment:

> . . . We commend to the Churches for their earnest consideration the following points of immediate practical importance:
>
> (1) The possibility, pending the solution of the larger and more important difficulties referred to,[137] of some provision at future Conferences for united or simultaneous celebration of the Sacrament, in a form consistent with the

[136] See *Faith and Order: Proceedings . . . ,* pp. 461-463.

[137] The report had rehearsed the disagreements which prevented unity at the Lord's Table.

present law of the several Churches, which could express to the world the spiritual unity to which we have already attained.

(2) The possibility, without prejudice to the doctrinal position of each Church, of providing in communities where no other [opportunity] of partaking of the Sacrament exists for the admission to communion, under proper safeguard, of members of other Christian bodies resident in or visiting those communities.

(3) The possibility, under similar safeguards, of making early provision for some form of intercommunion or, if that be not possible, joint or simultaneous celebration in the new Churches in non-Christian lands.[138]

Bishop Charles Gore of Oxford declared from the floor that the motion was out of order and asked that it be withdrawn. Dr. Brown replied that he was "conscientiously unable" to do this but agreed to interpose no objection if the Conference wished to withhold action, provided the resolution and the disposition made of it were recorded in the minutes. This offer was accepted.[139]

The 115 members of Section IV, on "The Church's Common Confession of Faith," heard at their first meeting, according to Canon Tissington Tatlow, their Chairman, "some vigorously-worded opinions" which "generated a good deal of heat." [140] An example of this was the remark of an Orthodox delegate, "We must declare our loyalty to the Nicene Creed," and the rejoinder from a Congregationalist, "Well, I think we should clear all that old lumber out of the way!" There were in the group those who thought they needed only the Scriptures and wanted no traffic with tradition; but others considered tradition essentially a part of the Scriptures. A limited agreement was reached on acknowledgment of the Ecumenical Creeds as acceptable statements of Christian doctrine, the substance of which was believed even by those regarding no man-made confession as a test of faith, and on the right, at the same time, of any church to make its own supplemental declarations of belief.

The Conference and the sections worked in the English, French, and German languages, but the discussions were mostly in English. This was a serious disadvantage for many, and a hindrance to the progress and success of the business. It may have accounted, in part, for the presentation by various delegations of declarations setting forth their theological positions and their views on the proceedings. A statement signed by Evangelical Lutheran representatives from France, Norway, Sweden, Germany, Latvia, and the United States expressed sympathy with the aims and spirit of the Conference but desired that it should take no final vote on the measures before it, referring them instead to the churches for decision. There were similar declarations by members of the Reformed Churches of Europe and of the Society of Friends. The Orthodox dele-

[138] *Faith and Order: Proceedings . . .* , pp. 393-4.

[139] *Ibid.*, p. 393. See also William Adams Brown, *Toward a United Church*, p. 106.

[140] *A History of the Ecumenical Movement*, p. 422.

gation stated that it could vote for the report of the section on "The Church's Message to the World—the Gospel," but not for the others, because it found "the bases assumed for the foundation . . . of their conclusions . . . inconsistent with the principles of the Orthodox Church."

There was some confusion concerning the purpose of the Conference, many of the conferees apparently thinking that it was to consider plans for the reunion of the churches. The Orthodox and some of the American delegates were slow to accept the repeated assurances from the chair that this was no part of the business.

The agenda carried no provision for a Communion service. On the second Sunday of the Conference, the authorities of the Cathedral invited the members to a celebration according to the Reformed rite of the national Church of the Canton of Vaud, at which the presiding clergymen were Bishop H. Ostenfeld of the Lutheran Church of Denmark, Rev. August Lang of the Reformed Church of Germany, Dr. Henri Monnier of the Reformed Church of France, and Dr. William Adams Brown of the Presbyterian Church in the United States of America. Professor Wilfred Monod of Paris preached the sermon. The sacramental prayers were offered in Danish, French, German, and English. The public filled the Cathedral, and more than a thousand persons communicated.

This did not satisfy all the delegates. An appeal by Dr. Peter Ainslie to the Conference officials to arrange for an observance of Holy Communion at the concluding service on the last Sunday, as "an expression of the equality of all Christians before God," received earnest support. Dr. Peter Hognestad, Bishop of Bergen, Norway, and Dr. William Adams Brown were among those seconding the proposal. No action, however, was taken by the Conference.

Before dissolving, the Conference elected a Continuation Committee of ninety-five members, of which Bishop Charles H. Brent became Chairmain, Dr. Alfred E. Garvie Vice-Chairman, George Zabriskie Treasurer, and Ralph W. Brown General Secretary.

On the adjournment of the Conference, the Continuation Committee became the organ of the Faith and Order Movement. Its first task was editing and transmitting the reports of the sections to the churches.[141] At the same time, a letter was sent asking for their "considered judgment upon the steps which should . . . be taken in furtherance of the work of the Conference, and, if possible . . . assurance that they were prepared to continue co-operation."

At its first annual meeting,[142] which was held in Prague, Czechoslovakia, in the summer of 1928, the Committee appointed a subcommittee

[141] The report of Section VII on "The Unity of Christendom" was revised and included with the others.

[142] A Business Committee consisting of denominational leaders in the United States was responsible for the work of the Continuation Committee between its annual meetings.

on reference to handle the replies from the churches to the Lausanne reports, and requested Canon H. N. Bate to act as its convener and adviser. Archbishop Germanos, Dr. Deissmann, Pastor Charles Merle d'Aubigné, and Archbishop Söderblom were made Associate Vice-Chairmen.

Bishop Charles H. Brent died in Lausanne on March 27, 1929, of an illness already apparent at the time of the Conference there, and at a meeting in August of that year the Committee elected William Temple, Archbishop of York, Chairman of the Continuation Committee.

Persons acquainted with Bishop Brent knew that what he was as a man and what he accomplished as a missionary, an official of his Church, and a servant of the ecumenical movement could not be told fully by the tributes of friends who wrote of his passing.[143] He had made himself truly a citizen of the world, and it was said of him that he had more friends than any man of his time. For nineteen years it had been his hand that guided the work of Faith and Order.

The office was transferred from Boston, Massachusetts, to Geneva, Switzerland, in 1930, and Dr. Floyd Tomkins was made Assistant Secretary, with headquarters in New York. At its annual meeting that year, the Continuation Committee decided that a second World Conference on Faith and Order should be held not later than 1937.

At High Leigh, Hoddeston, England, in 1931 the Continuation Committee received the first report of the Theological Committee, which had been created in 1929. Dr. A. C. Headlam, the Chairman, described the work which had been done in the preparation of a series of papers on "The Doctrine of Grace," the subject which had been chosen for study.[144]

This meeting received the report of Archbishop Söderblom's death. Though best known for his guidance of the Life and Work Movement, he had given distinguished service also to the cause of Faith and Order. His work was known wherever Christians aspired to translate their unity in Christ into a corporate ministry on behalf of the kingdom of God.[145]

George Zabriskie also died in 1931. He had earned the gratitude and confidence of both the clergy and the laymen of the Faith and Order Movement, of which he was Treasurer. He gave an inspiring example of the devotion of business ability and experience to the furtherance of Christian benevolence. The loss of his service was felt the more for the fact that most of the money for the work up to this time had been provided by American individuals and churches. Dr. Floyd Tomkins was asked to assume the added responsibility of soliciting financial support from those sources.

The world-wide economic depression had necessitated severe curtail-

[143] Alexander C. Zabriskie, *Bishop Brent, Crusader for Christian Unity.*
[144] See *The Doctrine of Grace,* edited by W. T. Whitley.
[145] N. Karlström, *Archbishop Nathan Söderblom;* also *Nathan Söderblom: in Memoriam.*

ments of activities; the Continuation Committee did not meet in 1932 or 1933. Ralph W. Brown resigned as General Secretary, and the office in Geneva was closed.

Canon Leonard Hodgson of Winchester, England, who had been appointed Theological Secretary, consented to become responsible temporarily for the duties of General Secretary. Actually this arrangement was continued until the Faith and Order Movement was merged with the Life and Work Movement in the World Council of Churches. He made his own house the office, first at Winchester and then at Oxford when he became Regius Professor of Moral and Pastoral Theology in Christ Church. Besides being a scholar, he had a genius for organization and a large capacity for work. The burden of preparations for the second World Conference on Faith and Order fell mostly upon him.

At this time an effort was made with considerable success to promote knowledge of the Faith and Order Movement through study of its publications and discussion particularly of questions suggested by the comment of the churches on the Lausanne reports. Groups which were formed in many countries for this purpose drew into their programs pastors and leaders from the official ranks of the clergy and representative men and women of the laity. Classes for young people also proved popular.

At Hertenstein, Switzerland, in September of 1934, the Continuation Committee, resuming its annual meetings, took up questions relating to the agenda for the second World Conference on Faith and Order, for which, it was reported, 52 denominations had already appointed 173 delegates. In the place of the Theological Committee it set up three commissions, as follows: "The Church and the Word," Dr. Wilhelm Zöllner, Chairman; "The Ministry and the Sacraments," Bishop A. C. Headlam, Chairman; and "The Church's Unity in Life and Work," Dean Willard L. Sperry, Chairman, and Dr. Floyd Tomkins, Secretary.

The last of these commissions was created at the request of the American members, who thought the work of Faith and Order should be related to living issues before the churches. For some years a group of theologians in the United States had been studying this problem, under the chairmanship of Dean Willard L. Sperry, with Dr. Angus Dun of the Episcopal Theological School in Cambridge, Massachusetts, acting as Secretary and Dr. H. Paul Douglass as Historian. They had considered five subjects—"The Nature of Unity," "A Decade of Progress toward Unity," "Non-Theological Factors Affecting Unity," "The Communion of Saints," and "Next Steps"—and published their conclusions. Their spokesmen had come to Hertenstein with a strong case for recognition of the empirical approach to unity at the next World Conference.

In 1935, at Hindsgaul, Middlefart, Denmark, it was decided to hold the second World Conference on Faith and Order at Edinburgh, Scotland, in August, 1937. The Committee appointed Professor Henri

Clavier of Montpellier, France, Travelling Secretary for the Faith and Order Movement. Representing at the same time the forthcoming Oxford Conference on Life and Work, he visited during the next ten months Czechoslovakia, Hungary, Yugoslavia, Germany, Rumania, Bulgaria, Turkey, Syria, Palestine, Egypt, Italy, Greece, Albania, Poland, Lithuania, Latvia, Estonia, Finland, and Austria, in each country having interviews with church authorities and addressing gatherings of the people they had assembled to hear of his mission. The work of informing the American churches about the two conferences fell to Dr. Floyd Tomkins and Dr. Henry Smith Leiper.

The American denominations raised the money for their delegates' expenses to Edinburgh, and the sum needed for the Conference itself was subscribed in Great Britain.[146]

As early as 1933, the opinion that the Continuation Committee on Faith and Order and the Universal Christian Council for Life and Work were engaged in work which they could do more effectively together than separately had become so general in the churches that the two bodies decided a consultation was advisable. The joint committee which they appointed to study their objectives and programs brought in a report favoring the cultivation of friendly cooperation but making no mention of any plans to unite them.

However, there was a movement on foot at the time which was shortly to bring them together in the World Council of Churches. How the merger was managed has been told by William Adams Brown in *Toward a United Church* and merits retelling as a significant episode of the birth of the World Council of Churches and incidentally as an example of ecumenical method at that time.

In the summer of 1933, according to Dr. Brown, William Temple, Archbishop of York and Chairman of the Continuation Committee on Faith and Order, invited a small company of churchmen to Bishopthorpe, his official residence, for two days of conversation on possible ways of uniting parallel ecumenical bodies, particularly the Life and Work and the Faith and Order Movements. He had acted, apparently,[147] at the suggestion of Dr. Brown, who, with eight other persons, accepted —Dr. J. H. Oldham and Dr. William Paton of the International Missionary Council; Dean H. N. Bate of the Faith and Order Movement; Dr. Samuel McCrea Cavert of the Life and Work Movement; Bishop Valdemar Ammundsen and Rev. H. L. Henroid of the World Alliance

[146] A balance was left of the amount raised in Britain sufficient, with the contributions of the churches in various countries, to finance the Faith and Order Movement until it became part of the World Council of Churches and provide four thousand pounds for the Commission on Faith and Order of the World Council of Churches. (*A History of the Ecumenical Movement,* p. 431.)

[147] See *Toward a United Church,* p. 136. Dr. Brown was at this time Chairman of the Administrative Committee of the Universal Christian Council for Life and Work.

for Promoting International Friendship through the Churches; and Charles Guillon and Dr. Willem A. Visser 't Hooft of the Youth Movement. It was an unofficial meeting, and all present understood that they had no authority to speak for their organizations. The discussion ranged widely but came to no agreement.

Two years later Dr. Temple, while in the United States, was asked to address a group of American church leaders at the home of Dr. J. Ross Stevenson, President of Princeton Theological Seminary, on the aims and experiences of the "consultative committee"—as the original ten had come to style themselves—and on that occasion it was voted to recommend that the Universal Christian Council for Life and Work and the Continuation Committee on Faith and Order make this committee their own. The membership, thereupon, was increased to thirty-five persons, among whom were William Temple, M. E. Aubrey, Leonard Hodgson, W. F. Lofthouse, Walter Moberly, J. Hutchinson Cockburn, W. A. Visser 't Hooft, Marc Boegner, Yngve T. Brilioth, Alphons Koechlin, Hans Schönfeld, James C. Baker, Albert W. Beavan, Samuel McCrea Cavert, Fred F. Goodsell, John R. Mott, Lewis S. Mudge, G. Ashton Oldham, Edward L. Parsons, William P. Merrill, William Paton, Germanos Strenopoulos, and William Adams Brown.

The next meeting was at Westfield College in London in July, 1937. After three days of conference, the consensus was "that only a complete merger of the Life and Work and Faith and Order Movements in a single comprehensive body would provide the ecumenical movement with the unifying center it needed." It was voted to ask the second World Conference on Faith and Order, which was scheduled to be held at Edinburgh, Scotland, the following month, and the Conference on Church, Community, and State at Oxford, England, the delegates of which were already gathering, to recommend to their constituent denominations the organization of a "World Council of Churches"[148] to carry on as a united enterprise the work for which the Universal Christian Council for Life and Work and the Continuation Committee on Faith and Order were, respectively, responsible.

"The wisdom of the procedure followed became immediately apparent," wrote Dr. Brown. "When the Oxford and Edinburgh Conferences met, each was presented with an agenda which crowded every available moment with business of the highest importance. Had not a definite plan for unification been ready for consideration before each . . . met, it is most unlikely that an agreement on a workable plan could have been reached in time."[149]

[148] According to Dr. William Adams Brown, Dr. Samuel McCrea Cavert suggested the name "World Council of Churches."

[149] For William Adams Brown's full account of the circumstances leading to the merging of the Universal Christian Council for Life and Work and the Continuation Committee on Faith and Order, see *Toward a United Church,* pp. 134-141.

The Oxford Conference, which acted first, had referred the proposition to the national groups in its membership early in its sessions, giving them in this way time for unhurried discussion. At Edinburgh the Chairman of the Conference appointed a committee representing, so far as possible, all opinions on the question, to present a recommendation, which was considered with the report of the section on "The Church's Unity in Life and Work."

32. The Second World Conference on Faith and Order—Edinburgh

Three hundred forty-four delegates from 123 denominations enrolled for the second World Conference on Faith and Order, which convened at Edinburgh August 3, 1937. In addition, there were 84 alternates, who, with fraternal visitors, members of the Continuation Committee not included among the official representatives of their churches, and 53 young people, brought the total of the company to 504.

Ninety-five of these had been at the first World Conference on Faith and Order, at Lausanne, Switzerland, August 3-21, 1927. A few of them had attended the World Missionary Conference of 1910 at Edinburgh, which had met in the Assembly Hall of the Church of Scotland, now opening its hospitable doors again to Christians from the ends of the earth. William Temple had been one of a group of students who served as stewards at the former gathering.

The Conference commenced with worship in St. Giles' Cathedral, at which Dr. J. Ross Stevenson read "The Church's Message to the World—the Gospel," [150] and Dr. William Temple preached the sermon.

At the first business session, the next day, Archbishop William Temple was elected Chairman; Archbishop Germanos Strenopoulos, Bishop Gustav Aulén, Pastor Marc Boegner, Professor Alfred E. Garvie, and President J. Ross Stevenson Vice-Chairmen; Canon Leonard Hodgson General Secretary; Dr. Floyd Tomkins and Professor Henri Clavier Associate Secretaries; and Canon Tissington Tatlow Financial Secretary.

The members of the Conference who had shared the interests of the Faith and Order Movement through the years were mindful as they gathered of the absence of its early leaders removed by death, among them Bishop Charles Henry Brent, Archbishop Nathan Söderblom, Bishop Charles Gore, Professor Adolf Deissmann, and Dr. Wilhelm Zöllner. The last two had died during the previous year. Dr. Zöllner had assisted with preparations for the program, serving as Chairman of the Commission on "The Church of Christ and the Word of God."

The preponderance of older men in positions of leadership in the ecu-

[150] The report of the commission at Lausanne headed by Professor Adolf Deissmann, who was the author of the "Message."

menical movement had long occasioned concern in the boards of the various organizations, and it was consideration for the future needs of the work that led the Continuation Committee in 1929 to adopt the plan of inviting to its annual meetings young people of the churches, to give them opportunity to observe its business and, if they should be so led, to become interested in the Faith and Order cause.

There was general regret that the German delegations, which had been appointed by their churches, had not been allowed by their government to come. It was realized that they could have made an important contribution to the Conference, had they been present; also that the German churches suffered a distinct loss in their forced separation from the Faith and Order Movement.

There were seventeen Orthodox delegates, who represented the Ecumenical Patriarchate of Constantinople; the Patriarchates of Jerusalem, Alexandria, and Antioch; the Churches of Cyprus, Bulgaria, Greece, and Latvia; and the exiles of the Russian Church.

Archbishop Germanos was given permission to present a statement on their behalf, explaining their inability to concur in many of the actions. They took part in the discussions and profited in a spiritual way from the fellowship, they said, but found uncongenial and embarrassing the generalizations in the reports, which tended to give the impression that substantial agreement had been reached where it did not exist. They repeated what they had suggested at Lausanne, "that the general reunion of Christian Churches may possibly be hastened, if union is first achieved between those Churches which present features of great similarity with one another."

The Conference organized in four sections to study simultaneously for ten days the subjects presented by the Commissions: "The Grace of Our Lord Jesus Christ"; "The Church of Christ and the Word of God"; "The Church of Christ—Ministry and Sacraments"; and "The Church's Unity in Life and Work." The last section was divided, at its own request, so that there might be an additional Commission to study "The Communion of Saints."

The sectional discussions ended, reports of the conclusions reached were duly considered in plenary sessions, after which they were referred to a redrafting committee before being submitted for action.

The report on "The Grace of Our Lord Jesus Christ" was introduced by the statement "There is in connection with this subject no ground for maintaining division between the Churches." The others had not been able to speak so encouragingly, though the section on "The Church of Christ and the Word of God" had made progress in defining the relation of the Bible to tradition.

The study on "The Church of Christ—Ministry and Sacraments" had clarified somewhat the several meanings of the term "intercommunion," which was blurred in the thoughts of many members of the Conference.

Intercommunion, the report explained, might be: a united celebration of the Lord's Supper by two, or more, churches of different denominational connections; participation at a service in any church practicing what was called "open Communion"; communing "spiritually," as in the Roman Catholic Church, without communicating in any physical way; or receiving the elements when the minister, by some special dispensation, invited authorized members of a different order to do so, as in the service of Holy Communion in St. Mary's Church in Oxford at the close of the Conference on Church, Community, and State, to which the authorities of the Church of England welcomed all the delegates who were regular members of the churches represented.

But the Commission could not report any real advance toward the solution of the stubborn problems of order as they related to the ministry and the sacraments. They were deeply involved in the nature of the Church, and all that could be done at this stage was to recommend that the Church itself be chosen the subject of the next conference on Faith and Order; and the Continuation Committee was instructed to make preparations accordingly.

Considerable interest was manifested in the report of the fifth section, on "The Communion of Saints," the subject, perhaps, on which the majority of the conferees were least informed. Undoubtedly the testimony of John R. Mott in this connection reflected the experience of many other delegates. He had had no clear understanding, he confessed, of what the creedal declaration "I believe . . . in the Communion of Saints" meant, and went on to say that the Commission's study had made this doctrine an inspiration and comfort for him.

A happy discovery was that time had all but reconciled the fancied conflict between the Faith and Order and the Life and Work Movements, which at Lausanne had led to the rejection of the report of Section VII [151] because of its strong appeal for collaboration by the churches in the field of applied Christianity, as a legitimate form of unity. The undertaking of common tasks was now advocated as the surest way toward eventual reunion. There had been in the Conference on Church, Community and State at Oxford the month before a complementary shifting of emphasis to the theological implications of so-called practical cooperation. Some delegates there had complained of what they thought was preoccupation with doctrine.

The impelling logic of the almost unanimous concurrent action to unite the two Movements was clear. The members of the two Conferences were, in large part, the same people. In their interlocking capacity they had attempted to act for the same churches. They were responsible for provid-

[151] Archbishop Nathan Söderblom was Chairman of Section VII. As the principal creator of the Life and Work Movement, he understood well the inseparableness of its ultimate objectives from those of the Faith and Order Movement, to which also he had given full support. The clumsy handling of his report at Lausanne in his absence had contributed to its rejection, as well as to the dissent from its thesis.

ing for the financial maintenance of both causes. They had now the sense of affirming the oneness of that which God had already joined together.

The resistance at Edinburgh to this course was allayed, for the most part, by the assurance that the independence and autonomy of the Faith and Order Movement should be preserved through its Continuation Committee, until such time as the proposed World Council of Churches was organized, and that further appointments to the membership of the Committee should be of persons only who belonged to churches qualifying theologically, according to the "basis," [152] for membership in the Faith and Order Movement.

Opposition on the floor of the Conference was maintained to the end by the Bishop of Gloucester, Dr. A. C. Headlam, who, defeated in all attempts to bring about its rejection, succeeded in having added to the report on "The Church's Unity in Life and Work" the sentence, "Some members of this Conference desire to place on record their opposition to this proposal." [153]

The Conference had early elected a committee to observe the proceedings and to prepare an "affirmation of union in allegiance to our Lord Jesus Christ in view of the world-situation," naming as its Chairman the Rev. Dr. Robert A. Ashworth of the Northern Baptist Convention in the United States (later American Baptist Convention). The "Affirmation" presented on the last morning "represented the unanimous mind of the committee" and was adopted, without debate or changes, by a standing vote. The Conference recognized it at once as one of the memorable documents inspired by the ecumenical movement.

After electing a Continuation Committee, the Conference adjourned to St. Giles' Cathedral for a service of Thanksgiving, "at which, in the presence of a great company of worshippers, the chairman led in a recitation of the Affirmation of Unity."

We are one in faith in our Lord Jesus Christ, the incarnate Word of God. We are one in allegiance to Him as Head of the Church, and as King of kings and Lord of lords. We are one in acknowledging that this allegiance takes precedence of any other allegiance that may make claim upon us.

This unity does not consist in the agreement of our minds or the consent of our wills. It is founded in Jesus Christ Himself, Who lived, died and rose again to bring us to the Father, and Who through the Holy Spirit dwells in His Church. We are one because we are all the objects of the love and grace of God, and called by Him to witness in all the world to His glorious gospel.

Our unity is of the heart and spirit. We are divided in the outward forms of our life in Christ, because we understand differently His will for His Church. We believe, however, that a deeper understanding will lead us towards a united apprehension of the truth as it is in Jesus.

[152] Acceptance of "Our Lord Jesus Christ as God and Saviour."

[153] Dr. George Craig Stewart of Chicago, who had led the opposition at Lausanne to unite the two movements, voted for the report, helped later to draft the constitution of the World Council of Churches, and moved its approval by the Convention of the Protestant Episcopal Church.

We humbly acknowledge that our divisions are contrary to the will of Christ, and we pray God in His mercy to shorten the days of our separation and to guide us by His Spirit into fulness of unity.

We are thankful that during recent years we have been drawn together; prejudices have been overcome, misunderstandings removed, and real, if limited, progress has been made toward our goal of a common mind.

In this Conference we may gratefully claim that the Spirit of God has made us willing to learn from one another, and has given us a fuller vision of the truth and enriched our spiritual experience.

We have lifted up our hearts together in prayer; we have sung the same hymns; together we have read the same Holy Scriptures. We recognize in one another, across the barriers of our separation, a common Christian outlook and a common standard of values. We are therefore assured of a unity deeper than our divisions.

We are convinced that our unity of spirit and aim must be embodied in a way that will make it manifest to the world, though we do not yet clearly see what outward form it should take.

We believe that every sincere attempt to co-operate in the concerns of the Kingdom of God draws the several communions together in increased mutual understanding and goodwill. We call upon our fellow-Christians of all communions to practise such co-operation; to consider patiently occasions of disunion that may be overcome; to be ready to learn from those who differ from them; to seek to remove those obstacles to the furtherance of the gospel in the non-Christian world which arise from our divisions; and constantly to pray for that unity which we believe to be our Lord's will for His Church.

We desire also to declare to all men everywhere our assurance that Christ is the one hope of unity for the world in face of the distractions and dissensions of this present time. Yet we are one in Christ and in the fellowship of His Spirit. We pray that everywhere, in a world divided and perplexed, men may turn to Jesus Christ our Lord, Who makes us one in spite of our divisions; that He may bind in one those who by many worldly claims are set at variance; and that the world may at last find peace and unity in Him; to Whom be glory for ever.[154]

[154] *The Second World Conference on Faith and Order, Edinburgh, August 3-18, 1937,* edited by Leonard Hodgson, pp. 275-276.

Part Two

THE WORLD COUNCIL OF CHURCHES IN PROCESS OF FORMATION

I

THE PROVISIONAL COMMITTEE

1. The Continuation Committee and the Universal Christian Council United

The Conference on Church, Community and State and the second World Conference on Faith and Order each appointed seven members of a joint committee to place before the churches their recommendation that the Universal Christian Council for Life and Work and the Continuation Committee on Faith and Order be merged in a new comprehensive organization of the nature of a "world council of churches." [1]

The representatives of Life and Work and their alternates were:

Dr. Marc Boegner and Dr. Alphons Koechlin
Dr. William Adams Brown and Dr. Samuel McCrea Cavert
Dr. George Kennedy Allen Bell and Sir Walter Moberly
Archbishop Germanos Strenopoulos and Bishop Irenei of Novi Sad
Bishop Marahans and Archbishop Erling Eidem of Sweden
Dr. John R. Mott and Charles P. Taft
Dr. Joseph H. Oldham and Dr. M. E. Aubrey

Those named for the Faith and Order Movement were:

Dr. William Temple and Canon Leonard Hodgson
Bishop George Craig Stewart and Dr. A. R. Wentz
Dr. J. Ross Stevenson and Very Rev. George C. Pidgeon
Professor J. Nörregaard and Dean Yngve Brilioth
Professor Georges Florovsky and Archimandrite Cassian
Professor S. F. H. J. Berkelbach van der Sprenkel and Professor Bela Vasady
Dr. George F. Barbour and Professor George S. Duncan

Meeting in London on the day after the adjournment of the second World Conference on Faith and Order, the Committee of Fourteen, as it came to be styled, elected Dr. William Temple Chairman and Dr. John R. Mott Vice-Chairman.

The Committee voted to request the churches which had been repre-

[1] The name "World Council of Churches" had been suggested by the Westfield Conference (July) but was not part of the motions.

sented at Oxford and Edinburgh to choose delegates for another conference to act on the recommendation, and agreed that a draft of a constitution embodying the outlines of a suggested structure for the proposed new body should be enclosed with the letter for their study and criticism.

Not feeling competent to undertake by themselves the preparation of such a communication, the Committee decided to ask the churches to help first with the forming of a preliminary advisory conference. In this way—and by the co-option of representatives of various ecumenical organizations—ninety-odd persons were designated to meet with the Committee May 9-12, 1938, at Utrecht, Holland. Among those invited to serve as consultative members were Dr. Luther A. Weigle of the International Council of Religious Education; Miss Van Asch Van Wyck of the World's Council of the Young Women's Christian Association; Tracy Strong of the World's Alliance of the Young Men's Christian Association; and Dr. Adolf Keller of the Central Bureau of Relief. Mrs. Henry Hill Pierce of the Protestant Episcopal Church in the United States was the only woman delegated a member of the Conference.

The Westfield Conference had suggested that the new federation be called the "World Council of Churches." Some of those at the Utrecht Conference would have chosen a less ambitious title. There was objection to the word "Council" because of its traditional connotations of legislative functions. But the vote was to adopt.

Practical considerations behind this action were that it would please many who were accustomed to association through councils of churches, particularly in America, and would continue a name familiar from frequent use in discussions in ecumenical meetings and descriptive of the character of the organization, which would be composed of churches themselves, rather than of individuals or boards.

Delegates belonging to denominations with congregational polity called for a definition of "churches" in this connection, and the Conference, on a motion presented by Professor Kenneth Scott Latourette of the Northern Baptist Convention in the United States, added to the constitution a footnote which read: "Under the word 'churches' are included such denominations as are composed of local autonomous churches."

There was unanimous agreement that the World Council of Churches should have no legislative power. "Any authority . . . it may have," explained the Chairman, "will consist in the weight it carries . . . by its wisdom."

Opinion divided on the question of doctrinal conditions of membership in the Council. A majority favored retaining the "basis" of the Faith and Order Movement, which was a simple confession of faith in "Jesus Christ as God and Saviour." The fact that this formula had proved reasonably acceptable in practice influenced the decision more than considerations of its theological adequacy.

On the latter point, William Adams Brown had this to say in *Toward a United Church* (p. 146):

This phrase "God and Saviour" has an heretical flavor which would have led to its rejection by any one of the Ecumenical Councils. It expresses only half of the Christian doctrine of the Incarnation, namely, the deity of Christ, while his complete humanity is an equally essential doctrine. To Christian faith, Jesus is not God pure and simple, but God incarnate, the Word made flesh. To ignore the human factor in the Incarnation is to be guilty of what is technically known as Docetism, or, in other words, of reducing the humanity of Jesus to mere appearance. Had the phrase "God incarnate" been used, it would have raised no difficulty and avoided many misunderstandings.

By the action of the Conference, the first article of the proposed constitution read: "The World Council of Churches is a fellowship of churches which accept our Lord Jesus Christ as God and Saviour. . . ."

Statements by officials of the Continuation Committee on Faith and Order during the debate at Utrecht met to some degree the objection in the Universal Christian Council for Life and Work to anything resembling a creedal condition of membership. Canon Leonard Hodgson said that Faith and Order desired only to be able to continue its work on the basis it had had from its beginning; it had no wish to impose its standard upon the World Council of Churches as a whole. And Dr. William Temple urged that it would be necessary "to keep the door open for co-operation in some form" with ecumenical bodies that could not accept the Faith and Order formula. The implication of these remarks appeared to be that the World Council of Churches should be free to follow in its program outside the area of Faith and Order the policy of Life and Work of cooperating with "all men of goodwill," and the constitution, as adopted, confirmed this interpretation of the intent. It provided that the Council might "call world conferences on specific subjects . . . empowered to publish their own findings," and that commissions might "add to their membership clerical and lay persons, approved for the purpose by the Central Committee,"[2] while specifying that "in . . . appointments to . . . the Commission on Faith and Order, the persons appointed [should] always be members of the Churches which [fell] within the terms of the Faith and Order invitation as addressed to 'all Christian bodies throughout the world which accept our Lord Jesus Christ as God and Saviour.' "[3]

The constitution adopted for submission to the churches was understood to be subject to amendment by them when they came together to organize the new body. Studying it, they could decide whether or not they would participate in the founding assembly, and have opportunity

[2] See Article III (6); and Article VI.
[3] See Article VI (b).

to give notice of changes they might desire to propose.[4] The proposed constitution was as follows:[5]

I. Basis

The World Council of Churches is a fellowship of churches which accept our Lord Jesus Christ as God and Saviour. It is constituted for the discharge of the functions set out below.

II. Membership

All churches shall be eligible for membership in the World Council which express their agreement with the basis upon which the Council is founded.

After the Council has been organized the application of churches to become members shall be considered by the Assembly or its Central Committee as it may be advised by national or confessional associations of churches. (Under the word "churches" are included such denominations as are composed of local autonomous churches.)

III. Functions

The functions of the World Council shall be:

(1) To carry on the work of the two world movements, for Faith and Order and for Life and Work.
(2) To facilitate common action by the churches.
(3) To promote co-operation in study.
(4) To promote the growth of ecumenical consciousness in the members of all churches.
(5) To establish relations with denominational federations of world-wide scope and with other ecumenical movements.
(6) To call world conferences on specific subjects as occasion may require, such conferences being empowered to publish their own findings.

IV. Authority

The World Council shall offer counsel and provide opportunity of united action in matters of common interest.

It may take action on behalf of constituent churches in such matters as one or more of them may commit to it.

It shall have authority to call regional and world conferences on specific subjects as occasion may require.

The World Council shall not legislate for the churches, nor shall it act for them in any manner except as indicated above or as may hereafter be specified by the constituent churches.[6]

V. Organization

The World Council shall discharge its functions through the following bodies:

(1) An Assembly which shall be the principal authority in the Council,

[4] For the constitution as finally adopted at Amsterdam in 1948, see Appendix A at the end of this volume.

[5] See *Ten Formative Years,* p. 7.

[6] In matters of common interest to all churches and pertaining to Faith and Order, the Council shall always proceed in accordance with the basis on which the Lausanne (1927) and Edinburgh (1937) Conferences were called and conducted.

and shall ordinarily meet every five years. The Assembly shall be composed of official representatives of the churches or groups of churches adhering to it. It shall consist of churches adhering to it and directly appointed by them. It shall consist of not more than four hundred fifty members who shall be apportioned as provided hereafter. They shall serve for five years, their term of service beginning in the year before the Assembly meets.

The membership shall be allocated provisionally as follows:

Eighty-five representing the Orthodox Churches throughout the world, allocated in such manner as they may decide;

One hundred ten representing the churches of the Continent of Europe, allocated in such manner as they may decide;

Sixty representing the churches of Great Britain and Eire, allocated in such manner as they may decide;

Ninety representing the churches of the United States of America and Canada, allocated in such manner as they may decide;

Fifty representing the churches of Asia, Africa, Latin America, and the Pacific Islands, to be appointed by them as they may decide;

Twenty-five representing the churches of South Africa, Australasia, and areas not otherwise represented, to be appointed by them, such places to be allocated by the Central Committee;

and, not more than thirty members representing minority churches, which in the judgment of the Central Committee are not granted adequate representation by the above provisions of this section, such churches to be designated by the world confessional organizations.

The Assembly shall have power to appoint officers of the World Council and of the Assembly at its discretion.

The members of the Assembly shall be both clerical and lay persons—men and women. In order to secure that approximately one third of the Assembly shall consist of lay persons, the Central Committee, in consultation with the different areas and groups, shall suggest plans to achieve this end.

(2) A Central Committee which shall consist of not more than ninety members designated by the churches, or groups of churches, from among persons whom these churches have elected as members of the Assembly. They shall serve from the beginning of the Assembly meeting until the next Assembly, unless the Assembly otherwise determine. Any vacancy occurring in the membership of the Central Committee shall be filled by the church or group of churches concerned. This Committee shall be a committee of the Assembly. The Assembly shall have authority to modify the allocation of members of the Central Committee as herein provided, both as to the manner and as to the ratio of the allocation.

The membership shall be allocated provisionally as follows:

Seventeen, of whom at least three shall be lay persons, representing the Orthodox Churches throughout the world, allocated in such manner as they may decide;

Twenty-two, of whom at least five shall be lay persons, representing the churches of the Continent of Europe, allocated in such manner as they may decide;

Twelve, of whom at least four shall be lay persons, representing the churches of Great Britain and Eire, allocated in such manner as they may decide;

Eighteen, of whom at least five shall be lay members, representing churches of the United States of America and Canada, allocated in such manner as they may decide;

Ten, of whom at least two shall be lay persons, representing the churches of Asia, Africa, Latin America and the Pacific Islands, to be appointed by them as they may decide;

Five, of whom at least two shall be lay persons, representing the churches of South Africa, Australasia and areas not otherwise represented, to be appointed by them, such places to be allocated by the Central Committee;

and, not more than six members representing minority churches, which in the judgment of the Central Committee are not granted adequate representation by the above provisions of this section, such churches to be designated by the world confessional organizations.

The Central Committee shall have the following powers:

(a) It shall, between meetings of the Assembly, carry out the Assembly's instructions and exercise its functions, except that of amending the Constitution, or modifying the allocation of its own members.

(b) It shall be the finance committee of the Assembly, formulating its budget and securing its financial support.

(c) It shall name and elect its own officers from among its members and appoint its own secretarial staff.

(d) The Central Committee shall meet normally once every calendar year, and shall have power to appoint its own Executive Committee.

Quorum: No business, except what is required for carrying forward the current activities of the Council, shall be transacted in either the Assembly or the Central Committee, unless one half of the total membership is present.

VI. Appointment of Commissions

The World Council shall discharge part of its functions by the appointment of Commissions. These shall be established under the authority of the Assembly, whether they be actually nominated by the Assembly or by the Central Committee acting under its instructions. The Commissions shall, between meetings of the Assembly, report annually to the Central Committee which shall exercise general supervision over them. The Commissions may add to their membership clerical and lay persons approved for the purpose by the Central Committee.

In particular, the Assembly shall make provision by means of appropriate Commissions for carrying on the activities of "Faith and Order" and of "Life and Work." There shall be a Faith and Order Commission which shall conform to the requirements of the Second World Conference on Faith and Order, held at Edinburgh in 1937.*

* The requirements of the second World Conference on Faith and Order, held at Edinburgh in 1937, referred to above, are the following:

"(a) That the World Council's Commission on Faith and Order shall, in the first instance, be the Continuation Committee appointed by this Conference.

"(b) In any further appointments made by the Council to membership of the Commission on Faith and Order, the persons appointed shall always be members of the churches which fall within the terms of the Faith and Order invitation as addressed to 'all Christian bodies throughout the world which accept our Lord Jesus Christ as God and Saviour.'

"(c) The work of the Commission on Faith and Order shall be carried on under the general care of a Theological Secretariat appointed by the Commission, in consultation with the Council and acting in close co-operation with other secretariats of the Council. The Council shall make adequate financial provision for the work of the Commission after consultation with the Commission.

"(d) In matters of common interest to all the churches and pertaining to Faith and Order, the Council shall always proceed in accordance with the basis on

VII. Other Ecumenical Christian Organizations

World confessional associations and such ecumenical organizations as may be designated by the Central Committee may be invited to send representatives to the sessions of the Assembly and of the Central Committee in a consultative capacity, in such numbers as the Central Committee shall determine.

VIII. Amendments

The Constitution may be amended by a two-third majority vote of the Assembly, provided that the proposed amendment shall have been reviewed by the Central Committee, and notice of it sent to the constituent churches not less than six months before the meeting of the Assembly. The Central Committee itself, as well as the individual churches, shall have the right to propose such amendment.

2. Provisional Committee of the World Council of Churches

The Utrecht Conference addressed itself, further, to establishing a temporary organization to oversee the work of the merging bodies until such time as the proposed World Council of Churches should be officially constituted. The interval was not expected to be longer than two or three years.

The decision was to create a Provisional Committee, using as its nucleus the members of the Committee of Fourteen and their alternates, and enlarging it, as might become necessary, by appointments from the Continuation Committee on Faith and Order and the Universal Christian Council for Life and Work. This action was approved by both these organizations, which agreed also to cooperate with the Provisional Committee in such plans as might be adopted "to secure from or through the churches the budget necessary for carrying on the work."

Dr. William Temple was elected Chairman of the Provisional Committee, and Dr. Marc Boegner Chairman of the small Administrative Committee which had been designated "to act on its behalf until the next meeting."

Dr. Willem A. Visser 't Hooft was chosen General Secretary, and the establishment of a central office in Geneva, Switzerland, was authorized.

Dr. William Paton of the International Missionary Council and Dr. Henry Smith Leiper, American Secretary for Life and Work and Secretary of the Commission on Relations with Churches Abroad of the Fed-

---

which this Conference on Faith and Order was called and is being conducted.

"(e) The World Council shall consist of official representatives of the churches participating.

"(f) Any Council formed before the first meeting of the General Assembly shall be called Provisional and the Assembly, representing all the churches, shall have complete freedom to determine the constitution of the Central Committee."

eral Council of the Churches of Christ in America, were added to the staff, the one as a General Secretary with an office in London, and the other as Associate General Secretary with headquarters in New York City.

At a meeting in St. Germain, France, in January, 1939, the Provisional Committee approved the action of the World Missionary Conference of 1938 empowering the International Missionary Council to nominate representatives of the younger churches for election to the Provisional Committee. The assembly of the churches to constitute the World Council of Churches was discussed at length, and later the same year, at a session in Zeist, Holland, the decision was taken to convene it during 1941 somewhere in the United States.

Until that time the task of gathering money for the movements which were being united necessitated area cooperation in reaching the churches. The establishment in 1939 of the Council on the Christian Faith and the Common Life[7] took care of this need in Great Britain. Agencies already in existence on the Continent offered their services. In the United States a Joint Executive Committee consisting of the American members of the Provisional Committee and representatives of the Universal Christian Council for Life and Work and the Continuation Committee on Faith and Order was formed for promotional work. It functioned until 1944, when it was succeeded by the American Committee for the World Council of Churches, the members of which were appointed by the denominations which had signified their intention to join the World Council.

The Provisional Committee had been given the duty, further, "to maintain relations with other ecumenical organizations whose relation to the . . . World Council [had] not yet been officially defined."

Ecumenical opinion had been favorable to proposals to include the International Missionary Council with the Universal Christian Council for Life and Work and the Continuation Committee on Faith and Order in the merger forming the World Council of Churches. It was felt that the churches could not maintain their spiritual vigor and practical effectiveness in an association of the kind contemplated if they left outside it such an important area of their work as the International Missionary Council represented. And the missionary movement clearly needed, for its health, a closer contact with the churches. The unwillingness of the International Missionary Council at the time had not alone prevented the taking of this step. Structural differences had seemed to pose extremely complicated problems which only time could resolve without the danger of serious impairment of the work of the two movements. The International Missionary Council was made up of regional and national confer-

[7] The Council on the Christian Faith and the Common Life was merged in 1942 with two other interdenominational societies to form the British Council of Churches, which then became the area organ of the World Council of Churches.

ences of missionary societies and national Christian councils, whereas the World Council of Churches was to be constituted, as the name implied, of churches—or denominations—as such. The wise course appeared to be the establishment, at least for the time, of some cooperative relationship, and the Provisional Committee joined with the Council in working out a policy on these lines.

There had been talk also of incorporating the World Alliance into the World Council of Churches, for its relationship with the Life and Work Movement had been especially close. Dr. Henry A. Atkinson, Secretary of the Church Peace Foundation, the supporting agency of the World Alliance, had served as Organizing Secretary of the Universal Christian Conference on Life and Work at Stockholm in 1925, and afterwards—until 1930—he was Secretary of its Continuation Committee. The two organizations through their commissions on social and political affairs had continued in successful cooperation, the World Alliance on occasion providing money for important activities of Life and Work.[8]

But, granting a willingness on the part of the Alliance to be included in the World Council of Churches,[9] there was, again, the well-nigh insuperable obstacle of structural differences. The membership of the Alliance consisted of individuals, among whom, because of the terms of the Foundation under which it operated, were Jews and Roman Catholics, as well as Protestants. There really was no way to relate it organically to the Protestant-Orthodox-Anglican-Old Catholic World Council in process of formation. Under the constitution which had been prepared provisionally for the latter, they could collaborate in the interests which had been the care of the Life and Work Movement.

At St. Germain, in January, 1939, the Provisional Committee had authorized a letter to the Vatican informing Roman Catholic authorities of the plans for founding a World Council of Churches. Dr. Temple wrote on February 10 to the Cardinal Secretary of State. "From previous communications, the Committee understood," he said, "that the Church of Rome would not desire to be formally associated with the Council"; but it felt that courtesy required the Holy See be apprised of what was proposed. The Committee hoped "that it might be permissible to exchange information with agencies of the Church of Rome on matters of common interest," the letter continued, "and that [it] should have the help, from time to time, of unofficial consultation with Roman Catholic theologians and scholars." The following July, the Apostolic Delegate of the Roman Catholic Church in Great Britain wrote assuring the Archbishop, on the authority of the Secretary of State for the Vatican, that there would be no objection to his consulting English Roman Catholic

[8] E.g., the Alliance met the expenses of Orthodox delegations at important Life and Work conferences.

[9] Some European churchmen would have made the Alliance a part of the World Council of Churches.

bishops and the Apostolic Delegate, or to the exchanging of confidential information and opinion with Roman Catholic theologians.[10]

3. The Second World War

During the early weeks of 1939, the Provisional Committee followed with growing concern the conflict in Germany between the Church and the government. It endeavored to maintain "the policy of . . . Life and Work . . . in giving spiritual support to the Confessing Church, which was felt to represent the whole Church of Christ in its battle for the purity and truth of the Christian message." [11] When a group of German church leaders, who were subservient to the government, issued a declaration condemning "every supranational or international Church structure, whether in the form of Roman Catholicism or of World Protestantism, as a political distortion of Christianity," it replied in a message on "The Church as an Ecumenical Society in Time of War," which drew its inspiration largely from the statement on this subject by the Conference on Church, Community and State. The German pronouncement had carried overtones of anti-Semitism, and the Committee made clear the insistence of ecumenical Christianity on the spiritual unity of all who were in Christ, of whatever nation or race. The storm which had long been brewing was even then about to break, and it was destined to sweep all before it; but in the blinding destruction of the long war years the word of Oxford on the relation of church and state was a light the darkness could not extinguish.

> We recognize the state as being in its own sphere the highest authority. It has the God-given aim in that sphere to uphold law and order and to minister to the life of the people. But as all authority is from God, the state stands under His judgment. God is Himself the source of justice, of which the state is not Lord but servant. The Christian can acknowledge no ultimate authority but God; his loyalty to the state is part of his loyalty to God and must never usurp the place of that primary and only absolute authority.
>
> The Christian sees distinctions of race as part of God's purpose to enrich mankind with a diversity of gifts. Against racial pride or race antagonism the Church must set its face implacably as rebellion against God. . . . Similarly the Christian accepts national communities as part of God's purpose to enrich and diversify human life. . . . National egotism tending to the suppression of other nationalities or minorities is, no less than individual egotism, a sin against the Creator of all peoples and races. The deification of nation, race or class, or of political or cultural ideals, is idolatry, and can lead only to increasing division and disaster.

[10] See G. K. A. Bell, *Documents,* Vol. III, pp. 298 ff., for text of the correspondence of Dr. Temple and the Cardinal Secretary of State; also *A History of the Ecumenical Movement,* p. 707.

[11] Willem A. Visser 't Hooft, in *A History of the Ecumenical Movement,* p. 707.

> The universal church, surveying the nations of the world, in every one of which it is now planted and rooted, must pronounce a condemnation of war unqualified and unrestricted. War can occur only as a fruit and manifestation of sin. . . . If war breaks out, then pre-eminently the church must be . . . the church, still united as the one body of Christ, though the nations wherein it is planted fight one another, consciously offering the same prayers that God's name be hallowed, His kingdom come, and His will be done in both, or all, the warring nations. This fellowship of prayer must at all costs remain unbroken. The church must hold together in one spiritual fellowship those of its members who take different views concerning their duty as Christian citizens in time of war. . . .[12]

In July, 1939, the Department of International Justice and Goodwill of the Federal Council of the Churches of Christ in America organized at Geneva, Switzerland, a conference on the international situation, under the auspices of the Provisional Committee of the World Council of Churches and the World Alliance for Promoting International Friendship through the Churches, "to consider what action [was] open to the churches and individual Christians with a view to checking the drift toward war and to leading [us] nearer to the establishment of an effective international order." The thirty-five delegates came from eleven countries,[13] and the fact that they could meet and formulate a memorandum to the churches was witness of the growing reality of the ecumenical spirit, as well as of their personal strength as Christians.[14] The statement dealt with the task of the churches in time of war; the need for true Christian prayer and for preaching centered on the righteousness of the kingdom of God; the duty to maintain brotherly relations between the churches in spite of propaganda, and to work for a just and lasting peace; and the opportunities for ministering to prisoners, soldiers under arms, and the rapidly increasing numbers of refugees.

Surveying the economic and political causes of the deepening crisis, the Conference said:

> Whatever judgment may be formed upon these factors, and however many others may be added, it will not be denied that behind them all lies the human element. Men lost their hold on spiritual realities and have too often not even realized their need for them. . . . They have been brought to accept as substitutes the supremacy of nation, race, or class, rather than the sovereignty of God and the brotherhood of man as taught by Christ.[15]

[12] *The Message and Decisions of Oxford on Church, Community and State,* pp. 76-88.

[13] Among them were John Foster Dulles of the United States, Max Huber of Switzerland, Charles Rist of France, Dr. van Asbeck of Holland, and Dr. von der Gablenz of Germany.

[14] This was the last ecumenical gathering attended by Germans until after the war.

[15] *The Churches and the International Crisis,* pp. 9, 10-13.

Among the conclusions reached were the following:

> Political power should always be exercised with a full sense of responsibility.
>
> Since all human beings are of equal worth in the eyes of God, the ruling power should not deny essential rights to human beings on the ground of their race or class or religion or culture or any such distinguishing characteristic.
>
> Since there can be no government without law, and no law can exist without an ethos, that is to say, a sense of obligation in the conscience of the members of the community, there must be some form of international organization which will provide the machinery of conference and co-operation.
>
> It is both necessary and possible to place international economic life upon a more assured basis.
>
> . . .
>
> We believe that no decision secured by force of arms will be just and that out of the evil forces thereby set in motion, more evil is bound to come. We believe that decision by negotiation, conference, and methods of conciliation should always be an available alternative method. We believe that such procedures should be adopted free of the menace of force.[16]

The Continuation Committee on Faith and Order, at a meeting in Clarens, Switzerland, in August of 1939, elected Professor R. Newton Flew of Cambridge, England, Chairman of the Theological Committee to succeed the Bishop of Gloucester, Dr. A. C. Headlam, who had resigned, and chose for the subject of its study "The Nature of the Church." [17] To a group of theologians named by the American representatives of the Faith and Order Movement it assigned "The Practice of the Churches in the Matter of Inter-Communion." Dr. George W. Richards was appointed Chairman of this study group.

An announcement by telephone of the signing of the Russo-German pact brought a sudden end to the sessions midway in the program.

4. The Provisional Committee in Wartime

The Provisional Committee had sent to the churches which were represented at Oxford and Edinburgh in 1937 the request that they appoint delegates for an assembly to constitute the World Council of Churches, and by the outbreak of World War II fifty or more had complied.

The invasion of Poland by German forces on September 1, 1939, ended whatever hope remained of holding an organizational meeting in 1941, and preparations for it ceased. But the Committee found itself with tasks not unrelated to its original main assignment, for its work

[16] *Ibid*. p. 12 ff.
[17] See Part One, Section III, *32*.

in connection with needs growing out of the war had the unforeseen effect of strengthening the sense of unity in the churches. It brought home the realization of their common need of an international body through which cooperation could be established upon a permanent basis, and put them more in readiness for the organization of the World Council of Churches when the opportunity finally came.

What could the Provisional Committee do about the war itself? There were conflicting views on this question in the Administrative Committee when it met in January, 1940, near Apeldoorn, Holland. Some of the members proposed issuing a statement condemning aggression and the suppression of freedom. Others stood with the representatives of the Scandinavian churches, who favored concentrating on bringing about mediation and held that a pronouncement would be ill advised from that standpoint.[18]

These matters were discussed outside the Committee's regular sessions, and Archbishop William Temple drafted a memorandum setting forth the conditions under which, in the opinion of the British members, negotiations could be opened, a statement which later appeared in the newspapers of England.

The Committee, as such, was never able to agree on a declaration of any kind. There were many attempts, but the judgment that it was not competent to speak for the World Council of Churches prevailed. In a letter to the General Secretary, Dr. Willem A. Visser 't Hooft, dated May 20, 1940,[19] Archbishop Temple expressed his advocacy of a policy which was followed apparently by common consent:

> If we speak corporately we may find that we have erected fresh barriers to the reconstruction of fellowship. Christians from one country can meet Christians from another country with which they have been fighting in an organization which has not corporately taken sides; it will be difficult, almost impossible, to do this in an organization which has officially condemned, directly or by implication, their own country. . . . I want us to prophesy individually and to do this in contact with one another through your office: so the same message will be given ecumenically though with a variety of emphases.

Commenting from the standpoint of the last suggestion, the General Secretary said:

> This was precisely what happened. . . . Church leaders in different countries spoke individually, but sought to remember that they spoke as members of a supranational fellowship.[20]

[18] Bishop Eivind Josef Berggrav of Oslo had visited statesmen in Berlin and London in the interest of mediation.

[19] See *A History of the Ecumenical Movement*, p. 710.

[20] *Ibid.* p. 711.

An official statement concerning the problems with which the Provisional Committee had to cope from the early months of the war until well into 1945 said:[21]

> It seemed at first that the war would not merely slow up the process of formation of the Council, but might well lead to its complete disintegration. The staff became smaller and smaller. . . . The provisional structure of the Council, which had not yet been authorized by the churches, seemed altogether too shaky to stand the strain. It appeared for a time that hardly any contacts could be maintained with the churches.
>
> But in the midst of the war years the tide turned. Instead of a period of stagnation, the war proved to be a time of deepening and intensifying ecumenical fellowship.

So it was that Bishop Eivind Josef Berggrav could say as the war came near an end, after having himself suffered imprisonment for his faith: "In these last years we have lived more intimately with each other than in times when we could communicate with each other. We prayed together more, we listened together more to the Word of God, our hearts were together more."[22]

Continues the official description of the wartime situation, quoted above:

> The struggle to be the Church, which was essentially one and the same struggle in many countries, the common defence against the ideological attack on the Church Universal, the common suffering, the opportunity to serve war prisoners and refugees from other nations—these proved more powerful factors in building ecumenical convictions than conferences, committees and journeys.
>
> In these years churches and individual churchmen proved willing to pay a price for their membership in the *Una Sancta*. The churches which declared openly their faith in the Holy Catholic Church over against pagan or semi-pagan nationalistic distortions of Christianity; the men and women who shared the life of the refugees and fought to save them from death; the men of all nationalities and positions who as officers, as civilians, or as "illegal" couriers kept the churches in touch with each other, were at that time the real builders of the ecumenical fellowship.
>
> It was the privilege of the World Council headquarters in Geneva to become one of the main centres of this creative movement. It proved possible to maintain relationships in various unusual ways with most of the churches of Europe and . . . the United States. Geneva was a city in which servants of the philanthropic societies, diplomats, resistance-leaders, refugees, and church leaders of many nations met and helped each other to keep the lines of communication open. In some cases documents crossed the frontiers in diplomatic bags; in other cases through the courier-service which the illegal press of the resistance movements had established between the various countries. Much of the material came in the form of tiny microfilms which

[21] In *Ten Formative Years;* and, somewhat revised, it is printed in *A History of the Ecumenical Movement*, pp. 709-710.

[22] *A History of the Ecumenical Movement,* p. 709.

might be hidden in a piece of shaving soap or a fountain-pen. In this way information constantly streamed through the World Council office and was passed on to the churches through the Ecumenical Press Service or in less official ways. Much of this information found its way into the illegal press. The story of the spiritual resistance of the churches in one country encouraged and strengthened those of other countries. It made all the difference to men in the dangerous and lonely sections of the Church's battlefront to know that they were surrounded by the whole company of the faithful. A special tribute is due to Dr. H. Schönfeld, whose untiring and perilous labours opened up lines of communication with many who otherwise could never have been reached. Specially significant were the visits of Dietrich Bonhöffer of Germany to Geneva and Stockholm, as occasions for the thorough discussions concerning the specific responsibility of the Church for the future international order. In spite of instructions given by the National Socialist authorities to watch the World Council of Churches and its emissaries, its relationships with the Confessing Church in Germany were never interrupted.

During these years, the Provisional Committee could meet only in sections—in Geneva, with Dr. Marc Boegner acting as Chairman (Dr. Alphons Koechlin replaced Dr. Boegner after the occupation of France by the Germans); in London, at the call of Dr. William Temple; and in New York, where Dr. John R. Mott presided. From each of these divisions messages went out regularly to the churches which could be reached by it. Under Dr. Henry Smith Leiper in the United States and Dr. William Paton in Great Britain, the work of raising funds for the Committee's administrative expenses and for its wartime services proceeded with remarkable success. From necessity, the Committee accepted, so far as it could, the responsibilities of the unprecedented emergency which would have fallen to the World Council of Churches.

The spiritual welfare of the prisoners of war was an immediate concern. The Ecumenical Commission of Chaplaincy Service to Prisoners of War, which was created in 1940, concentrated on organizing active Christian congregations in the camps where they were confined and providing a pastoral ministry of visitation and counseling. At the same time, it looked after distributing Bibles, hymnbooks, and religious tracts and securing equipment and materials for use in the administration of baptism and the Lord's Supper. Its work was closely coordinated with that of the various other agencies—the Young Men's Christian Association, the Young Women's Christian Association, the Red Cross, and others. For example, the Y.M.C.A. accepted as its task educational and recreational programs for the prisoners. The Bible Societies made available quantities of Bibles and portions of Scripture.

The Emergency Committee of Christian Organizations at Geneva and similar bodies which were set up later in other places also served usefully as centers of information. Through the collaboration of these and other agencies the churches were able to minister to persons belonging to all the nations at war. Many lonely men in the scattered camps discovered a new meaning in the world-wide Christian fellowship which embraced its members wherever they were.

Work for refugees, which had been begun prior to the war, increased as many fled, or were deported, from Germany and occupied areas. Money for its support came mostly from the United States, Sweden, and Switzerland.

The Department of Reconstruction and Inter-Church Aid was established in 1942, when the possible extent of the war's destruction could be foreseen, with the certain prostration of the churches in many of the European countries. Dr. Samuel McCrea Cavert went to Geneva to represent the American members of the Provisional Committee in this important move. The hope was to lay a foundation and perfect plans for a work of salvage and relief beginning immediately upon the coming of peace.

The Department outlined the steps which it proposed to take, as follows:

To survey the needs of all churches and Christian organizations which are members of, or collaborate with, the ecumenical movement.
To bring these needs to the attention of churches able to give help.
To register and co-ordinate all projects of aid from one church to another.
To formulate and develop relief projects in cases with which the help of several churches is needed.
To act as an executive agency in cases in connection with which it may be asked by one or more of the contributing churches to serve.

In time, the European Central Office for Inter-Church Aid, which had been founded in 1922 under the leadership of Professor Adolf Keller of Switzerland, was merged with the Department, which profited greatly from the experience of the older organization and its relations with the churches of Europe.

The Ecumenical Refugee Commission, which had been set up in England in 1934 (at first as the Christian International Committee for Refugees), also was absorbed by the Department after the scope of its program had been expanded to include work for refugees.

The parallel relief measures on behalf of the "orphaned" missions of European churches during and after the war, which in their cooperative phases proceeded under the direction of the International Missionary Council, have already been described as a triumph of ecumenical service. (Part One, Section I, 5)

Many persons assisted with the preparations which enabled the Department of Reconstruction and Inter-Church Aid to commence its work in Western Europe the moment any territory was liberated. Among them were Dr. A. L. Warnshuis, who in the midst of the war in 1944 made a trip from America to the Continent; Dr. Ralph Diffendorfer, who was so largely responsible for arousing the churches in the United States to the need of Europe; and Dr. William Paton, whose experience of the devastation and suffering which spread into his own nation taught him the importance and the urgency of the mission of relief.

The function of the Study Department of Life and Work under the Provisional Committee had been defined before the war. The Department had been given the subject "The Living Church in Modern Society" for development under the four sub-titles "The Ethical Reality and Function of the Church," "The Christian Ethos: Its Source, Nature and Authority," "The Church and Freedom," and "The Ecumenical Nature and Tasks of the Church." But because of the sudden turn of events it was decided to confine the study to the first and relate it to "The Responsibility of the Church for International Order."

The Department could not convene any meetings, but scholars in various places, upon invitations from its scattered members, addressed themselves to the subjects. The papers produced by a group in the United States who studied "The Ethical Reality and Function of the Church" circulated widely in Europe, in both the Allied and Axis countries. The Northern Ecumenical Institute, which had been established under the directorship of Dr. Nils Ehrenström at Sigtuna, Sweden, early in the war, managed in one way and another to maintain contact throughout the conflict with the churches on the Continent, which, with the disappearance of nearly all religious publications, eagerly welcomed any means of communication with one another.

Harking back to the Conference on Church, Community and State at Oxford in 1937, the churches of a number of countries, without any prompting from the outside, held meetings to consider their wartime responsibility; and reports of their findings traveled beyond their own borders. One such gathering was the Conference (1942) on a Just and Durable Peace at Delaware, Ohio, under the auspices of the Department of International Justice and Goodwill of the Federal Council of the Churches of Christ in America, which resulted in the constitution of a Commission on a Just and Durable Peace whose studies and pronouncements had wide influence.

Study under the Continuation Committee on Faith and Order followed during the war years about the same course as that of Life and Work. The plan after the Edinburgh Conference of 1937 had called for the production of four studies on the nature of the Church which it was hoped would help resolve the conflict on this crucial theme, at which all doctrinal approaches to unity halted. One would be concerned with the biblical idea of the Church, a second the history of the doctrine of the Church in Christian theology, a third statements by the major confessional groups of their doctrines of the Church, and another an attempted synthesis of the variant conceptions and a formulation of a doctrine of the Church which might be generally acceptable.

What happened in America has been reported officially, as follows:[23]

> Advantage was taken of the fact that the churches in the United States represented a wide variety of denominational traditions. It was the only country in the world where so widely representative a group could meet for Faith and Order discussions. From October, 1939, onwards the American Theological Committee[24] met twice yearly. Papers were read and discussed on the biblical teaching about the Church, on its historical origin and development, and on the conceptions of the Church held in different denominations.
>
> In 1945, a Report was published, containing an introductory survey of the questions discussed by Dr. Clarence T. Craig, eleven denominational statements by members of the different churches, and a summary of the proceedings of the Committee by its Chairman, Dr. George W. Richards.
>
> An American section of the Commission on Intercommunion was also formed, with Dr. Hugh Thompson Kerr as Chairman and Dr. Charles W. Lowry as Secretary. A questionnaire was drawn up and meetings [were] held to discuss the answers and prepare a report, which was printed in 1942.

Near the end of hostilities a meeting was held in London for the members of the Provisional Committee who found it accessible, to consider plans for postwar work. Representing the European constituency, Dr. Marc Boegner, President of the Federation of the Protestant Churches of France, Dr. George Kennedy Allen Bell, Bishop of Chichester, England, and the General Secretary, Dr. Willem A. Visser 't Hooft, attended a similar conference in May, 1945, in New York City. On these occasions it was agreed that steps should be taken at once to re-establish, so far as possible, normal relations with the churches of the Axis countries.

The following October a delegation of American, British, French, Dutch, and Swiss churchmen went to Stuttgart, Germany, to discuss this problem with the Council of the Evangelical Church of Germany. They were received warmly. The results of the mission outstripped all hopes. The members of the Council volunteered at the outset an admission of their own implication in the guilt of the nation, clearing the way for quick and full reconciliation. To it were added expressions of their purpose to join in earnest striving for the spiritual recovery of the Church and of their desire to have part in the fellowship of the World Council of Churches and other ecumenical bodies. In return, they were given every assurance of Christian goodwill and help.

While it met with violent opposition in some quarters,[25] the Stuttgart

[23] *Ten Formative Years,* p. 22.

[24] Appointed at Clarens in August, 1939.

[25] The opposition, which was within Germany, arose mostly from fear that the Stuttgart Declaration would be used to the political disadvantage of the nation.

Declaration made possible an immediate beginning of the reconstruction of church life in Germany through the World Council of Churches and other interchurch agencies.

The sessions of the Provisional Committee at Geneva in February, 1946—the first fully attended meeting in seven years—brought together representatives from the churches of both the victorious and the vanquished nations. Quite in contrast to the attitude of Christian leaders of the hostile countries after World War I, whose estrangement had been felt in ecumenical gatherings for many years, they appeared to accept one another as spiritual brothers. In a cabled report, an official in the Geneva office described as characteristic of the spirit the first encounter between Dr. Martin Niemöller and the Archbishop of Canterbury, Dr. Geoffrey Fisher: "The British prelate came up to the famous German pastor during a recess in the sessions. . . . The two men grinned as they shook hands and all but embraced. The Archbishop apologized because he could speak neither German nor French; so, talking English, they began to chat like old friends about the church situation in Germany." There was much evidence of this kind that the labors of those who had striven in all possible ways to preserve the unity of the churches during the years of strife had not been without effect.

The roll of those who had died during the war included, among others, William Temple, William Paton, William Adams Brown, J. Ross Stevenson, Alfred E. Garvie, George Craig Stewart, V. S. Azariah, Dietrich Bonhöffer, and Theodore Carswell Hume.

Chairman of the Continuation Committee on Faith and Order since the death of Bishop Charles Henry Brent in 1929, William Temple was at home equally in the missionary and the Life and Work movements. He had attended their meetings and followed their fortunes. The eloquent messages of the World Missionary Conference at Jerusalem in 1928 and the Conference on Church, Community and State at Oxford in 1937 had been written largely by him. No one had seemed so well qualified by experience for the chairmanship of the Provisional Committee, which, appointed to organize the World Council of Churches, would have to become, as the event proved, the "World Council of Churches in Process of Formation" and bear the burden of all its coalescent concerns through the years of war.

Like Temple, William Paton died in the fullness of his powers, which also were of the first order. Whether serving under the International Missionary Council, the Faith and Order Movement, or the Provisional Committee, he was always the missionary, whose hope was in the world-wide outreach of the Christian Church, to which all organizations and their resources were to be dedicated.

J. Ross Stevenson and Alfred E. Garvie alike had seen as one cause the manifold paralleling endeavors of the interchurch movement and worked with singleness of purpose, wherever assigned, to make their unity manifest in fellowship and cooperation.

As an early prophet and apostle of ecumenism of the younger churches, V. S. Azariah of India had in his own ministry pointed the way to the meeting of Christian minds, East and West.

Opposing at first the merger of the Faith and Order and Life and Work Movements, George Craig Stewart had later confessed that he acted under a misapprehension of the facts and not only cast his vote for it but moved approval of it by his own Church.

Dietrich Bonhöffer, "ambassador of the Confessing Church in Germany," had died in a concentration camp shortly before the war ended, having willingly risked his life to preserve the ties of his people with the ecumenical movement.

The first American representative on the staff at Geneva, and younger than the others, Theodore Carswell Hume had been lost on a mission to Sweden, when the airplane on which he had taken passage was shot down above the battlefields of Europe where so many men of his generation had fallen.

William Adams Brown was among the foremost architects of the ecumenical movement, bringing to this task the wisdom of long and varied experience. He had not the reward of seeing the World Council of Churches he helped to build; but he "died in faith, not having received the promises, but having seen them afar off, and [was] persuaded of them," as the concluding lines of his last book, *Toward a United Church,*[26] witness:

In every age it has been the joy of devout souls to explore the possibilities of fellowship with the present Christ, and the writings of the great saints, Catholic and Protestant alike, testify both to the reality of his presence and the joy and peace with which it is accompanied.

The possibility of such a personal fellowship is recognized in all the Churches. Its boundaries are not identical with those of any ecclesiastical body. Christ has his own outside of any Church. Wherever in humility and penitence before God the devout soul forgets self in the quest of the best it knows, there the living Christ is present to add his blessing, furnish his guidance and impart his peace. This company of the redeemed, often unrecognized but always present, is the true Church of Christ, that soul of the Church recognized in Catholic theology, that Church invisible to which devout Protestants in time of discouragement turn for hope.

This Church in the Churches, the continuing evidence of the present Christ, is the fact on which the Ecumenical Movement is founded, which it is its central purpose to make explicit in the consciousness of all sincere believers and to furnish with the instruments required for its most efficient spiritual life.[27]

[26] Published posthumously.
[27] *Toward a United Church,* p. 193.

Vacancies in the Committee were filled by the election of Bishop Eivind Josef Berggrav of Norway, Bishop Theophilus Würm of Germany, and Bishop G. Bromley Oxnam and Dr. John A. Mackay of the United States. Instead of appointing a chairman in the place of Archbishop William Temple, it was decided to name five Presidents to serve until the World Council of Churches should be constituted. Those chosen were Dr. Geoffrey Fisher, Archbishop of Canterbury; Dr. Marc Boegner, President of the Federation of Protestant Churches of France; Dr. John R. Mott of New York; Archbishop Germanos of Thyateira; and Archbishop Erling Eidem, Primate of the Church of Sweden.

After the long period of uncertainty, the Committee thought that the time had come when it could with some assurance fix the date for an assembly to act on the proposal to found a World Council of Churches, and it appointed the second half of August, 1948. The choice of Amsterdam, Holland, for the place of meeting was made later. In this connection, it was announced that during the war fifty-odd denominations had voted to send delegates, making the total of those which had acted to date well over one hundred.

The resolutions passed at this meeting emphasized the disorder and distress in the world, to which the work of the Committee was, in large part, the churches' response. Confronted with millions of refugees and displaced persons without homes, food, fuel, and employment, the Committee urged that every possible measure be taken by governmental and voluntary agencies to mitigate suffering, and to resettle and rehabilitate the uprooted populations without discrimination. It noted with gratitude the action of certain of the governments, especially those of Great Britain and the United States, to limit the supply of foodstuffs for their own people in order to give more aid to the devastated countries.

With regard to the dislocated, attention was called to the stipulation of the Potsdam Conference that their relocation should be carried out in an orderly and humane way, which had not been observed. "Transfers . . . had brought great hardship . . . and suffering," it was declared, "to millions of persons, including large numbers of women and children, and [had] resulted in disease and death for an appalling proportion of them." The situation had become "an offence to the Christian conscience." The United Nations Organization was asked to take immediate steps to assure that provision for the relief of those already moved would be made and that further transfers would be in accordance with the terms of the Potsdam agreement.

Concerning Jewish refugees, the Committee, as reported in the minutes of 1946, said:

The Provisional Committee of the World Council of Churches records its deep sense of horror at the unprecedented tragedy which has befallen the

Jewish people in consequence of the Nazi attempt to exterminate European Jewry. . . . It recognizes with thankfulness the faithful witness of many Christians, who, at great peril to themselves, made their protest against anti-semitism and gave shelter to victims. It also acknowledges with penitence the failure of the churches to overcome . . . those factors in human relationships which have created and now contribute to this evil which threatens both Jewish and Christian communities. It therefore urgently calls upon Christians throughout the world to combat this evil. . . . (a) By testifying against the . . . practice of anti-semitism as a denial of the spirit and teaching of our Lord; (b) By ministering . . . to the needs of those who still suffer the consequences of anti-semitism . . . ; (c) By giving support to efforts to find suitable homes for Jews who have been displaced or can no longer remain where they are; (d) By co-operating with Jews in reciprocal attempts to remove causes of friction in personal and community relationships; (e) By promoting understanding and goodwill between Christians and Jews, so that they may bear a common witness to the obligations of neighborliness. . . .

Dr. Theodore F. Adams of the First Baptist Church of Richmond, Virginia,[28] who attended the sessions as an invited guest, wrote the following estimate of the experience:

The most significant thing . . . was the fellowship. . . . As I looked about the conference table, there were representatives of the allied nations, the enemy countries, and the occupied lands. Only the Spirit of God and the church of Christ could bring such a group together in a spirit of love and goodwill so soon after hostilities had ceased. The spirit of repentance and humility was marked, coupled with the realization that we were bound by spiritual ties that had never been broken and . . . shared the responsibilities for building anew a world that was hungry and cold and that had suffered beyond description. . . .

. . . One can hardly imagine the promise and possibilities of such a gathering. . . . I came away impressed by one tremendous fact—that the World Council of Churches, though still in process of organization, is indeed a going and growing concern. It has served during the critical war years as a source of comfort and strength for the churches in many lands, and its future promises much.[29]

The message issued to the nations at the close of the meeting was in part as follows:[30]

An illusory peace is little better than war. No peace can be lasting unless it is built on true spiritual foundations. We appeal to all men of goodwill and all who believe in spiritual values and forces to work together for an order of justice and humanity.

[28] Later President of the Baptist World Alliance. His denomination, the Southern Baptist Convention, had declined the invitation to become a member of the World Council of Churches.

[29] As quoted in *Landmarks,* p. 23. While not accepting the invitation to join the World Council of Churches, the Southern Baptist Convention cooperated in the postwar relief program, and Dr. Adams at the time of the Committee's meeting at Geneva was in Europe on a mission for his denomination.

[30] See Minutes of the Provisional Committee, Geneva, 1946.

All nations are under the judgment of God. Those that have been defeated are suffering a fearful retribution. But springs of their recovery are within; and if they turn to God and heed the voices of those among them who, even in darkest days, withstood the forces of evil, they can yet take their proper place in a world community. The victorious nations have suffered greatly, but their victory brings with it a new responsibility to God. They should combine justice with mercy. To seek vengeance against their former enemies by depriving them of the necessities of life, or by mass expulsion of their population, or in any other manner, can only bring fresh disaster. There must be a new beginning in the relationships of all nations. The nation has its own place in God's purpose for mankind, but national egotism is a sin against the Creator of all peoples. . . . There is a mutual interdependence between social order and international order.

We therefore appeal to the governments of the five great powers to rise to their responsibilities to the world. It was by the union of their forces that they won victory in war. We ask them to unite their whole strength in a common purpose now for the establishment of justice, for the relief of hunger, and for the development of a world community of free peoples. . . .

5. Postwar Actions of the Provisional Committee

The two years between Geneva and Amsterdam were crowded ones for the Provisional Committee and its growing departments and commissions.

The work of the Department of Post-War Reconstruction and Inter-Church Aid increased in its proportions and urgency. In the beginning it was concerned with what, for want of a less ambiguous word, came to be called "spiritual aid"—that is, help which would strengthen the churches primarily for their religious ministry. But it soon became necessary, because of the impoverished condition of the people in many places, to provide "material aid" as well; eventually the scope of operations had to be extended to embrace service to refugees and displaced persons, whose numbers in Europe, with the shiftings of populations at the close of the war, multiplied steadily until by 1948 they stood at the appalling total of "at least twelve million."

The guiding principles under which reconstruction would be attempted were defined by the Committee as follows:[31]

The paramount principle is that which is implied in the very existence of the World Council, namely that the task of reconstruction is to be conceived as an ecumenical task in which all the churches participate to the limit of their ability, and that the common objective is to rebuild the life of the whole fellowship of churches which finds expression in the World Council.

If this ecumenical principle is taken seriously, this will mean that the churches will agree to co-ordinate their policies and activities in order to make certain that all needy churches receive adequate help, that the churches will not confine their help exclusively to the churches belonging to the same

[31] *Ten Formative Years,* p. 33 ff.

denomination or confession, and that the autonomy and desires of the receiving churches are taken in full consideration. . . . The primary question will not . . . be how to re-establish the *status quo ante* in this or that church, but rather how to help each of the churches to fulfill its special mission as a church of Christ in this or that country. Our efforts must be directed not to the replacing of what has been destroyed, but to construct what is necessary to revive the church. To draw up the catalogue of losses sustained by the churches in the war because of foreign oppression will not be enough; we must give practical expression to the new vision granted to us of the church's mission in the world.

The primary object of the reconstruction and interchurch aid program was again made clear by the vote to appeal for "material aid"—food, clothing, medicine, etc.—which stipulated that supplies would be sought "so long as they [did] not hinder the main . . . effort, which none [would] care for if the churches [did] not."

Thousands of church buildings had been destroyed in Europe, some six thousand in Germany alone; comparatively few of them could ever be rebuilt. The immediate problem was providing for worship and routine church activities. Prefabricated wooden army barracks, which could be bought from the Swiss government, were chosen as best meeting this need, and within two years 140 of them had been distributed in seven countries. Some congregations requiring more room were helped to construct sanctuaries from the rubble of ruined buildings, in which they could worship while using the barracks for other purposes.

Finding that many churches preferred to treat the aid given them as a loan which they would repay, the Department created a substantial revolving fund to be administered in this way. The amount made available was not, of course, proportionate to the enormous needs.

The shortage of ministers, theological instructors, and other workers presented a serious problem, which called for aid in the form of scholarships for study abroad, as well as in schools still open at home. Such help came as a great boon to hundreds of younger pastors and ministerial students after long war-enforced isolation.

With their people impoverished and some currencies devalued to the point of worthlessness, the churches could not maintain the salaries of their pastors at the level of barest subsistence. The supplemental assistance by the Department made it possible for many ministers to continue in their work who otherwise would have been obliged to turn to other employment.

Libraries, public and private, had been among the casualties of war, and their loss could not be repaired fully. Had there been money to pay for printing, paper was unavailable. The Department allotted some of its resources for publishing hymnals, prayerbooks, religious magazines, literature for Sunday schools, and theological works, "the hunger for which equalled almost that for food."

With the wide prevalence of malnutrition, poor housing, and general unsanitary conditions, disease took heavy toll among those working for the churches, as well as of the people they served. The increased incidence of tuberculosis became especially alarming, calling for immediate remedial measures. Steps were taken to provide food packages for those ill at home. Arrangements with sanatoria enabled those requiring it most to receive treatment. And vacation or rest houses were provided in a number of countries for others needing only opportunity to renew their strength in the midst of healthful environments away from the burdens of their work.

For funds the Department had to depend mainly upon the churches of the United States. Those of Europe which were not actually receiving aid had been reduced to an economic state making it impossible for them to provide for their own requirements; and, because of restrictions on exchange, little of what they might have given could have been sent abroad. The United States alone had emerged from the war solvent.

The bulk of the money from North America—some six or seven million dollars during the years from 1945 to 1948—passed through Church World Service. Individuals and churches also sent large sums independently. John D. Rockefeller contributed a half-million dollars. In addition to the money which was raised, large quantities of food and clothing were collected and forwarded by Church World Service and other agencies.

Finding persons competent to administer the relief program was as difficult, in its way, as gathering the means for it. The denominations and other religious bodies of the United States and Europe, including Great Britain, helped at this point by lending members of their staffs for duty in the Department of Reconstruction and Inter-Church Aid. Under the senior Secretary, the Very Rev. J. Hutchinson Cockburn of the Church of Scotland, the corps of workers at Geneva during these years reached a total of more than 140.

Along with his gift for reconstruction and interchurch aid, John D. Rockefeller sent another half-million dollars to establish an "ecumenical institute" for training Christian leaders, lay and clerical, for service under changing postwar social and religious conditions. The aim of this new adventure in education was amplified in an official statement, as follows:[32]

> In the struggle with totalitarian ideologies the churches have begun to realize their own grave responsibility for the de-Christianization of their countries and have discovered again that their evangelistic task is not merely to bring men and women into the church, but to make them witnesses of the Lordship of Christ in all realms of life. They have become aware of the need to reoccupy the many fields of thought and life from which they have

[32] Minutes of the Provisional Committee of the W.C.C., 1947, p. 19 ff.

retreated. But, as they are confronted with the great vacuum left by the ideologies and seek to help the uprooted war-generation to find an anchor in the Christian faith, they are gravely handicapped by the lack of leadership. What is therefore needed, particularly in Europe, is the training of leaders, both theological and lay, a training which gives both a strong foundation in Christian doctrine and a vision of the present reality of the world-wide *ecclesia militans*.

The memorandum on the purpose of the Institute and its guiding principles issued by the Provisional Committee stipulated, among other things, that:[33]

It should be founded on a definitely Christian basis and embody in its instruction the Christian convictions for which the World Council of Churches stood, giving students a solid knowledge of the foundations of the faith and life of the church;
It should be thoroughly ecumenical, so that among its staff and student body all denominations that were members of the World Council of Churches should be represented and feel at home spiritually;
It should be missionary-minded and therefore concerned with all classes and types of people, and all tendencies of thought and life which were relevant factors in the spiritual and social situation, standing for the evangelization of those who had lost touch with the church, particularly the younger generation, and seeking to help its students to find Christian solutions to the problems which they had to face in the various professions;
It should be a center where the new insights and new life which had come to the churches would be transmitted from one church to another, and stand especially for the re-awakening of the church through the spiritual mobilization of the laity;
It should foster in its teaching that understanding between nationalities and races which is based on a sense of common membership in the family of God and expressed in a community life in which persons of all nations live together on a basis of mutual respect.

Chateau de Bossey, an estate conveniently situated on the lake, ten miles or so from Geneva, became available for leasing as the seat of the Institute, which was established in 1946[34] Dr. Hendrik Kraemer of Holland was appointed Director, and a schedule was organized for visiting professors from universities and theological seminaries in various countries who would assist, in turn, with the instruction. The response on the part of students was encouraging from the start; and the campus quarters were found suitable for the entertainment between terms of ecumenical committees and boards meeting at Geneva.

[33] *Ibid.* p. 93.
[34] The purchase later of Petit Bossey nearby increased accommodations.

6. The Commission of the Churches on International Affairs Founded

In August, 1946, "a conference of men prominent in church affairs, representing seventeen nations," was convened at Cambridge, England, by the Provisional Committee of the World Council of Churches and the International Missionary Council [35] "to set up the Commission of the Churches on International Affairs to act on their behalf in the field of international relations." [36] The chairmanship of the new body was left vacant for the time. John Foster Dulles was elected Vice-Chairman; Kenneth G. Grubb Director; and Dr. O. Frederick Nolde Associate Director. The intention was that the Commission, when fully organized, should have between thirty and sixty members, and that they should be chosen by the sponsoring bodies.[37] Its "general purpose," as defined in the charter, was "to serve the constituency of the parent bodies as a source of stimulus and knowledge in their approach to international problems, as a medium of common counsel and action, and as their organ in formulating the Christian mind on world issues and in bringing that mind effectively to bear upon such issues."

"Particular responsibilities" of the Commission were outlined, as follows:

To call the attention of churches to the problems especially claimant upon the Christian conscience at any particular time and to suggest ways in which Christians may act effectively upon these problems, in their respective countries and internationally.

To discover and declare Christian principles with direct relevance to the inter-relations of nations, and to formulate the bearing of these principles upon immediate issues.

To encourage in each country and area and in each church represented in the parent bodies the formation of organisms through which the consciences of Christians may be stirred and educated as to their responsibilities in the world of nations.

To gather and appraise materials on the relationship of the churches to public affairs, including the work of various churches and church councils in these fields and to make this material available to the churches represented in the parent bodies.

To study selected problems of international justice and world order, includ-

[35] Authorized by the Provisional Committee at its meeting in Geneva in February, 1946, when it concurred in action taken previously by the International Missionary Council.

[36] See Minutes of the Provisional Committee at Buck Hill Falls, Penna., April, 1947, p. 33.

[37] The Commission was constituted a permanent agency by the First Assembly of the World Council of Churches in 1948 at Amsterdam, and by the International Missionary Council at Oegstgeest, Holland, the same year.

ing economic and social questions, and to make the results . . . widely known among all the churches.

To assign specific responsibilities and study to committees or special groups, and to claim for them the assistance of persons especially expert in the problems under consideration.

To organize conferences of church leaders of different nations.

To represent the parent bodies in relations with international bodies such as the United Nations and related agencies. In particular, the Commission should maintain such contacts with these bodies as will assist in:

(a) the progressive development and codification of international law and the progressive development of supranational institutions;

(b) the encouragement of respect for and observance of human rights and fundamental freedoms; special attention being given to the problem of religious liberty;

(c) the international regulation of armaments;

(d) the furtherance of international economic co-operation;

(e) acceptance by all nations of the obligation to promote to the utmost the well-being of dependent peoples, including their advance toward self-government and the development of their free political institutions;

(f) the promotion of international social, cultural, educational and humanitarian enterprises.

To concert from time to time with other organizations holding similar objectives in the advancement of particular ends.[38]

Immediate attention was given to "the formation of organisms through which the consciences of Christians [would] be stirred and educated as to their responsibilities in the world of nations," and within two or three years a dozen or more national committees on international affairs had been organized and brought into a working relationship with the Commission, and correspondents had been appointed in some sixteen additional countries, through whom information could be channeled to the churches.

Some of the issues which were in this way brought to the knowledge of the churches were:

The revision of original trusteeship agreements to include more adequate safeguards for religious liberty and missionary freedom;

Provision for human rights, with special reference to religious freedom in treaties with the Axis and satellite pwers;

Consideration of the Palestine problem, making available important information and stressing especially the historical and contemporary interests of the Christian community;

Investigations of the refugee problem, with a view to possible representation by the Commission when the basic information had been compiled by the Ecumenical Refugee Commission;

Provision for religious freedom in the Italian constitution and the import of this in face of restrictive articles in the Lateran Pact;

The alleged mistreatment of natives in Southwest Africa;

[38] See "The Commission of the Churches on International Affairs," 1949-50, p. 7. New York and London.

Violations of religious freedom in Spain;
Protection of German missionary property and the status of German missionaries;
General problems of the peace settlement with Germany, with special reference to human rights.[39]

7. First World Conference of Christian Youth

The Universal Christian Conference on Life and Work at Stockholm in 1925 established a Youth Commission, which later joined with a corresponding group in the World Alliance to form the Ecumenical Youth Commission. The young people had been active independently in their own programs of international Christian work. The Conference on Church, Community and State and the second World Conference on Faith and Order in 1937 turned this interest more particularly toward the churches and helped open the way for the World Conference of Christian Youth at Amsterdam in 1939, which was convened under the auspices of the Ecumenical Youth Commission (representing now the Faith and Order Movement, as well as the Life and Work Movement and the World Alliance), the International Missionary Council, the World's Alliance of Young Men's Christian Associations, the World's Young Women's Christian Association, and other Christian organizations represented through their national branches, including the World's Student Christian Federation.

To Amsterdam came some thirteen hundred young people from seventy countries to meet together in what was reported as "the first completely representative international conference of Christian youth . . . ever . . . held."[40] The announcement described the meeting as "aiming at confronting youth with the results of the world gatherings of the Christian churches and the Christian youth movements in the years of 1937 and 1938 . . . [and] to mobilize youth to witness to the reality of the Christian community as the God-given supranational body to which [had] been entrusted the message of victory over the world's spiritual, political and social confusion. . . ."

> A joint enterprise of this size and character has never before been attempted [the statement continued]. Only the gravest circumstances could persuade the experienced collaborating movements of the necessity and indeed the feasibility of such an . . . adventure of faith in the midst of the present world crisis. The prevailing world disunity and lack of direction has aroused increasing demand for such a manifestation. If it is to face this disunity creatively, Christian youth will need more than ever that sense of deeper solidarity which, it is hoped, the Conference will help to bring into being.

[39] Consult Minutes of the Central Committee, W.C.C., 1948-61.
[40] William Adams Brown (who was present), in *Toward a United Church,* p. 160.

Responsibility for organizing and directing the Conference rested with R. H. Edwin Espy of the United States, and the delegates heard eminent ecumenical leaders in stimulating addresses—Reinhold Niebuhr, George MacLeod of Iona, John R. Mott, and others. "In spite of the limitations, it is not too much to say that the . . . Conference was one of the most notable in the long series of ecumenical gatherings. . . ."[41]

Three weeks after the Conference had dispersed Europe was aflame. The delegates had returned to their homes, every one of them to become involved in the holocaust. No one could know or estimate the effect upon them of the experiences which they had shared in study and discussion, social intercourse and worship during the days at Amsterdam, especially of the great Communion service at the end in Nieuwe Kerk, where at the long tables arranged according to the rite of the Netherlands Reformed Church they sat down together and partook of the bread and drank of the cup of Christ before going out into the night then falling upon mankind. But the memory of it must have been for many of them a comfort in days of sacrifice and loneliness and a slender thread, at least, in the spiritual bond which God had seemed to be teaching them, with all who loved him, to weave against the sundering years of war.

Seven years afterwards, in 1946, the Provisional Committee of the World Council of Churches (in process of formation) set up the Youth Department; and the following summer the second World Conference of Christian Youth was held, in Oslo, Norway, with twelve hundred delegates present, half of whom had been appointed directly by their denominations. Francis House was Organizing Secretary of this gathering.

Miss Jean Fraser later succeeded Mr. House as Secretary of the Youth Department, and Rev. William Keys, who had been Co-Chairman with Mlle. Madeleine Barot of the Department, became Ecumenical Youth Secretary, with headquarters in the New York office.

8. Ecumenical Press Service

The Universal Christian Council for Life and Work and the World Alliance established in 1933 a press service (International Christian Press and Information Service) to circulate news of interest through the world-wide Christian community. They were joined soon in the venture by other bodies, including the World's Alliance of Young Men's Christian Associations, the World's Student Christian Federation, the International Missionary Council, the World Sunday School Association, and the United Bible Societies. After the Conference on Church, Community and State at Oxford and the second World Conference on

[41] *Ibid.*, p. 161.

Faith and Order at Edinburgh, both in 1937, the Provisional Committee of the World Council of Churches (in process of formation) took the place of the Universal Christian Council for Life and Work and gradually assumed responsibility for collecting and disseminating the news of the churches. It represented also, of course, the Continuation Committee on Faith and Order. Bearing the greater part of the cost of the Service, it gave to the Director, Alexandre de Weymarn, the status of a staff member. The bulletins appeared weekly in French, German, and English editions under the masthead "Ecumenical Press Service." Their file for the years from 1939 onward is a continuous record of ecumenical events.

This memorandum from one who had to do with the Service describes the problems of communication besetting the Provisional Committee and other religious organizations which labored to keep open the lines between the churches during the war:

> At first it seemed as if most countries of Europe would be out of reach "for the duration." But soon openings were found. The *Ecumenical Press Service* traveled around Europe in diplomatic pouches or in the form of microfilms hidden in all sorts of objects; and even if a few copies could reach each country the news of the World Council would travel from mouth to mouth or be reprinted in the clandestine papers which consisted largely of *Ecumenical Press Service* news and documents. Thus the *Service* could perform that indispensable task of keeping the churches in living touch with each other. The full significance of this information work became clear only after the war. A Chinese Christian leader who attended the first post-war meeting of the Provisional Committee in Geneva in 1946 reported that the *Service* had been "the only open window toward the world." The history of the church struggle in Holland underlines the importance which the *Service* had for the leaders of the Dutch churches, since it enabled them to keep in touch with developments in the churches of all countries.[42]

[42] *Ten Formative Years,* p. 63.

II
BUCK HILL FALLS, 1947

1. The Provisional Committee Meets

The Provisional Committee for its meeting in 1947—the third of plenary character[1]—went to Buck Hill Falls, Pennsylvania, where it was in session from April 22 to April 25.

Twenty-one members answered the roll call, ten from the United States, the other eleven from Canada, Great Britain, France, Germany, Sweden, Holland, Hungary, and Switzerland. The election to membership of four nominees of the younger churches of China, Korea, India, and Mexico increased those in attendance to twenty-five.[2] Eighteen denominations with seven different confessional connections were represented.[3]

Officers of the International Missionary Council and other ecumenical organizations, invited consultants, and seven members of the staff—altogether, twenty-six persons—sat with the Committee.

It had been nine years since the Utrecht Conference, and ten of the original twenty-eight members—principals and alternates—of the Committee of Fourteen,[4] who had there been constituted the "nucleus" of the Provisional Committee, were now at Buck Hill Falls. These were Marc Boegner, John R. Mott, S. F. H. J. Berkelbach van der Sprenkel, G. K. A. Bell, Georges Florovsky, Alphons Koechlin, Charles P. Taft, Bela Vasady, A. R. Wentz, and Samuel McCrea Cavert.

Since the meeting in Geneva, Dr. J. Hutchinson Cockburn had succeeded to the vacancy caused by the death of Dr. George F. Barbour, and Professor William Manson, upon the nomination of the Church of Scotland, had been elected his alternate.

[1] The meetings of the Committee as a whole were at St. Germain in 1939, Geneva in 1946, Buck Hill Falls in 1947 and Amsterdam in 1948. There had been sectional meetings during the war.

[2] G. Báez-Camargo of Mexico, T. C. Chao of China, Rajah B. Manikam of India, and Fritz Pyen of Korea. Michio Kozaki of Japan, who had been nominated, did not arrive but was elected.

[3] Some of the larger denominations were unrepresented: e.g., the Northern Baptist Convention.

[4] Appointed by the Oxford and Edinburgh Conferences of 1937 to arrange for the organization of the World Council of Churches.

In a prefatory statement the Chairman, Dr. Marc Boegner,[5] said that responsibility for the Amsterdam assembly, only fifteen months away, must dominate the Committee's deliberations. The agenda for that gathering must be got in hand fully in advance, or the churches might meet and fail to accomplish their purpose.

What this involved, especially in respect to coordinating the burgeoning departments of the provisional organization and making room for them in the structure of the World Council of Churches-to-be, became more apparent from the General Secretary's report, which he introduced by restating "the distinctive principles . . . the founders of the World Council had in mind in the formative years 1937 and 1938," as follows:

The movement for Christian unity and co-operation must be rooted in the life of the churches. The churches themselves must bear the main responsibility for the ecumenical movement.

It is not enough to arrange for occasional ecumenical meetings. We are called to manifest the unity which already exists between us by creating a permanent relationship between the churches and a specialized ecumenical agency which is constantly available to the churches for the performing of common tasks.

The ecumenical body which we need in the present state of our relationships must express at the same time the reality of the inability of the churches to achieve general organic union and the reality of their desire to have fellowship with each other. The World Council is therefore in no sense a super-church, but the servant of its member-churches for purposes of co-operation and unity.

The ecumenical task to be performed has two main aspects: the common study of and search for the essentials of faith and order on the basis of which the churches may unite, and the clarification of the common Christian attitude of the churches in society. These two tasks are interdependent and complementary, and the activities of "Life and Work" and "Faith and Order" must therefore be brought in the closest possible relationship to each other.

The basis of the ecumenical fellowship must be Christocentric—for it is only in common allegiance to the Lord of the Church as the divine agent of our unity that we can hope to be brought and held together.[6]

These principles had proved to be sound, the General Secretary thought, and had given a sure foundation to the work of the Provisional Committee. It had been "owing to their stability," he said, "that the provisional period, which was to have lasted three years but . . . will have lasted ten years, has been a period of growth and development,

[5] Of the other four Presidents of the Provisional Committee, only Dr. John R. Mott was present. The Archbishops of Canterbury and Uppsala could not come, and the arrival of Archbishop Germanos had been delayed by the lateness of his ship.

[6] Quoted from the General Secretary's report in Minutes and Reports of the Meeting of the Provisional Committee, Buck Hill Falls, Penna., April 1947, p. 43. Consult pp. 44-58 for information on other subjects covered by his report.

and that we have been able to stand the strain of the war years." The time had come "to build a more permanent structure on these foundations," and "the focus of attention" would have to be "the World Council which should emerge . . . from the Assembly."

The year ending had been a time of extraordinary expansion. Four new departments had been organized—the Material Aid Division, the Ecumenical Institute, the Commission of the Churches on International Affairs, and the Youth Department. The seven already at work, with the exception possibly of the department ministering to prisoners of war, had seen their "tasks increase by leaps and bounds." This had been the case especially with the Reconstruction Department and the Refugee Division.

The Ecumenical Press Service had tried to meet a fast "growing demand for . . . news" of the churches. In addition to its regular assignments, the Study Department had been working overtime on the preparation of discussion material for the Assembly, which it must complete and have in the hands of the delegates in advance of their departure for Amsterdam.

"Thus, the small band which had worked in the small buildings in Avenue de Champel in Geneva had grown to a staff of over one hundred working in three buildings, plus a wooden barrack, in Route Malagnou, Geneva." And the income "for all activities," which a few years before had not amounted to more than twenty-five thousand dollars, had risen to many millions.[7]

This growth was cause for gratitude, the more so because it had been in response to "the realities of the situation," and not to promotion "by artificial means." It meant that the World Council of Churches was needed. Its provisional organ was busy with tasks "in the name of the Church of Christ as a whole . . . which could not possibly be performed to the same extent and on the same level, if the churches acted separately."

But there was the danger that the Council's program might "grow faster than the degree of ecumenical awareness and understanding in the churches"; and a systematic education which was not "merely propaganda about the World Council's activities but the presentation of a new dynamic vision of the Church" was an immediate need.

"It must be explained to the church members," Dr. Visser 't Hooft continued, "that while interchurch collaboration does not imply interference with the autonomy of the churches, it does mean positively to think and act in terms of the Christian fellowship as a whole . . . and . . . that while ecumenical unity does not imply the denial of the confessional heritage . . . it means the attempt to manifest that unity which has actually been given the churches that take their confessions seriously."

[7] The larger total of millions included funds received for relief.

The future of the World Council of Churches, it must be understood, was believed to be bound up with the spiritual renewal of the churches.

"What the limits of the Council's task must be" was a question before the Provisional Committee. From different sources had come requests that the work be extended into new fields—evangelism, Christian education, women's work in the churches, the use of the radio, religious films, and religious literature. It would manifestly be "bad strategy to undertake any new tasks until those begun had been carried out in a sufficiently thorough and adequate manner."

The Committee had recommended in 1946 that attention should be given to evangelism, but "the only step taken to implement this resolution directly [had] been the Evangelism Conference of the Reconstruction Department." However, "various forms of evangelism" had been developed in the work with prisoners of war, and also in the youth program and the study of the Ecumenical Institute.

As with most religious organizations, the demands of the work were increasing faster than the income, and this would be "a difficult problem" for the World Council of Churches itself to solve.

Under "problems of relationships" the General Secretary spoke of "the confessional federations or alliances . . . entering on a period of intense activity . . . in and through which the attitudes of the churches to ecumenical questions were crystallized and defined." They should be associated as fully as possible with the World Council of Churches and encouraged to think of it, "not as a possible competitor, but as the instrument which [allowed] them to make their full confessional contribution to the whole ecumenical fellowship."

In twenty-three of the thirty-five countries in which there were churches intending to be members of the World Council national councils had been formed, and these could well be "one answer to the need . . . expressed earlier for strengthening ecumenical awareness and understanding in the churches." "In matters of reconstruction and of ecumenical education, in youth affairs and financial questions, and in other ways," the World Council should seek their fullest cooperation as a means of keeping in touch with the day-by-day needs of the churches.

Special thought would have to be given also to the relationship with the World Sunday School Association, the Y.M.C.A., the Y.W.C.A., and the World's Student Christian Federation. The Provisional Committee was already collaborating with these organizations in "general ecumenical tasks," and especially in youth work. They were participating in the second World Youth Conference, to be held in 1947 at Oslo, as they had in the first, at Amsterdam in 1939.

The Committee "was in the process of working out [the] relation with the World Sunday School Association which [sponsored particularly] church youth movements."

The question of . . . permanent relationships with the Young Men's Christian Association and the Young Women's Christian Association is more difficult [said the General Secretary], for although we have the closest . . . personal relations, there arises an important question of principle. . . . We consider the Youth Department, which represents the churches, as a body which should not concentrate exclusively on the youth . . . organized under the direct auspices of the churches, but should think in terms of the total Christian youth situation. . . . This implies that in whatever body is set up to serve Christian youth as a whole the Youth Department of the World Council would like to participate, not as though it were an organization parallel to the independent Christian youth associations, but as a body which has a wider function. . . . This does not mean that we should like to dominate the free movements, for we are deeply aware of the value of their independent status. It only means that we would like to manifest in a concrete manner the concern of the churches for all Christian youth.

"The gravest question" which the World Council faced, declared Dr. Visser 't Hooft, was "whether the churches [thought] of their relationships established in and through the Council as a point of arrival or as a point of departure. . . . Is the present form of co-operation . . . all that we should hope for in this generation, or is it only a step on a road which should lead us in the direction of full unity?" He believed that one's conception of the task before the Council depended on the answer to this question.

A Council which contents itself with interchurch co-operation and study may render great service to the Christian cause, but it might at the same time render the one great disservice . . . by freezing the situation—that is, by making the churches feel that they had done all that is required of them. . . . And in the last resort such a Council would not have that specific dynamism which exists where churches and church-councils point beyond themselves to the *Una Sancta*. . . . Co-operation is important, and we have to pray and work very intensively in order to maintain and increase the degree of co-operation which has at last been achieved. But our Lord prayed for more than this. Our basis in which we confess our common allegiance to him as God and Saviour must be a ferment in the lives of the churches and of the Council . . . and make us restless until we can manifest to the world the full meaning of unity in him. . . .

It is not the task of the World Council to unite the churches. That is the task of the churches themselves. But it is the task of the World Council to point beyond itself to the undivided body of Christ. . . . [It] should at all times be ready to decrease . . . that the *Una Sancta* may increase.

2. Report on the Orthodox Churches

The delegation appointed by the Provisional Committee at its meeting in Geneva to visit "the Orthodox and Eastern Churches of Greece and the Near East" reported a successful mission. It had consisted of Bishop Yngve Brilioth of Växjo (Sweden), who acted as Chairman; the Rev.

Oliver S. Tomkins, Assistant General Secretary of the World Council of Churches; the Bishop of Worcester (England); Dr. H. Alivisatos, Professor of Canon Law in the Faculty of Theology at the University of Athens; and Rev. Edward R. Hardy, Jr., Professor of Church History in the Berkeley Divinity School, New Haven, and a member of the Advisory Council on Ecclesiastical Relations of the Protestant Episcopal Church in the United States.[8] Their itinerary had included Athens, Nicosia (Cyprus), Istanbul, Damascus, Jerusalem, Cairo, and Alexandria. Jerusalem they had bypassed, because of the political unrest; but in all the other places they had been received favorably. In most of them they had seen, besides the resident ecclesiastical authorities, church officials from other cities who had been invited to meet them. They found the desire to cooperate with the World Council of Churches general, and were given opportunity to discuss its interests with those persons best qualified in each case to speak authoritatively for their churches. They received in this way much information that would be useful to the Council in correlating its departmental activities with corresponding functions of the Orthodox and other Eastern Churches, especially in the areas of youth and laymen's work. In Athens and Cairo they had made fruitful contacts with the Protestant churches. The Evangelical Church in Greece they could report ready to apply for membership in the World Council.

After a month of journeying, covering nearly seven thousand miles and touching ten countries in three continents, your Delegation is able to report, with gratitude, that its mission has been successful in its primary purpose. . . . The Provisional Committee can count upon the re-affirmed co-operation of the churches which we visited and their full participation in the Assembly of 1948. . . . We have seen again what riches they have to contribute to our common undertaking and where they need the brotherly assistance of fellow-members in Christ's Body: we have been the recipients of their generous hospitality and we record, with thanksgiving to God, these auguries of an increasingly close and heartfelt Christian fellowship with them. . . .

We are reminded of the historical roots of the Christian faith. We have lived in the company of names which are of the essence of Christian history; we have visited churches which were great before most of our countries had received the Gospel. It is with humility and gratitude that representatives of this very new "Ecumenical Movement" record their warm and loving reception by representatives of churches which first gave to Christendom the meaning of the word "Ecumenical."

We are reminded of the powerful pressure still exerted on many of our fellow-Christians by the compact and pervasive religion of Islam. In many places which we visited the bare fact of Christian survival is in itself a miracle of God's mercy, but cannot, for that reason, be taken for granted into an indefinite future. The fellowship of Christians is badly needed by those who continue to face that steady, relentless power.

[8] Rev. Floyd Tomkins of the United States, who had been one of the original members of the deputation, was unable to make the trip, and Dr. Hardy was appointed in his place.

In country after country, we were aware of the great importance of the U.S.S.R. . . . Our visit to these portions of the family of Orthodox Churches threw into greater prominence the importance of that part of the Orthodox family which lives even closer to Russia itself. We do not need to urge upon the Provisional Committee that this completed mission of ours is integrally related to the World Council's as yet uncompleted negotiations with the Church of Russia and our resumption of relations with the Churches of the Balkans. The churches which we have visited would be, and were, the first to remind us of the unity of the Orthodox tradition.

Therefore, we urge upon the Provisional Committee a reconsideration of effective means of contact with the Orthodox world. We are well aware of the difficulties, but we suggest that the time is ripe for the more effective encouragement of Orthodox participation by the appointment to the central staff of an Orthodox member. Such a person . . . could both act by correspondence and perhaps cover again the ground we have covered, fostering by personal contact the processes that have been set in train. He could be responsible for a special supervision of Orthodox contributions to the study process and facilitate the preparation of Orthodox delegates to the Assembly. . . . He could initiate the follow-up in the Orthodox world. Thereafter, it could be discussed whether a post like this should be a permanent feature of the secretariat. . . .[9]

The plans of the Provisional Committee had been to make simultaneous approaches to the Russian Orthodox Church and the Orthodox Churches of Greece and other Eastern Mediterranean countries. The Moscow Patriarch expressed himself as favorable to a conference with representatives of the World Council of Churches, but difficulties had prevented a meeting.

The Committee voted at Buck Hill Falls to renew the effort, and also to send small delegations to the Patriarchates of the Serbian and Rumanian Churches and the Church of Bulgaria "to re-affirm their cooperation in the ecumenical movement and to discuss with them their participation in the World Assembly."

Hopeful of general cooperation by the Orthodox Churches, the Committee decided to assign them eighty-five seats in the Assembly.

The General Secretary spoke of the Orthodox Churches in relation to the World Council of Churches, as follows:[10]

We know that the Patriarchate of Moscow is giving serious attention to the question of its relations with the World Council. And we have had very clear evidence of the desire of the church leaders in the Balkans to continue to participate in the ecumenical movement.

The great barrier to be overcome in this connection is the impression that the World Council is largely a Western, and more specifically Anglo-Saxon, organization which identifies itself consciously or unconsciously with the concerns and interests of the Western nations. We shall have to make it very clear in word and deed, that such is not the case and that we understand by

[9] Minutes and Reports of the Meeting of the Provisional Committee, Buck Hill Falls, Penna., April 1947, p. 104 ff.

[10] *Ibid.*, p. 53.

ecumenical fellowship the fellowship in Christ which includes but also transcends all nationalities and races and which must therefore be independent of all political constellations. If we do so we shall be in a strong position to ask for a similarly independent attitude on the part of the Eastern Churches.

The presence of the Orthodox Churches in the Council would create conditions which the other members should try to understand in advance, said the General Secretary.

We shall . . . have to ask ourselves whether we are prepared for the consequences of the entrance into the World Council of the churches of the Orthodox family. For their full participation will mean that in the composition of our committees and in our methods of work, in our programme of study and in our activities, full account will have to be taken of their tradition, which differs in so many respects from the tradition which is the largely unconscious common heritage of the churches of the West, and even of many of their daughter-churches in the East.

If, however, any would ask whether it is worth while to pay this price, the answer must be that the World Council loses its *raison d'être,* if it does not attempt to establish a deep, permanent contact between the churches of the West and those of the East. The Eastern churches have maintained a sense of the objective reality and the cosmic dimensions of the drama of salvation which the Western churches need to recapture. They are today going through a crisis which may well prove a crisis unto life and in which they must be able to count on the fraternal sympathy and help of their sister-churches of other confessions.

3. Report of the Joint Committee

The Joint Committee of the International Missionary Council and the World Council of Churches (in process of formation) presented a report at Buck Hill Falls, recommending that twenty of the younger churches[11] be given "immediate invitation" to join the World Council of Churches. This was a long step toward giving to this large potential constituency adequate representation at Amsterdam, as had been the election to the Provisional Committee of the five nominees proposed by the International Missionary Council from their membership.

The Joint Committee recommended, further, that the Provisional Committee consult the British and American Methodist Conferences,

[11] The Batak Church of Sumatra; the Minahassa Church of Indonesia; the Moluccas Church of Indonesia; the Churches in Java; the Methodist Church of Tonga; the Samoan Church; the National Presbyterian Church of Mexico; the Waldensian Church (River Plate); Jamaica Baptist Union; the Burma Baptist Convention; the Korean Methodist Church; the Presbyterian Church of the Gold Coast; the Ewe Presbyterian Church (Togoland); the Methodist Church of Italy; the Synod of the Nile (Evangelical Church in Egypt); the Evangelical Armenian Church of North Syria; the United Presbyterian Church of North India; the Church of the Brethren in India; the Church of South India; and the United Church of Madagascar.

the Lutheran World Federation, and the Baptist World Alliance for advice about other mission churches under the jurisdiction of denominations in their fellowship which might properly be invited to become members of the World Council of Churches; also that it ask the Archbishop of Canterbury to suggest, "in consultation with relevant missionary bodies in England and the . . . Anglican authorities in the United States and Canada, groupings of extra-provincial dioceses which might be considered as member-units of the World Council to be represented by delegates with vote in the Assembly: also . . . any other areas not ready for representation in this way which might be invited to send observers."[12]

Dr. Visser 't Hooft said it was important that the younger churches participate fully in setting up the World Council of Churches, that they might make their contribution and be able from the start to regard it as their own instrument of ecumenical fellowship and action.

Some had not received invitations because they did not appear in the original membership lists of the Oxford and Edinburgh Conferences. It was the duty of the Provisional Committee to determine which should now be invited.

The decision would not be easy, he explained. On the one hand, it was important to maintain the criteria for membership which had been formulated at the meeting in Geneva the year before; and, on the other hand, it would be necessary to avoid applying them in a way that would create division or interfere with sound missionary policy. The closest possible collaboration between the International Missionary Council and the World Council would be required. The appearance of competition between the "missionary and ecumenical relationships" must be avoided. The World Council desired to be missionary, and the International Missionary Council desired to be ecumenical. The common purpose, therefore, must be to build an integrated framework in which all churches, old and young, could meet on a basis of complete mutuality, but in which there would be scope for the carrying out of the abiding missionary responsibility of the churches.

The Committee listened with keen appreciation to a statement by Dr. Rajah B. Manikam of India concerning the interest of the younger churches in the first Assembly of the World Council of Churches. They thanked God, he said, for the manifestation of the spirit of unity in the Church of Jesus Christ the world over and rejoiced that it had extended to their own lands. They welcomed with great expectancy the new era in the ecumenical movement.

The churches of the East had come to the realization, he continued, that mere cooperation was not enough. In India particularly they had been planning and acting together in many undertakings for some time, as if they were one church; and lately they had decided to try experi-

[12] Minutes and Reports, Buck Hill Falls, pp. 54-5.

mentation in actual organic union. Within a few months, the United Church of South India, comprising the Congregational, Episcopal, Methodist, Presbyterian, and Reformed communions, would be constituted.

The younger churches hoped that the World Council of Churches would not content itself with being only an agency for cooperation, he said, but would lead the denominations unitedly to face their task in the world. They had been asking how the activities of the Council might bring Christians to the answer to the prayer of Jesus Christ that they might be one.

While they were churches in their own countries, they would not, he concluded, have the spirit of nationalism rob them of the sense of membership in the Body of Christ. So they hailed as of the greatest significance the birth of the World Council of Churches.

The Committee approved "in principle the establishment of a joint office in East Asia of the World Council of Churches and the International Missionary Council," the need for which had been "strongly expressed by the National Councils of India and China," and noted with satisfaction "that the younger churches [would] send strong delegations to the second World Conference of Christian Youth in Oslo."

The report called attention to the fact that both the International Missionary Council and the Provisional Committee of the World Council were using "the term 'evangelism' in its full sense as meaning both personal evangelism and the application of the Gospel to social life, and that both these aspects [were] being emphasized in the programme for the Assembly of the World Council of Churches."

The Committee reaffirmed the statement adopted in February of 1946 at Geneva, as follows:

> We deem it necessary that the International Missionary Council and the World Council of Churches shall make clear to all their identity of purpose and concern for the evangelization of the world, shall co-operate in every possible way, and shall draw progressively closer together in all their undertakings for Christian fellowship, witness and service.
>
> It is our judgment that the World Council of Churches cannot leave outside its purview the missionary enterprises of the churches; that, at the same time, the churches need a functional agency in this field such as the International Missionary Council, with its wider basis of membership and its particular responsibilities; and that the growing tasks of both these ecumenical bodies, and their common Christian interests and purposes, will require that they be increasingly united in vision, plan and sacrificial action.

However, the Committee believed that "for the time being the distinctive responsibilities and functions of the two bodies" required "the existence of them both as autonomous organizations." While the most important expressions of their complementary relationship would be in the field of action, the Committee proposed that the principle of their interdependence be acknowledged also in the use by them of the following titles: "The International Missionary Council, in Association with The World Council of Churches"; "The World Council of Churches, in Association with The International Missionary Council."

4. Youth Department Policy

Rev. William A. Keys, who had been elected Co-Chairman with Mlle. Madeleine Barot of the Youth Department, informed the Provisional Committee of its intentions to participate in the World Conference of Christian Youth at Oslo and the Assembly at Amsterdam. Plans were being considered, he said, for adding a secretary for reconstruction to the staff, or, if it seemed better, a secretary of youth work to the Reconstruction Department. He presented for approval a "Statement of Policy of the Youth Department," reported in the Minutes as follows:

1. The Youth Department of the World Council of Churches owes its origin to a resolution adopted by the Provisional Committee of the World Council of Churches in its meeting in Geneva from February 21 to February 23, 1946. The resolution is as follows:

The Provisional Committee approves the setting up of a Youth Department of the World Council with a special Committee. The task of this Committee and Department will be:

(a) to serve as the centre of ecumenical contact and inspiration for the youth movements directly related to the churches;

(b) to collaborate with the international Christian youth movements and other Christian agencies concerned with youth in ecumenical youth activities.

The Provisional Committee authorizes the Youth Department and its Committee to represent the World Council of Churches on the Ecumenical Youth Commission, which is the organ of collaboration between the various international Christian movements and agencies concerned with youth work.

2. The primary task of the Youth Department is to help the churches and in particular the youth organizations of the churches in giving to their youth a sense of participation in and responsibility to the Church Universal as it finds its provisional expression in the ecumenical movement.

The Youth Department fulfills this function in the following ways:

(a) By providing an avenue for co-operative study of the needs of youth throughout the world, for the planning of programmes for meeting their needs and for the advancement of the Christian faith among youth.

(b) By providing a medium for fellowship and exchange of experience among the leaders of the church youth organizations and movements of the world.

(c) By organizing international and ecumenical meetings for members of church youth movements.

(d) By publishing studies and ecumenical programmes and material for the constituent organizations and movements. A first undertaking of the Department should be a survey of all the existing national and international church or church-related youth organizations and movements.

(e) By assisting member churches anywhere in the world in the development of national ecumenical youth organizations where such organizations do not already exist and where such help is requested.

(f) By interpreting the convictions and concerns of church youth to the World Council of Churches and its constituent bodies and by arranging opportunities for young church leaders to follow closely the work of important ecumenical committees and conferences, thus carrying forward traditions established by the conferences on Faith and Order and Life and Work.

(g) By interpreting the life and work of the World Council of Churches and the ecumenical movement to the youth of the churches. This could be facilitated through visits, conferences and publications.

(h) By stimulating and co-ordinating financial and other types of assistance by church youth groups for the church youth agencies and movements in countries which need outside help.

(i) By collaborating with independent international Christian youth agencies and movements which are concerned with youth, in ecumenical activities which are of common concern.

3. The Youth Department shall be directed by the Committee appointed by the responsible bodies of the World Council, including representatives of the main confessional families and the main types of national or regional youth organizations and movements which are participating in the ecumenical youth movements.

4. The Youth Department shall sustain close working relationship with youth departments of its member churches and with national ecumenical youth agencies. Since the World Council is a World Council of Churches, the youth movements of the churches are organically related to the Council through their respective churches. The Youth Department of the Council, therefore, does not ask youth movements to affiliate themselves directly with the Youth Department.

5. In accordance with its statement of functions (Section 2 above) and on the basis of the resolution of the Provisional Committee (Section 1 above), the Youth Department will collaborate with international Christian youth movements which are concerned with ecumenical activities.

In doing so it takes its stand on the following two principles:

(a) that the Christian youth movements which are organized independently have made and are making special contributions in such realms as evangelism, ecumenical education and lay initiative;

(b) that, in recognition of these special contributions it is desirable that close collaboration be encouraged between the independent youth movements on the one hand and the churches and church youth movements on the other hand.

This collaboration between the Youth Department of the World Council and the independent youth movements finds its expression in:

(a) their common responsibility for the organizing and following up of the World Conference of Christian Youth;

(b) the organization of the Ecumenical Youth Commission as their common organ for consultation and planning.

6. In view of the fact that the independent Christian youth movements have among their affiliated movements a certain number which are in close organic relationship with member churches of the World Council of Churches, these movements are invited to accept a consultative relationship to the Youth Department and its Committee.

5. Action on Reconstruction

"In spite of the generally grim situation," the Department of Reconstruction reported "signs of hope in the dark picture." The churches had been "shaken wide awake" and saw "the precarious state of Christian culture." "From country after country" came word of new opportunity to preach the gospel. Churches were cooperating as never before, and the nations also. The Department was maintaining "the greatest effort in interchurch aid which the Christian Church [had] seen in its long history," laboring continually under the realization that "if Christ [was] to be enthroned over the lives of men in Europe, it [would] be through the revival of the Church by the grace of God and the working of the Holy Spirit." Concluded the report: "It is Christian civilization that is at stake, not merely in Europe but also in Great Britain and the United States."

The Provisional Committee adopted the following resolution, bearing upon conditions in the sphere of the Department's activity:[13]

1. In June 1946 the Ecumenical Refugee Commission, in session at Geneva, drew attention to the plight of Displaced Persons, Refugees and Expellees. Since then the condition of these people has deteriorated physically, socially and spiritually, and their present appalling plight, with so little apparent prospect of amelioration, is both a reproach and a menace to civilization. Each one is a brother or sister in the family of God, and this fact underlies our deep concern and our proposals for meeting the situation.

2. In the light of the above the Commission, in session at Copenhagen in March of 1947, calls attention to the deplorable fact that, neither separately nor through the International Refugee Organization have the nations yet made proper provision either for a long-term solution or for interim care and preparation for resettlement. The International Refugee Organization budget in particular is lamentably inadequate for these purposes.

3. We therefore urge redoubled efforts by the Governments and the International Refugee Organization towards

(a) Repatriation of those, and only those by whom this is desired, and for whom it is safe and practicable.

(b) Speedy resettlement elsewhere of as many as possible, with the assurance of economic opportunity, community welcome and eventual citizenship. We record our conviction that, in such transfers, family groupings should be preserved. We call upon Christian people in potential countries of reception both to make known to their Governments their own desire to help to rebuild these shattered lives, and also to rally public support for such a policy.

4. We would further call the attention of Governments and the International Refugee Organization to the need for after-care of resettled or repatriated families and individuals. We also remind the churches in all receiving lands, particularly at the moment in Belgium, Britain, France, Sweden,

[13] *Ibid.* p. 88, 89.

Canada, the United States and the countries of Latin America, of their opportunity and Christian obligation to supplement official measures. Especially valuable service can be rendered through alertness to the spiritual, educational, and cultural needs and opportunities of the newcomers, over and above the basic economic and social provision which it is the minimum duty of Government to guarantee.

5. Hundreds of thousands must inevitably wait a long time for repatriation or resettlement. During this period retraining and rehabilitation courses should be provided for them, along with an adequate service of information as to the possibilities and prospects of resettlement. At the close of the waiting period they should receive at least the minimum equipment and clothing appropriate to their destined home and occupation.

6. The overcrowded conditions of Germany and Austria with reduced territory, greatly inflated population and insufficient resources, make it imperative to resettle elsewhere the largest possible number of displaced persons and refugees. Further, we are bound to record our conviction that, unless these countries are economically rehabilitated, with due regard to the peaceful future of the world, and certain contemplated frontier adjustments are also reconsidered, such resettlement of Germans and German-speaking refugees on a large scale in other lands may be the only alternative to a further serious threat to world peace.

7. It appears inevitable, however, that a large proportion of these displaced persons and refugees will have to make permanent homes in the countries where they now are. This lays a tremendous obligation upon the governing authorities and the churches of such areas, to make optimum use of all available resources in the provision of work, housing, educational and cultural possibilities. The world-wide Church must welcome this opportunity to strengthen the hands of the local parishes, and to make such activities a truly ecumenical witness.

6. Commission of the Churches on International Affairs

Director Kenneth G. Grubb stated that the Commission of the Churches on International Affairs had been declared constituted on January 1, 1947, and had opened offices in London and New York. Its tasks were "defined by the nature of the international scene." It was hopeful of establishing "relationships with the United Nations and certain of its specialized agencies." Questions in the field of national trusteeships and human rights would be its special concern. The work of the United Nations Educational, Scientific and Cultural Organization was, on the whole, of a type in which the churches had experience in many parts of the world. The German Peace Treaty would raise "the perpetually recurring problem of freedom of religion." The Commission was already working on these and other related matters. It had begun its task as the fourth Study Committee for the World Assembly of the Churches at Amsterdam in 1948, in which it was having to give special attention to "the baffling problems raised for the Christian conscience by the accomplishments and policies of the U.S.S.R. in international affairs," the meaning of the modern doctrine of human rights from the standpoint of the essential demands of religious liberty, and the complex factors which the churches should understand in attempting to express the Christian conviction on critical world issues.

The financial requirements of this new department would run annually, it was brought out, to approximately fifty thousand dollars. In the discussion, it was emphasized that this money would be used to prevent such "damages of war" as the churches were at the time spending vast sums to repair. A small percentage of the reconstruction budget would provide the needed amount.

7. What of Faith and Order in the World Council?

Glimpses thus afforded of the extensive activities contemplated in the area of Life and Work under the approaching World Council of Churches revived concern lest other less public features of the program suffer eclipse. In the judgment of some of the members a counterbalancing stress was needed on the importance of Faith and Order in the World Council-to-be and on the sharply contrasting procedures necessary in its work.

Faith and Order was described by Dr. Floyd Tomkins as "a primary function of the World Council of Churches" and deserving of the status of a department, which would be permitted, because of the peculiar nature of its task, to operate more or less under its own direction, albeit reporting regularly to the Council. Whereas it would plainly be desirable to secure the widest possible discussion of many of the questions with which the Council would have to deal, progress toward the reconciliation of divisive doctrinal issues would be best achieved through consultations of small groups of persons with an intimate knowledge of the traditions and temperaments of their churches, whose competence and qualifications in other respects might well be independent of official denominational position.

Dr. Tomkins spoke approvingly of the statement by Dr. Leonard Hodgson in an article which had appeared in *Christendom,* that Faith and Order was "a movement created in order to perish." "With that final reconciliation of disagreements for which we work and pray, the Lausanne Movement will first sing *Laus Deo* and then *Nunc Dimittis.*"

8. The Constitution

The Sub-Committee on Constitutional Matters felt its duty was not to write a new constitution or to suggest all the changes which might seem desirable in the provisional constitution adopted nine years previously at Utrecht. It proposed instead "only such amendments as were indispensable in the light of altered circumstances and developments."

In response to the demand that evangelism be given a formal place in the program of the World Council of Churches, the Committee advised that a seventh function be added under Article III of the provisional constitution, as follows: "(7) To support the churches in their task of evangelization."

Aware of the dissatisfaction of some churches with "the basis," the Committee recommended "adoption of the procedure with reference to Article I . . . suggested in . . . the minutes of the Administrative Committee, meeting at St. Julian's (Horsham, England), August 2 and 3, 1946":

(a) The Provisional Committee should not initiate any revision of the basis of the first Assembly.
(b) If certain churches indicate an intention of submitting a revision of the Constitution as to the basis, the Provisional Committee should suggest to them that it would be preferable to have the question studied thoroughly during the interim between the first and second Assembly.
(c) If any church submits to the Assembly an amendment of the basis, the Provisional Committee should propose, as an alternative, that the whole question of the basis be made the subject of study and report to the second Assembly.

It was advised, further, that Article II be changed to read:

Those churches shall be eligible for membership in the World Council of Churches which express their agreement with the basis upon which the Council is founded and satisfy such criteria as the Assembly or the Central Committee may prescribe.

Election to membership shall be by a two-thirds vote of the Assembly, each member church having one vote.

Any application for membership between meetings of the Assembly may be considered by the Central Committee; if the application is supported by a two-thirds majority of the Committee, this action shall be communicated to the churches that are members of the World Council, and unless objection is received from more than one-third of the member churches within six months, the applicant shall be declared elected.

There were frequent references in the discussions at Buck Hill Falls to the prevalence of wrong ideas about the nature and work of the World Council of Churches, and the Committee approved the following statement for use in counteracting such misinformation:[14]

The World Council of Churches, composed of churches which acknowledge Jesus Christ as God and Saviour, owes its existence to the desire of its member Churches to express their unity in Him. The Council seeks to promote this unity among its members and to serve them as an organ whereby

[14] *Ibid*. p. 90.

they may bear witness together to their common faith and co-operate in matters requiring united action. The Council does not aim, however, to usurp the functions which belong to its constituent members, nor in any way to control or legislate for these bodies. Moreover, while earnestly seeking the co-operation and unity of all the churches that accept its basis, the Council disavows any thought of becoming a single unified church structure dominated by a centralized administrative authority.

The Christian unity for which the Council stands is of a different order. It strives after a unity in which Christians and Christian churches, joyously aware of their oneness in Jesus Christ their Lord, and pursuing an ever fuller realization and expression of that oneness, shall in times of need give help and comfort to one another, and at all times inspire and exhort one another to live worthily of their common membership in the Body of Christ.

With respect to public pronouncements, the Council regards it as an essential part of its responsibility to address its own attention in the realm of thought and action, "not as having dominion of their faith, but as helpers of their joy." The Council further considers itself responsible to Jesus Christ, the Head of the Church, to seek to know the Will of God upon important issues which radically affect the Church and society, and thereafter, in the name of Christ, in dependence upon the Holy Spirit, and in penitence and faith, to call upon churches, governments or men in general, as the situation may require, to deal with a given historical issue, in the name of Christ and in the light of God's revelation in Jesus Christ the Lord.

9. Concerning Public Utterances

With regard to public utterances, the Provisional Committee had been criticized both for speaking too much and for lacking courage "to give a prophetic witness in the face of . . . evils and injustices." There were those who, like William Temple, thought that the Committee should not issue any pronouncements, but should confine itself to encouraging and assisting the churches themselves on occasion to speak unitedly. The foregoing statement of policy adopted at Buck Hill Falls made it clear that this was not the judgment of the majority, who considered "the Council [15] . . . responsible to Jesus Christ, the Head of the Church, to seek to know the Will of God upon important issues which radically affect[ed] the Church and society, and thereafter . . . to call upon churches, governments or men in general . . . to deal with a given historical issue. . . ." It remained only to formulate the rules which should govern the promulgation of opinion, and these were set forth in the following resolution, April 25, 1947:

1. (a) In the performance of its functions, the Council in its Assembly or its Central Committee may make pronouncements as it may feel itself led by

[15] The World Council of Churches was not yet in existence, but the Provisional Committee in this, as in other matters, spoke as for the Council. In actual practice, it was not only the Provisional Committee appointed to make arrangements for the organization of the Council, but also the Provisional Committee *of* the World Council of Churches—"in process of formation."

the Holy Spirit upon any situation or issue with which it or its constituent churches may be confronted.

(b) While such statements may have great significance and influence as the expression of the judgment or concern of so widely representative a Christian body, yet their authority will consist only in the weight which they carry by their own truth and wisdom, and in making them the Assembly or the Central Committee assumes no constitutional authority over the constituent churches.

2. (a) The Administrative Committee or any Commission of the Council may recommend statements to the Assembly or the Central Committee for its consideration and action.

(b) No Committee or Commission of the Council shall publish any pronouncement or make any public statement until it has been approved by the Assembly or the Central Committee, except that in circumstances of urgent immediacy statements may be published by the Administrative Committee, or by any Commission of the Council on matters within its own field of concern and action if approved by the Chairman of the Administrative Committee and the General Secretary, and in these cases the Committee or Commission shall make it clear that it speaks for itself only.

(c) In cases of exceptional emergency statements may be issued by the Chairman of the Administrative Committee after consultation with the Vice-Chairman of the Administrative Committee and the General Secretary, provided that they are satisfied that such statements are not contrary to the established policy of the Council.

3. Nothing in these regulations shall contravene the special provisions of the Constitution regarding the Commission on Faith and Order.[16]

[16] *Ibid.* p. 87.

III

TOWARD AMSTERDAM

1. Arrangements for the First Assembly

The Report of the Committee on Arrangements for the First Assembly, presented by the Chairman, Dr. Samuel M. Cavert, at Buck Hill Falls, recommended "that the invitations from the Netherlands Reformed Church, the Bishops of the Old Catholic Church of the Netherlands and the Ecumenical Council of the Netherlands to hold the first Assembly in Holland be accepted with warm appreciation; and that Amsterdam be designated as the place of meeting," and proceeded to outline in detail the careful plans which had been made for all the appointments of what would certainly be one of the most notable gatherings in the history of the Christian Church.

The Assembly would consist, it was explained, of regular and alternate delegates of the denominations which had signified their intention of becoming members of the World Council of Churches, "fraternal delegates" of "world confessional associations" and "ecumenical organizations," and consultants, as prescribed by the provisional constitution.

The confessional bodies included in the invitation were:

The Lutheran World Federation
The Alliance of Reformed Churches
The Methodist Ecumenical Conference
The Baptist World Alliance
The International Congregational Council
The Disciples World Convention
The International Conference of Friends (Quakers)
The Lambeth Conference

The ecumenical organizations invited were:

The World's Student Christian Federation
The World Committee of the Young Men's Christian Association
The World's Young Women's Christian Association
The World Alliance for Promoting International Friendship through the Churches
The World Sunday School Association

The World Union of Christian Endeavor
The United Bible Societies

National and regional interdenominational societies[1] designated by the Administrative Committee might each send a consultant; and "members of the Provisional Committee, chairmen of permanent commissions and committees, members of the executive staff, officers and secretaries of the International Missionary Council and speakers," if not appointed as delegates by their churches, would have the privilege of attending in "consultative capacity."

Churches which had not acted on the invitation to join the World Council of Churches would be accorded the privilege of sending observers.

Invitations would be sent to the United Nations Organization, the United Nations Educational, Scientific and Cultural Organization, the International Labor Organization, and the International Refugee Organization to be represented by one observer each.

The Presidents of the Provisional Committee and the General Secretary were authorized to invite "a few individual Roman Catholics to attend the Assembly as unofficial observers."

The Youth Department Committee had been requested to arrange for the attendance of a delegation of from fifty to one hundred young people.

Members of the four preparatory study commissions who had not been appointed delegates by their churches would be given the status of consultants in the sectional meetings and the plenary sessions dealing with the reports of their sections.

It was recommended, further, "that provision be made for approximately six hundred accredited visitors, to be admitted by ticket, and that the churches of each area be authorized to accredit a number of visitors equal to the number of delegates, plus one third," who would have "the first claim on visitors' tickets," special consideration being given in the assignment of these to the wives of delegates, if designated as visitors.

The American Committee of the World Council of Churches and the Interseminary Movement were requested to make available the services of Rev. Robert S. Bilheimer (employed jointly by them) for a period of "from six to nine months immediately preceding the Amsterdam meeting, . . . one of his responsibilities [to] be the arranging of the programme for visitors at the Assembly."

The Committee on Arrangements submitted for approval the budget for the assembly as follows:[2]

[1] E.g., the Federal Council of the Churches of Christ in America and the British Council of Churches.
[2] Minutes and Reports, Buck Hill Falls, p. 123.

For additional staff, secretarial assistance and office expenses for the Study Department	$17,000.
For the meetings, office expenses and travel of the five study commissions	10,000.
For the translation and publication of the five preparatory volumes in three languages	13,000.
For the expenses of the Assembly, including staff travel, stenographic service, printing, publicity and publication of reports	20,000.
For partial travel expenses of certain delegates who come from great distances (such as representatives of the younger churches)	30,000.
For additional expenses of the General Secretariat for the Assembly	15,000.
For unforeseen emergencies	5,000.
Total	$110,000.

Of this amount, the churches of the United States were asked to raise $74,800, and those of other countries the balance of $35,200.

The Committee "felt that each member of the Assembly should have the opportunity to participate in a service of Holy Communion," but explained that no such service could be appointed as "an official act of the Assembly." There would be, however, a limited number of observances according to the different historical and liturgical traditions at such times as would make it possible for all desiring to attend to do so, whether as communicants or not, and these would be preceded by a preparatory service.

2. The Study Department

Director Nils Ehrenström stated that the Study Department had been seriously handicapped, because of its too small staff, but that the contributed services of Professor John C. Bennett of Union Theological Seminary in 1946 and of Professor Walter M. Horton of Oberlin Graduate School of Theology in 1947 had gone far toward making up the lack on this account.[3] The Provisional Committee commended him and his colleagues for "their excellent work despite many disadvantages."

The Study Department Commission, Chairman Henry Pitney Van Dusen explained, hoped to be able to place in the hands of the delegates to Amsterdam, prior to their leaving for the Assembly, "the quintessence of the vast amount of thought and criticism which had gone into the preparation of the material on the theme and its subsidiary subjects." The study was complicated, however, by the inability of the persons engaging in it to meet oftener for consultation and the consequent necessity of confining their exchanges largely to the mails. The Commission was aware of the danger that unless extreme care

[3] Professors Bennett and Horton had been given leave by their faculties to serve as they did without compensation.

was taken the results might be confusing to the Assembly. The desire was that the churches might be helped to see with clarity the few really crucial issues confronting them in a complex age, and, if this was to be accomplished, their representatives at Amsterdam should return with "a very clear impression of these."

The main theme chosen for the Assembly had been phrased "Man's Disorder and God's Design." It had been subdivided under four heads for sectional study: "The Universal Church in God's Design," "The Church's Witness to God's Design," "The Church and the Disorder of Society," and "The Church and International Disorder." The first of these subtopics was of special concern from the standpoint of Faith and Order; the second related directly to missions and evangelism; the third belonged in the traditional field of Life and Work; and the fourth embraced the general interests of both Life and Work and the World Alliance for Promoting International Friendship through the Churches, now the responsibility mainly of the Commission of the Churches on International Affairs.

The Continuation Committee on Faith and Order, the International Missionary Council, and the Commission of the Churches on International Affairs had collaborated with the Study Department in the development of these themes.

3. The Difficult Task

Concerning the Assembly at Amsterdam, toward which all reports and actions of the Provisional Committee were pointed, the General Secretary, Dr. Willem A. Visser 't Hooft, said:

> It will be the first official meeting of the churches in the ecumenical fellowship which is not an *ad hoc* meeting, but the beginning of a definite and permanent relationship between them. Moreover . . . [it] will be more comprehensive in scope than any of the former ecumenical conferences. The streams of Life and Work, of Faith and Order, of the younger churches and the missionary movement, and of the youth movement will flow into it. Then again, it will be the first representative post-war meeting of the churches and will therefore have to gather up the new insights which the churches have gained in the critical years.
>
> The Assembly will have no less than four distinct tasks:
>
> (a) To provide the opportunity for the thorough study of the main theme: "Man's Disorder and God's Design," with its four main aspects covering the nature of the Church, its witness and its social and international responsibility.
>
> (b) To adopt the Utrecht Constitution after full consideration of the modifications which will be proposed by the Provisional Committee or by the churches.
>
> (c) To decide what tasks the World Council should undertake during the next years and to agree on the main principles of the policy to be adopted.

(d) To provide an opportunity for the discussion of any matters which are of common concern to the churches.

The Assembly will meet after a period of isolation of the churches from each other, so that it will be difficult at first to understand each other. It meets at a time when there is not only ecumenical revival, but also a revival of confessional convictions and concerns. It meets, finally, at a time when men everywhere, with their acute sense of insecurity, are eagerly expecting a liberating word and feel critical towards the Church for not giving them that word in such a way that they can understand and receive it.

The Assembly faces, then, an almost impossible task. And we can only prepare for it in a very humble spirit, in the hope that it may be used in ways which we do not yet clearly see or comprehend. But we must also do all we can to avoid its performing the many secondary tasks, instead of the primary ones. . . . We must try to find the few essential things which through this Assembly the Spirit desires to say to the churches and, through the churches, to the world.[4]

4. The Invitation to Amsterdam

The subcommittee of the Provisional Committee drafting the "Call to the Churches concerning the first Assembly of the World Council of Churches" consisted of Bishop Bell of Chichester, who was Chairman; Dr. W. J. Gallagher of Canada, the Secretary; Bishop James C. Baker, Chairman of the International Missionary Council representatives at Buck Hill Falls, of the United States; Dr. Roswell P. Barnes of the United States; Dr. S. F. H. J. Berkelbach van der Sprenkel of Holland; Dr. T. C. Chao of China; Professor Georges Florovsky of Paris; Dr. John Alexander Mackay of the United States; Pastor Martin Niemöller of Germany; and Dr. Bela Vasady of Hungary.

On presenting the "Call" the Chairman suggested that the churches be asked to read it from their pulpits, and that a Sunday in May of 1948 be appointed as a "Day of Prayer for the Assembly."

I.

In August 1948 the first Assembly of the World Council of Churches will take place at Amsterdam, and all the member-churches will send their delegates. We are profoundly thankful that after long years of separation, and so soon after the most devastating war in human history, the Christian churches throughout the world will thus be able to express and to manifest their spiritual unity.

We know that this is due to no merit of our own, but is a gift, granted to the Christian churches by our Lord Himself against and beyond any human hope. Through the trials and persecutions of these last years, a new consciousness of fellowship has been awakened and made effective, and a flood of prayer has been released, overflowing all ecclesiastical barriers and national antagonisms. We have learned in a new way that "where one member suffers, all the members suffer with it." And we have been richly blessed by this ex-

[4] Minutes and Reports, Buck Hill Falls, p. 52.

perience. Thus, we have every reason to thank and praise God, "Who only doeth wondrous things."

But this graciousness of God reminds us all both of our responsibility and of our shortcomings. The main theme before the Assembly—"Man's Disorder and God's Design"—itself shows that the Churches of Christ have failed in preventing man's disorder, and will fail again, if we try to overcome it without God's grace, and without a renewal of our own lives. We have fallen short both in speaking the Word of Christ and in doing His healing and saving work.

II.

With the blessing of God, this Assembly can mark a new experience of the glory of God, and a new acceptance by Christians and Christian churches of their responsibility for seeking continually to bring the whole of human life and relations under the Kingship of Christ. But before attempting to make a new start, we ought to understand why we failed, and recognizing the cause of our failure, plead that the goodness of God may lead us to true repentance. The design of God declares itself in the new environment of our lives that has been created by the acts of God in Christ. In His life, death, and resurrection, and in the coming of the Church, a new beginning has been made in human history. "What is old has gone, the new has come." But at this crisis in the existence of mankind, we are compelled to confess that the contrast between the high calling of the Church and the visible institutions called churches is only too evident. We have failed because we ourselves have been partakers in man's disorder. Our first and deepest need is not new organization, but the renewal, or rather the rebirth, of the actual churches. May God grant that we may hear the call of the Spirit.

III.

We confess that because of the dividedness of the churches, also, we have fallen short in the witness we should have borne to Christ. Our churches are divided, and by their divisions the whole work of the Church, both in speech and in action, suffers most grievous harm. We long for the day when the Lord Jesus Christ shall recapture the churches and, manifesting His glory, lead them to speak with one clear voice and to act as those who serve Him only as their Lord. In that unity we desire to join our forces to do His work of feeding the hungry, clothing the naked, visiting the prisoner and healing the sick, to learn and to preach His truth and grace, and thus to proclaim His Kingdom.

IV.

The World Council of Churches is itself both a declaration of the spiritual unity of its member churches and a means through which they may express that unity in action. Already more than a hundred churches have joined it from the Old and New Worlds, from the East and the West—a clear sign of the longing of the churches for deeper fellowship in Christ. The Council stands on faith in our Lord Jesus Christ as God and Saviour and is a fellowship of churches which accept that faith. It serves the churches, and in no way seeks to legislate for them or control them. It aspires after an expression of unity in which Christians and Christian churches, joyously aware of their oneness in Jesus Christ their Lord, and pursuing an ever fuller realization of union, shall in time of need give help and comfort to one another, and in all times inspire and exhort one another to live worthily of their common membership in the Body of Christ. It also seeks increasingly to enable the churches to take united action for the furtherance of Christ's Kingdom. We trust that, by God's grace, through the meetings at Amsterdam, the World Council may be recognized by the whole membership of the constituent churches as a clear expression and a powerful instrument of their fellowship.

We therefore call upon all Christians to join us in earnest prayer that the first Assembly of the World Council of Churches may be used of God for a rebirth of the churches, and for their re-dedication in the unity of the faith to the common task of proclaiming His Word and doing His work among the nations.[5]

When the Provisional Committee adjourned it was to convene next at Amsterdam on August 21, 1948—the day before the Assembly of the World Council of Churches. Until then, the responsibility of implementing the resolutions at Buck Hill Falls would rest upon the Administrative Committee.

It is possible in a chronicle of this kind to trace only the main streams of the multifarious activities of the Provisional Committee, and this but swiftly. Yet these can hardly be evaluated or understood apart from the supposedly less important but often determinative happenings in the tributaries, which may as likely as not have gone unreported and unrecorded. Decisions by persons in official place in the face of suddenly developing situations, transactions by departments more or less self-governing, services on behalf of the movement by the multitude of voluntary workers in many countries, words spoken or written in the name of and about the emerging World Council of Churches—the influence of such incidents flowed into the swelling tide of the great events, which would be seen superficially as the grist of history.

5. Personnel, Offices, and Finances

Reference has been made to the establishment of the office of the Provisional Committee at Geneva, Switzerland. The personnel in 1940 consisted of five secretaries and four other staff members. With the increase of activities, particularly under the Department of Post-War Reconstruction and Inter-Church Aid and Work for Refugees, the number of employees had mounted by 1948 to 142.

An estate with a dwelling and a gatehouse, containing between them twenty-five rooms, was acquired on Route Malagnou in Geneva. As the volume of work continued to grow, the Committee bought an adjacent building accommodating twenty-six offices, the American and British Bible Societies and Church World Service helping with the purchase and taking over part of it for their headquarters. When still more space had to be found, the Department of Reconstruction and

[5] *Ibid.* p. 84.

Inter-Church Aid made available two wooden army barracks, similar to the ones supplied to the aided churches, which were converted into thirty-seven compartments, bringing the total number of rooms to eighty-eight.

For financial support for its enlarging operations, the Committee could look to only ten of the forty countries represented by the denominations accepting the invitation to join the World Council of Churches. Had the churches of the other thirty been able to contribute, restrictive currency regulations would have prevented forwarding the money. The greater part of the aid received came from the United States, where many of the member churches willingly accepted the necessity laid upon them by their favored economic position, "giving more than their proportionate part of the budget, on behalf of those unable to bear their full share."

The office in New York City became a center of vigorous and effective promotion, under the Joint Executive Committee which had been formed after the Oxford and Edinburgh Conferences of 1937 to look after the interests of the Life and Work and Faith and Order Movements in the United States. Dr. Henry Smith Leiper was its Executive Secretary. His assistant, Miss Eleanor Kent Browne, directed the clerical work, made arrangements for the ecumenical deputations arriving in New York from various parts of the world, and bore large responsibility for the soliciting and handling of funds. A well-organized and diligent subcommittee on education and promotion[6] gave its attention to supplying individuals and churches with information concerning the program and soliciting contributions. "Friends of the World Council" was incorporated under the laws of the state of New York for receiving and supervising bequests and other funds.

Most of the money which was made available for the work under the Provisional Committee had come as gifts from individuals, funds, and local churches. From the office in Geneva came acknowledgment that it had been "chiefly due to the consecration of those who raised the funds for the Council in America that it [the Provisional Committee] had been able to continue at all." "Dr. Leiper in New York has raised more funds for the World Council than anyone else," the memorandum stated, "and saved the situation at many critical moments."

The roll of its members in 1948 is evidence of the representativeness of the Provisional Committee:

Presidents

The Rev. Dr. Marc Boegner of France
The Most Rev. Archbishop of Uppsala, Dr. Erling Eidem of Sweden

[6] "Committee on Interpretation and Support," it was called, under the American Committee for the World Council of Churches, which succeeded the Joint Executive Committee after the Amsterdam Assembly.

The Most Rev. The Lord Archbishop of Canterbury, Dr. Geoffrey Fisher of Great Britain
The Most Rev. Archbishop of Thyateira, Dr. Germanos Strenopoulos
Dr. John R. Mott of the United States

Elective Members

The Rev. M. E. Aubrey of Great Britain
Professor Dr. Gonzalo Báez-Camargo of Mexico
The Rt. Rev. Eivind Josef Berggrav of Norway
Professor Dr. S. F. H. J. Berkelbach van der Sprenkel of Holland
The Rt. Rev. Yngve T. Brilioth, Bishop of Växjo, Sweden
The Rt. Rev. Bishop Cassian of France
The Rev. Dr. Samuel McCrea Cavert of the United States
Professor T. C. Chao of China
The Rt. Rev. the Lord Bishop of Chichester, Dr. George Kennedy Allen Bell of Great Britain
The Very Rev. Dr. J. Hutchinson Cockburn of Scotland
The Rev. Dr. R. Newton Flew of Great Britain
Professor Georges Florovsky of France
The Rt. Rev. H. Fuglsang-Damgaard, Bishop of Copenhagen of Denmark
The Rev. Dr. W. J. Gallagher of Canada
The Rev. Charles Guillon of Switzerland
The Rev. Canon Leonard Hodgson of Great Britain
The Rev. Dr. Douglas Horton of the United States
The Rev. Dr. Alphons Koechlin of Switzerland
The Rev. Michio Kozaki of Japan
President John Alexander Mackay of the United States
The Rev. Rajah B. Manikam of India
Professor William Manson of Scotland
Sir Walter Moberly of Great Britain
The Rev. Dr. Martin Niemöller of Germany
The Rt. Rev. Bishop of Novi Sad of Yugoslavia
The Rt. Rev. Dr. G. Ashton Oldham, Bishop of Albany, of the United States
The Rev. Dr. Joseph Houldsworth Oldham of Great Britain
The Rev. G. Bromley Oxnam of the United States
The Very Rev. Dr. George C. Pidgeon of Canada
The Rev. Fritz Hongkyn Pyen of Korea
Mr. Charles P. Taft of the United States
President Henry Pitney Van Dusen of the United States
Professor Bela Vasady of Hungary
The Rev. Dr. A. R. Wentz of the United States
The Rt. Rev. Bishop Theophil Würm of Germany

Consultants

The Rev. Henry Louis Henroid of Switzerland
Professor Adolf Keller of Switzerland
Mr. Georges Lombard of Switzerland

Members Deceased, 1938-1948

The Rev. Dr. George F. Barbour of Great Britain
The Rev. Dr. William Adams Brown of the United States
The Rev. Dr. John MacCracken of the United States
The Rev. Lewis Seymour Mudge of the United States
The Rev. Dr. J. Ross Stevenson of the United States

The Rt. Rev. George Craig Stewart of the United States
The Most Rev. The Lord Archbishop of Canterbury, Dr. William Temple of Great Britain

Members of the Secretariat in 1948

The Rev. Dr. Willem Adolf Visser 't Hooft, General Secretary, of Holland
The Rev. H. W. Newell, Assistant General Secretary, of Australia
The Rev. Oliver Stratford Tomkins, Assistant General Secretary, of Great Britain
The Rev. Dr. Henry Smith Leiper, Associate General Secretary in America, of the United States
The Rev. Canon Leonard Hodgson, Theological and General Secretary for Faith and Order, of Great Britain
The Rev. Floyd W. Tomkins, Associate Secretary in America for Faith and Order, of the United States
The Rev. Nils Ehrenström, Director of the Study Department, of Sweden
Mr. Frank Northam, Director of the Finance and Business Department, of Great Britain
Miss Jean Fraser, Secretary of the Youth Department, of Great Britain
The Very Rev. Dr. J. Hutchinson Cockburn, Director of the Department of Post-War Reconstruction and Inter-Church Aid and Work with Refugees, of Scotland
Professor Dr. Hendrik Kraemer, Director of the Ecumenical Institute, of Holland
Mr. Kenneth G. Grubb, Executive Chairman of the Commission of the Churches on International Affairs, of Great Britain
The Rev. Dr. O. Frederick Nolde, Director of the Commission of the Churches on International Affairs, of the United States
Mr. Alexandre de Weymarn, Director of the Ecumenical Press Service, of Switzerland
The Rev. Dean Halfdan Høgsbro, Representative in Germany, of Denmark

Church Representatives at the Geneva Office

The Rev. Dr. Benjamin Bush, Presbyterian Church in the United States
Bishop Paul N. Garber, Methodist Church in the United States
The Rt. Rev. J. I. B. Larned, Protestant Episcopal Church in the United States of America
The Rev. Dr. S. Michelfelder, Lutheran World Federation
The Rev. Dr. Edwin A. Bell, American Baptist Foreign Mission Society of the Northern Baptist Convention in the United States

Part Three

THE WORLD COUNCIL OF CHURCHES CONSTITUTED—AMSTERDAM

I

OPENING SESSIONS

1. MEMBERSHIP

The Assembly called to organize the World Council of Churches convened at Amsterdam, as appointed, on August 22, 1948. There were 351 official delegates and nearly as many alternates registered from 135 denominations in 44 countries. Consultants, fraternal representatives of various ecumenical and confessional organizations, accredited visitors, staff members, 242 press and radio reporters, and an undeterminable number of observers brought the total of those who had come for the meeting to approximately 1,500.

One hundred fifty churches had signified their intention to send delegates, and 450 places had been reserved, with an equal number for their seconds. The unoccupied seats belonged, for the most part, to the delegations of the Eastern Orthodox and younger churches. Eighty-five had been assigned to the former, which occupied only twenty-four; and fifty to the latter, which required but thirty-two.

Of the Orthodox in Europe, only the Greek Church and the Ecumenical Patriarchate of Constantinople were represented. Those of Russia and her satellite countries declined the invitation. Until a short time before the Assembly, the Russian Church had appeared inclined to participate; but the decision, in the end, was negative. The failure to cooperate was apparently due in part to the adverse attitude of a conference in Moscow in July, 1948, of Orthodox authorities, which charged that the aims of the World Council of Churches were political.[1] That the Patriarch, while feeling obliged to respect it, took this verdict with reservations was indicated by assurances from him shortly afterwards that he and his associates continued to be interested in the ecumenical movement and desired to be kept informed concerning its progress.

The Rumanian Orthodox Episcopate in America and the Russian Orthodox in Exile were represented, as were the lesser Eastern Churches

[1] See *A History of the Ecumenical Movement,* p. 716; also *Actes de la Conférence des Églises Autocéphales Orthodoxes,* Vol. II, p. 108; cf. *Ecumenical Review,* Vol. I, No. 2, pp. 188-197.

of the Levant, and the Protestant churches of the Near East and of southeastern Europe.

As for the other churches sending fewer than their quotas of delegates, when the difficulties in the way of obtaining passports and visas, in some instances, were taken into account, along with the cost of transportation and the monetary restrictions in force in most countries and the renewed threat of war from the Berlin blockade by Russia in effect at the time, it was surprising that not more of those expected had failed to arrive.

Two of the larger Protestant denominations rejecting the invitation were the Lutherans (Missouri Synod) and the Southern Baptist Convention, both of the United States. Four pastors from the latter, however, were, on their personal application, admitted as accredited visitors.

Recognizing that the Church of Rome could not take part in a meeting of the kind proposed, the Provisional Committee had not sent it an official invitation. Out of courtesy, the Pope had been apprised by letter earlier of the move to found the World Council of Churches; and it was expected that because of the interest of many Roman Catholics the Church might arrange to have observers at Amsterdam. Instead it issued a warning to all communicants not to attend the Assembly. Notwithstanding, certain Jesuit priests were reported to have observed the proceedings from the press gallery. The Roman Catholic Archbishop of Utrecht published a diocesan letter in which he explained the Church's position making cooperation impossible, but recognized that the ecumenical movement represented "the good intentions of many" and directed the priesthood and the laity to "pray fervently for all those participating in the congress, as well as for all other non-Catholic Christians."

The provisional constitution of the World Council of Churches limited membership to those denominations which accepted "Jesus Christ as God and Saviour"; but under this theological condition churches qualified [2] as different in liturgies as Friend and Orthodox, in polities as Congregationalist and Anglican, and in histories as Mar Thoma Syrian and Coptic, which traced their traditions to the apostolic age, and the United Church of South India, organized in 1947. The roll was as follows:

Australasia

Methodist Church of Australasia

Australia

Church of England in Australia and Tasmania
Congregational Union of Australia
Federal Conference of Churches of Christ in Australia
Presbyterian Church of Australia

Austria

Evangelical Church of the Augsburgian and Helvetic Confession

Belgium

Belgian Christian Missionary Church
Union of Protestant Evangelical Churches of Belgium

[2] See *The Christian Century*, September 17, 1948.

Brazil
- Methodist Church of Brazil
- Presbyterian Church of Brazil

Burma
- Baptist Convention of Burma

Canada
- Churches of Christ (Disciples)
- Church of England in Canada
- Presbyterian Church in Canada
- United Church of Canada
- Yearly Meeting of the Society of Friends

Ceylon
- Methodist Church in Ceylon (Minority Church connected with the Methodist Missionary Society of Great Britain)

China
- China Baptist Council
- Church of Christ in China
- Anglican Church in China
- North China Congregational Church
- Methodist Church in China (Minority Church connected with the Methodist Missionary Society of Great Britain)
- Provinces in China of the Methodist Church (Minority Church connected with the Methodist Church of the U.S.A.

Czechoslovakia
- Evangelical Church of Czech Brethren
- Evangelical Church in Slovakia, Augsburgian Confession
- Reformed Church in Slovakia

Denmark
- Church of Denmark

East Africa
- Church in East Africa (Minority Church—Anglican)

Egypt
- Coptic Orthodox Church
- Church of England (Minority Church)
- Synod of the Nile (Minority Church)

Estonia
- Evangelical Lutheran Church in Estonia

Ethiopia
- Church of Ethiopia

Finland
- Evangelical Lutheran Church of Finland

France
- Evangelical Church of the Augsburgian Confession in Alsace and Lorraine
- Evangelical Lutheran Church of France
- Reformed Church of Alsace and Lorraine
- Reformed Church of France

Germany
- Old Catholic Church in Germany
- Moravian Church
- Evangelical Church in Germany
- Mennonite Church
- Methodist Church in Germany (Minority Church)

Greece
Church of Greece
Greek Evangelical Church

Holland
General Mennonite Society
Free Evangelical Congregations
Evangelical Lutheran Church
Restored Evangelical Lutheran Church
Dutch Reformed Church
Old Catholic Church
Arminian Church
Union of Baptists

Hungary
Lutheran Church of Hungary
Reformed Church of Hungary

Iceland
Evangelical Lutheran Church of Iceland

India
Church of India, Burma and Ceylon (Anglican)
Church of South India
Federation of Evangelical Lutheran Churches in India
Mar Thoma Syrian Church of Malabar
United Church of Northern India
Provinces of India of the Methodist Church (Minority Church connected with the Methodist Church of the U.S.A.)

Indonesia
Batak Church
Protestant Church in Indonesia
Protestant Church in Timor
Moluccas Church
Protestant Church in the Minahassa
Protestant Church in East Java

Italy
Evangelical Church of Italy
Waldensian Church

Japan
Church of Christ in Japan
Anglican Church in Japan

Korea
Presbyterian Church of Korea

Lithuania
Reformed Church of Lithuania

Mexico
Methodist Church of Mexico

New Zealand
Associated Churches of Christ in New Zealand
Baptist Union of New Zealand
Church of the Province of New Zealand (Church of England)
Congregational Union of New Zealand
Methodist Church of New Zealand
Presbyterian Church of New Zealand

Norway
Church of Norway

Philippine Islands
United Evangelical Church of the Philippines
Poland
Evangelical Church of the Augsburgian Confession
Rhodesia
Methodist Church of North and South Rhodesia (Minority Church connected with the Methodist Missionary Society of Great Britain)
Rumania
Transylvania Reformed Church
Siam
Church of Christ in Siam
South Africa
Church of the Province of South Africa (Church of England)
Dutch Reformed Church of the Transvaal
Methodist Church of South Africa
Dutch Reformed Church of Africa
Presbyterian Church of South Africa
Spain
Spanish Evangelical Church
Sweden
Church of Sweden
Swedish Mission Covenant
Methodist Church of Scandinavia (Minority Church connected with the Methodist Church of the U.S.A.)
Switzerland
Old Catholic Church
Swiss Protestant Church Federation
United Kingdom and Eire
Baptist Union of Great Britain and Ireland
Churches of Christ in Great Britain and Ireland
Church of England
Church of Ireland
Church of Scotland
Church of Wales
Congregational Union of England and Wales
Congregational Union of Scotland
Episcopal Church of Scotland
Methodist Church
Methodist Church in Ireland
Presbyterian Church of England
Presbyterian Church of Ireland
Presbyterian Church of Wales
United Free Church of Scotland
United States of America
African Methodist Episcopal Church
African Methodist Episcopal Zion Church
American Lutheran Church
Church of the Brethren
Colored Methodist Episcopal Church
Congregational Christian Churches of the United States of America
Danish Evangelical Lutheran Church of America
Evangelical Lutheran Augustana Synod of North America
Evangelical and Reformed Church

Evangelical United Brethren Church
International Convention of Disciples of Christ
Methodist Church
Moravian Church in America (Northern Province)
National Baptist Convention
Northern Baptist Convention (American Baptist Convention)
Polish National Catholic Church of America
Presbyterian Church in the United States
Presbyterian Church in the United States of America
Protestant Episcopal Church
Reformed Church in America
Religious Society of Friends—Five Years Meeting of Friends
General Conference of the Society of Friends
Yearly Meeting of the Religious Society of Friends of Philadelphia and Vicinity
Rumanian Orthodox Episcopate in America
Seventh Day Baptist General Conference
United Evangelical Lutheran Church
United Lutheran Church in America
United Presbyterian Church of North America

West Africa
Church in West Africa (Minority Church—Anglican)
Methodist Church in West Africa (Minority Church connected with the Methodist Missionary Society of Great Britain)
Provinces of the Methodist Church in West Africa (Minority Church connected with the Methodist Church of the U.S.A.)

West Indies
Anglican Church of the West Indies
Methodist Church of the West Indies (Minority Church connected with the Methodist Missionary Society of Great Britain)

Non-National Churches
Church of the East and of the Assyrians
Ecumenical Patriarchate of Constantinople
Salvation Army
Union of the Armenian Evangelical Churches in the Near East

2. Amsterdam

Upon arriving at Amsterdam, the delegates found themselves in a gaily bedecked city; a reminder that they had broken into the nation's celebration of Queen Wilhelmina's golden jubilee, to end with her abdication and the enthronement of Princess Juliana, at about the time the Assembly was scheduled to adjourn. A holiday mood had already possessed the people, and many visitors were on hand for the festivities, adding to the crush in the crowded streets and public conveyances. Those arriving for the Assembly could consider themselves fortunate if they had made their reservations for lodging in advance.

Superficially, Amsterdam bore few marks of war damage. It had not suffered such destruction of its buildings as had some other Dutch cities, notably Rotterdam, the country's great seaport, the ruins of which were viewed with scarcely believing eyes by those arriving via transatlantic steamship routes from North America. But there had been deeper wounds.

For five years Amsterdam had been occupied and used as headquarters by the German army, which had appropriated its food and fuel resources, without due regard for the needs of the inhabitants, many of whom had died of exposure and malnutrition or hunger-induced sicknesses. The Germans had impressed its youth into military and other war services; assaulted its churches in the endeavor to seize their funds and to combine their youth organizations with those of the National Socialist government; exiled or thrown into concentration camps its citizens who had resisted, including some of the clergy; and led away to torture and traceless death its Jews to the number of 110,000.

All this was but three years past. But with their usual indomitable spirit the Dutch had risen to repair their city's loss. The only reminder to the delegates of its recent travail were the food ration-books assigned to them upon registering.

One evening on the occasion of a special boat trip for the delegates the lights shone again along the canals for the first time since the war; children, many of whom had never seen them shining, thronged the dikes and bridges with their elders. At the newly refurbished Rijksmuseum, in which the Dutch government tendered the Assembly guests a reception, the famous paintings of Holbein, Hals, Vermeer, Rubens, Rembrandt, and other masters had been returned to their accustomed places from hiding beneath distant sand dunes and in sealed barges at the bottom of canals.

Unchanged was the friendly courtesy of the people, wherever encountered—in tram, street, home, shop, hostel, or church. The burgomaster and the council made their welcome official at a reception in Town Hall.[3] The Crown Princess personalized the nation's goodwill and hospitality by attending a plenary session of the Assembly and sitting with the Presidents, in company with her consort, Prince Bernhard. And from the Queen at The Hague came the message: "Owing to the circumstance that the dates of this Assembly coincide with the preparation for the Jubilee, it is impossible for Her Majesty to give at the present moment such attention to the Assembly as she would desire to . . . give, since she follows the work . . . with very deep interest."

Evil as it was, the war had not been without blessing to the churches of Holland, as they themselves testified. It had driven them together to combat the tyrannous paganism which violated their liberties. It had opened their eyes to the more insidious and devastating enemy within their own life—the "universal scourge of secularism." The witness they

[3] Formerly the Royal Palace. When King of Holland, Louis Napoleon used it for his residence, and ever since it had been called Royal Palace. The seat of the present rulers is, of course, The Hague.

so courageously bore to their faith in time of danger and defection had kindled a fresh home missionary zeal. As Christians of different traditions united their forces in a common cause, they discovered that each denomination possessed something valuable to share with the larger fellowship, without which the preaching of Christ was incomplete. Mutual appreciation had grown with the practice of unity.

3. Worship at the Assembly

A leader of the Netherlands Reformed Church, the dominant Protestant ecclesiastical body, wrote:

> The Alliance of Free Evangelical Congregations in the Netherlands and the Union of Baptist Congregations in the Netherlands . . . are small autonomous groups of congregations, consisting of individual converts, confessing a personal belief in the Saviour, and adhering to baptismal confession. . . . They are a beneficial corrective to the churches, which, according to the ecclesiastical idea, are apt to lay too little stress on the necessity for personal conversion and confession of faith.[4]

These small communions, on the other hand, which before the war had stood aloof from the ecumenical movement, in the belief that their ministry would thus be more effective, changed their policy after having cooperated with the other churches in time of national disaster. Some of them voted to send representatives to the Assembly and to join the World Council of Churches.

The churches of Amsterdam brought to their role as hosts to the Assembly, therefore, besides a real spirit of Christian hospitality, the experience of a broad and fruitful ecumenical relationship with one another. The appointments for the occasion arranged by many committees proved that they were endowed also with genius of a superior order for organization.

Amsterdam's spacious Concertgebouw had been obtained for the business sessions, with the audience hall seating some 2,200 persons, and, in addition, numerous smaller rooms for offices, lounges, and exhibits. Short-wave radiophones, which had been specially installed by an American business concern, enabled the conferees to hear the proceedings simultaneously in German, French, and English translations. The great concert organ in hymn accompaniments and occasional interludes and recitals lent an appropriate churchliness to the meetings.

Those who had been at previous ecumenical gatherings had scarcely any recollection more inspiring or lasting than of the singing. The Amsterdam Assembly sang from *Cantate Domino,* the trilingual hymnbook of the World's Student Christian Federation. The occasion called for the

[4] From the *Official Handbook* of Assembly, p. 22, article by W. F. Golterman.

great hymns, in the universal testimony and majestic music of which unity is reached without struggle or retreat and the riches of the Christian tradition in all its variations of race, culture, and theology become a common possession. "Holy God, Thy Name We Bless," "All People That on Earth Do Dwell," "O God, Our Help in Ages Past," "The Church's One Foundation Is Jesus Christ Her Lord," "When I Survey the Wond'rous Cross," "Thine Is the Glory, Risen, Conquering Son," "Praise to the Lord, the Almighty, the King of Creation," "Christian Hearts in Love United," "We Gather, Dear Father, in Prayer before Thee," "For All Thy Saints Who from Their Labors Rest"—one joined in singing these sacred songs of many national and confessional origins, or listened and mused, and the experience passed description. He felt in them a mystic bond with all living believers and with past generations of Christians who had sung them. They called back familiar voices once heard upraised in them, now silenced. They reminded him of the transitoriness of life and its loves, but also of their eternity in God. They spoke courage to the soul in fear, and comfort in its solitariness.

Thou wast their Rock, their Fortress and their Might;
Thou, Lord, their Captain in the well-fought fight;
Thou, in the darkness drear, their one true Light.
Alleluia! Alleluia!

And when the strife is fierce, the warfare long,
Steals on the ear the distant triumphsong,
And hearts are brave again, and arms are strong.
Alleluia! Alleluia!

Several of the churches of the city had been designated especially as places of worship for use by the Assembly community. The days were to begin with half-hour services of devotion in Koepel Kerk, conducted by representatives of the various communions and countries according to their different traditions. The official handbook carried in the printed program the names of those who had been appointed to preside:

Rev. Michio Kozaki, Moderator of the Church of Christ in Japan
Dr. Ivan Lee Holt, Methodist Bishop of St. Louis, Missouri
Dr. Lajos Ordass,[5] Bishop of the Lutheran Church of Hungary
Rev. John A. Garrett, of the Congregational Union of Australia
Rev. M. D. Ratefy, of the Reformed Church of Madagascar
Dr. Elton Trueblood, of Earlham College, Religious Society of Friends, U.S.A.
Mrs. John Karefa-Smart, Evangelical United Brethern Church, Sierra Leone, West Africa
Dr. Melbourne Evans Aubrey, General Secretary, Baptist Union of Great Britain and Ireland

[5] Bishop Ordass on the eve of leaving for Amsterdam was placed under political arrest. At the service he was to have led prayers were offered for him in his affliction.

Bishop Chirakarottu Korula Jacob, Church of South India, Katayam, Travancore

4. Communion

The Assembly held no official Communion service. Each member had opportunity to participate in "Holy Communion, and to attend, in the fellowship of prayer, the Eucharistic worship of other traditions, even though, whether by reason of his own conscience or . . . of the [laws] of the church of which he [was] a member, or which [was] holding the service, he could not [partake] as a communicant." [6] There was a celebration of the Lord's Supper on a Sunday in Nieuwe Kerk, according to the rite of the Netherlands Reformed Church, with ministers of other denominations assisting and all baptized members of churches in the Assembly invited to communicate. On other days the Anglican, Old Catholic, Eastern Orthodox, Lutheran, and Methodist Churches celebrated Holy Communion in a Lutheran Church, according to their several liturgies. These gatherings were open to all as worshipers, with permission to receive the sacrament at the Lutheran and Methodist services.

Many of the churches opened their doors to the delegates for prayer meetings, and denominational groups in the Assembly were honored by invitations and other attention from the local congregations of their respective confessions.

Oude Kerk offered its impressive sanctuary for the presentation of "The Song of Unity," an oratorio which had been composed especially for the Assembly under the auspices of the Old Catholic Church of the Netherlands. Bishop E. Lagerway of Utrecht, head of the Church, had written the words; Dr. Alexandre de Johng, who had composed the music, conducted.

For the closing worship, the Assembly repaired to the venerable Wester Kerk, the first edifice erected in Holland for use by Protestants, at which there were addresses by Bishop Karl Friedrich Otto Dibelius, Dr. Philippe Maury and Dr. Ralph W. Sockman.

The celebration of the Lord's Supper in Nieuwe Kerk according to the practice of the Netherlands Reformed Church was an unusual experience for most of the eleven hundred or so persons communicating. Between the pulpit and the first row of pews had been set a long table draped in white linen. At the center of the table the celebrants took their places, facing the congregation, and about one hundred worshipers at a time were seated with them by the ushers, to be served by the officers of the Church. The table with each filling was presided over by different clergymen. Those receiving represented nearly all races and nationalities and denominations. An air of worshipfulness and manifest spiritual oneness

[6] Explanation from the *Official Handbook* of the Assembly.

pervaded the service, although some of those present did not partake of the sacrament. The Words of Institution were the familiar passages in the Gospels:

> He took bread, and when he had given thanks, He brake it, and gave it to His disciples and said: take, eat, this is My body which is broken for you; this do in remembrance of Me. In like manner also, after supper, He took the cup, gave thanks and said, Drink ye all of it; this cup is the new testament in My blood, which is shed for you, and for many, for the remission of sins; this do, as often as yet drink it, in remembrance of Me.[7]

5. Opening Service in Nieuwe Kerk

The opening service of the Assembly, on the afternoon of the preceding Sunday, with addresses by Dr. John R. Mott and Rev. Daniel Thambyrajah Niles of Ceylon, was held in Nieuwe Kerk. This Gothic structure, portions of which belong to the thirteenth century, is known as the Cathedral of the Netherlands. Occupying a site in the public square called Dam, hard by the Town Hall, it has formed part of the colorful backdrop of the changing pageant of history since the Middle Ages. Under ordinary circumstances it can accommodate about two thousand worshipers, but at the time of the Assembly an additional thousand could be admitted, temporary seats having been installed for the investiture of the new queen. Like most churches of the Old World, it is a mausoleum in which are buried the nation's great, remembered and forgotten. Delegates to an ecumenical conference wandering through its silent aisles might have reflected on the ecumenicity of death, in which the sons of men are not divided, for the stones beneath their feet and the memorials on the walls were inscribed with the names of Protestants and Roman Catholics alike, who had been honored by entombment there in the days of their alternating ecclesiastical and political ascendency.

Admittance to this first service of the Assembly was by ticket, and the members entered in a long procession, wearing their vestments of many designs and colors. Rev. James W. Kennedy took note of many of the details of the occasion which enliven, long afterwards, the record of it:

> The official four hundred delegates, on whom the burden of the Assembly's work rested, walked slowly and with great dignity, in spite of hidden photographers flashing bulbs in their faces. The arrangement of the procession was by church groups in alphabetical order, according to the name of the group. The costumes and dress were as varied as the denominations. There were colors of purple, blue, gold, violet, white, black, green, yellow, and all shades of red; garments academic and ecclesiastical with appropriate hoods, as well as business suits and cutaways, kilts and other native dress; there was some headgear, including a fez, a skullcap, and a golden metal

[7] As printed in the Netherlands Reformed Rite.

hood; there were starched bands and ruffles, and ornaments about the neck; and there were women as well as laymen and clergymen and young men: there were many colors of skin, all shades; and there were not a few beards.[8]

The five Presidents of the Assembly followed—Archbishop Erling Eidem of Sweden, Archbishop Germanos Strenopoulos of Thyateira, Archbishop Geoffrey Fisher of Canterbury, Pastor Marc Boegner of France, and Dr. John R. Mott of the United States—accompanied by Dr. Daniel Thambyrajah Niles and Dr. Koenraad Henricios Eskelhoff Gravemeyer, general delegate of the Dutch Reformed Church.

Dr. Gravemeyer (who had suffered imprisonment in concentration camps for his leadership in the resistance of the churches of Holland against Nazi encroachments during the war) had been appointed to preside. The Archbishop of Canterbury led in the recitation of the Apostles' Creed in unison; others on the platform assisted by offering the prayers and reading the lessons. This part of the service was simple and brief; then Dr. Mott proceeded with his address. Because of his advanced age and long experience in interchurch work, he deserved to be heard as honoring, even more than as being honored by, the Assembly, and evidence was not wanting that the audience gratefully recognized this. He said, in part:[9]

With hearts abounding in praise to God we come together today from all parts of the world to initiate formally the World Council of Churches. Hitherto he has led us; our expectation is from him.

The preparatory stages which have brought us to this hour have been truly notable. Memory throngs with experiences of divine favor and leadership as we recall the unifying vision-forming and creative power of the World Mission Conference of Edinburgh of 1910, of the Mount of Olives [in] 1928, and of Tambaram [in] 1938; likewise the tributary contributions of the Life and Work and Faith and Order Conferences of Stockholm [in] 1925 [and] Lausanne [in] 1927, and their subsequent consultations; and of the Christian statesman-like bodies meeting in 1937 . . . at Westfield College, London, at Oxford, and at Edinburgh, and . . . the following year at Utrecht, where we adopted our constitution.

At our culminating gathering today we would pay our grateful tribute to many colleagues and master-builders of different lands, races and communions who have passed on . . . [to] Archbishop Söderblom of Scandinavia; Archbishop Davidson, George Robson, Wardlaw Thompson, Archbishop Temple and William Paton of Great Britain; Peter Ainslie, Bishop Charles H. Brent, William Adams Brown, Grace Dodge, J. Ross Stevenson and Robert E. Speer of the United States of America; the Hon. S. H. Blake, Bishop M. S. Baldwin and the Hon. N. W. Rowell of Canada; Professor Gustav Warneck, Julius Richter and Professor Adolf Deissmann of Germany; Raoul Allier of France; Bishop Azariah, Pundita Ramabai, Isabella Thoburn and K. T. Paul of India; Chêng Ching-yi, Fletcher S. Brockman and D. E. Hoste of China; Joseph H. Neesima and Archbishop

[8] James W. Kennedy, *Venture of Faith,* p. 15-16.

[9] For this and portions of other Assembly addresses which follow, see *The First Assembly of the World Council of Churches,* 5 volumes, Geneva, 1948.

Nicolai of Japan; and Kwegyir Aggrey, Bishop Gwynne and Charles R. Watson of Africa.

One who has had the privilege of sixty years of world-wide travel and sitting at the feet of the various Christian communions and of different lands and races cannot but take notice of certain inter-racial, international and interdenominational bodies which have afforded the ecumenical experience and atmosphere so necessary for the wise development of the World Council of Churches.

First among these is one often overlooked, the Student Volunteer Movement for Foreign Missions which began its beneficent ministry in 1886. . . . Its work among students of North America, Europe, Australasia and South Africa has raised up and sent forth into the non-Christian world nearly, if not quite, twenty thousand students as missionaries of our various communions and indirectly has had a profound influence in drawing together the churches.

Speaking of students reminds us of another organization dealing with the future leaders of the nations—the World's Student Christian Federation, beginning in Vadstena Castle, Sweden, in 1895, with a small band of workers among students in North America, Great Britain, Germany and Scandinavia. This has spread the world over and embraces Christian societies of students in three thousand colleges and universities and constitutes the great fact of the weaving together of the future leaders of the nations.

A similar tribute might be paid to the Young Men's Christian Association and the Young Women's Christian Association which through their nearly three million members are weaving together the lay leaders of tomorrow.

The texture of our meeting here in Amsterdam reminds us of the great contribution being made by the International Missionary Council in fostering the ecumenical spirit and action. The uniting of the so-called Younger Churches constitutes one of the chief contributions of our gathering at Amsterdam. . . .

Our ecumenical gathering here . . . has assembled at one of the most fateful moments of the life of the world. There has been no time like it, not only in point of danger but of opportunity. . . . Never before have there been so many Christians who have had an authentic experience of the adequacy of Christ. . . . As this . . . Conference unfolds it will remind us increasingly of open doors, no matter in what direction we look. . . .

Let us not overlook the solemn fact that the cause of world-wide Christian missions and of the Christian Church in other relations is now called upon to face the greatest concentration of major unsolved problems that we have ever been called upon to confront. . . . Let us take heart from the words of Martin Luther. . . . "Before every great opportunity God sent me some special trial."

Above all, the reason why my heart beats high with hope in the present tragic . . . hour is the fact that we have a larger Christ. . . . He stands erect among the fallen, strong among the weak, clean among the defiled, living among the dead—the Fountain Head of Vitality, the Generating Source of all the greatest and most profound changes that have taken place or ever will take place. He is the Central Figure and Abounding Hope of our World Council of Churches.

The presence of the second speaker, Dr. Daniel T. Niles, a Methodist minister then serving at Point Pedro, Ceylon, reminded the congregation that the future of the Christian cause lay with the youth of the churches, and—more than in the past—with the leaders in mission lands. Dr. Mott had been an ambassador to the world and had won disciples for Christ wherever he went, and now these new recruits were taking their place in the ranks of leadership. The committees planning the Assembly had insured that representatives of the younger churches would take part in the deliberations on an equal basis with those from the founding denominations. The delegates understood this as they listened to the young Indian:

We . . . must begin at our place of self-revelation, and for us that place is the Cross. It was there that we saw God's inexhaustible resources—His love poured out without being emptied; and it was there that we lost the illusions about ourselves. We began there the life we live today, there we were shattered and stabilized, there we died and were born again, and still it is as we return that we see ourselves most clearly.

We are sent . . . [to] a world where the Christian faith is dispossessed of its hold on the mores of the people . . . a world that has sought to destroy the Church. . . . It seemed to be set for steady progress. . . . [It] was full of the stories of triumphs in many lands. And then in one war after another Christendom broke to pieces and hopes lay shattered. . . . Chaos remains.

Here we are as churches. Some were lost for years in the silence but did not lose their faith. Some were tested by fire but were not found unfaithful. Some were challenged by the need of their sister churches and proved not unmindful. Here we are, witnessing to the power of the risen Christ in all our churches and asking the question that lies nearest to our hearts, "Lord, is it now? When is the hour of fulfillment?"

The Christian witness recognizes no barrier and allows no partiality. We are witnesses to the Negro in the same way as to the White. We are witnesses with the western democracies as well as the eastern republics. We are witnesses among people of all religions and no religion. We are witnesses among the outcast, the refugee, the displaced person . . . witnesses unto the uttermost part of the earth.

6. First Meeting in the Concertgebouw

While the hour in Nieuwe Kerk was a memorable one, the thoughts of the delegates ran ahead to the plenary business session the next morning, when the action constituting the World Council of Churches would be the order of the day. For that mainly they had come to Amsterdam. But meantime they must make their way from Nieuwe Kerk to the Concertgebouw, where in a three-hour meeting that Sunday evening they would be briefed further on the history of the various movements tributary to the World Council of Churches.

There Dr. G. K. A. Bell, Bishop of Chichester, reviewed the Life and Work program since the Stockholm Conference in 1925, with its threefold objective: "common endeavor on behalf of international brotherhood and the organized unity of nations, common Christian principles and work for the renewal of society, and a common voice for the Christian conscience in social and political life."

Dr. Yngve Torgny Brilioth, Bishop of Växjö, Sweden, described the gifts of the Faith and Order Movement to the churches in their long search for unity as "a tradition of great leaders, a willingness to face differences in beliefs and to speak the truth in love, agreements reached through conversations, and fruitful collaboration in study." He referred to Bishop Charles Henry Brent as the father of the Movement and to Archbishop William Temple, with his "generous breadth of vision and prophetic gift of combining theory and practice," as its guiding genius.

With "The Missionary Heritage of the Church Universal" his subject, Dr. John Alexander Mackay, President of the Princeton Theological Seminary, reminded the Assembly that it could not have had the "world character which was its greatest strength," except for the success of the modern missionary movement, and suggested that the International Missionary Council should be called "the parent ecumenical body." "The Christian Church must be a missionary Church," he declared, "first, because its own health requires it; and, second, because the Lordship of Christ demands it . . . Who called [his followers] to move forward together on a world front, to fulfill that . . . task which he died to make possible and lives to make actual."

Dr. Marc Boegner, President of the Federation of Protestant Churches in France and a President of the Assembly,[10] confined himself to a report of the work of the Provisional Committee during the decade from Utrecht to Amsterdam, which, "without explicit authorization," had endeavored to act, he said, "for the World Council of Churches, in process of formation." Despite war, ecumenical contacts had been kept alive. Literature and letters had been sent through the battle lines. Commissions on study, aid to refugees, chaplaincy service to prisoners of war, reconstruction and interchurch aid projects, the establishment of an Ecumenical Institute at Céligny, Switzerland, and international affairs had been created and set to work. Property for headquarters had been acquired in Geneva, and the Committee had come to Amsterdam "debt-free and with all bills paid."

7. The World Council of Churches Constituted

When it met on the next morning, the Assembly was eager and ready for the business of the day. With the Archbishop of Canterbury in the chair, Dr. Marc Boegner submitted the resolution which had been prepared in advance by the Provisional Committee:[11]

[10] Dr. Boegner was a member of the Provisional Committee and the Chairman of its Administrative Committee.

[11] See *The First Assembly*. . . . Geneva, 1948.

That the first Assembly of the World Council of Churches be declared to be and is hereby constituted, in accordance with the constitution drafted at Utrecht in 1938 and approved by the Churches; that the Assembly consist of those persons who have been appointed as the official delegates of the Churches adhering to the council; and that the formation of the World Council of Churches be declared to be and hereby is completed.

The vote to adopt, though dissent had been voiced by at least one delegate, was unanimous, and likewise the prolonged applause. The Chairman then asked the Assembly to stand in silence for prayer, and after a moment gave utterance to the thanksgiving of all in the following words: [12]

Almighty God, here we offer unto Thee our thanksgiving of praise, that Thou hast brought us to this hour and this act in the faith of Christ and by the power of the Holy Spirit. As Thou hast prospered those into whose labors we enter, so we pray Thee, prosper us in this our undertaking by Thy most gracious favor, that in all our work, begun, continued and ended in Thee, we may set forth Thy glory for the well-being of Thy Holy Church and the salvation of all Thy people. Amen.

So had the World Council of Churches, long "in process of formation," become a reality. The date was August 23, the day Monday, and the hour ten-thirty o'clock in the morning.

The members of the Assembly, whose association with the ecumenical movement had begun prior to the proposal to found the World Council of Churches, were one in their judgment that the long delay of the consummation had, in all probability, been providential, the events of the intervening years having served to accelerate the growth of unity in the churches, and demonstrated in ways no one could have foreseen the imperative need of a comprehensive world organization for its expression.

From remarks overheard in the corridors, it was the sense of many of the delegates that with the adoption of the constituting resolution the climactic moment of the Assembly had been passed and that the rest of the program would, perforce, proceed upon a lower plane of interest. There was criticism of the "poor judgment" which had scheduled the action of greatest significance at the beginning. How the order of business could have been reversed, since a number of other essential transactions had to follow, rather than precede, the vote to organize, the critics probably could not have explained. The Assembly had been convened to form the World Council of Churches, but this involved much more than the founding motion. The provisional constitution adopted in this action had to be amended. Officers and committees were to be elected. Commissions on policy, administration, finance, and other organizational matters required time in which to reach and formulate conclusions and to report to the Assembly.

[12] *Ibid.*

Furthermore, only a superficial view of the program could have failed to discover the potential suspense and climax in the study of the themes which had been announced. There had been no doubt that the delegates would vote to organize. Most of them had come to Amsterdam instructed to do so. The churches had been working together ten years under the Provisional Committee for the World Council of Churches, a fact in itself tantamount to approval of making the relationship permanent. The actual constitution of the Council probably could have been effected by mail. The concern of the responsible leaders was less with the birth of the new body than with its survival. Could a foundation be laid underneath the structure that would make it secure? For the opportunity they afforded the conferees to become acquainted with one another and to reach some degree of consensus in their thinking about their agreements and differences, the study sessions, which were to occupy so many of the days at Amsterdam, could help greatly in arriving at an answer to this all-important question.

The growth of the ecumenical movement can hardly be understood apart from its emphasis on education. "Education" may not be the word best describing this aspect of its work. Others offer themselves—"propaganda," "promotion," "interpretation," "study," and possibly others. The process involves, first or last, the functions connoted by all of them.

The Amsterdam Assembly was to give an interesting demonstration of this. The program listed between forty and fifty instructional and interpretative addresses. Two hundred or more press and radio reporters broadcast what was said. "The statistical appraisal of the number of words written about the meeting . . . defies calculation," wrote Donald Boles, an experienced newspaperman. "Likewise, the number of papers throughout the world that daily brought to their readers an account of the Assembly can only be imagined. Eleven major press associations wrote from one to four thousand words around the clock each day, and many of their dispatches went by teletype, cable or wireless to papers on five continents. All of the sixteen hundred dailies in the United States carried stories of the sessions."

Some persons found such publicity objectionable. One prominent denominational official declared himself interested in an organization that would give expression to the unity already existing in the churches but would not turn itself into a "machine for propagandizing for more."

However, the educational method in the ecumenical movement has been more characteristically that of group study, with a searching together after knowledge about matters of common concern, in order that the unity actually existing may be enlightened and effective in its manifestation and grow to the fullest possible extent within the limits of mutual understanding and agreement. The procedure at Amsterdam mainly followed, in its intent, this pattern.

A great deal of care had been given to the preparation for the study.

"Man's Disorder and God's Design" had been chosen for the general theme nearly three years before the Assembly, and the Study Commission, of which Dr. Henry Pitney Van Dusen, President of Union Theological Seminary of New York City, was Chairman, had enlisted many eminent scholars in different parts of the world in its development. A very large amount of resource matter had been accumulated—enough to make, when it was published after the Assembly, an omnibus volume of nearly a thousand pages—from which information most germane to the sub-themes was culled and issued in printed form to the delegates and their alternates before they left for Amsterdam. And in some countries those expecting to attend the Assembly held meetings for consultation and further briefing on their duties by members or agents of the Study Commission.

The delegates were divided—so far as practicable, according to their own preference—into four groups to pursue their study under as many subheadings of the general subject, as follows:

Section I—"The Universal Church in God's Design." Chairman, Dr. Johannes Ernest Richard Lilje of the Evangelical Church of Germany, Bishop of Hannover; Secretary, Rev. Oliver Stratford Tomkins of the Church of England, Assistant General Secretary of the World Council of Churches.

Section II—"The Church's Witness to God's Design." Chairman, Dr. John Alexander Mackay of the Presbyterian Church in the United States of America, President of Princeton Theological Seminary; Secretary, Dr. Stephen Charles Neill of the Church of England, Assistant Bishop to the Archbishop of Canterbury.

Section III—"The Church and the Disorder of Society." Chairman, Dr. Constantijn Leopold Patijn of the Dutch Reformed Church, Counsellor of the Ministry of Economic Affairs of The Netherlands; Secretary, Dr. John Coleman Bennett of the Congregational Christian Churches of the United States, Professor of Theology in Union Theological Seminary of New York City.

Section IV—"The Church and the International Disorder." Chairman, Kenneth George Grubb of the Church of England, Executive Chairman of the Commission of the Churches on International Affairs; Secretary, Dr. O. Frederick Nolde of the United Lutheran Church in America, Dean of the Graduate School of the Lutheran Theological Seminary in Philadelphia.

The alternates, also in four divisions, studied the same theme simultaneously organized under the same subheads. The study sessions occupied the mornings of one week, and in the afternoons both groups of delegates were re-formed for work in committees to which they had been appointed, as follows:

Committee I—"Constitution, Rules and Regulations," Chairman, Dr. Alphons Koechlin, President of the Swiss Protestant Federation; Secretary, Dr. Leonard Hodgson of the Church of England, Canon of Christ Church and Regius Professor of Divinity in the University of Oxford.

Committee II—"Policies." Chairman, Dr. George Kennedy Allen Bell of the Church of England, Bishop of Chichester; Secretary, Dr. Albert Stanley Trickett of the Methodist Church in the United States.

Committee III—"Program and Administration." Chairman, Dr. G. Bromley Oxnam of the Methodist Church in the United States, Bishop of New York; Secretaries, Frank Northam of the Methodist Church in Great Britain, Director of Finance and Business Department of the World Council of Churches, and Dr. W. J. Gallagher of the United Church of Canada, Executive Secretary of the Canadian Council of Churches.

Committee IV—"The Concerns of the Churches."

1. "The Life and Work of Women in the Churches." Chairman, Miss Saroe Chakko of the Methodist Church in India, President of Isabella Thoburn College in Lucknow; Secretary, Mrs. Samuel McCrea Cavert of the Presbyterian Church in the United States of America.
2. "The Christian Approach to the Jews." Chairman, Dr. Angus Dun of the Protestant Episcopal Church in the United States, Bishop of Washington, District of Columbia; Secretary, Dr. Conrad Hoffman of the Presbyterian Church in the United States of America, Secretary of the International Missionary Council.
3. "The Training of Laymen in the Church." Chairman, Dr. Clarence Charles Stoughton of the United Lutheran Church in America, Director of the Lutheran Layman's Movement; Secretary, Dr. Hendrik Kraemer of the Dutch Reformed Church, Director General of the Ecumenical Institute at Chateau de Bossey, Céligny, Switzerland.
4. "Christian Reconstruction and Inter-Church Aid." Chairman, Dr. Arne Fjellbu of the Church of Norway, Bishop of Trondheim; Secretary, Rev. Elfan Rees of the Congregational Union of England and Wales, Director of the Refugees Division of the Department of Reconstruction of the World Council of Churches.

II

ASSEMBLY ADDRESSES

Some familiarity with the work of the study sections and the committees, as outlined, is essential to an understanding of the World Council of Churches. Further attention to these should be deferred, however, until after a glance at the addresses which were delivered to the Assembly, for many of the speakers had collaborated in the preparation of the study matter, and so had influenced the direction and conclusions of the discussions.

Fifty or more persons addressed the Assembly and the various meetings which were held under its auspices. Anyone listening to them all might reasonably have been permitted occasional moments of speculation about the considerations guiding the program committee in its appointments. Obviously some of the speakers had been chosen because of their fame, and others on account of their scholarship; but the invitation had gone to more, undoubtedly, for their prominence as administrators in the churches. The new organization was to be a council of churches and so would need the support and experienced service of the secretaries and the bishops. A number of those who spoke qualified through long association with the ecumenical movement. Certain strong denominations whose wavering interest must be encouraged may have received more than their quota of honors. At the same time, other speakers had been selected as a gesture of appreciation toward smaller churches. Special recognition had been shown the younger churches of the mission countries. The women had their places, and laymen and young people theirs. Some appeared to have been drafted because it was thought that their nations or denominations deserved to be represented, and they happened to be known to the committee or to be available. At least one speaker had been bidden at the last moment, because of a colleague's complaint that his communion had nobody on the published program.

Notice has already been taken of the earlier addresses before the Assembly. Now a summary of those at the sessions which followed may be added.

1. Karl Barth

Among the first to be heard was Dr. Karl Barth, Professor of Theology in the University of Basle, currently characterized as "probably the most influential living Protestant theologian." He had contributed to the symposium on the study program for the Assembly a paper entitled "The Church—the Living Congregation of the Living Lord Jesus Christ," and the delegates had some knowledge of his outlook. He himself considered his views contrary to the drift of thought in the Assembly, particularly in the American section, still influenced too much, he believed, by the discredited socially optimistic liberalism of the nineteenth century, against which his own theology was a protest.

He would have turned the study theme, "Man's Disorder and God's Design," about, he said, and made it read, "God's Design and Man's Disorder." It was important, he thought, to begin deliberations from above—from God. The world's disorder and our ideas of its causes and the ways of remedying it were from below; and he plainly believed that little could be done from that standpoint. "The care of the Church and of the world" was not man's. The kingdom of God had been established and given the victory in the resurrection of Christ. The Church had only to keep itself "the living congregation of the living Lord Jesus Christ" by the faithful preaching of the Word of God in the Bible. That was "its true concern." Beyond the witness of this regenerated and continuously renewed life of the spirit, he appeared to think, Christians could do little toward the improvement of society.

He thought of the Church, he had made plain in his pre-Assembly paper, as "the worshipping community meeting regularly in a given place and not constituted once for all but continually re-created by divine activity through Christ." The congregation existed when it lived by the act of the living Lord. The meaning of its life and calling consisted in being open continually to him and ready to perceive these signs of his coming. The period in which the congregation was living was that of the end, containing the final history of God and man which began with the resurrection of Christ and would close in the open manifestation of the reconciliation between God and the whole of creation already effected in Christ. In this last period the congregation was the event—that is, the ongoing creation of Christ—which consisted in gathering together those men and women whom the living Lord chose and called to be witnesses of the victory he had already won—the heralds of its future universal manifestation. The congregation was the event in which the communion of the Holy Spirit established a human fellowship derived from acceptance of the Word of Christ in and through the witness of the Bible, heard and perceived in common; in which the sacraments were powerful as the one reality by which men lived—baptism incorporated human beings into this special relationship with Christ, and the Lord's Supper kept them in this state of grace and enabled them to fulfill their mission to others; in which the divine mission of Christ was represented and attested through the preaching of his Word, through the invitation to believe on him, and also through the manifestation of the temporal, political, and social significance of the salvation that had appeared in him in the midst of the non-Christian world for which he died and rose again. The Church was this living congregation thus described, which consisted in the event by which it was being always gathered together—the decisive element in this final phase of the story of God's relations with men.

As will be seen from this brief summation of his teaching, Barth's theological outlook reflected the emphasis of the Reformed Churches on the relation of the Church to the Word of God, his distaste toward what he understood to be liberalism, and the results of his attempt to adjust his thinking to the collapse of Europe, which in so many places had carried the churches down in seemingly complete wreckage.

In 1918 he had been a country pastor at Safenwil, Switzerland. That year he wrote a book on *The Epistle to the Romans,* condemning the rationalization of Christ as a good man who came to enlist followers in work to make the world a better place. On the strength of the book he received a call three years later to become professor in theology in Göttingen University, from which he went after two years to the University of Bonn. Refusing to take the oath of loyalty to Adolf Hitler required of all teachers, he returned to Switzerland in 1933 to accept the chair of theology in Basle University, where students from many parts of the world gathered to hear his lectures on the Bible.

He was a man of rather massive person, whose manner of speaking bordered on gruffness; but under less formal circumstances he appeared approachable and friendly. A remark by him at Amsterdam concerning the place of women in the Church, which was understood as adverse to their claim to the right of full participation, unfortunately distracted attention from his main thesis. At a press conference he explained that he was not opposed to women having positions in the Church, as in society, but wished only to stress that there were differences of function between them and men, with whom nevertheless they could collaborate helpfully.

The disproportionate amount of space given here to Dr. Barth's ideas seems to be justified by their effect on the thinking of many leaders in the ecumenical movement, particularly those with Continental antecedents. Although he had little active part in the organization of the World Council of Churches, his theology influenced the orientation of its deliberations and pronouncements.

2. Emil Brunner

Also heard on the program of a plenary session was another renowned Swiss theologian, Dr. Emil Brunner of the University of Zürich, whose address dealt with "the de-personalization of man in modern society; and what the Christian must do . . . to help him maintain his true personality and community."

Like Dr. Barth, he had collaborated in the pre-Assembly preparation of study material. In addition, his books had exerted considerable influence upon Christian thought, which many members of the Assembly gratefully acknowledged. He looked to be more the professorial type than his fellow countryman and colleague.

For the dehumanization of man capitalism and communism were, he declared, equally to blame, although the latter in its totalitarian form was more dangerous because it eliminated the possibility of criticism and correction.

"Three factors . . . work[ed] together to modify . . . the capitalistic system—the labor unions, state legislation, and a growing insight among the capitalists themselves that they [were] responsible for and [had] to consider the public welfare."

Depersonalization had not been the result of the modern technological system but rather its cause. The evolution of civilization would have followed quite another course had it been guided by regard for personal values rather than for the production of material goods. The deep root of trouble had been the secularization of man's thoughts and will, he said, with the consequent estrangement from the Christian faith in which the worth of human personality and community were grounded.

Dr. Brunner's address followed the thought of his Gifford Lectures, *Christianity and Civilization,* which had treated of economic and political power, particularly in its warning against the centralized state toward which Western nations, because of their "crazy faith in the state," were heading. More and more they were appealing to the state for help whenever social evil needed to be cured, "instead of mobilizing the pre-state institutions and associations."

"Let me say that the Church is duty bound to postulate two things unconditionally—social justice and absolute negation of totalitarianism as implied in state socialism," which was "the real devil in our time" and "the grave of freedom," he declared.

He advocated keeping all enterprises which were not natural monopolies out of the hands of the state, the powers of which should be employed to oppose such concentration. Christians should work for decentralization as a bulwark against the destruction of the individual and for a "pluralistic social system" in which "immediate agencies" between the government and the citizens would afford the latter opportunity to participate in the affairs of community life.

But the Church's first responsibility was to make itself a community "in which the members [would be] brothers and every individual . . . valued as a person and mutual personal encounter [would take] place incessantly." Without such a brotherhood, "even the sacraments remained unintelligible mysteries."

"It is the Church alone," he concluded, "which really has a social gospel, being by its existence a testimony against all powers of depersonalization—such as irresponsible capitalism and totalitarianism."

While Dr. Brunner had more to say than Dr. Barth about social problems from the standpoint of the Church, their basic positions were not far apart. They concurred in the view that the responsibility of the Church was not the construction of "a system of social theory" but the building of its own life into a true community of spiritually reborn members which would set before the disordered world an example of the way of social salvation. Neither had any hope that society might in this way be saved, but such witness to God and his kingdom of love and peace, already established by Christ, it was the mission of the Church to bear. "There has never been, nor will there ever be, a Christian state or international order, but there ought to exist in every locality a Christian community imbued with the spirit of brotherhood and love. And where it exists, there alone can the world learn what real community is. 'See how these Christians love one another'—it was that persuasive, spontaneous example which opened the world of antiquity to the gospel." [1]

3. Martin Niemöller

The interest of both the Assembly and the community in Dr. Martin Niemöller brought overflow audiences when he spoke, as he did twice —once at a plenary session and again to a mass gathering of young people numbering some six thousand. Standing in the thoughts of all as the foremost symbol of resistance to Nazi tyranny, he received long applause. Because of his slight stature and ascetic appearance, he hardly looked the part of the hero of whose dramatic wartime role they had read. Seven years of imprisonment at the command of Adolf Hitler, four of them in solitary confinement, had left their mark upon him. Now, Sachsenhausen and Dachau behind, he was President of the Protestant Churches of Hesse and Rhineland-Palatinate, and likewise of the Council of German Protestant Churches.

He saw the world as "out of joint, not only here and there, but

[1] Brunner, in *Man's Disorder and God's Design,* an omnibus volume of the Amsterdam Assembly series, Vol. III, p. 180.

everywhere, and the disorder . . . increasing with alarming rapidity." "A paralyzing atmosphere of decline" was spreading, he thought.

> We do not know how the difficulties by which we are faced are to be overcome; we even doubt that they can be overcome at all. . . . We are already talking about a "post Christian era" . . . and we see the . . . decay affecting the Christian Church itself. . . . There is something fundamentally wrong . . . in Christendom. If we had . . . prayed humbly with the old Church, "May this world pass away, and let Thy Kingdom come," then we should be able to pray today, in the face of the present world situation, "Come, Lord Jesus!" and our ears would be open to the consolation and the promise of His words: "But when this begins to happen, look up and lift up your heads, for the day of your deliverance is at hand!" That is our common plight, that our ears are not open, that we ourselves share in the doubt and despair around us. . . . The fact that we cannot . . . say, "The world reaps what it has sown," but that we must . . . admit that we ourselves . . . Christians, are reaping what we have sown, shows our involvment . . . with the rest of the human race.

The churches in Germany, realizing "this state of affairs," he said, "had to make a clear confession concerning their involvement in guilt." In the "Stuttgart Declaration" they had charged themselves, before God and the world, for

> not having been more courageous in . . . witness, more sincere in . . . prayers, more joyful in . . . faith and more ardent in . . . love. . This declaration met with a wide response. . . . And if we meet here . . . representing Christians all over the world, and seek . . . for a way within the "Disorder of the World," it is not to draw up yet another plan . . . which we would propagate as our Christian plan. If we . . . ask and seek . . . for "God's Design" . . . there will be a broad basis of agreement in our realization that we are implicated in the trepidation because of the things that are to happen on earth. We ourselves stand under God's judgment. . . . It will not be given to us to speak a clear Christian message here unless we recognize this judgment that God has sent upon us and . . . we so richly deserve.

Christians in central Europe had felt "the effects of this judgment most of all," he thought. The foundations there of the Holy Roman Empire had all broken down, and two world wars had destroyed all the work of a century at repairing them. "The break-down is complete," he said, "and if anyone wanted to reconstruct these ruins, he would meet with nothing but derision."

> But we cannot simply turn away and start something else. And where could we find anything else? We live in the world; and if the world is falling into chaos . . . , our own lives are in peril. . . . If we lose our real nature, our special dignity as human beings (as is happening today) then we . . . shall sink back into chaos, into that meaningless existence in which there is neither good nor evil, no movement forward or backward, no distinction between what is above and what is beneath. We should not enter-

tain any more illusions: this nihilism is among us today—a deadly sickness that is taking hold of us and against which we have no remedy.

It was beyond the power of human plans to restore order and human dignity. By the grace of God, Christians in repentance should ask: "What wilt thou have us to do?" The answer to this question would be: "Witness to the mercy of God in Jesus Christ in all the world, by which all men, whatever their plight, can live as children of God." This was the sole function of the Church.

Try as they might, the delegates who had come from the more materially favored countries outside the theater of war could hardly realize the suffering those at its vortex had undergone or the effects of the experience upon them. It was observed that many representatives of these stricken areas bore in their person and mien evidences of the ordeal through which they had lived: the gauntness of physical under-nourishment; their poor—sometimes threadbare—clothing; a hesitation in speaking of the loss and pain which had set them apart from others; a lusterless expression in their eyes which arose, one felt, from deep weariness of spirit and hope too long deferred.

The churches of Holland were reported to have done, on behalf of these, one of those acts of kindness which help to keep alive faith in humanity. When it had become known that means were lacking or insufficient for sending the delegates of Germany to the Assembly, Amsterdam Christians had arranged for lodging and board for them on terms within their resources. Dutch families, it was said, had taken certain members of the delegation into their own homes as guests. This had been quite different from the reception the Germans expected, remembering the indignities and persecutions the people of Holland had so recently suffered at the hands of the Nazi army of occupation.

4. Bishop Eivind Berggrav

The Assembly heard Bishop Eivind Josef Berggrav, Primate of Norway, another churchman whose uncompromising stand against the assaults of totalitarianism on the Church had earned him long months in a concentration camp and made his name known throughout the world.

He began by saying he thought the statement in the United Nations Charter that "men are endowed by nature with reason and conscience" furnished a clue to the world's disorder. This conception stood in sharp contrast, he thought, to the words in the American Declaration of Independence "which spoke of rights and powers given to men by their Creator." Accepting it, nations followed war as the rule of life; set up governments by force, violence and threats; made aggression the aim and success of ambitious men. There could be no real peace, he declared, "without respect of a Ruler . . . above men."

He spoke strong words of faith and courage which one felt to be characteristic of the man.

> There is a living God whose will has been made known through Jesus Christ. . . . There is a foe who hates unity and loves division and iron curtains, especially between churches, who is fully satisfied so long as he can get them to exhibit their jealous rivalry, who delights in insults and incidents which cause churches, as well as nations, to be offended and to fight. . . . But there is also a victory in spiritual solidarity. This is God's will and way toward victory. The Christian witness in the disillusionment of international politics is to demonstrate solidarity in Christ.

5. Reinhold Niebuhr

Of Americans on the program, the one listened to with most general interest, perhaps, was Dr. Reinhold Niebuhr of the Evangelical and Reformed Church, Professor in the Union Theological Seminary in New York City, whose competence as a theologian many held to rival that of Barth and Brunner.

Like his compeers of the Old World, he summoned Christians to help mankind by their life and witness to find the answer to "the problem of community." The sins of the Church had been, he said, "sanctifying the existing social order, acting as if politics were irrelevant to the Christian life, approaching social problems with sentimentality, and invoking legalistic solutions." The fallacy in liberal culture, which had made itself an ally of capitalism, was the assumption that the good of the whole would be served by everyone's working according to self-interest. The civilization which had resulted might be faulty, he declared, but the alternative was worse, if one looked to communism with its horrible evils.

> There is so little health in the whole of our modern civilization that one cannot find the island of order from which to proceed against disorder. Our choices have become terribly circumscribed. . . . Must we finally choose between atomic annihilation or subjection to universal tyranny? If such a day should come, we will remember that the mystery of God's sovereignty and mercy transcends the fate of empires and civilizations. He will be exalted though they perish. However, he does not desire their perdition but rather that they turn from their evil ways and live. From us he demands that we work while it is day, since the night cometh when no man can work.

6. John Foster Dulles

The Honorable John Foster Dulles, American statesman, spoke on the role of the churches in international affairs. Because of his position as adviser of the Federal Council of the Churches of Christ in America in this field and his experience as a representative of the United States at the conference for setting up the United Nations, he was especially qualified to speak. He had collaborated in the preparation of reference matter for the study program of the Assembly. He had also contributed a paper on "Christian Responsibility in Our Divided World," which had been favorably received, on the whole, though not without some dissent from certain churches which were confronted by the immediate necessity of working out a *modus vivendi* with communist totalitarian governments.

Mr. Dulles thought that "the churches ought not to make authoritative pronouncements in respect to detailed action in political, economic or social fields. . . . Those who act in the political field must deal with the possible, not the ideal . . . ; [they] must try to get the relatively good, the lesser evil." For this reason, the churches should "exercise great caution in dealing with international political matters. They should not seem to put the seal of God's approval upon that which, at best, may be expedient, but which cannot wholly reflect God's will."

It did not follow, however, that Christian faith and Christian political action were unrelated, he said.

> All citizens have to act in relation to political matters, inaction being only a form of action, a clearing of the way for others to act. Also, Christian citizens, when they act, will try to be guided by Christian insight and . . . inspiration. . . . What the churches elect to say will have political consequences. What they elect to keep silent about will also have political consequences. So the churches, too, have a relationship to practical politics that is inescapable. . . . The churches ought to know what are the problems which Christian citizens face. "Thy word is a lamp unto my feet, and a light unto my path"—but churches cannot throw the light of the Word upon the Christian's path, unless they know where those paths lie and what are the obstacles that need to be illumined.
>
> Obviously, Christian citizens throughout the world do not face identical problems or have identical duties. . . . There are many paths . . . all leading . . . toward the doing of God's will on earth. Some paths lead from the East, some from the West; some from the North, some from the South. Each has obstacles of its own. These . . . constantly shift. What is described now may be irrelevant by tomorrow. . . . The churches should keep informed. Otherwise, they cannot keep each way illuminated with shafts of divine light.
>
> The churches should put more emphasis on Christianity as a world religion, remembering that God gave his Son because he loved the world, not merely the West.

Mr. Dulles recognized that the path he described led from the West and that it differed from other ways which also the Churches should know, for Christians concede "no priority or privilege to any nation, race or class."

He stood as an advocate of "a free society."

A free society, if it is to effect peaceful and selective change—and political change is inevitable—must be a society where, in addition to the right to vote, the people possess and use personal freedoms and access to information and the opportunity to exchange and propagate thoughts and beliefs; so that there is, on an individual basis, genuine reflection and sober choice of minds and spirits which are both free and developed by use of self-discipline. There is also need for tolerance, particularly in the sense that political power may not be used to promote any particular creed.

Turning to communism, he said:

A free society does not have to be a *laissez faire* society. . . . Few . . . today would put that belief wholly into practice. . . . In most countries there are important collective and co-operative enterprises. . . . There is no inherent incompatibility between the Christian view of the nature of man and the practice of economic communism or state socialism. . . . It is not possible to attach the Christian label to any particular political or economic organization or system to the exclusion of all others. . . . It is possible to condemn as unchristian societies . . . organized in disregard of the Christian view of the nature of man. This would include those which are totalitarian in the sense that they recognize the right of some men to seek to bring the thoughts, beliefs, and practices of others into conformity with their will by . . . coercion.

The world must work, he said, toward an institutionalization of change.

Today any world-wide system for institutionalizing change would inevitably be despotic. Either it would vest arbitrary power in a few individuals or . . . in the small fraction of the human race who have tested political processes for reflecting the individual choice. The great majority of the world's population will not, and should not, agree to be ruled by the "free societies." The free societies will not, and should not, go back to despotism. This impasse is a source of great peril.

The program the churches should support is, he urged, one for peaceful evolution to international unity.

The Soviet Communist party did not believe in such peaceful evolution, he pointed out. "It believes that only by violence and coercion can it secure its . . . ends."

It should be recognized, he suggested, that the long-range social ends which Soviet leaders professed to seek were in many respects similar to the ends which Christian citizens sought—"a higher productivity of labor, abolition of exploitation of man by man, 'from each according to his abilities, to each according to his needs.'" There was nothing in these long-term ends, he thought, irreconcilable with what Christians wanted. "Most of them have been sought by Christians long before there was a Communist party," he declared.

The great difference was that "Soviet thinking proceeded from a materialistic premise, whereas Christian thinking proceeded from a spiritual premise."

> Soviet leaders hold that the material life of society is primary, and its spiritual life secondary, being merely a "reflection" of the material life. Christians believe that material and social conditions on earth are primarily important as creating conditions needed for spiritual development. Christians believe in a moral law which derives from God and . . . establishes eternal standards of right and wrong. Soviet leaders do not believe in such concepts. These differences are important because they lead to differences in means and procedures.

Communism could not be crushed by force, he concluded. "It would be wrong and stupid to use violence in order to convince people that violence ought not to be used." The solution "is for those who have faith to exert themselves more vigorously to translate that faith into works." This needed to be emphasized, he said, "because even the good practices of the West no longer seem to be the expression of a great faith. Once the connection is broken between faith and practices, practices, however good, lose their moral significance and seem to be matters of expediency."

7. Josef Hromadka

Mr. Dulles was followed by Dr. Josef L. Hromadka of the Evangelical Church of Czech Brethren, Professor of Theology in the John Hus Theological Faculty of Prague, who also had written a paper on "Christian Responsibility in Our Divided World" for the collection of reference materials for the study sections of the Assembly. He was listened to with considerable sympathy, because of his difficult position as a Christian teacher in a country under communist domination.

Dr. Hromadka did not share the statesman's hope that necessary international adjustments might be reached through peaceful change. He said:

> The simple truth is that rapid changes of history are transcending our normal categories, that, lacking imagination and vision, we are unable to grasp the meaning of the present turmoil and so become either disillusioned and cynical, or angry and hostile toward the nations and the men who seem to thwart our plans so wantonly. Hence, it is essential that once again

we try to understand courageously and clearly the basic nature and issues of contemporaneous history. Courageously, that is—to go beyond our pleasant and popular clichés, to break through our accepted conventions, and to abandon ideas which are already out of date. We lack courage, but we likewise lack clarity which resists and withstands the intoxicating haze of comfortable simplifications.

The basic issue of our times, both in national and international life, is far more than freedom and democracy. It goes beyond the categories of capitalism and socialism, liberalism and communism, even beyond what we call the alternative of "a free society or a totalitarian system," the alternative of the democratic, free West or the communistic, regulated, controlled East. The whole of the civilized human race is sick, and none is justified to claim a monopoly of means and medicines for the cure of the disintegrated international order. We are living in a crisis that is more than a crisis of democracy and freedom, of liberalism and humanism. What is at stake is much more than modern civilization and free society. The ultimate principles and axioms of truth, justice, human personality, love, and the organic fellowship of men are at stake. Modern man, both in the West and the East, has lost a real understanding of the supreme authority and the supreme court of appeal to which all men, all nations, and races, ought to subordinate themselves in order to understand one another and to discover a common ground on which to start the construction of a new and better order.

It could hardly have been claimed that Dr. Hromadka made himself clear on what specific course he recommended for "the reconstruction of a new and better order." He seemed to believe that what existed of the old order should be brushed aside and a complete new beginning made; also, he appeared to be committed to the principle of collectivism and resigned to the necessity of some dictatorial authority. He said:

Many people have come to realize that what really matters is not primarily political freedom, but a well-thought-out, reliable plan of a new society based on social justice, human dignity, enduring peace. . . . There are peoples whose situation may be compared to a flood inundating and destroying villages and towns, to a fire sweeping across a city, to a volcanic eruption covering with dust and debris vast areas of a country. Millions of dead are heaped on the ground. How can we under these conditions expect a normally functioning democratic process? In such a situation, what matters is to help the people, to disarm wrong-doers, to organize reconstruction, not to thrive on individual freedom. . . . In certain circumstances discipline, service responsibility, self-control, self-dedication are superior to freedom and human rights.

While saying the West had moral and political values the East desperately needed, which he hoped might be saved from destruction, he plainly had no confidence in the leadership of the West. One could not see in his address anything but revolution and violence, albeit he did not seem to be a person of violent spirit. The charitable attitude was, one felt, to think that with the power of communist Russia closing its tentacles around his country he could scarcely speak or even know his mind. The same indefiniteness characterized his reference to the task of the Christian Church in the situation. It was "in 'the work of faith, and labor of love, and patience of hope' to make a new beginning," he said, "to start from the bottom and to work for a new society, a new order, that [would] stand in some continuity with the past, but which . . . [would] in a more adequate way respond to the real needs of the present moment and reflect more genuinely the invisible glory and majesty of the Crucified and Risen One."

One could understand the difficulty of the speaker's position. Realizing that Christianity would in many countries have to learn to live under communism, if at all, one could be thankful that there were Christians who, instead of fleeing the ordeal, determined courageously to find the way, if it should be possible. One wished them well in the hazardous adventure, whatever his misgivings as to the outcome for them and the Church.

8. Charles H. Dodd

The assignment to present "The Biblical Basis for the Preparatory Studies" for the Assembly sections had fallen to Dr. Charles Harold Dodd of the Congregational Union of England and Wales, Professor of Divinity at Cambridge University and a foremost New Testament scholar. He and Dr. Karl Barth spoke at the same plenary session, and the two suggested a study in contrasts. Of small stature, quiet manner and lucid expression, Dr. Dodd could have been called, it was remarked, "a still small voice" after the storm. The voice probably did not say what some would have liked to hear, but if the Assembly had less interest in clichés than in thought-provoking ideas, the address could not have been disappointing.

The Word of God was more, Dr. Dodd explained, than the inspired record in the Bible. The faith and deeds of those who wrote or were written about arose from what "the mighty acts of God" had said to them. God had led his people through the ages, and the record of what he had done for them had become their treasured revelation of him. In "the fullness of time," Jesus Christ by his incarnation entered into the historical scene, "the Word of God in luminous finality." In the experience of the Church from that point onward, God had been saying, "This is my beloved Son, hear ye him!" And he had been saying also, "Receive ye the Spirit of truth, who will take of the Word in Christ and show it unto you, guiding you into all truth."

The Bible belonged to the Church, he said. It came through the Church and could not be understood apart from the experience of the Church. This relation between the Bible and the Church was to be found in every congregation of Christian people, "under whatever ecclesiastical order." Thus, he concluded, "we have here a powerful medium of fellowship among the separated churches."

"All over the world," he reminded the delegates, "people are cherishing the hope that at this Assembly a word may be spoken to the desperate need of the nations. If so, it must be God's word and not ours. But we are to hear it as he speaks. We are now to try, in our deliberations and our worship, to bring our total situation and all the people caught up in it with us, in the place where history is made, into the presence of Christ, the living Word, and then to listen for what God will speak."

When the speaker referred to the Bible as "a powerful medium of fellowship among the separated churches," many doubtlessly were reminded that because of the widespread misunderstanding of its true nature the Bible had often been the cause also of division in the churches. At that very time, another group of Christians[2] who were meeting in Amsterdam were protesting "against the attempt which would be made under the auspices of the World Council of Churches to unite Christians without regard for revealed truth," and inviting "all true believers" to join under their banner with the slogan, "The whole Christ in the whole Bible." Delegates to the Assembly were receiving copies of a pronouncement from this other body denouncing them as "deniers of fundamental Bible doctrines" and the World Council of Churches as "anti-biblical," and calling upon "Bible-believers to separate themselves from this aggregation of religious negatives."

9. John Baillie

At a public meeting of the Assembly Dr. John Baillie of the Church of Scotland, Professor of Divinity in Edinburgh University, delivered an address on "The Christian Witness in the World," the general theme of the second study section. He stressed the need for a sacrificial Christianity, pointing out that martyrdom had an important place in the history of the Church and that present-day persecution under totalitarian dictators was an example of it. Quoting Friedrich Nietzsche, who said, "I will not believe in the Redeemer of these Christians till they have shown me that they are redeemed," he said that the defective Christianity of his followers had in every age been the most difficult hurdle Christ had to surmount in reaching the souls of men. Yet, there had been ages and places, he remembered, in which faith and charity walked hand in hand and profession was so matched by practice that men said not only, "Hear what these Christians believe!" but also, "See how these Christians love one another!" One result of the Assembly, he asserted, should be the recovery of such testimony.

[2] International Council of Churches.

He appealed for a more dynamic witness on the part of all Christians, but especially of the laity. Referring to evangelism, he said that "the lay apostolate is the hope of the Church in the modern world."

Dr. Baillie thought that the limited success of evangelism was due to the fact that multitudes thought of Christians, not as folk who enjoyed greater peace and joy in their hearts and loved and served their fellows with greater devotion than other men, but as people who believed a large number of things at which other minds balked. Under these circumstances, only "the witness of life" would be convincing.

10. Philippe Maury

Dr. Philippe Maury, a layman of the Reformed Church of France and Secretary of the World's Student Christian Federation, spoke next. The Christian message, he felt, often was ineffective because it was represented as consisting of teaching the world to live a pure, moral, respectable, and healthy life; to be free from all prejudice; to devote itself to the liberal struggle for a better social order and a fairer and lasting peace; to bring into the churches those who had not found their places there: when this was not the whole gospel, and the rest of it—what man needed to have God do for him—had not been preached. "The world is suffering from knowing too much about itself, and knowing only about itself," he said. "The testimony of the Christian is precisely to show that there is something else besides this world which is more important and true and definite."

11. Saroe Chakko

Miss Saroe Chakko of the Methodist Church in India, Principal of Isabella Thoburn College in Lucknow, who spoke on the same program with Dr. Baillie and Dr. Maury, said she thought that one of the most important needs in evangelism was to show the uniqueness of Jesus Christ. Indian Christians, who knew about the Buddha, Mohammed, and other holy men, were convinced that only Christ came to reveal God to man and to be their redemption. Like the other speakers, she emphasized life itself as the true and convincing witness, with the laity having an ever greater role. "Until India sees in those who bear the name of Christ the new life that is God's gift, the people will come to God not because of us, but in spite of us." One's vocation offered, she thought, the most fruitful evangelistic opportunity; she illustrated what she meant by telling of members of the government of India who were Christians and bearing witness to Christ as statesmen. She held that women had an important ministry which circumstances, partly of their own making but more because the churches had not opened the way, had prevented them from fulfilling.

12. Ernest Brown and Metropolitan Themistocles Chrysostom

At the public session of the Assembly at which Dr. Emil Brunner and Dr. Reinhold Niebuhr spoke, the theme of which was "The Christian Witness in the Social Order," there were addresses also by the Rt. Hon. Ernest Brown, President of the Baptist Union of Great Britain and Ireland and Privy Councillor in the British government, and Metropolitan Themistocles Chrysostom of the Ecumenical Patriarchate of Constantinople, in which was stressed, quite in contrast to the other discourses, the "individual gospel." The churches' responsibility, said the layman from London, was to prepare "individuals to live as Christians in a secular world, whether their calling be factory-work, politics, journalism, business or government." And the aged bishop advanced, in effect, the same view, declaring, "The task of the Church is primarily spiritual. . . . It should change individuals and set forth principles for the guidance of society, but not undertake to give social or political leadership itself."

Inattention on the part of the Assembly generally during these addresses might have been taken as the result of weariness from much speaking or the judgment that they did not merit reporting. But the fact that the speakers were well-nigh alone in raising their voices on behalf of the "individual gospel" seemed to give what they said significance in the midst of so many interpreters of the "social meaning of religion." The truth which they chose to emphasize most of the others on the program at Amsterdam probably would have considered so elementary as not to need restatement, especially in a conference concerned primarily with the problems of the world. But in stressing them the speakers may have done well, for the essentials of religious faith have a way of dropping from sight in preoccupation with the peripheral, and cannot always be taken for granted. Moreover, that a Baptist layman and an Orthodox priest agreed on what they considered most fundamental certainly was newsworthy—and a favorable augury for the organization of diverse elements they were helping to found!

13. Regin Prenter

The program committee had arranged for all four of the subdivisions of the general theme for study to be presented to the Assembly as a whole prior to the meeting of the sections. The first of them, "The

Universal Church in God's Design," occupied a lengthy session at which three speakers discussed various salient aspects of it.

Dr. Regin Prenter of the Church of Denmark, Professor of Dogmatic Theology in the University of Aarhus, spoke on "The Problems of the Ecumenical Movement," pointing out particularly those of nontheological character, such as history and tradition, organization and custom, racial and national differences, all of which were obvious enough as he described them but raised many obstructions to unity escaping the attention of the casual observer.

14. Clarence Tucker Craig

Dr. Clarence Tucker Craig of the Methodist Church in the United States, Professor of New Testament in Yale Divinity School, New Haven, discussed with special reference to the nature of the Church the main points whereon the theologians who had come to Amsterdam found themselves in agreement or disagreement.

They differed, he said, on the degree of the unity between the people of God under the old and new covenants; the sense in which the Church was the mystical body of Christ; the authority of tradition as normative, with the Scriptures, for the Church; the location of authority "within and among the congregations of believers"; and the nature of continuity in the Church, whether "horizontal or vertical."

In seven conclusions they had reached agreement, he said:

> We all believe that the Church is God's creation, not man's; that redemption centers in God's act in Jesus Christ; that the Church is marked by the presence of the Holy Spirit; that the Church has been set apart in holiness as a worshipping community; that the Church is related to two worlds—that forgiven sinners are at the same time heirs of the kingdom of God; that the ministry of the Church is equipped by God with various gifts of the Spirit; that the Church in its very nature is one.

15. Georges Florovsky

To those who had been at previous ecumenical gatherings Dr. Georges Florovsky of the Russian Orthodox Church, at the time Professor of Systematic Theology in the Orthodox Theological Institute in Paris, had become a familiar figure. Because of his fluency in several tongues and his competence as a scholar he was often chosen to present the views of Orthodoxy, and he had been appointed to speak to the Assembly on "The Experience of the Church in the World and the Problem of Unity."

It was impossible, he held, to give a formal definition of the Church. Strictly speaking, there was none that could claim doctrinal authority. The Fathers did not concern themselves much with the doctrine of the Church, because of the glorious reality. "One does not define what is self-evident." From the beginning, Christianity existed as a corporate reality—as a community. "To be Christian meant just belonging to the community." "One could not be a Christian by himself, as an isolated individual, but only with the brethren." *Unus Christianus nullus Christianus*. "Personal conviction or even a rule of life still does not make one a Christian. Christian existence implies . . . membership in the community." The Church was not a community merely of those who believed in Christ and walked in his steps, but of those who abided in him and in whom he dwelled by his Spirit. "Christians are set apart, 'born anew' and recreated. They are not given only a new pattern of life, but a new principle. . . . They are a 'peculiar people.' "

The unity of the Church, he explained, was effected through the sacraments. Baptism and the Eucharist were the two "social sacraments," and in them the true meaning of community was continually revealed and sealed. Even more emphatically, the sacraments constituted the Church. They could not be separated from the inner effort and spiritual attitude of believers. "Baptism shall be preceded by repentance and faith." The personal relation between the Christian and his Lord must first have been established by the hearing and the receiving of the Word—the message of salvation. By the Spirit Christians were united with Christ and constituted into his body—one body, according to St. Paul. The incarnation was being completed in the Church, and in a certain sense the Church was Christ himself in his all-embracing plenitude.

To recapitulate, "Christians are incorporated into Christ and Christ abides in them. This intimate union constitutes the mystery of the Church. 'The body of Christ is Christ himself. The Church is Christ, as after his resurrection he is present with us and encounters us here on earth.' In this sense, one can say Christ is the Church."

The primary task of the historical Church, he continued, was the proclamation of the gospel. "This it does by both word and deed. The true proclamation would be the practice of the new life in Christ, to show faith by deeds."

> The Church is more than a company of preachers, or a teaching society, or a missionary band. It has not only to invite people, but also to introduce them to this new life, to which it bears witness. . . . The aim of its missionary activity is not merely to convey to people certain ideas and convictions . . . but to bring them through their faith and repentance to Christ himself, that they should be born anew in him and into him by water and the Spirit. . . . Conversion is a fresh start, but only a start to be followed by a long process of growth. . . . The Christian has to be "a new creation."

"Christianity is not an individualistic religion," he concluded, "and it is not only concerned for the salvation of the soul. . . . The task of a complete re-creation or re-shaping of the whole fabric of life cannot and must not be avoided. . . . Christians have to transform the outer world, to make it the kingdom of God and introduce the principles of the gospel into secular transactions." All attempts at the direct Christianization of the world, in the guise of a Christian state or empire, had only led to the secularization of Christianity itself. "A practical program for the present age can be deduced only from a restored understanding of the nature and essence of the Church. . . . The failure of all utopian expectations cannot obscure the Christian hope: the King has come, the Lord Jesus, and his kingdom is come."

16. Bishop Stephen Charles Neill

Bishop Stephen C. Neill of the Church of England, in what was one of the most informative addresses of the Assembly, told of the evangelistic task before the churches as partially disclosed by a survey which had been begun in preparation for the study on "The Church's Witness to God's Design."

From the standpoint of evangelism, he said, there were three main types of area in the world:

> those countries in which the Christian tradition, though diminished in its hold on the national life, yet remains a factor of importance, influencing a great many who would not now be regarded as professing Christians; the countries in which the Christian tradition has been violently overthrown or so radically undermined that they must be regarded as belonging to the post-Christian . . . world; and the countries which have never been Christian at all, in which all the patterns of living have been worked out without reference to the biblical concepts of man's nature and his dependence on God."

In three main areas the churches had failed extensively, he said, in making the preaching of the gospel effective: the world of classical Hinduism and its offshoot, Buddhism; the domain of Islam; and the life of urban and industrial man in the great cities, which seemed to be producing a new type of humanity.

"It is right that we should start with our failures," he declared. "Yet even here the failure is not absolute." From each of the spheres mentioned, most encouraging evidence of the gospel as the power of God unto salvation had been received.

It had been found that there was no type of church that had not given evidence of the vitality of the gospel. From Roman Catholic sources had come the best studies of evangelistic situations they had found, and the most moving examples of sacrificial work; and, on the other hand, Pentecostal groups, which stood on the margin of the main Christian movement, had carried on some of the most successful pioneering enterprises in evangelism. "We find," he said, "that every conceivable variety of evangelistic method and approach has its triumph to record."

From our survey, we have reached the conclusion that the churches of the present day, whatever the difficulties of the task to which they are called, are not straitened in God, but only in their own faith and in the use they make of the resources that God has put at their disposal. . . . If we cannot assert that the evangelization of the whole world in this generation is possible, it is yet true that the gospel could be preached, within the life-time of men now living, to almost all the people of the world, if the churches would take seriously their responsibility, and would make evangelism the first and foremost of all their tasks. . . .

If this fuller concept of the work of evangelism is to be realized in practice, the lay members of the Church will have to be brought, more than they have been, into the work. There have at all times been zealous Christian laymen. Yet there is an almost ineradicable tendency for Christians to divide their lives into parts, the sacred and the secular, and to develop their religious activities in separation from their ordinary vocations. There have always been Christian doctors and lawyers. But in too many cases, professional life has not been penetrated by the Spirit of Christ . . nor been accepted as the sphere in which the meaning of the claim of Christ on human life is worked out.

17. Kathleen Bliss

Among the women appearing before the Assembly was Mrs. Kathleen Mary Bliss of the Church of England, Editor of *The Christian News-Letter*. Speaking on "The Church and the Disorder of Society," she said the Church had failed to understand that the fundamental problem of the technological society was power and its control.

If . . . we could look anew at the tragedy of our society which is going to live in disorder perhaps for decades, we might see that the renewal of the Church and the renewal of society come from one source, from the healing power of the love of God operating through men in open and courageous encounter with the world.

18. Anna Canada Swain

Mrs. Leslie E. Swain of the Northern Baptist Convention in the United States (who was later elected, to the Central Committee of the World Council of Churches and its smaller Executive Committee) emphasized the importance of interpreting to the people of all the churches the sense of oneness which had been experienced at Amsterdam, so that they would see that the similarities of Christians outweighed their differences and think of that first Assembly of the churches as only a beginning of larger cooperation. She urged that greater regard be had for lay responsibility in all the tasks of the kingdom of God. All Christians should be informed about the World Council of Churches and its aims, she said, so that they would know what it meant to belong to the larger household of faith.

19. Mildred McAfee Horton

At the session of which "The Christian Witness and the International Order" was the theme, Mrs. Douglas Horton of the Congregational Christian Churches of the United States, President of Wellesley College, addressed the delegates "from the point of view of the educational world." She said, in part:

> If you think the Church has a special weight of responsibility for bringing order out of chaos, you should hear what educators in America say about the responsibility of the school and college. . . . Politicians talk about the dignity of the individual, the inherent worth of personality, the moral obligation to build a better world, the importance of spiritual values to solving the problems of social disorder. . . . Many business men state their purposes, their sense of responsibility in almost the same terms as we are using here . . . and also young labor leaders. . . . Secularized Christendom is permeated with vast resources of idealism which could change the destiny of nations, if it were implemented and set to constructive action with dynamic power. Without that dynamic power geared to everlasting values, the very idealism may be more weakness than strength to a disordered world.
>
> It is for this reason that the secular institutions need to be supplemented by a virile Church, alert to its unique mission to keep man conscious of his relation to the loving, judging, living God. . . . Whatever else the Church can do and be, it will fail a needy world, unless it keeps vivid before men the awareness of the God whom Christ revealed. In doing that it performs its unique service and makes its unique contribution to the solution of the problems of the international disorder and the disorder of society in general. On behalf of . . . secular institutions dedicated to good works, I . . . say, with the enquirers of old, to every churchman among you, "Sirs, we would see Jesus."

20. Christian Kobla Dovlo

Christian Kobla Dovlo gave the Assembly a glimpse of Africa and its aspirations through the eyes of a native son. A divinity student in Edinburgh, he belonged to the Ewe Presbyterian Church of the Gold Coast. The Church in tropical Africa had the formidable task, he said, of existing and working in the midst of direst poverty, ravaging disease, and heathenism. Its successes would be a demonstration of the power of God. He saw need for evangelism among educated Africans, from whose ranks the ablest leaders might be drawn. His continent struggled in an environment entirely pagan, he explained, woefully ignorant of Christian truth; and the Church must find the patience and wisdom to lead it out into the light of Christ.

It is the Christian's immovable faith in the possibilities of all races and the power of God to use them that inspires his witness. Our Lord Jesus Christ himself was the greatest pioneer and author of this faith in humanity and God, in that he founded his church upon disciples whom he chose from the different walks of life—fishermen, tax-collectors, lawyers—both men and women. He knows that the sinner can be restored. . . . No human being is beyond the saving power of Christ. . . . We must, therefore, never despair of any . . . race . . . or nation. . . . It is this faith which is the motive power behind the adventure of missionaries to my own country. . . . It is the same witness of Christian faith that we need in international affairs—faith in the younger churches . . . faith in the so-called backward races . . . in the aggressive nations, yea, in all humanity.

There are still so-called Christians in this twentieth century who think that the mere color of the skin is a definite and permanent sign of inferiority or superiority. This is a complete denial of the definite teachings of the New Testament. It has two grave dangers, namely, that (1) the superiority complex of the advanced races blinds them both to their own shortcomings and the virtues of others, while (2) the inferiority complex enforced on the less fortunate races prevents them from contributing their special, unique gifts to the common welfare of all humanity. . . .

We as Christians today must learn applied faith from the communists. They believe and practice equality of all races, which is the most natural and greatest attraction for the colored races throughout the world.

On the days when the delegates and the alternates met apart for study, the unofficial members of the Assembly had opportunity to hear reports by distinguished speakers of the religious life of many of the countries which had representatives at Amsterdam.

21. Gordon Alfred Sisco

Dr. Gordon Alfred Sisco, General Secretary of the United Church of Canada, told of developments in Canadian church history. Beginning as a Roman Catholic colony, Canada became, he said, as a result of successive waves of immigration, strongly Protestant. Approximately 58 percent of the population now was Protestant and 42 percent Roman Catholic. The influence of the Roman Catholic Church had tended to strengthen the cohesiveness of Protestantism, and organic union had become a progressive goal, of which a result was the founding in 1925 of the United Church of Canada, comprising all Methodists, most Congregationalists, and about two-thirds of the Presbyterians.

22. Samuel McCrea Cavert

It fell to Dr. Samuel McCrea Cavert, General Secretary of the Federal Council of the Churches of Christ in America, to report for the United States. Never, he said, had a larger percentage of the people belonged to the churches, but, although seventy-five million—more than half the population—professed a church allegiance, there was a disturbing discrepancy between the numerical size of the churches and their positive influence on the nation's life. "The fact that Christianity is generally treated . . . as if it were irrelevant to the major interests of life, such as education and social welfare, and to business, industry and politics," he said, "forbids any complacency on the part of the churches."

The large number of denominations in the United States was accounted for, he explained, by the diversity of the population and the adoption of the principle of complete religious freedom. But 97 percent of the total church membership belonged to fifty denominations having each fifty thousand or more communicants. There were nearly five million Jews, one million Eastern Orthodox, twenty-five million Roman Catholics, and forty-five million Protestants.

Protestantism in the United States differed from that of Europe, he pointed out, in its rejection of the church-state pattern; its lesser interest in formal theological confessions and greater emphasis on personal Christian experience; its reaction against centralized ecclesiastical authority and concern for the independence of the local congregation; its preoccupation with the practical side of religion rather than the mystical and theological, which had brought upon it the criticism of being activistic; and its effort to make religion effective in the social, economic, and political life of the nation.

Referring to interchurch cooperation, he said, "The vision of the ecumenical Church has begun to capture the imagination and the loyalty of Christians in most of the churches. . . . There is a new appreciation of the Church, with less emphasis on the churches."

23. G. Báez-Camargo

It appeared incongruous, said Dr. G. Báez-Camargo of the Methodist Church and Secretary of the National Evangelical Council of Mexico, that "in spite of the fact that Latin American nations [were] among the most divided in and among themselves, there [were] still many people in them who regarded a religious minority as something of a crime against national unity, patriotism and loyalty." But he was able to report that increasing numbers of the people looked to evangelical Christianity for the satisfaction of their spiritual aspirations. Their churches were very poor. An evangelism was needed that would reach all social levels. Evangelical Christians in Mexico numbered around 250,000 in 31 sects. Still, interdenominational cooperation was growing rapidly.

24. Samuel Rizzo

Speaking for Brazil, Dr. Samuel Rizzo of the Presbyterian Church in that country, President and Professor of Greek and Theology in the Presbyterian Theological Seminary of Portugal,[3] said that it had more than a million Protestants—a greater number than in any other Latin nation. Brazil had religious freedom, and Protestant ministers were active in the nation's political life. The churches were growing, and large congregations evidenced their interest and activity. Roman Catholicism, although strong, had only one priest for each twenty thousand of the population, as compared with one for each four thousand in the United States, where the total number was twice that for Brazil. "I believe," he concluded, "that because of its phenomenal religious growth, the task of the Brazilian Protestant church is to lead—as far as one country can—the other peoples of Latin America into the fold of evangelical Christianity."

25. H. R. Høgsbro and Bishop K. F. O. Dibelius

From Europe, besides those who had already spoken at one or another session about conditions there, Dr. Halfdan Raunsöe Høgsbro of the Church of Denmark, Principal of the Practical Theological Seminary of the Danish Church in Copenhagen, and Dr. Karl Friedrich Otto Dibelius of the Evangelical Church of Germany, Bishop of Berlin, brought reports, confining themselves, for the most part, to Scandinavia and Germany respectively. Bishop Dibelius said that totalitarianism had placed all European churches in the same position; they must not compromise with the state but must stand against national and racial hatreds and give themselves unremittingly to evangelism. His own burden of responsibility was particularly for East Germany, where the churches had been beggared and were still in a precarious situation.

In Scandinavia, according to Dr. Høgsbro, the churches had full liberty for their work and security for person and property. Secularization was their most difficult problem. Because of it, the people did not understand the Church—did not leave it, did not fight it. The Church

[3] Dr. Rizzo was teaching at that time in Portugal.

must find a language for modern man. What he said further seemed to betray forebodings: "If the Church does not succeed in making its message understood and believed, if all good efforts are in vain, if the Old World breaks down in wars and revolutions, God then will give his Church grace to suffer with clemency, endurance and good hope, ready to join in building a new world on the ruins of the old."

26. G. K. T. Wu, Tsu-Chen Chao, and Rajah B. Manikam

Three speakers reported from East Asia, revealing bafflement and presentiment—Rev. George K. T. Wu of the Methodist Church, in China, General Secretary of the National Christian Council; Dr. Tsu-Chen Chao of the Anglican Church in China, Dean of the School of Religion, Yenching University, Peiping, who had been chosen as one of the Presidents of the World Council of Churches, representing the younger churches; and Dr. Rajah B. Manikam of the Federation of Evangelical Lutheran Churches in India, Executive Secretary of the National Christian Council of India.

All described vividly the difficulties under which Christian work had to be maintained in the Far East. Mr. Wu spoke with appreciation of the contribution of the missionaries and the institutions which they had built in China. Despite the uncertain prospects for the churches, because of growing opposition, the National Christian Council had launched a three-year forward movement, with emphasis on evangelism.

Dr. Chao dwelt upon the problem posed in education by the rise of communist ideology. Already the Christian schools had been restricted in their teaching. They hoped that some way could be found, without open conflict with the authorities, to continue their work on a Christian basis. (Dr. Chao was later to resign as a President of the World Council of Churches because of the conflict which he prayed might be avoided.)

Dr. Manikam described the non-Christian environment in which the churches of East Asia had to work. The "indigenous cultures and religions" forced them to fight for "religious liberty and freedom for missionary activities." They were generally poor and dependent on the West for financial support and leadership. War had destroyed their buildings in many places and reduced the people to want. In education, in the conquest of disease and superstition, in rural reconstruction, and in all works of mercy, the churches had rendered service "out of all proportion to [their] numbers."

27. S. A. Morrison and Johannes Apkarian

In the series of addresses on "The Condition and the Task of the Church" in the world, Stanley Andrew Morrison of the Church of England, Secretary of the Church Missionary Society in Egypt, and Rev. Johannes Apkarian of the Armenian Evangelical Union of the Near East, Minister of the Evangelical Church in Aleppo, Syria, reported for the churches of the Middle East.

Islam dominated this general region, Mr. Morrison said, and assigned "a permanent position of inferiority" to all non-Muslims—Jews and Christians alike. Religious freedom was guaranteed by law but was far from being realized in practice. He thought the churches of the West could help to remove this unfair disadvantage through the Commission on Human Rights of the United Nations and perhaps other channels. Evangelical churches in these parts had shown little interest in reaching non-Christians, directing their efforts to "expansion at the expense of the ancient churches." The latter might be assisted through the ecumenical movement, he suggested, to experience spiritual revival and to set up internal reforms which would add to their influence.

Mr. Apkarian estimated that of this area's seventy-odd million population not more than three million were Christians. These were distributed among a half-dozen denominations. According to him, they engaged vigorously in moral reform. He mentioned gambling, drinking, and white slavery as principal evils at which their attacks were directed. Other objectives of the churches included spiritual revival, closer cooperation, a greater degree of financial self-support, the preaching of honesty in business and of social and economic justice, and the promotion of understanding and reconciliation between the three monotheistic religions—Judaism, Christianity, and Islam.

Apropos of these presentations of the concerns of the churches in the Levant, a paragraph of the Assembly's survey of the world field of evangelism was recalled:

> Relations between Christians and Moslems are still in part determined by memories of the Crusades, and the Church has not yet made adequate reparation for that false start in its approach to the Islamic world. The Moslem is fully convinced of the superiority of his faith as the final word of God to man, and of the inferiority of Christianity as an earlier and now superseded revelation. The simplicity of the Moslem creed and the definiteness of its requirements make it intelligible and satisfying to the ordinary man. It is still difficult to obtain from the Moslem any serious, let alone sympathetic, consideration of the gospel.

28. J. M. Karefa-Smart[4]

The only way in which African life could be brought under the Lordship of Christ, declared Dr. John Musselman Karefa-Smart of the Evangelical United Brethren Church, physician in the missionary dispensary of Sierra Leone, was by an evangelism speaking "the language of community which the tribes understood" and by the Church's becoming itself a new community of the saved which would exist, not, as in the case of the old tribe, to save its own life, but to bring redemption to all tribes. The Church must understand the values in the old tribal community which enabled it to survive, he urged, the first of which was the surrender by the individual member of ambition for personal gain for its service. Within the Christian fellowship, this would mean that personal salvation should cease to be the all-important objective, that a Christian lived to serve and not to be served. As fear was the basis of the solidarity of the tribe, love would be the cord binding the members of the Church to one another, as it bound them to God. And the rigid discipline to which they had been accustomed would in the Christian society have its more spiritual counterpart in worship and work.

29. Ranson, Devanandan, Florovsky, and Horton on Priorities

"Priorities in the Ecumenical Movement, Present Issues, and the Future" engaged the Assembly at one of its more instructive sessions as it searched for broad and accurate information that would enable it to formulate realistically plans for the new Council. "Priorities in the World Mission of the Church" was discussed by Dr. Charles Ranson of the Methodist Church in Ireland, General Secretary of the International Missionary Council, and Dr. Paul David Devanandan of the Church of South India, Professor of Philosophy and History of Religions in the United Theological College at Bangalore. "Priorities in the Movement for

[4] At the time a student, Mr. Karefa-Smart finished his education in English and American universities, earning a degree in public health administration at Harvard. He married Miss Rena Weller of Waterbury, Connecticut, and they went to Freetown, Sierra Leone, Africa, as missionaries. He was descended from an African chieftain. They taught in the mission school in Freetown, and he served as a director of the Royal Connaught Hospital. Both were outstanding in Christian leadership and worthy representatives of the younger leaders of Africa. He became a member of the legislative assembly of the state and of the President's cabinet, with the portfolio of Minister of Lands, Labor, and Mines. From the time of its organization, he and his wife served the World Council of Churches and other ecumenical bodies in many capacities and situations. In 1959 they co-authored *The Halting Kingdom: Christianity and the African Revolution,* the book on Africa for students in the mission-study series which was published by the Friendship Press.

Unity" was dealt with by Dr. Georges Florovsky, Professor of Systematic Theology in the Orthodox Theological Institute in Paris, and Dr. Douglas Horton, Minister of the General Council of Congregational Christian Churches in the United States.

In the missionary enterprise first place should be given, suggested Dr. Ranson, to the training of an adequate leadership in the younger churches. Dr. Devanandan added to this point three objectives for special emphasis: the steady mobilization of the lay forces of the churches in the work of evangelism; attention to the Christian home as the center of religious education; and the promotion of the spiritual and material welfare of the Christian community in rural areas.

The priority in the movement for unity was always, declared Professor Florovsky, who had been heard at an earlier session, "Christian patience." He appealed to the various denominations of Christians to widen their horizon and learn to understand the inner spirit and purpose of one another. "We follow the same Christ," he said, "and, although he leads us by different ways, we are one in our faith and love toward him."

Dr. Horton said that "each denomination should have the will to unite with others, a knowledge of the faith and practice of the others, and the purpose to undertake union with other branches of the Church on such a scale as opportunity offered." "An effective welding of the Christian churches of the world into a single unit characterized by Catholic continuity and Protestant freedom in Christ is," he declared, "the burden of our hope as we gather here at Amsterdam."

30. John R. Mott

The shortest speech was made by Dr. John R. Mott, upon being elected Honorary President of the World Council of Churches:

"I will serve you as long as I live."

31. Archbishop Geoffrey Francis Fisher

Near the end of the Assembly, Dr. Geoffrey Fisher, Archbishop of Canterbury and one of the Presidents, made a brief statement during a session at which he presided. Although informal and apparently extemporaneous, it was received as a sagacious evaluation of the labors at Amsterdam:

> As I look back on the last fortnight's work, I am more than content. Some expected the New Jerusalem to descend the moment the World Council of Churches came into existence; these will be disappointed.
>
> A new power from heaven does reside in the World Council, and it has been tested out in discovering man's knowledge of God and how men are to live together on this earth.

We had our differences, but, as Dr. Barth said, they were within our agreements, and so could be discussed in a friendly spirit. People from all over the world have in a few days here become a brotherhood. We share a family likeness from our heavenly Father. The future lies in the churches and how well they take this power and use it in the local parishes.

The Archbishop thought the Church should not aspire to be "democratic," since that would mean that its power resided within the members, whereas the power of the Church never is the people's but God's Holy Spirit through Jesus Christ. He suggested that the Church seek to be "demo-practical," the people devoting themselves to all good works under the guidance of the Holy Spirit.

The foregoing résumés of the numerous addresses have been given to acquaint the reader with the Christian leaders to whom fell the education of the Assembly and to enable him to have some knowledge of the intellectual, as well as the spiritual, climate in which the World Council of Churches was born and set upon its way. One is in position to judge the prospects of an organization only when he knows the thoughts of those who created it and in whose hands rests its administration.

In this connection may be presented also part of an address by the General Secretary of the new World Council.

32. Address by the General Secretary

Dr. Willem Adolf Visser 't Hooft spoke mainly of the experience of the interim from Utrecht, where the first steps of organization had been taken, to their consummation at Amsterdam:

During the ten years which have passed since the plan for the formation of a World Council of Churches took definite shape, the Council lived in a time "between times"—in the twilight zone between existence and nonexistence.

This created . . . uncertainty. The question whether the Provisional Committee should go ahead and accept new responsibilities, even though the churches had not yet had opportunity to determine the policy and program of the Council, could not be answered satisfactorily. But from another point of view these ten years have proved a blessing in disguise. For they have been years of apprenticeship. The process of formation proved to be a formative process. . . .

We have learned much about the dimensions of our task . . . that they are far more formidable than we thought. . . . We have looked into abysses of ignorance and indifference which are to be bridged . . . up to mountains of misunderstanding which have to be removed. . . . Our patience with each other . . . in learning to live and work together must reflect something of God's . . . with our hardness of heart.

We have learned that the vitality of this Council depends wholly on the vitality of the churches which compose it. It is not merely that we cannot undertake tasks unless the churches support them. It is especially that our common witness in word and deed has no substance and no convicting power unless . . . rendered locally and nationally in all the churches. . . .

We have learned the simple lesson that the ecumenical Church is built where we act as members one of another . . . in the testimony of confessing churches speaking on behalf of the whole Church of Christ, in intercession for persecuted churches, in services of worship among prisoners of war and refugees, in fraternal aid given to suffering churches and orphaned missions, in relationships restored in the name of the common Lord. . . .

Our task is to make it clear to ourselves and to the world what our coming together does not mean. . . . The very fact that we are building a wholly new type of inter-church fellowship, for which there are no precedents . . . means that our plans are easily misunderstood.

The tenacious misunderstanding is that this Council seeks to become a super-church, a center of ecclesiastical power. . . . Our constitution makes it as clear as possible that the Council has no such intention and claims no such authority. . . . Anyone who has worked in the ecumenical field knows that the slightest attempt to exercise such control is bound to meet with determined resistance on the part of the churches which share the same strong sense of independence. . . .

A second misunderstanding is that the Council pursues political ends. . . . Our task is to prove in word and deed that we serve a Lord whose realm certainly includes politics but whose saving purpose cuts across all political alignments and embraces men of all parties, all lands.

We are a Council of Churches, not the Council of the one undivided Church. Our name indicates our weakness and our shame before God, for there can be and there is finally only the one Church of Christ. . . . Our plurality is a deep anomaly. But our name indicates also that we are aware of the situation, that we do not accept it passively, that we move forward toward the manifestation of the One Holy Church.

Our Council represents, therefore, an emergency solution—a stage on the road—a body living between the time of complete isolation of the churches from each other and the time—on earth or in heaven—when it will be visibly true that there is one Shepherd and one flock.

We are a fellowship in which the churches after a long period of ignoring each other come to know each other . . . in which the churches enter into serious and dynamic conversation with each other about their differences in faith, in message, in order . . . in which solidarity is practised, so that the churches aid their weak and needy sister-churches . . . in which common witness is rendered to the Lordship of Christ . . . in which we seek to express that unity in Christ already given us and to prepare the way for a much fuller and . . . deeper expression of that unity. . . .

With few exceptions, the churches which have been invited to participate in the constitution of the Council have accepted. . . . Some . . . which desired to be represented . . . have been unable to send their delegates, for reasons independent of their own will. . . . There are others . . . which have declined the invitation . . . others which refuse to join us or even attack us. . . .

We are not forming this Council in a spirit of ambition . . . to join in any struggle for power . . . [but] in a spirit of repentance for our failure to be the Church together and to render clearer witness together to the Lord who came to serve all. . . .

[We] ask . . . "What will he do to us and with us, if we consecrate ourselves and all that we have wholly to him and to the upbuilding of the Church, which is his body?" For the King who goes to war against the powers of darkness is not the World Council of Churches or any institution, but Jesus Christ to whom full authority has been given in heaven and on earth.

III

THE SECTIONS AT STUDY

We turn now to the reports of the study sections, which were each "received by the Assembly and commended to the churches for their serious consideration and appropriate action."

It is important, from the standpoint of a fair appraisal of the World Council of Churches, to read these reports for what they actually were: statements of opinion on the four sub-themes which a majority of the approximately one hundred members of the respective sections had been willing to approve—or acquiesce in. They were received by the Assembly for transmission to the churches. The vote to receive did not make them the voice of the Assembly. But this was not a distinction all persons could draw. They had, in popular thought, the weight of semi-official pronouncements.

It was partly for this reason that sagacious leaders had advised against releasing them. There were other quite as strong arguments for withholding them from immediate publication. They had been written for the churches to study and to approve or amend, as they would, and their disposition, once they had been received by the Assembly, belonged to the member denominations, until there had been time to study them carefully. They contained interpretations of issues on which there were sharp divisions in the churches; and their style and tone in places were such as would not strengthen confidence in the World Council of Churches. Moreover, their hasty composition, unavoidable under the circumstances,[1] could only increase the already too prevalent impression that the churches were given to muddy thinking and careless speaking. But the stage had been set for their broadcast, thanks mainly to the contriving of American churchmen, and the Assembly handed them to the world. It was a major instance of brilliant or inept use, depending on one's point of view, of propaganda in ecumenical "education."

[1] While the reports were submitted to the Assembly at plenary sessions, there was little time for amendments from the floor.

1. Section I: The Universal Church in God's Design

The general theme of the Assembly, it will be recalled, was "Man's Disorder and God's Design." Section I submitted its conclusions on the sub-theme "The Universal Church in God's Design"; it described the delegates who had come to Amsterdam "as Christians from many lands and . . . traditions . . . [and from] Churches which misunderstood, ignored and misrepresented one another," who believed that God had given his people in Jesus Christ a unity which was his creation and not their own achievement. But this oneness they had not been able to manifest as they would in organization and practice, mainly on account of "a hard core of disagreement between different ways of apprehending the Church of Christ." Characterized historically as "catholic" and "protestant," they emphasized, respectively, "the visible continuity of the Church in the apostolic succession of the episcopate" and "the initiative of the Word of God and the response of faith, focused in the doctrine of justification *sola fide*."

Yet their division at this point was far from absolute because the Catholic Churches, whether Anglican, Eastern, Old Catholic, or Roman, believed in the necessity of faith, and the Protestant in "the continuity of the Church in some form."

Whether or not this was their "deepest difference," as they declared, it had proved unyielding. Those who thought of the Church more in terms of the local congregation of believers—"the gathered community" —would have said that the difference between themselves and the others, the Catholics certainly, reached its extreme depth in sacramentalism, which understood the Church and its ordinances to be "channels by which divine grace was conferred and . . . inherently efficacious," and not "simply visible signs or symbols of the invisible spiritual blessing."

Though they could not agree, neither could they bring themselves to adjourn and go home. The nature of their relationship in Christ forbade this. "We cannot ignore one another," they said, "for the very intensity of our difference testifies to a common conviction which we drew from him."

While "genuine convictions and loyalty to truth itself" had helped to make and to perpetuate their divisions in the first place, "pride and self-will and lovelessness" had "played their part, and still did."

> Within our divided churches, there is much we confess with penitence before the Lord of the Church, for it is in our estrangement from him that all our sin has its origin. It is because of this that the evils of the world have so deeply penetrated our churches, so that amongst us too there are worldly standards of success, class-division, economic rivalry, a secular mind. . . . We are in danger of being salt that has lost its savor and is fit for nothing. . . . It is to our shame that we have so often lived in pre-occupation with

our internal affairs, looking inward upon our own concerns, instead of forgetting ourselves in outgoing love and service. Our churches are too much dominated by ecclesiastical officialdom, clerical or lay, instead of giving vigorous expression to the full rights of the living congregation and the sharing of the clergy and the people in the common life of the Body of Christ.

The Commission on Faith and Order had led in the development of the theme of Section I, and the report to the Assembly spoke, on the whole, for those who believed the will of God for the churches to be some form of corporate union.

We thank God for the ecumenical movement, because we believe it is a movement in the direction which he wills. . . . In many parts of the world, he is drawing long-separated Christians towards a closer approach to unity. Some notable unions have been achieved. For the courage, enterprise and vision which inspired them, we give thanks to our one Shepherd.

The report reflected, in this connection, a consensus of the members that the World Council of Churches was not to be an agent to negotiate union between the churches but was to help the denominations through fellowship, cooperation, and study to draw closer together, leaving the decision in respect of uniting to them. To this end the conferees prayed for the spiritual renewal of the churches, which was presupposed by any unity worth the effort to achieve it. "As Christ purifies us by his Spirit," they said, "we shall find that we are drawn together, and that there is no gain in unity, unless . . . in truth and holiness."

Their statement, "Because it is a Council of Churches, we must discuss them [i.e., their differences] in the full sense of responsibility to those who send us, not pretending to agreements which our churches as a whole would repudiate," seemed to suggest that many of them, if they could have acted only for themselves as individuals, would have gone farther in their expressions of accord. Indeed, they had already said, "To some of our members, issues which have been discussed here do not seem important or even relevant."

The report of Section I on "The Universal Church in God's Design" follows in full: [2]

I. Our Given Unity

God has given to His people in Jesus Christ a unity which is His creation and not our achievement. We praise and thank Him for a mighty work of His Holy Spirit, by which we have been drawn together to discover that, notwithstanding our divisions, we are one in Jesus Christ.

We speak, as Christians from many lands and many traditions, first of all to thank God for His goodness. We come from Christian churches which

[2] For this and the reports of the sections which follow, see the five-volume study series for the First Assembly, *Man's Disorder and God's Design*, London, Paris, and Zurich, 1949.

have for long misunderstood, ignored and misrepresented one another; we come from lands which have often been in strife; we are sinful men and we are heirs to the sins of our fathers. We do not deserve the blessing which God has given us.

God's redeeming activity in the world has been carried out through His calling a People to be His own chosen People. The old covenant was fulfilled in the new when Jesus Christ, the Son of God incarnate, died and was raised from the dead, ascended into heaven and gave the Holy Ghost to dwell in His Body, the Church. It is our common concern for that Church which draws us together, and in that concern we discover our unity in relation to her Lord and Head.

II. Our Deepest Difference

It is in the light of that unity that we can face our deepest difference, still loving one another in Christ and walking by faith in Him alone. It has many forms and deep roots. It exists among many other differences of emphasis within Christendom. Some are Catholic Orthodox in clearly understood senses; some are Protestant after the great Reformation confessions; others stress the local congregation, the "gathered community" and the idea of the "free church." Some are deeply convinced that Catholic and Protestant (or evangelical) can be held together within a single church. Yet, from among these shades of meaning, we would draw special attention to a difference to which, by many paths, we are constantly brought back. Historically it has been loosely described as the difference between "catholic" and "protestant," though we have learned to mistrust any oversimple formula to describe it. (Clearly "catholic" is not used here to mean Roman Catholic, and "protestant" in most of Europe is better rendered by "evangelical.")

The essence of our situation is that, from each side of the division, we see the Christian faith and life as a self-consistent whole, but our two conceptions of the whole are inconsistent with each other.

It is impossible to describe either tendency or emphasis briefly without doing it an injustice. Each contains within it a wide variety of emphasis and many "schools of thought." But in each case we confront a whole corporate tradition of the understanding of Christian faith and life. We may illustrate this by saying that the emphasis usually called "catholic" contains a primary insistence upon the visible continuity of the Church in the apostolic succession of the episcopate. The one usually called "protestant" primarily emphasizes the initiative of the Word of God and the response of faith, focused in the doctrine of justification *sola fide*. But the first group also stresses faith, and the second also stresses continuity of the visible church in some form. Moreover this difference of emphasis cuts across many of our confessional boundaries. Conversation and undertsanding between these traditions are often made even more difficult by the presence in each of many who are accustomed only to their own forms of expression, are ignorant of others' traditions and often hold beliefs about their separated fellow-Christians which are a travesty of the true situation. Yet even when the conversation is between those who deeply trust and understand each other, there remains a hard core of disagreement between different total ways of apprehending the Church of Christ.

Each of these views sees every part of the Church's life in the setting of the whole, so that even where the parts seem to be similar they are set in a context which, as yet, we find irreconcilable with the whole context of the other. As so often in the past, we have not been able to present to each other the *wholeness* of our belief in ways that are mutually acceptable.

III. Common Beliefs and Common Problems

It is not possible to mention all the points which have been raised in our discussion together, still less to mention those which have been discovered in other fields of work on Christian unity, especially the work of the Commission on Faith and Order. All that we do here is to indicate certain points to which we have given attention, and some of the ways in which we believe they can be pursued in the ongoing work for Christian unity. We consider that the book *The Universal Church in God's Design*, which was written in preparation for our studies, contains much helpful material and we commend it to the serious attention of our churches as they face these problems.

We group our agreements into those which concern the *nature* of the Church and those which concern its *mission*, each followed by some disagreements which are revealed by a closer examination of the agreements.

A. We believe that the Church is God's gift to men for the salvation of the world; that the saving acts of God in Jesus Christ brought the Church into being; that the Church persists in continuity throughout history through the presence and power of the Holy Spirit.

Within this agreement, we should continue, in obedience to God, to try to come to a deeper understanding of our differences in order that they may be overcome. These concern:

1. the relation between the old and new Israel and the relation of the visible church to "the new creation" in Christ. It appears from our discussion that some of our differences concerning the Church and the ministry have their roots here.
2. the relation, in the saving acts of God in Christ, between objective redemption and personal salvation, between scripture and tradition, between the Church as once founded and the Church as Christ's contemporary act.
3. the place of the ministry in the Church and the nature of its authority and continuity, the number and interpretation of the sacraments, the relation of baptism to faith and confirmation, the relation of the universal to the local church; the nature of visible unity and the meaning of schism.

B. We believe that the Church has a vocation to worship God in His holiness, to proclaim the Gospel to every creature. She is equipped by God with the various gifts of the Spirit for the building up of the Body of Christ. She has been set apart in holiness to live for the service of all mankind, in faith and love, by the power of the crucified and risen Lord and according to His example. She is composed of forgiven sinners yet partaking already, by faith, in the eternity of the Kingdom of God and waiting for the consummation when Christ shall come again in the fullness of His glory and power.

Within this agreement also, we should continue, in obedience to God, to try to come to a deeper understanding of our differences in order that they may be overcome. These concern:

1. the relation between the Godward vocation of the Church in worship and her manward vocation in witness and service.
2. the degree to which the Kingdom of God can be said to be already realized within the Church.
3. the nature of the Church's responsibility for the common life of men and their temporal institutions.

We gratefully acknowledge these agreements and we seek the solution of these disagreements. God wills the unity of His Church and we must be obedient to Him.

At many of these points, our problems cut across confessional boundaries, and we are grateful to God for the way in which we continually learn from our fellow-Christians and for the way in which He is making Himself more clearly known to us through our fellowship with one another. In some parts of the world and to some of our members, issues which have been discussed here do not seem important or even relevant. Yet, because they are vital to some, they ultimately concern all. Among others whom we represent, many of our difficulties seem either to have been overcome or are on the way to solution. We thank God for all that lights the path to visible unity.

IV. The Unity in Our Difference

Although we cannot fully meet, our Lord will not allow us to turn away from one another. We cannot ignore one another, for the very intensity of our difference testifies to a common conviction which we drew from Him. The Body of Christ *is* a unity which makes it impossible for us either to forget each other or to be content with agreement upon isolated parts of our belief whilst we leave the other parts unreconciled.

Yet we have found God, in His mercy, penetrating the barriers of our fundamental division and enabling us to speak, in the common language of the divine revelation witnessed to in the Scriptures, about the points at which we find we meet. Wherever we find ourselves thus speaking together of our unity, we also find ourselves faced by some stubborn problems. In dealing with them, we discover disagreements which are to be traced back into our different ways of understanding the whole and, beneath these disagreements, we find again an agreement in a unity which drew us together and will not let us go.

V. The Glory of the Church and the Shame of the Churches

The glory of the Church is wholly in her Lord. In His love, He stooped to redeem her and to crown her as His bride. We praise God for continually renewed signs of His love for the Church. In recent years, it has been given to many of our fellow-Christians to rediscover what it is to be a "Church under the Cross." There they discovered new life, found the Bible as a living, contemporary book, made a good confession of their faith and saw the Church come to life in the steadfastness of thousands of humble Christians. We praise God for many signs of awakened life in the churches in many lands. Christ is moving many to a more sacrificial identification with the homeless and desperate, to a more vigorous evangelism and to a deeper theological seriousness. In many parts of the world, He is drawing long-separated Christians towards a closer approach to unity. Some notable unions have been achieved. For the courage, enterprise and vision which inspired them, we give thanks to our one Shepherd.

Although genuine convictions and loyalty to truth itself have their part in the making and perpetuating of divisions, we confess that pride, self-will and lovelessness have also played their part and still do so.

Within our divided churches, there is much which we confess with penitence before the Lord of the Church, for it is in our estrangement from Him that all our sin has its origin. It is because of this that the evils of the world have so deeply penetrated our churches, so that amongst us too there are worldly standards of success, class-division, economic rivalry, a secular mind. Even where there are no differences of theology, language or liturgy, there exist churches segregated by race and colour, a scandal within the Body of Christ. We are in danger of being salt that has lost its savour and is fit for nothing.

Within our divided churches it is to our shame that we have so often lived in preoccupation with our internal affairs, looking inward upon our own concerns instead of forgetting ourselves in outgoing love and service. Our churches are too much dominated by ecclesiastic officialdom, clerical or lay, instead of giving vigorous expression to the full rights of the living congregation and the sharing of the clergy and people in the common life in the Body of Christ.

We pray for the churches' renewal as we pray for their unity. As Christ purifies us by His Spirit we shall find that we are drawn together and that there is no gain in unity unless it is unity in truth and holiness.

VI. The World Council of Churches

We thank God for the ecumenical movement because we believe it is a movement in the direction which He wills. It has helped us to recognize our unity in Christ. We acknowledge that He is powerfully at work amongst us to lead us further to goals which we but dimly discern. We do not fully understand some of the things He has already done amongst us or their implications for our familiar ways. It is not easy to reconcile our confessional and ecumenical loyalties. We also have much to gain from the encounter of the old-established Christian traditions with the vigorous, growing churches whose traditions are still being formed. We bring these, and all other difficulties between us, into the World Council of Churches in order that we may steadily face them together. Because it is a Council of Churches, we must discuss them in the full sense of responsibility to those who send us, not pretending to agreements which our churches as a whole would repudiate.

The World Council of Churches has come into existence because we have already recognized a responsibility to one another's churches in our Lord Jesus Christ. There is but one Lord and one Body. Therefore we cannot rest content with our present divisions. Before God, we are responsible for one another. We see already what some of our responsibilities are, and God will show us more. But we embark upon our work in the World Council of Churches in penitence for what we are and in hope for what we shall be. At this inaugural Assembly, we ask for the continual prayer of all participating churches that God may guide it in wisdom, saving us both from false claims and from faithless timidity.

2. Section II: The Church's Witness to God's Design

"The Church's Witness to God's Design" had special reference to evangelism, and the members of Section II agreed that this phase of Christian work was the end for which all else in the churches existed. What they were and what they did—their whole life and activity—bore testimony to faith in Jesus Christ and looked to the conversion and salvation of men.

It was not reported—and understandably—that some delegates could not bring themselves easily to approve the procedures which in certain quarters were considered most characteristically evangelistic, or that others found it equally hard to take seriously fellow members who discoursed on the effectiveness as means of evangelism of such Christian practices as liturgical worship.

A meeting of minds might have been facilitated by consulting a survey the Provisional Committee had caused to be made of the world, from the standpoint of its evangelistic need and opportunity. The survey had discovered that God was winning people to himself through all kinds of Christian groups, from the Roman Catholic Church to the latest peripheral sect, and by the employment of all varieties of technique. The fact appeared to be that any Christocentric theology, however untenable otherwise it might be, enabled evangelists to reach the hearts of sinners and turn them toward God. (See page 262.)

"Much in the purpose of God . . . to reconcile all men unto himself . . . is still hidden from us," admitted the report; but three things were "perfectly plain."

> All that we need to know concerning God's purpose is already revealed in Christ.
> It is God's will that the Gospel should be proclaimed . . . everywhere.
> God is pleased to use human obedience in the fulfillment of his purpose.

In the purview of the study of Section II, evangelism comprehended missions. "The evident demand of God . . . is that the whole Church should set itself to the total task of winning the whole world for Christ. . . . The present day is the beginning of a new epoch of missionary enterprise, calling for the pioneering spirit, and for the dedication of many lives to the service of the Gospel of God." This raised immediately the question of the churches' disunity.

> If we take seriously our world-wide task, we are certain to be driven to think again of our divisions. Can we remain divided? St. Paul told his Corinthian converts that he could not give them solid food, because their divisions showed that they were still carnal. God gives the gift of his grace to churches even in their separation. We are persuaded that he has yet additional gifts to give to a Church united in accordance with his will. The pressure for corporate union comes most strongly from the younger churches. . . . The path to unity is always beset by many difficulties. But the ecumenical movement loses significance, unless its constituent churches bear ceaselessly in mind the prayer of Christ "That they all may be one; as thou, Father, art in me, and I in thee, that they also may be one in us; that the world may believe that thou hast sent me," and are prepared to move forward, as God guides them, to further unity in faith, in fellowship, at the table of the Lord, and in united proclamation of the word of life.

The report elaborated four conditions of successful evangelism: worship, community, lay participation, and interdenominational cooperation.

"Worship and witness . . . belong inseparably together," it was stressed. But "effective witness becomes possible only as each worshipping group is so filled with the joy of the risen and living Lord that even the outsider becomes aware that . . . the Church speaks . . . of real things."

"The world . . . is hungry for community," according to the findings. "But a worshipping group of individuals is not necessarily a community." "It is essential that each group become a real fellowship, through acceptance by all of full Christian responsibility for mutual service, and by breaking down the barriers of race and class." The study concluded that it was "intolerable that anyone should be excluded, because of race or color, from any place of worship." From the evidence, it found that for many "the fellowship of the churches [was] . . . much less satisfying than that of their own secular or religious organizations and brotherhood."

"The work of God requires that every member of the Church, ordained and lay, be an active witness," declared the Section. "The layman has his duties in the Church. . . . He is charged also with a task in the world outside. . . . For most people, the field of witness lies in the place where they . . . work. The way in which they do their job or exercise their profession must be unmistakably Christian." But they were called also to bear courageously "that witness in word through which others" would be "confronted with the challenge of the living Christ."

As for cooperation, it was recognized that "most evangelistic work [was] carried out by denominational agencies in separation." While this was "the natural way" in many situations, there were conditions under which churches could successfully engage in evangelism together.

In some areas God had set new opportunities before the Church. "Millions of people are ready to listen to the Gospel, and are already considering whether it is their only hope. Such areas should be considered the responsibility of the whole Church, and not only of those at present . . . in them; adequate resources in personnel and money should be made immediately available to the local churches, so that what needs to be done can be done effectively and without delay." The younger churches were crying out "for the help of Christian colleagues from the West."

The churches are called today to be much more flexible in organization than in the past. They must deal with every situation in the light of the total task.

It is God himself who is showing us the inadequacy of those things to which we have been accustomed.

It is important that the constituent churches of the World Council . . . seek comity among themselves in all matters relating to evangelistic effort and to their respective spheres of responsibility.

The study concluded with a confession of a sense of urgency which the delegates had felt as they studied "evangelism in its ecumenical setting."

If the Gospel is a matter of life and death, it seems intolerable that any human being now in the world should live out his life without ever having the chance to hear or receive it.

It is not within the power of man alone to create a new evangelistic movement. But the Holy Spirit is at work in men and with men. In the past, he has from time to time quickened the Church with power from on high. It is our earnest hope and prayer that he will do a mighty work in our day, giving the Church again wisdom and power rightly to proclaim the good news of Jesus Christ to men.

The report of Section II, as received by the Assembly, was as follows:

I. The Purpose of God

The purpose of God is to reconcile all men unto Himself and to one another in Jesus Christ His Son. That purpose was made manifest in Jesus Christ—His incarnation, His ministry of service, His death on the Cross, His resurrection and ascension. It continues in the gift of the Holy Spirit, in the command to make disciples of all nations, and in the abiding presence of Christ with His Church. It looks forward to its consummation in the gathering together of all things in Christ. Much in that purpose is still hidden from us. Three things are perfectly plain:

All that we need to know concerning God's purpose is already revealed in Christ.

It is God's will that the Gospel should be proclaimed to all men everywhere.

God is pleased to use human obedience in the fulfillment of His purpose.

To the Church, then, is given the privilege of so making Christ known to men that each is confronted with the necessity of a personal decision, Yes or No. The Gospel is the expression both of God's love to man, and of His claim to man's obedience. In this lies the solemnity of the decision. Those who obey are delivered from the power of the world in which sin reigns, and already, in the fellowship of the children of God, have the experience of eternal life. Those who reject the love of God remain under His judgment and are in danger of sharing in the impending doom of the world that is passing away.

II. The Present Situation

Two world wars have shaken the structure of the world. Social and political convulsions rage everywhere. The mood of many swings between despair, frustration and blind indifference. The millions of Asia and Africa, filled with new hope, are determined to seize now the opportunity of shaping their own destiny. Mankind, so clearly called even by its own interests to live at peace, seems still rent by a fanaticism of mutual destruction.

The word "faith" has acquired a new content. For most men, it is now faith in the new society, now to be founded once for all, in which the "good life" will be realized. Even in the present-day confusion, there are still many who believe that man, by wise planning, can master his own situation. Such men are interested not in absolute truth, but in achievement. In face of many religions and philosophies, it is held that all truth is relative, and so the necessity of a costly personal decision is evaded.

A formidable obstacle to Christian faith is the conviction that it belongs definitely to a historical phase now past. To those who know little of it, it seems irrelevant. More thoughtful men, who hold that it enshrines some spiritual and cultural values, regard it as no longer honestly tenable as a system of belief. And yet there is an earnest desire for clearly formulated truth. The religions of Asia and Africa are being challenged and profoundly modified. In the period of transition, the minds of millions are more than usual open to the Gospel. But the tendency in these countries to press an ancient religion into service as one foundation for a politically homogeneous state already threatens the liberty of Christian action.

So the Church sees the World. What does the World see, or think it sees, when it looks at the Church?

It is a Church divided, and in its separated parts are often found hesitancy, complacency, or the desire to domineer.

It is a Church that has largely lost touch with the dominant realities of modern life, and still tries to meet the modern world with language and a technique that may have been appropriate two hundred years ago.

It is a Church that, by its failure to speak effectively on the subject of war, has appeared impotent to deal with the realities of the human situation.

It is a Church accused by many of having been blind to the movement of God in history, of having sided with the vested interests of society and state, and of having failed to kindle the vision and to purify the wills of men in a changing world.

It is a Church under suspicion in many quarters of having used its missionary enterprise to further the foreign policies of states and the imperialistic designs of the powers of the West.

Much in this indictment may be untrue; but the Church is called to deep shame and penitence for its failure to manifest Jesus Christ to men as He really is. Yet the Church is still the Church of God, in which, and in which alone He is pleased to reveal Himself and His redemptive purpose in Jesus Christ, in whom and in whom alone the renewal of man's life is possible.

It is a Church to which, through the upheavals of the modern world, God cries aloud and says, "Come, let us reason together" (Isaiah i, 18).

It is a Church that is, to millions of faithful people, the place where they receive the grace of Christ and are given strength to live by the power of His victory.

It is a Church awaking to great opportunity to enter as the minister of the redemption wrought by Christ into that world with which God has confronted us.

It is a Church that today desires to treat evangelism as the common task of all the churches, and transcends the traditional distinction between the so-called Christian and so-called non-Christian lands.

The present day is the beginning of a new epoch of missionary enterprise, calling for the pioneering spirit, and for the dedication of many lives to the service of the Gospel of God.

III. The Church's Task in the Present Day

The duty of the Church at such a time can be expressed simply in one sentence—it is required to be faithful to the Gospel and to realize more fully its own nature as the Church. But fulfillment of this duty involves a revolution in thought and practice.

A. Worship and Witness

Worship and witness have sometimes been held in separation, but they belong inseparably together, as the fulfillment of the great command that men should love God and should love their neighbour as themselves.

When the ordinary man speaks of the Church, he thinks of a group of people worshipping in a building. By what that group is, the Church is judged. Effective witness becomes possible only as each worshipping group is so filled with the joy of the risen and living Lord that even the outsider becomes aware that, when the Church speaks, it speaks of real things.

But a worshipping group of individuals is not necessarily a community. It is essential that each group become a real fellowship, through acceptance by all of full Christian responsibility for mutual service, and by breaking down the barriers of race and class. It is intolerable that anyone should be excluded, because of his race or colour, from any place of worship.

The world today is hungry for community. But to many it seems that the fellowship of the churches is much less satisfying than that which they find in their own secular or religious organizations and brotherhood. This cannot be put right, until the churches more recognizably bear the marks of the Lord Jesus, and cease to hinder others, by the poverty of the fellowship they offer, from coming to Him.

B. A People of God in the World

The Church must find its way to the places where men really live. It must penetrate the alienated world from within, and make the minds of men familiar with the elementary realities of God, of sin and of purpose in life. This can be done partly through new ventures of self-identification by Christians with the life of that world, partly through Christians making the word of the Gospel heard in the places where decisions are made that affect the lives of men. It can be done fully only if, by the inspiration of the Holy Spirit, the Church recovers the spirit of prophecy to discern the signs of the times, to see the purpose of God working in the immense movements and revolutions of the present age, and again to speak to the nations the word of God with authority.

C. The Ecumenical Scene

Each Christian group must be conscious of the world-wide fellowship of which it is a part. Each Sunday, as it comes, is a reminder of the innumerable company throughout the world who on that day are worshipping the same Lord Jesus Christ as God and Saviour. It can attain to fulness of Christian life only as it accepts its place in the great purpose of God that all men shall be saved, and takes up the responsibility for prayer, service and sacrificial missionary enterprise involved in that acceptance.

IV. Missionary and Evangelistic Strategy

The evident demand of God in this situation is that the whole Church should set itself to the total task of winning the whole world for Christ.

A. Lay Work and Witness

This is the day of opportunity for the lay membership of the Church. The work of God requires that every member of the Church, ordained and lay, be an active witness. The layman has his duties in the Church in worship and stewardship. He is charged also with a task in the world outside. The most obvious sphere of witness is the home, the place in which the Church of the coming generation is to be built up. Some are called to special ministries of preaching or intercession. For most people the field of witness lies in the place where they do their daily work. The way in which they do their job or exercise their profession must be unmistakably Christian. But also they are called to bear courageously, as God gives the opportunity, that witness in word through which others are confronted with the challenge of the living Christ. Christian service is to be conceived in the widest possible terms. The variety of forms of witness is just the means by which God can make known the fulness of the Gospel as His answer to all the needs of mankind.

B. Co-operation in Evangelism

A church may find a denominational framework too narrow for its work today. Most evangelistic work is carried out by denominational agencies in separation. In many situations this is the natural way. But there are places where the work can best be done through co-operation in evangelism. Many difficulties may have to be faced. It is important that the constituent Churches of the World Council of Churches seek comity among themselves in all matters relating to evangelistic effort and to their respective spheres of responsibility. But it is God Himself who is showing us the inadequacy of those things to which we have been accustomed. The Churches are called today to be much more flexible in organization than in the past. They must deal with every situation in the light of the total task.

There are parts of the world where the Church is holding on under great difficulties, and where its liberty of action is restricted or denied. Its witness is carried out more by suffering than by preaching. Such churches rightly claim that within the fellowship of faith they shall be supported by the prayers and succour of every member of the world-wide Church.

In other areas, God has set new opportunities before the Church. Millions of people are ready to listen to the Gospel, and are already considering whether it is their only hope. Such areas should be considered the responsibility of the whole Church, and not only of those at present engaged in work in them; adequate resources in personnel and money should be made immediately available to the local churches, so that what needs to be done can be done effectively and without delay. The younger churches are crying out for the help of Christian colleagues from the West. Churches older and younger alike call urgently for the dedication of lives to the ordained ministry, and other full-time vocations or service to Christ in His Church.

C. The Problem of Our Divisions

If we take seriously our world-wide task, we are certain to be driven to think again of our divisions. Can we remain divided? St. Paul told his Corinthian converts that he could not give them solid food, because their divisions showed that they were still carnal. God gives the gift of His grace to Churches even in their separation. We are persuaded that He has yet additional gifts to give to a Church united in accordance with His will. The pressure for corporate union comes most strongly from the younger churches; the older manifest greater caution. The path to unity is always beset by many difficulties. But the ecumenical movement loses significance, unless all its constituent churches bear ceaselessly in mind the prayer of Christ "That they all may be one; as thou, Father, art in me, and I in thee, that they also may be one in us; that the world may believe that thou hast sent me" (John xiv, 21), and are prepared to move forward, as God guides them, to further unity in faith, in fellowship, at the table of the Lord, and in united proclamation of the word of life.

V. "Now Is the Accepted Time"

As we have studied evangelism in its ecumenical setting we have been burdened by a sense of urgency. We have recaptured something of the spirit of the apostolic age, when the believers "went everywhere preaching the word." If the Gospel is a matter of life and death, it seems intolerable that any human being now in the world should live out his life without ever having the chance to hear or receive it.

It is not within the power of man alone to create a new evangelistic movement. But the Holy Spirit is at work in men and with men. In the past He has from time to time quickened the Church with power from on high. It is our earnest hope and prayer that He will do a mighty work in our day giving the Church again wisdom and power rightly to proclaim the good news of Jesus Christ to men. We rejoice that the World Council of Churches has included evangelism in its programme of development. Already we are seeing signs of renewal and fresh life.

Now, not tomorrow, is the time to act. God does not wait for us to be perfect; He is willing to use very imperfect instruments. What matters is that the instrument should be available for His use. The results of our efforts are not in our hands but in His. But He has given us the assurance that "it is required in stewards that a man be found faithful," and that where that faithfulness is found, He is able "to do exceeding abundantly, above all that we ask or think."

3. Section III: The Church and the Disorder of Society

The members of Section III, who studied the sub-theme "The Church and the Disorder of Society," won the distinction of having written the most newsworthy report, an achievement attributable mainly to what they said about capitalism and communism.

The study surveyed the disorder of society as a consequence of the "industrial revolution with its vast concentrations of power," in which it was manifest on a large scale, "not only in greed, pride and cruelty of persons and groups, but also in the momentum or inertia of huge organizations of men, which diminishes their ability to act as moral and accountable beings." The task was, therefore, "to find ways of realizing personal responsibility for collective action in the large aggregations of power in modern society."

"Man is created and called," it asserted, "to be a free being, responsible to God and his neighbor. . . . Any tendencies in state and society depriving man of the possibility of acting responsibly are a denial of God's intention for man and his work of salvation. . . . Man must never be made a mere means for political or economic ends. Man is not made for the state, but the state for man. Man is not made for production, but production for man."

A "responsible society" was defined by the report as "one where freedom is the freedom of men who acknowledge responsibility to justice and public order, and where those who hold political authority or economic power are responsible for its exercise to God and the people whose welfare is affected by it."

"For a society to be responsible under modern conditions, it is required that the people have freedom to control, to criticize and to change their governments, that power be made responsible by law and tradition, and be distributed as widely as possible through the whole community. . . . It is required that economic justice and provision of equality of opportunity be established for all the members of society."

On this basis, the report condemned

> Any attempt to limit the freedom of the Church to witness to its Lord and his design for mankind and any attempt to impair the freedom of men to obey God and to act according to conscience . . . freedoms . . . implied in man's responsibility before God;
> Any denial to man of an opportunity to participate in the shaping of society . . . a duty implied in man's responsibility towards his neighbor;
> Any attempt to prevent men from learning and spreading the truth.

The churches were implicated, and

> should not forget to what extent they themselves have contributed to the very evils which they are tempted to blame wholly on the secularization of society. While they have raised up many Christians who have taken the lead in movements of reform, and while many of them have come to see in a fresh way the relevance of faith to the problems of society, and the obligations thus laid upon them, they share responsibility for the contemporary disorder.
>
> Our churches have often given religious sanction to the special privileges of the dominant classes, races and political groups, and so they have been obstacles to changes necessary in the interests of social justice and political freedom. They have often concentrated on a purely . . . other-worldly or individualistic interpretation of their message and their responsibility. They have often failed to understand the forces which have shaped society around them, and so . . . have been unprepared to deal creatively with new problems as they have arisen in technical civilization.

"The social influence of the Church must come primarily from its influence upon its members through constant teaching and preaching of Christian truth in ways to illuminate the historical conditions in which men live and the problems . . . they face"; but "the greatest contribution that the Church can make to the renewal of society is for it to be renewed in its own life in faith and obedience to its Lord."

"Coherent and purposeful ordering of society has now become a major necessity," according to the report. "Here governments have responsibilities which they must not shirk," and the churches also. "There is no inescapable necessity for society to submit to undirected developments of technology, and the Christian Church has urgent responsibility today to help men achieve fuller personal lives within the technical society."

Pursuing this line, the study scrutinized directly the different types of social order, including, of course, communism and capitalism. Its advice with reference to these last was as follows:

> Christian churches should reject the ideologies of both communism and *laissez faire* capitalism, and should seek to draw men away from the false assumption that these extremes are the only alternatives. Each has made promises it could not redeem. Communist ideology puts the emphasis upon economic justice, and promises that freedom will come automatically after the completion of the revolution. Capitalism puts the emphasis upon freedom, and promises that justice will follow as a by-product of free enterprise; but that, too, is an ideology which has proved false. It is the responsibility of Christians to seek new, creative solutions which never allow either justice or freedom to destroy each other.

This statement followed a long and rather involved passage in the report, which probably few persons bothered to read and out of its full context appeared to pronounce a curse equally upon capitalism and communism. Actually, in a comparison of the two systems, with which the bypassed paragraphs were mainly concerned, capitalism came off the better, though what was said about it could have been taken by its partisans as faint praise of the kind that damns the recipient.

> Christians should recognize with contrition that many churches are involved in the forms of economic injustice and racial discrimination which have created the conditions favorable to the growth of communism, and that the atheism and the anti-religious teaching of communism are in part a reaction to the chequered record of a professedly Christian society. . . . The Church should make clear that there are conflicts between Christianity and capitalism. The developments of capitalism vary from country to country and often the exploitation of the workers that was characteristic of early capitalism has been corrected in considerable measure by the influence of trade unions, social legislation and responsible management. But . . .

The arraignment followed:

> (1) capitalism tends to subordinate what should be the primary task of any economy—the meeting of human needs—to the economic advantages of those who have most power over its institutions. (2) It tends to produce serious inequalities. (3) It has developed a practical form of materialism in western nations in spite of their Christian background, for it has placed the greatest emphasis upon success in making money. (4) It has also kept the people of capitalistic countries subject to a kind of fate which has taken the form of such social catastrophes as mass unemployment.

The presentment in turn against "atheistic Marxian communism" was couched in terms of its conflicts with Christianity, as follows:

(1) the communist promise of what amounts to a complete redemption of man in history; (2) the belief that a particular class, by virtue of its role as the bearer of a new order, is free from the sins and ambiguities that Christians believe to be characteristic of all human existence; (3) the materialistic and deterministic teachings, however they may be qualified, that are incompatible with belief in God and with the Christian view of man as a person, made in God's image and responsible to him; (4) the ruthless methods of communists in dealing with their opponents; (5) the demand of the party on its members for an exclusive and unqualified loyalty which belongs only to God, and the coercive policies of communist dictatorship in controlling every aspect of life.

The Church should seek to resist the extension of any system that not only includes oppressive elements, but also fails to provide any means by which the victims of oppression may criticize or act to correct it. It is a part of the mission of the Church to raise its voice of protest wherever men are victims of terror, wherever they are denied such fundamental human rights as the right to be secure against arbitrary arrest, and wherever governments use torture and cruel punishments to intimidate the consciences of men.

Criticism of the report's treatment of capitalism came largely from American sources. The United States was, of course, the leading capitalist country of the world. It had supported the economies of the free nations in two global wars and in 1948 stood as their hope in the desolate aftermath. Many Americans thought that a system enabling a nation to perform this feat deserved better than having its faults elaborated without more appreciative reference to its virtues. They felt that if it had been the will of God for the churches to pass judgment upon the sins of capitalism, their spokesmen should have been chosen with greater care. Capitalism of the kind described by the report belonged to a day that had passed.[3] This fact the Assembly had recognized, and had written *"laissez faire"* before the word "capitalism" in the inept paragraph which marked communist and capitalist ideologies alike for rejection. That amendment, with the further qualifying sentence, "The developments of capitalism vary from country to country, and often the exploitation of the workers . . . *characteristic of early capitalism*[4] has been corrected in considerable measure by the influence of trade unions, social legislation and responsible management," backdated the report, so far as its statements about capitalism were concerned, and to that extent qualified its relevance for Amsterdam. Unfortunately, they could not prevent its damage. Notwithstanding all that was said by apologists, during the Assembly and afterwards, the document's handling of these subjects seemed to many ill advised and unworthy of the occasion.

[3] Capitalism in 1948 would have been defined with greater accuracy as "regulated free enterprise." Those members of the Assembly who would have modified it still more through governmental action in the direction of socialism believed this policy necessary to prevent general acceptance by many nations of communism. This theory was widely held at the time. It was not questioned by the Assembly.

[4] Italics not in the original, but supplied.

That the churches should not accept as fully Christian any politico-economic ideology was undebatable but beside the question. In a world where perfect systems could never be devised, the problem was choosing the one, or ones, which in actual experience had proved best adapted to serve the interests of the people. The nations under the necessity in 1948 of reshaping their economic and political philosophies had been entitled to counsel from the Christian churches which would not add to their confusion but would help them assess the practical potentialities of democratic free enterprise at their true value.

The complete report of Section III was as follows:

I. The Disorder of Society

The world to-day is experiencing a social crisis of unparalleled proportions. The deepest root of that disorder is the refusal of men to see and admit that their responsibility to God stands over and above their loyalty to any earthly community and their obedience to any worldly power. Our modern society, in which religious tradition and family life have been weakened, and which is for the most part secular in its outlook, underestimates both the depth of evil in human nature and the full height of freedom and dignity in the children of God.

The Christian Church approaches the disorder of our society with faith in the Lordship of Jesus Christ. In Him God has established His Kingdom and its gates stand open for all who will enter. Their lives belong to God with a certainty that no disorder of society can destroy, and on them is laid the duty to seek God's Kingdom and His righteousness.

In the light of that Kingdom, with its judgment and mercy, Christians are conscious of the sins which corrupt human communities and institutions in every age, but they are also assured of the final victory over all sin and death through Christ. It is He who has bidden us pray that God's Kingdom may come and His will may be done on earth as it is in heaven; and our obedience to that command requires that we seek in every age to overcome the specific disorders which aggravate the perennial evil in human society and that we search out the means of securing their elimination or control.

Men are often disillusioned by finding that changes of particular systems do not bring unqualified good, but fresh evils. New temptations to greed and power arise even in systems more just than those they have replaced because sin is ever present in the human heart. Many, therefore, lapse into apathy, irresponsibility and despair. The Christian faith leaves no room for such despair, being based on the fact that the Kingdom of God is firmly established in Christ and will come by God's act despite all human failure.

Two chief factors contribute to the crisis of our age. One of these is the vast concentrations of power—which are under capitalism mainly economic and under communism both economic and political. In such conditions, social evil is manifest on the large scale not only in the greed, pride and cruelty of persons and groups; but also in the momentum or inertia of huge organizations of men, which diminish their ability to act as moral and accountable beings. To find ways of realising personal responsibility for collective action in the large aggregations of power in modern society is a task which has not yet been undertaken seriously.

The second fact is that society, as a whole dominated as it is by technics, is likewise more controlled by a momentum of its own than in previous periods. While it enables men the better to use nature, it has the possibilities of destruction, both through war and through the undermining of the natural foundations of society in family, neighborhood and craft. It has collected men into great industrial cities and has deprived many societies of those forms of association in which men can grow most fully as persons. It has accentuated the tendency in men to waste God's gift to them in the soil and in other natural resources.

On the other hand, technical developments have relieved men and women of much drudgery and poverty, and are still capable of doing more. There is a limit to what they can do in this direction. Large parts of the world, however, are far from that limit. Justice demands that the inhabitants of Asia and Africa, for instance, should have the benefits of more machine products. They may learn to avoid the mechanization of life and the other dangers of an unbalanced economy which impair the social health of the older industrial peoples. Technical progress also provides channels of communication and interdependence which can be aids to fellowship, though closer contacts may also produce friction.

There is no inescapable necessity for society to succumb to undirected developments of technology, and the Christian Church has an urgent responsibility to-day to help men to achieve fuller personal life within the technical society.

In doing so, the Churches should not forget to what extent they themselves have contributed to the very evils which they are tempted to blame wholly on the secularization of society. While they have raised up many Christians who have taken the lead in movements of reform, and while many of them have come to see in a fresh way the relevance of faith to the problems of society, and the imperative obligations thus laid upon them, they share responsibility for the contemporary disorder. Our churches have often given religious sanction to the special privileges of dominant classes, races and political groups, and so they have been obstacles to changes necessary in the interests of social justice and political freedom. They have often concentrated on a purely spiritual or other-worldly or individualistic interpretation of their message and their responsibility. They have often failed to understand the forces which have shaped society around them, and so they have been unprepared to deal creatively with new problems as they have arisen in technical civilization; they have often neglected the effects of industrialization on agricultural communities.

II. Economic and Political Organization

In the industrial revolution economic activity was freed from previous social controls and outgrew its modest place in human life. It created the vast network of financial, commercial and industrial relations which we know as the capitalist order. In all parts of the world new controls have in various degrees been put upon the free play of economic forces, but there are economic necessities which no political system can afford to defy. In our days, for instance, the need for stability in the value of money, for creation of capital and for incentives in production, is inescapable and world-wide. Justice, however, demands that economic activities be subordinated to social ends. It is intolerable that vast millions of people be exposed to insecurity, hunger and frustration by periodic inflation or depression.

The Church cannot resolve the debate between those who feel that the primary solution is to socialize the means of production, and those who fear that such a course will merely lead to new and inordinate combinations of political and economic power, culminating finally in an omnicompetent State. In the light of the Christian understanding of man we must, however, say to the advocates of socialization that the institution of property is not the root of the corruption of human nature. We must equally say to the defenders of existing property relations that ownership is not an unconditional right; it must, therefore, be preserved, curtailed or distributed in accordance with the requirements of justice.

On the one hand we must vindicate the supremacy of persons over purely technical considerations by subordinating all economic processes and cherished rights to the needs of the community as a whole. On the other hand, we must preserve the possibility of a satisfying life for "little men in big societies." We must prevent abuse of authority and keep open as wide a sphere as possible in which men can have direct and responsible relations with each other as persons.

Coherent and purposeful ordering of society has now become a major necessity. Here governments have responsibilities which they must not shirk. But centres of initiative in economic life must be so encouraged as to avoid placing too great a burden upon centralized judgment and decision. To achieve religious, cultural, economic, social and other ends it is of vital importance that society should have a rich variety of smaller forms of community, in local government, within industrial organizations, including trade unions, through the development of public corporations and through voluntary associations. By such means it is possible to prevent an undue centralization of power in modern technically organized communities, and thus escape the perils of tyranny while avoiding the dangers of anarchy.

III. The Responsible Society

Man is created and called to be a free being, responsible to God and his neighbour. Any tendencies in State and society depriving man of the possibility of acting responsibly are a denial of God's intention for man and His work of salvation. A responsible society is one where freedom is the freedom of men who acknowledge responsibility to justice and public order, and where those who hold political authority or economic power are responsible for its exercise to God and the people whose welfare is affected by it.

Man must never be made a mere means for political or economic ends. Man is not made for the State but the State for man. Man is not made for production, but production for man. For a society to be responsible under modern conditions it is required that the people have freedom to control, to criticise and to change their governments, that power be made responsible by law and tradition, and be distributed as widely as possible through the whole community. It is required that economic justice and provision of equality of opportunity be established for all the members of society. We therefore condemn:

1. Any attempt to limit the freedom of the Church to witness to its Lord and His design for mankind and any attempt to impair the freedom of men to obey God and to act according to conscience, for those freedoms are implied in man's responsibility before God;
2. Any denial to man of an opportunity to participate in the shaping of

society, for this is a duty implied in man's responsibility towards his neighbour;

3. Any attempt to prevent men from learning and spreading the truth.

IV. Communism and Capitalism

Christians should ask why communism in its modern totalitarian form makes so strong an appeal to great masses of people in many parts of the world. They should recognize the hand of God in the revolt of multitudes against injustice that gives communism much of its strength. They should seek to recapture for the Church the original Christian solidarity with the world's distressed people, not to curb their aspirations towards justice, but, on the contrary, to go beyond them and direct them towards the only road which does not lead to a blank wall, obedience to God's will and His justice. Christians should realize that for many, especially for many young men and women, communism seems to stand for a vision of human equality and universal brotherhood for which they were prepared by Christian influences. Christians who are beneficiaries of capitalism should try to see the world as it appears to many who know themselves excluded from its privileges and who see in communism a means of deliverance from poverty and insecurity. All should understand that the proclamation of racial equality by communists and their support of the cause of colonial peoples makes a strong appeal to the populations of Asia and Africa and to racial minorities elsewhere. It is a great human tragedy that so much that is good in the motives and aspirations of many communists and of those whose sympathies they win has been transformed into a force that engenders new forms of injustice and oppression, and that what is true in communist criticism should be used to give convincing power to untrustworthy propaganda.

Christians should recognize with contrition that many churches are involved in the forms of economic injustice and racial discrimination which have created the conditions favourable to the growth of communism, and that the atheism and the antireligious teaching of communism are in part a reaction to the chequered record of a professedly Christian society. It is one of the most fateful facts in modern history that often the working classes, including tenant farmers, came to believe that the churches were against them or indifferent to their plight. Christians should realize that the Church has often failed to offer to its youth the appeal that can evoke a disciplined, purposeful and sacrificial response, and that in this respect communism has for many filled a moral and psychological vacuum.

The points of conflict between Christianity and the atheistic Marxian communism of our day are as follows: (1) the communist promise of what amounts to a complete redemption of man in history; (2) the belief that a particular class by virtue of its role as the bearer of a new order is free from the sins and ambiguities that Christians believe to be characteristic of all human existence; (3) the materialistic and deterministic teachings, however they may be qualified, that are incompatible with belief in God and with the Christian view of man as a person, made in God's image and responsible to Him; (4) the ruthless methods of communists in dealing with their opponents; (5) the demand of the party on its members for an exclusive and unqualified loyalty which belongs only to God, and the coercive policies of communist dictatorship in controlling every aspect of life.

The Church should seek to resist the extension of any system, that not only includes oppressive elements but fails to provide any means by which the victims of oppression may criticise or act to correct it. It is a part of the mission of the Church to raise its voice of protest wherever men are the victims of terror, wherever they are denied such fundamental human rights as the right to be secure against arbitrary arrest, and wherever governments use torture and cruel punishments to intimidate consciences of men.

The Church should make clear that there are conflicts between Christianity and capitalism. The developments of capitalism vary from country to country and often the exploitation of the workers that was characteristic of early capitalism has been corrected in considerable measure by the influence of trade unions, social legislation and responsible management. But (1) capitalism tends to subordinate what should be the primary task of any economy—the meeting of human needs—to the economic advantages of those who have most power over its institutions. (2) It tends to produce serious inequalities. (3) It has developed a practical form of materialism in western nations in spite of their Christian background, for it has placed the greatest emphasis upon success in making money. (4) It has also kept the people of capitalist countries subject to a kind of fate which has taken the form of such social catastrophes as mass unemployment.

Christian churches should reject the ideologies of both communism and *laissez faire* capitalism, and should seek to draw men away from the false assumption that these extremes are the only alternatives. Each has made promises which it could not redeem. Communist ideology puts the emphasis upon economic justice, and promises that freedom will come automatically after the completion of the revolution. Capitalism puts the emphasis upon freedom, and promises that justice will follow as a by-product of free enterprise; that, too, is an ideology which has been proved false. It is the responsibility of Christians to seek new, creative solutions which never allow either justice or freedom to destroy the other.

V. The Social Function of the Church

The greatest contribution that the Church can make to the renewal of society is for it to be renewed in its own life in faith and obedience to its Lord. Such inner renewal includes a clearer grasp of the meaning of the Gospel for the whole life of men. The renewal must take place both in the larger units of the Church and in the local congregations. The influence of worshipping congregations upon the problems of society is very great when those congregations include people from many social groups. If the Church can overcome the national and social barriers which now divide it, it can help society to overcome those barriers.

This is especially clear in the case of racial distinction. It is here that the Church has failed most lamentably, where it has reflected and then by its example sanctified the racial prejudice that is rampant in the world. And yet it is here that today its guidance concerning what God wills for it is especially clear. It knows that it must call society away from prejudice based upon race or colour and from the practices of discrimination and segregation as denials of justice and human dignity, but it cannot say a convincing word to society unless it takes steps to eliminate these practices from the Christian community because they contradict all that it believes about God's love for all His children.

There are occasions on which the churches, through their councils or through such persons as they may commission to speak on their behalf, should declare directly what they see to be the will of God for the public decisions of the hour. Such guidance will often take the form of warnings against concrete forms of injustice or oppression or social idolatry. They should also point to the main objectives towards which a particular society should move.

One problem is raised by the existence in several countries of Christian political parties. The Church as such should not be identified with any political party, and it must not act as though it were itself a political party. In general, the formation of such parties is hazardous because they easily confuse Christianity with the inherent compromises of politics. They may cut Christians off from the other parties which need the leaven of Christianity, and they may consolidate all who do not share the political principles of the Christian party not only against that party but against Christianity itself. Nevertheless, it may still be desirable in some situations for Christians to organize themselves into a political party for specific objectives, so long as they do not claim that it is the only possible expression of Christian loyalty in the situation.

But the social influence of the Church must come primarily from its influence upon its members through constant teaching and preaching of Christian truth in ways that illuminate the historical conditions in which men live and the problems which they face. The Church can be most effective in society as it inspires its members to ask in a new way what their Christian responsibility is whenever they vote or discharge the duties of public office, whenever they influence public opinion, whenever they make decisions as employers or as workers in any other vocation to which they may be called. One of the most creative developments in the contemporary Church is the practice of groups of Christians facing much the same problems in their occupations to pray and take counsel together in order to find out what they should do as Christians.

In discussing the social function of the Church, Christians should always remember the great variety of situations in which the Church lives. Nations in which professing Christians are in the majority, nations in which the Church represents only a few per cent of the population, nations in which the Church lives under a hostile and oppressive Government offer very different problems for the Church. It is one of the contributions of the ecumenical experience of recent years that Churches under these contrasting conditions have come not only to appreciate one another's practices, but to learn from one another's failure and achievements and sufferings.

VI. Conclusion

There is a great discrepancy between all that has been said here and the possibility of action in many parts of the world. Obedience to God will be possible under all external circumstances, and no one need despair when conditions restrict greatly the area of responsible action. The responsible society of which we have spoken represents, however, the goal for which the churches in all lands must work, to the glory of the one God and Father of all, and looking for the day of God and a new earth, wherein dwelleth righteousness.

4. Section IV: The Church and the International Disorder

Surveying the chaotic conditions of the world, Section IV, which had studied "The Church and the International Disorder," under the direction of the Commission of the Churches on International Affairs, saw "the hopes of . . . recent war years and the apparent dawn of peace . . . dashed," and heard "men . . . asking in fear and dismay what the future held." "Exhaustion and disillusionment have combined with spiritual apathy," it said, "to produce a moral vacuum which would be filled either by Christian faith or by despair or even hatred." Its report (1) pronounced war "contrary to the will of God . . . and a consequence of the disregard of God"; (2) declared that "the churches must . . . attack [its] causes . . . by promoting peaceful change and the pursuit of justice"; (3) asserted that "no state [might] claim absolute sovereignty, or make laws without regard to the commandments of God and the welfare of mankind"; (4) denounced "all forms of tyranny, economic, political or religious"; (5) opposed "utterly . . . totalitarianism, wherever found, in which a state arrogate[d] to itself the right of determining men's thoughts and actions instead of recognizing the right of each individual to do God's will according to his conscience"; (6) resisted "in the same way . . . any church which [sought] to use the power of the state to enforce religious conformity"; (7) urged that "a positive attempt . . . be made to ensure that competing economic systems such as communism, socialism and free enterprise [might] co-exist without leading to war"; (8) called on Christians to support the United Nations Organization as an agency helping "to promote friendly relations among the nations" and to give "effectiveness to international law"; (9) deplored existing "flagrant violations of human rights" in many parts of the world; (10) reaffirmed "the equality of all men in the sight of God"; (11) appealed to the churches to "support every endeavor to secure within an international bill of rights adequate safeguards for freedom of religion and conscience, including the right of all men to hold and change their faith, to exercise it in worship and practice, to teach and persuade others, and to decide on the religious education of their children," and to "press for freedom of speech and expression, of association and assembly, the rights of the family, of freedom from arbitrary arrest, as well as all those other rights which the true freedom of man requires"; (12) declared "the establishment of the World Council of Churches . . . of great moment for the life of the nations . . . a living expression of . . . fellowship, transcending race and nation, class and culture, knit together in faith, service and understanding . . . to hasten international reconciliation through its own members . . . and the co-operation of all Christian churches and of all men of goodwill."

The Section submitted important practical proposals in resolutions on a ministry to "the uprooted peoples of Europe and Asia," the International Bill of Rights before the United Nations Organization, and a Declaration of Religious Liberty, which the Assembly could adopt with assurance of general approval.

I. Whereas the uprooted peoples of Europe and Asia are far more numerous than at the close of the war, and whereas this problem constitutes a challenge to the Christian conscience, be it resolved:

That the World Council of Churches give high priority to work for the material and spiritual welfare of refugees; and appeal to its member churches in countries capable of receiving any settlers, both to influence public opinion towards a liberal immigration policy and to welcome and care for those who arrive in their countries.

This priority in work for the material and spiritual welfare of refugees includes not only those within the care of the International Refugee Organization and refugees of German ethnic origin, but all refugees and expelled of whatever nationality.

Especial attention should be given to the needs of children, particularly in countries where children have been severed from family care.

II. That the International Refugee Organization, in pursuance of its task of re-settling refugees continue to urge governments which recruit able-bodied persons from among these displaced persons, to receive and settle their dependent relatives also, and thus respect the unity and integrity of family life.

III. That the Council authorize the World Council of Churches' Refugee Commission to take such steps as may be appropriate to bring persons of German ethnic origin within the protection of the United Nations International Refugee Organization. Further the Assembly directs the Ecumenical Refugee Commission to work for inclusion of all refugees and expellees within the mandate of the International Refugee Organization.

IV. That the World Council of Churches, having already requested its member churches to support the efforts of the United Nations' Secretariat on behalf of Arab and other refugees from the conflict areas of Palestine, appeal to the Jewish authorities throughout the world to co-operate in this work of relief, and to facilitate the return of the refugees to their homes at as early a date as practicable.

V. Whereas the World Council of Churches notes with satisfaction that the United Nations has accepted as one of its major purposes the promotion of respect for and observance of human rights and fundamental freedoms for all without distinction as to race, sex, language or religion, and whereas the Assembly, conscious of the magnitude and complexity of the task of placing the protection of human rights under the aegis of an international authority, regards a Declaration of Human Rights, which is neither binding nor enforceable, although valuable as setting a common standard of achievement for all peoples and all nations, as in itself inadequate, be it resolved:

That the Assembly calls upon its constituent members to press for the adoption of an International Bill of Human Rights making provision for the recognition, and national and international enforcement of all the essential freedoms of man, whether personal, political or social.

That the Assembly call upon its constituent members to support the adoption of other conventions on human rights, such as those on Genocide and Freedom of Information and the Press, as a step toward the promotion of respect for and observance of human rights and fundamental freedoms throughout the world.

VI. Whereas the Churches are seeking to promote the observance of religious liberty throughout the world, be it resolved:

That the World Council of Churches adopt the following Declaration on Religious Liberty and urge the application of its provisions through domestic and international action.

A Declaration on Religious Liberty

An essential element in a good international order is freedom of religion. This is an implication of the Christian faith and of the world-wide nature of Christianity. Christians, therefore, view the question of religious freedom as an international problem. They are concerned that religious freedom be everywhere secured. In pleading for this freedom, they do not ask for any privilege to be granted to Christians that is denied to others. While the liberty with which Christ has set men free can neither be given nor destroyed by any Government, Christians, because of that inner freedom, are both jealous for its outward expression and solicitous that all men should have freedom in religious life. The nature and destiny of man by virtue of his creation, redemption and calling, and man's activities in family, state and culture establish limits beyond which the government cannot with impunity go. The rights which Christian discipleship demands are such as are good for all men, and no nation has ever suffered by reason of granting such liberties. Accordingly:

The rights of religious freedom herein declared shall be recognized and observed for all persons without distinction as to race, colour, sex, language, or religion, and without imposition of disabilities by virtue of legal provisions or administrative acts.

1. Every person has the right to determine his own faith and creed.

The right to determine faith and creed involves both the process whereby a person adheres to a belief and the process whereby he changes his belief. It includes the right to receive instruction and education.

This right becomes meaningful when man has the opportunity of access to information. Religious, social and political institutions have the obligation to permit the mature individual to relate himself to sources of information in such a way as to allow personal religious decision and belief.

The right to determine one's belief is limited by the right of parents to decide sources of information to which their children shall have access. In the process of reaching decisions, everyone ought to take into account his higher self-interests and the implications of his beliefs for the well-being of his fellow-men.

2. Every person has the right to express his religious beliefs in worship, teaching and practice, and to proclaim the implications of his beliefs for relationships in a social or political community.

The right of religious expression includes freedom of worship, both public and private; freedom to place information at the disposal of others by processes of teaching, preaching and persuasion; and freedom to pursue such activities as are dictated by conscience. It also includes freedom to express implications of belief for society and its government.

This right requires freedom from arbitrary limitation of religious expression in all means of communication, including speech, press, radio, motion pictures and art. Social and political institutions should grant immunity from discrimination and from legal disability on grounds of expressed religious conviction, at least to the point where recognized community interests are adversely affected.

Freedom of religious expression is limited by the rights of parents to determine the religious point of view to which their children shall be exposed. It is further subject to such limitations, prescribed by law, as are necessary to protect order and welfare, morals and the rights and freedoms of others. Each person must recognize the right of others to express their beliefs and must have respect for authority at all times, even when conscience forces him to take issue with the people who are in authority or with the position they advocate.

3. Every person has the right to associate with others and to organize with them for religious purposes.

This right includes freedom to form religious organizations, to seek membership in religious organizations, and to sever relationship with religious organizations.

It requires that the rights of association and organization guaranteed by a community to its members include the right of forming associations for religious purposes.

It is subject to the same limits imposed on all associations by non-discriminatory laws.

4. Every religious organization, formed or maintained by action in accordance with the rights of individual persons, has the right to determine its policies and practices for the accomplishment of its chosen purposes.

The rights which are claimed for the individual in his exercise of religious liberty become the rights of the religious organization, including the right to determine its faith and creed; to engage in religious worship, both in pubilc and private; to teach, educate, preach and persuade; to express implications of belief for society and government. To these will be added certain corporate rights which derive from the rights of individual persons, such as the right: to determine the form of organization, its government and conditions of membership; to select and train its own officers, leaders and workers; to publish and circulate religious literature; to carry on service and missionary activities at home and abroad; to hold property and to collect funds; to cooperate and to unite with other religious bodies at home and in other lands, including freedom to invite or to send personnel beyond national frontiers and to give or to receive financial assistance; to use such facilities, open to all citizens or associations, as will make possible the accomplishment of religious ends.

In order that these rights may be realized in social experience, the state must grant to religious organizations and their members the same rights which it grants to other organizations, including the right of self-government, of public-meeting, of speech, of press and publication, of holding property, of collecting funds, of travel, of ingress and egress, and generally of administering their own affairs.

The community has the right to require obedience to non-discriminatory laws passed in the interest of public order and well-being. In the exercise of its rights, a religious organization must respect the rights of other religious organizations and must safeguard the corporate and individual rights of the entire community.

The report of Section IV follows in full:

The World Council of Churches is met in its first Assembly at a time of critical international strain. The hopes of the recent war years and the apparent dawn of peace have been dashed. No adequate system for effecting peaceful change has been established, despite the earnest desire of millions. In numerous countries, human rights are being trampled under foot and liberty denied by political or economic systems. Exhaustion and disillusionment have combined with spiritual apathy to produce a moral vacuum which will be filled either by Christian faith or by despair or even hatred. Men are asking in fear and dismay what the future holds.

The Churches bear witness to all mankind that the world is in God's hands. His purpose may be thwarted and delayed, but it cannot be finally frustrated. This is the meaning of history which forbids despair or surrender to the fascinating belief in power as a solvent of human trouble.

War, being a consequence of the disregard of God, is not inevitable if man will turn to Him in repentance and obey His law. There is, then, no irresistible tide that is carrying man to destruction. Nothing is impossible with God.

While we know that wars sometimes arise from immediate causes which Christians seem unable to influence, we need not work blindly or alone. We are laborers together with God, Who in Christ has given us the way of overcoming demonic forces in history. Through the Churches, working together under His power, a fellowship is being developed which rises above those barriers of race, colour, class and nation that now set men against each other in conflict.

Every person has a place in the Divine purpose. Created by God in His image, the object of His redeeming love in Christ, he must be free to respond to God's calling. God is not indifferent to misery or deaf to human prayer and aspiration. By accepting His Gospel, men will find forgiveness for all their sins and receive power to transform their relations with their fellow-men.

Herein lies our hope and the ground of all our striving. It is required of us that we be faithful and obedient. The event is with God. Thus every man may serve the cause of peace, confident that—no matter what happens—he is neither lost nor futile, for the Lord God Omnipotent reigneth.

In this confidence we are one in proclaiming to mankind:

1. War is contrary to the will of God.

War as a method of settling disputes is incompatible with the teaching and example of our Lord Jesus Christ. The part which war plays in our present international life is a sin against God and a degradation of man. We recognize that the problem of war raises especially acute issues for Christians today. Warfare has greatly changed. War is now total and every man and woman is called for mobilization in war service. Moreover, the immense use of air forces and the discovery of atomic and other new weapons render widespread and indiscriminate destruction inherent in the whole conduct of modern war in a sense never experienced in past conflicts. In these circumstances the tradition of a just war, requiring a just cause and the use of just means, is now challenged. Law may require the sanction of force, but when war breaks out, force is used on a scale which tends to destroy the basis on which law exists.

Therefore the inescapable question arises—Can war now be an act of justice? We cannot answer this question unanimously, but three broad positions are maintained:

(1) There are those who hold that, even though entering a war may be a Christian's duty in particular circumstances, modern warfare, with its mass destruction, can never be an act of justice.

(2) In the absence of impartial supranational institutions, there are those who hold that military action is the ultimate sanction of the rule of law, and that citizens must be distinctly taught that it is their duty to defend the law by force if necessary.

(3) Others, again, refuse military service of all kinds, convinced that an absolute witness against war and for peace is for them the will of God, and they desire that the Church should speak to the same effect.

We must frankly acknowledge our deep sense of perplexity in face of these conflicting opinions, and urge upon all Christians the duty of wrestling continuously with the difficulties they raise and of praying humbly for God's guidance. We believe that there is a special call to theologians to consider the theological problems involved. In the meantime, the churches must continue to hold within their full fellowship all who sincerely profess such viewpoints as those set out above and are prepared to submit themselves to the will of God in the light of such guidance as may be vouchsafed to them.

On certain points of principle all are agreed. In the absence of any impartial agency for upholding justice, nations have gone to war in the belief that they were doing so. We hold that in international as in national life justice must be upheld. Nations must suppress their desire to save "face." This derives from pride, as unworthy as it is dangerous. The churches, for their part, have the duty of declaring those moral principles which obedience to God requires in war as in peace. They must not allow their spiritual and moral resources to be used by the state in war or in peace as a means of propagating an ideology or supporting a cause in which they cannot wholeheartedly concur. They must teach the duty of love and prayer for the enemy in time of war and of reconciliation between victor and vanquished after the war.

The churches must also attack the causes of war by promoting peaceful change and the pursuit of justice. They must stand for the maintenance of good faith and the honouring of the pledged word; resist the pretensions of imperialist power; promote the multilateral reduction of armaments; and combat indifference and despair in the face of the futility of war; they must point Christians to that spiritual resistance which grows from settled convictions widely held, themselves a powerful deterrent to war. A moral vacuum inevitably invites an aggressor.

We call upon the governments of those countries which were victors in the second world war to hasten the making of just peace treaties with defeated nations, allowing them to rebuild their political and economic systems for peaceable purposes; promptly to return prisoners of war to their homes; and to bring purges and trials for war crimes to a rapid end.

II. Peace requires an attack on the causes of conflict between powers.

The greatest threat to peace today comes from the division of the world into mutually suspicious and antagonistic blocs. This threat is all the greater because national tensions are confused by the clash of economic and political systems. Christianity cannot be equated with any of these. There are elements in all systems which we must condemn when they contravene the First Commandment, infringe basic human rights, and contain a potential threat to peace. We denounce all forms of tyranny, economic, political or religious, which deny liberty to men. We utterly oppose totalitarianism, wherever found, in which a state arrogates to itself the right of determining men's thoughts and actions instead of recognizing the rights of each individual to do God's will according to his conscience. In the same way, we oppose any church which seeks to use the power of the state to enforce religious conformity. We resist all endeavours to spread a system of thought or of economics by unscrupulous intolerance, suppression or persecution.

Similarly, we oppose aggressive imperialism—political, economic or cultural—whereby a nation seeks to use other nations or peoples for its own ends. We therefore protest against the exploitation of non-self-governing peoples for selfish purposes; the retarding of their progress towards self-government; and discrimination or segregation on the ground of race or colour.

A positive attempt must be made to ensure that competing economic systems such as communism, socialism and free enterprise may co-exist without leading to war. No nation has the moral right to determine its own economic policy without consideration for the economic needs of other nations and without recourse to international consultation. The churches have a responsibility to educate men to rise above the limitations of their national outlook and to view economic and political differences in the light of the Christian objective of ensuring to every man freedom from all economic or political bondage. Such systems exist to serve men, not men to serve them.

Christians must examine critically all actions of governments which increase tension or arouse misunderstanding, even unintentionally. Above all, they should withstand everything in the press, radio or school which inflames hatred or hostility between nations.

III. The nations of the world must acknowledge the rule of law.

Our Lord Jesus Christ taught that God, the Father of all, is Sovereign. We affirm, therefore, that no state may claim absolute sovereignty, or make laws without regard to the commandments of God and the welfare of mankind. It must accept its responsibility under the governance of God, and its subordination to law, within the society of nations.

As within the nation, so in their relations with one another, the authority of law must be recognized and established. International law clearly requires international institutions for its effectiveness. These institutions, if they are to command respect and obedience of nations, must come to grips with international problems on their own merits and not primarily in the light of national interests.

Such institutions are urgently needed today. History never stands still. New forces constantly emerge. Sporadic conflicts East and West, the attainment of independence by large masses of people, the apparent decline of European predominance, the clash of competing systems in Asia, all point to the inevitability of change. The United Nations was designed to assist in the settlement of difficulties and to promote friendly relations among the nations. Its purposes in these respects deserve the support of Christians. But unless nations surrender a greater measure of national sovereignty in the interest of the common good, they will be tempted to have recourse to war in order to enforce their claims.

The churches have an important part in laying that common foundation of moral conviction without which any system of law will break down. While pressing for more comprehensive and authoritative world organization, they should at present support immediate practical steps for fostering mutual understanding and goodwill among the nations, for promoting respect for international law and the establishment of the international institutions which are now possible. They should also support every effort to deal on a universal basis with the many specific questions of international concern which face mankind today, such as the use of atomic power, the multilateral reduction of armaments, and the provision of health services and food for all men. They should endeavour to secure that the United Nations be further developed to serve such purposes. They should insist that the domestic laws of each country conform to the principles of progressive international law, and that they recognize that recent demands to formulate principles of human rights reflect a new sense of international responsibility for the rights and freedoms of men.

IV. The observance of Human Rights and Fundamental Freedoms should be encouraged by domestic and international action.

The Church has always demanded freedom to obey God rather than men. We affirm that all men are equal in the sight of God and that the rights of men derive directly from their status as the children of God. It is presumptuous for the state to assume that it can grant or deny fundamental rights. It is for the state to embody those rights in its own legal system and to ensure their observance in practice. We believe, however, that there are no rights without duties. Man's freedom has its counterpart in man's responsibility, and each person has a responsibility towards his fellows in community.

We are profoundly concerned about evidence from many parts of the world of flagrant violations of human rights. Both individuals and groups are subjected to persecution and discrimination on grounds of race, colour, religion, culture or political conviction. Against such actions, whether of governments, officials, or the general public, the churches must take a firm and vigorous stand, through local action, co-operation with churches in other lands, and through international institutions of legal order. They must work for an ever wider and deeper understanding of what are the essential human rights if men are to be free to do the will of God.

At the present time, churches should support every endeavour to secure within an international bill of rights adequate safeguards for freedom of religion and conscience, including the right of all men to hold and change their faith, to express it in worship and practice, to teach and persuade others, and to decide on the religious education of their children. They should press for freedom of speech and expression, of association and assembly, the rights of the family, of freedom from arbitrary arrest, as well as all those other rights which the true freedom of man requires.

In the domestic and in the international sphere, they should support a fuller realization of human freedom through social legislation. They should protest against the expulsion of minorities. With all the resources at their disposal they should oppose enforced segregation on grounds of race and colour, working for the progressive recognition and application of this principle in every country. Above all it is essential that the churches observe these fundamental rights in their own membership and life, thus giving to others an example of what freedom means in practice.

V. The churches and all Christian people have obligations in the face of international disorder.

The churches are guilty of both indifference and failure. While they desire more open honesty and less self-righteousness among governments and all concerned with international relations, they cannot cast a first stone or excuse themselves for complacency.

Therefore, it is the duty of the Christian to pray for all men, especially for those in authority; to combat both hatred and resignation in regard to war; to support negotiation rather than primary reliance upon arms as an instrument of policy; and to sustain such national policies as in his judgment best reflect Christian principles. He should respond to the demand of the Christian vocation upon his life as a citizen, make sacrifices for the hungry and homeless, and, above all, win men for Christ and thus enlarge the bounds of the supra-national fellowship.

Within this fellowship, each church must eliminate discrimination among its members on unworthy grounds. It must educate them to view international policies in the light of their faith. Its witness to the moral law must be a warning to the state against unnecessary concession to expediency, and it must support leaders and those in authority in their endeavour to build the sure foundations of just world order.

The establishment of the World Council of Churches can be made of great moment for the life of the nations. It is a living expression of this fellowship, transcending race and nation, class and culture, knit together in faith, service and understanding. Its aim will be to hasten international reconciliation through its own members and through the co-operation of all Christian churches and of all men of goodwill. It will strive to see international differences in the light of God's design, remembering that normally there are Christians on both sides of every frontier. It should not weary in the effort to state the Christian understanding of the will of God and to promote its application to national and international policy.

For these purposes special agencies are needed. To this end the World Council of Churches and the International Missionary Council have formed the Commission of the Churches on International Affairs. The Assembly commends it to the interest and prayers of all Christian people.

Great are the tasks and fateful the responsibilities laid on Christians today. In our own strength we can do nothing; but our hope is in Christ and in the coming of His Kingdom. With Him is the victory and in Him we trust. We pray that we may be strengthened by the power of His might and used by Him for accomplishing His design among the nations. For He is the Prince of Peace and the Risen and Living Head of the Church.

IV

OTHER REPORTS

1. Report on Life and Work of Women

The committees on "Concerns of the Churches" submitted reports of their findings, which, likewise, the Assembly received and commended to "the churches for their serious consideration and appropriate action." Miss Saroe Chakko presented the conclusions of the group which had studied "The Life and Work of Women in the Church."

The Present Situation

The Church as the Body of Christ consists of men and women, created, as responsible persons, together to glorify God and to do His will. This truth, accepted in theory, is too often ignored in practice. In many countries and churches it is evident that the full co-operation of men and women in the service of Christ through the Church has not been achieved. Yet the Church as a whole, particularly at the present time of change and tension, needs the contribution of all its members in order to fulfill its task.

In many spheres the witness of the Church can be effectively made only by men and women in co-operation: for example, in the Christian home, in the duties of Christian citizenship, in secular occupations, in social and community life. Lack of space prevents discussion of these important matters. Certain problems, however, relating to the life and work of women in the Church call for special attention.

1. Voluntary Organizations. Organizations of women within the churches afford rich opportunities for service and self-expression, and a valuable training-ground in Christian leadership. They do a great deal of work in teaching, in social and missionary service, and in the deepening of the spiritual life. In order that these organizations may not become independent movements or substitutes for a wider participation in the life of the Church, they must be integrated into its total structure.

2. Governing Boards. We urge that the experience of women should be further utilized for the central life of the Church through their inclusion in Church courts, committees, and boards, where policy is framed and decisions affecting Church life as a whole are made. We look to the World Council of Churches and the national Christian councils to give a lead in this direction, by the appointment of qualified women as members of their committees and as staff members in responsible posts.

3. Professional Church Workers. In order to secure the services of educated and well qualified women, with a sense of vocation, for professional work in the Church, e.g., as deaconesses, directors of religious education, parish workers, missionaries, youth leaders, attention must be given to improvement in standards of training, remuneration, status and security of employment. The study and teaching of the Bible, theology, and kindred subjects would be enriched by the co-operation of women.

4. Ordination of Women. The churches are not agreed on the important question of admission of women to the full ministry. Some churches for theological reasons are not prepared to consider the question of such ordination; some find no objection in principle but see administrative or social difficulties; some permit partial but not full participation in the work of the ministry; in others women are eligible for all offices of the Church. Even in the last group, social custom and public opinion still create obstacles. In some countries a shortage of clergy raises urgent practical and spiritual problems. Those who desire the admission of women to the full ministry believe that until this is achieved the Church will not come to full health and power. We are agreed that this whole subject requires further careful and objective study.

Information and guidance in connection with these and other problems might usefully be provided by the World Council of Churches, and it is therefore urged that the Life and Work of Women in the Church remain one of its particular concerns.

Recommendations

1. That the Interim Report on "The Life and Work of Women in the Church" be re-published with necessary corrections and additions.
2. That a longer report on "The Life and Work of Women in the Church" be prepared.
3. That an adequate supply of information about women's activities be provided through the Ecumenical Press Service and other channels.
4. That a greater number of women be chosen to serve on the Commissions, the major Committees and the Secretariat of the World Council of Churches.
5. That a Commission composed of men and women be appointed, with adequate budget and executive leadership, to give further consideration to the Life and Work of Women in the Church and to give guidance on important issues.

2. Report on the Laity

The committee on "The Significance of the Laity in the Church" reported as follows:

The Urgency of the Present Situation

The Committee was appointed to meet the wide-spread need expressed by the churches in many parts of the world for a consideration of the urgent question of the right use and training of the laity in the service of the Church. The evidence which has come before us makes it abundantly clear that while in some churches the laity are being used to a considerable extent, and some training provided, every church ought to be deeply dissatisfied with the present situation. The laity are there, and are waiting to become effective as members of the Church. It is at present incumbent upon the churches to make it clear to the laity that they have an essential place in the life and tasks of the Church. The lay members of the Church, however, are conscious of the fact that they are largely ill-equipped and that it is becoming apparent that the significance of the laity for the Church has new aspects which are being explored in experiments in various countries in Europe and in the United States. Many of these are described in one of the publications of the Ecumenical Institute.

Laity in the Church

There are obvious reasons why the churches should awaken to the importance of their lay members, both men and women, for every aspect of their life and work, in a way which they have not done hitherto.

The laity constitutes more than ninety-nine per cent. of the Church.

In the customary work of the Church (preaching, evangelising, teaching and social work) the latent spiritual resources of the rank and file are urgently needed. It is commonly assumed that this need is widely and sufficiently recognized, but in fact it is not.

There is, however, another aspect of this problem of the laity of even greater import for the Church in its relation to the world. Lay men and women spend the greater part of their lives in their homes, their occupations, and the public life of the community. It is essential that the churches should take note of this. For it is through the laity that the Church has the greatest and most natural opportunity to show in and to the world that the message of the Bible, and all that the Church is committed to by obedience to its Lord, are relevant to the real problems and needs of man in every age, and not least in our own. Only by the witness of a spiritually intelligent and active laity can the Church meet the modern world in its actual perplexities and life situations. Since one of the hard facts of the present time is that millions of people think of the Church as floating above the modern world and entirely out of real touch with it, the importance of this simple pronouncement cannot easily be over-estimated.

Basic Needs

The laity requires strengthening through biblical and theological study and discussion with special reference to the bearing of Christian faith upon daily life. This will include the study of "Christian stewardship," which means nothing less than faith in action. Without such a theological understanding of stewardship it may easily degenerate into a well-meant activism.

We need to think what it means to speak of the Church as "a royal priesthood, a holy nation, a peculiar people" (I Peter ii, 9), and as the "Body of Christ" (Ephesians iv, 16), to which every member contributes in his measure.

Laymen's retreats have proved of especial benefit, for it is not simply a question of more adequate training, or even of a new approach. It implies the age-old necessity of a complete personal commitment on the part of every member to Christ and His Church.

The Laity in the World

We have already indicated the great importance of this aspect of the problem as it presents itself to the Church today. We are thinking of the lay member of the Church not as a worker in the congregation, but as one living and working in the wider community. The question to be faced there is this: how can members of the Church be enabled to see the bearing of their Christian faith on their life in their occupation? How can men and women who stand in the stress and problems of life be helped to see how they can obey just there the will of God? The fact is that in their occupations, whether they are doctors, lawyers, industrialists, farmers, steel-workers, etc., they live in an increasingly secularized world. How to live and work there as Christians, as members of the Church; how to give witness to their faith, how to think about the bearing of the Christian faith on the economic, social, political and cultural realities and backgrounds, is for most of them a mystery. They are left to their own wits, which means that they largely live a life divided into two separate compartments, resulting in frustration and the weakening of spiritual vitality. The Church is for them not their source of strength and light, but a place for the satisfaction of a religious need isolated from the everyday realities of a modern world moulded by the effects of industrialism, technics and standardization. This is the more disquieting from the Christian point of view because it is in flat contradiction of the fact that the Lord Jesus Christ claims the whole of life and, therefore, the Christian faith necessarily demands expression in all realms of life.

It is cause for thankfulness that through the work of the World Council of Churches the churches have been summoned to realize and express their responsibility in social and international life and to recognize the need for a new kind of evangelistic approach. In the laity the Church has a body of men and women in which the real daily meeting of the Church and the world on its own ground takes place. This implies that the Church must see the great significance of giving guidance to her laity, trying to understand where exactly the intellectual, moral and religious issues lie which they have to face, and so giving them by these efforts the certainty that they are not isolated individuals, but are sustained by the experience of living and working as members of the living Body.

A vast field of new work opens up for the Church which will give a new direction to the expression of its evangelistic, cultural, social and political responsibility in the world. Especially in the field of missions, unparalleled opportunities are open for the participation of the laity. The Ecumenical Institute at Bossey, and the movements in various countries which have begun to take to heart this new endeavour to relate the Christian faith to the realities of life, are hopeful beginnings. It would be of great importance if this vision of the laity as part of the militant and living Church could receive adequate attention in the churches and the World Council.

Recommendation

In furtherance of this, this Committee looks with favour upon the proposal that has come from a conference of lay leaders at the Ecumenical Institute for not less than three area meetings, largely of laymen, for the purpose of further study of efforts for enlisting the full lay power of the Church, and the Committee recommends that the Central Committee of the World Council of Churches be asked to study this proposal and, if approved, to lay the plans for such meetings, including the designation of the areas (e.g., America, Asia, Africa, Europe), to draw up a skeleton outline for a programme for all such meetings, and to indicate how such gatherings shall be financed.

3. Christian Approach to the Jews

Bishop Angus Dun of the Protestant Episcopal Church presented the report of the committee on "The Christian Approach to the Jews."

Introduction

A concern for the Christian approach to the Jewish people confronts us inescapably, as we meet together to look with open and penitent eyes on man's disorder and to rediscover together God's eternal purpose for His Church. This concern is ours because it is first a concern of God made known to us in Christ. No people in His one world have suffered more bitterly from the disorder of man than the Jewish people. We cannot forget that we meet in a land from which one hundred ten thousand Jews were taken to be murdered. Nor can we forget that we meet only five years after the extermination of six million Jews. To the Jews our God has bound us in a special solidarity linking our destinies together in His design. We call upon all our churches to make this concern their own as we share with them the results of our too brief wrestling with it.

1. The Church's commission to preach the Gospel to all men

All of our churches stand under the commission of our common Lord, "Go ye into all the world and preach the Gospel to every creature." The fulfillment of this commission requires that we include the Jewish people in our evangelistic task.

2. The special meaning of the Jewish people for Christian faith

In the design of God, Israel has a unique position. It was Israel with whom God made His covenant by the call of Abraham. It was Israel to whom God revealed His name and gave His law. It was to Israel that He sent His Prophets with their message of judgment and grace. It was Israel to whom He promised the coming of His Messiah. By the history of Israel God prepared the manger in which in the fullness of time He put the Redeemer of all mankind, Jesus Christ. The Church has received this spiritual heritage from Israel and is therefore in honour bound to render it back in the light of the Cross. We have, therefore, in humble conviction to proclaim to the Jews, "The Messiah for whom you wait has come." The promise has been fulfilled by the coming of Jesus Christ.

For many the continued existence of a Jewish people which does not acknowledge Christ is a divine mystery which finds its only sufficient explanation in the purpose of God's unchanging faithfulness and mercy. (Romans xi, 25-29.)

3. Barriers to be overcome

Before our churches can hope to fulfill the commission laid upon us by our Lord there are high barriers to be overcome. We speak here particularly of the barriers which we have too often helped to build and which we alone can remove.

We must acknowledge in all humility that too often we have failed to manifest Christian love towards our Jewish neighbours, or even a resolute will for common social justice. We have failed to fight with all our strength the age-old disorder of man which anti-semitism represents. The churches in the past have helped to foster an image of the Jews as the sole enemies of Christ, which has contributed to anti-semitism in the secular world. In many lands virulent anti-semitism still threatens and in other lands the Jews are subjected to many indignities.

We call upon all the churches we represent to denounce anti-semitism, no matter what its origin, as absolutely irreconcilable with the profession and practice of the Christian faith. Anti-semitism is a sin against God and man.

Only as we give convincing evidence to our Jewish neighbours that we seek for them the common rights and dignities which God wills for His children, can we come to such a meeting with them as would make it possible to share with them the best which God has given us in Christ.

4. The Christian witness to the Jewish people

In spite of the universality of our Lord's commission and of the fact that the first mission of the Church was to the Jewish people, our churches have with rare exceptions failed to maintain that mission. This responsibility should not be left largely to independent agencies. The carrying on of this mission by special agencies has often meant the singling out of the Jews for special missionary attention, even in situations where they might well have been included in the normal ministry of the Church. It has also meant in many cases that the converts are forced into segregated spiritual fellowship rather than being included and welcomed in the regular membership of the Church.

Owing to this failure our churches must consider the responsibility for missions to the Jews as a normal part of parish work, especially in those countries where Jews are members of the general community. Where there is no indigenous church or where the indigenous church is insufficient for the task it may be necessary to arrange for a special missionary ministry from abroad.

Because of the unique inheritance of the Jewish people, the churches should make provisions for the education of ministers specially fitted for this task. Provision should also be made for Christian literature to interpret the Gospel to Jewish people.

Equally, it should be made clear to church members that the strongest argument in winning others for Christ is the radiance and contagion of victorious living and the outgoing of God's love expressed in personal human contacts. As this is expressed and experienced in a genuine Christian fellowship and community the impact of the Gospel will be felt. For such a fellowship there will be no difference between a converted Jew and other church members, all belonging to the same Church and fellowship through Jesus Christ. But the converted Jew calls for particular tenderness and full acceptance just because his coming into the Church carries with it often a deeply wounding break with family and friends.

In reconstruction and relief activities the churches must not lose sight of the plight of Christians of Jewish origin, in view of their special suffering. Such provision must be made for their aid as will help them to know that they are not forgotten in the Christian fellowship.

5. The emergence of Israel as a state

The establishment of the state "Israel" adds a political dimension to the Christian approach to the Jews and threatens to complicate anti-semitism with political fears and enmities.

On the political aspects of the Palestine problem and the complex conflict of "rights" involved we do not undertake to express a judgment. Nevertheless, we appeal to the nations to deal with the problem not as one of expediency—political, strategic or economic—but as a moral and spiritual question that touches a nerve centre of the world's religious life.

Whatever position may be taken towards the establishment of a Jewish state and towards the "rights" and "wrongs" of Jews and Arabs, of Hebrew Christians and Arab Christians involved, the churches are in duty bound to pray and work for an order in Palestine as just as may be in the midst of our human disorder; to provide within their power for the relief of the victims of this warfare without discrimination; and to seek to influence the nations to provide a refuge for "Displaced Persons" far more generously than has yet been done.

We conclude this report with the recommendations which arise out of our first exploratory consideration of this "concern" of the churches.

1. To the member churches of the World Council we recommend:

that they seek to recover the universality of our Lord's commission by including the Jewish people in their evangelistic work;

that they encourage their people to seek for brotherly contact with and understanding of their Jewish neighbours, and co-operation in agencies combatting misunderstanding and prejudice;

that in mission work among the Jews they scrupulously avoid all unworthy pressures or inducements;

that they give thought to the preparation of ministers well-fitted to interpret the Gospel to Jewish people and to the provision of literature which will aid in such a ministry.

2. To the World Council of Churches we recommend:

that it should give careful thought as to how it can best stimulate and assist the member churches in the carrying out of this aspect of their mission;

that it give careful consideration to the suggestion made by the International Missionary Council that the World Council of Churches share with it in a joint responsibility for the Christian approach to the Jews;

that it be resolved that, in receiving the report of this Committee, the Assembly recognize the need for more detailed study by the World Council of Churches of the many complex problems which exist in the field of relations between Christians and Jews, and in particular, of the following:

(a) the historical and present factors which have contributed to the growth and persistence of anti-semitism, and the most effective means of combatting this evil;

(b) the need and opportunity in this present historical situation for the development of co-operation between Christians and Jews in civic and social affairs;

(c) the many and varied problems created by establishment of a State of Israel in Palestine.

4. Reconstruction and Inter-Church Aid

The committee on Christian Reconstruction and Inter-Church Aid made the following report:

The Committee met on five occasions, and at each of the meetings the Liaison Officer reported the proceedings of the Alternates' Committee on the same subject, and, at its final meeting, the Committee recorded its appreciation of the valuable help it had derived from the deliberations and reports of the Alternates' Committee.

Reconstruction and Inter-Church Aid

The Committee commenced its work by a review of reconstruction achievements and continuing needs. After a comprehensive statement by Dr. J. Hutchinson Cockburn, Director of the Department of Reconstruction and Inter-Church Aid, the Committee received oral reports from Spain, France,

Germany, Czecho-slovakia, Poland, Belgium, Hungary, Holland, Norway and Greece. The burden of all these reports was a grateful recognition of the remarkable contributions towards church reconstruction that have been made since 1945 by the churches of various countries, acting either directly or through such inter-church bodies as Church World Service (USA) and Christian Reconstruction in Europe (UK). The Committee had to take into account that while much had been achieved, very much remained to be done. It considered that in view of the amount of reconstruction work already achieved, and the improvement in the general economic situation in Europe, some revision in the balance of future reconstruction programmes might be necessary. It believed that the Department might well consider whether the listed number of countries still needing help, and the number of projects to be assisted, should not be reduced. It was generally felt that there is an urgent continuing need for assistance in the maintenance of pastors, in the provision of theological training, and in the equipment of Christian institutions.

The Committee felt that while the need for material aid still continues, the emphasis of the future work of the Department should more and more take into account the basic and continuing necessity of inter-church aid. On details of policy that had been discussed under the Agenda, the Committee decided to take no definite action, but to refer such matters to the Department. It did, however, take into consideration the area of operation of reconstruction as a World Council of Churches project. The Anglican Bishop in Egypt made a special appeal for those churches, particularly in the Middle East, which benefited neither from the present European operations of the Reconstruction Department, nor from the channels of aid operated in the Far East through liaison with the International Missionary Council. He emphasized that by the withdrawal of numbers of Europeans from the Middle East, many of the churches outside Europe would lose the support that they had hitherto relied upon, and that some extension of the area of concern of the Department was essential if they were to be kept in the circle of fellowship and aid. The Committee agreed to refer to the proper committee of the World Council of Churches the consideration of the future areas of operation of the Reconstruction Department.

It also agreed that while material reconstruction in certain areas and in certain projects continues to be essential, it should not be allowed to obscure the developing need for spiritual regeneration and inter-church aid.

Prisoners of War

The Committee received a report from Professor Courvoisier, Chairman of the World Council of Churches Prisoners of War Commission, and resolved:

1. That the Council records its gratitude for the remarkable work of the Commission during the last eight years.
2. That, with the release and repatriation of POWs, the decision of the Commission to wind up its activities be approved, provided that the Refugee Commission assumes operational responsibility for any continuing problems of the rehabilitation and resettlement of those who return to their homes.
3. That a nucleus Commission should remain in being to meet as required, and consider the needs of those not yet released, maintain liaison with the churches of those who voluntarily remain in their countries of captivity, and to hold a watching brief for POW legislation and provision, particularly in regard to the Geneva Convention and kindred matters affecting legislation and agreements.

Refugees and Uprooted Peoples

The Committee then proceeded to a consideration of the problem of refugees.

Resolutions were received from the Methodist Conference of Great Britain and from the World's YWCA, emphasizing the need to give urgent priority to the refugee problem. It was agreed that these resolutions should be sent to Section IV with the request that this Section should draft a resolution in the general terms remitted to them.

The Committee then considered appeals which had been submitted to it from the Bishop of Jerusalem, and the United Nations' Mediator in Palestine, on behalf of refugees in the Middle East, and recommended the following resolution to the Assembly:

> The World Council of Churches, recalling that the origin of the Refugee Division was the concern of the churches for Jewish refugees, notes with especially deep concern the recent extension of the refugee problem to the Middle East by the flight from their homes in the Holy Land of not less than three hundred fifty thousand Arab and other refugees.
>
> It receives, with an urgent sense of its Christian duty, the appeal which originally came from Christian leaders in Palestine. It records appreciation of the prompt co-operation offered by the U.N. Mediator in Palestine with the projects of relief initiated by the churches and inter-church bodies, and in commending the actions in this field already taken resolves:
>
> to urge the churches to include in their provision for refugees additional emergency help for the urgent situation in the Middle East, and to channel this help in such a way as both to achieve a distinctive and maximum Christian effort in this field, and to ensure its co-ordination with the measures initiated,
>
> to recommend that, through its Refugee Commission the World Council of Churches should:
>
> 1. appeal for money, food, medical supplies, and blankets;
> 2. in conjunction with the International Missionary Council, appoint a special Field Representative to co-ordinate Christian action with the Mediator's programme;
> 3. urge and assist all Christians in Palestine and neighbouring countries to co-operate in this work in every way practicable.

The Committee expressed the view that Christian consideration of the refugee problem should not be confined to Europe and the Middle East. While recognizing that the operations of the Council's Refugee Commission were restricted to this area, it urged that the desperate plight of millions of uprooted peoples in the Far East should also be acknowledged as the concern and in the giving of the churches.

It studied with concern the working document "The Refugee Problem Today" and with the view of making as widely known as possible the alarming facts presented therein, resolved to ask the Council to publish this document with any current amendments, for wide circulation. It records the startling fact that, despite the repatriation of seven million displaced persons since the end of the war, the refugee problem is substantially larger today than it was in 1945. It especially deplores the fact that this increase has been mainly brought about by the expulsion of more than ten million persons from their homes by post-war Allied action. It would express to the Assembly its views that in terms of human misery and of deprivation of human rights, this problem is one of the most serious in post-war Europe, and that a failure to solve it not only involves untold misery for the victims, but seriously adds to the causes of international friction and war.

In view of the facts that only one million out of at least twelve million uprooted persons are at present eligible for United Nations' care under the constitution of the International Refugee Organization, and that the vast majority excluded from IRO care are exiled and homeless as the direct consequence of action by one or more member governments of United Nations, the Committee urges that strong representations be made to the United Nations, calling upon them to take effective steps to care for all these exiles, either by amendment of the constitution of IRO, and a consequent increase in its budget, or in some other effective way.

The Chairman invited Miss Marjorie Bradford, who was present as an official observer for the IRO, to speak to the Committee. Miss Bradford referred to the regression of public support for refugee work, pointing out that the resources and operations of some of the War Relief agencies had declined. She felt that the only enduring hope of continuing support for what is clearly a long-term need was through the churches and their agencies. Miss Bradford urged the Committee to think of the refugee not only as the object of compassion, but as a desirable and useful citizen in any country, and expressed the view that a better appreciation of the quality and character of the average refugee was essential if resettlement was to develop as it should. She also emphasized the religious and social importance of respecting the family unit. The Committee expressed its appreciation of the cordial working relationships which exist between IRO and Christian agencies operating in the field of refugee work.

The Committee decided that the refugee situation is so alarming in its size and implications, and so direct a challenge to Christian action, that the most urgent attention of the Assembly [should] be sought in this matter. Accordingly, it submits the following resolutions:

I. The Assembly of the World Council of Churches, having studied the continuing needs of reconstruction work, calls upon the member churches to support even more adequately the projects of the Department of Reconstruction and Inter-Church Aid of the World Council.

II. Sub-committee (d) of Committee IV, having reviewed the refugee situation, and being deeply concerned at its size and implications, and conscious of the need for urgent Christian action in this field, particularly in view of developing opportunities for resettlement, urges that, for the time being, the highest priority be given to the Refugee Division in the budgetary provision of the World Council.

5. Youth at Amsterdam

One hundred young people came from forty-eight countries to attend the Assembly as observers. They applied themselves to the study themes and listened to the proceedings. At the sessions they occupied seats reserved for them. They bore witness to their convictions and enthusiasms by frequent applause, even if they could not vote, and in this way contributed their quota of liveliness to the occasion. One expressed the sense of all, no doubt, when he said, "We want to have all the responsibility in the ecumenical movement we can be trusted with." Philip Potter of the Methodist Church in Dominica, a ministerial student at that time in Richmond College (England), presented their report on "Youth and the Assembly." In part, he said:

We, the Youth Delegation, welcome warmly this opportunity of expressing our deep gratitude for the privilege given us to take an active part in the First Assembly of the World Council of Churches. We represent many thousands of young people who are seeking in loyalty to Christ to serve the Church in the world, and who, during the last year or two, have been giving much prayer and thought to the Assembly. Indeed, we can claim to be a really representative group. There are one hundred of us who come from forty-eight different countries and who belong to a very wide variety of confessions. Further, there is a fair balance of sexes and callings among us which indicates more clearly the actual situation in the churches from which we come. We have lived and eaten together in the same place during these days and have realized the depth of our fellowship in Christ and with each other.

The Youth Delegation has been in session since August 20, and has spent much time, under the guidance of our Chairmen and Secretaries, in discussing the place of the Youth Department within the World Council of Churches. . . .

One of our first acts, on assembling together, was to read again the story of the first Pentecost. There we were reminded of the prophecy of Joel: "In the last days, saith the Lord, I shall pour forth my Spirit upon all flesh; your sons and daughters shall prophesy; your young men shall see visions and your old men dream dreams." In these words we read the promise of God to us all even as we waited upon Him in prayer and listened to His challenge to proclaim salvation to mankind. God has called us to another Pentecost here, not as spectacular perhaps as the first outpouring of His Spirit, but no less real and powerful. We young people have, throughout this Assembly, been waiting upon God and have not ceased to make intercession on your behalf that God may use both you and us in His great design for His Church and His world.

We want, therefore, to assure you that even though we have been aware of the rather considerable difference in years and experience between you, the fathers, and ourselves, we have nevertheless felt our oneness with you in the same Lord and in the same task. Your dreams and our visions find their source and center in the one Holy Spirit who united us in our diversities and who gives to us that humble love and obedience, which was the very character of Jesus Christ, our God and Saviour. . . .

. . . Like you, we have had some sessions on the main theme of the Assembly, "Man's Disorder and God's Design." During the last few months the Study Department has furnished us, not only with the preparatory volumes, but also with summaries of these volumes and brief statements on the four principal subjects—for all of which we are very thankful. Certain significant emphases emerged from our discussions.

Throughout we kept before our minds the centrality of God's Design, already mightily accomplished in Jesus Christ and appropriated by faith in Him and through the fellowship of the Holy Spirit. So that, although we were brought face to face with the grim disorder of mankind and the immense difficulty of making Christ known to men and accepted by them, we were all the time aware that Jesus Christ is Lord, to the glory of God the Father. Just because, too, Jesus Christ was the center of our thought we were able to hear His insistent call to be His witnesses in all the world. This sense of assurance in the ultimate victory of God's purposes and of urgency to make them known by life and witness, took away from us the prevailing despair and apathy. . . .

But along with the emphasis on Jesus Christ as Lord and Saviour, went our conviction that the Church, which is the agent of His redemptive purpose in the world, was in very urgent need of renewal both in life and thought. We cannot express too strongly how pained we are by the divisions of the churches. At every point in our discussions, whether on the Universal Church, the Church's witness to God's design, the Church and the disorder of society or international affairs, we were brought up against the inability of the churches to be clear and authoritative in these matters because of their disunity on the basic issue of the nature of the Church. . . . We are convinced that the time has come when the churches must speak to each other in love of the stumbling-blocks which mar our fellowship and which drive men and women, and especially youth, away from us.

We are also concerned about the general lack of Biblical preaching and teaching in the churches. . . . Nothing but a rediscovery of the Biblical view of life will enable a disordered world to learn and follow God's design.

However, we are sure that men cannot be persuaded to obey God's will unless they see in the churches that that will is for them in their condition and is being gloriously worked out there. The churches must be the centre of the living community of persons. This imperative task involves the continued loving witness of Christians in their daily work and intercourse with people. It is here that we young people feel that our vocation lies, and we urge the churches to a far more determined effort to encourage every Christian man and woman to pursue his and her evangelistic task.

We feel strongly that the way to finding new means of coming together as churches is not only through Faith and Order conversations, but most emphatically through corporate evangelistic endeavours. We need, not so much ecumenical understanding as ecumenical obedience. . . .

We gave particular attention to the plight of youth in the present disorder of the world. We were forced to lay far more emphasis than the Assembly Commission thought fit on the breakdown of family life. For we believe that the family is the first training-ground in mutual responsibility and understanding, and for the transcendent values of life. Anyhow, the communists in Russia are at present recognizing the primary place of proper family life for the stability of the classless society. A generation of youth is growing up today with a scanty sense of loyalty and responsibility. Moreover, we are persuaded that the present educational method with its pre-occupation with objective research and efficiency has failed to teach standards of values and to encourage responsible thought. The group which discussed "The Church's Witness to God's Design" was very deeply concerned that the evangelization of youth was being made extremely difficult for the spiritual demands of life are treated as merely optional. . . .

There can be no doubt that the task of the churches in the evangelization of the young people of this generation is an immense one. We are sure, therefore, that it cannot be attempted by the senior members of the churches without the young people, or *vice versa*. . . .

When the constitution of the Youth Department was in process of debate here someone stated that youth could be the explosive element in the Church. Very true. But we are reminded of the words of the sage bishop who, when called a "back number," retorted, "Yes, I am a back number. But, remember, you take back numbers to light the fire." . . .

What, then, is the place of youth in the ecumenical movement? Of course, we have already taken an active part in the movement in one form or another, whether in the WSCF, YMCA, YWCA, or other inter-denominational societies. And the work of such leaders of them as Drs. John R. Mott and Visser 't Hooft in the formation of this Council is well known, and we are humbly proud to be inheritors of such a crusading tradition. It is this same spirit of crusade that we are endeavoring to bring to the ecumenical movement. Many of us were delegates to the Second World Conference of Christian Youth at Oslo last year. Some of us have been among the more than three hundred young people from many lands who have been in the first eight work camps to be organized by the World Council of Churches through the Youth Department. We value very highly this vital experience of living and working with so many others in common projects of service in distressed areas of various countries, and are making plans for more widespread work of this kind in the coming years. . . .

. . . With you, therefore, we resolve to go forth from here with the vision of the compelling and consuming task before us, and yet with the firm assurance that our sufficiency is of God.

The young people were not more successful when it came to saying with brevity what they thought than the professors and the bishops who put out the official reports of the Assembly. Ecumenism seemed to run to prolixity, possibly to the hurt of the cause. Perhaps this was because it attempted to comprehend the whole world, a vast and involved subject indeed when approached from the standpoint of social and political disorder in the year 1948. But it was agreed that they had got together a very readable report of what they saw and felt at Amsterdam. No doubt it was, in some ways, the most significant statement presented. Even if it revealed the same bewilderment reflected by their elders and showed the authors headed for as yet unrealized perplexities and bafflements, it at least avoided the cocksureness to which youth is subject and manifested a becoming spirit of humility. In any case, it was the ecumenical movement of the future learning how to talk and doing very well. Those who tarried to listen knew that they were hearing voices to which time would soon give authority.

6. Program and Administration

The Committee on Program and Administration had found that the budget for the World Council of Churches during its first year would run close to a half-million dollars (later reduced somewhat), not including the requirements for relief, and urged that the money to meet it be sought of the churches as such, rather than of individual contributors, the Council being an organization of the denominations which should qualify immediately for the responsibility they had contracted, financially and otherwise. In a separate meeting the Chairman, Bishop G. Bromley Oxnam of New York, informed the delegates from the

United States that, because of the depressed economic state of the rest of the world, the churches of their country would be expected to provide approximately four-fifths of the required amount, which would be equivalent to about eight one-thousandths of their own annual current expenses, and found them willing to recommend to their several boards the assumption of this disproportionate part of the burden, until improved business conditions abroad were favorable for a readjustment.

7. Adoption of the Constitution

The Committee on Constitution, Rules and Regulations recommended certain amendments to the provisional constitution, which the Assembly adopted *nem. con.* (See Appendix A for text of the constitution.)

The Constitution vested in the Assembly power "to appoint officers of the World Council of Churches and of the Assembly at its discretion" and stated that the Central Committee should "consist of the President, or Presidents, of the World Council, together with not more than ninety members chosen by the Assembly from among persons whom the churches have appointed as members of the Assembly." During the latter part of the period between Utrecht and Amsterdam, there had been five simultaneous Presidents of the Provisional Committee. The Assembly continued this arrangement by re-electing Dr. Marc Boegner, Dr. Geoffrey Fisher, Dr. Erling Eidem, and Dr. Germanos Strenopoulos and choosing Dr. G. Bromley Oxnam for the vacancy created when Dr. John R. Mott declined to allow his renomination, and added to the presidium a sixth memeber, Dr. Tsu-Chen Chao.

The Central Committee consisted then of the six Presidents, the Honorary President, Dr. Mott, who had been so designated upon retirement from active duty, and the prescribed elective members. (See Appendix for list of the Central Committee.)

8. Statement of the Nature of the Council (Adopted)

The Assembly adopted the following statement regarding its own understanding of itself—its nature and its assumed obligations:

The World Council of Churches is composed of churches which acknowledge Jesus Christ as God and Saviour. They find their unity in Him. They have not to create their unity; it is the gift of God. But they know that it is their duty to make common cause in the search for the expression of that unity in work and in life. The Council desires to serve the churches, which are its constituent members, as an instrument whereby they may bear witness together to their common allegiance to Jesus Christ, and cooperate in matters requiring united action. But the Council is far from desiring to usurp any of the functions which already belong to its constituent churches, or to control them, or to legislate for them, and is indeed prevented by its constitution from doing so. Moreover, while earnestly seeking fellowship in thought and action for all its members, the Council disavows any thought of becoming a single unified church-structure independent of the churches which have joined in constituting the Council, or a structure dominated by a centralized administrative authority.

The purpose of the Council is to express its unity in another way. Unity arises out of the love of God in Jesus Christ, which, binding the constituent churches to him, binds them to one another. It is the earnest desire of the Council that the churches may be bound closer to Christ and therefore closer to one another. In the bond of his love, they will desire continually to pray for one another and to strengthen one another, in worship and in witness, bearing one another's burdens and so fulfilling the law of Christ.

With respect to public pronouncements, the Council regards it as an essential part of its responsibility to address its own constituent members as occasion may arise, on matters which require united attention in the realm of thought or action. Further, important issues may arise which radically affect the Church and society. While it is certainly undesirable that the Council should issue such pronouncements often, and on many subjects, there will certainly be a clear obligation for the Council to speak out when vital issues concerning all churches and the whole world are at stake. But such statements will have no authority save that which they carry by their own truth and wisdom. They will not be binding on any church unless that church has confirmed them, and made them its own. But the Council will only issue such statements in the light of God's revelation in Jesus Christ, the Lord, and the living Head of the Church; and in dependence on the power of the Holy Spirit, and in penitence and faith.

9. The Message from Amsterdam

The message adopted by the Assembly had been prepared by a committee under the chairmanship of Bishop Berggrav of Norway, who, in presenting it, said it was addressed "to our fellow-Christians in Christ who wait for his word. It is a letter to Christians, not for headlines in the press, of what is on our hearts. We have said only what we had a good conscience to say. Pray God to use even this small voice."

The World Council of Churches, meeting at Amsterdam, sends this message of greeting to all who are in Christ, and to all who are willing to hear.

We bless God our Father, and our Lord Jesus Christ Who gathers together in one the children of God that are scattered abroad. He has brought us here together at Amsterdam. We are one in acknowledging Him as our God and Saviour. We are divided from one another not only in matters of faith, order and tradition, but also by pride of nation, class and race. But Christ has made us His own, and He is not divided. In seeking Him we find one another. Here at Amsterdam we have committed ourselves afresh to Him, and have covenanted with one another in constituting this World Council of Churches. We intend to stay together. We call upon Christian congregations everywhere to endorse and fulfill this covenant in their relations one with another. In thankfulness to God we commit the future to Him.

When we look to Christ, we see the world as it is—His world, to which He came and for which He died. It is filled both with great hopes and also with disillusionment and despair. Some nations are rejoicing in new freedom and power, some are bitter because freedom is denied them, some are paralysed by division, and everywhere there is an undertone of fear. There are millions who are hungry, millions who have no home, no country and no hope. Over all mankind hangs the peril of total war. We have to accept God's judgment upon us for our share in the world's guilt. Often we have tried to serve God and Mammon, put other loyalties before loyalty to Christ, confused the Gospel with our own economic or national or racial interests, and feared war more than we have hated it. As we have talked with each other here, we have begun to understand how our separation has prevented us from receiving correction from one another in Christ. And because we lacked this correction, the world has often heard from us not the Word of God but the words of men.

But there is a word of God for our world. It is that the world is in the hands of the living God, Whose will for it is wholly good; that in Jesus Christ, His incarnate Word, Who lived and died and rose from the dead, God has broken the power of evil once for all, and opened for everyone the gate into freedom and joy in the Holy Spirit; that the final judgment on all human history and on every human deed is the judgment of the merciful Christ; and that the end of history will be the triumph of His Kingdom, where alone we shall understand how much God has loved the world. This is God's unchanging word to the world. Millions of our fellowmen have never heard it. As we are met here from many lands, we pray God to stir up His whole Church to make this Gospel known to the whole world, and to call on all men to believe in Christ, to live in His love and to hope for His coming.

Our coming together to form a World Council of Churches will be vain unless Christians and Christian congregations everywhere commit themselves to the Lord of the Church in a new effort to seek together, where they live, to be His witnesses and servants among their neighbours. We have to remind ourselves and all men that God has put down the mighty from their seats and exalted the humble and meek. We have to learn afresh together to speak boldly in Christ's name both to those in power and to the people, to oppose terror, cruelty and race discrimination, to stand by the outcast, the prisoner and the refugee. We have to make of the Church in every place a voice for those who have no voice, and a home where every man will be at home. We have to learn afresh together what is the duty of the Christian man or woman in industry, in agriculture, in politics, in the professions and in the home. We have to ask God to teach us together to say No and to say Yes in truth. No to all that flouts the love of Christ, to every system, every programme and every person that treats any man as though he were an irresponsible thing or a means of profit, to the defenders of injustice in the name of order, to those who sow the seeds of war or urge war as inevitable; Yes, to all that conforms to the love of Christ, to all who seek for justice, to the peacemakers, to all who hope, fight and suffer for the cause of man, to all who—even without knowing it—look for new heavens and a new earth wherein dwelleth righteousness.

It is not in man's power to banish sin and death from the earth, to create the unity of the Holy Catholic Church, to conquer the hosts of

Satan. But it is within the power of God. He has given us at Easter the certainty that His purpose will be accomplished. But, by our acts of obedience and faith, we can on earth set up signs which point to the coming victory. Till the day of that victory, our lives are hid with Christ in God, and no earthly disillusion or distress or power of hell can separate us from Him. As those who wait in confidence and joy for their deliverance, let us give ourselves to those tasks which lie to our hands, and so set up signs that men may see.

Now unto Him that is able to do exceeding abundantly above all that we ask or think, according to the power that worketh in us, unto Him be glory in the Church by Christ Jesus, throughout all ages, world without end.

Part Four

THE WORLD COUNCIL, THE ECUMENICAL MOVEMENT, AND THE CHURCHES

I

THE WORLD COUNCIL, THE ECUMENICAL MOVEMENT, AND THE CHURCHES

1. Influence of the World Council on Relations of the Churches with Ecumenical Bodies

The World Council of Churches brought the ecumenical movement closer to the churches, which had constituted it and would control it. Prior to its appearance, international interdenominational organizations had been almost altogether independent and autonomous. Their memberships had consisted of individuals or boards with little or no official representative authority. Such recognition as was accorded them by the denominations had been the nature of support for their work after it had been launched and proved, and then generally unofficial or, at most, semi-official. Under these circumstances, world interchurch bodies were largely beyond the view of the rank and file of church members, who seldom heard of them and felt no responsibility for their programs or policies.

In his *Ecumenical Foundations,* William Richey Hogg comments on the churches' lack of information concerning the International Missionary Council. Not only is the laity uninformed, he writes, but "few . . . clergymen can give an accurate answer to any inquiry about the Council."[1]

The International Missionary Council may be looked at somewhat closely as an example of this difficulty of ecumenical relationship, and along with it—for the purposes of illustration—a local American Baptist church.

This hypothetical church contributes to missions and sends its delegates annually to the American Baptist Convention, where they help elect the officers of the American Baptist Foreign Mission Society—one of the more than a hundred foreign mission boards of the United States and Canada forming the Foreign Missions Conference of North America,[2] a unit of the International Missionary Council. From the

[1] William Richey Hogg, *Ecumenical Foundations,* p. 355.

[2] The Foreign Missions Conference of North America was organized in 1893, with a membership of twenty-three denominational mission boards. The membership in 1948 had grown to 107.

Council—that is, from the Committee of the Council (its forty-five-member executive body which transacts all its business)—one may look back over the steps to be negotiated in making contact with the local church and see the improbability that a given report would reach members in the pews by the organizational route, or that a response from them would find its way by the same channel to the Council. In the American Baptist Convention, where the relation of the church with the Council originates, there is no opportunity to hear communications regularly from the Council or other such tangential agencies, the Convention meetings being monopolized by denominational matters. So the delegates from the local congregation hear little, if anything, about the International Missionary Council to carry back with them. What the Council may be doing touches the church only tenuously, and that without its awareness, through such influence as may be exerted by way, in turn, of the Foreign Missions Conference of North America, the American Baptist Foreign Mission Society, and the American Baptist Convention.

Under these conditions, the people of the churches, for the most part, know so little about the activities of the ecumenical movement that they can have no intelligent interest in them. At the same time, interdenominational agencies speak and act in other ways for the churches, which actually have no part in making their policies.

The first World Missionary Conference, at Edinburgh in 1910, whose action led to the organization of the International Missionary Council, was composed almost entirely of delegates chosen by mission boards rather than by denominations. The foundation of the Universal Christian Conference on Life and Work, at Stockholm in 1925, was projected by a few Christian leaders of Europe, and agents of the Federal Council of the Churches of Christ in America and the World Alliance and financed largely by the Church Peace Union. "Such official backing as it received from the constituted authorities (i.e., the churches)," according to Dr. William Adams Brown, who helped with its launching, "was given tentatively and sometimes in a roundabout way. It was only as the significance of what was done began to be perceived that this foster child of the churches was formally adopted and became a member of the official family." [3]

Bishop Charles Henry Brent first took his plan for uniting the churches through theological agreement and adjustment for approval to the Protestant Episcopal Church in the United States and, through it, to the Lambeth Conference. The result was that the first World Conference on Faith and Order, at Lausanne in 1927, and the Continuation Committee on Faith and Order which it set up to further its work had a closer connection with the denominations than most earlier ecumenical ventures. But the actions taken from 1932 to 1938 to unite

[3] *Toward a United Church*, p. 82.

the Faith and Order Movement with the Life and Work Movement to form the World Council of Churches had no official advance concurrence by the denominations which had sent representatives to Lausanne. The delegates from such of them as cooperated in the Conference on Church, Community and State at Oxford in 1937, and the second World Conference on Faith and Order at Edinburgh the same year, had known only by rumor of the motion to effectuate the merger, plans for which had been prepared beforehand by a self-appointed committee for submission at these gatherings. The Conference of Utrecht in 1938 was of the nature actually of approval after the event.

During the years between 1910 and 1948—from the first World Missionary Conference at Edinburgh to the World Assembly at Amsterdam—the spirit of unity had grown rapidly. The denominations had, however, generally been content to leave its expression to independent and unofficial agencies.

The ecumenical movement was fortunate in having leaders of ability and sound judgment, as well as of unquestioned loyalty to the churches. Some of them with considerable private resources served the cause without compensation, at times even paying their own expenses, while further contributing to the support of the work out of their personal funds. They were successful, moreover, in enlisting other persons of means in giving, and in these ways money was found for interchurch projects which would not have been available for denominational programs in this area.

This method had its obvious advantages. It got quick results. And time may be an important factor in Christian strategy. There are tides in religious movements which, if opportunity is not to be lost, must be taken at the flood. It also brought within the range of achievement some types of service the denominations could not have been deployed officially to undertake at all. But it had grave limitations and hazards, which many who had employed it successfully saw clearly. The work called for resources of human talent and of money greater than individuals alone could supply indefinitely. The system left too much to chance and placed too great responsibility upon the few. Unless it became a commitment of the churches themselves, the ecumenical movement would have no permanence. It belonged to the churches. God called them to own it as theirs. They required it for their education and in order to become fully the Church. Many of those who had given it long and steadfast support—Dr. John R. Mott, for one—were most fervent in their hopes for the World Council of Churches. They expected that some way would still be found under the new plan to give play to individual initiative. They believed the churches understood the need for this and would make a place for it in the more comprehensive new program.

A weighty consideration with those who founded the World Council of Churches was, therefore, that it should consist of the churches—or denominations—themselves and be altogether dependent upon and accountable to them. Its work would thus benefit from the greater interest of their congregations which could be looked for as a result of the closer relationship.

However, not all who knew the history of the ecumenical movement were convinced of the wisdom of linking it organically with the denominations. It was a cause in which pioneers had taken the lead and borne the burdens. It would not have been launched in the first place, let alone maintained in the face of many and formidable adversaries, had its dependence been upon the denominations. They had more often discouraged than helped. The modern missionary movement, in its foreign phase, had been started against official opposition from the churches. When God wanted the heathen converted, William Carey had been told, he would manage the task without man's planning. Christian conquest in other directions also had invariably been spearheaded by individuals with vision and the courage to obey it, ecclesiastical indifference and interdiction notwithstanding. Martin Luther, John Wesley, and many another had been each an example of this. It had been the way of the denominations immemorially to follow, rather than to lead, holding back at first and only eventually regularizing the works of clear-sighted and energetic pioneers who had forged ahead without the delaying encumbrance of slow-moving organizations and lethargic constituencies.

The founders of the World Council recognized that even an organization, constituted, as it had been, under a plan lodging in the churches authority and responsibility for its operations, would not be able easily to maintain itself in the thinking and favor of the congregations with their nearer and more pressing interests. Those who spoke to the Assembly vied with one another in reminding the delegates that the success of the Council would be in proportion to the extent to which "bodies of worshipping Christians" the world around gave meaning to the ecumenical spirit locally. They urged upon all who had collaborated at Amsterdam the duty of becoming sponsors of effective educational measures to this end in the communities for which they were in any way responsible. Plainly expressing the sense of the entire Assembly, Dr. Geoffrey Fisher declared: "The future lies in the churches and how well they take this power and use it in the local parishes."

2. Friends and Enemies

To those who had been associated with it over the years, the ecumenical movement seemed to bear the approval of God. They felt that many of its successes had been such as no body of men and women could have planned and achieved of themselves or in reason have anticipated, and could be regarded only as of the nature of miracles. They testified unanimously to the enriching effects in their own lives of the experience in its labors and its fellowship. They believed that through it they had been found anew of God. They were sure that the cause had been owned of him.

On the other hand, the movement had become the object of bitter and determined denunciation and attack,[4] not only from outside but from within the churches. Wrote a prominent American clergyman with reference to the World Council of Churches during the Assembly: "Should Christians tolerate the World Council of Churches . . . ? The simple answer is that no Christian who is intelligently informed can tolerate it . . . and at the same time be true to Christ. To tolerate the World Council of Churches is to tolerate the finest instrument the hand of Satan ever devised." The organization of churches[5] with which this critic was affiliated had made, and afterwards continued to make, the defeat of the World Council of Churches one of its chief aims, stopping at hardly anything which seemed likely to contribute to this end.

While more than 150 denominations had become members of the World Council of Churches, others had declined the invitation. If not denouncing it, they had not been able to see support of it as the will

[4] "The very fact that the ecumenical movement has come of age and has taken more definite and substantial form means in our present nervous and divided world that its purposes have been widely misunderstood and that it has been the object of attacks from different quarters.

"It is curious to notice that the Council is suspected at the same time of an over-emphasis on ecclesiastical centralized unity and of a lack of real concern about reunion; that it is considered by some to be a typical expression of the reactionary tendencies of the bourgeois world and by others as an organization which endangers the foundations of the capitalist system; or that it is attacked for its alleged modernism and for its static orthodoxy; and that it is alternatively considered as being manoeuvered by Social Gospel theologians, Barthians, Anglo-Catholics, and modernists.

"It is probably inevitable that such misunderstandings should arise when a complex movement without precedent in Church history comes into being. It would be wrong, however, to under-estimate the seriousness of many of these misconceptions." From Report of the General Secretary, 1949, to the Central Committee, Minutes for 1949, p. 63.

"The World Council is under fire. During this last year the attacks have been particularly violent. They deal with two aspects of our work: namely, our attitude to politics and our doctrinal position. And in both areas, the attacks come from two opposite directions. Thus the Bangkok Conference, under the auspices of the World Council of Churches and the International Missionary Council, has, on the one hand, been portrayed as part of a plan to subject the Eastern area to Western imperialism; but has, on the other hand, been described as paving the way for the advance of communism. Again, it is asserted in certain quarters that the World Council is essentially a modernist movement, but we are equally under attack for our so-called doctrinal intransigence and our Christo-centric basis. . . . It would be . . . a mistake to dismiss these wild statements altogether." From Report of the General Secretary, Minutes of the Central Committee, 1950, p. 66.

[5] International Council of Churches.

of God for themselves. And within some of the communions which had joined, groups of dissenters made membership the occasion of violent controversy and so only partially effective.

This simple statement of the fact of the devotion of some and of the hostility of others is, perhaps, all in this phase of the World Council of Churches that belongs properly in a chronicle of this sort. However, passing in silence over the debated issues might be considered unfair to those who read what is written in the hope of gaining help in forming a judgment of their own. The opposing sides have been represented generally by their partisans, who have done what those in such roles always do. They have said, in turn, the best and the worst about their subject. The views they have expressed could only confuse. No organization is perfect, nor can any built by well-meaning men be wholly bad. The truth lies somewhere between these extremes. A brief review of the principal arguments advanced for and against supporting the World Council of Churches may provide help to those interested in finding it.

3. Theological Differences

The severest critics of the World Council of Churches directed their attacks against its theology. These belonged, for the most part, to the conservative schools and looked upon the whole ecumenical movement as an issue between themselves and modernists. They carried on their opposition from outside the Council, with support from some dissidents in the denominations which had joined.

The theological position of the Council, although not defined in the Constitution, was deducible from Articles I and II. The first of these, captioned "Basis," read, "The World Council of Churches is a fellowship of Churches which accept our Lord Jesus Christ as God and Saviour"; the other, "Membership," explained that "those Churches shall be eligible for membership . . . which express their agreement with the basis upon which the Council is founded and satisfy such criteria as the Assembly or the Central Committee may prescribe."

While there was not any official interpretation of acceptance of Christ as God and Saviour, it was reasonably clear from the language that this act was understood as implying acknowledgment of the deity of Christ and a personal faith in his saving grace. The life of Christ in the soul of believers was thus made the bond of unity. The Constitution went no further than this, the Council apparently considering that those who were "in Christ" were already one and could begin to work together in his name. In their doctrinal beliefs—their understanding and description of their experience of God through Jesus Christ—they would differ at many points. But in much they would be agreed, and to the extent they were one they could commence to cooperate. Beyond that, they would wait for guidance, meanwhile carrying on "conversations" and seeking to learn from one another, as the Spirit of Truth taught them. The Study Department and the Commission on Faith and Order would afford them opportunity for study and consultation.

Differences in doctrine were not intended by the Council to be treated as of no consequence. It was the thought only that they should not be allowed to set in hostile camps those who were seeking to follow the same Christ, and that mistaken opinions were more likely to be corrected through fellowship and making common cause of the work of the kingdom of God than by denominational isolationism and controversy at long range.

It would have had to be said that, insofar as it had expressed itself theologically, the Council occupied a position consonant with general evangelical belief in the divine nature and saviourhood of the Lord Jesus Christ. Beyond this, its latitudinarianism toward diverse theological interpretations of the Christian experience would not satisfy those who demanded a creedal formulation of the particulars of doctrine, a basis on which there could never be, of course, an inclusive fellowship of Christians such as the Council aspired to be.

It will be observed that the bounds of membership prescribed by the article of the Constitution on the basis excluded nontrinitarian churches. But it was agreed that their members, and likewise those belonging to other denominations not in the Council, or to none, should not be regarded as debarred from appointment to commissions other than the one on Faith and Order. This last, it was expressly stated, should be composed of "members of the Churches which fell within the terms of the Faith and Order invitation [which had been sent to the churches in 1927 inviting them to appoint delegates to the Lausanne Conference] as addressed to 'all Christian bodies throughout the world which accept our Lord Jesus Christ as God and Saviour.'" According to Article VI, "the commissions may add to their membership clerical and lay persons approved for the purpose by the Central Committee"; and this provision, not prohibiting it, was construed as permitting the appointment to commissions not having to do with any Faith and Order function such individuals as might be useful in the capacity of consultants or agents, without regard to church affiliation—this, notwithstanding the fact that it conflicted in principle with the basis of membership in the Council as set forth in the Constitution.

This complicated situation arose from the divergent practices of the Faith and Order and Life and Work Movements prior to the organization of the World Council of Churches. The former from the start limited its purview to the reunion of those churches which it regarded as representing in their essential beliefs the traditional Christian faith, while the other worked for the application of Christian teaching to social problems and invited, without laying down any creedal test, the cooperation of any and all persons who might be interested. The Faith and Order Movement aimed to be a cause of the churches. Before launching it Bishop Charles Henry Brent and his associates obtained the approval of the Protestant Episcopal Church in the United States, which accepted responsibility for inviting other denominations to participate. On the other hand, the Life and Work Movement had been founded by persons and organizations without any formal mandate from the churches. These differences of policy between the two Movements had proved a serious obstacle to merging them in the World Council of Churches. Those who spoke for Faith and Order wanted the new body composed of churches—or denominations—themselves, with the Faith and Order condition and criteria of membership retained. While most of those supporting the Life and Work Movement were agreeable, on the whole, to this provision, they desired that the World Council of Churches should be left free, as the Universal Christian Council for Life and Work had been, to avail itself of the services of persons outside the denominations within its membership willing and qualified to help with the social phases of its program.

Finally, it had been agreed, as noted, that the Commission on Faith and Order of the World Council of Churches should be composed of "members of the Churches which fall within the terms of the Faith and Order invitation as addressed to 'all Christian bodies throughout the world which accept our Lord Jesus Christ as God and Saviour,'" and that the clause of the Constitution reading "The Commissions may add to their membership clerical and lay persons approved for the purpose by the Central Committee" might be made to cover, on occasion, others besides members of the denominations belonging formally to the Council.

It may be said that one should not turn to the Constitution of the World Council of Churches with the expectation of finding a superior example of logic and order. Those who wrote it were practical churchmen whose desire was to devise a scheme whereby the denominations might express their essential unity through an organization; and those who had been sent to Amsterdam to constitute the new body probably felt that, so long as the churches had a will to unite, the enabling instrument, if it was reasonably approximate, need not be scrutinized too critically.

Concerning the phrasing of the "basis" article of the Constitution, there has been persistent objection in some of the churches belonging to the Council. Dr. William Adams Brown, who over many years was a foremost figure in the ecumenical movement and did as much as anyone, perhaps, to bring to realization the plans for a World Council of Churches, wrote in his *Toward a United Church,* published after his death in 1946:

There was general agreement that there should be no creedal formulation of a test of membership [in the World Council of Churches] and that the same freedom of interpretation should be retained which had prevailed in the earlier forms of the Ecumenical Movement. At the same time, some phrase was needed which would indicate that the churches which were to be united in the proposed World Council stood in the tradition of the historic Christian faith. While many would have preferred a more biblical phrase, it was finally decided to retain the phrase used in the original invitation to the churches to the Faith and Order Conference, "which accept our Lord Jesus Christ as God and Saviour."

It is perhaps in order to point out that this phrase "God and Saviour" has an heretical flavor which would have led to its rejection by any one of the Ecumenical Councils. It expresses only half of the Christian doctrine of the Incarnation, namely, the deity of Christ, while his complete humanity is an equally essential doctrine. To Christian faith, Jesus is not God pure and simple, but God incarnate, the Word made flesh. To ignore the human factor in the Incarnation is to be guilty of what is technically known as Docetism, or, in other words, of reducing the humanity of Jesus to mere appearance. Had the phrase "God incarnate" been used, it would have raised no difficulty and avoided many misunderstandings.

The plea that this should be done was voiced in a moving letter which came to the Conference from a . . . Czechoslovakian Church . . . which had recently broken from Rome [and] desired to enter the fellowship of the Council. But it found difficulties in the phrase used which might make its membership impossible. It, therefore, raised the question whether it would not be possible to substitute a less controversial term. The pleas found sympathy among members of the Conference (at Utrecht, where the constitution was drafted provisionally), but it was felt that to substitute any other phrase for that used in the original invitation of Faith and Order would have made the consultative conference responsible for a doctrinal formulation which was beyond its authority. The question may still be dealt with by the full Council.[6]

Regarding the adjustments between the points of view of the Faith and Order and the Life and Work Movements, previously referred to, Dr. Brown commented as follows in the same book:

While the Trinitarian character of the proposed Council was thus assured [by the phrase "God and Saviour"], the way was left open—*except in questions concerned with Faith and Order*—for the new Council to include in its commissions those who could not accept the Trinitarian test and to call world conferences in the field of Life and Work in which men of every Christian background could join.

[6] *Toward a United Church,* pp. 145-46. The question of the "basis" was to be dealt with later. See Part Eight, Third Assembly, New Delhi, India, 1961.

4. Criticism of the Social Action Program

Another focus of criticism of the World Council of Churches was the social action program which it inherited from the Life and Work Movement.[7]

Assuming responsibility for Life and Work involved difficulties not presented by the companion movement. Faith and Order had brought to the Council a workable, if not fully acceptable, formulation of the theological terms of membership and a tried procedure in the comparative study of doctrinal disagreements not calling for experimentation outside the domain in which the authority of the churches was unchallenged. Life and Work could offer no comparable guiding principle of unity in the sphere of social and political affairs. It led into unfamiliar ways, with no promised land in sight. It called the churches to study the problems harassing men in secular life, and to pronounce the judgments of God concerning them, "without partisan bias." [8] This was a large order, indeed, and it marked the days ahead for trouble, which was not long delayed.

There were Christians who thought the churches should not busy themselves with such matters. For them to do so meant, in the eyes of these folk, turning from the clear divinely appointed mission of proclaiming the gospel of salvation for lost souls until Christ returned to judge the world. Believing this, they would have nothing to do with the World Council of Churches. They considered it a perversion to be shunned and denounced.

Many members in some of the churches which joined the Council shared these misgivings about its activities in the field of Life and Work but refrained from overt opposition. They were willing to abide the pursuit by others of the goals of "the social gospel," but looked for nothing helpful to come of it, seeing the world as evil beyond saving or changing. It was the nature of Christians, of course, to do good as they had opportunity; but the Bible made it plain, if contemporaneous events were not enough to convince everyone, that, all works of mercy notwithstanding, humankind was perdition-bent.

There were also those with Barthian sentiments, who declared it is the duty of the churches to set before the world an example in their own life of "the ideal society" created by the preaching of the Word of God and continually renewed by the living Christ. This would not

[7] Constitutional warrant derived from the first of its functions, defined in Article III "to carry on the work of the world movements for Faith and Order and . . . Life and Work," the latter of which had for its purpose the promotion of social Christianity.

[8] *A History of the Ecumenical Movement,* p. 724.

save society, they said; but it was the witness God willed his Church to give in this last period of human history.[9]

Those persons who demanded that the World Council of Churches deal with social issues fell, roughly, into two parties. Some wanted the evils of society condemned in language satisfying the Christian sense of righteousness and, that done, a good word spoken for the economic and political *status quo,* which, though not in all respects defensible, represented in their opinion the best attainable at the time in a social order. Dr. Reinhold Niebuhr spoke for them, after a manner, at Amsterdam when he said that, while the civilization which had risen under capitalism might be faulty and in manifold ways undesirable, the alternative would certainly be worse, if the nations embraced "communism with its monstrous barbarisms." [10]

The others wished the churches to crusade for reform using the methods of what had come to be known as "Christian social action," which called for radical revision of the existing economy.

In the United States, where there was a large degree of political and economic stability and a fabulous material prosperity, the former of these two classes was greatly in a majority. But in the rest of the world, which had suffered more from war and had not recovered from its impoverishment, those who thought change in order were undoubtedly the more numerous. And there were Christian leaders on the American side who sympathized with their demand, persuaded that only by radical readjustments could violent revolution be averted, and that, quite apart from such considerations of expediency, movement toward an equalization of the world's wealth was clearly the will of God.

Both these elements were represented in the World Council of Churches, in what proportion it would be impossible to determine. However, the latter controlled the Assembly and shaped the social policy of the World Council, which, it would be substantially correct to say, charted a course to the left of center in the thinking of the churches.

This is speaking from the standpoint of the United States and Canada but is less accurately descriptive of the orientation for the Eastern Hemisphere. In Europe, where state socialism had long been accepted, and in the other continents, with revolutionary unrest on the increase, "center" was farther to the left than west of the Atlantic, Latin America perhaps excepted.

With reference to this point, Dr. John Coleman Bennett of Union Theological Seminary in New York City, who was a member of the

[9] For the views of Karl Barth, see Part Three, Section II.

[10] See Part Three, Section II. Dr. Niebuhr was actually saying only that he approved capitalism in comparison with communism. He was apparently an advocate of a "planned society or state" of socialistic type somewhere between what was called capitalism and communism.

Preparatory Commission on the sub-theme "The Church and the Disorder of Society" and Secretary of Section III studying it at Amsterdam, has written:

> One thing that was clearly revealed at the Assembly is that the economic and political center among Christians in the world at large is much to the left of the center among American Churches. I believe that this report [the report of Section III] faithfully reflects that ecumenical center.
>
> It is most significant that in several hours of discussion of the unamended report in the section and the plenary session only once was there any suggestion that Capitalism should be less strongly criticized. Many of the delegates from Europe and from the younger Churches would have preferred an absolute condemnation of Capitalism. At no point was there any conservative pressure upon the Assembly except at the very end, when, because of criticisms outside the Assembly deliberation, the words *laissez faire* were added to the sentence about Communism and Capitalist ideology, not to change the meaning of the report, but to reduce the amount of criticism based upon the misunderstanding that the original draft put Communism and Capitalism on exactly the same level.[11]

Dr. Bennett's article in *The Living Church* confirmed the impression that the representatives of conservative social opinion at the Assembly were much in the minority, and that they had come to Amsterdam without adequate briefing for defending or explaining what was called capitalism.[12] At least, they were well-nigh inarticulate under the massive opposition. Concretely, they succeeded in doing little more than getting it written into the record that the capitalism which Section III had recommended, with communism, for rejection by the churches was the "early stage"[13] nineteenth-century *laissez faire* type, and that "the exploitation of the workers . . . characteristic" of it had been "corrected in considerable measure by the influence of trade unions, social legislation and responsible management." They allowed the capitalistic system to be dismissed thus as a mildly reformed culprit, without any word of commendation for qualifications it still might have had for serving the best interests of society.

The depreciation by the Assembly of the values of an economy which had been the nations' main reliance in their struggle toward social and political recovery was regarded by some critics as close to irresponsibility.

In the paragraph quoted above, Dr. Bennett mentioned the demand of "many of the delegates from Europe and from the younger Churches"

[11] *The Living Church,* Vol. X, No. 1, October 17, 1948, p. 15.

[12] All economic systems, socialist and communist included, had some form of capitalism. What the United States had, which those condemning capitalism were talking about, would have been best described as "regulated free capitalistic enterprise."

[13] John Strachey, in *Contemporary Capitalism.*

for "an absolute condemnation of Capitalism"; and the discussions showed the bias in that direction to be so completely blinding that few of the conferees to whom he referred could bring themselves to credit the material prosperity of the United States, the outstanding exponent among the nations of capitalistic free enterprise, to any condition other than the fortuitous advantages of geographical isolation and abounding natural resources, with which, they said, any politico-economic scheme would have been automatically successful.

If the churches believed it the will of God for them to deliver themselves on such social, economic, and political matters, they ought to have seen to it that the great body of conservative opinion represented in their far-flung constituencies would be set forth with fairness and competence.

As it developed, the World Council of Churches in its social action program became from its founding the organ of a party, and not of the whole Church.

The charge that those dominating the Assembly and the Council were communists, or were "soft" toward communism, could not be sustained, except perhaps in respect of a very small percentage of them.[14] Actually, they were, for the most part, socialists or collectivists, who, while rejecting communism's atheistic materialism and inhuman methods of promoting its ideology, accepted as essentially Christian its professed theoretical objectives of a classless society and economic equality. They believed that the cure for the defects of both Marxian communism and capitalism was more socialism. They had the doctrinaire assurance that the churches and the state would be able, working together in complementary ways, to control the "welfare order" which they envisaged and fix its bounds at any degree of leftness they might determine, and so to avoid the danger that the increasing momentum of socialism might deliver the world into the hands of communism. In ruling capitalism out as an adequate substructure for democratic political liberty, they were so sure of themselves that they saw no need to consider its usefulness even as a brake against possible sudden and uncontrollable veerings leftward.

Responsibility for the lopsided developments in social policy at Amsterdam rested, in the first place, upon the conservatives, who had held back from cooperation in the organization of the World Council of Churches because of their distrust of the conciliar movement, in the tradition of which it arose. Their refusal to collaborate left the field to the social liberals and radicals.

From the standpoint of the churches and of the world, a more unfortunate decision could hardly have been reached. Unnecessarily, it

[14] The Assembly was a "world" gathering, and churches in some communist countries were represented.

narrowed the witness of Christian unity, as stated, to the dimensions of a party. Conservatives and liberals could have taken their places together in the World Council of Churches—and would have, if they had acted in the true spirit of its nature and purpose. There was no reason why their sociological differences could not have been submitted for study with a view to reconciliation, after the method followed by Faith and Order in theological disagreements, or why, meantime, their respective positions on current issues could not have been maintained conscientiously and, in the event of division in the actions of the Council, fully set forth in both majority and minority reports. And in this way the Council would have spoken for the Church, and its testimony would have been fair, intelligible, and effective. Any division between conservatives and liberals would then only have emphasized their deeper spiritual unity in Christ. The world would have understood that Christians could differ in their opinions about the social application of the gospel, as about its theological explication, and felt the more, for their resolve to disagree in love, the strength of their brotherhood which withstood the tensions in human relations. That kind of oneness the nations and their peoples waited to see in the churches for guidance in their groping after an enduring bond of peace.

The liberals also stood to answer for the absence at Amsterdam of a constructive and effective conservative opposition, as later in the World Council of Churches. Counting crusading for a new social order more important than making good their profession of unity in diversity, they neglected their opportunity to encourage the enlistment of the forces of social conservatism.

In setting up the Preparatory Commission on "The Church and the Disorder of Society,"[15] the Study Commission of the Provisional Committee of the World Council of Churches (in process of formation) solicited generally the collaboration of scholars of liberal predilection. Had it acted with true ecumenical insight, it would have incorporated in the syllabuses for the sections full information also on the conservative position and arranged for its authoritative interpretation in the discussions and on the plenary programs.

The pre-Assembly procedure followed at the denominational level the over-all pattern of the Study Commission. For delegates those were chosen, for the most part, who had been active in some phase of the ecumenical movement or were known to be in accord with its objectives and methods. They were given the privilege of indicating the study sections to which they wished to be assigned and, before leaving for Amster-

[15] The main theme was "Man's Disorder and God's Design." It was divided into four sub-themes: "The Universal Church in God's Design," "The Church's Witness to God's Design," "The Church and the Disorder of Society," and "The Church and the International Order." The social thinking of the Assembly took shape in the development of the last two of the sub-themes. (See Part Three, Section I.)

dam, were supplied with printed summaries—"the quintessence" [16]—of the collateral study matter compiled by the researchers. On arriving at the Assembly, they found some of the authors of this briefing material on hand to act as consultants or as sectional chairmen and secretaries. In this way, it was insured that the discussion of the themes would proceed, more or less, on the lines pursued in their preliminary development in the Preparatory Commissions: which was almost necessary, it would be granted, if the sections were to reach a consensus and report their findings to the Assembly, since they had for all this barely a week. There was not time at the plenary sessions to debate the reports at length or to amend them in other than minor ways. It was emphasized that they would not be regarded as necessarily expressing the opinion of the Assembly on the various subjects, which would only "receive and commend them to the churches for their serious consideration." If there were members in the sections dealing with social questions who dissented from the conclusions of the majority, they could not have prepared, under the circumstances, a minority report giving their views. Only through arrangements by the Study Commission for thorough study in advance of their coming to Amsterdam could conservative delegates have made a statement worthy of themselves or of the Assembly.

If the mistakes made at Amsterdam were ever to be repaired, conservatives and liberals would have to learn to act together. There was reason to believe that the World Council of Churches had come to stay and would increase in power. External pressures and the urge of unity within the churches would support their declared resolve "to stay together." Many people shared the feeling of William Temple that the drawing together of Christians in the ecumenical movement[17] was the world's brightest hope, and were willing to bear with the weaknesses of its institutions and give them their blessing. Like all gifts of God, Christian unity could only be a "treasure in earthen vessels." Religious organizations were like the people belonging to them, and perfection could not be one of their attainments. That Christian was exceptional who could accept even his own church without at least inward protest because of its failings.

So the World Council of Churches would probably survive and become the voice of non-Roman Christianity to which the world would listen. The clear duty of the churches was to make it an organ of the Church, in which all parties would find place, because of the spiritual oneness of their members in Christ, and make their several contributions to the more ample knowledge of truth, for want of which the kingdom of God halted and the people perished.

[16] Minutes of the Provisional Committee's meeting at Buck Hill Falls, 1947, p. 28.

[17] William Temple was speaking "in the perilous years" between World War I and World War II—in 1938.

5. Unity in Love

The Scriptures supplied opponents of the World Council of Churches with a question which, lifted out of its context—as it often is, in other connections—seemed to many of them to hint at divine justification for their position. "Can two walk together, except they be agreed?" (Amos iii, 3). Here were some 150 denominations with their conflicting theologies and the problem of keeping intact their own internal unity saying, "We intend to stay together." [18] Did the experiment, however praiseworthy its intentions, not go in the face of reason and experience, as well as of the more explicit warning of God's Word?

Proponents were ready to explain that there was a large measure of agreement within the Council, quite as much, in fact, as men enjoyed in most of the ways wherein they walked together. The denominations belonging to it were one in their acceptance of "Jesus Christ as God and Saviour," according to the constitutional basis of membership. And they were agreed in their purpose to work together, in his name, at the things in which they found it possible to cooperate. They were united, too, in their hope that as they proceeded in this way and came to be better acquainted with one another God would enlarge the bounds of their common understanding and activity.

Some denominations which withheld their support on doctrinal grounds feared that association in the Council with those with whom they differed would seem to imply greater agreement than they actually admitted and thus compromise their testimony.

The reply from the other side was that this would not necessarily follow. Basically, the World Council of Churches was, as described, an organization for collaboration in Christian work that could be carried on happily and effectively together, the members being themselves the judges of what they could—and would—undertake, and not for demonstrating theological unanimity. There would be no occasion because of membership in it for any church to deny or to be hesitant about declaring its distinctive teachings. The Commission on Faith and Order would have the function to study and compare all Christian beliefs and practices.

The World Council of Churches did not bar membership, it was explained, to those Christians who thought they had a fuller grasp of the truth than others. In it there had been, from the start, some who held theirs to be the only true Church of Christ. No law or regulatory action of any kind forbade their doing this. Other members might have protested. If so, that also was a privilege freely granted. The general feeling in the World Council was that one should not be disturbed unduly by such exclusive claims by others. Concern on this account should be left

[18] From declaration in the Message from Amsterdam.

to the claimants. The burden of proof rested with them; and it was a very great responsibility they took upon themselves who insisted that their denomination alone was truly the Church. For support for their position, they would be tempted to point to history, tradition, theology, conformity to particular approved practices, organizational forms and successes, and other such things; but convincing evidence would be found, if at all, in the "more excellent way" commended by an apostle (I Corinthians xii, 31). Those who were of the true Church, whatever else they did, would surely love most; and if anybody was resolved to try to do that, he deserved the blessing of the others.

Indeed, notwithstanding all that the churches brought into it of the glory and pride of tradition, faith and good works, the World Council would only magnify their old sins unless they determined to vie with one another in manifesting the love that fulfilled itself in longsuffering and kindness, was not puffed up nor given to vaunting itself, did not behave itself unseemly nor seek its own, was not easily provoked, thought no evil, knew no envy, rejoiced in truth, bore all things, believed all things, hoped all things, endured all things; and that on the long journey through the half-light and shadows of this earth, where all else passed away—prophecy and tongues and knowledge and all other achievements of men—never failed.

There might well be rivalry in love! According to the exegetes, the burden of Amos when he believed that he heard God asking, "Can two walk together, except they be agreed?" was to impress upon Israel that moral obedience was the condition of divine fellowship. Transposed to the Christian scene and construed faithfully, the prophet's words, rather than warning the churches against trying to resolve their differences in the unity of love, suggested that in their resolution "to stay together" they could have been setting out upon the way God willed and in it would fulfill the condition of walking with him.

"This is my commandment, That ye love one another, as I have loved you" (John xv, 12).

6. Persecutions

Some churches had memories of persecutions at the hands of others, now members of the World Council of Churches, and this stood as a stubborn hindrance to their becoming members. It is not our nature to enjoy associating with those who have mistreated and punished us when they had the power, because we did what we believed the will of God and they considered the will of Satan—not even if they thought that they were obeying God and correcting us for our own good.

The solution of this problem seemed to be the commandment of Jesus that we love also our enemies. The control of the natural passions by higher disciplines was one of the marks for which the world looked in Christians, and if the cross of Christ was the design of God and not a horrible mistake, it was in patience and kindness toward those unwilling or unable to reciprocate that "immortal beauty in mortal things" was perfected.

"It hath been said, Thou shalt love thy neighbour and hate thine enemy. But I say unto you, Love your enemies, bless them that curse you, do good to them that hate you, and pray for them that despitefully use you, and persecute you; that ye may be children of your Father which is in heaven."

The argument, in this instance, was that those who chafed under past wrongs should be able to forgive, at least to the extent of joining an organization which, as in the case of the World Council of Churches, would do what it could, if occasion arose, to defend them against further mistreatment by their persecutors, standing as a tribunal pledged to respect human rights and liberties, before which they might come with every confidence for redress when abused or accused falsely.

The churches with grievances should remember, moreover, that they themselves were prone to mistakes and not always wholly right in conflicts with other Christians; and the knowledge that as they asked for a righteous judgment upon the deeds of others they also submitted to the same scrutiny their own would be salutary.

A minority Christian group in a European country, for example, suffered persecution over many years by the dominant church, which could invoke the power of the state against those whose teaching it considered dangerous or undesirable. One of the most resented contentions of these dissenters was that there should not be any governmental subsidization of the state church. In the councils of the denomination abroad which supported their work through missionary offerings reports were received from time to time of the sufferings of their people, because of their testimony against the evil practices of the establishment. Came the time when a political revolution unseated the national church and reduced it to the status of other religious bodies, making all eligible alike for grants from the public treasury. Whereupon, the erstwhile dissentients turned face about and accepted the subsidy. With this new source of income and the remittances from overseas, which had not been stopped, their ministers became the most highly paid in that country, not excepting the clergy of the disestablished church.

Furthermore, the churches with memories of persecution, if they thought they had been more Christian than their detractors, would do well to consider that they would not need more of the grace of God to join an organization to which their enemies belonged than the latter would to accept them as members. If they had actually been in the right, they should find it easier than these latter to forgive and to forget. And those who in the love of God went thus halfway for the sake of reconciliation would almost surely find that they had spanned the whole distance between enmity and friendship and between strife and peace.

How membership in the World Council of Churches could improve the position of a denomination whose members suffered disabilities because of their faith was demonstrated in the experience of a small nonconformist people in another European nation. These Christians were victims of serious discrimination. They were ineligible for public office. They could not qualify for teaching in the state schools. Their pastors were barred by law from performing marriage ceremonies. When the established church, which had upheld or countenanced these injustices, joined the World Council of Churches, this sect refused to apply for membership. Afterwards, it reconsidered this decision, made application, and was received. With this, the relations between it and the state church improved markedly, and likewise its status under the government.[19]

In a certain country, a small denomination which had remained aloof from the interchurch movement believed that its members had not received their proportionate share of the wartime relief supplies from overseas, and also that they had been subjected to other, more subtle kinds of discrimination, which was tolerated, if not actually instigated, by the more prominent churches. Its grievances received the attention of ecumenical authorities, who quickly righted matters. They found that the complainants had indeed not been given the help to which they were entitled, but that this had happened because of poor coordination between their own denominational organization and the committee on distribution of the national council of churches, with which they had not affiliated. The experience, and especially the attitude of the agents of the interdenominational bodies handling the problem influenced them to abandon their policy of isolationism and join both the national council and the World Council of Churches. This denomination's delegate at Amsterdam discovered that he had equal right to the floor and to the ear of the Assembly with those who represented the larger churches. And he had opportunity to see also that the World Council of Churches showed special consideration, whenever it properly could, for the interests of its weaker members.

7. Opposition to State Churches

Reference has been made to state churches as having at times persecuted dissenters; but, quite apart from criticism of them on this account, there had been objection to their presence in the World Council of Churches, on the ground particularly of their privileged status under the law. Even if accorded full freedom of worship, nonconformists had re-

[19] Other influences accounted, in part, for these developments. but the World Council of Churches had an important role in them.

sented having to pay taxes for maintaining the establishment, in addition to supporting their own communions. And they had protested against the polity under which the parishes of the state churches were assumed to embrace the whole population as a stumbling block and a hindrance to many people, who, connected with the state church only by the tenuous tie of baptism in infancy, with proper scriptural instruction and pastoral guidance might have found their way by conversion into a vital and fruitful church relationship. So, at least, those believing in the separation of church and state had insisted. They could not see how cooperation between themselves and the established churches would be profitable, if possible.

Some of the critics, not averse to judging motives, had attributed the willingness of the state churches to go into the World Council of Churches with separatists largely to the hope that they might in this way recover their declining prestige and so postpone "the day of reckoning for their failures at home."

The presentation of the other side could well have started at that point. If the state churches had become so anachronistic and their position so untenable that they were on the way to early disestablishment, what occasion was there for such concern as some denominations felt over their membership in the World Council of Churches? Moreover, if there was to be a truly ecumenical fellowship, commencing with the present situation in the church world, they would have to be included, whatever their past offenses and their present weakness.

Furthermore, membership in the World Council of Churches in no way implied approval of what might be adjudged errors in the conduct of any church. So long as there was agreement in the acceptance of "Jesus Christ as God and Saviour" and a purpose to cooperate, as far as possible, on the basis of democratic bylaws, the members could dismiss thoughts of one another's failures and give prayerful consideration, each of them, to their own, that they might justify their own presence in the Council.

No statement of the case of the state churches could with fairness have omitted acknowledgment of the able leadership which they had contributed to the World Council of Churches during its provisional period. It was hardly possible to conceive of the phenomenal progress of the ecumenical movement without the service of such men as Archbishop Söderblom of the Church of Sweden, Bishop Berggrav of the Church of Norway, Bishop Ammundsen of the Church of Denmark, and Dr. J. H. Oldham, Bishop Bell, and Archbishop Temple of the Church of England, to mention but a few of the more outstanding leaders for whom the World Council had established churches to thank.

The report of a commission of the Free Church Council of Great Britain, which had been appointed to inquire into the relationship of the Church of England with the state, might well have been consulted in weighing the criticism of the World Council of Churches for its inclusive policy in respect of national churches. "Disestablishment is not as simple and obvious a solution as might at first be thought," the commission said. "It is an open question whether any practicable alternative in the present situation would not be worse than the existing order with all its anomalies."

Though not favoring control of religion by the state, this representative group of Britain's Nonconformist churchmen saw "value in the recognition of religion by the state." It was desirable, the commission continued, that on important occasions, such as the coronation of a monarch, there should be "solemn acknowledgment for all the people of the ultimate sovereignty of God." The conclusion was that by "ill-considered proposals for disestablishment it would be easy to jeopardize the existing valuable co-operation between the church and the state," in which the free churches had come increasingly to share.

8. Separatists' Objections to the Council

There were denominations which because of their separatist history hesitated to join the World Council of Churches. They had had their origin in the action of spiritual forebears who left the older churches to form fellowships in which they could worship according to their faith and follow, unhindered, religious practices more in keeping, as they believed, with the Scriptures. To go into the Council with the very ecclesiastical bodies which had either thrust out their forefathers or made continuance of membership so uncomfortable that they had withdrawn of their own accord, sometimes to be persecuted for having done so, would be, they felt, to repudiate their heritage and to sacrifice principles which had been their strength and justification as separatists.

These Christians were reminded that their religious ancestors had left the established or dominant churches because, when not actually persecuted, they felt restricted in the exercise of their faith. If they had been allowed the liberty of disagreeing and of setting forth their reasons in the spirit of inquiry, they would not, in most instances, have gone in their dissent to the extent of withdrawing altogether from the Christian community.

Roger Williams, for an example, and those who joined him in Rhode Island, had no desire to leave Massachusetts or the other colonies, and did so only when driven out or when they had found that they could not remain without surrendering their freedom. The ecumenical movement stood for a different concept of Christian relations. It believed in a kind of unity which was consistent with diversity. The World Council of Churches welcomed all who accepted "Jesus Christ as God and Saviour" and asked for no abandonment of beliefs or practices held by them to be essential or otherwise desirable. It proposed cooperation within the recognized scope of agreement and study in areas of disagreement, that the measure of united action might be enlarged. In membership within this framework, it was contended, nothing could be found contradictory to an honest and honorable separatist tradition.

It was suggested, further, that the ecumenical way was really more in keeping with the spirit of the original separatists than the isolationism of their descendants who thought to honor them by aloofness from interchurch relations. They had been pioneers in the struggle for religious freedom, which in their day often necessitated individual and independent action. The fruits of their sacrifice had won appreciation and acceptance generally. The Assembly at Amsterdam had, for example, passed a resolution in support of religious liberty, and the World Council of Churches was throwing its full weight behind the movement in the United Nations to write an International Bill of Human Rights which would pledge governments to make constitutional provision for such freedom. Thus, the authentic pioneering spirit now led away from separation and individualistic action to a common quest for fundamental rights. Those of separatist inheritance were loyal to their fathers in the faith, therefore, when they accepted the opportunity to renew the broken fellowship with the older churches which now were acknowledging their share of the blame for the ancient breach and striving to do what they could to heal it.

9. Aversion to Church Union

The unwillingness of many of their members to encourage organic union had its part in keeping certain denominations out of the World Council of Churches and in causing strife and uneasiness in some that joined.

It was quite true, these Christians agreed, that by its constitution the World Council of Churches had not been committed specifically to working for union of the churches, but one of its functions[20] was "to promote the growth of ecumenical consciousness" in the member churches, and who could define what this meant? They thought that the denominations advocating corporate union as the ultimate goal would eventually write the interpretation of it.

They had in mind that the Faith and Order Movement had from its organization cherished the aim to "re-unite" the churches. And they knew that some of the denominations would have no interest in membership in the Council if it did not seem to them to hold out the promise of becoming a definite step toward that goal. So important a spokesman as

[20] Constitution of the World Council of Churches, Article III, Section IV.

the General Secretary of the Council, Dr. Willem Adolf Visser 't Hooft, had said at Amsterdam:

> We are a Council of Churches, not the Council of one undivided Church. Our name indicates our weakness and our shame before God, for there can be and there is finally only one Church of Christ. . . . Our plurality is a deep anomaly. But our name indicates also that we are aware of the situation, and we do not accept it passively, that we move forward toward the manifestation of the One Holy Church. Our Council represents, therefore, an emergency solution—a stage on the road—a body living between the time of complete isolation of the churches from each other and the time . . . when it will be visibly true that there is one Shepherd and one flock.

And in the same vein were the words of Bishop Lesslie Newbigin:

> All conceptions of re-union in terms of federation are vain. . . . They leave the heart of the problem untouched. . . . They do not grapple with the fact, which any serious reading of the New Testament must surely make inescapable, that to speak of a plurality of churches is strictly absurd . . . that our ecclesiologies are, in the Pauline sense, carnal. . . . The disastrous error of federation is that it offers us re-union without repentance. The result is the stalemate with which we are painfully familiar. As an organ of co-operation and conversation the World Council of Churches goes from strength to strength. But the visible re-union of the churches makes little progress and, indeed, denominational positions tend to harden. Thus, the Council, instead of being something transitional, tends to appear more and more as the permanent form of the churches' unity. Its ecclesiological neutrality is in danger of becoming a screen for ecclesiological federation. The World Council has a right to exist only as a means to something further, as a stage from disunity to unity; and . . . if it comes to be regarded as the proper form of the churches' unity in Christ, it will have become committed to a disastrous error.[21]

It could be held reasonably that there was room in the World Council of Churches for both those who believed in cooperation for its own sake and those who, like Dr. Visser 't Hooft and Dr. Newbigin, were interested in it mainly as a manifestation of unity that might grow into union. The latter surely were entitled to their hopes, and the others would not wish to close their minds to further revelation. If a united Church ever came to be seen as the will of God, all would wish to be in it.

But, despite the assurance with which the advocates of union spoke on the subject, it had to be said that the mind of God was not yet known. The meaning of the words of Christ when he prayed that his disciples might be one was still far from plain in the light of sound exegesis and Christian experience.

The Spirit of God had been in the midst of the churches through all their history, leading them, or suffering them to go, by different ways.

[21] Lesslie Newbigin, *Household of God*, p. 14.

Their greatest apparent successes had been more often in separate than united endeavors.

However, there had been for nearly a century an accelerating growth of fellowship among the churches, and the possibility that this presaged the approach of the fullness of time for a new and closer relationship could be admitted. Meanwhile, those who believed the will of God led through cooperation to the extent of agreement as to existing unity, whether beyond that or not, could walk together in the love of Christ and leave the issue with him.[22]

10. The Problem of Churches with Congregational Polity

Membership in the World Council of Churches had been regarded unfavorably by many persons in denominations with congregational polity as a violation of the autonomy of constituent churches.

This aspect of the problem was illustrated in a general way by the experience of the Northern Baptist Convention,[23] which will be reviewed briefly for the guidance it may give other denominational bodies in a similar position, including particularly those of the Baptist fellowship which have declined to join the Council.[24]

Like all such Baptist organizations, the Northern Baptist Convention was a voluntary association of churches; and many of these opposed its going into the World Council of Churches as an action without constitutional authority and contrary to the universally recognized Baptist principle of local church independence. From both a legal and a logical standpoint, this objection appeared to be well sustained.

Prefaced by the statement that "the Northern Baptist Convention declares its belief in the independence of the local church, and in the purely advisory nature of all denominational organizations composed of representatives of the churches," the articles of incorporation stated: "The objects of the corporation shall be to give expression to the opinions of its constituency upon moral, religious, and denominational matters, and to promote unity and efficiency in efforts for the evangelization of the world." There seemed to be nothing in this definition of purpose, nor could anything be found in the more lengthy bylaws, warranting taking this loose consociation of churches, each of which acknowledged no ecclesiastical power above its own will, into any interdenominational body.

The "efforts for the evangelization of the world," referred to in the

[22] It was generally agreed by all parties that the World Council of Churches was not to act as an agent in proposing and promoting the union of "specific churches."

[23] Later American Baptist Convention.

[24] The Southern Baptist Convention in the United States was the largest Protestant denomination not affiliating with the World Council.

articles of incorporation, consisted in the missionary program of the co-operating churches, in the interest of which they had formed the Convention.

Much earlier in their history, the American Baptist Foreign Mission Society, the American Baptist Home Mission Society, the American Baptist Publication Society, the Woman's American Baptist Foreign Mission Society and the Woman's American Baptist Home Mission Society had been organized independently of one another, though representing the same churches, to "promote the spread of the gospel among the unevangelized at home and abroad." Until 1907 they had carried on their work separately, except that they had adopted the plan of holding their annual meetings simultaneously in the same places and of scheduling their several financial appeals so as to give "breathing spaces" between them. The Northern Baptist Convention was formed to be a framework within which they would cooperate in fund raising and, to some extent, in policy making. It was regarded as itself an organ of missionary promotion, and not as in any sense a legislative body.

However, from almost the time of its founding, the Convention had belonged to the Federal Council of the Churches of Christ in America, and on essentially the same terms as were proposed for admission to the World Council of Churches. Prominent Baptists had helped as individuals with the formation of the Federal Council; but the Convention had sent official delegates to the World Assembly of Churches at Amsterdam. The churches opposing joining the World Council now also demanded withdrawal from the Federal Council (by this time called National Council).

The decision in favor of membership in both bodies was, roughly, two to one, and this ratio held in the voting afterwards, whenever questions relating to the Convention's continuing in them or to financial appropriations to them were put to ballot.

Looking at the matter from the side of the majority, it might have been suggested that local churches could not create an association for any purpose without limiting their independence in some degree. The new society would have to be given the right to define the conditions of membership, in case other churches wished to join it; and there would be other actions, from time to time, with similar restrictive effect. The Northern Baptist Convention had eventually required that churches, to be eligible for membership and for representation at its meetings, forward to it for the cooperating missionary societies a certain percentage of the funds raised by them for benevolences. Some of the member churches practiced "open membership," which meant that they received applicants, under certain conditions, without immersing them; and the Convention had changed its bylaws to disqualify "unimmersed persons" for sitting as delegates in its meetings. In various other ways, the authority of the local church had been modified by the Convention.

Turning to the declaration that the Convention had been formed to "promote . . . unity and efficiency in efforts for the evangelization of the world" and should confine itself to that objective, the reply might have been that a line of demarcation could not be drawn between the different kinds of endeavor to distinguish which were "evangelistic and missionary" and which were not. All forms of Christian work were in motive and ultimate result evangelistic and missionary. "The evangelization of the world" called for the entire program of every denominational agency.

In the Northern Baptist Convention other societies, besides the earlier missionary boards, had in time been formed: the Ministers' and Missionaries' Benefit Board for the aid of the clergy; the Retiring Pension Fund for all employed denominational workers, including the ministers; the Social Service Commission for the study of social problems and the Christian way of dealing with them; the Board of Christian Education for aiding the colleges and the theological seminaries in improving their facilities and teaching—and there were others. These all were missionary, broadly speaking, and essential to a successful prosecution of the worldwide evangelistic plans of the Convention.

And were the Federal Council of the Churches of Christ in America and the World Council of Churches not missionary agencies too? They were rooted in the modern missionary movement and had for their aim the evangelization of the world in all the areas of its life.

According to its articles of incorporation, the Convention should express "the opinions of its constituency upon moral, religious, and denominational matters." How would it go about doing that? Would it be with words only? If, in the judgment of the majority, it became the moral obligation of the Convention to associate itself with other denominations in forming organizations through which to cooperate in Christian work on a national or an international level, could this not be done consonantly with its original purpose and its developing practices? Was the Convention to be a discussion society supporting "moral" and "religious" causes only with resolutions?

It was agreed that the independence of the local church should be kept inviolate as a Baptist principle; but there were other equally important and cherished rights which, under given circumstances, stood to qualify it, one being that of majority rule. Individually, the churches in their day-to-day decisions determined by ballot what the will of God was for themselves. If they were going to work together as a denomination, by what other procedure would they decide questions arising in their common undertakings? If some two-thirds of the delegates to the annual meetings of the Northern Baptist Convention were convinced that it should join the World Council of Churches and duly implement its membership agreements, should that not settle the issue?

Those dissenting thought that this course would cause great hurt to the denomination. Many viewed it as aligning the churches with "theological modernism and sociological radicalism" in a relationship compromising "distinctive convictions of Baptists." They feared that it would divert the Convention and its societies from their own work. They objected to the cost of the new affiliation, which would, by so much, reduce what the denomination had to devote to its own missions, which as it was never got all the money they needed. And that was not the end of the list of probable ills which, they believed, would follow from the misalliance.

Those on the other side said the World Council of Churches brought Baptists an opportunity to serve the kingdom of God which they could not afford to reject. They believed it a duty to join with other Christians in giving such visible expression as was possible to the spiritual unity of the churches. In doing so, Baptists would be better able, it was contended, to fulfill their own destiny. They needed, more than they generally understood, perhaps, the advantages of the broader fellowship. It would help to save them from provincialism and a false sense of self-sufficiency. They had much to give and would certainly find much they could receive with profit and gratitude. The world was changing, and the advocates of membership in the Council believed that ecumenical experience would prove to be a requisite for the leadership of which Baptists were capable in the new order. The days of denominational isolationism were numbered, they said. Baptists had been pioneers, and the interchurch movement, in all its phases, called them to face forward, with other Christians, toward the unconquered and unexplored frontiers of the intellectual and social worlds in the name of Christ, bringing to the adventure the intrepidity that distinguished their confessional fathers, who belonged to the vanguard of the modern missionary movement and the crusade for religious and political freedom.

One recourse remained for those who could not bring themselves conscientiously to yield to the will of the majority, which all held in mind but hoped none would resort to. The Convention could not prevent withdrawal by a church. But even this step could not be taken without consequences demonstrating further that churches were unable to constitute themselves a denomination and avoid limiting their independence. For example, the pension system for ministers and other employed staff personnel which Northern Baptist churches had established together could not, by the terms of its charter, continue to serve those defecting, beyond the time of their withdrawal. They suffered no deprivation of benefits for the period of their membership.

So the controversy adjusted itself along these general lines. Some churches withdrew, albeit there were other circumstances also which strongly influenced many of them. The majority voted to take the denomination into the World Council of Churches and to retain its connection with the Federal Council of the Churches of Christ in America. Many who disapproved of the ecumenical affiliations acquiesced, after the traditional way of Baptists, because a majority had decided for them.

What happened beyond this? Besides the Northern Baptist Convention, the other denominational units of Baptists joining the World Council of Churches were the Baptist Unions of Great Britain and Ireland, New Zealand, Denmark, and Holland, and the National Baptist Convention and the Conference of Seventh Day Baptists, both of the United States. These, it can be said, distinguished themselves in the service of the World Council. Five of their representatives were honored by election to the Central Committee, and one of them was appointed also to the Executive Committee. It is not possible to say to what extent the fears or the hopes of those who took opposite sides in the controversy over membership in the World Council have been justified. Time only can afford the necessary perspective for that judgment.

That faith in God should not be rewarded with a less confused leading for Christians concerning the divine will is a mystery hard, indeed, to resolve, as the burden of it is to bear. Perhaps we may say this stands to remind us that love, as the apostle declared, is greater than faith, abiding all our misunderstandings and separations—which are the penalty of our partial knowledge—and, when obeyed, outreaching the gropings of our minds in the dark and awaking those ultimate insights which are self-authenticating and alone completely unitive. "For love is of God; and every one that loveth is born of God" (I John iv, 7).

Part Five

THE FIRST SIX YEARS OF THE WORLD COUNCIL OF CHURCHES

I

THE CENTRAL COMMITTEE

1. Organization

The authority of the Assembly of the World Council of Churches passed, upon adjournment, to the Central Committee, which met forthwith[1] at Woudscotten, Holland, and organized, choosing for Chairman Dr. G. K. A. Bell, Bishop of Chichester, and for Vice-Chairman Dr. Franklin Clark Fry, President of the United Lutheran Church in America.

The motion to elect Dr. Bell carried a provision that he be invited to serve five years. Dr. Willem Adolf Visser 't Hooft was appointed General Secretary of the World Council of Churches for the same term.[2]

The following members were named for the Executive Committee:[3]

Dr. G. K. A. Bell, Chairman
Dr. Franklin Clark Fry, Vice-Chairman
Dr. Eivind Josef Berggrav
Dr. Alphons Koechlin
Rev. Leslie E. Cooke
Dr. Georges Florovsky
Dr. Martin Niemöller
Mr. T. C. Luke
Metropolitan Panteleimon of Edhessa
Rev. R. Ambrose Reeves
Dr. Gordon Alfred Sisco
Mrs. Leslie E. Swain
Mr. Charles P. Taft
Rev. T. M. Taylor
Bishop Yngve T. Brilioth, *ex officio*

[1] Sept. 6-7, 1948. For the roster of the Central Committee, see Appendix B.

[2] It was expected that the next Assembly of the World Council of Churches would be held five years thence, and that Drs. Bell and Visser 't Hooft would serve until it convened.

[3] Like the other subcommittees, the Executive Committee was elected annually. In the interest of deliberative continuity and expeditious action, few changes in its membership were made during the first six years. See the Minutes and Reports of the Central Committee, covering its transactions since 1948, published annually, Geneva and New York.

The tenure of these appointments was for a year. The Executive Committee would meet semiannually and be responsible for the business of the World Council of Churches between the sessions of the Central Committee, subject to the authority of the Central Committee.

Other committees, boards, and commissions and their heads, chosen or approved at Woudscotten, were as follows:

Finance Committee—Bishop G. Bromley Oxnam, Chairman.
Study Department Committee—Dr. Henry Pitney Van Dusen, Chairman.
Board of Managers of the Department of Reconstruction and Inter-Church Aid and Service to Refugees, Dr. J. Hutchinson Cockburn, Director.
Board of the Ecumenical Institute, Dr. Reinhold von Thadden-Trieglaff, Chairman.
Board of the *Ecumenical Review,* Bishop Yngve T. Brilioth, Chairman.
Commission of the Churches on International Affairs, Baron F. M. van Asbeck, President, and Sir Kenneth Grubb, Chairman.
Youth Department Committee, Rev. Daniel T. Niles, Chairman.

The Continuation Committee on Faith and Order had become, according to a pre-Assembly agreement, the Commission on Faith and Order of the World Council of Churches, with Bishop Yngve T. Brilioth continued as Chairman.

Dr. Alphons Koechlin, Dr. T. C. Chao, President P. O. Bersell, Rev. Leslie H. Cooke, and Mr. T. C. Luke were elected to the Joint Committee of the World Council of Churches and the International Missionary Council.

The composition of a Commission on Women in the Church was referred for study to Bishop Bell, Dr. Visser 't Hooft, and Mrs. Leslie E. Swain, with the request that they report their findings to the Executive Committee.

Addressing itself to the implementation of Article X[4] of the Constitution of the World Council of Churches, the Central Committee voted at Woudscotten to invite the Lutheran World Federation, Alliance of Reformed Churches throughout the World Holding the Presbyterian System, World Methodist Council, International Congregational Council, Baptist World Alliance, World Convention of the Churches of Christ[5] and Friends' World Committee for Consultation to send one representative each to its meetings and the Assembly of the World Council of Churches; also the World's Alliance of Young Men's Christian Associations, World's Young Women's Christian Association, World's Student Christian Federation, World Council of Christian Education and Sunday School Association, and United Bible Societies. It was requested that

[4] Article X: "World Confessional Associations and such Ecumenical Organizations as may be designated by the Central Committee may be invited to send representatives to the sessions of the Assembly and of the Central Committee in a consultative capacity, in such numbers as the Central Committee shall determine."

[5] Called in the United States "Disciples of Christ."

the International Missionary Council be represented by its Chairman and Executive Secretaries. The British Council of Churches, Canadian Council of Churches, Federal Council of the Churches of Christ in America, National Christian Council of China, and National Christian Council of India were each given an invitation to designate one consultant to sit regularly with the Central Committee in its annual sessions.

It was agreed, further, that the Executive Committee should be authorized to arrange for a representative from some part of the Spanish-speaking world, if possible, to attend the meetings of the Central Committee. In the discussion mention had been made of eighteen Latin American countries in which there were "many important churches and at least two million evangelicals" without any voice in the World Council of Churches. Only two denominations in this large area had joined the Council, and a member of one of them had been elected to the Central Committee; but the opinion was that some means of contact with the unaffiliated majority should be sought.

The Baptist Union of Denmark, which had applied for membership in the World Council of Churches prior to the Assembly, but not in time for approval by the Provisional Committee, was admitted at Woudscotten. Favorable action was taken on applications also from the United Church of Christ in the Philippine Islands, the Church of the Central Celebes, and the Dyak Church of South Borneo.

The Finance Committee reported, among other matters, the decision that a diligent effort should be made to raise not less than $60,000 of the $300,000 budget of the World Council of Churches for 1949 in the churches of countries other than the United States, and suggested approximate assessments, as follows:

Africa	$ 2,000
Australia	5,000
Austria	250
Belgium	250
Canada	10,000
Ceylon	200
China	1,000
Czechoslovakia	1,000
Denmark	1,750
Eastern Mediterranean countries	250
France	1,000
Germany	1,000
Holland	2,000
Hungary	500
Iceland	250
India, Pakistan, and Burma	2,000
Italy	100
Japan	250
Mexico and Latin America	500
New Zealand	1,000

Norway	1,250
Sweden	5,000
Switzerland	5,000
United Kingdom	18,450
	$ 60,000
United States of America	240,000
Total	$300,000

Before putting the report of the Finance Committee to the members for adoption, the Bishop of Chichester expressed the gratitude of the Central Committee to the churches of the United States for their willingness to assume the task of raising so large a portion of the money required for the work of the World Council of Churches, and its hope that, with the improvement of economic conditions, those of the other nations might take over their proportionate part of the burden. He was confident, he said, that all of them would regard what they were able to do in this respect as a privilege.

It had been possible to make provision in the budget for the travel needs of members of the Executive and Central committees in only exceptional cases,[6] and it was agreed to ask the denominations to bear the expenses of their respective representatives who had been chosen for these important positions.

A memorandum in the minutes of the Woudscotten meeting stating that the budget included $10,000 toward the accumulation of a fund to defray the expenses of the next Assembly attested the faith of the founders in the future of the World Council of Churches; likewise the entry of an action to incorporate the Council under the laws of the United States and the United Kingdom, as well as of Switzerland.

2. Regional Offices and Their Staffs

The World Council of Churches having been constituted, it became necessary to readapt accordingly the provisional regional organization, which consisted of the offices in New York and London.

Under authority voted at Woudscotten, the American Committee of the World Council of Churches was succeeded by the Conference of the United States of America Member Churches, which bore the responsibility of interpreting the World Council to the denominations and the public at large and raising money toward its budget, plus some $50,000 annually for the maintenance of the New York office, through which it functioned. Under it were created committees to promote the plans of the

[6] Such as members from distant mission churches or small denominations experiencing severe financial reverses.

Study Department, the Commission on Faith and Order, the Ecumenical Institute, the Youth Department, and other interests of the World Council of Churches. It maintained close relations with other interdenominational bodies, especially the Federal Council of the Churches of Christ in America, the International Missionary Council, and the International Council of Religious Education,[7] and became one of three agencies sponsoring Church World Service.

At Woudscotten the Central Committee outlined the organization of the New York office as follows:

> The New York office is the headquarters of the Associate General Secretary for Promotion.
>
> Promotion in this case means such interpretation of the World Council by personal contact with congregations, with communions, and with individuals, as will produce moral and financial support for its operations, together with the use of all appropriate media to bring about that result. This function of the Associate General Secretary for Promotion is no longer to be considered as restricted to the United States, but is to be expanded to cover all those parts of the world where the constituent churches desire the service, or where the Christian Councils to which they belong request it.
>
> As the Associate General Secretary of Promotion, he is, of course, the senior officer at the New York office. But it is not expected that he will be charged with detailed administration of the New York office, especially as he will be away from the office, even more than previously as the Secretary of the American Committee for the World Council of Churches.
>
> The Program Secretary in the New York office will be the administrative head of the office, under the supervision of the General Secretary and the Associate General Secretary for Promotion. He will provide all necessary services for the staff of the World Council of Churches, when operative in the western hemisphere. He will be responsible for securing the co-operation of the communions in the program of the World Council as approved or authorized by the Assembly or the Central Committee.

The decision was taken to discontinue the London office and to transfer the management of the business of the World Council of Churches in that area to the British Council of Churches, the staff of which had already been assisting with it. This arrangement met with the approval of Dr. Oliver Stratford Tomkins, formerly Assistant General Secretary but now to become full-time Associate General Secretary with responsibility for the program of the Commission on Faith and Order.

The following appointments to the staff of the World Council of Churches were made at Woudscotten:

Dr. Henry S. Leiper, Associate General Secretary, with the portfolio of Promotion.
Rev. Oliver S. Tomkins, Associate General Secretary, with the portfolios of Faith and Order and relations with the Orthodox Churches.

[7] Later, Internationl Council of Christian Education.

Bishop Stephen C. Neill, Associate General Secretary, with the portfolio of Study and Evangelism, and with headquarters in Geneva.

Dr. Robert C. Mackie, Associate General Secretary with the portfolio of Reconstruction and Youth; also Director of the Department of Reconstruction and Inter-Church Aid, as of January 1, 1949, with headquarters in Geneva.

Dr. O. Frederick Nolde, Associate General Secretary, with the portfolio of International Affairs, and with headquarters in New York.[8]

Dr. Hendrik Kraemer, Director of the Ecumenical Institute.

Professor Nils Ehrenström, Director of the Study Department.

Mr. Frank Northam, Director of the Department of Finance and Business.

Miss Jean Fraser, Director of the Youth Department.

Dean H. Høgsbro, Representative of the World Council of Churches in Germany.

Rev. Robert S. Bilheimer, Program Secretary in New York.

M. Alexandre de Weymarn, Director of the Ecumenical Press Service.

Dr. Wolfgang Schweitzer, Secretary of the Study Department.

Rev. William Keys, Secretary in New York of the Youth Department.

Rev. Jan Mirejovsky, Reconstruction Secretary of the Youth Department.

The appointment of a Secretary of Evangelism was left to the Executive Committee.

3. Attention to Attacks on the World Council of Churches

Note was taken of the attack by the International Council of Churches at Amsterdam on the World Council of Churches, and it was agreed that the General Secretary should arrange for the preparation of a statement of the nature and aims of the World Council which would answer, so far as possible, the misrepresentations being circulated, whether from malice or ignorance, as well as the honest questions of persons interested in the ecumenical movement and desiring to know the truth about it.[9] The Chairman and other speakers urged all who understood the real character and purpose of the World Council to make it part of their service to give correct information concerning it in their personal day-by-day contacts with others.

4. The Central Committee at Work

The business coming before the Central Committee at its successive meetings during the six years between the first and second Assemblies involved, as the foregoing review of part of the proceedings at Wouds-

[8] Dr. Nolde was appointed at the same time Director of the Conference of the Churches on International Affairs.

[9] See Part Four, *4*, for reference to the attitude of the International Council of Churches to the World Council of Churches.

cotten shows, many details of organization and policy arising from the relations of the World Council of Churches with other ecumenical bodies, the varied activities of the departments of the Council, and the actions which the Committee itself felt called upon to take on social and political issues of world import. Some idea of the agenda, which generally required approximately a week for their proper consideration, can be gained from a glance at the indexes of the published minutes.

The following is the Table of Contents of the "Minutes and Reports of the Third Meeting of the Central Committee, Toronto (Canada), July 9-15, 1950":

A. Opening actions and the General Secretary's Report.
   1. Opening prayer.
   2. Presiding officers.
   3. Welcome.
   4. Roll call.
   5. Minutes of the last meeting.
   6. Adoption of the agenda and programme.
   7. Appointment of minutes secretaries.
   8. Arrangements concerning the press.
   9. Report of the Executive Committee.
   10. Report of the General Secretary.

B. The Central Themes.
   11. Dominant Religions and Religious Liberty.
   12. The Ecclesiological Significance of the World Council of Churches.
   13. The Nature and Theme of the Second Assembly.

C. Reports of Departments and Commissions of the World Council of Churches and Related Actions.
   14. The Commission of the Churches on International Affairs.
      a. Report of the Commission.
      b. Letter to Korean Christians, and prayer in regard to Korean situation.
      c. Statement on the Korean situation and World Order.
      d. Statement on Race Relations.
      e. Resolutions on International Law.
      f. Statement on the Refugee problem.
      g. Resolutions on peace studies.
      h. Stockholm Appeal.
   15. The Department of Inter-Church Aid and Service to Refugees.
   16. The Commission on Faith and Order.
   17. The Study Department Commission.
   18. The Ecumenical Institute.
   19. The Youth Department Committee.
   20. The Secretariat for Evangelism.
   21. The Commission for the Life and Work of Women in the Church.
   22. *The Ecumenical Review*.
   23. *The Ecumenical History*.

D. General Business.
   24. Election of a co-president of the Council.
   25. Report of the Nominating Committee.
   26. Report of the Finance Committee.

27. Applications for Membership in the Council.
28. The Joint Committee of the International Missionary Council and the World Council of Churches.
29. Relationships with National Councils.
30. Public Relations policy.
31. Appointment of Staff.
32. Proposal of the United Bible Societies.
33. Request concerning the Basis of the Council.
34. Place and date of next meetings.
35. Message from H.R.H. Princess Wilhelmina.
36. Report on Africa.
37. Expressions of Gratitude.

At its meetings the Central Committee studied, for its own information and guidance, "central" or "main" themes, among which, during the first six years, were:

What Should the Churches Expect from the World Council of Churches?
Contemporary Issues of Religious Liberty.
Christian Action in International Affairs.
Dominant Religions and Religious Liberty.
The Ecclesiological Significance of the World Council of Churches.
The Nature and Theme of the Second Assembly of the World Council of Churches.
The Calling of the Church to Mission and Unity.
The Role of the World Council of Churches in Times of Tension.
The Relevance of the Christian Hope to Our Time.
The Asian Situation as a Concern of Christians Everywhere.

The object of these inquiries was to arrive at guiding principles for the Committee's major decisions. The conclusions on certain of the subjects were printed and given to the churches for study.

Between the first and second Assemblies the Committee met six times: at Woudscotten, Holland, September 6-7, 1948; Chichester, England, July 9-15, 1949; Toronto, Canada, July 9-15, 1950; Rolle, Switzerland, August 4-11, 1951; Lucknow, India, December 31, 1952-January 8, 1953; and finally at Chicago, Illinois, U.S.A., August 12-14, 1954. The meeting which, by the regular schedule, would have been held in the summer of 1952 was omitted and its business combined with the agenda for Lucknow, so that the members; many of whom expected to attend other ecumenical gatherings in India at the end of the year and during January of 1953, might be saved the expense and inconvenience of the extra travel.

The Assembly had limited the membership of the Central Committee to "not more than ninety," not including the Presidents of the World Council, representatives of other Christian bodies, co-opted consultants, and members of the Council's staff. Attendance averaged about 65 percent of the membership.

Some important changes in the personnel took place during this early period. Archbishop Erling Eidem, upon his retirement as Primate of Sweden in 1950, resigned as President and was succeeded in the Presidium and the Central Committee by Bishop Eivind Josef Berggrav. In 1951 occurred the death of Archbishop Germanos and the election in his place of Archbishop Athenagoras of Thyateira. In the same year Dr. T. C. Chao resigned as President; Miss Saroe Chakko of India was appointed to fill the vacancy.

Dr. Eidem, who was elevated to the archbishopric upon the death of Dr. Nathan Söderblom in 1931, had proved himself worthy of his illustrious predecessor's example in the promotion of Christian cooperation. Dr. Germanos had been "a trusted leader in the ecumenical movement for more than a generation."

The occasion of Dr. Chao's resignation was a resolution by the Central Committee on the Korean conflict, responsibility for which he felt he could not share in his position under the communist regime in China. The Committee later received a report that he had been forced to give up his professorship in Yenching University in Peiping because he refused "to deny his faith in the ecumenical character of the Christian Church," and eventually that he had become a member of the Executive Committee of the Patriotic Protestant Chinese National Movement which condemned the World Council of Churches as "a tool of Anglo-American imperialism."

The untimely death of Miss Chakko on January 11, 1954, was cause for sorrow in the churches. Her leadership in the interchurch field had seemed to all who were associated with her of the greatest promise.

Five members of the Central Committee not of the Presidium had died before the second Assembly: Commissioner Alfred G. Cunningham of the Salvation Army in England; Mrs. Lillian Harrington of Houston, Texas, who represented the Presbyterian Church in the United States; Rev. E. Luka of the Coptic Church in Egypt; Dr. William Barrow Pugh, Stated Clerk of the Presbyterian Church in the United States of America, of Philadelphia, Pennsylvania; and Dr. Gordon Alfred Sisco, General Secretary of the United Church of Canada, of Toronto.

5. The Staff Between Assemblies

The Assembly authorized a secretarial staff of thirty-six members, but because a department of publicity, which had been voted, was not set up, and certain vacancies occurring in some of the divisions could not be filled readily, this number of persons was not at any time actually engaged. Those whose names appear below were appointed and served in the positions indicated:

Name	*Date*	*Department*
Rev. Paul Abrecht	1949-54	Study
Rev. James P. Alter	1953-54	Study
Miss Dorothy Asch	1953-54	Life and Work of Women in the Church
Rev. K. M. Baker, Jr.	1953-54	General Secretariat
Mlle Madeleine Barot	1953-54	Life and Work of Women in the Church
Rev. Robert Bilheimer	1948-54	Program Secretary, New York
Mr. Paul J. Bock	1949	Inter-Church Aid
Mr. George Booth	1949-51	Youth Department
Mr. Alan Braley	1948-53	Inter-Church Aid
Mr. Bernard Causton	1949-53	Publicity
Dr. Samuel McCrea Cavert	1954	Executive Secretary, New York
Miss Saroe Chakko	1950-51	Life and Work of Women in the Church
Dr. Edgar H. S. Chandler	1950-54	Inter-Church Aid
Mlle S. de Dietrich	1948-54	Ecumenical Institute
Dr. Nils Ehrenström	1948-54	Study Department
Miss Jean Fraser	1948-54	Youth
Mr. Alan Haigh	1948-54	Finance and Administration
Dr. H. H. Harms	1952-54	Study
Pastor Göte Hedenquist	1948-49	Inter-Church Aid
Mr. Charles Hein	1950-53	Youth
Pastor H. L. Henroid	1948-51	Ecumenical Institute
Dr. J. C. Hoekendijk	1949-52	Evangelism
Rev. Bengt Hoffman	1949-53	Inter-Church Aid
Dean H. Høgsbro	1948-50	Inter-Church Aid
Dr. R. D. Hyslop	1953-54	Evangelism
Miss Margaret I. Jaboor	1952-54	Inter-Church Aid
Rev. William Keys	1948-52	Youth
Dr. Heinrich Kloppenburg	1948-50	Inter-Church Aid
Mr. Wolfgang Kordon	1948-54	Finance and Administration
Dr. Hendrik Kraemer	1948-54	Ecumenical Institute
Dr. Laszlo Ledermann	1953-54	Inter-Church Aid
Dr. Henry Smith Leiper	1948-52	General Secretariat, New York
Dr. Robert C. Mackie	1948-54	Inter-Church Aid
Pastor H. Madsen	1953-54	Inter-Church Aid
Dr. Rajah B. Manikam	1951-54	East Asia Secretariat
Rev. Raymond E. Maxwell	1953-54	Inter-Church Aid
Pastor Dominique Micheli	1949-54	Inter-Church Aid
Pastor Jan Mirejowsky	1948-50	Youth
Pastor Bengt-Thure Molander	1951-54	Youth
Bishop Stephen C. Neill	1948-51	General Secretariat, Study
Dr. J. Robert Nelson	1953-54	Faith and Order
Rev. Daniel T. Niles	1952-54	Evangelism
Dr. O. Frederick Nolde	1948-54	General Secretariat and Director of Commission of the Churches on International Affairs
Mr. Frank Northam	1948-54	Finance and Administration
Rev. William A. Perkins	1953-54	Youth
Mr. Theodore Pratt	1953-54	Inter-Church Aid, Publicity
Dr. Elfan Rees	1948-54	Inter-Church Aid and Secretary of Commission of the Churches on International Affairs

Name	*Date*	*Department*
Dr. Heinrich K. Rohrbach	1952-54	Youth
Mr. James Ryberg	1950-52	Inter-church Aid, Publicity
Mr. Marc Sauter	1946-54	Inter-church Aid
Dr. Wolfgang Schweitzer	1948-52	Study
Mr. John Taylor	1953-54	Inter-church Aid, Publicity
Rev. Robert Tillman	1950-54	Inter-church Aid
Rev. Robert Tobias	1949-53	Inter-church Aid
Dr. Oliver S. Tomkins	1948-52	General Secretariat and Faith and Order
Rev. John W. Turnbull	1953-54	Study
Dr. W. A. Visser 't Hooft	1948-54	General Secretariat
Dr. H. H. Walz	1949-54	Laymen's Work and Ecumenical Institute
Count York von Wartenburg	1950-53	Inter-church Aid
Mr. Alexandre de Weymarn	1948-54	Ecumenical Press Service
Dr. Wayland Zwayer	1950-54	Inter-church Aid

The staff during this period represented in its composition some twenty denominations in fourteen countries. The work of its members was supplemented by the services of volunteers from some of the communions belonging to the World Council of Churches, particularly in the Ecumenical Institute, the Study Department and the Inter-Church Aid and Service to Refugees Department.

The general headquarters of the World Council were established permanently in Geneva, Switzerland, where they had been located during the provisional period, with branch offices, as previously noted, in London[10] and New York City. In 1951, an East Asia Secretariat was added, in cooperation with the International Missionary Council, with an office temporarily in Bangkok, Thailand.[11]

6. Growth in Membership

During the interim between the first and second Assemblies thirteen denominations joined the World Council of Churches, bringing the total membership to 162. The Baptist Union of Wales and Monmouthshire withdrew; but many of its churches were affiliated also with the Baptist Union of Great Britain and Ireland and through this connection continued to be represented in the Council. The new members were:

The Baptist Union of Denmark
The United Church of Christ in the Philippine Islands

[10] In the course of time, the business of the Council in Great Britain was turned over, as observed in the review of the Woudscotten minutes, to the British Council of Churches, and the London office was discontinued.

[11] Dr. Rajah B. Manikam, at the time Executive Secretary of the National Christian Council of India, became East Asia Secretary of the International Missionary Council and the World Council of Churches.

The Church of the Central Celebes
The Dyak Church of South Borneo
The Moravian Church in Great Britain and Ireland
The Methodist Church of Ceylon
The Synod of the Evangelical Churches of North Iran
The Church of Central Java
The Federacao Sinodal of Lutheran Churches in Brazil
The Presbyterian Church in Formosa
The Presbyterian Church of the Gold Coast
The Church of the Province of West Africa (Anglican)
The Russian Orthodox Greek Catholic Church of North America

The Central Committee received at its meeting in Toronto in 1950 a statement from the Evangelical Church in Germany, which had been accepted by the Synod on April 23 of the same year, relating to the membership of the German churches in the World Council of Churches, as follows:

In the list of member churches of the World Council of Churches, the name of the Evangelical Church in Germany is to appear, and beneath it the names of the twenty-seven constituent Churches in Germany are to be individually recorded. After the name of each Church which belongs to the United Evangelical Lutheran Church of Germany the indication Lutheran is to be printed with a reference to a foot-note which is to run as follows:

"This Church is directly a member of the World Council of Churches in accordance with the resolution of the General Synod of the United Evangelical Lutheran Church of Germany, dated January 27, 1949, which recommended that the member Churches of the United Evangelical Lutheran Church should make the following declaration to the Council of the Evangelical Church in Germany concerning their relation to the World Council of Churches:

"The Evangelical Church in Germany has made it clear through its constitution that it is a federation (Bund) of confessionally determined Churches. Moreover, the conditions of membership of the World Council of Churches have been determined at the Assembly at Amsterdam. Therefore, this Evangelical Lutheran Church declares concerning its membership in the World Council of Churches:

(1) It is represented in the World Council as a Church of the Evangelical Lutheran confession.
(2) Representatives whom it sends to the World Council are to be identified as Evangelical Lutherans.
(3) Within the limits of the competence of the Evangelical Church of Germany it is represented in the World Council through the intermediary of the Council of the Evangelical Church of Germany."

7. The Role of the Central Committee

To the Central Committee had been given an important and difficult role. It was responsible for coordinating and directing the activities of the departments of the World Council of Churches which had been established or authorized at Amsterdam. As occasion arose it would be expected to speak and to act for the Council. Not least, it must cultivate within the denominations constituting the Council an interest in participating in its development beyond the routine commitments of membership. With Amsterdam behind them, they would be tempted to think of their duty as limited to supplying their quotas toward the official personnel and raising their budgetary assessments. The pressure of their own programs would tend to compel this course. There would be little time in their crowded conventions or synods for ecumenical interests. The world confessional movements would demand more and more attention. There was the danger that the World Council of Churches would have, at most, but a peripheral place in their concern.

The need to relate the World Council to local congregations had been emphasized by the Assembly. Only so could intelligent cooperation be developed. Formidable under the most favorable circumstances, this undertaking would be especially hard, with the lack of organization in the denominations for channeling information to the churches and fostering understanding of the Council's aims and policies. But without such intercourse, the Council could not speak for the churches with any assurance or expect the approval necessary to give effect to its actions on their behalf. Its pronouncements would be binding on the churches and express their will, according to the Constitution, only as they acted to make its resolutions their own.

The records indicate that the Committee succeeded with its task beyond the expectations of at least most of those who knew from experience the hazards to be encountered. Through correspondence and the printed word it was able to maintain and to extend contacts with the churches. The officers and members of the staff visited [12] most of the forty-five countries in which there were churches belonging to the World Council, speaking in the pulpits, attending conferences, and meeting personally many of the laity and the clergy. The work of the several departments and committees, as it took shape, confronted the churches in numerous concrete ways with the reality of Christian unity and of the world organization which it had brought forth. Especially effective in this respect was Inter-Church Aid and Service to Refugees, with its

[12] For example, in 1950 Dr. Marc Boegner visited Latin America; Dr. W. A. Visser 't Hooft went to the Eastern Mediterranean Area and Asia; Bishop Stephen Neill was in the United States twice for university missions, and in Africa on behalf of the International Missionary Council to study theological education; Miss Jean Fraser went to the Near East and the Far East for the Youth Department; Dr. J. C. Hoekendijk was in South Africa to attend the Bloemfontein Conference; Dr. Martin Niemöller traveled to Australia and New Zealand; Bishop Bell also visited Australia and New Zealand, and India.

In 1951, Dr. Hendrik Kraemer made a journey to the Far East, also to the United States. He, in company with Dr. Reinhold von Thadden-Trieglaff, visited the United States again in 1952; Dr. H. H. Walz was also that year in the United States. Miss Saroe Chakko traveled into many countries in 1950 and 1951.

necessary appeals for material support and its wide ministry of relief. Moreover, in many countries voluntary committees busied themselves with spreading information about the World Council and its program.

Meantime, imponderable factors were at work. Social disintegration and the ever present threat of more war made men everywhere receptive to any suggestion of unity. Coming from the churches, the idea was especially welcome. The failure of education and science and government to unite the nations had turned the thoughts of mankind, perhaps more than ever before, to religion as a remaining hope.

To those who were closest to the World Council of Churches in these first years, the extraordinary progress of its work had many of the aspects of miracle. This is reflected in the records.

II

PRONOUNCEMENTS OF THE CENTRAL COMMITTEE

This review of the actions of the Central Committee may well commence with its pronouncements in the name of the World Council, particularly those which defined its nature and functions or dealt with social issues of international moment. They may be considered more or less chronologically.

1. Statements on Religious Freedom

The World Council of Churches was organized during a time of totalitarian hostility to the Christian faith, which had led in a number of countries to persecution of the churches and, in some instances, to the proscription of public worship and other normal religious activities. In certain nations the authorities of dominant churches joined with the governments in restricting the rights of minority Christian groups. Appeals to the Central Committee to speak on behalf of those so beset occupied much of the agenda of its second meeting at Bishop Otter College, Chichester, England (July 9-15, 1949) and prompted the issuance of a statement on religious freedom, as follows:

The Central Committee of the World Council of Churches, meeting at Chichester, is deeply disturbed by the increasing hindrances which many of its member Churches encounter in giving their witness to Jesus Christ. Revolutionary movements are on foot and their end no man can foresee. The Churches themselves must bear no small part of the blame for the resentments among the underprivileged masses of the world, since their own effort to realize the brotherhood of man has been so weak. But justice in human society is not to be won by totalitarian methods. The totalitarian doctrine is a false doctrine. It teaches that in order to gain a social or political end anything is permitted. It maintains the complete self-sufficiency of man. It sets political power in the place of God. It denies the existence of absolute moral standards. It moulds the minds of the young in a pattern opposed to the message of the Gospel. It sanctions the use of all manner of means to overthrow all other views and ways of life.

We call statesmen and all men who in every nation seek social justice to consider this truth: a peaceful and stable order can only be built upon foundations of righteousness, of right relations between man and God and between man and man. Only the recognition that man has ends and loyalties beyond the State will ensure true justice to the human person.

Religious freedom is the condition and guardian of all true freedom. We declare the duty and the right of the Church to preach the Word of God and to proclaim the will of God. We appeal to the Churches to interpret and apply God's will to all realms of life. We warn the Churches in all lands against the danger of being exploited for worldly ends.

In the countries where the State is antagonistic to the Christian religion or indeed wherever full religious freedom is denied, we ask all Christians to remember that the liberty which they receive from their Lord cannot be taken away by the violence or threat of any worldly power, or destroyed by suffering.

Therefore, we urge the Churches to bear clear corporate witness to the truth in Christ and their ministers to continue to preach the whole Gospel. We urge all Christians to stand firm in their faith, to uphold Christian principles in practical life and to secure Christian teaching for their children.

All who bear the Christian name must be true to the living God. God calls us all to pray earnestly for one another and to be faithful in all seasons in our personal witness. In loyalty to the word that sounded forth from Amsterdam we shall "stay together," in the certain knowledge that Jesus Christ is Lord. "Stand fast therefore in the liberty wherewith Christ has made you free."

The third meeting of the Central Committee, held at Emmanuel College, Victoria University, Toronto, Canada (July 9-15, 1950), addressed itself more concretely to the problems of religious liberty in a series of resolutions:

Whereas, the World Council of Churches and the International Missionary Council have formally adopted a Declaration of Religious Liberty wherein they set forth the conditions which are essential to the full exercise of religious freedom;

Whereas, in many countries restrictions upon the exercise of religious freedom are variously imposed by totalitarian governments, by dominant religious majorities, or by religious groups seeking dominance;

Whereas, the Central Committee of the World Council of Churches in July 1949 adopted a statement condemning restrictions upon religious freedom, particularly in countries where the state is antagonistic to religion and its manifestations;

Whereas, the attention of the Central Committee has now been called to serious infringements of religious freedom in certain countries in which the Roman Catholic faith is the dominant religion and in regions in which the Moslem faith is the dominant religion;

Whereas, from countries where the Protestant or Orthodox Churches are dominant, reports have been received concerning discrimination against religious minorities; and

Whereas, even if religious liberty is safe-guarded by constitutional processes, it may easily be neutralized by social and economic pressures;

The Central Committee of the World Council of Churches resolves:

(1) To declare its opposition to all practices by which governments, churches, or other agencies curb the exercise of religious freedom; to call upon the Churches to disseminate information and to take individual and collective action for promoting in their countries conditions under which religious freedom may be fully practised; and, further, to approve representations regarding infringements to governments or to the United Nations and to the religious authorities which have jurisdiction or influence in the countries concerned;

(2) To encourage the development of a comprehensive and coordinated programme of action, national and international, and thereby to pursue affirmative, preventive and remedial measures for promoting the observance of religious freedom for all men.

The Central Committee of the World Council of Churches also: emphasizes the vital importance of incorporating within national constitutions adequate guarantees of religious liberty; welcomes the recent enactment of such constitutional safe-guards in various countries; urges all governments when drafting or amending constitutions or laws to secure for all people within their jurisdictions the fundamental right of religious freedom; and, when adequate standards have been enacted, stresses the necessity of bringing local administration and practice into conformity with them.

2. Pronouncement on the Hydrogen Bomb

Between the meetings of the Central Committee at Chichester and Toronto, the Executive Committee issued from its February, 1950, session at Bossey, Switzerland, a statement concerning hydrogen bombs:

The hydrogen bomb is the latest and most terrible step in the crescendo of warfare which has changed war from a fight between men and nations to a mass murder of human life. Man's rebellion against his Creator has reached such a point that, unless stayed, it will bring self-destruction upon him. All this is a perversion; it is against the moral order by which man is bound; it is sin against God.

All men have responsibilities before God as they face the grave issues raised by the hydrogen bomb and other weapons of modern war. Let each ponder in his conscience, be he statesman or scientist or ordinary citizen, how far his own action or attitude contributes to the danger of world suicide; and what he must do to prevent it, and to bring the nations to understand and serve one another. The governments of the nations have an inescapable responsibility at this hour. The world is divided into hostile camps through suspicion and mistrust, and through the failure of the nations to bring their mutual relations within an agreed system of justice and order. As representatives of Christian Churches we appeal for a gigantic new effort for peace. We know how strenuously the governments have discussed peace in the past. But sharp political conflicts continue and the atomic danger develops uncontrolled. We urge the governments to enter into negotiations once again, and to do everything in their power to bring the present tragic deadlock to an end.

This is the hour to listen afresh to the Word of God Who is the Lord of history. And this is the hour for earnest prayer to Him. For the fate of mankind is in His hands. Those who trust Him do not need to fear, whatever comes. He is the God and Father of our Lord Jesus Christ. All are to appear before His judgment seat, and to give account of what they have done, or have refused to do, for their fellow men.

3. The Church, the Churches, and the World Council

The nature and mission of the World Council of Churches, which were not defined clearly at the time of its organization, became a cause of sharply conflicting views among the members and of hurtful misrepresentations by critics of the movement. The Central Committee was confronted immediately with the necessity of doing what it could to set these important matters in their true light. Realizing that it could not hope to speak the definitive word that would reconcile all differences of opinion and be accepted generally as a basis of agreement, it decided to explain its own conception of the World Council in a statement to the churches for study and criticism by them, preparing the way for such amendments as the broader consultation might reveal to be needed. The greater part of the time at its Toronto meeting was given over to the discussion and formulation of this message, which bore the title, "The Church, the Churches and the World Council of Churches."

The document, as recorded in the Annual Minutes and Reports for 1950, follows in full:

The first Assembly at Amsterdam adopted a resolution on "the authority of the Council" which read:

"The World Council of Churches is composed of churches which acknowledge Jesus Christ as God and Saviour. They find their unity in Him. They have not to create their unity; it is the gift of God. But they know that it is their duty to make common cause in the search for the expression of that unity in work and life. The Council desires to serve the churches, which are its constituent members, as an instrument whereby they may bear witness together to their common allegiance to Jesus Christ, and co-operate in matters requiring united action. But the Council is far from desiring to usurp any of the functions which already belong to its constituent churches, or to control them, or to legislate for them, and indeed is prevented by its constitution from doing so. Moreover, while earnestly seeking fellowship in thought and action for all its members, the Council disavows any thought of becoming a single unified church structure independent of the churches which have joined in constituting the Council, or a structure dominated by a centralized administrative authority.

"The purpose of the Council is to express its unity in another way. Unity arises out of the love of God in Jesus Christ, which, binding the constituent churches to Him, binds them to one another. It is the earnest desire of the Council that the churches may be bound closer to Christ and therefore closer to one another. In the bond of His love, they will desire continually to pray for one another and to strengthen one another, in worship and in witness, bearing one another's burdens and so fulfilling the law of Christ."

This statement authoritatively answered some of the questions which had arisen about the nature of the Council. But it is clear that other questions are now arising and some attempt to answer them must be made, especially in the face of a number of false or inadequate conceptions of the Council which are being presented.

The World Council of Churches represents a new and unprecedented approach to the problem of inter-church relationships. Its purpose and nature can be easily misunderstood. So it is salutary that we should state more clearly and definitely what the World Council is and what it is not.

This more precise definition involves certain difficulties. It is not for nothing that the Churches themselves have refrained from giving detailed and precise definitions of the nature of the Church. If this is true of them, it is not to be expected that the World Council can easily achieve a definition which has to take account of all the various ecclesiologies of its member Churches. The World Council of Churches deals in a provisional way with divisions between existing Churches which ought not to be, because they contradict the very nature of the Church. A situation such as this cannot be met in terms of well established precedents. The main problem is how one can formulate the ecclesiological implications of a body in which so many different conceptions of the Church are represented, without using the categories or language of one particular conception of the Church.

In order to clarify the notion of the World Council of Churches it will be best to begin by a series of negations so as to do away at the outset with certain misunderstandings which may easily arise or have already arisen, because of the newness and unprecedented character of the underlying conception.

(*1*) *The World Council of Churches is not and must never become a Super-Church*

It is not a Super-Church. It is not the World-Church. It is not the *Una Sancta* of which the Creeds speak. This misunderstanding arises again and again although it has been denied as clearly as possible in official pronouncements of the Council. It is based on complete ignorance of the real situation within the Council. For if the Council should in any way violate its own constitutional principle, that it cannot legislate or act for its member Churches, it would cease to maintain the support of its membership.

In speaking of "member Churches," we repeat a phrase from the Constitution of the World Council of Churches; but membership in the Council does not in any sense mean that the Churches belong to a body which can take decisions for them. Each Church retains the constitutional right to ratify or reject utterances or actions of the Council. The "authority" of the Council consists only "in the weight which it carries with the Churches by its own wisdom" (William Temple).

(2) *The purpose of the World Council of Churches is not to negotiate unions between Churches, which can be done only by the Churches themselves acting on their own initiative, but to bring the Churches into living contact with each other and to promote the study and discussion of the issues of Church unity.*

By its very existence and its activities the Council bears witness to the necessity of a clear manifestation of the oneness of the Church of Christ. But it remains the right and duty of each Church to draw from its ecumenical experience and consequences as it feels bound to do on the basis of its own convictions. No Church, therefore, need fear that the Council will press it into decisions concerning union with other Churches.

(*3*) *The World Council cannot and should not be based on any one par-*

ticular conception of the Church. It does not prejudge the ecclesiological problem.

It is often suggested that the dominating or underlying conception of the Council is that of such and such a Church or such and such a school of theology. It may well be that at a certain particular conference or in a particular utterance one can find traces of the strong influence of a certain tradition or theology.

The Council as such cannot possibly become the instrument of one confession or school without losing its very *raison d'être*. There is room and space in the World Council for the ecclesiology of every Church which is ready to participate in the ecumenical conversation and which takes its stand on the Basis of the Council, which is "a fellowship of Churches which accept our Lord Jesus Christ as God and Saviour."

The World Council exists in order that different Churches may face their differences, and therefore no Church is obliged to change its ecclesiology as a consequence of membership in the World Council.

(4) *Membership in the World Council of Churches does not imply that a Church treats its own conception of the Church as merely relative.*

There are critics, and not infrequently friends, of the ecumenical movement who criticize it or praise it for its alleged inherent latitudinarianism. According to them the ecumenical movement stands for the fundamental equality of all Christian doctrines and conceptions of the Church and is, therefore, not concerned with the questions of truth. This misunderstanding is due to the fact that ecumenism has in the minds of these persons become identified with certain particular theories about unity which have indeed played a role in ecumenical history but which do not represent the common view of the movement as a whole, and have never been officially endorsed by the World Council.

(5) *Membership in the World Council does not imply the acceptance of a specific doctrine concerning the nature of Church unity.*

The Council stands for Church unity. But in its midst there are those who conceive unity wholly or largely as a full consensus in the realm of doctrine, others who conceive of it primarily as a sacramental communion based on a common church order, others who consider both indispensable, others who would only require unity in certain fundamentals of faith and order, again others who conceive the one Church exclusively as a universal spiritual fellowship, or hold that visible unity is unessential or undesirable. But none of these conceptions can be called the ecumenical theory. The whole point of the ecumenical conversation is precisely that all these conceptions enter into dynamic relations with each other.

In particular, membership in the World Council does not imply acceptance or rejection of the doctrine that the unity of the Church consists in the unity of the invisible Church. Thus the statement in the Encyclical "Mystici Corporis" concerning what it considers the error of a spiritualized conception of unity does not apply to the World Council. The World Council does not "imagine a Church which one cannot see or touch, which would be only spiritual, in which numerous Christian bodies, though divided in matters of faith, would nevertheless be united through an invisible link." It does, however, include Churches which believe that the Church is essentially invisible as well as those which believe that visible unity is essential.

We must now try to define the positive assumptions which underlie the World Council of Churches and the ecclesiological implications of membership in it.

(1) The member Churches of the Council believe that conversation, co-operation and common witness of the Churches must be based on the common recognition that Christ is the Divine Head of the Body.

The Basis of the World Council is the acknowledgment of the central fact that "other foundation can no man lay than that is laid, even Jesus Christ." It is the expression of the conviction that the Lord of the Church is God-among-us who continues to gather His children and to build His Church Himself.

Therefore, no relationship between the Churches can have any substance or promise unless it starts with the common submission of the Churches to the Headship of Jesus Christ in His Church. From different points of view Churches ask "How can men with opposite convictions belong to one and the same federation of the faithful?" A clear answer to that question was given by the Orthodox delegates in Edinburgh 1937 when they said: "In spite of all our differences, our common Master and Lord is *one*—Jesus Christ who will lead us to a more and more close collaboration for the edifying of the Body of Christ." The fact of Christ's Headship over His people compels all those who acknowledge Him to enter into real and close relationships with each other—even though they differ in many important points.

(2) The member Churches of the World Council believe on the basis of the New Testament that the Church of Christ is one.

The ecumenical movement owes its existence to the fact that this article of the faith has again come to men and women in many Churches with an inescapable force. As they face the discrepancy between the truth that there is and can only be one Church of Christ and the fact that there exist so many Churches which claim to be the Churches of Christ but are not in living unity with each other, they feel a holy dissatisfaction with the present situation. The Churches realize that it is a matter of simple Christian duty for each Church to do its utmost for the manifestation of the Church in its oneness, and to work and pray that Christ's purpose for His Church should be fulfilled.

(3) The member Churches recognize that the membership of the Church of Christ is more inclusive than the membership of their own Church body. They seek, therefore, to enter into living contact with those outside their own ranks who confess the Lordship of Christ.

All the Christian Churches, including the Church of Rome, hold that there is no complete identity between the membership of the Church Universal and the membership of their own Church. They recognize that there are Church members "extra muros," that these belong "aliquo modo" to the Church, or even that there is an "ecclesia extra ecclesiam." This recognition finds expression in the fact that with very few exceptions the Christian Churches accept the baptism administered by other Churches as valid.

But the question arises what consequences are to be drawn from this teaching? Most often in Church History the Churches have only drawn the negative consequence that they should have no dealings with those outside their membership. The undying assumption of the ecumenical movement is that each Church has a positive task to fulfill in this realm. That task is to seek fellowship with all those who, while not members of the same visible body, belong together as members of the mystical body. And the ecumenical movement is the place where this search and discovery take place.

(4) The member Churches of the World Council consider the relationship of other Churches to the Holy Catholic Church which the Creeds pro-

fess as a subject for mutual consideration. Nevertheless, membership does not imply that each Church must regard the other member Churches as Churches in the true and full sense of the word.

There is a place in the World Council both for those Churches which recognize other Churches as Churches in the full and true sense, and for those which do not. But these divided Churches, even if they cannot yet accept each other as true and pure Churches, believe that they should not remain in isolation from each other, and consequently have associated themselves in the World Council of Churches.

They know that differences of faith and order exist, but they recognize one another as serving the One Lord, and they wish to explore their differences in mutual respect, trusting that they may thus be led by the Holy Spirit to manifest their unity in Christ.

(5) *The member Churches of the World Council recognize in other Churches elements of the true Church. They consider that this mutual recognition obliges them to enter into a serious conversation with each other in the hope that these elements of truth will lead to the recognition of the full truth and to unity based on the full truth.*

It is generally taught in the different Churches that other Churches have certain elements of the true Church, in some traditions called "vestigia ecclesiae." Such elements are the preaching of the Word, the teaching of the Holy Scriptures and the administration of the sacraments. These elements are more than pale shadows of the life of the true Church. They are a fact of real promise and provide an opportunity to strive by frank and brotherly intercourse for the realization of a fuller unity. Moreover, Christians of all ecclesiological views throughout the world, by the preaching of the Gospel, [have] brought men and women to salvation by Christ, to newness of life in Him, and into Christian fellowship with one another.

The ecumenical movement is based upon the conviction that these "traces" are to be followed. The Churches should not despise them as mere elements of truth but rejoice in them as hopeful signs pointing toward real unity. For what are these elements? Not dead remnants of the past but powerful means by which God works. Questions may and must be raised about the validity and purity of teaching and sacramental life, but there can be no question that such dynamic elements of Church-life justify the hope that the Churches which maintain them will be led into fuller truth. It is through the ecumenical conversation that this recognition of truth is facilitated.

(6) *The member Churches of the Council are willing to consult together in seeking to learn of the Lord Jesus Christ what witness He would have them bear to the world in His name.*

Since the very *raison d'être* of the Church is to witness to Christ, Churches cannot meet together without seeking from their common Lord a common witness before the world. This will not always be possible. But when it proves possible thus to speak or act together, the Churches can gratefully accept it as God's gracious gift that in spite of their disunity He has enabled them to render one and the same witness and that they may thus manifest something of the unity, the purpose of which is precisely "that the world may believe" and that they may "testify that the Father has sent the Son to be the Saviour of the world."

(7) *A further practical implication of common membership in the World Council is that the member Churches should recognize their solidarity with each other, render assistance to each other in case of need, and refrain from such actions as are incompatible with brotherly relationships.*

Within the Council the Churches seek to deal with each other with brotherly concern. This does not exclude extremely frank speaking to each other, in which within the Council the Churches ask each other searching questions and face their differences. But this is to be done for the building up of the Body of Christ. This excludes a purely negative attitude of one Church to another. The positive affirmation of each Church's faith is to be welcomed, but actions incompatible with brotherly relationships towards other member Churches defeat the very purpose for which the Council has been created. On the contrary, these Churches help each other in removing all obstacles to the free exercise of the Church's normal functions. And whenever a Church is in need or under persecution, it should be able to count on the help of the other Churches through the Council.

(8) *The member Churches enter into spiritual relationships through which they seek to learn from each other and to give help to each other in order that the Body of Christ may be built up and that the life of the Churches may be renewed.*

It is the common teaching of the Churches that the Church as the temple of God is at the same time a building which has been built and a building which is being built. The Church has, therefore, aspects which belong to its very structure and essence and cannot be changed. But it has other aspects, which are subject to change. Thus the life of the Church, as it expresses itself in its witness to its own members and to the world, needs constant renewal. The Churches can and should help each other in this realm by a mutual exchange of thought and of experience. This is the significance of the study-work of the World Council and of many other of its activities. There is no intention to impose any particular pattern of thought or life upon the Churches. But whatever insight has been received by one or more Churches is to be made available to all the Churches for the sake of the "building up of the Body of Christ."

None of these positive assumptions, implied in the existence of the World Council, is in conflict with the teachings of the member Churches. We believe therefore that no Church need fear that by entering into the World Council it is in danger of denying its heritage.

As the conversation between the Churches develops and as the Churches enter into closer contact with each other, they will no doubt have to face new decisions and problems. For the Council exists to break the deadlock between the Churches. But in no case can or will any Church be pressed to take a decision against its own conviction or desire. The Churches remain wholly free in the action which, on the basis of their convictions and in the light of their ecumenical contacts, they will or will not take.

A very real unity has been discovered in ecumenical meetings which is, to all who collaborate in the World Council, the most precious element of its life. It exists and we receive it again and again as an ecumenical gift from the Lord. We praise God for this foretaste of the unity of His people and continue hopefully with the work to which He has called us together. For the Council exists to serve the Churches as they prepare to meet their Lord Who knows only one flock.

4. Conflict in Korea

The Toronto meeting, at which the Committee's foregoing interpretation of the nature and mission of the World Council of Churches was adopted for communication to the member denominations, also issued a statement concerning the situation created by the conflict in Korea:

The conflict in Korea reveals the precarious nature of peace and security in the world today. The World Council of Churches expresses its deep concern and calls upon its members as a world-wide fellowship to pray for Korea, where guilty and innocent suffer or perish together, and to bear witness to Christ as Lord of all life and as Prince of Peace.

An act of aggression has been committed. The United Nations' Commission in Korea, the most objective witness available, asserts that "all evidence points to a calculated, co-ordinated attack prepared and launched with secrecy" by the North Korean troops.

Armed attack as an instrument of national policy is wrong. We therefore commend the United Nations, an instrument of world order, for its prompt decision to meet this aggression and for authorizing a police measure which every member nation should support. At the same time, governments must press individually and through the United Nations for a just settlement by negotiations and conciliation.

The enforced division of a people in Korea or elsewhere is a bitter result of the divided world. It violates fundamental rights and increases the threat to peace. The United Nations has attempted to establish a free, united and independent Korea within the community of nations. Every opportunity which may arise from the present tragic situation must be used to gain this end.

The Korean situation need not be the beginning of a general war. We must not regard world-wide conflict as inevitable. Any tendency to irresponsible fatalism should be resisted. We stand for a just peace under the rule of law and must seek peace by expanding justice and by attempting to reconcile contending world powers.

Post-war totalitarianism relies not only on military pressures but also upon a policy of exploiting the distress of the poor, the resentments of subject peoples, discriminations on grounds of race, religion or national origin, the chaos of badly governed nations, and the general disunity between nations. The Korean attack may well be one of possibly a series of thrusts at such weak points in world society. Since the world is still filled with these injustices and disorders, a mood of complacency is both wrong and politically dangerous. Overcoming these evils is therefore the most important means for rendering the world morally impregnable to totalitarian infiltration.

Such methods of modern warfare as the use of atomic and bacteriological weapons and obliteration bombing involve force and destruction of life on so terrible a scale as to imperil the very basis on which law and civilization exist. It is therefore imperative that they should be banned by international agreement, and we welcome every sincere proposal to this end. However, the "Stockholm Appeal," which demands the outlawing of atomic weapons only, without effective international inspection and control, both immediate and continuous, must be regarded as a strategy of propaganda rather than a genuine peace proposal. We must seek peace by cultivating mutual confidence and work for an increasing devotion to common moral principles.

We see the judgments and warnings of God in the things which are now being wrought. As Christians it must be our purpose to "redeem the time because the days are evil." Every temptation to ease any social indifference in so tragic an age, and every tendency towards hysteria amidst the perils about us, must be resisted. We must encourage each other to bear the burdens and face the tasks of our age in the faith of Him who abideth faithful, leaving what lies beyond our power to Him Whose power ruleth and overruleth the actions and passions of men and nations.

5. Letter to Korean Christians

From Toronto went also a letter to Christians in Korea, on behalf of the denominations which were members of the World Council of Churches.

Dear Brethren in Christ: The Central Committee of the World Council of Churches, assembled at Toronto, Canada, desires to express its profound sympathy with the people of Korea in their present ordeal. We wish, in particular, to convey to our Christian brethren, in all parts of Korea, our sense of unbroken fellowship with them in Jesus Christ, and to assure them of our acute concern and our prayers as they face the perils and sufferings of war.

In a world deeply divided, Christians everywhere are called to witness to the transcendent unity which is given by Christ to His Church. We affirm our faith in the liberty wherewith Christ sets men free. No violence or threat by any worldly power can rob us of that freedom. "Neither principalities nor powers, nor things present, nor things to come, nor height nor depth, nor any other creature shall be able to separate us from the love of God which is in Christ Jesus our Lord."

We pray that in your bitter trial God may guide you to do His will and give you strength to endure; that in the fires of your suffering faith may not falter; that in the midst of tumult and destruction you may be sustained by the sure knowledge that Christ has overcome the world. And "the God of all grace who hath called us unto His eternal glory by Christ Jesus, after that we have suffered a while, make you perfect, establish, strengthen, settle you. To Him be glory and dominion for ever and ever."

6. International Threats to Peace

In the months which followed the meeting of the Central Committee in Toronto, the international situation deteriorated rapidly. Fear of another war involving all the nations became acute. The Executive Committee, from Bièvres, France, where it had convened in February of 1951, sent a letter on the world disorder to the denominations in the World Council of Churches.[1]

The Executive Committee of the World Council of Churches, meeting at Bievres, January 30-February 1, gave much thought to the grave situation caused by the international crisis. In considering the many problems raised they had the advantage of the help of churchmen from different

[1] See Annual Minutes and Reports, 1951.

parts of the world, not belonging to the Committee, who had been invited to take part in a preliminary consultation. Amongst those to whom invitations had been extended were two from Eastern Europe, but to our regret they were not able to attend.

The Executive Committee gave consideration to a variety of problems which came up in the course of the discussion. And they decided to communicate the general result to the member Churches in the form of a letter, which we now offer as a guide to reflection with suggestions for action.

Throughout our discussions we felt keenly our limitations as representatives of the Churches of certain countries only. We did try constantly to bear in mind the Christian testimony of our absent brethren and their problems, so far as we are informed of them. But we have had to work within our limitations. This letter is ours and this fact should be remembered in reading it. It is not for us to judge others in the Church but each to pray for all.

In our conversation we kept in mind that the chief task of the World Council of Churches is to maintain and develop the fellowship between the Christian Churches. But we recognize that the World Council has also the important task of giving concrete witness to the Lordship of Christ and to the implications of His Lordship for national and international life. We were all the time conscious of these two obligations which, things being as they are, often enter into conflict. In all that follows we ask you to remember that we ourselves have at least tried our best to keep them fully in our minds.

We talked much about the critical points of the international situation. It has greatly changed since the Central Committee met in Toronto. The effort of the United Nations to contain and resolve the conflict in Korea has thus far proved unsuccessful. Our vice-chairman who has just visited Korea told us of the terrible sufferings of the Korean people which continue unabated. Need we speak of our real grief that no effective solution has been found and need we say that we are thankful that, through the United Nations, the lines of negotiations have been kept open and that it continues to seek an honorable and generally acceptable reconciliation?

But—and this is what brought a note of profound alarm into our meeting—the international situation has seriously deteriorated and mankind has been brought once more to the brink of a world war. Programmes of re-armament have rapidly increased and the world is still more vividly divided into two armed camps.

There is something underlying the explosive character of the world scene which constantly exercised our minds. It is the vast upsurge of peoples of every race, nation and creed. Some countries have been the scene of far-reaching social reform. Over seven hundred million people formerly dependent have recently attained independence. Other peoples are still seeking independence. At the same time the widespread and rightful demand for equality of personal status and for release from poverty and economic oppression remains unmet. Little wonder that the offer of civil rights and freedoms loses its appeal when people are wholly obsessed by the daily struggle against hunger and want.

Everywhere the victim is man. Often he is treated as no better than an object, or at best a tool, rather than as a responsible person. He hears much about peace, but for the sake of peace, he is told either to hate or to re-arm. He hears much about freedom, but in the name of freedom, he is in fact deprived of liberty, sometimes even from his childhood. He hears much about human rights, but he lives in a world of exploitation, deportations, concentration camps, arbitrary barriers and total war. To bring the comfort and strength of the Gospel to confused and threatened man, whatever his station in life, is the great task of the Church. Only thus can he find joy to live and to love, and learn anew the meaning of hope and peace. Whatever danger he may face, he will be sustained by the full assurance of the sovereignty of God and of man's worth in God's sight.

We believe that in these truths—truths which stand for ever in the Church, East and West—are the source and impulse of our endeavour. In the light of them we tried to face baffling and almost intractable problems. Uppermost in our minds were those of the totalitarian doctrine of man in society, the menace of peace, and the denial of social justice. We want to say a few words on each of them.

At Chichester in 1949 the Central Committee spoke of the totalitarian doctrine. "The totalitarian doctrine," it said, "is a false doctrine." It destroys human integrity and uses the means of slavery in the name of justice. In this respect there is a fundamental conflict between the Christian conviction and totalitarian ideology. These are hard words. But a system based on a false doctrine cannot be overcome by force alone and every effort must be made to meet the basic challenge of totalitarian communism by means other than war.

This brings us to the difficult question of arms and re-armament. Here we can only say this. Within the World Council constituency there are many different opinions about re-armament and indeed about the attitude of the Christian towards the use of arms.

Some of these difficulties were reflected in our discussions. We considered the conditions which have brought us to our present pass, but concluded that our attention should be centered on the existing crisis. It is this. The governments and many people of the West have come to fear that the more powerful of the communist nations are ready to extend the area of communist influence by means of force and, as a result, they are rapidly re-arming. In Eastern countries, there is a growing fear that these developments might lead sooner or later to the outbreak of a preventive war. Thus re-armament has become the main and general emphasis everywhere. Its declared purpose is peace, but it can in reality endanger both peace and security, and social justice is seriously threatened. In these circumstances, it is an urgent Christian concern—in fact, a concern of all men of goodwill—that armaments, whatever their necessity, do not dominate the whole life of national and international society. We are convinced that it is the duty of all the Churches to champion peace with justice. The Churches which still have real opportunities to influence government policies have a special duty.

We take the view that the Churches must urge that the new armament programme be exclusively devoted to the purpose of security. We must seek by constant vigilance to prevent the possession of power from precipitating violence. We must not allow the fabric of social justice to be destroyed.

Every chance for negotiations must be used. When military action is in question, the nations should not act unilaterally but heed the judgments of the United Nations. Everything must be done that can build up the authority of this instrument of world order, and the United Nations Peace Observer Commissions ought to be placed at every danger spot. All of us must be on our guard against hysteria, for fatal damage can be done by irresponsible and wild exaggeration.

We are convinced that the Churches in many countries could help along these lines, and we ask you, as we have asked ourselves, whether you are doing what you can. We must remember that we may all have to live for a long time in the presence of conflicting systems. This is a call to patient steadfastness and to the simple but difficult Christian virtues. But even in these circumstances we must use every influence we can to press for the objective of bringing all national armaments under international control.

Then there is the great challenge of social justice. One of the gravest dilemmas the nations are in consists in the danger that re-armament will itself drain the vigour out of social reconstruction. Thus governments will aggravate the very disease which they seek to heal. We must struggle that this shall not be the case. All nations which possess great economic and industrial resources must promptly afford economic and technical assistance on such a scale as will eventually assure an effective response to the needs of the under-privileged. Effective co-operation must be achieved in this field, too, through the United Nations and the Specialized Agencies.

This seems to us to mean imaginative thinking and action of a wholly new order. The peoples have seen the vision of social justice; it is for us to help to transform it into reality. All people in privileged countries, particularly Christians, must strive to enter sympathetically into the social demands of the needy. "From each according to his ability, to each according to his need" has its roots in the teaching of Jesus.

We are at a loss how to share with you the sense of urgency with which we were impressed as we discussed this matter. The Churches have by no means neglected social action, but they have fallen short of what they should have done and, often, of what they would have wished to do. It is clear to us that personal sacrifice must be accepted if the hungry are to be fed and the naked to be clothed, and Christians, above all, should accept it with joy.

We should assure our Christian brethren under totalitarian regimes that we rejoice with them in the evidence that the Word of God makes its power felt among them. As Christians in the East and the West think of and pray for each other, let them do so with the mind that was in Christ Jesus and therefore look not on their own things but on the things of others. (Phil. ii, 11.)

The ends of true peace and social justice must be the constant concern of all Christian men and of all Churches.

As we continue to face the perils and perplexities of our day, let us in humility and faith turn to the only source of abiding strength, praying from every corner of the earth: "Almighty God our heavenly Father, guide, we beseech Thee, the nations of the world into the way of justice and truth and establish among them that peace which is the fruit of righteousness, through Jesus Christ our Lord. Amen."

7. The Relation of Unity and Mission

One of the perplexing questions which early arose in the Central Committee was the relation of the unity of the churches to their mission. Notwithstanding that the World Council of Churches had incorporated evangelism in its Constitution as a major interest of the cooperating denominations, many persons thought the aims it proclaimed did not envisage the ecumenical missionary responsibility with sufficient explicitness or emphasis, and this problem had to be faced. After extended discussion in two meetings, it became the subject of a statement on "The Calling of the Church to Mission and Unity," which was adopted at the sessions of the Committee held at the Le Rosey School, Rolle, Switzerland, in August of 1951. The International Missionary Council had concurrently given consideration to the matter in its conference at Willingen, Germany, and was ready to act with the Committee in preparing the pronouncement. The statement was as follows:[2]

I. The Purpose of This Inquiry

(1) The problem of the relation of "Church" and "Mission" has been before the minds of Christians for many decades. The older churches have only slowly and painfully learned to accept the missionary obligation. The younger churches are slowly and painfully emerging from the period of tutelage under foreign missions into independence as churches. The words "church" and "mission" still denote in the minds of most Christians two different kinds of institutions. Yet we know that these two things cannot rightly be separated.

(2) The problem has taken a new shape through the development of the International Missionary Council and the World Council of Churches as two distinct organizations. These two organizations represent somewhat different constituencies and gather to themselves different enthusiasms. The time has come when the relation between them must be most carefully reconsidered.

(3) It must at once be said that it is impossible to say that the International Missionary Council represents the calling of the Church to evangelism, and the World Council of Churches its calling to unity. The situation is much more complex. On the one hand the missionary movement has been from the beginning imbued with a deep sense of the calling to unity. Because the Gospel is one and the world is one, those who were inspired to recall the Church to its duty to take the Gospel to the whole world could not fail to see a visitation of unity which transcended those divisions within which churches unmindful of their missionary calling had been so long content to live. The young churches which have grown up as the first fruit of this missionary movement have already in many areas formed regional unions of churches, and the fact that the Church is now—for the first time—world-wide has inevitably compelled Christians to think afresh about its unity. On the other hand, the movement towards unity has from the beginning concerned itself with the Church's witness to the world. Unity has been sought out of a deep conviction that only together can Christians give true witness and effective service to the world. By far the greater part of the total activity of the World Council of Churches is concerned with such witness and service to the world.

(4) The present situation is, however, one of real confusion. It is true that in some churches efforts have been made to present the missionary obligation and the obligation to unity in their interdependence, while in other churches there is so little concern about either obligation that the problem does not arise. But the following examples may be given of the failure to relate the two obligations rightly to each other:

(a) Among students and others in the older churches there is a wide-

[2] *Ibid.* 1951.

spread belief that the "missionary" ear has been succeeded by the "ecumenical" and that, as a consequence, the world-wide missionary obligation has lost something of its urgency.

(b) In the lands of the younger churches the word "mission" has been almost exclusively connected with organizations controlled from the lands of the Western nations. With the coming of a new era in which the younger churches have taken their place as equal partners with the older churches in the ecumenical movement, there is a danger that the whole concept of "mission" should be at a discount as belonging to a bygone day.

(c) There is a danger that the World Council of Churches, being in a position to leave "missionary" concerns to another body, should become an affair for ecclesiastics concerned simply with the Church itself, and should lose that character of openness and commitment to the world's needs which has characterized the "missionary" movement.

(d) It is a very serious fact that, on the above grounds, the World Council of Churches is rejected by considerable bodies of Christians who—in the name of missionary concerns—refuse to be bound up with a Council of Churches. These groups have increased greatly in recent years. Some of them are working deliberately against the Council, and are causing much confusion in some areas.

II. Terminology

It is necessary to point out that thinking on these issues is often confused by lack of clarity in the use of terms. It is extremely difficult to achieve uniformity because, quite apart from problems of translation, even the same English word carries very different overtones of meaning in different areas. The words "mission" and "community" are examples which have occurred during our discussion. We should especially draw attention to the recent confusion in the use of the word "ecumenical." It is important to insist that this word, which comes from the Greek word for the whole inhabited earth, is properly used to describe everything that relates to the whole task of the Church to bring the Gospel to the whole world. It therefore covers equally the missionary movement and the movement towards unity, and must not be used to describe the latter in contradistinction to the former. We believe that a real service will be rendered to true thinking on these subjects in the churches if we so use this word that it covers Unity and Mission in the context of the whole world. Both the International Missionary Council and the World Council of Churches are thus properly to be described as organs of the ecumenical movement.

Our concern in this study is the recovery in thought, in action, and in organization, of the true unity between the Church's mission to the world (its Apostolate) and the Church's obligation to be one.

III. The Biblical Basis for the Church's Unity and Apostolicity

The divisions in our thought and practice between "Church" and "Mission" can be overcome only as we return to Christ Himself, in whom the Church has its being and its task, and to a fresh understanding of what He has done, is doing, and will do. God's eternal purpose is to "sum up all things in Christ." According to this purpose He has reconciled us to Himself and to one another through the Cross and has built us together to be a habitation of God in the Spirit. In reconciling us to Himself in Christ He has at the same time made us His ambassadors beseeching others to be reconciled to Him. He has made us members of the Body of Christ, and that means that we are both members one of another and also committed thereby to partnership in His redeeming mission.

In more detail we may say that the Church's unity and apostolicity rests upon the whole redeeming work of Christ—past, present, and future.

(a) It rests upon His finished work upon the Cross. He has wrought the atonement between man and God—an atonement for the whole human race. As we receive the reconciliation we are both reconciled to one another, and also constrained by His love to bring all men the good news of reconciliation.

(b) It rests upon His continuing work as the risen Lord Who, having conquered sin and death, sits at God's right hand, and by His spirit communicates to us His own fulness. By His spirit we are joined as members in His body, committed to His redemptive mission. We are enabled to abide in Him, and so to bear fruit. We are given power to be His witnesses to all the nations and to gather together peoples of all races and tongues.

(c) It rests upon His promise that He will come again. In His final victory the kingdoms of the world will be His, there will be one flock as there is one Shepherd, and all things will be summed up in Him. But first the Gospel of the Kingdom is to be preached throughout the whole world. In His mercy He gives us time and strength to fulfill this task.

Thus the obligation to take the Gospel to the whole world, and the obligation to draw all Christ's people together both rest upon Christ's whole work, and are indissolubly connected. Every attempt to separate these two tasks violates the wholeness of Christ's ministry to the world. Both of them are, in the strict sense of the word, essential to the being of the Church and the fulfillment of its function as the body of Christ.

Note: There are two important matters in which we are not agreed as to the interpretation of the biblical revelation, and on these we consider that study is needed:

(a) While we are agreed that unity is of the essence of the Church, we are not agreed as to the visible forms in which this unity is to be expressed.

(b) While we are agreed in looking for Christ's final victory, we are not agreed as to the manner of His victory, and as to its relation to what we may rightly hope for within history.

IV. Implications for the Life of the Church

(1) We recognize with thankfulness all the signs of the Church's acknowledgment of its missionary nature—the witness of many congregations and groups, the great work of "home and foreign" missions, and the faithful witness of countless individuals.

(2) Yet we have to confess with deep penitence that the normal life of our churches does not express the truth that to be a Christian is necessarily to be involved in a mission to the whole world.

(a) The average congregation is apt to be an introverted community which does not think primarily of its obligation to bring the knowledge of Christ to its whole neighbourhood and to the whole world, and this introversion is apt to mark the life, thought and leadership of the whole Church. This applies to the younger churches as well as to the older.

(b) Even where the obligation is acknowledged and acted upon, such action tends to take the form of a separate "mission" supported by the congregation but not regarded as the responsibility of every member.

(c) Normal theological study and teaching does not sufficiently concern itself with the task of bringing the Gospel to those outside. It largely presupposes a static, rather than a missionary, Church.

(d) The great world missionary enterprise of the churches has naturally created its own instruments and organizations, and these tend to be somewhat separate from the rest of the life of the churches. It is too easy to be a church member without feeling oneself committed to the world-wide missionary task.

(3) We are thankful to know of many bold attempts to break through this situation and to develop new patterns of church life which will demonstrate the essentially dynamic and missionary character of the Church. We commend to the attention of the International Missionary Council and the World Council of Churches the studies carried on in this realm by the World Council of Churches through its Secretariat for Evangelism, and we hope that it will be possible to enlist the much more energetic participation of the churches in these studies.

(4) As we see how many churches in our own day are being stripped of many things which have been regarded as necessary—such as buildings, funds, institutions, and privileged positions—we are led to believe that God is in this way forcing His Church to come out into the open and to commit itself afresh in a dynamic encounter with the world. We pray that the Church everywhere may learn to abandon all trust in earthly securities and to face the world with that courage which is now the very condition of existence for some of our member churches.

V. Implications for the World Missionary Task

(1) The great missionary movement of the recent centuries has under God brought into being a Church which is in some respects world-wide. We confess with gratitude that this is a mighty work of God's Spirit working through His Church even when the Church's obedience was in many ways deeply imperfect. Despite all its limitations and imperfections this movement has been the greatest spiritual movement of its kind in history. It is a movement, moreover, which, even at the present time, engages the devotion and represents the sacrificial giving of a great multitude of Christian people.

(2) We have nevertheless to acknowledge with penitence that this great movement has in many respects been marred by the defects of the churches from which the mission went forth. In particular:

(a) There has been an unconscious confusion of the unchanging Gospel with the particular cultural, economic and institutional forms of the older churches.

(b) The result has been that missionaries of the older churches have often been instrumental in bringing into being churches which are too largely replicas of those from which they had come. We have, therefore, to admit that there has been an element of cultural domination in the work of missions, and that those engaged in the missionary enterprise have often relied too much upon their own precept, example and influence and have not given sufficient freedom to the younger churches to express their Christian obedience in new forms under the guidance of the Holy Spirit.

(c) This has inevitably resulted in the creation of churches which, even though technically independent, are yet compelled to depend upon the older churches for support in leadership and finance because they are too foreign in form.

(d) Moreover, because of the divisions in the older churches, the various missions of many denominations from many lands have created confusion and division of the Christian witness among non-Christian peoples.

(e) We have to admit that too large a proportion of the great volume of missionary giving and service which flows out from the older churches is at present required to prop up relatively static younger churches, rather than make them new advances for the Gospel.

(3) We are therefore led to urge that the time is ripe for a fresh study of missionary principles and practice, and especially for a very earnest reconsideration of our present methods in the light of the Bible. We trust that the present study programme of the International Missionary Council will be helpful to this end. Our aim must be a partnership between older and younger churches in which the strength of the former is not exhausted in the support of the latter, but in which older and younger churches together can devote their combined strength to the vast unfinished mission of the Church to all men and nations.

VI. Implications for the Future Structure and Relationship of the International Missionary Council and the World Council of Churches

(1) in recognition of the inseparability of the unity and the mission of the Church, the International Missionary Council and the World Council of Churches are constitutionally "in association" with one another. This formal interlocking is finding increasing expression, as in the creation of such common instruments of action as the Commission of the Churches on International Affairs and the appointment of an East Asia Secretary responsible to both bodies. Nevertheless, all that has been said in the foregoing paragraphs inevitably raises the question whether this association of two autonomous organizations adequately expresses the unity in calling and purpose which both bodies acknowledge. Should "association" now give place to a new and much closer relationship?

(2) This question cannot be answered without taking fully into account differences in the pattern and methods of the two organizations as well as some differences in the range and character of the constituencies which the two bodies at present represent and serve. These technical factors require more attention than can be given to them by the present meeting of the Central Committee. It is therefore suggested that the officers of the World Council of Churches and the International Missionary Council should be asked to examine this question afresh and (through the Joint Committee of the World Council of Churches and the International Missionary Council) make such recommendations to both bodies as may make their relationship the most convincing instrument and symbol possible of the unity affirmed throughout this statement.

(3) While this question of the future of two great ecumenical organizations follows inevitably from the principles formulated in this document, it cannot be emphasized too strongly that the real issues raised by this discussion have a far wider and deeper implication than that of organization.

8. Appeal on Behalf of Conscientious Objectors

At its meeting in Rolle, Switzerland, in the summer of 1951, the Central Committee adopted also a statement of principles in behalf of citizens objecting on the grounds of conscience to the requirements of military service:

The Central Committee of the World Council of Churches, having adopted the following resolution at its meeting in Toronto, Canada, 9-15

July, 1950: "Agreed: Whereas the Central Committee considers that the conscientious decision of Christians with regard to participation or non-participation in war are to be respected and that therefore all nations should make provision concerning conscientious objectors; Resolves: to appoint a committee to prepare a draft statement concerning the desirable principles on which such legislation should be based for submission to the Central Committee at its next meeting," receives with appreciation the report submitted to it by the Committee on Conscientious Objection and recommends:

I. That the following provisions designed to safeguard the right of conscientious objection be transmitted by the General Secretary of the World Council of Churches to Member Churches and by the Commission of the Churches on International Affairs to National Commissions of the Churches on International Affairs, as a provisional statement of principles which should be considered in this connection:

(1) Conscientious objection shall be recognized as objection to performing military training or service, and to performing combatant duties or activities in support of war, with the understanding that every conscientious objector has the duty to render equivalent service toward the safeguarding of the community.

(2) In countries where legislation provides for the recognition of conscientious objection, conscientious objectors should make use of such provisions, including registration and other arrangements for an orderly witness to conscience.

(3) In every country a conscientious objector shall be entitled to appeal to an impartially-constituted civilian tribunal established to deal with cases of conscientious objection.

(4) The proceedings of all civilian tribunals for conscientious objectors shall be open to the public.

(5) In no country shall the death penalty be imposed, in peace or in war, upon any civilian for conscientious objection. The conscientious objector as such shall suffer no derogation of human rights.

(6) A conscientious objector shall be entitled to exemption from the normal requirements of the laws of military training and service, it being understood that provision shall be made for exemption in one of the following ways: (a) exemption without conditions; (b) exemption conditional upon the acceptance of work of a civilian nature under civilian control, such work to be specified by a civilian tribunal; (c) exemption conditional upon the performance of non-combatant duties only.

(7) Every conscientious objector granted exemption shall receive a certificate of status and exemption for purposes of identification.

(8) An application for registration as a conscientious objector who is aggrieved by any order of a civilian tribunal for conscientious objectors shall be entitled to appeal to a higher tribunal.

(9) A conscientious objector shall be entitled at any time to request a civilian tribunal to change the classification of his examination.

(10) With due recognition of the sacrifices demanded of all citizens in time of crisis, the conditions of alternative non-military service to which a conscientious objector is directed shall not be different from current conditions of similar non-military employment.

(11) A conscientious objector performing alternative service of a non-military character shall be entitled to appeal to the tribunal if required to perform work which he deems to be of military nature.

(12) A conscientious objector shall be in the same position as a person

in military service in respect to re-instatement in his previous occupation after his period of service.

(13) The "non-combatant" conscientious objector shall be entitled to receive an official assurance that he will not be called upon at any time to bear arms.

Note: In every case these rights should be taken to apply equally to women as to men.

II. That member Churches and National Commissions be invited to study the above provisions and to report their proposals for modification and amendment.

III. That, when the reports of member Churches and National Commissions show sufficient agreement on a specific provision to ensure the right of conscientious objection, the Commission of the Churches on International Affairs be requested to seek their incorporation in international agreements.

IV. That meanwhile the Commission of the Churches on International Affairs in its governmental contacts be requested to continue its support of such general provisions to ensure the right of conscientious objection as are known to be widely endorsed within its constituency.

9. Social Conditions on Foreign Mission Fields

From Lucknow, India, where it had met simultaneously with gatherings of several other ecumenical bodies in December, 1952, and January, 1953, the Central Committee addressed a letter to the denominations of the World Council of Churches giving its impressions of social and political conditions in countries of southeastern Asia and of the responsibility of the missions of the churches which were confronted with them.[3]

Brethren: The Central Committee of the World Council of Churches has held its first meeting on Asian soil. While conscious of needs in many parts of the world, here at Lucknow we have been confronted with some of the vital problems of Asia today. Through our contacts with leaders of Church and State, through the reports of the East Asian Study Conference organized by the World Council prior to our meeting, and in discussion together, certain concerns have come to us with a new sense of urgency.

We are grateful for the fact of the ecumenical movement because it helps us to face the situation within a world-wide Christian fellowship. The fact that we are members one of another, and confront these difficulties together, places new obligations on us all.

As servants of One Who speaks to us of the cup of water and daily bread we must recognize that we are confronted in Asia by whole peoples in desperate need of food, clothing and shelter. We must support the efforts of those working for material and social welfare. The people of Asia are also seeking well-ordered political life and true community. Above all we see their need for an ultimate faith by which to live and for knowledge of Christ Who alone can impart this.

The struggle for, and the attainment of, national independence, the break-up of the old village structure of society and the attempt to build up a

[3] *Ibid.* 1953.

society based on industrial techniques, the challenge to old customs and traditions through new conceptions of fundamental rights, the transformations in the status of women and the pattern of the family, all these indicate the vast dimensions of the revolution.

I. The Imperative of Social Justice

Our meeting has brought home to us the poverty and distress of these peoples as well as their efforts to grapple with their problems. They are demanding social conditions which are worthy of human beings. Churches all over the world must ask how they can help the people of Asia in their efforts to attain a standard of living which meets basic needs, and in their search for a more just social and economic order.

The Church in Asia has the crucial task of helping to provide the true moral and spiritual dynamic for the people longing for social justice and peace. Without this dynamic their longing cannot be realized and may be betrayed by false hopes. To meet these needs, the full support of the Christian community in under-developed countries must be rallied behind the efforts of their governments and people to tackle their own economic problems. The churches in the more developed countries must urge these peoples and governments to do everything possible to strengthen programmes of technical assistance, without which such efforts in Asia cannot succeed. This assistance will be effective and welcome only when it expresses a concern for man and his needs wherever he lives, and is a manifestation of human solidarity. It must therefore be given with sensitivity to the economic, political and social goals of the people of Asia.

Re-armament and military tension seriously reduce the resources available for industrial development in Asia. They also create an attitude of mind which leads to national and international policies in which positive programmes of social reconstruction tend to be neglected. The Christian Churches must help their peoples and Governments to reckon with the threat to the social development of these countries, which is created by tensions and power rivalries.

II. The Christian Basis of Political Freedom

These countries which are attempting to construct political institutions that give form to their sense of freedom are forced to look for the cultural and religious foundations of responsible social life. In this situation the churches of Asia must continue to make clear that the fundamental rights of man will only be firmly grounded in so far as these are related to the Christian view of man as a child of God in spirit. Freedom can only be retained in a society which is based on the integrity of the individual.

The Christian understanding of man is directly relevant to the search for new foundations for society. Churches rooted in Eastern soil must be helped in making this witness real and effective. Only as the Church can offer actual demonstrations of the creation of Christian character, of community living, brotherly service and reconciling fellowship will it fulfill its redemptive task in the midst of the changes taking place in all aspects of Asian society. Here local congregations of the Church have an indispensable part to play.

III. The Call to Missionary Obedience and Unity

The missionary task of the Church is more important than ever in Asia today. Amid elemental hunger, the uprooting of life and the struggle to rebuild, the fundamental need is still man's need for God. It must be known that within the events of our time His Presence is to be discerned in judgment and blessing. Christ alone makes this knowledge possible in all its redemptive power. To preach Him and bear witness to Him amidst the claims of other faiths is a task of burning urgency. Yet we have scarcely begun to encounter and understand the other great religions of Asia on their own ground.

Again, the fulfillment by churches of their missionary task brings particular responsibilities in Asia. The churches are called to make their life a witness to social justice and political freedom. Only so can they find an opening in the hearts of these peoples for the greater treasure entrusted to the Church.

The overwhelming evangelistic task in Asia is the concern of the whole Church. This responsibility now falls primarily upon the churches in Asia. But the Western churches need to redouble, and not slacken, their missionary endeavour in Asia. Yet this contribution from the West must be undertaken in a spirit of partnership with the younger churches, and along lines which will strengthen them for their own missionary obedience.

No one can enter today into the Asian scene without realizing at every hand the urgency with which many of the churches and Christian people are crying for unity. While Christians find themselves as a small minority in the midst of vast communities of non-Christian peoples the call of God to all of us to seek for unity is powerfully re-inforced by the demands and circumstances of the situation, and by their own task of witness.

There are dangers in this very sense of urgency which cannot be disregarded. Unity may sometimes be looked upon as a solution of all problems. It may be sought without due regard for truth in doctrine and soundness in order. But, having said this, we feel bound to state that the churches of the West are called to show great understanding and a readiness to give full freedom and continuing support to their brethren in the East as they seek to find God's purpose for them in their own time and place.

"Prepare ye the way of the Lord, make His paths straight."

10. Letter to the United Nations

From Lucknow a letter was sent also to the President of the General Assembly of the United Nations, to convey the Committee's "deep concern at the growing deterioration in relations between the rival groupings of powers and to make an appeal to the United Nations."

Sir: The Central Committee of the World Council of Churches meeting at Lucknow has requested me as its Chairman to express to you as President of the General Assembly of the United Nations its deep concern at the growing deterioration in the relations between the rival groupings of powers and to make an appeal to the United Nations. It is profoundly distressed at the wide-spread sense of frustration over the increasing bitterness which affects relations between the powers. In addressing you it believes that it not only speaks for the delegates from the churches of many lands but also reflects the great body of Christian opinion throughout the world.

The World Council of Churches is appalled by the suffering and anxiety which the wars now raging inflict upon the peoples on whose soil they are fought and upon all engaged in the fighting. It assures you, Mr. President, that millions of people whom it represents are longing and praying for an honorable peace.

The Central Committee wishes me to say how greatly it appreciates the efforts of the United Nations to overcome what is apparently the one remaining obstacle in the conclusion of an armistice in Korea. It regrets that no plan has so far been found acceptable to all parties. It most earnestly urges the United Nations to persevere in its efforts to resolve the conflict by a truce which will safeguard prisoners of war against forcible repatriation or forcible detention.

The question of repatriation may not be the only obstacle to the conclusion of agreements to end fighting, and other steps may have to be taken. The Central Committee therefore welcomes the expressed willingness of the highest authorities of certain great powers to hold personal discussion and trusts that the essential preliminary conditions of successful consultation may be satisfied.

The immediate object for which the United Nations intervened has been fulfilled. There now remains the settlement of the Korean question with a view to the unification and independence of Korea. The Central Committee is far from underestimating the difficulties. But it is convinced that the only way to end the bloodshed in Korea and to hasten the solution not only of the Korean but also of wider questions is through negotiated settlements. A deep sense of responsibility therefore prompts this appeal to the United Nations to guard against any extension of the conflict and to persist unceasingly in the promotion of negotiations until success is achieved. It commends the more widespread use in international conference of an umpire.

The Central Committee of the World Council of Churches is also aware that the serious economic needs of many countries in different parts of the world, especially in Asia, cry out for attention. It appreciates the notable work done through technical assistance and in other humanitarian ways by the United Nations and urges the nations unitedly to devote their resources to meet this call. But in this grave and perilous hour the breaking of deadlock in Korea is the immediate and essential step to these wider constructive activities.

I am sending a copy of this communication to the heads of all delegations to the United Nations, and to the Secretary-General.

With much respect the Central Committee addresses this appeal to the General Assembly of the United Nations. On behalf of that Committee, I remain, Sir

Respectfully yours,
Bishop of Chichester
Chairman

Note: In sending this letter the Central Committee expresses its concern with the international situation and at the same time calls upon Christian people to pray for the establishment of a just and lasting peace.

11. Resolution on Korea

The Executive Committee at a meeting in Céligny, Switzerland, in August of 1953—after the conclusion of the Korean truce—took note in resolutions of the opening of the way thus for beginning political unification and economic rehabilitation in Korea, and urged the churches to call upon their governments to share fully in all relief measures and themselves to support liberally the Relief Committee of the National Christian Council of Korea.

12. Letter to the Berlin Conference

From its meeting in Königstein, Germany, on February 4, 1954, the Executive Committee addressed a letter through its Chairman, the Bishop of Chichester, to the "big four" conference of Foreign Ministers[4] then in session at Berlin:

Dear Sirs: The Executive Committee of the World Council of Churches which has been in session these days at Königstein has followed with its thoughts and prayers the deliberations of the Foreign Ministers' Conference at Berlin. In addressing this letter to you I reflect the concern and hopes not only of the leaders who are assembled from many lands but also of the churches and Christians whom they represent.

We are conscious of the difficulties and complexities which you face as you seek solutions of the problems before you. We know that a commonly accepted plan to restore Germany and Austria to the position of freedom and independence which they should now hold in a responsible world society is not easy to find. Yet we believe that this objective can and must be achieved in a way which will heed the legitimate desires of these nations and their people and which will not impose discriminatory restrictions upon them. Reconciliation will be most surely effected and safeguards for all parties against future aggression most securely provided by building a community of mutual responsibility and co-operation.

We are confident that substantial progress on concrete issues can be made at the Berlin Conference and that a better climate would thus be created for the solution of problems in various parts of the world. In view of previous negotiations we hope that difficulties will be overcome and an agreement reached on a Peace Treaty with Austria. We believe that the world is looking to the Berlin Conference for a conclusive decision on the steps leading to a Treaty of Peace with Germany. If an immediate and full agreement should prove impossible, the Conference ought certainly to offer a much more secure prospect of a German Peace Treaty and arrangements ought to be made promptly whereby the hitherto separated parts of the German people can be most naturally and closely related to each other.

In expressing these views to you we do not ask for agreements which are brought by forsaking sound principle and which would tend to build false hopes. We respectfully urge you to guard against despair and to persevere in the effort to move forward in concrete action for the relief of threatening tensions. The very atmosphere in which the four-power conference is concluded and the extent to which there is a commitment to further co-operation will largely determine whether the peoples of the world will regard the prospect of securing peace among the nations with or without hope.

We and our fellow Christians of many nations will continue to pray that God may grant you and your colleagues wisdom and understanding and bring your deliberations to a successful result.

Signed by "George Bell, Bishop of Chichester, Chairman of the Executive Committee."

[4] Georges Bidault of France, John Foster Dulles of the United States, Anthony Eden of Great Britain, and Vyacheslav Molotov of Russia. For letter, see Minutes, 1954.

III
EVALUATION OF THE PRONOUNCEMENTS

The public pronouncements given in the foregoing section do not exhaust the list reported in the minutes of the Central and Executive Committees for the years between the first and second Assemblies of the World Council of Churches; but they cover a sufficiently wide range to reflect fairly the thinking of the members of these bodies concerning the critical matters with which they dealt and other related subjects, and to afford grounds from which to judge the aims and principles guiding the Council during this formative period.

The Central Committee, with its Executive Committee,[1] was, it may be repeated, in effect the World Council of Churches. Upon it depended the confidence of the denominations which had constituted the World Council, in an unprecedented move to give expression to the spirit of Christian unity through an international organization of churches. The trust that might be accorded the effort in circles outside their constituencies hung upon its decisions. It had received from the Assembly at Amsterdam a charter, but no chart. However, it could draw upon the experience of the Provisional Committee which preceded it. A number of its members had been associated with the work in the decade prior to Amsterdam, most of which had been carried over into the program of the World Council of Churches. Moreover, they could hope justifiably for continued remembrance in the prayers of the churches which had chosen them for their exacting duties and believe that the Spirit of God, by whose guidance the movement now so much their charge had been brought to the present fateful days, would be also their help.

[1] Actions of the Executive Committee, unless authorized in advance, required approval by the Central Committee. The Central Committee, meeting annually, could deal with emergencies only through the Executive Committee. Though not regarded as ideally the best procedure, there seemed to be no other way to get the results desired. The Executive Committee had at all times the counsel of the other committees and the staff of the Council.

1. On the Nature of the World Council

Of the statements under consideration here, the one concerning "The Church, the Churches and the World Council of Churches" [2] fell undeniably within the province of the Committee's authority, setting forth, as it did, the nature and purpose of the Council for the information of the churches—its member denominations and others—and of interest mainly to them.

The fear had persisted that the Council, notwithstanding the constitutional definition of its functions, aspired to become a super-ecclesiastical body with control over the churches. This misapprehension had, if possible, to be laid.

To be dealt with also was the uneasiness some denominations felt on account of membership in the World Council with others which they could not treat as of equal status with themselves. So long as they remained silent, such latitudinarianism seemed to them likely to compromise their position.

There were in the Council, moreover, differing conceptions of Christian unity, and it had to make plain the fact that it offered room for all these and identified itself with none of them.

These were the main points calling for clarification.

The disquisition met generally with a favorable reception and went a good way to reassure those denominations which had joined the World Council of Churches but, afterwards—when critics leveled their arguments against it—wondered whether they had been ill advised. The document was commended to the churches for study and comment, with a view to amending it, if necessary, in the light of criticisms. The response indicated that it had satisfied the questions of many who had been uncertain or confused.

The results proved, further, that it was not impossible to develop in ecumenical discussion a workable two-way procedure whereby the World Council and its committees could ascertain the opinion of the denominations on important issues of concern to them and so speak with greater confidence for them.

No discussion of so complex a subject, however, could resolve all conflicts of thought, and some of the views expressed by the Central Committee in its interpretation had the effect, indeed, of creating new obstacles to agreement. For example, its disavowal of the intention on the part of the World Council of Churches to promote any particular concept of Christian unity seemed to some persons to imply acceptance of a static condition in interchurch relations.[3]

[2] See Section II, p. 374 ff.

[3] The purpose of the World Council of Churches, often stated, was to bring the denominations together in a fellowship of study and work, in which they would discover and manifest their unity and themselves initiate whatever attempts in the way of union they considered feasible.

The Central Committee itself had this to say:

> In spite of these efforts to define and interpret the nature of the Council, misunderstandings still persist. In some cases these are based on the *a priori* judgment that the encounter between the churches which do not have complete agreement on matters of faith is necessarily a denial of faith. We can only ask those who take that attitude to consider whether there is any other way to arrive at such agreement except the way of ecumenical conversation. In other cases the misunderstandings are due to the fact that the World Council is conceived in historical categories rather than in categories which are appropriate to a body which represents a new form of relationships between the churches. We have no example in history of a world-wide fellowship of churches which has fully respected the autonomy of every church. Thus it is hard to make it clear that the Council is not, and will not become, a super-church, or a structure dominated by a centralized administrative authority.

2. On Religious Liberty

"Revolutionary political and social movements" evoked the declaration by the Central Committee on behalf of religious liberty, which, with its assertion that "religious freedom [was] the condition and guarantee of all true freedom," could hardly have failed to make the dictators more determined, if that was possible, in their proscriptions and persecutions. But the indictment could not be limited to them. Others besides communists and fascists were against the free exercise of religion and not averse to using civil power to curtail or abolish it. There were persistent reports of such action by the Roman Catholic Church, particularly in certain of the Latin countries, by the Eastern Orthodox Churches in the Balkans and the Middle East, and by some Protestant communions in areas where they enjoyed pre-eminence in numbers and influence. These offenders had also to be admonished, if anybody had. The resolutions could not have been pleasant to pass, as they were not to read. They were a triumph for the so-called sects who could see in their promulgation the beginning of a new method in dealing with discriminations, harassments, and oppressions such as some of them were even then suffering. These groups had long cried out against their enemies, generally with little hope that anybody would hear or heed, but now a world association of the churches had raised its voice with theirs, not passing over the offenses of its own members who were guilty.

What the Committee said about religious liberty aroused criticism and could have been opposed reasonably enough, even by those believing in the general intent.

Christians under tyrannical governments ought, perhaps, to defy laws abridging or abrogating freedom of worship; but who within the secure bounds of nations which guaranteed the "unalienable rights" should venture to read this duty to them, especially when to do so would tend to justify the charge that the church authorities speaking on their behalf were only the mouthpiece of the false Western democracies, and to incite their oppressors to greater violence?

As for the religious bodies accused of being among the transgressors, they were entitled to a hearing. They had a case, even if it was inadmissible from the standpoint of those denouncing them. Not believing in the democratic idea that error and proselytism were to be countenanced as necessary to the progress of truth, they could justify to their own consciences the suppression of religious teachings they held to be false. And however mistaken they may have been, could it have been denied that those upon whom their repressions fell often had need of warning from their defenders against the practice of attacking and tearing down the work of Christian churches of a different confession and against other excesses of zeal?

Resolutions tempered by recognition of these facts would have been regarded by many persons as weakening the cause of freedom, but actually, because of their manifest fairness, they would have invited a more sympathetic hearing by those against whom they were directed, and, at the same time, would have helped the troubled Christian minorities at the point of their need of cultivating patience and moderation.

3. On Encouragement of Koreans

It should be said that only good could have resulted from such a letter as that "to Christians in Korea" [4] overwhelmed by the sufferings of war. It was in fellowship and prayer that the churches performed their most telling ministry. If they knew that other Christians remembered them in their distress, those who had to bear persecution would be strengthened and enabled better to know and do the will of God.

4. On the Korean Conflict and World Order

Those who thought the churches should not concern themselves with politics could only have felt unhappy over the statement of the Central Committee "on the Korean situation and world order." [5] But, if the duty to speak on such matters was granted, it probably would have been agreed that what was said well befitted an international body such as the World Council of Churches.

The assertion that "an act of aggression [had] been committed" was

[4] See Section II, p. 381.
[5] See Section II, p. 379.

based on the report of the Commission of the United Nations in Korea, the most objective testimony available, which had declared that "all evidence [pointed] to a calculated, co-ordinated attack prepared and launched with secrecy" by the North Korean troops, and bore otherwise the marks of fully responsible action. Its commendation of the United Nations, "an instrument of world order, for its prompt decision to meet this aggression and for authorizing a police measure which every member nation should support" had the backing of all but two members, conscientious objectors. The latter voted, however, for the remainder of the pronouncement with its plea to all governments to "press individually and through the United Nations for a just settlement by negotiation and conciliation" and to seek by international agreement a ban against the "use of atomic and bacteriological weapons and obliteration bombings," and with its warning against "any tendency to irresponsible fatalism" which accepted "world-wide conflict as inevitable."

The Korean War was to settle down into a stalemate in which the bitterness of its losses would obscure the principles on which the United Nations intervened, but a clear reading of history would seem to sustain the soundness of this course in the light of events in 1950. The conflict, through the action of the United Nations, affected many personally who might otherwise have escaped for the time, but if intervention prevented, as it may well have, another war on a larger, possibly a world, scale and established the will to deal in the future with attempted aggression through policing measures, these and other gains on the long road to security and peace should have helped those who bore the brunt of sacrifice, the men under arms and their families, to believe that their suffering would not be fruitless.

5. On Conscientious Objectors

The opposition of some in the Central Committee to the employment of military force against communist aggression in Korea raised questions concerning the position of conscientious objectors in the World Council of Churches.

The Conference on Church, Community and State at Oxford, England, in 1937 had considered at length the conflicting attitudes of Christians toward war. The conclusions reached and incorporated in its reports had since been accepted in practice as consonant with the principle of unity in diversity sanctioned by the policy of the World Council of Churches.

It had been agreed, in short, that there was room in the Church for both those who held it wrong for Christians to take part in war under any circumstances and those who, while recognizing its evil, thought nevertheless that when it stood over against an alternative course leading to worse offense war might properly command their cooperation; and that each group should accord to the other the right to be guided by conscience in the matter, without any breach of fellowship, both resolving to work together, so far as they might, for the peace of the world. In this spirit the Committee in its meeting at Rolle, Switzerland, in 1951 adopted the statement on "conscientious objection,"[6] the immediate occasion being the reported harsh treatment by certain governments of citizens who refused to render military service.

6. On World Unrest and Totalitarianism

The letter of the Executive Committee[7] to the churches from Bièvres in the early weeks of 1951 may be studied as an example of the difficulties the World Council of Churches encountered when it undertook to speak on political issues. The predicament arose inevitably from the presence in its membership of Christians from both the East and the West whose orientation could only follow the sharp division between the two spheres.

The conferees thought that the international situation had worsened to the degree that war had become imminent. They wished to awaken the churches to the danger, as well as to prayer and such other action as was possible.

Three causes contributed to the condition the world confronted, as they saw it: the totalitarian doctrine of man, the rapid increase of armaments, and the failure of social justice on behalf of the multitudes struggling for their rights. The Committee felt that it must speak against communism, which seemed to it so largely responsible for the acuteness of the tension. Could this be done without destroying the hope of the World Council to build a truly inclusive fellowship of Christians?

> The chief task of the World Council of Churches [wrote the Committee] is to sustain and develop the fellowship between the Christian churches. But we recognize that the World Council has also the important task of giving concrete witness to the Lordship of Christ and to the implications of His Lordship for national and international life. We are all the time conscious of these two obligations which, things being as they are, often enter into conflict. . . . We tried to face baffling and almost intractable problems. . . . Uppermost in our minds were those of the totalitarian doctrine of man in society, the menace [to] peace, and the denial of social justice. In this respect there is a fundamental conflict between Christian conviction and totalitarian ideology. These are hard words.

[6] Section II, p. 389.
[7] See Section II, p. 384.

The question thus raised was whether witnessing to the social implications of the Lordship of Christ, as one saw them, was the will of God for him, when what he must say would be "hard words" to another whose understanding of the Lordship of Christ in reference to the same matters was entirely different.

The Committee undoubtedly expressed the judgment of most of the churches of the World Council in what it said about totalitarianism, but whether in doing so it strengthened the fellowship of Christians, East and West, and helped those behind the Iron Curtain in their struggle was less certain.

This is a problem besetting the churches whenever and wherever they attempt to apply what they conceive to be the social teaching of the gospel. Christians of equally honest convictions differ in their interpretations. Shall they part and go their separate ways? Or shall they remain silent on controversial subjects and pray for one another, that in loyalty to Christ they may find his way together, which is by no means always plain from the record they have of his precepts?

The World Council of Churches was committed to speak on questions of this kind, and this policy must have rested on the presupposition that Christians united in love toward Jesus Christ would grant to one another freedom of speech in the discussion of the not always clear leadings vouchsafed them in regard to social issues, as of their doctrinal disagreements. The presence of representatives of churches in communist nations at meetings of the Central Committee and the World Council after the Bièvres letter seemed to imply admission on their part of the reasonableness of this assumption. Nevertheless, some members, whether of their own volition or under pressure, withdrew because of the criticism of the totalitarian way, particularly of communism.[8]

7. On Hydrogen Bombs

The Executive Committee's pronouncement from Céligny in 1950[9] on the hydrogen bomb was received with general approval. It was a most effective statement. In four short paragraphs it set forth with cogent eloquence the immorality of war with weapons for mass slaughter, the duty of every person to face his responsibility for trying to do something about it, the obligation upon governments to undertake new efforts on behalf of peace, and the background of religious faith with its consciousness of individual accountability to God. The World Council of Churches might well follow in all communications its example of brevity and perspicacity.

[8] E.g., Dr. T. C. Chao, who resigned as a President of the World Council.
[9] See Section II, p. 373.

8. On Missions and Social Action

The letter to the churches from Lucknow[10] conveyed the Committee's impression of the problems confronting Christian work in parts of the Orient, which was received from a close-up view and from reports of native leaders of both church and state. It had, incidentally, the significance of illustrating further the developing policy of the World Council of Churches in relation to Christian missions and social action.

The Committee found the people of Asia "demanding social conditions . . . worthy of human beings" and sensed how this exposed them to exploitation by the ambitious and unscrupulous who promised anything they asked for, in ignorance of the fact that in the last analysis, what they needed only they themselves could create. It thought "churches all over the world" had to ask how they could "help the people of Asia . . . to attain a standard of living which [met] basic human needs, and in their search for a more just social and economic order," and to "urge their . . . governments to do everything possible to strengthen programs of technical assistance . . . given with sensitivity to the economic, political and social goals of the peoples of Asia."

The churches of Asia themselves must see, the Committee said, that "the Christian understanding of man [was] directly relevant to the search for new foundations for society" and "offer actual demonstrations of the creation of Christian character, of community living, brotherly service and reconciling fellowship . . . in the midst of the changes taking place in all aspects of Asian society." In this "the local congregation" had "an indispensable part to play."

"The overwhelming evangelistic task in Asia is the concern," it said, "of the whole Church," though it fell "primarily upon the churches of Asia." Western churches needed "to redouble, and not slacken, their missionary endeavor in Asia. Yet this contribution . . . must be undertaken in a spirit of partnership with the younger churches."

9. On the Berlin Conference

It is not easy to evaluate statements like that in the letter[11] of the Executive Committee to the Conference of Foreign Ministers—Eden, Molotov, Bidault, and Dulles—in Berlin in 1954 on the status of Austria and Germany.

[10] See Section II, p. 391.
[11] See Section II, p. 395.

What the Committee said could only have accented the hopes of the West that agreement would be reached to reunite Germany and restore Austria; and this, like the assurance of prayers by Christians that the Conference might be successful, could only have seemed gratuitous to certain of the conferees and tended to stiffen their recalcitrance.

Whether it were better, under such circumstances, to leave the concern and the prayers of the churches to be assumed or to give them public expression was a question on which there would have been no unanimity. It is always in the minds of some religious folk that God may use what they say, even if resented, to bring conviction to the unregenerate. In this instance the Committee had possibly consulted some of the members of the Conference in advance on its contemplated action. Later, in speaking of its political pronouncements, the Central Committee recorded this observation in *The First Six Years:*

> It should . . . not be thought that these [pronouncements] are the only ways in which the Council has sought to bring Christian judgment to bear on international relationships. On several occasions officers of the Council, taking their stand on principles formulated by the Assembly or the Central Committee, have made their opinion known to the authorities concerned. And the Commission of the Churches on International Affairs, which is under the joint auspices of the International Missionary Council and the World Council of Churches, has constantly been watching international developments and has sought to implement the decisions of the Assembly or the Central Committee by interventions on specific points. The experience of the last years has shown that it is not through public pronouncements alone but through such pronouncements followed up by constant personal intervention in responsible quarters that concrete results are achieved.

10. On Unity and Mission

As noted already, the modern movement on behalf of Christian unity received its strongest impulse from foreign missions; but the World Council of Churches had no full organizational connection with this primary source of the inspiration which had created it, aside from the presence in its membership of a few of the so-called younger churches, and an associate relationship with the International Missionary Council.

The reasons for this anomalous development were quite obvious. In the first place, a majority of the leaders in the World Council were interested primarily in other phases of unity. Those associated with Faith and Order were deeply concerned for the attainment of closer theological agreement; others coming to the Council by way of Life and Work were as keenly interested in collaboration in the search for Christian solutions of social problems. In the second place, for more than a quarter of a century the International Missionary Council had been the organ for cooperation in the mission fields. And the hoped-for inclusion of this body—along with the Continuation Committee on Faith and Order and the Universal Christian Council for Life and Work—in the World Council was blocked by obstacles which seemed insurmountable at that time.[12]

Confronted by this impasse, the World Council made a place in its program for evangelism, which it conceived broadly as proclaiming the gospel through the whole life and endeavor of the churches. At the same time, it entered into a working "association" with the International Missionary Council on a partial basis, which grew into a pleasant and fruitful relationship.

But many persons on each side considered the situation as it stood unsatisfactory. They thought missions should be more explicitly a part of the work of the World Council, yet they feared that if the International Missionary Council were incorporated in the World Council the attention and the energy of the churches would be diverted from their commission of world evangelization to preoccupation with ecclesiastical matters. They could see also the difficulty of transferring the interest and loyalty of the younger churches, should a merger come about.

The thinking of the Central Committee and a special committee of the International Missionary Council was summarized in the summer of 1951 by their pronouncement entitled "The Calling of the Church to Mission and Unity."[13]

This document attempted to clarify the position of the two bodies and called for a careful re-consideration of their relationship. While recognizing the complexities of this relationship, it declared that the "unity" and the "mission" of the Church were inseparable. It warned that by confining itself solely to ecumenical matters, the World Council was in danger of losing "that character of openness and commitment to the world's needs which has characterized the 'missionary movement.'"

In the end, however, the problem was not resolved by this pronouncement of 1951. The Central Committee and the special committee of the International Missionary Council referred it to the officers and the Joint Committee of their organizations with the question: "Should 'association' now give place to a new and much closer relationship?"[14]

[12] One difficulty was the fact that the World Council of Churches was composed of churches as such, while the International Missionary Council consisted of regional mission bodies and national councils.

[13] For the text of this report see the preceding section, pp. 385-89.

[14] The International Missionary Council and the World Council of Churches were eventually merged at the Third Assembly in New Delhi, 1961.

11. Recapitulation

The letters and pronouncements of the Central Committee here reviewed reveal the activities of the World Council as:

Speaking whenever "vital issues concerning all churches and the whole world were at stake."

Urging peace by negotiation and conciliation, rather than resort to war.

Advocating reduction of armaments by the nations and the employment of those retained for security purposes only.

Counseling the abolition of such weapons of war as would cause the mass destruction of populations.

Supporting the United Nations Organization as the most promising instrument for promoting world order and peace.

Upholding the use of armed forces as a policing measure against manifest aggression.

Calling upon the churches and the governments for contributions for the technical assistance of economically undeveloped peoples.

Exposing the errors and inhumanities of communism and other totalitarian systems.

Espousing the cause of religious freedom.

Recommending the enactment by all nations of constitutional provisions for the just treatment of conscientious objectors.

Refusing to identify itself with any specific plan of church union, although working for the promotion of the spirit of Christian unity.

Sympathizing with the younger churches on the mission fields in their demand for greater unity, but recognizing the danger that corporate union might be looked upon mistakenly as a solution to all problems of Christian work and sought "without due regard for truth in doctrine and soundness in order."

Standing for the right of the younger churches to self-determination, with the counsel and support of the older sponsoring denominations acting "in the spirit of partnership."

Treating as the "chief task of the World Council of Churches" the maintenance and development of the fellowship of the churches, but insisting that witnessing to the lordship of Jesus Christ and to the implications of his lordship for national and international life was a duty not to be avoided when it seemed to conflict with brotherhood.

And calling the churches ever to prayer for peace, for governments in whose hands, humanly speaking, it lay, for Christian brethren in all walks and conditions, and for the unbelieving everywhere, that they might be led into the saving light of the gospel.

12. The Committees Criticized for Their Much Speaking

It is part of the record that, not unlike the Provisional Committee of the World Council of Churches (in process of formation), the Central and Executive Committees were criticized for their much speaking.[15]

[15] See p. 210, Part Two, Section II, *9*. It should be added that they were criticized also for not speaking enough.

But there were no signs of deviation by them from the purpose of the pre-Amsterdam body "to seek to know the will of God upon important issues which radically affect[ed] the Church and society, and, thereafter, to call upon churches, governments or men in general, as the situation . . . require[d], to deal with a given historical issue, in the name of Christ and in the light of God's revelation in Jesus Christ the Lord." And they apparently had the churches, on the whole, with them, even if many leaders would have been happier with fewer pronouncements or with silence.

They thought that to remain silent would be to speak. Encouraging this judgment, John Foster Dulles had declared to the Assembly at Amsterdam: "What the churches elect to say will have political consequences. What they elect to keep silent about will also have political consequences. So the churches . . . have a relationship to practical politics that is inescapable."[16]

When he urged the World Conference on Faith and Order at Edinburgh in 1937 to join with the Universal Christian Council for Life and Work in founding the World Council of Churches, William Temple said the new organization was needed to be "the voice of non-Roman Christendom," but afterwards he stated that the Council was expected, rather than to make pronouncements, to suggest to the churches what they might wish themselves to say together. And during World War II, when there were many appeals to the Provisional Committee to speak for the churches on various issues at stake, he adhered steadfastly to this principle, writing to the General Secretary, Dr. Willem A. Visser 't Hooft, as follows:

> If we speak corporately, we may find that we have erected fresh barriers to the reconstruction of fellowship. Christians of one country can meet Christians from another country with which they have been fighting in an organization which has not corporately taken sides; it will be difficult, almost impossible, to do this in an organization which has officially condemned, directly or by implication, their own country. . . . I want us all to prophesy individually and to do this in contact with one another through your office: so the same message will be given ecumenically, though with a variety of emphases.[17]

Remarking on the seeming dichotomy in the archbishop's position, Dr. Visser 't Hooft said:

> This duality lies in the very nature of the Council. Constitutionally, it is merely an instrument for the use of the churches, which leaves the initiative to them; but spiritually it is, as the Letter of Invitation[18] states, a way to manifest that unity in allegiance to our Lord which already exists among us.

[16] See Part Three, Section II, *6*. p. 251.
[17] *A History of the Ecumenical Movement*, p. 710.
[18] To the churches to join in founding the World Council of Churches.

The Council can, therefore, only speak if one or both of two conditions are fulfilled: firstly, when it is certain to speak on behalf of the churches in its membership; secondly, when the spiritual urgency of its message is such that it may be expected to *create* a united expression of the mind of the Church of Christ. In each specific situation the spiritual and organizational implications have to be weighed. It is impossible to arrive at precise rulings which cover all . . . situations. . . . But it is not impossible to arrive at some agreement concerning the degree of representativeness of statements made by various organs of the Council.[19]

Dr. Visser 't Hooft thought that a body such as the World Council of Churches could not be treated as "merely an instrument." Constituted by the churches, it possessed something of the nature of an organism, the Spirit of God indwelling it and working through it—the Spirit the churches knew and experienced in their own life. So was it one with them as no detached organ could be. Created for a special function, it would be much of the time, through its study and grasp of facts, better informed than the churches for the work expected of it. Withholding from it authority to speak, besides limiting seriously its usefulness, could have thwarted the will of the Spirit.

The confidence of those who believed the Council should be the "voice of the churches" was strongly supported by the philosophy of Christian social action as it was expressed by a high officer of the Study Department:

The Church is not any longer of a mind "to keep in its own sphere," as the saying is, and let the politicians, soldiers, businessmen and scientists run public affairs. It sees how badly they have managed. Two global wars in a generation: mankind faced with annihilation. . . . The Church can by study add to its always better understanding of the will of God a knowledge of and a competence in social and political matters as great surely as those have who are supposed to be practical experts in secular things. Churchmen could not do worse than they. At any rate, the time has come when the Church proposes to speak, as well as to act in other ways, and without apology.[20]

To those connected with established state churches, deliverances by the official clergy on issues of public concern were, of course, commonplace and quite in order.

The attitude of the World Council of Churches in respect of policy in such matters was influenced by the papal encyclicals on social questions.[21] At the meeting of the Central Committee in Chichester, Eng-

[19] Minutes of the Buck Hill Falls meeting of the Provisional Committee, 1947, p. 50.

[20] From an informal and unreported talk by an American ecumenical leader at a briefing conference for delegates to the Assembly at Amsterdam, which was held in the Fifth Avenue Presbyterian Church of New York City in 1948. (Transcribed from stenographic record.)

[21] The Study Department collaborated with a small group of scholars at Oxford University, Oxford, England, in a comprehensive study of papal encyclicals on social and political subjects.

land, in 1949, Bishop H. Meiser of Münich spoke of "the contrast between the utterances of the Roman Catholic Church, which were widely listened to, and the insufficient attention given to the witness of the World Council."[22] What he said led to a discussion of the need of "more adequate publicity" for the pronouncements of the Council. This became a recurring lament, which, however, never touched the real roots of the problem. The Church of Rome acted with an assumption of divine authority fully conceded by its millions, whose solidarity was, in itself, a factor to be reckoned with by secular powers. The weight carried by any "voice of non-Roman Christendom" consisted, on the other hand, only in the wisdom and truth of its words.[23] Between authoritarianism and democracy in the Christian religion was this fundamental difference, the limiting effect of which on statements or actions by the World Council of Churches no device of publicity could alter, least of all the explanation that the Council represented 161 churches—or denominations—with a total constituency of 170-odd millions, which usually accompanied ecumenical press releases from Geneva.

[22] Minutes and Reports of the Second Meeting of the Central Committee of the World Council of Churches, Chichester, England, July 9-15, 1949, p. 8.
[23] William Temple, in *A History of Ecumenical Movement,* p. 704.

IV

SPECIAL STUDIES BY THE CENTRAL COMMITTEE

1. The Church's Action in International Affairs

If it was to bear the authority and act in the place of the World Council of Churches during the interim between Assemblies, the Central Committee had to inform itself as thoroughly as possible concerning the various departments of the organization and the actual conditions under which they would have to function, which seemed to present nowhere a more serious problem than in international life. At its meeting in Geneva, February 8-10, 1949, the Executive Committee decided that the responsibility in this area should be a major consideration at the annual meeting of the Central Committee in Chichester the following July. Bishop Berggrav was asked to introduce the subject. He became ill in the midst of his preparation, and Sir Kenneth G. Grubb, Chairman of the Commission of the Churches on International Affairs, substituted for him, using his notes. The presentation and the questions it raised were the beginning of a study of the greatest importance to the World Council of Churches.[1]

Sir Kenneth explained that the paper necessarily touched at certain points the duties of the Commission of the Churches on International Affairs, but that the concern of the churches in this field was much wider than the purview of any single body. This was the first principle to grasp, he emphasized. Establishing a central agency with special functions was a sensible step, but it was churchmen themselves, who were citizens, as well as the churches as institutions and the governments as authorities, that were involved in world conflict. The whole life of mankind was at stake; indeed, the fateful doubt was, he thought, "whether existence on this planet could continue." Whether it could and of what quality it must be were intimately related. The answer to the former question depended on the latter. If the churches had anything to say at all, they were concerned with the quality of civilized life. In this sense,

[1] Minutes of the meeting of the Central Committee at Chichester, 1949, pp. 80 ff.

nothing international was alien to them. But it was also true that there were some questions in which they were more directly involved than others, and some on which they could speak more authoritatively, and "these distinctions of sphere, authority and appropriateness must be discovered and stated." Moreover, there were some issues which were "best handled through a central organ acting on behalf of all, and others . . . best left to multiple action or even to the conscience of thousands of individual Christians" proceeding as they felt impelled.

Section IV of the Amsterdam Assembly said nothing striking in its report, the paper stated. The paragraphs on the observance of human rights and the declaration on religious liberty were of greatest usefulness. Those on strengthening and extending world organizations were the most important.

Amsterdam had taken "insufficient account of the grave situation of the Church in the face of persecution or of pressure designed to secure political conformity." "Freedom was taken for granted in America and largely in Britain and certain other countries," as a "result of quite special historical conditions." In the world as a whole it was "rather exceptional, a social *rara avis.*" In consequence, the treatment of rights and liberties in Section IV had tended "to be somewhat formalistic and unrelated to the actual evolution of some of the churches."

Progress since Amsterdam had been slow, particularly in securing "important theological contributions to the ulterior problem of justice, power, peace and war," theologians generally being "too busy to attach much importance to what, to them, appear[ed] to be matters of inferior importance."

Bishop Berggrav had attended the Bossey Conference on International Affairs in April, 1949, and reported "a series of questions which, in its view, should have the attention of the Central Committee":

How can the World Council of Churches best help the churches whose liberties are infringed?

How can the churches help each other in propagating, maintaining, and implementing the religious freedoms defined by the Amsterdam Assembly?

How can the churches implement, in the light of recent developments, the attitude of the Amsterdam Assembly to all the ideological conflicts of our time and to the resulting power conflict?

What should be done to keep alive real ecumenical fellowship within the churches?

How can the World Council of Churches best help the Younger Churches which have to cope with the problem of communism, colonialism and nationalism? How can those churches which are not yet beset by any of these issues be best helped and counselled?

The Conference at Bossey recommended that information be supplied "by the churches concerned, on serious race tensions and racial discrimination in several parts of the world, with suggestions as to how the ecumenical movement could best promote a just solution of them."

The authors of the paper saw the danger that the churches and their organizations, having "so many international things to do," would not do any of them. Discussing "an order of priorities" for the Commission of the Churches on International Affairs, the observation was set down:

A distinction should, perhaps, be made between issues which are primarily domestic and those . . . primarily international. . . . Communism is an example. Communism as a social and political system is not for the Commission of the Churches on International Affairs to study: in its international policy and action it is. The two are connected, but unless a line is drawn somewhere the total might well be unmanageable.

There is a negro problem in the United States and a Bantu problem in Africa, and the churches are concerned with them, and Christians in the local church cannot say, "Hands off!" on the grounds of their . . . domestic character. It remains a matter of prudential calculation whether practical progress is likely to be made by regarding any problem as an international one because it disturbs the Christian conscience.

The paper took "a trip around the world" with the Bossey Conference, "noting some of the points and places where international friction was generated" and "their significance for the churches," as seen from the standpoint of such queries as:

Can the question under reference be usefully handled by international action?

Does it involve relations between the nations, so that it can be taken up between them directly or at the United Nations or elsewhere?

Is it a question in which the ecumenical conscience of the churches is roused, and to be handled by the churches in different nations supporting one another?

Is it a question which . . . can be handled by other bodies better than central ones like the World Council of Churches, the International Missionary Council or the Commission of the Churches on International Affairs?

Europe

The Peace Treaty with Germany, and the rights and prospects of the German missions; war trials and repatriation for trial; the place of Germany in Europe.

Positions and actions to be taken by the churches and the World Council of Churches in regard to alleged persecution of, or discrimination against, church leaders and members, e.g., Bulgaria, Hungary, Spain.

The attitude of the churches to the Council of Europe.

Near and Middle East

Palestine: the status of Jerusalem; the Holy Places; the property of churches and missions; freedom of religion and education.

Egypt and other Middle East countries: freedom of churches and missions and of religious confession, education and propaganda; the Anglo-Egyptian Sudan.

Africa

The race and color questions of South Africa and other countries—Bantu, colored and Indian; the future of protectorates.

Trusteeship, e.g., in Southwest Africa.

The African in areas of rapid economic development, e.g., Tanganyika.

Progress of religious freedom in areas of Italian influence and in the Portuguese colonies.

East Asia

The relations between China and the Western powers; status of the Church in China.

The future of Japan.

Indonesia and other new states in Southeast Asia. On this question the Bossey Conference recommended that the Central Committee might issue a statement covering:

a. The sympathy felt by the churches with nations trying to build up self-government and national life, remembering that this involves mutual responsibilities between nations;

b. The importance of complying with the demands of the rule of law, and the tolerance, the recognition of human rights and fundamental freedoms in the political, economic and social sphere;

c. The need for continuing responsibilities on the part of other nations to help such states as would welcome it, with technical assistance, personnel and finance, without trying to retain or to get any political supervision or control.

America

The status of the Negro in the United States.

The freedom of religion, the observance of human rights in certain Latin American republics.

The attitude of the churches to the Atlantic Pact.

The study considered "the general issues": (a) the ideological conflict and the international tension created by it; (b) war and power, peaceful change, and the pursuit of justice; (c) the rule of law and its recognition in, and by, international institutions; natural law as applied to international relations; (d) the building up of an international legal order by creating supranational, not purely governmental, agencies and institutions; (e) the definition and observance of human rights and fundamental freedoms, particularly religious liberty; action of the churches when these rights are flouted; (f) problems of social justice and economic order in the world; (g) problems of race and color, the progress of dependent people, including trusteeship.

The Ideological Conflict and International Tensions. The churches were declared by the authors to have approved the refusal of the Amsterdam Assembly "to equate the Christian cause with any political or social" system. "The World Council of Churches . . . must make clear that it desires, not only to confirm the position taken by the Assembly, but also to give it greater substance."

Communism created a specific problem for the churches, in that it claimed to provide a "complete answer to all questions of life" and in the present situation was fighting the churches indirectly. "The first answer of the Church to communism must be the renewal of the Church itself."

"The churches must claim and make use of the liberty to proclaim the gospel, to witness to all . . . the people, especially to youth, to organize their own life, and to maintain effective contacts with their sister churches." They "cannot accept the claim that all rights are to be granted and defined by the State."

The Church was "deeply concerned with the fate of man, and with his duties and rights," said the paper. Its freedom, therefore, must include the right to exercise "its prophetic ministry with regard to the condition of man in society."

The success of communism judged and challenged the churches and demanded "a response of repentance and of fruits of repentance." They "must recognize that through the inadequacy and social irrelevance of their witness they bear a heavy share of responsibility for the present state of society."

In all nations the basic problem was, according to the survey, "the spiritual and moral vacuum of the modern mass-society," in the presence of which the churches stressed "new and creative solutions." "The churches must stand for an order of society in which such constructive action is allowed and encouraged."

"Talk of preparation for war between two parts of the world dominates the international situation. In this struggle for power every nation becomes involved. There is at present no simple solution. Neither war, whether labelled 'aggressive,' 'preventive' or 'defensive,' nor the sacrifice of justice for the sake of a false peace is any solution. Since the Church recognizes the evils of both war and appeasement, it must support the statesmen in their search for provisional solutions which may pave the way for durable adjustment along peaceful lines."

Further, "the Church must resist the danger of exploitation for political and propagandistic purposes by both sides."

And "every possible effort must be made to maintain the ecumenical fellowship between the churches in the areas under different political systems. . . . Through the unity of the Church, God speaks to a divided world."

War and Power; Peaceful Change and the Pursuit of Justice. Amsterdam showed that, in spite of the limited common ground there discovered, a widening divergence of views existed. "There were those who remembered Munich, 1938, and resolved that they would never again be willing abettors of a betrayal of even relative justice," while others who could not forget Hiroshima were against war, under any circumstances.

The Rule of Law and Its Recognition. According to Bishop Berggrav, "the churches should adopt a declaration of the fundamental meaning and relevance of law in international affairs and force the nations to accept it." It should be asserted:

That the nations recognize the fundamental law of the Creator as the only basis and stronghold of human rights and order and of international law;
That this law of the Creator is supreme to all human law-making and not subject to approval or disapproval of political powers;
That the nations draw up a plan for written international law in paragraphs to be ratified by all nations and appealing to the conscience of mankind, and that they submit conflicts between nations to an International Court.

The churches must have, he held, a bold answer to the question "Shall fundamental human and national law be under God, or under Nature, i.e., under the rule of naked power?" Or "Is there a responsibility towards a rule above men and above the State?" Even if politicians were skeptical, he thought this argument would appeal to the people and create an atmosphere conducive to subsequent useful actions.

On the actual procedure of Christian action, the Bishop advanced four propositions:

The "Christian conviction" was in itself an active element in the life of society.
Christian action in international affairs might be either specifically Christian (e.g., prayer) or active promotion (e.g., reconstruction and relief).
Principles must be proclaimed and standards upheld.
Direct approach must be made, on the basis of these, to governments and authorities.

These views had elicited comment from various quarters, it was stated. John Foster Dulles was not in agreement with the Bishop. He had stressed, however, that the churches could render two services. They could get their members to realize that their moral judgments would, in the aggregate, be influential; and they could contribute to "a more accurate knowledge of the facts."

Professor Arnold Toynbee would have reformulated some of Bishop Berggrav's main positions and broadened the approach to the establishment of international law to admit of partnership in it with the adherents of other living religions—Jews, Muslims, Parsees, Hindus, and Buddhists.

"The proper formulation of Christian principles applicable to the field of international affairs is a considerable task," it was agreed, "but one which ought to be undertaken by the churches."

After considering the Bishop's principal proposal, the Bossey Conference minuted as follows:

They would not advise the Central Committee to discuss the diverse problems of natural law applied to international law[2] but would suggest that a group of specialists, including jurists and theologians, be invited to consider them. "The Bossey authorities," in consultation with the Commission of the Churches on International Affairs and the Study Department of the World Council of Churches, had decided, Sir Kenneth Grubb informed the Central Committee, to hold a conference of this kind in 1950, with "the terms of reference":

The evolution of the statement of Natural Law and its relevance to international society of today;
The Christian understanding of Law and Justice;
The confrontation of Natural Law and the Christian understanding of Law and Justice and their relationship.

Professor Kägi of Switzerland, Professor Ellul of France and Professor Baron van Asbeck of the Netherlands were proposed for appointment as a preparatory commission for this conference, to which should be added an English, an American, and a German member.

The Building Up of an International Legal Order. "It is not enough to examine problems of war and power and the pursuit of justice, or on the other hand those concerning the rule of law and its recognition, and related problems," the paper by Bishop Berggrav and Sir Kenneth Grubb continued. "Without providing the proper agencies . . . to uphold that rule of law and to aid in the realization of the precepts of justice in concrete cases, the rather loose society of nations will mark time, instead of moving forward to a more integrated community, dedicated to obedience to a legal order of its own."

The Definition and Observance of Human Rights. "Through the instrumentality of the Commission of the Churches on International

[2] The term "natural law" is variously understood. It is a Western conception, and, on that account, difficulty may be anticipated in any attempt to apply it universally. Two constructions are placed upon it. One derives from Stoic philosophy and posits the view that an understanding of right and wrong can be reached through man's own reason. More specifically Christian, the other advances on the assumption that from the basis of Christian faith it is possible to reach universally applicable principles of right and wrong.

While the term and its underlying idea are Western, there are reasons to believe that universal application may be possible. Societies do exist and hold together all over the world. They remain related by virtue of the good that is in them, and they become disintegrated by evil. We believe that God governs the world. Underlying the common forms of social organization, such as the family, are principles which hold our societies together. The proposed study can be useful in stimulating an investigation of the principles which underlie common social forms.

Note: The above is, in substance, a statement made by Bishop Stephen Neill, at the request of Sir Kenneth G. Grubb during the discussion by the Central Committee of "The Church's Action in International Affairs," here under review.

See the Minutes of the meeting of the Central Committee, Chichester, 1949, p. 17.

Affairs, and . . . the good work of Dr. Nolde, the position of the churches in the formal field of human rights has been ably advanced and well held, and definite results secured," the Committee was assured.

The recent trials of churchmen in certain countries reminded the churches that they faced a grave situation. Without becoming overly suspicious, they should seek a realistic knowledge of the tactics of communist penetration into their own ranks.

There was need also to analyze more closely the types of discrimination and persecution that were observable:

The persecution of the Church by the materialistic totalitarian state, which started usually with attacks on individuals and followed by seizing schools and property, controlling appointments, forbidding literature and confining preaching to churches and its censorship.

Discrimination against the Church, and sometimes persecution by a state which aspired in some sense and for certain purposes to be a modern theocracy, as in Islam. It might follow any of the previously mentioned steps, but was more likely to concentrate on control of schools, regulation of property, the status of foreigners and the laws of minorities.

Discrimination by one branch of the Church against another.

The vital question was how the churches could best mobilize for action, "if any member suffer." The facts were sometimes difficult to ascertain, it had been found. Messages, public protests, or official representations could worsen the lot of victims. The maintenance of a centralized system of information, presumably by the World Council of Churches, might, it was thought, be desirable. This could subject the Council to accusations of political interference; but it was important that such intelligence be available at short notice, with assurance also of accuracy. Competent legal advice and very skillful publicity would be necessary.

Problems of Social Justice and Economic Order in the World. Thirty years of the International Labor Organization and its activities must have convinced the world, the paper suggested, that international peace was dependent on the realization of social justice and the recognition of national cooperation. In this field churches could speak on a biblical basis. "The question of migration and of seeking to find a solution for the painful problem of uneven distribution of the world's population, and of the restraints put in some places on the free movements of colored peoples, must be of serious concern to the churches."

The churches had the task, it was held further, not only to proclaim that the earth was the Lord's and all that therein was, "but very much more to explore the consequences of that truth for the economic life of the world." They had "their own contribution to make in annulling the concept formerly prevailing of the autonomy of economic life, and to try to discover the just attitude between the two extremes of unfettered competition and deadening regimentation in international economic relations."

Problems of Race and Color, Dependent Peoples, Trusteeship. "The just distribution of the world's riches and aid to underdeveloped peoples constitute two living problems of acute actuality," the paper concluded.

> The development of non-self-governing peoples is of outstanding importance in this modern epoch. It exceeds by far the primarily emotional field of their independence or self-government, and the churches should avoid the temptation of extremism. The strengthening of the autochthonous peoples, each after their talents and gifts, their protection against abuses, the clash of industrialized and agrarian parties with all the grave conflicts and dangers resulting from it, and above all the combat against unchristian methods and feelings of superiority on the part of individuals as well as of groups and states, the exceptional role and duties of colonial powers in all these matters, constitute a heavy task for the world and for the churches, who here again have to speak a word of their own, coming from the Christian convictions on the dignity of man.[3]

2. What the Churches Expect from the World Council

The Central Committee, at its Chichester meeting in July, 1949, also heard statements by Dr. Franklin Clark Fry and the Bishop of Chichester, Dr. Bell, on "What the Churches Expect from the World Council."

The Council represented a "search for Christian unity," said Dr. Fry, which aim ranked first as its *raison d'être*. He believed that the Council had won the confidence of the churches because it had stated its method as well as its goal.

The purpose was not, he said, to dilute faith into a solution, not to reduce "our confessions into a shapeless amalgam." The Council needed "vertebrate religion in vertebrate churches—churches which knew what they believed."

The Council expected the churches "to meet each other around the Word of God." Its hope for achieving unity did not "rest upon any discovery of how to compromise, but upon a discovery of what the Scriptures" taught. "The deepest sin of all is not our separation from ourselves, but our separation from the full truth of the Word of God," he said.

"The World Council of Churches is an evidence," he continued, "of upsurging Christian life. . . . The drawing together of the churches in the ecumenical movement is not the result of a secret panic at inner weakness." Nor was it "to give false courage to hard-pressed present-day Christianity through artificial solidarity."

[3] *Ibid.* pp. 80-91.

The Council had been launched, he pointed out, in "the more confident days before 1939." If present threats were to be lessened, the churches would undoubtedly "stay together." Their "new fellowship corresponded to deeper impulses." The younger churches, which were brimming with vitality, were the most zealous for it.

The World Council of Churches reflected the fact that the churches had a new purpose: to guide, instruct, and reprove the "tremendous forces moulding the modern age." Institutional Christianity had contracted out of one after another realm, e.g., education and works of ministry. This would cause less anxiety if the secular authorities assuming such tasks "were suffused with a Christian spirit." "If the churches are not alert, they will forfeit their claim over most of the personalities of men." In the World Council they had an organ through which to make an effective impact. In their "fragmented state" that had been impossible.

Elihu Root had pointed out the insufficiency of sentiment without a supporting institution, he recalled, and the churches had found such an instrument in the World Council.

The churches were thankful, he believed, for the World Council's "oldest department and its newest activity—the Study Department and the Secretariat for Evangelism." Hard thought had not sufficiently characterized the Church in the past hundred years, he declared.

> We should remember that thought is action. Americans have been so busy applying the gospel, that they have insufficiently taught their people what it is. Europeans, if I may venture the opinion, have basked in tradition. Younger churches have been obsessed with their virile growth. We all rejoice that the World Council will continue to rally the ablest minds, in order to give a lead within the complex issues of our time.
>
> Moreover, the churches are increasingly conscious that they have had too narrow an appeal in their evangelism. We think of the priest and the Levite passing a bruised man by on one side, and are accused by the fact that our churches have often passed men by on both sides, leaving the intellectuals and too many workers alike untouched.

The churches expected the World Council to maintain a Department of Reconstruction and a Commission on International Affairs, he agreed; but it was a fallacy to suppose that the Church existed primarily to promote any subsidiary aims. When it lost sight of its main purpose of "garnering souls," the Church erred. This was true, he asserted, "even of such a worthy objective as world peace."

Dr. Fry expressed the hope that the World Council would not overemphasize "stratification in the Church according to age or sex," in organizing its Youth Department and the Commission on the Life and Work of Women in the Church. It would proceed fruitfully in these two areas in the degree to which it kept "churchmanship in the center."

The churches did not expect the World Council "to bring in the kingdom of God." God himself would do that. They hoped the Council would "exhilarate our common life, bring us closer together and challenge each to aim at heights others have attained."

The Bishop of Chichester, for his part, said there were indications that the theological interests of the churches grew steadily deeper, and, for this reason, the Council's usefulness would depend on the direction of the Study Department's activities, its ability to make and maintain contacts with the best minds of the Church.

There was need, further, he thought,

> of developing the religious basis of . . . ecumenical action: in other words, of deepening the life of worship and prayer, ecumenically speaking; partly by interchange of our churches' distinctive experiences and traditions; partly by the discovery of ways of common prayer in the ecumenical movement, both for ourselves at . . . Central Committee meetings, and for our churches in our home countries; in each case without contravening a particular church's laws or regulations.
>
> We have also, necessarily, to consider in the field of immediate action what the churches expect of the World Council in the light of the particular historic situation existing when it was founded in 1948.

Formed at a time when nationalism was on the increase and the world was acutely divided on political, economic, and spiritual issues, the World Council of Churches was a demonstration, in its very existence, he thought, of a supra-national unity, of "a living expression of . . . fellowship, transcending race and nation, class and culture, knit together in faith, service and understanding."[4] The churches would expect the Council "to do everything in its power to emphasize this supra-national unity," in the face, especially, of "another kind of supra-national unity," based on class or race. "The churches expect the Central Committee to be a unity in itself, a real fellowship in the personal relations of its members, in and out of its meetings. Its members ought also to convey the fact of this fellowship, wherever they are; standing not only for their own churches, but for the World Council."

The churches had a right to expect the Council "to promote the growth of ecumenical consciousness in the members of all churches," according to its fourth constitutional function; also to make plain "what the Christian faith had to offer toward 'a solid basis for international and supernational law,'" as implied in the declaration of Section IV of the Amsterdam Assembly: "The churches have an important part in laying that common foundation of moral conviction without which any system of law will break down."

Dr. Bell thought that the World Council would be expected to give "further guidance on the attitude which Christians ought to adopt towards communism"; and there were other issues on which it would be

[4] Quoted from the report of Section IV of the Amsterdam Assembly Study Series.

asked to "declare its mind in a definite way," such as "persecution and discrimination on grounds of race and color."

To sum up [said the Bishop], I believe that there is nothing more important for the future of the World Council than (1) a conviction on the part of all member churches that the fellowship . . . represented in the . . . Council is . . . living and . . . reliable, and that the churches will really stand together, whatever trouble comes; and (2) courage on the part of the Central Committee to apply Christian principles, especially those clearly defined at Amsterdam, in a definite way to a particular situation, should the facts warrant and the need arise.[5]

In the discussion on the papers by Dr. Fry and the Bishop of Chichester, Bishop Angus Dun of Washington, D.C., said that the subject "What the Churches Expect from the World Council" suggested "a dichotomy which was false." The implication was, he objected, that the World Council of Churches was an entity apart from the churches, whereas the fact was that the Council existed as a "meeting place of the churches." The real question which should be before the Committee, he thought, was how the structure of "this meeting place" might be "used by the churches in the service of the churches."

3. "The Basis"

"The Basis" of the World Council of Churches appeared in the agenda at two meetings of the Central Committee during the interim between Amsterdam and Evanston. This was in response to proposals by the Remonstrant Brotherhood of Holland and the Religious Society of Friends of Philadelphia and Vicinity, members of the Council, concerning changes in its phrasing. In 1951 the Committee adopted the following resolution:[6]

Agreed that

Whereas the First Assembly of the World Council of Churches adopted the following recommendation concerning Article I of the Constitution of the World Council of Churches:

"Whereas several delegates in the Assembly have expressed, either for themselves or for their churches, the desire for clarification or amplification of the affirmation of the Christian faith set forth in the basis of the Council (Article I), therefore it is

Resolved that this Committee recommend to the Assembly:

(a) that this Assembly of the World Council of Churches affirm its conviction that the basis set forth in the Constitution is adequate for the present purposes of the World Council of Churches;

[5] The Bishop's address, or the report of it, is on p. 77 of the Minutes of the Chichester meeting of the Central Committee, 1949.

[6] At Rolle, Switzerland. See Annual Minutes for 1951, p. 20.

(b) that any churches that may desire change in the basis be instructed to present their desires in writing to the Central Committee for study and report to the next Assembly;

(c) that the Central Committee be instructed to keep its study of possible changes within the Christological principle set forth in the present basis";

And whereas the Remonstrant (Arminian) Brotherhood of Holland and the Religious Society of Friends of Philadelphia and Vicinity have made proposals concerning a change in the basis, the Central Committee appoint a committee consisting of Dr. Douglas Horton (Convener), Professor Georges Florovsky and Bishop Anders Nygren to make a study of these proposals and any other proposals from churches, which may come in during the next year, and to report to the Central Committee at its next meeting.

It is understood that the study to be undertaken should be made in the light of the decision of the Assembly that the Christological principle set forth in the present basis shall be maintained.

The committee chosen to make a study of the proposals was instructed to complete its report in time for the Central Committee to examine it before its next meeting.

An entry in the records[7] of that meeting of the Central Committee, which was in Lucknow, India, December 31, 1952, to January 8, 1953, brought the transactions in regard to the Basis up to date, as follows:

Between the summer of 1951 and the summer of 1952 many memoranda, articles, and letters concerning the Basis were sent to the committee on the Basis.

The committee held several meetings during the Faith and Order Conference at Lund.[8] The three members were present and Dr. Visser 't Hooft also attended the meetings.

The committee studied the two proposals concerning a change in the Basis which had been transmitted to it by the Central Committee. A further proposal from the Presbyterian Church of Australia, which had arrived after the last meeting of the Central Committee, was also received.

The committee considers that the adoption of any one of the specific proposals submitted by member churches of the World Council (Remonstrant Brotherhood: "Jesus Christ [His Son], our Lord and Saviour"; Religious Society of Friends of Philadelphia: "Jesus as Lord"; Presbyterian Church in Australia: "God in Christ reconciling the world unto Himself," or "Jesus Christ as Lord," or "Jesus is the Christ, the Son of God") would not in fact be within the Christological principle set forth in the present Basis. This would be against the instructions given by the First Assembly to the Central Committee.

The committee has also considered whether the present Basis should be developed in one or two directions within its Christological framework. It has been suggested more than once that implicit reference to the humanity of our Lord be included in the Basis. It has further been suggested that reference be made to the Trinity.

The committee believes that it may be useful for the Assembly, without

[7] Minutes of the Central Committee's meeting at Lucknow, pp. 95-96.

[8] In August of 1952. This reference was to the Committee of Three.

amplifying the Basis itself, to state expressly that the fact of the Incarnation and the fact of the Trinity are both witnessed to, by implication, in the Basis. The Incarnation is affirmed in that the Basis speaks of *Jesus* Christ, that is of "Jesus of Nazareth," the Word who "became flesh and dwelt among us." And the Atonement and the Resurrection are implied in that the Basis speaks of Jesus Christ as Saviour. And the same words point to the Trinity, for historically the doctrine of the Trinity was developed through meditation upon the Divinity of our Lord.

In the light of the foregoing the committee has come to the unanimous conclusion that it is not desirable that the next Assembly should make a change in the present Basis.

The committee believes that in view of the many and widespread misunderstandings concerning the nature and function of the Basis of the Council it will be useful for the Assembly to state anew just what the World Council means by a Basis. The first statement on this subject in the "Explanatory Memorandum" drawn up by Archbishop Temple has not become an official document of the Council. The committee has drawn up a draft statement on this subject which is attached to this report.

The "Draft Statement on the Nature of the Basis of the World Council of Churches," which was appended by the subcommittee to its report on the Basis but not adopted by the Central Committee, was as follows:

The World Council of Churches is an instrument at the service of the Churches which enables them to enter into fraternal conversation with each other, to co-operate in various fields and to render witness together to the world. It is not a new Church (even less a super-church) and does not perform ecclesiastical functions.

Since the Council desires to make clear to the Churches and to the world what it is, what it does and who are its members, it has adopted a "basis." The first article of its Constitution formulates this Basis in the following words: "The World Council of Churches is a fellowship of churches which accepts Jesus Christ as God and Saviour." This Basis performs three functions:

(1) It indicates the nature of the fellowship which the Council seeks to establish among themselves. For that fellowship, as a fellowship of churches, has its own unique character. It has a specific source and a specific dynamic. The churches enter into relation with each other, because there is a unity given once for all in the person and work of their common Lord and because the Living Lord gathers His people together.

(2) It provides the orientation point for the work which the World Council itself undertakes. The ecumenical conversations which take place in the World Council must have a point of reference. Similarly the activities of the Council must be submitted to an ultimate norm and standard. The Basis provides that standard.

(3) It indicates the range of the fellowship which the churches in the Council seek to establish.

The acceptance of the Basis is the fundamental criterion which must be met by a church which desires to join the Council. The limits of each society are dependent upon its nature. By joining together the churches seek to respond to the call and action of their Divine Lord. The World Council must therefore consist of churches which acknowledge that Lord as the second person of the Trinity.

While the Basis is, therefore, less than a confession, it is much more than a mere formula of agreement. It is truly a basis in that the life and activity of the World Council is based upon it. And the World Council must constantly ask itself whether it is faithful to its Basis.

Each church which joins the World Council of Churches must, therefore, seriously consider whether it desires to participate in a fellowship with this particular basis. On the other hand, the World Council of Churches would overstep the limits it has set for itself, if it should seek to pronounce judgment as to whether any particular church is in fact taking the Basis seriously. It remains the responsibility of each church to decide itself whether it can sincerely accept the Basis of the Council.

The Central Committee took no action on this appendix of the report of the Committee of Three. No discussion concerning it was recorded in the minutes of the Lucknow meeting. It was probably as good an explanation of the Basis as anybody could have written, but it manifestly raised more questions than it answered. And it could have thrown open the floodgates to theological debate.

So long as the Basis could be interpreted legitimately in the light of its implications, as the committee suggested it might, just about everybody who believed in Christian cooperation and wished to practice it in the World Council of Churches could find ways of accommodating the statement to his own thinking. Those authorities of the Council were undoubtedly well advised who thought amendment and explication were better shunned.

When he brought the report of the subcommittee on the Basis to the Central Committee, Dr. Douglas Horton, the Chairman, was accorded the privilege of making "a personal statement" concerning it. He said:[9]

In presenting to the Central Committee of the World Council of Churches the report of its sub-committee on the Basis, I trust that you will allow me, in the interest of complete understanding, to say a word regarding my own position on the matter.

The report is entirely accurate in stating that the sub-committee has unanimously concluded that none of the specific changes in the Basis suggested by our constituent churches are acceptable. I personally am equally clear upon it that the whole matter of improving the Basis should, however, be kept open.

To say that the Basis is non-theological and should not therefore be subjected to theological criticism, as has often been done, is really to speak falsely. Please note that the report of the sub-committee does not do so. The Basis has obvious theological connotations. Indeed, if it had none, it would be unworthy of the World Council of Churches.

The theology expressed by the Basis is not, I think, bad theology: it is simply one-sided theology. It is designed to be Christo-centric, but the difficulty with it is that it is all centre and no circumference. It illustrates the nature of heresy: it is a choosing of part of the faith at the expense of that indispensable part not chosen. The statement on the content of the Basis offered by the sub-committee undoubtedly amplifies and ameliorates

[9] Minutes of the Central Committee's Lucknow meeting, p. 35.

the impact of the Basis, but at the same time is an acknowledgment of weakness, for a Basis which requires addendum cannot finally be acceptable for a World Council of Churches. Although the first and the third Persons of the Trinity are implied in the acknowledgment of the second Person, it will not do to consign them to a status of implication.

It is my conviction that there can be no substitute for a trinitarian formula. The wisdom of the Christian ages will hardly be improved upon at this point. This formula is at once broad and narrow—and the entire Church is used to it, understands it, and has conformed to it. I hope the Evanston Assembly will not close the door on the eventual possibility of altering our Basis to read (with the Apostles' Creed) ". . . Churches which acknowledge belief in God the Father Almighty, in Jesus Christ His only Son our Lord, and in the Holy Spirit," or something similar.

A recent long trip, in the course of which I have had occasion to talk with many World Council groups in different parts of the world, convinces me that satisfaction with our present Basis is far from universal. A group within my own communion, entirely apart from me, is already making plans to request an alteration of the Basis. No denomination desires to take action embarrassing to the Council, but there are many, I believe, which would like to have the whole matter studied at length and in the end see an enlarged Basis adopted.[10]

4. The Joint Committee of the W.C.C. and the I.M.C.

The associate relationship of the World Council of Churches and the International Missionary Council through the Joint Committee (which had been organized in 1946) continued during the years from Amsterdam onward with the same mutuality and with increasing fruitfulness. The two bodies were connected by interlocking memberships, many of the leaders and supporters of each having an active interest in the other; and in both there was general recognition of the complementary character of their programs.

At its first meeting after the formal constitution of the World Council of Churches, the Joint Committee decided that, with the responsibility of making "the association of the two parent bodies as meaningful as possible, it should not confine itself to questions of organization . . . but should consider the larger issues of common policy concerning world evangelization—the relationships between the older and younger churches, with a view to making recommendations on these subjects." [11]

The International Missionary Council had planned a conference of "the sending churches . . . to re-evaluate and restate the missionary task of the churches . . . ," and the Committee recommended to the Central Committee of the World Council of Churches that Dr. Johannes Christian Hoekendijk, its Secretary for Evangelism, be allowed to give

[10] By the Constitution of the World Council of Churches, a request for changes by three members, or more, must be heard by the Assembly.

[11] See Minutes of the meeting of the Central Committee of the World Council of Churches at Chichester, 1949, pp. 109 ff.

as much time to the preparations for this meeting as his other duties permitted, in which also close cooperation should be maintained by the secretariats of the International Missionary Council and the World Council of Churches.

The two Councils cooperated, as they had previously, in the publication of the Ecumenical Press Service and maintained their relations with the Commission of the Churches on International Affairs, which had been founded in 1946 under their auspices. They sponsored the East Asia Christian Conference in Bangkok in 1949 and shared its expense—some $15,000. Dr. Rajah B. Manikam became Secretary for East Asia of both bodies. The two Councils acted together in arranging for the Conference on Palestinian Refugees in 1950. Their Joint Committee worked with the Committee on the Christian Approach to the Jews in the study which the Amsterdam Assembly had committed to the World Council. They collaborated also in a survey by Bishop Stephen Neill of theological education in Africa. They agreed on a policy providing for the fullest sharing in their study programs of plans, resources, and counsel.

By the time of the meeting of the Joint Committee at Greyladies, Blackheath, London, June 30-July 2, 1952, it had become clear, according to Dr. John A. Mackay, the Chairman, that the International Missionary Council and the World Council of Churches must be brought together in some corporate form.[12] Said the report to the Central Committee at Lucknow:

> The movement of world events since 1948 has deepened the sense of need of unified ecumenical action in meeting the claims of human need and the challenge of formidable non-Christian forces. This reinforces the conviction that "association" is not merely expedient but imperative, and strengthens the determination of the Joint Committee to seek by every means to deepen and enrich the meaning of this relationship.
>
> The Joint Committee is at one in the view that the task of the immediate future lies in the strengthening of common witness and action, as autonomous but essentially interdependent bodies.

The report at Lucknow carried recommendations looking to closer collaboration:

Faith and Order

That the Executive Committee of the World Council of Churches arrange for formal representation of the International Missionary Council on the Faith and Order Commission.

That the International Missionary Council advise Faith and Order with reference to the establishment of theological commissions in the lands of the younger churches, or offer alternative suggestions for securing wider participation by these churches in Faith and Order.

[12] Minutes of the meeting of the Central Committee in Lucknow, pp. 46 and 123 ff.

Study

That no major study be projected by one body, without consultation with the other.

That from time to time there be regular consultation on approaches contemplated to persons or groups for participation in the study programs of either organization.

That the whole question of future working relationships of the two bodies in the field of study, and of the nature of the studies to be attempted by each, be carefully examined by the two study executives.

Constitutional Relationships

That the two bodies be asked to consider adjustments and additions to their rules and by-laws which would make association more specific.

Ecumenical Conferences

That in planning for the Second Assembly of the World Council of Churches and other major meetings of both bodies, care be taken to make association more manifest.

Public Relations

That the staffs of both bodies be asked to prepare an interpretative statement on the growing association of the International Missionary Council and the World Council of Churches, and that, as much as possible, both bodies act together in matters affecting their public relations.

Under "Emergency Inter-Church Aid and Relief," the recommendations had to do with the creation of a subcommittee to advise the two Councils on the manifold problems of a joint ministry in this field. The committee which was appointed consisted of Dr. J. W. C. Dougall, Chairman, Bishop H. Høgsbro, Dr. Charles Leber, Dr. Eugene Smith, and Canon Max Warren. Dr. Rajah B. Manikam, Dr. William Decker, and Dr. Robert Mackie were added to the committee as staff advisers.

5. The Eastern Orthodox Churches

The relations of the Eastern Orthodox Churches with the World Council continued throughout the period between the first and second Assemblies to be a subject of serious concern for the Central Committee. At its meeting in Chichester in 1949, the General Secretary,[13] Dr. Willem A. Visser 't Hooft, presented a statement concerning it:

> . . . The majority of the Orthodox Churches have not joined the Council. . . . We cannot say with certainty in how far this is due to circumstances beyond [their] control and in how far . . . to . . . basic ecclesiological assumptions. . . . But we do know that in all these churches . . . are men, often in very responsible places, who consider themselves spiritually as participants in our movement. . . .

[13] Minutes of the Chichester meeting, p. 66.

The official stand of the Conference of a number of Orthodox Churches . . . last summer at Moscow is that [they] should not enter the World Council. The documents and reports of the Conference have shown that this stand is mainly based on very serious misunderstandings concerning the nature and work of the World Council and on a conception of the relations between the Church and the world which conflicts with the common ecumenical convictions. . . . Unfortunately we have little opportunity to remove these misunderstandings or to discuss this deeper theological issue. . . . All that we can do is to maintain the few contacts which we still have . . . for a true interpretation of our intentions.

It is inevitable that this situation complicates the position of the Orthodox Churches which take part in the World Council. For it is owing to the absence of so many Orthodox Churches that Eastern Orthodoxy is not adequately represented in our meetings, in our discussions, in our activities. And this inadequacy can easily lead to the impression that our Council is in fact a Council of Western churches, together with their daughter churches in other parts of the world.

The situation is further complicated by the ecclesiological issue whether the World Council has room for a church which considers itself as "holding the whole truth and as being the only true Church on earth."

. . . What can the World Council say in this connection to the Orthodox Churches? . . . It has been the constant desire of ecumenical leaders to have fellowship with the whole of Eastern Orthodox Christendom. . . . The Council . . . will go out of its way to give the Orthodox within our movement that place to which they are entitled as spokesmen for the whole Orthodox world. . . .

The Council can state clearly and unambiguously that it has not prejudged the question of the nature of the Church. It is definitely possible for a Church which considers itself the true Church to enter into the Council. Nothing in the official documents contains the slightest suggestion that the Council takes its stand on an ecclesiology according to which each church is to think of itself as one of the many equally true churches. Ecumenism does not mean ecclesiological relativism or syncretism.

It is precisely the originality of the ecumenical movement that it invites churches, many of which are as yet unable to regard each other as branches of the same tree, to enter into fraternal conversation and co-operation with each other, so that they may come to know each other and, if the Lord wills, advance toward a wider manifestation of unity in Him. In this respect the situation of the Orthodox Churches is not fundamentally different from that of many other churches in our movement. . . .

Professor Hamilcar S. Alivisatos spoke at the Chichester meeting of the Central Committee concerning the position of Orthodoxy with reference to the World Council of Churches, pointing out that "from the very beginning the Greek Orthodox Church was favorably disposed towards the ecumenical movement," the Ecumenical Patriarchate having proposed in 1920 the formation of a league of churches" and cooperated "in its several stages and phases" during some thirty years.[14] Members of the Greek Church, including Archbishop Germanos, who represented the Ecumenical Patriarchate, had participated in the prep-

[14] *Ibid.*, p. 74.

arations for the formation of the World Council of Churches, he said, and by their presence confirmed the will of the Church to cooperate.

Professor Alivisatos explained that their position behind the Iron Curtain prevented most of the Orthodox Churches from sending representatives to Amsterdam. Temporary conditions in Greece had not permitted "a full preparation of the delegation" from the Greek Synod, and some misunderstanding had resulted, those members "inexperienced in international conferences" finding themselves "quite naturally in considerable difficulty, owing to the overwhelmingly Protestant atmosphere." He was glad to be able to say that "the isolated adverse opinions expressed about . . . co-operation with the World Council of Churches were repudiated even by those delegates at Amsterdam who had at the beginning misunderstood the spirit of the Assembly."

> In general I can assure you [he said], the co-operation of the Greek Orthodox Church of Greece . . . will continue. . . . The very facts (1) that . . . the Church . . . receives . . . thankfully the aid offered by the other churches for its reconstruction, (2) that we are . . . eager to use in our church work the young theologians at present (through the gracious help of the other churches) studying in this country [England] and in America, and (3) that we are preparing to celebrate in an ecumenical way the festival of the nineteen hundredth anniversary of the foundation of the Christian Church in Europe through the Apostle Paul's preaching in Athens and Greece, are evidence of the firm co-operation of the Greek Orthodox Church of Greece with the World Council, and I am sure I can say the same—in spite of sinister indications—for the Orthodox Churches behind the iron curtain, as soon as the outward pressure, with God's will, will faint away.

Dr. Visser 't Hooft advised the Central Committee at Rolle, Switzerland, in 1951, that relationships with the Eastern Orthodox Churches had improved.[15] The Holy Synod of the Church of Greece had confirmed its decision to "participate fully in the life of the World Council."

> This decision was implemented in a remarkable way when this Church invited many member churches of the World Council in all parts of the world to send representatives to the pilgrimage and festival in commemoration of St. Paul's coming to Europe. For the free and easy fellowship which grew up during those two weeks of common worship, of informal discussion, of sharing of deep impressions has probably done more to bring Eastern and Western church leaders together than formal conferences have done. . . .
>
> The Beirut Conference on Refugees also provided an unique opportunity for closer contact with the Oriental Churches. For the first time since the World Council was founded, the four ancient Patriarchates, as well as other Oriental Churches, were represented and the needs and the problems of these Churches were discussed. . . .
>
> Through its work among refugees the World Council has accepted a large share of the responsibility for the life of the Orthodox Churches in

[15] Minutes of the Central Committee meeting at Rolle, p. 59.

Western Europe with no fewer than a half million adherents. With the help of the late Archbishop Germanos, and since his death, of his successor, Archbishop Athenagoras, we try to arrive at the maximum co-operation and co-ordination of the Churches concerned and maintain constructive relations with all Orthodox jurisdictions. It should be added that we have been able to establish very good relations with the Orthodox Church in Yugoslavia.

6. The Roman Catholic Church

On December 20, 1949, the Vatican issued to its local ordinaries certain "Instruction" concerning the ecumenical movement, and the document was included for consideration in the agenda of the meeting of the Central Committee at Toronto the following summer, the Executive Committee presenting a digest of it for the information of the members.[16]

This "Instruction" commented on the growing desire for union on the part of many persons who were not members of the Roman Catholic Church, and enjoined upon bishops certain points in dealing with it. They were reminded of the duty of explaining the Catholic teaching "whole and entire," and of making plain to non-Catholics that, among other things, "true reunion could come about only by the return of dissidents to the one true Church of Christ." The bishops were instructed to give special attention to the manner in which the history of the Reformation was presented. Vigilance and control were to be exercised with regard to "mixed gatherings and conferences for the purpose of fostering union," and rules were given for obtaining permission from local ordinaries on behalf of the Holy See, and the provision for reports at the end of each year to the Supreme Congregation of the Holy Office. Opening or closing these gatherings with the common recitation of the Lord's Prayer or some other prayer approved by the Roman Catholic Church was not forbidden.

However, mixed gatherings in which Roman Catholics and non-Roman Catholics met to consider joint action in defense of the fundamental principles of Christianity and the natural law against the enemies of God were not made subject to the same strict requirements, nor were meetings concerned with "rebuilding the social order or similar matters." [17]

The Executive Committee had requested the General Secretary, Dr. Willem A. Visser 't Hooft, to remark upon the Instruction, which he did, with the explanation that his comments could be only of a personal

[16] *De Motione Ecumenico.*
[17] Minutes of the Central Committee, Toronto, 1950, p. 62.

and unofficial character, since the Central Committee had not yet considered the document:

> The very fact that such a document is issued at all is a clear indication that the ecumenical movement has begun to make its influence felt among the clergy and laity of the Roman Catholic Church. We can only rejoice that such is the case.
>
> As the document itself points out, meetings between Roman Catholics and representatives of other confessions are regularly held in many places. These meetings generally are of an informal character and are intended to lead to better mutual understanding and to frank discussion of points of friction.
>
> According to the new Instruction, all such meetings will henceforth have to be directed and supervised by the hierarchy. Thus they will lose that informal and spontaneous character on which much of their value depended. There will be less room for the pioneers.
>
> Moreover, these ecumenical contacts will be supervised from the viewpoint expressed in the document; namely, that the only purpose of ecumenical contacts can be the return of all Christians to the Church of Rome. At this point the document remains below the level reached by certain members of the Roman Catholic hierarchy who have declared that union cannot take place in the form of a victory of one body over another as happens in the secular realm. The Churches in the World Council have a different conception of true unity; namely, that, in the words of the Amsterdam Assembly, they are to be bound closer to Christ and therefore closer to one another.
>
> Unless I am mistaken, this document is the first in which the Holy See permits explicitly, though with certain restrictions, that Roman Catholics and Christians of other confessions may pray together. This is a step forward.
>
> It is also important that interconfessional meetings on social questions are allowed. This should facilitate effective common action wherever Roman Catholics and Christians of other confessions are ready to make a common stand for social justice.
>
> Christians outside the Roman Communion should continue to pray that the Roman Catholic Church may be led to a wider and deeper conception of Christian unity.[18]

7. Department of Public Relations

The Assembly had authorized the establishment of a department of public relations[19] but neglected to make adequate provision through the budget for its maintenance. The Central Committee had been able only to add an extra press officer to the Geneva staff.[20]

Other obstacles stood in the way of doing more, had sufficient

[18] *Ibid.* pp. 62, 63.

[19] Various designations for the department had been suggested—"publicity," "public relations," "ecumenical information," etc.

[20] See Minutes of the Chichester meeting of the Central Committee, p. 71.

funds been available. These included sharply different conceptions of what such a department would be expected to do. There were churchmen who objected to the kinds of newspaper publicity which some religious organizations employed, believing it hurtful to the Christian cause to treat it in this respect in the same manner as secular movements. In general, European church leaders disapproved of American techniques on this score. Conservative opinion within the Central Committee, and outside, held that the aim should be "to render theological and other technical vocabularies intelligible, without dilution and distortion," and this was recognized as a task requiring a special talent and training not easy to procure in persons with experience in the field of public relations. There was doubt in some quarters that the need for the dissemination of "ecumenical information" could be met under that limited outlook. Whether the work could be done more effectively from the World Council headquarters or national centers was a question on which, likewise, no agreement had been reached.

The Executive Committee, at its meeting in Geneva in February, 1950, took steps to convene a Conference on Public Relations Policy for the World Council of Churches in Emmanuel College of Victoria University, Toronto, Canada, the following July, in connection with the third annual meeting of the Central Committee. Memoranda on "public relations policy" prepared by the Geneva and New York offices of the Council and a questionnaire on the issues raised by them, "derived mainly from European sources," served as one basis of the discussion.

The Chairman of the Conference was Dr. George W. Buckner, Jr., editor of *World Call*.[21] Other representatives of the press, secular and religious, attended. One definite result was the suggestion of "a series of priorities . . . for the guidance of the publicity and information officers of the Council." It was agreed that the limitations of budget and personnel made it impossible for them to undertake more than "a minimal program," and that only the more important things should be attempted. Much, regrettably, would have to be left undone.

At that time, the publicity staff consisted of one press officer in the Council's Geneva and New York headquarters each, another in the Department of Inter-Church Aid in Geneva, and Dr. Alexandre de Weymarn, editor of the Ecumenical Press in Geneva. It was stressed, however, that others connected with *The Ecumenical Review* and the bulletins published by the various departments—the Youth Department, the Ecumenical Institute, and the Study Department—were "agents of information." The churches themselves could serve helpfully in this field through their journals circulating among their own constituencies, and through local newspapers and periodicals reaching the public at large.

[21] Publication of the Disciples of Christ.

The Executive Committee recommended to the Central Committee for consideration the following "priorities of public relations policy" suggested by the discussion in the Conference:

Information to the Churches

The Council shall account to the member churches on the stewardship of the study and action projects assigned to it, including reports of the inauguration of such projects, their progress, and conclusions reached; serve as a clearing-house through which information on programs and personalities may pass from one church to another, and one country to another; and inform the churches of the movements of outstanding church leaders when they are on missions of ecumenical concern and interest.

Information to the General Public

The Council shall seek to inform that percentage of the general public—perhaps 25% can be relied on for some modicum of sympathetic interest—of the existence and some of the activities of the World Council as an expression of the ecumenical idea; whenever possible, to interest newspapers and radio stations in material of general ecumenical import, with the hope of reaching that hypothetical 25%; and, at the time of the Assemblies and the issuing of pronouncements of wide public interest, to reach a far larger public through press and radio.[22]

8. Looking to the Second Assembly

The Second Assembly of the World Council of Churches was a concern of the Central Committee from the time of its first meeting after Amsterdam onward. Where and when it should be held, how it should be organized, and what its agenda should be were questions receiving long and careful consideration by proper subcommittees, which, from time to time, reported the progress they were making and the problems they had encountered. The meetings at Toronto, Rolle, and Lucknow heard and acted on their reports. The main theme of the Assembly provoked prolonged discussion in the Central Committee, which had chosen it and appointed the special committee on its development.

Experience had early shown the need for a revision of the organization of the World Council of Churches, and the Central Committee created a Committee on the Structure and Functioning of the Council to study the matter and make appropriate recommendations to the Assembly. The considerable amount of work this assignment entailed was indicated by the Committee's report at Lucknow, in 1953, which filled many pages of the printed minutes of that meeting of the Central Committee. Even so, there would be another year of study before the final draft would be presented at Evanston, the place of meeting chosen for the Second Assembly.

[22] Minutes of the Toronto meeting of the Central Committee, p. 129.

The Committee on the Structure and Functioning of the World Council of Churches consisted of:

Dr. Leslie E. Cooke, Chairman
Dr. Alphons Koechlin
Dr. Carl Lundquist
Dr. Pierre Maury
Rev. R. David Say

The Central Committee nominated as advisers to the Committee:

The Rt. Hon. Ernest Brown
Dr. Samuel McCrea Cavert
Dr. W. J. Gallagher
Sir Kenneth G. Grubb
Bishop H. Høgsbro
Bishop Hanns Lilje
Bishop S. K. Mondol
Principal T. M. Taylor

V

ACTIVITIES OF OTHER DEPARTMENTS

1. The Study Department

A primary function of the World Council of Churches was "to promote co-operation in study."[1] This emphasis represented no innovation. Approaching Christian work by way of study had become an accepted method in the ecumenical movement long before the Amsterdam Assembly.[2] The inclusion in the organizational structure of the World Council of a department to develop further and supervise this activity was a result of its already proved effectiveness. It was felt to be, aside from its practical helpfulness, a condition of the fullest guidance of the Spirit.

The Central Committee at Woudscotten[3] outlined the general duties of the Department, as follows:[4]

To initiate studies to be pursued under the auspices of the Department;
To stimulate and encourage study projects among the churches of the Council;

[1] Constitution of the World Council of Churches, Article III, Section iii. See Appendix A.

[2] "The work of this Department should be dated from the beginnings of preparation for the Oxford Conference, at Fanø in 1934. Two decades of continuous effort should have taught us much regarding the possibilities and procedures of effective ecumenical inquiry. . . . The stimulus of serious inquiry among one hundred fifty churches, scattered on every continent, seeking to communicate with one another in uncounted tongues and in almost as many structures of preconception and languages of discourse, is, by any account, a difficult task. Here, supremely, the Spirit bloweth where it listeth, and the fruitage certainly cometh not with observation. Clear conception of the ultimate purpose and firm and undiscouraged grip upon realistic possibilities of achievement are of the essence. It is our faith, rather than our assurance, that the effort is not wholly without result." Report of the Study Department by the Chairman, Henry Pitney Van Dusen, at the meeting of the Central Committee in Lucknow, India, December 31, 1952-January 8, 1953, Annual Minutes, p. 50.

[3] Minutes of the Woudscotten meeting of the Central Committee, p. 8; Minutes of the Chichester meeting, p. 95.

[4] According to "Recommendations of the Study Department Commission of the Provisional Committee on the Future Study Program."

To translate theological writings judged to be of importance and to disseminate in the constituency information concerning trends of thought;

To edit a series of documentary surveys[5] of trends in the life and thought of the churches;

To have charge of preparations for the Second Assembly, particularly such studies as might be undertaken for its program;

To co-ordinate all projects of study and research of the several departments of the World Council.

It had been agreed at Amsterdam that the Department could not carry forward successfully more than three major studies simultaneously, and the Assembly had directed that:

Questions emerging from Section I of the Assembly on "The Universal Church in God's Design" be referred to the Commission on Faith and Order for possible further study;

Questions proposed by Section IV of the Assembly on "The Church and International Disorder" be committed for consideration to the Commission of the Churches on International Affairs;

The attention of the Study Department be confined to questions reported from Section II on "The Church's Witness to God's Design" and Section III on "The Church and the Disorder of Society" and its pre-Amsterdam biblical research.[6]

Under these delimitations, the Department projected "three long-range inquiries"—"The Bible and the Church's Message to the World," "The Evangelization of Man in Modern Mass Society," [7] and "Christian Action in Society." The last was to be concerned with the meaning of "a responsible society" and the conflict between "communism and capitalism."

These "inquiries" were launched with the publication of a series of bulletins outlining the subjects for study, which were distributed widely among the churches, accompanied by an appeal from the Central Committee that they "give serious consideration, both in sustained study and appropriate action, to the issues raised," which were "of foremost importance for the life and witness of the churches today."

"Responsibility for the development of ecumenical thought lies with the denominations belonging to the World Council of Churches," resolved the Central Committee at its second annual meeting, at Chichester in 1949; and the Department followed from the outset the principle of encouraging "the promotion and organization of study in co-operation with related agencies and groups within the churches, rather than con-

[5] The *Ecclesia Militans* series.

[6] A symposium on "The Biblical Authority for the Church's Social and Political Message Today" had been organized prior to the Assembly. The new biblical study would be related to the work of evangelism.

[7] This subject was committed for development to the newly created Secretariat for Evangelism.

centrating on what [it] might be able to achieve through its [own] limited resources."

Where possible, the cooperation of national and regional councils of churches was sought, and in some countries study committees were organized to sponsor the Department's program or to conduct particular investigations. The Department "served chiefly as a centre of stimulation, co-ordination and exchange among people in all parts of the world . . . interested in the purposes of such study," facilitating "that kind of intercommunication and consultation between theologians, scholars and laymen" which enabled them "to think in terms of the needs of the whole Church."

"This network of study committees," which was begun in Europe and North America, was extended to the Orient with the holding of the East Asian Study Conference at Lucknow, India, in 1952. "National liaison committees" were set up in seven Asian countries, and a study secretary for the whole of East Asia was added to the staff.[8] In the United States, Great Britain, Germany, Hungary, and other nations groups pursued discussions on their own initiative, and some of them published findings. Reports were solicited from all participants, and the information obtained from them was wrought into composite statements of the churches' thinking.

The Study Department was administered by a committee of thirty members—theologians and a few laymen, representing twenty-odd countries and about the same number of confessions—of which Dr. Henry Pitney Van Dusen of the United States was Chairman and Dr. John Baillie of Scotland and Dr. Anders Nygren of Sweden were Vice-Chairmen. The committee held meetings in 1949, 1951, and 1953, and a small administrative subcommittee directed its activities during the interims.

The study on "The Bible and the Church's Message to the World" evidenced the intention of the World Council of Churches to found its work in all departments upon a scriptural basis.

"If ecumenical study were no more than intellectual activity, it would be condemned to barrenness," declared the General Secretary, Dr. Visser 't Hooft. "It is far more than that. Our studies begin with the Bible—that is, with hearing the Word of God; they move to evangelism—that is, to proclaiming the Word of God; they pass beyond to Christian action—that is, to doing the will of God."

"We are called to know the truth as it is revealed once for all in Christ," continued Dr. Visser 't Hooft, "to speak the truth as the Holy Spirit gives utterance, and—to use the Johannine phrase—to do the truth in a chaotic and rebellious world. We may humbly hope that, if God lends his aid in answer to our prayers, we may be led forward,

[8] Report of the Study Department in the Annual Minutes.

until we are able with courage, with confidence and with unanimity to make known his Word and his Will to a restless and troubled generation."

The report of the Study Department at the third meeting of the Central Committee, in Toronto, Canada, in 1950, contained this significant reference to the progress of the study concerning "The Bible and the Church's Message to the World Today":

> The three studies[9] forming an organic whole, the chief object of this particular inquiry is to provide a solid biblical grounding for the two others. But as the inquiry proceeded it became evident that deeper issues about the authority and interpretation of the Scriptural message had to be faced. Thus the inquiry, by its own logic, has been driven to enter some of the decisive battlefields in contemporary biblical thought, such as the principles of interpretation, the relation between the Old and New Testaments, Scripture and tradition.
>
> This is one of the most promising ventures in ecumenical study today; it has already proved its worth as a crystallizing factor, as evidenced by the statement on "Guiding Principles for the Interpretation of the Bible"[10] which has met with heartening response among scholars of differing denominational background, even Roman Catholics.
>
> The major event during the year[11] has been the completion of the symposium on "The Biblical Authority for the Church's Social and Political Message Today," initiated several years ago. Work is proceeding on three biblical monographs on "Justice and Law," "Work and Vocation," "Man in Society." The latter subject is in the hands of a group of scholars in Chicago. On the subject of "Justice" the Department is convening an international conference in Germany in August, to be preceded by a conference under German sponsorship on "The Bible and Natural Law." All three volumes are scheduled to appear in 1952. Systematic efforts have been made to supply interested groups and scholars with material (survey reports and bibliographies) on the state of discussion in regard to the problems under debate.[12]

One remembering the divisions in the Church over the Bible had to have great faith to speak of going forward "with unanimity"[13] on its message for mankind. The troubles actually encountered in this ecumenical "inquiry" on the message of the Bible were described by

[9] "The Bible and the Church's Message to the World," "The Evangelization of Man in Modern Mass Society," and "Christian Action in Society."

[10] Published in 1950.

[11] In the report of the Study Department at the fifth annual meeting of the Central Committee, which was held in Lucknow, India, December 31, 1952, to January 8, 1953, appeared this statement: "The current program has witnessed the publication of the notable volume *Biblical Authority for Today*, originally planned as a pre-Amsterdam preparation, but which has been received as a contribution of some permanent worth to a central problem for ecumenical thought." The Minutes, p. 49.

[12] Minutes of the meeting of the Central Committee in Toronto, July 9-15, 1950, p. 107.

[13] Refer to Dr. Visser 't Hooft's statement above.

Dr. Wolfgang Schweitzer, from 1947 to 1952 a study secretary, in *The Ecumenical Review.*[14] So great were they that he could write of the experience only in terms of "the problem of the Bible."

The former Study Department under the Provisional Committee had been asked "to organize an international symposium on the relationship between the Bible and the social and political questions of today," the findings of which might be available to those responsible for the themes for Sections III and IV of the Amsterdam Assembly.[15] A conference in London in August, 1946, developed into a three-cornered deadlock, as Dr. Schweitzer described it.

> The champions of Christian natural law, most of them from the Anglo-Saxon world, took up their position, as against the Continental emphasis on "Scripture alone" as the authority on social and political questions, as well as on matters of faith. . . . The Orthodox Churches . . . entered the fray, with the view that the essential nature of the Bible [was] such that it [could not] present any social and political message to the world, since it was written as a sacred book for the holy community of the New Covenant, that is, the Church.

It quickly became clear "that a number of preliminary questions must be settled before the publication of the proposed symposium could be taken in hand." It was hoped "that it would be possible to establish principles for the interpretation of the Scriptures" at a second conference, in 1947, at the Ecumenical Institute at Bossey, Switzerland; but there "a new difficulty appeared." Representatives of the Lutheran Churches of Scandinavia and of the Reformed Churches of Holland, Switzerland, and Hungary were in attendance, and "it became evident that any formulation of a message of the Church on social and political matters from a biblical basis [was conditioned] by the prior consideration whether such a formulation was regarded as a part of the Law or . . . of the Gospel." Discussion "raged, encounters between Karl Barth and Anders Nygren affording some exciting moments." Americans present were astonished that interpretations which had their roots in the sixteenth century should become so irreconcilable an issue, "while an English scholar . . . said that he felt like a fish out of water."

At a third conference, in the summer of 1947, "The Authority of the Bible for the Social and Political Message of the Church Today" was taken for the theme of an "international symposium" and assignments of study were made to members, but when a small subcommittee met at Zetten, Holland, in 1948 to collate the results, it was seen "that further study of principles was absolutely necessary, before the publication of the volume could be considered."

[14] Vol. II, No. 2, p. 123 ff.

[15] Previously referred to, p. 436, p. 438.

At a later gathering in Wadham College, Oxford, England, in 1949,[16] the "participants found themselves in a *cul de sac* from which there seemed to be no way out. We simply discovered how widely separated we were from one another. The difficulty appeared merely to have increased." When two English scholars engaged in a lengthy discussion of "the question whether the period of the Exile . . . or the deliverance of Israel from Egypt . . . should be considered as the key to the understandings of the Old Testament," it became the turn of the Continentals to feel "like fish out of water."

However, the atmosphere began to clear up immediately, when, by an inspiration, the symposiasts "opened the Old Testament itself and began to interpret it in fellowship with one another. . . . Divisions then appeared to be almost non-existent."

Thus it was discovered that principles of interpretation of the Bible were to be arrived at through practical cooperation. From this point those meeting at Wadham had undertaken, along with the divided and delayed symposium, scriptural studies on the everyday subjects of work, man's place in society, and justice. While the "problem of the Bible" could not be expected to be solved fully, the conclusion was: "As a result of such conferences, we can help one another to remove the difficulties which constantly prevent us from hearing and interpreting the Word of God together. . . . Not infrequently, real agreements are concealed behind differences in categories of thought and in the use of terms."

In its report to the Second Assembly—at Evanston in 1954—the Central Committee said concerning the inquiry on the Bible and its message: "Some of the results . . . are summed up in a symposium, 'Biblical Authority for Today' (1951), in which a number of distinguished scholars 'as members of different Christian confessions and

[16] This was an augmented meeting, or a meeting in conjunction with the Study Department Committee of the World Council of Churches, June 28-July 6. Minutes of the Central Committee, Chichester, p. 96.

In the report of the Central Committee for 1949, p. 97, appeared the following statement by the Study Department:

"The biblical scholars who have been engaged in this inquiry—'The Biblical Authority for the Church's Social and Political Message Today'—for more than three years are now projecting a series of studies in the biblical teaching on fundamental problems which underlie the two other areas of study (such as 'Work and Vocation,' 'Man in Society,' and 'Justice') and a further clarification of issues which have already been isolated by their previous work as the sources of sharp division among biblical interpreters, and which have made progress slower and more difficult in this than in any other area.

"In the meantime, the Wadham College Conference on the Bible has produced an agreed statement on 'hermeneutical principles' (or, in simpler language, the fashion in which the Bible may be used to guide the Churches in speaking and acting in the social and political realms) which breaks quite new ground, and furnishes an ecumenical consensus where previously there had been misunderstanding and disagreement—further proof that patient and persistent labor by representatives of seemingly irreconcilable viewpoints does yield a genuinely united witness."

denominations, living in different parts of the world, have made an attempt to read and interpret Holy Scripture together.' "

The Biblical Doctrine of Work had been published, the report continued, and *The Biblical Doctrine of Man in Society* was soon to be. The volume on *Justice and Law* was being written.

The inquiry on "Christian Action in Society" [17] was described by the Study Department as "bi-focal." On the one hand, it was concerned with the questions relating to the "East-West confrontation," or the conflict between communistic and democratic economies, which had been raised by the discussions in Section III at Amsterdam and afterwards had "evoked the widest and most vehement response . . . not only within but beyond the churches." The aim in this connection was "to define with [greater] detail and precision the characteristics of 'A Responsible Society,' to which Christians of the most diverse political and economic allegiances [could] render united support as furnishing norms by which all existing and projected systems [might] be judged, and pointing the directions toward which Christians should seek to influence the . . . varied societies in which they [found] themselves."

On the other hand, the study had its focus in "the concrete situations in which great numbers of individual Christians [found] themselves at their jobs within . . . secular society, the ethical dilemmas which confound[ed] them, whether artisans or managers or employers or labor leaders or professional men and women, and the decisions which, as Christians, they [were] constrained to face."

Explained the Department in its first report:

> At first thought, "The Christian Meaning of Work" may appear as a novel theme. Actually, a review of developments since Stockholm reveals that our minds have been moving steadily and with accelerated urgency in that direction. It will be recalled that one of the studies preparatory to the Oxford Conference bore the title "Christian Faith and the Common Life"; and that a serious and successful effort was made to enlist far larger participation by laymen in preparation for Oxford and in the work of the Conference itself, and to make the findings of that Conference convincing and relevant to the genuine concerns of Christian laity.
>
> We owe this orientation mainly to the persuasion of the principal architect of the Oxford Conference, and also of the World Council's study program, Dr. J. H. Oldham. . . .
>
> The immediate post-war years have witnessed, as one of the most hopeful signs of requickened spiritual vitality, the birth of "laymen's movements" in many churches and lands, the attention to the concerns of laymen at Amsterdam, the projected regional conferences under World Council auspices, and the Bossey Conference of last winter on the problems of Christian laymen in their work.
>
> It is clear that the time has come when this matter should be moved from

[17] "The Study Department exists . . . to make the churches better fighting churches, that is, to help them find Christian answers to the fundamental issues of the Church's relation to the world." Central Committee Minutes, Chichester, 1949, p. 69.

the periphery to the very center of concern, and when the Study Department should take it as a major theme.

The premises of this inquiry are quite simple, and in a sense axiomatic. They are that over ninety percent of the membership of the churches are laity; that the majority of them, especially men, are preoccupied throughout the greater part of each week by concrete demands of their secular vocations; that, for large numbers, the conditions of work in which they must seek to live as Christians have undergone far-reaching changes in recent times; that "in the minds of many Christians there is lacking any clear connection between their Christian faith and the decisions they have to make in their daily life, so that, either consciously or unconsciously, they live in a constant state of paralyzing schizophrenia"; that many feel that the Church is offering them scant guidance and support in the most baffling and harassing dilemmas of their existence; and that what they feel to be the Church's failure to aid them is due, in part, to the Church's blindness to these elemental facts, [and], in part, to the almost total absence within the churches of a doctrine of work or vocation, hewn out in the circumstances of contemporary life and directly relevant to the real issues which confront nine-tenths of their members through more than half of their waking hours.

Accordingly, the Study Department intends to undertake an investigation of this whole matter. Obviously, to be successful, it must aim mainly to assist laymen to find their own Christian answers to questions which they alone fully understand. The inquiry will move forward on two planes. Under the leadership of Dr. Oldham and Dr. Kraemer, and with the collaboration of the Ecumenical Institute (whose resources are being claimed by the Study Department for this and others of its projects), it is planned to enlist the consecrated efforts of a small group of carefully selected persons, mostly lay, with the purpose of working out a Christian statement on the meaning of work, which may hope to claim wide attention both within and beyond the churches. At the same time, efforts will be made to interest groups of laity in wrestling together with these difficult issues in the concrete situations which they confront. From this process, it is hoped to render to hard-pressed men and women the vital assistance of Christian faith for their own problems, to match the devotion which they are so readily offering to the Church in its problems.[18]

The Study Department was able, from year to year, to report encouraging growth of interest and participative response in the inquiry on "Christian Action in Society."

According to the minutes for 1951, study of the subject in the United States was "relatively far advanced." The project of the National Council of the Churches of Christ in the U.S.A. on "The Church and Economic Life" had progressed favorably. Findings of its Detroit Conference had been circulated internationally by the Study Department, and this had stimulated new activity in many countries. A group to discuss "Political Implications of the Responsible Society" and another "The Christian Significance of Work and Vocation," which had been formed under the direction of Rev. Robert S. Bilheimer, Program Secretary for North America, had held successful meetings.

[18] *Ibid.*, pp. 98 ff.

In Great Britain, the Social Responsibility Department of the British Council of Churches had promoted similar studies, using both its own resource matter on "Responsibility in Industry" and the pamphlets of the Study Department of the World Council of Churches. The movement had extended to Holland, and a report of an investigation there of the effects of industrialization was being prepared for publication. Germany was "bustling with Christian social and political initiatives, centering largely in the Evangelical Academies."

An important outgrowth of the inquiry on "The Responsible Society" was the Ecumenical Commission on European Co-operation, which had begun its work in 1951. Established as an independent body of economists and politicians and looking to the Study Department for secretarial direction, it gave attention especially to "the responsibility of Christians and churches for the common social and political problems of Europe." "European Issues," its first report, had "aroused considerable discussion."

The work of "drawing all these manifold efforts together in a real ecumenical conversation" was "as yet only in its beginning. But certain crystallization points" had emerged, "such as: co-partnership in industry [and] the ethical problems of the welfare state with its expanding control over life."

A number of documents on "Christianity and Communism" had been published,[19] and the Department was preparing "an analytical survey of the issues in the discussion" on this subject. There had been a "great demand, especially in Asia," for all these publications. The Department had established an Information Service to provide accurate reports of the "situation of the churches in communist-dominated countries."

The reason for the steady rise of interest in this direction was obvious. "The revolutionary changes . . . the interdependence of the nations," and related developments had made "it imperative for Christians to come to an understanding among themselves about the goals for which they should stand in society." "Most of the churches now realize," the Study Department had discovered, "how badly equipped they are to help their people meet the challenge of movements of world impact . . . based on non-Christian views of man and society. This inquiry is, therefore, a point where the discrepancy between the ever-increasing demands and the small resources available is especially marked."

The Study Department listed for the Central Committee's report to the Second Assembly "some of the particular projects . . . of significance in the pursuit of this inquiry," as follows:

"Moral Problems in Economic and Political Life Today," arising from rapid changes in economic systems and the many experiments with state

[19] One of these was John C. Bennett's *The Christian Answer to the Challenge of Communism.*

planning and control. The problem of state power both as a means of enlarging individual freedom and as a new threat to personal . . . liberty has been examined in numerous papers issued by the Department.

"The Responsible Society and European Problems," based largely on reports of the Committee on the Christian Responsibility for European Co-operation, a body of laymen from various countries of Europe.

"The Witness of Christians in Communist Countries," as reported in papers and studies from a number of different sources.

"The Responsibility of Christians for the Social Problems of the Undeveloped Countries," emphasized particularly by the East Asia Study Conference at Lucknow, India, in 1952.

"The Ecumenical Survey on Social Questions" and the memorandum on "The Responsible Society in a World Perspective," published by the Preparatory Commission, showing the present state of Christian thinking on the world-wide aspects of the topic.

It was an essential part of the Department's policy to establish broad bases of cooperation in the various countries and to "stimulate to self-activity." It recommended national ecumenical study committees for nation-wide promotion of study. The United States and Germany had, as noted, been forward in adopting this plan. Bishop Barbieri of Buenos Aires, a member of the Study Department Committee, had addressed himself to the work of organization on this line in South American nations. In Great Britain, Canada, and Japan the Department carried on its program through "the appropriate" committees of the national councils of churches, "or central correspondents." In consultation with the International Missionary Council and the Joint Asian Secretary, Dr. Rajah B. Manikam, it was "developing an extensive promotional project [with] the younger churches of the Far East."

Relations with the churches behind the Iron Curtain had become unilateral. "Various documents, relating especially to the inquiries on the Bible and . . . Evangelism, [were] still being sent to co-operative groups in some countries; and there [was] evidence that they [were] warmly appreciated and carefully studied, as a welcome testimony of spiritual fellowship across political and ideological barriers."

The aim of the Department had been, from the beginning, to orient "the whole study process in the coming period . . . toward action."

> To be sure [it explained], the word "action" appears in only one . . . topic, "Christian Action in Society." But it is intended that that emphasis should permeate the entire program. . . . We intend to concentrate attention upon concrete situations . . . what is being actually done, and left undone, in . . . evangelism; what action is required of the churches in the social and economic spheres toward the realization of a Responsible Society; the problems of laymen in their day-by-day activities.

This was to invite criticism, the Department recognized.

> Surely, it will be said, . . . emphasis on action is premature; the discovery and development of principles must precede action. Again, an em-

phasis upon action is bound to be superficial; it invites that damning word of ecumenical opprobrium, *"activismus."* [But] these are days which demand decision; the hour will not await leisured theoretical explorations. . . . We are not lacking in theory, in the articulation of fundamental principles. These have been a principal fruitage of four decades of ecumenical endeavor, of which we are heirs—Stockholm and Oxford; Lausanne and Edinburgh, 1937; Edinburgh, 1910; Jerusalem, Madras and Whitby. We intend to take full account of their achievements and to build directly upon their conclusions. The time has come to redress the balance in emphasis between theory and practice. . . . But, in the thought of some of us, a profounder consideration justifies . . . insistent attention to the concrete realities of Christian action. May it be that we shall discover sound theoretical principles only in the context of specific activities? May it be that we shall not achieve ecumenical unity save in a mutual confrontation of, and common wrestling with, the specific decisions demanded of churches and individual Christians amidst the fast-flowing events of these perilous days? In the fields both of evangelism and of Christian action in society, may it be that our efforts thus far have been relatively deficient in accomplishment, not only because disproportionate attention has been given to analysis rather than to experimentation, to diagnosis rather than cure, but also because the diagnoses have been conducted in an inadequate perspective. . . . Successful cure of disease is the ideal perspective, perhaps the necessary perspective, for diagnosis. . . . Only the physician who has witnessed and administered cure can be a trustworthy diagnostician. By the same token, only evangelism which has actually won men to Christ can furnish principles for "The Evangelization of Man in Modern Mass Society"; only proven results in social change can guide "Christian Action in Society." So we propose to focus attention upon "successful" evangelism upon "effective" Christian efforts to remould society, as furnishing the essential data for our inquiries.[20]

The problem was to enlist the churches. Cooperation by them had increased as the program proceeded. Soon after the Amsterdam Assembly, the Study Department had sent out a "set of communications . . . to one hundred fifty member churches" and had received only five replies. The response improved. But, "mid-way between the two Assemblies," the Department in its report to the Central Committee was asking:[21] "Are the churches really concerned with ecumenical study?"

This question is well worth pondering at this point. . . . "To promote co-operation in study" has been recognized as one of the functions of the World Council; and the Council has made provision for this task in various ways. In 1949 the Central Committee at Chichester, approving the present program of the Study Department, urged the member-churches and Christion groups "to give serious consideration, both in sustained study and appropriate action, to the issues raised in these inquiries, as they are of foremost importance for the life and witness of the churches today." Frequently, religious leaders have underscored the necessity of an intensive conversa-

[20] See the Minutes of the Central Committee meeting at Chichester, 1949, pp. 100 ff.

[21] At the meeting of the Central Committee in Rolle, 1951. See the Minutes, pp. 97 ff.

tion between the churches on their common mission in and to the contemporary world, if their ecumenical fellowship is to become a real unity of mind and purpose. . . .

Yet it is an undeniable fact that the member-churches, on the whole, show a disquieting apathy and unconcern as regards this aspect of their common enterprise. It is all the more disquieting, since today they find themselves in the midst of a world revolution of unprecedented dimensions, calling for joint efforts also of thought and mind, commensurate in many respects with the gigantic achievements of the Early Church in interpreting and communicating the mystery of Christ, and in out-thinking its pagan contemporaries.

True, there is today a large amount of spontaneous interpretation and cross-fertilization as from church to church, and from country to country. It is also true that an increasing number of individuals and groups are awakening to the significance of ecumenical study, and sharing it. But it remains a constantly vexing problem how to make ecumenical perspectives and issues a living ferment within the *regular* activities and processes of the churches. The ecumenical "conversion" of the churches has not yet gone deep enough to make them ready to pool their forces in *concerted* attacks on confronting problems. Nor do they possess adequate machinery for effectively participating in ecumenical study, and for translating its eventual results into terms of new policies and programs. . . .

Besides the "major inquiries" with which this review of its labors had been mainly concerned, the Study Department carried the continuous and often distracting burden of routine duties. Among these was maintaining coordination in study and research in the other several departments of the World Council of Churches. The dissemination of information about significant trends of thought in the constituency of the Council, another of its responsibilities, involved the preparation and publication of brochures and books, in addition to those outlining the main themes,[22] or growing out of them.

From time to time there were special assignments. A symposium on *The Christian Approach to the Jews* was projected jointly with the International Missionary Council, under the editorial direction of Bishop Stephen Neill, Dr. Hendrik Kraemer, and Rev. E. Brunner of Basle. Dr. Nils Ehrenström, Director of the Study Department, and Professor Georges Florovsky, a member of the Department Committee, collaborated on *The Orthodox Church Today*. A comprehensive survey of the important papal encyclicals on social and political subjects was made in cooperation with scholars of Oxford University,

[22] In English, German, and French, *The Bible and the Church's Message to the World, Evangelization of Modern Man in Mass Society, Christian Action in Society, The Responsible Society,* and *The Meaning of Work,* some 35,000 copies. In addition, *The Scope and Initiative of the Modern State,* by Principal T. M. Taylor; *Moral Problems in Economic Life Today,* by Denys Munby; and *The Christian Answer to the Challenge of Communism,* by Dr. John Coleman Bennett. Also, *The Biblical Doctrine of Work,* by Canon Alan Richardson and a symposium on *Biblical Authority for Today*. Other works were *Man and Society* and *Law and Justice*.

also "an exploratory inquiry" with the Press and Information Service on "public relation issues" before the World Council of Churches. With the Ecumenical Institute, the Department co-sponsored a conference at Bossey, Switzerland, in April of 1950 on *Foundations of International Law*.

The staff of the Department cooperated with the Ecumenical Institute in conducting "a survey on Christianity and social work in . . . fifteen countries," the results of which were to be published.

A special study on *The Encounter of Christianity with Communism* was completed in 1953. It was "a critical analysis of current trends in Christian thinking about communism."

Dr. J. H. Oldham's *Work in Modern Society*, described by the Department's report to the Central Committee at Toronto, Canada, in 1950 as "a basic document" on "the amelioration of industrial relations," had appeared earlier that year.

A revised edition of *The Life and Work of Women in the Church* had been added to the growing list of publications and had proved one of the most popular titles. Within a year after its announcement, nearly four thousand copies had been sold. Most significantly, they had gone into all parts of the world.

"Preparations for the Second Assembly" were one of the "six major types of activity" specified for the Study Department by the World Council of Churches, on the basis of recommendations by the pre-Amsterdam Study Commission,[23] and this task received immediate attention. From the important conferences of the study committees at Wadham College, Oxford, June 28-July 6, 1949, onward, it had a place in the agenda of all meetings of the Department and the Central Committee. Its importance and the difficulties it presented were recognized. "The determination of subjects for inquiry" was not, in the opinion of the Department, the hardest problem, "but the devising of effective ways and means" of study.[24]

The method commonly employed, which had been developed prior to the Conference on Church, Community and State at Oxford in 1937, consisted of the circulation by mail of memoranda by individuals and groups on the subjects under consideration, for reading and criticism; of revision, in the light of comment, and recirculation; and of the holding of occasional international study conferences. This procedure, "almost inevitably," had "yielded proven values—not least the 'conversion' to the ecumenical idea and task . . . of some of the most vigorous and influential Christian minds."

The Study Committee was not satisfied with reliance exclusively upon this plan. The years between Assemblies seemed to offer a chance "for leisurely and diversified experimentation in other methods," and it was

[23] Minutes of the Chichester meeting of the Central Committee, 1949, p. 96.
[24] See *Ibid.*, pp. 96 and 99.

resolved "to take advantage of the opportunity to pursue the most varied ways of conducting ecumenical interchange of thought toward the development . . . of an ecumenical mind."

The Central Committee, at its meeting in Toronto, Canada, in 1950, chose the main theme for the Second Assembly[25] and took steps to appoint an Advisory Commission on its development. Later, the six subsidiary subjects were assigned to preparatory commissions. The Study Department was given the responsibility of coordinating and supervising "the study preparations." Some of its members were elected to the Advisory Commission on the main theme, which, after three annual meetings, produced a 60,000-word report for discussion by the Assembly. Each of the other commissions prepared three documents: an introductory leaflet for general study by the churches, a descriptive survey of recent thought and activity in its field, and a working paper for the section of the Assembly studying its subject.

In connection with the publication of these studies, the officers of the Department said:

> In their present form the Surveys are the outcome of an extensive program of fact-finding and of consultation with denominational and interdenominational agencies and individual correspondents in many lands. During well over a year, the officers of the Commissions and the Study Department staff have been engaged in the complicated and often baffling task of collecting and digesting source data. The responses to the questionnaires and queries which were sent out have been uneven, both in quantity and in quality. The process has revealed how inadequately equipped the churches still are when it comes to investigating, and realistically assessing, facts and trends in their own situation. Yet judging from the wealth of statements and reports received (some of them well deserving separate publication in full), it would appear that the usefulness of such synoptic, ecumenical surveys has been fully recognized.
>
> Drafts of the Surveys were scrutinized and partly revised at meetings of the Commissions. . . . On the instructions of the Commissions, final editing was subsequently undertaken by officers and staff, who in several instances faced the painful task of drastically reducing valuable material in order to keep within allotted limits of space. Time has not permitted resubmission of the . . . texts to the members of each Commission . . . for approval.
>
> Such value and authority as they possess is intrinsic. It lies in the measure in which they acutely discern the signs of the Christian world scene, lift major issues into prominence, and thus offer sign-posts for the pilgrim Church.[26]

On presenting the report of the Study Department to the Central Committee at Lucknow in 1953—the year before Evanston—Dr. Nils

[25] Main Theme: "Christ—The Hope of the World." Subsidiary themes: "Our Oneness in Christ and Our Disunity as Churches," "The Mission of the Church to Those Outside Her Life," "The Responsible Society in a World Perspective," "Christians in the Struggle for World Community," "The Church Amid Racial and Ethnic Tensions," "The Christian in His Vocation."

[26] *The Christian Hope,* General Preface, pp. vi-viii.

Ehrenström, who had borne much of the responsibility for the preparatory work for the Second Assembly, remarked:

Ecumenical study shares in large measure that quality of the "things hoped for" of which Hebrews eleven speaks, namely, that they are "things not seen." It cannot be measured in dollars or rupees. It is a germinating seed sown in trust and hope, but it is impossible to predict whether the seed was good or the ground favorable, and rarely does it yield quick and spectacular harvests. Habits of mind and outlook, shaped over centuries and solidly entrenched in ecclesiastical traditions and practices, do not change overnight. The growth of an ecumenical mind among the churches is, as we all know, beset with immense difficulties: it is a road encumbered with untold stumbling-blocks. Indeed, perhaps more than most other forms of ecumenical activity, ecumenical study must be borne and carried forward by that active and patient expectation which characterizes the Christian Hope, or else it becomes a hopeless undertaking.

Yet, it would be incorrect to infer that it does not also show definite fruits. If we look at its growth over the years,[27] it has exercised no mean influence in drawing attention to crucial issues, in facilitating the process of mutual interpretation and of sharing, and in exploring new pathways of common witness and service. The preparations for the Evanston Assembly are, I would suggest, a telling example of the necessity and worthwhileness of such study.

At one point in the records of the Department was entered a memorandum saying that "the principle [had] been accepted that members of the staff of the Study Department should themselves occasionally have some leisure for study." The wisdom of this action will be apparent to anyone reading this record of their labors, which is, however, but a bare outline of them.

The staff consisted of three secretaries: Dr. Nils Ehrenström, who began his service in a similar position under the Universal Christian Council for Life and Work nearly twenty years before the organization of the World Council of Churches; Dr. Wolfgang Schweitzer, who served from 1948, after previous experience in the same field under the provisional departments of the World Council of Churches (in process of formation), to 1952; Rev. Paul Abrecht, who divided his time between the Study Department and the Ecumenical Institute; and Dr. Hans Heinrich Harms, who succeeded Dr. Ehrenström upon his retirement in 1954.

Dr. Harms came to the directorship from the Evangelical Lutheran Church of Hannover, Germany, having studied at the Universities of Göttingen and Bonn and Princeton Theological Seminary and served as lecturer on ecumenics at Göttingen and as *Oberkirchenrat* in the foreign office of his Church at Frankfürt, Germany, from 1950 to 1952, when he had assumed his duties at Geneva as Associate Director of the Study Department.

[27] Dr. Ehrenström had been associated with the study program of the ecumenical movement some twenty years, actually from its beginning.

2. The Secretariat for Evangelism

Another function of the World Council of Churches was "to support the Churches in their task of evangelism."[28]

Against the background of "the spiritual lostness of the post-war world," the Amsterdam Assembly in Section II addressed itself, as previously noted, to the sub-theme "The Church's Witness to God's Design" and in its conclusions stressed the "evangelistic mandate to the churches in the gospel." Before adjourning, it authorized the appointment of a Secretary for Evangelism, who should work under the direction of the Council's General Secretariat.

Dr. Johannes Christian Hoekendijk of the Dutch Reformed Church in the Netherlands was elected to this post and served from August 1, 1949, until December 1, 1952, when he resigned to join the Theological Faculty of the University of Utrecht.

The Secretariat for Evangelism had for its immediate responsibility developing the service of information and the study of special problems in evangelism begun by Dr. Elmer George Homrighausen of the Presbyterian Church in the United States of America. His report of visits to the churches in many parts of Europe and in the Near East during 1947 and 1948 had emphasized their need for "a new and living proclamation of the gospel" and their desire for guidance in the search for more effective methods of communication with the large groups outside their life, and so prepared the way for the discussion and findings of Section II of the Assembly. In addition, the Secretariat undertook the inquiry on "The Evangelization of Man in Modern Mass Society," which had been projected by the Study Department, as bearing directly upon this primary task.[29]

It was decided that in this field the Council could be of greatest help to the churches by leading them to study their work in the light of the actual conditions under which it had to be pursued, rather than by attempting itself to promote evangelistic efforts over the vast area marked for its attention.

The program thus conceived was launched with the supporting action at Amsterdam in mind:

> As we have studied evangelism in its ecumenical setting, we have been burdened by a sense of urgency. . . . If the gospel really is a matter of life and death, it seems intolerable that any human being now in the world should live out his life without ever having the chance to hear and receive it. . . . Now, not tomorrow, is the time to act. God . . . has given us

[28] Constitution of the World Council of Churches, Article III, Section vii. See Appendix A.

[29] See Minutes of the Chichester meeting, pp. 32 and 97 ff.

the assurance that "it is required of stewards that a man be found faithful," and that, where faithfulness is found, he is able "to do exceeding abundantly above all that we can ask or think."[30]

Those now girding themselves for the task saw many of the factors especially accenting its urgency: among them, the multitudes in every land who had not heard the gospel; those who, though they might have heard it proclaimed, had rejected it or come to no decision about it; and the "vast blocs of Christians" who felt no compelling concern and were blind to the problem and the opportunity, while others who had been awakened to the need were hesitant and uncertain as to the action demanded of them.

Basic to the study to be conducted with the churches was a series of reports describing the conditions and the outlook of evangelistic work in different countries—the United States, Great Britain, Finland, Holland, Sweden, Switzerland, France, India, Ceylon, Scotland, Germany, Burma, and others. Printed or mimeographed, these were circulated among the churches, which found them "a source of valuable information as they sought to understand the variety and complexity of the problems in any attempt to give the gospel to mankind."

"Modern mass society" in the context of the inquiry proposed by the Study Department of the World Council of Churches was presented as "an epiphenomenon of industrialization." "Evidence from all over the world" showed that "the Church was finding itself progressively less at home in the developing industrial society, . . . whether one looked at the unskilled laborer, at the artisan, at the clerk . . . in the suburbs, or at the managing and directing class. . . ." It had "increasingly been pushed aside." The problem was rapidly becoming universal, for industrialization, which had advanced on such a large scale in the West, was now developing with equal strides in the East and already disturbing the mission churches.

To make the conditions graphic, the study committee enclosed with the brochures sent to the churches a description of the situation in France, "written by one who [knew] the industrial world intimately from within," whose name was withheld:

> There exists a clearly distinct working-class in France, bound together by the fellowship of manual labor lasting for a life-time.
>
> Its milieu is determined by the factory, that world without miracles or mystery. It is at the same time an intensely human world, the fruit of man's will alone, and intensely inhuman, wholly artificial. Nothing unforeseen can happen here. Skill and routine limit the dangers. Here, there is an area where even the most despised of men and those most hardly treated by life can assert domination over matter. The factory is the sphere of the worker's domination, his responsibility, even of his freedom. At the same time, however, it is the place of his servitude. He is chained to the machine over which he asserts his domination.

[30] See p. 288 ff.

On analysis, however, the worker knows that it is not the machine but, in the ultimate issue, . . . the man who enslaves and exploits. His trust in things and his pride in the technical achievements that control matter are therefore combined with a deep distrust of man, of words, of values, and of "the spirit." In the world of human relations, feelings and ideas, the worker feels himself at a disadvantage and is ill at ease. He is continually aware of being treated as an asset, conscious of being exploited, because his work is being done for others. And this leads to that profound bitterness and to that exacting spirit which seems to be insatiable, and in fact is insatiable, unless radical change in the whole social fabric is effected. Marxist theories are generally accepted, not because they give an adequate explanation of the worker's actual situation, but because they do provide the working class, which is unable to express itself, with a means of expression.

Class-solidarity is cemented by the fact that the working-class is fixed in its social status. There is hardly any possibility of movement upwards in the social scale. Individual social differentiation is thereby checked. Either the worker accepts his status as such, not reckoning with the possibility of an improvement in his lot, short of any general improvement in workers' conditions, or he ceases to be a worker and seeks to get away from his status by way of total revolt and rejection of all society, or by escaping into the different class of small tradesmen and proprietors.

Inside the working-class its solidarity is expressed in a generosity, a readiness to help, a real camaraderie, and a common style of living. In relation to the outside world, the class-solidarity of the workers is expressed in a profound distrust and a complete rejection. The worker feels himself uncomfortable, often hurt, and occasionally scandalized in the bourgeois world. Memories of a long history of disappointment and frustration are alive. He knows that, as in the past, the worker can rely only upon himself and that at the crucial moment there will be not one single ally who is not liable to desert him. At every turn the worker has felt himself faced by the same fear and rejection of "out-groups." So he has learned the meaning of class-struggle. He rises in revolt against this society which has allotted him his unalterably inferior position. He can only spurn the entire legal and ethical structure through which that other world endeavors to establish its own justification, and he seeks to do away with all the "values" which appear indissolubly linked up with it.

Religion and the Church, as some of the dominant "values" in this bourgeois world, are for the same reason—more or less aggressively—rejected, because they are, in theory, at the bottom of the philosophical and ethical system that this world has built up.

The industrial order, however varied its superficial aspects in different countries, was found to pose certain general questions for those responsible for evangelism, and concerning many of them the committee of inquiry had, with frankness, to say, "We do not know the answers." It could only ask of the churches cooperation in gathering information which might become the basis of a hopeful approach to some of them.

The plan offered began with studies by local groups of the clergy and the laity in industrial communities of the conditions confronting their churches and of the kinds of evangelistic programs which were being followed in attempting to cope with them. Regional and national councils of churches, or their departments of evangelism, would be expected to promote the launching of such surveys as widely as possible and, as they proceeded, to provide for expert evaluation of the facts gathered.

It was desired that those participating should be engaged actively in the work of evangelization and committed to Christian witnessing in areas connected with industry. The information obtained would be printed, after a critical assessment, and made available to all the churches. If the project, as it evolved, should be found to require them, national and international conferences would be called to unify and give impetus to the cause of evangelism in its broader scope.

The committee of the Secretariat gave the following "tentative definition" of its aim:

To locate the problem, to find out where we are in relation to this new type of society that has been growing up for two hundred years, and in which the Church in many parts of the world has progressively failed to maintain its hold.

To make available as widely as possible tested and reliable information concerning successful attempts at Christian penetration of this world.

To facilitate contacts between those engaged in similar enterprises in different countries.

To challenge the churches to experiment and perhaps to help them by the inspiration of what, in different parts of the Church, is actually being achieved.

There were the "traditional procedures of evangelism" which the churches making the local surveys would wish, it was hoped, to re-evaluate: the baptism of children, Christian practices in the home, marriage in the Church, burial with Christian rites, churchgoing, the attendance of children at Sunday schools, the promotion of Bible-reading, personal contacts with the clergy and other religious workers, house-to-house visitation by the pastors and lay volunteers, open-air preaching, apologetic teaching, and campaigns of the older revivalist type—to mention some of them.

On the other hand, new experiments in evangelism in some countries had been reported as measurably successful, and a critical examination of them should be made, to determine whether or not their methods might be recommended for wider employment. Some of these were industrial chaplaincies, such as had become a part of denominational organizations in Great Britain; Christian workers' leagues, like those, for example, in Glasgow, Scotland; planned community life, after the pattern of Iona, Scotland; special religious orders, mainly Anglican in Great Britain; evangelistic service-centers, such as those of CIMADE[31] in

[31] *Comité Inter-Mouvements auprès des Évacués,* "an organization brought into being during World War II by the Protestant churches and lay youth movements in France." It was important particularly for its work with refugees and undercover operations therewith.

France; self-identification by Christian workers, including pastors and priests, with industrial life, through regular employment in factories; and attempts in various Roman Catholic countries to reach youth in industry, an example of which was the Jeunesse Ouvrière Chrétienne. It was probable, the Secretariat thought, that some of the most original and effective experiments were unknown, except in small circles, and that "fuller information . . . might be . . . useful for an interchurch cross-fertilization of evangelistic methods."

These unconventional adventures in evangelism seemed to have a fundamentally common methodology, which could be summarized as attempting to make the meaning of the gospel proclamation (*kerygma*) clear and appealing through life lived in fellowship (*koinonia*) and expressed in service (*diakonia*).

"It should not be forgotten," the inquiry committee admitted, "that there are flourishing parishes in industrial areas in Britain, the United States and elsewhere, in which the gulf between the industrial world and the Church seems to be bridged, or has never been allowed to develop." But such situations were exceptional, it said.

More fundamental to the task of evangelism than methods was the state of the Church, "the instrument of the gospel in this world." Some of those responsible for the study, as well as many persons engaged in evangelistic work in various countries, felt that every undertaking was neutralized by the sad state of the churches, "crying aloud that anyone desiring admission to them must accept conformity to their already outworn manner of life." "It would, therefore, be a tragic misunderstanding," these observers held, "if the churches, as they were, merely adopted some new evangelistic techniques and methods and essayed some fresh ventures in evangelism." "Nothing less than a revolution in the whole life of the Church," it was declared, "is needed to make it really an evangelistic Church." "The spiritual poverty and unpreparedness of the Church is such that no one can desire that a large number of those now outside should enter the churches as they are," agreed some workers in evangelistic programs in the areas described.

"The pressing question," wrote the Secretary of Evangelism[32] in *The Ecumenical Review* for the spring of 1950, "is how the Church can again become a *paroikia*—a company of strangers and pilgrims—a group of sojourners in the world—fully detached and so completely free to incarnate itself in every social structure."

In the same article Dr. Hoekendijk described the conception of the Church widely held by "the masses" and apparently shared by many nominally within its fold, as "a victim of sociological imprisonment, through which it is bound, and its manner of life ossified in the traditions of feudalism or of the bourgeois age. . . . Outside these areas of society . . . it is practically paralyzed." Traditional methods of evan-

[32] Dr. Johannes Christian Hoekendijk.

gelism, he pointed out, generally presupposed the existence of the *corpus Christianum*. John Hinrich Wichern, the father of the home missionary movement on the Continent, had said: "The task of evangelization is the winning back of the masses in Christendom who have fallen under the power of sin and are no longer reached by ordinary methods." It was a matter of reminding the lost of what they already knew and possessed. But in the decade following the outbreak of the Second World War Christendom seemed to many Christian leaders in Europe to have ceased to exist. It had given place to a non-Christian society in which religion was, for the most part, "primitive paganism with some survivals," chiefly in the seasonal observances of the churches and in social customs.

Such views had exerted a strong influence upon the inquiry into "the evangelization of man in modern mass society." Hence, the conclusion that nothing short of revolutionary changes in the life of the churches and an almost complete revision of evangelistic procedures offered any basis of hope that the Christian faith would be able to penetrate present-day society.

Those pursuing the inquiry seemed to be agreed, nevertheless, in urging the need for evangelistic activity while studying these seemingly almost hopeless problems. On "the local level" Christians talking about "witnessing for Christ should be prepared to work for the conversion of given persons known to them." On "the ecumenical level" discussion needed to be directed toward obedience to "the missionary obligation of the Church in the whole world." Again, action was considered a necessary element of the study, and not only an end, because the meaning of witnessing and its technique could be learned only by working at it with the light and opportunity one had. "It would be disastrous, if the study of evangelism, necessary as it is, were made a moratorium on a bold and courageous witness," declared the committee. The investigation could not be limited to a few experts. "Every Christian in the world has the facts under his eyes."

The summary of the Secretariat's survey was forwarded with a covering letter to all the denominations in the membership of the World Council of Churches. Such responses as there were came mainly from groups which organized for its study. They had value, particularly, in their disclosure of certain attitudes and conceptions which would have to be reconciled before there could be any united movement in evangelism.

They showed, for one thing, that there was serious confusion over the meaning and the aims of evangelism. On the one hand, there was continuous temptation to interpret evangelization as propaganda or proselytism, in which man was treated as a mere object—or a victim—to be molded by "our work, in our image and likeness." On the other hand, the whole process was likely to degenerate into making merely nominal church-members.

How could the Church avoid these superficial and hurtful results in this its primary mission? How could it in evangelism experience, through fellowship with the Holy Spirit, a continuous re-creation in its spiritual life?

> Connected with this uncertainty in the understanding of evangelization is a disagreement on the interpretation of conversion. . . . According to one school of thought, all evangelistic activity should be focused on conversion understood in a particular sense; according to another school, it should be detached from all attempts to convert individuals. One of the most urgent needs is a thorough study of the whole subject of conversion, in the light of the re-discovery of biblical theology and of modern psychological knowledge. Fear of a pietistic or semi-pietistic interpretation of conversion ought not to prevent our common attempt to recover the full and genuine biblical content of the idea of conversion, including the radical change of ideas and general outlook. We are called to consider also the significance of conversion as the penetration of the whole thought process of society by Christian ideas, in such a way as to produce a milieu in which the conversion of the individual can be real and significant.

There was evidence that the social approach to evangelism recommended by the inquiry discouraged a favorable response in the case of many. Revolution in the life of the churches such as the statement in the prospectus from Geneva seemed to envisage did not look like what older evangelists meant by their entreaty to men, "Get right with God!" Squaring oneself with the Almighty was expected to issue in a new moral attitude on the part of the convert which would be a very definite and enduring contribution toward the making of a better world. But linking a personal surrender to God with acceptance of new and untried patterns of social organization was another matter. There were many Christians who would have said that it looked in the direction of social as well as spiritual retrogression.

The Secretariat's hope that the response of the churches to the explanation of the inquiry would bring information concerning "new experiments in evangelism" was to be disappointed. Apparently there had been reluctance on the part of those engaging in such efforts to write about them, as they felt, perhaps, prematurely; or the silence may have indicated only that none of them had, in the judgment of the churches promoting them, met with sufficient success to warrant a recommendation for trial elsewhere.

"By its very nature the ecumenical study of evangelism is not likely to yield quick or very spectacular results," said the Secretariat in its report for 1950.[33]

> If such essentials are put under study (as has been done in the outline) as the structural reform of church life, a reconsideration of the churches' grand strategy, renewal of congregational life, an overhauling of religious vocabulary, evangelism as a function of eschatological expectancy (instead

[33] Minutes of the Toronto meeting of the Central Committee, 1950, p. 116.

of merely an attempt to extend the number of church members) . . . if, in other words, the total existence of the Church and the sum of all its activities are supposed to be brought under ruthless judgment, we cannot measure the results of this study by the kind of statements that will be produced. Attempts to do it better than before are the hoped-for fruits. . . .

These attempts may remain for some time to come rather unknown. It is the expressed desire of many of those, who are engaged in new experiments, not to draw attention to their efforts. They fear, and rightly so, that these . . . may be killed, if they hit the ecumenical headlines too soon or are glamorized as successful attempts at Christian penetration of modern mass society. . . . A great amount of reserve will . . . be required in the dissemination of information concerning these experiments.

Only a very few groups have until now been organized . . . to join in the ecumenical study of evangelism. There is, however, an impressive amount of study of some . . . aspects of industrial evangelism. . . . These local projects have the great advantage that they are rooted in concrete situations and have aroused the interest of the churches already. We expect to relate [them] to our over-all program. . . .

Some evangelistic movements in Europe showed "an ever-growing anti-ecclesiastical bias." There was a tendency to distinguish "rather sharply" between the "static church bodies" and the new "second church," composed of all these dynamic groups. It would have to be one of the main concerns of the Secretariat of Evangelism (in close cooperation with the secretary for laymen's work) "to prevent a widening of this gap, so that these . . . movements [would] not be canalized in a separate stream but [allowed to] vitalize the life of the churches."

In presenting the report of the Secretariat for 1951,[34] Dr. Hoekendijk commented on the continuing lukewarmness of the churches toward "ecumenical evangelism." So far, they had shown "very little interest in the matter." Theological faculties had replied concerning the inquiry, "one saying that we do not teach evangelism in our curriculum," and another indicating that its course of study was chosen "for the preparation of a pastoral task; that is, not an evangelistic one."

This lack of interest is in part explained [continued the Secretary] by the fact that the rediscovery of evangelism implies a revolution in the life of the Church. Such an orientation makes the study not only dangerous, but difficult to take hold of. . . . As we approach the Second Assembly, the most decisive question is whether we can combine the *charisma* of Christian imagination, in order that we may rethink the nature and structure of the Church in its evangelistic purpose with a new awareness of the great urgency in our concern for evangelism.

The action of the Assembly had been that, "to support the churches in their task of evangelization," a staff member be appointed "to set in the forefront of the World Council of Churches' work the task of evangelism and to make known to the constituent churches the effective new

[34] Minutes of the Rolle meeting of the Central Committee, 1951, p. 39.

approaches towards the problem of communicating with the unchurched."

The Central Committee at its Chichester meeting decided that the Secretary for Evangelism should work also for the Study Department, carrying chief responsibility for its inquiry on "The Evangelization of Man in Modern Mass Society," and, further, should give as much time as his duties to the World Council permitted to the promotion of the study initiated by the International Missionary Council on "The Missionary Obligation of the Church." [35]

Dr. Hoekendijk became secretary also of the joint committee from the two Councils conducting this last project. He was succeeded in 1952 as Secretary of Evangelism by Rev. Daniel T. Niles of the Methodist Church in Ceylon, who agreed to serve until the Second Assembly on a part-time basis. He could not take up residence in Geneva. His work consisted, for the most part, in visiting churches and attending evangelistic conferences in Europe and Asia.

Bishop Stephen Neill, as Associate General Secretary of the World Council of Churches, with responsibility especially for the promotion of evangelism, early in 1949 spent three weeks in the United States and Canada. He spoke at the biennial meeting of the Federal Council of the Churches of Christ in America on evangelism as the primary work of the churches and conducted a mission at the University of Toronto. According to reports, the Canadian effort in its results "surpassed the highest hopes of those who had set it in motion." The students, who had attended the meetings in overflowing numbers, declared that the Christian faith had become the principal subject of discussion in the University.

During 1953-54 Dr. Ralph D. Hyslop of the Congregational Christian Churches in the United States assisted the Secretariat for Evangelism at Geneva while on sabbatical leave from his professorship in the Pacific School of Religion at Berkeley, California. Dr. Arthur Mitchell Chirgwin of the Congregational Union of England and Wales, Research Secretary of the United Bible Societies, likewise spent considerable time at the Secretariat's headquarters gathering material for his book *The Bible in World Evangelism.*

Dr. Chirgwin's relations with the Secretariat led to a proposal by the United Bible Societies that collaboration be extended and broadened. The plan set forth in the following resolution by the Societies was agreed to and adopted, in substance, by the World Council of Churches and the International Missionary Council at Evanston in 1954:

Agreed that, convinced of the importance of Dr. A. M. Chirgwin's studies in the use of the Bible in world evangelism, and the value to the United Bible Societies of the contacts established in Geneva, the Council [of the United Bible Societies] has been led to consider desirable the continuance of these contacts and the making of further studies. Among the latter the most

[35] Minutes of the Toronto meeting of the Central Committee, 1950, p. 115.

important appear to be inquiries into the attitude towards the Bible on the part of people in and out of the Church under various current conditions, and studies of the Bible in the churches in order to discover the conditions and practices which are effective in securing full advantage of the Bible's great resources and to promote their effective application. The range of the investigation needed seems to the Council to be more extensive than it alone can properly deal with. They require a common endeavor by the leadership of the churches and of the missionary societies.

The Council of the United Bible Societies, therefore, suggests to the World Council of Churches and the International Missionary Council the formation of a joint Committee on studies in the place, relevance and use of the Bible in the present world situation, both in and beyond the churches. The Council suggests that such a joint Committee be composed of four representatives of each of the three bodies and be responsible for the planning and supervision of such studies, the enlistment of the organs or divisions of the three bodies carrying on the studies and in promoting such recommendations for action as may result.

On approval of such a plan in substance, the Council authorizes the appointment of a Secretary (with the necessary clerical assistance) to serve as the Secretary of such a joint Committee, and it is suggested that such a Secretary be recognized as a staff member of the United Bible Societies and the Division of Studies of the World Council of Churches and the International Missionary Council. . . .[36]

The Societies submitted for consideration an outline of studies and organization, in which a vital and discerning objective was "to stimulate expository preaching within the churches, to mediate constructively to pastors and people the new insights of fifty years of scholarship, to help teachers of religion in the right approach to Bible study and reading."

3. The Ecumenical Institute

The Ecumenical Institute, founded in 1946, continued its program uninterruptedly upon becoming a department of the World Council of Churches in 1948. Two new developments of special importance occurred.

Money donated by John D. Rockefeller, Jr., in 1946 enabled the Provisional Committee to lease the Chateau de Bossey at Céligny, Switzerland, for the Institute and to buy adjacent property, including a smaller building, known as Petit Bossey. Situated about ten miles from Geneva and overlooking the lake, these estates combined convenient quarters with a view unexcelled. Another gift from Mr. Rockefeller, in 1950, made possible the purchase of the Chateau, a rearrangement of its interior to accommodate more occupants, and the conversion of one of the lesser buildings into a chapel.

In 1952 the Institute established a Graduate School of Ecumenical

[36] Acted upon by the Council of the United Bible Societies at Eastbourne, England, 1954.

Studies, in cooperation with the University of Geneva, the aim of which, in the words of Dr. Hendrik Kraemer, the Director, was "to help a younger generation of university graduates to obtain first-hand knowledge [of] and insight into the ecumenical movement, its background, its goals and its problems, and thereby [to] become more effective workers for . . . interdenominational co-operation in their various countries."

The School's board of governors consisted of university professors, including a representative of the Theological Faculty of the University of Geneva; and the staff of instructors were to be mainly visiting teachers from educational institutions in different countries on temporary leave. The courses extended from the first of October to the middle of February and gave students opportunity each year to earn credit for a full semester of regular study at the University, which offered also examinations for a theological licentiate in ecumenics, conditional on two years of acceptable work in the School.

When the School started its third year, in 1954, it was with reasonable assurance from the outcome of the first two courses that its experiment "was full of encouraging potentialities." One problem it faced was enrolling, from year to year, a student body qualified by academic preparation for the study. Another was a disadvantage in the short tenures of visiting members of the faculty. Compensating for the latter in some degree was the introduction through the change of personnel of "a variety of churchmanship and experience into the life of the community."

In the Institute itself was maintained a full-to-overflowing schedule of courses and conferences, which, over the years, drew some four thousand representatives from churches in more than fifty countries.

The courses, which ran usually two or three weeks, offered studies in the history, fundamental issues, and ongoing features of the ecumenical movement. There were special classes for theological students of advanced standing and for missionaries on furlough or in transit to or from their posts, which often had more applications for admission than could be accepted.

Lay workers in the permanent service of the churches found courses to meet their respective needs, and pastors also their opportunity for specializing study.

The Institute cooperated as it could with the World's Alliance of the Young Men's Christian Associations, the World's Young Women's Christian Association, and the World's Student Christian Federation in conducting still other classes.

The conferences at the Institute, which were usually of shorter duration than the courses and devoted more to discussion than to formal instruction, served a number of more or less distinct groups:

Members of the same professions—such as educators, lawyers, artists, industrialists, managers, and others—who wished to consider how they might make their daily work more their Christian vocation.

Persons whose callings and training qualified them to cooperate with the churches in certain phases of their mission—as, for example, doctors and psychiatrists in evangelism, social workers in the pastoral ministries of the churches as they encountered the rapidly expanding secular oversight and care of the state, and specialists in problems of the family who brought to their service an intelligent religious concern.

Representatives of important areas of life with which the churches had little or no communication, who, in conference with Christian leaders, could help in bridging the gulf of separation and open the way for the gospel to penetrate their world—such as sociologists and philosophers, or experts in the multiplying problems of rural life which were of such urgent importance to the churches.

And, finally, those wishing to pursue discussions on the Bible and moral issues which linked themselves naturally with biblical principles and examples, under conditions affording more time and freer participation than the daily periods of Bible study at the Institute itself.

The Institute prospectus for 1953 showed something of the varied and timely character of its program of courses and conferences for a typical period:

(March and April) Conference for Social Workers, designed to help them to face the problems in their profession which are due largely to the increasing role of the state in the social services.

Conference on Pastoral Care, organized at the request of the Conference of Mental and Health Personnel, Ministers, and Theologians at Bossey in 1952, to bring together experts who will lead in the consideration of such topics as "The Theological and Priestly Foundation of Pastoral Care," "Pastoral Care and Psycho-therapy," "Training Theological Students for Pastoral Care."

Conference on Art and the Church, for study of some of the common problems of art as an expression of faith, the theology of art, the search of the churches for new art forms, and liturgy and worship as aesthetic form.

(May) Course for Missionaries, on reshaping the pattern of missionary activity, in the light of lessons learned from the withdrawal of the churches from China and "The Call to Mission and Unity" as based upon the reports of the Willingen Conference: for secretaries of missionary societies also, and principals of missionary training schools.

(June) Second Conference on the Problems of the Family, a follow-up of a similar conference in 1950, to consider especially the Church and marriage, and also material prepared by the consultation on birth control at Bossey in 1952: for a maximum of fifty persons—clergy, psychologists, lawyers, social workers, doctors, parents, and church workers.

(July) Vacation Course for Laymen, open to all lay members of churches and offering opportunity to come to Bossey and live in an ecumenical fellowship, while sharing their experiences as Christians in secular occupations.

Theological Students' Course, "The Nature of the Church," based on the preparatory documents and the report of the Third World Conference on Faith and Order and material prepared by the Study Department for the Second Assembly of the Churches.

(August) Conference on the Church and Rural Life, sponsored by the Division of Home Missions of the National Council of the Churches of Christ in the United States for twenty Americans and the same number of Europeans who will come to Bossey to discuss common rural interests in relation to the churches.

(September) Conference on the Relation between Philosophy and Theology, for a limited group of experts in these fields who will discuss how their attempts to deal with the problem of reality are related.

(October to February, 1954) Second Session of the Graduate School of Ecumenical Studies, in association with the University of Geneva.

(November) Consultation on the Theological Foundation of Laymen's Work.

An aim of the Ecumenical Institute was, in the first place, to help laymen in all walks of life to understand their Christian vocation and, by study and conference with one another under such guidance as the Church could give them, to prepare themselves as fully as possible for it. Said the Chairman of the Board, Dr. Reinhold von Thadden-Trieglaff: "It is urgent that the churches awaken to the need for making men and woman feel at home in the Church in a technological age, and to discover the meaning of the gospel for their daily lives." [37] This was fundamental to their own happiness and well-being, and also to the mission of the Church "to reconcile humanity in a world which had lost man because it had lost God."

From the beginning, the Institute cooperated closely with the ecumenical lay movement, Dr. Kraemer acting as the Institute's counselor until a secretary could be appointed, and thereafter taking the lead in working out a reciprocal relationship between his staff and the Secretariat for the Laity. However, because most of them could not be absent from their trades or professions for an extended time, the laymen were unable to avail themselves in as large numbers as some other groups of the advantages the Institute offered. The Iron Curtain barred the way of many to Geneva. For those of other continents distance proved, in most cases, an insuperable barrier.

The courses for theological students were the most popular. Not all applications for admission to them could be accepted. Some of the group conferences would have led to still larger ones had there been accommodations for them.

After the reconstruction in 1951 at Bossey, the Institute could announce that it had "about fifty beds in single and double rooms for its conferences, and thirty more beds in dormitories, of three to six beds each, for its larger courses." It had "housed this summer up to one hundred ten people, including the staff, and served meals to one hundred thirty." [38]

Twenty-four students registered for the Graduate School of Ecumenical Studies when it opened October 1, 1952, of whom six were from the

[37] Minutes of the Toronto Meeting of the Central Committee, 1950, p. 39.

[38] This was for the summer of 1952. See Minutes of the Lucknow meeting of the Central Committee, p. 122.

United States, one each from Australia, India, and Great Britain, and the other thirteen from Europe, with Germany sending five. Ten denominations were represented: Lutheran (and Uniate), eight; Eastern Orthodox, four; Mar Thoma, one; Anglican, one; Old Catholic, one; Reformed (or Presbyterian), five; Congregationalist, one; Methodist, one; Swedenborgian, one; and Baptist, one.

"It is gratifying," commented the Director of the Institute, "that, with hardly any exception, the students leave Bossey with a sense of having caught a new vision of the significance and essential oneness of the Church, and with a deep conviction that the concrete contact with a centre of ecumenical thought and action has changed their whole outlook and conception of being a member of the Christian Church." The Institute was, he said, literally "a seminary"—a place for sowing. "Perhaps the most influential part of its work lies in the study of the Bible," he said, "which is read to ascertain the Word of God for our time." [39]

The staff was too small—an insufficiency of which each of the departments of the World Council of Churches might have complained. The budget of the Council could probably never be increased to the amount needed for such a large work.

The faculty lacked balance, because its members were, for the most part, volunteers on leave from their regular duties. Their services had to be accepted when available.

While the Chateau de Bossey was undergoing reconstruction in 1951, Dr. Kraemer traveled to India, Pakistan, Burma, Ceylon, Thailand, and Indonesia. The trip was undertaken at the request of the Indian delegates to the Bangkok Conference in 1949, who wished him "to arouse in their country a real interest in the vocation of the lay members of the Church," and most of his time was spent there.

During these months, meetings could not be held at the Institute, and the scheduled courses and conferences were conducted in other places—Bièvres, France; Woudscotten, Holland; Berlin, Germany; and Gwatt, Switzerland.

The early weeks of 1952 the Director spent in the United States, visiting while there the new center for laymen's work at Parishfield, Michigan, founded by Rev. Francis O. Ayres of the Protestant Episcopal Church.

Most of the money required for the Institute during this period came from a fund provided by John D. Rockefeller, Jr., the World Council of Churches appropriating supplementally each year only a token amount from its budget. Since it was necessary to use both income and principal, the Institute would become—not later than the Second Assembly, it was expected—a charge entirely on the funds of the Council.

During the years between Amsterdam and Evanston, the staff of the Ecumenical Institute included Professor Hendrik Kraemer, Director

[39] Toronto meeting, Minutes of the Central Committee, 1950, p. 110.

from 1948 to 1954; Mlle Suzanne de Dietrich, 1948 to 1952; M. Henri Louis Henroid, 1948 to 1951; Dr. Hans H. Walz, 1949 to 1954; and Rev. Paul Abrecht, 1949 to 1954, part time. In addition to these were theological professors and other churchmen of various countries and communions who contributed their services as teachers and in other capacities. Professor William J. Wolf of the Episcopal Theological Seminary, Cambridge, Massachusetts, Professor William Pauck of the Divinity School of the University of Chicago, and Professor William Short of the College of the Bible, Lexington, Kentucky, were among the temporary members of the teaching staff in 1952.

4. Faith and Order in the World Council

When it was merged with the Universal Christian Council for Life and Work, in 1948, to form the World Council of Churches, the Continuation Committee of the Second World Conference on Faith and Order became, with only slight changes in structure and personnel, the Commission on Faith and Order of the new organization. In time the membership was found to be too large for the most effective functioning. Its work needed to be coordinated better at certain points with that of other departments and brought into closer relationship with the denominations in the Council. On a recommendation from the Third World Conference on Faith and Order (at Lund, Sweden, 1952) the Central Committee adopted a revised constitution for the Commission embodying these as well as other changes. The membership was reduced from 156 to 100 and an administrative subcommittee of 25 created to conduct the business of the Commission between its meetings. Bishop Brilioth continued Chairman, and Dr. Clarence Tucker Craig was elected Vice-Chairman, Archbishop Germanos, Bishop Aulén, Dr. Marc Boegner, Principal R. Newton Flew, and Dr. Douglas Horton, who had each been serving in this capacity, withdrawing. At the same time, Dr. Oliver S. Tomkins resigned the secretaryship and was appointed Chairman of the Administrative Committee, Dr. J. Robert Nelson being appointed to the office vacated. Dr. Floyd W. Tomkins became Associate Secretary for America, and Canon Leonard Hodgson, Theological Secretary.

The theological commissions, which had been set up by the Continuation Committee in 1938 to "pursue intensive study" of "The Nature of the Church," "Ways of Worshipping," and "Intercommunion," continued their work in the new status under the World Council of Churches.

The commission on the second of these subjects, under the chairmanship of Professor van der Leeuw, in 1951 published the results of its investigation in a report to the Third World Conference on Faith and Order, and in a book also with the title *Ways of Worship*. The findings on the last theme were in 1952 likewise reported at Lund and afterwards printed in the volume *Intercommunion.* This commission was chaired by Professor Donald M. Baillie of St. Andrews University.

The thirty-three scholars to whom the study on the Church was assigned, under the chairmanship of Principal R. Newton Flew of Wesley House, Cambridge, England, organized their subject in four divisions: the biblical basis, historic teachings concerning the Church, modern confessional positions, and constructive statements. *The Nature of the Church,* which appeared in 1952, contained a summary of what the group studying the third of these subtopics had learned about the beliefs and practices of the different confessions. The other sections of the commission did not finish their assignments, a fact attributable apparently to the difficulty of their subjects rather than to a lack of industry or purpose.

All the theological commissions were disbanded at Lund in 1952. The so-called Working Committee of the Commission on Faith and Order elected by the Third World Conference decided to have the uncompleted inquiry on "The Nature of the Church" carried on under the broader heading, "Christ and the Church," by a new commission. Bishop Anders T. Nygren, Professor of Theology at the University of Lund, and Dr. Robert L. Calhoun, Pitkin Professor of Historical Theology at the Yale University Divinity School, were asked to direct this.

At the same time, plans were set afoot for the organization of inquiries on worship in Asia, Europe, and North America. Committees were appointed also to study proselytism and tradition "in ecumenical perspective."

At the request of the Central Committee of the World Council of Churches, the Commission on Faith and Order prepared the preliminary background survey and the working paper for the section of the Second Assembly studying "Our Oneness in Christ and Our Disunity as Churches." For material it drew upon the earlier theological commissions' reports on the Church, worship, and intercommunion, and upon information supplied by the studies by various scholars and committees of the nontheological factors in disunity.

In 1950 Dr. Oliver S. Tomkins, at that time Secretary of the Commission on Faith and Order, had published his book *The Church in the Purpose of God*; and in another small volume with the title *Towards Church Union, 1937-1952* Bishop Stephen Neill "brought up to date the factual survey on church union negotiations which had been begun by the late Dr. Harlan Paul Douglas in 1937." The pamphlet *Social and Cultural Factors in Church Divisions* made public the report of a "Faith and Order Consultation" which took place at the Ecumenical Institute in 1951 and papers on nontheological causes of disunity by Professors C. H. Dodd, G. R. Cragg, and Jacques Ellul.

5. Faith and Order: The Lund Conference

The Third World Conference on Faith and Order, at Lund, Sweden, August 15-28, 1952, was the most conspicuous event in the ecumenical calendar during the interim between Amsterdam and Evanston. To it came some 250 delegates and consultants from 114 denominations, to spend two weeks searching through the theological wilderness in which Christians of different creeds and confessions followed their separate ways for the hidden trail upon which, perchance, they might walk together toward the City of God.

Though they may have "come with willing feet," as Dr. Yngve T. Brilioth said in the opening address, recalling the words of Bishop Charles Henry Brent describing the spirit of those who went with him to Lausanne a quarter-century before for the First World Conference on Faith and Order, it was no secret that most of them had little hope that their quest would be successful. The findings of the several theological commissions, which had already been engaged in the exploration for seventeen years, were not of much encouragement to them, nor was the report of the survey of the so-called nontheological factors in disunity.

These latter had been found to be many and formidable, and inextricably linked with the theological obstructions—contentment with the *status quo,* distrust of the new and unfamiliar, personal ambitions, national antagonisms, racial exclusiveness, historical isolations, resistance to the suggestion of compulsion, institutional pride, social customs, innate conservatism, memories of persecutions, psychological and personal incompatibilities, religious prejudices, "doctored" history, vested interests, ingrained habits and sentiments, political pressures, mental limitations, misrepresentations, revivalism, proselytism, traditions, indifference, and still many more.

Some of those who went to Lund had been at Edinburgh in 1937, and a few at Lausanne in 1927. Many of them had had something to do with later attempts to capture unity in a formula all could accept. They knew how slight the gain had been, how near to frustration earnest minds had been brought, how darkly obscured still seemed the path, which ought, logically, to be a highway none could miss. They remembered the elation and the gratitude at the Second World Conference on Faith and Order when it had been discovered that the differences dividing the churches could be brought into the open and talked over frankly, without any cooling of friendships. Such men as William Temple and William Adams Brown had set it down as perhaps the main accomplishment at Edinburgh that Christians had learned to love one another and to prize one another across barriers in thought and experience which they were trying to remove, and were able to attack squarely the disagreements, theretofore so provocative of passion, calmly and without hard words. But the gain in this respect had seemed to diminish in importance as time passed and, for all their talking with one another in the best of spirit, they found themselves little closer together in their thinking on the crucially divisive issues. Although they understood fully one another's positions, they could not find the elusive way to agreement. To what purpose would be their meeting again? Would it be only to do more talking?

Any optimism secretly cherished was subdued, moreover, by disappointment over the attendance. Representation by 114 churches in 30 countries, although not an unworthy response, hardly warranted styling the gathering a "world conference." While he could voice satisfaction because of the presence of the German Evangelical Churches, which in 1937 had not been permitted by the government to send their delegates to Edinburgh, of delegations from certain nations behind the Iron Curtain (Czechoslovakia and Hungary) and of the younger churches of mission lands, Archbishop Brilioth, the Chairman, had in his address of welcome to say:[40]

> There are lamentable blanks in our . . . membership. We know that there are many who would have desired to be with us . . . but . . . have not been able to come. . . . The younger churches in China are quite without representatives. Never have we had a conference with so few Orthodox. The Patriarchate of Moscow was, of course, invited, as were the Evangelical Churches of Russia, but . . . no delegates have been appointed. No delegations have been appointed by the Orthodox Churches in Bulgaria, Roumania or Poland. In these circumstances it was all the more sad that the Church of Greece, which had appointed a strong delegation, has in the end . . . no representatives. . . . It is similarly unfortunate that present circumstances in Egypt caused the delegate of the Patriarchate of Alexandria also to withdraw at a late stage. . . . That the Church of Rome has not found it possible to take active part in any of the gatherings which we have been used to call ecumenical . . . is a tragic fact which we have had to accept.

For those with long ecumenical experience, the absence of the towering personalities who had made Lausanne and Edinburgh milestones registering actual progress darkened the prospect at Lund. Had these men, Charles Henry Brent and William Temple, and a few others of scarcely slighter stature, pushed the movement for unity on theological lines as far as it could be carried? Or would unshaken barriers yet fall before the efforts of lesser men rallying with hope under the same Christ? The fifteen years since Edinburgh had left largely to faith an affirmative answer to this question.

However, the conferees arrived in goodly numbers in the quietly impressive setting of the old university city with its pleasant natural scenery and majestic Domkyrkan. Once the ecclesiastical capital of Sweden—

[40] See *Faith and Order: The Report of the Third World Conference, Lund, Sweden.* Published in London, 1952.

indeed, of Scandinavia—with its bishop the primate of the realm, it was still outranked in Sweden only by Uppsala. Here the delegates created another occasion for the eloquent expression of ecumenical fellowship and for binding with golden words the labors of a new generation to what had been wrought over the years by others who also walked by faith and not sight.

Said the Archbishop in his introduction:

It has been in the course of time one of the functions of the Christian Church to bridge over the chasms in the history of our civilization, and to preserve in times of turmoil and bewilderment a continuity, a holy tradition that cannot be broken by wars and revolutions—revolutions of war and social upheaval and revolutions in the realm of thought. It is our hope that it may be given to us to perform in this epoch a service similar to that which the Church performed at the end of the ancient world. This gives to the task of the whole ecumenical movement and also to our task a still greater importance and deeper significance, that we are called to carry on, under present conditions, that quest for unity which was begun before the great upheaval. It is a task which confronts each individual church. But that we are permitted to pursue it in common, with a common responsibility and a common hope, is a gift from the God of history which makes our responsibility greater, but also our hopes more secure. The traditions of a single church may be broken. But the united endeavor of all the churches, which take part in our movement, has a greater power of endurance. If they all strive to be faithful to their heritage, and to preserve the values which they together hold in trust for future generations, they will help each other and will . . . build the bridge from one historical epoch to another. . . .

The Edinburgh Conference took the decisive step in order to enter into co-operation with the other great ecumenical enterprise, the Life and Work Movement which has carried on the work of the Stockholm Conference of 1925, and which owns Archbishop Söderblom as its prophet and first leader. It appointed members in the committee of fourteen which in Utrecht in 1938 became the "Provisional Committee of the World Council of Churches." The World Council was definitely established through its first assembly in Amsterdam in 1948. The Continuation Committee of the Edinburgh Conference became the World Council's Commission on Faith and Order. It preserved its individuality, but the incorporation into the larger body gave it a new responsibility and placed it in a wider setting that should not hamper its freedom. . . . How the final integration into the World Council should take shape, and on what lines the Faith and Order Movement may best be carried on will be one of the most important questions . . . this conference has to consider. . . .

Our chief task, however, is not to consider organization and policy; it is to carry on the discussion of fundamental questions relating to Faith and Order. Looking back, I seem to discern several stages in the history of our movement. The first stage, represented by the preliminary meeting in Geneva (1920), and to a large extent by the Lausanne Conference, was characterized by a certain minimizing of the differences. The re-united Church was spoken of as a tangible reality, as something that might perhaps not be realized in the present generation, but still was an event to be reckoned with as possible in a not too far-distant future. A certain tendency to gloss over differences by formulas that could be interpreted differently was perhaps not wholly absent during this stage. During the second stage, the real depth of our differences became gradually more and more apparent. That was the result of answers which came in from the churches, and the very thorough work done by special commissions. . . . At Edinburgh the note of unity still seemed to dominate, particularly in the remarkable report on "The Grace of Our Lord Jesus Christ." Gradually, the tenacity of the confessional traditions, the different background and temper of the different churches became realized. . . .

It may be gathered from the very important material which is laid before this Conference that the problems of Faith and Order have become more difficult . . . [and] more urgent than ever before. At the same time, as the disagreements have become sharper, the consciousness of the different confessions and denominations [has become] more vivid than at any earlier time, [and] the will to unity has been strengthened, not least through the formation of the World Council. In spite of all that separates us, we that have gathered here to the Third World Conference on Faith and Order may well make our own the words of the Amsterdam message: "We intend to stay together."

It is the second time an event of great ecumenical importance has taken place in our country. [The other was the Universal Christian Conference on Life and Work in Stockholm, 1925.] We shall not be surrounded by the impressive pageantry that then symbolized the beginning of the ecumenical era. The unpretentious forms under which we meet will perhaps be felt in harmony with the task which lies before us and the nature of our deliberations. . . . We may differ in our discussions. But I trust that we shall feel united in our adoration.

Archbishop Brilioth had said, "Our chief task . . . is to carry on the discussion of fundamental questions relating to Faith and Order," and it now fell to Canon Leonard Hodgson, Theological Secretary of the Commission, to sketch this purview of the Conference in greater detail:

We are a gathering of representatives sent by their churches to confer . . . on questions of Faith and Order which keep us divided into separate churches. We are sent by our churches in the hope that by conferring . . . during these two weeks, by deepening our understanding of what others really believe, we may discover that some of the differences which have kept us apart need do so no longer.

"Our task is to confer," said the Canon. "Conferring means discussing, and I can best make clear what I want to say by drawing a distinction between discussing and arguing."

In arguing each party thinks he knows what he stands for; he is trying to put forward arguments which will not only enable the other to understand it but persuade him to change his mind and come around to holding it. In discussing, the different parties are aware of being faced by something which is a problem to them all; they are not trying to convert one another, each to his own view, so much as to help one another to a fuller understanding of the mystery which shall explain how the reality has looked so different to men coming to it by different approaches. It may be that this fuller understanding will lead to the reconciliation of different views as partial apprehension of the same truth seen from different approaches. It may be that it will lead to some changes of mind, the abandoning of some positions, some conversions.

It may be that some delegations have come to this conference briefed by their churches to stand up for certain positions, and that they will go back to their churches convinced that these briefs need revision. That is as the Holy Spirit may lead you. I cannot prophesy. But I beg of you to give the Holy Spirit the opportunity to lead you by entering upon your work here as men seeking through discussion for light on common problems, and not as men commissioned to defend tradition or position.

Canon Hodgson saw the issues to be discussed as centered around the Church:

Underlying all particular questions is that of the nature of the Church. . . . Our one aim is to inquire: How far are the various conceptions of the Church we bring with us reconcilable so as to be tenable together in one united Church? First, there is the laying side by side and explaining the positions from which we start as representatives of our churches. Then there is the attempt to see how far these can be related to one another as convergent approaches to the truth which is common to all, and by what revision or correction each may benefit through its intercourse with the others. . . .

I am asking you to pay first attention to the central question of the nature of the Church's unity, and to attend to this not as men arguing for the relative superiority of the ideas you now have, but as men seeking together for light on a wonderful mystery which God wills to reveal to those who earnestly seek Him. . . .

A month or two ago I received a letter in which were written the following words: "Some will come with rather high expectations, and there is great risk that they will be disappointed. . . . If we cannot look forward to something which carries us definitely beyond Edinburgh, the chief aim for the conference will not be reached."

This letter made me ask myself the question: "In what way can we 'look forward to something which carries us definitely beyond Edinburgh' while keeping within the terms of reference of a Faith and Order Conference?" It is not for us to take practical steps toward church re-union, nor even to form schemes and recommend them to the churches for their action. The Faith and Order Movement was founded to enable the churches to grow by discussion in mutual understanding and so to be in a better position to initiate action. The initiative must rest with them. What can we do except go on talking together as before?

I cast my mind back over the history of the movement. I saw how much growth there has been in this mutual understanding, how it has grown from small beginnings at the preliminary gathering in Geneva in 1920 through Lausanne, 1927, and Edinburgh, 1937. I tried to look to the future, and asked myself: "Can we go on forever and ever, round and round in the same circle, explaining ourselves to one another? If the time should ever come when we can take that for granted, what would our next step be? And can we begin to move on to that next step now?"

Then it came to me that it will be a real step forward if, on the basis of what we have gained in the way of mutual understanding, we join together in seeking light on mysteries which are common to us all, light which, reflected back on our present distress, may show the churches a way forward to unity. This is proper Faith and Order work, which seeks to help the churches by shedding light on their relations with one another. And it is a carrying forward of our own past work, for it is only as we bring with us our growth in mutual understanding from 1920 to 1952 that we can join together in this further inquiry. This conference meets at a moment of transition. It would be foolish to pretend that we have done all that we can or need be done in the stage of mutual explanation of where we as churches now stand. In these coming days you will find much of that still needing to be done. Do it as men for whom it is preparatory for a further advance on which you are already embarking.

At ecumenical gatherings it is often said, and rightly so, that church union will come to us as God's gift, that we shall best prepare ourselves for it not by devising man-made schemes of re-union, but by drawing nearer to Christ and so to one another in Him. So far, so good. But this must not be made an excuse for turning aside from the kind of work to which this conference is called, as though drawing nearer to Christ meant substituting some activity called prayer for the strenuous exercise of our minds in pursuit of truth. He to whom we are to draw near is the Lord who claims to be not only the way and the life, but also the truth. In every effort to grasp more fully the truth about the "I, yet not I" and the nature of unity, we are seeking to draw near to Him, as He stands above this conference saying, "Ask, and it shall be given you: seek, and ye shall find: knock, and it shall be opened unto you."

Into the preparatory statements presented to the Conference an address by Dr. Edmund Schlink, Professor of Theology at Heidelberg University, stressing further "the crisis of method" in Faith and Order study, injected the controversial subject of eschatology as bearing upon "the unity of God's people":

We are assembled here as divided churches. But before all of us stands the Lord who will come again. . . . [His] judgment is not only a future one, it is already taking place in many parts of the world and in many spheres of Christendom. . . . In such times of distress and the temptations which arise in them to save one's life by denying Christ's claim of kingship and the betrayal of the brethren, separations of final importance are already taking place. . . . [But] in the times of tribulation there will be a re-evaluation and change of the measures by which the divided Christian communities had measured each other hitherto. That which is great will come forth from the small, and the unessential, the One from the many. . . . This unity of the People of God is experienced everywhere where it appears in time of great distress, as a God-given reality, namely as the reality of the presence of Christ. Whoever experiences that will see it not as a desperate escape, nor as an eccentricity resulting from the extraordinary situation, but it will be to him an undeniable divine reality.

It is all the more astonishing how little the remainder of Christendom is touched by this event of the thinning of the walls which traditionally divide the churches. . . . It is even more astonishing how quickly that experience of the unity of the wandering People of God fades with many, when the time of persecution has ended. . . . How should we want to live in division who have known and confessed our unity in Christ? With every justification it has already been stated at Lausanne: "We can never again be the same as we were before." Have we really become different from what we were before? One cannot declare the unity again and again and at the same time remain divided.

The division which Christ will bring about at the end of the world will go through all churches. None of the churches assembled here can count upon remaining undivided then. . . . Let us hurry forward on our way through the world and not stand still and look back. Let us live by expectation, instead of digging ourselves into the past. Let us tear away our eyes from the hardened one-sidedness of those historical events in which the division of the Church took place. Let us direct our eyes toward the much deeper division which the returning Lord will effect in all the churches, and upon the unity of the eternal splendors which he will bring with him.

The work of Faith and Order finds itself in a crisis of the method employed so far. This method has been a planned and comprehensive inter-denominational comparison, whereby one endeavored to elaborate a maximum of that which we all have in common. This method has been improved at Amsterdam in so far as not only the agreements and disagreements were studied, but again the "agreements in the disagreements" and the "disagreements in the agreements." This method may be even further improved and it will also remain indispensable for the future. After leading at first to surprising results of far-reaching agreement with increasing exactness in its application, the depth of our differences was also revealed more clearly than had been the case in the enthusiasm of the ecumenical movement in its early days. It could not have been otherwise, because this method of comparison is a statistical method. It presumed a certain static structure of the churches which are to be compared with each other. It does not reckon with changes and does not demand sacrifices from the churches involved. On the contrary in the constitution of the World Council of Churches, each church has a certification of her rights to be and remain as she is. I am convinced that we have reached a quite natural limit with the comparative method in our Faith and Order work, and that on this way alone we can proceed no further—even that, on the contrary, this way, which does not demand any sacrifice from those involved, will present us with continually growing difficulties.

For the ecumenical work has meanwhile been faced with a crisis by what God himself is doing among the divided churches in many countries. This goes far beyond the terms of even a most careful statistical comparison. God himself has placed the work of Faith and Order in a crisis. On the one hand, [the crisis has come] through the new unity which has originated among our oppressed and persecuted brethren; and on the other hand, through the birth of the younger churches—[through all those] who are determined to "forget those things which are behind" and to "reach forth to those things which are before" and who, having left the historical traditions behind, strive towards unity as it corresponds with the One Lord, who is coming towards us. Actual changes are taking place. Traditional characteristics are [being] sacrificed. And, behold, these sacrifices prove the reception of riches—they prove themselves as such blessings that they cannot be called sacrifices.

The essential points of an address by Dr. Oliver S. Tomkins, Secretary of the Commission on Faith and Order,[41] filled in the background and the outline for the proceedings of the Conference. Referring to the declaration of the churches at the Assembly in Amsterdam in 1948, "We intend to stay together," he said:

[41] At Lund he resigned this office afterward serving as Chairman of the Working Committee on Faith and Order.

First, I would suggest this covenant-relationship brings us to the end of . . . the essential and pioneer task of Faith and Order to enable the churches simply to explain themselves to each other. . . . I am certainly not suggesting that this work of mutual explanation is no longer necessary. [There is need for the continued] education of those who have not begun to understand the beliefs of their separated fellow-Christians (or often, indeed, their own). [But if we merely go on explaining] we shall be in danger of cataloging dead issues instead of wrestling with living truth, and of giving the finality of a goal to that which was meant to be the starting point for fresh understanding.

In my second point, I would press yet further. By entering into this relationship with each other, we have already willed the death of our denominations. . . . We cannot simply "abolish denominations," for almost all of our knowledge of God has been mediated to us through them. . . . The ecumenical movement is the fellowship of those who have been compelled to admit that there is some kind of discrepancy, of which each may learn by paying serious attention to those who challenge them in the name of a common Lord, God's Word in His Son. Even if I believe, as I do, that my own church has been given the fulness of Catholic truth and life in potentiality, even so, the disparity between what my church is in practice and what God means the Church to be is already the death-warrant of my church as a sufficient, unself-critical denomination.

We all believe that the Church, which is the Body and Bride of Christ, is something more than our own particular church-tradition, and yet we know that we can only live in the Body of Christ by living faithfully in our own churches. The status of the World Council lies in accepting that paradox: its dynamic lies in refusing to accept it as final. The belief that enables the ecumenical movement to move lies in the unexplored territory of the sense in which the Body of Christ is more than our own church and of the meaning of living faithfully within our own churches. Of course, that territory is not wholly unexplored. The history of the modern ecumenical movement is the story of patient and fruitful exchange between us of that which we have inherited in our own traditions, of that which others have inherited in theirs, and of the relation of both to that which God has given us all in Christ.

The third implication of our now explicit relationship to each other as churches is that it demands new forms of life in each of our churches through which to respond to that relationship. . . . The implication of "Faith and Order" is clear in the word of our Lord that "He that doeth the will shall know the doctrine." There are truths about the nature of God and of His Church which will remain to us for ever closed, unless we act together in obedience to the unity which is already ours. . . . One of the things we share together as Christians is a common incomprehensibility to the mass of mankind. In the whole modern world, the language, thought, and tradition of Christianity are increasingly meaningless to millions of our contemporaries.

Fourthly, must we not recognize now that our continued association in the ecumenical movement has brought us to a new level of responsibility in common prayer . . . ? Whatever the value and the means of such common prayer, what I would rather stress now is our need to begin in Faith and Order a period of more sustained and adventurous experiment in supplementing our traditional methods with ways of meeting each other at the level of common devotional understanding.

Finally, I would suggest that we must now grasp more firmly the central problem of our relationship. We claim that we have a unity in Christ; we cannot show that we have unity in His Body, the Church. That is the heart of our dilemma, but it is also the ground of our hope. . . . We must face this together now as a common problem, allowing each other no escape from the rigorous demands of accepting the Lordship of Christ. . . .

We need have no fear that God has not prepared for us, as we meet in His name, new paths for us to walk in. We need only to pray for His grace to discern His ways and to walk in them.

The relation of the study of unity in the churches to the missionary movement was the theme of an address by Dr. Henry S. Leiper, Associate General Secretary of the World Council of Churches:

An ecumenical movement without a sense of world mission is a complete anomaly, and as of today it would be an anachronism. None of us who heard him say it will ever forget William Temple's words as he reminded the great congregation participating in his consecration as Archbishop of Canterbury, that out of the world missionary movement of the past one hundred thirty years has come the fellowship which corresponds to St. Paul's vision of the Church. This ecumenical fellowship was not planned by any human wisdom. In the providence of God, ruling and overruling the plans and activities of divided churches, this great fellowship has arisen and is, in his familiar phrase, the great fact of our time.

It is clearer now than it was ten years ago when the first president of the World Council Provisional Committee spoke these words, that there are two world missions, involving now literally almost all the world. The one is the communist world mission. . . . The other is the Christian. . . . The latter simply cannot operate without taking account of the former. In the former, the acceptance of the world-wide character of its mission is axiomatic. In the latter, it is too often, even now, subject to debate. That, however, would not be the case here among us, and I certainly need not here prove what is so obvious. In the communist world mission, there is enforced and almost undisputed unity: a unity of strategy and of command. In the Christian world mission we have no desire to emulate such a totalitarian scheme, but we do well to recognize the disadvantage which the Christian confronts in that neither the strategy nor the administration of its world mission is unified.

There is, however, justifiable comfort to be derived from the fact that the out-reach for unity in the sense of acceptance of community has been the distinguishing characteristic of this generation. It is no accident that those most deeply concerned with the world mission of the Church have been equally concerned about its unity. Several times this meeting has been reminded of the fact that Bishop Brent was a missionary of the Protestant Episcopal Church in the United States. Humanly speaking, he, more than any other person, was the founder of the Faith and Order Movement. Dr. John R. Mott, who laid so many of the foundations of the present movement for co-operation and unity, had his first introduction to the ecumenical idea as a leader of the Student Volunteer Movement for foreign missions. These two great champions of unity are among the many who have seen that wholeness of spiritual life in the churches is the only ultimate thing which the world can take as a promise that the Church can minister to a divided world desperately sick because of its lack of wholeness.

It has been said repeatedly of the ecumenical movement that it is a re-assertion of Christian community, not for its own sake but for the sake of the world for which Christ died. That clearly implies a sense of mission. As my colleague, Dr. Frederick Nolde, the able director of the Joint Commission of the International Missionary Council and the World Council of Churches on International Affairs, has said, "We are undertaking our tasks and doing these varied things in the ecumenical movement not simply because they are good for the Church; if they are not good for the world, then, in a basic sense they are not good for the Church.". . .

The World Council and the International Missionary Council both represent attempts to make the existing spiritual oneness of a great cross section of Christendom visible. We are engaged in an attempt to fulfill the conditions for the realization of our Lord's dying wish that His followers might be one. We are engaged in an attempt to recover both the sense and the substance of that community which was so real to the first Christians.

The world will best understand what that community should be like, if we take every opportunity to remind ourselves and others that Jesus found the pattern of spiritual world community in that primary human community in which He spoke of God, and even the form of His Great High Priestly prayer is proof of this. We are to be as common members of God's one family united as the Father and the Son are united. That is quite clearly a family relationship. We do not create family relationships. We manifest them. Or what is more common—we fail to manifest them effectively to an unbelieving world. . . .

. . . Happily we are at last able to speak to one another across the national and racial, as well as the confessional, divisions of our shrinking world. In this fellowship we speak as those already conscious of the oneness which we have in Christ, our common Lord.

On the connection of unity and mission, Rev. Daniel T. Niles said:

One does not understand the Gospel unless one shares in it; and one does not share in it except as a confessing Christian, one who is seeking to lead persons to Jesus Christ. . . . The distinction between Christianity and the Gospel is a distinction we must constantly maintain and live by. It defines the evangelistic position. Unless Christianity is seen as standing under the Gospel, the ecumenical task becomes an impossibility. The Gospel is what God has done for us. Christianity is what we do for God in response.

According to Dr. Rajah B. Manikam, Joint Secretary in East Asia of the World Council of Churches and the International Missionary Council, it was "only together that Christians gave their true witness and rendered effective service to the world." He continued:

The vastness of the unfinished task of the Church in East Asia has compelled the denominations to think in terms of co-operation, pooling of resources, sharing experiences and insights, and coming together in unity. . . . Divisions in the Church, when unreconciled, distort its true nature and unity and frustrate its mission. . . . It may be that, in the providence of God, the younger churches, untrammeled by the weight of history and tradition, may lead the way to unity in Christ. While the older churches may engage in theological discussions as to whether church union is desirable or necessary, to the younger churches it has become an imperative, a necessity, a matter of life or death. The eighteenth and nineteenth centuries witnessed the great missionary expansion of the Church, but the signs of the twentieth century make it clear that the Holy Spirit is leading the churches, not only to proclaim the gospel to the whole world, but also to manifest in and to that world the fellowship and unity which is in Jesus Christ. One rejoices to find that the Holy Spirit is moving in the hearts of Asian Christians today and bringing them together as never before. In Japan there exists the United Church of Christ in Japan (Kyodan) in which have merged fifteen denominations. It is often said that church union there has been the result of the totalitarian policy of the former Government, but this is only a half-truth, since church union negotiations under the National Christian Council of Japan date as far back as 1935. Some churches which joined the Kyodan have withdrawn but they formed only three percent of the churches in the Kyodan. A few are still considering withdrawal. The question centers on questions of a creedal basis and decentralization. About sixty to seventy percent of the entire Protestant Church membership in Japan is found in this Church which has a baptized membership of one hundred fifty-one thousand nine hundred sixty-five, with fourteen hundred ninety-nine congregations and evangelistic centers. The Kyodan has come to stay.

In the Philippines since 1948, the United Church of Christ . . . [has been] functioning. The United Evangelical Church of the Philippines, the Evangelical Church, and the Philippine Methodist Church are members of this United Church. But within this unity each of the uniting Churches preserves its own special heritage of faith and witness. This Church is episcopal but does not adhere to the historic episcopal succession. It has a membership of about one hundred twenty-five thousand.

While these two United Churches retain still some of the characteristics of a federation, we have in the Church of South India real organic church union. The Church of India, Burma and Ceylon (Southern Anglican dioceses), the South India United Church (Congregational, Presbyterian and Reformed) and the Methodist Church in South India united to form one Church of South India in 1947. This Church has over a million members, with fourteen dioceses. It has now three types of ministry—those episcopally ordained before the union, those not so ordained, and those ordained after union by bishops. After a thirty-year period, the Church is to decide whether any exceptions to the rule of episcopal ordination should be allowed. The Lambeth Conference in 1948 welcomed the formation of the new Church, but did not recommend terms of full intercommunion between Anglican Churches and the Church of South India. The Church of India, Pakistan, Burma and Ceylon has recognized as valid the ordinations that had taken place in the Church of South India since union. Conversations are going on between the Church of South India and the Lutherans and the Baptists with some degree of hope in the former case. It is significant that a union, motivated from the beginning by the missionary calling of the three separate churches, has resulted in a deepening sense of the mission of the Church and new boldness in evangelism.

Negotiations are under way in Ceylon. While in the Church of South India we have for the first time an Episcopal Church in Asia in union with non-Episcopal Churches, in Ceylon the Baptists are considering union. The negotiating churches are the Church of South India, the Church of India, Pakistan, Burma and Ceylon, the Methodist and the Presbyterian Churches. In North India, negotiations are proceeding among churches which include the Church of India, Pakistan, Burma and Ceylon and the Baptists. In Indonesia there exists a Protestant Church of Indonesia with a membership of six hundred ninety-seven thousand. This Church has retained still some of the characteristics of a federation. An Indonesian Council of Churches is in existence today, and its avowed aim is to further the cause of church union in Indonesia.

Conditions revealing sharply the relation between the evangelistic mission of the Church and its unity were portrayed by Rev. Farid Audeh, President of the Supreme Council of the Evangelical Churches in Syria and Lebanon, who spoke from the standpoint of his observations in the Near East:

> The Near East is the birthplace of the three great monotheistic faiths of Judaism, Islam and Christianity. Nowhere else in the world are these religions brought into such close contact and competition. . . . There now lies buried in the hearts of the peoples of the Near East more fear, frustration and hatred than has been found since the crusades. So the churches and missions . . . have to face these great forces of Islam, world Jewry, communism, and nominal Christianity. . . . The hope and peace of the Near East lies with the Christian Church. But what kind of Church? Certainly not the type we have at present—poor, weak, torn by schisms and divisions. It must be missionary and united. . . . In the words of Mr. S. A. Morrison of Egypt, "There is little likelihood that the non-Christians of the Near East would listen seriously to the Christian claim that Christ is the answer to all human problems until they see more co-operation and closer unity between the Christian Churches themselves. The problems of the Near East are too great for one church to attempt to solve them alone."

With these and other briefings, the delegates formed in five sections to study the subjects which the theological commissions had been exploring during the fourteen years since their appointment: "Christ and His Church," [42] "Ways of Worshipping," and "Intercommunion," the first of which had been divided into three parts and submitted to as many groups—"The Church as the Mystical Body of Christ and a Congregation of Sinners," "The Continuity of the Church," and "The Form of Unity for Which to Seek." The accumulated matter on nontheological factors in disunity, which had been summarized in addresses by Dr. Winfred E. Garrison and Dr. Josef Hromadka, was to receive attention collaterally by all the sections at the points where it had relevance to their discussions.

Meanwhile, committees of the Conference attended to the organizational details—among them, revision of the constitution of the Commission on Faith and Order of the World Council of Churches, preparation of a message to be sent to the churches, and recommending an appropriate and timely theme in the field of Faith and Order for study at the Second Assembly of the World Council of Churches at Evanston,

[42] Originally "The Nature of the Church," but changed by the new Commission to "Christ and His Church."

two years thence. And, of course, there were the usual business, press, and worship subcommittees.

In due order, the findings of the several sections were reported, discussed, and accepted. Of special significance as carrying Faith and Order consultations "beyond the consideration of . . . immediately apparent disagreements and [exploring] the underlying theological problem" was the statement on "Christ and His Church":[43]

We believe in Jesus Christ our Lord, who loved the church and gave himself for it, and has brought the church into an abiding union with himself. Because we believe in Jesus Christ we believe also in the church as the body of Christ.

I

We confess that without Christ we are lost, and without him we are subject to the powers of sin and death, but that God has not abandoned us to the powers of destruction. He has given to us and all men his only begotten Son as Saviour and Redeemer. Through his life, his suffering, his death and his resurrection, Jesus Christ as the mighty Victor has overcome sin and death, brought the ungodly powers to nought, and has given us freedom. When we believe in Jesus Christ these powers can no longer exercise lordship over us. Thus we stand under a new Lord. It is Jesus Christ who is our Lord.

For he, in his incarnation, death and resurrection, has entered into oneness with man in his estrangement and in his existence under the judgment of God, and by making atonement for man's guilt has consecrated a new way in which man, reconciled with God, may live in union with Jesus Christ. Through him God has given to lost humanity a new beginning, for in that Jesus Christ died and rose again, all who believe in him die and rise again to a new life.

Jesus Christ is the King of the new people of God. He is "the chief cornerstone in which the whole building, fitly framed together, grows up into a holy temple in the Lord." He is the head of the Church which is his body. Through his Spirit Jesus Christ himself is present in his Church. Christ lives in his Church and the Church lives in Christ. Christ is never without his Church; the Church is never without Christ. Both belong inseparably together, the King and his people, the keystone and the temple, the head and the body. As members of his body, we are made one with him in the fellowship of his life, death and resurrection, of his suffering and his glory. For what concerns Christ concerns his body also. What has happened to Christ uniquely in his once-and-for-all death and resurrection on our behalf, happens also to the Church in its way as his body. As the Church is made a partaker in the crucified body of Christ, so also it is given to be a partaker in the risen body of the same Lord. This means that the Church is called to continue the mission of Jesus Christ to the world, so that the way of Christ is the way of his Church.

II

On the ground of the apostolic witness to Jesus Christ, the Lord of the Church, and in obedience to him, we seek to penetrate behind the divisions

[43] The Second World Conference on Faith and Order (Edinburgh, 1937) had decided that "The Church" should be the main theme for study at the next Faith and Order Conference.

of the Church on earth to our common faith in the one Lord. From the unity of Christ we seek to understand the unity of the Church on earth, and from the unity of Christ and his body we seek a means of realising that unity in the actual state of our divisions on earth.

We believe that many of our differences arise from a false antithesis between the Church's being in Christ and its mission in the world, and from a failure to understand the Church in the light of Jesus Christ as God and man, and in the light of his death and resurrection. In the following paragraphs we seek:

(1) To speak of the nature of the Church in terms of a double movement (its being called from the world and its being sent into the world) through which it is ever being built up into Jesus Christ its Head;

(2) To speak of the Church as the new creation which, while it continues to live on earth as a community of forgiven sinners expecting the redemption of the body, is already given to participate in the new life of the risen Christ.

The Faith of the Church in the Father, the Son and the Holy Spirit

In his eternal love the Father has sent his Son to redeem creation from sin and death. In Jesus Christ God's Son became man. By word and deed he proclaimed on earth the arrival of God's kingdom, bore away the sins of the world on the Cross, rose again from the dead, ascended into heaven, the throne of his kingdom, at the right hand of God. At Pentecost God poured out his Spirit upon the Church, giving all who believe in Jesus Christ the power to become God's children. Through the indwelling of his Spirit Jesus Christ dwells in the midst of his Church. As Lord and King he will come again to judge the quick and the dead and to consummate the eternal kingdom of God in the whole creation.

The Nature and Mission of the Church

(a) The Lord Jesus Christ, through his Word and Spirit, calls his Church from the world. He forgives sins, delivers men from the lordship of the powers of destruction and gathers out of this broken world the one people of God, the community of the justified and sanctified whose citizenship is in heaven and whose life is hid with Christ in God.

(b) Jesus Christ through his Word and Spirit sends his Church into the world to be the salt of the earth and the light of the world. That is, as Prophet, Priest and King he gives his Church to participate in his ministry of reconciliation, constraining it by his love to enter into his passion for the redemption of the world, and empowering it by his Spirit to proclaim the Gospel of salvation to all nations, calling them to obey the will of God in all areas of political and social and cultural life and to live out in the divisions of the world the life of the one people of God, so that through its witness Jesus Christ is at work among men as Saviour, and brings all things in subjection under himself as Lord and King of the World.

(c) By calling and sending his people, by granting them manifold spiritual gifts for the ministry, Jesus Christ builds up his Church as the living temple of God. Thus the Church as the body of Christ "grows up into him in all things who is the head, from whom the whole body fitly joined together and compacted by that which every joint supplieth according to the effective working in the measure of every part, maketh increase of the body unto the edifying of itself in love."

The Church between the First and the Final Coming of Christ

(a) At the same time the Church is a community of forgiven sinners, eagerly expecting and patiently watching for the final consummation of its redemption. It continues to be a pilgrim people in a strange land, so that all its life and work on earth is incomplete. Ungodly powers and forces are still rampant in the whole creation in an alarming way, and they seek to confuse the Church and defeat its mission. But the Church continues to live and work by the power of Jesus Christ.

(b) At the end of its pilgrimage Jesus Christ, the Crucified and Risen, will come again to meet his Church in order to complete his work of redemption and judgment. Out of all peoples and ages he will gather his own who look for his appearing and for a new heaven and a new earth, and he will consummate the union between Christ and his Church in the eternal kingdom of God.

(c) Through the indwelling of the Holy Spirit the new age of the future is already present and through union with the risen Jesus Christ the Church on earth is already given to participate in the power of the resurrection. The Church of Jesus Christ in history as at once the congregation of sinners and the new creation, for although it continues to live and work within the brokenness and estrangement of this world and to share its divisions, the Church belongs essentially to the new age and the new creation. As such the Church is summoned to perpetual renewal, to put off the old life, and by the renewal of its mind to be conformed to Christ, looking beyond its historical forms to the full unveiling of its new being in the coming Lord.

III

We have sought to declare in these brief paragraphs the inseparable relation between Christ and his Church. To these convictions about the Church we are led by our faith in Jesus Christ and by our shared acceptance of the authority of the Holy Scriptures. We cannot build the one Church by cleverly fitting together our divided inheritances. We can grow together towards fullness and unity in Christ only by being conformed to him who is the Head of the body and Lord of his people. And he manifests his fullness, however brokenly, in the gifts he has given to us even in our separations. Wherever two or three are gathered together in his Name he is in the midst of them. Whenever men are met in obedience to him, he is known. He may be found in the midst of those from whom we are separated and in the midst of those to whom we are sent.

When we place ourselves in our churches under his judgment and in obedience to his calling and his sending, we shall know that we cannot manifest our unity and share in his fullness without being changed. Some of us who have been assured that we possess the true order and the true sacraments will find ourselves called to give its rightful place to the preaching of the Living Word. Some who have neglected the sacraments will be confronted by him who humbled himself in baptism and broke bread and shared the cup to make us partakers of his passion and death. Those who have sought to show forth the glory of the Church as the body and bride of Christ must stand under the judgment of his simplicity and servanthood. Churches which have valued little his prayer that the oneness of his people be made manifest to men will be summoned to make his prayer their own. Churches complacent in the face of racial divisions in the body will be brought to repentance by him in whom bond and free, Jew and Gentile, Greek and barbarian, are one. Churches which have stressed onesidedly that God in his Church gives himself to men will be reminded that Christ in his humanity offered himself to the Father. Those who are ever looking backward and have accumulated much precious ecclesiastical baggage will perhaps be shown that pilgrims must travel light and that if we are to share at last in the great Supper, we must let go much that we treasure. Churches settled and self-assured will have to hear again the Lord's heartbroken concern for the sheep without a shepherd and know that to be his Church is to share in his world-embracing mission. Churches too much at home in the world will hear themselves called out of the world. Churches too wrapped up in their own piety or their own survival will see again him who identified himself with the deprived and the oppressed.

We cannot know all that shall be disclosed to us when together we look to him who is the Head of the body. It is easy for us in our several churches to think of what our separated brethren need to learn. Christ's love will make us more ready to learn what he can teach us through them. The truth we would hold fast is that because Christ is the Head and Lord of the Church, his way is the Church's way. He calls, he sends, he judges. The shape of his life is the shape of the Church's life. The mystery of his life is the mystery of the Church's life.

IV

In our work we have been led to the conviction that it is of decisive importance for the advance of ecumenical work that the doctrine of the Church be treated in close relation both to the doctrine of Christ and to the doctrine of the Holy Spirit. We believe that this must occupy a primary place in the future work of this movement, and we so recommend to the Faith and Order Commission, and to its working committee.

Those who were at Lund disagreed in their estimates of the results of the Conference, some declaring that it registered no advance beyond Lausanne and Edinburgh, and others claiming, while admitting disappointment, that there had been definite progress. This latter view was expressed in the Preface to the official report:[44]

Our work is "not to formulate schemes and tell the churches what they ought to do, but to act as the handmaid of the churches in the preparatory work of clearing away misunderstandings, discussing obstacles to reunion, and issuing reports which are submitted to the churches for their consideration." This has called for great self-restraint on the part of those of us who, in this direction or that, would have liked to see more positive recommendations to action. But where such recommendations would present to any churches a choice between disloyalty to their convictions and a withdrawal from ecumenical fellowship in discussion, they would do more harm than good.

Nevertheless, we feel that in this Conference we have ourselves gained much, and can issue a Report which bears witness to an advance upon what has gone before. At Lausanne in 1927 and at Edinburgh in 1937 it was impossible directly to approach the fundamentally important subject of the nature of the Church. Too many more immediately obvious differences surrounded that central theme, demanding much in the way of mutual explanation. Here at Lund we have met in a spirit of mutual trust and confidence which has enabled us to find fellowship in exploring together

[44] *Faith and Order: The Report of the Third World Conference at Lund, Sweden: August 15-28, 1952,* Preface, p. 1 B.

the deepest and most controversial issues. We go back to our churches as men who have entered into a rich experience of deeper understanding of one another. We go back to bring that understanding to those whom we represent, and in this Report, as we speak of the Church, of Ways of Worship, and of Intercommunion, we speak of issues deeper and more controversial than have been so spoken of before.

In two ways in particular these pages make an advance on previous Faith and Order Conference Reports:

(i) It . . . does not record agreements and disagreements on subjects at present dividing the churches, but seeks to initiate a . . . study of the biblical teaching about the relation between Christ and the Church. We have had no time to do more than make a first approach, but we believe that this first attempt to pass beyond the consideration of our immediately apparent disagreements and to explore the underlying theological problem . . . opens up fertile lines of further study. . . .

(ii) The bearing on the problem of unity of social, cultural, political, racial and other so-called "non-theological" factors was hardly so much as mentioned at Lausanne in 1927. At Edinburgh in 1937 some attention was paid to it in one section of the Conference. Since then there has been an increasing realization of its importance, and as part of the preparation for this Conference a group was convened to consider it at the Ecumenical Institute at Bossey, Switzerland, in November, 1951. Its Report, "Social and Cultural Factors in Church Divisions," was not assigned to any particular section of our Conference, but its influence was felt throughout. . . .

One other document that we have had before us is "Towards Church Union, 1937-1952." This survey of approaches to closer union among the churches, compiled by Bishop Stephen Neill, describes unions achieved and negotiations entered into by churches since the Edinburgh Conference. It is a factual record, which was given to us for information, not for discussion. It tells of much for which we have to thank God, much from which we have drawn encouragement in our work. We submit our own Report to the churches in the hope that what we have done together here may be used by God to make possible the writing of further chapters in this story according to his will.

It was clear from the foregoing statement that those whose experience in ecumenical work had been longest did not take a pessimistic view of the Lund Conference. The statement of purpose in the new constitution of the Commission on Faith and Order reflected their confidence:

To proclaim the essential oneness of the Church of Christ and to keep prominently before the World Council and the churches the obligation to manifest that unity and its urgency for the work of evangelism.

To study questions of faith, order and worship, with the relevant social, cultural, political, racial and other factors in their bearing on the unity of the Church.

To study the theological implications of the existence of the ecumenical movement.

To study matters in the present relationships of the churches to one another which cause difficulties and need theological clarification.

To provide information concerning actual steps taken by the churches toward reunion.

In the Message of the Conference to the churches also could be detected a distinct note of admonitory hopefulness:

> We have been sent to Lund by our churches to study together what measure of unity in matters of faith, church order and worship exists among our churches and how we may move towards the fuller unity God wills for us. We give thanks to the Lord of the Church for what he has wrought among us in and through our fellowship of conversation and prayer and for evidence that in several parts of the world churches are drawing closer together. We have made many discoveries about one another's churches and our perplexity in the face of unresolved differences has been surpassed by our gratitude for the manifold grace of God which we see at work in the life of the churches all over the world.
>
> We have seen clearly that we can make no real advance towards unity if we only compare our several conceptions of the nature of the Church and the traditions in which they are embodied. But once again it has been proved true that as we seek to draw closer to Christ we come closer to one another. We need, therefore, to penetrate behind our divisions to a deeper and richer understanding of the mystery of the God-given union of Christ with His Church. We need increasingly to realize that the separate histories of our churches find their full meaning only if seen in the perspective of God's dealings with His whole people.
>
> We have now reached the crucial point in our ecumenical discussions. As we have come to know one another better our eyes have been opened to the depth and pain of our separations and also to our fundamental unity. The measure of unity which it has been given to the churches to experience together must now find clearer manifestation. A faith in the one Church of Christ which is not implemented by acts of obedience is dead. There are truths about the nature of God and His Church which will remain forever closed to us unless we act together in obedience to the unity which is already ours. We would, therefore, earnestly request our churches to consider whether they are doing all they ought to do to manifest the oneness of the people of God. . . .
>
> Obedience to God demands also that the churches seek unity in their mission to the world. . . .
>
> The word "penitence" has been often on our lips here at Lund. Penitence involves willingness to endure judgment—the judgment of the Lord to whom has been given the power to sift mankind and to gather into one the scattered children of God. We await His final triumph at the end of history. But, in God's mercy, tokens of judgment which are also calls to a new and active obedience come to us in our day also, here and now. Surely we cannot any longer remain blind to the signs of our times and deaf to His Word.
>
> The Lord says once again: "He that gathereth not with me, scattereth."

The days at Lund had been, in any case, a rare opportunity for fellowship, and for the orientation of those for whom the Conference was an initiation into the ecumenical movement. If they had shown that the point had been reached where it was impossible for the churches to proceed farther in their quest of unity under Faith and Order, that was in itself a gain. From such an impasse they could turn to other ways.

Examination of what was said at Lund—in the addresses, the study groups, the reports, the Message to the churches—verifies the claim of a veering in new directions in the thinking of those who organized and directed the Conference. The decision to turn back to the Bible and explore "more deeply the mystery of the God-given union of Christ and His Church" was regarded by the theologians themselves as one new tack of especial promise.

The intention was not, they explained, to discontinue examining the agreements and disagreements between the beliefs and practices of the denominations. For a multitude of Christians, the study of these would be necessary for a long time, they said, but it need not engage the attention of the entire Conference or of a whole section. While those new in ecumenical experience were bringing themselves up to date in these elementary lessons, others who had exhausted them could withdraw and probe behind the traditions and formularies of the churches for possible new meanings in the Scriptures.

Those who suggested this new procedure in theological study had grounds for hopefulness as to its results, perhaps, which do not appear readily to others not present or sharing the decision. It sounded well to say that there had been a return to the Bible, to examine more carefully its meaning. But optimism concerning this course could only be tempered when it was remembered that the Bible had more often divided than united Christians. Was there a denomination that did not think its doctrinal tenets scriptural? The problem was arriving at acceptable principles of biblical interpretation. Lacking agreement in this, the Bible would only continue to sanction whatever anyone desired to believe; and there was not any evidence in what Lund accomplished that Christians could come to unanimity on how the Scriptures should be read for their true teaching any more readily than an apostolic succession in the ministry or the other lesser questions dividing them in their church life.

The appeal of the Conference to the churches to commence at once to cooperate with one another more fully in the ways open to them, while the efforts to achieve closer doctrinal accord proceeded, certainly had good warrant in Scripture and, by the axiom that learning comes by doing, commended itself as practical and sound. The Message to the churches spoke on this point, it will be recalled:

> The measure of unity it has been given to the churches to experience together must find clearer manifestation. A faith in the one Church of Christ which is not implemented by acts of obedience is dead. There are truths about the nature of God and His Church which will remain for ever closed to us, unless we act together in obedience to the unity which is already ours.

The emphasis which the Conference placed upon the practice of unity at the parish level, though not in any sense a new idea, raised fresh hopes that the Commission on Faith and Order might succeed where other ecumenical attempts had failed, or been only partially successful, in trying to get an effective response from the churches.

While the Conference was calling for action "in obedience to the unity already ours," the younger churches had their representatives present and could have answered then and there, as in effect they did: "This we have done and, if permitted, would do yet more." But it was not certain to what extent the Conference wished the churches to act in this direction. Influential members were known to fear too precipitate movement by the missions. Proposals of union by some of them in the years immediately before the Conference had not been received with ananimous approval, seeming to certain of the authorities to have gone beyond "the unity already ours." Small wonder that the theologians had begun to talk about "a crisis of method" in their study, having found themselves trailing events and hard put to regularize what was happening!

The following is "A Communication to the Members of the Lund Conference on Faith and Order from Some Representatives of the Younger Churches":

We, the representatives of the younger churches present at this Conference from lands where church union negotiations have either been completed or are in progress, desire to say a word in love to those who have been used of God to send us holy baptism.

We are now much more fully alive to our responsibilities and opportunities in our own lands. Far more than any material gift, we need from you the gift of prayerful understanding and trustfulness.

We desire church unity primarily because it is the will of our Lord. In this matter the parent churches must resist the temptation to measure everything by their own standards. We well realize that the hope for a united church lies in maintaining all those elements of Faith and Order which were the fundamentals of the church before that unity was broken by the sins of men who could not maintain those elements in a just balance. As we go forth, under the Holy Spirit, to restore that balance, let it be remembered that unprecedented situations cannot be dealt with in every detail by the precedents of church history: and further, where all the fruits of visible union cannot be had at the inception of a scheme of union, our friends in the West must for the peace of the church apply a self-denying ordinance to themselves in certain particulars where they expect more of us than they are ready to demand of themselves.

Also, we would plead with you to use your influence to encourage similar schemes of union amongst yourselves and your kindred overseas, so that the inevitable crop of anomalies on the way to union would be reduced. While we appreciate the place given to Asia to occupy in such creative tasks, we ourselves must guard our honour against the possibility of our services to Christian unity being mistaken for a by-product of Asian nationalism. Many doubts and hesitations may be resolved if a number of similar schemes, affecting a wider variety of peoples and continents could be brought to fruition about the same time. Synchronisation, were this possible, would greatly reduce the number of anomalies and confusions.

May we also bear witness to our experience under God as we have worked together as churches actually negotiating for organic church union, and also as churches which have already come into being as a result of such union.

(i) We have seen how, as we resolutely held to that on which we were united and sought to give form to such unity, God himself drew nigh to us and fulfilled among us his promise that they who do his will shall learn of the doctrine.

(ii) We have also experienced the guidance of the Holy Spirit in the way in which He has led us into greater wholeness of truth as we, having reached the limits of discussion, ventured in faith trusting one another into life together in a united church.

(iii) We can testify with gladness that we have seen the vision of a church in which the episcopal, presbyteral and congregational elements have each their structural place in the life of a united church; and we humbly seek to bear this testimony before you and share our vision with you if you so desire it.

In our different lands, we are God's people, called by him, and commissioned by him to win our several nations for Jesus Christ. We must obey him as we can, trusting that he will confirm our obedience, overrule our mistakes, and perform his holy will. Brethren pray for us, as we pray for you.

A. Thakur Das	United Church of Northern India and Pakistan
D. T. Niles	Methodist Church, Ceylon
Augustine Ralla Ram	United Church of Northern India
J. R. Chandran	Church of South India
David Wilson	Methodist Church, Ceylon
P. D. Devanandan	Church of South India
Farid Audeh	Evangelical Churches in Lebanon and Syria
Aubert Rabenoro	Reformed Church, Madagascar
Rajah B. Manikam	Tamil Lutheran Church, India
E. C. Bhatty	United Church of Northern India
Takeshi Muto	United Church of Christ, Japan
Ernest John	Church of India, Burma and Ceylon
Lakdasa Kurunagala	Church of India, Burma and Ceylon

The statements of honest men at ecumenical gatherings show sometimes how difficult it is, when espousing an ideal, to keep an eye upon reality. The temptation becomes strong to grow rhapsodic over "the divine far-off event" and leave the listener struggling with the intervening delays and wondering whether the speaker is insincere or inexcusably visionary. The delegates to Lund were, for the most part, officials of the churches or persons chosen at the nomination or indicated approval of the executives, and one might have asked how they could feel otherwise while listening to the Secretary instructing them in their duties and saying, with reference to the discussion in which they were about to participate:

It may be that it will lead to some changes of mind, the abandoning of positions, some conversions. It may be that some delegates have come . . . briefed by their churches to stand up for certain positions, and that they will go back . . . convinced that these briefs need revision. . . . I beg of you to give the Holy Spirit the opportunity to lead you by entering upon your work here as men seeking through discussion for light in common problems, and not as men commissioned to defend tradition or position.

Ecclesiastical leaders are chosen, if not to defend "tradition and position," because they are believed to be "sound" and steadfast in such matters; and conversion in the sense of leading to a questioning or repudiation of the historic teachings of their communions would mark the end, in most cases, of their acceptableness for office. Imagine the reckoning a Baptist delegate to an ecumenical conference would face on returning home, who had announced himself convinced that the Lambeth Quadrilateral was a reasonable and scriptural basis of church union, or an Anglican that he had seen the light and now rejected the conditions of the ordination of ministers in that instrument.

Most of the members of the Conference at Lund were men in the middle years or beyond. Burdened with responsibilities for their respective denominations which had first claim upon them, they could hardly have brought themselves to take a step, such as retreating from some theological position believed by their constituencies to justify the separate existence of their churches, which would have added to the load of administrative duties they were already carrying criticism for doctrinal irregularity and the distraction of controversy and possibly division.

It was this unrealistic approach to unity on the part of some of those who were supposed to set the course of Faith and Order that compelled many members of the Conference and others interested in its success to question again the assumptions upon which the Movement appeared to proceed: for one, that the unity God willed demanded to be expressed through "one Church of Christ," meaning a visible organization comprising all denominations.

In the thought of many Christians, the World Council of Churches had been conceived primarily as an instrument of cooperation. The proposal to study and compare the theological positions of the churches which joined it had been adopted as a promising way of extending the areas in which they might work together. The principle of "unity in diversity" had been recognized as governing their relationship. But before the Council could be constituted prominent leaders had begun to explain that its formation represented only a first step toward union in one church and had no meaning apart from that end; and some denominations had confessed to having no sufficient interest to continue as members, unless it could be made a means of reunion. Earlier, there had been in ecumenical councils voices proclaiming the value of cooperation for its own sake. But at Lund these were muted, if raised at all. The other view dominated the thinking. Anything short of union, anything interfering with it, was sin to be repented.[45] "By entering into this relationship with each

[45] It was not held that the World Council of Churches should itself become a church comprising all denominations, but that it should make its main objective the fostering of a spirit of unity that would lead the communions ultimately to unite.

other,"[46] declared the Secretary of the Commission on Faith and Order, "we have already willed the death of our denominations."

If one asked on what scriptural grounds such assertions as this rested, he was reminded of the prayer of Christ that his disciples might be one; or of the borrowed metaphor of the physical body and its members employed by St. Paul to suggest the spiritual unity of Christians with Christ and with one another in him. When he spoke of the oneness of his followers, Christ had envisioned their "union in one church," it was said; and likewise the Apostle in his comparison. The correctness of these interpretations was assumed; but when they became the authority for sweeping dogmatic statements in support of as yet untried policies and practices, they could only be challenged.

Questioning them did not mean, of necessity, that the unconvinced opposed union in one church, if God could be shown clearly to will it. They could see that some denominations might, without radical revision of their doctrines and polities, unite, and probably should do so. It was obvious that the field of cooperation for all churches could be enlarged greatly by comparatively simple changes in the rules governing orders to admit of intercommunion and intercelebration, and of interministry by their clergy in other ways as well; and that some steps could be taken without doing violence to vital convictions. Not many were against some action of this kind, whatever the attitude of their denominations. But they believed that more real unity and good results could be achieved by a loose plan of federation, whether or not there were modifications in the rules of church order, than by corporate union.

As for the argument that the success of the Christian world mission waited upon the consummation of union, it also did not appear to be conclusive beyond re-examination. On the contrary, the thought could reasonably be indulged that mankind, harassed by the repeated irresponsible acts of monolithic states, might look with greater favor upon a democratic association of the churches, which, while having an effective unity in the love of God, would offer opportunity for freedom in which to realize their individual selfhood in service according to their own predilections and methods, than upon an all-embracing "great church" with a centralized system and its concomitant uniformity.

At Lund there must have been insights which did not break through the carefully channeled program to illuminate, or possibly confuse, the discussion, those to whom they came judging that the time for them was not yet. Among the members of the Conference were scholars who brought to the deliberations learning and understanding born of long and varied experience. They could hardly have been unaware of the profound implications for religious thought in the swift advances of scientific method and discovery, which seemed so remote from what most of the briefing speakers were saying. The President did speak of the

[46] Referring to the Amsterdam statement, "We intend to stay together."

Church's mission in times of revolution—"in revolutions of war and revolutions of thought." But he did not elaborate. The earth writhed in the throes of such social upheavals as had never been witnessed, and well might some have suggested, as they did, that the churches turn back to the Bible and investigate anew such fundamental questions in theology as Christology and its meaning for the Church and the Christian mission. But what promise was there that a searching of the Scriptures would produce more than a reaffirmation by rival theological groups of the clashing dogmas "most surely believed"?

Some delegates consoled themselves with the thought that the Conference had "time on its side." Ten years might be required, it was said, for what Lund had written to become the possession fully of the churches. Was there any apprehension of the rapidity with which change was making "ancient good uncouth," or of the probability that the next decade would disclose to the churches truth not perceived at Lund? There was no way of staying social and political revolutions, the swift overturnings of which brought disaster in the end to those hailing them and the defeated alike; and the breaking up of static traditions and thought molds in religion could proceed with equal suddenness and calamitousness.

Some of those at Lund must have asked whether such an earthquake in the ecclesiastical world, for all that it would mean great distress, should not be welcomed, in preference to the greater disaster its delay might be building up. One of the causes of the breakdown of morality in the modern world had been its inextricability from religious concepts which masses of the people had found not only incomprehensible but, as they believed, demonstrably false. There was reason to think that this condition had opened the way, in large part, for the most devastating phases of the debacle of the 'thirties in central Europe, which could be repeated easily there or anywhere else in the world. If the churches would not unfetter truth and let it become a support, instead of a hindrance, to the peoples in their struggle for emancipation from outmoded theological dogmatisms, then the strong man and those ready to rally to him as messiah could be depended on to attempt it, if it would further their ambitions; and, of course, they could do it only profanely, bringing deeper darkness and heavier shackles.

It had been the clergy whose duty was to reinterpret the gospel. Their first responsibility in evangelism had been to show that the Christian faith still was relevant and to make a beginning of proving it so by preaching it in the idiom of the time. But they had seemed to suffer from an inhibiting paralysis which left them able to speak only in clichés. There had been too few with the knowledge or courage to say simply and straightly that theology, over which Christians wrangled, was only the explanation, so far as men were able to explain it, of the believer's experience of God in Jesus Christ and needed in every generation to be recast according to the unfolding revelation of God; that the "givenness" of "the faith once for all delivered to the saints" was in the saving encounter with God through faith in Christ, and not in the terminology of its description, and Christianity was, in consequence, always more at home in the common way than in the lecture room; and that the way in which the spiritual reality of salvation was to be described and mediated through rites and symbols, for all the importance such things might have in systematic education, could never rationally be allowed to become cause of divisions. Study and comparison of its variant theological expressions might make for orderly thinking; but this, though not without its value, was not of sufficient importance to be permitted to interfere with wholehearted cooperation by Christians in proclaiming the good news.

A delegate to the Conference on Church, Community and State at Oxford in 1937 sat drinking a cup of tea in the lounge of the old Mitre Hotel in High Street on an evening, after a plenary session in Town Hall, when the editor of one of the well-known religious journals joined him, asking what he thought of the progress of the Conference. With his reply that the action seemed to him confused and halting because, chiefly, there was no agreement on the fundamental nature of the Christian revelation the journalist agreed, and asked: "Who is there that could write an authoritative article on the meaning of revelation for us to print?"

At that moment John R. Mott entered and sat down at the table with them. They told him of what they had been talking. He expressed himself as thinking they had touched the crucial problem besetting all ecumenical gatherings and, looking up, said: "Here comes the man who is best qualified to write your article."

The newcomer was William Temple, whose book *Nature, Man and God* had appeared a few years before. The Archbishop (of York) protested that not he but a certain theological professor in one of the colleges at Oxford, who at the moment was working at a book on revelation, was the person most competent to prepare the desired paper. Seated around the table, they discussed the subject well into the night. The delegate who had started it was never to forget the conversation because of the notable personalities present and of their confirmation of his conviction, long held, that the nature of the Christian revelation was the rock on which the ecumenical movement stood always in danger of foundering.

Fifteen years had passed when the third World Conference on Faith and Order met at Lund. Temple was untimely dead, and Mott aged and ready to retire. Already retired were the journalist and the anonymous parish minister, the fourth member of the group at the Mitre in Oxford. Still unexplored was the problem of Christian revelation, except in its traditional meaning, while theological commissions discussed the secondary questions dividing the churches.[47] Would they ever get to it —the churches' real "deepest difference"? Probably not. Christians who could not agree on parochial matters were hardly to be expected to discover truth of continental proportions. Union, federation, or any other plan for the manifestation of unity would be practicable only on the principle of oneness in widest diversity. Would Christians ever learn that they could be "together in one accord," as were their earliest predecessors on the day of Pentecost, only in their common experience of God in Jesus Christ, each explaining it and trying to share it with others in his own way, but with brotherliness and confidence toward those with different "tongues"; that only such discerning love could transcend all differences and persuade the world? Not until they approached one another in a true knowledge of the nature of the Christian revelation.

6. Youth Department

"Since its beginning the ecumenical movement has been concerned with youth." So began a statement from Geneva in 1948 on the relation of the World Council of Churches, soon to be constituted, to young people. The statement could have been turned about and written with equal truth: "Youth has been concerned with the ecumenical movement since its beginning." The sons and daughters of the church fathers had not waited for invitations to accompany them to the conferences. They had let it be known that they would like to go, if not forbidden, and followed. They had arranged their own simultaneous programs. When permitted, they had looked in upon the meetings of their elders. They had filled the sittings assigned for their use, on occasion, in observing the proceedings, and had been grateful—and industrious and dependable—when given even small responsibilities. They had proved themselves capable of thinking and working with ecumenical spirit. The ideals of unity and cooperation had appealed to them for what seemed their rightness and inevitability. In the gathering of representatives of their generation from lands the world around they had seen signs of hope for the ending of confessional separations and geographical isolations. They had had a good time, in every right meaning of the words. The experience had included the adventure of travel to far places, of foregathering with strange peoples and learning about their customs, of encounter with new and challenging ideas, of being part of a fellowship reaching across the ages and of the work of a kingdom that knew no

[47] *Revelation,* with chapters by T. S. Eliot, Karl Barth, William Temple, Sergius Bulgakoff, M. C. D'Arcy, Walter Horton, and Gustav Aulén, had been published in April of that year by Faber and Faber Limited, London, under the editorship of John Baillie and Hugh Martin.

national bounds and no end. There had not been any doubt that youth's collective mind was made up to go along and to belong.

Where could the movement have got without the young people of the churches? It could never have started, in fact, but for their vision, enthusiasm, and dedication.

The Youth Department originated in the action of the Provisional Committee in 1946 in response to the growing desire of the young people to be given a definite place in the program of the World Council of Churches, and to the natural purpose, as well, of their communions to have them assume responsibility as they were ready and prepare themselves for leadership. They had qualified in many ways for this recognition.

The Youth Commission, which had been set up by the Universal Christian Conference on Life and Work at Stockholm in 1925, had early joined with the corresponding body in the World Alliance for International Friendship through the Churches in forming the Ecumenical Youth Commission. This body, in turn, had collaborated with the World's Alliance of the Young Men's Christian Associations, the World's Young Women's Christian Association, the World's Student Christian Federation, and the World Sunday School Association[48] in conducting the first World Conference of Christian Youth, at Amsterdam in the summer of 1939, its Secretary, Dr. R. H. Edwin Espy, acting as the executive officer of the Conference. And the wartime Emergency Committee of Christian Organizations, of which the Ecumenical Youth Commission was one, with sections in Europe and North America, had succeeded notably during the sundering years from 1939 to 1946 in keeping alive the interest and fellowship which had marked the preceding decade and a half, so that, even before World War II ended, the young people, in cooperation with the same international organizations that sponsored the Amsterdam meeting, had begun plans for a second World Conference of Christian Youth, to be held in Oslo, Norway, in 1947.[49]

The establishment of the Youth Department had brought this latter project under the auspices of the Provisional Committee, and to it the first Secretary, Rev. Francis House, gave most of his time.

Because of restrictions on travel and of the very large number of delegates attending—some twelve hundred—this had been a laborious task. But the results justified the effort, and more, demonstrating how the confidence of youth could succeed where more experienced judgment would have hesitated to act at all. The Conference had been successful to an unusual degree in rallying and unifying Christian young people for their ecumenical mission. The Department had been organized somewhat as an experiment, but when the denominations gathered at Amsterdam two years later to form the World Council of Churches, it was

[48] To become eventually the World Council of Christian Education.
[49] Part Two, Section II, *4*. p. 204.

made a permanent part of the structure, with the functions as outlined in the beginning by the Provisional Committee: "(a) To serve as a center of ecumenical contact and inspiration for the youth movements directly related to the churches; and (b) to collaborate with the international Christian youth movements and other Christian agencies with youth in ecumenical . . . activities;" and with latitude "to develop its program in such other ways as the Spirit of God might direct."

By its constitution, the Department had the freedom to welcome the cooperation of all young people, whether members of denominations belonging to the World Council of Churches or not, and the duty to maintain close relations through the World Christian Youth Commission with all international organizations in the field of youth work having representation in that body. A committee of young people and leaders of youth, on which there were members appointed by the International Missionary Council and the World Council of Christian Education, guided the activities of the Department.

Upon the retirement of Rev. Francis House, after the Oslo Conference, Miss Jean Fraser was chosen Secretary of the Department, with headquarters in Geneva, and Rev. William A. Keys Secretary for the United States, with an office in New York City.

A world-wide study of youth work in the churches had been conducted during 1948, 1949, and 1950 by Dr. Everett Stowe, with the International Missionary Council and the World Council of Christian Education cooperating. It yielded information enabling the Department to pursue its task with an understanding of needs and opportunities in the different countries and with some assurance of a hospitable reception by the churches, which had been found "generally aware of the inadequacy of much of the traditional programs for youth."

In Europe the immediate need was to bring together the national church leaders to discuss common problems and make a beginning, at least, in breaking down the wartime isolation which had persisted after the cessation of hostilities. In many places the churches required material as well as spiritual aid, and the Department helped with obtaining and administering a certain proportion of the relief and reconstruction funds. It aided, and in time took over, the work camp program, through which young people, usually in companies of from twenty to thirty members of different nationalities, "cleared ground and dug foundations in the realm of human relations, as well as in terms of physical buildings." "Pick-and-shovel ambassadors," they came to be called.

The gatherings for these and other purposes under the auspices of the Department afforded opportunity for the young people to discuss their Christian obligations in relation to civic enterprises as well—e.g., the developing European Movement, which was an attempt outside the churches to bring the nations into closer political and economic association.

"A visible sign of the new ecumenical consciousness," according to the report at Amsterdam, "is the great meeting-place for the youth of the world at Agape, in the Italian Alps, built by young people of many nations and offered by the Waldensian youth as an open house for the youth of all countries."

In the eastern Mediterranean area the Department found it necessary to make available such material aid as could be gathered, particularly to Greece, which had suffered most from the ravages of war. The countries of this region had strong youth movements in both the Eastern Orthodox and the Coptic Churches, which were encouraged to join with others in different parts of the world working through the Department. In Egypt and Lebanon, the Orthodox and the Evangelical Churches had evolved a cooperative relationship which could be held up as an example to the leaders of their communions in other nations. In 1951 the Department organized and took part in a pilgrimage to Greece on the occasion of the celebration of the nineteenth centennial of the landing of St. Paul in Europe. In Lebanon, Greece, and Cyprus it helped with the establishment of work camps under Orthodox auspices.

Rev. Daniel T. Niles of Ceylon served the Department as Chairman from 1948 to 1953, an arrangement reflecting the interest of the World Council of Churches in the extension of Christian work in Asia. But many conditions combined to delay the inauguration there of an ecumenical program for church youth. At the Conference of Christian Leaders of East Asia, at Bangkok in 1949, nine young people from as many countries of southeastern Asia were brought together for consultation on this problem. The discussion emphasized the fact that the work of international bodies there—of the Young Men's Christian Association, the Young Women's Christian Association, and the Student Christian Mission, chiefly—touched mainly those in the educational institutions who could speak the English language, and that the needs of other young people in the churches, who were greatly in a majority, called especially for attention. But for anything that might have been attempted on their account very little indigenous leadership would have been obtainable. There was agreement that the situation offered opportunity for work of possible far-reaching effect but demanded, if it was to be entered with any hope of success, the wisest strategy. In the course of time, the results of conferences which were held with youth workers in both North and South India gave encouragement to proceed, and a three-months' training course for leaders proved fruitful in its discovery of talent and serious purpose. When it was decided to hold the third World Conference of Christian Youth at Kottayam, in Travancore-Cochin State, the Secretary of the Department transferred her headquarters to India and spent upwards of a year visiting among the churches, counseling and in other ways cooperating with them as they organized and marshaled their resources for their contribution to the Conference and their own youth program.

In 1953 Rev. Philip Potter, a young pastor in the West Indies, who had succeeded to the chairmanship of the Department, spent some weeks in the Gold Coast region of Africa, visiting Nigeria, Angola, Sierra Leone, and Liberia. He found the churches of these parts greatly concerned about the effects of the rapid economic and political changes on the life of their youth and eager to inquire concerning what might be done to relate Christian work more dynamically to their interests. As a step toward seizing this opportunity, training and setting apart youth organizers were under consideration, and the churches welcomed the counsel of ecumenical leaders in developing their program.

In the Union of South Africa contacts had been established through the Youth Committee of the National Council of Churches. The work camp sponsored by the Department at Wilgespruit had significance as an experiment in interracial cooperation and community living. Two leaders of the youth movement of the Dutch Reformed Church were helped to plan a tour in 1953 of Europe and North America, for observing Christian work there with young people.

One result of the second World Conference of Christian Youth had been the formation of a youth committee by the New Zealand Council of Churches and the holding of a national conference after the pattern of the Oslo program. In Australia a provisional youth committee was organized in 1952, the physical character of the country, which created many problems of travel, having delayed the full development of ecumenical work. Both New Zealand and Australia had been led to give special thought to their Christian duty in relation to Asia. Thus they welcomed the more gladly a visit by D. T. Niles during his incumbency as Chairman of the Youth Department.

The world survey of youth work in the churches had discovered in Argentina, Brazil, Chile, Colombia, Cuba, Mexico, Puerto Rico, Peru, and Uruguay national federations of young people, working together in the Union of Evangelical Youth of Latin America, under the auspices of which regional conferences had been held with conspicuous success in 1941 and 1946. The churches in the several cooperating nations were developing an ecumenical outlook, although with little contact with what was going on in this field outside Mexico, South and Central America, and the West Indies. The approach of the Youth Department of the World Council of Churches and the World Council of Christian Education was welcomed by the young people of these areas as offering an opportunity to establish a wider fellowship. An almost immediate result was the development of an active relationship with Christian youth work in Latin countries of Europe closely linked in their history and culture with the peoples of Latin nations of the Western Hemisphere.

The natural basis of common interests of youth in American and European Latin nations was apparent from the themes and the message of a conference at Agape, Italy, in September, 1952, of forty leaders from the Continent under the auspices of the Department. In effect, this was a continuation of a meeting of the churches from the same general region at Torre Pellice in 1950. The study covered such subjects as "The Problems of Minority Churches in Catholic Countries" and "Is It Possible to Hold a Protestant Position between Catholicism and Communism?" The drift of the thinking was indicated by the statement issued at the close of the gathering:

> Meeting . . . to study the conditions for the bearing of faithful witness in our respective countries, we would, first of all, express our gratitude to our Lord who has enabled us to hold this encounter in gladness and brotherhood.
>
> In a common will to place our whole existence under the authority of Christ, we who are members of his universal Church feel and affirm our absolute solidarity with those who are refused full freedom to express their faith.
>
> After exchanging our experiences regarding the different methods of evangelism, we have arrived at a clearer conception of our relations with the young people of our time who are Catholics or Communists.
>
> Christ is the sole Lord of the Church and the one and only Truth. His cross forbids us to impose the gospel upon men by any political of clerical pressure whatsoever.
>
> Our faith in Christ is not an idealistic evasion, but a joyful release from all bondage: it [integrates] us in an active search for human justice.
>
> To all those who are seeking a reason for existence, to those who are indifferent and those who are discouraged, we say that hope in Christ alone gives the joy of being men.
>
> We implore all our fellow-Christians, all those who call upon the name of the same Lord, to overcome their divisions and join together in the service of the young to whom Christ must be proclaimed.

In response to the desire of the young people in these lands for ecumenical news, the Department began publication of a bulletin in Spanish, which attained a wide circulation.

The action of Christian youth of the United States had a very great influence upon the work of the Department. It was in this country that work camps had their origin, and they were a characteristic expression of the altruism and energy of youth. Concerning them, the report of the Central Committee of the World Council of Churches entitled *The First Six Years*—from Amsterdam to Evanston—had this to say:

> Following early post-war experiences in work camps at the Collège Cévenol, France, the Congregational Christian Service Committee offered the Youth Department in 1947 a budget and staff member to establish work camps on an ecumenical basis. In 1951, the programme was officially adopted by the Youth Department, and was recognized as a project of the Inter-Church Aid Department. The Administrative Budget is included in

the Service Programme of the latter. The finance of the camps themselves is largely met locally, and by campers' contributions. The programme has developed from six camps in four European countries with three hundred campers in 1948 to twenty-nine camps in sixteen countries on three continents, with over one thousand campers of thirty-eight nationalities, in 1953. Responsibility is divided between committees in Geneva and New York.

The work camps sponsored by the World Council of Churches provide opportunities for young people to participate practically in the ecumenical movement. The life of the camp itself, international and inter-confessional, involving work, worship, Bible-study, discussion and relations with the local community, is in itself a miniature ecumenical encounter. The projects chosen all relate to some concern of the World Council of Churches—for refugees, for the evangelism of industrial workers, for the strengthening of the Church's ecumenical life and witness. Young people who have taken part in such camps go back to their home communities with a new awareness of the task of the Church in the world, and the eagerness to translate it into local terms.

By 1954 the number of countries in which work camps had been organized under the auspices of the World Council of Churches had increased to twenty-five. The enrollment had reached about fifteen hundred. The camp locations on the map of three continents "formed an arc reaching from the Philippine Islands on the East through Thailand, India, the Middle East and Europe into South Africa."

World Youth Projects, as they came to be called, had their origin in "The Call to United Christian Youth Action" which the United Christian Youth Movement in the United States launched in 1951, on the strength of evidence that work with young people in many parts of the earth languished for lack of sufficient resources and of ecumenical vision and experience. Their incorporation by the World Council of Churches and the World Council of Christian Education in the joint program of their Youth Departments in 1953 led to the tentative selection of thirty-two tasks in twenty-two countries which appeared to lend themselves favorably to the abilities and schedules of young people, one special qualifying factor being that each showed potentialities for becoming self-sustaining.

The following statement of principles, which was adopted by the two Councils, suggested the spirit and the scope of the new venture:

> That in a truly ecumenical exchange all give to one another what each is able to give; that giving should, therefore, in every case, be a mutual exchange of resources; that the resources should include those of money, leadership, literature, correspondence, prayer; that the object of this interchange be primarily the strengthening of the ecumenical conscience and co-operative work of youth in the nations concerned.[50]

During the years from Amsterdam to Evanston the Youth Department gave much thought to the training of leaders, cooperating with

[50] *The First Six Years,* p. 46 and p. 51.

the Ecumenical Institute in 1947, 1948, and 1949 to organize special courses for this purpose and conducting its own instruction conferences for European countries. It assisted, likewise, with many nationally sponsored efforts of the same nature in both Europe and Asia.

For the guidance of the growing number of regional, national, and local youth organizations preparing their own training courses, the World Christian Youth Commission in 1953 defined what it considered to be the essential subjects in the instruction of leaders. The Department, as one of the several constituent bodies of the Commission, shared responsibility for the statement, which recommended study of the Bible, worship, the Christian mission, the Christian movement, personal relationships, the Christian society, leadership of youth, and the organization and administration of youth work.

The Department acted jointly also with the World Christian Youth Conferences in the issuance of various kinds of printed material for use by study and discussion groups and, likewise, with the World Council of Christian Education's Youth Department in the publication of subject matter of help to young people in program building. Some three thousand subscribers in different parts of the world received *News Sheet,* the Department's bulletin, which was published monthly in English and Spanish, and quarterly in French.

Examining the records of the years here under review one comes upon many organizations working with young people in the ecumenical field with names so similar that they are confusing, as are also the entries of mergers and coordinations of their activities. Their main significance lay in the fact that they represented a new beginning of effort to implement the ideal of world fellowship for youth through Jesus Christ. The considerable number of persons who, in one way or another, took part in their programs reminds the reader, by contrast, of the vastly greater body in the churches not touched by them, and indeed scarcely aware of them. But faith in the day of small things was a quality of the ecumenical mind, and those who led the vanguard of the movement thought that they glimpsed beyond the difficulties and discouragements of the present a triumphant kingdom which marched toward them upon the feet of youth out of all nations but having one King and one loyalty, and pressing steadfastly forward.

The largest gathering of young people during this period was the Fourth Baptist World Conference at Rio de Janeiro in the summer of 1953, and it emphasized the divisions and tensions within the ranks of Christians over the ecumenical youth movement. Some denominations of the Baptists belonged to the World Council of Churches and others did not, and representatives of the young people of all went to the meeting in Brazil. The numerical strength of those whose churches opposed interchurch cooperation overbalanced that of the others and gave full effect to their plan to devote the program altogether to Baptist concerns; but the voices of the latter, and, without doubt, of some of the majority, were heard in the message of the Conference to the Youth Department of the World Council of Churches:

> As Baptist young people, although divided as to matters of ecumenical participation, we want to take our share of the work God has assigned to the Christians of the world at the present moment. We wish that God's richest blessings may rest on every young Christian of every denomination.[51]

This swift sketch of the program of the Youth Department during the first six years of the World Council of Churches may be concluded fittingly with a report of the third World Conference of Christian Youth at Kottayam, in Travancore, India, in December, 1952, to which reference has been made.

Like the previous international gatherings of young people,[52] this Conference was sponsored by the World Council of Churches and the International Missionary Council, with the World Council of Christian Education, the World's Student Christian Federation, the World's Alliance of the Young Men's Christian Associations, and the World's Young Women's Christian Association cooperating. It was part of "a concentration of ecumenical programs in India during December, 1952, and January, 1953," and, with the action of the other bodies meeting at the same time, it helped to give strong emphasis to the strategic role of India in the Christian movement. Its sessions, which extended through two weeks, had been preceded by a preparatory retreat for the leaders. Following hard upon its adjournment came the Rural Work Conference of the Young Men's Christian Association in South India and the meeting in Madras with men of non-Christian faiths arranged by the World's Alliance of the Young Men's Christian Associations and the Council of Young Men's Christian Associations of India, Pakistan and Ceylon. Simultaneously, in Lucknow, the East Asia Study Conference proceeded under the Study Department of the World Council, and in Ootacamund, the Post-Travancore Conference of the World's Young Women's Christian Association, while at Lucknow, also, the Executive Committee of the World Council of Churches was in session—and at Alwaye the Youth Department Committee of the World Council of Churches and the World Council of Christian Education. Then followed in swift succession the Young Men's Conference of the Young Men's Christian Association in Madras, the sessions of the Central Committee of the World Council of Churches in Lucknow, and the meetings of the General Committee of the World's Student Christian Federation in Bombay, while during nearly the whole of January an ecumenical work camp carried on at Barapani, Assam.

[51] Communicated through the Secretary of the Conference, Dr. Joel Sorenson of Sweden.

[52] At Amsterdam and Oslo, in 1939 and 1947, respectively.

More than three hundred delegates and leaders from fifty-five countries came to Kottayam for the Conference of Christian Youth, the first such event in the East. Half of them had been appointed by their churches, the others by various units of the Y.M.C.A., the Y.W.C.A., and the student Christian movements. Two-thirds of them were Asians.

His Highness the Rajpramukh of Travancore-Cochin inaugurated the Conference. With him on the dais, which had been decorated in typical Oriental splendor, were the Chairman, Lakshman Perera; the India Committee Executive Chairman, Dr. P. V. Charian; His Holiness the Catholicos of the East, Moran Mar Baselios Geevarghese II; Metropolitan Juhanon Mar Thoma and other prelates of the Syrian Church; and the bishops of the Church of India and the Church of South India.

"The world today is torn with fear and anxiety," said Professor Perera in greeting the Conference, "and drives people to dark despair or blind indifference. But amidst all this our hope is Jesus Christ, and our faith is in him as the Lord of history. We pray that from this Conference will issue not only a fresh appreciation that Jesus Christ is Lord, but also a firm conviction that [he] is the answer to every problem." "Jesus Christ the Answer" had been announced as the general theme.

Mr. M. A. Thomas welcomed the delegates, on behalf of the Kerala Ecumenical Youth Committee, the regional organization of young people in that part of India, saying, "Never did we dream, when we met in Oslo in 1947, that this quiet corner of the world would be chosen as the venue of the Third World Conference of Christian Youth." And Miss Saroe Chakko, Principal of Isabella Thoburn College for Women, a President of the World Council of Churches, and Chairman of the Conference planning committee, described the coming to Kottayam as a "pilgrimage."

> We are on a journey, and to us comes God's question, "Adam, where is thy brother?" On the spirit we show and the imagination we display depends the fruitfulness of our coming together. Let us not be too clever in our cleverness, nor yet too fearful in our littleness. But let us be humble in our ignorance, depending on "the foolishness of God which is wiser than the wisdom of men." Like the Magi, let us seek the King with confidence, bringing as royal gifts the best of body, mind, soul and strength. Let us cast aside with courage our preconceived notion as to where he can be found. Let us be ready to be sent forth from his presence to wherever he may send us.

Others addressing the Conference included Miss Anne Baëta, a barrister of Accra and Chairman of the Juvenile Courts; Leo Marsh of the program staff of the National Council of the Young Men's Christian Association in the United States; Tsunegoro Nara, a secretary of the student department of the Young Men's Christian Association of Japan; Dr. Visser 't Hooft, General Secretary of the World Council of Churches; and Dr. Martin Niemöller of Berlin-Dahlem, representing the Confessional Church of Germany.

Sectional meetings had for study topics "Interpreting the Gospel of Jesus Christ," "Jesus Christ and the Search for Personal Freedom and Social Justice," "The Church's Witness to Jesus Christ," "The Claims of Christ in Personal and Family Relationships," and "Christ in a World of Tensions." Nine workshops, conducted by experts in each of these fields, demonstrated techniques in making the study of the Bible relevant to the daily life of young people; helping youth to enter into the worship of the churches; building and conducting programs with a variety of interests that appealed to youth and securing continuity in them; teaching the value and use of music for young people; preparing and displaying filmstrips, posters, and other such visual aids; expressing ideas through drama; orienting activities to rural life; planning and managing work camps, caravans, and service projects in towns and villages; writing for newspapers on religious subjects; and creating literature young people would appreciate and use.

Committees prepared summations of the findings of the various groups for presentation to the plenary sessions and circulation after approval.

The festival commemorating the nineteen-hundredth anniversary of the arrival in India of St. Thomas the Apostle fell at the time of the Conference and brought together all the Christian churches of Travancore in characteristic Oriental pageantry and parade. The Conference members marched four abreast attired in their national costumes through throngs lining the streets and the common. Twenty thousand people, it was estimated, had come from surrounding regions to swell the local crowd. His Holiness Moran Mar Baselios Geevarghese II, Catholicos of the East, presided at the public meeting, flanked by bishops of the Orthodox Syrian Church, Mar Thoma Syrian Church, Chaldean Church, Church of South India, and the (Anglican) Church of India, Pakistan, Burma and Ceylon. Three Roman Catholic bishops presented messages from their Church. Dr. Visser 't Hooft was heard in one of the principal addresses, along with speakers from the Mar Thoma, Orthodox Syrian, Jacobite Syrian, and Roman Catholic Churches. *The Ecumenical Review,* reporting the event, said:

"The festival at Kottayam, attended by tens of thousands of people and by all delegates of the World Conference of Christian Youth, included many features . . . not often encountered in church ceremonies. Among these, the elephants were not the least noteworthy. . . . In happy contrast to the outward display of splendour, the addresses were characterized by great soberness." The speakers gave thanks to God for "the astonishing fact" that in spite of its almost complete isolation the Christian Church in Travancore had not shared the fate of other ancient Christian communities in various parts of Asia, but had survived. Now this providential preservation meant surely that God had a plan for the Church in this part of the world. Said Dr. John Matthai, former Minister of Finance in the Indian Government: "The Church should, therefore, re-vitalize and Christianize itself in order to respond more effectively to the call made upon it."

> Due to God's great mercy, I see before me a replica of the ecumenical movement. This Assembly is a great reminder to us of the divinely-ordained purpose toward which we have to strive. I expect that these friends who come from afar will carry to their homes the message of this century. This message is the high priestly prayer of our Master, "that they may all be one." During the nineteen centuries of our existence we have not been blessed with an occasion like this. Let this be a prologue to the fulfillment of our Lord's desire. St. Thomas came to preach the Gospel. Nothing will be a more fitting memorial to St. Thomas and this centenary than our resolve to undertake the long-delayed task of evangelization of this country.

The Kerala Ecumenical Youth Committee, representing all the churches and missions, had arranged a program of parish visits by the members of the Conference, which proved to be an interesting and profitable feature. Congregations with which these "ambassadors of Christendom to the local churches," as they were introduced, met were of the Orthodox Syrian, Jacobite Syrian, Mar Thoma Syrian, South India Churches, and the Church of God. In addresses they brought greetings, described their own home church life, and shared with the people their experiences and convictions as Christians. Declared one appraisal:

> The outstanding characteristic of [the Conference] was certainly not only that it was held in the fascinating setting of Travancore, with its beauty and its remarkable church history, but that it was, as it were, in continuous contact and conversation with the people of Travancore. The daily meetings attended by many thousands who never seemed to tire of the messages of fellow-Christians from other parts of the world, the visits of the delegates to the congregations all over the area and the discussion with the Communists of Kottayam were not just additional and extra-curricular activities, but an integral part of the life of the Conference.

The exchange of letters between the Conference and communist youth leaders had significance as bringing into focus the critical issue of communism's challenge to the bid of the Christian faith for the allegiance of the youth of the world. What was said on each side had wide circulation through the East and deserved to be made a permanent part of the record. (See Appendix E.)

Youth had a larger stake in the conflicts of this troublous age than others and accordingly suffered most. In its natural buoyancy it felt the anguish of its plight less perhaps than those—parents and teachers—who worried on its account; but the damage of the repression, deprivation, and misguidance which it experienced, in many cases never to be repaired, made a vaster total, if such balances can be computed, than the ravages upon adult life. It would endure longer and affect more deeply the shape of mankind's future. No one could see how the minds and spirits of those victimized might ever be renewed and fitted for life under normal conditions, except by a miracle of God's grace; and the realization that such divine healing would never be brought to many of those needing it most desperately gave an urgency to all Christian work.

There was reason for gratitude that the churches had leaders who arose to comfort their people in the distress of these dark years, heeding not the peril to themselves. Conspicuous among them was Bishop Otto Dibelius, Chairman of the Evangelical Church in Germany, who withstood the persecutions of Christians in East Germany by the communist regime and fearlessly and eloquently championed the cause of the *Junge Gemeinde*. Words spoken by him to the youth of his country and their parents in the spring of 1953 helped greatly to strengthen all Christian work with young people. In part, he said:[53]

The news of the persecutions which have come upon the *Junge Gemeinde* in the German Democratic Republic is running through the whole Christian world. . . . Services have been disturbed by members of the Free German Youth movement, Young Pioneers have been told that they should not attend Christian instruction any more, one attack is following another on Christian teaching, great Christian institutions have been commandeered, and the number of pastors, deaconesses, catechists and other church workers who have been arrested is rising all the time.

All this speaks for itself. No palliations or hushing-up can conceal it. . . . I send greetings to those who have kept their faith even in very great stress. To the others, who have yielded to constraint and signed against their conscience and conviction, I say, "God's pardoning mercy is greater than our human frailty." By that mercy we, all of us, live. But signatures obtained under duress have not value in the eyes of God. You are free to act according to his Word and commandment. . . .

The *Junge Gemeinde* is not an organization, and most certainly not an illegal one. It is part of the total *Gemeinde,* or community of the faithful, situated both in particular localities and in the Church as a whole. Nobody can *leave* the *Junge Gemeinde,* because nobody can *enter* it. You can only either take part in its functions or not take part in them. And it is the free and inalienable right of each individual Christian boy or girl to decide which. . . .

To the parents I say this. I know how hard it is for you to have to look on while your children are victimized for the sake of the faith, and how natural it is to want to protect them from further persecution. But bear in mind that nothing will bring your children in later life so much confidence as the fact that they stood by their Church when they were little. Above all, bear in mind that a clear conscience is better than a smooth path through life. . . . God takes his Church often enough into ways that we find it hard

[53] Excerpt from a broadcast of a pastoral letter.

to understand. But it is the two-thousand-year-old experience of the Church that his ways are just and true. . . .

To the grace of God I commend you and your children.

In her report to the Central Committee at Chichester in 1949, Miss Jean Fraser stated that the Youth Department existed to remind the churches of their responsibility for youth, and youth of its responsibility to the ecumenical movement. She was asked whether or not there could be youth representation on the Central Committee. It was explained by the Chairman that this would require action by the Assembly itself. Dr. Visser 't Hooft thereupon pointed out that the Committee had power to invite "consultants" to attend its meetings and could secure the presence of young people by including them in the invitation. Thereafter it acted on this suggestion, and representatives of youth became interested observers of its proceedings. They had earlier been admitted to meetings of the Study Department, the Commission on Faith and Order, the Board of Directors of the Ecumenical Institute, and the Commission on the Life and Work of Women in the Churches. Ten young people attended the Bangkok Conference in 1949, and twenty the third World Conference on Faith and Order, at Lund in 1952.

Staff workers during the interim between Amsterdam and Evanston included Rev. Jan Mirejovsky, who was appointed Reconstruction Secretary in 1948; Mr. George Booth, Secretary of Work Camps from 1949 to 1951; Mr. Charles Hein, who, assisted by Mr. Heinrich Rohrbach, carried on the work camps after Mr. Booth's resignation; Mr. Bengt-Thure Molander, who succeeded Mr. Mirejovsky as European Secretary; Miss Frances Maeda, Secretary in the New York Office; and Dr. K. M. Simon, a deacon of the Syrian Jacobite Church of Travancore, who served as Organizing Secretary of the Third World Youth Conference, in 1952.

Mlle Suzanne de Dietrich wrote *"Discovering the Bible"* for the Department's study program.

Rev. William A. Keys was Secretary for the United States from 1948 to 1952. He had "kept in touch with the Caribbean and Latin American countries and made two visits there on behalf of the Youth Department, his itinerary including seven countries." He had also carried supervisory relations with certain Asian areas and "been largely responsible for the good basis on which the Work Camp program developed." In addition, he had "given endless time to working out study visits for European and Asian students of youth activities in America." The Department said, in accepting his resignation: "We are indeed grateful for the wholehearted conviction about the ecumenical movement which . . . inspired his work." [54]

The Department was invited by the Church of Greece to recruit the

[54] Minutes of the Central Committee, 1952-1953, p. 115.

youth delegates from the constituency of the World Council of Churches to the festival celebrating the nineteenth centennial of St. Paul's landing in Europe. In this it had the close cooperation of the World's Student Christian Federation. The group organized for the journey consisted of forty young people from a number of different countries. Besides them, there were twenty-five Greeks and fifteen Roman Catholics.

The Department was fortunate in receiving, in addition to its inadequate budgetary allocations, substantial contributions from the Rockefeller Fund for its varied activities. The Congregational Christian Churches in the United States gave liberally toward the support of the work camps program.

This survey of youth work under the World Council of Churches between Amsterdam and Evanston may be concluded with mention of the Department's representation, through its Secretary, Miss Jean Fraser, at the conference of young people's leaders convened by Princess Wilhelmina of the Netherlands at the palace of Het Loo at Apeldoorn in September, 1953. An expression of the nation's gratitude for the world-wide help it had received during the flood disaster of the previous year, the conference was attended by delegates from European countries and various ecumenical youth bodies. It was in Amsterdam during the reign of Wilhelmina, who abdicated as queen in 1948, it will be recalled, that the World Council of Churches had been organized, and the Executive Committee of the Council sent greetings to the conference. The program included discussion of Christian responsibility in relation to European unity, united action by the churches, and government and industry. In its findings, the conference called for more ecumenical action on the local level, especially in service to those in need, and for closer fellowship and consultation on the part of youth leaders in the countries of Europe.

The First Assembly of the World Council of Churches authorized the constitution of a Youth Department, and the instrument, known as "Charter of the Youth Department," embodied, in substance, the "Statement of Policy of the Youth Department" adopted by the Provisional Committee at Buck Hill Falls, in 1947.[55] The Central Committee at its first meeting approved a document setting forth a constitution (see Appendix) as well as the policy of the Department:

The Policy of the Youth Department

We affirm with thanksgiving our belief that the formation of the World Council of Churches and of the Youth Department within it is a significant part of the answer of Christ's prayer "that they all may be one . . . that the world may believe." We agree that on this basis the Youth Department must

[55] See Part Two, Section II, *4*. p. 204.

always have as its ultimate aim the development of the means for the united witness in speech and action of all younger members of the Christian churches. It also means that the Youth Department should encourage young people to participate fully and responsibly in the life and witness of their own churches and of the World Council.

In practice the Youth Department is charged by the World Council with direct responsibility for developing the ecumenical concern of the younger members of the churches and for providing channels for united ecumenical action on the world level. The Youth Department will not confine its activities either (a) to Christian youth organized in church youth groups or movements, or (b) to the younger members of the churches which are formally members of the World Council. In the widest sense, the Youth Department is intended to be an instrument (a) for expressing the concern of the churches for youth, and (b) for expressing the concern of Christian youth for the ecumenical movement which finds a partial but rich expression in the formation of the World Council of Churches.

Hence, it is the clear duty of the Youth Department to be the means whereby (a) Church youth may help each other, and (b) Christian youth work within the various churches may be strengthened. It is the policy of the Youth Department to work always for the creation of the widest possible fellowship of Christian young people within the Universal Church.

Since the World Council is a World Council of Churches, the younger members of these churches are organically related to the Council through their respective churches. The Youth Department will constantly seek to develop among younger church members the sense of belonging to the ecumenical movement and of participation in the work of the World Council, but the Department as such has no membership. The Department will also co-operate with interdenominational youth organizations which desire to relate themselves to the ecumenical work of the World Council.

It is the policy of the Youth Department to encourage the largest possible measure of participation by young people themselves in the formulation of policy and direction of activities at the local, national, regional and world levels.

7. The Laity

The main emphasis of the laymen's program under the World Council of Churches was on obeying the Christian calling in daily work. In a report at the First Assembly on "The Significance of the Laity in the Church," a special committee, "which had been appointed to meet the widespread need expressed by the churches in many parts of the world for a consideration of the urgent question of the right use and training of the laity in the service of the Church," went beyond the somewhat restricted scope of its assignment and said that men should be not only used to a much greater extent in the churches but also helped to understand and render a true Christian stewardship in the affairs of the world outside, with which they perforce spent most of their time. Concerning this kind of mission, it spoke of "experiments in various countries" with "new aspects of the significance of the laity for the Church," and suggested holding "area meetings, largely of laymen, for the purpose of further study of efforts for enlisting the full lay power." The question to be explored for a full and clear answer was, it declared: "How can members of the Church be enabled to see the bearing of their Christian faith on their life in their occupations . . . [and] to obey just there the will of God?"

While not new, the idea that Christians should serve the calling of God in the secular sphere was in the ecumenical context carried beyond the traditional teaching of mere loyalty to principles of honesty and fair dealing in business and given a social application involving endeavor by them to change the conditions under which they worked, as well as the motives which many workers brought to their tasks, so that their regular occupations would become a means of spiritual, and not only material, blessing and of witness to the Christian way of life.

The leaflet with the title "The Christian in His Vocation" prepared by the study commission on the laity, of which Dr. Hendrik Kraemer was Chairman and Dr. Hans Hermann Walz Secretary, later developed this view in comparison with others. It asked the question "What is the relevance of the Christian faith to the world of work?" and proceeded to discuss possible answers. There were those, it recognized, who held that the churches had no particular message beyond the general injunction to be upright, sober, and industrious, and no technical competence to advise people concerning their jobs, and so should not attempt to deal with the problems of this sphere.

However, others understood that all kinds of work raised ethical questions for which instruction and counsel were needed and that the churches had a duty to take cognizance of these. A third school went farther and proposed that the Christian message should "assess all social relationships and supply motive power for re-moulding society, including its vast domain of labor." "All those activities in the economic, political and cultural fields, which help man in one way or another to maintain and enrich his life upon this earth, must be examined," they said, "in the light of the Christian faith." And these last represented in a general way the theory on which the laymen's work under the World Council of Churches proceeded.

What it came to, when translated into practical terms under ecumenical auspices, appeared in resolutions adopted by a conference of "prominent laymen" on "The Christian in Industry" under the sponsorship of the Australian Council for the World Council of Churches in 1952:

To encourage the growth of Christian fellowship in . . . industry;
To put loyalty to Christ first in daily work and relationships with fellow-workers;
To see our own jobs as avenues of Christian service;
To act within our own industry in the conviction that industry was made for man, and not man for industry;

To encourage active Christian participation in all groups concerned with industry—employers' organizations, management institutes, and trade-unions;
To strive for regular consultation at all levels between management and men for the purpose of achieving mutual respect and common service;
To seek the facts in all industrial disputes and help in every possible way towards their solution;
To promote lay conferences in . . . industrial centers to have these points put into effect;
To stand ready to follow up this program in local churches or lay organizations.

While there was nothing new in this construction of the Christian vocation, events in the world at the time had for increasing numbers of people seemed to invest with fresh urgency the social responsibility of religion it set forth. Two global wars within a generation had left the churches stunned by the near collapse of civilization over vast areas of the earth and by the realization of their own apparent impotence to stay the downward rush of the nations toward worse disaster. As the committee reporting at Amsterdam had found in its investigations, churchmen in many countries, clergy and laity, had been driven to consultation on possible ways of making the power of the Christian faith effective again in the economic and political realm, as it once had been—at least to a degree giving some security to life in Christendom, which had, they felt, all but ceased to exist.

With its founding in 1946, the Ecumenical Institute had become "a center of interest in the re-awakening of the Church through the spiritual mobilization of the laity." It had convened at Chateau de Bossey in 1947 such leaders of European lay groups as could be brought together. According to a report of the meeting, those who came "were filled with amazement to see to what extent this was a gathering of fellow-workers who had been, without knowing it, engaged for years on what to all intents and purposes was the same work," i.e., bridging the gulf the cataclysms of revolution and war had shown to exist between the churches and the world.

The Amsterdam Assembly had received the report on "The Significance of the Laity in the Church" but taken no action to constitute a department of work with laymen. "The right use and training of the laity in the service of the Church" had been one of the "concerns" during the provisional decade, and it remained so, with the experience of the Ecumenical Institute during the past two years suggesting a first step in the acceptance of responsibility for it.

Whatever might be done to mobilize and educate the men of the churches would have an important bearing upon the programs of all the departments of the World Council of Churches, and it was seen that a logical action would be to set up a committee representing them to supervise the movement. This was done, with the appointment of Dr. Kraemer of the Institute as Chairman. Soon thereafter, Rev. Denis Baly, on furlough from missionary duty in Palestine, was made Secretary for one year. In 1949 Dr. Hans Hermann Walz succeeded him, and the financing of the office became, with his administration, a project of the Department of Inter-Church Aid, toward the support of which special gifts were received "from certain interested churches."

Dr. Walz had been instrumental in the founding of the Evangelical Academy at Bad Boll, Germany, near the close of World War II, which provided for prisoners of war a chance to study during their internment, and had served as secretary of the study association of all the Evangelical Academies of that country. Although a clergyman, he was experienced in laymen's work. In 1952 he became Assistant Director of the Ecumenical Institute, on a half-time basis, and thenceforward carried the duties of that post with the secretaryship of the Council for work with the laity.

A serious question of policy early arose. The Ecumenical Institute, through its Director, Dr. Kraemer, and his associates, had interested itself helpfully in the lay groups of the churches near and far. Dr. Kraemer had become President of the European Laymen's Conference. Should the Secretary, Dr. Walz, or whoever might in future be called to that position, be the representative of the general lay movement at the headquarters of the World Council of Churches? Many thought he should and hoped he might. The Committee on Laymen's Work decided against this proposal, in favor of the establishment of a distinctive program for men under the Council. This, it must be said, was more in keeping with the character of the Council as an organ of the churches as such, and it was wise from the standpoint of practical considerations, when the great diversity of ideas, aims and circumstances presented by the 150 or so lay organizations "from Ceylon to Norway and from India to the United States of America," which would have been involved, was taken into account. The World Council could more properly limit itself to the largest practicable degree of unofficial counsel than undertake to become the organ of a movement to gather them into a world body. Like the women and the young people, laymen had representation in the Council through their denominations and would be entitled to every consideration that could be given their interests.

The Committee on Laymen's Work had three general objectives: Fundamentally, it aimed to establish the view that the spiritual renewal of the churches depended on the laity's serving the calling of God in their secular work. The chasm between the churches and the world could be bridged in no other way. There could be no really effective evangelism without it. The moral reclamation of society waited upon it. This became the burden of pronouncements, conferences, and study programs for laymen.

In the second place, the Committee sought to make contacts with national and regional lay groups of the various countries. It knew and had record of 150 or more—*Kerk en Wereld* in Holland, the Evangelical Academies and the *Kirchentag* in Germany, *Associations Professionelles* in France, *Zoē* and *Aktinēs* in Greece, and similar institutes, associations, and conferences in many other nations. It began in 1951 the publication of a semiannual bulletin with the title *Laymen's Work* as a means of keeping alive its relations with them and of providing them with information about one another, practical suggestions for lay programs, and reports of significant ecumenical activities at the headquarters of the World Council of Churches in Geneva.

As a result of its efforts in these directions, the Committee felt justified in saying in a report recording its activities during this early period of the World Council's history:

> It is certain that in these years thousands . . . all over the world, have experienced anew the living truth of the Christian message through the discovery that . . . [it] is related in an astonishing way to the facts of everyday life . . . and to the problems, perplexities and "achievements of our age."

In 1949 the Central Committee began action toward implementing the recommendation of the committee on "The Significance of the Laity in the Church" that "area meetings" be arranged "for the purpose of further study of efforts for enlisting the full lay power of the Church." Two conferences were held—one at Bad Boll, Germany, in 1951, and the other at Buffalo, New York, in 1952. Each gathering was attended by approximately four hundred persons, including a considerable number of clergymen.

The American meeting was organized under the joint auspices of the National Councils of Churches of the United States and of Canada and marked a somewhat new departure in this respect. "Whilst in Europe the meeting was more in the nature of a confirmation of what had been done by the various groups, so far . . . ," explained the report from Geneva, "the meeting in America . . . started a process of re-thinking the relations between the Christian faith and the daily work of ordinary people which is being followed up by various undertakings."

Dr. Walz attended the Buffalo Conference and wrote later in *The Ecumenical Review* (Fall, 1952) concerning lay activity in the United States:

> A dynamic new interest in religion is evident among laymen and lay women in the United States. . . . You find this interest coming to life, for instance, in the conferences which have been held in Buffalo and elsewhere under the sponsorship of the Department of Church and Economic Life of the National Council of Churches. . . . Groups of laymen of many trades and professions have been meeting to give serious consideration to the impli-

cations of their Christian faith in relation to their various daily vocations, as engineers, teachers, doctors, house-wives, farmers, salesmen, industrialists. Groups of office managers, . . . store-owners, . . . lawyers have been meeting to explore in what ways their avowed Christian belief puts new and different responsibilities upon them in relation to these everyday occupations. Many people think that this means new life and energy for the whole Church, and that through this renewal the Church will re-energize and re-Christianize a society which [was] slipping . . . rapidly into secularism.

Another channel through which Dr. Walz found religion influencing the life of the United States was the retreats for laymen, such as Parishfield in Michigan and the Faith and Life Center in Austin, Texas. "Here laymen have an opportunity to explore their responsibility as Christians to the whole of life, including politics, patterns of economic development and cultural contacts," he wrote. "Since religion deals, not with one compartment, but with the whole of life, such an over-all view is most important."

Dr. Walz commented on the "unlimited potential of the United States, as to both land and churches." Drawing a parallel with the countries of Asia, in which Christian minorities gave public leadership much out of proportion to their numbers, he suggested that "the Christians of America must not only form the leaven of their own society, but must exert the kind of influence which would help the United States to realize her responsibility for world leadership, and to interpret it, not in terms of political power, but of Christian service."

The sociological orientation of laymen's work under the World Council of Churches had its explanation in a complex of factors, which included the Study Department's need of somebody to develop the subject "The Meaning of Work," the second half of the "divided inquiry on 'Christian Action in Society,'" and the ready availability of the Ecumenical Institute, which had been—at least semiofficially—sponsor of the interchurch lay movement. Progress in Christian social action depended on the enlistment and education of the laity. The conferences and courses for men at Bossey had made liberal use of the Report of Section III of the Amsterdam Assembly on "The Church and the Disorder of Society" and of the influential book by Dr. J. H. Oldham on *Work in Modern Society*. These source writings elaborated the theory of social Christianity the Department wanted promoted.

Most of the leaders in the laymen's program were clergy of European background, who, whether from predilection or force of circumstance, regarded as nearest to the Christian ideal the types of socialistic state to which they were accustomed. While they would have agreed that no socio-political system could be equated with the kingdom of God, they believed that all the nations would have eventually to come to some kind of collectivistic economy; and with this opinion, it should be said, not a few prominent American ecumenical leaders concurred.[56]

At Amsterdam there had been considerable shaking of heads by laymen, particularly those from America, when they encountered these ideas, but with bishops and archbishops advancing them as of the gospel and other clerics of all degrees of authority assenting, they had acquiesced. Only scattered voices had been raised in protest or questioning; and by the passing of "the first six years" the social philosophy and policy of the World Council of Churches had, in their broad outlines, been developed and accepted.

In this conception of what was called "a responsible society," evangelism was linked with action looking to improvement of the material conditions of life. Besides fulfilling the requirements of justice, this approach, it was suggested, would demonstrate to the unevangelized that the Christian religion offered something of immediate tangible advantage, and so would encourage them to give attention to the gospel, which, they had been misled to think, promised "only pie in the sky."

There were in ecumenical councils those who thought they saw in this reasoning a misplaced emphasis, if not an unconscious fallacy. Did it not contradict, they asked, both the teaching and the experience of Jesus? They recalled that the multitudes he had fed rejected him as decisively as those plotting his death, turning from him when they found that he would not consent to be "king" or "divider"; that these were not more disposed than the Pharisees to "seek first the Kingdom of God," and asked first for those things that would, he explained, "be added"; and that the penalty for gainsaying them was, a little way thence, the cross. Would the churches at Amsterdam not better have said "No" and gone, if they must, to their Calvary? The program of social amelioration stood always in danger of self-defeat, for the reason that human needs and desires always increase with their satisfaction. Even the dispensation of Christian charity was challenged constantly by this threat. The policy now evolving would inevitably carry the churches to the point beyond which they could not go and remain the Church. The time would come when they would have to say "No" and take up their cross. Then, for all that they had made the cause of the people their own, their social ministry would not save them. It would be misunderstood, as was their Lord's. ("Ye follow me because I fed you"—John vi, 26.) In the eyes of the masses, they would suffer then as defenders of the *status quo* and dissemblers who had thought to win them by outbidding the kingdoms of the world.

"Labour not for the meat that perisheth, but for that meat which endureth unto eternal life, which the Son . . . shall give you" (John vi, 27-35). This gift it was the mission of the churches to proclaim.

[56] An evolutionary movement toward socialism was by many considered necessary to forestall violent revolution.

Only as men received it would the problem of "all these things" be solved. All needed it alike, the "haves" and the "have-nots." Without it, the new nations that were asking for independence, self-government, industrial development, education, and the rest of "these things" could only multiply their own sorrows and add to the strife and chaos of the earth; and the older nations, if they continued to reject it, could look forward to no peace. East and West could never meet except in common disaster, falling to their doom in the ever widening gulf sundering them.

So it seemed to some of the voiceless at Amsterdam and in the years that followed. It was certain that the lostness of mankind called for a witnessing with power. Although hoping that they were wrong, they had in honesty to put a question mark after ecumenical social evangelism.

8. Women and the World Council of Churches

The denominations limited voting representation in the Council to delegates appointed officially by them. They made it strictly a council of churches. Under this plan, the clergy continued predominant numerically, as they had been during the provisional period. From their ranks came the majority of the members of the First Assembly, and the range of selection had been narrowed, in most instances, largely to those who held offices in their denominations. They presided. They did most of the talking. They elected, to run the World Council of Churches, officers mainly from their own contingent.

The laymen, whose number was very small; the women, who were fewer still; and the young people, with only a delegate or so, talked about "the tight clerical control." They understood, however, that it could hardly have been different. In an organization of denominations, who if not the bishops and secretaries and their aides would have been best qualified to serve? Their appointment had been tantamount to a vote of confidence by their churches and had been anticipated. Without them the World Council of Churches could not have been set upon its way or got anywhere.

The young people were quite content with their position in the Assembly. With time on their side, they could wait. The average age of delegates must have been as reported, close to sixty. The laymen generally coveted no special recognition. Most of them had come because of the urging of the clergy, who thought the movement needed them. For what it wanted them they were themselves uncertain. Much of the discussion was "over their heads," and the actions were often of little practical meaning from their point of view. This suggested that somebody would have to translate what went on into the language of the streets, but they were not attracted to that job, not understanding it very well themselves.

But the women had another mind. They desired to be in the Council. They thought that they knew what it was about or at least could learn. They had done what they could, in advance, to open the door. And they succeeded beyond their own hopes, and certainly beyond the expectations of others. With fewer than a dozen delegates, they went home from Amsterdam with two places in the Central Committee and one in the small Executive Committee.

The noteworthiness of this accomplishment was emphasized by an official statement which had been issued a short time previously by the Central Committee:

> For some years . . . a certain number of women have been able to participate fully in the ecumenical movement, thanks to the Youth Movements—World's Student Christian Federation and the World's Young Women's Christian Association—but when they pass the age limit of youth organizations, their churches are hesitant to associate them with ecumenical work, or barely tolerate their participation.[57]

Many ecumenical leaders, including some of the clergy, thought that a status of equality with other members should be given to women, but the women did not leave their fate in the hands altogether of their advocates. "As early as 1946, the General Secretariat was eager to make the churches aware of the aspirations of women to give more complete service, and also of the work done by women in the Church, often without appreciation. Mrs. Samuel McCrea Cavert was, therefore, asked to initiate an inquiry on 'The Life and Work of Women in the Church.' "[58] This announcement from Geneva may be taken at its face meaning, but behind it had been strong prompting. The appointment of Mrs. Cavert revealed the main source of the importunity. The women of the United States, accustomed to their separate societies and broader responsibilities in the management of their churches, looked with unconcealed disapproval upon the prospect of having to confine themselves in the World Council of Churches to the traditional role of inspiring others who would actually do the work. They wished to lend a hand. Some women of other countries shared increasingly this desire. Said Miss Saroe Chakko of India, "What is happening to women in the world . . . is an urge toward usefulness." They thought, moreover, that the Council needed them. They were aware of their possession of powers men lacked. Were they not more adept at grasping the practical elements of problems and finding solutions? And were they not less bound by stereotyped procedures, traditions, theologies? A doubtful recommendation,

[57] *The First Six Years,* p. 53.
[58] *Ibid.,* p. 54.

those who would have restrained their enthusiasm said! But they had their own opinion, and, for all that an apostle with followers at Amsterdam had bidden women keep silent in the church, they expressed it. So, they were invited, eagerly or not, "to initiate an inquiry."

All things in the ecumenical movement began with inquiries, and some died with them. But this time there was not to be any casualty. "A questionnaire was sent out to the authorities of all World Council member churches, and to a number of women outstanding for their work in their own churches. Of all the inquiries issued by the World Council of Churches before the Assembly this questionnaire evoked by far the greatest number of serious, thoughtful and varied answers." So runs the record. "A temporary secretariat" had to be formed, it is added, "to sort out and file the replies and present them . . . to the Assembly." There the whole matter might have ended, but it did not. "As only a few women were to be present there [at the Assembly], it was decided to hold a 'consultation' of women at Baarn [Holland] before the Assembly convened." [59]

Here occurs a hiatus in the report which we are consulting, and next we read, "In compliance with the wish expressed at Baarn and agreed to by the special committee entrusted with this question at Amsterdam, the Assembly recommended the establishment of a Commission." The women had demonstrated their power of practical initiative and persistence.

This action of the Assembly did not establish a women's department in the World Council of Churches, as the impression generally was. It only continued the inquiry, with the possibility of a widening of its scope. The way was opened, however, for the development of some services of ecumenical nature to women.

The Central Committee had been authorized to implement the action, and this it did at its meeting in Chichester a year later, to the extent of choosing the personnel of the Commission and prescribing its functions. The work of the Commission, at least to start with, was defined as follows:

To publish a book based on the responses to the 1946 inquiry, and to stimulate the thinking of the churches on the question of the place of women in the Church;

To institute a special study on man-woman relationships in the light of biblical teaching and of the traditions of the Church;

To give help to women by encouraging the exchange of information and experience between various groups, and by inviting more women to participate directly in ecumenical work.[60]

The Commission met as a complete body only once—at Oxford, England, in September, 1952, three years after its appointment. There

[59] *Ibid.* p. 54.
[60] *Ibid.* p. 54.

had been a conference of some of the members at the Chateau de Bossey, Céligny, Switzerland, in February, 1950, at which Mrs. Kathleen Bliss had been chosen Chairman of the Commission and Miss Saroe Chakko Secretary. Here a schedule of activities had been projected "as definite and clear-cut," whoever wrote up the meeting for *The Ecumenical Review* said, "as that of any department of the Council."

Mrs. Bliss had been asked to write the book authorized by the Central Committee, and it had been published before the Commission met at Oxford under the title *The Service and Status of Women in the Church.* A pamphlet entitled *A Study of Man-Woman Relationship* also had been brought out and was being translated into a number of languages, there being a considerable demand for it for use in study programs.

At Oxford Miss Chakko reported her visits in Canada, the United States, Scandinavia, the Middle East, Greece, Great Britain, Germany, and France. In all these countries she had made pleasant and fruitful contacts with women and their organizations. It had been necessary for her to relinquish the secretaryship of the Commission in August, 1951, but she had accepted the chairmanship, Mrs. Bliss having resigned. She presided at Oxford and, although now a President of the World Council of Churches, accepted re-election. Mlle Madeleine Barot was appointed Secretary, her duties to begin in January, 1953. Between Miss Chakko's resignation in 1951 and Mlle Barot's assumption of office, Mrs. Bliss served as Secretary on a part-time basis.

By the time it met at Oxford, the Commission had succeeded, despite its inability to hold regular meetings, in arriving at a consensus on the principles that should govern the development of its program. These stemmed from the fundamental agreement which had been reached, that woman's place was alongside man in a complementary relationship, not in the background merely supplementing what he might do, nor conducting on her own a more or less parallel effort with essentially the same aims.

An address by Miss Chakko before a conference on "Men and Women in Church and Society" at St. Andrews, Scotland, at about the time of the Oxford meeting of the Commission reflected the thinking leading to this conclusion, and what she said may be summarized.

In earlier agricultural and craft societies, she pointed out, women worked beside men, each undertaking the phase of the task at hand for which he or she was especially endowed. With the arrival of industrialization, man came to be thought of as the wage earner and woman as "a decorative adjunct." Although woman had power, in both the church and the community, she missed the interest of creative work and the satisfaction of having responsibility and a feeling of worth in the sense of being useful. Even her function of homemaking had been given over largely to others. Schools, playgrounds, motion-picture houses, and clubs of various kinds relieved her of the children's care.

Women could take one of three attitudes regarding their place in the church and community, continued Miss Chakko. They could assume a strictly supplementary role in relation to men, concerning themselves with protecting and serving husbands and children, and wielding power by influencing them, rather than by bearing responsibility themselves. Or they could try to be like men and equal to them, in which case they would often imitate the worst rather than the best in them. If man and woman got the same kind of education and entered into the same fields of work, a competitive relationship would inevitably result. Or they might seek to establish a complementary relationship which would allow for individual differences and, with careful planning, give both a chance to make their best contributions and enjoy the highest sense of individual well-being.

From this point of view, it became clear, in the first place, that woman's status in the church could not be determined apart from man's. If it was the will of God that their relationship should be complementary, they would have to work it out together. The problem belonged to both, not to woman only.

The Commission had consisted originally of women. Some men had been added, at its request; and in 1953 it was asking that the next chairman be a man, and that a second executive secretary, if money to employ one could be found, also be a man. Further, it was recommending that its name be changed, "to remove the impression that it [was] the 'Women's Department' of the World Council of Churches," to "Department on Co-operation of Men and Women in Church and Society."

It was seen, also, that the right man-woman relationship, as it appeared in the reasoning of the Commission, presented problems the solution of which would be influenced by conditions in the world outside the Church. In the shaping of its life the Church had often followed the patterns of the social order, when its duty had been to demonstrate God's design. Where, if not in its fellowship, could there have been an example of the truly Christian partnership between man and woman? This was part of its witness. The teaching of the Bible needed to be re-examined and religious traditions consulted for the light they would give. But the study the Commission must develop would have to take into account many more factors—the biological, psychological, sociological, economic, political, racial, and others. Indeed, there was no phase of life unrelated to this central concern.

The work of the Commission as it unfolded in this perspective grew to forbidding dimensions. Mrs. Bliss spoke at Oxford of "the enormous size of the phenomenon with which we are dealing." Where could be found the time and the resources for it, especially the time? The kingdom of God was long and the years fleeting. If there was not to be some kind of world organization of church women, with offices to be filled, meetings to attend, and money to be raised, could interest in such a long-term and unspectacular program as that called for be created and sustained? There were the books for study. They had been prepared, as requested by the Central Committee. And the invitation to women "to participate directly in ecumenical work" would be given in every possible way, as the Committee had directed. But there were already too many study books, and the only place in which the average woman could do ecumenical work was the home parish, which as often as not was indifferent or hostile. There, of course was where such work needed most to be done, had to be done, in fact, if the ecumenical movement was to succeed. But could women be got to see their opportunity to make this large contribution to the cause, and the enrichment of life it held out to them?

Much would depend on the attitude of pastors and laymen—on their cooperation or the lack of it—and cultivating them would be part of the Commission's responsibility. But that, also, would be slow work, with many obstacles. Not all had faith to endure while seeking "a city which had foundations"; and, although many were able to look back to those who had been steadfast and say with rejoicing, "They, without us, were not made perfect," only the solitary few could find joy for the struggle in the thought that their work would be made complete in the greater successes of those who would come after them.

Then there would not be, by any means, universal acceptance of the Commission's reasoning on the status of woman or her relationship with man. Neither those who believed the traditional role of woman in the church as helper and inspirer of man should be continued nor those who thought that women should have their separate organizations and programs would admit as valid the differentiation which had been drawn between what had been called supplementary, competitive, and complementary relationships between the sexes. What the Commission had described as supplementary help by women was really, in the opinion of many, complementary in the ways divinely intended. Both man and woman gained by it, they believed, as did the church, and, though women might have their own work apart, they would be perfectly able and willing to coordinate it with whatever else the church might do. It would not be, in any sense, competitive with what men did. Nor was it accurate, in the view of many, to say that for the ministries of man and woman in the church to be made complementary they would have to be recast on such sweeping lines as those proposed.

It is easy to understand how those responsible for encouraging and finding ways for the participation of women in the ecumenical movement came to the end of this first period of the World Council of Churches with mingled feelings of discouragement and hope, as their statements and actions appear to show. The report of the Commission for inclusion in the survey of the Central Committee for the six years intervening, evidently prepared by its executive officials, contained this paragraph, which probably reflected the sentiments of others as well:

"It is difficult to say whether this re-examination [the study by the Commission since the Amsterdam Assembly] of the situation of women in the Church will procure for them wider openings in the service of the churches, or whether, on the contrary, it will result in a renewed and stricter subordination of woman's ministry to that of man's."

Less discouraged—or more expressive of the attitude in time of doubt of reaffirming judgments and staking out new endeavors—was the report of a meeting of "a small group of members of the Commission on the Life and Work of Women in the Church" at Bossey in September, 1953, "to plan the work of the Commission up to the time of the Evanston Assembly":

All the discussions . . . were undergirded by the re-affirmation of . . . basic principles which have always governed the work of the Commission. . . .

(1) Woman's place in Church and society is not just a woman's problem. . . . It is just as wrong to leave it to women, as is so often done today, as it was to have men make all the decisions . . . , as was too often the case in the past.

(2) The Church needs the full employment of all its resources in the fulfillment of its mission, therefore the spiritual gifts of all its members are needed. The Church cannot afford to miss the opportunity which would follow from harmonious collaboration of the two sexes.

(3) The churches must re-consider the place of women, not only for the sake of their own inner life, but also to give an answer and a witness before the world which is very much aware of this issue. It is not enough for the churches just to let things drift along, either clinging to their old traditions on the one hand, or merely following the present-day trends in the secular world on the other. . . .

It was decided that, as a sequel to the study outline on "Man-Woman Relationship" . . . the churches should be invited to join in an enquiry into "The Biblical Message Regarding the Co-operation of Men and Women": (i) In the life of the Church; (ii) in the life of society; (iii) in the life of the family.

In order to carry . . . further . . . the earlier survey which resulted in the publication of Kathleen Bliss's *Service and Status of Women in the Church,* the Commission considered making a survey of all the existing women's organizations in the . . . churches of the World Council; but it became apparent at once that there was a parallel question which also needed examination: "The Place of Man in Church and Society." For this reason it was decided that the study envisaged should be broadened to include the various types of Christian organizations which are specifically masculine or feminine, the reasons for their existence, their present-day activities, etc. . . .

The Commission is looking forward eagerly to the kind of response that the member churches will make in choosing their delegations to the Evanston Assembly. The official invitation to the Assembly asked the . . . churches to consider including women among the delegates. It is still too soon to tell just how many women will actually be present at Evanston, but first indications are that much work still remains to be done before the Commission on the Life and Work of Women in the Church has achieved its aims!

It was of interest that the investigations of the Commission discovered less agitation over ordination for women than was generally supposed to exist. More than forty denominations of the United States ordained women, it had been found, among them several of the major ones. A number of others licensed them. The question had come to be considered as not of first importance in relation to women's position in the churches, but as only part of the general problem. "In many countries women have been ordained for both preaching and administering the sacraments," reported Mlle Madeleine Barot, "without really altering the status of the average woman in the churches in any way."

Bishop Fjellbu, a member of the Commission, of Trondheim, Norway, had given the problem of women's work in the Church much study at the experiential level and spoke helpfully, on more than one occasion, concerning it, from the standpoint particularly of the principle of "complementary," or "integrated," relationship between woman and man. He emphasized the special gifts women had for pastoral counseling and ministry to the sick, the need for which was greater than the average pastor could meet. This situation in the churches offered opportunity, he thought, for cooperation by men and women in very essential work. "The more crowded life becomes, the greater the problems of the lonely," he said. "But the Church is a community—a family in which those alone must be able to find their place, knowing that God never forgets anyone." The three problems which, more often than all others, were brought to the pastor, he suggested, were suffering, loneliness, and sex; and they were intertwined in all kinds of patterns. To persons troubled by them man and woman in a joint ministry could give better guidance, he believed, than either working singly. "If men and women will serve as Christian fellow-workers," he concluded, "the Church could again become the leaven of society."

The philosophy at which the Commission arrived with substantial unanimity, as set forth in two reports, or memoranda, on the discussion at its Oxford conference in September, 1952, will repay study by those who follow the ecumenical interest of women with special concern. (See Appendix D.)

9. Inter-Church Aid and Service to Refugees

The Department of Inter-Church Aid and Service to Refugees continued in the World Council of Churches the Department of Reconstruction and Inter-Church Aid of the provisional period. The new double title indicated something of its functions and history.

The original purpose had been to repair the damage to church buildings in bombed zones of World War II and to provide material relief for their people. By 1948 this work had begun to give place to aid of more permanent character aimed at enabling the churches to prepare themselves better for their mission of spiritual reconstruction and meeting the more or less long-term needs of the homeless displaced millions adrift in the war's wake.

This change of emphasis the Central Committee recorded at its meeting in Chichester, England, in 1949:

> The Central Committee decided to remind the member churches that Inter-Church Aid is a permanent obligation of a World Council of Churches which seeks to be true to its name; that many of the churches of Europe are in dire need of assistance as they take their part in the great spiritual struggle of our day; that the millions of refugees in Europe have an urgent and incontrovertible claim upon the help of the churches; and, therefore, that a fresh approach must be made by the churches which are in position to help to their members for renewed and generous giving on behalf of their fellow-Christians in Europe.[61]

During its first years, at the outset under the Provisional Committee and later under the World Council of Churches, the Department's main activity had related to Europe. By the time of the Central Committee's meeting at Chichester in 1949, however, attention had begun to turn to the urgent need for a like ministry in other continents. The Joint Committee of the World Council of Churches and the International Missionary Council by a resolution at Chichester began "a study of the strategy of inter-church aid on a world scale." The results of this inquiry were to take definite shape three years afterwards at the meeting of the Central Committee in Lucknow, India, as outlined by the report of a special Reference Sub-Committee from the Joint Committee and recorded in the Annual Minutes (p. 54) for 1953:

> The Reference Sub-Committee has studied the proposed plan for co-operation between the International Missionary Council and the World Council of Churches for emergency inter-church aid and relief in countries outside Europe. It welcomes the suggestion that the Department of Inter-Church Aid and Service to Refugees should be entrusted with this responsibility. . . . At the same time, the Reference Sub-Committee realizes that this plan will only become a reality in so far as member churches, mission boards and Christian relief agencies enter into the fullest ecumenical co-operation; it would, therefore, ask the members of the Central Committee to do everything in their power to ensure that this new approach to the pressing emergency needs of the churches in countries outside Europe may receive the cordial support of all who are in a position to make it effective.

[61] Minutes of the Central Committee, Chichester, 1949, p. 26.

The broader work thus conceived would be, outside Europe, mainly on the mission fields, and care would have to be taken lest it interfere with the churches' regular missionary giving and administration. It would have to do, as stated, with "emergency needs," such as those arising from wars and natural disasters, for which the regular funds and organizations of the mission boards would not be adequate.

The provisional Department of Reconstruction and Inter-Church Aid at the beginning of the postwar program acted as an agency for receiving and administering both money and materials for relief, alongside and, when possible, in cooperation with the numerous other bodies working in the same field. By the time it had become the Department of Inter-Church Aid and Service to Refugees—that is, after the organization of the World Council of Churches in 1948—it had found itself drawn more and more by changing circumstances into the role of coordinator, in which its "principal function" had become "to provide, on the basis of mutual study and consultation, a total strategy of Inter-Church Aid and Service to Refugees in which the initiative and programmes of the churches and national committees [could] be related to one another, and thus be given maximum usefulness." [62]

From 1948 onward, an "annual consultation" brought to Geneva representatives of the churches, where they could get from one another's reports a general view of need throughout the world and guidance in determining where and in what ways they could lead their organizations to serve most effectively and with least overlapping. From that point, leadership in the over-all plans for the rest of the year passed to the Administrative Committee of the Department, meeting quarterly with a staff consisting of a director, an associate director, and executive and publicity secretaries. This small corps of officers stood at the center of the process of interchurch aid, by travel, conferences, and correspondence "facilitating the practical help which churches [might] render one another," and taking responsibility for their cooperative action on behalf of refugees in Europe and for emergencies, of whatever nature, as they arose.

Of these latter there was a steady succession—civil war in Greece; harvest failures in Yugoslavia, Pakistan, and India; war and famine in Korea; an earthquake in the Ionian Islands; floods in Holland and Japan; and sudden influxes of refugees into Germany, Hong Kong and other places, which overtaxed facilities that could be furnished locally.

While aid toward the reconstruction of churches damaged by wars and natural catastrophes had in some measure, of necessity, to be continued, as had the feeding of the hungry and the serving of all the other elemental human needs, the sense of the very great importance of providing also what came to be called "spiritual aid" increased. Churches asked, not only for new buildings, but for assistance in

[62] See *The First Six Years*, p. 64.

creating new life, and discovered the deeper significance of mutual help, it was reported, when they joined efforts to strengthen one another's internal structure and ability to bear their full Christian witness in the world.

The work looking to the inner renewal of the churches began with measures to safeguard the health and further the education of their leaders. The high incidence of disease from malnutrition, particularly of tuberculosis, had begun to drop after the ending of hostilities and the returning availability of food for normal diet, so that the resources which had been employed in caring for the sick could be applied increasingly to preventive steps, such as supplementing inadequate salaries and means for vacations in the case of underpaid priests and pastors. Casa Locarno, the rest home for ministers and other church workers maintained jointly with the Swiss Inter-Church Aid Commission, brought holidays and the opportunity for recuperation within the reach of many who otherwise could not have afforded them. And the fellowship there with colleagues from different countries and confessions had its renewing power, no less than the invigorating air and warm sunshine of the mountains and lakes of the Southern Alps.

As for theological training, help had, of necessity, been given at first to the churches isolated by war and unable to keep up their schools and seminaries. Some twelve hundred scholarships had been made available to students at institutions outside their own countries. With the return of more nearly normal conditions, it had become possible to select candidates for supplementary training abroad, with special reference to their ability to share with their congregations their new experiences and impressions. Some attended seminaries of other confessions than their own, which had the effect of furthering their ecumenical education.

With the ending of World War II, a plan had been inaugurated for opening to young people, mainly from the United States, the opportunity to serve as fraternal workers "within the framework of European countries." They responded in considerable numbers and, on the whole, gave a good account of themselves. The interest on the part of the volunteers and of the churches served was such that they mutually desired to continue the relationship when the actual need out of which it developed had largely passed. According to an ecumenical leader in a position to appraise what had been accomplished, "the presence of the young people in work of this kind can be a guarantee of the health of other interchurch aid transactions: it translates interchurch aid out of purely financial terms into those of personal relationships."

In the same way the work camps, which have been described in the chapter on the Youth Department, proved to be a cumulatively creative movement. They undertook and carried through needed projects which otherwise, because of their expense and personnel requirements would not have been attempted; and in each instance they became schools of practical ecumenical experience, the effects of which proved far-reaching.

The Department early saw in the lay movement a direct channel through which to work for the spiritual rebirth of the churches. It believed that the laity, if enlisted and trained for the Christian vocation in daily life, would be able to interpret the true meaning of the gospel to the world in clear and compelling terms, and so to give special power to the churches' evangelistic mission. From designated gifts by persons and denominations in agreement with this view, it made available funds for the support of a secretary of laymen's work (H. H. Walz) under the World Council, with an office at Geneva, who, at its nomination in 1949, was duly elected by the Central Committee.

In these and other ways the World Council attempted to respond to the appeal of the churches for assistance with the work of spiritual reconstruction to which they felt themselves especially called in societies whose moral collapse had almost eclipsed even their physical devastation. What could be done was generally not of spectacular nature and never of adequate proportions, in comparison with the massive problem confronting them, but the chosen principle of approach, as time passed, commended itself with increasing assurance as the condition on which they could depend upon the power of God, to supplement their efforts as necessary.

Concerning the policy pursued in this work and the money and supplies involved, the Department in its report (See *The First Six Years*) for the interim between Assemblies had this to say:

Inter-Church Aid in Europe is multifarious in character. The Department has continued to put forward a programme of Inter-Church Aid Projects especially for those churches which seek advice on the use of available funds. There has also been the extensive programme of the Lutheran World Federation. Other confessional bodies, individual churches, and special societies have raised funds and administered them through the European churches. The Department has had neither the desire nor the power to direct all this spontaneous action into one channel. But it has endeavoured to be a reliable source of information on needs and gifts, and to provide an informal voluntary system of co-ordination. While some churches pass their Inter-Church Aid Funds through the accounts of the Department, and the Department is always ready to perform this service, the majority of transactions are carried out independently between the churches.

The task of co-ordination is not an easy one, and it has never proved possible to publish a document which would contain complete information. But each year a "Year-End Report" has been produced, showing, not the details, which would simply be confusing, but the variety and extent of Inter-Church Aid operations within the knowledge of the Department. Behind this Report lies a great deal of correspondence and advice which prevents overlapping and confusion. It is interesting to note that the figures recorded by the Department for total Inter-Church Aid and Service to

Refugees amounted in 1949 to fourteen million five hundred thousand dollars, in 1950 to ten million dollars, in 1951 to nine million, and in 1952 to eight million five hundred thousand dollars. These totals include Inter-mission Aid given on behalf of the work of the European churches in the area of the younger churches.

It will be noted that not all of this giving is in cash; at least half of it is in the form of contributed supplies of food, clothing and medicaments. In the early days of post-war reconstruction, material aid was obviously prominent in the minds of the churches. There was indeed a material aid section of the Department and essential help was brought not only to the churches but through the churches to men and women of every kind who were in need. At the Amsterdam Assembly the Committee on this work of the Department "felt that while the need for material aid still continue(d), the emphasis of the future work of the Department should more and more take into account the basic and continuing necessity of inter-church aid." This distinction was made in order to help the churches to understand that spiritual needs were not answered by the provision of food and clothing. At the same time, one of the ways in which some churches can best be helped in their main task of witness is in the provision of certain material goods which make their spiritual work possible.

In recent years a balance has been struck between the need for funds and the need for clothing and food. Indeed the work for refugees and the emergencies which have occurred have called for all the assistance that could be found at the material level. The Department is responsible each year for preparing a Contributed-Goods Programme for the whole of Europe. Special emphasis is placed upon areas of national disaster and upon refugees and refugee church groups. Through this programme church people do help to meet basic human needs, as well as contribute material aid to the churches. One good feature is that appeals for material aid in kind do not militate against appeals for inter-church aid funds. Often such material aid comes from people who would not contribute in cash to an inter-church aid or relief programme.

Reports at the Amsterdam Assembly estimated the total of dislocated persons in the world in 1948 variously at from twelve to twenty millions, a number by its very size discouraging attempts at remedial action. But common humanitarianism and the fact that many, perhaps a majority, of these unfortunate people belonged to the churches laid upon the World Council the obligation to do whatever it could to relieve their plight.

As a matter of fact, the Provisional Committee (before Amsterdam) had accepted this responsibility on behalf of the churches. At its first meeting, in January, 1939—before the actual outbreak of World War II—it had been brought to "face the challenge of the increasingly tragic situation of the refugees" and, with Dr. William Paton and the Bishop of Chichester, who was Chairman of the International Christian Committee for Refugees, urging immediate action, had appointed Dr. Adolf Freudenberg[63] to undertake the task of coordinating the work of

[63] Dr. Freudenberg was a trained diplomat of experience and so especially qualified for such work as the Council called him to.

the various church committees organizing to provide relief for refugees. Caught in Switzerland later that year by the sudden onrush of war, Dr. Freudenberg had been in a position to keep in touch with the countries where the refugee problem would become most acute and, with funds supplied largely by the churches of Switzerland, Sweden, and the United States, to organize a ministry of spiritual and material aid, at first mainly for Christian Jews fleeing from Germany, but also, by autumn of 1940, for the larger deportations of non-Aryans to southern France.

At the end of the hostilities there had been nine or ten million displaced persons in Europe to be resettled under the United Nations Refugee Repatriation Authority. Of these some million and a half had been unable or unwilling to return to the countries of their origin. In the face of such misery and spiritual isolation the Provisional Committee had in 1946 established a refugee division in the Department of Reconstruction and Inter-Church Aid under the administration of the Ecumenical Refugee Commission, which it had set up at the same time, with the Rev. Henry Carter of Great Britain as Chairman. The International Refugee Organization, upon succeeding to the work of the United Nations Refugee Repatriation Authority, had mandated the Commission "as a special agency for the welfare and spiritual care of Protestant and Eastern Orthodox Refugees."

With this heavy commitment, the Commission had also been obliged to accept responsibility in connection with the greater problem created by the expulsion under the Potsdam Agreement of the Sudeten Germans and the *Reichsdeutsche* of Poland and East Prussia and the *Volksdeutsche* of Austria and Hungary, which added to the already swollen streams of homeless many millions, with more still to come from the Danube basin and the countries of eastern Europe. Bereft of their possessions and destitute, denied citizenship and nationality, and adjudged ineligible for assistance by the United Nations for their care or resettlement, these people had been recognized as having a first claim on the conscience of the churches, some six million of them belonging to the Protestant and Eastern Orthodox confessions. A new organization, the World Council of Churches Refugee Commission, was set up as a joint agency through which the Department of Reconstruction and Inter-Church Aid, the Lutheran World Federation, and Church World Service, the main bodies in the field at this juncture, might minister to them.

The Provisional Committee had come to the Assembly at Amsterdam, therefore, with an almost overwhelming assignment of work on behalf of the dislocated and dispossessed for the World Council of Churches there to be founded. A brief résumé of a statement submitted with it will give some idea of its dimensions:

The present operations in the field consist of three distinct phases:

(1) The provision of a Christian ministry to refugees in the countries and camps of their temporary asylum. . . .

(2) Provision for the spiritual care and welfare of refugees resettling in new countries. . . .

(3) Recognizing that the only solution is re-settlement, the Commission is now giving increasing attention to the positive task of finding new homes for those looking to it.

The refugees . . . fall into three main groups. . . .

For the majority . . . under the mandate of the International Refugee Organization ultimate re-settlement can hopefully be regarded as a matter of time. . . . Meanwhile the Commission brings the Church to these people while they wait. The tragedy is that this category represents less than one-tenth of the total.

The second category comprises . . . nationals from ex-enemy satellite countries for whom repatriation is out of the question: Hungarians, Roumanians, Ukrainians and the like. They are both ineligible for United Nations care and incapable of settling in the Germany where they now live as pilgrims and strangers. . . . In many ways theirs is the most desperate situation of all. Re-settlement in new homes is its only solution, and what governments will not do for them men of goodwill must surely set their hands to.

The last and by far the largest group consists of the Reichsdeutsche and Volksdeutsche expellees. No realist would pretend that the problem of so many millions can be solved by re-settlement. The absorption of the vast majority of them into the German and Austrian economy is inevitable and may prove desirable. Meanwhile, they present a picture of destitution and despair, of . . . separated families and of a serious mal-distribution of ages and sexes which is a daily challenge to the Christian conscience. The burden that they constitute for the Churches in Germany is indescribable, and the Commission is convinced that it is the duty of all Churches for years to come to see to it that Churches in Germany which have the will to meet this need shall not be without means.

It is, of course, most earnestly hoped that a Refugee Commission need not be a permanent feature of the World Council of Churches' administration. For the moment, however, its continuance and, indeed, its development is essential, for the most reliable and optimistic estimates for the future suggest that this story of a decade can only be the prelude to at least another decade of . . . endeavour.

For something over three years after its founding, the World Council of Churches, through the Department of Inter-Church Aid and Service to Refugees, had collaborated with the International Refugee Organization in the service to those displaced persons who could not, or would not, return to their homelands under the administration of the United Nations Refugee Repatriation Authority. An excellent spirit of cooperation and significant results had marked this period, notwithstanding the somewhat premature liquidation of the International Refugee Organization in 1952. The number of dislocated persons in this category had by that time been reduced to approximately 400,000.

Extensive programs of resettlement, welfare, and support of churches in exile had been built up in Germany, Austria, France, Belgium, Italy, and Greece. With the help of Church World Service in the United States and of the national church committees elsewhere, the Department of Inter-Church Aid and Service to Refugees had assisted more than 100,000 displaced persons in migrating to new homes and finding self-sustaining employment.

The Lutheran World Federation,[64] with headquarters in Geneva and working in close coordination with the Department, had helped relocate some 75,000 more. In these operations, as in the welfare program and other services, the responsibility of the World Council of Churches was, as previously explained, for those particularly with Protestant or Orthodox connections and those without confessional relationships.

During the first part of this period the American churches had their own work in Europe, the Protestant and the Orthodox under Church World Service, in which they helped more than 350,000 refugees to find homes and employment under the Displaced Persons Act in the United States. In this extraordinary accomplishment, agencies of the Roman Catholic Church, the several groups of Jewry, and the Protestant and Eastern Orthodox churches had worked together.

When, in 1950, the work of Church World Service was merged with that of the Department of Inter-Church Aid and Service to Refugees, this wider policy of cooperation was continued, the World Council of Churches in its activities maintaining through its office at Geneva a close relationship, not only with the Lutheran World Federation, but also with the World's Alliance of the Young Men's Christian Associations and the World's Young Women's Christian Association, and a consultative exchange with the National Catholic Welfare Association, the Friends' Service Committee, and the Joint Committee of Jewish Organizations. It was one of the bodies on whose representations of existing need the Ford Foundation in 1952 made available some three million dollars for refugee projects. Moreover, it received part of this fund to be used in its own work with refugees.

After the discontinuance of the International Refugee Organization, the Council had established a satisfactory relationship with its successor, the Office of the United Nations High Commissioner for Refugees, in which its most manifest opportunity for service was helping the new agency "to be informed of . . . problems as they [arose] throughout the world and to act as one of the operative agents in providing solutions which [depended] for their success on the action of voluntary organizations." The experience in this connection had proved most happy. In the opinion of the Department of Inter-Church Aid and Service to Refugees, the relationship had been "one of the finest in-

[64] Many of the refugees were from countries in which Lutherans had strong churches.

stances of the value and necessity of co-operation in the humanitarian field between the churches and an inter-governmental agency."

The Council was able to evolve a practicable pattern of cooperation also with the Inter-governmental Committee for European Migration, which, while not specifically an agency for refugees, provided for them, as well as for others, certain of the services and skilled techniques of the program of the International Refugee Organization for emigrants. And under the United States Escapee Program it received substantial funds for the welfare of refugees of certain categories for whom it was especially responsible.

A large proportion of the refugees for whose problem no solution could be reached under the International Refugee Organization had been of the Eastern Orthodox faith. They were scattered in small communities in many countries of asylum. Because of the extensiveness of its operations in the field of relief, as well as of its peculiar relationship with the Orthodox churches, the World Council of Churches became the "residuary legatee" of the responsibility for them.

The World Council gives a succinct summary of its efforts on behalf of these and other International Refugee Organization "residual" groups, as reported in *The First Six Years* (p. 73 ff.):

For thousands of these refugees, the aged and the physically handicapped, there was no permanent solution, and the efforts of our service were devoted to establishing them in church homes and institutions, many of them especially opened for the purpose, in a number of countries of goodwill. Most of them are by now (in 1954) assured of care for the remainder of their days at the hands of fellow Christians, frequently of another confession, but remain, of course, a special concern for the World Council of Churches and the co-operating churches.

A group of one hundred thirty European refugees from China left in temporary asylum on the island of Samar in the Philippines presented a spectacular and seemingly intractable problem. They were individuals for whom it was particularly hard to find homes, but by mid-1953 their re-settlement or establishment in permanent homes was completed.

There remain three areas in which our on-going operation continues to be concerned with the International Refugee Organization cases. There are thousands of European refugees, largely of Russian origin, in China, for whom re-settlement is an urgent necessity and the only solution. Their problem is the daily concern of the joint office in Hong Kong of the World Council and the Lutheran World Federation, and its solution will depend on the success which attends the rapid expansion of our Migration Service to South America and other parts of the world. At the time of writing, Trieste remains another danger spot on the refugee map. The re-settlement of the refugees from that zone is an urgent priority, and at the end of 1953 half of the total of four thousand were the peculiar responsibility of the World Council of Churches.

Finally, in Turkey, Ethiopia, Egypt, Iran and other countries of the Near East there are isolated pockets of European refugees whose precarious circumstances make special and difficult demand upon our service.

This is perhaps the place to note that this work of re-settlement since the war has greatly aided the growth of Orthodox churches in countries where previously their hold was slender. The World Council has followed the refugees, and helps them in their new homes with the establishment of new parishes.

It should be recognized that in inheriting the unsolved problems of the International Refugee Organization the World Council, in common with other voluntary agencies, also inherited its unspent funds to assist in providing solutions. Other official sources provide funds for specific purposes. The World Council has been in a position to accept their funds because the gifts of the churches enabled it to create the basic organizational structure of a Service for Refugees. An anxiety of the future lies in the possibility that public funds may cease to be available with only some of the problems solved.

The millions of refugees of German ethnic origin constituted a problem that would not lend itself to any quick solution. It belonged peculiarly to the churches of Germany and Austria but was also of international concern in that, aside from its humanitarian aspects, the absorption of this great mass of uprooted people into the economies of these countries had an immediate bearing on the peace of the world.

In February, 1949, the World Council of Churches had convened at Hamburg representatives of the churches most directly concerned and of the Allied and German governments to consider the matter as it related to Germany. In the extended range of its results, this meeting had proved of great importance. The ecclesiastical and political authorities with responsibility had for the first time faced in it together the situation as a whole. While the latter had attended only unofficially, the plans followed in later governmental and intergovernmental action had borne its stamp.

Early in 1950 a conference of similar character at Salzburg had studied the problem of the *Volksdeutsche* in Austria. It likewise had resulted in fruitful decisions and was especially notable for the presence of delegates from both the Protestant and the Roman Catholic Churches.

An added ecumenical aspect was given this work by the churches of other countries, which had helped those of Germany and Austria, not only with material gifts, but also with staff members and other personnel "in all the work they . . . carried out for the housing, welfare and general integration of . . . refugees. In particular, the Lutheran World Federation . . . enabled Lutheran churches in other countries to help, with great generosity, their fellow Lutherans in Europe."

As it came up to the Assembly at Evanston in mid-1954 the Department described its work in this sphere as mainly "public representation and negotiation on behalf of refugees."

"If the refugee tragedy is not to be worsened," it said, "the Church must be permanently vigilant. . . . New groups of refugees are created almost every month in different parts of the world; old problems are left unsolved and become more insoluble; injustices are committed and maintained; family life is destroyed by inadequately planned schemes of re-settlement."

The Department's staff had worked with the United Nations High Commissioner for Refugees and other governmental bodies. In 1953 Dr. Elfan Rees, who had begun work with the World Council of Churches in 1947 and was familiar with all the stages of the developing ministry to refugees, had been transferred to the staff of the Commission of the Churches on International Affairs, through which the most logical and direct contact could be maintained with these agencies. From 1950 onward his work had been supplemented "on the operational side" by the service of Dr. Edgar Chandler.

The entire operation had come to the practical test of finding homes for refugees, as stated in its report in *The First Six Years*:

There is no final solution to the human problem of being up-rooted, other than being able to put down roots again. Consequently, it was decided by the Administrative Committee, early in 1952, that, even after the discontinuance of the International Refugee Organization, the Department should remain fully involved in questions of migration.

Many of the refugees whom we are seeking to help in this way have been homeless for a decade. Others have newly come from Eastern Europe to what they believe is a life of freedom in the West. This work is carried on in daily relationship with the Inter-governmental Migration Committee and with a score of governments or governmental agencies, but it primarily depends for its effectiveness upon the co-operation of the churches in the different countries.

Here it has been proved that the creation of a World Council of Churches was most timely. It has enabled the Department to rely upon the immediate response and steady co-operation of church leaders in countries where . . . refugees could be settled. In 1953, for example, the Service for Refugees has helped to settle eight thousand eight hundred eighty-one refugees from twenty countries in forty-two [other] countries, during a period when there was little immigration into the United States of America. This has called for field workers in twenty-two countries and correspondents in nineteen others.

Particular mention should be made, on the one hand, of the American churches which again have taken up their self-appointed task of making a new immigration bill work through efforts of hundreds of local congregations, whereby tens of thousands of refugees may become American citizens and, what is more, members of American churches in the next two years.

Mention must also be made, on the other hand, of the sacrificial aid given by churches throughout the world, notably the churches of Europe, and very especially by the minority churches. The hardest problem in connection with the Samar refugees, the refugees passing through Hong Kong and the refugees in Trieste has only been solved by the imaginative aid given by the churches in Belgium and France. One is led to conclude that where there is a really insoluble human problem the only people to turn to for help are those whose own situation is precarious. The task of finding new homes does not always lie in distant lands. Much of the work of the World Council of Churches' staff is in helping to integrate refugees in the communities where they find themselves. Extensive plans of this nature are being developed at the present time in co-operation with European churches.

The Amsterdam Assembly received a report of the growing numbers of displaced Arabs in Palestine and directed the Department of Inter-Church Aid and Service to Refugees to help as it might toward their relief. The Near East Christian Council had formed a refugee committee, and the Department established with it a satisfactory relationship for a joint approach to the task. As the program developed, they had the cooperation of the International Missionary Council in arranging for a conference at Beirut in May, 1951, of delegates from the churches of Great Britain and the United States with representatives of the churches of the Middle East for a careful exploration of the problem.

Those coming for this meeting first spent several days at refugee camps of the area observing conditions. Published widely, the findings of the conference stimulated giving for work with refugees in the Levant, particularly by the churches of England and the United States. They also influenced public opinion in many countries which were members of the United Nations and made it possible for the Commission of the Churches on International Affairs to support with good effect the undertakings of that organization's Relief and Works Agency. The increased giving by the churches had enabled the Department to guarantee funds for employing an executive secretary for the Near East Christian Council Refugee Committee. Rev. S. A. Morrison of the Church Missionary Society of Great Britain had served in this capacity two years and been succeeded at the end of 1953 by Mr. A. Willard Jones of the American Friends Mission. Dr. Elfan Rees had represented the Department in the Near East during 1949 and 1950.

It will have been noted that the World Council of Churches had extended its ministry through the Department of Inter-Church Aid and Service to Refugees as needs of an emergency character for which it had responsibility arose—to European refugees in China who had fled to Hong Kong, Japan, and the Philippine Islands; to those from other countries seeking asylum in Turkey, Iran, and Egypt; to displaced and dispossessed non-Europeans, such as the Arabs who had been expelled from Israel and the Chinese crowding into Hong Kong and other places of refuge in southeastern Asia.

With other agencies undertaking to serve in these areas the Department encountered problems of the most baffling complexity, such as, for example, those presented by the nearly 400,000 Chinese refugees in Hong Kong and the 300,000 or more "dependents," as they were called. The latter regarded themselves as Chinese, but they had been born in Hong Kong and so were British subjects. The others, since

Britain recognized Communist China, were not refugees in a technical sense, being entitled to the protection of Chinese consular authorities of Hong Kong, who, however, were communists. Moreover, it was the Nationalist government of China that belonged to the United Nations; and it prevented that body from declaring that those designated Chinese had no state to protect them and so required protection by it. When it came to being helped, they were in a more unfavorable position than they would have occupied without any nationality at all. The report of a study of aid to refugees from Communist China for the United Nations in 1954-55 by Dr. Edvard Hambro of Norway suggested that the High Commissioner's mandate be extended to cover the Chinese refugees in Hong Kong, or that a special agency of the kind created to deal with Palestinian Arab refugees be set up. Failing in this, an international appeal for funds would be the only recourse.

When it succeeded the International Refugee Organization, in 1952, the United Nations Korean Reconstruction Agency used some of the workers who had been employed by the disbanded body and invited the cooperation of church representatives who had been engaged in the relief program. Dr. Elfan Rees had visited Korea in 1953 and written a report on conditions there, which had been read widely in governmental and church circles. The same year, while "cease-fire" consultations were in progress, Dr. O. Frederick Nolde, Secretary of the Commission of the Churches for International Affairs, also had twice been in Korea. Mr. Arnold Vaught of Church World Service; Mr. James Atkinson, who had been engaged in refugee work in Austria; and Dr. Edgar Chandler of the Geneva office had represented the World Council of Churches in the organization of a relief program for the churches under the Committee of the Korean National Christian Council.

In its report to the second Assembly at Evanston, the Department of Inter-Church Aid and Service to Refugees could speak of "the beginning of an Asian programme." The churches of Australia, New Zealand, Great Britain, and the United States had "responded to an appeal issued by the World Council of Churches and the International Missionary Council to help the churches in Indonesia with a work of reconstruction too long delayed." Dr. Rajah Manikam, East Asia Secretary of the two Councils, had visited India and Pakistan and taken steps to relate the work of relief and rehabilitation in those countries to the Department.

"Development of a co-ordinated programme for such a vast area in which there are so many different existing initiatives must be inevitably slow," stated the report. The Department had been "hampered by being unable to find immediately an additional member of the staff to carry the administration and travelling work involved." The Director of the Department, Dr. Robert Mackie, had been in Asia and could conclude the report with the promise that "the year 1954 should certainly see the drawing up of a first tentative co-ordinated programme on an ecumenical scale for the great emergency needs of the churches and peoples of Asia."

10. Publications

Publication of *The Ecumenical Review* began in 1948, under the editorship of the General Secretary of the World Council of Churches, with offices at the headquarters in Geneva. Dr. Visser 't Hooft had for associates in this new responsibility Dr. Nils Ehrenström, Bishop Stephen Neill, and—for a short time—Dr. H. Paul Douglass, Editor of *Christendom,* the quarterly published in New York under the auspices of the World Council of Churches Conference of United States of America Member Churches, which was in the way of being incorporated in the new journal.

While it has never had more than 3,500 subscribers, *The Review* has served an important need as a chronicler of ecumenical developments and a medium of communication between those upon whom the World Council of Churches depend for leadership in the different countries. Their interest in the work has led them to write for it or—if not having this opportunity—to read it and give what currency they could in the churches to news from its pages.

It will be the task of this review [wrote Bishop Brilioth, Chairman of the Editorial Board] to be the continuous record of the World Council's history. On these pages its decisions are to be registered, the events in its evolution are to be reported and commented on. Here also the ecumenical discussion is to be carried on. The review should be an open forum, a permanent "conference" for questions of Faith and Order, as well as for Life and Work, and transcending both for the evangelistic and missionary activity of the Church.

Financially, it proved substantially self-supporting, although to accomplish this the printing had to be confined to one language, which undoubtedly restricted the circulation. From 80 to 85 percent of its subscribers were in Great Britain, Canada, Australia, New Zealand, and the United States, and this made advisable the use of English.

The editorial pages of the first number set forth at some length the aims and hopes of *The Review* and may be quoted as defining also the general objectives of the World Council of Churches itself.

This *Review* is not an end in itself. Its one and only purpose is to help in the creation of true fellowship between the Churches. . . . For several centuries the Churches have not been on speaking terms. . . . They ignored each other or spoke against each other. In the various pioneering movements of the nineteenth century, and above all in the earlier stages of the ecumenical movement, individual leaders and members of different Churches have begun to learn how to overcome this estrangement and to enter into an ecumenical conversation with each other. Yet the churches as such have not yet participated in this conversation. The launching of the World Council means that in principle they now agree to listen and to speak to each other.

What are the characteristics of a truly ecumenical conversation between churches? We shall gradually discover the full answer to this question. But this much can be said already. A conversation between churches is a conversation about the truth of God and His purpose for men. The rules of diplomacy and politeness which have their use in the intercourse between states are overruled by the one fundamental concern with ultimate realities. We hope, therefore, that the pages of this review will reflect that common struggle for that truth which transcends all churches and all men. We therefore ask our readers not merely to tolerate but to welcome uncompromising frankness of speech, even if at first reading it may hurt. Churches cannot afford to deal with each other on any lower plane than the plane of truth. How . . . can we ever hope to come closer to each other, if we do not say to each other openly what we really believe?

Churches which enter into conversation with each other can do so meaningly, however, only if they are willing to listen to each other—not merely in order to learn more about each other, but in order to learn more about their common Lord and about His will for the Church. The ecumenical conversation presupposes both a fundamental readiness to receive from sister-churches in the fellowship the gifts of grace which have been bestowed upon them, and a willingness to face the challenges and questions with which they confront us, not in their own name but in the name of the Lord. We would therefore ask our writers and readers to consider this *Review* not merely as an interesting record of events and tendencies of thought in the ecumenical world, but as a common spiritual adventure, leading to unexpected and surprising discoveries.

This *Review* will reflect the weaknesses of the ecumenical movement. We shall see that in so many ways it appears as a movement of disharmony and inner contradictions. It is weak also in that it lacks a clearly defined theology and presents therefore an easy target to shoot at from the trenches of a specific theology. The ecumenical movement is not a finished product and should not be judged as such. It is a meeting place of theologies and no one can know beforehand to what degree an "ecumenical theology" will emerge as a result of the conversation, or what its content may be.

This *Review* should, however, also reflect the true strength of the ecumenical movement. This strength lies in the fact that it is essentially a *humble* movement . . . of those who stretch out their hands to receive from God a fuller knowledge of His truth and a fuller manifestation of His Church. We hope that it may be said of the writers and readers . . . "People who speak in this way plainly show they are in search of a fatherland. . . . That is why God is not ashamed to be called their God; He has prepared a city for them."

The Review was not alone or first in the field of ecumenical journalism. Behind its advent lay a century of experience by pioneering periodicals which had carried forward the thinking of the churches on Christian unity and preserved the most nearly complete historical record that existed of significant interdenominational and interconfessional events.

As early as 1847 the Evangelical Alliance, which has been referred to earlier in these pages as among the interchurch organizations providing channels for the unitive work of Christians, had brought out *Evangelical Christendom,* from its beginning a medium of information about world religious conditions and movements toward cooperation or union.

Following its world conference at Lucerne in 1892, the Old Catholic Church had launched a monthly, first in German as *Internationale Theologische Zeitschrift,* then in 1895 in French as *Revue Internationale de Théologie,* and from 1911 in German again as *Internationale Kirchliche Zeitschrift.* Always ably edited, it had preserved unbroken a record of ecumenical news and constructive thinking on Christian unity, especially as bearing on questions of Faith and Order.

During the period from 1847 to the close of the century several other religious journals had appeared. Each of them—although published for only a short time—had made an important contribution to ecumenical files. They included, among others, *The Christian Union and Religious Memorial,* 1847-50, edited by Dr. Robert Baird, a Presbyterian; *The Evangelical Catholic,* 1851-53, founded in America by William Augustus Muhlenberg, an Episcopalian, "to promote union with the Protestant bodies of Christendom"; *The Re-union Magazine,* 1877-79, launched in England by F. G. Lee, an Anglican; *La Revue Anglo-Romaine,* 1895-96, a weekly issued by Abbé Portal to publicize his and Lord Halifax's efforts on behalf of union between the Anglican and the Roman Catholic Churches; and *The Review of the Churches,* 1891-96, published by Sir Henry Lunn, a Methodist, as an ecumenical forum for the churches.

Inspired by the World Missionary Conference of 1910 at Edinburgh and the experiences of a journey with John R. Mott the following year through the Near East, Dr. Silas McBee of the publishing department of the Protestant Episcopal Church in the United States started *The Constructive Quarterly* in 1913. Continuing publication until 1922, it had given wide coverage to ecumenical interests, particularly those relating to Faith and Order.

Two years earlier, also in the United States, Dr. Peter Ainslie of the Disciples of Christ had founded *The Christian Union Quarterly.* It appeared until his death in 1934, when it was succeeded by *Christendom,* under the editorship of Dr. Clayton C. Morrison, also of the Disciples of Christ, which now was to be continued in *The Ecumenical Review.*

In 1924 Sir Henry Lunn had revived *The Review of the Churches* in connection with another of his series of reunion conferences in Switzerland. It discontinued publication in 1930.

Following the Universal Christian Conference on Life and Work in 1925, Dr. Adolf Keller of Switzerland had edited a magazine called *Stockholm,* 1928-31, with special emphasis on cooperation in the social application of the gospel.

In Scandinavia *Kristen Gemenskap* (*Christian Fellowship*) had met with growing favor under the editorial guidance of Dean Nils Karlström, from 1928 onward.

In Great Britain *The Peacemaker,* under the editorial management of Dr. J. H. Rushbrooke, had been a voice from 1911 to 1914 for Christian collaboration in international affairs. After the outbreak of World War I, it had become, under the name *Goodwill,* the mouthpiece of the English branch of the World Alliance for International Friendship through the Churches.

From 1913 to 1933 Dr. F. Siegmund-Schultze had made his *Die Eiche* (*The Oak*) a medium of ecumenical news and documentary records, as also his *Oekumenisches Jahrbuch* from 1934 to 1937.

Societies and communities devoted to ecumenism had issued their bulletins: *Irenikon,* of the Benedictine Prieure d'May in Belgium, begun in 1926; *Vers l'Unité Chrétienne, Bulletin Catholique d'Information Mensuel,* of Istina Centre in Paris; *Unitas* in Italian, French, and English editions, of the Association Unitas and the League of Prayer for the Return of the Separated to the Unity of the Church; *The Christian East,* issued by the Anglican and Orthodox Association; and *Sobornost,* of the Fellowship of St. Alban and St. Sergius.

Other religious periodicals of a more general character had given an ever increasing amount of attention to interchurch questions, such as: *Le Christianisme Social* and *Foi et Vie,* of France; *La Vie Protestant,* of Switzerland; *The Christian Century* and *Christianity and Crisis,* of the United States; and *The Christian News Letter* and *Theology, of* England, eventually to be merged to form *The Frontier.*

Notable among ecumenical publications which had preceded *The Review* and survived to be its contemporaries were *The Student World,* organ of the World's Student Christian Federation, which had been founded in 1908, and *The International Review of Missions,* the journal of the International Missionary Council, established in 1911, which had made itself an authoritative source of information about the younger churches and supplied a continuous survey of ecumenical literature in its department on "Comity, Co-operation and Unity."

Periodicals under denominational auspices had kept their readers informed on developments in the interdenominational field and so helped to prepare leaders in their respective constituencies for the responsibilities to come later with the establishment of the World Council of Churches and other ecumenical organizations.

The history of the growth of Christian unity in the past century could not be written without reference to these publications and to many others which lack of space forbids listing here. While few of them were read by any large number of persons, together they reported chronologically the cooperative activities of the churches and significant developments in the thinking of Christian leaders and became an indispensable part of source records. *The Ecumenical Review* would take its place in their succession, events were to prove, as a worthy example of the best in religious journalistic endeavor.

The *Ecumenical Press Service* in October of 1953 marked its twentieth year, having been established in 1933 by the Universal Christian Council for Life and Work and the World Alliance for International Friendship through the Churches as *International Christian Press and Information Service*. In time it was adopted also by the International Missionary Council, which substituted it for its own periodic news notes, the World's Alliance of the Young Men's Christian Associations, the World's Young Women's Christian Association, the World's Student Christian Federation, the World Council of Religious Education, the United Bible Societies, and the World Council of Churches. From 1948 onward, the World Council of Churches had assumed most of the expense of publication, adding the director, Alexandre de Weymarn, to its own staff at headquarters, where an editorial committee could be gathered from the several international Christian organizations with offices in Geneva. This advisory body had in its membership representatives of some fifteen or sixteen confessions and more than thirty nationalities.

The *Information Service* had kept the individuals, churches, and other organizations receiving it informed concerning significant events in the religious world and supplied material for use by the ecclesiastical and secular presses and radio commentators. It appeared weekly in German, French, and English, with an American edition issuing from the office of the World Council of Churches in New York City. Its news sources were the several hundreds of church circulars and periodicals in more than a dozen languages which came to the Geneva office and special correspondents in various parts of the world. Its circulation from week to week was around 2,500 copies, which went, for the most part, to organizations and editorial offices, where their contents were broadcast further by printed page and over the air. By general agreement, it was between Amsterdam and Evanston one of the most successful and useful features of the work of the several organizations responsible for it, and its files are a valuable record of current church history.

A History of the Ecumenical Movement was published in April, 1954, on the eve of the Second Assembly, the delay of two years beyond the date set by the original schedule having been caused apparently by a miscalculation of the time a work of this kind would require.

The plan projected in 1946 and 1947 called for two volumes of about 200,000 words each, covering the period from 1517 to 1948—the three and a quarter centuries, roughly, from the Protestant Reformation in Europe to the Assembly at Amsterdam—to be written by scholars who would be chosen from various parts of the world, as befitted a labor of such ecumenical character.

Those appointed for this work had, of course, their own private duties; the new assignment added to these, besides the actual writing, the necessity for extensive research and study. If the book (it finally came out as one volume) was to be a history and not merely a collection of more or less detached essays on various phases of ecumenism, the authors would have to give time also to real collaboration, and this meant attendance at conferences and, for most of them, travel. They would also have to submit what they wrote to special consultants for reading and criticism, and, in most instances, revision and rewriting. While agreeable to this procedure and willing to comply with it as they might, not all could finish the parts promised, and substitutes had to be found. Fortunately, the editorial management had been entrusted to the competent hands of Miss Ruth Rouse and Bishop Neill, who themselves, in addition to carrying their executive responsibilities, wrote important chapters and assisted with others.

Some two hundred persons helped with the undertaking as authors, consultants, research historians, executives, editorial secretaries, office assistants, or members of the general committee in charge. It proceeded under the sponsorship of the Ecumenical Institute, whose Director, Dr. Hendrik Kraemer, and board of directors, under the chairmanship of Dr. Reinhold von Thadden-Trieglaff, gave it strong support. It was made financially possible by the Disciples of Christ denomination in the United States, which at the start gave $20,000 to meet the estimated cost and later, when the work ran beyond the time schedule, added other substantial grants. The first edition, printed in English, carried in the Foreword a promise of early translations into French and German, and, if the demand became great enough, into other languages.

The *History* was "in no sense an official publication of the World Council of Churches," according to the Foreword. But the Central Committee had appointed the commission which, under the chairmanship of Dr. Adolf Keller, supervised its production and regularly received reports from that body of its progress. Moreover, the whole project was carried out, as noted, under the auspices of the Ecumenical Institute, the officers and directors of which gave to it freely of their time and labor. It contained a chapter entitled "The Genesis of the World Council of Churches" by Dr. Willem Adolf Visser 't Hooft. A report of its publication appeared in the official résumé of the work of the first six years of the World Council of Churches which was submitted at Evanston, with reports of the Council's accomplishments during this initial period.

11. Ecumenical Library

With the founding of the World Council of Churches, it was desired that available information on the origin and development of the ecumenical movement be collected and preserved, and a library for this purpose had been established at Geneva. Valuable bequests of books, periodical files, and documents of many kinds had been acknowledged prior to the Assembly at Amsterdam, and the hope there expressed that the churches and friends of the Council would be pleased to augment the collection had borne fruit, according to the report at Evanston. "During the last six years," it stated, "much progress has been made, so that the collection of books, periodicals and brochures on Christian unity . . . and kindred subjects is now probably the most complete existing anywhere."

The committee appointed to write *A History of the Ecumenical Movement* informed the Central Committee in 1950 of its discovery that much material essential to completing the records of the movement had already been lost or destroyed.

> Even this very recent past of forty years is falling into oblivion. Facts concerning some aspects of the period are already buried almost beyond . . . resurrection. . . . Large numbers of men and women who have made ecumenical history have died: concerning not a few of them, we possess neither autobiographies nor biographies; their collections of . . . documents and correspondence have been destroyed, lost or dispersed by relatives and fellow-workers. The same is true of societies, movements and organizations: their committee minutes, annual reports . . . , not to speak of their correspondence, have, in case after case, . . . disappeared without trace.

"The World Council of Churches," added the committee, "is in gravest danger of loss of memory."

Reporting good progress in the development of the library at the Geneva Headquarters, the statement at Evanston concluded with an expression of hope that there might be cooperation generally by those who were able to add to its shelves.

12. The Budget

In the first years particularly, the World Council of Churches found the financing of its multifarious work, which had been inherited, for the most part, from the provisional organization, a problem of great difficulty. The Assembly at Amsterdam had approved an operating budget of $363,000, but the contributions for 1949 amounted to only $319,000, and the Central Committee had found it necessary to limit drastically the expenditures of most of the departments and to delay some authorized extensions of activity, "adhering to the more or less self-imposed policy of keeping the income and the out-go in balance, whatever the curtailments required."

At Amsterdam it had been anticipated that the receipts likely would not be sufficient to cover the budget voted, and the Assembly had made permissible the withdrawal annually for the needs of the Ecumenical Institute of not more than $60,000 from the fund established earlier by John D. Rockefeller, Jr., for this department. The Committee acted to keep the draft on this source, from year to year, at the figure of the Institute's actual expenses, as follows: for 1949, $53,390; for 1950, $45,144; for 1951, $40,469; for 1952, $44,954; for 1953, $56,504.30; for 1954, $59,784.93; for 1955, $58,657.77.

The World Council of Churches commenced its career with operating reserves amounting to less than $7,000. By the end of the first six years, about $128,000 had been accumulated in this account by annual appropriations from current income—this, notwithstanding that the income was never adequate for the work. At the same time, budgetary allocations toward the expenses of the forthcoming Second Assembly had by 1954 reached the sum, approximately, of $130,000, nearly one-half of what was needed for that purpose.

When it adopted a budget of $363,000, the Assembly asked for contributions from churches and individuals to cover $300,000 of the total, but only $265,000 had been forthcoming, and the higher figure had not been reached until 1951. A hindering factor had been the devaluation in 1949 of currencies in the sterling area, which had the effect of reducing by 30 percent the value of receipts from these countries.

Not all the denominations belonging to the Council had contributed to the budget, and some of those giving could hardly do more than send token sums. The bulk of the support had come from the United States of America, as the Assembly in adopting the budget knew it must. United States churches had been asked to accept responsibility for raising $240,000 which was to be solicited from denominations and individuals. While they had consented, through their representatives, to undertake this assignment, they had not succeeded in attaining the goal until 1951, when they exceeded it, as they continued to do in 1952, 1953, and 1954.[65]

These results probably had seemed to follow more or less automatically from the fact that Christians of the United States could give out of an abundance other countries did not possess. A principal reason actually had been the active work of the World Council of Churches Conference of the United States of America Member Churches and its Committee of Interpretation and Support, under the energetic leadership of Dr. Henry S. Leiper, Associate General Secretary of the World Council of Churches in the United States.

A comparative statement of the operating budget of the Council voted at the Amsterdam Assembly and during the inter-Assembly period follows:

[65] Total from churches and individuals: 1949, *$265,770*; 1950, *$274,096*; 1951, *$302,771*; 1952, *$306,316*; 1953, *$311,112*; 1954, *$314,720*; 1955, *$408,942*.

General Secretariat	*1949*	*1950*	*1951*	*1952*	*1953*	*1954*
Geneva	$72,900	$52,450	$37,860	$42,020	$42,550	$54,554
New York	42,000	36,890	38,640	41,350	42,570	41,073
London	4,000	4,360	2,670	2,890	2,760	2,587
Germany		2,320				
Far East			120	1,420	3,000	3,344
Publicity	17,000	11,130	12,790	11,420	12,750	12,811
Faith and Order Department						
Europe	19,500	10,630	13,310	14,570	10,970	11,331
United States	6,000	5,570	5,970	5,940	6,000	4,442
Study Department	31,000	28,220	28,370	31,680	35,560	36,191
Youth Department						
Geneva	17,500	17,920	16,770	19,100	20,650	23,272
New York	12,500	14,800	16,000	16,050	16,000	14,697
Secretariat for Evangelism	9,000	4,800	6,800	7,840	8,570	5,176
Life and Work of Women	6,000		5,970	6,610	7,440	8,133
Library	3,000	3,570	3,660	3,560	3,770	3,932
Ecumenical Review	4,000	2,700	1,600			
Ecumenical Institute	65,000	58,400	55,140	55,470	59,960	59,784
Comm. of the Churches on Int. Affairs	33,000	32,960	27,530	32,030	32,030	32,029
Ecumenical Press Service	600	600	600	2,000	2,000	3,000
General Reserve	10,000	10,000	20,000	20,000	20,000	5,000
Assembly Reserve	10,000	10,000	15,000	20,000	20,000	35,000
Allocation of Surplus						
Ecumenical Press Service		770	2,120	1,110	1,010	
Assembly Reserve			5,000	4,700		
Comm. of the Churches on Int. Affairs				2,500	2,500	
Faith and Order (Lund)					1,180	
General Reserve		11,070	3,320	980		

The funds for Inter-Church Aid and Service to Refugees, before the Amsterdam Assembly, had been controlled by the administrative committee of the department. After the organization of the World Council of Churches, this business, which involved the handling of more money than was required for the operating budget of the Council, had been brought under the centralized management, along with that of the other departments. Meantime, the nature of the operations had undergone important changes, as described by the Central Committee in its report *The First Six Years:*

The Department receives and transmits funds for Inter-Church Aid projects. No financial risk is involved, since payments are made only after receipt of the funds from the giving organization. This type of operation has declined from the high level reached in the years immediately following the war. In the immediate post-war period military and financial controls were such that the Department was able to render valuable service in transferring, either in cash or by purchasing and shipping needed supplies, gifts which churches could not send direct to their sister churches. As conditions have become more normal an increasing part of inter-church aid support has been sent by direct remittance from the giving to the receiving church. Thus the total amount handled by the Department for operations of this type in

1947 was about three million dollars, whereas the annual level is now (1954) a half million dollars.

The Department operates under the general title of the Service Programme a number of activities. . . . These operations, under the headings of Administration of Inter-Church Aid Work, Health and Scholarships Programmes, Fraternal Workers, Work Camps, and particularly the Service to Refugees, are of such nature as to create on-going financial responsibilities. The total expenditure from such contributions to the Service Programme in 1952 amounted to six hundred thirty thousand dollars, but the total, including expenses against special funds made available to the Service to Refugees by inter-governmental and other bodies, amounted to one million two hundred thousand dollars. The main sources of these special funds were the International Refugee Organization (IRO), the Inter-governmental Committee for European Migration (ICEM), the United States Escapee Programme (USEP), and a special grant from the Ford Foundation for refugee projects to be carried out by voluntary agencies. The operations under the Service Programme are controlled by the Administrative Committee of the Department and are subject to the control of the Executive Committee of the World Council of Churches. In accordance with the decision taken by the Central Committee at its meeting at Toronto in 1950, only the budget for the administrative expenses of the Department is submitted for approval to the Central Committee itself.

The travel loan fund had been "a growing activity of the Refugee Service" involving considerable administrative work. It had not been possible to continue the practice of the International Refugee Organization and its predecessor, the United Nations Refugee Repatriation Authority, of providing free transportation for migrating displaced persons, government funds for this no longer being available. The voluntary agencies inheriting this problem had undertaken to meet it through loans to the persons aided, to be repaid after they had become established in their new homes. A fund for the purpose had been created, mainly with the help of the Inter-governmental Committee for European Migration.

During 1952 and 1953, nineteen thousand emigrants had been helped with some three thousand loans to individuals and families. Their expenses had often been incurred in several countries, and it had been necessary to put them together in the currencies of the nations where the loans were to be collected, a transaction involving much detail in bookkeeping. It had been necessary also to set up offices in the lands of destination through which the repayments could be handled; and, having extended its organization in this wise, the World Council of Churches had consented to serve also in collecting loans which had been made by such intergovernmental bodies as the International Refugee Organization and the Inter-governmental Committee for European Migration, the money recovered in this way becoming available for lending to others.

Commented the Central Committee in its report for the inter-Assembly years:

> In the work of the Department [Inter-Church Aid and Service to Refugees] there is a constant tension between the desire . . . to bring the greatest possible help to those in need, and . . . the requirements of a sound financial policy. During the period since the Amsterdam Assembly, controls have been exercised in such a way as to ensure financial solvency and to build up the reserves available for the various sections of the Service Programme to a total of slightly exceeding one hundred thousand dollars.

The Department of Finance and Administration had acted as accountant "for all divisions and departments of the World Council," prepared the annual financial reports, and, with the General Secretary's advice, set up the budget schedules. These routine procedures presented many complexities, as the Service to Refugees would again illustrate. The Department had established field offices in twenty-seven countries, all operating in the national currencies, as well as in dollars, and having to be kept supplied with working funds in both dollars and the local tender. The controls exercised by the nations over monetary transactions had interposed many difficulties. "This task would have been vastly more difficult, if not impossible," explained the Central Committee, "if the World Council had had its headquarters in a country of Europe other than Switzerland, since foreign exchange operations [in Switzerland] are . . . subject to permits in all other European countries, except Portugal."

Moreover, during these years, the Department had purchased and transported the supplies required for the World Council and related organizations in Geneva, a seemingly commonplace duty, but one full of problems, according to the Central Committee's report:

> The regular activities include the buying of medicines to be sent to the church workers needing and unable to secure them, and buying books for theological libraries. During 1953 about one thousand orders were passed for medicines and about seven hundred orders for books from many countries. The following examples illustrate the variety of other articles needed: a printing press was purchased in England for a church publishing house in Greece; the first of what may well become a number of prefabricated wooden buildings was purchased in Austria, after prices were checked in a number of European countries, for experimental erection as a temporary church in one of the islands suffering from the Greek earthquake disaster; fifty pedigreed goats were purchased in Switzerland and shipped to a church college in Egypt as a part of a programme for improving the stock of goats in that country; motor vehicles of all kinds have been bought regularly for Inter-Church Aid work and the operations of the Service to Refugees.

The Finance Department had supervised the headquarters property in Geneva and the reconstruction of Chateau de Bossey, seat of the Ecumenical Institute, involving an expenditure of more than $180,000 contributed by John D. Rockefeller; also the purchase of a building adjoining the headquarters needed to provide more office space. It had handled the insurance on all the properties and the shipments of supplies. Its responsibility included oversight of the personnel, the payment of salaries, the organization and administration of all meetings of the Council, and all arrangements for travel.

The World Council followed the policy of assisting related organizations, when requested, without making any charge, and in many instances acted as agents for those engaging in relief work, such as the Lutheran World Federation, the Overseas Inter-Church Service of the Presbyterian Church in the United States of America, the World Presbyterian Alliance, the United Bible Societies, and the Brethren Service Commission. All these transactions had devolved upon the Department of Finance and Business Administration, which operated at the headquarters in Geneva "on the basis of self-balancing budgets under which the expense of the services for the Council's divisions and departments and the 'related bodies'—e.g., the handling of mail, telephones, telegrams, duplicating, lighting, heating, cleaning, repairs, etc.—were charged to each according to their [several] requirements."

13. Joint Secretariat for East Asia

It had been recommended by the East Asia Conference at Bangkok in 1949 "that a Joint Secretary of the International Missionary Council and the World Council of Churches, to work among the churches and Christian councils of East Asia, be appointed . . . by the parent bodies, after consultation with their constituent organizations and member churches of East Asia." In April, 1951, Dr. Rajah B. Manikam, the Executive Secretary of the National Christian Council of India, had been chosen for this position.

The churches of East Asia being mostly weak minority groups scattered among vast non-Christian populations adhering to Hinduism, Islam, Buddhism and other religions, it had been decided that the Secretary should give especial attention to the pastoral function of his office. Accordingly, during the first year he had visited the national Christian councils and many of the churches belonging to the World Council in Malaya, Indonesia, and India. At Singapore he had held an East Asia Christian Literature Conference, which brought together for the first time representatives of the publishing agencies of the churches of this area to share experiences. He had attended the Asian University Professors' Conference at Bandung, which had been arranged by the World's Student Christian Federation, and the Asian Student Leaders' Training Institute at Djakarta, where an all-Indonesian theological conference had been convened at his request.

He had continued his journeys in 1952, going to the Celebes, the Moluccas, Timor, Bali, Java, Hong Kong, Japan, South Korea, Formosa, and to Singapore and India again. At the end of the year he had attended the World Conference of Christian Youth at Kottayam and the meeting of the Central Committee of the World Council of Churches at Lucknow and had chaired the East Asia Study Conference which was meeting at Lucknow.

His travels in 1953 had taken him to Burma, Thailand, Indo-China, Singapore, Indonesia, Malaya, India, East and West Pakistan, and Ceylon; and in 1954 his plans called for trips, after the second Assembly of the World Council of Churches at Evanston, to the Philippines, Australia, New Zealand, and the Fiji Islands.

In addition to visiting the Christian councils and churches of East Asia, he had gone each year to Europe and Great Britain to meetings of committees of the World Council of Churches and the International Missionary Council which required his presence, and to confer with mission boards having work in the Orient.

It was the judgment of the Central Committee, expressed in its report of his work at Evanston, that Dr. Manikam had helped through these contacts to create a sense of fellowship among East Asian churches that had not existed previously, given greater reality to their place in the ecumenical movement, and brought the World Council of Churches and the International Missionary Council closer to their people.

Headquarters of the World Council of Churches and the International Missionary Council for the East Asian work had been established temporarily at Bangkok.

14. The World Council in the United States

After the Amsterdam Assembly the American Committee for the World Council of Churches had given place to the World Council of Churches Conference of the United States of America Member Churches.

Dr. Henry S. Leiper, Executive Secretary of the American Committee, had become Associate General Secretary of the World Council of Churches "for promotion," with headquarters in New York City. Simultaneously, he had been appointed General Secretary of the new World Council of Churches Conference of the United States of America Member Churches. The work of this body was mainly to acquaint the churches of the United States with the program of the World Council and to help them raise their quotas toward the budget. A Committee on Interpretation and Support had been formed to assist with these duties under Dr. Leiper's direction.

It had been expected that the denominations would provide the money required from their treasuries, and a number of them had responded accordingly; but some had been unable, for one reason or another, to meet their assessments in this way, and the New York staff and the Committee on Interpretation and Support had been obliged to continue the solicitation of contributions from individuals, local churches, and foundations, much as during the provisional period before Amsterdam. The annual budget of the Conference of Member Churches had also to be raised, as had the balance needed, in addition to the reserve accumulated at Geneva, to finance the Second Assembly, which was approximately $150,000.

Rev. Robert S. Bilheimer had been added to the New York staff of the World Council as Program Secretary. His duties had been broadened soon to include assisting the General Secretary of the World Council at meetings of the Central and Executive committees; and in 1951 he had been appointed Executive Secretary in charge of arrangements for the Evanston Assembly.

Rev. William A. Keys, who had served as Director of Youth's Work under the American Committee for the World Council of Churches, had continued on the staff in the same capacity until the end of 1952, at which time he had been succeeded by Miss Frances Maeda.

In 1950 the Conference had formed an advisory committee for the Department of Inter-Church Aid and Service to Refugees, and this necessitated the appointment of an additional staff member. Dr. Wayland Zwayer had been chosen for this post, the duties of which he carried with his responsibilities as Secretary of the Central Department of Church World Service of the National Council of the Churches of Christ in the U.S.A.

During the inter-Assembly period, the New York office had arranged many itineraries for representatives of the World Council of Churches and other visitors coming to the United States on ecumenical missions to the churches. It had published *Christendom* until this journal had been combined with *The Ecumenical Review; The Ecumenical Courier,* the bimonthly news bulletin, which was mailed to members of Friends of the World Council and others in official positions in the churches; and the American edition of *Ecumenical Press Service,* which the Conference subsidized.

Friends of the World Council of Churches, Incorporated, constituted under the laws of the state of New York to receive and administer gifts and bequests, had been continued after the Amsterdam Assembly, its membership consisting, as previously, of contributors to the World Council, who, in virtue of their giving, were enrolled as "Friends of the World Council." It was through this organization that John D. Rockefeller had made his several gifts to the World Council of Churches for the Ecumenical Institute and the Department for Reconstruction and Inter-Church Aid and Service to Refugees.

Dr. Leiper had resigned in 1952 as Associate Secretary of the World Council of Churches and General Secretary of the Conference of Member Churches. He had been succeeded by Dr. Samuel McCrea Cavert upon his retirement in February, 1954, as Executive Secretary of the National Council of the Churches of Christ in the U.S.A.

At the recommendation of the Committee on Structure and Functioning, the name of the auxiliary organ of the World Council of Churches in the United States, which had been under the provisional organization first "Joint Executive Committee" and later "American Committee for the World Council of Churches," and after Amsterdam "World Council of Churches Conference of the United States of America Member Churches," was in 1954 changed once more—this time to "United States Conference for the World Council of Churches."

15. The Commission of the Churches on International Affairs

The Commission of the Churches on International Affairs had been founded, according to its charter, "to serve the churches and councils which were members of the World Council of Churches and the International Missionary Council as a source of stimulus and knowledge in their approach to international problems, as a medium of common counsel and action, and as their organ in formulating the Christian mind on world issues and in bringing that mind effectively to bear upon such issues." It had been composed of forty-five members of twenty-seven nationalities, two-thirds of whom were "laymen with specialized competence and experience in the field of international affairs." Having only a limited budget, the Commission had met as a whole only once—at Woudscotten, Holland, after the First Assembly at Amsterdam—for organization; but there had been yearly meetings of the Executive Committee, and at some of them the attendance had been augmented by invitations to other members of the Commission and to special consultants for whom the sessions were accessible without extended travel. Offices had been maintained in London and New York, and in 1952 a third, by arrangement with the Department of Inter-Church Aid and Service to Refugees, had been opened in Geneva. "Four officers, serving largely in a voluntary capacity and three secretaries at the executive level" had looked after the responsibilities of the Commission "in close consultation with the officers of the parent bodies."

One of the aims of the Commission, as set forth in its governing regulations, as they were called, had been "to encourage in each country and area and in each church represented in the parent bodies the formation of organisms through which the consciences of Christians [might] be stirred and educated as to their responsibility in the world of nations." The obvious practical relation of this objective to the entire program gave it immediate and continuing priority. In whatever way it could the Commission had proceeded to establish contacts with the churches, not only to give them the results of its own thinking on issues of international import, but also to learn theirs and so to be able to speak and to act in other ways for them. The "organisms" formed had been, for the most part, national and area committees on world affairs, and the Commission had met with some success in promoting their organization. Under its encouragement and assistance, their number had grown from a half-dozen or so to twenty-one in 1954. Bodies already existing which had served a like function in relation to the Commission included the several national councils of churches and a number of regional groups. Other connections had been established through "a system of special correspondents." Altogether, officials of the national and area commissions and of Christian councils, leaders of the denominations belonging to the World Council of Churches and, through their mission boards, to the International Missionary Council, the special correspondents, and the members of the Commission itself made a mailing list at the office of nearly four hundred persons in more than seventy countries.

Some idea of the scope of the Commission's activities can be got from a glance at the schedule of conferences and other meetings at which, during the first two years, it had official representation through one or another of its officers or members:

1949

February-March, at Lake Success: United Nations Economic and Social Council, Eighth Session.

March 21-23, at Evanston, Ill., U.S.A.: The World Council of Churches United States of America Conference of Member Churches.

March 31-April 2, at Cleveland, Ohio, U.S.A.: Second National Conference, United States National Commission for United Nations Educational, Scientific and Cultural Organization.

April 1-5, at Bossey, Switzerland: Discussion Group on International Affairs, arranged by the Commission.

April 4-8, at Lake Success: Conference of Non-Governmental Organizations, under the auspices of United Nations Department of Public Information.

April-May, at Lake Success: United Nations General Assembly, Third Session, Part II.

May-June, at Lake Success: United Nations Commission on Human Rights, Fifth Session.

June, at Elsinore, Denmark: United Nations Educational, Scientific and Cultural Organization Conference on Adult Education.

June 29-July 2, at Geneva: Second General Conference of Consultative Non-Governmental Organizations.

July-August, at Geneva: United Nations Economic and Social Council, Ninth Session.

August-September, at Lake Success: United Nations Scientific Conference on the Conservation and Utilization of Resources.

September, at Paris: United Nations Educational, Scientific and Cultural Organization's Fourth General Conference.

September 20-December 10, at Lake Success: United Nations General Assembly, Fourth Session.

October, at Oslo, Stockholm: Consultation with religious leaders of Norway and Sweden.

November-December, at Washington, D.C., U.S.A.: Food and Agriculture Organization, Fifth Annual Conference.

December, at Lake Success: Social Commission of the United Nations Economic and Social Council, Fifth Session.

1950

January 9-27, at Lake Success: Sub-Commission on the Prevention of Discrimination and the Protection of Minorities, Third Session.

January 10-16, at Geneva: Conference of Non-Governmental Organizations Interested in Migration, Joint Sponsorship of United Nations and the International Labor Organization.

January 19-April 4, at Geneva: United Nations Trusteeship Council, Sixth Session.

February, at Bangkok, Thailand: United Nations Department of Public Information, Non-Governmental Organizations.

February 7-March 6, at Lake Success: United Nations Economic and Social Council, Tenth Session.

February, at Geneva, Switzerland: World Council of Churches, Executive Committee.

March 27-May 20, at Lake Success: United Nations Commission on Human Rights, Sixth Session.

April-May, at Lake Success: Social Commission of the United Nations Economic and Social Council, Sixth Session.

April 11-17, at Bossey, Switzerland: Conference on the Christian Approach to International Law, arranged by the Commission of the Churches on International Affairs and the World Council of Churches Study Department and the Ecumenical Institute.

May, at Bangkok, Thailand: United Nations Economic Commission for Asia and the Far East, Sixth Session.

May, at Montevideo, Uruguay: United Nations Sub-Commission on Freedom of Information and of the Press, Fourth Session.

June 26-28, at Geneva, Switzerland: Fourth Conference of International Non-Governmental Organizations on United Nations Information.

January, 1949-June 1950, at New York City, U.S.A., Geneva, Switzerland, and Lake Success, New York, U.S.A.: Twenty meetings of the Interim Committee of Eighteen Members of Consultative Non-Governmental Organizations.

Note: Those attending these meetings as representatives of the Commission of the Churches on International Affairs included the following: Dr.

O. Frederick Nolde, Director of the Commission; R. L. Steiner, Jr.; Kenneth Grubb; E. P. Eastman; A. A. Wyckoff; Dr. Johannes Magelund; Rev. Robert Tobias; Rev. Dominique Micheli; Dr. Ira W. Moormaw; Ellen Jarden Nolde; Baron F. M. von Asbeck; Dr. John H. Reisner; Miss Marion V. Royce; Alan Braley; Raoul Bossy; Elfan Rees; Dr. Horace W. Ryburn; Sr. J. Emilio Gillardo; Rev. Paul Abrecht; Dr. W. A. Visser 't Hooft.

The Commission had been directed by its charter "to represent the parent bodies in relations with international bodies such as the United Nations and related agencies." It will have been noted from the foregoing calendar of activities for 1949 and half of 1950 that most of the meetings attended by its agents had been appointed under the auspices of organizations connected with the United Nations, which is partially explained by a statement in the Commission's report prepared for the Second Assembly, as printed in *The First Six Years*:

The necessity of concentrating its resources to secure maximum results has thus far prevented the Commission from undertaking the full programme outlined in its aims. . . . The major substantive work . . . can be summarized under the six objectives listed in Aim VIII of its charter. . . . The Commission has pursued these objectives at the inter-governmental level, and has maintained contacts with the United Nations and other international agencies.

More specifically, the report says:

Formal consultative relations are maintained with the United Nations Economic and Social Council and its Commissions, the Food and Agriculture Organization, and United Nations Educational, Scientific and Cultural Organization. Particular attention is devoted to the United Nations General Assembly where major decisions are made. Contacts are maintained with the Trusteeship Council, Technical Assistance Board and Administration and there are close relations with the Office of the High Commissioner for Refugees. There are also formal contacts with the International Labour Organization, the World Health Organization, the United Nations Korean Reconstruction Agency, the United Nations Relief and Works Agency for Palestinian Refugees in the Near East, the United Nations Children's Fund, the Inter-Governmental Committee on European Migration, and the Council of Europe.

Through such channels, the report added, the Commission had attempted to keep under scrutiny aspects of the work of international agencies which were of particular concern to the churches. It had developed "a small but rather flexible mechanism for following . . . international decisions at the formative stage, for alerting Christian leaders, for giving evidence of Christian concern, and, as occasion invited, for bringing a specific Christian influence to bear on such decisions."

The significance of the Commission's actions can be seen best, perhaps, from its own explanation of the method followed:

The procedure . . ., still essentially experimental in its efforts to make the Christian witness in international affairs more relevant and effective, has benefited from cumulative experience and periodic ecumenical review. Starting with an initial concentration on the question of international safeguards for religious liberty and related human rights, the Commission has been able to build step by step a procedure for action on a wider front. The growing confidence accorded . . . by leaders of the ecumenical movement has enabled [it] to act more flexibly and promptly in a variety of critical international situations than was possible at the initial stage. . . . However, [it] has remained aware of the restraints imposed by the need to build solidly, to use limited resources effectively, and to develop a clearer ecumenical consensus.

The frame-work of policy is provided by the Aims of the Commission . . . and the decisions of the parent bodies, such as the joint Declaration on Religious Liberty of 1948. Within this framework, the Commission . . . Executive is gradually building a body of policy directives to guide the officers in their representative work. The officers consult with each other and the executives of the parent bodies on issues involving the application of principles to concrete situations as they emerge. When the pace of events permits, a wider consultation is carried on with Commissioners, officers of national commissions and correspondents. In this process lies the beginning of a method for encouraging world-wide Christian participation in international affairs.

The work in connection with the sessions of the United Nations General Assembly provides the most comprehensive example of [the] procedure. Prior to the Assembly an effort is made to ascertain actions relevant to agenda items taken by Christian bodies within the World Council of Churches and the International Missionary Council. Against this background, policy directives are formulated by the Commission . . . Executive and subsequently embodied in a memorandum summarizing selected agenda items and the Commission's . . . position. This is circulated both to Christian contacts and United Nations delegations. On certain items there may be concerted or parallel action by various national commissioners and Christian councils. At the United Nations, the follow-up takes varied forms: personal consultations with delegates and officials, formal communications by the Commission's . . . officers, suggestions for textual amendments, or efforts to win support for decisions considered of vital importance to the churches. A characteristic of the Commission's . . . procedure is the amount of attention devoted to the follow-up of policy statements at the international level.

In the years since Amsterdam, some procedural patterns have emerged . . . which have been found helpful in the interest of faithful representation and effective action. When there is substantial agreement, approaching unanimity, as in the case of religious freedom, the Commission . . . can reflect this relatively common mind. During the drafting of the Universal Declaration of Human Rights, the Commission's . . . officers undertook a study of the components of religious freedom, in which Christian leaders from many parts of the world participated. The result was a fairly precise representation flowing from common Christian conviction and experience. This contributed to the evolution of the draft article into an acceptable text. . . . On the other hand, where there is obvious disagreement, as was found in regard to an instrument for the internationalization of Jerusalem, a frank statement of differing view can render a service to inter-governmental agencies and provide a background for more effective presentation of points of agreement.

The value of an international Christian agency on international affairs for keeping issues in an ecumenical perspective has particular relevance when there are substantial Christian groups in two contending countries. At the time of the Netherlands military action in Indonesia, officers of the Commission . . . asked colleagues in the two countries to prepare memoranda interpreting the situation, which were subsequently circulated among Christian leaders. . . .

It is possible for the Commission . . . to bring about a concerted impact on governments when they are attempting to shape a common policy. When the conflict in Korea was enlarged in November, 1950, church leaders in the United States and Britain, at the suggestion of the Commission's . . . officers, were able to bring a simultaneous influence to bear on their representative governments, in behalf of policies of moderation and restraint, immediately before a meeting of the heads of government. The conference of the Commission's . . . Director with church and governmental leaders in the United States and Korea in June, 1953, on the desirability of an early armistice on honorable terms may be cited as an example of a different procedure with a similar end in view.

The presence of church representatives at inter-governmental meetings has a value beyond any direct impact on specific issues. Delegates have tangible evidence of Christian concern and those who share our faith become aware of the Christian fellowship even when dealing with political issues. The observer is a reminder of the principles for which the churches stand, and an indication of the churches' concern for Christian vocation at the political level. His presence, moreover, often provides opportunity for informal discussions of religious questions and of the work of the ecumenical movement. The importance of such indirect methods of Christian witness should not be under-estimated, for the moral climate of international conferences helps to shape their decisions.

While the Commission had met with increasing support from church leaders, there had been in some quarters sharp criticism of its policy of cooperation with the United Nations and related agencies, and its Executive Committee, at a meeting in Céligny, Switzerland, in August, 1953, responded with a statement, "Christians Look at the United Nations," later included in its report in *The First Six Years*:

The United Nations has been created because of the longings of the peoples for a just and durable peace and their sense of need for collective security. It was born out of the sacrifice and tragic suffering of a global war. Its work is, in many respects, directed toward goals which Christians believe to be in accordance with God's will for justice among his children.

An understanding of the substantial contributions which the United Nations has thus far made must reckon with the handicaps under which it is forced to operate. The United Nations reflects the disorder of this interdependent world. In its structure it is an association of sovereign states. Its members in many cases have been unable or unwilling to co-operate fully, and their representatives normally look at international questions not so much on the basis of merit as on grounds of national interests and ideological points of view. It operates on the frontier of international anarchy. It is threatened by a jungle of clashing nationalism, social systems, and power blocs. Indeed, its decisions are at times influenced, if not determined, by these same forces. The development of its limited powers has been hindered, especially in the realm of security, by the abuse of the veto.

Nevertheless, the United Nations, as well as related agencies, including the International Court of Justice, provide the nations with an instrument for the development of international law, the just regulation of common interests of nations as well as for the peaceful settlement of disputes and the discouragement of threats of peace. It also provides a world forum for the interchange of thought between diverse cultures and view-points. Through such co-operation these institutions offer now an effective means of developing conditions essential to the rule of law in the world.

Moreover, the United Nations offers the best means for co-ordinating the activities of the nations for human welfare. Through its related organizations it is rendering valuable service in combatting ignorance, want and disease, especially in under-developed territories. It is helping to create a common mind on the subject of Human Rights, and to provide those services essential for refugees and migrants.

Therefore, the United Nations needs and deserves the discerning and active support of Christians. The valid purposes of the Charter can be served neither by utopian illusions nor by irresponsible defeatism, but only by the constructive support of all people of goodwill. The tremendous task of developing effective international machinery cannot be performed within a few years, but only by patient and cumulative effort of generations. To aid in this task is a Christian duty.

If it is to live, the United Nations must grow. There are, of course, grave obstacles to any fundamental revision of the Charter, so long as post-war fears and antagonisms corrode the confidence and obscure the moral basis prerequisite for this. But the present structure is flexible enough to permit more adequate procedures, if public opinion can be sufficiently informed and aroused. The growth of the United Nations requires fuller co-operation on the part of member states in honoring their common commitment.

We therefore call on Christians everywhere to study, pray and work for a better fulfillment of the purposes of the United Nations Charter.

Said *The Ecumenical Review* (October 1953) concerning this subject:

It is natural that questions should be asked about this new approach of the churches to international affairs. One of these is why the churches should be concerned at all with the United Nations. The answer is that the United Nations provides the only existing framework of inter-governmental action, that its membership consists of governments in all parts of the world and that it deals with matters on which the peace of the world and the establishment of justice depend. That does not mean, however, that the Commission of the Churches on International Affairs or the World Council is in any sense committed to the United Nations. In this, as in all other relationships, we maintain our full independence. There are occasions when the Commission . . . backs specific actions of the United Nations; there are other occasions when it criticizes such actions. The scope of the Commission's activity in this respect is very wide. It ranges from such obvious questions of human concern as the plight of Arab refugees and the question of Human Rights to such a very intricate question as disarmament. . . . It is clear that the ultimate effect of this . . . approach to international affairs will depend to a very large extent on the clarity with which the churches voice their convictions concerning international questions. The spokesman cannot speak if the body for which he is to speak is silent or confused. It is therefore urgent that all churches in the ecumenical movement should accept their responsibility with regard to the grave international situation and keep the officers of the Commission . . . informed about their convictions.

A predominant purpose of the Commission during its provisional phase (1946-48) had been to rally Christian influence in support of the United Nations Commission on Human Rights. All meetings of this body had been attended, and at them representations had been made, under the direction of the executives and after consultations with Christian leaders in many countries, of the mind of the churches concerning proposals arising for consideration.

In December, 1948, the Commission, now a formally constituted adjunct of the World Council of Churches (in association with the International Missionary Council), had turned its attention to the problem of getting the nations to respect and enforce observance of the standards raised in the Declaration, urging particularly the incorporation of "binding instruments" to that end in international covenants.

At the request of the Central Committee of the World Council of Churches, the Commission had in 1949 undertaken a study of "Religious Freedom in the Face of Dominant Forces," which had resulted in the submission of "a comprehensive plan for promoting the observance of religious freedom." In this connection, it had stressed, in answer to an inquiry from the United Nations on the subject, the importance of safeguards for human rights, including religious liberty, in any plan for the internationalization of Jerusalem; expressed regret over the refusal of Bulgaria, Hungary, and Rumania to cooperate in an investigation of charges of treaty violation of human rights in their territory; initiated governmental negotiations to facilitate the return of church and mission property which had been confiscated or seized; urged repeatedly the repatriation of Greek children dislocated by war; manifested concern because of the unsatisfactory position of the Indian minority in the Union of South Africa; given special attention to alleged discriminations against evangelicals in Colombia and to like situations in other countries where the actions or the attitudes of dominant churches or religions had led to complaints by smaller Christian groups, as in Italy and Spain, Pakistan and Indonesia; and brought to the cognizance of governments attacks from communist quarters upon the churches in East Germany. The Commission had gone on record with the declaration that "every denial of fundamental rights should be made known and resisted."

With respect to the "furtherance of international economic co-operation," as enjoined in its charter, the Commission had worked in a consultative relation with the Food and Agriculture Organization, the United Nations Educational, Scientific and Cultural Organization, and the agencies of the United Nations especially responsible for what had come to be known as "technical assistance." It had suggested what it considered sound guiding principles in this last-named area: respect for the rights of the people of underdeveloped regions; cultivation of the desire for self-development; selection of experts with integrity and insight; training native leaders until they became experts; concentration on improvements affecting the masses; encouraging cooperation by all assisting agencies; and perseverance in long-range programs.

The churches had been reminded of the dependence of such work upon a favorable moral climate which they might help to create, and qualified laymen had been counseled to consider finding in its program their Christian vocation. Also stressed had been the possibility of improving the effectiveness of technical assistance as given through the regular avenues of missions.

Apropos of the announcement in 1952 of the United Nations Expanded Technical Assistance Program, the Commission emphasized the need for more sufficient resources, the importance of integrating projects at the field level, a long-range evaluation of programs, and the value of supplementary undertakings by private agencies to relate such schemes "more quickly to human needs at the local level through the training of indigenous leaders for community reconstruction." Later (in 1953) it had supported, with a growing sense of the greater resources available through regular business channels, "adequate planning for international financial assistance for economic and social development, particularly when its aim was to help establish conditions in less developed regions which would enlist expanding capital investments, both private and public, both domestic and foreign."

On the same general lines, the Commission had given attention to the advancement of dependent people toward self-government—another of the objectives of its charter. Taking into account "the limits as well as the potential value of action at the international level," it had tried to make clear the necessity of work by responsible Christian agencies within the nations involved. It had urged that each country must accept for itself "the obligation to promote the utmost well-being of dependent peoples (under its mandate or otherwise subject to it), including their advance toward self-government and the development of their free political institutions," associating itself, as it found opportunity, with the activities of the Trusteeship Council and the General Assembly's Committee on Information from Non-Self-Governing Territories of the United Nations. South-West Africa, Morocco, Tunisia, and Cyprus had been among the areas of special concern, from the standpoint of their aspirations and struggle for statehood.

Under "the promotion of international social, cultural, educational, and humanitarian enterprises" (Charter: Aims, VIII, [f]), the principal work of the Commission, aside from its continuous consultative relationship with UNESCO had been on behalf of refugees and migrants. By 1952 this problem had increased so much that the Department of Inter-Church Aid and Service to Refugees had considered that it required an additional secretary and had appointed Dr. Elfan Rees to the staff, with the provision that he have an office in Geneva. The Commission had endeavored in every way to help with establishing and strengthening the Office of the United Nations High Commissioner for Refugees and had the satisfaction of seeing adopted a number of its suggestions for improving the draft statute; supported action authorizing the raising of a voluntary International Assistance Fund and providing for a larger administrative budget for the High Commissioner; influenced the governments, as it could, to sign and ratify the United Nations Convention on Refugees and otherwise to take generous action to meet the refugee problem; participated in several intergovernmental and other conferences on broader aspects of the problem of migration by dislocated persons; and stressed the need for continuing support of the relief activities of the United Nations Children's Fund.

The plight of Palestinian refugees also had engaged the Commission, which as early as 1949 had supported a United Nations relief plan on their behalf. "In line with the recommendations of the Beirut Conference in 1951, the Commission . . . [had] supported the plan, later adopted by the General Assembly (of the United Nations), for a fund of two hundred fifty million dollars and the provision of 'homes and jobs for refugees, without prejudice to their rights of repatriation or compensation.'" It had done this, however, recognizing "that the political and economic conditions necessary for a lasting settlement [had] not been achieved."

Liaison had been maintained with the United Nations Korean Reconstruction Agency, and in 1953 representatives of the Commission had visited that country to consult with officials on behalf of the churches.

The Commission had been able to do nothing directly to promote "the progressive development and codification of international law," as outlined in the aims of the charter. It had been one of the sponsors in 1951 of a conference at Céligny, Switzerland, on "Foundations of International Law," which had brought together eminent churchmen, among them jurists and statesmen, and left with them a desire to continue the discussion at a later meeting. Apparently the desire was frustrated by demands more immediate and pressing than its splendid distant goals, since there is no record that a second gathering was held.

By supporting the program of the United Nations in the name of the churches to the extent that circumstances permitted, the Commission was helping to lay the foundations of law and to create a habit of mind for orderly and peaceful relations in international life, as well as making possible the perfecting of the only supranational instrument on the world's horizon for its expression and ultimate triumph over anarchy and chaos.

How effective concerted action by the churches might be in international affairs was shown by an entry in the records of the Commission for 1950. The Commission had sent a letter to national commissions and church leaders throughout the world urging consideration of the "observer commission plan," which proposed to the General Assembly of the United Nations the setting up of a network of observers covering all the danger spots in the world where war might develop. In a number of countries approaches to the governments were made as a result of this communication. Some months afterwards, the General Assembly adopted a resolution entitled "Uniting for Peace," which included a provision for establishing "a Peace Observation Committee which should observe and report on the situation in any area of international tension." This proposal had been the only one in the entire resolution accepted by Russia and the Communist bloc.

The Commission concluded its report of "the first six years" under the World Council of Churches (in association with the International Missionary Council) with some practical references to the "needs" it faced. These must be included in any survey seeking to foster a true understanding of its accomplishments and its interpretation of the mission for which it was founded:

> The work of the Commission of the Churches on International Affairs has been carried on with a sense of the limitations inherent in such an effort, the modest achievements in the face of immense needs, and the challenging potentialities to which the brief history of the Commission clearly points.
>
> The study and clarification of the theological pre-suppositions of the churches' witness in international affairs is a task which the Commission has not attempted and for which it is not qualified. But the Commission . . . recognizes the need for such an effort to undergird its work.
>
> A more vigorous effort to stimulate and help national commissions of the churches on international affairs is a clear need for which the Commission . . . presently lacks personnel and budget. The importance of broadening the base of ecumenical work in this field through education and action programs at the national level is evident, in view of potentialities presently untapped in many countries.
>
> The task of securing more adequate background studies of current international problems is another unmet challenge. It is recognized that continuing study groups with specialized competence and knowledge of church experience in different countries would provide a valuable asset to the work of the Commission.
>
> The concern of Christians everywhere over denials of human rights merits a mechanism for first-hand investigation and report. There are opportunities here which can be seized only if substantial new resources are provided.
>
> Justification for the kind of work which the Commission . . . has under-

taken must in the final analysis lie beyond any success or failure which has attended its efforts. The Christian who has experienced the peace of God which passes all understanding must seek peace among the nations and peoples of the world. The Christian who by faith apprehends the righteousness which God in his mercy has wrought must in the spirit of brotherhood seek justice for all men. The Christian who has experienced the liberty with which Christ has set men free must press for a society in which God's children may fulfill the destiny which he has fixed for them. The Christian witness for peace, justice and freedom is an imperative implication of the Christian Gospel.

At the organization at Woudscotten, Holland, in 1949, Baron F. M. von Asbeck had been elected President of the Commission, Sir Kenneth Grubb Chairman, and Dr. O. Frederick Nolde Director. Dr. Elfan Rees had been added to the staff in 1952, as noted. Among the distinguished members of the Commission representing the World Council of Churches had been Dr. Charles Malik of Lebanon, Hon. John Foster Dulles of the United States, Dr. Arnold Toynbee of Great Britain, Hon. Francis B. Sayre of the United States, and Professor Hamilcar S. Alivisatos of Greece.

It is clear that the influence of the Commission had amounted to more than the effect of its formal pronouncements and negotiations. Quite as important had been the emphasis given what it said and what it endeavored to do by the association of its personnel with the representatives of governments, international political organizations, and other ecumenical religious bodies, a ready example of which had been the presence of Director Nolde in Korea in 1953 during the conversations of President Syngman Rhee and Envoy Walter Robertson of the United States, at the Berlin Conference of the foreign ministers of Great Britain, France, Russia, and the United States in 1954, and later the same year at the Conference of the Great Powers on the Asian situation at Geneva, Switzerland.[66]

The Ecumenical Review, in its first number for 1952, touched on this point, as follows:

As they read the rather gloomy reports of the meeting of the Assembly of the United Nations many churchmen will ask themselves, What are the churches doing about this grave situation? One answer . . . is that the Commission of the Churches on International Affairs is "on the job." Its two representatives, Dr. O. Frederick Nolde and Rev. Elfan Rees, who are present at the Assembly as consultants, do not merely observe the Assembly, but participate very actively in the process of discussion out of which its decisions . . . will grow.

The full significance of the work of these spokesmen for the churches is perhaps not yet sufficiently realized. The Churches and the ecumenical movement have of course been concerned with international affairs for many years. But it is only recently that they have learned to follow inter-

[66] See Appendix G for the constitution of the Commission of the Churches on International Affairs.

national developments through day-to-day consultation. And it is clear that such continuous participation is incomparably more effective than statements or resolutions which are not followed up by personal contact. Much depends on the competence of the representatives . . . and their ability to inspire confidence. In this respect the Commission . . . has made a very real place for itself, as anyone who visits the Assembly and talks with [its] delegates can ascertain.

Part Six

THE SECOND ASSEMBLY

INTRODUCTION: EVANSTON

The Second Assembly of the World Council of Churches was held August 15-31, 1954. Those attending it agreed that Evanston came near fulfilling the specifications of an ideal meeting place. Its lake-tempered climate, shaded streets, hospitable homes and cloistered atmosphere, and its situation somewhat off the main transcontinental thoroughfares invited withdrawal for work or rest, the necessity of which the arduous demands of the Assembly would lay upon the conferees.

Northwestern University, with the cooperation of Garrett Biblical Institute and Seabury-Western Theological Seminary, provided ample and convenient housing. Dormitories for the delegates' quarters, administrative halls and libraries for offices and exhibits, and auditoriums, large and small, for meetings left no facilities to be desired. The churches of the community, commodious and accessible, afforded appropriate accommodations for daily worship.

Chicago, ten miles distant, had in its mammoth Soldier Field nearly room enough for the multitude, estimated at 125,000, who came on a Sunday evening to participate in the "Festival of Faith," presented under the auspices of the Assembly. Other suburban cities joined in their several ways with Evanston in promoting the success of this first major ecumenical gathering in North America.

It was especially advantageous for the Assembly to be so near the center of the continent where its presence and influence would be most broadly felt. The nations had come, at the promptings of faith, to the American scene and had not stopped, as foreign visitors did so often, at the seaboard where it began but proceeded into its midst. This undoubtedly accounted, in part, for the wide popular interest in the event.

The news-gathering organizations responded to the public's eagerness for information about the Assembly by sending to Evanston the largest number of reporters ever assigned a religious meeting. There were 646 accredited press and radio representatives, including both secular and church contingents. At the end of a fortnight the Assembly was informed that it had received the widest coverage ever given a gathering of any kind, with the possible exception of the latest Democratic and Republican national conventions, which had been held in Chicago two years previously.

"Official participants" numbered 1,298. They came from 197 communions in 54 countries. First among them were 502 delegates who had been sent by 132 of the 161 denominations belonging to the World Council of Churches. Next were 499 "accredited visitors" who served as their alternates. In addition, there were 241 consultants, 31 fraternal delegates, 25 observers, and a very large number of "general visitors" of whose presence no complete record was kept. A staff of 376 persons—executives, secretaries, interpreters, translators, stewards, and aides—managed the Assembly business from their stations at the different levels.

The preparatory plans for the Assembly had been developed, as had the program, under the direction of the Central and Executive Committees of the World Council, which had delegated to various subgroups most of the actual work.

The Study Department had supervised the collaboration on the main theme. The Faith and Order Commission, the Commission of the Churches on International Affairs, and four appointed commissions had similarly planned the six subjects for study by the sections.

The United States Conference for the World Council of Churches had borne the responsibility for local arrangements. Besides the organization for the Assembly while in session and manifold incidental duties, this task required negotiations with the Department of State for the entry of persons from foreign countries, cooperation with theological seminaries in Greater Chicago in conducting an Ecumenical Institute for ministers during the two weeks immediately preceding the opening of the Assembly, and raising $150,000 toward the expenses of the Assembly, to supplement the approximately equal sum which the World Council of Churches had accumulated in its reserves for this purpose.

The organization of the Assembly, into which had gone a very great deal of labor, was to draw criticism on two accounts. Some delegates thought the program was too crowded for the most profitable results. Others objected that the arrangements and the day-to-day management, which extended to the minutest details, left too little freedom for guidance by the Spirit at junctures where human designs and discussions seemed to need new direction.

This meant to the more easygoing and deliberate members from abroad that the event could only have been pronounced successful from the standpoint of the characteristically activistic Americans, who would ask at any suggestion of complaint, "Was not something happening all the time?"

The agenda of the Assembly fell, roughly, into four parts: the presentation of the main theme; the study by sections of the six subthemes; the consideration of organizational changes proposed by the Committee on the Structure and Functioning of the World Council of Churches; and the routine business arising from official reports, which included the adoption of a budget and the election of officers and committees for the ensuing seven years.

Following the Assembly through these several phases, the observer was able to view more clearly the work of the World Council during its first six years and was helped to a better understanding of the policies and methods likely to give shape to its course in the days ahead. Evanston saw also the appearance of certain new theological and sociological emphases, particularly during the debate and action on the main theme. It would be quite impossible to enter fully into the spirit of the World Council at that time, or to reach a realistic judgment concerning its prospects, without knowledge of the conception and development of the theme. For this reason, it will be necessary to review some of the meetings in preparation for the Assembly as well as actions and debate at Evanston.

I

"CHRIST—THE HOPE OF THE WORLD"

1. The Main Theme Conceived and Developed

The main theme for the Second Assembly of the World Council of Churches was originated in the summer of 1950 at the Toronto meeting of the Central Committee. The Bishop of Chichester, Dr. Bell, opened discussion with the question "How do we envisage this Second Assembly?" and proceeded to suggest that "it should help the churches in their relations with one another, and in their relations to the contemporary world. It must help them to face the world's problems and make clear to the world that its problems are being faced."

The problem of man himself was plainly fundamental, he suggested: his very existence as a spiritual free being was in danger. Because of depersonalizing circumstances in society, not only in the totalitarian state but in the mass processes of democracy as well, the whole structure of present-day society militated against the significance of the individual. The issue might be stated, he proposed, in some such terms as "Man's Quest for Significance." The problem presented many facets. Not only the material condition of the masses of Asia, Africa, Russia and the Balkans, and other underdeveloped countries and of workers in the industrial democracies, but also their mental, moral, and spiritual needs, had been too long neglected. It had to be recognized, he continued, that one reason why communism had made such a strong appeal was its promise to meet some of these needs, though it had, of course, a false and tragic answer, for while claiming to set the masses free economically, it actually enslaved them. The main reason why communism failed was its denial of God. The materialistic philosophy of history and of human life was false, and it was of utmost importance to show that man's quest for significance could be "met by the transcendent God."

The Bishop referred to race relations as presenting another aspect of the subject with which the churches would have to deal in concrete ways, "showing not only where communism, imperialism and nationalism [were] wrong, but what [were] the indispensable musts of a Christian policy." Declaring that evangelism and education were needed for the task, and to be effective had to be reorientated, he concluded:[1]

> "Let me sum up man's quest for significance in laymen's language." What is it that the masses of men . . . most lack? Freedom. Freedom from poverty, hunger, insecurity, war. Freedom to speak, believe, print, assemble, persuade. Freedom of body and spirit. . . . Could we, therefore, think of the theme of the Second Assembly on the lines of a general title like "Christianity and the Freedom of Man," "Christ and Man's Freedom," or "The Freedom with Which Christ Sets Men Free"?

The discussion proceeded from this point, Sir Kenneth Grubb expressing doubt that laymen would recognize their problem of insecurity in terms of freedom and Dr. Pierre Maury maintaining that the churches should not "take their lead from the world," in which position he was seconded by other members of the Committee.

Dr. Reinhold Niebuhr proposed that the doctrine of redemption be considered, which, he explained, combined the eternal message of the gospel with the immediate needs of the world. "We are confronted actually with false schemes of redemption, which contain proximate solutions but are not based upon any ultimate solution," he said. "We tend to deal with the ultimate and disregard the proximate. In the Christian doctrine of redemption we should be confronted with both."

Dr. Benjamin Mays thought "Christianity and the Salvation of Man" would be a timely theme. It should be shown that men needed to be saved from economic insecurity, imperialism, race domination, and war, he said, and how Christianity affected life in these areas.

The counsel from the venerable Dr. John R. Mott was that the Assembly should "give a sense of direction, of mission, and of the presence of God leading us"; and Mr. F. W. Gilpin expressed the hope that it would deal with the spiritual factors of life, with some such theme as "God and the Need of the Individual."

Dr. Martin Niemöller said: "We must show that the ultimate redemption is relevant. . . . There is an absolute responsibility to take the relative needs of the people seriously. Communism or race may or may not be the issue, but it will be necessary to be specific. We must get our immediate issues from the world situation, but we must speak from an ultimate responsibility."

Bishop Geoffrey Allen urged the need for the churches to study communism and scientific humanism to discover what in them appealed to men and made them more successful than Christianity. This, he declared, would set evangelism in a central place in the program of the World Council of Churches, where it ought to be.

Professor Georges Florovsky said: "What is needed is a positive central statement which may be directed toward the concrete issues of the time."

[1] Minutes of the Central Committee, Toronto, 1950.

The problem in all the questions they were discussing, suggested Dr. Edwin T. Dahlberg, whether international relations, labor, race, or family, was enmity. "We tend to attack the enemy," he said, "but Christ attacked the enmity between people. The Assembly should direct itself to this issue."

Dr. Henry Pitney Van Dusen hoped that the Assembly might deal with the concerns, not of the individual, but of civilization. In his view neither redemption nor freedom would be a subject lending itself to such treatment as effectively as others that might be chosen. He felt that the Christian message, or evangel, should be considered, with strong emphasis on evangelism, and with special reference to the collective problems which beset men.

As a layman, Dr. Charles P. Taft considered redemption, freedom, and the Christian message "too smooth" and lacking grip. He proposed that, whatever the phrasing, a main element in the theme chosen be the idea of "the adventurous spirit of spiritual risk-taking, in order that the Assembly might make clear to large and small groups a line of action upon faith and trust beyond what could actually be seen."

Dr. Rajah B. Manikam asked that the Assembly be allowed to deal with questions which concerned the East, suggesting three that were most urgent—the meaning of freedom, especially in its spiritual as distinguished from its political aspects; race, particularly from the standpoint of the appeal of communism; and church union, which was a matter of increasing pressure upon the churches.

From the standpoint of his position of leadership in the *Kirchentag* movement, Dr. Reinhold von Thadden-Trieglaff hoped that the Assembly, whatever its theme, would send out a positive and clear statement that would challenge laymen.

Dr. Visser 't Hooft noted in what had been said in the discussion the emphasis on witnessing. He was favorable toward the suggestion but saw a serious difficulty in dealing with evangelism:

> It is that we think we know all about evangelism. In reality, there is very little "break-through" evangelism; that is, evangelism which is converting communists, existentialists and scientific humanists. Could we go to the Assembly in the spirit that we don't know much about evangelism? There would be great promise for us, if we could go asking how we could break out, seeking the answer to how we may meet the despairing, the seekers, those outside the Church.

One of the consultants, Mr. E. J. Bingle, offered the opinion that it would be unwise to start from problems such as had been brought forward by various speakers. Remembering the despair in the churches, he believed that a more suitable and helpful subject for the Assembly would be Christian hope. The World Council of Churches had become a symbol of hope to many, he said, and the theme "Christian

Hope" would face in the same direction as the International Missionary Council's study, "Expectant Evangelism."

Summing up, Dr. John Baillie expressed the judgment that the "situation called for a common theme, rather than a single specific problem, with emphasis upon the essential Christian gospel message."

From this point, the Toronto *Minutes* continued: "After full discussion of the problem, it was agreed that the following statement be adopted:"

> The time has come when the World Council of Churches should make a serious attempt to declare, in relation to the modern world, the faith and hope which are affirmed in its own basis and by which the Churches live. The world is full of false hopes, of fear and of despair. Religious indifference is widespread. In the churches, spiritual power and triumphant hope are not clearly manifest. Though there is much active evangelism, the old paganisms still maintain their power in many parts of the world, while on the other hand there are very few points at which the Church is breaking out of its isolation into the world of those who hold to such modern substitutes for the Gospel as communism and other political messianisms, scientific humanism, and certain forms of existentialism, or are indifferent to every religious or quasi-religious faith. The presence of secularism within the churches is deeply marked. Now, as always, man's greatest need is God's greatest opportunity. We think therefore that the main theme of the Assembly should be along the lines of the affirmation that Jesus Christ as Lord is the only hope of both the Church and the world; and that the subsidiary themes of the Assembly should be considered in relation to this central theme.

Looking to the implementation of this decision, the Committee agreed further,

> that the main theme [should] be considered in the first week by the whole Assembly, divided in the first instance for that purpose into groups . . . that the Study Department Committee be authorized to take the initiative in preparations for the study of the main theme . . . that the proposed themes [main and subsidiary] of the Assembly be communicated immediately to the member churches with a request for comments on them, and that their final form be determined after consideration of the comments of the churches . . . that the Study Department Committee take steps to form a commission of not more than twenty-five of the most creative thinkers of the churches to work on the preparation of the document, which will be the basis for the consideration of the main theme . . . and that the material issued in preparation for the Second Assembly should consist of [among other documents] a statement of perhaps ten thousand words on the main theme.

Those chosen to collaborate on the preparation of the main theme were later designated the Advisory Commission on the Main Theme of the Assembly. They were:

* Bishop Lesslie Newbigin, Chairman, India
Dr. W. A. Visser t' Hooft, Secretary (ex officio), Holland

Professor Hamilcar S. Alivisatos, Greece
Miss Leila Anderson, United States
* Rev. C. G. Baëta, Ghana
* Professor John Baillie, United Kingdom
* Professor Karl Barth, Switzerland
* Mrs. Kathleen Bliss, United Kingdom
Professor Emil Brunner, Switzerland
* Professor Robert L. Calhoun, United States
* President Edgar M. Carlson, United States
Professor Paul Devanandan, India
Mr. T. S. Eliot, United Kingdom
* Professor Georges Florovsky, United States
Professor Josef L. Hromadka, Czechoslovakia
* Professor Hendrik Kraemer, Switzerland
Professor Donald Mackinnon, United Kingdom
Dr. Charles Malik, Lebanon
* Professor Roger Mehl, France
Mr. Francis P. Miller, United States
* Dean Walter Muelder, United States
Professor Reinhold Niebuhr, United States
* Rev. Daniel T. Niles, Ceylon
* Professor Edmund Schlink, Germany
Professor G. F. Thomas, United States
* Professor Henry P. Van Dusen, United States
* Professor H. Vogel, Germany
* Professor Gustav Wingren, Sweden
* Professor C. H. Dodd, United Kingdom
President John A. Mackay, United States
* Professor V. E. Devadutt, India
* Professor Paul Minear, United States
* Rev. Owen Chadwick, United Kingdom

* Members who took part in the third meeting in which the report to the Assembly was drawn up.

The Central Committee at its meeting a year later—in 1951 at Rolle—heard a report by Bishop Lesslie Newbigin of the Advisory Commission. While many of the members had been skeptical that it could "accomplish its objective," he said, all at the conclusion of their first meeting felt that "they had been given a profound and meaningful ecumenical experience." The decisive word in the theme chosen at Toronto the Commission had thought was "hope." How Christian hope could be adequately stated was a difficult but important question:

We speak on the one hand of immediate hopes for our children, for peace, for the evangelization of the world, for our sister churches. Although we speak thus of hope, we live in a world where many hopes do not materialize. We know that we must ultimately depend upon a final hope which cannot be exhausted by these lesser hopes and lies beyond them. Yet the ultimate hope for the victory in Christ has in fact been split into two parts. On the one hand, many Christians have entertained hope in progress in history, and on the other hand hope in immortality. Recent history has shattered hope in historical progress so that in fact many are left only with hope for personal immortality, frequently vaguely conceived and by itself wholly inadequate. It is essential that we recover a sense of the great hope which is involved in the simple statement of the Apostles' Creed: "He shall come again."

When this question is opened in any representative gathering, large difficulties appear. This has happened in the meeting of the Advisory Commission. . . It is apparent that many . . . find this report unacceptable. It will be certain to cause discussion. We are convinced, however, that it will not be possible to hold an assembly of representative Christians, unless we can tell the world what to hope for. If the Central Committee decides that it can continue the work of the Advisory Commission, the Commission will desire to proceed to the full. It plans three additional meetings and extensive correspondence together with individual written contributions to the development of the whole.

The Bishop ended with this personal testimony:

In the new liturgy of the Church of South India there occurs a prayer in which the following is said by the whole people: "Thy death we commemorate; Thy resurrection we confess; Thy second-coming we await. O Lord, have mercy upon us." As I have said this in many congregations in South India I have come to know that the health of the Church depends upon our ability to say with our whole heart: "Thy second-coming we await." [2]

The Central Committee noted with appreciation the work of the Advisory Commission and authorized the General Secretary to send "the substance of this first report" to the churches for criticism and comment.

After a lengthy discussion over the wording of the theme, during which strong sentiment was expressed that the title should refer to Christ as "Risen Lord," the Committee voted that for the time two versions be accepted—"The Crucified Lord, the Hope of the World," and "The Crucified and Risen Lord, the Hope of the World"—with the understanding that it could see no basic difference between them and that they would "provide suitable direction for the preparatory work of the Assembly."

The final decision on the phrasing of the title was taken at the Central Committee's next meeting the following year at Lucknow. At that time "Christ—the Hope of the World" was adopted.

Addressing the Central Committee at Lucknow on "The Relevance of the Christian Hope to Our Time," Dr. John A. Mackay stressed the importance of getting the main theme of the Assembly "into perspective and stimulating discussion" of it, so that the views expressed might "be passed on to the Advisory Commission."

How to formulate the Christian hope was, he said, the important question. He recalled the disagreement at Rolle over the phrasing of

[2] *Ibid.*, Rolle, 1951.

the title and approved the action accepting the simple statement "Christ—the Hope of the World." Two criteria should guide the Commission, he recommended, in its exposition. The formulation, he elaborated, should be "biblically founded" and "ecumenically unifying."

Christ was the hope of the world in two respects, he continued.

In the New Testament there is, first, the hope that is grounded in Christ's coming again. Christ will come. He will come at the end of history, or within it, to inaugurate the new order of things. There will be the resurrection of the dead, a judgment in which secrets will be laid bare and by which injustice will be righted, and the triumph of the Church, the Bride of Christ [consummated]. This is a real hope, with important implications. It means that the historical process is not endless change or meaningless drift. It means that humans should not construct utopias as things in themselves to be realized within history. It means that we should not absolutize anything that is merely historical. This hope, moreover, makes a special appeal to millions of Christians who are politically and culturally homeless. For them the hope at the end of history becomes more real than it has been for centuries.

Yet, if our interpretation places exclusive emphasis upon this aspect of Christian hope, we cannot expect that there will emerge out of it any crusading missionary movement. This hope can infuse tremendous courage into Christians; it can produce sensitivity and saintliness in Christians. But it could not produce crusaders, because it tends to create pessimism regarding the future and the significance of historical movements as such. Only when Christ is regarded as coming to establish a millennial era within history does the specifically eschatological hope produce a crusading spirit.

The other phase of the New Testament hope is the hope of Christ's calling, as set forth in *The Epistle to the Ephesians*. In this epistle, St. Paul does not speak of Christ's second coming, but rather "the hope of his calling." It is thus equally native to the New Testament so to experience the power of the living Christ, or of the Holy Spirit, that one is filled with a buoyant hope concerning possibilities in history. When the hope of Christ's coming in this sense is real, the words, "Follow me," become real. Christ is a road companion moving towards history's frontiers. He says also, "Go, make disciples of all nations; and, lo, I am with you alway, even unto the end of the world." Christ's command and promise are the ground of the missionary hope. Some believe that what is achieved in history is a prelude to Christ's coming again. So they "prepare the way of the Lord." However that may be, they find themselves under a compulsion which they must obey. For us this means that millions in and outside the Church must be evangelized. A revived Church which is mastered by the Holy Spirit of promise is the key to the Church's fulfillment of its missionary mandate.[3]

The theme must be ecumenically unifying, he added. It would be disastrous to turn Evanston into a forum in which rival viewpoints on the Christian hope were aired. Presentation of the hope must rather be a fountain of inspiration. This could be assured only if, alongside the ultimate eschatological hope which was real and basic, justice were done to the equally real and biblical hope which related to Christ's calling.

[3] *Ibid.*, Lucknow, 1952-53.

In our time, he pointed out, the hope of Christ's calling was at the heart of great spiritual movements such as the *Kirchentag* in Germany and striking evangelistic movements in East Asia and the Western Hemisphere. The hope which rested upon the Lordship of Christ in history and was a manifestation of the presence in time of the kingdom of God and its supernatural powers must be given equal status with the ultimate hope at history's close; otherwise, Christians would be disloyal to what Christ offered to his Church in the way of supernatural power, and the nerve of the missionary movement would be cut.

Dr. Paul Devanandan contributed a paper entitled "The Relevance of the Christian Hope to Our Time," which appeared in the April (1953) *Ecumenical Review*. The first report of the Advisory Commission on the main theme for the Second Assembly had been printed and circulated among the churches in 1951 for their critical comment, and a second report was now before the Central Committee. Dr. Devanandan explained that a final statement had yet to be written for submission at Evanston. He went on:

> Meanwhile, this report and the previous one represent the efforts of the Advisory Commission to clarify its own thinking, and to arrive at some common understanding of the scope and significance of the subject. The intention is also to initiate an ecumenical conversation . . . among the churches; and to create general interest among Christians everywhere in this much neglected aspect of the Christian creed. Such ecumenical conversation will provide the Advisory Commission with valuable material for further consideration, so that the final formulation of the theme . . . will be in a real sense the fruit of the common experience and considered thinking of the ecumenical movement.

The second report was a great improvement on the first, he believed, because of the suggestions received from the churches and many individuals. Although the criticisms expressed radical dissent on certain points, there had been agreement that the theme of Christian hope was "eminently suitable and challengingly relevant."

There was difficulty, he said, in the way of reaching an agreement on the nature of Christian hope, which had its cause partially in the outlook of Continental theology and the socio-political situation of European Christians. "To many people the Commission's treatment of the theme gave the alarming impression of being concerned primarily with the second-coming of our Lord," he said. "It looked as though the Evanston Assembly were being urged to take easy comfort in a future . . . which will somehow break upon the dismal, sorry state of things in this present world for which the Church has no message of buoyant courage nor any counsel for action."

The use of strange terms like "eschatology" and "apocalypticism" had also "further clouded the issue." Continued the paper:

Many re-acted violently to what appeared to be a lop-sided emphasis on a Christian doctrine of last things, which sounded far too pessimistic and world-denying. In fact, the fear was expressed that the first report's treatment of the theme was not only misleading but unsound. It looked as though it advocated a millennarianism which might not only seriously affect the inner life of the Church, but might also adversely counteract its evangelistic mission.

Concern especially was expressed whether such futuristic over-emphasis on the coming victory of Christ and the final establishment of his reign would provide the needed dynamic for an active program within and outside the Church to meet the crying needs of our time. Would such an interpretation of Christian hope, it was further asked, furnish a Gospel for the evangelist in non-Christian lands? Grave doubts were also expressed that any futuristic over-stress on the Christian hope would lead to serious misconceptions of the Christian faith in the minds of the adherents of non-Christian religions, especially in Asia.

While it had not succeeded fully, the second report of the Advisory Commission represented, Dr. Devanandan said, a conscientious attempt to amend the criticized portions of the first.

The Commission wanted to make perfectly clear that our hope is Christ Jesus, the Crucified and Risen Lord. . . . "Jesus Christ died and is risen from the dead. By this event the world has been re-constituted and the human situation re-defined. . . . In Christ there is a new creation. . . . The Christian hope is hope in God in Christ . . . the confident affirmation that God is faithful, that He will complete what He has begun."

At present the Lordship of Christ is discerned only by faith [the second report declared] . . . but Jesus himself has promised that he will return in glory and . . . will judge the earth. And yet it is true that we do not simply hope for Christ's return as an event in the distant future. The Christ who is to come is already the boundary of our lives, he who meets us at each step forward, to whom every tomorrow belongs.

In the life of the Christian believer, therefore, there needed to be the dynamic of the dual affirmation of faith, which maintains at the same time that in Christ Jesus the New Age has already come, and that the new life in Christ awaits fulfillment at the end of history. In Christ we are given new hope, not for escape from the world, but for a share in his victory over the powers of evil in the world and in our lives—a participation that is real, though not completed here and now. At the same time, we must not lose sight of the supreme hope of eternal life beyond judgment and resurrection. If we do we blur our criteria of action and are in danger of confusing Christian with merely human satisfactions.

The Commission had revised the first report, he continued, to set forth that Christian hope had a very direct bearing on the earthly calling of Christ. "If we say that the deepest level of our existence lies in the love of God made concrete in Jesus Christ, it is ours to show this forth, not only in word but in deed." The revised report directed attention, he said, to five areas in which there was need for Christian action: Christians were urged to work for peace, righteousness, freedom, truth, and fullness of life. And it had concluded with strong emphasis on evangelism.

But it had become clear, he admitted, that still further work would have to be done by the Commission before the statement of hope for the Assembly would be acceptable. He reviewed some of the difficulties which stood in the way of writing something all Christians could accept. One was terminology, particularly that of the Bible. "The members of the Advisory Commission were conscious of this," he said, "at every turn of the discussion. All the terms which are used in connection with Christian hope . . . defy translation or create misunderstanding. This task of making biblical words and concepts intelligible to the modern mind, whether in Europe and America or in Asia, is an undertaking to which we need seriously to address ourselves."

A second major obstacle arose from the idea that God's purpose for the world in Christ had been fulfilled in the incarnation, but the ultimate triumph of his will for the destiny of man in the world still awaited completion. This many Christians found utterly confusing.

Nor had the second report resolved the difficulty in the first over the emphasis on apocalypticism, which seemed to rob the present of all purposive significance and to invest the future with a glory unrelated to and divorced from the stress and strain of the realities of life here and now. This, he thought, was to some extent the result of failure to understand the Christian meaning of history, in which it is recognized "that God is with us at all times . . . so that the certainty of God's final purpose invests any living present in human history with a purpose which is partly derived from the fulfillment that is yet to be and partly also from the unrealized imperfections striving toward the end."

The Commission was aware, he said, that the first report had given the impression of visualizing the nature of Christian hope in such a way that it did not urge Christians to a prophetic ministry of informed action in a world where so much evil was rampant. "Perhaps this criticism . . . that greater emphasis should be laid on Christian responsibility for action should be given serious thought."

Dr. Devanandan appended to his paper a paragraph on the relevance of Christian hope to the missionary movement:

> In Asian lands resurgent religions put forward four main claims. They maintain that religious truth cannot lay claim to absolute validity here and now. This is . . . the basis of the prevailing temper of religious universalism and the common tendency towards syncretism. Secondly, they tend to define religion as self-realization, a mystic experience of ultimate absorption in the Ultimate Reality. This makes religion purely a matter of individual preference, both subjective and relative. Thirdly, resurgent faiths in Asia talk of a "secularity that is spiritual," and in doing so they seek to invest world life with a more tangible sense of reality, although metaphysically they cannot provide substantiations for it. Finally, they are evolving a new interpretation of their traditional ethics so as to encourage a sense

of responsibility in social action. In fact, this is really an attempt to re-define the nature and destiny of man. [Over against these philosophies has to be set] the claim of the Gospel, which is that it is . . . valuable not only here and now, but that it is true for all times, and therefore true now.

Many of the members of the Central Committee joined in the discussion which followed the dissertations of Drs. Mackay and Devanandan at the Lucknow meeting.

Dr. Martin Niemöller said:

The hope of final things and the hope of Christ's calling are basically one, the unity lying in the fact that Christ has come and that we are on our way to meet him; and his coming is the strongest incentive to work, as the parable of the talents suggests. The time is short in which Christians can prove that they are true husbandmen. The wholeness of Christian hope and its relevance lie in the fact that Christ's appearing is shown in and through Christians—"Inasmuch as ye have done it unto one of these the least of my brethren, ye have done it unto me."

Dr. Ivan Lee Holt submitted a statement of personal criticism of the reports in which he believed he represented the opinion of the Methodist Church in the United States:

The report . . . is . . . still too pessimistic. The optimism of divine grace, at least as it expresses itself in the present temporal order, is almost entirely overlooked. The stress of the document is either upon what has taken place, once for all, in the mighty acts of God in the biblical dispensation, or upon what will take place at the end of history, when the sheep will be separated from the goats. But what God is doing redemptively in this present time is seen only under the ugly aspect of judgment and not in the bright and encouraging calm of moral and spiritual reconstruction, the bringing of peace and justice among men. Though the theme may be the crucified and risen Lord, Calvary still dominates Easter, and the suffering Lord takes precedence over the victorious Saviour, who is able to do exceeding abundantly above all that we can ask or think.

The world now needs desperately to be encouraged by the Church. The Church itself needs to take heart by considering its own superlative gains. The cause of Christianity and more especially Protestantism in the United States will be greatly injured if Evanston sounds the pessimistic and uncertain note that runs through the revised document.

Dr. Holt then proceeded to suggest the principles which "must be stressed."

The world needs Christ now as its Saviour. . . . Those who have accepted him and serve him, individually and collectively, are the sons of God and shine in good works like the sun. . . . They are the leaven in this world of sin; the whole creation can rise to new life through the power of creative goodness. . . . The Church must not be so concerned with its own future and destiny. It can never become what God wants until like its Lord it loses itself in an anxious concern and effort to save the lost. . . . Like Paul, we must boast in what God has enabled us to do so far, and through that take courage for the future. . . . We can best prepare ourselves and watch for his coming by living now and encouraging others to live as if he had already come.

Rev. Clifford Urwin proposed that the thinking of the Commission be altered to bring out the connection between faith and hope. "Hope springs out of the present experience of the believer," he stressed. There was need, he thought, to distinguish between Christian hope and the hopes to which "the masses" had turned only to meet disappointment.

Commenting on the reference in the revised report to "the Crucified Christ [as] the hope of the Utopian," Mrs. Douglas Horton pointed out that, while the statement might be true, it spoke about Christ as Christians knew him but as humanist utopians did not know him. "Our real task is to make utopians want to know what the Christian hope is," she added, "so that they will then come to understand both concept and language."

Bishop Janos Peter of Hungary stated that the Churches under his care had found the reports satisfactory.

"The fact that we can formulate our hope in the same way as the Advisory Commission gives us encouragement and hope in the actual situation of our churches and the world. We are all united in the conviction that there is a connection between the oneness of the world and the unity of the Church, as well as between the disunity of the world and the disunity of the Church. The more we serve church unity, the more we bring near to solution the seemingly insoluble problems of our time."

It was not enough to criticize and destroy utopian hopes, Dr. M. M. Thomas asserted. Concern for human beings and justice must be put in their place.

Evangelism and social action should be emphasized, declared Dr. Edwin T. Dahlberg, who hoped that at neither point "should we become resigned or weary."

Mr. P. Mahanty said that it would help if the Bible Societies would prepare a document on the meaning of the word "hope" in the Bible and in the various languages into which it had been translated, and Mrs. Norwood M. Phelps remarked that the scriptural statement "Christ in you the hope of glory" gathered up what they were trying to say.

While expressing appreciation of the second report, Dr. Henry Pitney Van Dusen spoke of "deep disquiet in certain circles . . . concerning it." This centered, he explained, around "the degree to which the expectation of Christ's return within the historical process determine(d) the Christian hope." He summarized three positions held by Christians on this issue:

Some feel that the whole of the Christian hope must be defined in reference to the ultimate eschatological hope. Some maintain that Christ will come and bring the fulfillment and the terminus of history, but do not believe that this defines the whole Christian hope; for them additional elements of the Christian hope are found in the presence of Christ now and of the Holy Spirit. Thirdly, there are those for whom a confident affirmation of the coming of Christ at the end of history has no essential place in Christian hope. They do not deny the coming of Christ, but they do not believe it to be essential. They point to the biblical expectancy regarding the immediate return of Christ, and to the fact that this has not happened, and to the consequent danger of a misuse of biblical eschatological terms.

The Advisory Commission had been asked, Dr. Van Dusen said, to set forth "the essential common message of the Churches concerning Christian hope," and if it did this, it had either to arrive at a statement to which all could agree or to say frankly that there were differences and indicate what they were.

There was biblical and historical evidence, Dr. Franklin Clark Fry reminded the Committee, that "the propulsive quality of Christian faith was exhibited in times of tragedy," and that the absence of a strong sense of mission in the report could be dealt with at that point. He thought the relation of Christian hope to the Holy Spirit had not been made clear. Neither had the real danger in democratic utopianism been indicated, which was its menace to "the integrity of the individual." "Christian faith must be zealous," he said, "not so much for equality as for the preservation of individuality." He noted that "peace" had been referred to in a way that was confusing, "the peace which comes from faith in God" standing "parallel to international peace, and so with freedom."

The discussion led to the appointment of a committee to summarize for the Advisory Commission the views which had been expressed. It consisted of Bishop Angus Dun, Dr. V. E. Devadutt, Bishop Ivan Lee Holt, Bishop J. E. R. Lilje, the Bishop of Malmesbury, Dr. Martin Niemöller, Mr. M. M. Thomas, Dr. Paul Devanandan, Dr. Norman Goodall, Dr. John A. Mackay and Dr. Henry P. Van Dusen.

Toward the end of 1953, the Advisory Commission on the main theme finished its third and final report. It was sent to the Assembly participants in May, 1954, and made available a month later to the public. "Probably not less than four hundred people contributed directly or indirectly to the writing," declared the Chairman, Bishop Lesslie Newbigin. Speaking on the report at Evanston, he suggested that the Assembly might take any of three courses with reference to it: bury it, with or without ceremony; adopt it, after amendment, as a report of the Assembly; or send it to the churches for study and such action as they chose to take concerning it. The Assembly decided to follow the third suggestion, which was in consonance with the policy of the World Council of Churches with reference to such pronouncements.

2. The Theme Presented and Debated

Before referring the final report on the main theme to the churches, however, the delegates spent four days in a study of it. They were organized into fifteen groups, and their findings were presented by Bishop J. E. R. Lilje, who served as chairman of a coordinating committee for the study. His report, as amended by the Assembly, follows:[4]

We are profoundly grateful for the work of the Advisory Commission. The Report exhibits a substantial ecumenical consensus. It indicates the direction in which we must all move: away from ourselves towards Christ, our only hope, away from human desires, doctrines and ideologies towards the Word of God which alone has eternal authority and power, away from the godless self-centeredness of this world towards the kingdom of Christ.

As we discussed the Report at this Assembly, sharp differences in theological view-point were expressed among us. In view of the greatness of the theme, this fact should occasion no surprise. The nature of our disagreements and their reference to the contents of the Report are described in brief here and more fully in the précis of our discussions. But even our difficulties provided us with a common bond, as, confronted by this great theme, we saw our differences and disagreements become diverse insights into its richness.

Our major criticism of the Report relates not so much to its substance as to its mode of expression; not to what is said, but to what is not said. We find that the note of joyous affirmation and radiant expectancy which should mark a statement of the Christian hope does not sufficiently illuminate the Report. We find certain important omissions: the present work of the Holy Spirit in the Church and the world; specific reference to "signs of hope"; adequate treatment of the theme of creation and cosmic redemption.

We are not agreed on the relationship between the Christian's hope here and now, and his ultimate hope. As the précis of our discussion clearly reveals, we are not satisfied with the presentation in the Report of the so-called "rival hopes." Some hold that a too sympathetic account has been given of these hopes, some ask for a more understanding treatment of them and many point out that the list is incomplete and should certainly include hopes which falsely bear the Christian name. We are not wholly satisfied with the treatment of the non-Christian religions and are not agreed on the correct definition of our hope as it applies to all who, while believers in God, do not know him as revealed in Christ. There are many who feel that the Report should emphasize more strongly the solidarity between the people of the Western world and those of other continents. And some think that too sharp a distinction is made between the Church and the world.

The Report has engaged the full attention of the Assembly. It moved us not only to agreement and disagreement, but to testimony. It is our desire that all who read it will be moved to give utterance to the Christian hope in their own words and with the additions which their thought and prayer

[4] *The Evanston Report: The Second Assembly of the World Council of Churches, 1954,* edited by W. A. Visser't Hooft. pp. 70-72.

discover. Our witness will thus become our united response to the Report, for by its aid, and with the guidance of the Holy Spirit, we shall then speak together of the living Christ, the hope of the world. The joyous word rings across the world and through all time: "Christ is risen!" We cry: "Christ is risen indeed!"

Because Jesus Christ died and rose again for the world and will come again to renew it and judge it in his glory and grace, this world is anchored to him with unshakable hope. He rules over all history by the power of his cross and resurrection and nothing can pluck this world out of his hands. His eternal purpose of redemption will be brought to its complete consummation. Because Christ is the living Christ, he is able to meet us in every circumstance of life and every mood of our hearts.

The Holy Spirit is living and working within men. The steadfastness of Christian men and women in their daily work and their courage in times of trouble are tokens of our hope in Christ. The fruits of the Gospel when it is proclaimed in the world, the winning of the hearts and lives of men by Christ, are tokens of hope. A society which seeks to recognize human dignity, where there is an attempt to distribute justly the burden and benefit of labour, where there is effort to banish hunger, war, and despair, is a token of hope.

All these witness to his coming in our time where the Gospel is preached and the sacraments administered and the Holy Spirit descends and dwells in us; and to his coming in glory and triumph at the end of this age.

The Church witnesses to this hope when it seeks, in unity with its Lord, to be *his* Church; when it is in the world as he is in the world to seek all, to save all, to serve all; when it manifests growing unity in its fellowship; when in its sacramental life the bread and cup are truly shared across all barriers of class and race, culture and wealth.

It is in this perspective that the Report of the Advisory Commission is presented to the churches. It cannot be represented as the only word of the Assembly on this subject. It is, however, a creative and provocative ecumenical statement of Christian hope for this day. And it is, therefore, forwarded to the churches, with the commendation of this Assembly, for their study, prayer and encouragement.

A précis was compiled from secretarial notes of the discussions on the main theme in the fifteen groups and in the plenary sessions of the Assembly, and made public. While not attempting to give a detailed statement of all comments, or "to assess the importance of the points argued," it was found useful for the additional information it contained on the thoughts and feelings with which the delegates received the report of the Advisory Commission.

"The fact that the Assembly commended the report . . . to the member churches indicates general support for it," according to the précis. "Criticism was vigorous and frequently far-reaching. Nevertheless, it was clear from group and plenary discussion that the Assembly wished to take a generally favourable action upon it. Discussion revealed the following four specific points of approval:"

(a) The report is biblical in its source of authority and its scheme of thought and expression.

(b) The report rightly bases Christian hope not on human expectations but on God's promise attested in Scripture and on the fact of Christ's active presence.

(c) The report sets forth the unity of the Christ of history, His presence in Word and Sacrament, and His coming again in glory and judgment, thus correctly discerning the eschatological character of Christian hope.

(d) The report recognizes that the Church is the sign and witness of God's mighty acts, the means of His working and the field wherein His glory is to be revealed.

"The general approval given to the report was reflected in all of the discussion groups . . . ," said the précis. "Yet it is of the nature of discussion groups that they should be able to express their approval briefly and . . . spend more time on criticism. For that reason this précis of necessity devotes more attention to comments of a critical nature. But it should not be forgotten that these criticisms were always made within the general frame-work of deep appreciation for the report as it was prepared by the Advisory Commission."

Omissions of important aspects of hope were noted. Some felt that the work of the Holy Spirit had not received due attention. Others thought the report relied too much on biblical and revealed theology, with not enough attention to natural theology, and so weakened its message of hope for the world. "The personal hope of Christians of life and resurrection after death was too little stressed," many thought, "and the relation of these to the final manifestation of the Kingdom of God." It was pointed out a number of times that the supposed relationship of the Christian hope to the destiny of the Jews was not made explicit.

The language of the report came in for severe criticism as "heavy," "too theological," "too biblical and therefore unintelligible to many." "It is a vibrant theme but a lugubrious document," ran one comment. "There is missing the joyful trumpet sound which belongs to the words about hope in the New Testament," declared another.

On the "Basis and Ground of Hope," many called for a clearer statement of the relationship between the final revelation of eschatology and that which was being unfolded in history. The report did not seem to them to deal sufficiently with those elements of Christian life which were "hope-producing" and clues to an understanding of the ultimate hope. "The work of the Holy Spirit in creating hope as well as faith, the hope-giving side to forgiveness of sins, and historical vindication of Christian truth, were all felt to be a part of the Christian hope, but neglected by the report," according to the précis.

Certitude and joy seemed to many to be wanting. Belief in the risen Christ should give the words and deeds of Christians "a unique and authoritative quality, without which statements about hope are dead."

There was disappointment that in the eschatological interpretation of hope Christ was not related to the world in a way "to make either our experience of him or our proclamation of hope in him meaningful." A more immediate and understandable reason for hope in Christ is "the new humanity which is the result of his death, resurrection and ascension. The present experience of Christ being the basis of our hope, the link between hope and action is found in the neighbour in whom Christ crosses our path repeatedly. The report failed to provide understanding of this vital connection between hope and obedience."

Another comment pointed out, quoting the précis further,

> that the treatment of "other hopes of our time" seemed often to be tinged with self-righteousness because of a failure to keep ever in mind the fact that Christ is indeed the centre of world history, not simply of church history. This failure is then reflected in the tendency to forget that, on the one hand, there may be serious manifestations of false hopes within Christianity, and, on the other, searching evidences of true insight and valid witness elsewhere.
>
> At points of seeming contradiction in the discussion, light is cast upon the significance of this criticism. While many complained that full justice was not done to the other hopes of men, others held that these had been too positively presented with inadequate indication of the Christian answer. Similarly, many spoke of the document as being insufficiently universal, while others felt that non-Christian religions were dealt with too sympathetically. The treatment of Marxism was criticized both as too severe and too easy. Many felt strongly that natural hopes for health, family and so on had not been adequately treated. Others asked for a fairer treatment of sober-minded scientists and scientific thought, as distinguished from naive "scientific humanism."
>
> Careful analysis of the discussion indicates that these contradictions are themselves clues to a consensus regarding this section: that it fails adequately to relate all hopes and all tasks in the clear light of the revelation of God and the purpose of God for the world he created and rules. Because of this failure, rival hopes are defined without sufficient understanding of their dialectical nature as both revealing and concealing the truth of God.

The report itself must, of course, be read if it is to be appraised fairly and its significance seen in relation to the thinking of the World Council of Churches, and in its bearing on the ecumenical work of the churches. (See Appendix H.)

Papers prepared by Dr. Edmund Schlink and Dr. Robert L. Calhoun on "Christ—the Hope of the World," at the request of the Advisory Commission, were the most exhaustive explanation from the platform of the main theme. They stood in the program before the reports of the Commission and the committee appointed to coordinate the findings of the fifteen groups of delegates which had been organized to study the theme.

Professor Schlink spoke concerning hope in Christ from the standpoint of those who are at home in the traditional terms of eschatology. In the New Testament, the end of the world is linked with Christ's coming. How, then, can he be the hope of the world? Manifestly, he will not bring social salvation to man.

If . . . we place emphasis on the preservation of this threatened world, we miss the point of our . . . theme completely. If we expect Christ to insure this world, so that men can continue undisturbed their pursuit of liberty . . ., carry on their business and seek an improvement in their standard of living, then Christ is not the hope of the world, but rather the end of all . . . hopes; for he is the end of the world. The name of Christ is taken in vain, if it is used as a slogan in the world's struggle for its own preservation.

Our real problem is what we shall do when Christ returns to judge the world, as the Scriptures say he will; and the answer is clear enough.

He who died for the world intercedes at the throne of God for those who cry unto him. It is to the crucified Lord we must cling, and in him we must hope. Only through faith in him will we find salvation in the Day of Judgment. . . . For God has made him . . . our righteousness.

Jesus Christ, then, is the hope of the world, not because he guarantees the preservation of this world, but because he liberates us from all the binding ties of this world . . . because he calls men out of the world. . . .

Christ is the hope of the world, insofar as the world no longer remains the world, but is transformed through repentance and faith. Christ is the end of the world with its joy and sorrow, and for just that reason he is the world's hope; for as the world passes away, he will bring to birth a new creation.

Christ, therefore, comes again into the world as its judge and . . . redeemer. He will accept some and reject others. He will raise some to life and others to death. To some he will say, "Come, ye blessed of my Father"; and to others, "Depart from me, ye cursed." He will smash the rule of the mighty, the rich and those self-contented in their unrighteousness. He will destroy the comfort of the satisfied, the happy, and those who are at home in the world. But the poor in spirit, they that mourn, they that hunger and thirst after righteousness, the peacemakers—all these will he save.

Thus, future separation is already happening. By the preaching of the cross, God is already putting to shame the wisdom, virtue and power of this world, and saving the foolish, the unworthy and the helpless. Even now the coming redemption is taking place through the gospel. . . . Through baptism and the Lord's Supper the believer participates even now in the power of the coming resurrection. He who is born again to a living hope through the Holy Spirit is even here and now a new creature. . . . In the Church the coming new creation is already a present reality. . . . Behold, all things are become new.

For this reason, the days in which we live are the last days. In his resurrection Christ has broken through the limitations of this world and has been raised to become Lord over the world. All men and all powers are subject to Christ, whether they know it or not, whether they recognize him or revolt against him. When he returns he will make his victory apparent to every eye and bring to an end the revolt of this world.

This world's time, then, is tightly hemmed in by the victory of Christ. It is quite impossible to break out of this encirclement. Into this hopeless situation comes the call of the gospel through which the world is bidden to recognize its Lord. . . . "Today if ye will hear his voice, harden not your hearts."

What does hoping in Christ mean? Not sleeping, but watching with the utmost alertness. From the time of the apostles until our own day, it has not been paralysis but action that characterized the life of those in whom Christian hope dwells.

Dr. Schlink asked what the actions of hope were. The first, he said, was preaching the gospel to the whole world. That the gospel may be preached "in truth and purity," study was important. The Assembly had been wise in choosing for two of the sub-themes evangelism and the Church's unity in faith.

Another action of hope was accepting responsibility for the just ordering of society. For this reason, the Assembly had appointed the third, fourth, and fifth sub-themes for study, these having to do with important social questions—economic justice, peace, and racial accord.

But those who hope in Christ do not preach the gospel and work for justice and peace with the thought of saving the world thereby. They work for order, that they may preach the gospel and men may hear and be saved. God gives time for all men to decide.

We do not preach the gospel in order that the world may be preserved. Rather we accept our responsibility for the preservation of the world, in order that many may be saved through the gospel. God preserves this world, in order that through the gospel salvation may be offered. . . . We try to establish justice, that we may preach the gospel.

There has always been misunderstanding of this fact. The World Council of Churches is undergoing this temptation.

We do not know what results our evangelism and our struggle for a just society will accomplish, said Dr. Schlink, but we know the most important thing we need to know—that our work is not in vain in the Lord. "If God be for us, who can be against us?" This is not the hope of the world; it is the hope of the Church. To this hope the Church must call the world.

Professor Schlink's paper was followed by that of Professor Robert L. Calhoun of Yale University:

Our theme, as all the world knows by this time, requires that we seek some common understanding of Christian eschatology. This is by no means the whole meaning of the theme, but it defines an essential perspective in which the meaning must be interpreted.

The difficulty is not merely that the word "eschatology" is a somewhat formidable one, less familiar in some parts of the Church than in others. . . . The real trouble has been that [it] . . . is all too easily misinterpreted by omitting or under-emphasizing essential aspects of its meaning. The ordinary popular paraphrase, "doctrine of the last things," actually favors such misinterpretation. It suggests much too simply either some "far-off divine event" at the end of a long, vague future, without direct bearing on our life today; or else an end of the world at a particular date, calculated by methods for which most of us find no good warrant in either Scripture or Christian experience, and in which most of us do not believe.

Pre-occupation with "the end" as if it were a date on the calendar—the final date, the only crucial one that still awaits us—and neglect of "the present" as comparatively trivial in importance leads to one sort of distortion. Pre-occupation with "the present" and refusal to take seriously the significance of "the end," in its biblical and Christian sense, leads to another sort. Both these errors are made easier when we over-simplify the admittedly difficult concept of Christian eschatology into a static "doctrine of the last things."

Happily, there is a better reading of the word, closer both to the classical and to the biblical meaning of its component parts. Eschatology is the doctrine concerned with *the limits or boundaries* of our living, in time and existence, toward which at every moment our whole lives tend.

For Christian faith, God revealed in Jesus Christ is the boundary of our time and existence, at once infinitely beyond us and immediately near. For us he who is our Creator, the First, the Source of our being, is at the same time the Last, the End that gives significance. Time is our name for one order of the living relationships in which his presence and his acts are known to us and bear upon our lives. Time thus understood is neither illusory nor merely abstract or ideal. It is as concrete and actual as anything in the physical world. But it has no independent reality apart from the living God, Creator and Sustainer of the world, who makes himself known in Jesus Christ as Redeemer, who as Holy Spirit acts ceaselessly in human affairs.

Past, present and future are not separate segments of an endlessly outstretched line, a kind of space to be filled, but dimensions and directions within the living interaction of God and men. The future is not a kind of inverted past, nor an endless repetition of "tomorrows," but the homing of our unfinished lives to the One who gives them direction, meaning and fundamental security. He is the One who comes to meet us at every moment, yet who lives and promises that we can live beyond the limits of earthly time and space.

Hope is then not a mere expectation of things wished for, but the powerful, deep impulse with which we face joyfully and confidently toward the living boundary, the true end of our lives and of our world, at once here-now and yet-to-be. . . .

To think of eschatology in these terms is to re-affirm with full vigor the basic insights of a theology that finds the Kingdom of God, the lordship of Jesus Christ and the power of the Holy Spirit very present living reality. The Kingdom of God is of all present realities the most real, the providential order full of vital tensions, the cleansing flame of judgment and the stillness of grace, the steady swell of sustaining power and the incessant denial of rest here, that gives meaning to our life on earth. The Lord Jesus Christ and the Holy Spirit are at work now with the incalculable power of truth and love, transforming both Church and world. But the Kingdom and the Power are not restricted to the earthly doings of men. They work in judgment and mercy toward such glory for both Church and world as we can neither foresee nor achieve. In all this is our hope, despite all the forces of evil here and hereafter. . . .

The fundamental reality is God, his Kingdom and his righteousness, ever present and ever coming to judge and to bless his creatures. He is our hope, because in Jesus Christ he has come down into the midst of earthly history, taken our cross upon his shoulders and our wounds into his heart, met death and hell face to face for our sake, and filled the human scene with a vast new light in which we men are judged and blessed as never before. He is our hope because in Jesus Christ, died and risen, he gives us promise of strength to endure the stress of earthly battle, and of life with him beyond all earthly bounds. . . .

Christians' understanding of the gospel, Professor Calhoun said, is "mediated, in large measure, through living historical involvements; and for each, not the whole gospel as God knows it, but some aspect or version of it as man can know it 'in a mirror dimly,' is disclosed." All, while affirming with conviction what their own eyes have seen and their hands have touched concerning the word of life, should speak with humility and charity, studying to be aware always of possible misplaced emphases and fallacies in their own views.

From this standpoint, he spoke of American "activism," declaring that the "theology of the Kingdom of God" which actuates it "does not forget the final judgment nor the life everlasting; but its chief confidence has been in God's grace from day to day, and its stress on the duty of every Christian to live as a devoted follower and servant of Jesus Christ." Though "sound and basic doctrine," he said,

it is neither proof against distortions nor free of shortcomings. . . . We tend to confuse the will of God with our way of life, and to suppose that our version of the gospel of hope is the only one that is meaningful and true. . . . It is perilously easy for us to identify God's promises with the peculiarly American way of life; to suppose that the Kingdom of God is, at least in principle, our republican form of government, the economic system we call free enterprise, the social and cultural heritage we cherish. . . . Like fellow Christians in every country and in every part of the Church, we are apt to regard our own understanding of the gospel as both correct and sufficient.

This bore immediately, he thought, upon the treatment of the main theme. In at least two ways American activism could hamper understanding of the gospel of hope. For one thing, centering attention on human effort, it stood in danger of thinking of Christian hope as primarily assurance that the Church's best efforts would succeed, with God's help. There was need, he suggested, to keep in mind that God's ways were not man's ways. "Christ, our hope, was crucified before he was raised in glory. . . . God's will, not ours, is to be done."

A second limitation often regarded as typical of our thought is the supposition that the Kingdom of God will be fully realized within earthly history. Here, again, a valid insight is involved. This is God's world. His Kingdom enfolds it and his will is being done in the midst of it, overcoming its evils with the redeeming power of good. But . . . there is no sign that earthly history is being progressively purged of evil and steadily nearing perfection. On the contrary, new achievements bring new perils and new forms of corruption. . . . Death, "the last enemy," armed with terrible new weapons, . . . stands across the path of every person and people. . . . Again, it is God and not we who can know what new order will be.

In the discussion on the main theme, which followed its presentation to the Assembly, there was more criticism by the delegates of what seemed to them serious faults in its development.

Professor Ernest Kinder disliked the disproportionate emphasis it put upon the present reality of Christian hope, as against the ultimate hope. He insisted that his judgment was biblical, rather than merely European. In the Bible what was ultimate gave vitality, he said, to the present.

The terms "they" and "we" in the report met with objection in the remarks of Mrs. John Karefa-Smart, from Freetown, Sierra Leone. They gave it a Western tone, she pointed out. "Sober and urgent rather than basically joyous" described the hope of Africans, she said, addressing herself to the criticism of the document because of its lack of the note of joy.

A statement of dissent from the Orthodox delegates on the main theme drew praise from Anglican quarters, the Bishop of Durham declaring that the report of the Advisory Commission "ill bore comparison with it."

Describing himself as a Christian humanist, Rev. Kenneth Henderson expressed the hope that the report might inspire the laity with greater self-confidence.

Dr. Henry P. Van Dusen, as Chairman of the Study Department committee which had appointed the Advisory Commission and as a member himself of the Commission, said that none of the latter body was "wholly satisfied" with the text of the report, but he felt that it was a fair consensus.

During the discussion, the Anglican Bishop of Jerusalem objected to certain references in the report to Israel. Every statement of that sort was likely to become, he said, bitterly controversial. He emphasized that many hopes other than that of Israel had been fulfilled in Christ's coming. And the deletion of all mention of Israel was urged by Father Makary El Souriany of the Coptic Church, who thought that the World Council of Churches ought not to single out any nation for special concern. Dr. Charles P. Taft also decried the references to the Jewish people, which were, he said, "an addition to the report of the Advisory Commission." They should not be foisted on a minority not agreeing with them, he protested. They did not represent, in his opinion, "the right way to start a mission to the Jews" and would certainly impair the relations of members of the Assembly with their Jewish friends.

Continuing this phase of the discussion, Dr. Farid Audeh of Beirut asked whether Christ was less the hope of all peoples than of one and

said he did not think the Assembly wished to make the position of the churches in the Near East more difficult. He read a telegram from Dr. Charles Malik disclaiming as a member of the Commission any suggestion that political events at present involving the Jews were connected with the fulfillment of Christian hope.

Dr. Aziz Suryal Atiya of Egypt expressed himself as persuaded that the mention of Israel would be a "disservice to the World Council of Churches" in the Near East.

The opposite side was taken by Dr. Hendrikus Berkhof of the Netherlands, who said that Jesus Christ was born of Israel as the fulfillment of God's promise to his people, and there was no political implication in the wording of the report.

The steering committee of the Assembly had decided, Dr. Franklin Clark Fry announced eventually, that the "hope of Israel" should be made a subject of further study under the guidance of the Central Committee and presented a resolution, which was passed, as follows:[5]

> In view of the major divergence of views revealed in the action of the Assembly amending the Statement on the report of the Advisory Commission on the main theme by omitting all references to "the New Testament concepts of the ultimate fulfillment of God's promise to the people of ancient Israel," the steering committee is convinced that this is the type of issue that calls for further study and ecumenical conversation, and therefore proposes that the Central Committee be instructed to make suitable arrangements for such study and conversation on this subject.

A statement on "The Hope of Israel" signed by twenty-four delegates who thought that this subject should have been treated as a part of the report on the main theme was received by the Assembly to be printed in the minutes:[6]

> In view of the decision of the Assembly . . . to omit any reference to the hope of Israel in its Statement on the Main Theme, we feel it our duty to offer an explanation of our convictions in the hope that it will help toward closer understanding with those from whom we differed.
>
> Our concern in this issue is wholly biblical and is not to be confused with any political attitude toward the State of Israel.
>
> We believe that Jesus Christ is the saviour of all mankind. In Him there is neither Jew nor Greek, but we also believe that God elected Israel for the carrying out of His saving purpose. Jesus Christ as Man was a Jew. The Church of Jesus Christ is built upon the foundation of the Apostles and Prophets, all of whom were Jews, so that to be a member of the Christian Church is to be involved with the Jews in our one indivisible hope in Jesus Christ. Jesus, the Messiah of Israel, was accepted by Gentiles but rejected by His own people. Nevertheless God is so gracious and mighty that He even makes the crucifixion of His Son to be the salvation of the Gentiles (Romans xi, 11). Whether we are scandalized or not, that means

[5] *The Evanston Report,* p. 79.
[6] *Ibid.,* p. 327.

that we are grafted into the old tree of Israel (Romans xi, 24), so that the people of the New Covenant cannot be separated from the people of the Old Covenant.

The New Testament, however, speaks also of the "fulness" of Israel, when God will manifest His glory by bringing back His "eldest son" into the fold of His Grace (Romans xi, 12-36; Matthew xxiii, 29). This belief is an indispensable element of our one united hope for the Jew and Gentile in Jesus Christ. Our hope in Christ's coming victory includes our hope for Israel in Christ, in His victory over the blindness of His own people. To expect Jesus Christ means to hope for the conversion of the Jewish people, and to love Him means to love the people of God's promise.

In view of the grievous guilt of Christian people towards the Jews throughout the history of the Church, we are certain that: "the Church cannot rest until the title of Christ to the Kingdom is recognized by His own people according to the flesh." [Findings of the Pre-Evanston Conference of the American Committee on the Christian Approach to the Jews, at Lake Geneva, August 8-11, 1954.]

We cannot be one in Christ nor can we truly believe and witness to the promise of God if we do not recognize that it is still valid for the people of the promise made to Abraham. Therefore, we invite all men to join in praising and magnifying that God who "concluded them all in unbelief that He might have mercy upon all" (Romans xi, 32).

Signed:

H. Berkhof—Holland	H. d'Espine—Switzerland
M. Boegner—France	R. S. Louden—Scotland
A. Koechlin—Switzerland	H. F. Schuh—United States
P. Maury—France	A. E. Haefner—United States
T. F. Torrance—Scotland	J. Hromadka—Czechoslovakia
H. Vogel—Germany	G. J. F. May—Austria
J. Sittler—United States	J. P. Van Heest—Holland
O. S. Tomkins—England	M. Niemöller—Germany
J. Smemo—Norway	A. H. Ewald—United States
E. Schlink—Germany	L. Pap—Hungary
H. L. Yochum—United States	S. B. Coles—Canada
N. A. Winter—United States	G. Stratenwerth—Germany

Dr. Georges Florovsky presented the statement of the Eastern Orthodox delegates concerning the report of the Advisory Commission:[7]

Being entrusted with the responsibility of representing the Orthodox member churches at this Assembly of the World Council of Churches, we are in duty bound to present the following comments on the Report of the Advisory Commission on the Main Theme: "Christ, the Hope of the World."

(1) We are happy to express our general agreement with the Report of the Advisory Commission. Ever since Pentecost, the Orthodox Church has been proclaiming to the world that Christ is the Hope and especially in our own time she is persistently re-affirming that all human hopes must be interpreted and judged, condemned, or amended, in the light of this hope. That at this decisive moment of its life the World Council of Churches unanimously felt that Christians should proclaim this hope to the world,

[7] *Ibid.,* pp. 329-31.

and should alert themselves to their responsibilities in a world full of distress and suffering makes us rejoice exceedingly.

(2) But this general agreement makes it even more necessary to state clearly, on the one hand, what we regard as not fully acceptable from the standpoint of the Orthodox Church, and, on the other, what we consider as requiring further development in the Report, and formally to draw attention to certain points which are not touched upon in the Report at all. Obviously, in these few remarks we cannot give a full confession of the Orthodox conception of the Christian Church. It must be affirmed, to begin with, in stronger terms, that the Christian Hope is grounded on Christian Faith. It is grounded on the belief that God takes a personal interest in human life and human history. God so loved the world as to give His only begotten Son. The Christian Hope is grounded in the belief that Jesus Christ, Incarnate Lord, came down from Heaven to save men. He accomplished the work of salvation on the Tree of the Cross and He manifested the new life for humanity in His glorious resurrection. He established upon earth His Holy Church which is His Body in which by the power of the Holy Spirit He abides with man for ever. The Church of Christ is one loving Body of Christ in which all generations of believers are united in the new life in Christ.

It is misleading to describe the Church simply as "the pilgrim people of God" and to forget that the Church Triumphant and Church Militant are but One Body. It is precisely in this unity that the Christian Hope is grounded. The Church is the great Communion of Saints. We upon earth live and strive in communion with the glorious "cloud of witnesses" revealed through the ages and are strengthened by the intercessions of the Theotokos and the Saints with whom we join in adoration of Christ our Redeemer.

(3) The Report justly stresses the importance of the belief in the second coming of Christ for the Christian Hope. However, we strongly believe that it is necessary to place an adequate emphasis on the actual presence of the Kingdom of God in the Church. The Kingdom has been founded by God through the Incarnation of His Son, the Redemption, the Resurrection, the Ascension of Christ in glory and the descent of the Holy Spirit. It has been existing on earth since Pentecost and is open to all men, bestowing to all who enter the power transforming and renewing human existence now on earth. Life eternal is not only an object of future realization; it is given to those who were called by the Word of God in the Sacrament of Baptism (Romans vi) and is continuously renewed through participation in the Holy Eucharist. Nothing has been left undone by God for our salvation and for the immediate transformation of human existence. Thus our participation in the renewed life of the Kingdom of God is a present reality as well as a future fulfillment.

(4) The hope in Christ is itself a gift of the Holy Spirit and no one can confess Him as Lord and Saviour except by the Holy Spirit. It would be in vain to preach Christ as the Hope of the World without mentioning divine action and acknowledging the reality of grace which is the sole source of this hope. The tragedy of the fallen world consists precisely in its inability to hope in Christ without the help of grace. Moreover, this hope is meaningful and fruitful only inasmuch as it leads man into the real life in Christ which pre-supposes the continuous action of the Holy Spirit within us.

(5) The paragraphs of the Report dealing with the unity of the Church raise serious doubts. This subject will be treated in full in the Section on

Faith and Order, but it should be noted that some of the ideas expressed in the Report lead to interpretations which cannot be accepted from the standpoint of the Orthodox Church.

The power of God is operating in the midst of human weakness. We never can fulfill all the demands which Christ makes upon us and in humility and repentance we must acknowledge our limitations and short-comings, applying steadfastly for an increase of our faith and strength. And yet it is in the Church that we find this strength. The reality of the New Life is never compromised or annulled by our failures. Thus, the Church of Christ, as the realized Kingdom of God lies beyond Judgment, whereas her members being liable to sin and error are subject to Judgment.

(6) In proclaiming that Christ is the Hope of the world, we must not lose sight of the reality that Christ is not separated from His Father and the Holy Spirit. Hope in Christ cannot be separated from the hope in God, the Father, and God, the Holy Spirit. Of all the promises of Christ, the most precious is when He asserts that the Holy Trinity will abide in us (John xiv, 23; xv, 26; xvi, 13-17; xvii, 21-26), Eternal life is but fellowship with the Divine Trinity.

(7) Hope in Christ must be interpreted in its true content. We place our hope in the Incarnate Son of God, in Whom we also have become sons of God, the Father, and co-heirs with Christ. This sonship constitutes the foundation, the content, and the aim of our Christian Hope. Adoption by the Father renders a man a "new creation." In Christ the Fatherhood of God has been revealed to us and communion with Him has been given. Through Jesus Christ, the Son of God, the Father bestows upon us the knowledge of truth, divine love, sanctification, eternal life, and ultimately participation in the divine nature (*theosis*).

(8) Hope in Christ means hope in the Blessed Trinity. The Orthodox Church gives clear expression to this truth in one of her prayers: "My Hope is the Father; my Refuge is the Son; my Shelter is the Holy Spirit; Holy Trinity, glory to Thee."

(9) Finally, we do not believe that the analysis of false hopes given in the Report is adequate and complete. False doctrines, which are mentioned in the Report, especially that of communism, threaten the whole human existence, threaten human personality as such. All of these de-humanize life. It is this aspect of false hopes with which the Church is primarily concerned. The danger for man which these false doctrines present appears to be sorely under-estimated in the Report. If we seek at the present time in our troubled and distorted world, a true basis for human hope, we must profess emphatically that it is only in the Church of God, Holy, Catholic, and Apostolic, that this basis can be found, since the Church is the "pillar and ground of Truth."

A large amount of space is being given in these pages to the report of the Advisory Commission, and for this there seems to be sufficient reason. At Evanston the main theme occupied nearly half of the time and overshadowed and qualified the remainder of the program. For three years it had aroused more general and intense interest in the churches than anything the World Council of Churches had presented to them. The discussion of it during months of preparation and in the Assembly revealed, as had nothing previously, the religious outlook of Christians the world over of different social and theological inheritances.

Disclosures in connection with it of obstacles and limitations besetting organized Christianity in both its denominational and its ecumenical contexts raised many questions concerning its future. Certainly, it must be reiterated, one is not fully prepared to judge the prospects of the World Council of Churches unless he has taken time to ponder the multifarious aspects of the experience into which this conventional theme, "Christ—the Hope of the World," plunged the churches.

It is clear that the choice of the theme had been unmanipulated and democratic. The suggestion of hope came as we have seen, from a lay consultant at the meeting of the Central Committee at Toronto in 1950, where the theme was scheduled to be chosen. Various ideas had been introduced. The Bishop of Chichester had opened the discussion by pointing to pressing social questions currently before the world, speaking in particular of the depersonalizing effects of life in modern society. "Man's Quest for Significance" might be, he thought, a suitable subject for the Assembly to consider; or it could be phrased "Christianity and the Freedom of Man." Others had followed with proposals, with here and there emphasis on the need to keep to a definitely spiritual point of view in the development of whatever theme was chosen. In the midst of the conference, Mr. E. J. Bingle of the staff of the International Missionary Council, who had been a teacher in Madras Christian College and was to become editor of *The International Review of Missions,* dropped his suggestion about hope. The World Council of Churches had become for many, he explained, a symbol of hope, and hope as the theme for the Assembly would carry something of the orientation of "Expectant Evangelism" which the International Missionary Council (at its Whitby meeting in 1949) had made its special study. And soon the Committee had agreed "that the main theme of the Assembly should be along the lines of the affirmation that Jesus Christ as Lord is the only hope of both the Church and the world; and that the subsidiary themes of the Assembly should be considered in relation to this central theme."

The criticism afterwards that the theologians had dictated this action had apparently no basis in fact. Once it had been chosen, however, the theme had almost unavoidably to be passed to them for development. The origin and meaning of Christian hope were to be explained, how it differed from other hopes had to be defined, and its implications for the life of man at the point of every relationship needed to be set forth. Who could be asked to undertake this task, if not those who by training and experience were most competent and trusted in the field of theology? Those in other walks who might have been chosen as ablest, aside from technical knowledge, to attempt it would have been quickest to decline because of their realization of their own incompetence. As a matter of fact, a majority of the thirty-two persons appointed to the Advisory Commission on the main theme were theologians, and the naming of the others who were not was probably a concession to the anticipated complaint that the pulpit and the pew had been omitted. However, the first draft of the Commission's report went to the churches in the World Council for study and suggestions for its revision, and amateurs from the rank and file of their constituents, as well as scholars and experts, had ample opportunity to try their hand at revising what had been written. Not a few responded, and the Commission apparently endeavored to give fair consideration to all the amendments proposed.

If one had reflected on the manner of the selection of the main theme, he might have been slow to say, as some did, that a different one should have been chosen. The presumption would have been that good men, duly chosen representatives of the churches, seeking prayerfully to reach a decision, would have been led of God. If the churches had come to a place where there could be in such matters no confident reliance upon divine guidance, one could but ask what became of the validity of prayer and of belief in God's presence in the midst of his people.

The assertion of others that there should not have been any main theme may have been, from a practical point of view, hasty and ill advised. Those who had been at Amsterdam in 1948 and, back of that, at other ecumenical conferences—Stockholm in 1925, Jerusalem in 1928, Oxford in 1937, Tambaram in 1938, and others—could not without misgivings look forward to another Assembly at which the familiar socio-religious themes would have further going over. These themes could be counted upon always to arouse discussion, but the process had already got to be too much like beating old straw. Many of those officially responsible for leadership in the various areas of social Christianity under the World Council of Churches had come to feel keenly the necessity of infusing into their work a more real and obvious spiritual meaning. From the standpoint of the Commission of the Churches on International Affairs, for example, Dr. O. Frederick Nolde, the Director, in his report of that organization's activities, mentioned as one need "study and clarification of the theological pre-suppositions of the churches' witness in international affairs . . . to undergird its work."

If the main theme had been dropped from the Evanston agenda, the Assembly certainly would have lost the richer part of its experience.[8]

[8] Dr. Nils Ehrenström, who had been associated with the study program of the ecumenical movement over twenty years, actually from its beginning, spoke of the main theme before the Central Committee at Lucknow in 1953, as follows:

"Looking back, I doubt whether any previous ecumenical gathering has ever been focused on a more central and timely theme. It concerns the very foundation of our Christian faith, and it pointedly speaks to our human condition today. It has already become a powerful crystallization-point in the thinking of the churches. Those of you who took part in the sub-committee at Toronto in 1950, which drew up the Assembly program, may remember how the discussion moved about among various alternative proposals, until it finally, as if by accident, crystallized around the subject of Hope. It was one of those inconspicuous decisions which, unknown to the actors, have a tremendous influence. In fact, the Toronto decision has released an expanding movement of thought and reflection far beyond anything the participants in that meeting could imagine or

This, notwithstanding the incongruent handling of it at times—as, for example, in the attempts "to decide questions of theology by popular vote," which properly enough drew criticism.

However, we may easily magnify unduly the hurtful effects upon the public mind of this sort of thing. There is enough religious literacy in the nonchurch multitudes to enable them to understand that language is only one of many symbols by which religious faith is expressed and—like the others—carries variant meanings for different people of equal conscientiousness and uprightness. The world, when it gives thought to such things, is not looking for Christians to think alike, so much as for them to learn the length and breadth of the love they profess, which, when taken seriously, makes room enough for brotherhood and cooperation, in spite of conflicting doctrinal formulations.

Protests on account of the theology of the report on the main theme were really misdirected. The Commission had understood that its statement should be, in the words of Dr. Mackay before the Central Committee, "biblically founded" and "ecumenically unifying," and these conditions evidently determined its substance and form. Its scripturalness had to pass traditional tests. It could have been biblical in a different and, for many, a more acceptable sense by following less closely the letter and emphasizing more the spirit, but it then would not have been, because of the theological conservatism of some of the churches and their representatives in the Assembly, ecumenically unifying.

What many of the critics really would have liked to see was a revision of the methods of scriptural exegesis; but Evanston was no place for that kind of undertaking, which, in itself, would have developed into the proportions of a main theme. Most of the members of the Commission were undoubtedly familiar with the modern criteria of scientific historical criticism, and many of them probably were accustomed to read the Bible with due regard for these; but any attempt to revise accordingly traditional views on such subjects as eschatology (to mention but one) would have begun an educational process needing time and another environment for its development and possibly inviting disaster for the Assembly. How far apart the scholars of the old and new schools were in their hermeneutical approach to the Scriptures was amply revealed by the addresses of Dr. Edmund Schlink and Dr. Robert L. Calhoun.

The World Council of Churches could not avoid being a meeting place of traditionalist and modernist; and a working unity between the two could be achieved, if at all, only on the basis of the former's vocabulary,

foresee. The World Council was led to this subject, as it were, blindfolded; it was of more than human choosing. . . . But the very significance and timeliness of the subject is the measure of our responsibility. Here the World Council . . . has been entrusted with a task of spiritual leadership of the first magnitude. To fail here would make the Evanston Assembly a landmark of frustration instead of inspiration."

which often causes their differences to appear greater than they really are, as the latter knows and is, for this reason, better able usually to make necessary allowances. There is a good deal of such theological accommodation in the ecumenical fellowship, as in the churches, by those who think the work Christians can do together justifies it and hope that cooperation and the educative influences of time will remove the need for it.

The liberal has another reason also for being less assertive theologically. He knows the possible harmful effects of a sudden disclosure of new truth on the faith of those who would have difficulty in making the readjustments in their thinking it might demand. A generation ago, a distinguished editor[9] of a religious journal wrote that if the facts known to science should be broadcast, with an explanation of their full import for traditional religious belief, the assurance of multitudes of Christians would be shaken. Informed Christians do not believe that any truth rightly interpreted would be found incompatible with faith, but the fact is that many earnest persons do not have the understanding in such matters to orientate themselves anew in their religious views.

Most of the members of ecumenical, as well as of denominational, bodies are responsible, moreover, for the organized programs of Christian work and fear the disruptiveness of theological controversy. By way of avoiding this danger, some think it best to keep to the language of the creeds, written or unwritten. It affords a common and familiar vehicle of communication and at the same time allows latitude for private interpretation. It enables Christians to pray and serve together and to grow in their apprehension of truth according to their varying powers and opportunities.

Some consider this course unwise, it should perhaps be added. They fear that the sense of the relevance of the churches' teaching to present-day life will be lost in the multiplying contradictions between reality and the traditional conceptions, even when there is much show of applying religious principles to everyday social problems. "Why not trust truth and speak it, whatever the casualties?" it is asked. Truth is of God, they argue, and if we respected it more, we should probably discover that he has ways of repairing its wounds and making it further, rather than hinder, the health of his work.[10]

[9] L. P. Jacks in *The Hibbert Journal*.

[10] "There is a strong feeling that the question of Scripture and tradition must be much more deeply studied. This question has great ecumenical significance, and many are convinced that no deep agreement can be hoped for, until some measure of understanding about it has been reached. The rise of historical and scientific criticism has wrought a revolution in the concept of the authority of the Bible, and of the relationship between Scripture and tradition. *Even those who maintain in words the traditional positions very rarely maintain them completely in their own deepest thinking.* Is this not a realm in which careful self-criticism is necessary, and in which we may find that the logic of events has driven us to seek for new solutions, or at least for a re-statement of the tra-

But this all concerns, in the first place, the churches, as already suggested. The World Council of Churches is their creation and can hardly escape their limitations.

The revision of Christian theology, if demanded, may not reasonably be looked for at the hands of theologians berthed in church-controlled schools or positions of ecclesiastical leadership. It must come, if at all, from outside the governing councils of the churches, or from those prophetic persons inside who are willing to be put out, if that penalty must be suffered for nonconformity. At least, it may have its beginning within, with the sacrifices to which it will expose those hardy enough to undertake it. When the truth has been made known, with its enlarging and enriching implications for faith, and its light seen by enough of the people, the churches then will follow, as will their leaders, with the sense of having themselves discovered the way God was leading.

Criticism of the theology of the Assembly missed the target. Changing the metaphor, the stream at that point was turbid from causes which lay back in its tributaries.

3. The Theme Reviewed

Anyone at home in the poetry of the Scriptures and the creeds, whether he understands its imagery literally or symbolically, will be likely to find the report of the Advisory Commission on the main theme profoundly moving. (See Appendix H.) In its way, it is a truly notable document, deserving of being read by every Christian, whatever his theological predilections. If one accommodates himself to its mood, it can but stir anew within him deep unvoiced longings whose source and end are, he knows, beyond him and yet a part of him, and invite him to return to its pages to keep alive remembrance of the eternal things revealed through faith, which eye has not seen nor can see. Many of its passages will fix themselves unforgettably in his memory. For example:

> In the new age that now is God has disclosed to eyes of faith what is the character of the age that is to come. We must speak of matters which, in the nature of things, defy direct expression in explicit speech, for which the language of inspired imagination employed in the Scriptures is alone adequate, for those are things that can be discerned and communicated only by the Spirit. The pure in heart shall see God as He is and know Him as they are known by Him. Those who are now sons of

---

ditional positions?" *The Bible and the Church's Message,* an ecumenical inquiry published by the Study Department of the World Council of Churches, Geneva, and printed in the United States, October, 1949, p. 6. (Italics above added.)

Note: Dr. Edmund Schlink spoke in his address to the Assembly on the main theme of demons. Asked afterwards by reporters whether or not he believed in demons, he replied, "Of course, but not in the sense of the conception of them prevalent in Bible times."

God will receive the fullness of their inheritance as joint heirs of Christ. There will be a new heaven and a new earth. We shall all be changed. The dead will be raised incorruptible, receiving a body of heavenly glory. The agony of the created world will be recognized as the travail of child-birth. Blind eyes will see, deaf ears will hear, the lame will leap for joy, the captive will be freed. The knowledge of God will cover the earth. The Holy City will appear, made ready as a bride adorned for her husband. The choir which no man can number will sing hallelujahs to the praise of the Eternal. God's people will enter into the sabbath rest, and all created things will be reconciled in the perfect communion of God with His people. It is in such visions as these that the Spirit enables us to point to the splendour of the salvation that is ready to be revealed in the last days. It is toward this salvation that God guides us in hope. This hope is not seen, or it would not be hope; but it is promised to us as suffering, sinning, dying and believing men. Therefore we wait for it with patience.

Our hope is grounded in one great Event, comprising the incarnation, ministry, death and resurrection of Jesus Christ. In this Event the purpose of God for mankind, foreshadowed in His dealings with Israel and declared by the prophets, found fulfillment, and His Kingdom was inaugurated on earth, to be consummated hereafter.

The tremendous Event occurred within a brief epoch which soon passed, leaving the broad scenery of history ostensibly unchanged. One concrete result alone was to be discerned: the Christian Church. It appeared as a small, obscure community, unwelcomed and almost unnoticed by the great world.

It knew itself to be a colony of the heavenly fatherland planted in an alien territory, and looked forward to an end lying beyond this earth and a day when the fullness of what God had done in Christ would be finally disclosed. It also knew itself to bear responsibility for the world for which Christ died, a responsibility that drove it to action and to suffering. This Church still exists. It is a historical society living among other societies in the world, and yet not of the world.

. . . .

We must all die, one generation after another. But Christ died—and is risen again. Christ's own people are still members of His living Body. They are with Him. Within the communion of saints they remain united with one another. In the resurrection they will be manifested, each and all, in a new mode of being. They will know God, for they will see Him. In the fellowship of those who are made perfect they will know and love one another. All of them, even those who died immature and undeveloped, the despised, the failures, the defeated, will, in the communion of saints, draw upon the inexhaustible treasury of life which is God's gift to them all in Christ. . . . Beyond all defeat and persecution, beyond their own sin and guilt, beyond death and hell, the people of Jesus Christ will raise the hymn of triumph. . . . Their highest blessedness will be that God is God; and He will be all and in all.

The report had, of course, to be studied critically, and there was much in it that could be criticized, albeit such failures as marred it generally rooted, as already indicated, in the churches.

Criticism might well have started with the title, "Christ—the Hope of the World." Actually, the "hope of the world" for the Christian is God, as the report itself says in the first page; and the broader accurate phrasing would have invited wider attention to the body of the statement.[11] By greater care in the use of words, ambiguities and contradictions in other places also could have been eliminated. However, such faults are almost unavoidable when so many hands work at the composition of a document.

The position of Christ in relation to God in the thinking of Christians could have been defined with more persuasiveness, at least for those outside the churches. This would have called for less of the tone of affirmation and more of the manner of reasoning. There may have been a time when those prevailed who declared their beliefs with loudest voices and with least appearance of doubt, but it was different in 1954. In a scientific age treating conviction as knowledge was a sure way of losing the audience. Christian witnessing must learn and manifest a different temper if it is to have any chance of breaking through the barriers of the modern mind. To win a hearing, the faith must be declared in a way showing that the evangelist understands the obstacles life with its expanding horizons raises to belief and has himself found, in spite of them, solid grounds for acceptance of the Christian hope.

It could be said, further, that the report accented too strongly the objective bases of hope, or dealt with them almost to the exclusion of the subjective. According to its exposition, the Christian hope rested largely upon the acts of God in history. It rehearsed the cosmic drama with the crucifixion and the resurrection of Christ at its center and his coming again at the end of time as hope's sufficient support.

The trouble was that such acts are not self-authenticating. How does one determine whether an event was of God or not? How does one satisfy himself that God *is* at all, or, if he is, has anything to do with history?

The report assumed, of course, the dependableness of the scriptural witness. Its formulation of Christian hope was "biblically founded." "Look at the world and its panorama of past revelatory events through the eyes of the Scriptures," it said, "and rest your hope on God and 'his mighty acts.' " But many have to question the trustworthiness of the Bible when so interpreted.

Jesus apparently sought to meet the queries of men at this point by proposing a subjective test. The mightiest act of God, according to the Scriptures, was the creation of man "in his own image," and everyone came closest to God in the inmost recesses of his own being: therefore, Jesus said, "Look within." His reported words were: "If any man will to do his will, he shall know of the doctrine whether it be of God."

"Our obedience is one measure of our hope," declared the report; but obedience not only shows how much or how little we hope, but also

[11] Of course, according to the theology of the Basis of the World Council of Churches, Christ is "God and Saviour."

limits our power to hope, for it is the organ of hope. Apart from works, hope is dead, even as, the Scriptures say, faith is.

Here is an emphasis which the world can understand better than cosmological and eschatological conditions of hope; and it is "biblically founded."

Apparently seeking to avoid encouraging the notion that salvation was through good works, the report treated doing the will of God as following from the incentive of hope which had been inspired by God. We are under the compulsion to serve him, it declared, because of what he has done for us, especially at the cross and the empty tomb. And we would better serve him, seeing that as the crucified and risen Lord he is coming again to judge the works of every man. The report is slow to turn the problem around and look at it where heaven meets man in the common way with intimations of the ultimate, from which direction it is seen that hope is given as one serves, because in obedience he finds himself walking with God. "He that loveth is born of God and knoweth God: God is love." "We know that we have passed from death unto life, because we love the brethren." Nor does it speak of the danger of disobedience in terms of the loss of fellowship with God, and so of hope. "He that loveth not his brother abideth in death." At that point it might have confronted the reader with the true cause of hopelessness in our class-ridden society, in which there is so little love, and touched the need at which its message should have been aimed, whether in oppressor or oppressed.

Those who believe in Christ know that they already have eternal life, according to the report, and their hope looks forward mainly toward events in the eschatological future when he will come to consummate his kingdom. Without doubt, there are many who find comfort and encouragement in contemplation of "the last things" and should have the privilege of sharing this experience with others; but many also to whom eschatology has little or no meaning believe that they have fellowship with God in Christian worship and work. They think that they have eternal life now through spiritual union with God, as the report declares, and that this is the sufficient basis for their hope. For them it is enough to leave what is to be in his hands, who has loved them, they believe, with a love that is everlasting.

The report was criticized for its seeming joylessness. Whether justified by the facts or not, there is an impression that the early Christians possessed a radiant happiness and that this quality has been lost. What the Advisory Commission on the main theme had written was taken by some who studied it as supporting this supposition.

In the history and anatomy of Christian joy the Assembly would have had a subject with the potential dimensions of the main theme itself. Obviously, a document which had reached the stage of cold print could not be charged with an emotion that had not originally suffused its writing. However, the Commission, by the grace of the Chairman, who headed also the committee which prepared the Message of the Assembly, appended to this latter pronouncement to the churches the exhortation: "Therefore, we say to you, Rejoice in hope!" [12]

Had there been occasion to deal with this criticism more fully, the true reply would have been that joy, like hope, was born out of the obedience of love. Anyone who looked upon the world only cosmologically or theologically was likely to see little that made for rejoicing. The satisfaction some found in the promises of the Bible that the wicked should "utterly perish" could hardly be regarded as a part of Christian joy.

The Bible speaks of "joy in heaven," and one may feel that only God, who is omniscient, can be joyful in contemplation of the plight of humanity. Our guiding light perhaps is the fact that those who in the ways of Christian service come closest to the tragedies of earth are happiest, because therein they are convinced that God in Jesus Christ comes to meet them, whose word was, "Go . . . and I am with you alway."

In the opinion of many, the worst fault of the report was that, as already intimated, it made so little of the validated insights of Christian experience, which would have been a more intelligible and winning approach to the modern mind than the transcendent acts of God emphasized by the theologians and which seemed, after all, to afford the convincing grounds of belief in the doctrines of the Church.

4. The Message of the Assembly to the Churches

Concurrently with the consideration of the Advisory Commission's report on the main theme, a committee consisting of Bishop Lesslie Newbigin, of the Church of South India, Chairman; Dr. Charles W. Ranson, General Secretary of the International Missionary Council, Secretary; Dr. Kathleen Bliss, a member of the National Assembly of the Church of England; Professor Pierre Burgelin of the Faculty of Theology at Strasbourg; Archimandrite James Coucouzis of the Ecumenical Patriarchate of Constantinople; Bishop Gottfried Noth of the Lutheran Church of Saxony; with Dr. Nathan Pusey, President of Harvard University, Professor Robert L. Calhoun of Yale University and Mr. M. M. Thomas, Youth Secretary of the Mar Thoma Syrian Church of Malabar, serving as consultants, prepared the Message of the Assembly to the churches, which, after discussion at a plenary session and an open hearing, was adopted in the following form: [13]

[12] See p. 602.
[13] *The Evanston Report,* pp. 1-3.

To all our fellow Christians, and to our fellowmen everywhere, we send greetings in the name of Jesus Christ. We affirm our faith in Jesus Christ as the hope of the world, and desire to share that faith with all men. May God forgive us that by our sin we have often hidden this hope from the world.

In the ferment of our time there are both hopes and fears. It is indeed good to hope for freedom, justice and peace, and it is God's will that we should have these things. But He has made us for a higher end. He has made us for Himself, that we might know and love Him, worship and serve Him. Nothing other than God can ever satisfy the heart of man. Forgetting this, man becomes his own enemy. He seeks justice but creates oppression. He wants peace, but drifts toward war. His very mastery of nature threatens him with ruin. Whether he acknowledges it or not, he stands under the judgment of God and in the shadow of death.

Here where we stand, Jesus Christ stood with us. He came to us, true God and true Man, to seek and to save. Though we were the enemies of God, Christ died for us. We crucified Him, but God raised Him from the dead. He is risen. He has overcome the powers of sin and death. A new life has begun. And in His risen and ascended power, he has sent forth into the world a new community, bound together by His Spirit, sharing His divine life, and commissioned to make Him known throughout the world. He will come again as Judge and King to bring all things to their consummation. Then we shall see Him as He is and know as we are known. Together with the whole creation we wait for this with eager hope, knowing that God is faithful and that even now He holds all things in His hand.

This is the hope of God's people in every age, and we commend it afresh today to all who will listen. To accept it is to turn from our ways to God's way. It is to live as forgiven sinners, as children growing in His love. It is to have our citizenship in that Kingdom which all man's sin is impotent to destroy, that realm of love and joy and peace which lies about all men, though unseen. It is to enter with Christ into the suffering and despair of men, sharing with them the great secret of that Kingdom which they do not expect. It is to know that whatever men may do, Jesus reigns and shall reign.

With this assurance we can face the powers of evil and the threat of death with good courage. Delivered from fear we are made free to love. For beyond the judgment of men and the judgment of history lies the judgment of the King who died for all men, and who will judge us according to what we have done to the least of His brethren. Thus our Christian hope directs us towards our neighbour. It constrains us to pray daily, "Thy will be done on earth as it is in heaven," and to act as we pray in every area of life. It begets a life of believing prayer and expectant action, looking to Jesus and pressing forward to the day of His return in glory.

Now we would speak through our member churches directly to each congregation. Six years ago our churches entered into a covenant to form this Council, and affirmed their intent to stay together. We thank God for His blessing on our work and fellowship during these six years. We enter now upon a second stage. To stay together is not enough. We must go forward. As we learn more of our unity in Christ, it becomes the more intolerable that we should be divided. We therefore ask you: Is your church seriously considering its relation to other churches in the light of our Lord's prayer that we may be sanctified in the truth and that we may all be one? Is your congregation, in fellowship with sister congregations around you, doing all it can to ensure that your neighbours shall hear the voice of the one Shepherd calling all men into the one flock?

The forces that separate us from one another are strong. At our meeting here we have missed the presence of Chinese churches which were with us at Amsterdam. There are other lands and churches unrepresented in our Council, and we long ardently for their fellowship. But we are thankful that, separated as we are by the deepest political divisions of our time, here at Evanston we are united in Christ. And we rejoice also that, in the bond of prayer and a common hope, we maintain communion with our Christian brethren everywhere.

It is from within this communion that we have to speak about the fear and distrust which at present divide our world. Only at the Cross of Christ, where men know themselves as forgiven sinners, can they be made one. It is there that Christians must pray daily for their enemies. It is there that we must seek deliverance from self-righteousness, impatience and fear. And those who know that Christ is risen should have the courage to expect new power to break through every human barrier.

It is not enough that Christians should seek peace for themselves. They must seek justice for others. Great masses of people in many parts of the world are hungry for bread, and are compelled to live in conditions which mock their human worth. Does your church speak and act against such injustice? Millions of men and women are suffering segregation and discrimination on the ground of race. Is your church willing to declare, as this Assembly has declared, that this is contrary to the will of God and to act on that declaration? Do you pray regularly for those who suffer unjust discrimination on grounds of race, religion or political conviction?

The Church of Christ is today a world-wide fellowship, yet there are countless people to whom He is unknown. How much do you care about this? Does your congregation live for itself, or for the world around it and beyond it? Does its common life, and does the daily work of its members in the world, affirm the Lordship of Christ or deny it?

God does not leave any of us to stand alone. In every place He has gathered us together to be His family, in which His gifts and His forgiveness are received. Do you forgive one another as Christ forgave you? Is your congregation a true family of God, where every man can find a home and know that God loves him without limit?

We are not sufficient for these things. But Christ is sufficient. We do not know what is coming to us. But we know Who is coming. It is He who meets us every day and who will meet us at the end—Jesus Christ our Lord.

Therefore we say to you: Rejoice in hope!

II

"TOGETHER IN HIS LOVE AND HOPE"

A dominant note throughout the Evanston Assembly was a subdued, yet assured, consciousness of fellowship through Jesus Christ of all who call upon his name.

1. The Assembly Sermon

Bishop G. Bromley Oxnam of the Methodist Church in the United States preached the Assembly sermon at the opening service in the First Methodist Church. For his subject he had chosen the declaration from the Message of the First Assembly (Amsterdam, 1948), "We intend to stay together." He proceeded to develop this theme in the light of the closing verses of the eighth chapter of the Book of Romans, in which was declared the inseparableness of Christians from the love of God in Jesus Christ. "There can be no separation from the Eternal," he said, "nor from each other when we stand in his love." He recalled the testimony of Adolf Harnack in his presence in response to the question "Upon what do you base your hope for immortality?" Harnack had replied, without hesitation, "Nothing can separate me from the love of God."

"It is easy to affirm such a faith," said Dr. Oxnam, and confessed,

> I have done so again and again. But in deep humility I must confess my faith has cost me nothing. . . . I have never suffered for the faith. I have never been hungry. I have not been in prison. I have never had a stone thrown at me. I have not been persecuted. My faith has cost me nothing. I was born in a free land, and possess a freedom won for me by my fathers. I have inherited a faith for which others died. I have read of faggots and of lash and of the goodly company of martyrs. But for me it has been too much a matter of appropriating the benefits of Calvary rather than sharing in Calvary that the world might be redeemed. I bow in respectful

homage before my colleagues in this presence who know the meaning of prison cell, of fetters, of hunger.[1]

The love of God demanded unequivocal acceptance of the fact that "we who . . . are children of one Father are also brothers," he said. "As children of God, we are beings of infinite worth. . . . Personality flowers in freedom and . . . freedom must be preserved. . . . We are morally obligated to maintain freedom and in co-operation to extend it until at last all men are free. Together, we stand for the free mind in the free society, seeking the truth that frees."

Discovering the concrete means by which the ethical ideals of religion might be translated into the realities of the common life were, the preacher thought, the most compelling obligation placed upon clergy and laity alike.

When competent Christians seek to express the worth of personality in political institutions they speak of "government of the people, by the people, for the people." They declare "all men are created equal and endowed with certain unalienable rights." They insist that "government derives its just powers from the consent of the governed." They hold that their institutions shall be conceived in liberty. Thus they affirm that the state does not confer our liberties, it merely confirms them. They belong to us, because we are sons of God. We are endowed with these rights. . . . In this insistence, we intend to stay together. . . . We reject all forms of tyranny . . . [and] repudiate the assumption that the state has the right to determine the philosophy to which every individual who lives within [it] must give assent. . . . Together, we reject once and for all those theories that command us to conform or die, and affirm that dissent is treason and deviation disloyalty. . . .

But freedom is not enough. Justice must be established. Christians must face the issues of power and justice. Power must be brought under democratic control, justice established by the democratic process.

It is not enough for us to repudiate, as we do, the atheism of orthodox communism . . . to reject, as we do, a philosophy of materialism . . . to repel, as we do, the fallacious theory of social development and an abhorrent concept of dictatorship. Men who affirm that nothing can separate them from the love of God must renounce the practical atheism that lies in the affirmation that God is not relevant to all the activities of men. . . .

It must be made clear that we dare not identify the Gospel of Jesus with any historically conditioned political, social, or economic system. [It] stands in judgment upon them all. . . . The Gospel is not to be found in Adam Smith's *Wealth of Nations* nor in Karl Marx's *Das Kapital,* [but] . . . in Matthew, Mark, Luke and John, in The Acts of the Apostles, the Epistles of the New Testament, and in . . . The Revelation. It is to be found in the Hebrew prophets, in the lives of saints and martyrs, in the service of faithful followers of Christ, and in the continued revelation of God.

Stating that the per capita annual income in China was twenty-three dollars, in India forty-three, in Great Britain six hundred sixty, and in

[1] Dr. Oxnam's sermon is taken from the mimeographed text issued to delegates and visitors at the Second Assembly.

the United States fifteen hundred, the preacher said "brothers must face together" these disparities in living standards. "It is well nigh blasphemy to talk about the love of God and to declare that such issues are not the concern of the sons of God. . . . Upon these issues of freedom and justice, we intend to stay together."

"We are out for peace," the Bishop concluded. Christians were not to be deterred in their role as peacemakers by "spurious and even sinister appeals for peace to discredit this sacred word." They worked "in harmony with the moral law written into the nature of things," he declared. The universe was with them. "It was not made for madmen . . . not created for the lie."

2. Report of the Central Committee[2]

Bishop G. K. A. Bell presented the report of the Central Committee of the World Council of Churches, which bore the title *The First Six Years* and summarized the activities of the various departments since the First Assembly, and gave his impression of the conduct of the central executive body during this period.

The Committee had been confronted with many difficult issues, he said, but a harmonious relationship between the churches had existed, and their leaders on the Council's staff and in its committees had been able to proceed with "a working unanimity."

> What has engraved itself so clearly on my mind in the six years has been the steady growth of mutual trust, and deep understanding, as well as a greater sense of urgency. In subjects which ordinarily afford ample ground for controversy, whether political or theological, complete freedom, frankness and charity have prevailed. There has been no thought, even in the most difficult matters, of one bloc lining up against another; but always the sense of being an instrument of a World Council of Churches, not of a Council of the West or of the East, or of the North or of the South, and of a common desire to know the mind of Christ and to follow its leading to the best of our ability in all our relationships.

"I make bold," he added, "to say that this fellowship of churchmen from countries in eastern Europe with churchmen in the West, and of churchmen from Asia and Africa with churchmen from Europe, America and Australia is . . . of real significance for the future of the nations."

3. The General Secretary's Report

Introduced by World Council President G. Bromley Oxnam as "a man who was prepared providentially for this high task," the General

[2] Many of the actions of the Central Committee have been incorporated in the survey of the work of the World Council in Part Five.

Secretary, Dr. Visser 't Hooft, prefaced his report to the Assembly with a brief interpretation of the World Council of Churches:[3]

As we look back . . . we can see clearly that the emergence of the World Council idea was far more than an attempt to unify and simplify the organization of the ecumenical movement. It was also more than a new approach to the problem of co-operation and unity of the churches. The unofficial slogan of the Life and Work Conference [Conference on Church, Community and State] at Oxford in 1937 had been: "Let the Church be the Church." That slogan did not mean: "Let the Church live unto itself in ecclesiastical self-sufficiency," but: "Let the Church be the Church as it was intended to be by its Lord." In other words, the real motivation of the ecumenical movement was a sense of repentance that in the actual life of the churches the holiness, the apostolicity, the unity of the Church had been obscured and a determination to manifest more clearly the true nature of the Church of Christ. It was discovered that in order to demonstrate these fundamental characteristics of the Church the churches needed each other. For how could they "make all men see what is the fellowship of the mystery" (Ephesians iii, 9), how could they convince men that "the middle wall of partition" had been broken down (Ephesians ii, 14), if they continued to live in isolation from each other?

The churches also needed to speak and act together, in order to reveal that the Church depends on God alone and is independent from men. For it is only in their togetherness that they can manifest clearly how their fellowship in Christ transcends the barriers of nation, race, class or culture. They require each other's help to render a prophetic witness to the world in all realms of life. For how could they expect the world to listen . . . as long as they spoke with many and discordant voices? They had a common responsibility for the unfinished missionary task among those who have never heard the Gospel and for the pressing evangelistic task among those who had turned away from it. And they were called to go as far as conscience would permit them to go in showing that fundamentally there is one and only one Church of Christ.

It was this deep and comprehensive concern for the removal of all that obscured the true nature of the Church and for a clearer manifestation of its glorious mission which brought the World Council of Churches into existence. It is this same desire which has made it possible for us to stay together and to work together since the beginnings in 1937 and then again in 1948.

The World Council of Churches is therefore essentially an instrument at the service of the churches to assist them in their common task to manifest the true nature of the Church.

When churches come together . . . they do not meet as self-contained organizational structures. They are gathered together by the Lord. The economy of the *charismata,* the spiritual gifts, begins to operate. They learn from each other. They see anew the full dimensions of the Church Universal. They feel compelled to render common witness . . . undertake common tasks. . . . There is born among and between them a *koinonia,* a fellowship of participation in the work of the Holy Spirit.

It is important that we should neither overrate nor underrate the nature of this fellowship. . . . There is unity, but it is not the full unity for which our Lord prayed. It does not help to declare that our divergences in faith

[3] Quoted from mimeographed report issued at Evanston.

and order are merely accidental and unimportant. For unresolved disagreements have a way of reasserting themselves in unexpected ways. The World Council does not stand for a general relativism, but for an honest and respectful confrontation with the ultimate issues of the faith and refuses to . . . promote the cause of unity at the expense of the cause of truth. But it would be a lack of realism . . . if we should under-estimate the reality of the fellowship . . . given us. While recognizing its imperfection, we must render thanks to God that through the witness which we have been allowed to render together in many fields, through the common tasks which we have been permitted to undertake, the meaning of the wholeness, of the universality, and of the unity of the Church have become clearer to many.

Seen from the angle of its power or authority, the World Council is an extremely modest undertaking. Seen from the angle of the purpose which it serves, its task is one of unrivalled importance.

Dr. Visser 't Hooft at this point took up the fear of some that the formation of the World Council of Churches had been premature. The churches had themselves answered this anxiety, he asserted, by "the remarkably faithful attendance at meetings of our governing bodies, by the attendance at this present Assembly and the widespread process of preparation which had preceded it . . . , by financial contributions to the general budget . . . and . . . for interchurch aid and service to refugees."

This did not mean, he said, that the problem of rooting the Council in the life of the churches had been solved. "It is one thing to have the support of the church leaders, . . . another to strike roots in the life of the local congregations. . . . And the ecumenical movement can only live, if it lives in the intercession . . . convictions . . . sacrificial actions of church members."

There had been concern also, lest the Council might have undertaken too many and great responsibilities, which the General Secretary thought had been quieted. The heaviest single undertaking had been the care of refugees, and the churches by their extraordinary response had made it successful beyond expectations and finely expressive of Christian solidarity in the face of human need.

The criticism of some that the organization of the World Council of Churches would "freeze the ecumenical situation," the denominations being structurally "unable to produce that pioneering spirit which had characterized the . . . movement," seemed to Dr. Visser 't Hooft to have been met with "impressive signs of renewal of life" in the churches, as evidenced by "the new approach of the Commission of the Churches on International Affairs to the problems of international life . . . the new ground broken by the Ecumenical Institute, the Laymen's Secretariat, and the Youth Department, . . . the development of ecumenical work in East Asia through the East Asia Secretariat, . . . the pioneering in ecumenical understanding through the Advisory Commission on the main theme, and of progress in . . . association with the International Missionary Council." These new activities did not give the impression, he thought, "that the period of the hardening of the arteries" had begun.

It was in "the realm of church unity" that "the decisive actions" ought to have been taken, the General Secretary said. Had any progress been made there? He recalled the function "to proclaim the essential oneness of the Church of Christ and to keep prominently before the World Council and the churches the obligation to manifest that unity and its urgency for the work of evangelism," as set forth in the constitution of the Faith and Order Department, and explained that the Council had been giving attention conscientiously to it.

This did not mean that the Council promoted a specific conception of church unity. The "task in this realm can only be two-fold": he explained,

> first, to remind the churches again and again that co-operation or friendly relations are not enough, for unity means at least complete and unrestricted fellowship; second, to create the conditions in which the churches come to know each other, enter into searching conversation . . . and learn from each other, so that the walls of partition become transparent and finally disappear altogether. . . . The greatest service . . . the . . . Council can perform . . . is . . . indirect rather than direct. The Council cannot and must not negotiate unions between churches. . . . But the Council can and must work to create a situation in which there is so much in common between the churches, that there is no adequate reason for them to remain separate. . . .

With most of those who had journeyed to Evanston, the General Secretary realized that the Second Assembly would become a test of "the inner strength of our . . . cause." "The tremendous tensions of the present-day world, not only the gravest of all between the two groups of great powers, but also those between the continents" were bound to be reflected. "At the same time, the ecumenical development of recent years" had "inevitably led to a reconsideration by each confession of its specific heritage and of its place in the ecumenical situation and thus produced a stronger confessional consciousness."

> The state of the world public opinion is one of nervousness, irritation, suspicion and uncertainty, so that it will be hard to get a fair and patient hearing for all that we want to say together. Again, this Assembly will be under pressures from different sides with a view to get support for various causes.
>
> Thus we seem to be up against an almost impossible task. What reason have we to think that it can be performed? No other reason than that all that we know of God's plan of salvation in Christ and all that we know of the needs and sufferings of mankind . . . convinces us that the churches of Christ are called . . . to render a clear, common, independent and concrete witness to the healing and saving power of Christ and to his Lordship

over all human relationships. . . . We may confidently expect that in a real measure our divisions will be transcended, and that beyond and above the loud voices of this world we will hear . . . the eternal word of God.

Dr. Visser 't Hooft expected the main theme, "Christ—the Hope of the World," to be "uniting and inspiring." It could save the churches from self-centeredness, he thought, by calling them to look beyond themselves to the kingdom of God and their mission to announce its coming in acts of justice and love. It challenged them to answer "the world-wide cry for a convincing message of hope." If would help to orientate the Assembly in the study of the sub-themes by showing "how the whole life and witness of the Church must be determined by its dependence upon the Kingdom, rather than by the demands of the world."

With regard to the attendance at this Second Assembly, we have reason to be greatly encouraged. With very few exceptions, the member churches have eagerly responded to the invitation, and the vast majority have sent their full quota of delegates. It is especially remarkable that we have this time very much larger delegations from a number of countries in Asia. We can also note progress in the participation from Africa, though we must confess that the representation from this continent, as also that from Latin America, is not yet what it ought to be, in view of the strength and growth of the churches concerned. . . .

We are one in our conviction that all churches should have full freedom to participate in ecumenical assemblies through their officially appointed delegates. We deplore, therefore, that certain churches do not enjoy that freedom. But while they may not be in direct contact with us, they remain more than ever part of the fellowship of Christ. From one of those Churches we have received word that it remembered fellow Christians in other countries in its prayers and hoped that Christians elsewhere would remember [it] in their prayers. We shall certainly want to respond to this desire and try to remember in all that we say and do that we have a very special responsibility for those who are absent against their will. . . .

We express the hope that other Christian churches which share our faith in Christ as God and Saviour and as the Hope of the world, but which have had no contact with the World Council, will come to see that our one and only purpose is to be servants of the Kingdom of God and of Christ's Church on earth. We are ready at any time to enter into conversation with them, so that they may come to know our true intentions and, if possible, join our fellowship.

Concerning the Church of Rome, the General Secretary said:

No unofficial observers from the Roman Catholic Church will be present among us. In view of the 1949 Instruction of the Vatican and of the presence of such observers at the Faith and Order Conference in Lund in 1952, it had been expected that some observers would be allowed to attend this Assembly. Later on it was found that the necessary permission would not be given. The pastoral letter from the Archbishop of Chicago has stated the reasons for this refusal. It is surprising to find that this letter makes no reference to the Vatican Instruction and shows a serious lack of understanding of our true purpose. On the other hand, it is significant that a number of well-known Roman Catholic theologians in Western Europe have issued a substantial memorandum on the main theme of our Assembly which is a valuable contribution to our discussion. Introducing that document, the review *Istina* expresses its sentiments of fraternal sympathy with the effort made in the ecumenical movement to render a common witness to Christ as the only Hope of the world. It is good to know that in spite of deep divergencies there remains this precious link.

Dr. Visser 't Hooft concluded his report with a confident note of optimism. "It is conceivable," he said, "that the Assembly will become an impressive demonstration of the power of the Spirit which gathers the children of God together."

4. The Problem of Intercommunion

Nevertheless, it remains the ironic fact that the Lord's Supper has not been brought, as yet, within the area of full ecumenical fellowship. Not all those representing their denominations at meetings under the auspices of the World Council of Churches and other interchurch bodies are willing to sit down with one another at the Table of Christ, a fact both resulting from and explaining the failure of the churches to agree on the meaning of Holy Communion—how and by whom it shall be administered, by whom it may be received, and what it is supposed to do for those partaking.

As hard as it is to understand how Jesus, if he had the divine prescience with which he has been credited and expected his followers to manifest their spiritual oneness in a visible way, as it is held, could have instituted a memorial rite which would expose their disunity in such a conspicuous manner before the world, this is the apparently unresolvable situation; an observance of his Supper could have no official place on the Evanston program, as it could not at Amsterdam.

No one spoke of desegregation in this connection. It would indeed have been very much in order and its delay not more excusable on the grounds of conscience than in social spheres, where opposition to it by many who felt they were moved just as surely by Christian conviction was denounced.

However, Holy Communion was celebrated in Evanston at five services, announcements of which were carried by the Assembly bulletins.

In the morning of the second Sunday of the Assembly, Bishop Ivan Lee Holt, President of the Methodist World Council, was celebrant at a service in the First Methodist Church of Evanston, which had been authorized by the Council of Bishops of the Methodist Church in the United States of America, with the provision that all members of the Assembly might, if they chose, participate.

The following morning the Rt. Rev. Henry Knox Sherrill, Presiding Bishop of the Protestant Episcopal Church in the United States of America, administered Holy Communion in St. Mark's Episcopal Church of Evanston, which was "open to all baptized communicant members of the member Churches of the World Council of Churches," by an action of the House of Bishops in 1952 placing "gatherings for a responsible ecumenical purpose" under a special dispensation.

A celebration of the Lord's Supper according to the Lutheran rite took place the next day in the Immanuel Evangelical Lutheran Church of Chicago, Dr. O. V. Anderson, President-Elect of the Illinois Conference, officiating, to which the Augustana Synod issued to members of the Assembly the invitation: "In the name of the Lord Jesus Christ, our Redeemer, we invite to the Lord's Table this morning all who believe in His Actual Presence and that we receive His true Body and Blood in this Sacrament."

The Greek Orthodox Archdiocese of North and South America invited "all participants of the Second Assembly . . . to attend the Divine Liturgy of Saint John Chrysostom" in the Greek Orthodox Cathedral of the Annunciation in Chicago on Wednesday morning, at which Archbishop Athenagoras of Thyateira, assisted by Bishop John Shahovsky of San Francisco, presided.

On the following Sunday—the last during the Assembly—the sanctuary of the First Methodist Church of Evanston was again the scene of a Holy Communion Service, under the auspices of the Church of South India, at which the Rt. Rev. C. K. Jacob of Kottayam, officiated and Rev. J. R. Chandran, Principal of the United Theological College, Bangalore, preached. About a thousand persons communicated, participating in the liturgy of the Church of South India, a composite of parts of the rituals of the Anglican, Methodist, Congregational, and Presbyterian denominations which united in 1947 to form the Church of South India. The Supper began with the "Kiss of Peace," a rite preserved by the Mar Thoma Syrian Church of Malabar "since the earliest days of Christianity," in which each member of the congregation clasps another by the hand and says, "The peace of God be with you." The bread and the wine were brought from the rear of the church, along with the plates containing the alms of the worshipers, continuing an early Christian practice which originated in the custom of the people to provide these as a part of their offering.

At a service of preparation for this week's observances of Holy Communion in their several ways, Dr. Ernest A. Payne, General Secretary of the Baptist Union of Great Britain and Ireland, said:[4]

We are gathered to prepare ourselves for the service which sets forth, as does no other, the ground of our hope. As we do so, we are aware that

[4] From the mimeographed report circulated at the Assembly.

we shall not . . . be fully united in our observance, or able to participate together. . . . Who with the New Testament open before him or the long and devious story of the Christian Church in mind, would dare to assert that the mind of Christ is necessarily or fully expressed by either the majority or the minority in any particular Christian assembly, or even by the whole Church at any one moment in its pilgrimage? . . . The truth is that on the question of the ordering of the Lord's Table, on the question who should celebrate the Holy Supper and who should partake, Christians—even the Christians associated in the World Council—remain divided. . . . Each must obey his own conscience, standing himself answerable to his Lord. To try to force the conscience of another is as wrong as it is fruitless. Even to hint at such a thing as we approach this sacred service would be an act of sacrilege.

Invitations will be issued which will cause embarrassment, will not be accepted, from sincere convictions cannot be accepted. Barriers will be raised, must be raised, because of loyalty to what is apprehended as truth, and some will be hard put to it not to resent them.

We come perplexed, frustrated, in danger of being impatient with one another, inclined to charge those from whom we differ with obstinacy, or blindness or carelessness. Some are tempted to press for majority decisions and try to force issues. But who shall decide how heads are to be counted?

Tomorrow, and on other occasions during this Assembly, we must go together as far as we can and then go our own ways, in sincerity and charity, seeking each one of us that we may "discern the body," as the apostle has said it, and praying that this discernment may, by the mercy of God, be granted not only to us but to all those with whom we are united in this Assembly. . . . After the Communion services, we shall go out with Christ re-committed to a great adventure, to a great task; to the making of disciples, to the building up of the body of Christ, "until we all attain to the unity of the faith and of the knowledge of the Son of God, to mature manhood, to the measure of the stature of the fulness of Christ." We cannot but be aware that so long as we cannot meet together at the Lord's Table we have gone only a small part of the way towards our appointed goal.

III

THE STUDY SECTIONS

When the Central Committee had chosen the main theme for the Second Assembly at its Toronto meeting (1950), it had also "provisionally accepted" six subsidiary themes to be "considered in relation to this central theme: (1) A subject in the realm of Faith and Order, if desired by the Commission on Faith and Order; (2) Evangelism, with special reference to the evangelization of men in modern mass society, and to the missionary obligation of the Church; (3) The Responsible Society, with immediate reference to communism and other secular messianisms; (4) The Churches' responsibility for international justice and peace; (5) Race relations; and (6) The responsibility of the laity for the Church."

Eventually six topics of study by the Assembly were framed from these suggestions.[1]

I. Our Oneness in Christ and Our Disunity as Churches
II. The Mission of the Church to Those Outside Her Life
III. The Responsible Society in a World Perspective
IV. Christians in the Struggle for World Community
V. The Church Amid Racial and Ethnic Tensions
VI. The Christian in His Vocation

1. Our Oneness in Christ and Our Disunity as Churches

The Central Committee had perhaps shown—by leaving the decision on Faith and Order up to the 1952 Lund Conference—some uncertainty about the inclusion of a theme relating to Faith and Order. This may have arisen out of any number of circumstances. For one thing, the Lund Conference could be expected to cover thoroughly the prob-

[1] The six study surveys were published as separate booklets by the SCM Press, London, and in one volume *The Christian Hope and the Task of the Church: A Source Book for the Second Assembly,* Harper and Brothers, New York.

lems confronted by the churches in the area of Faith and Order and to report its findings; and the Commission might consider another inquiry so soon unnecessary. Furthermore, many in ecumenical circles had concluded that about all that could be said helpfully on theological issues dividing the churches had been said; and it could be foreseen that any need for discussion in this sphere of interest that might exist at the Assembly would probably be satisfied by the sessions in which the delegates addressed themselves to the main theme.

The Conference decided, however, that the subjects which had engaged it should have the wider attention of the churches through their larger and more representative Assembly of the World Council itself and proposed its theme accordingly. At the same time, it appointed to serve as a Preparatory Commission with responsibility for organizing and supervising the study the following scholars:

Dr. Oliver S. Tomkins, *Chairman,* United Kingdom
Dr. J. Robert Nelson, *Secretary,* United States
Mr. Percy W. Bartlett, United Kingdom
Professor J. Russell Chandran, India
Dr. Clarence T. Craig, United States
Bishop Angus Dun, United States
Professor H. d'Espine, Switzerland
Dr. R. Newton Flew, United Kingdom
Professor Georges Florovsky, United States
Dr. Herbert Gezork, United States
Dr. Perry E. Gresham, United States
Professor R. R. Hartford, United States
Dr. G. Jacob, Germany
Metropolitan Juhanon, India
Professor T. A. Kantonen, United States
Professor C. Konstantinidis, Turkey
Dr. John Marsh, United Kingdom
Dr. Ernest A. Payne, United Kingdom
Dr. Edmund Schlink, Germany
Dr. K. E. Skydsgaard, Denmark
Dr. T. F. Torrance, United Kingdom
Professor L. J. Trinterud, United States
Professor Gustav Wingren, Sweden

Addresses by Bishop Anders Nygren of Sweden, Professor V. E. Devadutt of India, and Professor Georges Florovsky of New York introduced at plenary sessions the Faith and Order subsidiary theme, "Our Oneness in Christ and Our Disunity as Churches." [2]

Bishop Nygren described the Third World Conference on Faith and Order at Lund in 1952 as "a turning-point" in study and discussion in this field. He said, in explanation:

[2] Quotations are from mimeographed texts of the three addresses.

The churches have come to realize that ecumenical labors must have a new focus. When we speak of the unity of the Church we speak of Christ and His Spirit. For that reason Lund set up its Commission on "Christ and the Church." This means that in their conversations the churches are moving from the periphery to the centre. Instead of registering our various conceptions—with eventual agreement or disagreement—we are led to the centre of Christian faith and required, not to present the peculiar conceptions of our denomination, but together to learn from the divine word. The Church of Christ is already a unity, and only because that is true does ecumenical work have promise. Just as there is only one Christ, so there is only one body of Christ, only one Church of Christ. .

Looking to the future, the distinctive element of our present situation is, as it appears, that to ecumenical study has been granted the privilege and responsibility of giving to Christianity this deeper insight into the essence of the Church. When the understanding of the Church as the body of Christ, which has now been discerned theoretically, becomes a mighty reality in the life of the Church, then the decisive step to the unity of the Church will have been taken.

"Church union means primarily two things," declared Dr. Devadutt, "the unity of the ministry and the unity of the sacraments." In elaboration of this idea, he said:

The fellowship of believers suffers a reduction when there is no common ministry and no common Eucharist. . . .

There is a paradox in the life of the empirical churches. . . . We are indeed one in Christ, but as churches we are divided. This paradox is of serious import. . . . As a Baptist, I subscribe to the conviction underlying the . . . practice of believer's baptism. But I have often felt a concern for the way in which this excellent practice has led many a Baptist to forget . . . a fundamental fact. While the conscious faith of the believer in the saving grace of Christ and the believer's experience of it are fundamental to his Christian growth, his faith were of no effect and his experience would not occur, if antecedently . . . something had not happened. It is the redemptive work of God in Christ . . . that makes that faith possible. . . . The objective ground for my being a Christian is not my decision or my response . . . but . . . the gracious act of God. . . . This is the one foundation of the Church and no man can lay another. Church membership is not based on the pursuit of an ideal agreed to as desirable by its members . . . [but] on an historic and intractable fact—the life, death and resurrection of Jesus Christ. We are indeed one, for we are all delivered and saved by one objective fact. This is our objective unity. Our oneness in Christ is therefore not a pious affirmation; not an idealistic hope; and not a theological inanity.

If the basic justification for calling ourselves Christian believers is this one objective fact, if the reason for the existence of the Church is this one objective fact, then our divisions on the empirical level are an alienation from that which alone justifies our existence as Christians and churches. If in all conscience some feel that the Christ whom they worship and whose sacrifice for their redemption they commemorate with an exultant gratitude at the celebration of the Eucharist bids them to exclude other believers in

Christ from participation . . . then the Christ they worship and the Christ others worship . . . [are] not the same Christ.

There are certain confusions with regard to the movement for church union.

The first confusion is that serious divisions are complacently identified with a desirable diversity.

The second confusion follows from the first—that church union implies the destruction of diversity and the achievement of a dead uniformity.

A third confusion is that union means an elaborate unified organizational structure with a central authority and an authoritarian government.

Church union . . . means the unity at least of two things—the ministry and the sacraments. The unity of the ministry would imply that in its exercise the God-given vocation of a minister shall have no delimitations set for it by man-made divisions, excepting such as are necessary for a proper and orderly exercise of that vocation. The unity of sacraments will imply that the members of the body of Christ will have the privilege to participate in the sacred feast whenever and wherever it is duly set. Once such a unity is achieved, the question whether there should be a federation or an organic structure of administrative unity will be . . . of little moment.

I am aware that the unity of the ministry and sacraments is organically connected with the question of the unity of doctrine. Lund found, however, that twenty-five years of discussion of these questions . . . has only brought [us] to an impasse. If I understand the spirit of Lund, the desire was to start afresh on the basis of Christology. I take this to mean that we are now bidden to re-orientate our thinking to . . . the centrality of Christ in the Christian Faith. . . . In Christ we are one. In him we have an objective unity which cannot be invalidated by anything we do in actual practice.

A church that lives out of communion with another church is taking upon itself a dreadful responsibility, for it is saying in effect to its sister church, "You are not founded on Christ." . . . The call to find in our actual relations an expression of the objective and given unity is a call to obedience.

Professor Florovsky's address bore the title "The Challenge of Disunity," which indicated its main emphasis. "No Christian can ignore the fact of Christian divisions," he said, and proceeded to characterize the condition of disintegration in Christendom, as follows:

There is but one Church, as there is but one Lord. . . . Yet, Christians are divided. The Christian world . . . is split into antagonistic camps. . . . There is no common mind among Christians. . . . There is no common "Christian language." . . . The use of Scriptural language . . . is often ambiguous and unreal. . . . Christians of different persuasions meet each other very often . . . as foreigners and strangers. The years of the modern ecumenical movement may have improved this situation, but not to any considerable extent, simply because the movement itself was confined rather to an advanced minority in the churches. . . .

Asking what the sub-theme "Our Unity in Christ and Our Disunity as Churches" meant exactly, Dr. Florovsky said:

It may mean that Christians are united by Christ, in his redeeming love, from which no human being is excluded, as Christ died for all men.

The phrase may suggest that Christians are at one in their common allegiance to the same Lord. Surely, this link . . . is very real . . . supernatural . . . as no man can confess Jesus to be Lord, except by the Holy Spirit. We must gratefully acknowledge this bond of peace, this community in hope and allegiance. . . . Still, this allegiance is so variously and divergently interpreted and understood . . . as not to secure a sufficient ground for our unity as churches.

When Christians of various traditions and persuasions meet in an ecumenical setting . . . they always have to face the fact of their conscientious disagreement, in spite of their earnest desire to agree. The greatest achievement of the modern ecumenical movement is in the courage to acknowledge that there is a major disagreement . . . which cannot be exorcized by any appeal to unity or toleration.

Taking cognizance of those who say "that all Christian divisions are, as they always have been, just human misunderstandings, conditioned ultimately by a lack of charity and comprehension, by an excessive emphasis on certain secondary matters, by a narrowness of mind and heart, by . . . inherited and inveterate prejudices, by rivalry and pride," Dr. Florovsky said:

It is simply unfair to trace all divisions and disagreements . . . to various "non-theological factors" . . . or to certain "social sources," as weighty and hypnotizing as they might have been in certain cases. The very sting of Christian tragedy is in the fact that, in the concrete setting of history, many divisions have been imposed, as it were, precisely by the loyalty to Christ and by a sincere zeal for the true faith. It is . . . in the name of the true apostolicity of the teaching and of the true holiness of life that many Christian groups persist in their mutual separation even now. . . . Tragically enough, in many situations separation or schism seems still to be the demand of Christian loyalty and conscience.

In our ecumenical conversation and fraternal exchange of convictions we have reached a stage at which it is becoming increasingly difficult to speak with a common voice, or to make agreed statements, or to engage in united action.

It can be objected at this point that what has been said amounts to a recognition that the ecumenical movement has reached a dead-end, and that further discussion cannot be profitable and cannot lead anywhere. In fact, it only means that some *new way* must be discovered, if only we earnestly believe that unity is God's will and not just a human project.

The goal is distant, the path is narrow. But a sure and infallible guide is given to us who search with humility and devotion, the Comforter, the Spirit of Truth. He will lead the faithful believers into the fulness of Truth.

Canon Oliver S. Tomkins, who had been Associate General Secretary of the World Council of Churches until 1952, speaking in explanation of the work of the Commission on Faith and Order, dealt with the several functions set forth in the Revised Constitution (adopted at Lund), which were:[3]

To proclaim the essential oneness of the Church of Christ and to keep prominently before the World Council and the churches the obligation to manifest that unity and its urgency for the work of evangelism;
To study questions of faith, order, and worship with the relevant social, cultural, political, racial, and other factors in their bearing on the unity of the churches;
To study the theological implications of the existence of the ecumenical movement;
To study matters in the present relationships of the churches to one another which cause difficulties and need theological clarification;
To provide information concerning actual steps taken by the churches towards re-union.

The first of these constitutional objectives went "right to the heart of our purpose," Dr. Tomkins explained, "revealing both our profoundest agreement and our most serious difficulty. We are united in the conviction, which we proclaim, that in some profound sense the Church is one. We are divided and stultified over defining that unity." The problem was semasiological as well as theological.

We struggle continually to find words in which to describe this disagreement within an agreement which is yet paradoxically an agreement within a disagreement. . . . When the constitution was being formulated, the language in use was English, and we were forced into a distinction which in most other languages could not even be a verbal difference. We had said "essential unity" and had to change "unity" into "oneness," because the word "unity" suggested to some a degree of outwardly expressed cohesion which they neither desired nor believed in. Similarly, there were many committee-battles before our present formulation of the Faith and Order subject for this Assembly was agreed on, "Our Unity in Christ and Our Disunity as Churches."

"And yet—there is something," he said, "which we find it impossible to agree in defining, which we are determined to unite in proclaiming!"

The fourth and fifth functions, which concerned, respectively, the "relationships of the churches to one another which cause difficulties and need theological clarification" and providing "information concerning actual steps taken by the churches towards re-union," introduced into the recondite studies in the area of Faith and Order some very human and practical considerations.

"We have decided to plunge right in at the deep end," said Dr. Tomkins, "and grapple with one of the oldest problems of relations between churches. It is normally called proselytizing—but the mere word creates difficulties because it is one of those words which we always use

[3] The Commission on Faith and Order became a department in the Division of Studies in 1954.

to describe something which other people do and . . . we never do ourselves! Obviously it raises the whole question of the religious liberty to change one's faith. But it also involves trying to analyze when improper pressures are being used to bring about a change of allegiance."

As for reunion, Faith and Order had always been clear, the speaker said, on the fact that its work was "not to formulate schemes and tell the churches what they ought to do, but to act as the handmaid of the churches in the preparatory work."

"Yet unions do go forward," he continued. "Bishop Neill's survey, published in preparation for Lund, lists thirteen organic unions achieved, four achievements of full inter-communion and sixteen organic unions under discussion, in the period 1937-1952. Churches cannot afford to ignore those facts, for they are manifest signs of the work of the Spirit. Only churches as such can negotiate unions; but the World Council is clearly the place in which they can learn from one another's successes and failures."

He concluded:

> Such, then, are the functions of Faith and Order as an integral part of our whole Council. It is one of the pillars upon which the World Council was founded, and it remains fundamental. Every kind of co-operation between Christians is good and we may be thankful for the way in which God has blessed our common witness and our common service. But built into the whole structure of our Council is this part of itself which bears witness to the whole that we may not rest content with co-operation. It may be that, by every standard of human achievement, the unity of the Church is an impossible task and that to think of it is an idle dream. But we are not limited to human achievements. "Christ, the Hope of the world," has made us His own—and He is not divided. Men can neither create nor destroy the unity of the Church; to do that belongs to the Lord of the Church alone. We can choose only to deny it or affirm it. By the grace of God, we have chosen: so may His grace fulfill our choice.

A paper by Bishop Berggrav of Norway, although not included with those introducing the first of the subsidiary themes, may well be read with the report of Section I, because of its clear and forthrightly expressed insights concerning the unity of Christians. Its title was "The Tensions of the World and Our Unity in Christ." [4]

Dr. Berggrav said that in his presentation he was not considering "the world to be the secular place as distinguished from the sacred soil of the Church," for the Church found itself "exactly where mankind was living." He thought it fair to ask to what extent the churches were contributing to the tensions of the world. If there was any area where the churches had to confess their solidarity with the world, he thought it was "in sharing the charges of creating tensions within mankind." "I think all of us . . . feel conscience-bound to confess that we are pri-

[4] The Address was mimeographed and issued at the Assembly.

marily the culprits," he said. "He to whom much is committed, of him the more shall be demanded. . . . The churches have been committed by Christ . . . with the message to tell, not in mere words, but by a complete self-sacrifice, how much God loves men. The Christian community even ventures to call itself the Body of Christ. . . . This means that very much is committed to the Church, and therefore the more shall be required of her. How stands our account with God when we face the question concerning tensions in the world and in the Church?"

> It may suffice to mention just one point in passing. Christ proclaimed his hearty desire to all his followers to gather with them around his communion table. Now consider what is the actual situation today. . . . The churches have succeeded in producing the very strongest tensions and divisions among themselves and in the world precisely by means of what Christ offered them as his own life's heritage to make bonds of unity strong among them. This Assembly might be called upon simply to confess shamefulness as to such tensions in the Church. But even if the churches did so, I am sorry to say that in all probability they would let it stay at that and do nothing further. . . . Even in this World Council of Churches we have not realized up to now our unity in Christ at this very point . . . where He himself asked us to start.

Turning from "this sore point" to the strife of the world, the Bishop suggested that somehow tensions were included in the purpose of God, because they were necessary to the growth of life. "Life without any sort of tension could not be alive any more," he said. "God did not create a friction-free life . . . [nor] any sort of uniformity of this life." He thought that the experience of Christ in Gethsemane showed that tension had "heavy reality" even in his relation with God. "[He] surrendered to the will of his Father, but it demanded a hard struggle." Therefore, tensions between Christians might be, in some sense, Christian, becoming destructive only when sin entered. Tensions between men or nations also might be according to God's plan for vitality, inspiration and growth. "All this might be right, except for sin."

There were creative and destructive moods, the speaker said. Fear and anger were of the latter, and love the chief of the former. Nations like Canada and the United States or Denmark and Norway, because they had a neighborly spirit toward each other, could "have healthy discussion without anger or fear. Between other nations there may be some . . . mutual respect or even good will, but they . . . harbor suspicions toward each other and get irritated . . . easily. . . . If they are able to do so, they keep apart. A new word has entered the language of mankind . . . 'apartheid,' meaning to keep away from fellowship to avoid . . . tensions. Up to the first decade of this century it might even be true of the churches that they preferred apartheid—each for itself. A tendency for isolation . . . might be noticed, but nothing can conceal that tensions in fact are at work."

Let us take the bull by the horns: Is there not in many of our churches anger, sometimes also fear, towards the Church of Rome? And is there not only very, very seldom a bit of respect, not to speak of a sense of love? I know that you want to interrupt me here and ask: How could we love Rome? My answer would be by means of a question: Does Christ love them? Has he sacrificed himself for them? Not, of course, for the organization of the fabric of that Church, but for all its members. . . .

What about our own member churches confessing their unity in Christ? I have been looking around to find church bodies fond of each other. I think the most we could achieve would be to tolerate each other in "co-existence," which means that we keep the tensions down, but there they are. . . .

There is nothing to this unity [in Christ] if it does not work and makes its effect felt in our church life as well as in our human life as a whole. We may feel happy when we talk of this unity, but if it is not changing the churches and the world, the reason can only be that we ourselves are paralyzing the power of it by . . . our destructive moods.

Has "this unity" not been working at all? Dr. Berggrav asked, and answered that it had "to some extent," but not with "any big results." That Christendom as a whole was "having a bad conscience about unity in Christ" was one indication of progress, he said. Another was "a fresh respect among us, not at all concealing differences or divisions of truth and thought, but . . . creating a hitherto unknown willingness to listen to each other, no longer in the old self-conceited way, but nearly in a humble mood." Moreover, "our unity in Christ, if taken seriously, prevents us from self-aggrandizement," he said, "and the feeling of having a monopoly of truth and wisdom, or of being entitled to be the judges of our fellow-churches rather than . . . their brethren. Any church prestige is doomed by Christ himself. There exists no master church above the others. What we have is a 'church family' in Christ."

So he thought it could be said that unity in Christ had started to change the world's church atmosphere and put the tensions of evil on the defensive. But, returning to "fruitful tensions," he said:

Our unity in Christ does not call upon us to become one uniform church. Divisions in thought or tradition, as well as those divisions provoked because truth has been revealed to us differently, do not in themselves cut us off from each other if we are in this unity of Christ. . . . God loves differences and nuances quite as much as he puts judgment on isolationism (as opposed to fellowship and communion) as well as on self-complacency. . . . The spirit of Christ never is a spirit of discord. Where black discord enters . . . the power of the unity in Christ is at once paralyzed. . . . It does not become paralyzed by differences in attitude or even in creed as long as the love of Christ guides our hearts.

Could such Christian unity as he had described exert an influence in the world outside the churches? the Bishop asked. And he declared his belief that it could, provided that it first dominated the Church itself. "Today every breath of every human being is co-influencing the global atmosphere."

> True, the tensions of nations are of a political quality, while our unity in Christ is . . . religious. These two qualities may seem to be as different as fire and water, but that is not . . . the case. . . . The mind or mood of mankind is a common ground of Christ as well as of the United Nations, of churches as well as of governments.
>
> If Christians took seriously their unity in Christ, they would become engaged in that very quality of love to man which was characteristic of Jesus Christ. . . . Christ loves even the communist peoples. . . . This does not mean that we should make sweet soup of all the mess we are in. . . . Jesus spoke out distinctly about injustice and violation . . . took a firm stand against lies and falsifications, against God-denying wickedness of all sorts. He was in solidarity with sinful men, but not . . . with sin. He was the Prince of Peace, but never a prince of war, disguised in a mantle of peace. . . . As Christians we are duty-bound to keep the glasses of his lighthouse clean. The red signals war against wickedness and injustice, the green ones guide us to good will and peace. Those two lights on our course over the oceans of time must always be shining, both of them. Never can justice or law be left alone, never love be left to itself.
>
> It is no easy job we have. . . . Start in your own mind and sanctify Christ in your hearts as Master and Lord. Every Christian, not only every church, is responsible for the effective power or for the destruction of the power, embodied in our unity in Christ. We are all responsible for the fate of mankind.

From its report, Section I appeared not to have progressed much beyond Lund in resolving the theological differences between the churches. It broke no new ground. It had made evident to some Christians whom the Faith and Order Movement had not previously addressed the fact that the quest for unity, insofar as corporate union and doctrinal agreement under any kind of organizational relationship were concerned, had come to an impasse; and that could be set down as at least a modest accomplishment.[5]

The members of the section had begun their study, the report stated, with awareness of the oneness of Christians which had been heightened by their association with one another in the World Council of Churches and other ecumenical bodies. Their fellowship was "no mere unity of sentiment," they were convinced: it resulted from their re-creation spiritually by Christ and the indwelling of his life. It was "a given unity." And this view they were able to buttress with many scriptural references.

The dilemma confronting them was that the churches had not realized the fullness of this close spiritual bond, "discord from the beginning having marred the manifested unity of Christ's people." They asked, as

[5] Realizing that the long search for a theological basis on which the denominations could unite had not succeeded, the Faith and Order movement could turn its attention more to other important tasks.

many before them had, whether Christians could learn to live in oneness in Christ.

At this point, they recalled what they had read in the brief supplied to them by the Preparatory Commission:

> Impelled by a strong enthusiasm to see the divine love and righteousness become fully effective in the affairs of men, with the undivided, harmonious Church as the perfect social expression of that divine reign, many Christians yield to two temptations: they underestimate the tenacity of man's sin, which persistently confounds efforts to achieve both church unity and a "Christian" world; and they ignore the New Testament's distinction between the Reign of God as partially experienced within history and as fully consummated beyond history.
>
> A renewed concern about the meaning of history, the Kingdom of God and eternal life is now being expressed increasingly by theological leaders of various confessions. Prompted by recently recovered biblical insights, as well as [by] the social and political exigencies of the present time, many Christian thinkers are rejecting the concept of God's Kingdom as a social order evolving progressively toward perfection. They realize that the consummation of the Kingdom necessarily involves judgment upon mankind generally and the Church in particular. They are less disposed therefore to expect the full and perfect unity of the Church as an easily achieved historical possibility. . . . The separations within the Church are kindred in cause and kind to the separations within mankind as a whole. The same Judge and Saviour of mankind will judge and save the People of God. This aspect of Christian faith gives to the Church the dual attitude of both fear and joy; fear for its infidelity, and joy in realization that its labors are not in vain. While theologians dispute whether the consummation of God's purpose for mankind and the Church shall take place within or beyond the end of history, there is much agreement that the perfect unity of the Church cannot be expected apart from the final coming of Jesus Christ as Judge and Saviour.
>
> What bearing does this hope have on present relationships of the Churches? On the one hand, this kind of faith delivers us from frustration and despair when we consider the seemingly irreparable damage which has been done to the Church by schism and separations. At the same time, it may lead those who misapprehend its meaning into an attitude of total irresponsibility, if they think nothing can now be done about our divisions and that God will ultimately take care of them anyhow.
>
> Two things still confront the divided Churches: the Lord's urgent demand that the unity He has granted them now be expressed in church life; and the hope that He will gather His divided People into one at His final coming.

The members of Section I skirted past the temptation to try disposing of the problems of disunity by referring them to eschatology for solution. Christian hope, when these matters were looked at in the light of the main theme, meant more for the churches as they faced their divisions, one gathered from the general tone of their report, than waiting for the return of Christ at the last day; rather, it gave courage to face the conditions they saw weakening their efforts, with faith in the already present Christ and his power to help with changing them.

> The undivided Christ is present amongst us, pouring His life into us all, in spite of our divisions. . . . We all wait upon one Father through the one Holy Spirit, praying that we may be ready to hear and obey when He takes of the things of Christ and shows them to us. We all read the Holy Scriptures and proclaim the gospel from them in the faith that the Word speaking through them draws us to Himself and into the apostlic faith. We all receive His gift of Baptism whereby, in faith, we are engrafted in Him even while we have not yet allowed it fully to unite us with each other. We all hear His command to "do this" and His word "This is my body . . . this is my blood" in the Sacrament of the Eucharist, even whilst our celebration of the Lord's Supper is not yet at one Table. We all receive a ministry of the Word and Sacraments, even whilst our ministries are not recognized by all and not understood in the same sense. We are all called to be imitators of Christ and to follow Him in moral obedience as we confess Him before men. . . . We give thanks to our Father for these evidences that our unity in Christ is a present reality, both in the World Council of Churches and in relation to other Christians whose fellowship we do not yet fully enjoy. But the very fact that, in every case, our benefit from these mercies is marred by our separation from each other, compels us to examine seriously how it is that our disunity as churches contradicts our unity in Christ.

The report reviewed the historical cleavages between the churches which had been caused and were perpetuated, to a large degree, "by sincere concern for the gospel," and suggested that honest convictions, as they were responsible for divisions, should bring Christians together "at the foot of the Cross." "By planting the Cross of Christ in the midst of our divisions," the report said, "we believe he will over-rule all their sin and make them serve his purpose of unity." The World Council of Churches provided a fellowship in which they were ready to bring their convictions under scrutiny, "in the presence of . . . fellow-Christians and . . . of the living Christ."

"Concretely, this means that when the churches, in their actual historical situations, reach a point of readiness and a time of decision, then their witnessing may require obedience unto death. They may then have to be prepared to offer up some of their accustomed, inherited forms of life in uniting with other churches without complete certainty as to all that will emerge from the step of faith. . . . When churches have been ready in this sense 'to die with Christ,' they have found that He who raised Jesus from the dead is faithful and powerful still."

The report concluded with the same positive note, by suggesting ways in which, "being both united and divided," Christians must seek to be obedient.

They should try to understand the theological implications of their oneness and "to implement it in the . . . relations of neighbor churches."

They should listen together in the midst of their disunity to the one Lord speaking through the Holy Scriptures—a hard thing to do. "Yet whenever we are prepared to undertake together the study of the Word of God and are resolved to be obedient to what we are told, we are on the way to realizing the oneness of the Church in Christ in the actual state of our dividedness on earth."

They must try to understand also the influence of social and cultural differences upon matters of Faith and Order which caused divisions, and how the events and developments of current history made disunity a most urgent question.

They must speak the truth in love with one another and practice that love toward those with whom they disagreed, even if it involved them in judgments which fellow Christians could not recognize as having been reached in love.

There was need, moreover, that Christians learn afresh the implications of the one baptism for their sharing in the one Eucharist.

They should acknowledge each ministry beyond the bounds of their own churches that preached the gospel of reconciliation as a means whereby Christ performed his saving deeds.

They should seek healing for their divisions, to the end that their witness might be more effectual.

All should pray for the unity of the churches, praying together across theological and ecclesiastical lines when there was opportunity.[6]

The delegates of the Eastern Orthodox Churches submitted a statement concerning the report, declaring that its "whole approach to the problem of re-union" was "entirely unacceptable from the standpoint of the Orthodox Church." [7]

As delegates of the Orthodox Church participating at this Assembly of the World Council of Churches, we submit the following statement concerning the report of Section I:

1. We have studied the document with considerable interest. It falls into three parts: the first contains an able exposition of the New Testament doctrine of the Church. The organic character of the Church and her indissoluble unity with Christ are adequately stressed in the document. We feel that this at least provides fruitful ground for further theological elaboration. The second and third parts of the document deal with the divided state of Christendom and suggest practical steps toward union. It is our conviction that it does not follow logically and consistently from the first part and indeed if we do actually accept the New Testament doctrine of the Church we should come to quite different practical conclusions which have been familiar to us Orthodox for centuries. The whole approach to the problem of re-

[6] For full report, see Appendix I and *The Evanston Report,* pp. 82-91.
[7] *The Evanston Report,* pp. 92-95.

union is entirely unacceptable from the standpoint of the Orthodox Church.

2. The Orthodox conception of church unity implies a twofold agreement:

(a) The whole of the Christian Faith should be regarded as one indivisible unity. It is not enough to accept just certain particular doctrines, basic as they may be in themselves, e.g. that Christ is God and Savior. It is compelling that all doctrines as formulated by the Ecumenical Councils, as well as the totality of the teaching of the early, undivided Church, should be accepted. One cannot be satisfied with formulas which are isolated from the life and experience of the Church. They must be assessed and understood within the context of the Church's life. From the Orthodox view-point, reunion of Christendom with which the World Council of Churches is concerned can be achieved solely on the basis of the total, dogmatic Faith of the early, undivided Church without either subtraction or alteration. We cannot accept a rigid distinction between essential and non-essential doctrines, and there is no room for comprehensiveness in the Faith. On the other hand, the Orthodox Church cannot accept that the Holy Spirit speaks to us only through the Bible. The Holy Spirit abides and witnesses through the totality of the Church's life and experience. The Bible is given to us within the context of Apostolic Tradition in which in turn we possess the authentic interpretation and explication of the Word of God. Loyalty to Apostolic Tradition safeguards the reality and continuity of Church unity.

(b) It is through the Apostolic Ministry that the mystery of Pentecost is perpetuated in the Church. The Episcopal Succession from the Apostles constitutes an historical reality in the life and structure of the Church and one of the presuppositions of her unity through the ages. The unity of the Church is preserved through the unity of the Episcopate. The Church is one Body whose historical continuity and unity is also safeguarded by the common faith arising spontaneously out of the fulness (*pleroma*) of the Church.

3. Thus when we are considering the problem of Church unity we cannot envisage it in any other way than as the complete restoration of the total Faith and the total episcopal structure of the Church which is basic to the sacramental life of the Church. We would not pass judgment upon those of the separated communions. However, it is our conviction that in these communions certain basic elements are lacking which constitute the reality of the fulness of the Church. We believe that the return of the communions to the Faith of the ancient, united and indivisible Church of the Seven Ecumenical Councils, namely to the pure and unchanged and common heritage of the forefathers of all divided Christians, shall alone produce the desired re-union of all separated Christians. For, only the unity and the fellowship of Christians in a common Faith shall have as a necessary result their fellowship in the sacraments and their indissoluble unity in love, as members of one and the same Body of the One Church of Christ.

4. The "perfect unity" of Christians must not be interpreted exclusively as a realization of the Second Coming of Christ. We must acknowledge that even at the present age the Holy Spirit dwelling in the Church continues to breathe in the world, guiding all Christians to unity. The unity of the Church must not be understood only eschatologically, but as a present reality which is to receive its consummation in the Last Day.

5. It is suggested in the report of the section that the road which the Church must take in restoring unity is that of repentance. We recognize that there have been and there are imperfections and failures within the life and witness of Christian believers, but we reject the notion that the Church herself, being the Body of Christ and the repository of revealed Truth and the

"whole operation of the Holy Spirit," could be affected by human sin. Therefore, we cannot speak of the repentance of the Church which is intrinsically holy and unerring. For, "Christ loved the Church and gave Himself for it, that He might sanctify it and cleanse it in the washing of water and the word, that He might present it to Himself as a glorious Church, not having spot or wrinkle or blemish or any such thing, but that it should be holy and without blemish" (Ephesians v, 26-27).

Thus the Lord, the only Holy One, sanctified His Church for ever and ordained that her task be the "edification of the saints and the building of the body of Christ." Her holiness is not vitiated by the sins and failures of her members. They cannot in any way lessen or exhaust the inexhaustible holiness of the divine life which from the Head of the Church is diffused throughout all the body.

6. In conclusion, we are bound to declare our profound conviction that the Holy Orthodox Church alone has preserved in full and intact "the faith once delivered unto the saints." It is not because of our human merit, but because it pleases God to preserve "his treasure in earthen vessels, that the excellency of the power may be of God" (II Corinthians iv, 7).

Those who had been at previous ecumenical gatherings had become accustomed to the claim of the Orthodox Church to being the one and only true Church and to the habit of its representatives of dissenting from actions on questions relating to theology and ecclesiology. There was every reason to think that their course in this respect was marked by charity toward other Christians and their churches. Much of what they said was edifying. Though criticized for their ecclesiastical exclusiveness, they had continued from the earliest days of the ecumenical movement to give a good example of the way in which a denomination, even if it did not agree altogether with the views of the others constituting interchurch organizations, could make membership in them profitable for itself and for its associates.

No denomination is so self-sufficient as not to be able to reap benefit from intercourse with others, and the health of an interdenominational body like the World Council of Churches will be sounder and its work more effective for the influence of honest and forthright dissent. The ecumenical movement owes much to the Orthodox Churches, and they are, in turn, greatly indebted to it.

It would be quite impossible to represent, except in a very general way, the thinking of the Assembly concerning the theme of Section I and the report, which "was received . . . and commended to the churches for study and appropriate action."

The oneness of Christians consists, it may be said, in their common possession of eternal life through Jesus Christ. It is spiritual in essence, though it may be characterized by correspondence at other levels. The disunity of the churches is in doctrines and organizations which set them apart from one another and hinder or prevent interrelations. It does not destroy the essential unity of Christians belonging to them.

It is believed by many, however, to interfere with witness by the churches on behalf of Christ.

From his prayer in the seventeenth chapter of the Gospel according to John, Christ appears to have considered a relationship approaching union on the part of his disciples prerequisite to the evangelization of the world. When he prayed that they might be one, he was asking, many think, for more than unity in a spiritual sense, which they enjoyed already, in virtue of their conversion, and so had not to pray for. The growing impatience with sectarianism, especially on the mission fields, seems to bear out in a practical way this construction of his words.

Many Christians who believe sectarianism destroys or weakens their witness, while robbing them of the full richness of unbroken religious fellowship, are committed to the cause of church union. And they are well represented in the World Council of Churches. They believe in the union of Christians as a matter, not only of principle, but of practical necessity for the Church, if it is to do its work in the world and give its people the spiritual nurture to which they are entitled. They support the efforts of the Department on Faith and Order and consider them justified, whether or not they register visible gains. The study by the Assembly of the sub-theme "Our Oneness in Christ and Our Disunity as Churches" was well advised, they would have said, even if the report appeared to leave the problems considered no nearer to solution. The reunion of the people of God was so completely right and to be desired that he could only reward the search for a way to achieve it, if not with immediate concrete success, then in other ways agreeable to his will; and they were resolved to bring to the quest their best thought and most patient and prayerful collaboration.

In the Assembly were others, of course, whom the disunity of the churches did not disturb so much. They thought it unlikely that all Christians could ever agree sufficiently on matters of doctrine and practice to unite organically. They remembered, too, the nontheological obstacles to corporate union, which seemed to them hardly less stubborn than the theological. Conversion, through which they became one spiritually, left believing people individuals still, who would have inevitably their differing opinions concerning the doctrinal expression and organizational implementation of their common experience.

Moreover, it was not certain that Christians, even if permitted the freedom of retaining their cherished beliefs and ways of worshiping, could work as successfully or be as happy in one church as in their accustomed state of separateness. The kingdom of God had advanced through the independent work of the several denominations, their overlapping, and sometimes conflicting, programs notwithstanding; and it was a question whether, if union were attained, there might not develop from it disadvantages counterbalancing the apparent gains.

Those inclined to these views were naturally lukewarm in their support of the work of Faith and Order, although not necessarily opposing it. They were willing generally that others should have the privilege of promoting it, who could do so with conviction and more hopefulness. Meanwhile, they were for continuing cooperation in such undertakings as agreement by the churches made possible, and were waiting for clearer revelation concerning amalgamation.

2. The Mission of the Church to Those Outside Her Life

No phase of the program of the World Council of Churches received greater attention at Evanston than evangelism, which took its place in the list of "subsidiary themes" under the title "The Mission of the Church to Those Outside Her Life."

In the early sessions, the entire Assembly had an introduction to the subject in the report of the Secretariat for Evangelism and addresses by Canon Theodore O. Wedel of Washington Cathedral and Rev. Daniel T. Niles of Ceylon, Chairman and Secretary, respectively, of the Preparatory Commission for Section II; and later, when the study was in progress in the sections, heard Dr. Charles W. Ranson, Executive Secretary of the International Missionary Council, on "World-Wide Evangelism in This Generation." When, finally, it had received the report of Section II, it extended the time for discussion into a second period in order to hear, if possible, all wishing to speak on the subject.

In its report, which was presented by Rev. Daniel T. Niles, the Secretariat for Evangelism said that the major concern had been "to keep the churches reminded of their double duty to the Gospel—to be true to it and . . . to commend it." To this end, they had promoted studies in redefining the theology of evangelism and reappraising evangelistic methods.

The Secretariat had discovered that the Christian community in many parts of the world was "isolated and indistinguishable"—isolated "in the sense that where Christians and non-Christians [met] in the normal business of life the Christian witness [was] not being rendered and the evangelistic encounter not taking place," and indistinguishable because "nothing mark[ed] it off from the general community" and it blended smoothly with its environment and shaded off into its background.

The Secretariat had endeavored to "keep the challenge of an evangelistic Church" to the fore. "Communication had broken down between the Church and some of the main groups of society," it said, and referred to industrial workers and intellectuals among Hindus, Buddhists, and Muslims as among these.

Rural evangelism, in Asia and Africa particularly, had been found to have parallel problems. "It is essential to find out how the breakdown of communication has come about," the report continued, "and what must be done to restore it."

The Secretariat was engaged in "an on-going study of the problems of evangelism among industrial workers." In association with the research division of the International Missionary Council, a conference was being considered for reopening discussion on the Christian message to a non-Christian world, which had been a subject of the Third International Missionary Conference at Tambaram, India, in 1938.

As for rural evangelism, some churches had been invited to undertake case studies in this area.

The Secretariat had sought to give encouragement through fellowship and prayer to lay workers and ministers engaged in evangelism at "the frontiers" between social groups, who were working to "restore lines of communication where they [had] broken down or . . . to find access for the Gospel into still unoccupied areas of . . . life." Most of these felt themselves alone, many had little sympathetic support from their churches, and all stood in danger of seeing the experiments in which they were employed out of true focus.

"Every human soul over the face of the globe has as much right to the Gospel as we have," declared Canon Wedel, and "every chiselled stone in our Gothic shrines, every carving on our pews, every cushioned parish house stands under God's judgment, if it is not serving the apostolic calling of the Church . . . on mission sent." Christians are "indeed God's people," but "woe unto us if we enjoy our citizenship in heaven as if we had earned it," he warned. Some Christians act as if they think they are "a family enjoying a rich inheritance on an ancestral estate," or "islands of the saved in the midst of the lost," or "an aristocracy among the future citizens of heaven," he said. But the Church is "an evangelizing army on the march and a haven of rest only between campaigns when it returns to home base to renew its strength and to receive fresh orders." "We have no right," he asserted, "to our Sabbath ease and our promised end before the Gospel will have been preached throughout the world."

Carrying the gospel to others does not mean, said Dr. Wedel, "merely opening our doors and welcoming those who find us attractive enough to join our fellowships." Rather, it means "moving out into the slums of our great cities, among the poor and down-trodden, the social and racial minorities, the sceptics and unbelievers, let alone the unevangelized multitudes of distant lands."

Not even the race to produce hydrogen bombs, he thought, was equal in urgency to Christ's command, "Go, therefore, and make disciples of all nations."

Dr. Niles stressed in his address the social dimensions of evangelism. Those knocking at the doors of the churches were not "merely the hungry, the homeless, the refugee, the displaced person, the outcast," he said; "there are at the Church's door also every type of community—nations, races, classes, political groupings." He took issue with those who thought the churches should answer only the "call of private personal need or the call for salvation after death," asserting that when the Church cease[d] to be concerned with the world, it ceased to hear God speak." "It is the world which is the direct object of God's action," he held. "He made it . . . loved it . . . saved it. He will judge it through Jesus Christ. . . . The church that is disobedient to its commission to go to the world becomes a menace to the world. . . ." It had a duty, he continued, to speak on "such matters as international affairs, racial and ethnic tensions, social and economic questions, the issues of church unity and disunity—all topics before the Assembly." Its mission was not to offer solutions to such problems, he said, but "to incarnate the Word in every human situation." "Evangelism means that the Christian Community, by all that it does and says and is, brings to bear the truths of the Gospel on the torments of the world. . . . It means that thus the pressure of the Gospel upon the world is maintained, so that the solution to every human problem . . . may be worked out under that pressure by those whose responsibility it is."

Declaring that Christians did not "care enough about people as people," he explained that church members were concerned about evangelism largely out of a desire to fulfill what they regarded as a Christian duty. In order to be true to its divine meaning, he concluded, "evangelism must cease to be a duty and . . . become an inevitability."

In the background of the presentation of the study on evangelism were the conclusions reached by the Preparatory Commission for Section II in its survey of the subject, which consisted of the following persons:

Canon Theodore O. Wedel, *Chairman,* United States
Principal David G. Moses, *Vice-Chairman,* India
Rev. Daniel T. Niles, *Secretary,* Ceylon
Rev. Thomas Allan, United Kingdom
Bishop S. U. Barbieri, Argentina
Rev. Benö Bekefi, Hungary
Rev. J. P. Benoit, France
Dr. Jerome Cotsonis, Greece
Dr. Edwin T. Dahlberg, United States (Consultant)
Dr. S. E. Engström, United States
Professor J. C. Hoekendijk, Netherlands
Principal C. H. Hwang, Formosa
Dr. Hajime Inadomi, Japan
Professor T. E. Jessop, United Kingdom
Mrs. John Karefa-Smart, Liberia

Rev. P. Mahanty, India
Dr. Jesse J. McNeill, United States
Bishop John S. Moyes, Australia
Professor H. Richard Niebuhr, United States
Rev. Chandu Ray, Pakistan
Professor H. Rendtorff, Germany
Professor Richard C. Smith, United States
Canon E. R. Wickham, United Kingdom
Rev. Eric W. Nielsen, Consultant, International Missionary Council

Wrote the Commission,[8]

Acknowledging the difference of situations in various parts of the world, we find almost general agreement on the following emerging patterns of evangelism:

Evangelism is the participation of the total Christian community in Christ's mission in the world.

Every single aspect of the Church's life and activities is of evangelistic significance.

In proclamation, fellowship and service, the Church must demonstrate the Gospel in the actual life context of men.

Laymen are on the front-line, served by the ministry whose function it is to equip the people of God for its mission.

Laity and ministry together should strive to be of the mind of Him who "emptied Himself" in service to the world.

Study of evangelism in the context of an ecumenical body such as the World Council of Churches raises the question of the extent to which cooperation in evangelistic effort is today possible and fruitful, and the Preparatory Commission had the following to say on this point:

There is ample evidence that united evangelism is a fact, and there are persuasive indications that it may be the answer to some of the difficulties faced by the churches as they seek to reach great segments of society now untouched by their influence.

The Committee on Evangelism of the British Council of Churches had commented in the report of a survey in England:

To stop short of united evangelism is to countenance the conclusion that Christians do not experience a unity in Christ strong enough to enable them to join in bringing Christ to men and women and men and women to Christ. To effect an entry through the countless doors at present barred to Christianity is a task of too great magnitude for anything less than a united approach.

On the theological difficulties involved in cooperation in this area, the Preparatory Commission in its briefing of the members of Section II had remarked:

[8] See report in *The Christian Hope*.

No service is rendered to the cause of evangelism . . . by attempts to evade the serious questions raised in the realm of "faith and order" by proposals for united evangelism. Such proposals imply agreement by the participating churches concerning the content of the Christian message and the nature of the Church. That such agreement is not a reality among all the churches having membership in the World Council of Churches is clearly indicated by the statement in the Toronto Declaration, holding that "membership does not imply that each Church must regard the other member Churches as Churches in the true and full sense of the word." It is therefore true that there will be those who, on doctrinal grounds, are unable to participate in such endeavors. But it is also true that the discipline of preparation in study, prayer and shared experience, so essential for the work of united evangelism, may become a major factor in drawing closer together those churches which venture in the common proclamation of the Gospel. . . . Uniting for evangelism may thus hasten the coming of the day of full Christian unity.

Dr. Ranson dwelt in his address before the Assembly on the nature, opportunity, and problems of evangelism in its world scope.[9]

The one great task which has been given to the Church is to preach the Gospel to the ends of the earth and to the end of time. It is this task which gives meaning to the existence of the Church. . . .

Between the birth of our Christian hope in the first coming of Christ and its final consummation when "he shall come again with glory to judge both the quick and the dead" there lies the unfinished task of world evangelism. This missionary obligation is not simply a task laid upon the Church. It is a gift from God to the Church. It is not we who offer salvation to men. It is God who has visited and redeemed His people. He has spoken in Christ the word of redemption for all mankind. What has been done for the whole world must be made known to the whole world; and to the Church is given the task of world-wide proclamation.

The Church's own foundations rest upon that universal mission. We live by the word we give. The missionary calling of the Church is not only integral to its own life, it is interwoven into the texture of God's design for the world. It is the only means by which, in the obedience of faith, we enter the creative context of God's action in history. The Bible compels us to say no less than this. God leads the world to its consummation through the mission of the Church. Apart from this basic biblical truth this great Assembly can have little meaning. Our discussions on the nature of the Church and the content of Christian hope will be barren if they do not result in an inescapable summons to proclamation and a new obedience which will thrust the Church forth into all the world as an expectant and evangelizing community, in this generation.

In this generation we have seen the fantastic development of modern scientific invention and have felt its impact on human experience in both total war and partial peace. We have witnessed the swift contraction of human society, the uneasy intermingling of isolated and divergent cultures, the heightening of age-long tensions and the awakening of new conflicts of nations and races and classes. We have watched with alarm the advent of the armed barbarian and, with anxiety, the creeping menace of the mass mind. We look back upon a rapid succession of catastrophic events the full mean-

[9] From mimeographed text issued at the Assembly.

ing of which we cannot understand. We are confronted with possibilities which we cannot measure and certainly cannot control. We know that in this generation we are at one of the turning points of history. But there are many things that we do not know and cannot know. It is not our business here to speculate upon the course and the limits of human history. . . . To the question: "What is the meaning of the present time?" there is but one certain answer. It is that this is the time given to the Church for the prosecution of its apostolic mission to the world.

The Church is summoned to encounter with the world. . . . This must mean a more determined grappling with the issues raised by the great religions of the Orient. It must mean a quickened sense of Christian responsibility for the Jewish people. . . . They represent the home base which has too often been ignored or forgotten by the Christian Church. For the world of industrial society . . . largely divorced from Christian presuppositions, there is also a call to fresh encounter. We have to re-learn the meaning of evangelism in the contemporary world.

This means, primarily, the re-discovery of the art of Christian communication—the translation of the Gospel into an idiom which the people can understand. . . . We rightly rejoice that the Bible has been translated into more than a thousand tongues. . . . We are much less concerned than we should be as to whether the Word thus made available speaks to the mind and heart of the peoples of the world. We rejoice in the growth of literacy. We invest heavily in Christian schools and colleges. We have not yet begun to take with due seriousness the task of providing a Christian literature to meet the hunger and need for books. . . . But communication is more than proclamation by word and pen. . . . It is encounter with people—people who are foolish and frightened, baffled and self-confident, sinful and self-righteous, bored and hopeless—people for whom Christ died . . . to whom we are sent as Christ's ambassadors with His word of reconciliation and hope.

The whole life and endeavor of the churches came to a practical focus in evangelism, declared the report of Section II. "Evangelism is no specialized or separable or periodic activity, but is rather a dimension of the total activity of the Church. Everything the Church does is of evangelizing significance. Through all the aspects of its life the Church participates in Christ's mission to the world, both partaking of the Gospel and seeking to communicate it. Evangelism is the place where the Church discovers itself in its true depth and outreach."

At this point, the report faced the problem of disunity. "This witness of the Church to its Lord is weakened by our unfaithfulness—not least by our divisions," it said. "Therefore, will the Church deal with these divisions with holy impatience, and passionately strive for unity? Unity is destroyed where there are confessional antagonisms, nor will unity of faith and life among Christians be achieved except as churches increasingly work together to bring the gospel to the whole world."

The report underscored among "the concerns of evangelism" proclaiming the gospel with the aim of transforming "the groupings and patterns of society in which men and women are involved, to the end that human institutions and structures may more nearly conform to the divine intention, and respect the limiting prerogative of God." "We who think ourselves converted to the Christian Gospel, and who have entered into many of its blessings, should beware lest whole areas of our thought and outlook remain unregenerate, so that it is after all not the whole gospel to which we have been converted," it warned.

"Still another aspect of evangelism," it continued, "is the attempt to bring people into the full life of the Church as expressed in a local congregation."

Underlying all concerns of evangelism, it urged, "is the bringing of persons to Christ as Saviour and Lord, that they may share in His eternal life. Here is the heart of the matter. There must be personal encounter with Christ. It is not enough to present Him merely as an example to follow. The Gospel proclaims a living Christ. . . . On his relationship to God in Christ depends the eternal destiny of every man."

The report contained a section on "Exploring Frontiers" which listed practical suggestions concerning "areas of evangelism." The first was "our own inner life." When Jesus gave his commission, he commanded his disciples to wait for the power of the Holy Spirit. The minister and the congregation equally needed this renewing and strengthening for their evangelistic mission.

The second area was secular life, where the laity stood at the very "outposts of the Kingdom of God as missionaries."

Childhood and youth were another "frontier" at which in every generation there must be a fresh presentation of the gospel.

The specialized ministry of chaplaincies, in the support of which the denominations could cooperate, had been found effective, according to the report, in serving hospitals, prisons, military forces, industry, universities, schools.

Where family life or geographical areas were disintegrating, "it was urgent that the Church come to life in 'street or house churches' where neighbors, church and non-church, might gather to think and pray . . . and thence to enter the churches' continuing life."

Again: "Literature and arts play an increasing part in the shaping of men's outlook; but we face today the overwhelming impact of the cinema, radio and television, as well as the greater perfection of posters, newspapers and magazines. The result is that the convictions and decisions of individuals in many countries are reached under a common mental climate which these media of mass communication tend to create." All these the Church must learn to employ.

The report called for a more realistic training of ministers. Experience in agriculture, industry, and social work should be incorporated, it suggested, in the curricula of theological seminaries.

"Conditions of communicating the Gospel" were discussed: The first "is to be possessed by the transforming power of Jesus Christ" and the second to "love our neighbor as he is, even as Christ has loved us." In the third place, the Church should be a fellowship through which the love of Christ will be manifested. And the Church must "break out of its isolation and introversion" and go to those outside its life. It must learn, also, how to speak to the problems that beset men in a way to convince them that God cares for them. It must go farther and serve their needs as this may be possible. Lastly, "in order to possess the power to evangelize, the Church must nourish its life on the Bible," which "speaks to all, provides a common language for the Church, transcending our divisions."

In a concluding passage with the caption "Come, Lord Jesus," the drafting committee oriented the report to the main theme of the Assembly.

> The messenger of the unlimited grace of Christ looks towards the consummation of the Kingdom, in which His redeeming love shall have achieved its full intention. How thoughtless they speak who say, "Where is the promise of His coming? For ever since the fathers fell asleep, all things have continued as they were from the beginning of creation." To them the answer has been given, "The Lord is not slack concerning his promise, as some men count slackness, but is long-suffering to us-ward, not willing that any should perish, but that all should come to repentance."
>
> The time of expectation is the time of evangelism, even as the time of evangelism is the time of expectation. For He who comes as our Judge is also our Redeemer. . . . The tragedy of the world is that it knows no judge, no lord of history. To the Church it is given to know that man is not condemned to an endless succession of meaningless nights and days, to never completed toil, to uncomforted mourning or ever-disillusioned hoping. It possesses, or is rather possessed by, the hope of a glorious fulfillment. . . . In this hope we are saved and by it we live.
>
> The time of evangelism will not last for ever; it will be succeeded by the time of the Kingdom fulfilled. The good news will not remain for ever a promise made: it will become a promise kept. The gospel will not be the knowledge of a privileged few: it will be revealed to all. Seeing in a glass darkly will not be our ultimate vision of God: we shall know even as we are known until we say, "We are complete in Him." Therefore are Christians under constraint to declare this hope to the world until the consummation of the Kingdom and the coming of the King.[10]

Some of the conclusions the Assembly reached in its exploration of the subject give a fairly clear view of evangelism in the ecumenical context:

> The whole life and endeavor of the churches come to a focus in evangelism. Evangelism is not a specialized, separable or periodic activity, but a dimension of the total work of the church.
>
> To effect an entry through the countless doors at present barred to Christianity is a task of too great magnitude for anything less than a united approach.

[10] The official text is printed in Appendix J and *The Evanston Report,* pp. 98-108.

There is ample evidence that united evangelism is a fact, and there are persuasive indications that it may be the answer to some of the difficulties faced by the churches as they seek to reach great segments of society now untouched by their influence.

That evangelism is "a dimension of the total work of the church" is a conception at which most churches have arrived, perhaps, and the World Council of Churches has been instrumental in its development.

When considered in its missionary outreach and from the standpoint of its social objectives, at home and abroad, such evangelism is seen to be a task of obviously too great magnitude for anything less than a cooperative approach, but the statement that there is ample evidence that united evangelism is a fact needs to be qualified.

The churches have made common cause of surveys which defined more clearly what the possibilities and the problems of the evangelistic responsibility were. And Christians have disregarded denominational lines in their observance of special seasons of prayer for missions and other phases of evangelism. They have collaborated also in disseminating the Scriptures and Christian literature, as they have in manifold charities. They have worked together in movements for social reform. Many of them have joined in meetings for the proclamation of the gospel. But all such efforts have been more or less restricted. There are churches which will not share the pulpit or the instruction room where the invitation to "accept Christ" is at issue. At this crucial point, ecumenical evangelism comes to a halt. It is blocked by the seemingly unresolvable conflict arising from the conviction of some churches that others do not understand or teach the whole gospel and that it is beyond them to do so. These latter generally feel much the same way toward those not recognizing their competence, and evangelizing becomes, logically, persuading people to leave one church for another, or, if they are new converts to the Christian faith, to choose one church in preference to another.

A glimpse of the complicated situation may be got by turning to the report of the evangelistic survey which was made by the Secretariat on Evangelism after the organization of the World Council of Churches, in which the churches were circularized for their opinions.

The replies had value in their disclosure of certain attitudes and conceptions which would have to be reconciled before there could be any united movement in evangelism. There existed, for one thing, serious confusion about the meaning and aims of evangelism, which had been encountered in the course of the enquiry, and was characterized as follows:

On one hand, there is continuous temptation to interpret evangelization as propaganda or proselytism, in which man is treated as an object or a victim, to be moulded by our work, in our image and likeness. On the other hand, evangelization is likely to degenerate into merely making churchmembers. How can the Church avoid this proselytism and mere "churchification"?

Connected with this uncertainty in the understanding of evangelization is a disagreement on the interpretation of conversion. . . . According to one school of thought, all evangelistic activity should be focused on conversion understood in a particular sense; according to another school, it should be detached from all attempts to convert individuals. One of the most urgent needs is a thorough study of the whole subject of conversion, in the light of the re-discovery of biblical theology and of modern psychological knowledge. Fear of a pietistic or semi-pietistic interpretation of conversion ought not to prevent our common attempt to recover the full and genuine biblical content of the idea of conversion, including the radical change of ideas and general outlook. We are called to consider also the significance of conversion as the penetration of the whole thought process of society by Christian ideas, in such a way as to produce a milieu in which the conversion of the individual can be real and significant.

It can be said, of course, that a beginning of united evangelism has been made, long since; and "it is true," as the Evanston report stated, "that the discipline of preparation in study, prayer and shared experience, so essential for the work of united evangelism, may become a major factor in drawing closer together those churches which venture in the common proclamation of the gospel."

Perhaps the most significant fact ever presented to the World Council of Churches, in connection with the subject of evangelism, was the discovery in a survey conducted by Bishop Neill that "God had blessed with good results all kinds of efforts to win people to an acceptance of the Christian faith." [11] The theological implications of this may be very great. Some think it proves that God comes to those who seek him in the name of Jesus Christ, even if their understanding of the doctrinal interpretation of what they are doing is inadequate; and that all evangelistic methods, from the informal, even ignorant, preaching of the gospel in a conventicle or a tent to the symbolism of a "high church" liturgical service of worship, are, in some degree, valid. They would have people come to God in their own way, so long as they are enabled to know Christ who is "the way, the truth, and the life."

But others would say that the evangelistic effectiveness, on occasion, of groups outside the true Church is only evidence of the overflowing grace of God. Even the Roman Catholic Church must accommodate its rigid teaching to the inescapable fact that some of the lost are saved thus without the fold. But the fullness of salvation cannot be realized, so it is held, apart from life within the true Church, which must, in conscience, keep free from relationships in evangelism which mislead those outside and confuse its own members.

It is not impossible, we may say, that the Spirit of God will resolve even these most intractable problems, in his own time, and bring the churches to "a day of full Christian unity." Meanwhile, the World Council of Churches, by its original charter, invites them to cooperate,

[11] See pp. 262 ff. and pp. 281 ff.

to the extent that is possible, in evangelism, as in other types of Christian endeavor.

3. The Responsible Society in a World Perspective

The study of Section III on "The Responsible Society in a World Perspective" was introduced by an address by Dr. C. L. Patijn, a layman of the Netherlands Reformed Church and, at the time, a member of the Dutch delegation to the United Nations, who had served as one of the co-Chairmen of the Preparatory Commission and the Chairman of Section III.[12]

Taking an historical approach, he said that it was "a matter of life and death for our generation whether the Church [would] be able to permeate . . . the vast network of commercial and industrial relations of financial capitalism and . . . an increasingly powerful State" which had arisen in the industrial revolution "outside the sphere of influence of the Church and traditional morality," or would "remain at the other side of the gap over against the bad world, throwing an occasional stone or yielding to all sorts of escapism."

For all that had been written on social affairs by exponents of the ecumenical movement, only a beginning had been made, he thought, in elaborating "a new social ethos which was truly Christian and relevant to modern society."

Tracing the "Christian concern for social and political affairs," he considered that it had begun, so far as the ecumenical movement had to do with it, at the Universal Christian Conference on Life and Work at Stockholm in 1925, where "a re-encounter between the Church and the world, after three centuries of pietism, took place." This had been the "first major attempt to draw the churches together in a united effort of social renewal," and, following it, Life and Work had taken the lead in studying the implications of Christian teaching for social and political affairs. The beginning had been hesitant, the Stockholm Conference defining the position of the Church in public life in "curious words": "The mission of the Church is above all to state principles, and to assert the ideal, while leaving to individual consciences, and to communities the duty to apply them with charity, wisdom and courage."

The Jerusalem Conference of the International Missionary Conference had three years later formulated "some criteria by which the Christian could test the social and economic system," which were "extremely elementary and clearly hostile towards the essentials of economic activity," including "the validity of individual profit and the profit motive itself." But it had made, he suggested, a forward step in dealing with social problems of the underdeveloped countries.

[12] Quotations are from mimeographed text issued at Evanston.

"The Oxford Conference of 1937 [Church, Community and State], more than its predecessors, stood under the immediate impact of history," he said, "which led the churches to some clear and forthright statements." Its findings "deeply influenced the social and political thinking of the Church." "Even today the more general and introductory parts . . . are fully relevant to our work here and in many respects far ahead of the actual social thinking of the churches." One could say in retrospect, he felt, that the Oxford Conference "laid the foundations for a new Christian social ethos." But it had had its shortcomings, having been "far more explicit in proclaiming the desirable than in indicating how the undesirable could be checked." Its "statements regarding the economic order were . . . still remote from the battlefields. They bore witness to great academic reflection, but did not always breathe the atmosphere of active wrestling with actual problems in social and economic life."

By the time of the Amsterdam Assembly in 1948, he continued, a shifting of emphasis had occurred in ecumenical thinking.

> For many years the ecumenical movement had stressed the dangers of economic life for the soul . . . and indicated some general tendencies . . . as social sins. Now for the first time, in the preparatory studies for the Amsterdam Assembly, an attempt was made to give cohesive appraisal of our technical civilization in its complexity and intractability. Society no longer appeared under a moral aspect only. . . . Out of some analytical studies appeared a picture of society—of a technical civilization of things, of forces and powers which man has called into being, but which dominate him as a second nature . . . , in many respects far more hostile . . . than original nature itself.

"Against this background of a robot-like civilization, which threatens mankind in its spiritual, social and political freedom, the Amsterdam Assembly attempted to present an equally comprehensive word—'responsible society,'" which "expressed concern for the adequate protection . . . of the economically weak" and "the churches' concern for a social order which provides democratic ways of living for 'little men in big societies,' which does not regard man as a cog in a machine, but as a free and responsible person, able to act responsibly in social, political and private life."

The Amsterdam report had also proclaimed "the independence of the Church with regard to structures of political and economic life," he added. In its view the Christian conception of justice transcended history, and the Church all systems. "Accordingly . . . , the report was critical of both communism and laissez-faire capitalism, while seeking to draw the churches away from the false assumption that in society there was no alternative to their ideologies."

Amsterdam had been significant, he believed, "but more in terms of general attitudes than specific issues," and at Evanston the task was, in his opinion, "to cross the borderline from the general to the specific, from the clergy to the laity, from the ideal to the existential, from academic reflexion to the actual struggle for justice in society, from ethics to the daily round in which faith, hope and love are burning faintly."

Indicating some of the trends reflected in the study report prepared for Section III, he said: "There is more interest in the problems of production and efficiency than before. At the same time, it is more generally accepted that the state has an important part to play in economic life, although the extent of state intervention is still a controversial point. Since there is also a better understanding of the significance of private initiative and the dangers of centralization and rigidity in the economic system, it seems as though the old controversy between socialism and capitalism is beginning to lose its sting. . . ." The question of the underdeveloped areas of the world and the problem of communism had been much to the fore in the section's discussions.

"It is a long way indeed from the mere concern for the soul and the moral person of Stockholm, via the scientific prolegomena of Oxford, to the realistic appraisal of conditions in society which will be our task here," he said.

In attempting to write a report both Christian and relevant, the drafting committee had kept in mind two points: the Church "should see the dangers and sins of society, not as an object for mere criticism, but as an object for responsible action"; and "should base its word with regard to society not on fear, but on hope."

"The real service which the Church can render is to understand society better than society understands itself. . . . It is for the Church to give power, motivation and courage for Christian action in society by proclaiming that God reigns and that we are called to participate in his ministry of reconciliation."

In the introduction Section III attempted to relate its report to the main theme of the Assembly. "The centre of world history is the earthly life, the cross, and the resurrection of Jesus Christ," it began.[13]

In Him are revealed the present plight of man, and the end toward which the world is moving.

He has established with men a living relationship of promise and commandment in which they are called to live in faithful obedience to His purpose. The promise is the gift of abundant life as children of God for those who hear and follow the divine call. The commandment is that men should love God and their neighbors. In the call to responsible social action, the promise and the commandment of the righteous and loving God require us

[13] See Appendix K and *The Evanston Report,* pp. 112-126.

to recognize that in every human being Christ Himself comes to claim our service. Responding to God's love in Christ, and being aware of His final judgment, Christians will act responsibly.

. . . .

Our hope in Christ does not offer technical answers or specific solutions which statesmen and experts have not found. But in the context of Christian faith we gain new insights into our dilemmas and ways to overcome them.

This orientation of the report to the main theme drew criticism during the discussion in a plenary session, because of what some who spoke of it described as "its artificiality."

By way of definition, the Assembly was reminded that, in the words of the report at Amsterdam on "God's Design and Man's Disorder," "a responsible society" was one in which freedom was "the freedom of men who acknowledged responsibility to justice and public order, and those who held political authority or economic power were responsible for its exercise to God and to the people." "Christians are called to live responsibly, to live in response to God's act of redemption, in society, even within the most unfavorable social structures," declared Evanston.

While it dealt "mainly with large-scale institutions, . . . the art of social living had to be learned in small groups," the report explained—in the family, the Christian congregation, and young people's, workers' and tribal communities.

The churches had been obliged, in recent years, to give fresh thought to the nature and function of the state, and the definition of these by the Conference on Church, Community and State[14] had served them well, which Section III had recalled in its study:

Since we believe in the Holy God as the source of justice, we do not consider the state the ultimate source of law, but rather its guarantor. It is not the lord but the servant of justice. There can be for the Christian no ultimate authority but very God.

Justice is dynamic and meets changing needs. . . . It involves continuous effort to overcome those economic disadvantages which are a grievous human burden, and which are incompatible with equal opportunity for people to develop their capacities. Justice requires the development of political institutions which are humane as they touch the lives of people, which provide protection by law against arbitrary use of power, and which encourage responsible participation by all citizens.

Christians should work for political institutions which would afford protection against "arbitrary arrest or other interference with elementary human rights," continued the report, among which were mentioned "the right to express . . . religious, moral, and political convictions." They should work also for the establishment of channels of political action, by which the people could, without recourse to violence, change their governments; and for the guarantee against state control in their inner

[14] Oxford, England, 1937.

life in associations within society, such as churches, families, and universities, which had their own foundations and principles. "At all stages of political development, and in the face of all problems, . . . a Christian community must act as a conscience for the nation, and ceaselessly remind all who hold power of God's purpose for the nation and of God's judgment upon their use of power."

Under "Problems of Economic Life," the report spoke of the extensive removal of the control in economic affairs from the sphere of "automatic responses," and of the fact that the new initiative on the part of the state had increased recognition "of the importance of relative freedom in enterprise and of the regulating role of the price system." "Many socialists have come to appreciate the importance of the private sector of the economy," it said, "and the necessity for the energetic, enterprising, and expert businessman, as well as being aware of the dangers of centralized government."

This represented, the Assembly noted, a distinct change in the attitude of socialists as reflected in the Amsterdam discussion of the responsible society.

The report claimed that disputes over capitalism and socialism disguised the more important issues in the field of economic and political policy, since each word was applied to different "social forms and economic systems." "It is not the case that we have merely a choice between two easily distinguishable types of economic organization," it explained. "In some countries the 'welfare state' or the 'mixed economy' suggests a new pattern of economic life; others may be regarded as 'capitalist,' but the capitalism of today is very different from that of even twenty or thirty years ago."

"The Church is concerned with economic life," the report stated, "because of God's concern for human beings who work to produce goods and services, who use them, and for whom business exists," and "cannot uncritically support any particular form of organization." Its interest is "especially . . . the . . . moral implications of economic life."

"Much Christian social thought in the past has tended," it was admitted, to ignore in its stressing of fair distribution the importance of production. "Laziness and waste are sins before God no less than selfishness and greed." The churches had been properly critical of monopolistic practices, but they also needed "to understand and lay stress on the valuable contribution which the skilled executive [had] to make to society, irrespective of the form of ownership or organization. At its best the business system [had] provided incentives for the responsible initiative and hard work which produce[d] economic progress, and . . . embodied the wisdom of decentralized decisions and widely distributed power . . . virtues needed in any system."

Among those workers who "should have a status in society which accord[ed] with . . . responsibilities and . . . human dignity" were mentioned farmers especially, whose "demand for a reasonable measure of security of income" should be supported. However, they were warned against exhausting the soil, exploiting those who worked for them, and taking "unfair advantage of the consumers."

The warning of the Bible against the danger in the possession of riches was timely, the conferees thought, "for everyone in a rich society," who was faced continually by the temptation "to overemphasize material values."

"Not only increased production but a stronger regard for equity in the distribution of wealth and income is required," according to the report. "Every society should recognize the extent to which great contrasts between rich and poor destroy fellowship and undercut the political institutions of a responsible society."

It was the duty of the churches "to promote adequate assistance on the national and international level for children, the sick, the old, the refugees, and other economically weak groups, by means of church organizations, voluntary societies, and local or national governments. It is the duty of the Christian to work for improved national or local welfare legislation and for the provision of adequate medical care. It may be his duty to fight against any tendency for the state to monopolize social welfare activity."

Trade unions and the associations of employers, farmers, and professional people "must be responsible to the whole of society." Their members must participate responsibly in their organizations, and leadership must be responsible to the members.

"Christians have a duty to bring to the attention of their governments that national policies have effects on the . . . welfare of peoples in other countries," the report insisted. "The richer countries particularly must remember that one test of their policies is their effect on the under-developed areas of the world."

An entire section of the report was given over to an analysis of the problems of these "under-developed areas" and of the responsibility of the churches to them. They comprised, it was pointed out, most of the continents of Asia and Africa, the Middle East, and large parts of South and Central America. In them lived close to a billion and a quarter people—nearly half the world's population.

The findings of the Ecumenical Study Conference at Lucknow, India, in 1952 had been consulted by the section for information to guide the churches in their action with reference to these parts of the earth especially in need of help, and the following problems were outlined: the building of political institutions, which called for a redefining of democratic, political and economic social values; land reform and rural improvement, in which the churches were in position to "give concrete assistance" by reason of the missionary program; industrial development, for which capital needed to be obtained under terms which would not interfere with social progress; overpopulation, which posed "family planning and birth control" as "burning questions"; the difficulty of new independent nations in becoming stabilized, because of the withdrawal of capital by the former colonial powers and the hesitation of private investors to come to their aid without guarantees hard to give; the interference by cold and hot wars in the progress of social reconstruction; the need for the extension of educational opportunity, especially for the training of experts in public administration and technology.

"The Church in Relation to Communist-Noncommunist Tension" occupied another section of the report. "Only as Christians work for social justice and political freedom for all, and rise above both fear and resentment, will they be fully able to meet the challenge of this conflict," it was declared. But this approach did "not alter the mission of the churches to bear witness in the face of all atheistic and self-righteous ideologies."

What the churches at the Oxford and Amsterdam Conferences had said concerning the points of opposition between the Christian faith and Marxist ideology and totalitarian practice was reaffirmed:

> The communist promise of what amounts to a complete redemption of man in history;
> The belief that a particular class by virtue of its role as the bearer of the new order is free from the sins and ambiguities that Christians believe characteristic of all human existence;
> The materialistic and deterministic teachings, however they may be qualified, that are incompatible with belief in God and with the Christian view of man as a person, made in God's image and responsible to Him;
> The ruthless methods of communists in dealing with their opponents.
> The demand of the party on its members for an exclusive and unqualified loyalty which belongs only to God, and the coercive policies of communist dictatorship in controlling every aspect of life.

Said the report: "There are Christians who think that they can cooperate with the communist movement in their countries because they see it as the way to a new order of material abundance and greater justice: We must ask: 'Can communism be an effective instrument for these limited purposes or must we give warning that, where such social and economic methods are introduced, the . . . communist scheme will come to dominate the minds of men as well as their institutions?' "

"Pre-occupation with the real dangers of subversion . . . has led to a less widely recognized and more subtle danger . . . from those who identify as subversive any unpopular opinions or associations," it was suggested by the report, which feared that nations might emphasize unduly the military aspects of defense against communism "and fail to see the need for reform in political, social, and economic institutions as an important part of their response to its challenge." It would be the task of the churches to point out the dangers inherent in the present situation: "on the one hand the temptation to succumb to anti-communist hysteria and the danger of a self-righteous assurance concerning the political and social systems of the West; on the other hand the temptation to accept the false promises of communism and to overlook its threat to any responsible society."

In any event, "Christians in communist and non-communist countries [were] called to hold each other in special brotherly concern and prayer across all barriers."

"Because Jesus Christ is Lord in earth and heaven, the call to responsible social action which God addresses to His Church does not present us with an impossible task. We are not called upon to shoulder the burden of this world, but to seek justice, freedom and peace to the best of our ability. . . . The Church knows that in obedience and prayer our efforts will bear fruit. . . . 'Faithful is he that calleth you, who also will do it.' "[15]

Members of the Preparatory Commission for Section III were as follows:

Professor John C. Bennett, *Co-Chairman,* United States
Dr. C. L. Patijn, *Co-Chairman,* Netherlands
Rev. Paul R. Abrecht, *Secretary,* United States
Dr. Walter Bauer, Germany
Mrs. L. Chevalley-Sabatier, France
Mr. Tilford E. Dudley, United States
Mr. John P. Edwards, United Kingdom
Rev. John Garrett, Australia
Bishop Gerald Kennedy, United States
Dr. John Matthai, India
Mr. Irwin Miller, United States
Mr. Charles C. Parlin, United States
Bishop J. Peter, Hungary
Professor André Philip, France
Professor Mikio Sumiya, Japan
Dr. A. M. Tambunam, Indonesia
Mr. M. M. Thomas, India
Rev. John W. Turnbull, United States
Professor H. D. Wendland, Germany
Bishop A. Fjellbu, Consultant, Norway
Rev. H. J. Lazarus, Consultant, India
Rev. E. C. Urwin, Consultant, United Kingdom
Mr. Edwin Barker, Consultant, United Kingdom
Professor Pierre Burgelin, Consultant, France

The significant fact about the report of Section III was not anything it said or did not say but its reception by the Assembly without serious questioning. It proposed for the churches a policy of social reform through economic and political action in line with "the way . . . society

[15] The complete official report is given in Appendix K.

had increasingly taken the control of economic affairs out of the sphere of 'automatic responses,' " and of seeking a more nearly equal distribution of wealth and income, an expansion of the benefits of the "welfare state" on both a national and an international scale, and governmental supervision of business and finance to the degree necessary to compel their compliance—all this without any reference to the increase it would cause in the already crushing tax burden of most of the solvent nations, and with only a casual intimation of the danger in such a program to the initiative of the responsible leaders in commerce and industry and to the spirit of self-reliance and independence of those who would be encouraged to look more and more to the state for support and security. And there was no audible dissent.

Nobody criticized the theological rationalization of this sweeping policy as the will of God in the orientation of the report to the main theme, "Christ—the Hope of the World," except to suggest that it could have been done less "artificially," a criticism of the phrasing rather than of the philosophy.

There was none to point out that such reliance upon politico-economic power in the attempt to implement what was presumed to be the social teaching of the gospel was tantamount to confessing that the churches had failed to win their own members to an acceptance of the obligations of Christian charity. If they had learned to live in the sacrificial spirit they extolled in Jesus Christ, the churches could themselves, with the vast wealth and influence they possessed, do many of the good works their leaders at Evanston marked for the state, and in doing them make the Christian religion a force more to be reckoned with in the world.

When the drafting committee admitted, through its spokesman, that the report in its interpretation of the social principles of the gospel ran far ahead of the thinking of the churches, no one asked whether the people of the pews and their pastors were to be regarded as uninformed and indifferent, or the ecclesiastics who were in the habit of attending ecumenical conferences as misinformed and misled.

Questions such as this could have been raised, without impugning motives, and ought to have been, because of the momentous issues at stake for the churches and free society.

The plain fact was that the statement submitted to the Assembly by Section III, to be relayed to the denominations, approved, on the whole, the procedures of collectivism, notwithstanding its mild warnings against certain socialistic pitfalls, such as the tendency to disregard the dangers in the centralization of economic control in government and the failure to recognize that, at its best, capitalistic business had provided, despite monopolistic practices, "incentives for the responsible initiative and hard work which produce[d] economic progress, and . . . embodied the wisdom of decentralized decisions and widely distributed power . . . virtues needed in any system."

It appeared that those who had written the report thought to negotiate the difficult passage between the Scylla of irresponsible individualistic capitalism and the Charybdis of the collectivist state and had been wooed dangerously in the direction of the latter.

The Rev. Shin Hong Myung did not like the paragraph decrying "anticommunist hysteria" and spoke out vehemently against any appearance of compromise with communism. Ten years of firsthand experience of it in his native Korea and elsewhere had convinced him, he said, that it was a "world-wide imperialism" which intended "to stamp out all religions."

Like the others, the report was "received by the Assembly and commended to the churches for study and appropriate action." Unfortunately, there was little likelihood that it would be studied widely. One could only believe that a general reading of it in the churches would lead to its revision at many points. What would actually happen could be predicted from the usual experience in such matters. Departments of social action of denominations and councils of churches would study it and see that it got into the educational literature prepared by them for use in the churches, and into the resolutions passed by their conventions in the rush of final sessions. In this way it would become the recorded voice of the churches.

And thus would be made still clearer the need in the World Council of Churches for a sociological, as well as a theological, "opposition," whose voice could be raised, on occasion, against the majority opinion on socio-political issues, making the actions and the pronouncements of the body more truly representative of the total thinking of the churches, and serving to silence the growing criticism that the Council spoke for only one school or party.

4. Christians in the Struggle for World Community

An address by the Honorable Dag Hammarskjold, Secretary-General of the United Nations, on the churches in relation to that body and an interpretation of the work of the Commission of the Churches on International Affairs by Director O. Frederick Nolde preceded the presentation by Sir Kenneth Grubb, Chairman of Section IV, of the report on "Christians in the Struggle for World Community."[16]

By speaking for justice, truth, and trust in public affairs, and helping "to explain how world affairs are run and what is the responsibility of everyone," the churches could be a decisive force for good in both national and international life, said Dr. Hammarskjold, without assuming a political role or trying directly to influence politics. "In spite of . . . differences in character and responsibility, the churches and . . . the

[16] From mimeographed text issued at Evanston.

United Nations have," he declared, "an aim in common and a field of action where they can work side by side."

The ideals of the United Nations "run parallel to the . . . aim and beliefs of the common man who wishes to live in peace with his neighbors, with freedom to build his own little world in human dignity," he explained, and it and the churches "stand side by side as participants in the efforts of all men of good will, irrespective of their creed or form of worship, to establish peace on earth."

"What is required from the United Nations, and from the governments and peoples represented therein," he continued, "is renewed faith every day, expressed in a never abandoned, every day newly initiated, responsible action for peace." While it "necessarily stands outside confessions," the United Nations is, nevertheless, an instrument of faith, he asserted, and "is inspired by what unites and not by what divides the great religions of the world."

The present world conflict was "a war fought in the hearts of men," he said, and could be waged successfully only by those speaking directly to men; because of this, the churches had an "overwhelming task . . . in the work for peace."

"Looking for explanations of the situation we are facing, we will find beneath the surface," he declared, "forces which are in themselves to a large extent both natural and constructive." But, "permitted to develop outside a system of legal order which is inspired by a will to peace, these same forces threaten with destruction."

"In broad terms, our time is characterized by two prominent trends," he said, "one in the direction of social and economic equality within the nations, the other . . . in the direction of equal rights and opportunities for all nations." He felt that both these trends should be welcomed as reflecting "an urge for . . . greater justice—such justice as is necessary for lasting peace." But we should also recognize, he added, that, "if no means are provided for an orderly development, these trends may lead to cataclysms like those . . . we have seen."

A first need, he emphasized, was "practical action helping underdeveloped countries to achieve such economic progress as would give them their proper share of the wealth of the world." Political arrangements should be worked out for independence and self-determination "for peoples attaining to maturity as nations," and the "leaders of such people should be helped to master the new forces in their hands for evolution and not revolution."

Ideological tensions could not be overlooked, he warned, but added, "let us not exaggerate their significance." Especially, we should not let ourselves get caught in the belief that divisions of the world between the righteous and the wrongdoers, between idealism and materialism, between freedom and slavery, coincided with national boundaries. "The righteous are to be found everywhere, as are the wrongdoers. Those whose only ideal is material well-being meet us in every country, as those whose ideal is selfless service. We would lack in historical sense and psychological insight, if the experience we have gathered during our short span of time would lead us to believe that this people or that is to be considered as an enemy forever of our ideals, or if we were to believe that ideals which we feel should dominate our own society will survive without an honest and continued fight for their supremacy in our public life."

The main task of the United Nations was mediation, negotiation, and reconciliation in concrete cases of conflict, the Secretary-General explained, but it was not to be expected to help the governments in attempts to direct "the social and political forces behind the conflicts and to meet the widespread demands . . . these . . . reflect."

"When we go beyond the great social and economic trends to the underlying ideological tensions, the contribution the United Nations can make is more limited," he said. Looking to the churches for participation in this sphere, he urged that work for peace "should be pursued with the patience of one who has no anxiety about results, acting in the calm self-surrender of faith." In this struggle, "the Cross, although it is the unique fact on which the Christian churches base their hope, should not separate those of Christian faith from others," he thought, "but should, instead, be that element in their lives which enables them to stretch out their hands to peoples of other creeds in the feeling of universal brotherhood which we hope one day to see reflected in a world of nations truly united."

Following Dr. Hammarskjold, Dr. Nolde spoke to the Assembly. "Christians recognize that the main contribution of the churches to peace among men and nations lies in the steadfast proclamation of the gospel at home and to the uttermost parts of the world," he said, reporting on the work of the Commission of the Churches on International Affairs, "and in the growing solidarity of a Christian fellowship which transcends race, class, and national frontiers. But the tragedy of two world wars in a single half century with peace still not secured has convinced churchmen that new and more direct methods also must be tried and developed."

"The Commission . . . faced a two-fold task: to build an organization which would express an effective and timely Christian witness to the world of nations, and to offer such help for the solution of international problems as may be derived from the Christian faith and the experience of the churches."

From this viewpoint, Dr. Nolde described the procedure followed by the Commission in ascertaining the mind and will of the churches concerning international issues and in presenting its conclusions to the agencies in position to profit from them. "I venture to say that in this co-operative witness . . . a new world peace movement is progressively developing, a movement which is rooted in the life of the churches and which seeks to express the meaning of the Christian faith for relations among nations. . . . It is not yet, unfortunately, a popular movement but ultimately it must become so, for its success depends upon study and support by Christians in every walk of life."

Looking upon "the road ahead," Dr. Nolde characterized "the confusion of our times" as resulting largely from "a vast upsurging of peoples of every race, color and creed . . . clamoring for equality of personal and national status, and for an opportunity to live in a manner befitting human dignity," over seven hundred million of whom had attained political independence and statehood; and from the "clash of interests" between Russia and the United States, the two dominant nations, rendered more menacing in its explosiveness by the invention of atomic and hydrogen weapons. We must "choose between two fateful alternatives," he declared. "Do we believe that deep-rooted international problems can be solved only by war, or are we convinced that their solution can be found, and must unwaveringly be sought, in a framework of peace?" "Many would claim," he said, "that the choice is obvious" and the repudiation of war unnecessary. "Let not complacency or over-simplification delude us," he warned. "The demand for a preventive war is not completely stilled . . . and in every walk of life there are those who yield to defeatism and take the position that 'an end with horror is better than horror without end.'" He held that Christians "must be in the forefront proclaiming that a third world war is not inevitable. It can be avoided. It must be prevented."

The speaker felt himself driven to advocate coexistence as a point of departure to the road of peace, explaining that he did not use this term as carrying "the implication of a world divided into compartments with an apparent commitment that both parties will respect existing geographical and ideological boundaries." There can be no such "geographical compartments, from the standpoint of the Christian faith," he asserted. "There is one world. . . . The ecumenical movement is . . . demonstrating that there is a Christian fellowship which recognizes no frontiers. . . . A variable form for 'coexistence' must manifestly reveal the opportunity for a release of the dynamic forces which are known to exist. . . . The alternative to war can only be found in peaceful competition with commitment to growing co-operation."

Competition will . . . require the clear recognition of a fundamental ideological conflict. Marxist communism in its orthodox philosophy is atheistic in its conception of ultimate reality and materialistic in its view of man and his destiny. Its violent revolutionary strategy and its totalitarian practices disregard the sacredness of human personality. On issues of faith the Christian cannot compromise, and those who on other than Christian grounds hold to the dignity and worth of the individual man will not yield.

The World Council of Churches has taken the position that totalitarianism is false in doctrine and dangerous in practice. This applies to totalitarianism wherever it appears and in whatever form.

Speaking of attitudes that would block "peaceful competition," Dr. Nolde mentioned especially "powerful groups in the United States and . . . Western Europe" who "oppose legislation to authorize support for any international enterprise," even if it be "intrinsically right," if it is not anti-communistic. He referred to those also who objected to negotiations with Russia "as in essence appeasement," but held that "notwithstanding past experiences of failure . . . , it must be obvious that if international issues are not to be settled by war, they must be . . . by negotiations or similar methods prescribed by the United Nations Charter."

The ending of imperialism in its colonial aspects was to be welcomed, the director continued, with due recognition of the good in it. But he drew attention to "a more direct form of imperialism found in the practices of various countries but particularly ascribed to the United States," which "is exercised by economic power." "By credits, trade agreements and like measures," he said, "control has been attempted from outside a country and in order to protect vested interests measures have been taken to keep a friendly government in power. Military and ideological conditions have at times been coupled with economic assistance to an unwarranted extreme." Soviet Russia exercised control of an imperialistic character in other countries, he explained, through the subversion of indigenous minorities and the use of military threat or force.

In the midst of the world's confusion, "no greater responsibility rests upon the Christian citizen," he concluded, "than to put his own house in order. . . . In . . . competing societies, it is easy for people to repent of each other's sins. It is far more difficult to remove the beam from one's own eye. . . . The domestic community where men and women can determine their faith by conscience and freely express it, subject only to the rights of others" is a magnet to attract men everywhere, and "to build it is our first task."

The report of Section IV echoed these sentiments. "The Assembly of the World Council of Churches proclaims the Christian hope in an hour of grave international crisis. This troubled world . . . is still God's. . . . We commit ourselves to seek . . . justice, freedom and peace for all men." Christians "face the fact that . . . peace will not be easily or quickly attained. . . . Basically the problem is . . . spiritual . . . , and economic and political measures alone will not solve it. Men's hearts must be changed. This is always the supreme evangelistic challenge of the Church."

"It is not enough for the churches to proclaim that war is evil," it continued. "They must seek out, analyze, and help to remove the psychological and social, the political and economic causes of war." They must go farther and "plead with their governments to be patient and persistent in their search for means to limit weapons and advance disarmament."

"An international order of truth and peace would require," it was suggested, "the elimination and prohibition of atomic, hydrogen and all other weapons of mass destruction, as well as the reduction of all armaments to a minimum," and "the development and acceptance of . . . peaceful change to rectify existing injustices."

The report called upon the nations to forswear the threat and the use of hydrogen, atomic, and other weapons of mass destruction, as well as all other means of force against the territorial integrity or political independence of any state, and urged that, in the event pledges given to that end should be broken by a nation, the United Nations and its own government limit military action recognized as the right of national self-defense "strictly to the necessities of international security."

In this connection, the report condemned "the deliberate mass destruction of civilians in open cities by whatever means and for whatever purpose" and said that experimental tests in the development of hydrogen bombs should be made only in the nation's own territory, or, "if elsewhere, only by international clearance."

In a divided world nations had to learn to live together, it declared, and proceeded to outline further the responsibilities of Christians in making this possible; but it avoided explicitly using the term *coexistence* "because of its unhappy historical significance and some of its current political implications." [17]

"Coexistence" as conceived by Christians cannot imply any willingness to disguise from themselves or others the vast difference which lies between the search for an international order based on belief in Christ and His reconciling work, and the pursuit of aims which repudiate the Christian revelation. . . .

We stand against submission to, engulfment by, or appeasement of totalitarian tyranny and aggression. We also stand against the exploitation of any people by economic monopoly or political imperialism. In the world community we must stand for the freedom of all people to know the truth which makes men free and for the basic civil liberties of all people to struggle for a higher freedom.

Christians claim the right to propagate their faith, by proclamation and persuasion, by example and suffering, just as they uphold the same right for others. Nevertheless, conflicts of conviction about the origin and destiny of man have long existed within societies essentially peaceful, and Christians must continue to condemn totalitarianism as false in doctrine and dangerous in practice. They will be no less firm in continuing to oppose atheistic materialism. Yet however deep the conflict may be it is not necessarily an insuperable bar to living together in a divided world. The same

[17] The Report of Section IV may be found in *The Evanston Report,* pp. 130-144.

may be said of methods of political and economic organization, whether they be democratic or dictatorial.

Such living together does, however, require that certain minimum conditions be met on both sides:

1. A conviction that it is possible for nations and peoples to live together. . . .

2. A willingness not to use force as an instrument of policy beyond the existing frontiers. . . .

3. A vigorous effort to end social and other injustices which might lead to civil, and hence international, war.

4. A scrupulous respect for the pledged word.

5. A continuing effort to reach agreement on outstanding issues, such as . . . peace treaties and disarmament, which are essential to a broader stabilization. . . .

6. Readiness to submit all unresolved questions of conflict to an impartial international organization and to carry out its decisions.

"The world community has become interdependent," the report reminded. "The legitimate right of the self-determination of peoples must be recognized. Specific assurance of independence or self-government should be given."

"We welcome the development of international responsibility in place of the old colonialism, and the principle of international study and review, exemplified by the United Nations Trusteeship System," it added.

"The response of more developed countries through expanded international programs of technical assistance is one of the brightest pages of recent history," according to the report; "but the effort thus far has been small in comparison with the needs of the less developed countries and the resources of those more developed."

In the opinion of the section, the United Nations, despite "the critical post-war tensions," had made significant contributions to order and justice, its defects reflecting mainly the divisions within the international community."

The report endorsed the creation of regional organizations of nations for collective self-defense and pursuit of common interests, so long as they were clearly defensive in character, were subordinate to and reinforced the aims of the Charter of the United Nations, and served the genuine mutual interests and needs of their people. It also strongly upheld "the proclamation of international standards in the Declaration of Human Rights" and emphasized that "the importance of attempts to secure international legal safeguards for [those standards was] not diminished by the obstacles."

The report called for measures by the governments and the churches to continue relief for refugees, migrants, unrepatriated prisoners, and other groups of oppressed and suffering people, whatever their origin, race, or religion.

Considerable space was given to a statement of the need to help the nations to develop "an international ethos" embodying a common view of moral principles, and the following declarations were suggested for study:

1. All power carries responsibility and all nations are trustees of power which should be used for the common good.
2. All nations are subject to moral law, and should strive to abide by the accepted principles of international law. . . .
3. All nations should honor their pledged word. . . .
4. No nation in an international dispute has the right to be sole judge in its own cause or to resort to war to advance its policies, but should seek to settle disputes by direct negotiations or by submitting them to conciliation, arbitration, or judicial settlement.
5. All nations have a moral obligation to ensure universal security and to this end should support measures designed to deny victory to a declared aggressor.
6. All nations should recognize and safeguard the inherent dignity, worth, and essential rights of the human person, without distinction as to race, sex, language, or religion.
7. Each nation should recognize the rights of every other nation, which observes such standards, to live by and proclaim its own political and social beliefs, provided that it does not seek by coercion, threat, infiltration or deception to impose these on other nations.
8. All nations should recognize an obligation to share their scientific . . . skills with peoples in less developed regions, and to help the victims of disaster in other lands.
9. All nations should strive to develop cordial relations with their neighbors, encourage friendly cultural and commercial dealings, and join in creative international efforts for human welfare.[18]

Four resolutions dealing with international matters were submitted at the same time as the report of Section IV and adopted by the Assembly, as follows:[19]

Resolution I

God is the God of justice and peace, and the Lord of history. He calls us all to repentance. It is in obedience to Him, and through the eyes of the Christian faith, that we look at the problems of this troubled world.

It is not our purpose in the present statement to pass judgment on past actions. We seek rather to contribute to a new spiritual climate in which a fresh start can be made by all governments and peoples.

The world is so broken up and divided that international agreement seems remote at the moment. Everywhere fear and mistrust prevail. The very possibility of good-neighborly relations between nations is denied.

We believe that there are two conditions of crucial importance which must be met, if catastrophe is to be avoided:

1. The prohibition of all weapons of mass destruction; including atomic and hydrogen bombs, with provision for international inspection and control,

[18] The complete official draft of the report of Section IV, as received by the Assembly, appears in Appendix L.

[19] *The Evanston Report,* pp. 146-49.

such as would safeguard the security of all nations, together with the drastic reduction of all other armaments.
2. The certain assurance that no country will engage in or support aggressive or subversive acts in other countries.

We believe that a sound international order is possible only to the extent that peace, justice, freedom and truth are assured.

We are convinced that peace will be gravely endangered so long as the armaments race continues, and so long as any nation seeks to extend its power by the threat of military force.

To meet the demands of justice, whether in a particular nation, or in the assistance of peoples in under-developed countries, is our moral duty. We recognize that progress in raising the standard of living in under-developed countries is discouragingly slow; and that increasing sacrifice on the part of richer nations is essential. Freedom means man's opportunity to realize his worth in God's sight, and to fulfill his God-given destiny. All nations have a duty to secure for their citizens the right to criticize or approve, as conscience dictates. Moreover fear and suspicion cannot be replaced by respect and trust unless powerful nations remove the yoke which now prevents other nations and peoples from freely determining their own government and form of society. Freedom and justice in their turn depend upon the steady proclamation of truth. False propaganda, whether to defend a national policy or to criticize the practice of another government will increase international tension and may contribute to war.

The World Council of Churches bears witness to Christ as the Hope of the World. In the strength of that hope, and impelled by the desire to help in the relief of present tensions it makes the following appeal:

We appeal to the governments and the peoples to continue to speak to one another, to avoid rancor and malice, and to look for ways by which fear and suspicion may be removed.

We appeal to the governments and the peoples also to devote their strength and their resources to meeting the peaceful needs of the citizens of their countries, and above all a determined common effort to secure a decent standard of living among poorer and underdeveloped countries.

We appeal to the statesmen and the leaders of public opinion and the press to refrain from words and actions which are designed to inflame enmity and hatred.

We appeal to the representatives of the churches in those countries between which tension exists to visit one another, so that they may gain a better understanding of one another, and of the countries in which they live, and thus strengthen the bonds of fellowship, and promote the reconciliation of the nations.

We appeal to the churches to bid their members recognize their political responsibilities, and also to ask Christian technicians and administrators to find a vocation in the service of U.N. Agencies engaged in meeting the needs of economically and technically under-developed countries, thus bringing a Christian temper of love and understanding to bear upon the immensely difficult task of mutual assistance in the encounter of different cultures.

We appeal to all members of all churches to unite in a common ministry of reconciliation in proclaiming Christ as the Hope of the World, in intercession for one another and in mutual service.

Finally, we call upon all Christians everywhere to join in prayer to Almighty God, that He will guide the governments and the peoples in the ways of justice and peace.

Resolution II

That the Central Committee be requested to appoint a delegation or deletions (i) to communicate the foregoing statement to the member churches of the World Council of Churches, (ii) to take such steps as seen most suitable with a view to the presentation of the same statement to the churches not related to the World Council of Churches, including the churches in the U.S.S.R. and in other lands, (iii) to invite these churches to consider ways in which they might communicate the statement to the governments of their countries.

Resolution III

The World Council of Churches, at its Second Assembly in August 1954, records its concern and sorrow over the continuing sufferings and disabilities of fellow Christians in many parts of the world.

It knows that the Assembly is incomplete because the World Council cannot communicate with many churches over whose life and testimony a veil of silence has been forcibly drawn. We assure these fellow Christians and those who stand with them of our prayers and we earnestly look forward to the day of freedom and reunion.

Christians must stand together with all who, in the struggle for freedom, suffer pain and trial. We thank God for the steadfastness of our fellow Christians who, in trial and tribulation, gave so much—even their lives—for Christ's sake and for ours, and we humbly pray that we may not be unworthy of their sacrifice.

The Assembly also deeply regrets that in certain countries from which information can be gathered with reasonable accuracy, Christians are suffering many disabilities and even violence; and human rights and liberties, albeit acknowledged in official protestations, have in practice been denied.

To all such the Assembly extends the assurance of the prayers of its member churches, that those who are absent from its fellowship may be sustained by the presence of Christ. The World Council will continue to work for a new day of fellowship and liberty of witness.

We thank God that His Church is worthy to follow its Lord in suffering.

We rejoice—with our brethren who suffer in the faith—in that fellowship in Christ which nobody and nothing can destroy. We know that their fidelity and ours will prevail.

Resolution IV

Having received representations regarding a number of specific and serious cases of religious persecution and repression, this Assembly of the World Council of Churches re-affirms previous declarations regarding religious liberty and expresses its grave concern regarding the situation in a number of lands and continents. It also calls attention to the statement on religious freedom in the United Nations' Declaration of Human Rights. The Assembly instructs its officers and the Commission of the Churches on International Affairs to continue to use every effort in representations to the governments concerned and, where they are involved, the religious authorities; and appeals to its member churches to make direct representation in certain cases to continue in prayer for those suffering from persecution and repression.

Members of the Preparatory Commission for Section IV were as follows:

Sir Kenneth Grubb, C.M.G., *Chairman,* United Kingdom
Dr. Richard M. Fagley, *Secretary,* United States
Dr. K. A. Busia, Gold Coast, Africa
Professor W. Grewe, Germany
Dr. J. L. Hromadka, Czechoslovakia
Professor Werner Kägi, Switzerland
Dr. J. Leimena, Indonesia
Dr. Charles Malik, Lebanon
Dr. Philippe Maury, France
Mr. S. A. Morrison, United Kingdom
Dr. O. Frederick Nolde, United States
Mr. Wesley F. Rennie, United States
Miss Marion Royce, Canada
Mr. Soichi Saito, Japan
Professor Arnold J. Toynbee, United Kingdom
Professor Baron F. M. van Asbeck, Netherlands
Mr. Maurice Webb, South Africa
Mr. Erling Wikborg, Norway
Rev. M. Kozaki, Consultant, Japan
Dr. Alice Arnold, Consultant, Switzerland
Rev. E. Philip Eastman, Consultant, Switzerland
Dr. Whan Shin Lee, Consultant, Korea
Rev. Philip Potter, Consultant, Haiti
Rev. W. Menn, Consultant, Germany
Professor R. B. Y. Scott, Consultant, Canada

Whether in a political body like the United Nations or an ecclesiastical conference such as the Assembly of the World Council of Churches, men endeavoring to find a way to security and peace in the midst of this world must always by the little that they can do accentuate the contrast between their own meagre powers and the massiveness of the forces against which they contend.

Greatest of all the obstacles which combine to thwart them is the failure in the modern world of international law, with its sanctions, resulting from the deterioration of its all too unstable foundation in a common morality. Classical international law developed, as the ecumenical Conference on the Foundations of International Law at Céligny, Switzerland, in 1950, pointed out, "among a plurality of more or less equal nations, all acknowledging much the same unifying tradition," but today large blocs of powers face each other "with hardly any common ethos binding them to one another."

It is not only that there is no generally accepted basis on which an understanding can be reached across ideological and cultural frontiers but that agreements, when entered into without moral supports, become at the first clash of private interests only "scraps of paper." With the repudiation by nations of their pledged word, trust is destroyed and anarchy unloosed.

Chaos is increased by the proved willingness of some nations to give lip service to the moral code and to diplomatic usages founded upon it, with the purpose only to deceive and thus to gain the advantage over others in ways which, when the mask of dissimulation is thrown off, expose those acting in good faith to sudden and possibly disastrous attack.

The rise of totalitarianism in its modern forms has introduced the code of gangsterism into international life, under which the first concern of those conspiring to bind and plunder the world must be to maintain their usurped positions as the rulers of nations, and this is a necessity that knows only the law of the jungle. Not to obey this primitive code would invite their own destruction, a prospect more forbidding to them than the wasting of the whole earth. If they must go down, they would not hesitate to attempt to take with them the temple of mankind.

These latter day tyrants are militant and professed atheistic materialists, not content to reject spiritual values themselves but determined that others, who are to be bent to their wills, shall also. Their philosophy reduces man to little more than a beast. He has no soul. Whether he shall be allowed to exist or not is to be determined by his usefulness to those who have made themselves his masters. At the same time, with their lives exposed to constant jeopardy at one another's hands, these ruthless men must learn to hold their own destruction—and even that of the world—in contempt. So is created in the midst of civilization a disorder no persuasion can touch.

Christians see in the gospel of Jesus Christ hope for the struggle to build a solid foundation under international relations. But many ask whether the day is not too far spent for this. They believe in the reality of conversion, but they cannot bring themselves to look for a quick transformation of nations flouting Christian morality.

The Pope in Robert Browning's *The Ring and the Book* could with some reason pray that the villainous Guido might, by a miracle, suddenly be enabled to see the truth and so be saved through repentance, as he himself remembered having on a dark night beheld Naples as in daylight by a flash from erupting Vesuvius; but in that case the sinner was a solitary individual. Changing a nation is another matter.

The kingdom of hope in which the churches trust is like "leaven that is hid in three measures of meal," according to its King. Its power for social regeneration is evolutionary, rather than revolutionary. Meanwhile, the momentum of the forces of world destruction appears to accelerate.

It should cause little wonder that in the face of such portents war seems the only recourse to some, and they would welcome its coming as more to be desired than peace under endless intolerable tension.

With the lawless at large in a city or a countryside, safety lies in their apprehension and punitive control. The difference between that kind of operation in local and international spheres, however, is that in the latter, with the ever present probability of war, it may result in the destruction of the community and not only of the offenders.

Christians of Hungary, who live under a totalitarian government, differ with what appears to be the consensus of those outside the Iron Curtain, that, in the words of the Congregational Union of Great Britain, "there can be no world peace until both East and West acknowledge the existence of a law higher than that prescribed by their own emphases and interests." The Hungarian Ecumenical Commission, studying the problem, concluded that no international ethos was needed in order to reach a reconciliation of a "temporal, relative and provisional kind," the cross of Jesus Christ having provided, it said, all the necessary conditions, and that God might purpose using for his own ends those who did not know him.

Christians of democratic countries think, however, that this position would involve the churches in compromises which would vitiate their witness. Those speaking through Section IV at Evanston declared that they were unwilling to disguise from themselves or others the vast difference which lay between the search for an international order based on belief in Christ and his reconciling work and the pursuit of aims which repudiated the Christian revelation. "There can be no abandonment," they wrote, "of the right to assert this fundamental difference and the faith on which it rests. We stand against submission to, engulfment by, or appeasement of totalitarian tyranny and aggression. . . . In the world community we must stand for the freedom of all people to know the truth which makes men free and for the basic civil liberties of all people."

It was in the conflict between the anarchic international disorder, which seemed to be beyond remedying, and the conviction that the gospel must be preached in all the earth without compromise in its social application that the apparent dichotomy in the sociological and theological outlook of the Assembly at Evanston had its roots. In concluding his address on the work of the Commission of the Churches on International Affairs, Dr. Nolde said:

> The tensions and difficulties by which we are now beset in all probability will continue for some generations, and then new problems will arise. Peace and justice are never won with security and finality. They are the object of continuous striving. I have tried to show . . . that in this struggle . . . Christians and churches have a distinctive contribution to make. I do not claim that their effort will, of necessity, prove successful, but I am convinced that the effort must be made.

There are Christians who feel that, in order to make the effort, they must have assurance of its ultimate success, and who seem to find comfort in the idea, confusing to many others, that Christ has already won the victory and will upon his second coming share it with his people.[20]

On the other hand, there are those who do not think that, in order to keep on with the struggle, they have need of such eschatological solace. They are not sure that God intends the conflict to end in a victory on the earthward side. They do not know, and are content not to know. They keep on because it seems to them in the nature of their Christian commitment. God keeps on, and they know no duty but to go with him. Not to do so would be to lose him, and to fail others who are bound up in the bundle of life with them. They can see that to keep on heads them toward sacrifice, and that from this standpoint there may have been deeper implications than at first appeared in the statement of the Hungarian Christians when they said that Jesus Christ had provided in his suffering on a cross all the necessary conditions of reconciliation between man and man. They can only believe that the important consideration is what happens to themselves spiritually when they take up their cross and to those for whom it is borne. The reconciliation which can be wrought in this way, perhaps only in this way, may be so completely the will of God that he stays the day of doom for it. Facing in that direction, they could not think of abandoning the effort for peace, in which is to be found thus also "the peace of God which passeth understanding." They may have to give up talking about security as a condition of either kind of peace, because neither can be attained without risking all, and those concerned only for safety, persons and nations alike, invite thereby the loss of all. There are profounder meanings than have been fathomed, they suspect, in the ancient insight that "without the shedding of blood, there is no remission of sins," and so also no hope.

5. The Church amid Racial and Ethnic Tensions

Race relations had at Evanston the status of a separate study under the theme "The Church Amid Racial and Ethnic Tensions"—the fifth in the subsidiary list—and the program committees had arranged for its ample presentation to the Assembly at large and also at the special meetings for accredited visitors, who were actually alternates to the delegates. A half-dozen or more addresses dealt with it exclusively, and many of the other speakers took occasion, whatever their subjects, to remark on it.

Dr. Benjamin E. Mays and Dr. B. J. Marais, both members of the Preparatory Commission for Section V, introduced the theme at plenary sessions of the Assembly.[21]

The burden of what Dr. Mays said was the evil of segregation, which he condemned as penalizing one for being what God made him, and

[20] See report of Section IV: "Assured the final victory is Christ's, we can work for that reconciliation which we believe to be God's will."

[21] Their addresses were issued in mimeographed form.

as "tantamount to saying to God, 'You made a mistake, God, when you made people of different races and colors.'"

"If the Church can find no support in science for ethnic and racial tension, none in the Bible for segregation based on race or color, none in the practice of the ancient and medieval Church, and no basis for it in Christian theologies, the question naturally arises: How can segregation and discrimination in the Church be justified?" If the churches could not practice "full Christian fellowship in worship and membership, how could they preach the prophetic word to secular organizations that discriminate on grounds of race, color and caste?" he asked.

He pointed out that local churches, as a matter of fact, "permitted secular bodies, such as the state and federal courts, the United Nations, big league baseball, professional boxing, colleges and universities, the public schools and theatres to initiate the change," and then, whether Negro or white, "follow slowly or not at all."

"It will be a sad commentary on our life and time," he said, "if future historians can write that the last bulwark of segregation . . . in the United States and South Africa was God's Church."

Addressing himself to the "demands of justice in the matter," he declared:

> Even if we laid no claim to a belief in democracy, if the whole world were at peace internationally, if atheistic communism had never developed, if fascism had never been born, if nazism were wholly unknown, a non-segregated church and social and economic justice for all men are urgent, because we preach a universal gospel that demands that our deeds reflect our theory. To proclaim one thing and to act another is sheer hypocrisy. It weakens the influence of the Church, not only in its own fellowship but throughout the world. . . . It is not communism, not fascism, not the struggle between the East and West, but the gospel itself which demands interracial justice and an unsegregated church.

"It has been the responsibility of the Church always," he asserted, "to plow new ground, smash traditions, break mores, and make new creatures. Such was the role of the Hebrew prophets, of Jesus and Paul, of the early Church, of Savonarola and Martin Luther, of Livingstone and Albert Schweitzer." The task had become in modern times, he continued, to show how the gospel of Christ could be "presented and lived so as to make new creatures of men and women in the area of race, and bring hope and abundant life to all men—not only beyond history but in history." "We refuse to believe that God is limited in history and that we must wait until the end of history before his mighty works can be performed."

Following his address, Dr. Mays, who lived in Atlanta, Georgia, where he was President of Morehouse College, an institution sponsored by the American Baptist Home Mission Society for the education of Negroes and a beneficiary of the Spellman Fund established by the first John D. Rockefeller, explained his position,[22] as follows:

> All church doors [should be] opened in membership and worship to all who serve and love the Lord. For the Church is God's creation and not man's, and it belongs to God. And in God's domain all men are equal. . . . I don't think a man should be denied the privilege to worship in a church because of his race. If he is of the same faith, I do not believe he should be denied membership in the church because of his race.
>
> I have never advocated that a Negro church or a white church should be abolished. The doors should be open to people who like to worship and to those who would like to join. A white person may be an atheist, and a Negro may be an atheist, but he can worship in a white church or a Negro church without embarrassment. In most churches in the South a Negro cannot even worship without being segregated. . . . If I could join a white church in Atlanta, I would not. I would still keep my membership in the Negro church near Morehouse [College]. But quite often I would like to worship in some white church in Atlanta, but I dare not try. Even if I wanted to join, I think I should be permitted.

Dr. Marais, who belonged to the Dutch Reformed Church in South Africa and came from Pretoria to the Assembly in the capacity of a consultant, having served as a member of the Preparatory Commission on the theme for Section V, began his address by saying that he thought those studying race relations were dealing with "one of the most difficult areas in the life of the Christian Church of the twentieth century." His manner, as well as what he said, made it plain that he felt the gravity of the subject, understood the prejudices it aroused, knew the issues it embodied could not be settled in a day, and wished to talk about it dispassionately; and his attitude in this respect—this should be reported if the temper of the Assembly is to be described fairly—caused some shaking of heads by those who thought the occasion called for strong words and immediate and vigorous action.

"In different branches of the Church Universal Christian men and women work and think in local situations," he said, "where an accumulation of racial and ethnic tensions has brought about explosive [conditions] which may at any moment flare . . . into eruptions and even disasters."

"This problem is made more difficult," he added, "by the fact that it is so heavily loaded with emotion and clouded with a great variety of fears and suspicions. Straight thinking is often at a premium and rationalization at the helm. Though I have lived in one of these most difficult human situations where tensions have . . . heightened with the passing of every decade, I want to speak to you humbly as one who is himself a seeker . . . who has not succeeded in discovering all the answers for his own situation."

[22] In a letter to the author, published by permission.

He often listened, the speaker confessed, "with some twinge of envy" to people in his own and other countries "who spoke with absolute certainty on these matters and had no doubts in their minds." Part of the problem lay, he thought, in the fact that groups of these people who had such full assurance gave "diametrically opposed solutions and even scriptural interpretations." "It behooves us," he said, "to seek the will of God humbly and with minds free of human pride and intolerance, in the knowledge that, wherever we live, our thinking is to some degree at least . . . conditioned by our special circumstances. . . . Nobody lives and thinks *in vacuo*."

We easily take the *status quo* for granted. When I was a boy in the Great Karroo in South Africa nobody . . . ever questioned social segregation or segregation within the church. It was . . . accepted as a normal human and Christian relationship. Only in later years when I tried to relate this social heritage to the totality of my Christian thinking, deep doubts . . . were born in my mind. It was no longer adequate to be told: "He must be separate because he is black."

Today we all face this problem. Great upheavals and vast social and political changes, new ideologies and even the growth of the Christian Church itself, have brought men and women in all countries face to face with the problem of race and color, as perhaps never before in history. Christian men and women in many lands look towards the church for guidance. Even the secular world takes note. While we are gathered here the problem is literally world-wide. As we learn the intricacies of . . . scattered communities or travel from land to land, a disturbing awareness makes itself felt that racial and ethnic problems . . . are not confined to two or three so-called "hot spots" but are part of the . . . experience of many peoples and . . . churches. . . . Therefore, it is becoming that we face this problem in a calm Christian spirit . . . not . . . in a spirit of judgment and recriminations.

Perhaps we must all come with repentance—repentance for an often un-Christian and unbrotherly attitude towards fellow-Christian groups of another background, color, or race, or a spirit of censure towards, and a lack of understanding of, the often extremely complicated problems of these groups or churches who follow a very different course from our own. It is just possible that they are not primarily motivated by fear, pride, prejudice and selfishness.

Dr. Marais turned to "the long history of the Church which," he suggested, had "many lessons to teach," and gave a summation of its salient experiences in race relations. The primitive Church was "an integrated . . . many-hued society of believers," without "any form of segregation on the basis of race, color or ethnical differences. So closely were Christians of all nations linked together . . . they were . . . called a 'third race' over against pagans and Jews." However, the "great negroid, caucasian and oriental groups of the modern world" were not so closely connected culturally, he pointed out, as the peoples around "the Mediterranean basin among whom the early Church grew up." Furthermore, "after the vast sweeps of Islam from the seventh century onwards, the Christian Church was a more or less 'white' Church and included only relatively small colored groups. It was only after the great discoveries of the Americas and the new trade routes to India and the East, and, for Protestants, after the . . . missionary movements' beginning in the eighteenth century, that the . . . Church was once more confronted with great groups of colored people. . . . This fact that Christianity was for almost a thousand years a white man's religion has placed the modern church in a situation where it has, to some degree, to face this problem of race and color *de novo*." And, "amid the storms and stresses of often almost overwhelming actualities, it has few historical decisions to fall back upon and from which it can draw guidance."

It was a part of the development of this history, he recalled, that the dealings of European nations with colored people greatly complicated the problem of race for the churches. "These contacts were not normal," he explained, but those of conqueror with the conquered, superior with inferior, and, in many cases, master with slave; and out of them developed definite social patterns quite disparate from those of democracy. The churches, perforce, lived and moved within these patterns, not only influencing them but influenced by them, for they were deep and rigid.

The results of the investigations of the Preparatory Commission indicated, he observed, that most churches no longer justified segregation. Their policy rested upon "a fairly generally accepted interpretation of Scripture which in the light of the great acts of God in the incarnation, the crucifixion and Pentecost, the reality of the brotherhood of all believers and the records of the primitive Church, posits the conviction that in the Church of Christ all believers must be at home and no barriers like race or color may divide" them. "Whether black or white, rich or poor, all, as the Body of Christ, are one." Many who hold this point of view conceded, however, he said, that "if a group, on account of language, for instance, wishes to worship separately, they are free to do so, on condition . . . that nobody is excluded on any other ground than faith."

"But within the Universal Church there is a small body of opinion," he wished it recognized, "which bases a policy of racial segregation within the Church on Scripture." The Preparatory Commission had had to face this fact, and he asked leave of the Assembly, as one who did not hold this view but had daily contact with honest and sincere Christians who did, "in fairness to all concerned, to sketch the main lines of reasoning" these latter followed. "Knowledge of each other's insights is a pre-requisite," he said, "to better understanding, though it may in no way pave the way to agreement"; he would confine himself to quotations from documents that were representative, one of which had been recently affirmed by a synod. (The churches alluded to, it should be said, were not members of the World Council of Churches.)

One apologetic beginning with the division of humanity at the Tower of Babel "by an act of God," reasoned:

It is clear that God willed the existence of separate nations and that he wills to perpetuate the divisions into races and nations. Because a nation (*Volk*) is divinely ordained (*göttliche Ordnung*), it must be honored and guarded against every possible menace. The Scriptures teach . . . that the restoration of the unity of mankind can be effected only through the conquest of sin. According to God's Word there is only one unifying element which can bridge, without removing, the gulf between nations and races, and that is the Gospel of Christ.

We learn from God's Word that the solution to the problem of racial relationships cannot be found in efforts on the part of man to wipe out divinely instituted differences, but that it is possible, while faithfully preserving national identity and cultural character, to practise Christian brotherly love among nations and races in a spirit of thankfulness towards God.

De Quervain points out the necessity for each nation to safeguard its language, ethical code and country with great reverence and loyalty against every threat. If a nation regards these things with indifference, it is lacking in gratitude towards God and wholly irresponsible. He states furthermore that it is from the manner in which people live and conduct themselves that we learn what is characteristic of a nation and who should be regarded as belonging together. According to this principle, it would certainly not be un-Christian for Christians of different races to associate at international congresses . . . , but in ordinary social intercourse, especially where national mores are involved, each should preserve his national character by withdrawing into his own particular circle. True Christianity is certainly not displayed in a common social intercourse in which the national identity of each racial group is threatened, but much rather in proper recognition of, and respect for, the national identity which God has given each. The Christian nations which have pursued a policy of equality and fraternization in their "social intercourse" with other nations have, even after centuries of contact, failed in their efforts at unification, as is evidenced by the history of Indonesia and India. The concept of apartheid, or rather the maintenance of the racial identity of each nation, can for that reason not be regarded as a temporary measure of an undeveloped or immature people, but is a constant obligation of every nation out of respect for God's dispensation.

Dr. Marais quoted "a leading South African churchman" also, as follows:

The easiest way to extinguish the light of the cross in South Africa would be a policy of total fusion of the races. Therefore, in order to remain faithful to his divine calling and to continue proclaiming the Gospel of God's love in Christ, the Afrikaner had to retain his identity. This obligation rested on him. He had to love himself, that which he had become through the grace of God, in order to be able to love his neighbor. He had to prepare himself, in order to be a blessing to the millions of non-whites. Thence he derived his apartheid idea.

Mankind desired a unity that was sinful in the eyes of the Lord. The Lord intervened and caused an increase in peoples which, according to Scripture, must continue until the completion of all things, and possibly even after (Revelation viii, 8; xxi, 24). The rise and continuance of separate peoples and nations is, according to Scripture, in accordance with the will of God. Attempts at unification, the equalitarian idea, is a revival of the Babylonish spirit that had already said, right at the beginning of man's history: "Let us make us a name lest we be scattered abroad upon the face of the whole earth" (Genesis xi, 4). It is fruitless to speculate on the question whether the organic development of mankind would have led to the same result, had sin not come. We have to deal with the factual position, such as we experience in this sinful world. There can be no doubt that God willed the separate existence of nations, and that even in the Church of Christ, as it exists here in its instituted form, the Gospel did not abolish the differences in endowment, nature, culture, etc., between the different racial groups. Any attempt to ignore this will be an attempt to build another Tower of Babel. And it is significant for the Christian Church that the products of such attempts in the political field are called "beasts" in the Revelation of St. John (Revelation xvii, 13).

It is, therefore, not only for practical reasons, as is sometimes stated, that the Nederduitse Gereformeerde Churches in their mission policy aim at the establishment of separate non-white churches which must finally become completely independent. The missionary policy of these churches has sufficient scriptural grounds for us to feel justified in saying that the creation of separate churches is not only permissible but essential.

But then what of the unity which we as Christians profess? Is not the Church the body of Christ? And must not all members be knit together in this one body? These questions are asked with compelling seriousness, and then reference is made to the well-known pronouncements of St. Paul in Galatians iii, 26 and Colossians iii, 11. It must strike every unprejudiced interpreter of Scripture that in Galatians iii, St. Paul three times uses the expression "in Christ." In St. John xvii, 21, 22, the Lord Jesus six times uses the expressions "in Me" and "in Thee." The unity that is advocated there is to be found only in Christ and in God. Outside Christ . . . there is no unity, in any case no unity in the sense in which the New Testament understands it. Notwithstanding all pleas to the contrary, and in spite of Galatians iii and other scriptural passages to the same effect, there still exist Jews and Greeks and men and women and circumcised and uncircumcised, even within one and the same communion. These earthly distinctions have remained in existence within the Church of Christ, and we can only conclude that the intention of the Apostle is that whoever are in Christ are spiritually one, in spite of all . . . national, language, sex or other differences.

This does not mean that the Church can escape its responsibility to demonstrate to the world the oneness we confess in Christ. We therefore note two possibilities. There is the first possibility that the truths of the Christian religion can be used to build an artificial, unnatural, sinful unity out of all sorts of heterogeneous elements. . . . This way holds the dire possibility that man, and even the Church, however well-meaningly, will convert the natural order, the cosmos willed and brought into being by God in such rich diversity, into a chaos, an interfusion of species and types, where no order can any longer exist. The other possibility is to respect God's handiwork, to pay heed to all natural distinctions and to strive to come to the oneness of the spirit of Christ, being all informed by the same Spirit. The characteristic of this oneness is described in the prayer of the Lord Jesus: "That all may be one as Thou, Father, art in me and I in Thee" (John xvii, 21). . . . It is not a question of uniformity in the institutional sense. It is . . . oneness of faith. Oneness in Christ is not to be conceived apart from oneness with the body of Christ. And that is a matter of faith much more than of external demonstration.

The Church as the body of Christ exists here within all the limitations of space and time; it is subject to these. Only when the Kingdom of God comes in perfection will these limitations pass away and will a great multitude that no one can count appear before the throne of the Lamb from all nations and tribes and peoples and tongues. In the meantime, we walk by faith, not by sight. The fact is that the unity in Christ is a community of soul transcending anything that man can plan or think. It belongs to those things that "eye hath not seen, nor ear heard, neither have entered into the heart of man, the things which God hath prepared for them that love him," that can be accepted only in faith.

After presenting thus at length some of the conflicting views of Christians on race relations, the speaker concluded:

We may never lose the ideal of a Church in which all men who believe in Christ will be at home. But while we struggle towards the attainment of that ideal different churches based on language or race may be useful and even preferable in some extreme cases, always on the understanding, however, that nobody who wishes to join a Christian church may be excluded on other ground than that of faith. . . . But the fact that this is still necessary must lead us . . . to repentance. . . . Judgment can start at no other place than the house of God. The Church of Christ may not remain indifferent to a fundamentally wrong conception, however firmly it may be imbedded in our very structure. . . . Accommodation must be seen clearly as a temporary measure . . . adopted only as the better of two evils . . . justified only on the ground that the ultimate goal may be missed if we proceed over-hastily. . . . It is obvious that such a change cannot be brought about immediately . . . but . . . only step by step, sometimes after failure and disappointment.

Dr. Marais said that in submitting the report with Dr. Mays he acted as one who believed that the Christian knew only one *apartheid* (separation) and that was separation from sin. "Let condemnation in these things be far from us and understanding, prayer and hope motivate and characterize our discussions and actions as men and churches."

It is to be presumed that Dr. Marais chose the points of special emphasis in his address, which we have reviewed, with the knowledge and approval of the Preparatory Commission for Section V, of which he was a member. In that case, the Assembly was to be commended for its fairness and sound practical sense in listening to variant views on the racial question known to be held by Christians.

The United Nations Educational, Scientific and Cultural Organization had issued a series of publications on "The Race Question in Modern Science," which included the titles:

Race and Culture, by Michel Leiris
Race and Psychology, by Otto Klineberg
Race and Biology, by C. L. Dunn
Racial Myths, by Juan Comas
The Roots of Prejudice, by Arnold M. Rose
Race and History, by Kenneth L. Little
The Significance of Racial Differences, by G. M. Morant

Race Mixture, by Harry L. Shapiro
The Race Concept: Results of an Inquiry

These books had enjoyed some circulation in the churches and been recommended by Christian leaders for study. They had become part of the body of research materials for sociological surveys by denominational and interchurch organizations, such as the Preparatory Commission for Section V, which had made use of at least some of them. They were announced on the inside of the cover pages of the volume on *The Ecumenical Movement and the Racial Problem* by Dr. W. A. Visser 't Hooft, also published by the United Nations Educational, Scientific and Cultural Organization as one of its series on the race question and the churches, which was exhibited at the book tables of the Second Assembly. Whatever, therefore, any church had to say on the subject was entitled to a hearing.

There are those who stress the duty of the churches to speak with one voice on great issues, such as race relations; but it is less to be desired that they set forth their views in unison on any subject than that they keep before the world an authentic example of unity in love toward God which allows room to differ. An institution that learns to do this will certainly influence the future of mankind. When it seeks to act for all the churches, the World Council suffers a diminution of the power it exerts if it reports what even a majority agree to and is silent about what the rest think. Dissent emphasizes the wisdom of official actions if they are wise. In any case, it is witness of a tolerant spirit, which, if it were learned, would make the earth habitable in peace —something of vastly greater importance than an opinion to which all the members of an organization may subscribe.

In turning to the report itself,[23] it is well to recall that in all the study groups the members and drafting committees were briefed on the "terms of reference" within the general scope of which they should pursue their inquiry. The first of these guiding—and delimiting—suggestions was the main theme of the Assembly. They were expected to orientate their thinking to Christian hope. The second was ecumenical history. They would be working, it was explained, "in the main stream of the ecumenical conferences" which had considered the same problems in their day. The other qualifying consideration was the task of the Christian Church in their own time—the faithful discharging of its stewardship for the souls and lives of men. Thus, the sections did not start *de novo* with their work. They had to look backward, in order to look forward. They would build upon the foundations of others.

[23] The Report of Section V is printed in Appendix M. See also *The Evanston Report,* pp. 151-158.

"Racial and ethnic fears, hates, and prejudices are more than social problems with whose existence we must reckon," the report declared; "they are sins against God and His commandments that the Gospel alone can cure." And it stressed that no greater opportunity had ever been offered the Church "to be the creative instrument of our God of love in a restless and changing world and the faithful servant of our Lord who is its hope."

"It is our Christian belief that our Lord is concerned for all just hopes of men," the report continued, "but in Himself He offers the hope that transcends them all. The Bible teaches us that God is the Sovereign Creator of all men, and by Him they are sustained and have their being. When He made the world, He saw that it was good. But man by his sin—by his disobedience and pride and the lifting of his arm against his brother—has filled it with division and distrust." The hope in this disunity of unrighteousness, it reiterated, was in "Jesus Christ, who revealed God as Father and . . . died for all men, reconciling them to God and to each other by His Cross. From every race and nation a new people of God is created, in which the power of the Spirit overcomes racial pride and fear."

"So to us is given the gift of sharing in and working for the Kingdom even now. Assured that the final victory is Christ's, we can work actively, continually repentant and . . . forgiven, for that reconciliation which we believe to be God's will. . . . This is the calling of the Church with regard to race, to witness within itself to the Kingship of Christ and the unity of His people, in Him transcending all diversity."

The report continued:

> Their calling requires Christians to . . . strive through social and political action to secure justice, freedom, and peace for all. . . . All churches and Christians are involved, whether they recognize it or not, in the racial and ethnic tensions of the world. But it is in communities where segregation prevails that they face the plainest difficulties and the most challenging opportunities; for such segregation denies to those who are segregated their just and equal rights and results in deep injuries to the human spirit, suffered by offender and victim alike.
>
> The great majority of . . . churches affiliated with the World Council have declared that . . . separation within the Church on grounds of race is a denial of spiritual unity, and of the brotherhood of man. Yet such separation persists within these very churches.

The churches sought to justify this on other grounds than race, because, otherwise, it would be "abhorrent in the eyes of God." "The Church is called upon, therefore, to set aside such excuses and to declare God's will both in words and deeds."

The report recognized that some churches had abolished segregation in their worship and membership. If obedience to God in this led to suffering, it was part of the cost of being Christian, even as Christ "endured the Cross, despising the shame, for the joy that was set before Him."

The churches had the twofold duty, the report asserted, "to obey and to proclaim the word of judgment, to repent and to call to repentance. It is their task to challenge the conscience of society."

The churches should support in every possible way "those of their members who [felt] called to challenge actively the conscience of society, and who thus [offended] against custom, and [incurred] loneliness and suffering," the report urged. Moreover, it declared them duty bound to "protest against any law or arrangement . . . unjust to any human being or . . . [making] Christian fellowship impossible, or . . . [preventing] the Christian from practising his vocation."

In this connection it was suggested that some church members might feel it their duty to break unjust laws. Said the report: "The Church does not contemplate lightly any breaking of the law, but it recognizes the duty of a Christian to do so when he feels that he has reached that point where the honor and glory of God command him to obey God rather than man."

"The Church of Christ cannot approve of any law which discriminates on grounds of race, which restricts the opportunity of any person to acquire education to prepare himself for his vocation, to procure or to practise employment . . . , or in any other way curtails his exercise of the full rights and responsibilities of citizenship and of sharing in the responsibilities and duties of government."

Taking up the subject of marriage, the report stated that the members of the section could not "approve any law against racial or ethnic intermarriage." What it said in explanation of its position was tantamount to approval of such marriages, albeit not without warning about the unhappy social consequences which might ensue, because, as it said, of "the hardness of men's hearts" and "cultural differences."

While it [the study group] can find in the Bible no clear justification or condemnation of intermarriage but only a discussion of the duties of the faithful in marriage with partners of other religions, it cannot approve any law against racial or ethnic intermarriage, for Christian marriage involves primarily a union of two individuals before God which goes beyond the jurisdiction of the state or of culture.

A minister of the Church should advise young people, when preparing them for the grave responsibilities of intermarriage, both of the potential richness of such marriages and of the painful consequences in some situations, which . . are often caused by the hardness of men's hearts and by cultural differences. There is no evidence that the children of such marriages are inherently inferior, and any treatment of them as such should be condemned.

The report took note of the fact that the churches were "not alone in their concern for the welfare of society and the need for resolving the tensions within it between racial and ethnic groups." Many international agencies were at work in this field, and in "nearly every country" there were governmental, civic, and private bodies seeking the solution of racial problems. Some of these, it recognized, accused "the churches and their members of being preachers of love, but lukewarm in their passion for justice, slow in action, and afraid of public opinion and unpleasant consequences. The courage of some of these bodies, and the success of some of their experiments, often put the churches to shame." Some churches felt that they could not cooperate with them because of their political views. Then they "should take action of their own."

The Assembly received also a statement by delegates from the Dutch Reformed Churches in South Africa for inclusion in the Minutes, as follows:[24]

> On behalf of all the delegates from the Dutch Reformed Churches in South Africa we wish to state that we would have felt happier if the report of the Committee on Inter-group Relations (Report of Section V) and the proposed resolutions attached thereto had been put to the Assembly to be received and referred to member churches for their consideration and report to the Central Committee. We appreciate the agreement that no resolution of this Assembly has mandatory power over member churches and that certain recommendations, and especially number one, are intended to stimulate the independent thought and action of certain churches in specific situations. But we feel constrained to say that, at this stage of our ecumenical discussions on these matters, it may have the opposite effect by so prejudicing the issues at stake for some churches that fruitful action for them will be gravely jeopardized. We would deplore it deeply if the impression were created that this report and these resolutions are intended as the last word in a matter that vitally affects the mission of some churches and which, we feel bound to say, has not been considered in all its aspects during our talks at Evanston.
>
> However, we are not offering an amendment, nor do we intend to record our votes against what is being proposed. At this stage we dare not commit our churches either way, but wish to keep the door open for further conversation. We wish to place on record that we have experienced at Evanston much evidence of what we truly believe to be real Christian goodwill and an attempt to understand the peculiar difficulties we have to face. In response to that we now pledge ourselves personally to the task of urging our respective churches to apply themselves as urgently as possible to the study of the report and to communicate their findings to the Central Committee as soon as possible.
>
> Signed:
> W. A. Landman, Ned. Geref. Kerk van Suid-Afrika
> C. B. Brink, Ned. Herv. of Geref. Kerk van Suid-Afrika
> A. J. G. Oosthuizen, Ned. Herv. Kerk van Afrika

Members of the Preparatory Commission for Section V were as follows:

[24] *The Evanston Report,* pp. 328-29.

Dr. Roswell P. Barnes, *Chairman,* United States
Professor G. Báez-Camargo, *Vice-Chairman,* Mexico
Rev. Robert Bilheimer, *Secretary,* United States
Professor S. P. Adinarayan, India
Professor J. H. Bavinck, Netherlands
Rev. Charles Bonzon, France
Rev. Gerhard Brennecke, Germany
Professor Uhla Bu, Burma
Mr. L. B. Greaves, United Kingdom
Dr. John Karefa-Smart, Liberia
Dr. B. J. Marais, South Africa
Professor Z. K. Matthews, South Africa
Dr. Benjamin E. Mays, United States
Rev. Allan T. McNaughton, New Zealand
Mr. Alan Paton, South Africa
Dr. Liston Pope, United States
Professor Margaret H. Read, United Kingdom
Dr. Channing Tobias, United States
Bishop M. H. Yashiro, Japan
Dr. Norman Goodall, Consultant, United Kingdom
Dr. Leslie E. Cooke, Consultant, United Kingdom
Bishop L. Dia, Philippine Islands

The ecumenical movement owes much of its growth to the hope of the churches to achieve through cooperation a more effective implementation of Christian social teaching. This has been the case, particularly, with councils of churches.

From its beginning, a dominant aim of the Federal Council of the Churches of Christ in America was "to secure a larger combined influence for the churches of Christ in all matters affecting the moral and social condition of the people, so as to promote the application of the law of Christ in every relation of human life." This objective was in 1908 elaborated in sixteen "articles" which came to be known as the "Social Creed of the Churches," calling for such reforms as "abatement and prevention of poverty," old age pensions, minimum wage guarantees, shorter working hours, and not least of all "equal rights for all men." [25] Although revised somewhat over the years, the purposes embodied in the "Social Creed" never changed in their essentials, and the Federal Council's pursuit of these ends attracted considerable popular interest, within and outside the churches. By 1954 state and city councils, organized under the auspices of the Federal Council and inspired largely by the principles of social Christianity, had grown to nearly one thousand—not including the two thousand or more councils of church women, sharing the same motivations.

World War I made clearer the need to broaden the ministry of the churches under this social manifesto. The field had now become the world. The churches, not only of one nation but of many, joined in

[25] The "Social Creed" is outlined fully in Part One, p. 34.

organizing the Universal Christian Council on Life and Work in Stockholm, Sweden, in 1925. The words "Life and Work" in the title located the area of their special concern, as "Universal" indicated the boundary of their vision. More than twenty years were to pass before they would arrive at Amsterdam, by way of Oxford,[26] with its searching studies in social Christianity, to establish an organization commensurate with the scope of their mission. There had been, also, collateral groups which shared their hopes and worked toward much the same goals; notably the International Missionary Council,[27] with its contribution of fresh insights in the application of Christian social principles from the younger churches of the mission fields; and the Faith and Order Movement,[28] which led the churches through theological study to closer understanding and in 1948 merged with the Life and Work Movement to form the World Council of Churches.

Throughout, there had been encouraging evidences of growing strength and popular interest, and the ecumenical movement, as it had come to be called, seemed to those whose dreams and toils had helped to create it to be lifted and borne forward upon "the wave of the future," the more so because they saw it as rising out of elemental needs and aspirations of the human spirit.

The delegates to the Evanston Assembly in 1954 had been instructed, by those who had come up through these stirring events and had helped to bring them to pass, to key their discussion to what had gone before them. History should be one of the "terms of reference," in the perspective of which they would seek inspiration and direction. And in this respect they did their work well indeed. The study reports from Evanston were found, on analysis, to fit into the lengthening succession of documents expounding and elaborating the philosophy of the program of social action to which the denominations had set themselves in the World Council of Churches, gathering up the threads of previous deliberations and decisions and weaving them into the now familiar pattern.

Ecumenical sociological thought had arrived at a consensus in its major conclusions so generally consonant with the prevailing practices of what now passed for Christian democracy in the Western world and so nearly unanimously validated by the theologians that its acceptance was unquestioned in the World Council. Nevertheless, there were those —many of them persons friendly toward the movement—who thought that in no area of its activity was there stronger reason for the World Council to take to itself the scriptural admonition "Let him that thinketh he standeth take heed, lest he fall." They thought that the theories

[26] Conference on Church, Community and State, 1937.

[27] Its conferences were: Jerusalem, 1928; Tambaram, 1938; Whitby, 1948.

[28] First World Conference on Faith and Order, Lausanne, 1927; Second World Conference on Faith and Order, Edinburgh, 1937.

underlying its social policy, which in their development reached back, as noted, across half a century, ought to be re-examined, from the standpoint particularly of certain questions that were being raised concerning them.

There was cause for uneasiness, they thought, lest the emphasis by the Council on the state's responsibility in the general sphere of social welfare divert the attention of the churches from what they should themselves be doing and become, in their thinking, compensatory for their own failures.

Representatives of an interchurch body, who had been appointed to interview governmental authorities on a legislative proposal increasing appropriations for aiding "underdeveloped nations," met with the objection that much of what they were asking the state to do their own churches were able to do—if they would take seriously their own teaching about charity and sacrificial service. It was well within their power to raise the money they were asking for, they were told, if they would "sell the proposition" to their constituencies. And in their own ranks could be found persons with technical skill and training who might be persuaded to volunteer for the task of administering the funds. Just or not, the implication of what they had to listen to was that their churches were attempting to hand the government a job which, in the first place, belonged to them.

The committee were reminded, further, that granting the increases would necessitate raising the tax rate, and asked whether they thought the churches had a right to press an appeal which, if it prevailed, would impose an added burden upon all citizens, many of whom were not Christians or, Christians or not, did not favor the policy of aiding foreign nations in the way proposed. The churches would be more faithful to their distinctive mission, it was suggested, if they applied themselves to tapping the vast resources in the control of their members for the humanitarian work they wished to promote.

"The law of Christ" enjoins Christians to "bear . . . one another's burdens," and the churches have a good deal to say about it; but no one could gainsay the imputation that there has not been a dedication of money and life by Christians worthy of the preaching of the cross of Jesus Christ, borne for their sakes. Why is organized Christianity failing at this crucial point? Many who are interested in the ecumenical movement were asking this question, and they thought that its answer had a bearing on the turning of the churches to more and more social action. They feared that it was a case of taking what seemed to be the easy way—of detouring past the cross. They believed it a yielding to the illusion that the kingdom of God could be gained without suffering. And they could only look upon it with misgivings. They saw in it the passing of true charity, without which the Christian religion had little right to the name, and for which there was nothing in social action to compensate, if both Christians and non-Christians were compelled to pay in the name of justice what neither would willingly give in response to the love of God.

What had happened, it was asked, not only to the "law of Christ," which was fulfilled in mutual burden-bearing, but to its ancient sanctions—that is, the rewards and the punishments which were set down in the Scriptures? Had these vanished with the fading of hell and heaven from actual places into "spiritual states"? Had they been erased for plain folk by the discoveries of astrophysics and the other sciences to which they could not accommodate their religious thinking? As someone who helped with the writing of the treatise on the main theme of the Second Assembly, "Christ—the Hope of the World," said, if the eschatology of the Bible had been set before the churches by that document to restore their vision of heaven and hell, it might have been asked whether it was supposed that men by grateful contemplation of "the mighty acts of God" in redemption or by a fearful looking for his judgment in the end upon the parsimonious would be constrained to practice Christian stewardship. How could human hearts be charged with love, which alone invested the biblical symbolism with meaning, until the law of Christ supplanted the law of nature? It was at this point, many feared, that Christianity suffered defeat no show of busy social concern by the churches could mask.

And what of the complementary law under the ecumenical program—namely, that "every man shall bear his own burden"? Obedience to it was discouraged by the multiplying unearned governmental benefits which the churches led in advocating and approving, even turning over to the state, in part, the responsibility of providing for the old age of their pastors. Many thought they saw developing a society in which more and more of the citizens would inevitably be habituated to dependence on the state for their economic support; those who wanted to maintain their financial independence would find it impossible to do so, because of the mounting taxation with its inevitable inflation; and the incentive to work and to acquire, not only in order to bear one's own burden, but also to help those who were weaker with theirs, which had been the mainspring of Christian philanthropy, would disappear. Many who contemplated the possibility of these developments could not see in them any promise of the coming of the kingdom of God.

When they declared it to be the will of God that they work through political measures for what they called "justice for all men," the churches, in the opinion of many of their loyal members, were embarking upon a course with still other hazards which they little understood.

In this direction, they encountered on every side men contending against one another for what they considered their rights, and justice as between them called for the judging of persons and causes, and the support of one embattled group against another. In no such conflict was either of the opposing sides wholly right or wrong. More basically, both were composed of sinners; and if the victory went to those who were adjudged to be preponderantly in the right, there was no assurance that they would not be, in their new power, as unjust as were the vanquished. And the churches would not have improved their opportunity to save either group spiritually. Indeed, they could consider themselves fortunate if they had not forfeited their evangelistic approach to both.

What the churches had actually to offer of worth in the cause of human justice was the word of Christ: "Repent!" All were asking for recognition of their rights. The Christian way was putting "the things of others" before one's own, and by this method only could disputes be settled. This was the justice of love—love born of the grace of God in true repentance and conversion. If the churches had a mission, it was to make plain this way of salvation, whether for the individual or for society. This truth was confused and obscured, many Christians thought, when the churches attempted, or acceded to the demand, to become advocates in the world of strife—in the disputes of nations, the contentions of classes, the warrings of races.

The call to repentance had never been what men wished to hear, and it would not be now. They would ignore it, and the churches sounding it, until Christians themselves began to repent and to take up their cross. Then there would be a new accession of power in the churches. They would be in the way of creating in the hearts of the people—rich and poor, whites and blacks, Orientals and Occidentals, employees and employers, all men—the conditions of justice. The miracle of God's grace would happen through them, because it had happened in them.

6. The Christian in His Vocation

Several addresses at plenary sessions and at meetings of the accredited visitors introduced the last of the six subsidiary themes, "The Laity—the Christian in His Vocation," as the section took up its study.

Speaking on "The Specific Task of the Christian Layman in Society," Mr. Francis P. Miller, a delegate of the Presbyterian Church in the United States, said he believed that God had "a grand design for human society" and was calling all men to serve him in its realization. "A man of faith called of God to his service will be shown," he declared, "what he has to do when confronted with choices and decisions in the concrete circumstances of life." [29]

> God is changing things. As his judgment falls societies disintegrate and disappear. As he transforms man and makes him a new creation he changes man's relations—with his family, neighbors, business partners . . . and society to that extent is changed.

[29] From mimeographed text circulated at the Assembly.

> Men of faith are citizens of two worlds . . . their own country . . . and God's eternal Kingdom; and their citizenship in his Kingdom determines what kind of Americans they are striving to be, or what kind of Asiatics or . . . Europeans. In other words, human society furnishes the Christian with raw material . . . on which he can leave the imprint of his eternal citizenship. The Christian life is thus an effort to express the meaning of citizenship in God's Kingdom through our duties, responsibilities and opportunities as citizens of a particular human society. In this sense, the Christian is an advance agent of the coming Kingdom. And the Kingdom . . . is at hand . . . even now knocking at the door. The Kingdom is not remote in either time or space. It is continually breaking in upon us and . . . our affairs.

"God rules," he declared. "The government is not in Moscow, London or Washington" but "upon his shoulders." "God is at work in the world, destroying by his judgment, redeeming by his love and grace and recreating men and nations from the inexhaustible stores of his mercy and goodness."

But, he warned, so also do "the principalities and the powers, the world rulers of this present darkness" work. "A fateful struggle is engaged for the souls of men." "All men enlist on one side or the other," each being responsible for the side he chooses.

The speaker thought the struggle approached "a climax of some kind."

> We have seen the Father of Lies himself appear in human guise in various parts of the world. . . . He has corrupted great nations, threatened whole civilizations and established hell on earth. Wherever men are used as pawns and not persons . . . , ends are said to justify the means . . . , people live in . . . mistrust, hatred, fear and confusion, there we know his minions have been at work. . . . The battle will be fierce and long. But we know that final victory will be won (as in one sense it has already been won) by Jesus Christ our Lord. . . . And it is he who is calling us now to go . . . with him . . . to meet the challenge of the Father of Lies. . . . He is our Captain . . . and will assign to each of us our specific task and mission. Regardless of what the assignment of each may be, he calls us all to stand for truth, . . . purity of personal life, . . . decency in human relations, . . . community, . . . justice and . . . peace, . . . not just within our . . . churches, but every day and at every place where we find ourselves working members of human society.

Referring to his own experience in political affairs, Mr. Miller said he was convinced "that one of our greatest weaknesses as a world-wide Christian community [was] our failure to provide our laymen with the kind of education that [made] them think of their work in secular society as being the place to which God has called them to serve him." Many tended to think of the Christian life as a separate existence from their work, he had observed. "The Christian life is not flight from the world," he urged, "but assumption of responsibility in the world. . . . Every honorable job, no matter how mechanical or trivial, can become a vocation the moment the man who holds [it] understands the full meaning of being a Christian."

At this point, the speaker was touching upon the fundamental thesis of the study in Section VI, which was that the laity should carry a sense of vocation—that is, of the calling of God in Christ—into their occupations and there make the ministry of their churches effective in society and find themselves the true meaning of work. The report from Section VI may be read in this connection with profit.

The title, "The Laity—The Christian in His Vocation," the report explained, "is here taken to signify Christian vocation in the sphere of daily work."

We must understand anew the implications of the fact that we are all baptized, that, as Christ came to minister, so must all Christians become ministers of his saving purpose according to the particular gift of the Spirit which each has received, as messengers of the hope revealed in Christ. Therefore in daily living and work the laity are not mere fragments of the Church who are scattered about in the world and who come together for worship, instruction and specifically Christian fellowship on Sundays. They are the Church's representatives, no matter where they are, It is the laity who draw together work and worship; it is they who bridge the gulf between the Church and the world, and it is they who manifest in word and action the Lordship of Christ over that world which claims so much of their time and energy and labor. This, and not some new order or organization, is the ministry of the laity. They are called to it because they belong to the Church. . . .

. . . "Layman" and "laity" are used to indicate those members of the Church, both men and women, who earn their livelihood in a secular job and who therefore spend most of their waking hours in a "worldly" occupation (not excluding housewives). . . . Accordingly, the theme of *work* is prominent in this discussion, not because it is the only aspect of life in this world, but because it is a very important one and one which has not received from the churches the attention it deserves, although some important attempts to redress this situation have been made. God calls the whole Church to a life of faith, obedience, service and worship; this is the meaning of Christian vocation in the teaching of the New Testament. Every Christian has a vocation in this biblical sense. In modern usage, however, the term is frequently employed to mean "occupation" or "profession"; and, though we cannot prevent this secular use of a great biblical word, we shall here use "vocation" in the Christian meaning of God's call which comes to each member of his household, the Church. The principal object of this discussion is, therefore, to make clear the true meaning of Christian vocation in all the occupations or professions in which Christian lay-folk engage.

"Many people are asking," the report continued, "whether Christianity has any relevance to their daily work," feeling that there is "a gulf between the Church and its worship and their workday lives." It discussed some of the developments in modern society which caused this sense of separation, such as industrialization, which thrust many persons out of their home and church environment into work in a different community; the lingering separation of the Church from the world in the thinking of many from the day when the Church through the clergy controlled great areas of life which now stood altogether outside its realm; the current evaluation of different kinds of work which reckoned some occupations of greater dignity than others; the attitude of some Christian leaders who thought of "man only as a soul to be saved without regard to his physical, mental, and social welfare" and of work "only as a field for evangelism."

"The gulf between the Church and the life of the world can be bridged," according to the report, "by those who have a Christian view of work." They will find that "doing one's work not as men-pleasers but as unto our Master in heaven is a deliverance from the frustration of men's efforts." They will find satisfaction in the sense that "all honest work is service rendered to society." Every situation in daily life will provide "opportunity to respond to [the] call of God" to witness to the redemptive and creative work of God through Christ in men.

The report discussed some of the "serious conflicts" which "arise as Christians seek to relate their divine vocation to their daily work," dealing particularly with agriculture and industry. It found special need "for Christian consideration of some of the new problems in a highly organized industrial society," in which individuals had not yet been helped by their churches to think out "the ethics of group responsibility" in decisions, whether in the sphere of management or labor. Those who work together may be drawn into a community and become opposed to the wider society around them in seeking to promote their own ends.

Here again it is necessary that the traditional concern of Christian ethics with personal morality should be widened so that the insights of Christian faith may be brought to bear upon . . . group behavior. The working community must be seen to be neither an end in itself, nor a means to the ends of the state, and its true . . . . character must be defined in the light of the Christian understanding of man.

Because work is a divine ordinance . . . there is an obligation upon society to provide all its members with opportunity to work. Unemployment is not only a problem for economists but for all Christian people. . . .

Thus, all human life and work are transformed by hope in Christ. All work honestly done, whether undertaken for the sake of earning a livelihood, or for the sake of the community, or out of spontaneous joy in creative effort, has genuine value and meaning in the purpose of God. . .

The time has come to make the ministry of the laity explicit, visible and active in the world. The . . . battles of the faith today are being fought in factories, shops, offices, and farms, in political parties and government agencies, in countless homes, in the press, radio and television, in the relationship of nations.

The churches have failed to give their members the support they need to make them their effective representatives in the world. There ought to be "a change of emphasis and of prevailing atmosphere in many churches."

The churches should not become so preoccupied with their internal organization and activities that they fail to grasp the importance of Christian witness in and through secular organs of society, and to encourage their members to participate fully in them, the report urged. There was need, moreover, to change the social atmosphere in many churches which otherwise could not offer a congenial fellowship to newcomers, especially in those attended by people mostly of one class or those still conformed to traditions of a culture of a past generation. There should be also a single standard of faithfulness for clergy and laity in the Christian calling.

The report ended with suggestions for the training of the laity for the kind of ministry it had envisaged. New converts—and many members of long standing—needed, it said, basic Christian teaching "in the faith, in prayer, worship and Bible-reading" and in witnessing in the home and daily work. Those with responsible positions in the church should receive theological instruction. The clergy should have "a better acquaintance with present-day working society, both by study and experience, in order that they [might] help their laity and follow them with their prayers. . . . The home should [be] a place where children grow up to regard work and occupation as a sphere of Christian vocation." Laymen should be encouraged to use the pastoral gifts which many of them possess. "Mutual care of members by each other as well as by the clergy is needed." "Christians from the same or related occupations should have some opportunity to meet occasionally," to "discuss common concerns, including problems of the structure of their occupation, in the light of Christian faith." When a single parish was not large enough to provide for this, "a regional and ecumenical basis" might serve the purpose.[30]

Upon receiving the report of Section VI on "The Laity—The Christian in His Vocation," the Assembly adopted the following resolutions:

i. We commend this report to the churches in the hope that they will make it a part of their thinking and encourage adventurous experiments.

ii. We commend this report to those engaged in such experiments in order to strengthen their efforts and to draw their attention to certain criteria which may help them and to certain dangers which they may encounter.

iii. We commend this report to organizations of laymen and women in the Church asking them to consider how their activities can be co-ordinated so as to contribute to a better realization of the ministry of the laity in the Church and in the world.

iv. We recommend that the World Council of Churches continue the study of the Christian understanding of work, begun before Evanston, and

[30] The complete text of the report of Section VI appears in Appendix N. See also *The Evanston Report*, pp. 160-170.

that it be jointly undertaken by the Department of Church and Society and the Department of Laity.

v. We recommend that the Central Committee provide for the adequate staffing of the Department of Laity and that the Central Committee take care that it remain a flexible instrument able to assist, by every possible means, the emergence of a true ministry of the laity.

Members of the Preparatory Commission for Section VI were as follows:

Professor Hendrik Kraemer, *Chairman,* Netherlands
Dr. Hermann Hans Walz, *Secretary,* Germany
Mr. David W. K. Au, Hong Kong
Professor Jacques Ellul, France
Mr. Joseph W. Fichter, United States
Dr. O. H. von der Gablentz, Germany
Dr. Cameron P. Hall, United States
Rev. Olov Hartman, Sweden
Mrs. Douglas Horton, United States
Dr. A. W. Kist, Netherlands
Mr. Rajaiah D. Paul, India
Miss B. Nancy Seear, United Kingdom
Dr. E. Somasekhar, India
Professor Douglas V. Steere, United States
President Clarence C. Stoughton, United States
Mr. W. G. Symons, United Kingdom
Dr. Reinhold von Thadden, Germany
Professor A. N. Tsirintantes, Greece
Mrs. J. A. Tumanken-Gerungan, Indonesia
Dr. Paul Limbert, Consultant, Y.M.C.A.
*Principal Saroe Chakko, Consultant, India
Principal T. M. Taylor, Consultant, United Kingdom
Miss Madeleine Barot, Substitute and Consultant, France
Professor Walter M. Horton, Substitute and Consultant, United States

* Deceased

"The Laity—The Christian in His Vocation" was, perhaps, the least piquant of the subsidiary theme titles. At first glance, it might have been dismissed as another invitation to exhort the laity to improve the opportunity afforded by their weekday jobs to practice the virtues of honesty and industry and to evangelize their fellow workmen. But this would have done it less than justice. The interpretation of it by those responsible for its development presented a broader and more provocative conception of the role of laymen. From their standpoint, it could well have had a significance more vital than any of the other subjects which came before the Assembly.[31]

It was the prayer of Christ that his Church might be in the world, as

[31] Dr. Hendrik Kraemer said at Evanston that in his view the work of Section VI was the most important of all the Assembly's studies. See *The Evanston Report,* p. 49.

he was in the world. Whatever may have been its position in this respect in other centuries, in modern times the church is separated from the world to a degree which seems to make impossible discharging the mission he gave it. Between it and "the field" are raised barriers the gospel appears powerless to surmount. Whole segments of society lie beyond the farthest reach of its ministry.

There are, for example, the large areas of scientific discovery and the practical uses to which the new knowledge has been turned, particularly in the development of industry and the creation of wealth which have brought about fundamental changes in the external conditions of men's lives and their relations with one another.

Yet the members of the churches have their occupations and spend most of their time during waking hours in this religious "no man's land"; and it is the burden of the report of Section VI that the laity by obedience to "the calling of God" in their daily work shall answer the prayer of Christ for his Church according to its deeper intent. They are the Church in the world and must learn to think of themselves as such; and they must be trained for their responsibility.

Beyond seeking to live uprightly and to win those with whom they work to the Church, they must undertake to change the ideas and practices of secular life which hold a grave threat to religious faith and the spiritual foundations of civilization. It is their duty to gird themselves as the Church in the world into which they have been thrust by the common necessity of earning a livelihood and to give effect to the prayer "Thy kingdom come, thy will be done on earth as it is in heaven."

Dr. J. H. Oldham was credited with having been first in the ecumenical movement to set forth in a way to awaken general interest the importance of this lay ministry. He wrote of it in *The Church and Its Function in Society,* a book which as co-author he had helped to prepare for the Conference on Church, Community and State at Oxford in 1937. In the years that followed he had elaborated the theme in the small volume *The Meaning of Work* and in articles which had appeared in various publications, including, notably, his contributions to the body of research materials for use by the First Assembly of the World Council of Churches, at Amsterdam, in 1948.

Meanwhile, totalitarianism had taught the churches the indispensability of the laity's witness. Alongside the Young Men's Christian Association, the Young Women's Christian Association, the World's Student Christian Federation, the numerous organizations of men and women in the churches, the Sunday School Associations, and other older lay societies, many new movements had sprung up in Europe, the United States, India, and Australia, with the purpose of exploring the implications of the Christian faith for social and occupational life. Among these were the *Associations Professionnelles Protestantes* in France and Belgium, the Christian Frontier Council in Great Britain, centers like Sigtuna Foundation in Sweden, the Evangelical Academies in Germany, the *Kerk en Wereld* Institute in Holland, *Zoe* and *Aktines* in Greece, and in the Roman Catholic Church *Actio Catholica.*

By the time of the Second Assembly of the World Council of Churches, in 1954, interest in this phase of Christian ministry had reached such proportions as to entitle it to a place among the study themes.

Dr. Kathleen Bliss, a member of the National Assembly of the Church of England, chaired Section VI of the Evanston Assembly. She had been associated actively with the Commission on the Life and Work of Women in the Church, which had taken the position that, rather than organize their separate programs, women should develop their work as an integral part of the broader ministry of the Church, and so of the World Council of Churches, insisting on some structural arrangement in the latter body which would make it possible for them and men to collaborate freely in the discharge of their complementary religious functions. The Assembly gave the Commission on the Life and Work of Women in the Church the status of a department, under the Division of Ecumenical Action, with the title "Department on Co-operation of Men and Women in Church and Society," and the following aim and duties:[32]

The aim of the Department shall be to help the churches to work towards such co-operation between men and women as may enable them both to make their full contribution to church and society.

The functions of the Department shall be:

(i) To promote among men and women, through the Division of Studies, and directly, the study of questions affecting the relationship, the co-operation and the common service of men and women in the churches and in society;
(ii) To help women to make their contribution to the total life of the churches and at the same time to encourage the churches to accept the contribution of women to a fuller extent and in more varied ways;
(iii) To foster an ecumenical outlook in women's organizations in the various churches and countries, to promote co-operation among them and to secure their participation in the ecumenical movement as a whole;
(iv) To advise and co-operate with the Ecumenical Institute, the Department on Work for the Laity, the Youth Department, and any other ecumenical body on the work of the Division of Ecumenical Action;
(v) To keep actively in touch with other divisions of the World Council of Churches and with other bodies whose work may have a bearing on the work of the Department.

At Evanston was created also the Department on Work for the Laity, the aim of which should be "to keep before the churches their responsibility for helping the laity to serve their churches and to witness before the world, to strengthen work for the laity in the churches, to promote

[32] *The Evanston Report,* p. 204.

fellowship between church-related organizations of laity throughout the world, to foster ecumenical understanding among the laity." The functions of the Department should be:[33]

(i) To assemble and disseminate information about developments in work for the laity in different countries;
(ii) To consult with national institutes and organizations for the laity on topics requiring study, and to arrange for the ecumenical consideration of these topics;
(iii) To provide a news bulletin, surveys, bibliographies and particular studies as may be required.
(iv) To arrange for regional conferences of the laity;
(v) To arrange for the visitation of laity in different countries by persons able to advise on the development of work for the laity and to stimulate new experiments;
(vi) To co-operate with the Ecumenical Institute, the Department on Co-operation of Men and Women in Church and Society, the Youth Department and the Division of Studies in all matters concerning the work of the Department.

[33] *The Evanston Report,* p. 205.

IV

NEW STRUCTURES AND PAST PERFORMANCES

1. Committee on Structure and Functioning

The business at Evanston, aside from routine Assembly matters, had to do with adjusting the organization of the World Council of Churches to the framework erected by the Committee on Structure and Functioning. Its report, already approved by the Central Committee and occupying a dominant place in *The Assembly Work Book*, was presented by the Chairman, Dr. Leslie E. Cooke, at an early plenary session. Outlines of the work proposed for the divisions and departments under the new scheme had been assigned for study and criticism to seven committees—Committees on General Policy, Division of Studies, Division of Ecumenical Action, Division of Inter-Church Aid and Service to Refugees, Department of Information, Department of Finance and Administration, and Commission of the Churches on International Affairs—under instructions to present their findings later, according to the schedule in the agenda.

The official *Evanston Report* explained the appointment of the Committee on Structure and Functioning, as follows:

> At Amsterdam much attention had been given to these matters, but largely on the pre-supposition that existing departments, committees and relationships between them would continue, save with the recommended addition of a very few others. As, however, the Central Committee took up its work in the years following 1948, it became convinced that the Second Assembly should consider the basic pattern of the World Council's structure, and the manner of its functioning. In part this conviction grew out of the need to rethink relationships between departments, commissions and committees which had been created at different times and in response to various needs. In part it arose from the need to complete in a final and satisfactory way the merger of Faith and Order and Life and Work into a World Council of Churches. In part also it was required by the growing closeness of association between the International Missionary Council and the World Council. Also it was needful because of certain additions to the World Council programme which were necessary and which would have to be put into proper relationship to

other World Council structures. Finally, there was a desire to give the whole a careful scrutiny in the light of the experience of the first six years.

Accordingly, the Central Committee at Rolle (Switzerland) in 1951 appointed a Committee on Structure and Functioning, charged with reviewing World Council organization and making such recommendations as might seem wise. An extremely careful and exhaustive survey resulted, with periodic reports to the Central Committee, culminating in the Report on Structure and Functioning presented by the Central Committee to the Assembly, and adopted with only a few amendments.[1]

Prior to its adoption by the Second Assembly, the Report, which was submitted by the Central Committee, provoked some criticism among the delegates during their deliberations. In the discussions on the Report on Structure and Functioning, strong objection was voiced to a proposal limiting the Presidents of the World Council of Churches to one term, unless re-elected after retirement for a period between Assemblies, but a motion to eliminate the proposal was not sustained.

The plan to make the Ecumenical Institute one of the departments within the Division of Ecumenical Action evoked criticism, because of what looked to many delegates like "a threat of subordination" to this body. Dr. Kathleen Bliss spoke on this issue: The Institute was equally linked with Evangelism and Studies. Annual expenditure on its work was the largest single item in the World Council's budget. The office of Director was a very important one. The present Director[2] was a man of high caliber, and his successor should be. The Institute occupied a unique place in the ecumenical movement which should not be impaired. A motion to re-commit this provision of the report to the Central Committee carried.

The Report on Structure and Functioning was adopted with only minor amendments. The final version is printed in Appendix O.[3]

Supplementing the Report on Structure and Functioning, as approved by the Central Committee, were the findings of the seven committees assigned to study organizational changes relating to their departments. Summaries of their reports to the Assembly follow.

2. Committee on General Policy

The Committee on General Policy, the Chairman of which was Bishop William C. Martin of the Methodist Church in the United States, confined its report largely to discussing amendments to the constitution of the World Council of Churches. The need for this arose from the changes

[1] *The Evanston Report,* p. 8.
[2] Dr. Hendrik Kraemer.
[3] See also *The Evanston Report,* pp. 174-214.

at Lund in the constitution of the Commission on Faith and Order which had been approved by the Central Committee.[4]

From "Article III. Functions," the following words were dropped:

In matters of common interest to all the churches and pertaining to Faith and Order, the Council shall always proceed in accordance with the basis on which the Lausanne (1927) and Edinburgh (1937) Conferences were called and conducted.

Under "Article VI. Appointment of Commissions," the third paragraph was deleted, and in its place was substituted:

There shall be a Faith and Order Commission of which the following shall be the functions:

(i) To proclaim the essential oneness of the Church of Christ and to keep prominently before the World Council and the churches the obligation to manifest that unity and its urgency for the work of evangelism;

(ii) To study questions of faith, order, and workship with the relevant social, cultural, political, racial, and other factors in their bearing on the unity of the churches;

(iii) To study the theological implications of the existence of the ecumenical movement;

(iv) To study matters in the present relationships of the churches to one another which cause difficulties and need theological clarification;

(v) To provide information concerning actual steps taken by the churches towards re-union.

The Commission shall discharge these functions in accordance with a constitution approved by the Central Committee.

In invitations to world conferences on Faith and Order, it shall be specified that such gatherings are to be composed of official delegates of churches which accept Jesus Christ as God and Saviour.

"Article VIII. Amendments" was interpreted, on a recommendation by the Committee, to mean that "the sending to the constituent churches of the notice of a proposed constitutional amendment is the responsibility of the General Secretariat and should be mandatory, unless, as a result of review by the Central Committee or for any other reason, the member church making the proposal should withdraw it more than six months before the meeting of the Assembly."

The Committee apprised the Assembly that the Arminian Church in Holland (Remonstrant Brotherhood) had withdrawn its request for a change in the Basis, "because it desired to further an informal theological discussion on the Basis rather than to promote a constitutional decision."

The Church of Norway had submitted a proposal for amending Article I of the constitution of the World Council of Churches, so that it would read: "The World Council of Churches is a fellowship of churches

[4] For the Report on General Policy, see *The Evanston Report,* pp. 215-220.

which, in accordance with Holy Scripture, confess our Lord Jesus Christ as God and Saviour." The request had been received too late for consideration by the Second Assembly and would be reported by the Central Committee, after careful study, to the Third Assembly.[5]

The Committee recommended for adoption a "Statement on the Purpose and Function of the Basis," as follows:[6]

The World Council of Churches is an instrument at the service of the churches which enables them to enter into fraternal conversation with each other, to co-operate in various fields, and to render witness together to the world. It is not a new church (even less a super-church) and does not perform ecclesiastical functions.

Since the Council desires to make clear to the churches and to the world what it is, what it does, and who are its members, it has adopted a *basis*. The first article of its Constitution formulates this Basis in the following words: "The World Council of Churches is a fellowship of churches which accept Jesus Christ as God and Saviour." This Basis performs three functions:

(1) It indicates the *nature* of the fellowship which the churches in the Council seek to establish among themselves. For that fellowship, as a fellowship of churches, has its own unique character. It has a specific source and a specific dynamic. The churches enter into relation with each other, because there is a unity given once for all in the person and work of their common Lord and because the Living Lord gathers His people together.

(2) It provides the *orientation point* for the work which the World Council itself undertakes. The ecumenical conversations which take place in the World Council must have a point of reference. Similarly the activities of the Council must be submitted to an ultimate norm and standard. The Basis provides that standard.

(3) It indicates the *range* of the fellowship which the churches in the Council seek to establish.

The acceptance of the Basis is the fundamental criterion which must be met by a church which desires to join the Council. The limits of each society are dependent upon its nature. By joining together the churches seek to respond to the call and action of their Divine Lord. The World Council must therefore consist of churches which acknowledge that Lord as the second person of the Trinity.

While the Basis is therefore less than a confession, it is much more than a mere formula of agreement. It is truly a basis in that the life and activity of the World Council are based upon it. And the World Council must constantly ask itself whether it is faithful to its Basis.

Each church which joins the World Council must therefore seriously consider whether it desires to participate in a fellowship with this particular Basis. On the other hand, the World Council would overstep the limits it has set itself if it should seek to pronounce judgment as to whether any particular church is in fact taking the Basis seriously. It remains the responsibility of each church to decide itself whether it can sincerely accept the Basis of the Council.

[5] The constitution required that notice of any proposed amendment must be sent to the constituent churches "not less than six months before the meeting of the Assembly."

[6] Refer to Part Five, Section IV, 3.

3. Committee on the Division of Studies

The Committee on the Division of Studies reported through its Chairman, Dr. H. Meyer. It had begun, but had not carried to any conclusion, "a discussion of the question whether all studies . . . might be carried out in relation to a general theme and whether this . . . theme should be 'The Mission of the Church into the World,' emphasis to be put on its Christological interpretation and an ecumenical biblical approach," which seemed to reflect an awareness of certain crucial theological problems calling for more serious attention than they had received.[7]

The need for additions to the staffs of the East Asia Secretariat and the Department of Evangelism, if the work proposed for the Division of Studies was to be done effectively in these important areas, was stressed. At these and other points in the program more money would have to be supplied by the churches. Recommending "that additional resources and personnel be sought," the Committee suggested particularly, "because these studies are undertaken on behalf and in the service of the churches,"

A. that the World Council of Churches ask the churches to put at the disposal of the Division of Studies from time to time scholars interested in ecumenical studies and to bear as much of the cost thereof as they are able to do,
B. that the attention of the churches be drawn to the necessity of carrying out specific ecumenical studies on a regional basis,
C. that the theological faculties be approached also by the Division of Studies with regard to particular study topics for which one or the other professor might be especially equipped,
D. to draw the attention of theological faculties, seminaries and professors to the unique facility that students desiring to write a thesis for a degree might work on topics contained in the study programme of the Division of Studies and thus aid ecumenical studies.

The emphasis on study in the World Council of Churches gave special significance to the report of Dr. Nils Ehrenström, who was retiring as Director of the former Study Department, and to the accompanying "Recommendations Concerning the Division of Studies" emanating therefrom.

Dr. Ehrenström began with the statement that "ecumenical study is a novel and daring adventure."

"Practically for the first time in history, Christians from various walks of life, denominational traditions, and cultural backgrounds throughout the world, are enlisted in a common effort to rethink their faith and its implications for personal and corporate life. No wonder, then, that it still is in an exploratory and experimental stage. Yet it has already borne

[7] *The Evanston Report*, pp. 221-226.

sufficient fruitage to substantiate the claim that, henceforth, to think Christianly is to think ecumenically."

Four words described the work of the Study Department "and of ecumenical study in general," Dr. Ehrenström said: priorities, cross-fertilization, integration, and partnership.

The selection of priorities was important, he explained, because the churches were tempted "to concentrate their forces on secondary battle-fields or to maintain them on front-lines of yesterday—unresponsive to the demands of the present hour." "To discern and to point up . . . decisive issues upon which the churches should focus . . . attention," he declared, was a primary function of ecumenical study. He considered the choice of "Christian hope" by the Central Committee for the main theme an example of this.

As for cross-fertilization, he suggested that "at first glance it might appear as if the nascent world Christian community already possessed sufficient media of communication and exchange to make deliberate efforts of this kind superfluous"; and it was true, he said, that there existed a growing volume of intercommunication from church to church at various levels: but on the whole it remained accidental and limited. "Fresh, illuminating insights into the Word of God, novel experiments in Christian advance, convictions forged in the crucible of persecution, often remain in seclusion behind denominational, national or linguistic walls," he thought, and thus were prevented from helping to revitalize the whole Church.

Dr. Ehrenström spoke of the surveys and consultations on the Assembly topics as illustrative of the cross-fertilizing function of ecumenical study.

To make the churches aware of common problems and front-lines, however, was not enough in itself, nor was the intensification of exchange between them: the movement looked, he said, toward the rebirth of the churches through the experience characterized by the words of St. Paul, "Be ye of one mind in Christ." "The ultimate aim of ecumenical study is precisely to assist the churches in recovering that 'one mind in Christ,'" he declared, "in their ways of belief and thought, in their testimony and polity." The growth of the churches toward such integrated thinking was, he believed, a patent fact, although its present limitations were equally so. He referred to the collaboration on the main theme of the Assembly and the cooperative study on "The Bible and the Church's Message to the World," which issued in the statement entitled "Guiding Principles for the Interpretation of the Bible," as encouraging results.

Concerning the element of partnership in ecumenical study, Dr. Ehrenström pointed out that over the years there had been a steady growth in the number of denominational and interdenominational agencies and of Christians in different walks of life who in one way or another had cooperated. "In fact," he said, "one could cite a score of world-famed theologians and men of public affairs who have been converted to the ecumenical cause through their association with some particular study project." He continued:

> This partnership involves a sharing of the spiritual and intellectual gifts of the whole church throughout the world. In practice, however, owing to the great inequality of resources among the churches, it imposes a special obligation upon better equipped churches and groups to regard their participation in ecumenical study as a vicarious service, for the benefit of all. It is significant that appreciative comments on the value of such ecumenical exchanges mostly come from isolated or poorly endowed churches. On the other hand, it is equally true that the freshest and most provocative contributions often come from churches living dangerously on the frontiers of Christendom. Here it becomes manifest that ecumenical study, too, is an authentic form of inter-church aid.

Dr. Ehrenström concluded by proffering some recommendations. He thought those charged with the responsibility of the study program should be provided with "a center where basic and long-range inquiries could be carried forward in circumstances of sustained and quiet reflection . . . denied to a small staff committed to day-to-day tasks of stimulating study activities among the member churches." He recalled an early proposal by the Provisional Committee, that "an ecumenical centre of study and research, which in intellectual calibre and its material resources would be worthy of the World Council, be established at the earliest possible moment," and said he thought the time had come when such resolutions should issue in action.

He suggested that in the light of the favorable results in the study of the main theme of the Evanston Assembly it would be well for the World Council to "invite the churches to explore together the central affirmations of faith, one after the other, seeking to deepen and to extend the areas of their common witness."

"One of the most intractable obstacles to ecumenical study is . . . the fact that, with few exceptions, . . . the member churches of the World Council are not equipped to participate effectively," he declared. They should set themselves to provide more adequate organization for educational interchange.

"The present world situation cries out for Christian discernment," he said, "for . . . illumination of the dark road ahead." He asked whether the World Council and its constituent churches were willing to pay the price "of spiritual perceptivity and of sharing the prerequisite resources for the accomplishment of this part of their ecumenical mission to the world."

The Committee submitted the following report entitled "Recommendations Concerning the Division of Studies":[8]

[8] *The Evanston Report,* pp. 307-313.

Introductory

The Evanston Assembly will open up new and larger opportunities for the development of ecumenical and missionary thinking. A chief factor in this situation is the proposal to set up a Division of Studies, which will also serve the International Missionary Council and include four departments: Faith and Order, Evangelism, Church and Society and Missionary Studies. This last Department will be sponsored by the International Missionary Council.

This proposal marks a new departure in two ways. It takes account of the increasing convergence in thought and outlook of the ecumenical and missionary movements, thus facilitating closer co-operation between older and younger churches. It provides a framework which will make for greater flexibility in the shaping of study programmes and will enable departments—if so desired—to join forces in a concerted approach to given problems.

The aim of the Division has been defined as follows: "to serve the churches by promoting ecumenical studies on the fundamental issues of their faith and life, so that they may increasingly think together, advance in unity, render common witness, and take common action in the social and international field."

The programme of the Division for the coming years must obviously be determined in the light of the deliberations of the Evanston Assembly and the meeting of the Executive Committee of the International Missionary Council. The Department on Faith and Order has already had its major projects fixed by the Faith and Order Working Committee in August, 1953. Broadly speaking, the programme will include two distinct though closely connected stages: (a) the follow-up of Evanston by promotion of study of the Assembly reports in the churches; (b) the development of new long-range projects. The latter task in particular will require a period of careful exploration and planning by the Division, working in close association with the Ecumenical Institute and the other departments in the Division of Ecumenical Action.

The Assembly Committee dealing with the Division of Studies may therefore wish to formulate its recommendations to the Assembly in broad terms, authorizing the Central Committee and the Committee on the Division of Studies to shape a detailed programme which will take full account of the varied interests of the Council and its member churches.

The proposals listed below are thus merely to be regarded as a basis for discussion, illustrating possible priorities. They are the outcome of a considerable volume of consultation with advisers and correspondents in many countries. For the sake of brevity, the proposals are simply listed without developing arguments favouring their selection. It will be profitable to consider them against the background of the ecumenical surveys prepared for the six sections of the Assembly, and their analysis of the tasks confronting the churches at the present time.

The following questions should be kept in mind in examining these proposals:

What should be the objectives of ecumenical study?

How should priorities be chosen?

What methods have proved most fruitful in the past?

What new methods may be envisaged?

What can be done to make ecumenical study more truly an enterprise undertaken by the churches for the churches?

Should each department promote its own programme? Or should the Division as a whole centre its programme around one or more themes, exploring them from the different angles of the several departments?

How should the study projects of the departments within the Division of Ecumenical Action be integrated with the programme of the Division of Studies?

Projects

1. *General Projects of the Division.* The executive staff of the Division will carry a broad range of responsibilities. These will include stimulation of ecumenical thought among the churches, planning and co-ordination of the Division's own activities, and maintenance of relationships with other divisions and departments. It is moreover essential that the Division should have sufficient staff resources to enable it to carry out important projects, which do not fall within the confines of its specialized departments. The following have been recommended:

I. An Ecumenical Approach to the Interpretation of the Bible

A good deal of work has already been done on this subject, which is so fundamental for all ecumenical studies. So far the main focus has been the interpretation of the biblical teaching on social questions. These studies could be continued in a wider context and with particular reference to evangelism and the presentation of the gospel to modern man.

II. The Training of the Ministry

A long-range enquiry to be conducted in conjunction with the enquiry undertaken by the International Missionary Council in selected younger church areas. An important aspect of such study would be the furtherance of ecumenical outlook in theological education. Initial step: an exploratory conference of theological educators to advise the Division on issues and methods for this enquiry.

III. Editing of a Series of Ecumenical and Missionary Surveys

2. *Department of Faith and Order.* The primary task of the Commission on Faith and Order is to carry on basic studies of questions pertaining to Christian unity. Following the Third World Conference on Faith and Order at Lund, 1952, plans for the study of the following questions during the coming years have already been formulated, and partially implemented, by the working committee of the Faith and Order Commission:

I. The Church as understood in the light of the doctrines of Jesus Christ and the Holy Spirit
II. The ways and meaning of Christian worship
III. Christian tradition and the various church traditions
IV. Proselytism as a problem within the World Council of Churches
V. Social and cultural factors affecting church unity

With these studies already under way, the Commission on Faith and Order seeks counsel, not on what shall be studied, but on how its work is to be related directly to the churches in their common concern to express their unity in Christ.

The following questions need to be discussed:

I. How can reports prepared by study commissions of the Faith and Order Commission be given wider circulation among the churches, and how can churches make effective responses to such reports?

II. How can the numerous centres of experiment and study on matters of unity be connected by channels of communication which pass through the Faith and Order Commission and its secretariat?

III. What specific problems of inter-church relations may be illuminated by a study of proselytism?

IV. How may occasions be promoted, where permitted, for the common worship of Christians from various confessions and denominations? Is this a proper responsibility of the Faith and Order Commission? (See Lund Report, p. 35.)

V. How may the social and cultural factors affecting church unity be brought to light, examined, and dealt with by the Faith and Order Commission as well as by divided churches?

3. *Department on Evangelism.* To what extent would it be desirable and feasible to shape joint projects with the Department of Missionary Studies?

It is suggested that the Department—in addition to its assistance to the churches in planning their evangelistic activities—should concentrate on two types of study: surveys of evangelism in different situations or areas, and a thorough enquiry on one or two problems of particular importance in the field. Here the question needs to be faced whether the conditions and problems confronting the churches in different parts of the world are not in fact so different that the Department should promote enquiries on a regional basis (e.g. the emphasis on industrial evangelism in certain countries, and on rural evangelism in others).

I. Descriptive and Evaluative Surveys
- (a) Continuation of the present series of national and regional surveys. Projects under way or envisaged: South America, the United States, Scandinavia, Germany, Ceylon, Burma, a Muslim country.
- (b) Problem surveys on:
  - (i) The use of the Bible in evangelism (in collaboration with the United Bible Societies).
  - (ii) The evangelistic emphasis and practice of the "sects" (in collaboration with the International Missionary Council and the United Bible Societies).
  - (iii) The needs and problems in rural evangelism.

II. The Mission of the Church to Workers

Combining study and pioneering experimentation, the project would include:
- (a) A series of case studies on:
  - (i) Approaches actually used in evangelism among workers;
  - (ii) The religious assumptions and convictions of workers, and their attitude toward Christianity;
- (b) An information bulletin carrying regular reporting of experiments, projects and studies in this field, which would give a sense of fellowship in common endeavour.

III. The Christian Approach to the Jews

It has further been suggested that the World Council—through the Department of Evangelism—should associate itself more closely with the projects of the International Committee on the Christian Approach to the Jews. If so, in what ways?

4. *Department on Church and Society.* The primary task of the Department on Church and Society is to carry on basic studies of "the crucial problems of society about which the churches should declare their common mind and take action."

In the first place, it is proposed that the Department sponsor a number of regional study conferences and consultations as soon as possible after Evanston. The purpose of these meetings would be to discuss the Assembly report on social questions in relation to concrete situations, and to determine the principal projects for further study. It is suggested that there be:

(a) Three regional consultations, one in South America, one in Africa, and one in East Asia. These three meetings would take as their general theme: "The Christian Responsibility for the Social Problems in the Regions Concerned," discussing this in the light of the Evanston report. (The first two especially would be in the nature of consultations seeking to concentrate on fact-finding and on crystallizing the issues which need to be considered in the churches.)

(b) Two study conferences dealing with the issues in the Evanston report which specifically concern Western countries. One of these meetings would be held in Europe and the other in North America (unless it is felt that more would be gained by a joint meeting of Europeans and Americans).

Specific Issues

In the studies carried on since Amsterdam certain issues have emerged which will undoubtedly receive major attention at the Second Assembly, and are likely to become the subject of these post-Evanston meetings and the basis of the programme of the Department. These are as follows:

I. The Christian Responsibility for the Social Development of the Under-Developed Countries, including:
  (a) Appraisal of the moral problems involved in changing economic and political conditions in the under-developed countries.
  (b) The problem of creating a social ethos conducive to responsible social living.
  (c) The encounter between Christian and non-Christian ethics.

II. The Christian Responsibility for the Political and Economic Problems of Western Countries, including:
  (a) Christian thinking about political ethics in relation to the growth of the social planning state (special problems in Europe due to the development of supra-national economic and political integration).
  (b) Relation between domestic social policies and international economic and political responsibilities (e.g. the contribution of Western "privileged" countries in supporting efforts to achieve a responsible society in under-developed countries).
  (c) The appeal of communism to workers, intellectuals and youth, in some countries of the West.

III. Church and Society in Communist Lands
  Survey of the moral and spiritual problems faced by people living in communist societies.

Whether or not these or other issues are selected for emphasis, the regional meetings proposed above will be the chief means for carrying forward study in the year following Evanston. The preparation of reports and studies on such topics is envisaged in preparation for, or as an outcome of, the various conferences and consultations. For the topic "The Christian Witness in Communist Countries," it is proposed that the Department continue to issue reports similar to those issued by the present Study Department on the subject.

Publications

The Department on Church and Society is also expected "to disseminate the results of these studies," "to keep the churches informed about important developments in society," and "to acquaint the churches with action taken by other churches in this field." For this purpose it is proposed to publish occasional study documents on the projects outlined above, and a quarterly information bulletin on *Church and Society*.

Additional Projects

The following projects have been proposed as important study topics, if the help of additional staff should be offered by interested churches:

I. The Church as a Social Institution in a Changing Society—a sociological study of the ways in which the life of the Church is shaped by the prevailing social, economic and political structures of the particular societies in which it lives, and the problems this raises for Christians in a period of great social change.

II. Racial and Ethnic Tensions—in pursuit of the issues raised by the Evanston section on this topic.

III. Basis of an International Ethos—jointly with the Commission of the Churches on International Affairs, the staff members in charge to be related to the Commission . . . and the Division of Studies.

IV. Human Relations in Industrial Life—the Christian witness in relation to industrial tension and in particular to the labour movement.

V. Sex and Family Life—an exploratory survey of the thought and activities of the churches in this field, possibly leading to a more permanent enquiry. Undertaken jointly with the Department on Work for the Laity and the Department on Co-operation between Men and Women in Church and Society.

VI. The Christian Understanding of Work (jointly with the Department on Laity).

5. *Department of Missionary Studies.*

I. Life and Growth of the Younger Churches

A long-term enquiry focussed on the understanding of their task by the younger churches, as missionary churches which represent the Universal Church in a local setting (with field studies, promotion of discussion, and experimentation).

(a) New ways of worship (jointly with the Department on Faith and Order).
(b) Presenting the gospel to adherents of other faiths (continuing the discussions of the International Missionary Council Conferences at Tambaram, 1938, and at Willingen in 1952; jointly with the Department of Evangelism).
(c) The inter-action of the Church, and its cultural and religious environment in non-Christian societies; the need for new patterns of church life (jointly with the Department on Church and Society).
(d) Re-shaping missionary strategies.

II. Reform of the Training of the Ministry

Continuation of the current fact-finding and interpretative surveys undertaken in selected younger church areas.

III. Christian Missions in China—and attempt at an appraisal

Preparation of a volume incorporating relevant material and the circulation of papers.

IV. A Projected Series of Missionary Research Pamphlets

—Toward a Theology of Missions
—Missionary Vocation
—African Marriage and Family Life

—The Bible in the Life of the Younger Churches (by the United Bible Societies)
—Healing in the Church's Mission—a discussion of principles and problems of modern medical missions
—The Responsibility of Churches and Missions in the Field of Education, particularly with regard to Africa
—Urban Evangelism in Africa

4. COMMITTEE ON THE DIVISION OF ECUMENICAL ACTION

The report of the Committee on the Division of Ecumenical Action was placed before the Assembly by Bishop Angus Dun, who reviewed briefly the functions of the four departments in the Division—the Ecumenical Institute, the Youth Department, the Department on Work for the Laity, and the Department on Co-operation of Men and Women in Church and Society. Speaking as Chairman for the members of the Committee, he said: "It is our conviction that the four departments under consideration correspond to needs widely recognized, or calling for recognition, in our . . . churches. All of us wish to express our indebtedness to their heavily burdened staffs for the devotion and ability they have brought to our common cause. Let us not forget that the whole executive staff of these four far-reaching undertakings . . . number only nine persons." [9]

Formally the Commission on the Life and Work of Women in the Church, the Department on the Co-operation of Men and Women in Church and Society "is concerned," he said,

> with certain quite special problems of dislocation and unbalance in the life of the Church, now seen as urgent in many areas, but which we dare hope may prove to be transitional. Its task is to promote among men and women the study of questions affecting the co-operation and the common service of men and women in the churches and in society. It seeks to help women to make their contribution to the total life of the churches, and to urge the churches to enable and stimulate women to share fully in the opportunities and responsibilities of church membership. In view of the strength of women's organizations in many countries and churches, this Department is inevitably called upon: (1) to foster an ecumenical outlook among them; (2) to encourage their participation in the ecumenical movement as a whole, and (3) to provide for women church members information on the life and work of women in churches everywhere and to encourage contacts between them. We commend this Department to the confidence and support of the Assembly, until its task shall have been substantially fulfilled.

The Committee was "not satisfied with the name of the Division," and thought it detected "some tendencies to over-elaboration and artificiality in the plan, resulting from a commendable effort to put on paper a tidy

[9] *The Evanston Report,* pp. 226-233.

and rational scheme." Not advising any immediate attempt to alter the structure or to revise the definition of the aim and functions of the Division, the Committee expressed its confidence that the Central Committee would "view the scheme as somewhat provisional and experimental and as subject to revision in the light of experience with its workings."

The churches should be asked, the Committee recommended, to review most carefully their own administrative structures, to make sure that within each adequate provision was made for cooperation with the different departments of the World Council of Churches. They should be reminded that ecumenical education was not one particular activity within the life of a church but concerned the Church in all its ministry, including preaching and teaching on major doctrines.

Special attention should be given "to the urgent question of the approach of the churches, severally and jointly, to industrial workers."

Churches and mission boards should be asked to consider earnestly "the development of new patterns of co-operative ecumenical youth work in different parts of the world."

"The member churches should be asked to note the fact that the Department on Work for the Laity is not concerned with lay *men* only, but with the laity, i.e. *lay men* and *lay women* generally."[10] They should "be asked to recognize *the seriousness of the problem of the co-operation of men and women* in various areas of church life, and to seek ways in which this problem can be solved so that both men and women can give their full contribution to the life of the Church. It should be [understood] that these are not questions for women only, but for men and women to consider together."

The report suggested that "the member churches" should be helped to understand the importance of the Ecumenical Institute and urged to explore ways of encouraging and financing the enrollment of selected mature students. The opportunities presented by the Institute for "following up special problems and concerns which [had] been the subjects of ecumenical gatherings and conferences held elsewhere" should be brought to the attention of the churches, and likewise the numerous courses and conferences at the Institute "for the developing of an ecumenical consciousness among members of the churches."

The Committee would have the World Council of Churches also "help the . . . churches to make better use of delegates to ecumenical conferences and meetings, and of visitors . . . for the ecumenical education of their membership, especially at the local level."

Cooperation with the World Council of Christian Education and other interested bodies in exploring ways of providing ecumenical education for boys and girls under eighteen also was recommended by the report.

The Central Committee, moreover, "should consider whether and how

[10] The title of the Department was referred to the Central Committee for further consideration.

the World Council could give more assistance to the churches in promoting ecumenical prayer and worship."

"An early study [should be made] of the possibility that regional institutes on parallel lines (with the present Ecumenical Institute) should be brought into existence, so that church members in all parts of the world may have the opportunity to share in consultations, conferences and courses of the type now available at Bossey," the Committee concluded.

5. Committee on the Division of Inter-Church Aid

The report of the Committee on the Division of Inter-Church Aid and Service to Refugees, of which Dr. E. Emmen was Chairman, stated that inter-church aid had become a permanent obligation of the World Council of Churches. By accepting the privilege of sharing in this work the member churches bore witness to their hope in Christ and manifested the reality of the fellowship and wholeness of the Church.[11]

The relationships in this field, it explained, could be sustained only by mutual trust and confidence, every church being responsible for its own area and members and at the same time impelled by Christian compassion to suggest and initiate assistance to other churches.

The Division declared its acceptance of the functions for it set forth in the report of the Committee on Structure and Functioning.

The Committee on the Division reaffirmed, on behalf of the World Council of Churches, its deep concern for the millions of refugees who represented in 1954 "an even greater claim upon the Christian churches than confronted them at Amsterdam in 1948 when its First Assembly resolved to 'give high priority to work for the material and spiritual welfare of refugees, and appeal to its member churches in countries capable of receiving any settlers, both to influence public opinion towards a liberal immigration policy and to welcome and care for those who arrive in their countries.' "

It was the recommendation of the report that the World Council of Churches should:

(a) Urge upon the United Nations and its member governments the need for continuing and maximum support for the United Nations High Commissioner for Refugees and particularly for financial support to his programme of integration and emergency relief;

(b) Call upon governments to support the Inter-Governmental Committee for European Migration both by membership of that body and by generous provision of immigration opportunities for refugees and to maintain their financial support to such agencies as the United Relief and Works Agency for Palestine Refugees, the United Nations Korean Reconstruction Agency, or other agencies as may be needed;

[11] *The Evanston Report*, pp. 233-238.

(c) Press for the conditions which will make possible the repatriation of those refugees who wish to return to their homes;
(d) Negotiate with the authorities involved to secure the reunion, in accordance with their wishes, of families now separated;
(e) Maintain and extend its service to refugees and migrants in Europe, the Near East, and Asia, especially in Japan and Hong Kong and other areas where refugee needs may rise;
(f) Keep before the member churches the need for providing resettlement opportunities for refugees within their local communities;
(g) Ensure that the spiritual needs of refugees are adequately provided for and continue to hold all refugees within the fellowship of prayer.

Appended to the report was the following extract of a letter from the High Commissioner for Refugees:

It seems to me to be one of the greatest achievements of the Christian churches in recent times that they have started increasingly to translate their faith and their hope into terms of practical programmes and projects in fields in which they bear responsibility. I do not think that I have any right to compare, but I would be surprised if there were any field in which the Christians have achieved so much as they have in the field of the refugee problem. During my travels I have met the programmes of the World Council and of the Lutheran World Federation literally everywhere and I have the greatest admiration for those men and women who, with unflagging courage and belief in what they are doing, fight day by day for the solution of a problem which is still with us and unfortunately will remain with us for many years to come.

Over the borders which separate freedom from oppression refugees come every day walking into the unknown with a poor little bundle on their shoulders. They have been led to believe that the free world will restore their basic rights and their human dignity. They come to us with confidence and hope and the one thing which Christians cannot afford to do would be to let them down. Fortunately so far they never have, but it is human nature to get tired of a problem as the years go by and it is therefore indispensable to remind people of goodwill time and again that there is still a task ahead as long as the problem has not been really solved.

6. Committee on the Department of Information

Dr. Ernest A. Payne of Great Britain reported for the Committee on the Department of Information. "The co-ordination of resources made possible by the Assembly's action (in establishing the Department) should be conceived," he said, "as requiring more than efficient technical processes. The Department should seek a distinctive 'style' and way of dealing with its problems so as to be of service to all parts of the Council's structure and to the member churches in interpreting the ecumenical movement."[12]

In all forms of information [he continued] it should be the aim . . . to render theological and other technical vocabularies intelligible, without dilu-

[12] *The Evanston Report*, pp. 238-244.

tion and distortion. The Department should also aim at securing as well as providing information, and it should endeavor to reach people outside the churches. . . . The primary problem before the Department is clearly that it is meant to be an agency to facilitate the processes whereby the World Council of Churches may become real both to the rank and file membership of its constituency and to people who at present take little or no notice of the Church. . . . The penetration of language barriers must . . . be a concern, especially in such important smaller areas as Scandinavia, and in the case of Spanish.

In assessing the value of current ecumenical publications, the Committee indicated that "consultation with Dr. Rajah B. Manikam, Joint East Asia Secretary of the World Council of Churches and the International Missionary Council, might well lead to the publication of a periodical East Asian Newsletter or a supplement of the Ecumenical Press Service."

Direct communication with member churches is a first call on the Department's resources for disseminating information. The official heads or designated executive offices of the churches should receive specimens. Ecumenical committees or other designated agencies should then be provided with quantities. Provided this direct communication is safeguarded in the first place, the Department should be free to work through national ecumenical bodies, local councils of churches, interested ministers and clergy, theological seminaries, organizations for men, women, and youth, and the church press. In countries where member churches are preponderantly in the majority of the population, the appropriate world confessional alliances may be consulted on questions of public relations; for instance, in Scandinavia it might prove convenient to incorporate ecumenical information in publications in the national language as they go out from the Lutheran World Federation.

The report commented on the probability that the budgetary allotment for the Department would be inadequate, particularly in view of the large cost of service through some of the media of information it would need to employ, which should include radio and television.

7. Committee on Finance

The report of the Committee on the Department of Finance and Administration, of which Dr. Eugene Carson Blake of the Presbyterian Church in the United States of America was Chairman, summarized the finances of the World Council of Churches during the first six-year period ending with the Evanston Assembly. It recommended:[13]

(a) That the Assembly approve the continuance of the policy of building up the General Reserve by annual allocations from the revenue until in the judgment of the Central Committee or a subsequent Assembly an adequate General Reserve has been established;

[13] *The Evanston Report,* pp. 244-252.

(b) That the Assembly ask the Central Committee to investigate whether or not it may be desirable, as an insurance against inflation, to invest some part of its permanent reserves in equities;

(c) That the Assembly approve the plan of retaining approximately $50,000 as a special reserve for the Ecumenical Institute, in view of the large properties at Bossey and the type and scope of the programme (this will mean that the whole support of the Institute will in future necessarily come from current revenue);

(d) That the Assembly give approval for a request to be made from the Department of Inter-Church Aid and Service to Refugees to member churches for the provision of an operating fund for the Service to Refugees, by either (i) an advance payment against future contributions to the Service Programme or (ii) special non-recurring gifts.

The Committee reported that sufficient money had been raised for the World Council budget of $267,000 for the Evanston Assembly and the originally approved public relations budget of $40,000.

The operating budget for the World Council of Churches recommended by the Committee for the ensuing year called for income from churches of $420,000, which represented an increase of over 30 per cent above the total amount raised in 1953. This sum was not sufficient to cover all requests by the divisions and departments, and, "in view of the unmet requests . . . for strengthening the staff and increasing the work," the Committee recommended "that the Central Committee be authorized to continue to seek from all the member churches a proper proportion of support for the work of the World Council and, if income allows, to initiate such advances in programme as in its judgment are the most pressing and promise to be most fruitful."

In the discussion incidental to the adoption of the budget, Bishop Fuglsang-Damgaard of Denmark expressed gratitude, on behalf of the Council's members outside the United States, for the generosity of the churches of that country which during the period from Amsterdam to Evanston had contributed some 80 per cent of the money raised. He remarked that postwar conditions had made it impossible for many churches to give adequately during these first years and voiced their determination to assume a larger part of the financial responsibility thenceforward.

8. Committee on the Commission of the Churches on International Affairs

The Committee on the Commission of the Churches on International Affairs, Dr. Erling Wikborg, Chairman, considered the work of this Department of such strategic importance that it should be not only maintained but substantially strengthened. The Commission, in common with most of the other departments, needed additional funds. Financial limitations notwithstanding, the Committee expressed the view that the work of the Commission was of such paramount importance that the churches should be urged to give it the highest priority in their planning.

The Committee recommended:[14]

I. That the urgency and international significance of the problems of Europe were such as to require much more specific attention and study than they had hitherto received and urged that the staff be increased by the appointment of a European secretary.

II. That the increasing importance of Asian action and opinion in international affairs emphasized the comparative inactivity of the churches in Asia in international action and representation and called for the early appointment of an officer—an Asian—responsible for Asia and for the mobilization of concerted action by the churches of Asia.

The Committee thought the addition of a European and an Asian member to the staff was necessary to balance the Anglo-Saxon predominance in the present composition of the Secretariat.

The report recognized that the Commission had evolved a successful technique of fact-finding study but thought that there was need for further attention to major world issues and the theological bases of its policy. Issues urgently requiring study, it was suggested, included:

An International Ethos
Religious Liberty and Proselytism
The Background of the United Nations Educational, Scientific and Cultural Organization
The Application by Governments of the Principle of Reciprocity, Particularly in the Admission of Missionaries
The Problem of Germany
Issues in the Near East
An Asian Security Pact

The Committee recognized the Commission's need of a definition of "the Christian bases" for its actions but could see no way, because of the limited resources, of instituting the desired program of theological study in its field of operations.

The dangers of overlapping and the possibilities of cooperation, particularly in study, by the Commission and other departments of the World Council of Churches handling social matters had been discussed, and it was agreed that assignments to the Commission should be limited by the distinctive purpose for which it had been established.

In addition to the foregoing reports, submitted by the seven com-

[14] *The Evanston Report,* pp. 252-255.

mittees within the framework of Structure and Functioning, the Assembly heard reports of the Credentials and Nominations Committees.[15]

9. Credentials Committee

The Credentials Committee, Dr. M. E. Aubrey, Chairman, commented in its report on the cases of two delegates who had been appointed to represent two or more churches which were closely related and of the same faith and order:

> Your Committee feel that all member churches should be represented by delegates who belong to them and are in the fullest way acquainted with their life, problems, views and aspirations. But we realize that this may be difficult for some churches remote from the meeting-place of the Assembly, which have scanty financial resources, or cannot find among their members those who have the time and opportunity to travel a great distance. We consider it would be wrong to disfranchise them under such conditions and appreciate that the only way for them to be represented at all, and to make their membership of the Council effective, is to appoint from outside their membership, and we consider that each church should be allowed to appoint such a delegate as it may be able to approve with confidence.
>
> We recommend therefore that a delegate be permitted to represent more than one church if he is properly accredited by each of them; and, further, that when votes are reckoned by churches (as, for example, in the admission of new members) he should be entitled to vote in behalf of each; but that when votes of individuals are counted, as usually on a motion after discussion in the Assembly, he should have only one vote.

On the late substitution of a delegate for another, the Committee remarked as follows:

> Nothing is said in the Constitution concerning the latest date when names of delegates may be received by the World Council office. It would be hard to make a satisfactory rule, since death, illness or some other unavoidable cause may create at the last moment a gap which cannot be filled to the advantage of the Assembly as well to the church concerned.
>
> No problem arises when the substitute is appointed by his church or some duly authorized committee or person designated by it and the usual form is sent in. . . . But your Committee feel that last-minute substitutions, even from among accredited visitors, should not be allowed unless any such substitution is authorized through the usual church channel of communication, or by a delegation or leader who has been definitely appointed to make it and the authorization made known to the World Council office through the appropriate channel.
>
> In receiving delegates it is felt that the Council should act only on instructions of the churches communicated through normal intermediaries. . . . We recommend therefore that no delegate be recognized as such, unless he has

[15] See *The Evanston Report*, pp. 256-263.

been appointed by the governing body of his church, or by some body or person authorized by it, after due notice of such authorization has been sent to the World Council office.

10. Committee on Nominations

The report of the Nominations Committee, Dr. J. Earl Moreland, Chairman, was presented by Rev. David Say. Care had been taken, it stated, "to follow . . . the rules of procedure governing the action of the Committee," which provided that "the maximum number of presidents shall be six and that in making nominations the . . . Committee shall have regard to the following principles: (a) the personal qualifications of the individual for the task for which he is to be nominated; (b) fair and adequate confessional representation; (c) fair and adequate geographical representation."

Compliance with the last two of these provisions was shown by the following statements submitted by the Committee:

Confessional Representation by Those Nominated for the Central Committee

Anglicans	11
Baptists	4
Congregationalists	4
Copts	2
Disciples	1
Lutherans	16
Methodists	10
Old Catholics	1
Orthodox	12
Orthodox Syrians	1
Reformed	16
Salvation Army	1
United	10
Brethren	1
Total	90

Geographical Distribution of Those Nominated for the Central Committee

North America	22
Europe	22
United Kingdom and Eire	10
Eastern Orthodox	12
Asia	12
Africa and Latin America	6
Australia and New Zealand	5
International	1
Total	90

Twenty-three members of the former Central Committee were nominated for re-election. The membership of the new Committee consisted of seventy-three clergymen, eleven laymen, and six laywomen, representing thirty-one countries.

Dr. G. K. A. Bell, Bishop of Chichester, who had served as Chairman of the Central Committee chosen at Amsterdam in 1948, was elected Honorary President of the World Council of Churches, and Dr. John R. Mott, who had been voted this honor at the First Assembly, was re-elected.

Those who were elected, on the Committee's nomination, to the Presidium and the Central Committee were:

Presidents

The Very Rev. Principal John Baillie, Edinburgh (Church of Scotland)
Bishop Sante Barbieri, Buenos Aires (Methodist)
Bishop Otto Dibelius, Berlin-Dahlem (Evangelical Church in Germany)
Metropolitan Juhanon, Tiruvalla (Mar Thoma Syrian Church of Malabar)
Archbishop Michael, New York City (Greek Orthodox Archdiocese of North and South America)
Bishop Henry Knox Sherrill, New York City (Protestant Episcopal)

Central Committee

Australia—Archbishop H. W. K. Mowll, Sydney (Anglican); Principal Robert B. Lew, Burwood (Methodist); Rev. C. D. Ryan, Killara (Congregationalist)
Austria—Bishop Gerhard J. F. May, Vienna (Evangelical Church of the Augsburgian and Helvetic Confession)
Brazil—Rev. J. A. do Amaral, Petropolis (Methodist)
Canada—Canon W. W. Judd, Toronto (Church of England in Canada); Principal Clarence M. Nicholson, Halifax (United Church)
Ceylon—Bishop H. Lakdasa De Mel, Kurunegala (Anglican).
Czechoslovakia—Bishop Jan Chabada, Bratislava (Evangelical Church in Slovakia); Professor Josef L. Hromadka, Prague (Czech Brethren)
Denmark—Bishop Hans Fuglsang-Damgaard, Copenhagen (Church of Denmark)
Egypt—Professor Aziz Suryal Atiya, Cairo (Coptic Orthodox); Archimandrite Parthenios-Aris Coinidis (Greek Orthodox Patriarchate of Alexandria)
Ethiopia—Bishop Abouna Theopolis, Addis Ababa (Ethiopian Church)
Finland—Professor Aimo Tauno Nikolainen, Helsinki (Church of Finland)
France—Dr. Philippe L. E. Maury, Paris (Reformed); Inspector P. T. Poincenot, Montbéliard (Lutheran)
Germany—Bishop J. E. R. Lilje, Hannover; Bishop Gottfried Noth, Dresden; Professor Volkmar Herntrich, Hamburg (EKID: Lutheran); Dr. Martin Niemöller, Wiesbaden; Dr. Reinhold von Thadden-Trieglaff, Fulda (EKID: United); Dr. Wilhelm Niesel, Schoeller/Dornap (EKID: Reformed)
Gold Coast—Rev. Peter Zwei Dagadu, Accra (Methodist)
Greece—Professor H. Alivisatos, Athens; Professor Panayotis Bratsiotis, Athens; Archimandrite Jerome Cotsonis, Athens; Professor Basil Ioannidis, Athens; Bishop Panteleimon, Salonika (Church of Greece)

Hungary—Professor Laszlo Pap, Budapest (Reformed); Bishop Lajos Vetoe, Budapest (Lutheran)

India—Bishop Lesslie Newbigin, Tallakulam; Mr. Rajaiah David Paul, Mylapore (Church of South India); Rev. Gnanajayam Paul David, Tambaram (Lutheran); Rev. Korah Philipos, Kottayam (Orthodox Syrian Church of Malabar)

Indonesia—Rev. Karimuda Sitompul, Tampanuli (Batak Church of Sumatra: Lutheran); Rev. C. Mataheru, Ambonia (Church of the Moluccas: Reformed)

Japan—Dr. Enkichi Kan, Tokyo (Anglican); Dr. Michio Kozaki, Tokyo (Kyodan)

Lebanon—Professor H. Aharonian, Beirut (Armenian Evangelical); Dr. Charles Malik, Washington, D.C. (Greek Orthodox Patriarchate of Antioch)

Netherlands—Dr. Hendrikus Berkhof, Dreibergen (Dutch Reformed); Archbishop Andreas Rinkel, Utrecht (Old Catholic)

New Zealand—Bishop Alwyn K. Warren, Christchurch (Anglican); Mrs. F. O. Bennett, Christchurch (Presbyterian)

Norway—Bishop Johannes Smemo, Oslo (Church of Norway)

Pakistan—Dr. Andrew Thakur Das, Lahore (United Church of Northern India and Pakistan)

Philippines—Bishop Enrique C. Sobrepena (United Church of Christ)

South Africa—Dr. Cornelius B. Brink, Johannesburg (Dutch Reformed)

Sweden—Archbishop Yngve Brilioth, Uppsala; Mrs. Margit Lindstrom, Lundsberg (Church of Sweden)

Switzerland—Professor Henri C. W. d'Espine, Geneva (Swiss Protestant Federation)

Turkey—Archbishop Athenagoras of Thyateira, London, England; Archimandrite James Coucouzis, Boston, U.S.A.; Metropolitan James of Philadelphia, Istanbul (Ecumenical Patriarchate of Constantinople)

United Kingdom and Ireland

Ernest A. Payne, London (Baptist Union of Great Britain and Ireland); B. J. Hartwell, Southport (Congregational Union of England and Wales); Dr. Kathleen Bliss, Bromley, Kent; Archbishop Geoffrey F. Fisher, London; Bishop Richard A. Reeves, Johannesburg, South Africa; Bishop Ivor Stanley Watkins, Bristol (Church of England); Mrs. Ernest Jarvis, Glasgow; Professor William Strang Tindal, Edinburgh (Church of Scotland); Dr. Eric Baker, London; Professor Harold Roberts, Richmond (Methodist); Rev. James Rowland Boyd, Belfast, Northern Ireland (Presbyterian); Commissioner Gordon Simpson, London (Salvation Army, European Secretary, classed as an international member of the Committee)

United States of America

Bishop D. Ward Nichols, Philadelphia (African Methodist Episcopal); Dr. Reuben E. Nelson, New York; Mrs. Leslie E. Swain, Craigville, Mass. (American Baptist); Dr. Henry F. Schuh, Columbus, Ohio (American Lutheran); Dr. P. O. Bersell, Minneapolis (Augustana Lutheran); Dr. M. R. Zigler, Geneva, Switzerland (Church of the Brethren); Dean Liston Pope, New Haven, Conn. (Congregational Christian); Dr. George W. Buckner, Indianapolis (Disciples of Christ); Dr. James E. Wagner, Philadelphia (Evangelical and Reformed); Mrs. Frank G. Brooks, Mount Vernon, Iowa; Bishop William C. Martin, Dallas, Tex.; Bishop G. Bromley Oxnam, Washington, D.C.; Charles C. Parlin, New York (Methodist); Dr. Joseph H. Jackson, Chicago (National Baptist); Francis P. Miller, Charlottesville, Va. (Presbyterian in the United States); Dr. Eugene C.

Blake, Philadelphia; Dr. Ralph Waldo Lloyd, Maryville, Tenn. (Presbyterian in the United States of America); Bishop Angus Dun, Washington, D.C.; Dr. Nathan M. Pusey, Cambridge, Mass. (Protestant Episcopal); Dr. Georges Florovsky, New York; Bishop John Shahovsky, San Francisco (Russian Orthodox Greek Catholic); Dr. Franklin Clark Fry, New York (United Lutheran)

At its first meeting, in Evanston, the Central Committee elected as Chairman Dr. Franklin Clark Fry and as Vice-Chairman Dr. Ernest A. Payne.

The Executive Committee, which was appointed at the same meeting, consisted of the Chairman and the Vice-Chairman of the Central Committee, the six Presidents of the World Council of Churches, and twelve elective members from the parent body, as follows: Dr. Eugene C. Blake, Archbishop Yngve Brilioth, Rev. Peter Z. Dagadu, Bishop H. Lakdasa De Mel, Dr. Georges Florovsky, Dr. Josef L. Hromadka, Metropolitan James, Dr. Martin Niemöller, Bishop G. Bromley Oxnam, Dr. Rajaiah D. Paul, and Dean Liston Pope.

The Central Committee elected the nominees for the staff of the World Council of Churches who were proposed by the staffing committee, as follows:

General Secretariat

Dr. Willem Adolf Visser 't Hooft, General Secretary

Dr. O. Frederick Nolde, Associate General Secretary (while he remains Director of the Commission of the Churches on International Affairs)

Dr. Robert S. Mackie, Associate General Secretary, with special responsibility for the Division of Inter-Church Aid and Service to Refugees (for one year)

Dr. Leslie Cooke, Associate General Secretary, with special responsibility for the Division of Inter-Church Aid and Service to Refugees (for five years, beginning in mid-1955)

Dr. Robert S. Bilheimer, Associate General Secretary, with special responsibility for the Division of Studies (for five years)

Rev. Francis H. House, Associate General Secretary, with special responsibility for the Division of Ecumenical Action (for five years, beginning in mid-1955)

Rev. Kenrick M. Baker, Assistant to the General Secretary (for an additional year)

Division of Studies

Dr. H. H. Harms, Associate Director (for three years)

Dr. J. Robert Nelson, Executive Secretary, Department on Faith and Order (for three years)

Rev. Paul Abrecht, Executive Secretary of Department on Church and Society (for three years)

Rev. Daniel T. Niles, Part-time Secretary, Department on Evangelism (for one year)

Dr. Erik Nielsen, Executive Secretary, Department on Missionary Studies, with full-time status as a staff member of the World Council of Churches during term of appointment

Division of Ecumenical Action

Dr. Hendrik Kraemer, Director, Ecumenical Institute (for one year)
Rev. Robert Paul, Assistant Director, Ecumenical Institute (for three years)
Mr. Bengt-Thure Molander, Executive Secretary, Youth Department (for period to be decided by the Executive Committee)
Rev. Philip Potter, Secretary in Youth Department (for three years)
Miss Frances Maeda, Secretary in Youth Department (for two years)
Mr. Heinrich Rohrbach, Secretary in Youth Department for Work Camps (for one year)
Mr. William Perkins, Secretary in Youth Department for Work Camps (for two years)
Mlle Madeleine Barot, Executive Secretary, Department of Co-operation between Men and Women (for three years)

Division of Inter-Church Aid and Service to Refugees

Dr. E. H. S. Chandler, Associate Director (for three years)
Rev. Robert B. Tillman, Administrative Secretary (for two years)
Miss Margaret Jaboor, Assistant Director of Service to Refugees (for three years)
Rev. Harold Bonnell, Administrative Secretary of Service to Refugees (for three years)
Rev. Raymond Maxwell, Secretary in the Division (for three years)
Rev. Dominique Micheli, Rev. Harold Madsen and Rev. Laszlo Ledermann, Secretaries (for one year)

Department of Information

Rev. John Garrett, Executive Secretary (for three years)
Dr. Alexandre de Weymarn, Editor, Ecumenical Press Service (for period to be decided by the Executive Committee)
Mr. Theodore Pratt and Mr. John Taylor, Members of the Staff (for one year)

Department of Finance and Administration

Mr. Frank Northam, Director (for three years)
Mr. Alan Haigh, Member of Staff (for three years)
Mr. Wolfgang Kordon, Member of Staff (for three years)
Mr. Peter Smallwood, Member of Staff (for three years)

New York Office

Dr. Samuel McCrea Cavert, Executive Secretary (for three years)
Miss Eleanor Kent Browne, Part-time Secretary for Department of Finance and Administration (for three years)
Mrs. Elsie Culver, Part-time Secretary for Department of Information (for one year)

Joint Appointments

Dr. Elfan Rees (with Commission of the Churches on International Affairs), Secretary in the Department of Inter-Church Aid and Service to Refugees (for three years)
Dr. Rajah Manikam (with International Missionary Council), East Asian Secretary (for three years, beginning January 1, 1955)
Dr. Normal Goodall (with International Missionary Council), Secretary of the International Missionary Council and World Council of Churches Joint Committee

Note. Dr. H. H. Wolf was to be invited to become Director of the Ecumenical Institute in 1955. If he declined, the Executive Committee was authorized to name a Director. The new staff of the Institute would then be appointed.

The Executive Committee was given authority to name an Executive Secretary for the Department on Work for the Laity.

11. Joint Committee of the International Missionary Council and the World Council of Churches

In July 1954, a month prior to the Second Assembly, the Joint Committee of the I.M.C. and the W.C.C. had prepared a report for presentation to the delegates at Evanston. Significant among its recommendations was the proposal that one Division of studies serve both organizations, and further, that there be closer ties in areas of public relations and information. The report follows in full:[16]

The Joint Committee at its last meeting, in July 1952, "saw more clearly than ever before that the inseparable oneness of mission and unity, as the deep meaning of the Church's existence, is basic to all the issues the Church has to face in the ecumenical movement." The Committee, therefore, put certain key questions on this subject to the conferences at Willingen and Lund. Thus, in this and other ways, the original impetus of the document on "The Calling of the Church to Mission and Unity," issued by the Central Committee of the World Council of Churches at Rolle in 1951, is passing into the thinking of a wider constituency.

Meanwhile another impetus had come from the East Asian Study Consultation which met in December 1952 at Lucknow. That meeting called for still more serious consideration of the relationships between the World Council of Churches and the International Missionary Council. The Central Committee of the World Council of Churches, meeting immediately afterwards at Lucknow, referred this request to the Joint Committee. This was the direct origin of the meeting at Königstein, Germany.

The work of the Spirit, we believe, is found in the total ecumenical movement of which the World Council of Churches and the International Missionary Council are two organized manifestations. In reflecting on this, and in the light of recent developments in the relationship of the two bodies, the Joint Committee believes that their association is also a witness to the work of the same Spirit. This association has already been worked out practically in a number of instances with signal success. It has been found possible to arrange for many common tasks to be performed through joint action. The Commission of the Churches on International Affairs was established by both bodies and is dependent upon them, while at the same time enjoying considerable freedom in carrying out its functions. The East Asia Secretaryship is a significant expression of our association and an effective instrument of joint action. The responsibility for co-ordinating emergency inter-church aid and relief outside Europe has been entrusted by both bodies to the Department of Inter-Church Aid and Service to Refugees of the World Council of Churches. It has now been proposed that the Division of Studies of the

[16] *The Evanston Report,* pp. 322-327.

World Council of Churches should also be the Division of Studies of the International Missionary Council, and that it should include a Department of Missionary Studies of which the Executive Secretary would be the Research Secretary of the International Missionary Council. Measures are being taken to ensure closer ties in public relations and information.

While welcoming these developments "in association," and the deepening conviction in many quarters that the two bodies belong together in one calling and purpose, the Joint Committee realizes that it has not yet become clear whether this association should necessarily lead to a single organization or whether it can best be furthered by the joint action of two "autonomous but inter-dependent councils." The Committee is aware that within the constituencies of both bodies there are divergent views on this question. These divergencies indicate the necessity for deeper thought on the whole matter and for a willingness to be led to conclusions which cannot yet be defined.

At the same time the Committee has become increasingly conscious that there are great issues and intractable problems which vitally concern the evangelistic outreach and world mission of the Church, and which are not being adequately faced by either the International Missionary Council or the World Council of Churches. Political regionalization, the destruction of familiar patterns of life, the vitality of non-Christian faiths are problems which call for attention. The Committee is clear that such matters should not be delegated immediately to an existing department of either body or to a special committee. They require in the first instance careful study to find out how the combined resources in thinking and action of both bodies may be most effectively applied to them. Further, within the world-wide Christian fellowship itself there are new movements which must urgently occupy the attention of both bodies, for example manifestations of Christian missionary zeal outside the life of the older denominations, and the new awareness among the denominations themselves, partly due to the influence of the ecumenical movement, of their own world-wide confessional groupings. These are matters which call for joint consideration.

The Joint Committee has increasingly become an effective instrument for dealing with matters of common concern. Consequently it has decided to ask the parent bodies to strengthen its membership, and to provide it with a secretariat, so that it can itself undertake this new phase of joint consideration of common problems.

Proposed Constitution of the Joint Committee

(1) The International Missionary Council and the World Council of Churches shall each officially appoint six representatives to the Joint Committee. In order to secure the best possible coverage of confessions and areas, the officers of both bodies shall consult with each other before nominations are submitted to their respective governing committees.

(2) The officers of the International Missionary Council and the World Council of Churches, in consultation, shall appoint the chairman of the Joint Committee, who shall be an additional member.

(3) The officers of the International Missionary Council and the World Council of Churches, in consultation, shall make recommendations to their respective bodies concerning the appointment of the secretariat of the Joint Committee and the methods of financing the appointment.

(4) The General Secretaries of the International Missionary Council and the World Council of Churches, and such other members of the staff as may be required, shall sit with the Joint Committee.

Proposed Functions of the Joint Committee and Its Secretariat

The Joint Committee shall be an advisory committee to the International Missionary Council and the World Council of Churches. It shall have no authority to act independently in its own name. Its functions shall be:

(1) To help the two bodies to keep prominently before their member churches and constituent councils their common responsibility for the evangelistic outreach and world mission of the Church.

(2) To study major aspects of the common tasks confronting the two bodies, and to make specific recommendations concerning the policies to be followed by the two bodies.

(3) To keep under review the ways by which the two bodies are co-operating, and to suggest new ways.

(4) And, in so far as may arise from the above, to continue to study the organizational implications of their developing relationships. Examples are: (a) the study of ways and means whereby the member councils of the International Missionary Council may be constructively related to the work of the World Council of Churches and the national councils of churches in countries of the older churches related to the missionary movement; (b) the study of the advantages, disadvantages, and implications of a full integration of the International Missionary Council and the World Council of Churches.

Proposed Plan for the Division of Studies

Consideration was given to the best way of relating the study work of the World Council of Churches and the International Missionary Council. A plan was submitted which had been carefully studied by the staff of both bodies and after discussion and modification was passed for submission to the Executive Committee of the World Council of Churches and the *Ad Interim* Committee of the International Missionary Council, as follows:

(a) The Division of Studies of the World Council of Churches as outlined in the Report of the Committee on Structure and Functioning shall also be the Division of Studies of the International Missionary Council.

(b) In addition to the present provisions for Faith and Order, Church and Society, and Evangelism, there shall be a Department of Missionary Studies of which the Research Secretary of the International Missionary Council shall be the Executive Secretary.

(c) The Central Committee of the World Council of Churches, in appointing the members of the working committees for Faith and Order, Church and Society, and Evangelism, shall consult with the International Missionary Council. The administrative committee of the International Missionary Council, in appointing the members of the working committee of the Department of Missionary Studies, shall consult with the World Council of Churches. The Central Committee of the World Council of Churches, in appointing the additional members of the divisional committee, shall consult the International Missionary Council.

(d) The Associate General Secretary of the World Council of Churches responsible for the Division, and the Executive Secretaries of Faith and Order, Church and Society, and Evangelism, shall be appointed, and their salaries and expenses paid, by the World Council of Churches. The Executive Secretary of the Department of Missionary Studies shall be appointed, and his salary and expenses paid, by the International Missionary Council. The expenses of the working committee of the Department of Missionary Studies shall also be met by the International Missionary Council.

(e) The members of the staff of the Division shall work under the leadership of the responsible Associate General Secretary, but the location of the Department of Missionary Studies shall be left for the International Missionary Council to decide.

Report on East Asia, Africa, and Latin America

East Asia

(1) The decisions of the Bangkok Conference which led to the appointment of a Joint Secretary of the World Council of Churches and the International Missionary Council for East Asia have been justified by the experience of the past three years. The Secretary has rendered effective pastoral service to the churches and the Christian councils of the region and has established his position as the accepted interpreter and symbol of the two bodies which he represents.

(2) The work of the East Asia Secretary in the next phase should continue the pastoral emphasis but include the task of relating the various activities of the World Council of Churches and the International Missionary Council to the life and work of the churches and councils in the region.

(3) Less continuous travel will be required than during the past three years. Such travel as is undertaken should normally be related to specific tasks or occasions.

(4) It is, therefore, desirable that an office of the East Asia Secretary be established in a suitable centre. In the present circumstances this might, for the time being, be located in India.[17]

(5) The parent bodies should consult and decide regarding any budget adjustments which may be necessary.

(6) The Committee recommends the nomination of Dr. R. B. Manikam[18] for appointment as Joint East Asia Secretary for a further period of three years from 1st January 1955.

Africa

(1) In reviewing the total situation in Africa (south of the Sahara) the Committee noted the following facts.

(a) The growth of a new African self-consciousness.

(b) The acuteness of the racial problem in many parts of Africa and the need for the Christian Church to play a constructive role in relation to it.

(c) The rapid increase in industrialization and the consequent disintegration of African patterns of life.

(d) The need for education in responsible Christian citizenship.

(e) The intensity of the encounter between advancing Islam and a growing Christian community.

(f) The necessity for a deeper understanding of what an indigenous church should be.

(2) These facts point to the urgent need for a regional approach to Africa and closer co-operation between churches and between Christian councils in Africa.

(3) The Joint Committee recommends that the International Missionary Council be asked to take the initiative (on behalf of both the World Council of Churches and itself) in assisting councils of churches and missionary societies to discover what further co-operative action, especially on a regional basis, may be taken to meet these needs.

[17] Headquarters were established in Madras, India.

[18] At the beginning of 1956, Dr. Manikam succeeded Dr. Johannes Sandegren, third Lutheran Bishop of Tranquebar. He was consecrated January 14 at Tamil.

(4) In the judgment of this Committee it is advisable that a special Africa Committee (or Commission) be set up, administratively related to the International Missionary Council, but with adequate World Council representation, and that this committee should report from time to time to the Joint Committee.

Latin America

(1) Looking at the Christian task in the world, the Joint Committee is aware of the need in Latin America for increased regional co-operation, and for relating such co-operation to the world Christian fellowship.

(2) The Committee recognizes that this must be worked out in Latin America—possibly by a conference convened and held within the region. It is therefore recommended that Dr. John Mackay and the Rev. Rudolfo Anders, as Chairman and Vice-Chairman of the International Missionary Council, be asked to consult with Christian leaders in Latin America as to the best means of achieving a comprehensive consultation in Latin America on these matters, or alternative means for achieving the ends in view.

The Commission of the Churches on International Affairs

The Joint Committee received from Dr. Nolde a report on the recent activities of the Commission of the Churches on International Affairs. It recommended strongly to the two bodies that this Commission should be continued on its present basis, which had proved so satisfactory. It noted the need for increased income to the Commission . . . in order to deal more realistically with the present obligations as regards staff; the need to strengthen the international character of the officers and staff; the inevitable limitation of the range of the Commission, even in the matter of denials of religious liberty; and the new possibilities of co-operation with the Division of Studies and the Department of Information in securing wider participation on the part of the membership of the churches in the issues dealt with by the Commission.

The Christian Approach to the Jews

The Joint Committee noted:

(a) that this subject would appear on the agenda of the Section on Evangelism of the Evanston Assembly;

(b) that the symposium to be published on this subject was to be made available to the members of that Section;

(c) that the World Council is now represented by three members on the Committee on the Christian Approach to the Jews;

(d) but that it had not proved possible to give such full and concentrated attention to this subject as it deserves in view of its inherent importance; and decided that this subject should be fully discussed at one of the first meetings of the Joint Committee after the summer of 1954 and that the Committee on the Christian Approach to the Jews be asked to prepare for the Joint Committee the documentation required for this discussion.

V

THE COUNCIL'S MEMBERSHIP

The Assembly voted to admit to membership the Dutch Reformed Church in South Africa of the Cape Province and the Bantu Presbyterian Church of South Africa. The former, with a membership of approximately 290,000, was the largest of its communion in the Cape Province. The other had submitted its application in 1953 as "a daughter of the Church of Scotland." It had about 50,000 communicants. It was described as "the one church in South Africa in which European missionaries served an African congregation."

These new accessions brought to 163 the number of denominations in the World Council of Churches. At the adjournment of the Second Assembly, the membership role included:

Australasia

Methodist Church of Australasia

Australia

Church of England in Australia and Tasmania
Congregational Union of Australia
Federal Conference of Churches of Christ in Australia
Presbyterian Church of Australia

Austria

Evangelische Kirche A. u. H. B. in Oesterreich (Evangelical Church of the Augsburgian and Helvetic Confession)

Belgium

Église chrétienne missionaire belge (Belgian Christian Missionary Church)
Union des Églises évangéliques protestantes de Belgique (Union of Protestant Evangelical Churches of Belgium)

Brazil

Federaçao sinodal (Federation of Lutheran Synods)
Igreja methodista do Brasil (Methodist Church of Brazil)

Canada

Churches of Christ (Disciples)
Church of England in Canada
Presbyterian Church in Canada
United Church of Canada
Yearly Meeting of the Society of Friends

Ceylon

Methodist Church in Ceylon

China

China Baptist Council
Chung Hua Chi-Tu Chiao-hui (Church of Christ in China)
Chung Hua Sheng Kung Hui (Church in China)
North China Kung Li Hui (North China Congregational Church)

Cyprus

Church of Cyprus

Czechoslovakia

Ceskobratska Cirkev Ecangelicka (Evangelical Church of Czech Brethren)
Evangelicka Cirkev A. V. na Slovensku (Evangelical Church in Slovakia, Augsburgian Confession)
Ref. Cirkev na Slovensku (Reformed Christian Church in Slovakia)

Denmark

Baptist Union of Denmark
Den Evangelislutherske Folkekirke i Danmark (Church of Denmark)

Egypt

Coptic Orthodox Church
Patriarchate of Alexandria

Ethiopia

Ethiopian Church

Finland

Suomen Evangelis-luterilainen Kirkko (Evangelical Lutheran Church of Finland)

Formosa

Tai-oan Ki-tok Tiu-lo Kau-hoe (Presbyterian Church in Formosa)

France

Église de la confession d'Augsbourg, d'Alsace et de Lorraine (Evangelical Church of the Augsburgian Confession in Alsace and Lorraine)
Église évangélique luthérienne de France (Evangelical Lutheran Church of France)
Église réformée d'Alsace et de Lorraine (Reformed Church of Alsace and Lorraine)
Église réformée de France (Reformed Church of France)

Germany

Altkatholische Kirche in Deutschland (Old Catholic Church in Germany)
Evangelische Brueder-Unitaet (Moravian Church)
Evangelische Kirche in Deutschland (Evangelical Church in Germany)
Evangelische Kirche von Berlin-Brandenburg
Pommersche evangelische Kirche
Evangelische Kirche von Schlesien
Evangelische Kirche der Kirchenprovinz Sachsen
Evangelische Kirche von Westfalen
Evangelische Kirche im Rheinland
[1]Evangelisch-lutherische Landeskirche Sachsens

[1] These Churches are directly members of the World Council of Churches in accordance with the resolution of the General Synod of the United Evangelical Lutheran Church of Germany, dated 27th January 1949, which recommended that the member Churches of the United Evangelical Lutheran Church should make the following declaration to the Council of the Evangelical Church in Germany concerning their relation to the World Council of Churches:
"The Evangelical Church in Germany had made it clear through its constitution

*Evangelisch-lutherische Landeskirche Hannovers
*Evangelisch-lutherische Kirche in Bayern
*Evangelisch-lutherische in Thüringen
*Evangelisch-lutherische Landeskirche Schleswig-Holsteins
*Evangelisch-lutherische Landeskirche im Hamburgischen Staate
*Evangelisch-lutherische Landeskirche Mecklenburgs
*Evangelisch-lutherische Kirche in Lübeck
*Baunschweigische evangelisch-lutherische Landeskirche
*Evangelisch-lutherische Landeskirche in Schaumburg-Lippe
Evangelische Landeskirche in Württemberg
Evangelisch-lutherische Kirche in Oldenburg
Evangelisch-lutherische Landeskirche Eutin
Evangelische Kirche in Hessen und Nassau
Evangelische Landeskirche in Kurhessen-Waldeck
Vereinigte evangelisch-protestantische Landeskirche Badens
Vereinigte protestantische Kirche der Pfalz
Evangelische Landeskirche Anhalts
Bremische Evangelische Kirche
Evangelisch-reformierte Kirche in Nordwestdeutschland
Lippische Landeskirche
Vereinigung der deutschen Mennonitengemeinden (Mennonite Church)

Gold Coast
Presbyterian Church of the Gold Coast

Greece
Ekklesia tes Ellados (Church of Greece)
Greek Evangelical Church

Hungary
A Magyarorszagi Evangelikus Egyhaz (Lutheran Church of Hungary)
A Magyarorszagi Reformatus Egyhaz (Reformed Church of Hungary)

Iceland
Evangelical Church of Iceland

India
Church of India, Pakistan, Burma, and Ceylon
Church of South India
Federation of Evangelical Lutheran Churches in India
Mar Thoma Syrian Church of Malabar
Orthodox Syrian Church of Malabar Catholicate
United Church of Northern India and Pakistan

Indonesia
Geredja Kalimantan Evangelis (Church of Kalimantan)
Gredja Keristen di Soelawesi Tengah (Toradja Church)
Gredja Kristen Djawi Wetan (East Java Church)
Geredja Masehi Indjili di Minahasa (Church of Minahassa)

---

that it is a federation (Bund) of confessionally determined Churches. Moreover, the conditions of membership of the World Council of Churches have been determined at the Assembly in Amsterdam. Therefore, this Evangelical Lutheran Church declares concerning its membership in the World Council of Churches:

"(i) It is represented in the World Council as a Church of the Evangelical Lutheran confession.

"(ii) Representatives which it sends to the World Council of Churches are to be identified as Evangelical Lutherans.

"(iii) Within the limits of the competence of the Evangelical Church of Germany it is represented in the World Council through the intermediary of the Council of the Evangelical Church in Germany."

Gredja Masehi Indjili di Timoer (Protestant Church of Timor)
Hoeria Kristen Batak Protestant (Batak Church of Sumatra)
Geredja Keristen Djawa di Djawa Tengah (Javanese Christian Churches in Central Java)
Geredja Protestant Maluku (Church of the Moluccas)
Protestantse Kerk in Indonesie (Protestant Church in Indonesia)

Iran
Synod of the Evangelical Churches of North Iran

Italy
Chiesa Evangelica Methodista d'Italia (Evangelical Methodist Church of Italy)
Chiesa Evangelica Valdese (Waldensian Church)

Japan
Nippon Kirisuto Kyodan (United Church of Christ)
Nippon Sei Ko Khai (Anglican Church in Japan)

Jordan
Greek Orthodox Patriarchate of Jerusalem

Korea
Korean Methodist Church
Presbyterian Church of Korea

Lebanon (see also Syria)
Union of the Armenian Evangelical Churches in the Near East

Mexico
Iglesia Methodista de Mexico (Methodist Church of Mexico)

Netherlands
Algemene Doopsgezinde Societeit (General Mennonite Society)
Bond van Vrije Evangelische Gemeenten in Nederland (Union of Free Evangelical Congregations)
Evangelisch Lutherse Kerk (Evangelical Lutheran Church)
Nederlands Hervormde Kerk (Dutch Reformed Church)
Oud-Katholieke Kerk (Old Catholic Church)
Remonstrantse Broederschap (Arminian Church)
Unie van Baptisten Gemeenten in Nederland (Union of Baptist Congregations in the Netherlands)

New Zealand
Associated Churches of Christ in New Zealand
Baptist Union of New Zealand
Church of the Province of New Zealand (Church of England)
Congregational Union of New Zealand
Methodist Church of New Zealand
Presbyterian Church of New Zealand

Norway
Norske Kirke (Church of Norway)

Philippine Islands
United Church of Christ in the Philippines

Poland
Kosciol Ewangelicko-Augsburski w Polsce (Evangelical Church of the Augsburgian Confession in Poland)
Polski Naradoway Kosciol Katholicki (Catholic Church of Poland)

Rumania
Biserica Lutherana Ungara din Romania (Hungarian Lutheran Church in Rumania)
Biserica Protestanta Evangelica di Romania dupa Confesiunea dela Augsburg (Protestant Evangelical Church, Augsburgian Confession)

Biserica Reformata din Romania (Transylvanian Reformed Church)

South Africa

Bantu Presbyterian Church of South Africa
Church of the Province of South Africa (Anglican)
Congregational Union of South Africa
Methodist Church of South Africa
Ned. Gereformeerde Kerk van de Kaap Provinsie (Dutch Reformed Church of South Africa of the Cape Province)
Ned. Hervormde of Gereformeerde Kerk van Zuid-Afrika in Transvaal (Dutch Reformed Church of South Africa in Transvaal)
Nederduits Hervormde Kerk van Afrika (Dutch Reformed Church of Africa)
Presbyterian Church of South Africa

Spain

Iglesia Evangélica Española (Spanish Evangelical Church)

Sweden

Svenska Kyrkan (Church of Sweden)
Svenska Missions Förbundet (Mission Covenant Church of Sweden)

Switzerland

Christkatholische Kirche der Schweiz (Old Catholic Church)
Schweizerischer Evangelischer Kirchenbund (Swiss Protestant Church Federation)

Syria (see also Lebanon)

Evangelical Synod of Syria and Lebanon
Greek Orthodox Patriarchate of Antioch

Thailand

Church of Christ in Thailand

Turkey

Ecumenical Patriarchate of Constantinople

United Kingdom and Eire

Baptist Union of Great Britain and Ireland
Baptist Union of Scotland
Churches of Christ in Great Britain and Ireland
Church of England
Church of Ireland
Church of Scotland
Church of Wales
Congregational Union of England and Wales
Congregational Union of Scotland
Episcopal Church in Scotland
Methodist Church
Methodist Church in Ireland
Moravian Church in Great Britain and Ireland
Presbyterian Church in England
Presbyterian Church in Ireland
Presbyterian Church in Wales
Salvation Army
United Free Church of Scotland

United States of America

African Methodist Episcopal Church
African Methodist Episcopal Zion Church
American Baptist Convention
American Evangelical Lutheran Church
American Lutheran Church

Augustana Evangelical Lutheran Church
Christian Methodist Episcopal Church
Church of the Brethren
Congregational Christian Churches of the United States of America
Evangelical and Reformed Church
Evangelical United Brethren Church
Holy Apostolic Catholic Church of the East (Assyrians)
International Convention of Disciples of Christ
Methodist Church
Moravian Church in America (Northern Province)
Moravian Church in America (Southern Province)
National Baptist Convention, U.S.A., Inc.
Polish National Catholic Church of America
Presbyterian Church in the United States
Presbyterian Church in the United States of America
Protestant Episcopal Church
Reformed Church in America
The Religious Society of Friends:
Five Years Meeting of Friends
General Conference of the Religious Society of Friends
Religious Society of Friends of Philadelphia and Vicinity
Rumanian Orthodox Episcopate of America
Russian Orthodox Greek Catholic Church of North America
Seventh Day Baptist General Conference
Syrian Antiochian Orthodox Church (Archdiocese of New York and all North Amreica)
United Evangelical Lutheran Church
United Lutheran Church in America
United Presbyterian Church of North America

West Africa
Church of the Province of West Africa

West Indies
Anglican Church of the West Indies

Yugoslavia
Reformed Christian Church of Yugoslavia

Other Churches
Eesti Ev. Lut. Usu Kiriku (Estonian Evangelical Lutheran Church)
Lietuvos Ev. Reformatu Baznycia (Lithuanian Reformed Church)

Part Seven

AFTER EVANSTON

INTRODUCTION

Evanston was further evidence that the denominations in the World Council of Churches had grown into an international community with cohesion to maintain itself and to carry on an extensive work, in spite of tensions within its membership and attacks from without.

Anyone who understood the nature of the ecumenical movement could only have credited the Second Assembly with having been, on the whole, an extraordinarily successful achievement. It demonstrated that the churches could discuss controversial questions of theology and social philosophy frankly and fully, without organizational disruption or failure of goodwill. It accomplished a far-reaching revision of the framework of the World Council of Churches and made provision for implementing the new structure. It disposed of an agendum covering the Council's numerous concerns with greater dispatch and unanimity than might have been expected of a gathering of such size and diversity. It created by its actions a more widespread interest in interchurch movements, giving them a larger place in the day-to-day news reports and lifting the World Council of Churches in particular further on the way of becoming "like a city that is set on a hill." [1] Most importantly, it stimulated in many local congregations responsiveness and initiative in cooperation to a degree not previously manifest. That it marked the beginning of a new accession of confidence on the part of ecumenical leaders could be seen increasingly as the months passed and the results of its decisions appeared. Five years after Evanston—in 1959—Bishop Henry Knox Sherrill, Chairman of the United States Conference of the World Council

[1] "Activities of the World Council of Churches are news. The Council can no longer be kept out of the papers, even if it wishes to be." (New York Office Report, Central Committee Minutes, 1960, p. 151.)

"The goodwill generated by the Assembly makes our task easier. Even fierce criticism constitutes a point of interest, a negative area to be filled with accurate information. There may never be a meeting as big as Evanston again. Yet Evanston has set the stage for on-going daily work. The result is an increasing comprehension of 'what the ecumenical movement is all about.'" (Central Committee Minutes, 1955, p. 112—Department of Information.)

of Churches and a member of the Presidium of the Council, was moved to write, "It cannot be said too strongly that the World Council is a growing concern." [2]

[2] In a New Year's message to American Friends of the World Council of Churches.

I

THE CENTRAL COMMITTEE

1. Program and Activities

The expanding program came to focus in the deliberations and transactions of the Central Committee, the governing body of the Council between Assemblies, which continued the practice of going for its annual meetings to different countries, with the purpose of forming living contacts with as many of the churches as possible and so strengthening their sense of belonging to the larger fellowship.

The Executive Committee, which met semiannually, followed the same plan.

On these occasions, local, national, and regional interchurch bodies usually joined in providing the facilities for entertainment, governments sometimes assisting. The latter joined also in welcoming the conferees with appropriate ceremonies.

Members of the committees, divisions, and departments accepted invitations to speak in the churches accessible to the places of meeting and thus to meet their clergy and people.

When necessary, representatives of the World Council could confer with local denominational officials on problems growing out of their relations with the ecumenical movement. In one instance, at least, the government of the country was involved. In Hungary officers of the Council discussed with the political authorities the removal by the state of certain ecclesiastical leaders from office and the disadvantages this action had created for the Hungarian churches, from the standpoint of their relations with the World Council of Churches.

The calendar of post-Evanston meetings of the Central Committee was as follows:

1954—Evanston, Illinois, U.S.A.
1955—Davos-Platz, the Grisons, Switzerland.
1956—Galyatetö, Hungary.
1957—New Haven, Connecticut, U.S.A.
1958—Nyborg Strand, Odense, Denmark.
1959—Rhodes, Greece.

1960—St. Andrews, Scotland.
1961—New Delhi, India.

The Executive Committee met during this same period at

1955—Geneva, Switzerland.
Davos-Platz, Switzerland.
1956—Gibulla, Australia.
Vienna, Austria.
1957—Geneva, Switzerland.
Greenwich, Connecticut, U.S.A.
1958—London, England.
Nyborg Strand, Odense, Denmark.
1959—Geneva, Switzerland.
Kifissia, Greece.
1960—Buenos Aires, Argentina.
St. Andrews, Scotland.
1961—Geneva, Switzerland.
New Delhi, India.

The Executive Committee was composed of twelve members elected by the Central Committee from its own membership and, in addition, the Chairman and Vice-Chairman of the Central Committee.

The Central Committee itself consisted of the ninety elective members, as provided by the Constitution, and the six Presidents of the World Council; but its sessions were attended also by appointive consultants, fraternal delegates, and invited observers from other religious bodies, interchurch and confessional.

The divisions and departments of the World Council, and likewise the various subcommittees, adopted the plan of holding their annual conferences simultaneously at, or within easy reach of, the Central Committee's meeting places, having—as they did—to consult one another on interrelated matters and to submit reports of their proceedings and plans to the governing body.

When convened thus, these groups, with their staff representatives, constituted from year to year a temporary community of several hundred members, as at Rhodes in 1959, when more than four hundred persons were present. Their gathering was, in itself, always newsworthy and frequently was accorded front-page mention by the press in many parts of the world, with occasional significant editorial comment.

2. Personnel Changes

Evanston marked the beginning of a period of many changes in World Council official personnel.

Of those elected to the Central Committee by the Second Assembly, only twenty-three had previously served as members of that body; and in the other rosters of the World Council the replacement of old names by new became the order.

The founders and first officials of the World Council had belonged, for the most part, to the senior administrative echelons of the member denominations, and retirement and death consequently took a heavy toll during the early years. By 1957 two decades had passed since the organization of the Provisional Committee; and 1958 was the tenth anniversary of Amsterdam. In the septennium between Evanston and New Delhi, the names of John R. Mott, John Foster Dulles, George Kennedy Allen Bell, Eivind Josef Berggrav, Pierre Maury, Archbishop Michael, John Baillie, Ingve Torgny Brilioth, Max Huber, Hans Scofield, Walter Freytag, Walter W. Van Kirk, Peter Dagadu, Ulrich van Beyma, and Henry A. Atkinson were added to the necrologies.

Fear was felt lest the loss of so many leaders interrupt the continuity of the work and have other hurtful effects. It was found, however, that successors generally brought to their appointments capability and loyalty productive of counterbalancing gains. The meeting of the Central Committee at Davos-Platz in the summer of 1955 gave some immediate assurance on that score. The number of persons on committees of one kind or another and in the various other official posts was much larger under the new plan of organization adopted by the Second Assembly than formerly, and there had been doubt that nearly two hundred individuals living in widely separated parts of the world could be got together for necessary briefing and consultation. The fact that all committees and other groups were present at Davos-Platz with working quorums—some with their entire memberships responding to roll call—greatly strengthened the confidence the Evanston Assembly had inspired.

The retirement of other prominent leaders—such as Alphons Koechlin and Robert C. Mackie of the Division of Inter-Church Aid and Service to Refugees, Hendrik Kraemer of the Ecumenical Institute, Nils Ehrenström of the Division of Studies, Oliver Stratford Tomkins of the Faith and Order Commission, and Henry Smith Leiper and Samuel McCrea Cavert of the General Secretariat[1]—could be accepted, if regretfully, with gratitude that their counsel would still be available to the World Council.

Among those chosen to fill vacancies caused by retirals were Leslie Cooke, General Secretary of the Congregational Union of England and Wales; Francis House, who had served on the staff of the World Council of Churches prior to the Amsterdam Assembly; H. H. Wolf of the School of Theology, Bielefield, Germany; Roswell P. Barnes of the National Council of the Churches of Christ in the United States of America; R. Keith Bridston; and Hans-Rudi Weber. In the order as named here, these became Associate General Secretary of the World Council of Churches and Director of the Division of Inter-Church Aid

[1] There were other retirals, of course, from time to time during this period.

and Service to Refugees; Associate General Secretary and Director of the Division of Ecumenical Action; Director of the Ecumenical Institute; Executive Secretary in the United States of America; Executive Secretary of the Department of Faith and Order;[2] Executive Secretary of the Department of Work for the Laity.

Bishop James of Malta, who had been the Orthodox representative at the Geneva headquarters of the World Council, was elected by the Central Committee to the vacancy in the Presidium resulting from the death of Archbishop Michael, whom he had succeeded in the Archbishopric of his Church for North and South America.

The General Secretary recalled in his report to the Central Committee at New Haven in 1957 an entry in the minutes of the historic Westfield College meeting,[3] to the effect that the World Council of Churches, at that time still to be organized, must deserve and win, if it was to be successful, the respect of the denominations to the degree that their members of greatest ability and influence would be willing to support and serve it," and asked whether this condition had been fulfilled.

> The fact that we are now holding the tenth annual meeting of the Central Committee must not tempt us to make congratulatory speeches [he said], but we should be ungrateful, if we did not answer that question affirmatively. It is no small thing that it has proved possible to bring together year after year—and that in the one period when busy men deserve holidays—the leaders of so many churches. And if we add those churchmen who participate in our committees, conferences and study-courses, we can say that for a large number of men and women in responsible positions in the churches or in various professions the existence of the World Council has meant a . . . change in their lives . . . which adds considerably to their burdens.

Continuing, Dr. Visser 't Hooft spoke of the importance the meetings of the Central Committee had "for the whole life of the Council," aside from the discharge of executive functions:

> They enable the Council to keep in close touch with . . . many of its member churches; they protect the staff against the danger of "Genevese secretariocracy"; and, what is even more important, through the discussion of central themes . . . and through worship they form that ecumenical ethos and . . . theology which we find it so hard to define, but which is very real, and without which there would no longer be an ecumenical movement, but only ecumenical machinery.

[2] Dr. Bridston resigned toward the end of this septennium and was succeeded by Dr. Paul S. Minear.

[3] At Westfield College in London, England, in July of 1937, thirty-odd ecumenical leaders met and decided to recommend to the Oxford Conference on Church, Community and State, about to be convened, and the Second World Conference on Faith and Order, which would be held in August of that year in Edinburgh, Scotland, that steps be taken to merge the Life and Work and Faith and Order Movements in one organization to be called "World Council of Churches," or some such name (Part Two, Section I, *1*).

3. Central Themes

The "central themes" for these years, to which the General Secretary referred, included

1955—"Implications of Christian Unity for Inter-Church Aid and Assistance to Under-developed Countries."
"The Various Meanings of Unity and the Unity Which the World Council Seeks to Promote."
1956—"Christian Witness, Proselytism and Religious Liberty in the Setting of the World Council of Churches."
"The Churches and the Building of a Responsible International Society."
1957—"The Calling of the Church to Witness and to Serve."
"The Significance of the Eastern and Western Traditions within Christendom."
1959—"The Role of the World Council with Regard to Unity."
"The Population Problem."

The meeting of the Central Committee in 1958 was given over to the discussion of reports on some of the special subjects assigned to divisions, departments, or committees for investigation. In this rather long list appeared

"Christians and the Prevention of War in an Atomic Age."
"The Nature and Limits of the World Council's Program."
"The Lordship of Jesus Christ over the World and the Church."
"The Theology of Evangelism."
"The Place and Use of the Bible in the Life and Activities of the Churches."
"The Word of God and the Living Faiths of Men."
"The Christian Concern in Economic and Social Developments."
"Our Common Christian Responsibility toward Areas of Rapid Social Change."

The studies undertaken related to emphases of the World Council's program and were helpful in preparing the Central Committee for effective deliberation. The method of inquiry and discussion made for unanimity in decisions, or—when agreement could not be reached—for clear definition of differences. At the same time, the themes chosen looked to the theological orientation of contemplated tasks.

Examinations of the functions and problems of divisions and departments also proceeded generally within a theological frame of reference; or, at least, there was the growing sense that they must do so if real progress was to be expected.

The views of General Secretary Dr. Visser 't Hooft on this point appear to have been widely shared.[4]

[4] Minutes and Reports of the Central Committee, 1956, p. 71.

It seems to me that the main issue is whether theology and policy, reflection and action, are in step or out of step in our life. . . . We have important theological commissions of "Faith and Order"; we have biblical study of the Lordship of Christ, and these fulfill an important function. But we give little, if any, time to the serious study of the theological problems arising in the life of the World Council itself. . . . It is increasingly clear that many of our structural and organizational problems are essentially theological. The relation of the World Council to the missionary movement, the relation between interchurch aid, on the one hand, and the evangelistic and missionary task, on the other; or the task of the Church in areas of rapid social change, or the vocation of the laity, or the co-operation of men and women, or the question of our Basis, or the whole problem of the ecclesiological implications of the existence of the World Council, or a host of other seemingly practical issues, cannot be clarified, if we do not arrive at a . . . theology concerning the nature and mission of the Church.

That this emphasis came to be accepted generally was shown by the repeated insistence of divisional and departmental committees on their need of theological guidance. The biblical authority for the work expected of them should be defined more clearly, they urged unanimously and repeatedly. In the field of Life and Work particularly was this felt to be imperative.

But an adequate answer to their demand could not be arrived at quickly, if at all. Had the World Council a large enough budget to attempt and carry through the studies required? More important, had it, or could it enlist, the scholars? If found, would the theologians be able to agree?

On this last point, ecumenical experience was far from reassuring. The Bible could be depended on to draw Christians together devotionally. Whatever their denominational persuasions, each claimed its spiritual authority. In any case, its deep religious and moral insights answered to their own. When the delegates to Lund [5] could not make further progress toward unity by talking about doctrinal differences, they found it a relief to read the Bible together. This they could do as they might have joined in singing a great hymn. In its pages of tragedy and hope the voice of the Eternal became audible above the dry rustle of commentaries. But this experience could easily have been misleading. It suggested that they should "return to the Bible" and make it central in their study; and this could only head them again into the old controversies over exegesis and doctrine, in which no common understanding would probably ever be reached. That way they would only learn once more that the Bible became a book of confusion when men insisted on trying to make it more than a sanctuary of the Voice, where all might wait together in humility to hear what the Lord God would speak.

To many of the most earnest workers, a pragmatic approach to the problem of authority appeared, for this reason, to promise more. Might

[5] The Third World Conference on Faith and Order in 1952.

it not be the way of the Spirit of the Scriptures, they asked, to reveal the dynamic and unifying interpretation as the churches took up the ecumenical task together?

From this standpoint, it was believed that participation by the churches in the study programs would prove productive of new insights. In any case, the pulpit and the pew would have to be helped to advance with the World Council, or it would not get far on the way to its goal. There may have been some impatient and self-confident leaders of the Council who were not unwilling for the cause to be identified with their own theological and sociological theories; but it would apparently have to be said that the more responsible wished the people of the churches at large to have opportunity to make their contribution and endeavored to bring them into the study process.

To this end, reports of important discussions in the Central Committee were made available to them through denominational offices and other channels, for reading and criticising. Such attempts at much-talked-about "grass-roots" education revealed, however, that it was a long way from Geneva to the local parishes, and that when this distance had been negotiated the problem of getting an informed response still remained unsolved. It called for means of two-way communication, largely non-existent, and for instruction, for which there were not enough interested and competent teachers. The task would be long—discouragingly so—and time would not be less fleeting for the fact that it was the Lord's work. There had been encouragement, as observed, in the readiness at the local level since Evanston to listen and even to ask for information; but this was augury more for the longer future and eased but little the immediate frustration.

II

MAJOR AREAS OF TENSION

From the beginning of the ecumenical movement four major areas of tension had been noted in its relation to the churches and to the world. Within the World Council were unresolved problems between Protestant and Orthodox members—between the Eastern and Western traditions of Christianity. Between the World Council and Rome there continued to exist the massive separation that had marked the relation of Rome to Orthodoxy since the first millennium of the church's history and of Rome to non-Roman Western Christianity since the sixteenth century.

For the World Council and its member churches, as indeed for the entire world, there were two main centers of social and political tension. One was the remarkable growth in power and dimension of world communism. The other lay in the explosive quality of so much of twentieth-century life—most marked in Asia and Africa, in what have come to be singled out as "areas of rapid social change," but noticeable everywhere. What had the churches to say to these problems? Indeed, in what ways were the churches themselves being modified by such rapidly accelerating dissolution of familiar patterns of human cooperation?

1. The Churches and Rapid Social Change

From Lucknow, in 1953, the Central Committee had sent a letter to the denominations belonging to the World Council of Churches, drawing attention to the acute social problems of Asia. In the Second Assembly, the following year, both that continent and Africa had been spotlighted by reports and addresses descriptive of their needs.

Acutely aware of the fatefulness for the rest of the world of what would happen in the immediate future in these vast and populous continents, the Evanston program committee had scheduled a number of informative addresses to bring the delegates up to date on what was happening in the thinking and movement of their peoples. Some of these throw light upon the developing policies and activities of the World Council of Churches.

We turn first to the report of Dr. Rajah B. Manikam as Secretary of the World Council of Churches and the International Missionary Council for East Asia. "To declare that the multitudes which inhabit East Asia are today caught in the terrific maelstrom of a gigantic revolution may sound trite," he said, "but it is the stark and stirring truth." In elaboration of this condition he spoke as follows:[1]

More than half the world's population living in the area between Karachi and Tokyo is today involved in a major political, economic and social revolution. Probably the greatest single development of the twentieth century, this revolution has broken the hold of the West over the countries of Asia and is now rapidly changing the conditions of life in these countries. Never before have so many millions of people taken part in such a rapid and radical social upheaval.

Within the last ten years, six new nations have been born—the Philippines in 1946; India and Pakistan in 1947; Burma and Ceylon in 1948; and Indonesia in 1949. The combined populations of these lands amount to something over five hundred seventy millions. . . . Struggle for independence is going on in other parts of East Asia which are not yet free.

Asia is a crucial area . . . with regard to economic development, for on this depends the achievement of a higher standard of living and a greater measure of social justice for hundreds of millions of people. Asia has the lowest per capita production and income levels in the world. The threat of population outstripping food resources is ever present. The East Asian nations are fast becoming industrialized. Five-year and ten-year plans are being implemented with material and technical aid from the West and the United Nations organizations. Yet rapid industrialization brings in its wake many serious problems, both human and economic, similar to those that Europe faced in the early years of its industrial revolution.

The ancient East, instead of "letting the legions thunder past and plunging into slumber again," has become wide awake. The candle and the cocoanut oil lamp are yielding to the electric bulb. This alone is enough to transform the life of a people who went to bed with the fall of the night. But now the "talkie" and the dance hall, the cocktail party and the night club characterize the life after sunset in all the cities and most of the towns. . . . It is not the king nor the clan . . . that is assuming importance . . . , but the individual. Asian collectivism is fast yielding place to individualism, and often to modern utilitarianism.

We are also witnessing a gigantic process of revolutionary change in the indigenous cultures . . . consequent upon the impact of ideas and institutions of the West. The rigid social structure built upon the acceptance of the vertical lines of family authority is being challenged. In most countries . . . where women had been in virtual bondage, women's movements have registered phenomenal growth. Public education is receiving more attention; the importance of the village school . . . cannot be over-emphasized. The crucial problems of health and better provision of medical facilities are being tackled vigorously. Caste and class distinctions are losing their hold on the people. The radio is bringing the village new information, ideas and insights. . . . The growth of the vernacular press is another recent significant development. The Church . . . has a glorious role to play in this setting. In itself, the Asian Church is an interesting sociological unit, as it has

[1] The text of Dr. Manikam's report and the other statements at Evanston included in this section, were issued on mimeographed sheets at the Assembly.

drawn into itself converts from all castes and classes, and is therefore best fitted to create a classless society.

Dr. Manikam spoke of "the religious aspects of the Asian context in which the churches . . . find themselves, and the chief issues arising for them."

> With the single exception of the Philippines, the churches . . . Roman and non-Roman, are small minorities amidst vast non-Christian communities. In three of the large countries . . . , India, China and Japan, the proportion of Christians to their population stands at two, one, and a half of one per cent, respectively. In Vietnam it reaches ten per cent, in Ceylon eight and eight-tenths, and in Indonesia four. Out of twelve hundred thirty millions of people who inhabit East Asia, roughly only forty millions are Christians. . . . Out of one-hundred East Asians, only three are Christians, and of these only one is a non-Roman. The Roman Church is larger than the non-Roman in the Philippines, Vietnam, Ceylon, East Pakistan, China, Malaya, and Thailand. . . . The non-Roman Church is larger in Japan, Korea, Taiwan, Indonesia and Burma. The two are approximately equal in India and West Pakistan.
>
> One of the surprising facts . . . is that there is a Christian church in each of the major countries of East Asia. . . .
>
> In spite of the strong forces of opposition to Christianity in many countries of East Asia, everyone recognizes that it has come to stay. It is in the process of being domesticated. . . . Christians, on the whole, now command the respect of their non-Christian brethren.
>
> The Christian congregation, whether in Calcutta, Djakarta or Tokyo, is a unique social phenomenon. There is nothing like it in any of the non-Christian societies. . . . Proclaiming the transcendent Word of God and being a community of grace in tension with the political, economic and social orders . . . the Christian congregations have a revolutionary significance. . . . Not many of them give today evidence of that quality of life that is expected of them. . . . Yet, they have taken root . . . and in many countries withstood persecution and even martyrdom. Many of their members have been in the forefront of movements for national liberation, social reform and economic uplift.
>
> East Asia is the home of Hinduism, Buddhism and Confucianism. It contains four great non-Christian cultures—Hindu, Buddhist, Confucian and Islamic. . . . It has also . . . one-half of the Christians of all mission lands, and more than eighty-five per cent of mission colleges, high schools and hospitals.
>
> Hinduism holds sway over three hundred millions in India. Buddhism is . . . dominant . . . [in] Ceylon, Burma, Thailand, China, Korea, Formosa and Japan. Pakistan and Indonesia are Muslim. . . . In recent years these age-old religions have become resurgent. Nationalism has taken on a religious coloring. . . . The churches . . . have now to confront those who look upon their traditional religion with a new understanding and attempt to re-think it in modern terms, discarding what is untenable and proclaiming boldly that which is of value as being the equal of any other religion, especially Christianity. . . . The churches . . . should no longer ignore these modern developments in non-Christian religions but establish centres for their study.

Dr. Manikam referred to the feeling of Asians that Christianity is an appendage of Western sovereignty and civilization and said that "some governments had begun to limit the entry and work of foreign missionaries," demanding that they leave their primary calling to native Christians. "A sadly divided Protestant Christianity is a severe handicap in East Asia," he said, "and becomes an enigma to non-Christians." This condition has been increased by a new influx of sects in recent years. In Japan alone, the presence of more than fifty such groups has been reported since the Second World War. Taiwan, Hong Kong, and Singapore and India have had a similar visitation. These Christians exhibit great evangelistic zeal, but their divisive tendencies make more difficult a united witness. "However, it is a matter for rejoicing," he said, "that under the guidance of the International Missionary Council national Christian councils in each of the major countries . . . enlist and bind together Christians of different denominations in common projects of . . . co-operation and witness." For the average Asian Christian, the ecumenical movement as exemplified by the World Council of Churches and the International Missionary Council has, he asserted, a powerful attraction.

Dr. Manikam concluded by referring to "the unfinished task."

> There are vast areas in Asia with five to ten million people who have never heard the Gospel, nor have had a church built among them. Relatively few from Islam, Buddhism and higher Hinduism have come to the Christian Church. Most of the accessions to the churches have been from the lower strata of society. A number of ethnic and racial groups have not been reached by the Christian message. Many areas of life in East Asia have not been Christianized. Afghanistan, the Asiatic regions of the U.S.S.R., and some areas bordering on the Himalayas are closed to Christianity. The Church in China has been cut off from fellowship with the rest of the Church. . . . Ancient religions have taken on a new lease on life and defy the exclusive claims of Christianity. A militant communism preaches that religion is the opiate of the people and wills to destroy it. Secularism and atheism are gaining ground alongside the revival of ancient religions.
>
> Against these tremendous odds the Church . . . does not have adequate resources either in personnel or finance, and therefore it cannot but beckon to its partners to come to its aid.
>
> A new chapter in the missionary history of East Asia is being written . . . and . . . fills one with hope. In recent years, . . . churches have sent their own sons and daughters to other Asian countries as missionaries. . . . The Church in China in its early period sent its missionaries to the tribes known as Mias and Lolos . . . , to minister also in Malaya and Indonesia. The work of the Chinese and Foreign Missionary Union is well known. Before the last war, the Church in Japan sent . . . ministers . . . to the churches in Manchuria, the South Sea Islands, Korea, Taiwan and Okinawa. There existed also in Japan some overseas missionary societies, such as the East Asia Missionary Society, the Overseas Missionary Society and the South Seas Island Mission.
>
> Recently the Tamil Lutheran Church of India sent an Indian doctor as a

medical missionary to the Bakak-land in Sumatra, and an Indian theological professor to the Sipoholon Seminary of the Batak Church. The Church of South India has sent an Indian couple to Papua as its missionaries. There is an Indian working in the Y.M.C.A. in Indonesia. The United Church of Christ in the Philippines has sent a Filipino couple to Indonesia and another couple to Thailand. The United Church of North India has revived its plan to send an Indian couple to East Africa. The Methodist churches of the Philippines and Malaya are doing missionary work in Okinawa and Borneo, respectively. Several Christian Bataks, Ambonese and Minahassans are working . . . in the neighboring islands of Indonesia. The Church of Vietnam has nine couples . . . among the tribes in Indo-China. A Cambodian Christian is preaching the Gospel among . . . fellow Cambodians in Surin, Thailand. The Episcopal Church in Japan has opened missionary work in Okinawa. The Kyodan of Japan is making arrangements to send a missionary to Amami Ooshima, an island . . . between Japan and Okinawa. . . .

Churches in . . . the West have frequently urged their governments to give economic and technical assistance to Asian nations. These are significant beginnings in ecumenical co-operation, but they are only beginnings. The needs of Asia are so overwhelming, the tensions so acute and the human resources of the churches so meagre, that nothing less is needed than the fullest possible use of ecumenical funds and personnel in an ecumenical way.

In an address to the accredited visitors (alternate delegates) on "Christians in the Struggle for Responsible Society in India Today," Rev. M. M. Thomas, describing briefly "fundamental changes in the structure and conception of every aspect of social life" in his country, asked what the responsibility of Christians was in "such a revolutionary situation" and discussed the answer to this question by the churches, insofar as it had been agreed upon.

Christians constituting a minority in India of some two percent—about eight millions in a population of four hundred millions—resisted successfully the temptation "to follow the path of fear of the non-Christian majority and to become exclusive and narrow and seek special safeguards for the Christian community as a minority in the nation," because they considered that attitude "both unChristian and unwise." They had chosen, he said, to work with non-Christians "for the good of the whole nation and for justice for man as man, and not to be an exclusive community concerned with its own rights." They were "concerned with social justice; that is to say, with the development of social conditions in which human dignity and freedom can find their expression as befits the nature and destiny of man as a child of God." They believed that they could "present the Christian understanding of man as directly relevant to the search for the new foundations for society and exercise their prophetic ministry, only if they [were] concerned primarily, not with themselves, but with justice to all men and co-operate with all men of good will in their struggle to build a more responsible society."

"It was this attitude," he explained, "that led the Christian community in India to give up voluntarily all special minority rights of communal representation they were offered, and to ask to be considered citizens without any special protective safeguards, along with the rest of the people." Action from this standpoint had been their "contribution as Christians to the building up of a secular state as opposed to a Hindu state . . . based on the fundamental rights of the human person as a person, whatever . . . his religion, . . . and . . . conceiving all citizens, Hindus, Moslems or Christians, as . . . having equal rights under the law."

"In a country where militant Hindu communalism and an equally militant Muslim communalism have led to Hindu-Muslim riots at the dawn of independence causing the massacre of thousands, Christians have the first and foremost duty," he declared, "to strengthen the hands of those working for the establishment of a secular state." They "must make their . . . witness, not through a Christian political party . . . , but in and through secular parties in which they are free to bring their . . . faith to bear upon the problems of society. . . . If the Christian faith has a more realistic understanding of man and society, as we do believe, it must express itself in the insights Christians as citizens bring to the common pool in the . . . struggle of a responsible society where human freedom and social justice are real."

Mr. Thomas proceeded to show how this approach had "shaped the Christians' attitude to two specific problems, namely, religious freedom and economic revolution."

The fact that the Constitution of India recognized the right of every citizen to "preach, practise and propagate" his religion had resulted, he thought, from the action of Christians who had been able to convince "the important leaders of the nations that religious freedom [was] the condition and guardian of all other freedoms," and, with help from the churches outside the nation, when faced with the stupendous task of relief and rehabilitation of the refugees in the early days of independence, had demonstrated that they were a patriotic community prepared to forget themselves in the service of the country.

"The demand of the awakened people for a higher standard of living and for a . . . realization of equality and community" called, he said, for radical changes in the economic structure. There would have to be a liquidation of "landlordism and other feudal property-relations," to satisfy the hunger of peasants for land.

The problem of unemployment and under-employment raises in a technically under-developed and largely agricultural country, the whole question of industrialization and the means for it. All these revolutions—the liquidation of feudalism, the development of industrialization, the realization of social welfare—pressing simultaneously raise the one question that everyone is asking. . . . Can we effect these revolutionary changes through democratic means? Will democracy and revolutionary dynamics mix? Communism says they cannot and asks the people to choose the Chinese way as the only effective way of making the revolution. Extreme anti-communists like the aggressive Hindu nationalists fight both political democracy and economic change, because both are revolutionary forces which threaten feudal vested interests.

Democratic social revolution is the only answer to the totalitarianism of the right and the left. . . . And Christians . . . are getting more . . . convinced about this. A group of Christians produced a book recently under the auspices of the National Christian Council . . . called *Communism and the Social Revolution in India—a Christian Interpretation*. The main point they make is that the basic social revolution . . . should be distinctly differentiated from communism, and that it is the positive Christian concern for the revolution seeking social justice that leads Christians to oppose communism; that we should oppose communism, not because it is revolutionary, but because it betrays the revolution by turning it into a new oppression.

. . . .

Concluding, let me say a word about India's role in international politics. India feels that both for itself and for many other nations, this is a period of positive social reconstruction; and that the only effective way of fighting against totalitarianism of any hue, fascist or communist, is in the long run to remove the social causes that make totalitarian solutions attractive. Even in the short run, one cannot depend too much on the military solution of problems created by the revolt of whole nations and peoples and classes. So we are not convinced that the polarization of the world into two armed camps achieves the objectives of strengthening democracy in the world. On the contrary, it weakens the forces of reconstruction and reduces the resources for developing positive social health among the nations. And Christians in India, in their very concern for freedom and justice, support Nehru in his striving for a Third Area of Peace in the world, . . . in which a positive social alternative to war and tyranny may be worked out.

One of the oldest Christian councils is that of the West Africa Gold Coast, and its General Secretary, Rev. Peter Dagadu, addressed the Assembly at a plenary session on questions "raised in the minds of Africans by their contact with the West," which had to be answered, he said, if the churches and the governments were to prevent "racial, economic and political forces from moving toward further conflict."

"Africa is no more a continent of dark mystery peopled with primitive folk," he said. "It has hit the headlines of the world's press because of its contact with the West. . . . It has tasted the fruits of Western civilization and Christianity, and the effect on its life has been tremendous." Agricultural, educational, political, economic, industrial, military, and religious elements of the West "have poured in a flood-tide upon Africans," he explained, "and under the impact of these forces the external and spiritual features of . . . life have already been profoundly changed."

Africa was appreciative and grateful, he declared, "above all for the light of Christianity," which was dispelling superstition, fear of the unknown, "and many other things which in the past [had] cast a shadow on the continent." But there was a woeful misunderstanding of the African, he held, which had been caused by representatives of the West engaged in commercial, political, and missionary enterprises who had too often left in their reports the impression that he was "an indolent fellow, lying under a cocoanut or a banana tree, shaded from the tropical sun and waiting for the fruit to ripen and fall." Actually, he said, Africans do "all the unskilled and semi-skilled work and much of the skilled work as artisans, except where the color bar and discrimination prevent this." They drive cars, trucks, and tractors; increasing numbers are teachers, doctors, lawyers, ministers of religion, and public officials, while hundreds hold college and university degrees from leading British and American institutions. In addition, Africa provides the world with great quantities of its rich gifts of gold, diamonds, copper and cocoa "because Africans do the work." And their resources of materials and labor could be matched, he declared, "by their potential moral and spiritual contributions."

While Europe and America had won their freedom by war and were trying to gain peace through the use of force, he said, Africans had sought to win peace and freedom by patience and goodwill, except when forced by stress of circumstances to employ means of violence.

> The care of each other for the family, his clan and his tribe, and the concern of the whole tribe for each member are facts of African life imperfectly understood and difficult to adjust to Western individualism. Christian churches through the missions have found great resources of faith, zeal and sacrificial service in African personal, family and communal life. To many Africans, Western ignorance of this picture of . . . life is very bewildering. He feels that he has not been well interpreted . . . and . . . this situation makes it impossible for the average man of the West to estimate the true worth and value of the African, thus denying him the basic consideration for vital relationships which adequate knowledge and understanding could establish.

Mr. Dagadu commented on "the wonderful achievements of the West toward more civilized living. However, he said, Africa had been "sorely disappointed" by the "destructive wars in every generation" in which the West had involved her people. "Western science having made the world a small place by its facilities of transport and communication, it has become impossible for Africa to live in peaceful isolation when the West is involved in war." Because it "cannot escape the devastating effects of the atomic and hydrogen warfare any more than people in New York, London or Hiroshima," Africa often asks, "Are these material things we see in Western civilization for the good of mankind or for human destruction?"

More than that, he said, Africa is dissatisfied because, while the repercussions of war affect her equally with the rest of the world, she is not allowed to share fully in the discussions relative to war affairs. "We are still treated as primitive people who must always be patronized," he complained. "The leaders of the West discuss the grave problems of war at conference tables in Washington, London, Paris, Berlin and Geneva. Africa will no longer be contented with this sort of patronage. Her political, religious and commercial leaders want to sit side by side with the Western leaders to decide their future and the future of the world." Africans want to have "a full share in the management of their own affairs."

In his opinion, the political struggle which was going on in different parts of the continent had been "prompted by the suspicion that the patronage of the Western world [was] fraught with unbridled elements of superiority and imperialism." The African realized, he continued, that in spite of all the proof he had given of his ability to develop his talents, when allowed full opportunity, various types of discrimination against his color and prejudice were noticeable in varying degree in French West, East, and South Africa. This, added to the treatment of the Negro in the United States, constituted, he thought, "a negation of the basic Christian Gospel of the Fatherhood of God and the brotherhood of man."

While he did not have sufficient knowledge of the facts, he confessed, to arrive at a confident judgment in the matter, the speaker expressed the opinion that the primitive organizations of the Mau Mau had been able to withstand the most modern weapons of war for many months mainly because they believed they were fighting against the arrogance of the West, toward which bitterness had piled up to unlimited dimensions and which they were prepared to try to overthrow at any cost.

Africa shared the West's disapproval of communism, according to Mr. Dagadu; but he warned the Assembly that the economic and industrial approach to life in his country by the Westerner provided the conditions under which communism would thrive, if it came to Africa. In this connection, he spoke specifically of the exploitation of natural resources, the poor circumstances of laborers on account of low wages, the color bar, and wage discrimination in industry and trade.

> As Christians we know that communism is evil, but such practices . . . water the soil for the seeds of communism to germinate, were they to be scattered. . . . They [the African people] are asking which system of philosophy or religion and which government will help them get a larger share of the benefits that arise from their land and their labor. The Christian way of life and the democratic order of society must meet that critical choice. Colored people all over the world are watching what is being done in Africa.

The speaker discussed the position of the churches in African life, which in his opinion left much to be desired. "It is in the light of Christianity that we can measure our true advancement growing out of our contact with the West," he said; but the division of Christian forces was a great weakness giving his people impressions of strife and competition when they needed examples of unity and cooperation. He described the split between Protestants and Roman Catholics as a great scandal and declared that the disunity of the Protestant churches failed in fostering the spirit of love and mutual helpfulness on a basis equal even to that of the African communal system. Christianity was being called in some quarters the servant of the policy of divide-and-rule imported by the West for political ends and was regarded "as having small value for Africa's new spiritual life." He dwelt on denominational competition in missionary activity and the rise of numerous sects in Africa as examples of "the cost of disunity," for which his country was "paying a high price."

It was "painful to the Africans," he continued, that Christians of the West regarded some things as spiritual and others as secular, when for themselves life was one and all life sacred. It was discouraging, he thought, "to accept a religion with all the power and promise of Christianity and then to find that this Gospel as so generally practised in the West [was] expected to control only a part of life and not to enter into what [were] called secular aspects of life"—politics, industry, labor, and "other examples of oppression."

The acquisition by the Western churches of land in Africa for missionary purposes "exercise[d] the mind of the average native Christian," Mr. Dagadu remarked, because the local churches were permitted to use it only by agreement in "Edinburgh, London or Basle." "If this Christian Gospel cannot deal effectively with these urgent problems of politics, industry, labor, wages and land acquisition," he declared, "then it is not relevant to the life of the present-day African."

Concluding, he urged missionaries to "hasten their Africanization policy," in order to overtake political advances. "The training for Christian leadership," he said, "must now be a peculiar duty of the Church so as to capture the initiative from the secular forces. . . ." Church members of the West must live more convincingly by Christian standards, he urged, so that African youth studying abroad would not return home with scientific training but no sense of Christian responsibility. Otherwise, he warned, "they will be the very people who will go back to Africa to undermine all for which you are sending men and money. . . . The hope for Africa is with men and women of the West and of Africa who are living witness of the miracle of conversion to Christ. They alone can unlock the doors of the Continent of the future, and answer the questions Africa is asking of the West."

At the same plenary session Dr. Charles Malik, Ambassador of Lebanon to the United States and a delegate of the Greek Orthodox Patriarchate of Antioch, addressed the Evanston Assembly, having for his subject "Asia and Africa Ask Searching Questions."

"The relation of Asia and Africa to the outside world" presented "problems of political freedom, economic development, and social and racial justice," he said, for which there was no "neat solution," every one requiring "profound political, social and scientific analysis" and even then often defying all efforts to find "a way out." "The duty of the Christian is . . . to identify himself with the cause of truth, justice, and being everywhere, as best he sees and understands these . . . , leaving the issue to God. . . . If the Christian of the West cannot always determine policy, he certainly . . . should help promote . . . a more adequate knowledge of the facts."

Asia and Africa will develop their own social and political forms. These will not be the same as those known in the West. The place and mode of existence of the individual, . . . the family, . . . the corporate organization, . . . government and law, and . . . the production and possession of wealth, all these will vary . . . from the Western norms. Asia and Africa demand that they enjoy the necessary freedom to develop their own institutions . . . to be themselves. . . . The important thing is not uniformity of culture but the growth of an international and intercultural order wherein every people and every culture will freely develop its own genius as much as possible, . . . subject . . . only to four conditions:

That no culture or nation encroach upon another;

That . . . they all voluntarily enter into some universal juridical order;

That there be free interchange of ideas and goods among them; and

That the enjoyment of a certain indispensable minimum of fundamental human rights be guaranteed within each of them.

The point of free interchange of ideas and goods is that this is the only way of avoiding putrefaction, stagnation, error, false self-sufficiency, for cultures have a chance to correct themselves and grow and truth has a chance to assert itself only in an atmosphere of exposure to freedom and light. And the point of human rights is the . . . question whether there is not a fundamental, natural core of . . . freedoms defining our very dignity as human beings, . . . which cannot be derogated from, no matter how compelling the circumstances or diverse the cultures. . . . And foremost among the freedoms to be ensured . . . is [that] of thought and conscience . . . that no arbitrary, external, social or political impediment be placed before man in his . . . quest after truth. The freedom needed is not the questionable [one] of being, but the genuine freedom of becoming. It is a mockery of man, of truth and of God if after much suffering a man sees in freedom more light and still . . . cannot open the window and let it in.

The important question he said, is "what is going to happen to the mind and soul of Asia and Africa." Political, social, and economic problems are as "nothing compared to the intellectual and spiritual. . . . The greatest fallacy of the present age" is "that the mind, the spirit, the soul of man, the fundamental bent of his will is derivative from, subordinate to, and a function of his economic and social existence. . . . The real challenge of Asia and Africa is of an intellectual and spiritual order."

Like the other reporters and interpreters of Asia and Africa, Dr. Malik considered science and technology indispensable to their development, disciplines which they lack and must learn from Europe and "the two offshoots of Europe—America and the Soviet Union." They "must ultimately depend upon one or more of these three homes of science. It will be decades, and in some cases centuries . . . before [they] can liberate themselves from this scientific dependence. Nor is it certain that such a liberation would be a good thing, even if it were possible. Why should we set continent against continent, race against race, culture against culture in these matters? Why should it not be a good thing to have scientific interdependence in the world?"

The Ambassador here reduced the problem to its theological meaning.

> These matters are ultimately grounded in the fallen nature of man. This is where religion, and especially the Cross and salvation of Jesus Christ, come in. Nations and cultures seek complete self-sufficiency, even in scientific matters, because of the ultimate facts of power, pride, and fear. . . . Only then as people feel they belong to a larger whole which they trust and . . . can call their own . . . will Asia and Africa accept their scientific dependence. . . . All these are spiritual conditions belonging ultimately to the province of God and Christians magnifying the Lord . . . and obeying his commandments to love him with all their hearts and . . . their neighbors as themselves.

However, because "the children of men . . . are not going to be remade tomorrow, despite the presence of the Church in their midst, neither the West is going to reveal to the East its scientific secrets without a price, nor is the East going to acquiesce in a position of permanent scientific inferiority vis-à-vis the West. And this situation is . . . big with tensions. . . ."

On the face of it, the importance of liberal education, of the cultivation of intellectual virtue for its own sake for Asia and Africa is not sufficiently appreciated by Christians, Dr. Malik thought.

> There are tremendous intellectual values, both in the local traditions of Asia and Africa and in the authentic traditions of the West, which . . . should be revived and cultivated, and which can have a great bearing upon the future. The revival of Avicenna and Averroës alone in the Middle East [would] produce an intellectual revolution in one generation. The responsible publication of the world's greatest classics in the major local vernaculars [would] produce an intellectual revolution in less than two generations. A concentrated and sustained attack upon the problems of language so as to close the gap between the language of higher thought and the language of daily life [would] produce in time a considerable economy in the wasteful spiritual agony which creative thinkers in the East . . . undergo. Thousands of Asian and African students come every year to Western centers of learning where they are practically never required to go through and participate in the great banquet of being which is liberal education. They go back proficient in this or that technique, but with hardly any knowledge of the deepest things the Western world . . . has to offer, and with even less critical appreciation of the deepest values of their own culture. . . .
>
> The mind of Asia and Africa demands original and independent atten-

tion. The aim should not be to propagandize this mind or to win it to a particular cause, whether political or religious. If the intention is to indoctrinate it with a view to using it, even if for the best of causes, it will rebel. In any event, such intention is not the way of the Christian. The aim should be to cultivate the highest intellectual virtue, in freedom and equality.

Western secular leadership had failed the world intellectually and spiritually, Dr. Malik declared. It was too encumbered with problems and with the consideration of means.

If it be said that it is not its office to lead in these realms, then I answer: let those whose office this is come forward and speak. Let them articulate the long-awaited message and carry it in mighty works beyond the confines of their study. For it is a fact that, for the most part, only spiritless secularism reaches the world.

In their demand for a message, a living message dealing with the final things, Asia and Africa pose their greatest challenge. This is the test at once of our faith, of our hope and of our charity. For if we really believe, if we really hope, and if we really love, then God's will will be done on earth. The shrivelling up of the genuine universal is the greatest agony of this age.

Communism can never be opposed in Asia and Africa by a mere negation. The cultural and racial continuities between the Communist world and Asia and Africa, and the cultural and racial discontinuities between Asia and Africa and the Christian world, these two things are too great and too mutually re-inforcing for communism to be swept back only by negation. At the present rate of spiritual impotence, with the protective covering of the hydrogen bomb, it is only a matter of time before the whole of Asia and Africa, and maybe even Europe, will be engulfed by communism.

What is desperately needed, besides the highest political wisdom, is a ringing positive message, one of reality, of truth and of hope. Communism exposes the inadequacy, if not indeed the bankruptcy, of the Western-imperialistic and the smug-Christian approach of the past. Something infinitely more humble, more profound, more positively out-reaching, something touching the hearts of men, touching their need for fellowship and understanding and love, for being included and . . . trusted, something providing them with real hope . . . for themselves and their children, hope in this life as well as in the next . . . is needed. This something is Jesus Christ, the Risen Lord.

The missionary movement must be intensified. The Eastern churches must be loved and helped. . . . The spiritually rich must come down and carry the Cross. And there should be faith in the sufficiency of the simple story of the Gospel, without the embellishments of dialectics and philosophy.

It was announced after the Assembly that John D. Rockefeller, Jr., had made available $250,000 [2] to finance a survey by the World Council of Churches and associated ecumenical organizations of social and religious conditions in underdeveloped areas where the problems growing out of rapid change were most acute. The continents of Asia and Africa would come within the scope of this vast project, according to

[2] This amount was increased in 1958 to $2,000,000.

the report, the study probably commencing with certain African communities.[3]

A widely representative consultation in New York, in January, 1955, which had been arranged by the Division of Inter-Church Aid and Service to Refugees, reached certain conclusions relative to the general conditions in Africa and Asia, as recorded in the reports of the Central Committee for the year:

The churches of Asia and Africa are being profoundly affected by the rapid and revolutionary changes in the society of which they are a part. No relief action should be taken which is not related to this fact.

There are great needs in many areas today, created, not only by natural causes, such as floods and droughts, but also by the changing structure of society, due to the rapid advance of industrialization. The churches throughout the world have a responsibility to help in these areas of need.

While no relief action must be taken without consultation with the churches in the area, . . . they must not be asked to undertake actions which would cause them to be regarded as identifying themselves with foreign interests.

Emergency Inter-Church Aid and Relief must always be regarded in the light of the permanent witness of the church, and should be linked with the study of the Christian responsibility for the social development of economically under-developed countries.

The Department on Church and Society had already launched a study of these areas, from the standpoint of the Christian responsibility. The report of the Division of Inter-Church Aid and Service to Refugees to the Central Committee at Davos-Platz in 1955 suggested that "the pursuit of this study, nationally and regionally, as well as internationally, should provide guidance for those dealing with emergency problems . . . and throw light upon the whole missionary task." It added, "For the moment, we can surely say that it is folly to concentrate on ameliorating the worst effects of social change, and not to enable the churches to see the part they must play within that process, so alarming in its rapidity and so overwhelming in its results."

The Department on Church and Society submitted, at the same time, a statement on "Our Common Christian Responsibility toward Areas of Rapid Social Change," which included Latin American countries with those of Asia and Africa and outlined this "main study" to which it would address itself during the next three years. The document bore the subtitle, "A Study of the Meaning of Responsible Emancipation," which,

[3] "The Council's newly organized Division of Studies assumed special responsibility in relation to such 'areas of rapid social change' as Asia, Africa and Latin America. With the help of a substantial grant (the major part of a total of $250,000 to the World Council from John D. Rockefeller, Jr.) the Division set up a three-year survey of the problems of 'bread, freedom and dignity' as they concern people on every continent. The study was to be closely integrated with several units of the Council, such as the Division of Inter-Church Aid, the Department of Missionary Studies and the Commission of the Churches on International Affairs." (*The Ecumenical Courier,* January and February, 1956, p. 2.)

it was suggested, reflected the ecumenical view that the social awakening in these designated troubled parts of the world, having "come about through the impact of Western technology, education and religion," would "find its creative fulfillment in the development both of a better community life and of human solidarity" only if the West recognized an obligation to support in every way it could the constructive forces working in the revolutionary ferment. "Bread, freedom and dignity for the large masses of people who are denied them," the conclusion was, "can be faced as world problems." The Davos-Platz Minutes continued (p. 103):

> Of special concern is the contrast between prosperity and poverty in the world. . . . Two-thirds of the world's population are living in . . . poverty, disease and misery. The new realization that a better life is possible makes the disparity a question of moral injustice, and the economic and social well-being of the peoples of the world comes as a fundamental moral challenge to the whole world. . . . And the Christian Gospel has a direct . . . relevance to this obligation of world community. . . .
>
> The churches in the lands of rapid social change have the task of making their witness to the lordship of Christ . . . from within the revolutionary process. The responsibility of the churches in Western lands is no less fundamental. It is in this context that the churches in every land can make use of the ecumenical movement, because it helps us to face the situation within a world-wide fellowship. The fact that we are members one of another and confront these difficulties together places new obligations on us all. . . .
>
> The churches and the ecumenical movement have become increasingly aware in recent years of the social implications of their faith and have stated on numerous occasions their concern for responsible society in a world perspective. Through missions, . . . programs of interchurch aid and work for international assistance and peace, the ecumenical movement has sought to give practical expression to this concern. However, there is today a further need for interpreting Christian concern in relation to particular social issues. . . . Therefore, the World Council is launching this study of the common Christian responsibility toward areas of rapid social change.

The inquiry would have two objectives:

- To enable the indigenous churches to make a concerted investigation under their own native leaders of the developing new social problems, in order to see more clearly the Christian responsibility for political, economic and social life, and to guide any alterations that needed to be made in the Church's structure in the light of its social missions; and
- To help Christians in the West understand their responsibility in the evolution of healthy political institutions, the development of the economic welfare and the building of a new community life in the countries concerned.

These aims could be achieved best, the assumption was, through the ecumenical fellowship, within which the search for the truth in social issues could proceed in a world perspective and an atmosphere of mutual confidence.

It was necessary, according to the statement, to recognize that the churches in many places were weak and confronted by hostile ideologies, secularist forces, or dominant non-Christian religions and therefore could exert only a limited influence on political and social developments; but also that the strength of the Christian witness lay in the knowledge that "the Christian Gospel was mighty, because true."

The plan set forth called for the study of four main phases of the general problem:

The Meaning of Responsible Citizenship.
The Problems of Interrupted Village and Rural Life.
The Problems of Industrialization and Consequent Urbanization.
The Impact of Foreign Enterprise and International Assistance.

In a number of countries, churches and other groups had by 1955, already organized inquiries.

The Working Committee of the Department on Church and Society reported to the Central Committee at Nyborg Strand in 1958 that the program outlines had been "welcomed in churches throughout the world, often in places where a response to the initiative of the World Council might have been least expected." The Department, said its Committee, did not regard this development as "on the periphery of the Church's concern."

Where Christians become more sensitive to what is happening in society, the life of Christ in the Church becomes manifest to men. . . . Where Christians awake to the human impact of city life and industry, where in politics they learn to show forth their witness from day to day, and where men learn to see the hand of God in the midst of unceasing changes that disturb almost every society in the world, there we find action central to the mission of the Church and an essential part of the Church's evangelism.

The study had enlisted social scientists, theologians, and many persons equipped for it by practical experience in their respective spheres. "We believe that this continuous dialogue has been of immense value," said the authors of the report. "We expect it to continue. . . . Many of its fruits are already visible. . . . It involves every concern of the World Council of Churches . . . the changing role of women, the aspirations and frustrations of youth, altered family patterns and rapid population growth."

Study projects had been organized in twelve countries: Brazil, the Cameroons, Egypt, Ghana, India, Indonesia, Japan, Kenya, Lebanon, Liberia, Northern Rhodesia, and the Union of South Africa. In addition, smaller programs had been undertaken in several other nations of Asia and Latin America. In the West—Europe, the United States, Australia, and New Zealand—interest had led to the organization of conferences and study classes.

To effect a coördination of programs and secure exchanges of information and ideas on the issues of rapid social change, several regional meetings had been held. There had been "a consultation" on "The Social Goals of the New Asia" in March, 1957, at Siantar, Sumatra, Indonesia. The All-Africa Church Conference at Ibadan early in 1958 had served the same purpose for that continent; and the "Consultation on Specific European Responsibilities in Relation to Asia and Africa" had occurred in August of the same year at Odense, Denmark, prior to the meeting of the Central Committee of the World Council of Churches at near-by Nyborg Strand.

The European consultation had been attended by "many churchmen from the United States," and the discussion had dealt with matters of common concern in Western nations in relation to the situation in Africa, Asia, and Latin America created by rapid social change. The Department on Church and Society proposed studying the Christian response to social change in the West itself and recommended a conference, to be held in 1960, on "The Impact of Social Change in the Western World."

The reports from the various regional conferences were, without exception, valuable contributions toward a reliable documentary record of conditions characterizing social change, East and West, and an intelligent understanding of the Christian responsibility with reference to them. Especially worthy of mention was the one prepared by the Social Problem Committee of the National Christian Council of Japan on that country and submitted to the World Council's Department on Church and Society as preparatory material for the broader ecumenical study.

The Asian Study Conference at Siantar published its discussions and findings under the title "The Social Goals of New Asia." A full record of the Rhodesia Conference, including major addresses and the Bible studies on race, was prepared for circulation by the Christian Council of Northern Rhodesia.

The Consultation on Specific European Responsibilities in Relation to Asia and Africa discussed ethical issues in the political, economic, and cultural relationship of Europe to the countries comprising the major areas of rapid social change, as well as problems of church and missionary cooperation in these regions. Included in its report were the addresses and a summary of discussions which were of especial importance as presenting in a broad way the point of view of Western churches.

Dr. Egbert de Vries, Director of the Institute of Social Studies at the Hague, had rendered a noteworthy service, it was agreed, as Chairman of the Department on Church and Society, which originated and supervised the general plans of study.

The international conference on "Christian Action in Rapid Social Change: Dilemmas and Opportunities" in Salonika, Greece, July 25-

August 2, 1959, brought together the findings of the many regional and national inquiries and considered further, in a world perspective, the nature of the responsibilities of Christians. With 146 persons in attendance, "it was the largest . . . ecumenical conference since the Evanston Assembly." It was also the most representative gathering of that period, approximately one-half of the participants coming from Asia, Africa and Latin America, and the rest from Europe and North America. The fourteen Africans enrolling were the largest delegation ever to attend an ecumenical meeting from their continent. Locating the Conference at Anatolia College provided new and intimate contacts with the Greek Orthodox Church. The conferees were cordially received by the clergy, the government, and the people. Dividing into three groups, they studied the sub-topics into which the main theme had been divided: "Man in Rapid Social-Cultural Change," "Christian Responsibility in Economic Development," and "Christian Responsibility in Political Action in Rapid Social Change."

In the findings, it was emphasized by Asians and Africans that nationhood was the means by which all peoples had come "to express their own group individuality and make what they considered to be their special contribution to the world." Agreeing, the Conference added that "even a legitimate movement of nationalism expressing the urge for political freedom or for nation-making had in it the seeds of perversion . . . Even the most constructive nationalism needed to be guarded from the domination of destructive tendencies . . . and very often the struggle of the idea and methods of responsible nationalism against irresponsibility within is as acute as its fight against external enemies."[4] Concerning the Christian evaluation of the methods of economic development in communist countries, the Conference said:

> The results already achieved in Russia and the gigantic effort to transform a nation in China make communism appealing as a quick method of achieving economic development, securing structural social changes and satisfying national pride, albeit at a high cost in terms of the dignity and freedom of the human spirit. It is indeed a tragedy that Marxist Communism, which is in so many ways effective in securing social and economic changes, should involve such total ideological claims. These . . . Christians must reject.

The statement then presented over against the communist method the possibilities and problems in truly democratic procedures.

Spokesmen for the Department on Church and Society directing this engrossing study movement felt that it had become "an essential part of the work" of the World Council of Churches. It had renewed the Church's understanding, they said, of the link between evangelism and social action. Bringing Christ to men found expression, they believed,

[4] Minutes of the Central Committee, 1959, pp. 80-82.

in meeting the challenges confronting them in changing societies. One happy result, it was pointed out, had been a redressing of the balance between ecumenical givers and receivers. "Those who came to teach have stayed to learn, and those who learned have become teachers." Study was affecting the life and outlook of many individual Christians. An understanding of social change was bringing a new vitality in meeting the demands of Christian solidarity.

One of the most significant results had been the urge to translate informed concern into practical projects, a number of which had already been begun. This was in the historic tradition of the Church in pioneering to meet change, and not merely following after it. The Committee of the Department was, therefore, confident that the movement would have continuing life, that it was "the beginning of something much greater."

2. The World Council and Communism

The issue of communism had confronted the World Council from the time of its organization at Amsterdam in 1948.

The Russian Orthodox Church, which had been considering favorably the invitation to participate in the First Assembly, was unrepresented, as were the other Eastern Churches in communist countries on the European salient. Twenty-seven delegates and alternates from Protestant communions in these Russian satellites registered, but some of their fellow churchmen who had been designated to attend were denied passports, and at least one was reported to have been detained by what bore the marks of political arrest.[5]

The number of denominations joining in the founding of the World Council of Churches was thus reduced by communist interdiction or influence, as the churches of China which took part were soon afterwards to be cut off and isolated even more completely.

Of the 450 official delegates who had been expected at Amsterdam only 352 arrived. Difficulties arising from currency regulations accounted for the absence of some, and a few may have remained at home because of the widespread fear that the Berlin blockade by the Russians, in progress at the time, might lead to war. But about two-thirds of the ninety-eight vacant seats had been reserved for representatives of Orthodox Churches who did not come.

By its handling of the sub-theme "The Church and the Disorder of Society," Study Section III of the Amsterdam Assembly made communism more explicitly an issue. Its report drew a comparison between capitalism and communism which assessed their promises and failings

[5] Lutheran Bishop Ordass of Hungary, who had been tried and convicted on a charge of violating the currency regulations in transactions with the Lutheran World Federation. See pages 767 and 787.

and advised the churches that it was their Christian duty to reject both systems and to "seek new, creative solutions."

The mention of capitalism turned attention to the United States, as the reference to communism pointed to Soviet Russia, and to many citizens of the former nation at least the comparison was odious, notwithstanding the report's conclusion that capitalism—because of its more civilized treatment of opponents and its openness to correction through democratic processes—was preferable to communism. While granting that it had its faults, many Americans did not think free capitalistic enterprise[6]—which had been the mainstay of most of the countries represented at Amsterdam in their recent life-and-death struggle against totalitarianism—could fairly be put into the same category with a system which was notorious for its despotic expropriations, slave labor, and murderous intrigue. That smacked, they felt, of the easy, undiscriminating judgments by some Europeans that had become rather too common.[7] For example, an article in *The Christian News-Letter* a few months previously had typically thrown the United States and Russia together into the same class of spiritual backwardness, as follows:

> The resemblance [between the United States and Russia] is rooted in certain fundamental characteristics of the modern world which neither has escaped. They both suffer from giganticism. They both show unquestioning confidence in the scientist and the technocrat. They both accept a materialist conception of civilization. They both tend—one consciously and the other unconsciously—to exclude from life the personal, the spiritual and the mystical elements without which man's hold even on his essential humanity seems to grow feeble.[8]

Estimates of this kind were sometimes influenced by personal dislike of Americans, who came in for criticism because of the financial gain of their country from wars which had impoverished other peoples, including its allies. The United States had, admittedly, bestowed upon the ravaged much in the way of charity and financial help of other kinds, but its motive had been misunderstood, even by many of those benefited. In any case, the help which had been given amounted to only a bagatelle, it was said, compared with what the United States had been able to do. What if the American denominations had pledged themselves to underwrite four-fifths of the budget of the World Council of Churches? They could give the whole of it, it might have been said, with less actual sacrifice than the churches of the rest of the world could their one-fifth. In the nations which had been assisted in a material way there were,

[6] It was brought out in the discussion at Amsterdam that capitalism in the United States was no longer of the *laissez-faire* type, and that private enterprise was governmentally regulated.

[7] It was not generally known at the time that the paragraph on capitalism and communism in the report of Section III had been conceived and, for the most part, written by certain American theological professors.

[8] Article by Barbara Ward in the number for July 9, 1947.

undoubtedly, many persons who took a different attitude, but resentment at having had to accept aid affected even some of these; and the fear was universal lest, becoming dependent upon the economy of the United States, their countries might be carried by its rivalry with Soviet Russia into another world war.

In its counsel to the churches to reject capitalism, as well as communism, and to "seek new, creative solutions," the report of Section III at Amsterdam appeared to be prescribing more state socialism of the non-totalitarian kind, and for that most of the people of the United States had no stomach, having already been given large doses of it during wartime and the great depression. At the same time, they were convinced that this kind of prescription had made postwar Europe sick and was fast destroying the resistance of the whole world to the virus of communism. They were frankly rebellious when their social and political doctors, among whom were some of their own ecclesiastical leaders, told them that more of the same treatment was indicated for creating an immunity against epidemic Marxism. They feared that socialism in Europe had already gained a momentum—to change the metaphor—which would be impossible to brake short of communism.[9]

Again six years later, the presence of delegates at Evanston from behind the Iron Curtain caused much questioning in the Assembly and throughout the free world. That they had been permitted to come, while some of their compatriots who had been chosen were refused clearance, seemed to show that they enjoyed the favor of their governments, if they had not actually yielded to them and undertaken the role of "red emissaries." The Assembly accepted them as loyal Christians, in the absence of evidence to the contrary, and accorded them honor for having persevered in the calling of God under adverse circumstances.

It could only have been expected that such consideration toward them would be regarded as softness toward communism. The presence in the Assembly of some delegates from nations outside the Iron Curtain who were suspected of sympathy with communism because of their membership in its so-called front organizations, among them churchmen of eminence in the ecumenical movement as well as in their own denominations, could also only have added to the disquiet.

It was difficult to obtain authoritative information concerning the status of Christian churches in the various communist countries. Their representatives apparently could do little to supply this lack. The Assembly could only suppose that their silences and their imperspicuity when they spoke were attributable to restraints inherent in, if not overtly imposed by, their political involvements.

Dr. Josef L. Hromadka of Czechoslovakia was listened to hopefully

[9] There was general acceptance of the Russian belief that the logical and eventual end of all socialism was communism.

in a main address at one of the plenary sessions. In his charge that Western leadership had failed mankind spiritually and that this failure explained the social and religious crisis he was explicit enough, but on the duty of Christians in the situation he spoke with much less clarity. He appeared to think that communism, if it did not itself promise social salvation, was the inevitable next step. What might come after it he could not see, or did not attempt to predict. He likened the state of the world to that of a local community overwhelmed by sudden disaster which, if it was to be dealt with effectively, called for the surrender of personal freedoms in the interest of the larger public welfare and for consecrated service under such authority as could be established immediately by other than the slower democratic procedures. If he did not favor communism, what he said implied that he did not despair because of it. He wished it understood, he said, that he had not found renunciation of his faith as a Christian necessary under a totalitarian regime.[10]

How could the swift advance of communism be successfully resisted? The Evanston Assembly recommended indirect action. It bade the churches "make Christianity work." By this was meant more than intensifying conventional activities. It envisaged the churches' addressing themselves to a program of social reconstruction which would ameliorate the conditions supposed to be driving into the ranks of communists the faceless multitudes of the world who despaired of getting relief from any other source.

"It is not enough for us to repudiate . . . the atheism of orthodox communism, . . . to reject a philosophy of materialism, . . . to repel . . . the fallacious theory of social development and an abhorrent concept of dictatorship," declared Bishop Oxnam in the opening sermon at Evanston, interpreting the original and accepted policy of the World Council of Churches. "Men who affirm that nothing can separate them from the love of God must renounce the practical atheism that lies in the affirmation that God is not relevant to all the activities of men."

Reduced to terms of social action, the slogan "Let the Church be the Church," which came out of the Conference on Church, Community and State at Oxford in 1937, looked to making "Jesus Christ Lord of all life."

Negatively, the First Assembly in 1948 had warned the churches

[10] In February, 1956, Dr. Hromadka was quoted as having said while on a visit to Australia that "if you mean by communism a certain method of political action and reconstruction on a socialist basis, I believe it is possible to be both a communist and a Christian." (*New York Times,* August 6, 1957.) At the meeting of the Central Committee at New Haven, Connecticut, in August, 1957, his reelection to the Executive Committee was opposed. More than half of the seventy-five members present abstained from voting. He received a majority of the thirty-five votes cast. On this occasion he was charged by fellow delegates with being "an outspoken apologist for communism." It was stated that he had said his allegiance would be to the East, in the event of war between Russia and the Western powers. He denounced the protest of the World Council of Churches against Russia's military suppression of the Hungarian uprising in 1956.

against the counsel from various quarters that communism should be resisted by military measures. Such a course would only increase, it said, the tenacity of the ideology attacked and the misery on which it thrived (See Dulles' remarks, Part Three, Section II).

This advice was widely rejected, Dr. O. Frederick Nolde of the Commission of the Churches on International Affairs reminded the churches as late as 1954 in an address to the Second Assembly. "The demand for a preventive war is not completely stilled, . . ." he said, "and in every walk of life there are those who yield to defeatism and take the position that 'an end with horror is better than horror without end.' Christians must be in the forefront proclaiming that a third world war is not inevitable. It can be avoided. It must be avoided."

Communist and Nazi totalitarianisms were more instrumental than any other factors in presenting the World Council of Churches with its heaviest immediate task: its work with refugees cast adrift in many parts of the world during a generation of hot and cold wars.

This burden had, in fact, assumed large proportions during the Council's provisional period—prior to Amsterdam. While the conditions out of which it developed had begun with the dislocation of whole populations by Naziism and its military actions, the communist powers by their political conquests after World War II, especially in Central Europe and in Asia, had enlarged the streams of these homeless dispossessed with the millions fleeing their tyranny. The knocking of exiles at the doors of the free world for bread and shelter, and for admission—if it might be gained—to new life in settled abodes, was not to cease for many years, perhaps never for the generation then alive. More than a decade after the Amsterdam reports, refugees still were pouring from behind the Iron Curtain into Western Europe at the rate of some three hundred thousand annually. Of the flight into Southeast Asia from the terror inside the Bamboo Curtain accurate records were not available, but observers on the ground spoke of "the migrant millions."

With the full responsibility of the World Council, the Central Committee, after the adjournment of the Assembly at Amsterdam, took up the service to refugees and the work of the several other departments, to find that communism, more than any other external condition, would shape the course it must pursue. It was soon to become evident that scarcely any action could be taken in the name of the World Council of Churches without regard for this massive and all-pervasive pressure upon the society of the whole world, and upon every human concern, from the unending struggle for physical survival and subsistence to the search of the soul for God. At every turn stood communism to challenge the churches—a distorted religion in itself whose mission was the destruction of all other religions; which denied the spiritual being of man, proclaimed a philosophy of materialistic determinism, walked rough-shod over human rights, violated human dignity, showed no pity or forgiveness, turned churches into museums of atheism, or, when suffering them to live, forced upon them restraints calculated to accomplish their ruin without making martyrs of the faithful (subjecting them to governmental control, forbidding the religious education of their people, indoctrinating their youth in its own godless teachings, restricting or abolishing theological training for their ministers, and prohibiting all public and even postal appeals for their financial maintenance).

The Central Committee adopted the policy of supporting through the United Nations and in other ways all efforts to gain recognition and protection by the nations of human rights. This brought it directly into conflict with the totalitarian powers. Of the major subjects engaging its meeting in Chichester, England, in 1949—within less than a year of the Amsterdam Assembly—"the most urgent," as the Chairman, Bishop Bell, reported in *The Ecumenical Review* (October, 1949), "was the position of the churches in communist-controlled countries."

The General Secretary's report made special reference to the deterioration of the situation since September, 1948, to the Communist State's policy of regimentation, and, amongst other things, the complete isolation of the churches in the several countries concerned from their sister churches abroad. The . . . Committee agreed that this subject must be given the first priority. . . . The fact of a common pattern in all the States involved was undisputed [in the debate which ensued]. This was directed at the withering away of Christianity, and the creation of a new type of man through the education of the young in the spirit of Communist ideology and Marxist-Leninist theory, by whatever name, harsh or smooth, but fitted to the particular condition of the place and time. . . . Attention was also called to the background of the general revolutionary situation and the tremendous tensions which had to be faced by people both within and without the churches, the danger of the Church's being turned to as a shelter in which the old world could be recaptured, and the atmosphere of crisis. There was a common conviction that the World Council of Churches had no mandate to make a judgment on the merits of particular economic systems (e.g. Capitalism and Communism, looked at on the economic level), and that the churches could be exploited by quite opposite political interests. Nor was the feeling absent that the churches were themselves often to blame for failure in the achievement of social justice in different parts of the world where the Christian gospel had been preached. . . . There was besides a strong sense of the necessity of maintaining fellowship with all the churches in both East and West, and of consideration for the complex and difficult character of the problem involved for those who had to live on a razor's edge. It was no easy matter to find the right expression when so many elements were involved; and the whole process of reaching the unanimous and representative statement was in itself a valuable experience. But the . . . Committee . . . believed the issue to be [one of] conscience. It felt compelled to declare its deliberate condemnation of totalitarian doctrines and . . . methods, as in fact a denial of absolute moral standards and a moulding of the minds of the young in a pattern utterly opposed to the message of the Gospel.

The pronouncement of the Committee from Chichester had said:[11]

The totalitarian doctrine is a false doctrine. It teaches that in order to gain a social or political end everything is permitted. It maintains the complete self-sufficiency of man. It sets political power in the place of God. It denies the existence of absolute moral standards. It moulds the mind of the young in a pattern opposed to the message of the gospel. It sanctions the use of all manner of means to overthrow all other views and ways of life. . . . We call statesmen and all men who in every nation seek social justice to consider this truth: a peaceable and stable order can only be built upon foundations of righteousness, of right relations between man and God and between man and man. Only the recognition that man has ends and loyalties beyond the State will ensure true justice to the human person.

From its meeting at Biévres in 1951 the Executive Committee said of totalitarianism, referring specifically to communism, "It destroys human integrity and uses the means of slavery in the name of justice. In this respect there is a fundamental conflict between Christian conviction and totalitarian ideology."

In a statement "on the Korean Situation and World Order," issued from Toronto in 1950, the Central Committee spoke, of necessity, directly against the communist powers involved:

An act of aggression has been committed. The United Nations' Commission in Korea, the most objective witness available, asserts that "all evidence points to a calculated, co-ordinated attack prepared and launched with secrecy" by the North Korean troops.

Armed attack as an instrument of national policy is wrong. We therefore commend the United Nations, an instrument of world order, for its prompt decision to meet this aggression and for authorizing a police measure which every member nation should support. . . .

It [the division of Korea] violates fundamental rights and increases the threat to peace. The United Nations has attempted to establish a free, united and independent Korea within the community of nations. Every opportunity, which may arise from the present tragic situation, must be used to gain this end. . . .

Post-war totalitarianism relies not only upon military pressures but also upon a policy of exploiting the distress of the poor, the resentments of subject peoples, discriminations on grounds of race, religion or national origin, the chaos of badly governed nations, and the general disunity between nations. The Korean attack may well be one of a possible series of thrusts at such weak points in the world society.

It was in the Toronto declaration (1950) that the Central Committee (acting with the Commission of the Churches on International Affairs) also branded as "a strategy of propaganda rather than a genuine peace proposal" the Stockholm Appeal for Peace which called for "the outlawing of atomic weapons only, without effective international inspection and control, both immediate and continuous," and admonished

[11] See earlier references to the Central Committee's pronouncements on the subject, 1949-53, Part Five, Section II, p. 371 ff.

those sponsoring it in the words "We must seek peace by cultivating mutual confidence and work for an increasing devotion to common moral principles."

The Stockholm Appeal had been issued in March, 1950, at a meeting of the World Peace Committee, originally called the "World Committee of Partisans for Peace," which had been set up under communist auspices by the First Peace Congress in Paris in April of the previous year. The Stockholm Appeal stated in part:[12]

We demand the total banning of the atomic weapon, the arm of terror and the mass extermination of populations. . . .

We demand the establishment of strict international control to ensure the implementation of the ban. . . .

We consider that any Government which first uses the atomic weapon against any country whatsoever would be committing a crime against humanity and should be dealt with as a war criminal. . . .

We call on all men of goodwill to sign this appeal.

The Central Committee discussed the Appeal at its meeting in Toronto four months later and referred to it in a statement to the churches on the Korean situation and world order:

Such methods of modern warfare as the use of atomic and bacteriological weapons and obliteration bombings involve force and destruction of life on so terrible a scale as to imperil the very basis on which law and civilization can exist. It is, therefore, imperative that they should be banned by international agreement, and we welcome every sincere proposal to this end. However, the "Stockholm Appeal," which demands the outlawing of atomic weapons only, without effective international inspection and control, both immediate and continuous, must be regarded as a strategy of propaganda, rather than a genuine peace proposal. We must seek peace by cultivating mutual confidence and work for an increasing devotion to common moral principles.

Officials of the Commission of the Churches on International Affairs had sent a letter to Christian leaders in many countries, explaining the differences between the positions of the World Peace Committee and the World Council of Churches on desired peace measures. "Strict international control" in the Appeal did not mean, it was pointed out, "continuous control," which the churches believed necessary and evidence of good faith.

The President of the "World Peace Council," M. Joliot-Curie, approached the Presidents of the World Council of Churches in January, 1951, with a bid for support for the appeal by the Second World Congress of the Defenders of Peace that "all kinds of atomic, bacteriological, chemical, toxic, and radio-active weapons, and all other means of

[12]See Minutes and Reports of the Central Committee, 1950, Section 14 h.

mass-destruction be entirely prohibited; and that during 1951 and 1952 there should be a gradual reduction simultaneously and in the same proportion of all armed land, sea, and air forces." The reply of the Council through the Commission of the Churches on International Affairs in February of that year emphasized the necessity of adequate international forces under the United Nations to safeguard the nations against aggression and to enforce international law.

M. Joliot-Curie, in June of the same year, wrote again to the Presidents of the World Council of Churches, apprising them of a new proposal by the World Peace Council of a peace pact by the five great powers.

All these propositions were then considered by the Central Committee at their meeting in Rolle the following August (1951), and the reasons for their rejection were set forth in a communication in the name of the World Council of Churches:

> The churches of the World Council of Churches loathe war. They realize to the full the ruinous consequences with which the world is threatened, should war break out. They, therefore, believe that the utmost efforts should be made at every point possible to prevent war starting, and that, as such efforts are made persistently and sincerely, their cumulative effect in promoting peace will be great. But peace is not a magic condition which can be conjured up by a stroke of the pen. The present acute international tension has lasted too long, and is too complex in origin, to admit of a quick termination, or a simple solution. Nor are they true friends of peace who, while crying out for peace, create strife and so intensify division.

While the Central Committee did not think the issuing of a general peace appeal "a practicable policy or one that would help the general situation," it instructed the Executive Committee and the Commission of the Churches on International Affairs "to watch for opportunities of co-operation on concrete issues where there was some promise of a fruitful intervention on just grounds." These bodies prepared the following formulation of principles for the churches, as recorded in the Annual Reports:

> As Christians it is our duty to seek both peace and justice. We no less than others detest war, and we shall do everything in our power to prevent tensions and limited conflicts from leading to a third world war. Yet, we must neither purchase peace at the price of tyranny, nor in the name of justice look on war as a way to justice or as a ground of hope.
>
> We stand opposed to every form of oppression and aggression. We condemn any extension of oppression, carried on behind a façade of propaganda for peace. We condemn equally the proposal of a preventive war, or the use for aggressive purposes of atomic weapons.
>
> We do not believe that peace will come merely by new pacts or disarmament. There must first be sufficient mutual trust and good faith between nations to ensure that agreements will be honored. Peace and disarmament will follow from mutual trust; they will not automatically create it.

In present world conditions peace and justice require international organs of law and order. We, therefore, fully support all forms of co-operation between the nations which will serve this purpose. Believing that the United Nations and its agencies present now the best means to develop the rule of law over the nations, we condemn unilateral military action in defiance of decisions under the Charter of the United Nations.

We press urgently for the most generous assistance by the wealthier to the poorer nations of the world in their economic and social development, and for the immediate sharing by all nations in responsibility for the millions of refugees.

We believe that it is the duty of all Governments and of the United Nations to recognize the dignity of man as a child of God, and to protect the right of the individual. Every denial of fundamental rights should be made known and resisted.

Christians can witness convincingly to peace only if they and their churches, in their relations with one another across all frontiers, put loyalty to their common Lord above any other loyalty.

There followed on November 24, 1951, a conference in Paris between M. Joliot-Curie and Baron van Asbeck, Chairman of the Commission of the Churches on International Affairs, and certain of their colleagues, at which the matter of their correspondence was discussed and a communiqué issued:

They [the persons present] proceeded to an exchange of information and a clarification of their respective positions on the leading international problems and on their respective modes of approaching these in the total setting of the problem of peace and justice. They examined more particularly the disarmament question, that of the control of atomic weapons and of all weapons of war, and that of peaceful co-existence of different political and social regimes; and other questions, such as the importance which must be attributed for the maintenance of peace to the protection of human rights and to technical assistance for underdeveloped areas.

They decided to proceed to the exchange of documents, and they will consider the advisability of meeting again.

The conference revealed the differences between the conceptions of peace and its attainment held by the representatives of the two movements and removed some misunderstandings. There were no further discussions.

The 1950 Toronto message of the Central Committee to the churches on the Korean action brought about the resignation of Dr. T. C. Chao of the Yenching School of Religion in Peiping, China, as a President of the World Council of Churches. He wrote:

In July last year the Central Committee of the World Council of Churches issued a statement condemning North Korea as aggressor and questioning the motives of the Peace Appeal of the World Peace Congress held at Stockholm. It placed me in a very strange position, for I am one of the presidents of the World Council of Churches, on the one side, and a loyal citizen of the Republic of the Chinese People, on the other. Only recently I came to realize how impossible this position was. As a patriotic Chinese, I must protest against the Toronto message, which sounds so much like the voice of Wall Street, and as a president I should have to endorse the statement. I can no longer be one of the presidents of the World Council. Therefore, I resign from the office and request that my name be deleted from all the Committees of the Council, in which it has been placed. In so doing I want to say that I have complete freedom to affirm my faith in and my loyalty to Jesus Christ, my Lord and Savior. Yours under Christ's grace.

To Dr. Chao, the Central Committee sent the following reply, as recorded in the Minutes for 1951 (page 55):

The World Council accepts your resignation with very real regret. We must add that we do not believe that you have understood the true nature of all the various actions which our Council has taken during recent years. We regret that we cannot discuss these matters with you personally and give you a personal impression of that very real spiritual struggle through which we have gone together as we seek at the same time to voice the implications of Christ's Lordship over the world and to maintain our ecumenical fellowship in which so many different viewpoints are represented. . . . We rejoice that we can together affirm our common faith and . . . loyalty to Jesus Christ, our Lord and Savior. And we express the hope that in spite of all that has happened and [that] may happen we will remain united in the oneness of Christ and in intercession for each other. (Signed by W. A. Visser 't Hooft, General Secretary.)

The pronouncement on the Korean situation drew criticism from the churches of central European countries in the communist orbit. In the meeting of the Central Committee at Rolle, Switzerland, where Dr. Chao's resignation was acted upon (August, 1951), Bishop Albert Bereczky of the Reformed Church of Hungary denounced the course which the World Council had elected to take. The decision had precipitated a crisis for the Council, he said; and he thought there was little hope that the other side could be heard and understood. He continued, in substance:

We take it for granted that there was pressure on Dr. Chao. I do not know him personally, but I am sure that the World Council of Churches did when it elected him President. I am certain that Dr. Chao must have been regarded as a real Christian to be elected to such a high position. He is under pressure, but not the pressure you think. A Christian always acts under God's pressure. Dr. Chao is a Christian, but a Chinese Christian who lives with his people. When he has to decide whether to stay with them or with the World Council the answer is not difficult. Let us not forget that the World Council of Churches is not the Una Sancta, and that remaining in it is not proof of one's loyalty. Why did Dr. Chao make this decision? The source of the decision does not come from Dr. Chao or from Chinese Christians. It comes first because the churches of the West and the World Council of Churches in the West have not understood the world situation accurately. . . .

Secondly, after the great socialist revolution all Christianity has become suspect. Why should it be otherwise? Do we understand that people fighting against the colonial system associate it with Christianity, and if we do understand this do we do so in a spirit of repentance?

If I were Dr. Chao, I could not do otherwise than he has done, in view of the Toronto action.

It must have been very difficult. His decision requires us also to make a decision as a World Council of Churches. We have to decide whether it was a mistake to elect Dr. Chao as President, or whether we do not understand what is happening in China.

It was courageous, right and Christian for him to do what he did. . . . An individual lives in a political and social tension, and we cannot view him without seeing humanity itself. Our task is to achieve what has not been achieved [in] two thousand years—to find a just and peaceful way for the community life of man.

This problem must be understood dialectically: each man has a value, but can live according to God's will only in a community. I am glad that the World Council of Churches tries to work in all parts of the world. But is it not only an illusion? Is it not so that the Oikumene has kept effective contacts in Asia only with countries which are, more or less, Western-minded?

I agree that the main problem of all humanity and of Christendom is the problem of peace. I think that we shall have to discuss this question seriously in the coming days. But now my hope is small. . . . Can we make a statement when we are not united? . . . The report [of the Executive Committee] repeats the Toronto statement, in spite of attacks; the report says nothing about our protests, and does not say a word concerning the fact that the Lutheran and Reformed Churches in Hungary—still members of the World Council of Churches—have protested against the re-militarization of Germany and press for the recognition of China.

Bishop Bereczky concluded: "I, therefore, have three requests to make: that my name be removed from the Commission of the Churches on International Affairs; [and] . . . from the Sub-Committee on the Missionary and Ecumenical Calling of the Church; and that I be listed not as a member of the Central Committee, but as an observer."

Three years after his statement at Rolle, Bishop Bereczky of Hungary was among a group of Iron Curtain churchmen who were granted permission by the United States Department of State to attend the Second Assembly at Evanston. His presence and that of the other Hungarian delegates was the cause of some controversy. In addition to Bishop Bereczky, the other four delegates from Hungary were Bishop Laszlo Dezsery and Bishop Lajos Vetoe of the Lutheran Church, and Dr. Laszlo Pap and Bishop Janos Peter of the Reformed Church of Hungary.

Granted permission at the same time were six delegates from Czechoslovakia: Dr. Josef L. Hromadka and Dr. Victor Hajek of the Evangelical Church of Czech Brethren; Bishop Jan Chabada, Dr. Jan Michalko and Generalinspektor Andre Ziak of the Evangelical Church of Slovakia, Augsburgian Confession; and Bishop Emerich Varga of the Reformed Christian Church in Slovakia. Admitted also were Bishop Karol Kotula and Professor Victor Niemczyk of the Evangelical Church of Poland, Augsburgian Confession. From East Germany came Bishop Ernest Hornig of the Evangelical Church in Silesia and Dr. Guenter Jacobs, General Superintendent of the Evangelical Union Church in Berlin-Brandenburg. There were also six delegates, three consultants, and an accredited visitor from West Berlin, most of whom were in some way associated with churches in eastern Germany, among them Bishop Otto Dibelius of the Evangelical Union Church, President of the Evangelical Church in Germany.

Four denominations in China and three in Rumania were not represented.

Of those from churches behind the Iron Curtain, Bishop Jan Chabada and Dr. Josef L. Hromadka of Czechoslovakia and Bishop Lajos Vetoe and Professor Laszlo Pap of Hungary were elected to the Central Committee. Bishop Dibelius, whose jurisdiction extended into East Germany, was chosen a member of the Presidium.

The Department of State restricted the privileges of Bishop Janos Peter to the journey to Evanston and participation as a delegate in the Assembly. There was no explanation of this action.

The Honorable Alvin Bentley, Chairman of the Sub-Committee of the House of Representatives on Communist Aggression, invited the Hungarian delegates to testify at a hearing in Washington. Their statement at Evanston to the effect that Hungary enjoyed complete religious freedom was in direct conflict, his telegram stated, with testimony by witnesses before the Sub-Committee. "We would like the benefit of your testimony, under oath," he added, "believing that the best way to attain peace . . . is by telling all the people the entire truth." On advice from Assembly authorities, the Hungarian delegates declined the invitation, which Dr. Franklin Clark Fry, Vice-Chairman of the Central Committee of the World Council of Churches, had characterized as "highly improper and unfair." Dr. Fry explained that he was not interested in "protecting Bishop Bereczky or any other person," but was concerned only that the "focus of public opinion might [not] be diverted from the proper objectives of the Assembly."

Bishops Peter and Bereczky and Professor Hromadka were heard in addresses to the Assembly and interviews by newsmen for such information as they might give concerning their experiences as Christian leaders in communist-controlled countries.[13] Said Bishop Peter:

Some impressions gathered during our deliberations and stay here compel us to make some remarks concerning our general attitude with regard to these experiences, and about the relationship of the Hungarian member churches of our World Council. . . . We come from the other side of the world, but not from the other side of the Church. At home, and here, too, we proclaim against all divisions and tensions the unbreakable oneness of the Church. It

[13] See earlier reference to Dr. Hromadka, pp. 754-55. The Hungarian Bishops' remarks appeared in mimeographed form.

is in the conscience of our fellowship—yes, it was in joy and readiness to talk to you that we came here. . . . In the present moment, it would not suit the spirit of our fathering to touch any details of those experiences which have almost eovershadowed these feelings of ours since we arrived. . . . I wish to thank you in the name of our delegation for the profound signs of love we experience here whenever we meet gatherings of church delegates. You know that it is not always easy to understand each other in the actual world situation, but the very fact of our staying together is one of the encouraging signs of the realization that in the churches we already do live in the effective powers of our Lord's coming world. . . .

Expressing his faith that in Christian contacts most of the urgent international problems could be solved, the Bishop continued:

In this connection, I realize that we, coming from the other side of the world, are tempted to represent to you not only the message of the church, but also the way of life we are learning to practise. On the other hand, we often feel also that you, living on this side of the world, are tempted to represent not only the message of the Word but also the way of life to which you are accustomed. We have to learn in the World Council of Churches to speak on political and social issues of international life with more ecumenical-mindedness and in more ecumenical language.

I wish to tell you in the name of my fellow-delegates, also, that we are not very strongly interested in what anybody may say here in criticism of certain human tendencies. We are very much more interested in what we might say in common in a positive way for the solution of our most urgent problems. The reason for this attitude . . . is recognition of the fact that whenever Christianity influenced, or even changed, the trends of history it always happened not so much through its negative statements but rather through its positive witness and service, through which it was able to give a solution to generations living in sorrow. There are signs in the deliberations of these plenary sessions and group meetings which show that this meeting of ours may move toward such influential witnessing and service.

Our churches are thankful for the existence of the World Council of Churches. We have recognized with gratitude that this Council . . . has greatly contributed to strengthening the Christian witness in the Church and around the Church, and in connection with this effect we have also recognized that the World Council has had its heart in lessening international tension. . . .

I am sure we will stay together in order to be free from all misunderstanding, from all thoughts which are not thoughts of our Lord, and in this freedom of our hearts we will hear together what we should tell the world in the face of these problems. We hope that not only our actual staying together but, above all, our moving together in our resolutions and in our worship following our meetings, we will be able to give testimony to the world of the fact that the World Council of Churches is really a World Council and that the member churches are united in the same fellowship, in spite of all tensions and with the effect of lessening the tensions.

Speaking more informally on another occasion, the Bishop asserted that "the Christian church was not bound up with any social system." He admitted that the Hungarian Church was subsidized by the government under an arrangement whereby the amount received was reduced

5 percent every fifth year, thus encouraging the hope of eventual self-support by the Church. The first reduction had gone into effect early that year, he said, and the congregations had increased their contributions in order to make up the difference.

In an interview by the press, he answered many questions. He said, among other things, that "in a certain sense of the word," one could be a communist and a Christian at the same time, and that Christianity could co-exist with communism. He stated that communism was taught in the Hungarian public schools and that religion was too. The newspapers carried religious news and church advertisements, he said, and there were regular broadcasts by radio of religious services. He insisted that he would be free, when he got home, to report objectively the actions of the Assembly. He expressed appreciation, on behalf of the delegation from Hungary, of the "brotherly Christian feeling" which had been manifested toward them by American churchmen at Evanston.

At a meeting of accredited visitors, the Bishop dwelt upon the emphasis of his churches on evangelism. They were better equipped for this work than they had been, he thought, because "the spiritual pattern of . . . divinity students, as reflected in their vocational consciousness and life," was "much better . . . than it was ten or twenty years" earlier. The improvement in this respect had been effected by "replacing the former representatives of theologically indifferent, liberalistic and rationalistic trends" with professors "deeply rooted in the Holy Scriptures, in the historic creeds of the Church, in the present service of the Church, and in the wide fellowship of world Christendom." He noted that "evangelical Christendom" in America assigned "a different task to evangelism than the churches of Europe," which, he explained, lived "amidst the signs of the dissolution of the *corpus Christianorum* [the whole body of Christians]." He said further:

> Evangelism is such a peculiar work of the Church that to have it for discussion in a gathering of various denominations we need the same ecumenical-mindedness that we require when speaking of the sacraments, the conception of the Church, the order of the Church, or apostolic succession. . . . If the Church is actually nourished by the Word of God, . . . its entire life is evangelism—that is, the life-giving sharing of the Gospel of redemption wrought by Jesus Christ and of the new creation with men within and around the Church.

By the "entire life" of the Church, he said he meant preaching, administration of sacraments, charitable work, church discipline, finances —in fact, all activities.

> The cause of evangelism and the cause of ecumenism belong together in Hungary. I may tell you that there is no pulpit in our churches which has failed to voice, in the last months, the grand message of the Word: Christ is the hope of the world.

Proclaiming the Gospel of repentance and sanctification, let us practise together the love of God and the love of our fellow-men, amidst the everyday events of our congregations, and let us have a place in our prayers and service for every true cause of universal Christendom and universal human society.[14]

Appearing before the Assembly at his own request, Bishop Albert Bereczky, whose withdrawal from the Commission of the Churches on International Affairs and the Central Committee in 1952 has been noted earlier, spoke as follows:

In the fellowship of the member churches, which extends over the whole world, the Hungarian Protestant churches prepared expectantly and hopefully for the Second Assembly of the World Council of Churches. We have received many encouraging signs that these hopes will not be unfulfilled. As Bishop Janos Peter expressed it, in the name of the Hungarian delegation, we are coming from one-half of a divided world, but not from another half of the Church. During the course of the last six years, we have never forgotten that promise, which we expressed in Amsterdam—when I had the privilege of taking part in the First Assembly—that we shall remain together. In accordance with our common conviction, we owe this, beyond all doubt, not to our own merits, that we have been able to keep our promise up to now, but to the loving help of God. The very fact that we are in Evanston together obligates us to deep gratitude and to new hope. And the fact that we, after Evanston, not only will remain together, but seeking and recognizing the will of our Lord in healing the most burning problems of our generation, and together in our good works we shall ever go forward. That is the fervent hope of each one of us.

Mr. President, in this spirit I report with joy in the name of the Hungarian delegation, . . . to the effect that we in Hungary are looking forward in the immediate future to an important ecumenical meeting of the World Council of Churches. Details of this matter are the concern of the competent official organs of the World Council of Churches. Without doubt, the members of the Assembly understand the far-reaching significance of the fact that such an opportunity for an ecumenical meeting is offered in Hungary where, within the framework of the World Council of Churches, the churches of the western and eastern parts of the world may confer with full freedom. Permit me to plead fraternally with all of you for your love and prayers in behalf of this good cause. We on our part should like in this way to express our esteem and unbroken hopes for the World Council of Churches.[15]

Long a controversial figure in ecumenical circles, Dr. Josef L. Hromadka of Prague in an interview by newsmen spoke with vigorous assurance of the relation of the Christian churches and communism. He con-

[14] That there were grounds for calling Bishops Peter and Bereczky collaborationists was disclosed by the Hungarian revolution in 1956. With the overthrow of the regime, both were immediately deposed by their Church. Thereupon, Bishop Peter was made head of the Hungarian Cultural Relations Institute. He was denounced as "the worst kind of Stalinist" by some of his fellow churchmen. Bishop Bereczky was replaced by Dr. Ladislaus Ravascz. Later came the announcement that he had "withdrawn from ecclesiastical activities."

[15] See report of the meeting in Hungary, p. 781 ff.

fessed that he was "a man of very definite convictions" and of devotion to the reconstruction of his country, but added, "I have come here to meet my brethren."

He explained that Czechoslovakia was "not a communistic or Marxist state, according to its constitution," but was "presently led by the communist party," which felt "a strong mission to lead the nation toward a new classless society," and admitted that he had "very much to say in favor of this aim." He defended the view that Christians might well discuss their problems with Marxists in a friendly way.

The modern technological world found itself in a spiritual vacuum, because man could make everything and did not believe in anything, and this was where Marxist ideology "stepped in," he said. He saw the danger that some people might regard this new teaching as a religion and declared it was here that the theologians must say, "Stop!"

Questioned whether it was true that he had said that communism was "the wave of the future," as reported, he asserted that he had been misquoted. "I do believe that communism anticipates many things to come," he qualified, adding that this statement should not be oversimplified.

He expressed himself as believing that Christianity might not only prevail against communistic materialism but advance in its social conquests if Christians took their faith seriously. He spoke earnestly in defense of the possibility of co-existence "in a world in a status of civil war—divided on social, economic and political questions." "We are still men," he said, "created by God for unity, and the world is one, despite temporary differences." He called upon Christians "to move forward," unless they would face "a terrible catastrophe."

Speaking to the Assembly on "The Church's Dependence on God and Its Independence from Men," Dr. Hromadka said that "human, civil and political categories of freedom" could not be applied to the Church, which "marches through our secular world avoiding and rejecting self-identification with any human absolute." The Church had no right, he held, "to yield to human standards, to political, social or cultural divisions, to stop before the barriers established by human traditions, prejudices, privileges, aspirations, cultural snobbery and pride. . . . It looked in a majestic freedom, across the divisions of nations, races, political or social systems, struggling against permanent dangers of becoming sterile or senile, petrified and servile." He described all "human absolutes" as "idols, myths and spurious, false truths" and urged that the Church reject "any efforts to look for an absolute evil in any secular institution, in any man, being afraid not so much of a godless world as a godless, Christless altar, pulpit and worship."

The Czech theologian warned of "a terrific danger of religious or metaphysical self-deception" concerning faith in God and his Church.

> The God of Abraham, Isaac and Jacob is the God of sovereign, free grace, bound to no human ideas and institutions, to no temples and orders,

to no human aspirations and achievements, to no theological, dogmatic and moral criteria. There is no sacred place, no human institution that can contain him, get hold of him. However, there is no darkness, no corruption, no wretchedness, no sin, no misery and destitution that can prevent him from being, in his gracious love and compassion, present exactly where no man would dare to expect him. The God in whom we believe according to the prophets and the apostles is beyond all the most sublime thoughts and speculations, beyond all human religions, cults and pious sentiments, beyond all human norms and moral judgments. And yet he is, in his mercy and grace, so near to us as nobody else.

All this meant, he explained, that "the thesis of the dependence of the Church on God [had] nothing to do with . . . academic, theoretical 'truth.'"

. . . Any human ideology, no matter how idealistic and theistic it might be, is nothing else than a human effort to get hold of God, to subordinate him to our thoughts and systems, to use him as our ally in ideological, political and social struggles, to make him a basis of our culture and our way of life; in other words, to make him, through a very subtle and sublime reasoning, dependent on ourselves. The most imperceptible temptation the Church lives in lies in the avowed desire to use God for human ends, to profit from what we call religion, to attain a false security, to convert the faith and cult into safeguards of human earthly treasures and possessions. . . .

The Church could claim "only one genuine freedom and independence," he concluded—"that of self-consecration unto the Lord [and] self-dedication unto men, both of them in the love which casts out fear."

To believe in Jesus Christ is to be where he is and do his work, to be on his side in his continuous struggle with human sin and suffering, with injustice and death, with bigotry and selfishness, with pride and religious self-assurance. . . . The Church's freedom is the freedom in service. Her glory is the glory in humility. Her majestic independence rests in her self-identification with poor, weak, destitute, despised, forsaken men.

Evanston heard another voice from behind the Iron Curtain, that of Dr. H. G. Jacobs, General Superintendent of the Evangelical Union Church in Germany, who came from Cottbus and spoke on "Possibilities for Christian Witness in East Germany."

"The question is how far there is real freedom for the life of the churches today in East Germany," he began. "By East Germany we understand the land situated between the border of the zone and the Oder-Neisse line, and officially designated as the German Democratic Republic." At least 80 percent of the population in this area belonged "organizationally to a Christian confession, most of these to the official Evangelical Church," he said, adding that conditions were "much easier for the churches under 'the new policy' than they were even eighteen months previously." But "the question about the possibilities for Christian witness" could not be confined, he thought, "to the practical life of our Church communities at the present moment. Whatever be the outward manifestations of the confrontation of Church and State, we must go to the heart of the matter." His remarks, as printed in "Selected Addresses from the Accredited Visitors Program," continued:

> Our State consciously embraces the communist ideology. It has a clear-cut program and definite goal: to establish, step by step, the communist social order. It is common knowledge that the communist ideology does not hold the place of a personal *Weltanschauung* of a few citizens; it does appear as a dogma which cannot bear any opposition. . . . Adherents . . . must . . . be intolerant of anybody who does not acknowledge its absolute relevance in matters of life and death. They must be particularly intolerant of . . . Christians who are bound in faith to God . . . and can never approve the communist dogma . . . [which] is faith in mankind's self-redemption through . . . social progress. . . . It is impossible to believe in both our Christian dogma and . . . the . . . communist dogma, which reduces God to a product of a primitive mankind's anxieties and Jesus Christ, at best, to a revolutionary who tragically failed. It is an either-or proposition for any single-minded person: . . . the gulf cannot be bridged. There can be no synthesis.
>
> According to official statements, the Government has no intention of attacking . . . individual religious convictions, provided the believers accept the communist practice and refrain from stirring up public opinion by their confession of faith and their behavior. The State does not want to take any administrative measure against the Christian churches. The communists believe the existence of the Christian religion to be so entangled with certain stages of sociological evolution that education out of these backward stages by gradual scientific and ideological propaganda will necessarily eliminate the basis of existence.
>
> What has been said makes it clear that the soil on which the Christian communities live is volcanic. . . . However, there are not always . . . eruptions. There are also periods of relative stability during which the State postpones attaining a goal on tactical grounds and stops a necessary development from pragmatic considerations. It is at this point that the Church has great opportunities. . . .

Special difficulties in the way of the Church's work were, he explained:

1. The fact that the state schools, which all children must attend, "are explicitly based on the communist creed. . . . Imagine a child who learns in his religious instruction class that God is creator of the world, whereas at school he is assured of the scientific knowledge that the world is all material and as such without beginning or end."
2. The limitations on missionary service, which was reduced to work within the walls of the churches.
3. The governmental monopoly in the opportunities of professional life, "not only for officials, teachers, and members of the police force, but also for workers, peasants . . . shop-keepers, doctors, artisans, technicians and artists. . . . Many people who would like to be

Christians are driven into a conflict which they cannot ultimately sustain."

The Assembly heard also Bishop Otto Dibelius, a President-elect of the World Council of Churches, on the conflict between Christianity and communism. As Bishop of the Evangelical Union Church of Berlin-Brandenburg, he had a jurisdiction three-quarters of which lay in East Germany. In messages to his churches and in other actions he had opposed the police state's methods, violations of justice, the arrest of pastors, and persecutions and threats of suppression of church youth groups. He had also traveled widely in the Soviet zone, in defiance of the communist authorities.

In his address, the Bishop recalled that in 1934 the Confessing Church of Germany had placed itself on record as opposing Adolf Hitler and his National Socialist state as "a God-sent liberator." Although called upon to "place itself clearly and unequivocally at the state's disposal," the Church had "refused to do it." "It did not identify itself and its task with a nationalistic movement," he said. "It knew itself obliged to proclaim the Word of God, regardless as to whether this proclamation pleased or displeased those in power." And members of the Lutheran, Reformed, and United Churches in both East and West Germany still stood behind the statement of Barmen, he said. "The Church has but one Master: Christ. It acknowledges but one authority: the Word of God. The Church has to obey God rather than men. . . . For this conviction we went to prison and to concentration camps."

Because it depended solely upon the Word of God, he continued, the Church was independent of the state. However, its independence could be threatened also, he said, if it became "dependent upon the mercy of rich people, feudal powers, modern slogans or similar pressures." But the Holy Spirit could help the Church through these trials which were "its acid test," he continued. The destiny of the Church would be decided by its being subservient to or remaining steadfastly independent of the state's propaganda and political will.

The Bishop admitted that it was easier to state principles than to live by them, and that the less the Church allowed itself to become dependent on state financial aid, the easier it was for it to keep itself otherwise independent. But a totalitarian state, he warned, would not permit the church to "organize the freedom of its members to sacrifice in the ways common, for example, in the Anglo-Saxon countries. . . . In a totalitarian state the church is not permitted to print even the smallest slip of paper which urges sacrifice, [or] . . . to enter the homes to collect the contributions of the faithful." For this reason, he said, the church in the totalitarian state "will always have limited material assets."

In order to preserve its independence, he continued, the church must rely upon the Word of God. "Daily and urgently it must pray to God

. . . to be at [its] side. Only after [it] becomes independent from the worry over daily bread . . . from the danger of conceit, and . . . from every aspiration toward external power . . . can it rest assured that the Spirit of Jesus Christ is with it still." Living thus, it witnessed that "there is another world, a world over which the state possesses no power and which sets a limitation to its totalitarian demands. *The totalitarian state is really totalitarian only when the church, as a church, no longer exists within its orbit*. If God grants his grace, this shall nowhere happen; this must never happen."

Bishop Dibelius then spoke of the problem for the church when the state demanded compliance with its wishes which were contrary to Christian principles. An example of this was the "elaborately planned propaganda programme for peace" (referring to the recurring "peace" offensives of Soviet-controlled powers). It was remembered in this connection that he had recently refused the invitation of the authorities in East Germany to support their peace crusade. The Church could not join the state, he said, in promoting a "political campaign for peace." Rather, it should say: "Perform your task! As for us . . . we will work for peace within the ambit of our own resources, retaining our loyalty to the word of him who is our peace and our hope, thus holding fast to our independence from you, the state." Although "the state will not understand," and "even among Christians, many will not understand," for the sake of her independence, the Church must remain steadfast. No one who has not lived in a totalitarian state "has any conception of how heavily this burden rests upon the churches," he said, and they can only "pray again and again to God to keep them free from fear of men while making their decisions, so that it becomes apparent to the opponent that the Church does not act out of political reflection, but under the word of God."

Recognizing that there was little "outward help" that could be given the Church in such a struggle, the Bishop concluded with the request of the Apostle Paul to the congregation of Christians in Rome, "that ye strive together with me in your prayers to God for me."[16]

Dr. Gustav W. Heinemann, Mayor of Essen, Germany, and President of the Evangelical Church in Germany, who on invitation of the Patriarch of the Russian Orthodox Church had visited Russia, addressed the accredited visitors of the Assembly. He gave his impressions of the condition of the churches in that country under communism, prefacing his remarks with the statement that the resistance to Hitler had made close allies, in many countries, of Christians and communists, and, while they now were in separate camps, "personal, human solidarity between them

[16] Cf. *Ecumenical Review,* Vol. VIII, No. 4, July 1956, p. 384. Bishop Dibelius retired in 1960 because of age.

need not . . . be severed." His observations touched mainly upon the Orthodox churches, of which there were thought to be some twenty thousand within the Soviet Union:

After years of . . . violent persecution, the Russian Orthodox Church has been living—since 1943—under legally controlled conditions. . . . Three things are forbidden . . . it—instruction of its youth, charitable work, and religious propaganda. Services in church rooms and official acts of the priests (baptisms, weddings, funerals, prayers of intercession) are permitted. . . . After the Revolution of 1917, the Orthodox Church developed the sermon, and . . . reading of the Bible in its services, more than at any time previously. From a singing and praying church it became also a speaking church. . . . It is under the jurisdiction of a particular state bureau, which constitutes the liaison between church and society. All requests . . . for materials [building materials, gasoline, newsprint, etc.] must be cleared by this bureau. Anything . . . other agencies have to settle with the church likewise passes through this bureau. . . .

Church services . . . were crowded. . . . Juveniles . . . can participate . . . and actually do. . . .

Since all real estate . . . belongs to the state, the church can . . . own no property. The state leases the grounds . . . without compensation and for an indefinite period. . . .

The number of baptisms is surprisingly large . . . in the Ukraine . . . ninety percent of . . . newly-born children. On an average it is supposed to be far more than half. Our translator, . . . a confirmed Marxist and atheist . . . whose wife shared his convictions, also had his child baptized. . . . As in the United States, the church lives from voluntary contributions alone. It sells candles for the adoration of the icons, . . . takes up collections in its services, and accepts donations for the official acts of its priests. . . .

The Orthodox Church . . . until 1917 a state church . . . supported the Czaristic regime and . . . exploitation of the peasants. . . . The anti-religious propaganda continues. Schools, universities, newspapers and television . . . all serve Marxism. . . . The Church refrains from every expression concerning official industrial or cultural life . . . and has transferred the loyalty it once showed the Czaristic state to the Bolshevist, . . . apparently more in accordance with their history and theology than any other attitude. I don't believe . . . we should apply our . . . church attitude toward nation and state . . . as a criterion for the Russian Church. . . . The main thing is that Christianity . . . exists in the Soviet Union. . . . It has a hard time. . . . The ecumenical movement is being followed with interest by the Church. . . .

In his report in the 1956 Minutes as Secretary for East Asia of the World Council and the International Missionary Council, Dr. Rajah B. Manikam described the situation relating to communism as follows:

That China . . . is under a communist government is a fact that cannot be ignored. The Church there is cut off from the rest of us. Communist influence has also infiltrated the life of churches elsewhere in Asia. In Indo-China, Christians have been divided into two camps by the struggle going on there. . . . In Burma, some of the leaders of the Karen rebellion, among whom a few Christians are to be found, have been associating themselves with the communists, in order to bring about the downfall of the government. In

Thailand, Indonesia and Japan, there is little open alliance between Christians and communists. . . . In India, elections have revealed that in areas where Christianity is strong the communist party is also strong, and some of the communist leaders are Christians. In Thailand, Pakistan and Formosa, communism has been outlawed. At the other end stands the Church in South Korea with its determined opposition to communism. To some Asian Christians, communism has a great appeal, since they too, like the communists, are fighting for social and economic justice in an area where in general poverty rules the masses. . . . It is imperative that the rank and file of the Christian community . . . should be thoroughly educated as to the real nature of communism. . . .

The Rev. M. M. Thomas, in an address at the Second Assembly with reference to India, maintained that "democratic social revolution is the only answer to the totalitarianism of the right and the left." Christians must oppose communism, he said, "not because it is revolutionary, but because it betrays the revolution by turning it into a new oppression." [17]

In an address to the accredited visitors, Rev. Charles C. West, a former missionary of the Presbyterian Church in the United States of America to China, described the status and circumstances of the churches in that country:

There is no delegate from the churches on the mainland of China . . . to speak with his own voice. . . . Although four of China's largest denominations—the Baptist Council, the Episcopal Church, the Congregational Church, and the Church of Christ in China—have been members of the World Council from the beginning, there is no letter of greeting or goodwill from them, no sign whatever of their participation in our labors here.

For over three years the only news which has come to us of their doings has been brought by departing missionaries and refugees, and the communist-censored church publications which come into our hands. . . .

There continues to be a Church . . . in China. By this I mean not simply that external conditions allow religious worship. The evidence on this is quite ambiguous. On the one hand, the Common Program under which the communist government operates and the draft of the new constitution guarantee "freedom of religious belief," which has generally been interpreted to mean the right of church groups to meet for worship and other religious activities, so far as these are co-operative with government projects and propaganda, or at least not offensive to the government. It has meant the right of churches, under government license and guidance, to organize nationally, hold synods, conduct theological education, publish materials, and the like, so far as these have no foreign contact or finance. . . .

Freedom has been made dependent on the churches' proving themselves "anti-imperialists." Some . . . leaders are in prison, and some have been executed, or have disappeared. . . .

In 1950 a group of pro-communists in the Church prepared under govern-

[17] For the struggle of the youth of India over communism, see the letter of the Democratic Christian Youth of Travancore (Communist) to the World Christian Youth Conference in 1952-53 and the reply of the latter (Appendix E). Rev. Thomas' discussion appears more fully on p. 738.

ment guidance a "Christian Manifesto" denouncing American imperialism and pledging the Church to purge itself of elements unfriendly to the communist government. Signaturing this statement has become practically a test of loyalty among Christians.

. . . Yet there exists a Church of Jesus Christ in China today, not because it is permitted, but because there are men and women who in the midst of the insecurity, the fears, the pressures on their freedom, their time, and on their daily bread, continue to live from the nourishment of the Word of God, and to gather around the table of the Lord. . . .

The Church . . . in China . . . faces problems which we can share. The first . . . is . . . finding an expression of the Gospel which is genuinely free from the charge that it is part of the imperialism of Europe and America. . . . Christianity came to China with the help of imperialist power. Its worship, its theology, its education and its social service have been part of the revolution which has changed the fundamental patterns of Chinese life. China has been in this revolution for over a hundred years. Her leaders have long since ceased to think in terms of the ancient Confucian culture and have sought the new pattern of China's life in some western system of thought . . . which at the same time will be China's answer to western dominance. Communism has become that system. It is the first power in centuries which has given China relatively incorrupt and efficient government. It has covered the land with great projects, both industrial and military, and has shown its force in aggressive war. It has gripped the imagination and changed the lives of millions of Chinese youth. It has left those who are oppressed by its power and repelled by its total claim no place to turn. . . . Allegiance to the communist state and to communist plans for society has become a test of patriotism. This is the dilemma with which the Chinese Christian is confronted.

Mr. West quoted from a statement by "a student body in Peking" which revealed the feeling of many of their generation, it was suggested, who weighed the claims of Christianity and communism together:

As we began to enter through prayer into the deep place of faith, we began to see that Christian faith is essentially a life obedient to Jesus Christ; that its chief task is to bring men to repentance, to belief in the Gospel, and to reconciliation with God. We began to see that to obey Christ meant a total denial of self and a total love for others; that to bring men to repentance involved taking part in the construction of a new China; that to spread the Gospel involved entering the Church, creating an indigenous theology related to China's own cultural background, and going in with the whole heart and mind for every kind of service to men.

"This was the message of the former President of the World Council of Churches, Dr. T. C. Chao," said Mr. West.

His one . . . plea as long as he was free to write and speak in communist China was for the inner reform of the Church, in order that the quality of its fellowship might outdo both the communist ideal and practice and bear witness to the love of Christ. This meant for him church union as quickly as possible, mutual open criticism in love between pastor and people, and between classes and the Church—a thing rare in old China. It meant leadership through service in an age which could not tolerate individual heroes.

. . . It meant evangelism through the example of Christian life. It meant preparation for a ministry to the communists themselves. In his words:
"Communists are human beings, like fragile Christians. They are groping for appropriate policies, for economic development, for political and social structures, for educational methods, and for industrial advancement. Are Christians groping for something in organization, in church unity, in evangelistic methods, in creative fellowship, to match them? Just at this moment, and for some years to come, communism is too full of passion and self-confidence to be tackled. But like everything else in this ever-changing world, the romance will die down and the hard facts of human sin and selfishness, along with the human need of a spiritual redemption and the human yearning for God in Christ, will stare in the eyes of the erstwhile enthusiasts. Then the time will come, perhaps in the not too far distant future. Then, not a few of the communists will knock at the door of the Church for admission and for salvation."

"There is, of course, an illusion lurking in words such as these," observed Mr. West. "The Christian who accepts the communist definition of loyalty to his country and who tries to prove himself anti-imperialist by those standards will never succeed."

An effect of the communist conquest of China had been the multiplication of sects, Mr. West concluded, "largely at the expense of the established denominations." They were "a natural response of simple Christians to the chaos of both the world and the Church." Between the sects and the Church there was no clear line of distinction, he explained, and he saw the danger that in sect religion contact would be lost with both the Church and the world, while prayer and the Word of God were still taken seriously. If this happened, the sects of today might, he thought, become the Church of tomorrow.

Among those speaking of communism was Archbishop Michael of the Greek Archdiocese of North and South America, who characterized it as "the greatest rival to Christianity that has yet been seen in the world, a new religion whose fundamental principle is the denial and the annihilation of every other religion." [18]

But he saw it also as "the greatest challenge [to the churches] since the appearance of Christianity on earth." It wanted and asked for the whole man, he pointed out, as Christ did. And "the communists, no matter where they find themselves, no matter what country or nation or race they belong to, consider themselves comrades and brethren; precisely as the first Christians whom we . . . should imitate . . . considered themselves brothers, no matter where they met. . . . The sign of the cross was their emblem. . . . If all of us who call ourselves Christians were to act toward Christ and . . . one another as faithfully as

[18] Dr. Henry Smith Leiper at the Third World Conference on Faith and Order spoke of communism as a rival of Christianity in respect of its sense of world mission, as follows: "It is clearer now than it was ten years ago . . . that there are two world missions, involving now literally almost all the world. The one is the communist. . . . The other is the Christian. The latter simply cannot operate without taking account of the former." (Part Five, Section V, *2*.)

the communists with their system act toward one another, then certainly the Kingdom of God would come."

The Archbishop exalted Christian love as the first need. It would keep the churches from "the sin of proselytism," he said, which fomented dissension among Christians, growth of differences and enmity, and generally "the intensification of hatred among men." "Those who proceed in this fashion . . . ," he held, "but aggravate the situation."

The ecumenical movement should be encouraged, he believed, because it enabled Christians to know one another better through cooperative service, and so to manifest more fully their spiritual unity in Christ.

"The first and most important responsibility we have toward . . . our brethren behind the Iron Curtain, whether they be Orthodox, or Roman Catholics, or Protestants, or Jews," he urged, "is prayer in their behalf—regular and systematic prayer—such as moves mountains, accomplishes miracles, makes possible the impossible," adding that "conscientious Christianity and the pure life in Christ can cure the world of every evil vestige of totalitarianism."

"Exiled leaders of the Protestant and Orthodox Churches of the Baltic States" addressed to the Assembly an appeal on behalf of their people, who, as they said, were "enslaved by the godless and cruel communist terror regime."

> Our people are in constant danger of thinking, acting, or talking counter to the official line . . . , even of simply being suspected of not following the official line. They are in constant danger of being deported, arrested, or tortured. . . . The official line being one of . . . atheism, to worship God means endangering one's life.
>
> We implore you . . . to hear us, and to help the Estonian, Latvian and Lithuanian peoples in their humiliating frustration. . . . Belief in Christian solidarity encourages us to approach you, our brethren, asking you to join us in our prayers and to include in the resolutions . . . the following:
>
> The communist way of life is the incarnation of the anti-Christ. . . . The systematic corruption of youth . . . is contrary to the teachings of Christ. . . . The communists' use of church leaders in occupied areas as propaganda tools for their "peace conferences" should be regarded as an outrage against the Church. . . . Co-existence between the godless communist regime and Western Civilization based on Christian principles must be recognized as an unholy way.

This plea appeared over the signature of Rev. Aleksander Hinno of the Evangelical Lutheran Church of Estonia, a delegate, who said that "Estonian refugees . . . in the free world must not be considered as immigrants who are looking for a new and better home, but as temporary exiles until the time comes when their home country will be freed from . . . dictatorship."

Speaking from the standpoint of Latin American countries, Dr. Gonzalo Báez-Camargo of the Methodist Church in Mexico declared, "A simple policy of repression will not stop communism. Socially progressive governments are the best bulwark of democracy." Referring to the Dominican Republic, Cuba, Nicaragua, Honduras, Venezuela, and Peru as dictatorships, he raised the question whether the concept of continental defense was not being used to keep bad governments in power. "We should beware," he cautioned, "of the danger of supporting regimes just because they claim to be anti-communist."

What Section III of the Second Assembly said about communism in its report on "The Responsible Society in a World Perspective" may be summarized for the purposes of this general survey:

The conflict between communists and non-communists not only divides the world: it creates divisions in the free half over the issue of the right attitude toward communism which strikes even into the churches.

The report reaffirmed the statement of the First Assembly on the points at which communism was found to be at variance with the Christian faith, as follows:

The communist promise of what amounts to a complete redemption of man in history.

The belief that a particular class, by virtue of its role as the bearer of a new order, is free from sins and ambiguities that Christians believe characteristic of all human existence.

The materialistic and deterministic teachings, however they may be qualified, that are incompatible with belief in God and with the Christian view of man as a person, made in God's image and responsible to him.

The ruthless methods of communists in dealing with their opponents.

The demand of the party on its members for an exclusive and unqualified loyalty which belongs only to God, and the coercive policies of communist dictatorship in controlling every aspect of life.

The conflict over communism had important consequences for the political and economic life of nearly every nation. In some regions communism had a specially strong appeal, particularly in Asia, Africa, and Latin America, where poverty, misery, the newly-aroused aspirations for freedom and security, doubts as to the effectiveness of democracy, and the tendency of those in power to brand all reforms as communistic combine to make its promises attractive, in spite of the totalitarianism which accompanies it.

For many, there seemed to be no alternative which would bring essential social change quickly enough.

There were Christians who thought that they could cooperate with the communist movement in their countries because they saw it as the way to a new order of material abundance and greater justice. Here, the question became: "Can communism be an effective instrument for these limited purposes, without eventually dominating the minds of men and their institutions?"

The report reaffirmed the idea rather generally accepted in ecumenical circles, that "the growth of communism was a judgment upon . . . modern societies . . . for the past and present indifference to social justice, in which the Church was also involved," and added that "only as Christians worked for social justice and personal freedom for all, and rose above fear and resentment, would they be fully able to meet the challenge of this conflict."

"In this way Christians living in different parts of our divided world may contribute," it thought, "to the creation of the necessary conditions for different systems to live side by side."

"It is our concern for the brother for whom Christ died that should impel us to fulfill" this obligation. But "this concern . . . does not alter the mission of the churches to bear witness in the face of all atheistic and self-righteous ideology."

Among the "serious effects the conflict with communism is already producing," the report warned, "is the tendency in democratic societies to lower their standards of civil liberties, and sometimes to strengthen reactionary forces abroad. . . . Pre-occupation with the real dangers of subversion in many situations has led to less widely recognized and more subtle danger to society from those who identify as subversive any unpopular opinions or associations.[19]

"It will be the task of the churches to point to the dangers inherent in the present situation: on the one hand, the temptation to succumb to anti-communist hysteria and the danger of a self-righteous assurance concerning the political and social systems of the West; on the other hand, the temptation to accept the false promises of communism and to overlook its threat to any responsible society."

The report stressed the danger "that nations will over-emphasize the military aspect in their defense against communism and fail to see the need for reforms in political, social and economic institutions as an important part of their response to its challenge." These nations could have greater influence on the course of the present world conflict, it insisted, if they showed their ability to deal justly with the legitimate aspirations of the dependent peoples, to cope successfully and creatively with their own problems, and to remain self-critical.

"Christians in communist and non-communist countries are called," declared the report, "to hold each other in special brotherly concern and prayer across all barriers. Those of us in non-communist lands affirm our unity with these churches in the ecumenical fellowship and the bond of the Spirit, and our confidence in their loyalty to Christ. We rejoice with them in the Christian witness which they make in these new circumstances and seek to understand and affirm our fellowship with them in their temptations and in their Christian hope, for this witness and these temptations are relevant also to our social responsibility."

The report of Section III, like those on the other sub-themes, was only "received" and "recommended to the churches for study and appropriate action. . . ." The official word of the Assembly was heard in the Message, which did not mention the communist movement by name but contained allusions to it: "the forces that separate men from one another," the absence "of Chinese churches which were with us at Amsterdam," "other lands and churches unrepresented," thankfulness "that, separated as we are, by the deepest political divisions of our time, here

[19] The report here reflects the disapproval of investigative procedures followed by the Congress of the United States in inquiries into the activities of communists, which certain members of the clergy prominent in the ecumenical movement had expressed publicly prior to the Evanston Assembly.

at Evanston we are united in Christ," and rejoicing "also that, in the bond of prayer and a common hope, we maintain communion with our Christian brethren everywhere." "From within this communion," the Message spoke further "about the fear and distrust which at present divide our world" and pointed to the ways toward unity:

Firstly, Jesus Christ. "Only at the Cross of Christ, where men know themselves as forgiven sinners, can they be made one."

Secondly, work for social reconstruction. "It is not enough that Christians should seek peace for themselves. They must seek justice for others —great masses of people in many parts of the world . . . hungry for bread" and living "in conditions which mock their human worth, . . . millions of men and women . . . suffering segregation and discrimination on the grounds of race."

Thirdly, evangelistic missions. "The Church of Christ is today a world-wide fellowship, yet there are countless people to whom He is unknown."

There was confidence at Evanston that the churches had in the gospel of Jesus Christ the antidote to communism, but also the feeling that to administer it effectively they needed more time than the revolutionary masses were in a mood to give the Christian—or any other—appeal on behalf of evolutionary progress in human betterment.

"At the present rate of spiritual impotence, with the protective covering of the hydrogen bomb, it is only a matter of time," warned Dr. Charles Malik of Lebanon, "before the whole of Asia and Africa, and maybe even Europe, will be engulfed by communism." He frankly expressed the foreboding of many minds. He added:

> What is desperately needed, besides the highest political wisdom, is a ringing positive message, one of reality, of truth and of hope. Communism exposes the inadequacy, if not indeed the bankruptcy, of the Western-imperialistic and the smug-Christian approach of the past. Something infinitely more humble, more profound, more positively out-reaching, something touching the hearts of men, touching their need for fellowship and understanding and love, for being included and being trusted, something providing them with real hope, hope for themselves and their children, hope in this life as well as the next, something of this order is needed. This Something is Jesus Christ, the Risen Lord.

But could the offering of the gospel of Christ by the churches, however prayerfully and sacrificially, stay even momentarily the surge of the multitudes toward the quicker political and material gains they demanded, without submission to the moral disciplines of the Christian faith?

Speaking apparently to this point, the Message said, "Those who know that Christ is risen should have the courage to expect new power to break through every human barrier."

Faith had in such times to make allowance for imponderable factors, one of which was the fate always driving evil to self-defeat. "Seek ye first the kingdom of God and his righteousness, and all these things shall be added unto you." The Church had in these words of Christ the divine order; he who reversed it after the fashion of any worldly philosophy would find the stars in their course against him.

Nevertheless, the tribulations which might be loosed upon the earth before the attempt again proved its futility could be such as to cause those mankind had known to pale into oblivion.

The confrontation of communism by the World Council of Churches after Evanston added important new pages to the earlier chapters on this subject.

In the summer of 1956 the Central Committee went to Galyatetö, Hungary, for its annual meeting, the first to be held in communist territory. The invitation had been extended by the Hungarian Ecumenical Council in 1954. At Galyatetö, Dr. Visser 't Hooft, the General Secretary of the World Council, explained the attitude of the Committee in coming to Hungary:[20]

By accepting the invitation, the World Council showed once again that it lives its own life in complete independence from any particular political or economic system or ideology, and desires to render its witness in all parts of the world, wherever it can get a chance to do so.

At the same time, we believe that churches living under differing systems can and must learn from each other. There is a mutual correction in seeing ourselves as others see us, which is one of the most precious things in the ecumenical movement. If all of us remember that we may have a beam in our own eyes, we shall be more humble in asking about the speck we seem to notice in the eye of our brother; and we may in this way help to make sure that our own specks do not become beams.

"This does not mean a general relativism with regard to the forms of political and social life," he continued.

What we have said together in Amsterdam and Evanston about these matters is everything but relativistic. Whenever we meet, we stand for certain great fundamental truths concerning man as a creature of God and a brother for whom Christ died, concerning his right and duty to serve God and to witness in full freedom to the lordship of Christ over all aspects of life. One of our main themes in these days will be: "The Churches and the Building of a Responsible International Order." In this concept of a responsible society to which we are committed ever since our First Assembly, we proclaim together that society has a responsibility for the well-being of its members, that every person in society has a right to participate as a responsible member in that society, and that society is not an aim in itself but is responsible to God. In our discussion on this main theme we will surely seek to apply these convictions to the international life.

[20] For the General Secretary's address and others at Galyatetö, see Annual Minutes and Reports for 1956.

It had been six years since the Central Committee, acting on these principles, condemned as aggression Red China's attack on Korea, and T. C. Chao had resigned as a President of the World Council of Churches. Bishop Albert Bereczky, who had, in protest, withdrawn from membership in the Central Committee, was now Chairman of the Hungarian Ecumenical Council and of its welcoming committee.

Meantime, events had woven unpredictable and strange new patterns of international and interchurch life.

Bishop Rajah B. Manikam, erstwhile Joint Secretary of the World Council of Churches and the International Missionary Council for East Asia, was at Galyatetö, to report on his visit to the People's Republic of China on an invitation from the Chinese churches, which had not been cooperating with either of the Councils since Chao's resignation. He had attended the "Three-Self Movement" in Peking and there met 150 church leaders. He had found the churches, he said, "self-supporting, self-administrating and self-propagating," having no longer to provide funds for their schools and hospitals, the state having taken them over, and being themselves exempt from tax on other mission properties. Such income as they received could, under these circumstances, be devoted "altogether to the Church's purpose and ministry."

The churches enjoyed freedom of worship, according to their leaders, though they might not hold open-air meetings or speak against the government.

Theological education in the seminaries had been put on a union basis. While not yet united organically, the churches cooperated in many other ways. He had heard criticism of the World Council of Churches, because of what the Chinese called "its political activities."

The familiar voice of Professor Josef Hromadka of Prague was raised in appeal to the World Council to help the churches in coping theologically, as he put it, with the fact that the ecumenical center of gravity had shifted to Asia, "by giving them a lead through open-minded study and discussion."

Professor Albert Maksay of the Reformed Church of Rumania spoke for the churches in that communist country. The Reformed Church of Rumania had been in the World Council since its formation in 1948 but had not been permitted by the government to send representatives to its meetings. The three denominations belonging nominally to the World Council—the Reformed, the German-speaking Lutheran, and the Hungarian-speaking Lutheran—had altogether a million members.

"It is nineteen years since we took part in ecumenical work," Dr. Maksay said, recalling the Second World Conference on Faith and Order at Edinburgh in 1937. "We are grateful to our government," he said, "for making it possible for us to come; but, above all, we thank God for this opening of the doors. Something bigger, mightier, has done this thing than simply the changed atmosphere in human relationships."

By invitation, Bishop K. H. Ting of the Episcopal Church in China attended as an observer. Requested to speak, he said it was "no secret that the Chinese churches had not been too satisfied with certain positions the World Council of Churches had taken in recent years." This accounted for the existing estrangement. He was glad, however, that the Chinese churches had taken the first and second steps toward reconciliation, by inviting Bishop Manikam to China and by sending himself to Hungary. He hoped that the relationship could be "normalized" soon.

What the Chinese regarded as liberation had not been, Bishop Ting said, "a political or diplomatic accident." It had marked "a turning-point in history that was overdue," and the people would not like it reversed. They did not think of it as "an act of God's wrath, but of his love." Christians in China did not pretend to agree with communists in their views on matters of faith, but this did not keep them from recognizing the value of the good things the People's Government was doing. They were "humbled and gave thanks to God for this."

There was, admittedly, the temptation for Christians in China to put their new loyalty to the country first, because they were impressed by the remarkable progress that had been made. But this problem existed in all countries, those claiming to be Christian being by no means excluded.

The open atheism of communism made the "evangelistic situation" in China less confusing. Frankness about religion was a guarantee that subtle use would not be made of it under the guise of religiosity. The right of citizens to enjoy religious freedom was guaranteed by the national constitution. They could freely worship, evangelize, educate their children in religion, and publish books and periodicals.

God had been leading the Christians of China during a time of social upheaval, declared the Bishop, to learn many new lessons. They had abandoned "the various types of pragmatic Christianity . . . and the crutches of human power, prestige and wealth, which could give only a false security, and had found that Christ's grace was sufficient for them." They had proved the truth of Pascal's words, "It is a blessed state for the Church to be dependent on God alone."

At the same time, the churches had been "more ecumenical." The hundred denominations which Christians in China had formed under outside influence had been "on bad relations with one another." Now they were in close association. Though there had been no discussion of church union, their present relationships would be a promising basis for that step in the future.

Chinese Christians had been brought, moreover, "to a very acute awareness of their lack of love for their own people, and were learning the lesson of love."

The divorce between doctrine and life, the Bishop thought, was in the way of being overcome by the Chinese Christians. Theology had been oriented to their "own situation, rather than to that of Western Christianity." While it had much to learn from the West, the Church in China had first to be itself. The "Three-Self Movement"—i.e., the effort toward self-administration, self-support, and self-propagation—was aimed at this. The Chinese wished to avoid the dangers of a nationalistic church "but were not apologetic for wanting to make the Church of China as national, for instance, as the Church in England was English."

Chinese Christians knew that colonialist interests made use of missionary work to serve their own purposes. The harm they had caused had to be taken seriously. "But for all the good things missionaries had done they were grateful, and these would remain."

The best missionaries worked to make themselves dispensable and were only glad that the Church in China "was standing on its own." Unfortunately, a small number of former missionaries were saying "untrue and slanderous things" about China and their former colleagues. Though not hurting the work of Chinese Christians, they put obstacles in the way of the "normalization of relationships between Christians in China and elsewhere."

The Chinese had in their work many defects, of course; even some of the good things they did had been done awkwardly. But they were ready to learn from all other Christians.[21]

The meeting concluded its session with Bishop Ting with the following resolution, as reported in the Minutes for 1956:

> The Central Committee desires to give expression to its deep sense of satisfaction, that through the visit of Bishop Manikam and through the presence of Bishop K. H. Ting, as observer at our present meeting, the churches in the People's Republic of China and the World Council of Churches have again entered into contact with each other. It rejoices in the evidence reported to it concerning the vitality of church life in that country.

[21] Early in 1959 the Standing Committee of the Conference of Missionary Societies in the U.K. and the Division of Foreign Missions of the National Council of the Churches of Christ in the U.S. reported under way in China a process of compulsory unification of the major denominations, reduction in the number of local congregations, and expropriation of unused church property by the government. Of sixty-five buildings in Peking, only four remained. All but about a score of the two hundred church buildings in Shanghai had been closed. The Standing Committee warned that all the facts were not known and that it was not easy to interpret the meaning of those that were known.

At the All-Christian Peace Assembly at Prague in 1961, Bishop Ting delivered what was described by Milton Mayer in *The Christian Century* for August 16, 1961, as a "ferocious attack on the United States," which he charged with "moral and religious degeneracy." At the same time Bishop Ting praised the People's Republic of China, where, he said, "beggary, robbery, prostitution, gambling, and all other kinds of vices and evils have been done away with forever."

The Central Committee believes that a visit of representatives of the World Council to the churches within the People's Republic of China, whenever such a visit were welcomed, would increase goodwill, understanding and fellowship within the world-wide community as represented by the World Council of Churches.

The Central Committee expresses the additional hope that such a deepened fellowship will aid the building of a peaceful world of freedom, truth and justice for all peoples.

A few months before the Galyatetö meeting of the Central Committee, a report of representatives of the British Society of Friends who had visited China had been published and read widely in ecumenical circles, undoubtedly influencing the thinking of some Christian leaders. Declaring that "only a miracle could save Chinese Christians from slow but sure diminution of influence and ultimate extinction," it nevertheless summed up the Chinese Christians' more optimistic estimate of their situation, as follows:

The guarantee of religious freedom is not only written into the constitution but is fully respected in practice. It works. We have freedom of worship, freedom to evangelize and to publish the Scriptures and Christian literature, freedom to manage our church affairs in our own way.

The Bureau of Religious Affairs, a department of government, has been uniformly helpful to us. It exists not to control us but to assist us. It has protected us from over-zealous governmental agencies or persons who would have denied us our rights. It has helped us materially in building new churches.

. . . The Christian church in China today . . . is a Chinese church. It is our own, and we run it ourselves. . . . The former church could have no future, because it had no independence. We are free and independent, and our future is secure. Our Christianity is a much healthier and more genuine thing. . . . The rice Christians have left us, and that is no loss. It is no longer necessary to come to church . . . to get something to eat. . . . There is infinitely more co-operation between the churches than formerly. . . . The National Christian Conference has gone from strength to strength—from an attendance of one hundred eighty delegates in 1953 to six hundred this year (1956).

As for our attitude to the new regime, no government and no system is the kingdom of God, but this is, we believe, a real people's government. We have a voice in it, even as Christians, and it does our will. . . . This is . . . a much more Christian country than old China. . . . Public corruption and personal dishonesty . . . have largely . . . disappeared; prostitution and gambling have been eliminated. . . . The government is taking care of the social evils of our country. We can concentrate on preaching the gospel to the people in the language they understand. We are not asked to be Marxists. . . . We believe something more is required than social ethics . . . , that the Christian has to go further than the communist in personal and social responsibility, in understanding and living the good life. Our task is to nurture Christians, believing that one day . . . China may become a truly Christian nation.

Chairman Franklin Clark Fry expressed the Central Committee's gratitude for the hospitality shown the members in Hungary:

To the People's Republic of Hungary, and especially President Janos Horvarth of the State Office for Church Affairs, for the many facilities offered the Committee, and for the welcome accorded the Committee; to the National Council of Trade Unions of Hungary for the use of the excellent facilities of Galyatetö, and to the manager of the Hotel; to the Hungarian Ecumenical Council and its member churches, and especially to Bishop Bereczky, Chairman of the Council, for their welcome and many happy arrangements for the meeting; to the Reformed Theological Seminary for hospitality on journeys of the Committee to and through Budapest; to the congregations and churches of Hungary which received the Committee members in their midst and sent them gifts.

From Galyatetö the Central Committee issued, on behalf of the World Council of Churches, the following statement, the significance of which was chiefly that it was published from within a Communist country:

The Central Committee of the World Council of Churches, meeting in Hungary, has been once more impressed by the way in which barriers of race, ideology and tradition are overcome in Christ.

Among the matters specially considered has been the part of the churches in the building of a responsible international society. This means a society where all men can act in freedom with consideration for the needs and rights of others; and where the several members have regard for the well-being of one another and that of the whole family of men. Such a society will recognize its allegiance to God who is the Sovereign Ruler of the Nations.

In the light of its discussion, the Committee claims the attention of the churches to certain matters which are of the greatest importance for the welfare of the peoples of the world.

Man is in danger physically, morally and spiritually. As followers of the One who loved men and bore the burden of their sin and suffering, we cannot be indifferent to man's peril.

A great gulf separates rich and poor on an international scale. In this the churches cannot acquiesce, but must strive with all their power to bridge this gulf. Therefore, the processes of economic growth must be understood and aided, in order that rapid social change may be so guided as to advance the interests of the peoples.

Social justice must be pursued between the nations, as well as within each nation. The churches in countries with more favorable economic and social conditions have a particular responsibility to express in deeds their common humanity with all poor, oppressed and suffering people, and to urge their governments to base their policies upon recognition of the justice of this principle.

When one nation dominates another politically or economically, the dependent or subject people is deprived of the possibility of developing a fully responsible society. Many dependent peoples are demanding self-government and independence for their countries. The churches within and without these lands must appreciate the urgency of this demand and must stand with the people in orderly progress towards these goals. In multi-racial societies they must recognize the claims of justice and boldly exercise a reconciling and constructive influence.

Mankind is fearful of actual and potential danger from experimental tests of nuclear weapons. We call upon the churches to appeal to their governments and the United Nations to negotiate such an agreement for the discontinuance, or limitation and control, of these tests as to end any . . . danger. Provisions must be made to safeguard both the health of the people and the security of the nations. In order that human resources may be directed towards constructive ends, the churches should continue insistently to press for an adequate system of disarmament and a peaceful settlement of the unresolved issues which confront the world.

The world wants peace, but will not gain it, unless men are ready to make sacrifices for peace and to abandon practices which make for war. To move out of a state of "cold war" into one of real peace requires respect for truth under all circumstances. People must not be subjected to deliberate misrepresentation and false propaganda. They must have access to information and be free to discover the truth for themselves.

People must be free to travel, to meet and to know their neighbors, through personal encounter to seek understanding and create friendship, and thus to achieve mutual confidence and respect. They must also be free to choose by whom and in what way they wish to be governed. They must be free to obey the dictates of their consciences. They must be free to worship God, to witness to their faith and to have their children educated in it in church, school and youth meetings.

We call upon all Christians to lay these matters to heart and to seek these ends in a spirit of prayer and of penitence for past failures and in the name of their Lord and Master, who is the Way, the Truth and the Life.

Included in the minutes of the Galyatetö meeting of the Central Committee was a statement concerning conversations by representatives of the Lutheran World Federation and Dr. Visser 't Hooft with the State Office for Church Affairs of the Hungarian government and a committee of the Hungarian Lutheran Church about the case of Bishop Lajos Ordass, who had allegedly been fraudulently arrested and imprisoned in 1948, when he resisted the government's move to take over the schools of the church, and deprived of his office. The agreement had been reached, it was stated, that action should be taken by the civil courts to release him from prison and clear him of the conviction, and that his innocence and integrity should be attested by the publishing of a new verdict. He should be given deferred compensation, and his eligibility to serve as bishop should be restored. The understanding was that, following his reinstatement, he should resign and have the status of a bishop in retirement, but with the right to return to an active bishopric at some later time, if he desired. If unable or not wishing to assume the regular duties of a bishop again, he should be appointed to a professorship in theology, under which he would enjoy the right to preach, or to some other suitable position. (See earlier reference, page 752.)

This action was characterized, though not by the negotiating committee members, as "a smashing end to a great meeting," which went far to justify the Central Committee's decision to meet in Hungary. But approaching events were soon to temper exultation.

Within two months Hungary was aflame with revolution, and Protestants were hastening to balance the scales of justice in their churches. While the fighting raged, Laszlo Dezsery and Lajos Vetoe, who owed their offices as bishops to the will of the government, were forced to resign, and Lajos Ordass was reinstated as sole bishop in the Hungarian Lutheran Church.

In the Hungarian Reformed Church, Albert Bereczky, holder of the Hungarian communists' Order of Labor, was replaced immediately by Ladislaus Rauascz as bishop of the Danubian district and ministerial president of the Church. Rauascz had been forced to withdraw in 1948 in Bereczky's favor. The Reformed clergy demanded the resignation of Bishop Janos Peter[22] of the Trans-Tiscian district, calling him "the worst kind of Stalinist," and nominated as his successor Bela Papp, who had been in prison.

In fact, all church officials who had been appointed by the government contrary to the will of the churches since 1948 were compelled to resign, so that the posts held by them might be filled in new elections.

Imre Kadar quit as editor of the communist-controlled Hungarian Church Press. A new religious journal, *Reformacio,* was planned. The State Office for Church Affairs was closed. Church schools, hospitals, the Young Men's Christian Association, the Student Christian Movement, the Boy Scouts, and other organizations, long under ban, made ready to resume operations. Protestantism, still vital and vigorous despite years of repression, rose to reorder and manage its own work, dispelling any illusions Christians inside or outside the Soviet orbit may have had about adjustments by any church to criminal communism. Bloody brutality would soon put an end to the revolt and its hopes, but in blazing events the truth had stood revealed.

Attempts by Laszlo Dezsery and Lajos Vetoe to regain the offices from which they had been ousted failed for the time, although the latter was eventually reinstated.[23] Dezsery, with Sandor Fekete, who had been superintendent of the Reformed Church's North Budapest Presbytery, received appointment to the staff of the Budapest Radio, and Janos Peter became head of the Ministry to Cultural Affairs and later a Hungarian delegate to the United Nations. Declining reinstatement as bishop, Peter in 1958 was appointed Deputy Foreign Minister.

Nine pastors of the Reformed Church of Hungary were imprisoned on the charge of having encouraged the revolution.

The victory of the churches was short-lived.

It appeared that other denominations than the Reformed, the Lutheran and the Roman Catholic had not been seriously involved in the

[22] Bereczky and Peter had represented their Church at Evanston in 1954 and had there been charged with being communist collaborators. They obtained visas on the representation of the World Council of Churches that they would be seated as delegates.

[23] Vetoe continued as representative of his Church on the Central Committee of the World Council and retained his membership in the Commission of the Churches on International Affairs.

struggle with the government. They were numerically weak. About 20 percent of the population were Reformed and 6 percent Lutheran. The Church of Rome was larger than all the others together. Its troubles with the state had dramatic culmination in the arrest of Cardinal Mindszenty. On October 31, 1956, after imprisonment lasting more than seven years, he returned in triumph to Budapest. With the failure of the revolution he sought and was given asylum at the American Embassy.

The private promise of the government to formalize the churches' freedom went unfulfilled. Excuse could be found easily in the illegality of the actions of the denominations during the revolt.

Janos Horvarth of the State Office of Church Affairs moved quickly to act on a statement of the Lutheran Church's case submitted by Bishop Ordass by appointing four church officials ejected during the uprising, among them Lajos Vetoe. Although Bishop Ordass rejected them, when he appeared at the hearing, in company with Bishops Zoltan Turoczy and Joszef Szabo, he found them sitting in judgment for the state. As evidence of his desire to get along with the government, he accepted election to the National Council of the Patriotic Popular Front but refused to approve the removal of Bishop Turoczy and the appointment of Lajos Vetoe in his place, demanded by the State Office of Church Affairs. The political authorities had their will, however, adding to the choice of Vetoe the reinstatement of Erno Mihalfi and Joszef Darvas as inspectors of the Lutheran Church.

The Reformed Churches Janos Horvarth warned "to revise their international relations and pay more attention to churches in the 'People's Democracies.'" Connections with ecumenical organizations, he said, must "exclude influences of imperialist policies." As a result of this demand, Professor Laszlo Pap, since Amsterdam a member of the Central Committee of the World Council of Churches and a leader clearly held in highest regard by fellow churchmen who hoped for closer cooperation with the World Council and with Christians in other lands, was not permitted by the government to come to the Committee's meeting in New Haven in 1957. His rustication followed soon.

In the Lutheran Church, Lajos Vetoe became primate, "because Bishop Ordass had taken over the functions of a bishop after him, and the Presidial Council of the People's Republic had not yet approved of his episcopal prerogatives."

The restoration of the pre-revolution order was signalized by an agreement between the regime and the Lutheran Church, in which it was affirmed that the state granted freedom of worship to pastors and church members, in accordance with the constitution, and that the Church recognized the government as the supreme organ of the state and would educate its members in the spirit of obedience to the political authorities. The Church pledged itself also to support their efforts to promote the cause of socialism.

Spokesmen of the Lutheran and Reformed denominations outside Hungary and of the ecumenical movement appealed to the Hungarian powers to grant to the churches full liberty to conduct their own spiritual affairs, only to be rebuked by the Director of the State Office for Church Affairs for "interfering in a purely internal matter." The four Scandinavian Lutheran primates—Archbishop Yngve Brilioth of Sweden, Bishop Fuglsang-Damgaard of Denmark, Archbishop Ilmari Salomies of Finland, and Bishop Johannes Smemo of Norway—expressed concern over the removal of Bishop Zoltan Turoczy as a bishop of the Hungarian Lutheran Church and the displacement of Bishop Lajos Ordass as presiding bishop. In reply the Director explained that these Hungarian dignitaries had been acting illegally within the Church and had found themselves in collision with "the majority of the clergy and the mass of Christians" before their relations with the state had deteriorated. Bishop Turoczy's rejection was described as "a consequence of the stubbornness of these selfish church leaders who [were] not at all representative of the true interests of the Church." The Director accused Bishop Ordass of having made the settlement of important issues impossible, including the definition of Bishop Turoczy's position. He observed that in Scandinavian nations, England, and "other capitalist countries" governments frequently brought influence to bear on the appointment of bishops. He accused the Lutheran World Federation and "certain foreign church leaders" of making statements that went beyond the limits of interested goodwill. Their utterances were, he held, really attempts "to exercise pressure on the Hungarian Government and the progressive personalities in the Church and to interfere in an unwarranted way in personal problems within the Hungarian churches."

As might have been anticipated, the World Council of Churches was criticized because of the Central Committee's meeting in Hungary. Going to Galyatetö was regarded in the free world as "playing into the hands of the communists," and inside the Iron Curtain as "deliberately planned by imperialism." The revolution's coming hard upon the event seemed to lend the color of truth to these charges—to the latter particularly; and communists were quick in exploiting their opportunity.

What had occurred, according to the communist point of view, was reported in *Tieng Feng,* a Chinese periodical (December 23, 1957), under the caption "Counter-Revolutionary Events in Hungary and the Utilization of Christianity by Imperialism," as follows:

> The Hungarian events were counter-revolutionary events, carefully conceived and deliberately planned by imperialism in close collaboration with the counter-revolutionaries within Hungary.
>
> The General Secretary of the World Council of Churches and his company utilized their ecclesiastical connections with Hungary to have a hand

in the Hungarian events and rendered harm to the Hungarian nation, the Hungarian people and the Hungarian churches.

Even after the failure of the counter-revolution, the small clique controlling the World Council of Churches has not learned any lesson. They have shown no sign of repentance, but are still conducting activities for the interests of imperialism.[24]

These and other more specific accusations were answered by officials of the World Council of Churches directly to representatives of the Hungarian government, who, in some instances, undertook, so far as they could, to transmit their denials to "publications concerned."

Some critics giving no credence to the charges against the World Council said that, although nothing overt had been done, the Central Committee's going for its meeting to Hungary and there by its actions and pronouncements upholding the ideals of religious and political freedom could only have encouraged the revolutionaries in their hope of receiving support from the West. The considerable material aid given to the refugees from Hungary by the churches, they added, while not measuring up to the expectations of leaders of the revolt, furnished ground for the contention that they had been backed by the World Council.

Finding it quite impossible to deal adequately with all these criticisms, the Central Committee requested its Vice-President, Dr. Ernest A. Payne, to prepare an article covering them for publication in *The Ecumenical Review*. It appeared in the April, 1958, number.

Dr. Payne, referring to a speech by Bishop Bell in the House of Lords in July, 1957, mentioning "what the churches [were] doing in order to penetrate the Iron Curtain and to link up persons of a similar religion with persons of the same religion on the other side," which communist propagandists had cited as evidence of ecumenical designs against the People's Republics, said:

No one who knows Bishop Bell and his life-long services to the cause of Christian fellowship . . . would dream of his ever becoming "a tool of cold war." . . . Such penetration is in the interests of peace, not of war. It is this Christian encounter which is the aim of the World Council. In the case of Hungary, it has been accompanied by a wave of Christian sympathy and generosity which has brought practical help to thousands of refugees and also, with the encouragement of the Hungarian Government, to thousands of needy persons within Hungary. . . . In the light of all this we cannot but declare that it is a grievous illusion and error to suggest that the World Council of Churches has aimed at, or has been used by others to assist in, "the overthrow of the revolutionary government and the socialist

[24] "Similar statements have been made in Hungary itself. In more elaborate form, they are the theme of a book by Dr. Imre Kadar, the former editor of the Hungarian Church Press, and the substance of them is contained in a letter of October 17, 1957, from the acting-officers of the General Convent of the Reformed Church in Hungary to the presidents of the World Council." (*The Ecumenical Review*, Vol. X, No. 3, p. 298.)

social system." On the contrary, it has consistently sought Christian fellowship and understanding.

Continuing, Dr. Payne said that the spirit in which the World Council had acted found "impressive verbal expression" in the report of "The Responsible Society in a World Perspective: Section II, The Church in Relation to Communist-Non-Communist Tension" (*Evanston Report*, pp. 120-123). "Christians in communist and non-communist countries," stated this report, "are called to hold each other in special brotherly concern and prayer across all barriers."

Hungary had been a swift and terrible example of the trials in store for those who were committed to the ideal of building "a responsible international society."

Whether or not the Central Committee had acted wisely in accepting the invitation to Hungary was, after the event, useless to debate.

The action led to a regrettable experience within the World Council. Josef Hromadka of Czechoslovakia tried to justify Russia's bloody suppression of the revolutionaries, on the ground that their leaders were reactionaries and fascists who had to be removed to save Hungary "from terrible bloodshed and disintegration, and, furthermore, from national, chauvinist and social reaction, which would have taken the first step in Hungary toward a broader military conflict in Central Europe and perhaps in Europe in general." His statement of the matter, in which the foregoing words appeared, had been printed in *Witness* and widely read. He was on the Executive Committee of the Central Committee of the World Council, and when the time came at New Haven in 1957 to choose its members for the ensuing year, the Committee on Nominations proposed the re-election by one ballot of all who had served during the previous term. Dr. Petrus Olaf Bersell of Minneapolis thereupon announced that he would be unable to vote for Dr. Hromadka because of his record and the statements made by him after the Hungarian rebellion in November. A motion by him that the nominees be acted upon individually failed to carry, and the entire slate was elected by a vote of twenty-eight to seven. More than half of the members of the Central Committee abstained from voting. Seven opposed the re-election of Dr. Hromadka, Dr. Bersell not casting any ballot: Bishop Johannes Lilje of Germany; Dr. Harold Roberts, Vice-President of the World Methodist Council; Colonel Francis Pickens Miller, Presbyterian layman of Virginia; Mrs. Leslie E. Swain and Rev. W. Hubert Porter of the American Baptist Convention; Archbishop Michael of the Greek Archdiocese of North and South America; and the Very Rev. Georges Florovsky of the Russian Orthodox Church in exile.

The experience of the Central Committee in the Hungarian situation had made it clear, if there had been any doubt, that dealing with the churches in communist countries immediately involved the national governments. In each of them the churches were under the authority of a state office for religious affairs. President Janos Horvarth could say to the Central Committee that, under Hungarian law, no ecclesiastical appointment could be made without the sanction of the state, which had the ultimate authority; and the case was not essentially different in any of the other communist nations.

The negotiations of the World Council of Churches with the Russian Orthodox Church proceeded within this same general frame of reference. The churches of Russia could, of course, do only what the government would approve and permit.

The Russian Orthodox Church had in 1948 considered with favor the invitation to take part in the Amsterdam Assembly of the World Council, until the convocation of Orthodox Churches in Moscow in July of that year. There G. G. Karpov, Chairman of the Commission on Russian Orthodox Affairs in the Ministerial Council of the Union of Soviet Socialist Republics, appeared and explained to the delegates that their presence indicated their purpose to oppose "efforts from abroad" against their position. Other church authorities followed with representations that the World Council of Churches, because of its political aims and methods, was an influence inimical to true religion and international peace. The delegates to Amsterdam arrived to find the seats which had been designated for the Russian Orthodox empty.

Upon adopting Resolution I submitted by Section IV,[25] the Evanston Assembly voted:

> That the Central Committee be requested to appoint a delegation or delegations (i) to communicate the foregoing statement to the member churches . . . , (ii) to take such steps as seem suitable with a view to the presentation of the same . . . to the churches not related to the World Council . . . , including the churches in the Union of Soviet Socialist Republics and in other lands, (iii) to invite these churches to consider ways in which they might communicate the statement to the governments of their countries.

Pursuant to this action, Bishop Otto Dibelius of Germany and Dr. W. A. Visser 't Hooft, acting for the Central Committee, addressed the Moscow Patriarchate through Archbishop Boris of Berlin on October 18, 1954, bringing to its attention the resolution and other germane matters. The Patriarchate replied on February 21, 1955. The Central Committee, at its Davos-Platz meeting in August, 1955, authorized an answer, and in January of 1956 it received another letter from the Patriarchate.

The correspondence showed the Russian Orthodox Church to be interested in exploring the theological disunity of Christians and willing apparently to consider cooperating with the World Council of Churches

[25] For Resolution I of Section IV of the Evanston Assembly see page 655 ff.

in the area of Faith and Order, if it could do so without seeming to approve the ecumenical program of social action. The Russian Church and the Soviet state had obviously arrived at an accommodation that allowed the former more freedom than it had previously enjoyed, and it would not wish to risk disturbing this relationship by "mixing in politics." The dispensation for activity in that sphere extended only to causes initiated or favored by the government, such as the crusade of the World Peace Council, which followed faithfully the communist line of propaganda.

The epistolary encounter did not encourage hope that the Russian churches, the Orthodox or the others, would try to act in any way to bring about a change in Soviet social and political policies. The Russian churchmen wrote in platitudes concerning peace, without giving any evidence that they linked the subject in their thinking with justice. From anything they said or their words implied, they could not have been expected to advocate a so plainly just and humane action on the part of Russia as consenting to the reunion of severed Germany or the liberation of Czechoslovakia and other satellite states.

Nikolai, who signed the letters of the Patriarchate to the World Council, was the liaison official between the Russian Orthodox Church and the government, by report standing highest among the clergy in the favor of the Kremlin. While in the United States in 1956, he was quoted by the Associated Press as having said in a conference with American churchmen, when Christian and Marxist moral views were being discussed:

> We [the Russian Orthodox Church] are opposed to the materialism of the communist party in our churches and journals, and . . . reject the teachings of the party. . . . We say openly that between materialistic and Christian outlooks on morality, ours is the Christian. . . . Materialism denies all that we regard as holy. . . . We consider the communist party as materialistic.

Nikolai explained that the party conducted its anti-religion propaganda and the Church its teaching, and that "nobody was forced to listen to atheistic propaganda." The Church's means of counteracting communistic thought were sorely limited, he admitted, consisting of only the pulpits and a few religious periodicals with small circulations. These seemed inadequate, he recognized, in contrast to the massive program of indoctrination by the communists.

His words were taken generally as suggesting that the Russian government felt secure enough in its control of the churches to allow them the freedom of dissenting from its principles, so long as there was no move on their part to implement criticism through political action. This probably defined the extreme extent of the additional liberties which had been granted them under the latest concordat with the state. No freedom had been given them to concern themselves with changing the *status quo.*

It should be remembered, in this connection, that the Eastern Church has always interpreted its relation to the state mainly as a spiritual service, and has never sought secular authority itself. "In its conception of 'the symphony between the Church and the state,' the Church has affirmed its spiritual power by renouncing all secular power."[26]

In 1956 a delegation of American churchmen—clergy and laymen—visited Russia under the auspices of the National Council of the Churches of Christ in the United States of America and were guests there of officials of the churches. Their report described the conditions which formed the background of the correspondence of the Russian prelates with the World Council of Churches and may be included in this study of the confrontation of the ecumenical movement with communism, since the visit was prompted by the Evanston Assembly of the World Council. It was, in part, reported in *The Christian Century,* as follows:

Our mission was to church leaders in Russia.[27] We knew in advance . . . that it would not be easy to achieve understanding, let alone agreement. But we believed that in a time of world tension, with deep cleavage between East and West, Christians of varying backgrounds and traditions should talk with one another with frankness, in an endeavor to clarify differences and to seek areas of agreement. . . .

The experience was profitable. We understand the Russian churchmen better. . . . We are also confident that our clear statements face to face enabled them to understand us better.

This visit should be understood as a first step toward future correspondence and other exchanges. . . .

We were received with generous hospitality. . . . We visited many churches and shared in the worship of the Orthodox as well as of the Baptists. Lutherans from the Baltic states and Armenian Orthodox joined in the discussions. We were taken to theological seminaries and academies, and to monasteries.

In addition, we held two conferences with the Council of the Soviet Government which deals with religious affairs. As we went for a definite church purpose, we make no comment on economic and political conditions in the Soviet Union, except as they apply to the situation of the churches.

[26] Edmund Schlink in "The Significance of the Eastern and Western Traditions for the Christian Church," *The Ecumenical Review,* Vol. XII, No. 2, p. 138.

[27] This mission was organized in response to the Evanston resolution directing that the appeal to the member churches of the World Council on behalf of measures be sent also to other denominations, with mention particularly of those in Russia, in which it was proposed that reciprocal visits by churchmen be arranged between countries in whose relations there were manifest tensions. (See Resolution I, Section IV, pp. 655 ff.

The delegation included Paul B. Anderson, Roswell P. Barnes, Franklin Clark Fry, Herbert Gezork, D. Ward Nichols, Charles C. Parlin, Henry Knox Sherrill, Walter W. Van Kirk, and Eugene Carson Blake.

Dr. Nichols and Dr. Blake were members of the Central Committee of the World Council of Churches, as was also Mr. Parlin.

Later in 1956, a group of Russian church leaders, headed by Metropolitan Nikolai, spent ten days in the U.S. as guests of the National Council of Churches.

It is apparent that Church and State have reached at least a temporary accommodation.

It was stated again and again that Church and State are separate. In a limited sense, this is true, by our standards. There seems to be no interference with worship. Congregations are large and devout in the relatively few available churches, with a preponderance of older people and of women. Enrollment in the few theological seminaries that are open is at capacity. Some churches have been repaired and a few new ones are being built, though there are far from enough.

The most severe limitation of the church is in the area of education; for there seems to be no religious education, except in the home by parents and by priests or ministers on occasional visitations. . . .

It is clear that the churches generally are confined within themselves. They regard their function as . . . saving souls and preparing them for heaven. They show little concern for the social or intellectual life of their people. . . . Educational, economic and political life are the concern of the state. . . .

This sharp division of function, in a population rapidly receiving scientific education biased toward atheistic assumptions, constitutes perhaps a greater danger to the church than political control of the church itself.

This . . . prevailing concept of the mission of the church is in our judgment inadequate. . . . We hope that future conversations will bring both to them and to us a deeper understanding of the church's mission. . . . We are grateful for a deepened appreciation of the elements of devotion and mystery in Christianity. We hope that further contacts will lead them to increased concern for the totality of life.

During the last several years, the policy of the Soviet Government has discouraged persecution of the churches and regarded the clergy and other believers as loyal citizens. At the same time, it has increased the aggressiveness of scientific education as a means ultimately to eradicate religion. Thus, the church has more freedom . . . but at the same time confronts a more subtle challenge. . . .

In return for freedom of worship, the leaders of the churches have apparently inclined to go along with Soviet communist leadership in important areas. Perhaps the most distressing illustration is in the area of peace propaganda.

We had frank discussion of that matter. We are convinced that the . . . churches and the people ardently desire peace. However, the statements of the church leaders were almost uniformly identical in making vague appeals for "the defense of peace," without taking into consideration the realities of the world situation or the facts of history.

It appeared to us that their concept of peace was derived not only from the Soviet Foreign Office, but also from an inadequate concept of the mission of the church.

We pointed out that the World Peace Council, in which the church leaders from Russia have given conspicuous leadership, has consistently taken the same line as that of the Soviet Government, and that participants from the West have not been truly representative of Western churches. We emphasized the necessity of finding some other basis than their past position, if we are to work together for peace.

We made it clear that the means to peace are as important as the end. Specifically, we set forth certain positions taken by the National Council of Churches (USA), for example: (1) Peace cannot be achieved, apart from justice, human rights, and fundamental freedoms; (2) The reduction and abolition of atomic weapons cannot be separated from effective inspection and control, nor in isolation from other armaments; (3) The goal of independence and freedom for subject and colonial peoples is best reached through processes of law and order and by free election under international control. . .

During 1955 and 1956 various other religious groups visited Russia. A company of Quakers, under the sponsorship of the American Friends Service Committee, said that their "strongest impression" was of "the fluid quality" of Soviet society. They noted Russia's intensive educational program, her sharp class distinctions, the spiritual vigor of her people, and the evidence of a relaxing of internal controls. They thought the theories of Marxism were proving inadequate and made these observations in *The Christian Century*:

> A whole nation has been taught to read. . . . An increasing number are being taught to think . . . and to think, according to American scientists, very well. But education, once provided, is not easy to control. How long will men well trained in the scientific process accept, without question, party pronouncements?
>
> Another force that refuses to fit neatly into the Marxist doctrine of scientific human relations is religion. We found enough evidence of spiritual vigor to suggest that the communist concern over a religious revival is well-founded. The church and synagog and mosque labor under difficulties, but neither persecution nor persuasion has yet succeeded in removing them from the Soviet scene, and, in our opinion, they are gaining rather than losing.

The government might try to reverse these trends, the observers thought, but the farther they were permitted to develop, the more difficult it would be to restore the earlier patterns. They urged that "the West should seize every opportunity to encourage decentralization and relaxation and to exploit every chance for increased contact." They cited these —and other—reasons why "men of goodwill should not despair of eventually breaking through" the Iron Curtain:

> Communists could not avoid being human beings, even if they wished to, and as human beings they are far too complex to be explained by their own doctrines.
>
> The very emphasis they put on the cult of science and the dialectical nature of all phenomena may make it easier for them eventually to recognize the contradiction between their Marxist interpretations of reality and reality itself.
>
> The Marxist-Leninist official religion "already showed evidence of producing the same antithetical force that has so often corrupted state religions—the force of indifference."

While in Russia as a member of the American delegation of churchmen (1956), Dr. Franklin Clark Fry, at the request of the Executive Committee of the World Council of Churches, conferred with Metropolitan Nikolai on the proposal that a meeting of representatives of the

Russian Orthodox Church and the World Council of Churches be held. Later, when the Metropolitan was in New York with a company of Orthodox clergy returning the visit of the Americans, the conversation was continued. The result was that a meeting in Paris at the end of January, 1957, was agreed on, "for the purpose of broader mutual acquaintance and to discuss topics suggested by either conferee and agreed to by both."

Unable to make the necessary arrangements for that date, the Russians asked for a postponement of the conference. It was finally held in Utrecht, August 7-9, 1958, and from it was issued a communiqué, reported in the Minutes (p. 80) as follows:

The basis which enabled us to meet was our brotherhood in Christ, and so we have spoken frankly with each other about the real nature and aims of the church bodies we represent.

We found that we shared the Christian concern for the unity of Christians and the manifestation of their unity in the life of the churches.

The delegates of the Holy Orthodox Church of Russia explained how their Church prays and works for the reunion of all Christians. The delegates of the World Council of Churches described how the World Council . . . seeks to promote church unity, both by the theological work of the Faith and Order Commission and in many other ways involving Christians at all levels of church life.

We share a deep concern for world peace with justice and freedom. The two delegations expressed the determination to work toward this objective. They feel the solemn responsibility of the churches in every country to call upon their governments and their people to do everything in their power to prevent war. During recent years, the World Council of Churches and the Moscow Patriarchate have exchanged their convictions about the great international problems of our time, such as disarmament, atomic warfare and nuclear weapon testing. At this meeting we have continued this conversation about our respective positions. Further contacts will be needed, in order to achieve agreement about the different ways toward peace which each is following.

The fundamental importance of the liberty with which Christ has made men free commanded our attention, and each delegation expressed its views on the manner in which religious liberty should find expression in society.

We gave consideration to a number of specific problems which the churches encounter as they seek to manifest their faith in life and work. Our discussion contributed to a better understanding of these problems.

With regard to the future, the delegates of the Holy Orthodox Church of Russia declared that they would give a report to the Patriarch and the Holy Synod of their Church, and that they would do so in a spirit of full sympathy with the fundamental principles of the ecumenical movement.

The World Council of Churches' delegates declared that they would report to the Central Committee of the World Council . . . , and that they would propose that, if this would be agreeable to the Holy Orthodox Church of Russia, observers should be invited to attend meetings of the Central Committee.

The delegates expressed gratitude to the Lord for the privilege of meeting together in the spirit of Christian love.

The Patriarchate was represented by Metropolitan Nikolai of Krutitsky and Kolmos, Bishop Michael of Smolensk, and Alex Buevsky; the World Council by Dr. Franklin Clark Fry, Metropolitan James of Melita, and Dr. Visser 't Hooft.

The Patriarchate accepted the invitation to send observers to Geneva and the Central Committee's meetings. Two delegates from Moscow spent the month of June, 1959, at the headquarters of the World Council of Churches, acquainting themselves at first hand with the office activities and afterwards attending the sessions of the Central Committee at Rhodes.

The World Council of Churches reciprocated by sending a delegation, the following winter, to visit the Church of Russia, at its invitation.

Those accompanying the General Secretary included Rev. Francis House of the General Secretariat, Dr. O. Frederick Nolde of the Commission of the Churches on International Affairs, Dr. Nick Nissiotis of the Greek Orthodox Church, and Rev. U Kyaw Than of the Burmese National Church Council.

The Geneva deputation held conversations with Patriarch Alexei and Metropolitan Nikolai and made contacts with leaders of the Russian Baptists, the Lutheran Churches of the Baltic States, and Vazgen I, Supreme Catholicos of the Armenian Church.

At a farewell dinner in Moscow on December 17, 1959, attended by many Orthodox clergy, Metropolitan Nikolai, head of the Russian Church's Department of External Relations, and representatives of the Baptist churches and of the Soviet government's Council of Religious Affairs, Patriarch Alexei spoke of his joy in welcoming "the dear guests of the Russian Orthodox Church, our brethren in Christ, representing the Christian churches united around the World Council of Churches, on Russian soil at the altars of ancient Orthodox shrines." The Russian Church looked with sympathy upon the efforts "of [our] Christian brethren to overcome centuries-old divisions and to re-unite men who worshipped God in different ways," he said. The Church of Russia would, he promised, help them in "that task." His remarks, as reported in *The Ecumenical Review* (Jan. 1960), continued:

Your already considerable achievements in that good work have been to us a source of consolation and deep spiritual satisfaction. We shall invoke God's blessing upon your efforts in the future. . . .

You have had the opportunity of seeing yourselves the piety and devoutness of the faithful people of God in our crowded churches. You have been able to see how important liturgical life and common prayer is to us, Orthodox Christians. Our strength lies in the sacraments of the Church, through the mystery of which comes the unseen but real presence of the Lord. . . . This remains perhaps beyond the comprehension of those observers who, seeing the Russian Church from outside, express . . . astonishment at its vitality. That strength does not come from ourselves. It proceeds from the quickening grace of the Holy Ghost, and is due to the guidance of Divine

Providence . . . thus we believe that separation of our Church from the state has been . . . for the good of the Church.

The relations of the Russian Church with the Christian world . . . have been strengthened in recent years. . . .

Our Church welcomes and supports . . . all things that help to strengthen world peace, to improve mutual understanding between men and to build human society on love, freedom and justice. . . .

Remaining, above all, in communion of prayer and canon law with our sister churches, the autocephalous national branches of the Universal Orthodox Church, we pray for the re-union of all Christian churches. . . .

In response, Dr. Visser 't Hooft thanked His Holiness "for a number of benefactions which have been bestowed on us"—"the invitation to visit the Church of Russia, . . . the truly fraternal reception, . . . the opportunity to come to know the spiritual life of the Church, . . . the privilege of meeting also the Lutheran, Armenian and Baptist churches, . . . above all, the fact that wherever we went we were received as brethren."

"It is the purpose of the World Council," the General Secretary said, "to be an instrument of that gathering together of the children of God for which . . . our Lord gave his life. And we hope that our little delegation, representing . . . five different churches, has been a sign and token of the realization of that purpose."

Remarking that Christians, whatever their differences in language, culture, and national history, had a common basis enabling them to recognize one another as children of one God and brothers for whom Christ died, Dr. Visser 't Hooft said:

We leave with deep thankfulness . . . for the . . . devotion of Christians in whose worship we have shared. Our hope for the future of the Church of Christ in Russia is based upon the scriptural truth that the Word of God is not bound and will continue its saving work, . . . as in the past. . . . Your Church, as well as the other churches in the Soviet Union, have shown in troubled times that they live by that power which comes from the Holy Spirit . . . eternal and ever creative. All churches . . . have entered into a period . . . in which their faith will be tested. The changes in the social and cultural situation create new conditions in which the faith once delivered to the saints will have to be expressed in new forms. We will, all together, have to find the right answers to these new needs, and we cherish the hope that your Church, with its age-old tradition, may in that process be found to renew its strength.

Our visit to the Holy Orthodox Church of Russia has no political purpose. Nevertheless, the very fact that personal contacts have been established in a spirit of friendship and Christian understanding is an important contribution to better international relations. The World Council of Churches reflects the concern of its member churches . . . for the promotion of peace, justice and freedom. Through the Commission of the Churches on International Affairs, it maintains day to day contact with government officials who are responsible for international decisions and seeks to make constructive proposals concerning the solution of international problems.

In offering this Christian testimony, the World Council steers its course between two unacceptable extremes. On the one hand, it refuses identification with any political ideology or national position, and it avoids political entanglements. On the other hand, it cannot rest content with vague generalities, because it knows that men have often cried, "Peace, peace," when there is no peace. The Christian witness must, therefore, be addressed to the concrete realities of the ever-contemporaneous situation, in order to express more fully in human relations God's will for peace, justice and freedom on earth. And the churches are called to teach that only when all nations are willing to make sacrifices in the cause of peace do they have the right to expect that they will enjoy the fruits of peace.

In all their work together in the World Council the member churches seek to share with one another the diversity of spiritual gifts which they have been given by the One Spirit for their mutual enrichment and correction, . . . and [they] especially value the rich contributions already made by the Orthodox Churches. They ardently desire to receive from the Russian Orthodox Church also the fruits of its rich history and contemporary Christian experience. We thank God for all the treasures of mystical experience and practical obedience in daily life; of liturgical community life and personal commitment; of the inheritance of the certainties of the Faith and of interpretation of the eternal verities in ways which are meaningful for this generation. Our prayer, as we part, is that all that has passed between us during the last eighteen months, and especially during this visit, may lead to a fuller sharing of all these treasures for the peace and unity of the whole Church of Christ and the fulfillment of its mission in the world.

Returning to Geneva, Dr. Visser 't Hooft described "the songs and shouts of welcome, the waving of handkerchiefs," with which the ecumenical deputation had been received, and "the joy of Russian Christians in being with Christians of other churches, and their sincere desire for closer contacts with those from other lands."

Speaking to the question "What of Christianity in Russia?" he said that Orthodox leaders estimated the membership of their Church at about twenty-five million, in the total population of over two hundred million. The theological seminaries were filled with "high-caliber students." Congregations were large, but the question was whether they could continue so, under the communists' strict policy of cutting off young people from the churches. There were no Sunday schools, no religious youth movements; and most of those seen at church were over thirty-five years of age. A majority of these were women. Church authorities were under close supervision by officials of the government's Council for Religious Affairs, who were, of course, "full-blooded Marxists."

"But some of these atheist supervisors have developed a real liking for their job, and show a deep interest in church affairs and history," Dr. Visser 't Hooft added. "After all, there may be found in England and Sweden and elsewhere government functionaries in charge of church affairs who are agnostics as well!"

The year 1960 brought a number of observers from the Russian Orthodox Church to ecumenical gatherings. They attended meetings of the Faith and Order Commission, the Executive Committee of the Commission of the Churches on International Affairs, the World Council's Central Committee, and the European Youth Assembly at Lausanne. Bishop Nikodim, successor to Bishop Nikolai as head of the Patriarchate's Department of Foreign Church Relations, paid visits to the World Council at Geneva in November, 1960, and February, 1961.

The Geneva office made public on April 27, 1961, its receipt of an application for membership in the World Council of Churches from the Russian Orthodox Church.

The letter, signed by Patriarch Alexei, stated that the Church found itself in accord with the Council's requirement that all members "accept our Lord Jesus Christ as God and Saviour," and added:

> The Russian Orthodox Church has always attached the utmost importance to the problem of mutual rapprochement between all Christians, the deepening of mutual understanding among divided Christians and the strengthening of universal brotherhood, love and peace among the nations on the basis of the Gospel.
>
> In this respect, we count on the efforts made by the World Council of Churches to strengthen the spirit of ecumenical brotherhood, as well as the contacts with the Russian Orthodox Church.
>
> Believing in the One, Holy Catholic and Apostolic Church, and being herself an integral part of that Church, the Russian Orthodox Church has not only always prayed for the welfare of Holy Churches of God and the union of all, but is fully determined to make her contribution to the great task of Christian unity on the lines of the previous movements of faith and order, life and work and international friendship through the churches; which now find their common expression in the different forms and aspects of the World Council of Churches.

The announcement from Geneva stated that the application would be submitted, with others, to the Third Assembly in November of 1961. If approved, the Russian Orthodox Church would be seated. This would require an affirmative two-thirds vote.

Commenting on the matter, Dr. Visser 't Hooft observed that the action of the Russian Church could be regarded as an act of faith in the World Council of Churches and its present members. The World Council had not changed its basic view about ecumenicity since Amsterdam, but the Russian Church had changed its attitude toward the Council.

Nothing had occurred in the Russian Church, he said, to make it less acceptable as a member in 1961 than it would have been in 1948, when it was invited to cooperate in the founding of the World Council of Churches. Receiving it would meet with fewer "questions and hazards" than would have been encountered in 1948. The World Council was an entity with established characteristics and methods of procedure, he noted. There were abundant precedents out of the formative years. There was assurance that every study and activity would be based on biblical theology, not political casuistry. If the application should not be accepted, the World Council would "itself give occasion and provocation for the formation of an Eastern equivalent of the Council, with unhappy consequences . . . to present members and the Christian cause."

One grave problem for the World Council of Churches in its attempt to obtain the cooperation of the Russian Orthodox Church had been the passionate resentment of Christians who believed that members of the hierarchy had been responsible for their persecution, including Metropolitan Nikolai, who as Vice-Regent of the Moscow Patriarchate handled the correspondence with the Geneva office.

During his mission to the United States, in company with representatives of other Russian churches, he was openly charged by Professor Nicholas D. Chubaty, editor of *The Ukrainian Quarterly,* in a letter in *The New York Times,* June 9, 1956, with having acted with the state against the Ukrainian Orthodox Autocephalous Church and the Ukrainian Greek Catholic Church. The accusation was, in part, that

> He persecuted the Ukrainian Orthodox Autocephalous Church by trying Metropolitan Polykarp *in absentia* before the church court in Moscow. He then issued a proclamation which was full of distortions and slanders on the Ukrainian Orthodox who favored autocephaly. This proclamation was a guide for the terroristic action of the M.V.D. against the Ukrainian Orthodox Church when the Red Army in 1944 started to occupy the Ukraine. Metropolitan Nikolai became expert in Ukrainian church affairs for the Moscow Patriarchate.
>
> But a totally un-Christian persecution was started in 1945 against the Ukrainian Greek Catholics in the western provinces of the Ukraine, in Galicia and Carpatho-Ukraine, occupied by the Soviets. This Church of over four million followers was condemned to destruction by fire and sword. In this barbaric action we see the harmonious co-operation between the Moscow Patriarchate and the Soviet police.
>
> In April, 1945, in one day in Soviet-occupied Galicia were imprisoned all five Ukrainian Catholic hierarchs. Simultaneously, a group of three renegade clergy was created to liquidate the Ukrainian Catholic Church and bring it under the Russian Orthodox Patriarchate in Moscow.
>
> In May, 1945, the Moscow Patriarch issued a proclamation to the Catholic Ukrainians . . . to abandon the Catholic Church and join Russian Orthodoxy. The appeal was . . . without results. . . . The Soviet Government came to his assistance . . . issued an official decision approving the . . . three renegade priests as the church authority . . . in Galicia, demanding registration of all the dissidents and their denunciation. . . . In June, 1945, . . . three hundred priests were arrested.
>
> The Moscow Patriarchate . . . called a mock synod in St. George Cathedral, Lvov, composed of two hundred four priests and twelve laymen assembled with the support of Soviet authorities. They proclaimed the separation of the Ukrainian Catholic Church from Rome and its dependency upon Moscow. . . . Hundreds of priests and thousands of the faithful were deported to the concentration camps as martyrs of the faith.

Whether or not such charges as these represented the facts accurately and fully, they emphasized the impossibility of effectively uniting Christians for an assault upon communism. Ancient mutual hatreds and distrust would give the victory in advance to the enemies of Christianity, whom many professing Christians seemed to endure more happily than they could one another.

Criticism of ecumenical councils and of denominations belonging to them for certain phases of their policy on communism gathered increasing force in the free world during the post-Evanston years, and all such bodies, because of their interlocking relations, were implicated whenever any of them were attacked.

The damaging effects of this opposition were attributable, in part, to the failure of the interchurch organizations and their member denominations to keep their constituents informed concerning their objectives and the principles which guided their actions in this area. Had information been adequate, there would still have existed room for honest differences of opinion on the wisdom of the course taken with the problems posed by communism; but much confusion might have been avoided, and the wildly imaginative charges which arose from ignorance and half-knowledge. Better communications with the pulpit and the pew and more attention to public relations would at least have created conditions favorable to constructive discussion and the correction of mistaken reports.

The World Council of Churches afforded in its experience illustration of the complicated nature of the controversy. From the start, the Council had in its membership denominations in communist countries, whose survival depended on acknowledgment of the authority of the state and obedience to its decrees. Many of their members might individually reject the communist philosophy, but they had, with their churches, to accommodate themselves to governmental requirements. The World Council had been unwilling to deny membership to such churches, understanding their need of Christian fellowship and hoping that they would in time regain their freedom.

Some of the churches behind the Iron Curtain had been permitted by the political authorities to participate in ecumenical gatherings, including Assemblies of the World Council, and delegates from them had been elected to various offices. They had representation on the Central and Executive Committees of the World Council.

Not only had membership not been denied to these "captive churches," but they had been invited and encouraged to join the Council, as witnessed the meetings and conversations over many years with the Russian Orthodox Church.

At the same time, the World Council declared its rejection of totalitarianism and reserved to itself the right at any and all times to criticize all political systems. The application of this principle to communist states from time to time had made it the target of condemnation. On the same account, the churches of some communist countries belonging to the World Council had withdrawn from active participation in its work.

The denominations which were members of the World Council of Churches stood, of course, in essentially the same position with reference to communism. They not only were the Council and responsible for its policies; they had themselves—many of them—churches scattered through communist lands, which they felt obliged to keep in fellowship and to help in other ways. Moreover, most of the denominations were members of world confessional bodies which embraced churches in all nations, East and West.

Other conciliar organizations, besides the World Council of Churches, were similarly involved in the tangle with communism. The International Missionary Council had in its membership of national and regional councils churches in more countries than any ecumenical body. Councils of smaller areas found themselves bound in this same bundle of life through their relationships with the denominations and the councils with international constituencies: for example, the National Council of the Churches of Christ in the United States, which through its Division of Foreign Missions had ties with Christians in nearly all lands, as it had also through its relations with the World Council of Churches.

While there was no evidence at any time of conscious concealment of connections with churches in communist-controlled countries by the religious bodies having interests on a world scale, the education of their own people and the public at large concerning the reasons for the policy which was being pursued left much to be desired. As stated already, even with the fullest information, there would have been room for disagreement on the soundness of the policy. There were Christians who, knowing the reasons influencing the decisions of the denominations and their conciliar agencies, believed that the attempt to bring into the world program of the denominations churches owning allegiance to communist states could only result in compromising Christianity. They objected to the World Council's acceptance of the credentials of delegates from Hungary who had been appointed by the government contrarily to the will of the churches, as described above.

If many of those who knew what was being done and were familiar with the explanations were disturbed, it could hardly have been surprising that others altogether uninformed should have given credence to the charges of "softness" toward communism against the World Council of Churches and its denominations and other ecumenical bodies related to them.

Whether it would have silenced criticism or not, the only answer was to be found in the facts. But, strangely enough, Christian leaders generally were content to assert their personal innocence of sympathy with communism and to represent the critics as seeking only to discredit and destroy the ecumenical movement.

Since churches in communist countries could exist only in some degree of collaboration with, or submission to, the governments, the Lutheran Church in Hungary, after the revolution of 1956, entered into agreement with the political powers, as previously noted, to recognize the state as supreme and to instruct its members in obedience to the laws "in all things." At the same time it submitted to the authority of the state's Office for Religious Affairs in all matters, including even its internal administration. (See p. 789.)

Baptists and other free-church groups, whether in Hungary or Russia, thrived, after a manner, by yielding to the state's demand that they confine themselves to the promotion of "spiritual religion" in its private and other-worldly aspects, except when directed by the government to support its social and political programs, such as the Stockholm Peace Appeal.

How long Christianity could live under these conditions was a question that would grow ever more pressing for the World Council of Churches and other ecuminical councils, the denominations which were members of them and had at the same time their own separate international missions, the confessional bodies with their global memberships, and the churches themselves in communist countries.

Would there not have to be eventually a decisive stand for the full freedom of the Gospel, even at the risk, for the captive churches, of martyrdom and for the World Council of Churches and other missionary agencies of the churches of having to abandon their international programs at the frontiers of communistic totalitarianism? Otherwise, would not the Gospel cease to be of effect and the work of the World Council and of the denominations in their individual capacities be reduced to the dispensing of charity?

Here was a "main theme" needing, in the opinion of many friends of the Christian movement, to be probed to its depths.

3. The World Council and the Roman Catholic Church

In 1938 William Temple, then Chairman of the Provisional Committee, had informed Pope Pius XI unofficially of the intention to hold a conference to implement the concurrent action of the Conference on Church, Community and State (Oxford, 1937) and the Second World Conference on Faith and Order (Edinburgh, 1937) looking to the founding of a World Council of Churches. Recognizing that by its policy the Roman Catholic Church could not join in the meeting, the Committee forwarded no formal invitation. It was hoped, however, that because of the considerable interest of Roman Catholics in the ecumenical movement the Church would send observers.

This expectation was to be disappointed. The Church issued a warning to its communicants not to have anything to do with the proposed Assembly. According to reports which were regarded as reliable, several hundred Roman Catholics had applied to their authorities for permission to attend.

The interdiction of the Church notwithstanding, the Bishop of Geneva was known to have "gone out of his way to express his goodwill as the time for the Assembly approached," and the Roman Catholic Archbishop of Utrecht, in a diocesan letter explaining why the Church could not cooperate, recognized that the movement represented "the good intentions of many" and directed priests and laity to "pray fervently for those participating in the congress, as well as for all other non-Catholic Christians." Certain Jesuits, apparently on their own initiative, observed the Assembly closely, some as journalists from the press gallery and others from seats reserved for the general public.

The Amsterdam Assembly and the World Council of Churches which it organized received extensive attention in periodicals and books published in Roman Catholic countries. Some of the writers dismissed with disdain the efforts of non-Roman Christians to find in their so-called ecumenical movement the unity Roman Catholics had always possessed. But there were those who with more irenic purpose attempted to discern and represent the true inwardness and spiritual significance of the World Council of Churches. Among these was Father Robert Rouquette, who contributed an article to *Études* for April, 1949, which for its mood and penetration was commended by many reviewers.

By way of introduction, the author commented on the problem Roman Catholics had in trying to project themselves "into the position where sympathetic understanding of the non-Roman world becomes possible." He said:[28]

> Perhaps the greatest difficulty for us is in the psychological realm. Accustomed as we are to catholic unity, to a definite expression of the faith, to discipline with firm outlines, we are naturally inclined to underestimate an attempt to achieve Christian unity, which starts simply by seeking it. . . . We must react against this tendency; we must attempt to measure not only what is lacking in non-Roman Christianity, as seen at Amsterdam—and that indeed is infinite—but also to feel the dynamic energy which springs from it. This dynamic energy has not yet been able to find expression in concrete forms of unity, or to express a common faith; nevertheless, it is a powerful potency, which tends to pass over into act.

Turning to the theological basis of the World Council of Churches, he wrote:

> I cannot find words to express the decisiveness, from our point of view, of the fact that these Churches, mainly Protestant, assembled at Amsterdam, have, before everything else, solemnly and unanimously professed faith in the divinity of our Lord, the primary foundation of the Christian faith.

[28] From translation in *The Ecumenical Review,* Vol. VII, No. 3, p. 279.

Remarking on methods of approach in the search for unity—doctrinal compromise, the reduction of theologies to the lowest common denominator, cooperation in Christian work, and the frank attack on differences—he said:

> Amsterdam has introduced a formulation describing the tension, instead of trying to conceal differences. This marks immense progress over former ecumenical conferences.

And concerning what he called "the pragmatic approach by practical action":

> This . . . method is sound, if regarded only as a means to prepare for a unity, which for the moment it is impossible directly to promote. But if the means becomes an end, it is a way of illusion and positively harmful. . . . At Amsterdam, it was found possible to register at certain points a real and relative unity, which is more than a mere verbal agreement, but within which an essential disagreement is recognized.

Father Rouquette saw it as

> . . . of importance that the churches, by the very fact of undertaking to consider great social problems, have in practice recognized that the Church has the right and the duty to judge the world, to act within it, to improve it and to direct it towards the kingdom of heaven, not indeed in order to realize the kingdom here below, but in order to make it, even here on earth, the goal of our efforts. It is good that pragmatism and pietism have been held in equilibrium.

He explained why it was impossible for the Roman Catholic Church to cooperate in the ecumenical movement and the World Council of Churches.

> If the Roman Church agreed to take part in the ecumenical movement, she would be bound to regard herself as one Christian communion among others, seeking the Body of Christ, unaware where and how that Body expresses itself; this would be tantamount to admitting that Christ has deserted his Church, and has denied it the means of recognizing and expressing itself as his Body. . . .

During the interim between the First and Second Assemblies, interest in the ecumenical movement continued to grow among Roman Catholics, and a memorandum by a group of their European theologians on the main theme of the Evanston Assembly, "Christ—The Hope of the World," was described by Dr. Willem Adolf Visser 't Hooft as "a valuable contribution to our discussion."

Many non-Roman Christians had hoped that "An Instruction to Local Ordinaries" issued by the Vatican in 1949, to the effect that "mixed gatherings," while "not to be held without the previous sanction of the competent ecclesiastical authority," were "not forbidden outright," left the way open for at least occasional limited cooperation. Not a few Roman Catholics would have liked to see their Church act to show its sympathetic interest in the effort to increase collaboration by the Christian communions. They were encouraged by the fact also that in 1952 some of their theologians attended the Third World Conference on Faith and Order, in Lund, Sweden, as observers. But a pastoral letter of Cardinal Stritch of Chicago forbidding "the faithful of the Church . . . to attend the assemblies or conventions of non-Catholic organizations or councils," which went out "to the clergy and laity" of the archdiocese in advance of the Evanston Assembly of the World Council of Churches (apparently with the approval of the Vatican, as well as of the American hierarchy) rudely halted all such aspirations. It said:

> There are men outside the church professing the Christian name who deplore the divisions which exist among them. . . . They gather in international organizations; they hold congresses, conventions and assemblies. . . . Quite naturally the question arises in your minds, What should be the opinion of a Catholic, what his attitude with regard to these organizations and their activities?
>
> The answer of the church to this question is: The Catholic Church does not take part in these organizations or in their assemblies or conferences. She does not enter into any organization in which the delegates of many sects sit down in council or conference as equals to discuss the nature of the church of Christ or the nature of her unity, or to propose to discuss how to bring about the unity of Christendom, or to formulate a program of united Christian action.[29]
>
> She does not allow her children to engage in any activity or conference or discussion based on the false assumption that Roman Catholics too are still searching for the truth of Christ. . . . Such an admission she can never make, for she is now, as she has always been, the one and only Spouse of Christ, the one and only mystical Body of Christ, the one and only church of Christ. . . .
>
> If we are asked, does the Roman Catholic Church desire the unity of all believing men, our reply is that she by all means desires unity, but not a unity forged according to fallible human conceptions. . . . If the Catholic Church does not take part in these international and national councils, conferences and assemblies, it is not because she is not interested in co-operating with our Lord in bringing his other sheep into his fold. . . . This attitude of the church with regard to our separated brethren is not one of arrogance and pride. Far from it. It is rather that of a loving parent toward erring children. She knows her duty to Christ. She mingles love with firmness. . . .

[29] In *Irenikon* Father P. C. Lialine mentioned the presence at Evanston of six Roman Catholic journalists and described the attitude of the Assembly toward them and their Church, as follows:

"I believe I can summarize the position in this way: much friendliness and courtesy on the part of the delegates to the Assembly and of its staff for individual Catholics—little sympathy, to say no more, towards the Catholic Church as an institution, as little as towards the totalitarian regimes which exist today in the world! Its unity is always considered as being at the opposite extreme of the unity sought ecumenically." (*Ecumenical Review*, Vol. VII, No. 3, p. 278.)

In the World Council of Churches were denominations, it should be said, as reluctant about encouraging cooperation by the Roman Catholic Church as that Church was to be encouraged. Some of them would have favored a pan-Protestant, if not an anti-Catholic, policy for the Council. They had joined chiefly because of the opportunity it afforded for participation in useful and needed joint ministries and could not see how a communion accustomed to speak infallibly would be able to accommodate itself to ecumenical democratic relationships and procedures. Moreover, they objected to the political aspirations of the Roman Catholic Church, and other activities including reported persecution of religious minorities, especially in countries where it enjoyed ascendancy, as in certain of the Latin states. Some of these denominations had many constituents who, whatever the official attitude of their leaders, were definitely affected by the ancient feeling of hostility between Protestantism and Romanism, which in 1954 was still strong enough to be mentioned by Bishop Berggrav of Norway in an address at Evanston along with the tensions disturbing the peace of the world:

A new word has entered the language of mankind . . . "apartheid," meaning to keep away from fellowship to avoid . . . tensions. Up to the first decade of this century it might even be true of the churches that they preferred apartheid—each for herself. . . . Nothing can conceal that tensions in fact are at work. . . . Is there not in many of our churches anger, sometimes also fear, toward the Church of Rome? And is there not only very, very seldom a bit of respect, not to speak of a sense of love? I know that you want to interrupt me here and ask: How could we love Rome? My answer would be by means of a question: Does Christ love them? Has he sacrificed himself for them? Not, of course, for the organization of the fabric of that Church, but for all its members . . . ?

In some of the other addresses at Evanston, strong statements were made about alleged actions by the Roman Catholic Church against Protestants in certain countries. Accredited visitors (who were deputy or alternate delegates) heard Professor Manuel Gutierrez-Marin, President of the Spanish Evangelical Church, on the situation in this respect in Spain.

The Spanish state is a Catholic state and the leading men are serious about this. . . . They are anxious to prevent all trends which would prejudice Catholic unity. . . . In [the last concordat] . . . the state declares itself to be partisan protector of the Catholic Church . . . , pledges to provide opportunities for worship and to pay the salaries of the clergy. . . . Ecclesiastical buildings and institutions are tax exempt. . . . The concordat recognizes the canonical celebration of marriage as being valid in civil law. . . . All . . . baptized Catholics have to contract this canonical marriage, even if they have become indifferent or joined another confession. . . . The concordat provides that lessons in the Catholic religion shall be obligatory from grade school to university. . . .

None of the evangelical churches in Spain is legally recognized. No local congregation is recognized even as an association. . . . "Propaganda" or "proselytizing" is strictly prohibited, and colporteurs are not permitted to circulate any literature at all. Even the Protestant Bible is not permitted to be printed. . . . Spanish Protestantism is denied the right to make itself known to a broader public.

Bishop Sante Uberto Barbieri of the Methodist Church in Argentina reported on the conflict between Protestantism and Roman Catholicism in Latin American countries:

Parallel to the despotic authority of the imperial powers, the Roman Catholic ecclesiastical authority grew up and asserted itself on totalitarian lines, true to the underlying Catholic philosophy of *"Ubi Roma, ubi Ecclesia"* (Where Rome is, there the Church is), by which there is no other way to become and to remain a Christian except through the agency and the ministration of the Church of Rome. Outside her fellowship there is either paganism or apostasy, and both these, . . . in the multiplicity of their manifestations, have to be eliminated by whatever means are at hand, if not by persuasion, then by force, if force can be exerted either directly or indirectly. This philosophy has been at work since the beginning of the Conquest, through the whole Colonial period, and after the wars of independence, despite the liberal constitutions of almost all of the Latin American countries. These constitutions are not the result of the influence of the Roman Catholic thought and action. Those who fought for the independence of the Latin American countries had to face the opposition of the high ecclesiastical hierarchy, allied to . . . Spain and Portugal. . . . After the victory of the Revolution for Indepedence, we find the Roman Church siding always with the most reactionary political forces, because these are more akin to her ecclesiastical philosophy, and because they are the most natural allies to a system which, by nature and constitution, is the most totalitarian of all.

We understand, therefore, why the Roman Catholic Church feels that Latin America is her natural heritage and possession, and why she cannot admit or tolerate the presence of other Christian bodies, and why she is, in one way or another, trying to obstruct, to eliminate, or to persecute them. For more than three centuries she was the only and undisputed religious force with tremendous economic and political power, and so could never accept the liberal spirit of the Latin American constitutions, which were written mainly under the inspiration of the thinkers who were responsible for the French Revolution and the influence of the North American Constitution. . . .

If the Roman Catholic Church could have as tolerant a spirit as that shown to her by the Protestant majorities in traditionally Protestant countries, . . . I am quite sure that many of the religious disturbances and persecutions we have had in Latin America would not have existed nor could exist. . . . At the bottom of every curtailment of religious liberties, we . . . find the direct or indirect influence of the Catholic Church.

Bishop Barbieri, continuing, declared that "the attack on Protestantism by the Roman Catholic Church" followed the lead of the Spanish hierarchy as represented by Cardinal Pedro Segura y Saenz, Archbishop of Sevilla, who in a pastoral letter in 1952 said: "In our times the worst kind of liberty is presented as the success of our times, because liberty of thought, of teaching, of the press . . . in reality are liberties for perdition, whose origin is a poisoned fountain from which the worst evils of the world flow. . . . The liberty of worship is reckoned as a privilege or prerogative of the modern world. . . . This the Church condemns in a decisive and energetic way."

As illustrative of the sequent evils of this incitement to the suppression of Protestantism, he referred to the appeal of the Executive Committee of the Evangelical Confederation of Colombia, of April 17, 1954, to the United Nations and the Organization of American States:

> During the last six years, in violation of constitutional provisions which guarantee liberty of worship and teaching, Protestant Christians have been victims of a persecution largely instigated by elements in the Roman Catholic clergy. The religious persecution has resulted in the death of fifty-three Protestants because of their evangelical Christian faith, the destruction by fire and dynamite of forty-three churches and chapels, the forced closure of one hundred sixteen primary schools, and the displacement of thousands of church members.[30]

However, by the time the World Council of Churches arrived at Evanston there was general acquiescence in, if not approval of, the open-door policy toward the Roman Catholic Church, which had for its main sponsors those denominations whose interest was in the first place in union.

This solicitude in the direction of Rome was strongest in the churches of the Anglican group, generally speaking.[31] But it was shared by many churchmen in other communions; one of the best-reasoned statements

[30] Bishop Barbieri was charged by Roman Catholic writers with unfairness for not having spoken of the indebtedness of the nations of Central and South America to the Roman Catholic Church. (See *The Christian Century*, October 20, 1954.)

[31] It was the churches of the Anglican communion that conceived and led in founding the Faith and Order Movement, the purview of which from the beginning included the Roman Catholic Church. The committee sent by the Protestant Episcopal Church of the United States to confer with British and European churchmen on the proposal to hold a world conference on faith and order at Lausanne paid a call upon Pope Benedict XV and laid the plan before him. It has been noted that Archbishop William Temple of York felt it an amenity due the papal incumbent (Pius XI) in 1938 to inform him unofficially of the decision to call a conference to organize a World Council of Churches. Prior to the inception of the Faith and Order Movement, it was because of the objection of churches and officials of the Anglican group to inviting representatives of the Protestant missions in predominantly Roman Catholic countries that the Latin nations had no part in the World Missionary Conference at Edinburgh in 1910, and the holding of the Pan-American Missionary Conference at Panama in 1916 was considered necessary.

Archbishop Nathan Söderblom, Primate of the Swedish Church, supported the Anglican position, declaring that an ecumenical conference which excluded the Church of Rome was a contradiction in terms.

The Church of England took no part in the First World Missionary Conference at Edinburgh in 1910, because the Church of Rome was not invited. This was in keeping with its policy.

expressive of it was an article by Dr. Ernest Kinder, Professor of Systematic Theology at the University of Münster, Germany,[32] in *The Ecumenical Review* (July, 1955). Speaking of those Protestants who "can no longer see any basis for reaching an understanding with the Roman Catholics, and regard further discussions as futile, pointless and hopeless," he wrote:

Although one can readily understand this kind of reaction, as far as human feelings and considerations of expediency are concerned, on a deeper level it seems to me this reaction is wrong and even dangerous. Just in the present situation, and in spite of everything, I am convinced that it is our duty to maintain as much contact as possible [with Roman Catholics], to listen to one another and to carry on discussion, for the sake of the Roman Catholic Church and of Christendom on the one hand, and for the sake of the ecumenical movement and genuine ecumenical thought on the other.

The Roman Catholic Church is a fact, and it embraces a considerable number of Christians in the world. That alone is sufficient reason for true ecumenical thought not to ignore it, whatever its own attitude may be. . . . Any ecumenical thought and action which definitely excluded the Roman Catholic Church because of the difficulties involved would no longer be truly ecumenical. . . . It is not the mission of the World Council to become the official censor of the churches and of Christianity . . . , granting admission only to churches which we like and which make things easy for us. The World Council has to reckon with the churches as they are. . . . The problem posed by the external existence of the Roman Catholic Church is basically exactly the same as the problems which the member churches present for one another within the World Council. . . . Do we not find many of the other member churches incomprehensible, strange and annoying? Does not the whole thing sometimes look like the square of the circle, so that the only thing which holds us together, and enables us to venture further, is faith? If we were to shirk facing the problems posed by the Roman Catholic Church, it would have permanent repercussions on the relations of the churches within the World Council. . . .

It is essential that true ecumenical thought should not restrict its own outlook by taking serious account only of a legally-defined group of churches. It would be contrary to the nature of the World Council, if it were to claim the exclusive monopoly of ecumenism. For it to seal itself up would be thoroughly unecumenical.

Pointing out that this "is just the difference between the World Council of Churches and other movements today which pretend to be 'ecumenical' (like the movements instigated by Rome or Moscow or by the International Council of Christian Churches—nor should the strength of these be under-estimated!), that [it] . . . does not claim to have the monopoly in ecumenism and does not pretend to be the only possible legitimate model for a future world church," he continued:

The member churches of the World Council desire, on the contrary, to leave room for Christ himself to make the unity of the church a historical

[32] Dr. Kinder was a delegate of the Evangelical Church in Germany to the Second Assembly at Evanston.

reality. . . . They want to face the implications of the fact that they recognize at least certain *"vestigia ecclesiae"* in one another, and acknowledge one another to be members of the Body of Christ. . . . And there are quite a number of people in the Roman Catholic Church, some of them influential, who are seriously prepared to discuss the subject in the light of Jesus Christ, who is Head of the Church; and many Catholics want to discuss the matter as representatives of their Church, and are making more serious efforts than many Protestant churches do to ensure that Christ is the basis for the special characteristics of their Church.

Professor Kinder thought that Protestants should not "ignore the repercussions which a definitely anti-Roman attitude and a future development along anti-Roman lines would have on the ecumenical movement."

Even if we did not wish it, an anti-Roman attitude would very probably (in accordance with the law of opposites) send the pendulum swinging in the opposite direction and drive the World Council into a radicalism which would be just as undesirable as "Romanisation." Slamming the door in the face of the Roman Catholic Church would turn the ecumenical movement more and more into a world Protestant movement, in which Protestants would discuss things together. . . . But it is part of the nature of Protestantism that . . . in spite of the many indispensable things in it, it is not capable singlehanded of carrying on a truly ecumenical discussion nor a really ecumenical movement. We cannot do without the Roman Catholic Church. . . .

The author felt that a new spirit working in Catholicism and Protestantism was drawing them together.

The rigid attitude resumed [since war times] by many official Roman Catholic authorities must not deceive us. . . . The old historical barriers between them [Protestantism and Catholicism] have crumbled from within, and they are being drawn together by a renewal of the Christian spirit; that is a spiritual fact which we simply must recognize. . . .

The phenomenon that confronts us is this: the more seriously, positively and faithfully Catholics and Protestants concentrate upon the *essence* of the Christian message and remain true to the heart of their own confession (notwithstanding the all-too-human and secular-historical elements in their churches), the more they will feel drawn to one another. . . . They will be forced to take each other seriously, to listen to one another, and to learn from one another's spirit and theology. . . .

Referring to "the intense interest with which Roman Catholics are following developments in the ecumenical movement," Dr. Kinder emphasized again "that there are many essential things which . . . Protestants must learn from the Roman Catholic Church and from their comments on what we do." He suggested that

If we are horrified by many dangerous secular and even pagan elements in the Roman Catholic Church, we should be equally horrified by similar elements in our own church—instead of going to the other extreme (secularism and humanism). . . . Our first task is not to judge the Roman Catholic Church, but to judge ourselves. . . .

On both sides many far-reaching changes must be carried out and many accretions removed, so that that which is truly Christian . . . can develop more freely and truly. We cannot "create" this; only God can do that. But we can at least remain together. In obedience to God and with a sense of real responsibility we must do so.

Those less philosophical and theological than Professor Kinder could find, perhaps, practical grounds for rationalizing his conclusion that the World Council of Churches should maintain contact, so far as possible, with the Roman Catholic Church, in the hope that eventually some degree of rapprochement might be reached.

They could see, for one thing, that it would be easier to deal with the serious problems arising out of hostile attitudes of Protestants and Roman Catholics within an organization to which both belonged than in their present state of complete separation. There would be a forum for the discussion of differences and the submission of grievances which, if the ties of Christian fellowship could be kept intact, would open the way to fairer results than could be arrived at by the usual method of charge and countercharge between them, with no opportunity ever for confrontation. And whatever capacity for Christian love Protestants and Roman Catholics possessed would under such conditions have a better chance for development. When those who were Christians had become acquainted, they would already have taken a long step toward the discovery of their essential unity and of their mutual advantage in a state of peace and brotherhood, and possibly of actual cooperation.

Moreover, the addition of the weight of the Roman Catholic Church to the undertakings of the World Council of Churches in the area of social action[33] would tremendously increase their effectiveness. And collaboration in the sphere of interchurch relief would give a demonstration of Christian charity which would heal many wounds and go farther toward winning the attention of the world than the customary preachments of either side. The imagination could be stirred deeply by contemplation of what might be accomplished by Protestants, Anglicans, Orthodox, Old Catholics, and Roman Catholics united and working together for all the interests of the kingdom of God on the basis of their common faith in Jesus Christ.

Short of miracles, such things could never happen: but did not Christians believe in miracles?

Roman Catholic officials generally construed as an attack on their Church a motion in the Central Committee at New Haven in 1957

[33] Roman Catholicism was experienced in social action, the term *Catholica actio* itself probably having originated with the lay movement within the Church for applying Christian teachings to the problems of society. Behind this development were the encyclicals of the Popes dealing with social questions.

instructing the Executive Committee "to arrange for studies to be made of the problem of religious liberty arising from the Roman Catholic and other countries," contending that "great damage had been done to Catholic-Protestant relationships throughout the world."

The action referred to, which was moved by the Archbishop of Canterbury, had been aimed mainly at the Latin countries, particularly Spain and Colombia. It followed upon a demand by Methodist Bishop Uberto Barbieri of Argentina, Bolivia, and Uruguay for a strong condemnation of persecution of Protestants in predominantly Catholic countries.

The Bureau of Information of the National Catholic Welfare Conference in Washington, D.C., thought it "regrettable that the discussions of the leaders of the World Council of Churches . . . devoted so much time to criticism of another religion, when so much more might have been accomplished, had they addressed themselves entirely to matters of common spiritual and moral concern." This statement came from Rev. Martin J. Work, Executive Director of the National Council of Catholic Men.

Rev. John E. Kelly, Director of the National Welfare Conference of the Church, published the rejoinder that the World Council's studies of "other countries" should include those in which Roman Catholics suffered disabilities at the hands of Protestant majorities—for example, Denmark, Norway, and Sweden, where Lutheranism was the "established religion."

Actually, the resolution, which was mildly phrased, was less the provocation than some of the persons who discussed it, who had on other occasions and in other capacities been involved in controversy with the Roman Catholic authorities.

The study, which was conducted by Dr. A. F. Carrillo de Albornoz and published on a grant from the Fund for the Republic, must have commended itself for competence and fairness to many Roman Catholics, as well as Protestants. The printed report was factual and irenic, bearing none of the odor or noise of conflict.

In his 1960 report to the Central Committee, the General Secretary of the World Council said of the relation of the Roman Catholic Church and the ecumenical movement:[34]

> If I analyze the present situation correctly, the road which the World Council of Churches will have to find, in this respect, is a road between two abysses.
>
> The one danger which we shall have to avoid is that we should consider ourselves or become generally considered as an opposite number of or a counterweight to the Roman Catholic Church. This is a real danger, for there are many Roman Catholics who *compare* the World Council of Churches with the Roman Catholic Church as if they were comparable entities, and there are those on our side who think too easily in terms of the

[34] Minutes and Reports of the Central Committee, 1960, p. 110.

formation of ecclesiastical power constellations. The natural Adam in us and the political categories which are current in the world can easily drive us in this direction.

But that would be a spiritual disaster, because we exist to work for unity, and not to replace a division between many groups by a division between a few large groups. We must, therefore, remind ourselves that the World Council of Churches is a body *sui generis,* which refuses to become the adversary of any church or groups of churches and stands for the unity in Christ of all who recognize him as God and Savior.

On the other hand, there is the danger that, in order to facilitate contacts with the Roman Catholic Church, we should give up convictions and principles which belong to the very essence of our movement.

In saying this, I think particularly of the advice that a certain number of Roman Catholic ecumenists are giving us. This advice amounts to saying that the one and only valid activity of the World Council of Churches is theological study and conversation about the issues of reunion of the Church. Everything else is considered by them as a dangerous deviation from the true task of the Council.

Now, we have made it abundantly clear that full unity is and must be the goal of the World Council of Churches, but we believe at the same time that there are urgent common tasks to be performed even now, and that the performing of these tasks will help us to advance toward unity. We come from Edinburgh and Stockholm, as well as from Lausanne, and we are not ashamed of our ancestors.

There are other things in our living tradition which we are not prepared to give up for any price—our convictions about religious liberty, our concern for an ecumenical relationship between the churches in which there is a real listening to each other.

To avoid both dangers will take much wisdom and practice. But the purity of our cause is at that price.

Apropos to the announcement in 1959 that Pope John XXIII would the following January call an Ecumenical Council in the interest of unity, the Executive Committee devoted a section of its report to the Central Committee at Rhodes to matters having to do with the relationship of the World Council with the Roman Catholic Church:

It is well known that during recent years informal contacts have existed between the World Council staff and the group of Roman Catholic theologians who collaborate in the Roman Catholic Conference on Ecumenical Questions. These contacts have provided opportunity, during recent months, for us to gain clearer understanding of the plans concerning the [Ecumenical] Council and to explain what are the hopes and desires of the World Council with regard to relationships among the churches.

On the basis of the discussion, the Executive Committee emphasized that relations could be greatly improved: if opportunity were given for greater co-operation in social service and in working for just and durable peace, if there could be more discussion among theologians, and if the churches would join in securing full religious liberty for all peoples in all lands.

The Executive Committee and the staff have been mindful that in this, as in other matters, they have no authority to speak on behalf of the churches or, indeed, for the World Council itself, except insofar as the official organs of the Council have laid down the principles of World Council policy.

The Executive Committee will continue to follow the developments with regard to the Ecumenical Council with interest. As leaders of a movement which stands for church unity, we cannot be indifferent to an event which affects so large a number of Christians, and which cannot avoid having a bearing on relations among the several churches. We hope and pray that that bearing will be of a constructive nature, and that it will serve the cause of unity according to the will of God. [1959 Minutes, pp. 93-94.]

The impression given by the secular and religious presses that the Ecumenical Council announced by the Pope would be concerned mainly with church unity, proved incorrect. While representatives of other churches were invited as observers, Rome emphasized that it would be a Council of Roman Catholic bishops, and that its main purposes would be "that the Church should attain new vigour for its mission and consolidate its own life and cohesion."

Nevertheless, it was meant to have a considerable indirect influence on the issues of Christian unity in ecumenical discussions. Interest in the subject had been growing steadily among Roman Catholics and had reached a stage making it necessary to have at the Vatican an organ to deal directly with it. In the *motu proprio, Superno Dei nutu,* the Pope stated that a new Secretariat for the unity of Christians would be organized, with Augustin Cardinal Bea its head, and Monsignor J. G. M. Willebrands the secretary.

From the Cardinal came the statement that the Secretariat would have the double function of enabling non-Roman Catholics to follow the work of the Second Vatican Council and of helping the churches not in communion with Rome to arrive at unity with the Church.

The Vatican had made its first official statement on the ecumenical movement in the encyclical *Mortalium animos* of 1928, which revealed a negative attitude toward it. The new announcement clearly indicated that the Church had decided to enter the conversation on unity. It could no longer leave the initiative in this area to individual Roman Catholics but must begin to act and speak for itself.

At a meeting in Riedböhringen, Germany, his home, Cardinal Bea said that it was most important for the unofficial dialogue between the confessions, which had been in progress before his Secretariat was set up, to continue. These meetings of theologians had resulted, he believed, in "a certain amount of agreement." He thought that "a two-way conversation" could be established between his Secretariat and the World Council of Churches on some questions of Christian faith, albeit each church in the World Council would have to make its own decision independently as to closer relationship with the Church of Rome.

In a later interview, the Cardinal said that he saw no obstacle to co-operation with the World Council of Churches, composed of 178 Anglican, Protestant, and Orthodox churches, in such areas as social and charitable work and the promotion of world peace. "What would it not mean to mankind, for instance," he said, "if all Christians would proceed unitedly with regard to such essential questions as atomic war, disarmament and the preservation and promotion of peace!"

The Cardinal expected his Secretariat to keep Protestant and Orthodox clergymen informed on the progress of the Ecumenical Council, later tentatively appointed for sometime in 1962, and to receive suggestions from non-Catholic churchmen. The Council would have to work slowly toward Christian unity, he said, with a long-range view. Apart from doctrinal differences, there were practical difficulties in the fact that Protestantism had no authoritative counterpart to the Secretariat for talks and action. To an evangelical theologian who had suggested that the Secretariat should negotiate with a group of Protestant clergymen, he had been forced to reply, he stated, "that this would be practical, if he could tell me who on the Protestant side would have the authority to delegate such theologians and to make the possible results . . . acceptable to the Protestant world."

Monsignor Willebrands told a study conference of the Ecumenical Centrale at the Evangelical Academy in Arnoldshain, Germany, that Christian unity, in his opinion, would have to be a gradual new historical process, and not simply "a restoration of the unity which the Church lost centuries ago." He did not think that the Roman Catholic Church was preventing Christian unity by claiming to be "the one authentic Church which Christ established." The Toronto Statement of the World Council of Churches (1950) had declared that the ecumenical movement would not be furthered by insistence on the abandonment of principles of beliefs; and Protestants, or others, ought not to ask or expect Roman Catholics to give up their belief in the primacy of the Pope and the Church. It was neither conceivable nor desirable at present for the Church of Rome to become an official member of the World Council of Churches. By organizing the Secretariat it had created eyes and ears for observing and listening during what must be a long period of unofficial relationships with other Christians. The Secretariat was also a mouthpiece, he said, through which the Church "might speak to them."

On the constitution of the Secretariat's membership, Cardinal Bea announced that it would consist of at least two members from each country where there were considerable non-Catholic Christian communities, to facilitate "a two-way flow of information"—from local non-Catholic groups to the Secretariat, and from the Secretariat the facts about Roman Catholicism.

Reporting to the Central Committee at St. Andrews, the Executive Committee said:

The fact that a dialogue with the Roman Catholic Church becomes possible is to be welcomed.

It is to be hoped, however, that this new development will not mean that the informal discussions which have been going on between Roman Catholic theologians and those of other churches will henceforth be entirely superseded by more official discussions, for at the present stage it is precisely the informal discussions which can best contribute to the removal of misunderstanding.

No church should fear that the World Council will in any way seek to act or speak for its member churches in matters concerning church union. . . .

The World Council may, however, use such opportunities as may present themselves to make known to the new Secretariat certain basic convictions which have been expressed by the Assembly or the Central Committee (e.g., issues of religious liberty, Christian social action, etc.).

It should be remembered that the creation of the Secretariat does not mean that any of the fundamental differences . . . between the Roman Catholic Church and the churches in the World Council have been solved. . . . The change is in procedures and climate. The opportunity for dialogue is to be grasped, but . . . the real problems will come to the fore. Our task . . . will be to represent the insights which God has given us . . . in the fifty years since our movement started.[35]

The Pontiff in a speech to the Central Preparatory Commission for the Second Vatican Council amplified the aims of the latter as being to inspire the clergy, instruct the people in the truths of the faith and Christian morals, provide hope of better times for youth, promote concern for social evangelism, and urge all Christians to be missionary at heart. In reference to unity, he said:

What should we do for our separated brethren whom we love? What should we do for those who do not bear on their foreheads the sign of Christ, but who are nevertheless sons of God? Believe me, our hearts are very responsive to what they are saying. . . . From this aspect also, the Vatican Council is not a speculative assembly, but a living, sensitive body which longs to embrace the whole world in the light of Christ's love. The house is adorned ready for a festival. . . . It is the Church which invites all men to enter it.

The encyclical *Mater et magistra* by Pope John XXIII was released July 14, 1961, though it bore the date of May 15, 1961, the seventieth anniversary of the *Rerum novarum* issued by Pope Leo XIII. Like *Rerum novarum* and its restatement, *Quadragesimo anno,* the new 26,-000-word pronouncement was, because of its reference to social, economic, and political problems, of special interest to the ecumenical movement of non-Roman churches. It amplified at great length what the Church of Rome called, in the words of the Pontiff to the Central Preparatory Commission for the Second Vatican Council, quoted above, "social evangelism." It touched upon a number of subjects to which the World Council of Churches had addressed itself—communism, labor, birth control, private property, farming, and international relations. It referred to "relations between economically developed political communities and political communities in the course of economic development" as "perhaps the biggest problem of modern times." If cooperation by

[35] Minutes and Reports of the Central Committee, 1960, pp. 103-04.

the Roman Catholic Church with the World Council of Churches "in such areas as social and charitable work and the promotion of world peace," to which Cardinal Bea said "he saw no obstacle," ever got beyond talk, this latest encyclical would be studied as demarcating where collaboration might begin and where it would have to end. However, like other papal letters, it was not infallible and so would have in this respect a certain flexibility.

4. The World Council and Eastern Orthodoxy

The serious interest of the Orthodox Churches in ecumenicity was of record as early as 1919. The deputation of the Protestant Episcopal Church to promote in Europe the proposed Conference on Faith and Order was received by the Ecumenical Patriarch (Constantinople) and the bishops of the Balkans and the Near East with ready assurances of favor and the purpose to cooperate. In August of 1920 eighteen Orthodox delegates attended the preparatory consultation of Faith and Order in Geneva, some of them staying for a similar meeting of Life and Work which followed.

In January of 1920 the Ecumenical Patriarch had issued an encyclical letter *Unto the Churches of Christ Everywhere,* suggesting that the time was "most favorable for bringing forward" the question of rapprochement "and studying it together," and requesting the churches to state in reply their opinion of this proposal.

Orthodox Churches had strong delegations at the Universal Christian Conference on Life and Work in Stockholm (1925) and at the First World Conference on Faith and Order in Lausanne (1927). Their representatives served with distinction in the years that followed on the Continuation Committees and the various commissions of these bodies. Their scholars and theologians made particularly valuable contributions to ecumenical study.

Some forty Orthodox dignitaries, representing the Ecumenical Patriarchate, the Patriarchates of Alexandria and of Antioch, the Churches of Cyprus, Greece, Rumania, Yugoslavia, Bulgaria, and Poland, and including some Russian Church emigrants, were at the Conference on Church, Community and State in Oxford (1937). Seventeen from the Ecumenical Patriarchate; the Patriarchates of Jerusalem, Alexandria, and Antioch; the Churches of Cyprus, Bulgaria, Greece, and Latvia; and the Russian Church in Exile were in attendance at the Second World Conference on Faith and Order in Edinburgh the same year. (The so-called Lesser Eastern Churches, which sent delegates, are not included in the Orthodox list for either Conference.)

Mainly because of abnormal political conditions, only the Ecumenical Patriarchate and the Church of Greece in Europe and the Rumanian Orthodox Episcopate of America were represented officially in the Assembly at Amsterdam founding the World Council of Churches in 1948. (Again, not including the Lesser Eastern Churches.) A few members of the Russian Orthodox emigrant colony in Paris attended.

The Church of Greece, the Ecumenical Patriarchate, and the Rumanian Orthodox Episcopate of America joined the World Council of Churches at Amsterdam. Later the Russian Orthodox Greek Catholic Church of North America and the Syrian Antiochian Orthodox Church—Archdiocese of New York and all North America—joined, as did also the Church of Cyprus and the Patriarchates of Alexandria, Jerusalem, and Antioch.

The circumstances limiting participation by the Orthodox Churches at Amsterdam in 1948 likewise reduced greatly the number of their delegates at Lund in 1952 for the Third World Conference on Faith and Order. "Never have we had a conference with so few Orthodox," observed Archbishop Brilioth, the Chairman. The Patriarchate of Moscow had been invited but had declined, as had also the Churches of Bulgaria, Rumania, and Poland. Something had happened to prevent the "strong delegation" appointed by the Church of Greece from coming, and the delegate of the Patriarchate of Alexandria "had withdrawn at a late stage."

The Holy Catholic Apostolic Orthodox Eastern Church is not one body in its organization, but a consociation of some nineteen or twenty independent, autonomous Orthodox Churches which maintain full communion with one another, recognize the authority of the first seven ecumenical councils and accept the Niceno-Constantinopolitan Creed without the *filioque* clause. The tradition of subserviency to the state, which goes back to the Constantinian revolution in the fourth century, when Christianity was made the official religion, still involves these churches in the intrigues and divisions of national and international politics to an extent that interferes with their cooperation with one another, as well as with other churches. The largest and most powerful of them is the Holy Russian Orthodox Church, and its policy naturally exerts a strong influence on the others.

The Orthodox Churches taking part in the ecumenical movement gained thereby very definite advantages. Apart from the stimulating association with other Christians, the movement afforded them a common meeting ground at a time when they had none. Prior to the organization of the World Council of Churches and for over a decade following, they found it impossible to hold a pan-Orthodox conference.[36]

Orthodoxy welcomed the support of the broader Christian fellowship in the impoverishments and persecutions suffered by some of its Churches during and after the two world wars. The Ecumenical Patriarch's letter of 1920 coincided with the expulsion from Asia Minor of

[36] The first pan-Orthodox meeting in modern times was held at Rhodes in 1959.

the Christian population, which consisted mainly of a million and a half Greek Orthodox, and was an appeal for the creation of "a league of Churches to promote Christian unity and solidarity against the growing power of anti-Christ menacing the whole Hellenic Christian civilization."

However, the impression should not be given that the Orthodox Churches interested themselves in the ecumenical movement out of considerations of selfish advantage. They believed deeply in the unity of the Church and, unlike Rome, were willing to talk about it and to work for it with any and all Christians. They had a long record of readiness in this policy, plainly seeing that it afforded missionary opportunity and fulfilled a duty they owed to the cause of union and to all inquirers seeking truth in sincerity.[37] While maintaining firmly their contention that the Holy Catholic Apostolic Orthodox Eastern Church was "the one and the only true Church," they held that, as the patriarchal encyclical asserted, such "rapprochement between the various Christian Churches and fellowship between them" was "not excluded by their doctrinal differences."

This was clearly the temper of Dr. I. Koman's study of the invitation to the Orthodox Churches to participate in the World Council of Churches, which was presented at the anniversary of Russian Orthodoxy's autocephalicity in Moscow a month before the Amsterdam Assembly:[38]

> The representatives of Orthodoxy have always maintained a proper attitude toward ecumenical meetings, and have repeatedly upheld with success the standpoint of their Church. They not infrequently prevented the adoption of hasty or mistaken resolutions, without at the same time making the smallest compromise of a dogmatic or liturgical nature. . . .

[37] "The Eastern Orthodox Church is sure of its ecclesiology; it is convinced that its doctrine is sound. It takes part in the ecumenical movement, not because it seeks a fuller church life; but because of its basic optimism. Realizing its own fulness and the wealth of its own heritage, it would like to share them with its Western brethren who are seeking and who are not spiritually satisfied. The Orthodox Church does not participate in ecumenical conferences merely out of courtesy. It is its response . . . to a highly estimable and idealistic initiative on the part of the Protestant world." (Antoine Kartachoff, "Orthodox Theology and the Ecumenical Movement," in *The Ecumenical Review,* Vol. VIII, p. 32.)

"The churches of the East, following in the footsteps of the Founder of the Church Universal, have always responded to calls for church unity from whichever source or initiative they came. History itself since 1054 bears witness to this incontestable fact. . . . Since 1920 we have made manifest our will to co-operate with all churches in a 'league of churches,' and we have been ready to confront together the social, moral and cultural problems created by the war or through internal upheavals and revolutions. . . . We are still, and more so, willing and anxious to meet together with the different churches, branches of the One Church, and to discuss in real humility . . . how a united Church of Christ may serve, influence and reform our society and world. . . . Instead of involving ourselves in endless debate, we believe that our time calls for united action. . . ." (Metropolitan James of Melita, "The Significance of the World Council of Churches for the Older Churches," in *The Ecumenical Review,* Vol. IX, p. 16.)

[38] *Ibid.* See also G. K. A. Bell, *The Kingship of Christ,* p. 60.

Participation . . . in the ecumenical movement thus seeking to ensure the re-uniting of the churches is wholly in accordance with the true tradition of Orthodoxy, dating from the times of the Saviour, of the Apostles and of the early Fathers. The churches taking part in the ecumenical movement must join together in the One Church, by turning again to the mystic oneness of the Body of Christ. . . . This ideal is such a sacred one that it merits the most vigorous struggle for its realization, and justifies every sacrifice.

Like most of Orthodoxy's ecumenical utterances, the Patriarchate's message of 1920 to the churches well repays, from this standpoint, a careful reading:[39]

Our own church holds that rapprochement between the various Christian Churches and fellowship between them is not excluded by the doctrinal differences which exist between them. In our opinion, such a rapprochement is highly desirable and necessary. It would be useful in many ways for the real interest of each particular church and of the whole Christian body, and also for the preparation and advancement of that blessed union which will be completed in the future in accordance with the will of God. We, therefore, consider that the present time is most favorable for bringing forward this important question and studying it together.

Even if in this case, owing to antiquated prejudices, practices or pretensions, the difficulties which have so often jeopardized attempts at re-union in the past may arise or be brought up, nevertheless, in our view, since we are concerned at this initial stage only with contacts and rapprochement, these difficulties are of less importance. If there is good will and intention, they cannot and should not create an invincible and insuperable obstacle.

Wherefore, considering such an endeavor to be both possible and timely . . . we venture to express below in brief our thoughts and our opinion regarding the way in which we understand this rapprochement and contact, and how we consider it to be realizable; we earnestly ask and invite the judgment and opinion of the other sister churches in the East and of the venerable Christian churches in the West and everywhere in the world.

We believe that the following two measures would greatly contribute to the rapprochement which is so much to be desired and which would be so useful.

First, we consider as necessary . . . the removal . . . of all mutual mistrust and bitterness between the different churches which arise from the tendency of some of them to entice and proselytize adherents of other confessions. . . . So many troubles and sufferings are caused by . . . Christians and great hatred and enmity are aroused, with such insignificant results, by this tendency of some to proselytize. . . .

After this essential re-establishment of sincerity and confidence between the churches, we consider,

Secondly, that, above all, love should be rekindled and strengthened among the churches, so that they should no more consider one another as strangers and foreigners, but as relatives, and . . . part of the household of Christ. . . .

For if the different churches are inspired by love, and place it before

[39] For the full text of the message, see *The Ecumenical Review,* Vol. XII, p. 79. The translation here printed is the *Review*'s.

everything else in their judgments of others and their relationships with them, instead of increasing and widening the existing dissensions, they should be enabled to reduce and diminish them. By stirring up a right brotherly interest in the condition, the well-being and stability of the other churches, and to obtain a better knowledge of them, and by willingness to offer mutual aid . . . many good things will be achieved for the glory and benefit both of themselves and of the Christian body.

"Friendship" and "kindly disposition" toward one another could be demonstrated by the churches, it was suggested, in the following ways:

By the acceptance of a uniform calendar for the celebration of the great Christian feasts. . . .
By the exchange of brotherly letters . . . on the great feasts of the churches' year. . . .
By close relationships between the representatives of all churches. . . .
By relationships between theological schools and the professors of theology, and the exchange of theological and ecclesiastical reviews and other publications of the churches.
By the exchange of students by the seminaries. . . .
By convoking pan-Christian conferences . . . to examine questions of common interest to all the churches.
By impartial and deeper historical study of doctrinal differences. . . .
By mutual respect for the customs and practices in different churches.
By allowing each other the use of chapels and cemeteries for the funerals and burials of believers of other confessions dying in foreign lands.
By the settlement of the question of mixed marriages between the confessions.
. . . By whole-hearted mutual assistance for the churches in their endeavors for religious advancement and charity. . . .

Such a course will be profitable "for the whole body of the Church," the message said, "because manifold dangers threaten not only particular churches, but all of them."

Alcoholism, which is increasing daily; the increase of unnecessary luxury under the pretext of bettering life and enjoying it; the voluptuousness and lust hardly covered by the cloak of freedom and emancipation of the flesh; the prevailing unchecked licentiousness and indecency in literature, painting, the theatre, and in music, under the respectable name of developing good taste and cultivation of fine art; the deification of wealth and the contempt of higher ideals; all these and the like, as they threaten the very essence of Christian societies are . . . timely topics requiring . . . common study and co-operation by the Christian churches.

. . . .

For all these reasons, being ourselves convinced of the necessity for establishing a contact and league between the churches, and believing that the other churches share our conviction . . . at least as a beginning we request each one of them to send us in reply a statement of its judgment and opinion on this matter, so that common agreement . . . having been reached, we may proceed together to its realization. . . .

East-West tensions, ideological and political divisions, and fear lest the ecumenical movement by its pronouncements and actions should further endanger their position explained very largely the reluctance of most of the Orthodox Churches to join the World Council of Churches.

This version of the circumstances seems to be supported by the official report of a meeting of Orthodox ecclesiastics in Moscow, July 8-18, 1948, at which the invitation to the Orthodox Churches to take part in the Amsterdam Assembly came up for consideration.

According to the announcement, the occasion was the five-hundredth anniversary of Russian Orthodoxy's independence. In his inaugural address, Patriarch Alexei, who presided, observed that the gathering had been organized "at the united petition of those taking part" and was to be regarded as "a testimony" and "a pledge of their strength in the face of the enemies of Orthodoxy."[40] The chairman of the commission representing Russian Orthodox Church affairs on the Ministerial Council of the Union of Socialist Soviet Republics, G. G. Karpov, explained to the delegates that their presence in Moscow indicated their purpose to oppose "efforts from abroad" against their position.

Later in the sessions, the Bulgarian Metropolitan, Stephan of Sofia, declared that collaboration with the ecumenical movement over many years had brought him to the realization that its program as a whole had "fallen under the influence of political tendencies prejudicial to its aims, which had been originally in accordance with the Gospel spirit"; and that the loss of its ecclesiastical character had made impossible the Orthodox Church's taking any further part in it. Bishop Nestor, referring to the friendly attitude of some members of their fellowship toward it as "scandalous," followed with an appeal to the 150,000,000 faithful of their confession to stand aloof from the movement.

When the invitation to send delegates to Amsterdam was put to a vote, the decision stood in the negative, fourteen to three.

However, cooperation in the ecumenical movement had its advocates, among them Dr. I. Koman of Rumania, quoted above, who had prepared the report introducing the subject. He had studied the development of the movement from its beginnings to the Conferences at Oxford and Edinburgh (1937) and, with certain reservations "proper to Orthodoxy," concluded that it had a sound ecclesiastical and ontological basis and should be recognized as an effort "to emerge from the crisis of a thousand-year-old schism and to rediscover the unity that had been lost"—an almost superhuman task, but one in which Orthodoxy "had avowedly a decisive share to take." Participation in the ecumenical movement seeking a reunion of the churches was, he said, "wholly in accordance with the true tradition of Orthodoxy, dating from the times of the Saviour, of the Apostles and of the early Fathers." Protestantism

[40] On the agenda were the subjects "The Orthodox Church and the Papacy," "The Validity of Anglican Ordinations," "The Church Calendar," and "The Ecumenical Movement and the Orthodox Church."

realized that uniting the churches demanded of it the fulfillment of certain prerequisite conditions. Should these be duly respected, he concluded, there was hope that "the efforts of a World Assembly such as that of Amsterdam would in the ultimate issue be crowned with success." [41]

Lay voices were raised in support of Dr. Koman's position. "Withdrawal from contacts with other Christians would only deprive them of the opportunity to approach Orthodoxy," argued a layman[42] from the Netherlands, adding that refusal to cooperate with the ecumenical movement because it occupied itself with social and political questions, to the possible detriment of the kingdom of God, would lead to the same result. How could the spiritual be separated from the social? He regretted the suggestion that Orthodoxy should, on the grounds indicated, have no part in the quest for unity.

Professor G. I. Rasumovsky of Russia, who had opposed taking any part in the World Council of Churches, said, nevertheless: "We live side by side with many non-Orthodox, unacquainted with their peculiarities. Let us pay heed to one another . . . devote thought to one another, and it may be that they will then come to see Orthodoxy, and, with it, miracles."

The considerable show of favorableness toward the ecumenical movement, the evidence that opposition arose partly from political interference that could conceivably in time lose its force, the obvious grave misunderstanding of some phases of the program reflected in the report of the Moscow meeting and in the communications from the Orthodox authorities that might with patience be corrected—these considerations, together with the strategic position of the Orthodox Churches in relation to the problem posed by militant communism and the earnest and helpful cooperation already of a number of their influential leaders, caused the World Council of Churches to persevere in its efforts to maintain and extend contacts with Orthodoxy, even in the face of much skepticism within its own ranks concerning the hoped-for results.

Persistence was encouraged by the qualifying language of the response from the Moscow Conference and of the covering letter by Metropoli-

[41] Some World Council officials thought that the presentation of the matter by one with no "personal knowledge" of it gave "an entirely misleading account and created a quite false impression of" the ecumenical movement and its work. Likewise, they felt that "those taking part in the discussion had had no first-hand experience of the movement, with the result that its method and purpose were woefully misunderstood." (G. K. A. Bell in *The Kingship of Christ,* p. 64.) This criticism seems not to have taken sufficient account of the political inhibitions under which the question was considered, because of which the "few lonely voices which sought to explain its [the ecumenical movement's] true character were not heard." (*Ibid.*) Represented, besides Moscow, were the Churches of Constantinople, Antioch, Alexandria, Georgia, Serbia, Rumania, Bulgaria, Greece, Albania, Poland, and Armenia, with representatives of "the Moscow Patriarchate from other countries." Nearly all of these Churches had, from experience, some knowledge of the ecumenical movement. A majority of them had been connected officially with it.

[42] Delegate van Ephenhuizen.

tan Nikolai on behalf of the Russian Patriarchate. The resolution embodying the action stated that the Orthodox Churches were obliged to decline participation in the ecumenical movement *"in its present form."* The patriarchal letter said:

> Refusal on our part does not mean that we shall not be interested in the activities of the ecumenical movement. The Russian Orthodox Church, besides, has not lost confidence in the possibility of re-union in grace with her, by God's help, of any Christian confession or body. . . . In view of this, we would ask you to continue to keep us informed regarding the activities of the World Council of Churches, sending to us suitable literature, reports on the assemblies and conferences, papers on all questions, and so forth.

This did not sound as if the last word had been spoken. Would the Conference have gone to the trouble of detailing in the minutes it forwarded what it saw as the defects and errors of the ecumenical movement, which compelled it to decline the invitation to cooperate, if the consulting Churches had felt that they saw no grounds for rapprochement and were dismissing the matter with finality? [43]

The policy with reference to the Orthodox Churches, to the acceptance of which, it must be said, the World Council as a whole came only slowly, was to be credited to the perseverance of those leaders who were convinced that it was necessary to have their cooperation to give the movement a true ecumenical character and to compensate weaknesses inevitably inherent in it because of its strongly pan-Protestant character.

"The full participation of the Orthodox Churches is a matter of great moment to the World Council of Churches," declared Dr. G. K. A. Bell, Chairman of the Central Committee during the period between Amsterdam and Evanston, expressing a judgment increasingly, if slowly, shared. "On no account ought the World Council to be allowed to give the impression of being either an organization of Protestant Churches, or

[43] The Conference, according to the preamble of the resolution, looked upon the proposal to form a World Council of Churches as indicating the purpose to found an "Ecumenical Church," which through "social and political activity" would seek to exercise "an international influence." This was "not in accord with the ideals of Christianity and the aims of the Church of Christ as . . . understood by the Orthodox Churches."

The ecumenical movement had "too early lost faith in the possibility of union in one Holy, Catholic, and Apostolic Church," it said.

The movement had given up "discussion on the idea of union of the Churches on dogmatic and confessional grounds . . ." and reduced "requirements and conditions for unity to the simple recognition of Christ as Our Lord."

Note: There was no purpose to set up an "Ecumenical Church," of course, or to achieve a union of any kind. The union of churches on doctrinal and confessional grounds, on their own initiative, was advocated. Unity in Jesus Christ as Saviour and Lord was the basis of fellowship and cooperation in the World Council. "The social and political activity" of the ecumenical movement had been questioned by others besides the Orthodox and might well stand in need of explanation, if not amendment. It was of a nature that exposed it at all times to misunderstanding.

largely a Western, and, more specifically, an Anglo-Saxon organization, which identifies itself, consciously or unconsciously, with the concerns and interests of Western nations." [44]

At the time he wrote this, Dr. Bell apparently had before him a statement concerning the Orthodox Churches which Dr. Visser 't Hooft made to the Provisional Committee in 1947,[45] when it was known that the Patriarchate of Moscow was giving serious attention to the question of its relations with the World Council and there was evidence that Orthodox leaders in the Balkans desired to continue their cooperation in the ecumenical movement. Said the General Secretary:

> The great barrier to be overcome in this connection is the impression that the World Council is largely a Western, and more specifically Anglo-Saxon, organization which identifies itself, consciously or unconsciously, with the concerns and interests of the Western nations. We shall have to make it very clear in word and deed that such is not the case, and that we understand by ecumenical fellowship the fellowship in Christ which includes, but also transcends, all nationalities and races, and which must, therefore, be independent of all political constellations. If we do so, we shall be in a strong position to ask for a similarly independent attitude on the part of the Eastern Churches.

Raising the question whether the World Council was prepared for the consequences of the entrance into its membership of the churches of the Orthodox family, with their traditions differing in so many respects from those of the West, Dr. Visser 't Hooft said: "The World Council loses its *raison d'être,* if it does not attempt to establish a deep, permanent contact between the churches of the West and those of the East."

"The Eastern Churches," he added, "have maintained a sense of the objective reality and the cosmic dimensions of the drama of salvation which the Western churches need to recapture."

It was realized that their differing conceptions of the Christian faith and their diverse ecclesiastical practices made discussion between Orthodox and Protestant churches difficult, and agreement more so. But, this notwithstanding, many ecumenical leaders thought that the attempt had not been without a theological advantage, at least to the latter, and that much greater gain in this respect might be expected from continued interchange. It was, they believed, a relationship large with opportunity for profitable theological cross-fertilization, and, for their own sake as well as the World Council's, Protestants should be alert to its possibilities.

Churches of all confessions would find enriching elements, for example, in Orthodox worship. Orthodoxy's appreciation of the interaction of faith and love, reflected in the call to confession, "Let us love one another, in order that we may confess," might be seen balancing the

[44] In *The Kingship of Christ,* p. 57.
[45] See Minutes of the Provisional Committee, Buck Hill Falls.

tendency to legalism in connection with the Protestant teaching of salvation by faith alone. Orthodoxy's position that true Christian individualism and soul liberty could be realized only within the community and fellowship of the Church stood to discourage the irresponsible and fragmenting type of religious freedom which strewed its wreckage across the earth. Orthodox insistence on the responsibility of the Church, by sound instruction, to give force to the authority of the Bible as a basis of unity faced toward the need the World Council felt for a formulation of the principles of biblical interpretation for ecumenical study. The emphasis of the Orthodox on the unchanging character of the Church as constituted by Christ and the Apostles could well set Protestants to examining the foundations of hope for continuity and permanence in their churches which rejected institutional succession and conformity. And the Orthodox eucharistic doctrine of the *metabolē,* or mysterious mutation taking place in the bread and the wine on the altar, which differed in its conception from both transubstantiation and consubstantiation, might be found, if understood, to throw light upon ways not inconsonant with the Protestant tradition to save the Communion from its present barrenness in those churches which denied the possibility of any change in the sacred elements or of any special Presence.

So the Protestant churches might look forward to the fellowship with the Orthodox as an experience sufficiently rewarding intellectually and spiritually to justify every attempt at accommodation by way of making them feel at home in the World Council of Churches.

Eleven Orthodox Churches were represented at Evanston, including the Lesser Eastern group. Of the forty-five delegates, fifteen were from the Church of Greece and eight from the Ecumenical Patriarchate. American branches of Orthodoxy sent eight delegates.

"Instead of involving ourselves in endless debate," wrote Metropolitan James of Melita, representative of the Patriarchate at Geneva, "we believe that our time calls for united action; not for theoretical or doctrinal disputes which lead to disunity." His remarks, as reported in *The Ecumenical Review* (Jan. 1954), continued:

> It is at this point that the World Council of Churches acquires an extraordinary significance for the older churches, for it pursues the same goals, namely, to bring churches together and to make them conscious of their responsibility to face the Lord and to meet adequately the spiritual needs of the world. . . .
>
> The World Council of Churches has shown that it is inspired by the spirit of prayer, and has demonstrated real Christian solidarity. The member churches . . . echo the continuing prayer of the older churches that all may be one. . . .
>
> The ancient churches are offered through the World Council opportunity of telling Christians all over the world what is not sufficiently known to them: that they have been and are ready always to enter into conversation with both Roman Catholics and Protestants, and to discuss church union and co-operation in what is their common duty to Christ and the world.

Moreover, the older churches find in the World Council of Churches the spirit which is needed for revitalizing the past and restoring the wholeness of the Church.

Finally, the older churches see in the World Council . . . a true friend . . . deeply concerned with their fate, which is still in the hands of the non-Christian environment in the midst of which many of them live.

The churches of the East hold steadfastly to the biblical assertion that nothing happens without the knowledge or the will of our Father in heaven. They believe that the World Council of Churches is a sign, through which God intends to say something to the world. It must be understood as an instrument of divine providence and economy, the purpose of which is that all Christians eventually become alerted to seek together Him who is the way. . . .

The World Council of Churches must have been entrusted with the same command with which the older churches have been entrusted; i.e., to voice to Christians their duty to let themselves be gathered within the one fold and recognize no other but the One Shepherd, who has given his life for the sheep. Its understanding of this command . . . makes [it] an important ally for the older churches in the common search for Church unity and peace. . . .

The older churches turn their eyes gratefully to the World Council of Churches and thank the Lord for its existence. . . .

The older churches can, therefore, glorify the name of the Lord, in that he has given them the World Council of Churches . . . rekindling faith in God, charity among men, and hope for new understanding and unity.

Attempts at further understanding and closer rapprochement continued after Evanston. The Central Committee had for a main theme at Rhodes (1959) "The Significance of the Eastern and Western Traditions within Christendom." The appropriateness of this study, the members being guests of the Eastern Orthodox Churches, was at once apparent. Remarked also was the fact that a Faith and Order theological commission had been working for some years on the same general subject, under the title of "Tradition and Traditions." Moreover, the Department of Faith and Order had cooperated in arrangements for a three-day consultation of Orthodox, Anglican, and Protestant theologians at Kifissia, Greece, immediately preceding the meeting of the Central Committee, at which had been presented and discussed treatises on the "principles and characteristics" of the churches, East and West.

The opportunity thus afforded for Orthodox scholars to expound their theological and ecclesiological views was fruitfully exploited, with the Western churchmen encouraging them in every way.

Professor C. Konstantinidis of the Theological School of Halki, Istanbul, spoke for Orthodoxy, setting forth lucidly its understanding of tradition; and Professor Edmund S. Schlink of the University of Heidelberg, Germany, the Protestant spokesman, concerned himself, for the most part, with "the values of the Eastern tradition for Western Christendom." [46]

[46] See *The Ecumenical Review,* October, 1959.

"Our main concern must be," Dr. Schlink said, "to discover the spiritual wealth concealed in the different traditions, and to seek the unity of the Church, not in uniformity, but in a fellowship of different traditions."

Professor Konstantinidis explained that for Orthodox Churches Scripture of the canonical New Testament and the Holy Tradition were of equal authority. Both had been inspired by the Holy Spirit and were together necessary to faith and salvation. He recalled that Athanasius the Great had said, "There is a primary tradition and teaching and faith . . . . which the Lord Jesus gave, the apostles preached and the fathers preserved: on it the whole Church has been founded." "This Tradition," Professor Konstantinidis said, "is the ecclesiological element of our Christian unity, and the uniting element of the undivided Church."

"The principal forms of Holy Tradition" are, he continued, (1) the valid and authentic interpretations of Scripture in the Church; (2) the official formulations and confessions of faith; (3) the definitions and creeds of the Ecumenical Councils; (4) the larger accords of the teaching of the Fathers and ecclesiastical authors, in other words, the *consensum Patrum;* (5) the forms, acts, and institutions of worship and liturgies of the early Church, which constitute the living expression of the apostolic spirit in the ways of worship in the Church. Everything outside these forms of the *depositum* of faith can be tradition in the Church, but it cannot be Tradition of Dogma—the Holy Tradition. "This integral and undivided Tradition . . . projects the divine and continually living substance of the Church . . . becomes also the most secure criterion of its unity." [47]

All Protestant churches have their own traditions, Dr. Konstantinidis suggested. These presented some common points with the Holy Tradition of the Church but were more a reflection of the world from which they arose. They were, in general, Western traditions. They included many historical, racial, national, rational, and linguistic elements, but with these also clearly theological ideas and forms common to the whole of Christianity.

> This Protestantism, with its varieties and ramifications . . . its historical confessions and statements of faith . . . its contemporary tendencies and currents . . . its inter-confessional and unionist dispositions and desires . . . its mutual repulsions and rivalries . . . its missionary experiences . . . its special way of thinking and living the commandments of the Holy Gospel, and finally . . . its proper theology is the most inclusive conception of what we define as Western traditions. These are not the One Tradition, but the teaching of their communities, their message to the world.

[47] Professor Konstantinidis explained that the early Church had only one tradition the Gospel being preached by word of mouth before anything was written. The canonical Scripture was drawn from the oral. There were other scriptures not included in the canon. He differentiated between them by spelling the first with a capital "S"; likewise between Holy Tradition and the great body of oral tradition.

Here, as the Orthodox see it, is the most essential "crisis" of contemporary Protestantism. It is not the Tradition of the "One, Holy, Apostolic and Catholic Church" which safeguards the integrity of revealed truth. It is a kind of symphony of individuals under the grace of Christ, a kind of accord which is quite subjective and elastic . . . an . . . accord of each member of the Church, illuminated by the Holy Spirit in the reading, understanding and interpretation of the Bible. This accord pre-supposes the presence of the Paraclete, but there is no criterion to render this presence more tangible . . . it is constrained to find non-biblical criteria for the correct interpretation of revealed truth.

Would it not be of great utility for our Protestant brothers to emphasize here that these criteria lie in what we call Tradition . . .? Would not this consensus of individuals be more positive and theologically more concentrated, if accepted as a *consensus Traditionis?* And the Grace of Christ, which assists and illuminates individuals, can it not be considered as the Grace which acts upon . . . Fathers of the Church, and upon the Church itself, when it interprets and formulates its dogmas and its saving truth? Does not this accord of individuals have a greater value when it has the character of catholicity, antiquity and of larger numerical agreement?

Professor Konstantinidis concluded with an appeal to Protestants to consider the impossibility of "ecclesiological restoration" under their long "de-traditioning" and seek reunion through sincere effort for "re-traditioning."

Professor Schlink indicated three basic forms of the Eastern Church which were, in his opinion, of special importance for Western Christendom:

1. The worship service. In all churches, the great acts of God in history and the promise of the coming redemption are expressed, he said, through Scripture reading, preaching, the Lord's Supper, and prayers; but in none are the pronouncements so strongly determined by the hymnology and doxology as in the Orthodox. He suggested, by way of illustration:

In its Canons, Stichera and Troparia, the Gospel of the day is developed in ever-new forms of praise. . . . The message of God's act of salvation in history is drawn into the worship of the Eternal God and Christ, so that this act . . . is experienced in the liturgy as if it were actually taking place among the congregation. In the doxological attitude, the lapse of time between then and now disappears. . . . In praising Christ's victory on the cross and in the resurrection, and in the adoration of the Eternal Trinity, the glory to come is experienced as a present reality. The worshippers are translated into that glory, and the menace of the material world grows dim. In no other church does the liturgy so triumphantly unfold the victory of Christ with its implications for the whole cosmos, or laud and magnify in such rapturous way the presence of the Creation that is to come.

2. The embodiment of dogma in the liturgy. It is characteristic of the Eastern Church that its dogma has not become separated from its liturgy but is formulated as a liturgical statement. "Unlike the Western

Church, it has always had an aversion to separating dogmatic statements from the liturgy; it has never turned them into binding dogmas isolated from the doxological frame-work. . . . While adhering strictly to the dogma of the early Church . . . it in principle left open opportunities for free theological thought."

3. The special relationship between Church and ministry. Notwithstanding its emphasis on hierarchy, this relation is not merely one of higher and lower grades, because it is enclosed within the framework of fellowship. The ministry and the congregation are likewise one fellowship, as the worship attests. The supreme authority is not a single dignitary but the Ecumenical Synod, and the decisions of the Synod are not valid unless confirmed by the congregation.

By renouncing any legally secured authority with jurisdiction over the whole Church, the Eastern Church shows a more reverent attitude than the Roman Catholic Church towards the free action of the Holy Spirit. . . . Jesus Christ is honored as the sole Lord of the Church, and this leaves room for a number of different autocephalous churches. For the incarnate Son of God, as the ascended Lord, wishes to permeate through the Holy Spirit the historical reality of every nation and language. . . . In accordance also with the doxological nature of its worship service and its dogma, and with the congregational form of its church order, the Eastern Church has always interpreted its relation to the state mainly as a spiritual service, but has never sought to possess secular authority itself. In its conception of the symphony between the Church and state, it has affirmed its spiritual power by renouncing all secular power.

Western churches have sometimes regarded the Eastern Church's concentration on the holy liturgy as evading responsibility in the world, and its hymnic emphasis on the eschatological presence as tantamount to abandoning this world to its own devices, without attempting to influence society or promote justice. On considering these criticisms,

. . . we must in all justice take due account of the fact that for hundreds of years the Eastern Church was unable to exercise any influence upon its environment, because it lived under the oppression of Arabs, Mongols and Turks. . . . Every dimension of church life is concentrated in its liturgy in such a way that the Church has not only been protected during times of oppression; from this focal point it can also receive fresh power to push out into the world. This is proved by the history of its missionary effort. . . . It is true, the Eastern Church interprets its ethical task . . . to be the transformation and sanctification of men rather than the passing of new social and legal ordinances. But where there is a genuine renewal of men and women to faith, hope and love, this is bound to have its effect on the social order.

Concluding, Professor Schlink said:

Every church tradition is exposed to its special dangers, especially if it claims to be exclusive. But the basic structures of preaching and doxology, historic-personal and ontological statement, complement one another; the expectation of Christ's return also complements the assurance that he is already present. . . . I am convinced that on essential points the Eastern and Western traditions complement one another, and can warn and protect one another against the specific dangers inherent in their respective positions. . . . The Western Church should be restrained from proselytizing within the Eastern Church, out of respect for the fact that the latter not only survived centuries of oppression . . . but has during the twentieth century suffered the bloodiest persecution ever experienced in the history of the Christian Church, and in the face of that ordeal has shown a spiritual strength which quickened the vitality of the whole of Christendom.

I have particularly mentioned the importance of the Eastern tradition for Western Christendom. . . . I could have spoken much more convincingly about insights and impulses which spring from the Reformation, which, in my opinion, are of tremendous importance for the Eastern Church. For . . . it is an undoubted fact that some important and essential pronouncements of the Apostles are less developed in the Eastern Church than in the West. But during the course of the centuries the different Christian traditions have become and still are so estranged from one another, that the first step must be for each of us to try to understand the importance of the other tradition.

In the discussion, Professor Georges Florovsky suggested that a study of tradition in a historical sense would bridge many of the present separations. "The place of meeting is not in the future," he said, "but in a common past—in the shared history of Christendom."

Professor Panayotis P. Bratsiotis re-emphasized that Scripture was not an exhaustive expression of the Word of God. The books of the New Testament expressed the Word of God in specific situations, and this required historical interpretation. "The Church must help at this point. And who decides that the New Testament is to be limited to only certain Scriptures?"

III

THE POST-EVANSTON STUDY PROGRAM

No phase of the World Council's work was more ecumenically characteristic than the study program, nor in any were successes and failures more significant in their bearing upon the Council's progress. For this reason, as well as for their inherent interest, the subjects explored and the conclusions reached should be taken into account in any realistic assessment of the fortunes of the movement.

In his report to the Central Committee at Davos-Platz, Chairman Walter Freytag of the Division of Studies said that the process of study was itself more important than the knowledge arrived at; the exchange of ideas leading often to their revision and setting free the deeper values of common spiritual heritage, of which the participants, if they remained imprisoned in their own traditions, might never become aware. So would the historian, and the reader as well, miss something essential to an understanding of the World Council of Churches if he passed up its studies and concerned himself altogether with its actions, of which research and reflection were actually an indispensable, if a more or less hidden, part.

The thematic areas overlapped, and it was one function of the Division of Studies to coordinate the plans of the study groups and help them each become part of "a process of the whole." The interlocking inquiries ranged widely in their exploration of accessible sources of information, supervising committees sometimes working together or sharing their findings. Ecumenical files back of Evanston were reopened for whatever assistance earlier investigations would yield, which was often valuable. Other interchurch bodies and certain of the denominations which were not members of the World Council collaborated on some of the subjects in which they were especially interested and competent.

1. The Bible in the Churches

Appropriately enough, the United Bible Societies cooperated on the inquiry "The Place and Use of the Bible in the Life and Activities of the Churches," providing a secretary, Edwin S. Robertson, to conduct it. Because of the Societies' world-wide work and their contacts with virtually all the denominations and ecumenical organizations, this proved to be a particularly advantageous arrangement.

In some countries, the Bible societies and councils of churches in their national capacity contributed the services of secretaries from their own staffs toward extensive surveys of the uses of the Bible in the churches and of their methods of study.

It was in connection with this theme that the Missouri Synod Lutheran Church in the United States, various Assembly of God congregations, and a number of Pentecostal Churches,[1] although not members of the World Council of Churches, gave valuable and appreciated help, as did certain Roman Catholic scholars of France, Belgium, and Holland.

The Department of Missionary Studies of the International Missionary Council had been incorporated in the Division of Studies of the World Council of Churches prior to the launching of the post-Evanston study program, and representatives of the older ecumenical body assisted with the development of this theme on the Bible.

In his report to the Central Committee at Rhodes, Secretary Robertson explained that the study would have to be, on account of its wide scope, "an on-going process, with no specific date-line for its completion." For this reason, and the fact that the undertaking required a coverage more extensive than the operations of the World Council of Churches itself, the collaboration of the United Bible Societies would, he suggested, continue to be needed.

The survey, which had been extended to many countries, had shown that "the divided Church heard only dimly the Word of God through the Bible," and that "the insights of the various parts of the Church must be brought to the service of the whole Church." It had disclosed, moreover, "utter confusion" in the attempts of the churches to "apply the Bible to the problems of modern life," as evidenced by pronouncements on public questions and statements of faith "in contemporary terms." Most confused were their interpretations of "the ethical teaching of the Bible for an industrial society." Many persons interviewed had betrayed a sense of frustration, saying, "Since we have passed beyond the era of proof-texts, we are hesitant to try to use the Bible at all."

However, the committee had found that, while "the modernist crisis of the nineteenth century had discouraged study of the Bible in the churches," events of the twentieth century, particularly in countries exposed to totalitarian dictatorship, had helped to bring about "a Bible revival," the effects of which could be seen in all denominations, including the Church of Rome.

This recrudescence of interest had produced many new books on

[1] Mainly of Latin American countries.

the Bible and increased phenomenally the circulation of the Scriptures. East and West, publishers, sometimes solely from business motives, were adding to their lists of publications the Bible and books on it. In India and certain other Asian countries, correspondence courses were successfully promoting study of the Scriptures, even outside the membership of the churches. The East Asia Christian Conference was helping with the survey in this general area, having provided financial support for a regional secretary to direct it.

The study had encountered all the conflicting conceptions of the Bible as a book and as a divine revelation. There were literalists who regarded it as *verbatim* the Word of God. Neo-orthodox views, which represented an attempt "to absorb the truth of modern biblical criticism without losing the authority of the Scriptures," treated it rather as a medium of the Word of God. These and other theories in many gradations had their exponents in, and outside, ecumenical circles. The discovery that Christians holding diverse ideas about the Bible could read it profitably together, and with a sense of their unity, had been one encouraging result of the study, justifying the observation of Chairman Freytag at Davos-Platz, "The exchange of thoughts crossing the borders of nationalities and denominations not only shakes the ideas we have about others, but at the same time . . . sets free the deepest values of our own spiritual heritage, of which we sometimes are not aware, if we remain imprisoned in our own circles." [2]

The traditionalist considered his own views of the Bible and its revelation of God essentially contradictory to those of other schools. Actually, there was not the conflict he imagined. For example, the illumination of the written Word for him by the Spirit of Truth was not so different as he thought from the Word communicated by the same Spirit through the Bible to his modernist brother. The Bible was for both a sanctuary of the Voice. Listening, both gathered from its pages new meanings. However explained, the explicit in the text was being amplified, and sometimes qualified, by the implicit. The literalist, haunted by the fear that treating the Bible as a channel of revelation would undermine its authority, might wisely have had more regard for this fact. His rallying slogan, "The Bible says," meant to him, "God says," and God was, without doubt, speaking also to others. This none could dispute, whether the Bible was the Word or a medium of the Word.[3]

[2] Minutes of the Central Committee, 1955, p. 29.

For sources of other statements and reports quoted in this section on the Post-Evanston Study Program consult the Annual Minutes, 1955 through 1960.

[3] "How do Christians from different traditions approach the Bible? This question presents itself with more and more urgency as the ecumenical conversation develops. There is agreement that further progress in ecumenical biblical and theological work will depend upon a frank facing of the different ways in which the Bible is interpreted. This is particularly true for theological conversations with members of the Church of Rome. But let no man believe that the churches of the Reformation are themselves agreed on this point!" (Commission on the Lordship of Christ, *The Ecumenical Review,* July, 1959, p. 447.)

2. The Lordship of Christ

Implementing an action of the Second Assembly, the Central Committee at Davos-Platz appointed a commission of "twenty-five biblical scholars, theologians and laymen," to study the theme of the lordship of Christ, under the chairmanship of Canon Alan Richardson of Durham.

The choice of this topic, which was phrased eventually "The Lordship of Christ over the World and the Church," was likewise dictated by the often-urged need to develop a supporting and direction-giving theology for the burgeoning program of the World Council of Churches. It was agreed that the doctrine of the lordship of Christ offered a promising approach to this problem. The Bible affirmed his sovereignty over "all things." He was Lord, not only of the Church, but of the world. True, the world had shown little inclination to own his authority. But it was the Church's calling to declare him Lord and to work to make him regnant. If it could not do this with hope that mankind would be brought to acknowledge his lordship, it would, nevertheless, be able to ameliorate wrong social conditions in some degree and have, meanwhile, the assurance that Christ would return to earth at the end of history to make manifest his victory, already won in his death and resurrection, and to share his triumph with all his faithful followers. In any case, while in the flesh, he "went about doing good," and Christians accepting his lordship had no alternative to obeying his example.

There were in the ranks of ecumenical scholars, perhaps, those who would have characterized the lordship of Christ in other ways, but this was, roughly, the statement of it that seemed to be generally accepted or acquiesced in. In a study memorandum, the Commission conducting the inquiry suggested:

> Since Christ's lordship cannot be restricted to the community of those who gladly acknowledge his rule, the Church must participate in responsible and faithful action in the world in his name. Christ's lordship over the Church and the world provides the proper basis for a Christian social ethic. The living Lord does not restrict the political and social responsibilities of the Church to those which were accepted by his people under either the Old or New Covenants. In different historical situations the Gospel impels the Church to assume tasks which differ from those of biblical times. In every situation the Lord of the world is actively at work exercising his sovereignty over nations and peoples.
>
> The nature of the Church's own internal life makes effective declaration to the world . . . concerning Christ's power to overcome social antagonisms, create international community and reconcile hostile racial groups; concerning also the power of the Cross to reverse all purely human estimates of greatness and power. . . .
>
> Both by open criticism and voiceless patient endurance of injustice and tyranny, the Church confesses the lordship of Christ over all political and

social institutions. Whether or not invited to speak, it warns men against idolatries of every sort and testifies that all these agencies are . . . but authorities receiving their proper functions from God. . . .

In the judgments of God implied in present events the Church recognizes the foreshadowing of the Last Judgment and the signs of the new order where blessing, peace and righteousness will prevail.

As for the implications for the mission of the Church of the doctrine of the lordship of Christ thus formulated, the World Council had already demonstrated in its policy of Christian social action something of what they were supposed to be.

In this connection, more questions could have been raised than this proclaimed version of the doctrine evoked. For example, could a commission have laid under the program of the World Council of Churches a different theological foundation, if its study had led it to reject the old one as unbiblical? Could there have been any extensive alteration of the existing one, without toppling the superstructure? Would the World Council have been prepared to tear down and reconstruct what it had begun, if the Commission had found that its house had been built theologically upon sand?

The answer to all these questions would, undoubtedly, have been "No." The World Council obviously felt at this point quite secure in its original theological improvisations and had authorized the study on the lordship of Christ with expectation that the Commission's findings would confirm them. The main function of such studies was "to educate and unite"—probably justification enough of the procedure.

Upon the launching of the program of the Division of Studies after the Second Assembly, Chairman Freytag had said frankly that the inquiries projected would be less important for the new knowledge they turned up than for the changes they would bring about in the self-realization and the relationships of the persons participating in them, who would be the whole constituency of the World Council of Churches, if they could be got to cooperate.

At the end of two years the Commission had reached the conclusion, according to Professor Freytag, that, however convinced they may have been that Christ's lordship over the Church and the world provided a "proper basis for a Christian social ethic," they had found "in the Bible no direct and literal basis for what [we have today] to recognize as the political and social responsibility of the Church."

If he demanded biblical authority for what the World Council of Churches was doing in the field of social action, the literalist would have to continue searching the Scriptures in the hope that the Spirit of Truth might yet make explicit the Word of God implicit in them, while others looked to find support for the program in the Word of God which came through the Bible or from beyond it through the prayers and deliberations of faithful churchmen—clergy, laymen, administrators, and theologians.

Unfortunate but inescapable was the fact that the Bible conveyed to equally devout and conscientious students different meanings. In his New Haven report in 1957 Professor Freytag cited examples of this which had arisen in the current study of the lordship of Christ. One concerned "the prophetic ministry of the Church" and another "the task of the Church." There were at least two opinions of what constituted a prophetic ministry. Some conceived it to be a ministry related to public affairs, like that of the Hebrew prophets. Others thought that it had to do more with interpreting the prophetical passages of the Bible which seemed to set forth what God was doing and what he had revealed of his plans for the future. As for talking about "the task of the Church," many objected to the misunderstanding of Christian work it reflected. It seemed to shift initiative and responsibility from God to man and to encourage a superficial and ineffective activism, of which there was already too much in the ecumenical movement. "It was common opinion that the term 'prophetic ministry' or even 'task' needed careful biblical study," stated the minutes of the New Haven report.

During the discussion, it was asked what practical outcome could be expected of the study on the lordship of Christ. Dr. Robert S. Bilheimer, Associate General Secretary, explained that the work of the Commission would have "a direct bearing upon the deliberations at New Delhi." Meantime, the study was providing a focus for the work of the Division of Studies, and there was hope that it would contribute to the "formulation of a common mind in the areas of biblical and theological inquiry." According to a statement by the Associate Director of the Division of Studies to the Central Committee at Nyborg Strand in 1958, he said, it had proved of help to "other studies carried out under the auspices of the Division . . . e.g., 'The Theology of Evangelism,' 'The Word of God and the Living Faiths of Men,' 'Our Common Christian Responsibility for Areas of Rapid Social Change,' 'Christians and the Prevention of War in an Atomic Age.' " Actually, the fundamental nature of the doctrine of the lordship of Christ made it "relevant to all ecumenical concerns and inquiries."

3. Christianity and Other Faiths

Among the studies authorized by the Central Committee at Davos-Platz was "The Word of God and the Living Faiths of Men." At the Committee's request, the Departments of Evangelism and Missionary Studies had accepted responsibility for it, finding that, because of its dimensions and complexities, it required "a longer period of incubation" than some other inquiries.

The International Missionary Council had established study centers "in a number of countries in Asia, from which a continuing process of research into the contemporary character of non-Christian religions could be maintained." The Division of Studies, through the two assisting departments, would use the information obtained in "a biblical and theological discussion on the relation of the Gospel to the phenomenon of man's religion and the resurgence of non-Christian faiths." Dr. David Moses of India would head a commission to initiate and organize the movement.

The object, further outlined by the Division of Studies, would be to inquire into:

> The nature of the living faiths and the elements in them of appeal and power;
> The nature of the Word of God which is addressed to men living by these faiths;
> The nature of the relation between the Christian message and these faiths;
> The ways by which the Church may be enabled to communicate this message to those living by these faiths.

There appeared to be good reason to agree with the Division's statement that this would be "a major study" and that it would probably have a place among the agenda of the Third Assembly, if it progressed far enough by 1961. The knowledge it would seek surely was a condition of responsible missionary work. If conducted open-mindedly and with thoroughness, it could be perhaps a beginning of new and fruitful relations between the greater religions and of revolutionary changes eventually in missionary strategy.

The world needed nothing so much as an easement of tensions, which had been growing steadily more intolerable in their threat of overt international conflict. Some of the most bitter and irreconcilable of them were rooted in religion. The various faiths stood to confirm the biblical declaration that God had not left himself without witness in any nation. All had sprung from some apprehension of him by men and had many elements in common. Each needed to have its attention directed to what all possessed that could be made a basis for amity and, if God willed, for cooperation in the cause of world brotherhood and peace. A study of the kind proposed might discover how a start in that direction could be made and induce a mood for it. Even the slightest hope that the religions might, in the God-given unity they deeply shared, see their way to act urged all possible haste.

It was quite certain, of course, that many adherents of each would have nothing to do with such a movement. They would look upon it as being impossible—or, if possible, likely to prove damaging to their respective claims of superiority and authority. Many Christians could be expected to adopt this attitude. But some men and women of goodwill and public spirit in the vast followings of all the faiths would undoubtedly respond if theological arguments and attempts to evangelize were banned and attention centered, in tolerance and brotherliness, on the objective of summoning the peoples and the governments of all nations to work together in humility and justice for the establishment of a stable world order.

Whether qualified leadership would be available for such consultation and action, only the trial would show. Whether there would be time for it might be determined by the response. If religious peoples manifested the will to act for such ends, the God of them all might give the time.

The objectives of this inquiry were closely related to several other studies projected by the Division. "The Theology of Missions" would fall quite definitely within the same scope, as would "The Theology of Evangelism" and "The Calling of the Church to Witness and to Serve." The Commission responsible for it and the Commission on "The Lordship of Christ over the World and the Church" would need to consult each other at many points. "The Churches and the Building of a Responsible International Society," "Christians and the Prevention of War in an Atomic Age," and "Our Common Christian Responsibility toward Areas of Rapid Social Change" likewise involved cognate issues. It might be said, in fact, that none of the investigations scheduled could, apart from this one, fully achieve its end.

If religious men could not find in their experience common ground for attacking the problem of their insecurity in the world, they would fail the God in whom they believed, and all endeavor on behalf of peaceful and fruitful life would be of little avail. The claim that any one religion was destined to overwhelm the rest and win universal acceptance was hardly less irrational or frightening than the megalomania of dictators aspiring to world domination. Dedicated to faith in God, the major religions held in their power the fate of their peoples. As they drew nearer to God, they would find themselves closer to one another. So would they turn their nations—from the East and the West, from the North and the South—toward their true center, and into their ordained spheres of complementary service and influence. Any hope or plan envisaging less than this would be irrational and futile.

4. Missionary Obedience and the Word of God

When it decided to work with the Division of Studies of the World Council of Churches, the Department of Missionary Studies of the International Missionary Council brought to the union plans for inquiries on a number of subjects, including the greater ethnic religions of the East, the so-called younger churches, the training of the ministry, and the theology of missions. These were added to the list of the Division of Studies authorized at Evanston and in process of implementation by the Central Committee.

Research on the non-Christian religions went forward, as noted, under the title "The Word of God and the Living Faiths of Men." The study of the mission churches was designated "The Life and Growth of the Younger Churches" and that of the theology of missions "The Word of God and the Church's Missionary Obedience."

When it turned to the development of the last of these subjects, the Central Committee decided to explore first the plans for an inquiry into the theology of evangelism which had been announced by the Department of Evangelism. It seemed likely that the two topics would be found to cover much the same ground. Investigation discovered "The Word of God and the Church's Missionary Obedience" to be definitely related to the other themes, including the one on evangelism, but, in the opinion of those conducting the examination, to have "substantial justification as a separate study."

At the meeting of the Central Committee in New Haven in 1957, the undertaking, though begun in 1955, was reported to be "still in the planning stage." The following year, at Nyborg Strand, Chairman Freytag of the Division of Studies explained that the committee had noticed with particular interest the statement in a report of the Department of Missionary Studies that "at the Ghana Assembly[4] it was recognized that in the conditions of these times, God is leading the Christian Mission into a deep re-consideration of the present expressions of the traditional missionary enterprise." The statement had continued: "Neither the new obstacles nor the new opportunities which confront us can be met with a comfortable repetition of traditional lines of thought and activity. . . . [They] demand of us a return to the original springs of our missionary action and a re-thinking of its deepest foundations. Out of such a reconsideration, we hope, will come a renewal in missions suitable to our time." In view of the importance of the task when thus conceived, the Central Committee had urged the Department of Missionary Studies, he said, to proceed "with the plans with all vigor," first organizing "a commission of high competence" for its prosecution.

Preparations for the study had moved slowly, the Central Committee was informed at Rhodes in 1959, "because of the difficulty of formulating the precise delimitation of the subject"—which only emphasized the need for it. "If the Mission of the Church were interpreted as the total work of the Church in the world," the Rhodes report elaborated, "the study might easily become a vast essay in general ecclesiology or even in

[4] The Assembly of the International Missionary Council, University College, Ghana, December 28, 1957-January 8, 1958.

systematic theology at large—an undertaking far too great for such a project, and unnecessary. On the other hand, if the study were confined to the area in which the need for it is most practically felt, i.e. the theological basis for 'foreign missions' as a specific facet of the total Mission of the Church, then its very terms might seem to beg the real question, and the project might appear to be an apologia for the past, instead of a new, creative approach to the future."

"A certain sense of confusion and frustration descended upon these drawn-out preliminary stages," said Professor Freytag. However, at Nyborg Strand, "certain plans" had evoked considerable interest and discussion, and out of them had evolved a new proposal which had been favorably received. Dr. John Baillie of Edinburgh had consented to serve as Chairman of the Commission to implement it; and Dr. David M. Stowe, Educational Secretary of the American Board of Commissioners for Foreign Missions, had been released to serve as Secretary. Prominent theologians had accepted appointment to the Commission, and the International Missionary Council had agreed to underwrite the inquiry in the sum of twenty thousand dollars. The development of the new plan had proceeded successfully in the meetings of the Working Committee of the Department of Missionary Studies at Spittal, Austria, in the summer of 1959, and unanimous approval by the Division of Studies and acceptance by the Central Committee had followed immediately at Rhodes.

There was full agreement, according to the record, that a sharp focus should be given to the Commission's work and that "what was needed was a real blending of theological insight based on biblical study with practical insight into the nature of the real problems which arise empirically in the actual experience within the missionary enterprise." There was a strong feeling that the ecumenical movement had demonstrated "the limitation of agreed statements produced by a large number of persons, and that the needed fire and guidance were less likely to be gained by this method than by the work of individual authors." Accordingly, "a scheme was drawn up" for "gaining the best from both ways of working used in combination." In the first place, someone with knowledge of recent work of "theologians and missiologists" would be asked "to write a . . . study on the basis and meaning of the Church's mission to all nations, including a constructive and critical appraisal of recent work in this field, to be used as study material by the Commission and regional groups." A second person with missionary experience and theological competence would "initiate and carry through a series of study conferences and consultations in different parts of the world, consisting of people responsibly engaged in the actual life and mission of the Church, which would study, on the basis of biblical material and of the present situation of the Christian mission, the following question: 'What does it mean in theological terms and in practice in this ecumenical era for the Church to discharge its mission to all nations?' "

Involved would be many ancillary questions requiring attention. How did the Apostolic Church conceive and discharge its universal mission? What is the meaning of "the nation" biblically, theologically, and sociologically, and the implication of this for the Christian mission? What is the validity of "international" as a Christian concept, similarly considered? What is the relation of the Gospel and human cultures? What meaning has the new world-wide base of missions for "the nature of the unity we seek"? With what authority does the individual engage in missions which cross national and cultural frontiers? Must missions be totally recast in ecumenical terms? Is this possible while churches are themselves divided?

The Division of Studies made it clear that a volume of work had been assigned that would "consume years of time," if the pace of the inquiry itself was not swifter than that of the preliminary decisions, which had taken four years or longer.

5. The Life and Growth of the Younger Churches

The study of "The Life and Growth of the Younger Churches" aimed to understand their "inner life" and to promote "a constructive conversation between them and the missions regarding their relationship." How they engaged in the encounter with their environments and the effects of this experience on their own life were other phases of the subject to be examined.

The exchanges between the younger churches and the missions were of especial importance to the survey because of what they would reveal of the acute feeling of the native Christians about "Westernization." Do we really allow these new churches to be what they are? Do they consider themselves what they actually are—churches created by God to be instruments for his mission? Such questions would have to be discussed with all candor.

The complicated milieu of the new churches, involving nationalism, communism, and secularism, could be understood "in the West, but not in Western terms."

Many of these churches were young in a historic sense, and this stage of their experience would present impossible problems if they were asked to give the kind of witness expected of the older churches.

The method of study called for research on the field in connection with the life and growth of specific churches. This work had begun with the Anglican Church in Uganda, under the direction of Rev. John Taylor, and would be continued, according to tentative plans, in Nigeria, the Gold Coast, and a French or Belgian area of Africa. The hope was that it might be extended to Northern Rhodesia, in cooperation with the Department on Church and Society, and beyond into India, in cooperation with the Indian National Council of Churches.

The results of such "pilot projects" would be expected to afford guidance for later phases of the program. Area and local churches would be encouraged to conduct studies of their own. "The plan is bold and far-reaching," it was agreed, "and should form the main work of the Department of Missionary Studies for several years to come."

One series of studies of the Department concerned China alone. It sought information on what had happened in the Chinese churches and missions under communism. The findings would be published for the light they might throw upon the problem of the Christian mission in that country. Dr. Miner Searle Bates, an authority on China, had consented to write a book interpreting the conditions disclosed by the inquiry.

6. Theological Education

At Davos-Platz the Central Committee authorized "the Division of Studies to act as a clearing house and centre of exchange for various studies . . . in process concerning theological education; and to convene a consultation at Bossey of people connected with [such] studies, . . . if possible, within the next year." So began in earnest the inquiry on "Theological Education and the Training of the Ministry."

During the year, the staff of the Division organized for the collection of information on theological education in America, Britain, Europe, and the nations of the younger churches.

The consultation was arranged jointly with the World's Student Christian Federation, which had studied the subject for some years, and held at Arnoldshain, Germany, July 15-18, 1956, under the chairmanship of Professor William S. Tindall. It was not able to finish its work or to form a specific recommendation to the Committee of the Division of Studies. Those present agreed to continue their discussion by mail, in the hope of issuing a report by December. In this purpose they were successful, and their conclusions were submitted to the Executive Committee in February, 1957, and by it to the Central Committee in New Haven in August of the same year. They proposed a five-year study on "Theological Education and the Training of the Ministry" by the Division of Studies of the World Council and the World's Student Christian Federation, with special attention to three areas of the subject:

1. What is the true function of theological education, and how is it related to the Church and its mission?

This should be both a normative and descriptive part of the program. . . . It will need to inquire as to the way in which theological education should serve the Church and its mission; the terms in which the relationship between theological education, the Church and its mission should be conceived; and the degrees and ways in which . . . [it] should be responsive to the state of the Church and the world in which it is set. . . . Various . . . issues will appear: e.g. the adequacy of present theological training for the needs of the Church, the use of a non-professional ministry and the problem of training for it, specialized preparation for meeting immediate needs, and others.

The survey should have regard for the specific needs of different geographical and cultural parts of the world and gather "facts concerning the current theory and practice of the churches and theological schools." Notes should be taken of "the various concepts of the work and function of the minister . . . in different countries and churches."

2. Of what basic elements should theological education consist, and what is the proper relationship between them?

Is it true to say, specifically, that theological education must involve a theological discipline in the intellectual sense of that phrase, a spiritual training, and a practical training for some specialized aspects of the ministry?

3. The significance of the ecumenical movement to theological education should be examined.

To be considered especially under this heading was whether "ecumenics" should be a specific discipline within the theological curriculum, "or the ecumenical movement provided a general perspective" for the orientation of all subjects of the curriculum—or both.

This program was approved by the Central Committee for a five-year period, on condition that funds for financing it must be in hand before it was begun. Its results should be reported, possibly "in connection with a concluding international conference."

Gifts amounting to four million dollars for the development of theological education in the lands of the younger churches were announced by the International Missionary Council at the end of 1957. Two million dollars was contributed by John D. Rockefeller, Jr., and an equal sum by eight mission boards of the United States of America.

Dr. C. W. Ranson of the International Missionary Council had in 1956 led a team conducting a study of the training of the ministry in Madagascar; and Dr. Bengt Sundkler had written a book on the Christian ministry in Africa. The work of these men had done much to prepare the way for the larger inquiry on "Theological Education and the Training of the Ministry," and others also, in different countries, had made valuable contributions.

7. Evangelism

The Department on Evangelism informed the Central Committee at Galyatetö (1956) that during the previous year it had completed a survey of evangelism in Germany. The report, which had been prepared in German, would be translated and published in English.

The records of a recently finished study of evangelistic work in Latin American countries had already been sent to the printer for publication in English.

Other surveys would be conducted in Greece, Formosa, the United States, Japan, and Great Britain. In the last two of these countries, attention would be given particularly to industrial evangelism.

A beginning had been made "to get surveys from Holland, Burma, South Africa, Northern Rhodesia, and certain other countries."

The Department issued monthly letters from October to June of each year about "outstanding efforts in evangelism in particularly difficult areas of the Church's witness—mines, slums, prisons and the like—" which went by mail to seven hundred or so addresses in forty-four nations.

These investigations in many widely separated parts of the world were a means of gathering information for the Department's studies. The main theme could be summarized, the report stated, in six questions under the heading "Faithful Evangelism."

What theological convictions are necessary for faithful evangelism?

What are the means and disciplines of the Christian community which is the instrument of faithful evangelism?

What is the relation between the three-fold characteristics of the Christian community—its *kerygma,* its *diakonia* and its *koinonia?*

What elements in the Gospel make our task urgent and decision necessary?

What kind of analysis of the culture in which men live is required, if communication of the Gospel is to be effective?

In what forms and in what way will an evangelizing Church as it prosecutes its task expect the powers of the new age to operate?

Dr. Daniel T. Niles, who before becoming General Secretary of the East Asia Christian Conferences had served in a part-time capacity as Executive Secretary of the Department on Evangelism, reported at Rhodes on the Department's progress with its studies.

Following the Amsterdam Assembly, he said, Dr. Hoekendijk, the Secretary of Evangelism, had raised issues concerning theology and evangelism for study in the churches and the World Council; and the Department had since 1949 concentrated on this subject. A document titled "A Theological Reflection on Evangelism" had been produced for release to the churches after further editorial revision and upon approval by the Central Committee. It was, in part, a result of a consultation in March, 1958, at Bossey of about forty persons engaged in evangelistic work, special experimentation, and doctrinal discussion concerning evangelism. It dealt with the subject from the standpoint of such questions as:

Authority and Urgency

What is our authority for evangelism?

What authority have we for intruding into other people's lives?

What "credentials" must the Church have as evidence of the fact that it actually possesses the authority it claims to have?

What is the urgency of evangelism in relation to the work of Christ among men, in relation to death, in relation to the final end?

The Wider Dimensions of Evangelism

What are the true dimensions of evangelism?

In what terms should we think of evangelism's three-fold witness—*kerygma, koinonia* and *diakonia?*

The Dilemma of the Evangelist

What does "the dilemma of the evangelist" mean for the content and method of his work? The dilemma consists in the following: Ultimately Christ alone is the evangelist, not man; yet men feel the duty to evangelize. How does one plan to do something which ultimately he does not do? And what does this mean for the method of evangelism?

What methods of "successful evangelism" should not be used, because they are incongruous with the Gospel?

Structure

What changes in the structure of church life are required by the task of evangelism today?

From its organization, the World Council of Churches had stressed the importance of evangelism and had been criticized for not itself engaging in evangelistic endeavors of conventional type. The situation of the Council, in this respect, had not been generally understood. In its membership were represented about all the commonly held conceptions of evangelism, some of which differed so greatly that no common ground could be found for cooperation. Many of the member denominations could not, outside the World Council, work with one another in this area of the Christian task; and sharp divisions over it existed within some of them, which limited their individual evangelistic efforts. These conflcts could hardly be expected to be resolved by the establishment of a department on evangelism in an ecumenical body such as the World Council.

The Department had early decided that, quite apart from these difficulties, the World Council hadn't a working force, nor could it employ one, large enough to conduct "evangelistic campaigns," had it seemed wise to attempt them; and that it could best serve the cause by organizing studies on the meaning and the objectives of evangelism, such as those reported, and gathering for dissemination among the churches information on methods of proved effectiveness. It had been hoped that the churches could be brought in this way into closer agreement and, eventually, at least limited cooperation in their evangelistic mission.

In the characteristic ecumenical view, all phases of Christian work looked to evangelizing as their logical result. Social action was not excepted: through it the laity, with the clergy, witnessed to the power of God to save men's lives as well as their souls. In no other way, it was believed, could the Gospel of redemption be proclaimed convincingly to the masses of an industrial age.

8. The Relation of Witnessing and Serving

In the study on "The Calling of the Church to Witness and to Serve" by the Central Committee, the theology of evangelism occupied much of the discussion. Particular attention was given to the implications of "social services" for the work of evangelism. Professor H. Berkhof of Holland and Principal Russell Chandran of India prepared dissertations on the theme for presentation at the meeting of the Committee in New Haven. (Minutes, 1957, pp. 85-93.)

The purpose of the World Council to help the churches with their evangelistic mission was explicit enough, if words could make it so. "The Council desires to serve the churches which are its constituent members," the First Assembly (Amsterdam, 1948) had resolved, "as an instrument whereby they may bear witness together to their common allegiance to Jesus Christ." And a principal aim of the Commission on Faith and Order, according to its constitution, was to "keep prominently before the World Council and the churches the urgency of the work of evangelism."

"The two main elements in the Christian mission," Dr. Chandran said, were preaching, or witnessing to Jesus Christ, and "ministering to the needs of men."

Agreeing, Dr. Berkhof elaborated the complementary relation of these two functions:

Jesus Christ is the Word of God, in which the Kingdom is at hand. In him God proclaims our adoption . . . appoints us as his children. And what happens in him as the Word can be transferred only by the human word. . . . It has to be said—what God has said to us in the life, the acts, the death and the resurrection of Jesus Christ. The forgiveness of sin, the liberation from guilt, the elevation to sons of God can only be told—a message urging acceptation or rejection. . . . The human word is the image and analogy of the divine Word.

The Hebrew *dabar* is not a mere word; it is a creative act. . . . "He spoke and it was done; he commanded, and it stood fast." And in Jesus the

Word became flesh. . . . God's Word is also deed. As Word of forgiveness of sin, it was far more than a mere word; it is a creative act; it is in itself the beginning of the restoration of the divine order, which will be complete in the new society of the coming world.

The Word of God's grace is full of an eschatological reality, to which it not only points, but . . . is the gate, and for which it is the vehicle. But because it is just that, it can never be expressed in human words only. That these words mean a divine *dabar* can become evident only when they are accompanied by acts which show that really all aspects are included, that we have to do with a totalitarian reality, which embraces the whole man and the whole world. God's *dabar* is more than information. The Word is the shape in which the Kingdom now and here appears. So it can never be represented by the Word only; it has to be represented by word and act.

This duality by which the *dabar* is present in the world is seen in the Word and the Sacraments, by which Christ rules his Church. . . . The Sacraments are acts. . . . For our subject, the Holy Supper is of special importance, because it has to be repeated, just as preaching; and these two together accompany the life of the congregation. The Holy Supper is primarily the image of the coming Kingdom, in which we shall live in complete communion with the Host and with the other guests. . . . In the preaching we receive the forgiveness of sin and the promise of eternal life, and at the Holy Table we celebrate what we heard in the sermon, as the ultimate reality. . . .

We act out in hope the total glorification of our lives, of which we are sure by the adoption in Jesus Christ. . . .

Churches which neglect the sermon are threatened by impersonal objectivism; and churches which neglect the Holy Table are in danger that the word they preach may become abstract. Word and Holy Supper are the two eyes through which we see salvation in its full proportions.

In his development of the same thesis, Dr. Chandran drew upon the Scriptures for illustrations, referring particularly to Luke iv, 16-21; John vi; Acts vi, 1-6; and II Corinthians viii. "Summing up the references to the New Testament," he concluded, "we may say that witnessing to Christ, preaching the Gospel, challenging . . . unbelief in the world and rendering Christian service to suffering humanity, both within and outside the Church, are two necessary functions of the Church. . . . They belong together in the obedience of the Church to the one Lord."

The duality of word and act characterized not only the means of grace by which the Church was led and fed, it was agreed, but also the answer which the Church gave to grace. Christ charged his disciples to "underline" their preaching of the Gospel by "deeds of healing and charity." As early as the primitive Church, we find the two kinds of ministry: a ministry of teaching and preaching—a ministry of the word; and a ministry of aiding and serving—the ministry of the deed. The twofold ministry of *presbyterate* and *diaconate* reminds us of the two ways by which Christ's Church gives actuality to the *dabar* of the Lord in the midst of the congregation and to those outside—in witness and service, in word and deed.

A preaching Church, without the life and works of love and mercy, has no winning power . . . [declared Dr. Berkhof]. But it is impossible to imagine a Church which serves only in silent acts. . . . Our deeds are always partial and sinful. To mankind in suffering and despair, they can never offer the ultimate ground for peace and hope. Not our deeds are saving, but the deeds of God in Jesus Christ, whose love is infinitely greater than ours, and whose restoration will far outdo all our weak attempts to restore something in the world. So, the Church needs the Word to say what her deeds mean. She will show God's love in her serving. At the same time, she must say: "Don't look to my deeds, but to my words!" . . . Witness, without service, is empty; service, without witness, is dumb.

Although stressing the primacy of evangelism in the mission of the Church, the World Council was not in a position to witness through preaching, in the ordinary sense; nor could it give a place in its program to the celebration of Holy Communion, which showed forth "the acts" that followed upon the Word of God in Christ. It was able to help the churches in their witnessing, it thought, by leading them in studying the nature and meaning of biblical evangelism, and in gathering information throughout the world concerning evangelistic endeavors and methods. Beyond this, it could serve as a channel for their works of charity, which were vital in giving concreteness to their proclamation of the Word.

It was evident from the discussion that "not all humanitarian and philanthropic activity" gave expression to the true witness. "It cannot be the primary task of the Church to contribute in the general work of supporting, developing and improving . . . human life." This was, admittedly, a good and necessary work, to which Christians and non-Christians were equally called—or so it was held. But when the Church served those outside, what it did had to be "a sign of the Kingdom, an echo of God's saving and restoring work."

At this point, the discussion reflected the fear of many in the ecumenical movement that too much emphasis would be put upon "building the Kingdom" and not enough upon giving God the opportunity to do the building.

Simultaneously with this study on "The Calling of the Church to Witness and to Serve," the interest of the World Council was being focused upon another theme, "Our Common Christian Responsibility toward Areas of Rapid Social Change," in the study of which it would have to come to grips with political and economic questions of international dimensions as they affected the life and mission of the churches. There was concern because of the difficulty foreseen of carrying on the ministry of the Word under the conditions to be encountered. The comment of Professor Berkhof voiced this uneasiness:

There are circumstances under which life is in such material or social distress that many Christian workers are seduced to defend the opinion that our service can only be carried out for the time being without words—

in silence, in wordless deeds of love; so that we can only hope that in the long run people will grow curious, and after two or ten or a hundred years will ask by what power we do our works of love. However noble this attitude may be, it is a mistake. History of Christian service is there to contradict it. Though this attitude is right to a certain degree, we cannot give our witness as long as people mistrust our meaning and feel that "we want something of them." Only when they know that we act from an unselfish love, can we tell them about the reality of the Kingdom. . . . It would be loveless to show only our partial and sinful love, and not lead them to the source, the everlasting love of God for all poor sinners.

This, in the highest measure, is the concern of the serving work of the Church in areas of rapid social change. The territories, almost all, have an old naturalistic pattern of life. . . . The new structure . . . imported by Western civilization, is anti-naturalistic and deeply influenced by Christianity. Most of the Western workers are not conscious of this fact. They feel that they bring only technical and social developments which are quite natural for any reasonable man. They don't see the underlying ideas about good and evil—sex, marriage, education, government, labor, human personality, social justice, etc.—as branches from the Gospel-tree. One cannot graft all this on a naturalistic tree, without uprooting a whole society or without causing the heaviest fevers of hidden hatred, on the one hand, and, on the other hand, secularism and nihilism. If anywhere, then here, we can discover the need of the two-fold service of the word and deed. Without the Gospel itself, the Western derivatives will do more evil than good.

"The calling to serve" presented some problems when it brought the discussion down to the welfare state. Under collectivistic schemes, governments were assuming "many philanthropic functions . . . before a privilege of the churches." Some felt that this development ought to be resisted as "an attack on the realm of the Church." The consensus was that "the only realm of ecclesiastical service was the poor, the oppressed —those without rights." There should be rejoicing over their getting governmental rights for help, it was agreed, so that they would not be dependent on the mercy of others. "The government or the society then consciously or, far more often unconsciously, does the will of God, whatever the motives. . . ."

"The Church need never be afraid that she will not have a realm. . . . No social system, no welfare-state will ever in this sinful world eliminate the oppressed and helpless. They will leave painful gaps, and the Church must be where the gaps are. There her service is a witness of the saving Lord."

The service of the Church, therefore, bears, more or less, "the nature of protest against the dominating system, is revolutionary, in a sense, an attack on the closed social and political organization, on lovelessness and formality and guilty forgetting of those who suffer. It is a protest against collectivism and ideological thinking, a plea for the forgotten. There is no society that does not offer full opportunity and obligation for this witnessing service."

"The world-wide service to which the Church is called in the second half of our century cannot be . . . put over against the 'mission' of the previous century . . . ," said Dr. Berkhof. "As nations and governments think they discover the helpless of the world, the Church has to understand this helplessness far more deeply and to know that all help will leave people more helpless than they ever were, unless it is the help of the Kingdom of the new Ruler, the Lord Jesus Christ."

The inquiry considered evangelism in the larger context of the missionary movement, in which evangelistic work was accompanied by "a great measure of humanitarian service—education, medical aid and the like." It had to be asked whether the institutional framework in which the missionary program had been carried on was adequate for expressing the intimate relationship between witness and service. The organization of the World Council should be such as to do this; and "every unit of the Church." Distinctions ought not to be made between so-called "sending and receiving churches"—"a terminology reflecting an inadequate institutional patterning of missionary enterprises." All churches should "send" and "receive," expressing their commitment to witness and to serve in obedience to Christ.

Oppositions to the Christian faith in non-Christian lands made it most necessary for the relation between witnessing and serving to be understood. While paying tribute to the humanitarian works of the Church in their country, leaders of the Hindu renaissance in India were opposed to the propagation of Christian teachings. The Niyogi Committee, which made a study of this problem from the standpoint of Hinduism, recommended that the government control the funds for all such activities, to insure that they would not be used to support evangelistic effort. Many Indians, according to Principal Chandran, would like the Church to continue its humanitarian ministry as an end in itself, subscribing to "the general syncretistic belief in the unity of the great religions." The Church is confronted by this attitude, he said, "not only in India, but also in other Asian—and African—countries, where non-Christian religions and philosophies are revived."

On the other hand, the work of the Church was restricted in communist countries to "the purely religious life." Social service there belonged to the function of the state, and the Church was denied freedom to work out the social and political implications of the Christian faith. In them the Church was a worshiping community, but little more.

In the discussion, Dr. John Baillie suggested that the Church had a responsibility "to convince the state to uphold justice"—a bigger job than "filling the gaps with deeds of charity." The Church should work as "a symbol and sacrament" for fair treatment, and "not merely for charity," he said.

The thought also was advanced that "service should never be used consciously as a means of witness." The Christian concern was "to serve the whole man."

Peter Dagadu, a native representative of the "areas of rapid social change," so much in the thoughts of the conferees, believed that "witness and service" were not enough by themselves; they needed "to be supplemented by worship in which the Church received the direction of the Holy Spirit."

Dr. Fisher, the Archbishop of Canterbury, called attention to "the danger of setting up a dichotomy between Word (that which is said) and Sacrament (that which is done)—which is a magical conception of the Sacrament." The New Testament spoke, he remarked, of "doing the truth." Referring to the relation between Christian work and the social service of the state, he said that when government entered this field—for example, in education—it made the responsibility of the church more important. Pastoral care had a part in every kind of social justice, he suggested, and "it is always the calling of the Church to 'feed the sheep and tend the lambs.' "

9. Concerning Proselytism

At Evanston the Central Committee, following the Second Assembly, authorized the appointment of a commission "to study further proselytism and religious liberty." Its purpose was to find, if possible, some way to resolve the complicated and bothersome problem of proselytism, which had plagued the World Council of Churches from its beginning. The title of the inquiry was later changed by the Commission itself to "Christian Witness, Proselytism and Religious Liberty in the Setting of the World Council of Churches," a phrasing suggesting the relation of the prime subject to important qualifying aspects of religious and ecclesiastical life and indicating the somewhat restricted scope of the study.

Certain denominations in the ecumenical fellowship, the Orthodox in particular, had long been asking for an end to proselyting activities. The Ecumenical Patriarchate had in its historic 1920 encyclical on Christian cooperation stressed the need for a cessation of such practices. Later the same year, at preliminary conferences on Faith and Order and Life and Work in Geneva, Orthodox representatives had renewed the demand. On various occasions in succeeding decades the subject had been revived, but without any action beyond discussion and the formulation of admonitory suggestions to the churches, as at Toronto in 1950, when the Central Committee, in the statement on "The Church, the Churches and the World Council of Churches," said: "The positive affirmation of each church's faith is to be welcomed, but actions incompatible with brotherly relationships toward other member-churches defeat the very purpose for which the Council has been created."

The issue had caused more misunderstandings, it was felt, than would have arisen, had it been faced in a forthright and serious way. In the confusion over it, the World Council had been criticized both for encouraging proselytizing tendencies and for obstructing the full exercise of religious liberty.

The Commission, under the chairmanship of Bishop Angus Dun of Washington, proceeded forthwith to its work. Two years later at Galyatetö (1956) it brought to the Central Committee "a provisional report," which, after some revision by a special committee, was "submitted to the member churches for their consideration."

At Rhodes, three years later, it was decided by the Central Committee that the churches had not made sufficient response to warrant final action on the provisional report, and its transmission to them again was ordered, with the request for a reply by March 1, 1960, so that, on the strength of their advice, the Commission might prepare a statement of policy "for consideration, adoption and recommendation to the Third Assembly" in time to be authorized by the Central Committee at St. Andrews. "A substantial volume of careful responses from a variety of member churches" had been received and the report revised, after further consultation, accordingly.

"As our study has proceeded," declared the Commission in 1960, "it has become increasingly clear that the poles of our problem are to be found in the right and duty of free Christian witness, on the one hand, and in the obligation of ecumenical fellowship to manifest the visible unity of the Church as the Body of Christ, on the other hand. The tension is between the two, and we must deal justly with both in trust and love."

The study, presented by the Commission at St. Andrews, had taken note of "historical causes" encouraging proselytism:

The contacts of missionaries, particularly in the Middle East, with adherents of the ancient churches.

Renewed emphasis of Christian freedom as basic to securing all liberties.

Evangelistic programs by "free churches" in areas previously the exclusive provinces of national, or state, churches.

The increase of Christian groups working for individual conversions, without church-consciousness or interest in co-operation.

The rise of totalitarian movements and governments, which gave new significance to religious liberty and freedom in Christian witness.

The emergence of an organized ecumenical movement affording a focal point to the struggle for religious freedom and the claims of unity and fellowship.

The coming of the modern technological age which gave all these issues new and larger dimensions, through increased means of communication and mobility, and the enlargement of educational opportunities for the masses.

The extension of religious and cultural communities beyond their own national and ethnic borders, into all the continents.

"Churches all over the world," said the report, "find themselves confronted with the necessity of carrying out their tasks in this new situation.

It is sometimes thought that the issue of 'proselytism' arises only in a few areas, and that not many churches are involved. As a matter of fact, there are very few . . . which are not affected by it, one way or another."

Witness—or evangelism—which "is the essential mission and responsibility of every Christian and of every church," seeks to persuade people to accept the authority of Christ as supreme and to commit themselves to him for loving service in the fellowship of his Church.

Proselytism is not something entirely different from witness, but is rather a corruption of it.

> When cajolery, bribery, undue pressure or intimidation is used—subtly or openly—to bring about seeming conversion; when we put the success of our church before the honor of Christ; when we commit the dishonesty of comparing the ideal of our own church with the actual achievement of another; when we seek to advance our own cause by bearing false witness against another church; when personal or corporate self-seeking replaces love for every individual soul with whom we are concerned—then witness has been deformed into proselytism.

The Universal Declaration of Human Right claimed "for everyone . . . the right of freedom of thought, conscience and religion . . . freedom to change his religion or belief, and freedom, either alone or in company with others, and in public or in private, to manifest his religion or belief, in teaching, practice, worship and observance." However, liberty is not absolute, for it is not to be exercised in ways that impair the freedom of others or infringe the Golden Rule.

Among "basic considerations" advanced by the Commission was "the proposition that every Christian church" was "not only permitted, but required, freely and openly to bear its witness in the world, seeking to win adherents to divinely revealed truth."

The commandment respecting this "ministry of love . . . to mankind" was "valid in relation, not only to non-Christians, but also to all only nominally attached to Christian churches." The Commission thought that "churches ought to rejoice whenever fresh influences quickened the faith of those committed to their pastoral care . . . , even if . . . from outside their own structures." Should errors or abuses within a church distort or obscure the central truths of the Gospel and jeopardize men's salvation, other churches might be "bound to come to the rescue with a faithful witness to the truth lost to view." But they should humbly look in the unfortunate church for "hopeful elements of the real Church" that might be revived through "frank fraternal contact and co-operation" with it.

"No church, by virtue of its membership in the World Council was under an obligation to suppress, truncate or alter its full confession of truth, by which it stood or fell in its being and ministry as a church."

This agreement had been reached in the Toronto Declaration of 1950, which also stated that membership in the World Council "did not imply that each church must regard the other member churches as churches in the true and full sense of the word."

"The more frankly a church states its views in the Council . . . the less will be the need to express them in undesirable ways. . . . It is within the ecumenical fellowship that this exchange should proceed to the fullest extent, and without minimizing the difficulty and seriousness of the issues." (Cf. Toronto Declaration, III, 4.)

Membership in the World Council laid upon the churches, according to the Declaration, a moral obligation to "observe a particular attitude in this discussion." "It would be inconsistent . . . for one member church altogether to deny another . . . the status of a church, or to regard it as entirely heretical or hopelessly given over to abuses, so that its members could only be helped by being rescued from it. On the basis of their common confession of Jesus Christ as God and Saviour, and as the one Head of the Church, member churches jointly recognize 'hopeful signs' in each other." (Toronto Declaration IV, i.)

Witnessing within the ecumenical fellowship should take place in the following ways:

Unofficial, personal and private discussion between individuals seeking truth.
Official discussion between one church and another, each giving full weight to its confession.
Through Inter-Church Aid, when churches help one another in agreed ways "to carry out work of an evangelistic, catechetical or educational character, or some other service on behalf of the members, with the aim, not only of leaving them in their own church, but of enabling them to be more faithful to it and to become better Christians there."

Where there were problems in the relationships of churches, the Commission believed that solutions would be found, not so much by rules and regulations as by "right attitudes and reconciling actions." Even if rules and regulations were desirable, the World Council by its nature, and according to its Constitution, had neither the authority nor the intent to exercise control over the member churches or to legislate for them, "and was indeed explicitly prevented by its Constitution from doing so."

It was even more obvious that the World Council could not control churches or religious groups which had no relation to it. The influence of its statements "derived from their intrinsic merit and from the fact that they expressed the convictions of responsible representatives of the churches."

"Having due regard for the nature of the ecumenical fellowship represented by the World Council of Churches," explained the Commission, "we at the same time recognize certain principles which we believe should guide churches in their mutual relationships and, if followed, might provide objective and generally applicable standards of practice. . . . They lay no claim to finality. . . . However, they are already receiving sympathetic consideration in many of the member churches." They were "set forth in the hope and belief that they might be helpful to the churches as they examined their own situation, and that they might provide churches and councils of churches with a useful basis for further study:"

That we in our churches respect the convictions of other churches whose conception and practice of church membership differs from our own, and consider it our Christian duty to pray for one another and to help one another rise above our respective shortcomings through frank theological interchange, experiences of common worship and concrete acts of mutual service; and that we recognize it as our obligation, when in exceptional cases private or public criticism of another church seems to be required of us, first to examine ourselves and always to speak the truth in love and to the edification of the churches;

That we recognize it as the primary duty of every awakened Christian to strive prayerfully for the renewal of that church in which he is a member;

That we recognize the right of the mature individual to change his church allegiance, if he becomes convinced that such change of allegiance is God's will for him;

That, since grave obstacles to brotherly relationships between churches are created when some churches are denied the religious liberty which is accorded to others, all Christians should work towards the establishing and maintenance of religious liberty for all churches and all their members in every land;

That we disavow any church action by which material or social advantages are offered to influence a person's church affiliation, or undue pressures are brought to bear on persons in times of helplessness or stress;

That, while it is proper for churches to make clear their position with regard to marriages between persons belonging to different communions, the conscientious decision of marriage partners as to their future church allegiance should be respected;

That before a young child is received into the membership of a church other than that of the present affiliation of the parents or guardian, a due pastoral concern for the unity of the family should be exercised; and where the proposed change of affiliation is contrary to the desire of those directly responsible for the child's nurture and upbringing, he (or she) should not be received into the membership of another church, unless there be reasons of exceptional weight;

That due pastoral care should be exercised before receiving anyone into the membership of a church, if he is already, as the member of another church, under discipline by that church, or if there is evidence that his reasons for seeking membership in a different church are worldly or unworthy;

That whenever a member of one church desires to be received into the membership of another church, direct consultation should be sought between the churches concerned; but if conscientious motives and sound reasons are apparent, no obstacle should be placed in the way of such change of membership, before or after its accomplishment;

That, while there may be situations where a church already present in a given area seems to be so inadequate in its witness to Christ as to call for more faithful witness and proclamation of the Gospel to its members, the first effort of other churches should be patiently to help that church towards its renewal and the strengthening of its own witness and ministry;

That we should aid churches in areas where they are already at work, by offering fraternal workers and exchanges of personnel, as well as by sharing knowledge and skills and resources, rather than by establishing a competing mission of some other church.

"In our relationships in the World Council of Churches, the member churches are all called to show such restraint in their exercise of religious liberty as to avoid the causing of offence," concluded the Commission, "and in the fullest possible measure to respect the convictions of other churches. We, therefore, call upon the member churches to disavow proselytism as defined in this report."

In the discussion on the provisional report in the Central Committee at Galyatetö, one member, Dr. John Baillie of Scotland, expressed "uneasiness" about the Commission's idea of the causes of proselytism, which resulted, he thought, from wrong conceptions of truth and mistaken zeal more often than from the conditions mentioned—desire for prestige or self-aggrandizement or the intention to do wrong.

Others felt that this point was well taken. It seemed to indicate awareness of the incentive to proselytism hardest to overcome, which the study had not dealt with directly; namely, the conviction of many Christians and churches that their peculiar interpretations of the Bible and their traditions were necessary to salvation, in the true meaning of the experience, and that not giving their witness would be tantamount to betrayal of Christ and his Gospel. Misapprehended truth could be as imperious for the misled, it was agreed, as truth itself for the informed.

The circumstances thus created could be changed only by fundamental education of a kind proselyters of this genre would, for the most part, be incapable of comprehending, or, if they understood it, reject.

The sense of the Central Committee seemed to be, on the whole, that the adoption of the Commission's report at St. Andrews would prove of historic significance.

IV

PROGRESS AND PROBLEMS

1. The Marvel of the World Council

A group of Christian denominations taking for a corporate name "World Council of Churches" and for a program "building a responsible international society," and, while working for this goal, ministering to the victims of the existing irrational and inhuman order would not, if it were itself acting responsibly, expect to experience again any burden-free days. It would surely find itself in the way of learning something of what the Christian apostle meant when he spoke of "the care of all the churches," and perhaps much more besides; for St. Paul apparently felt it to be his duty to "become all things to all men," only that he "might *win some.*" Well might it ask who was equal to such things; also whether God willed that men, even Christian men, should undertake them. In his omniscience, he would know, it might be assumed, what a "responsible society" of world dimensions would be like, if it could ever be achieved, and would be able to look upon the totality of human woes without being crushed by its weight. But would he call men to face such trial, who could never be sure that the very actions they thought likely to further such a society might not in the end work to make it more remote and more nearly impossible, and who, if given compassion equal to the demands of their mission, could never again have any peace of mind?

To be taken into account, of course, was the strange paradox that in every age there were those people who thought that they could find happiness and fulfillment only by taking upon themselves the burdens of mankind, which, viewed humanly, so plainly belonged to the gods. Christians heard Jesus Christ saying, "Take my yoke upon you . . . and ye shall find rest unto your souls," who identified himself with the suffering multitude and owned the dreamer's hope of a better day. So had we in this century of many marvels a World Council of Churches.

Said Dr. Visser 't Hooft to the Central Committee at Davos-Platz, under the realization that new doors had recently been opened for the Christian mission by a great Assembly: "It is characteristic of our time that so many of the grave human problems which we face are created by forces which operate on a world-wide level. . . . Issues challenge the churches to think in world-terms, to render a common witness, to act on the basis of world strategy." His words underscored what was perhaps the most striking aspect of the ecumenical movement: its audacity, or—some would have said—its visionariness.

With reference to these possible alternatives—whether it was inspired insight or self-delusion that drove men to concern themselves with the herculean problems of world strife and suffering—those who judged would undoubtedly continue to stand divided. But on the fact that the World Council's program put upon those appointed to execute it an almost insuperable handicap there could hardly be any difference of opinion. The organization, deliberations, and actions of the Council were a composite of the thinking and experience of some 170-odd denominations—its members—which fact set it at once beyond the comprehension of most persons who might wish to understand it. Activities were carried on by it, or in its name, the earth around, many of them—perhaps most of them—going unrecorded in the official files. One could not see the whole of its works. Few persons could enumerate, let alone describe, them.

The history of the World Council cannot, therefore, be written: it can only be written about. Anyone essaying to do this feels that what he writes can be hardly more satisfactorily informing than those aerial photographs of the earth which are taken from some distant point in outer space. Looking at small areas of the ecumenical program under the magnification, so to speak, of the recorded minutes of the Central Committee's meetings and of the occasional Assemblies, one finds that he must concentrate on a few of the seemingly important actions, passing up the rest—by far the greater numerically, and possibly, in many instances, the more significant. But, wherever he turns, wherever he pauses, he will discover that the way the World Council of Churches leads him lies always within sound of the unceasing "ebb and flow of human misery," and that therein are for many its greatness and its fascination.

2. Inter-Church Aid and Service to Refugees

Interchurch aid had its beginning under the Provisional Committee (1946-48), before the organization of the World Council, in response to the need of churches in devastated European countries at the end of World War II. Earlier chapters of this book dealing with that period describe its development.[1]

As therein explained, the purpose of interchurch aid was to help, in the first place, with the restoration of damaged church properties and to provide ordinary necessities for the members of impoverished parishes

[1] See p. 178 ff.

and congregations. However, its scope was soon broadened to include "spiritual aid,"[2] as it was called, and later work with refugees was added. Eventually, it was decided that relief supplies for churches should be shared by them, when possible, with the needy outside their membership.

The program of the Department of Inter-Church Aid and Service to Refugees grew thus into a ministry of the churches to one another and, in their corporate capacity, to human want, wherever encountered. It quickly became the largest operation of the World Council, as it was the first, and the most influential in winning for the Council general acceptance with the churches and the wider public.

The Evanston Assembly in 1954 instructed the Division[3] to extend its work to other continents, designating for assistance particularly certain countries of Asia, Africa, and Latin America, many of whose churches lacked resources for even their own support, let alone an effective ministry to teeming populations in the throes of social upheaval.

The launching of an ecumenical relief movement of this kind was a venture prudence alone might have rejected. The vastness of the need dwarfed, by comparison, the means which could be amassed for its alleviation, especially after the extension of aid beyond Europe.

Writing from observation on his travels through Asia, the late Dr. Ulrich van Beyma of the Division of Inter-Church Aid and Service to Refugees said in 1955, "The ways of helping are so small, in comparison with the millions who suffer, that there is almost no use of inciting help to let a drop fall—not in a bucket, but in a cosmic ocean."

The problem of the refugee also was one of overwhelming dimensions. The number of the homeless increased in the first decade of the World Council's work with them, according to the most reliable estimates,[4] from about twelve millions to over forty millions. During the fifties, around seven hundred persons, on an average, were still crossing nightly from East into West Germany, which had already given asylum, since 1945, to approximately twelve million refugees and expellees of German nationality or origin.[5]

The separation of Pakistan from India displaced between thirteen and fourteen millions of their inhabitants—part of the heavy cost of independence.

In these same years of political convulsion, several millions of Chinese fled revolution in their own land into southeast Asia. Hong Kong, the most accessible stopping place for them, was overrun. Unable to find shelter, many camped in the streets and on the hillsides.

[2] Help toward maintenance of worship and the conventional ministry of the churches.

[3] The Department of Inter-Church Aid and Service to Refugees became, with the revision in 1954 of the organizational structure of the World Council, the Division of Inter-Church Aid and Service to Refugees.

[4] Elfan Rees, *The Ecumenical Review,* July, 1956.

[5] During the Berlin crisis of 1961, those crossing from East to West Germany numbered from one to two thousand daily.

The partitioning of Viet Nam in 1954 set more than a half-million people moving from the north to the south of that country, as in Korea, when a like shift of population had occurred under communist pressures.

Meantime nearly a million dispossessed Arabs squatted on Israel's frontiers, and in Austria the economic and political assimilation of some 600,000 *Volkdeutsche* was far from having been accomplished.

Crises of one kind and another yearly swelled the stream of the uprooted. Suez, Cyprus, Lebanon, Hungary, Jordan, Ceylon, Morocco, Algeria, Turkey, Tibet, Indonesia, Burma, Laos, Congo, Angola, Puerto Rico, Cuba—in these countries, and others, revolutionary violence or unrest set multitudes adrift; and in some of them natural disasters aggravated the condition.

The settlement in Italy of evacuees from the nation's former colonies and the destitute survivors of earthquakes and civil war in Greece made it necessary for many in these countries to seek employment or other obtainable relief elsewhere. Such movements of population from one land to another created problems similar to those presented in the case of refugees.

The World Council of Churches deemed it advisable to have a commission study the whole subject of migration, with special attention to apparent responsibilities of the churches.

After three years of preparation, which embraced careful investigation, the World Council convened at Leysin, Switzerland, June 11-16, 1961, an international conference of "some two hundred experts in the field of migration," among them representatives of seventy-five of the denominations belonging to the Council from thirty-odd countries of Africa, Asia, Australasia, Europe, Latin America, and North America; a number of non-member churches, including the Roman Catholic Church; fourteen governments; and intergovernmental and other agencies.

Topics considered touched upon the emigration of Puerto Ricans to the United States, West Indians to Great Britain, Japanese to Latin America, and migrations within the continents of Africa, Asia, and Europe. The immigration policies of important "receiving countries," such as the United States, Canada, Australia, and New Zealand, were brought under review.

Among the speakers were M. Felix Schnyder, United Nations High Commissioner for Refugees; Marcus Daly, Director of the Intergovernmental Committee for European Migration; Francis Blanchard, Assistant Director General of the International Labor Office; and J. J. Norris, President of the International Catholic Migration Commission. Dr. Franklin Clark Fry, Chairman of the Central Committee of the World Council of Churches, presided and gave the opening address; and four subcommittees reported the results of a study of as many phases of the experience of the churches with migrants in different parts of the world.

A series of statements and recommendations was adopted for presentation to the Third Assembly of the World Council of Churches at New Delhi.

Two mutually countering positions advanced in ecumenical consultations on the problems of migration for the churches were, on the one hand, that those contemplating changing countries ought to consider whether it might not be the will of God for them to remain where they were and there work out their destiny with their own people; and, on the other hand, that, the earth being the Lord's and the fulness thereof, his children should not be prevented from seeking its blessings wherever they felt led. The history and the religion of the Bible began with a migration to a promised land. Totalitarianism would decree where its subjects must live; but even the suggestion of such control seemed foreign to Christian freedom.

These references to the displaced give but a glimpse, so to speak, of a condition almost too vast and complex to be visualized.

The refugee and the church requiring aid were, in a sense, one problem. Many of the dislocated unfortunates belonged to the needy parishes. If not actually members, they were fellow countrymen caught in the same sweeping disintegration of the old order. And it was a world problem, in that it involved in its ultimate consequences all nations and peoples and called for ecumenical action by the churches.

The Division of Inter-Church Aid and Service to Refugees was an organization of international compass and constituency. The shocks of successive rendings of the fabric of world society were something no part of mankind could escape. But their full tidal force had not yet reached all nations, and from providentially protected countries help had to come for the others. This was the pattern of the Division's reasoning and of the churches' response. But care was taken to avoid, if possible, creating the impression that the relief operation divided into different categories those giving and those receiving aid. Circumstances compelled recognition of the greater ability of some than of others to contribute material gifts; but this must not be allowed to overshadow the even more urgently needed exchange of spiritual ministries in which all could join. The record showed, as a matter of fact, that the money and goods received by no means always came from the favored regions with abundant resources, many in other areas giving, as it was said of some in the earliest days of the Church, out of their poverty and "beyond their ability."

The projection of its work outside Europe involved the Division in new difficulties. The task undertaken in Europe had looked forbidding enough, but it had to do with communities and nations used to stable economies and having historical and commercial ties with the outside world which supported their efforts toward recovery. The service in other continents which had been designated for aid was, for the most part, to peoples for whom physical want was a continuing condition of long standing suddenly made worse by natural catastrophes or sweeping revolutionary social and political changes; foundations on which to build were broken and insecure or—in many cases—nonexistent.

The denominations had been working in these latter countries a long time through their mission boards; and, in order to avoid overlapping of services, the Division limited its operations to "emergency situations." The difficulty was determining when appeals, which came from all sides, fell into this classification. There were differences of judgment and occasionally misunderstandings. Happily, most of these could be, and were, resolved. Here the cooperative relationship between the World Council of Churches and the International Missionary Council gave under practical testing further proof of its essential wisdom and was, in consequence, strengthened. Indeed, experience in this area quickened the movement of these bodies toward their ultimate merger.

Under "the procedures for consultation and co-operation with the missionary agencies," the Division received authorization to concern itself with the needs caused by natural disasters, economic crises, and political upheavals; refugees and other homeless people; churches not in regular relations with any missionary society; urgent interchurch and ecumenical projects which the established boards could not finance; relief undertakings beyond the resources of local churches and missionary societies cooperating with them; and experiments aimed at helping churches or Christian communities, which had been "adequately examined and duly commended," to become self-supporting.

It could only have been expected that, under the broadened ministry, requests for help would exceed still more the Division's means. The insufficiency of the aid that could be undertaken with the available resources gave rise to criticism. Not all applicants could understand the meagerness of the relief supplies offered, or the denial of assistance when the stores were exhausted.

This was hardly surprising. The organizations appealed to belonged to the West and to nations rich almost beyond the imagination of the aided. How could the great disparity between that vast reservoir of wealth and the trickle of Christian charity in their desert of impoverishment be explained?

The common belief that colonialism had been a main contributory cause of their predicament tended to make those not helped resentful and those aided dissatisfied because they had not got more. Present at all times was the suspicion that the kindnesses rendered might be part of a subtle scheme to gain advantage of them in their extremity.

Even in prosperous countries there is little general knowledge of what a nation's actual financial competence comprises, aside from a fortunate inheritance and luck. The indispensable part that political leadership, business management, industrious labor, and the habit of thrift play is fully understood by comparatively few enjoying the fruits of prosperity. A superficial familiarity with the so-called welfare state encourages the notion on the part of many that in the solvent nations there are inexhaustible stores of wealth which could be opened for distribution to the poor of the earth, until none would want.

It is not to be wondered at that the administration of charity in this generation encounters all the old delusions and some new ones besides.

The World Council of Churches would "build a responsible international society" incorporating welfare-state features as popularly conceived, particularly the responsible sharing by the "haves" with the "have-nots," but its success depended quite as much upon educating the latter in receiving responsibly. The one condition could not be regarded as more important than the other.

The slogan "Not charity, but justice!" which had been taken up by the "underdeveloped" countries sounded ominous, because of the misconception it betrayed of both charity and justice. Could those who had not the capacity for gratitude know the meaning of justice?

Adding to the confusion and danger were the unrelenting machinations of some governments to discredit, for their own purposes, the efforts of those who sacrificed for the causes of relief and freedom for all peoples.

The sometimes impatient demands of the destitute could be understood and, for the most part, forgiven, as could their turning often to demagogic pretenders who promised them more than they might hope to get from those who cared for them for their own sake. Who could blame the shelterless sick for listening to anybody speaking to them of a home and rest?

Depending on the point of view, one might have magnified or minimized the value of the World Council's relief program.

Seen in relation to the massive need, it was indeed, as Dr. van Beyma had said, like a drop in an illimitable ocean. During the dozen years from Amsterdam to New Delhi, the Division of Inter-Church Aid and Service to Refugees was instrumental in helping with the resettling of nearly a quarter of a million refugees overseas, while assisting many thousands besides in finding asylum and employment nearer their own countries. These were not insignificant figures certainly; yet they approached the infinitesimal, in comparison with the millions of exiled who came to no such happy end.

The same was true of interchurch aid in its broader aspects. The churches gave annually sums running into many hundreds of thousands of dollars, and food, clothing, medicine, and other supplies amounting to even more. The spontaneous outpouring of Christian charity, year after year, was an achievement impossible to exaggerate. But the help it provided seemed, in proportion to the need, almost as nothing.

It was necessary in any appraisal of these good works to take into account the over-all policy of the World Council with reference to relief. It was not intended only, or even mainly, to raise and administer funds, but to serve the other agencies working in this field by gathering information on existing need, listing projects organizations wishing to cooperate might adopt, and stimulating interest on the part of secular bodies in a position to assist. On occasion it undertook, by request, to help directly with the application of aid provided by these last. In some years money turned over to the Division by governmental and intergovernmental departments to be expended according to agreement amounted to more than the total of gifts from the churches.

The United States Government in 1959 gave from its storehouses of agricultural surpluses grain and other foods of a value approximating $128,000,000, the churches raising, in cooperation with Church World Service and other boards, money toward the expense of shipment to the countries to which they were consigned.

An auditor's report would be needed for complete tabulation of the contributions—money and commodities—which passed through the books of the World Council from year to year. Figures of totals given by other bodies acting in cooperation with the Council could not be compiled from any single source.[6]

The World Council knew that for its own sake it must do what it could, whether much or little, toward the relief of world need. Work in this realm it saw to be an essential part of its program, from the standpoint of the churches' spiritual renewal. A body such as it could not play the Levite and take the other side of the road past wounded humanity. Scriptural compulsion was laid upon it—or so it believed—to lead its member churches in a continuing ministry of mutual aid and of service to others. It had regard for the admonition of St. Paul: "As we have opportunity, let us do good to all men, especially to them that are of the household of faith." It was as the Christian testimony was conjoined with works that it had power. The Division of Inter-Church Aid and Service to Refugees became thus, in its deeper meaning, a ministry to the souls of men. Its work brought illumination to the study of such central themes as "The Calling of the Church to Witness and Serve" and "The Implications of Christian Unity for Inter-Church Aid and Assistance to Underdeveloped Countries." The churches could be united really only in the doing of good. Without the deed, doctrine divided. The Word lived when made concrete in Christian compassion. Through the charity of the Church the Incarnation became a continuing reality. No phase of the World Council's program had scripturally more convincing justification.

This conclusion was set forth in a memorandum[7] by the Administrative Committee of the Division of Inter-Church Aid and Service to Refugees

[6] Interchurch aid comprised assistance through all church agencies. Inter-Church Aid was help channeled through the World Council of Churches, which served as coordinator, adviser, and stimulator also to ecclesiastical and governmental bodies with responsibility for providing relief, from whatever sources. While the Council knew about, if it had not to do directly with, most such aid given, its books properly carried a record only of its own transactions.

[7] Minutes of the Central Committee, 1959, pp. 148 ff.

"as a contribution to the discussion of the integration of the World Council of Churches and the International Missionary Council."

The task of the Division . . . has its origin in the spontaneous action of the churches in dealing with emergency situations caused by war on a world scale; but in, and through, the experience of ministering to churches and people in need, the churches have discovered the values of such service as an expression of the fellowship which they have found in the World Council of Churches, in the furtherance of their unity and the renewal of their life, as well as in their witness to the Gospel. . . .

The whole process of giving and receiving . . . [took] on a new complexion with the recognition that in the ecumenical movement churches had found a new sense of their interdependence, their partnership and their common life in the Body of Christ. . . .

There has been recognition from the earliest days that interchurch aid is more than a humanitarian activity, and that it has its source and sanctions in the Gospel. . . . Statements that interchurch aid is a permanent obligation of a World Council of Churches, which seeks to be worthy of its name, that it makes for the renewal of the Church, that it serves the cause of Christian unity, are examples of the recognition that this ministry has a significance beyond the immediate achievement of mutual aid by the churches to one another and beyond their corporate action in seeking to meet the need of men and women.

In recent years, the discussion of the relationship between Inter-Church Aid and Mission has led to a searching of the Scriptures. . . . into the meaning of *diakonia, marturia, apostole* and *koinonia* as elements of the total mission of the Church and of their relationship to each other in the fulfillment of that mission. . . .

Diakonia was . . . a ministry by one congregation to another, as by the Church at Antioch through the work of Paul and Barnabas to the Church in Jerusalem; or the ministry of a group of congregations to others, as by . . . the churches of the Gentile world through the collection organized by Paul to the Church in Jerusalem and Judea. . . .

Diakonia was also understood to mean a ministry . . . by a congregation to the needy in its own midst. . . .

By . . . the Master's teaching and example, and . . . his interpretation of his . . . ministry to those in need, *diakonia* was understood also in terms of . . . compassion to all in any way afflicted. . . .

The constraint to *diakonia* . . . was not simply . . . the Master's exhortation nor even his example, but . . . his person. The source of compulsion and inspiration . . . was seen to be in the Incarnation,[8] in the self-emptying of Christ, in his assumption of the form of a servant, and in his obedience as a suffering servant, even to the death of the cross. . . . The obligation to this ministry . . . has been recognized by the Church through the centuries as the only adequate response to the self-giving love of God in Christ.

Diakonia is, therefore, an obvious expression of *koinonia* related to *apostole* and *marturia.* It is, with them, indispensable as a manifestation of the reality of Christian fellowship. Through *diakonia* that fellowship is not

[8] We have come to see that these ministries are not only a preparation for the Gospel and a corroboration of its proclamation, but are themselves of the Gospel and integral to the life of the Church, whose task (to quote Canon Hodgson) "is not only to love the world with a love like Christ's, but actually to be his love expressing itself through his continuing earthly body." (Leslie Cooke)

only expressed; it is also strengthened. A World Council of Churches by nature and definition is a manifestation of *koinonia.* The expression of its life in *diakonia* is, therefore, essential. In the light of experience . . . it is also clear that as the churches have engaged in these ministries to one another and to the needs of men and women, *koinonia* has become for them an increasing reality.

It is clear that *diakonia* stands in relationship to the other activities of the Church. . . . [It] often paves the way for the preaching of the Gospel . . . is corroboration of the Gospel . . . , as shown by the Epistle of James. The ritual of a pure religion is to visit the orphans and widows in their affliction.

Diakonia, however, stands in its own right as a manifestation of the faith and life of the Church. Whether it prepares the way for *apostole* and *marturia* or not, whether it corroborates them or not, it is itself an essential element of the Church's mission. . . . The World Council of Churches, which must both be an expression of the quest of its members for the wholeness of the Church and at the same time a challnege to them to manifest the wholeness which Christ has already given them, cannot fulfill its purpose unless there is in its structure an identifiable, recognizable element devoted to the expression of all that is gathered up in the term *apostole* or mission. It is also true that it cannot fulfill this purpose unless there is in its structure a recognizable and identifiable element devoted to the expression of all that is gathered up in the term *diakonia* or . . . Christian service.

Among the agencies responsible for interchurch aid, broadly speaking, were the Lutheran World Service; the Central Executive Department of Church World Service of the National Council of Churches in the United States; *Hilfswerk* organizations of Germany, Switzerland, Sweden, and some of the other European countries; the Department of Inter-Church Aid and Service to Refugees of the British Council of Churches; the Relief Committee of the Near East Christian Council; the Pontifical Mission of the Ancient Churches of the East; the East Asia Christian Conference; the Hong Kong Christian Social Welfare Council; the relief departments of the various world confessional bodies; the international committees on relief of the Young Men's Christian Association and the Young Women's Christian Association; the United Nations High Commissioner for Refugees; the United Nations Relief and Works Agency for Palestine Refugees in the Near East; the United Nations Korean Reconstruction Agency; the Intergovernmental Committee on European Migration; the International Labor Organization; and the United States Department on Voluntary and Foreign Aid.

The Division of Inter-Church Aid and Service to Refugees of the World Council of Churches, besides administering such funds as it received of the churches, offered, as stated, its services as coordinator and adviser to such of the other organizations as desired them and also to individual churches with resources to invest independently in relief. By reason of its world-wide contact with churches of many denominations and its considerable experience in the field, it was in an advantageous position to gather reliable information and to counsel helpfully. Only occasionally did it undertake the responsibility of acting as agent for other bodies, as, for example, in 1955, when it entered into contracts with the United Nations High Commissioner for Refugees involving nearly a million dollars. It conceived its opportunity for highest usefulness to lie, as stated, in the role of stimulator, counselor, and coordinator to other agencies.

The Division was forward in promoting such movements as World Refugee Year (June, 1959–June, 1960); the Surplus Commodities Program, under which large quantities of foodstuffs and other materials worth hundreds of millions of dollars were contributed; the plan of the Food and Agriculture Organization of the United Nations to focus attention on the creation of food supplies and to conduct a Freedom-from-Hunger Campaign in 1963; conferences to draw the attention of the world to acute need calling for quick action, such as that of Palestinian Arab refugees; and appeals in sudden emergencies, like the Hungarian rebellion of 1956, when, approximately a million and a half dollars was raised for the aid of refugees and fellow sufferers unable to flee. Its seventy offices in some fifty nations, through which its own operations were administered, were placed at the service of other relief organizations. It took the initiative, as already explained, in appointing a commission and calling a world conference in 1961 on problems growing out of the migration of peoples in search of employment, better opportunities, and greater freedom and security.

Meanwhile, the Division administered the Ecumenical Church Loan Fund of about three million dollars of help from which more than eighty congregations had availed themselves by 1960, including one in Burma —the first outside Europe. And it found time for attention to smaller services, like providing scholarships for prospective Christian workers and managing its cooperative interests in Work Camps, a permanent and growing feature of the ecumenical program, in which, by the end of the present period, more than six thousand youths had been enrolled. It also established a number of institutional homes for aged and sick refugees, who could not be properly cared for otherwise, giving shelter and nursing to more than a thousand such wards in their last years.

Dr. Robert Mackie, who had been Director of the Division for seven years, retired in 1955, to be succeeded by Dr. Leslie E. Cooke. Mackie continued giving of his time to the Division as Chairman of its Administrative Committee. Other principal officials assocated with these during the period here under review were Dr. Edgar H. S. Chandler, Associate Director and Head of the Service to Refugees; Rev. Raymond Maxwell, Secretary for Orthodox Churches and Countries, and the Scholarship Committee; Dr. Elfan Rees, Adviser from the Commission of the Churches on International Affairs to the Division on Refugee Work; Dr. Howard Schomer, Inter-Church Aid Secretary for Europe, and Secretary of the Committee on Fraternal Work; Alan Brash, Secretary for Inter-

Church Aid in the East Asia Secretariat; Dr. Ulrich van Beyma, Secretary for Asia and Africa; and Dr. Sjollems, member of the staff of the Service to Refugees in Austria and Director of the study by the Committee on Migration.

The purview of the Division, which experience was continually broadening, was described further in the 10th Annual Report of the Central Committee for 1957 (p. 29), as follows:

It is to express through the ministry which the churches have in the World Council a fellowship in which all members stand as partners with equal status. It is to manifest that fellowship in mutual aid, which each member has the right to ask and to receive, without a sense of dependence or indebtedness, and which it is the privilege of each member-church to give. In this ministry of the churches to one another, the distinctions between giving and receiving churches, churches of the East and churches of the West, older churches and younger churches, will no longer have meaning or relevance. It is the purpose of this Division that the churches shall not only be joined in a partnership of mutual aid, but shall be increasingly engaged together in a ministry to human need whenever it is found, a ministry which crosses the boundaries of race, nationality and religion. In this ministry the churches not only give evidence that the coming Kingdom has come; they witness to the authority of their Lord who identified himself with the poor, the outcasts, the suffering and dying, in the service of whom he is to be found.

The report for 1960 stated that the Division had become "a means by which the churches could express their ecumenical solidarity by mutual aid of all kinds, and offer disinterested service on an ecumenical basis to men in any part of the world, not simply in emergencies but as a permanent part of their normal life." Inter-Church Aid remained "the fundamental basis of the Division's life." In Europe, where work had been in progress fifteen years, "the underwriting of projects . . . still flowed at the rate of one million seven hundred thousand dollars a year." Outside Europe, expenditures had risen from $185,000 in 1956 to over $800,000 for the first six months of 1960.

Initially, the churches had looked to the Division for help in sudden need, but now they expected the Division to alert them to emergencies as they occurred. In the previous five years, forty-four appeals had been issued by the Division, with responses known to it totaling over two and a half million dollars in cash, and "material aid greatly in excess of that figure in value." In the past eleven years, 220,000 refugees had been resettled overseas "and thousands more helped to find places in the societies of the countries where they had found asylum, while many hundreds . . . of aged and difficult-to-settle had been cared for in institutions."

The Division had worked diligently for the success of the World Refugee Year program, just concluded. This commendable project had not been without its dangers, in that it might have given the impression that the refugee problem had been solved, which would be disastrous.

Multitudes of refugees remained unhelped; their "plight was made worse because of disappointed expectations." The observance of World Refugee Year had revealed the immensity of the task. Meanwhile, refugees were still crossing frontiers. "It is imperative that a clear word be spoken to the churches that they must maintain their effort both in keeping the needs of these people before their governments and the United Nations, and in sustaining their own ministries to them."

In April, 1960, the Administrative Committee of the Division, meeting in Geneva, invited into consultation representatives of the associated agencies of the United Nations, the International Missionary Council, other ecumenical bodies, the Young Men's Christian Association, the Young Women's Christian Association, the World's Student Christian Federation, the Lutheran World Federation, the Presbyterian World Alliance, and Inter-Church Aid Committees related to the Division, as well as leaders of Christian work in Asia and Africa and officials of the Commission of the Churches on International Affairs and of other departments of the World Council of Churches, on the subject "The Christian Response to Areas of Acute Human Need." *The Ecumenical Review* (July 1960) summarized the conclusion reached, in substance, as follows:

Hunger has its root causes in maldistribution, inadequate methods of soil conservation and cultivation, population expansion, the principles governing policies and economies of nations.

While distribution programs have their place in meeting immediate needs, only the success of enterprises calculated to increase food production give hope of a permanent solution.

The needs of the unprivileged are to be met, not only by introducing new techniques of production, but by providing leadership.

The voluntary and governmental agencies require the help of one another, to make the best use of their resources; and everything should be done to strengthen their collaboration. The Freedom-from-Hunger Campaign of the Food and Agriculture Organization of the United Nations is to be welcomed and supported by the churches.

The emergence of new nations in Asia and Africa increases the need for technical assistance. Rapid political change is not accompanied by rapid economic change, and new nations urgently seek help to establish stable economies.

Though their resources are small, in comparison with the need, the churches have an indispensable contribution to make. They are in position particularly to supply volunteers for training for technical assistance as a Christian vocation. They are especially qualified also for pioneer experimentation needing intimate people-to-people relationships for success.

To render an effective service, the churches need to develop an ecumenical strategy that will facilitate the use of available resources to best advantage. No other procedure will be acceptable in some areas, because of the insistence on unity.

With these considerations in mind, the Administrative Committee and the other divisions and departments of the World Council of Churches decided to undertake the development of an ecumenical strategy on three main lines of action: the organization in carefully chosen areas of comprehensive demonstration projects in self-help; the supplying of adequate material aid until these experiments could be got under way; and the recruitment of Christian workers with technical competence to serve in them, after training.

These recommendations met with a favorable reception in the Central Committee at St. Andrews. It was explained that inquiries indicated "a surging of interest in the churches and the possibility of considerable resources being made available for this enterprise." While results from it could hardly appear before the churches met in New Delhi, the Division hoped for action by the Assembly making "this as much a continuing concern of the churches as . . . their concern for homeless people has been and still is."

Serious questions were raised by certain implications of interchurch aid in the context of "a responsible international society," some of which were touched upon in discussions initiated by other divisions or the Central Committee and in reports coming from them. Of the reports, one bearing the title "Christian Concerns in Economic and Social Developments" was especially timely and relevant.[9]

Obviously, Christians had the duty to give as they were able toward the relief of human need, which was the burden of the Inter-Church Aid program. The Gospels made it clear that this compulsion arose from both the teaching and the example of Jesus. That there were limits to what they should give was apparent from his experience and the conclusions to which he was driven. He found that the problem of physical want could be monopolizing; also that it presented dangers. He would not commit himself to continued miracle-working to feed the hungry, and dismissed the multitude with a rebuke when he saw that they followed him only because he had fed them.

Christians were a considerable element of the world's population; but if all of them gave as they were able, the needs of mankind would not be met. The abolition of poverty, if possible at all, would require more than Christian charity. There would have to be investments of capital by individuals, corporations, and governments in the underdeveloped countries. These would face many hazards. Christians might feel it their duty to take such risks. But should business concerns, which handled stockholders' money, or governments, which represented all their citizens, non-Christians as well as Christians? The losses of states fell upon all the people, having to be made up in taxes which all paid. Moreover, aid to foreign nations might be used, as under the Marshall Plan of the United States for Europe after World War II, to develop businesses which, to find markets, must compete with those in the befriending

[9] Minutes of the Central Committee, 1958, pp. 53 and 124-25.

country; and this might result in serious losses of income to the latter and unemployment or lower wages for their employees.[10] If one was willing as a Christian to accept such conditions of helping the world's underprivileged, had he the right to use his government, if he could, to force them upon fellow citizens?

The committee reporting the study on "Christian Concern in Economic and Social Development" said:

> International private investment has an important role to play. . . . Far more grants and generous loans are essential. . . . In pressing for further assistance, we are aware that this raises a number of economic difficulties for contributing countries. It may require an increase in private savings for foreign investment and . . . in taxation, where aid comes from public funds. . . . As Christians, we call on nations to make the necessary adjustments in their economic policies.

The argument in this connection that all—Christians and everybody else—ought to give, if not from a sense of religious duty, as a patriotic contribution to national defense against those who might be disposed to take what they needed by force, if it was not given voluntarily, could only be regarded as both foolish and unworthy, though one heard it advanced seriously in churches and ecumenical gatherings. Its unwisdom lay partly in the idea that friendship and goodwill could be bought, and partly in the advertising of fear and the branding of all that might be done through genuine Christian charity as only calculating expediency. It incited the unprincipled in underdeveloped countries to step up their demands. It was unworthy because it counseled submission to the tyranny of social elements who would destroy civilized society, and would have reduced those heeding it to the payment of what amounted to tribute.

Ecumenical study groups, who had searched the Bible for guidance on these and other related social questions, had reported that they found no definitive word. The Scriptures described many human situations fraught with timeless perplexities and reflected what men of faith thought God wanted done about them. They were, of course, a truly valuable record of experience, which society could ill afford to neglect. But the honest person who was competent in the Scriptures knew he could not say responsibly that the Bible taught this or that solution of any complex modern problem. He could say only, with reference to a given issue, that the Bible seemed to lend moral support to a certain course of action—a conclusion which might be of value if it had been reached with due regard to valid principles of scriptural interpretation and avoided dogmatism. He would seek a workable consensus with

[10] For example, factories built with Marshall Plan funds made it hard for some American businesses to survive and caused serious unemployment. The billions the United States gave abroad were raised by general taxation. They figured in the gold drain on the Treasury and the depreciation of the dollar.

others whose thoughts took them in the same direction. But he would be more than rash if he tried to impose his convictions upon them, or anybody else, by resolutions or legislation.

Progress toward a responsible international society would depend, then, on acceptance by those with this world's goods of the duty to share with the less fortunate. Giving would be prudent, not sacrificing the capacity to continue helping nor weakening the resolve of those aided to strive for self-help. Christians were under obligation to God to keep in mind that what they had they received of him, not to be dissipated through reckless use, even in charity, but to be husbanded with care, that it might increase and abound unto greater liberality. Without such stewardship on the part of all entrusted with wealth of any amount—individuals, banks and other businesses, and governments—the responsible society for which the World Council and the churches worked would remain only a dream.

However, a responsible society depended quite as much on the development of responsibility in receiving. Perhaps this was even more important, and what could be done about it might rest in the hands of the Church; for responsibility had to be taught—to the "have-nots" as well as the "haves"—and who but the Church could teach them?

The Church had the Gospel, which in its law of stewardship took account of both rich and poor. "It is required in stewards that a man be found faithful." In judgment, all were equal. "Unto whomsoever much is given, of him shall much be required," and "he that is faithful in that which is least is faithful also in much." Men were not equal in what they received of God. Equality could be achieved, and was expected by God, on the level of their spiritual response. "Everyone shall give account of himself to God."

Let this Gospel be preached to all, with its reminders of the deceitfulness of riches and of the poverty of all who were not rich toward God. Let it warn all against the destruction selfishness and covetousness visited upon individual and society. Let the Church believe the Gospel and practice it. Let the preaching of it be with the motive, not of prodding those who heard to give more money for budgets, but of saving their souls. Let the apostolic concern exercise its persuasion through the ministry of the Word: "Love not the world, neither the things that are in the world. If any man love the world, the love of the Father is not in him. For all that is in the world—the lust of the flesh, and the lust of the eyes, and the pride of life—is not of the Father, but . . . the world. And the world passeth away, and the lust thereof; but he that doeth the will of God abideth forever."

The Church should know that this Gospel would be taught by it or not at all. The Gospel was its unique responsibility, relating itself to everything worthy of a place in its mission. Interchurch aid gathered its impulse from the Gospel. Its supporters were those Christians who recognized their God-given stewardship. Unless a faithful effort was made at the point of distribution to awaken the same spirit in those receiving, the relief mission would hurt and not heal. The wisest and most earnest effort could fail for both giver and receiver who rejected the Gospel; but the attempt must be made. The churches aided or provisioned for giving to the destitute of their communities should be made to understand the spiritual meaning of the operation and instructed how they might represent this truthfully to the people served.

Churches, as well as nations, which managed to keep solvent were sometimes caricatured as greedy oppressors of the poor. Anything they gave was represented as coming out of an abundance which made sacrifice by them impossible and as aimed at quieting those aided in their misery or at gaining some further advantage over them.

Even churches and their leaders were not above this kind of misrepresentation. With the best of purposes, one could be persuaded, they sometimes justified by their methods the suspicions of the aided toward them. How often one heard it said in the giving churches that what Christians gave represented no actual sacrifice, and that they had better give more or they would lose all. If it was true that the giving of the churches stopped short of self-denial, it were better not talked about as a prod to more liberal giving. Likewise, if what had been given was in any sense a ransom against the day of revolution and expropriation. Christian leaders in the underdeveloped areas should have been briefed for dealing with these attitudes intelligently before they were entrusted with the distribution of interchurch aid.

The care taken by the World Council to cultivate a spirit of mutuality in interchurch aid tended to serve this end. No church was to think of itself as only receiving or giving. Regardless of their economic ability, all gave and all received. Right attitudes in the transaction—compassion, humility, appreciation, trust, gratitude, understanding—were more important than money and goods and were fruits of a relationship all were responsible for maintaining. They belonged to the results of a true Gospel ministry, and without the purpose to do everything possible to provide for their growth, the interchurch program had no real claim on anybody's support.

The promotion of interchurch aid drew attention continually to the economic disparities between the nations—a sore subject not always handled with the understanding and circumspection that might have been expected of the Christian Church.

Occupying a position in the world comparable to that of the rich citizen in a community, the United States was especially sensitive to criticism, which, as might have been expected, was not uncommon. "Could any country have amassed so much wealth fairly?" "Should any, under whatever circumstances, possess so much?" Such questions by others were, naturally enough, disturbing. The United States had provided, by the most reliable estimates, upward of forty billions of dollars for world relief and rehabilitation. But, give as it might, it could not do enough to hush questionings or to evoke much show of gratitude. What it had done was proportionately less than it ought to have been, in the eyes of those aided, and of the nature more of self-aggrandizement and self-defense than of true charity. Appeals continued without end, and ecumenical churchmen pressed for the policy of increasing foreign aid through all channels.

The problems were not confined to this area of the program. Human nature being what it was, other nations could not always resist successfully the ever-beckoning temptation of envy. After visiting the United States and making the circle tour from New York to California and back, with the glimpses it gave of the northern and southern tiers of states, a distinguished European said for the press, "In the American idiom, Uncle Sam Money-Bags ought to cough up," his assumption being the all too common one: that what the United States disgorged would go far to meet the deficiencies of the rest of the world; that the underdeveloped areas of Asia, Africa, and South America—and of Europe also—had their little because the Western Croesus had so much.

There were, of course, more perceptive foreigners who knew the case was not that simple. They secretly thanked Providence that the United States had been able financially to save itself and the Western economy from collapse during and following World War II. The fact was that the United States had by its aid exposed itself to the criticism of having bought control of the ecumenical movement, while its payment of a large share of the expenses of the United Nations had led to the similar charge of attempted political domination of the world.

Perhaps it was not to be expected that the nations or the churches would in their common confrontation of the events of these desperate years be able to treat one another with the wisdom and the charity that were their main hope of survival. Without intent to condemn, a passage in "The Report of the Director of the Division of Inter-Church Aid and Service to Refugees for the Year 1956-1957" [11] may be cited as showing the superficial and confusing manner of handling momentous issues into which leaders of ability and goodwill lapsed at times, if not under the blindness of unconscious bias, because of the pressures of enterprises too vast and burdensome to allow opportunity for reflection and careful statement:

> From time to time during the past year, the Administrative Committee and the staff have had their minds fixed on the great problem of hunger. . . . How enormous and appalling it is! . . .

[11] *The Ecumenical Review,* July, 1957, p. 429.

In his book, *Christianity and Economic Problems,* [The report continued] Dennis Munby[12] quotes the following statistics:

In 1949 the world's population was 2400 million.

In North America the population was 213 million—less than 10% of the total world population. But North America had 44% of the world's income.

Asia's population in 1949 was 1300 million—53% of the total world population, but it had only 10.5% of the world's income.

The citizen of the United States has an average of $1453 to spend each year. The citizen of India . . . $57; the citizen of China . . . $27.

Now in such figures there is no more than a statement of fact. There is no criticism intended or implied. Indeed, if there has to be such a preponderance of wealth in the hands of one people, we may be thankful that it is in the hands of such people.

The only moral to be drawn is the one which Munby himself draws, when he says: "When moralists tell the poor not to be envious, we must expect them to demand in reply a careful scrutiny of the moralists' bank account." The facts, however, are eloquent. . . . Such inequality is a challenge to the Christian conscience.

Whatever may have been the aim of this reference and the accompanying comment, they went far to prove the insight of an ecumenical writer who had observed that it would be better for all concerned if they stopped talking about human inequalities and set about doing what they could, both rich and poor, to relieve one another's burden, in silence and humility before the massive task none could fully understand.

At least those who undertook to interpret the work of the World Council of Churches were under obligation to remember that they were, in the first place, the appointed spokesmen of religion.

"If there has to be such a preponderance of wealth in the hands of one people, we may be thankful that it is in the hands of such people." In short, a good providence had canceled a bad one. But, if God had anything to do with events, were not the concentration of wealth in a place beyond war's destruction and the employment of its people, however unworthy and prone to mistake they may have been, in the defense of the free world things also of his willing?

"Such inequality is a challenge to the Christian conscience." Indubitably; but equally to the Christian intelligence. Could anyone think that the solution of the problem of inequality in respect of material riches at the middle of the twentieth century consisted in distributing the resources of the North American continent until all the nearly three billions of the earth's population shared alike? Could a more sinful dissipation of wealth have been conceived? It would have been like opening the sluice gates of a reservoir and letting the impounded

[12] Vice-Chairman of the Department on Church and Society of the World Council of Churches, and Lecturer in Economics in Aberdeen University, Aberdeen, Scotland. He was engaged for research in connection with certain studies conducted by the World Council of Churches in the field of social Christianity.

waters, life-giving so long as they were used wisely, flow over a desert-land to evaporate or disappear in the sand.

Competent leaders in the ecumenical movement had already come to see that hope for the underdeveloped nations lay in helping them do for themselves, which, of course, called for continued giving by the well-to-do countries, not only of money but of services. Knowledge of scientific techniques particularly must be shared with them, as the World Council of Churches had already agreed. Discussion, if it kept to this point, would be constructive and stimulating; but it only multiplied woes when it degenerated into vague deplorings of human inequalities. Economically backward countries had to be helped to believe in the better way of change through peaceful actions, which the World Council proposed, and with which it was girding to assist them, as against revolutionary violence which promised only greater suffering and want and might trigger a universal war of annihilation.

"The only moral to be drawn is the one which Munby himself draws, when he says: 'When moralists tell the poor not to be envious, we must expect them to demand in reply a careful scrutiny of the moralists' bank account.'" Was no moral to be drawn against envy? Was the Church accepting the characteristically worldly reaction to social disparity? Surely, it had been commissioned of old to speak against envy, not with complacency toward oppression of the poor, but because the death of all good walked in envy. "Envy is like a rottenness in the bones," warned the Bible. "Where envy is, there is confusion."

> Envy led to the murder of a brother [Abel]. . . . Through envy . . . Jacob fled from the face of . . . his brother. Envy made Joseph be persecuted unto death. . . . Envy compelled Moses to flee from the face of Pharaoh. . . . On account of envy, Aaron and Miriam had to make their abode without the camp. Envy brought down Dathan and Abiram . . . to Hades. . . . Through envy, David underwent hatred before Saul. . . . Through envy . . . the greatest and most righteous pillars [of the Church] have been persecuted and put to death. . . . Peter, through . . . envy, endured . . . numerous labors . . . and . . . martyrdom. . . . Envy has . . . overthrown great cities and rooted up mighty nations. . . . Wherefore . . . let us forsake all . . . envy, which leads to death.[13]

Who, if not the Christian researcher and the dispenser of Christian charity, would speak against envy when the destitution of multitudes cloaked the sin? Who would see that pity for the poor did not stifle the warning of the Gospel short of a more devastating evil than hunger? Those who demanded "a careful scrutiny of the moralists' bank balance" needed to be reminded that the envious poor had their reward, as well as the selfish rich.

[13] "The First Epistle of Clement to the Corinthians," *The Ante-Nicene Fathers* (Charles Scribner's Sons), iv, v, and vi.

Perhaps the greatest danger to the World Council of Churches was failure, in its enthusiasm for the distant goal of a responsible society, to deal with the personal sins of the spirit in those who must together live out their lives in the present social order. The quest for the far-off kingdom would have to begin in the hearts of the "haves" and the "have-nots" alike, or it held only frustration and disappointment.

3. Revision of the Basis of the World Council

There had been, from the outset, rather general dissatisfaction with the Basis of the World Council, which had been adopted mainly because it had been the Basis of the Faith and Order Movement, and the denominations had accepted—or acquiesced in—it without serious controversy. In both instances, its nature was regarded as functional rather than theological. It was not intended to be a creed, nor, of course, a full statement of the Christian faith. Its purpose, in the words of General Secretary Willem A. Visser 't Hooft, was "to say what holds us together in the World Council, what is the starting-point of our conversation and the foundation of our collaboration." Because it had "worked" in this way for the Faith and Order Movement, it commended itself to the World Council, particularly in the days of its beginning when nothing mattered more than keeping the denominations together until they could have time to decide whether or not they would commit themselves finally to the new venture. How it might be improved became a subject of general discussion, which produced many suggestions; but, with the acceptance of it, the disposition of the World Council was to leave well enough alone. Any attempt to change it would open the doors to all comers with proposals and might develop into an effort to write a confession of faith, which could only be divisive.

However, when the Church of Norway presented, in accordance with the constitutional provision, a request that certain changes, which it specified, be proposed to the Assembly, action had to be taken. The communication came to the Central Committee too late to be considered at Evanston. At Davos-Platz, it was referred to a subcommittee, consisting of Dr. H. Berkhof, Bishop James of Melita, the Bishop of Malmesbury, Dr. Liston Pope, Bishop Johannes Smemo and Dr. Ernest A. Payne (Chairman), who were instructed to bring to the Central Committee recommendations on not only the proposal of the Church of Norway but also any other suggestions about the Basis that might be forthcoming.

The Church of Norway objected to the Basis because it made no reference to scriptural authority—"the basis of the Basis." It desired the statement changed to:

The World Council of Churches is a fellowship of Churches who, according to Holy Scriptures, confess Jesus Christ as God and Saviour.[14]

The bishops presenting the matter explained that "the Christian way of expression" was "not that 'we accept' Christ, but that we confess him."

The subcommittee, in correspondence with theologians and in open hearings, invited an expression of views in regard to the Basis. There was criticism from various sources, the Orthodox Churches particularly, because of its omission of specific recognition of the Holy Trinity.

From the General Council of the Congregational Christian Churches in the United States of America came the suggestion:

The World Council of Churches is a fellowship of churches which profess belief in one God: the Father, the Son and the Holy Spirit."

Archbishop Michael concurred with this statement. Bishop James of Melita would have revised it as follows:

The World Council of Churches is a fellowship of churches which accept our Lord Jesus Christ as God and Saviour, in whom the Father was revealed and through whom the Spirit became manifest to the world.

The Bishop of Samos, in an article in *Ekklesia,* urged that the Basis be "faith in the Holy Trinity," and in *The Ecumenical Review* Professor H. Alivisatos appealed for an "explicitly trinitarian formula."

The Central Committee, at New Haven in 1957, received the subcommittee's report,[15] which was sympathetic to the proposal of the Church of Norway and also to the view that the Basis should be explicitly trinitarian. It did not think that the churches would desire the World Council to go on record as opposing either suggestion. Nevertheless, a redrafting of the Basis would open the way for the submission of other amendments than those received and might seem to move into the realm of full confessional or creedal statement, which should be undertaken only by churches. Other difficulties emerged when the attempt was made to combine in one brief sentence an explicit trinitarian affirmation and a reference to Holy Scripture. After "careful study of various alternatives," the subcommittee presented for consideration an "expansion" of the present Basis, which sought to make use of only biblical language, as follows:

The World Council of Churches is a fellowship of churches which, in accordance with Holy Scripture, confess our Lord Jesus Christ as the Son of God who was made man for our salvation, in whom the Father was

[14] The original Basis: "The World Council of Churches is a fellowship of churches which accept our Lord Jesus Christ as God and Saviour."

[15] Minutes of the Central Committee, New Haven, 1957, p. 132.

revealed, and to whom the Holy Spirit bears witness guiding us into all truth.[16]

Action on the subcommittee's report preparatory to its reference to the Third Assembly was taken at St. Andrews in 1960.[17]

The Central Committee has kept in mind the history of the present Basis, the important function it has fulfilled and the considered statement of its purpose and function adopted by the Evanston Assembly (Report, pp. 306-307). In that statement it is made clear that while the Basis is less than a confession, it is much more than a mere formula of agreement . . . also . . . that it has always been understood as implicitly trinitarian. The Basis has never been thought of as a creed. . . .

Not unnaturally, . . . there has been considerable reluctance to alter the Basis, lest its essential character be affected or the World Council become involved in an attempt to offer a formulation or definition of the faith. Nevertheless, it appears important to guard against any possible misunderstandings and to meet the widely supported requests for four specific changes: (i) The substitution of the word "confess" for "accept"; (ii) the use of "the," instead of "our," before "Lord Jesus Christ"; (iii) the addition of the phrase, "according to the Scriptures"; and (iv) making explicit the trinitarian character of the Basis.

"Confess" is a more decisive word than "accept" and is generally employed by all member churches in declarations regarding the Lord Jesus Christ. To speak of him as "the" Lord avoids the more subjective reference of "our" and emphasizes the lordship of Christ over the whole world. The phrase, "according to the Scriptures," used by the Apostle Paul on a number of occasions, has found a place in the ancient creeds and in later confessions, and directs attention to the authority the Scriptures possess for all Christians. To make explicit the trinitarian character of the Basis is in line with the statement adopted at Evanston. At the same time, it appears fitting by the addition of the phrase, "and therefore seek to fulfill together their common calling to the glory of God," to acknowledge the end and object of our fellowship together.

Accordingly, the Central Committee recommends that at the Third Assembly, due notice having been given, Article I of the Constitution be altered so that it will read:

The World Council of Churches is a fellowship of churches which confess the Lord Jesus Christ as God and Saviour according to the Scriptures and therefore seek to fulfill together their common calling to the glory of the one God, Father, Son and Holy Spirit.*

* *Der Oekumenische Rat der Kirchen ist eine Gemeinschaft von Kirchen, die den Herrn Jesus Christus gemäss der heiligen Schrift als Gott und Heiland bekennen und darum gemeinsam zu erfüllen trachten, wozu sie berufen sind, zur Ehre Gottes, des vaters, des Sohnes und des Heiligen Geistes.*

Le Conseil oecuménique des Églises est une association fraternelle d'Églises qui confessent le Seigneur Jésus Christ comme Dieu et Sauveur selon les Écritures et s'efforcent de répondre ensemble à leur commune vocation, pour la gloire du seul Dieu, Père, Fils et Saint-Esprit.

At its meeting in 1959 (Rhodes), the Central Committee requested the Faith and Order Commission to make a study of the proposed

[16] Translations in French and German also submitted.

[17] Minutes of the Central Committee, St. Andrews, 1960, p. 211.

substitute Basis submitted at New Haven and of "the real nature and function of the Basis of the World Council of Churches." If the Commission complied, the fact was to be reported by the Central Committee to the "member churches and . . the Third Assembly, together with an account of the study and discussion of the matter since the Second Assembly, and . . . at the same time it [was to] be made clear that the Central Committee is in no way opposed to the suggested additional affirmations, believing them to be in accord with the beliefs of the member churches."

4. The Future of Faith and Order

Various circumstances contributed to the ebbing of Faith and Order morale after Evanston.

The movement had not recovered altogether from the loss of its early leaders. Men of the stature of Charles Brent and William Temple do not appear in every generation, and those who look back to days when there were giants have often to pay for their inheritance from greatness with despair for their own inadequacy, until they learn—those who lead and those who are led—that dependence once placed in others can be transmuted through personal trust in God into Christian self-confidence.

The pioneers of Faith and Order had, after the genius of their kind, walked by faith. They had led out on the ecumenical trek, if with a conviction of knowing where they were going, with no chart of the way; and they had left none for the unfinished journey. When they died, it seemed that they had helped the churches explore all the conditions of unity that could be known until there were further revelations. The conferees at Lund in 1952 had decided that little was to be accomplished by keeping on with the discussion of the differences hindering reunion, beyond educating those members of the Conference who were new to the ecumenical experience and having their introduction to the problems of Faith and Order. Even these late-comers hardly needed to have pointed out the impasse which had been reached.

If there was no place left to go and nothing left to do, initiative and enthusiasm could only wane.

The relegation of the Commission on Faith and Order to the position of a department in the Division of Studies had added to the feeling of depression. The new status was regarded as tantamount to a downgrading. Before the reorganization, the Commission had been a major department of the World Council of Churches—when there were no "divisions"—with a considerable degree of autonomy and its own conditions of membership.

Sensing the dissatisfaction on account of the new order, Professor

Walter Freytag, Chairman of the Division of Studies, remarked to the Central Committee at New Haven:[18]

> During the last days, questions have been raised about Faith and Order and the Division, stating that Faith and Order has lost its prominence and . . . become a mere part of a larger organization.
>
> I must say that I was almost shocked by this statement . . . Faith and Order is a department among other departments; that is true, but in name only. In fact it is not true. Our departments are not what the name suggests: bureaucratic entities with strictly limited competencies. Our so-called departments, as well as our divisions, represent various aspects of the same body we serve. They have their very nature, not in any specialistic character, but in the responsibility they have for the whole.

The Commission on Faith and Order would have said that it understood the responsibility it had "for the whole" and for this reason coveted a divisional status.[19]

> Our deepest concern [it explained] is that the World Council as a whole should always serve that unity into which God calls his people. . . . We believe that in order for the World Council as a whole to be this effective organ in the cause of unity, Faith and Order should be at the center of its life and a major element in its organizational structure. . . . It is our conviction that not only to enable Faith and Order to accomplish its specific tasks within the total work of the World Council of Churches, and more particularly, to promote the original intention of the founding of the Council, that the concern for unity should be at the very heart of its life and penetrate all of its activities, the structural position of Faith and Order in the organization of the Council needs to be re-inforced, as well as its staff and financial resources strengthened.

To this end the Commission felt that it should have, through its representatives, a part in policy making at the highest level and, as intimated, the appropriation a divisional position would carry, to provide an adequate staff.

Withal, many concerned about the progress of Faith and Order thought that interest in unity was in danger of becoming satisfied with what they felt were superficial and misleading attempts at its expression, which ended with "brotherly collaboration" and a "federal type of union" and left the denominations each still independent.

So it was that, through uncertainty and weakness, after a manner of speaking, the Commission on Faith and Order came to the decision to define the kind of unity it conceived to be its duty to promote, and to describe how it would endeavor to proceed and the support it would need from the World Council. At the suggestion of the Executive Committee of the Central Committee of the World Council, the Working Committee of the Commission applied itself to the preparation of a

[18] Minutes of the Central Committee, New Haven, 1957, p. 19.
[19] *Ibid*. St. Andrews, 1960, p. 187.

statement setting forth the convictions it held about its function, for presentation to the Third Assembly.

The report, in the process of its shaping, came before the Central Committee for criticism in three successive years (1958, 1959, and 1960), and was cogently analyzed in a paper by Professor Henri d'Espine under the title "The Role of the World Council of Churches in Regard to Unity."[20] As finished, it was a document which both the Commission on Faith and Order and the World Council could freely approve, as the action of the Central Committee at St. Andrews attested.

> The Faith and Order Movement was born in the hope that it would be . . . a help to the churches in realizing the will of God for the unity of the Church. . . . We have become convinced that the time has come for a fuller statement of this purpose, and for a re-examination of the means by which Faith and Order should, within the World Council of Churches, seek its realization.
>
> The Commission on Faith and Order understands that the unity which is both God's will and his gift to his Church is one which brings all in each place (neighborhood) who confess Christ Jesus as Lord into a committed fellowship with one another through one baptism into him, holding the one apostolic faith, preaching the one Gospel and breaking the one bread, and having a corporate life reaching out in witness and service to all; and which at the same time unites them with the whole Christian fellowship in all places and all ages, in such wise that ministry and members are acknowledged by all, and that all can act and speak together as occasion requires for the tasks to which God calls the Church.
>
> It is for such unity that we believe we must pray and work. Such a vision has indeed been the inspiration of the Faith and Order Movement in the past, and we re-affirm that this is still our goal.
>
> We recognize that the brief definition of our objective, which we have given above, leaves many questions unanswered. In particular, we would state emphatically that the unity we seek is not one of uniformity, nor a monolithic power structure, and that on the interpretation and the means of achieving certain of the matters specified . . . we are not yet of a common mind. The achievement of unity will involve nothing less than a death and rebirth for many forms of church life as we have known them. We believe that nothing less costly can finally suffice.

In presenting his analysis of the report, Professor d'Espine mentioned that the General Secretary of the World Council had asked the advice of some fifty persons "particularly competent and representative of our different churches" in regard to its proposals in the paragraphs quoted above, and that "the great majority" of those consulted approved them in principle.

"The argument most frequently advanced in favor of approval," he said, "is that this conception has the merit of ruling out as insufficient a unity which is merely federal and co-operative, and prevents us from being content with the kind of unity which the World Council of

[20] One of the "main themes" for the St. Andrews meeting of the Central Committee, 1960. For Professor d'Espine's paper, see the St. Andrews minutes, p. 183 ff.

Churches represents at present. It is significant that none of the correspondents took upon himself to defend either a purely 'spiritual' . . . or 'federal' unity."

If the reference to "the kind of unity . . . the World Council of Churches represents" was found confusing or seemed derogatory to the Council, explained Dr. d'Espine, the words of the Archbishop of Canterbury, Dr. Geoffrey Fisher, who was among those whose views were solicited by the General Secretary, might put it in better light. "The report of Faith and Order speaks very confidently of 'the unity which is both God's will and his gift to his Church.' There is indeed a gift, but one not yet given or claimed in its fulness. On the way there are many stages." It had always been the position of Faith and Order that cooperation in the World Council of Churches could not be justified as an end in itself, but only as a means to unity "in its fulness."

Continuing his commentary before the Central Committee, Professor d'Espine said, "Since . . . the definition of unity proposed by Faith and Order as the final objective to be achieved appears to be received with such general agreement, it is necessary . . . once more to indicate as clearly as possible what this proposal implies:

> First, that there would no longer be in each locality several churches, but one church comprising all those . . . who confess the lordship of Jesus Christ; that their union would be based on the same baptism and express itself by the preaching of the same Gospel and by participation in the one bread.
>
> Second, that this local community would be linked to the whole Christian community of all times and of all places by the fact that its ministry and members would be acknowledged by all.
>
> By its very nature, such a unity would be visible, but it does not imply a single centralized ecclesiastical institution—which is very generally set aside as being undesirable. It is compatible with a large degree of institutional and liturgical diversity, but it is neither "federal" nor merely "spiritual." To adopt it would undoubtedly involve making a choice between the different possible conceptions of unity.
>
> But it should be said that this concerns the ultimate objective. The full realization of this objective will require a long period of time, since it implies that profound differences which still exist concerning baptism, the ministry, the common celebration of the Holy Communion, and perhaps also concerning the Gospel which should be preached, should first be eliminated.
>
> It seems that the time has come to ask our churches, without imposing upon them any conception of unity which they would be unable in conscience to accept, to examine without prejudice what Faith and Order proposes, in the hope that by common agreement certain clarifications may be reached concerning the nature of the unity to which God is calling us.

In making this proposal respecting unity, the Commission seemed to some persons to be giving official support to "a particular conception of unity," something which it had been pledged not to do. The

Central Committee at Toronto in 1950 had declared that the World Council had no intention to impose on its members any particular conception of unity. Commenting in 1955 on the Toronto declaration in an address to the Central Committee on "The Various Meanings of Unity and the Unity the World Council Seeks to Promote," the General Secretary of the Council had said, "It belongs to the very nature of the ecumenical encounter which the Council seeks to promote, that it holds the door open for every church which, accepting the Basis of the World Council, is willing to consider with other churches how the unity of the Church of Christ may be realized. And it is obvious that a Council which would promote one specific type of unity over against others would in fact close the door to the churches whose doctrinal pre-suppositions make it impossible to accept that type of unity." Would the present proposal of the Faith and Order Commission be, in effect, an abandonment of this fundamental principle?

The constitution of the Commission, which had been approved by the World Council of Churches, declared its function to be "to proclaim the essential oneness of the Church of Christ and to keep prominently before the World Council and the churches the obligation to manifest that unity and its urgency for the work of evangelism." "It is our strong conviction," said the Commission, "that to proclaim the essential oneness of the Church of Christ involves facing the question, 'What kind of unity does God demand of his Church?' We agree that no one definition of the nature of unity can be a condition of membership in the World Council of Churches, but Faith and Order exists . . . to stand for the unity of the Church as the will of God and for a ceaseless effort to know what obedience to that will means concretely. Only so can it be 'manifest.' The World Council of Churches can have no neutrality on whether that question is answered or not."

The Toronto statement (1950) had said, "As the conversation between the churches develops, and as the churches enter into closer contact with each other, they will no doubt have to face new decisions and problems. For the Council exists to break the deadlock between the churches." The Commission on Faith and Order felt that there was a conflict between this position and the statement that the World Council could promote no specific type of unity. How could a deadlock be broken if no type of unity were ever brought forward for discussion? Manifestly, no denomination could be pressured, but should all be denied the opportunity to consider any scheme because it was unacceptable to some?

All churches in the World Council confront each other under the demand of God himself that they should learn from him the nature of the unity which we seek [said the report]. It has been characteristic of Faith and Order to recognize that patience and thoroughness are needed for this task. But it is also necessary to recognize that in such matters we are not entirely free to proceed at our own pace, that events are forcing upon us various kinds of Christian cooperation, and that if we do not find true unity we shall find ourselves remaining content with a form of organizational unity which leaves unfulfilled many of the central requirements of the Church's life. There is, therefore, need for a proper sense of urgency, lest we lose the time that God gives us. Faith and Order must constantly press upon the Council and the churches the fact that the question of unity is one upon which an answer has to be given, and that to give no answer means to be shut up to the wrong answer.

Specifically, Faith and Order must raise this question (a) in Assemblies, so far as its program for the whole World Council of Churches allows; (b) in the Central Committee, from time to time, as best serves, as well as in Theological Commissions which all at least bear upon the answer. All these are ways in which Faith and Order makes its witness within the World Council of Churches, but in order ultimately to reach the churches themselves, for whose sake all this activity is organized. . . .

But within the Council, bearing in mind the . . . constitution, it is also important that every department should be concerned that unity is borne in mind as it does its work, and we should hope that the World Council secretariat would, from time to time, ask how far their respective departments are contributing to the fulness of unity.

As plans for the integration of the International Missionary Council proceed, the relation of mission to unity should be more clearly seen. We would ask that national Christian councils and councils of churches should be asked whether their work also makes provision for Faith and Order, so that this connection may be brought home in every region.

As our churches seek to obey God in the renewal of their confessional and liturgical life and in promoting their mission, they will be deaf to what God is saying to them in our day, if they do not constantly and specifically seek his guidance in how to translate all aspects of renewal and mission into manifestation of greater and growing unity.

Finally, in all this we must bring home the truth that our present differences and divisions hinder the mission and renewal of the Church, and may obscure, even if they do not actually contradict, the Gospel of reconciliation.

Professor d'Espine, commenting further on the issue,[21] said:

Faith and Order declares . . . that in formulating its proposal, so far from innovating, it is on the contrary being faithful to its original inspiration and aim. It is quite clear that there is not complete unanimity on this point.

For example, Professor R. R. Hartford, one of the veterans of Faith and Order, has no hesitation in saying "that the Faith and Order movement has always been concerned with the kind of unity about which Bishop Newbigin has written." But Professor Leonard Hodgson, who was for a long period the theological secretary of Faith and Order, and who knows the facts about its origin and development better than any, is . . . more reserved on this point. He thinks that while the pioneers were certainly concerned to restore Christian unity, they were also very much aware of the profound doctrinal divergencies between the churches, and did not judge that it was possible to define precisely what this unity ought to be.

Archbishop William Temple's formula "full union and communion,"

[21] See Minutes of the Central Committee, St. Andrews, 1960, pp. 114 ff.

which did not attempt to resolve all the questions in dispute but tried "to state what all were aiming at in such a way as to exclude contentment with any lesser goal," seems to Professor Hodgson to express the vision which Faith and Order had of unity.

But in the last resort the answer to the question whether the reports of the Lausanne, Edinburgh and Lund Conferences contain affirmations equivalent to the present proposal of Faith and Order, will be more decisive than the opinions of individuals.

It is clear that if at Lausanne in 1927 agreement was established on the necessity that "the one life of the one body should be manifest to the world," and that in consequence "existing obstacles to the manifestation of the unity in Christ should be removed," it was not possible to reach agreement on the nature of this unity and on the elements of faith and order which were essential for this manifestation. But then we must note that already at Lausanne some strongly expressed the fear that a merely federal type of unity would be substituted for organic union. . . .

Ten years later at Edinburgh, the duty of manifesting unity was forcefully asserted, but without reaching agreement on the mode of this manifestation:

"We are convinced that our unity of spirit and aim must be embodied in a way that will make it manifest to the world, though we do not yet clearly see what outward form it should take."

It is in the report of Lund (1952) that for the first time we find some more precise descriptions of the nature of unity:

"The nature of the unity towards which we are striving is that of a visible fellowship in which all members acknowledging Jesus Christ as living Lord and Saviour shall recognize each other as belonging fully to his body to the end that the world may believe."

It was noted, however, that not all the Conference shared the opinion that the unity of the Church ought to be organic.

If William Temple's formula "full union and communion" can truly be considered as expressing what was for the pioneers of Faith and Order the final objective to be achieved, then it seems to us that the present proposal of Faith and Order is less an innovation than a making explicit of what was already implied.

The report of the Commission proceeded with a "re-assessment of its functions" point by point as defined by its constitution, and dwelt at some length and effectiveness on "other concerns" it felt called of God to undertake. Though not specifically indicated in the present terms of reference, the latter were in keeping, it thought, with the spirit and tradition of the Faith and Order Movement: unity negotiations between churches, regional meetings, and relations with Christians outside the World Council, including Roman Catholics. The staff of the Commission and its whole organization should be adequate, it urged, to functioning intelligently and continuously in these and related areas.

The report was received by the Central Committee as evidencing an awakening in the ranks of Faith and Order. If it had not said what all the churches could approve, it had spoken with a clear voice of matters that provoked thought and demanded more serious study than they had received. It left none in doubt that Faith and Order had a future.

In the discussion, Professor Alivisatos, who had been associated with the movement from the beginning, expressed gratitude at "the revival of Faith and Order." Bishop Hunt of Canada approved the definition of unity. Professor Josef Hromadka, referring to the invisibility of Faith and Order for some time, said he rejoiced that a revival was taking place. Bishop Barbieri welcomed the special attention given to Roman Catholic relations and explained that 75 per cent of all Protestants of South America were in the category of those referred to in the report as "outside the World Council membership."

The Central Committee approved the definition of unity in the opening paragraphs, which should, it decided, be discussed by the Third Assembly. It also gave approval to the requests relating to measures for strengthening the Commission, agreeing that there should be a staff of three members. The senior secretary should have the title, it suggested, of director and be fully involved in the total work of the World Council of Churches, since "concern for unity pervades all the parts." Therefore, "he should be a member of the Staff Executive Group, in which the General Secretary takes counsel with the Associate General Secretaries and the Directors of Finance and Information on all matters of over-all strategy. . . . Here he would be responsible for bringing the concerns of Faith and Order to bear upon the total program of the Council, for forwarding the study of the theological implications of the existence of the ecumenical movement and for correlating all studies and functions in any unit of the Council which specifically relate to the concerns of Faith and Order."

Authority was given to increase the Commission from one hundred to two hundred members and to hold the "Fourth World Conference on Faith and Order in 1963," at a place to be decided later. (The meeting was held at Montreal, Canada.)

The budget appropriation for Faith and Order was increased from $18,600 in 1960 to $42,000 per annum.

The Commission had concurred with a recommendation of the Committee on Program and Finance, which had been adopted by the Central Committee, "that at the present stage, in the light of the total situation in the World Council of Churches, and in view of the importance of study in the program of Faith and Order, the Commission or its Working Committee should continue to be represented on the Committee of the Division of Studies and the Secretariat should continue to work, as at present, under the authority of the Constitution of Faith and Order within the Division of Studies."

Dr. Yngve Torgny Brilioth retired as Chairman of the Commission in 1956, because of failing health, and the vacancy was filled in 1957 by the election of Dr. Douglas Horton. Dr. J. Robert Nelson resigned as Faith and Order Secretary in 1957 and was succeeded by Dr. Keith Bridston.

Seven theological commissions, with an aggregate membership of more than eighty scholars, had during this period carried forward their long-range studies on "Christ and the Church," "Tradition and Traditions," and "Worship." An important new study on "Institutionalism" had been launched after Evanston under the chairmanship of Dean Walter Muelder and the secretaryship of Dr. Nils Ehrenström. The subject of baptism would be given special consideration, beginning in 1957.

A significant service of the Commission was its collaboration in 1957 with the North American Conference on "The Nature of the Unity We Seek" at Oberlin College, under the auspices of the World Council of Churches, the National Council of the Churches of Christ in the United States of America, and the Canadian Council of Churches.

Dr. Bridston submitted his resignation as Executive Secretary of the Faith and Order Department in 1961 to become director of a nation-wide study in the United States of pre-seminary education, and Dr. Paul S. Minear of Yale Divinity School was appointed his successor. He assumed the post on July 1, 1961. Dr. Minear was chairman of the committee which prepared the study guide on the themes of the Third Assembly of the World Council of Churches.

5. On Merger with the International Missionary Council

The Joint Committee of the International Missionary Council and the World Council of Churches, after a review of its functions under the new constitution,[22] informed the Central Committee at Davos-Platz (1955) that it would not concentrate immediately "on the question of the possible integration" of these Councils. While recognizing this issue as a "direct responsibility," it had agreed that the solution would probably be reached more effectively if time was taken to develop further cooperation between the two bodies. It should be understood, however, that "fresh thought" concerning the proposal to merge would accompany their continuing collaboration. The two Councils should understand that progress toward their union turned not only on their attitude to each other but also on the rapport between them and their constituencies "as to the meaning of mission-in-unity."

[22] (a) To help the two bodies to keep prominently before their member churches and constituent councils their common responsibility for the evangelistic outreach and world mission of the Church; (b) to keep under review the ways by which the two bodies are cooperating and suggest new ways; (c) to study major aspects of the common tasks confronting the two bodies and to make specific recommendations concerning policies to be followed; (d) to continue to study the organizational implications of the developing relationships.

With the passing of another year, the Joint Committee had decided that the time was ripe for action. Commenting on the five factors which, in his judgment, demanded the re-opening of the matter—the deepening awareness in both movements of parallel objectives and obligations, the growth of overlap in memberships, their increasing area of common action,[23] realization from experience in these joint operations of the greater intimacy in the life and work of the two Councils "and the wastefulness as well as danger of tension and misunderstanding in their present separation," and the importance of beginning a study of possible plans of integration if action was to be possible at the Third Assembly—Chairman Henry Pitney Van Dusen submitted to the Central Committee at Galyatetö (1956) "a statement on integration":

One of the most significant features in the Christian life is the deepening awareness of the churches of their missionary vocation. The calling of the Church to proclaim the Gospel to the ends of the earth and the obligation of the Church to bear witness in deed and word to all nations are once again being seen as belonging to the essence of the Church's life. This sense of mission is more and more pervading the ecumenical movement—as, indeed, this movement largely owes its origin to it.

Since the First Assembly at Amsterdam, the World Council of Churches and the International Missionary Council (itself an ecumenical expression of the churches' outreach through the historic witness of missions) have been in constitutional and practical "association" with each other. This association had its origin in the common calling and purpose of both bodies, and it was entered into in the hope that such a relationship would deepen and express "the missionary consciousness of churches and the church-consciousness of missions." Many aspects of the work of both Councils—study, international affairs and the work of the East Asia secretariat—have since become so deeply interwoven as to go beyond what was described in 1948 as the "inter-relatedness of two autonomous councils." Not least important, increasing recognition is being given to the bearing of the Church's unity—with which the World Council is specially concerned—on the fulfillment of its mission, while within the constituency of the International Missionary Council mission and unity are seen in their closest and most urgent bearing on one another.

In the membership of both the World Council of Churches and the International Missionary Council, there is an increasing overlap. On the one hand, the historic missionary societies or boards are working in partnership with, or as servants of, churches which are taking their place as members of the World Council of Churches. On the other hand, National Christian Councils, which are constituent members of the International Missionary Council, are entering into closer relationship with the World Council of Churches as "associated Councils"—a relationship which is proving to be of increasing significance for the National and for the World Council of Churches itself. Moreover, some of the most important tasks and opportunities before both Councils are necessitating more of these processes which

[23] At Davos it was noted that more than half of the total work of the World Council of Churches was then carried on jointly with the International Missionary Council.

go beyond "association." This is notably true of the expanding work of the Division of Inter-Church Aid and Service to Refugees and its transition from emergency to more permanent relationship of service between the younger and older churches. It is equally apparent in developments which are taking place in various parts of the world—especially in Asia—and which must profoundly affect the means by which the mission of the Church is fulfilled in and through the churches in these areas.

In the light of such considerations as these (and many of them arise from situations in which events are moving rapidly) the Joint Committee affirms its conviction that the time has come when the World Council of Churches and the International Missionary Council should consider afresh the possibility of an integration of the two Councils.

The Committee regards it as imperative that any such integration should be in a form which ensures that missions belong to the heart of the ecumenical movement. It should also be on lines which would bring the missionary forces into closer relationship with all phases of the Church's witness in the life of the world and engage the fullest resources of the churches in the task of formulating and fulfilling their mission in terms commensurate with the needs of the world today and with the nature of the "glorious Gospel of the blessed God."

The Joint Committee, therefore, asks the authority of both Councils to undertake the formulation—in the fullest possible consultation with all concerned—of a draft Plan of Integration for presentation to the World Council of Churches' Central Committee in 1957 and to the International Missionary Council Assembly at the Gold Coast in December-January, 1957-1958. Should the Plan, with such amendments as the . . . Central Committee and the International Missionary Council Assembly may wish to make, prove acceptable to these two bodies, it would be possible for it to be communicated to the member councils of the International Missionary Council for their consideration in time to be acted upon at the Third Assembly of the World Council in 1960.[24]

The Central Committee voted authority to the Joint Committee to proceed with the formulation of a Plan of Integration, and a report from the latter was received and studied at New Haven the following year. The Plan, which was submitted at that time, "endeavored," according to Dr. Van Dusen, "to provide for 'the union of two living realities,' not of 'two pieces of organizational machinery,' and sought to fulfill two ends; namely the permeation of the life of the integrated Council with missionary conviction and commitment, and the continuation of the life and program of the International Missionary Council in its full scope and strength." (See Appendix P. for the plan as finally adopted, 1961.)

To insure the accomplishment of this objective, "four means" were proposed:

The creation of a Division on World Mission and Evangelism.
The organization of a Commission on World Mission and Evangelism.

[24] The Third Assembly was postponed to 1961, to give time for the completion of the Joint Committee's work. For Dr. Van Dusen's statement, see the Galyatetö minutes, p. 110 ff.

Provision for representation within the Assembly and the Central Committee of those with special knowledge in the field of World Mission.

The re-examination and re-definition of all departmental and divisional activities of the World Council of Churches to the end that the missionary aim of the Council should find expression.

The discussion of the Plan in the Central Committee emphasized the sharp division of opinion on its merits.

Dr. Norman Goodall, Secretary of the Joint Committee, declared the necessity for the World Council to move increasingly into the "whole field of mission," and the importance to the International Council of continuing "its own distinctive work in an integral relationship with all for which the World Council stands."

Dr. John A. Mackay spoke in support of the recommendations as historically logical and theologically sound.

Canon Say thought that, although "a calculated risk" would be involved, integration was the next step indicated. There might be doubt on the part of some persons as to the extent to which the World Council would still be concerned with the unity of the Church, and fears on account of an enlarging organization and concentration of power; and financially, the change might be burdensome. But the risk should be taken, for the alternative would be disrupting.

Bishop Lesslie Newbigin viewed the Plan "as a serious and careful attempt to meet a complex situation" and declared that it should be supported. He would have liked the "process of integration to go even further than the actual proposal." Said he, "Integration should signify the restoration of unity which ought never to have been broken." Many of the problems arising in the relationship of the younger and older churches, he argued, could not longer be met by a bilateral structure of Church and Mission. They needed to be "worked at" within a single ecumenical structure that was "profoundly churchly and . . . missionary."

Metropolitan Juhanon Mar Thoma of India supported the proposal. Orthodox members, in general, opposed it. Archbishop Michael wished to know whether the World Council would remain autocephalous. Professor Georges Florovsky objected to integration on the grounds that it would change the character of the ecumenical movement. He saw it making the World Council responsible for Protestant missions, "which existed to propagate the Reformation and proselytize in the areas of the Orthodox Church."

If proselytism was a main fear, it could be resolved better within an integrated Council, in the opinion of Bishop Angus Dun. "Our responsibility for missionary activity would be confronted with the claims of our ecumenical relationships."

Dr. Thakur Das was in favor of discontinuing the use of the word "mission" in the titles suggested for the Commission and the Division, since in Asia it stood for separateness and had no real connection with evangelism.

Bishop Smemo, while not opposed to the principle affirmed in the introduction to the Plan, remembered fears held by some of the conferees that integration would weaken those spiritual forces embodied in the voluntary societies.

Dr. Ernest A. Payne disagreed on this point, replying that there were urgent critical reasons which made integration necessary. Difficulties in the present plan of "association" would increase, he said, especially as the World Council of Churches moved into more areas, as it must, in which the International Missionary Council was also working. He believed the step was necessary also in the interests of the historic missionary movement, which had to reshape its work in a situation fundamentally different from that of the nineteenth century. Postponing consideration of integration would not be a solution.

Professor Westphal explained that the hesitation of the Paris Mission and the missions of French West Africa and French Equatorial Africa about integration grew out of their position as non-denominational organizations and their fear lest the proposed action would result in disrupting relations of the Orthodox Churches with the World Council of Churches.

The Central Committee received the draft Plan and "commended it to the member churches for their study and prayerful consideration." It asked them to answer two questions: Are you, in principle, in favor of integration, if a satisfactory plan can be evolved? What comments have you to offer on the details of the proposed Plan?

With the draft Plan the Central Committee sent a covering memorandum on the fear expressed, that it would alter the basis of membership in the World Council of Churches and involve the member churches in responsibility for missionary and proselytizing activities of which they did not approve, and in "the scandal of competing evangelistic activities by rival bodies." Said the Committee:[25]

A distinction must be made between the missionary obligation to bring the Gospel to the whole world and proselytism (which the member churches of the World Council generally agree in condemning).

It is true that problems arise where missionary work is carried on in geographical areas where there are already established churches. These problems have already received the most careful attention of the World Council, and the document "Christian Witness, Proselytism and Religious Liberty in the Setting of the World Council of Churches," received at the last meeting of the Central Committee, gives solid ground for believing that these problems can be solved in a way that will be acceptable to all the churches in the Council.

The International Missionary Council has from the beginning been concerned to remove the scandal caused by competing missionary activities in

[25] Minutes of the Central Committee, New Haven, 1957, p. 116 ff.

the non-Christian world, and has been a powerful factor in the movement towards unity in missionary work and in the life of the Church.

The present proposal for integration with the World Council and indeed the modern ecumenical movement as a whole are in part the result of the long labors of the International Missionary Council for unity in the missionary task. Integration will, in turn, strengthen this movement for unity.

The International Missionary Council is not a body which itself conducts or supervises any missionary activity. It is a consultative body. The proposed new Division will have the same role. Moreover, the churches whose missionary activities are involved in the proposed integration are—for the most part—already members of the World Council.

The proposed integration will not change the principles which govern membership in the Council. It will remain a Council of Churches. All members of the Assembly will be delegates of member churches, and the membership of the Central and Executive Committees will continue to be drawn from these. The fact that some members of the new Commission (on Missions and Evangelism) may be members of the churches which are not members of the Council introduces no new principle, since this is already the case in other parts of the Council's organization. Moreover, the general lines of the Commission's policy will be subject to the approval of the Central Committee.[26]

Those churches which are concerned about the problems arising from the activities of missions carried on by other churches in their own areas will be in better position to deal with such problems in an integrated Council than they are at present.

In this communication to the denominations, the Central Committee dealt also with the objection to integration on the grounds that the World Council was not committed to the task of world mission and, therefore, could not provide a proper milieu for the work of the International Missionary Council. It pointed out that Article III (vii) of the Constitution showed that missions had from the beginning been accepted as part of the concern of the World Council; also that the discussions on integration had demonstrated the depth of interest within the World Council in the Church's missionary task.

With regard to the suggestion that more time should be given for deliberation before acting on the matter, the Central Committee explained that "more harm than good would result from further delay." "In view of the long discussions which have already taken place," the Committee said, "a decision to postpone . . . would be an extremely negative action." The only alternative to acting immediately was postponing the problem to the Fourth Assembly, which would probably not be held earlier than 1966. Such a long deferment the Committee considered fraught with "serious dangers."

The chairman of the committee presenting the Plan, on behalf of

[26] The International Missionary Council was composed, not of churches as such, but of national Christian councils and councils of churches. One object in forming the World Council had been to bring the churches directly under responsibility for the ecumenical movement. The integrated body would be a council of *churches.*

the Committee of Reference, was Bishop Lesslie Newbigin, also Chairman of the International Missionary Council and soon to become its General Secretary. His interpretation of the circumstances which seemed to urge favorable action on the proposal for integration reflected the thinking of many in ecumenical circles, though meeting with strong dissent on the part of others.

There is a very natural desire that things should always remain unchanged, but to succumb to this is death.

The fact that the present discussion puts all concerned with the missionary movement in the position of having to take difficult and perhaps costly decisions is one which should be accepted, not with resignation or resentment, but with gratitude and faith.

The missionary movement . . . stands in a critical situation. If we compare the mood of the present with that of earlier decades, it is difficult to escape the impression that there is today a certain hesitance, a certain loss of momentum.

It is true that there are certain areas of real growth. It is also true that there are some Christian bodies which claim large advances, as shown by their own statistics; one would need to make careful analysis of these to find out how far they refer to genuine missionary advance and how far to proselytism from among existing churches. It is true also that certain societies in some areas are able to secure large numbers of missionary recruits; one would have to ask how far the sending of these missionaries is really resulting in the penetration of non-Christian cultures by the Gospel and the building up of vital and stable indigenous churches.

In spite of the evidence of vigorous growth in certain areas, the facts remain that the churches of Asia are almost entirely from the loosely attached fringes of Asian society and have not penetrated into the ancient religious cultures to any significant extent; that Islam is—again with some exceptions—as completely resistant to the Gospel as ever, and in some areas advancing, relatively to Christianity; that world-wide Communism faces the Christian mission with an aggressive opposition undreamed of fifty years ago; and that it is extremely probable—in view of the rapid rise in the world's population—that the number of Christians relatively to the whole is decreasing, rather than increasing.

But, we are concerned [also] . . . with the attitudes of Christians.

There have been very wide-spread changes in theological conviction, which have undermined older forms of missionary motivation. I do not speak here of the complete loss of belief in the sufficiency and finality of the Gospel, which has taken many right out of the sphere of missionary concern, and therefore out of the context of the present discussion. Even for those who unhesitatingly acknowledge that being committed to a mission to the whole world, many older ways of stating the missionary obligation have become untenable. . . .

There have been changes in the world situation—partly the fruit of the missionary labors of earlier decades—which have made some former expressions of the missionary imperative impossible for many Christians.

The profound change in the balance of cultural and political power as between the nations of Europe and America and those of the rest of the world, and the development of much more effective means of contact between the different parts of the world have made it impossible to use many of the arguments for missions common in a former day. It is simply impossible to suggest to the intelligent western Christian that in going from Europe to Asia he is going from light to darkness.

The rise of the "younger churches" and their increasingly vigorous and effective participation in the ecumenical movement invalidates many older attitudes and raises the question, "Are missions still needed?"

The circumstances in which China became closed to western missions have raised very searching questions regarding the relation between "foreign missions" and the development of truly indigenous churches.

As a result, one finds that the Christian who in a former day would unhesitatingly have offered for service as a foreign missionary is today doubtful whether it would not be more in accordance with real Christian obedience to offer his service abroad in some other capacity.

The very name "missionary" is being abandoned in some quarters in favor of the phrase "fraternal worker."

Everyone who is concerned in the present discussion would agree that the fundamental religious grounds for mission remain unchanged; and yet the facts stated above are true. We are in a period of hesitancy. No good purpose is served by denying this.

Two wrong courses are open. . . . One . . . is to say . . . that the age of missions is over and the age of ecumenism has come. This is, of course, a hopelessly debased conception of ecumenism. A movement which is not missionary has no right to use the word "ecumenical."

The other wrong course is to try to escape from our hesitancy by going back, instead of forward, by trying to recapture both the method and the mood of the nineteenth century. It means looking round the world for areas which are still so backward that the nineteenth-century pattern can . . . be applied, or developing . . . a missionary work which acts over the heads of the younger churches of Asia and Africa as though they were not churches and could be ignored.

But there is a third possibility, another way which may not be easy, but which leads forward. It is that we should undertake the costly but exciting task of finding out what is the pattern for the Church's mission in the new day. . . .

This is not, first, a matter of organization . . . [but] of fundamental theological thinking, of Bible-study and of discerning the signs of the times.

Perhaps what we need above all—and only God can give it to us—is a vision, a symbol, a myth, if you like—which will evoke from the ordinary Christian the response which God wants of us in our generation. . . .

I do not think we have very far to seek for the essential outline of a symbol for the coming days. It is already present in the thinking and speaking of missionaries and churchmen. . . . It could be briefly stated as: "The Whole Church, with one Gospel of reconciliation for the whole world."

The unsolved problems of human togetherness hang over our generation with appalling menace. The Christian world mission holds the secret that can make mankind one family. This is its appeal to the youth of today.

It has been objected that the idea of unity is static and has no explosive power. Certainly, there are times and places at which unity has degenerated into uniformity and has to be challenged in the name of truth and life. But perhaps it is a significant symbol that—in our day, at least—the most tremendous explosions are produced by fusion, not by fission! [27]

[27] This statement by Bishop Newbigin was in substance drawn from an address at the Ghana meeting of the I.M.C. in 1958 and his *One Body, One Gospel, One World* (S.M.C., 1960).

During the next two years the churches were left to their study of the Plan of Integration.

The Central Committee at Rhodes (1959) received from the Joint Committee a report of its work containing in full "A Draft Constitution for the Proposed Commission on World Mission and Evangelism and the Division of World Mission and Evangelism" and "A Draft Constitution of an Integrated World Council of Churches and the International Missionary Council." The discussion concerned mostly the opposition of the Orthodox Churches.

Metropolitan James had said the year before at Nyborg Strand that the Orthodox delegates were instructed by the Patriarchate to ask for clarification of the "question whether the World Council of Churches would remain a council of churches and not become a council of churches, missionary societies and other organizations," and that no attempt should be made to reach a decision on the proposal for integration until it had been studied further. At Rhodes, the Bishop of Clemsford spoke of the close association of the Anglican and Orthodox Churches and stated that the former, although their reply on the Plan was warmly friendly, would not wish it adopted at the price of fellowship in the World Council of Churches with the latter. The kind of proselytism which was the cause of anxiety and uncertainty worried not only the Orthodox, he said, but Anglicans, Presbyterians, Methodists, and Baptists as well. It came from "free-lance organizations which had no intentions of co-operating with the International Missionary Council or the World Council of Churches."

Metropolitan James thanked the Bishop of Clemsford—and others—for their recognition of the Orthodox position and assured the Central Committee that he and those for whom he spoke wished to be "positive and helpful." They realized their duty "to make Christ known where he was not known." Hesitations about integration had been based on such questions as: Is the World Council of Churches, which is still a young organization, now being changed into something new? Does the membership of the International Missionary Council include missions unrelated to any church? The Orthodox Churches opposed, more especially, "what was supposed to be the theological basis of integration . . . the statement in the preamble to the draft Plan, that unity and mission belonged equally to the essence of the Church."

"We mean to stay in the World Council of Churches," concluded the Bishop, "and we appreciate what other churches are doing to propagate the Gospel."

Professor Ioannidis regretted the necessity of being "negative," but he felt impelled still to object to the proposal, because any step relating national councils to the World Council would raise serious questions about the nature of the Church, and because integration would overload an already big World Council of Churches and make it a mammoth organization. In his reference to national councils he made the point that "no religious organization could exist outside the Church." "St. Paul was not free to preach where he chose," he said, "but was subject to the control of the synod."

Bishop Newbigin said that he believed the integration proposal right from the standpoint of the theological principles the Orthodox were defending. The disputed preambular phrase had been an attempt to affirm that the Church was one, catholic and apostolic. God's will for the Church was that the Church itself should be the body carrying the Gospel to all nations. As for the procedural precedent set by the early Church, St. Paul certainly reported to Jerusalem, but he came back with new doctrine, which, though strange to Jerusalem, carried conviction through evidence of the Holy Spirit's blessing.

The Metropolitan of Carthage said, "Mission is a word we fear. I do not know why: it is my tradition. Integration has to be discussed; but postpone it for some years, and go slowly."

The Bishop of Gibraltar asked the Orthodox to think again about some of their statements. The World Council was not trying, he said, to be a super-church but a genuine meeting place for the churches. He and others who favored integration had no desire for large organizations. They supported the move because in their view it represented a step toward which God had long been leading the ecumenical movement. It was a challenge to the churches to take more seriously the world missionary obligation and to recognize the need for cooperation in fulfilling it. It made due allowance too for the right of religious liberty. Integration would provide an ideal setting for a more adequate discussion of the relation between mission and unity and the nature of the Church. "It is within an integrated organization," he concluded, "that these vital discussions . . . on such matters as cooperation and comity must go on. How glad Anglicans (and others) would be then to discuss the missionary policy of the Orthodox Churches, especially in Africa!"

In bringing the discussion to a close, Chairman Fry requested that the statement of Metropolitan James be put in writing and given to the Reference Committee, which would have the draft Plan under advisement, since what had been said was "at least a semi-official statement . . . and other Orthodox authorities had indicated their solidarity with the position of the Ecumenical Patriarchate."

In his report to the Central Committee at Rhodes, the General Secretary addressed himself, in part, to the integration issue:[28]

I should like to call attention to the fact that the conviction that cooperation in the realm of missions as a common concern of the churches is not a new idea, but . . . was advocated in the earliest days of the ecu-

[28] Minutes of the Central Committee, Rhodes, 1959, p. 95.

menical movement. . . . At the meeting in the Château de Crans near Geneva in 1920, at which it was decided to create the International Missionary Council, Dr. J. H. Oldham presented a memorandum in which he said: "It is becoming less and less possible to discuss missionary matters without representatives of the churches in the mission field, and any organization that may be created will probably have before long to give way to something that may represent the beginnings of a world league of churches."

And a few weeks later, at the preliminary meeting of Faith and Order, also in Geneva, the representatives of the Greek Orthodox Church, in presenting their plan to create a League of Churches, mentioned as two principal aims of such a body the avoidance of proselytism and "to secure definite mutual understanding and co-operation between all Christian communions for missions among non-Christian peoples."

The point was developed by Professor Alivisatos, the only participant of the 1920 meetings who is still actively engaged in ecumenical work. He said: "As a first request, we mention the suppression of all proselytism and the preparation of an agreement concerning missions among non-Christian people. . . . I want to say as a representative of the Orthodox Church, that the Orthodox Church will avoid in the future, as it did in the past, all proselytism among Christians; the Church is ready to help other churches to spread the Gospel among non-Christians, as long as she is not able to do this herself. Do you not think that the World Conference (on Faith and Order, 1927) will have made an important step toward unity when this step is generally accepted?"

These prophets from East and West saw that when the churches begin to co-operate they must of necessity co-operate in that fundamental task of the Church which is to obey the great commission . . . of our Lord himself. Dr. Oldham looks at the problem from the angle of the younger churches and comes to the conclusion—abundantly confirmed in the last forty years—that the emergence of these churches brings the missionary movement necessarily into an even closer relation to the churches than had existed. . . . The Orthodox delegates at the Geneva Conference look at the problem from the angle of the older churches and stress that the churches must help, rather than hinder, each other in their missionary work. Both point to the need for closer association between the concerns for mission and for unity.

Once again, we find that an insight given to some of the early fathers of the ecumenical movement has, after many years, become an insight shared by very many churches: for the answers which have been received from the churches concerning the proposed integration are nearly all favorable and positive.

The replies to the draft Plan and the memorandum of the Central Committee accompanying it, to which Dr. Visser 't Hooft refers in the paragraph next above, indicated that more churches talked about it than communicated their conclusions to headquarters. In 1959, forty-seven of the denominations which were members of the World Council of Churches had sent in their answers, and of these forty-four "affirmed their agreement with the principle of integration and their satisfaction with the general form of the draft plan." These reports were, according to the Joint Committee's statement, "widely representative, confessionally and geographically."

At the same time, twenty-two of the thirty-eight councils belonging to the International Missionary Council had signified their approval in principle, twelve had not expressed any judgment, three had voiced opposition, and one had withdrawn from membership in the Council because of the proposal to integrate with the World Council.

In July, 1959, the Administrative Committee of the International Missionary Council stated that, "in the light of this correspondence and discussion in its meetings, it felt assured that opinion within the Council was overwhelmingly in favor of proceeding further with negotiations toward integration." The announcement continued:

The Committee rejoices in the fact that at a time when preparations are in hand for celebrating the jubilee of Edinburgh, 1910, these significant agencies of the ecumenical movement—the World Council of Churches and the International Missionary Council—should be seeking to bring together their resources in a single instrument to further greater unity in the world mission of the Church. . . . After receiving from the Joint Committee, following its meeting in 1960, the final and constitutional form of the Plan, the Administrative Committee proposes to act upon the authority entrusted to it by the Ghana Assembly [1958]. On behalf of the International Missionary Council, the Committee will consider this document and, if approving, will resolve that the Council assents to the proposed integration.

The Joint Committee announced that, in the light of these reports, it was preparing a constitution for the proposed Commission on World Mission and Evangelism, a revision of the Constitution of the World Council of Churches in terms giving effect to the Plan of Integration, and a corresponding revision of the Rules of the World Council of Churches. In these actions, the Committee had taken into account the comments of the denominations in the World Council and of the constituent bodies of the International Missionary Council, as well as the various proposals for amending the draft Plan arising from consultations with the members of the two Councils.

The Central Committee took final action at St. Andrews in August, 1960, approving the Plan of Integration as revised in the light of the discussion at Rhodes and of consultations with other groups. Its decision was as follows:

In 1957, the Central Committee submitted to member churches a draft plan of integration of the International Missionary Council and the World Council of Churches, and asked the churches whether they were "in principle in favor of integration, provided a satisfactory plan is evolved." In 1959, the Committee took note of the replies to this question and recognized that they "reflect an opinion overwhelmingly in favor of the principle of integration."

The Committee, accordingly, submitted to member churches a definite proposal for effecting the integration of the two bodies by means of a series of constitutional amendments, and expressed "the hope that it might prove acceptable" to the member churches. The weight of opinion being clearly in favor of the proposal submitted, the Central Committee now recommends to the Third Assembly of the World Council of Churches that it approve the integration of the World Council of Churches and the International Missionary Council.

The Central Committee makes this proposal in the confidence and with the prayer that by this step the full purpose of the ecumenical movement shall be furthered.

Other resolutions by the Central Committee provided for the implementation of the Plan of Integration, if adopted by the Third Assembly, through a Division of World Mission and Evangelism with a secretariat and an annual budget of approximately $200,000.

In the background of these discussions and actions relating to missions was the fact that the modern missionary movement was a minority cause in the churches. Mission properties, budgets for their maintenance and manning, programs of education, ministry to the sick, and the relief of poverty represented the giving of not more than one-third of the members of the churches. This had long been the consistent record of those churches raising their missionary and current expense funds separately. Others grouping all their interests under a single appeal and making appropriations to missions from the general receipts might seem to enlist more givers to this feature of their work. But the average contribution of individual members, whether calculated on this basis or on the separate-pledge plan was found to be about the same; and it never exceeded what could only be regarded as a very inadequate sum, when the extent of the missionary operation and the need it faced were taken into account. Many of those who gave were motivated by loyalty to their churches more than by interest in missions, accepting it as a duty to help meet what amounted to denominational assessments, whether or not they considered them always wise.

Whatever the members of the churches thought about this branch of their activities, and whether they gave or not, they expected to leave the administrative responsibilities to the clergy.

Modern missions could hardly be said to have started through the initiative of congregations or parishes. Individuals felt the call to go as missionaries, and what support they received was provided largely from private means, their own and what a comparatively few interested persons gave and persuaded others to give.

Slowly the denominations accepted the work which had been begun in this way, and the obligation, at least in part, of supporting it financially, although there never was, as stated, any full enlistment of their members in giving.

Missions became, eventually, the most characteristic and demanding work of the churches. Many Christians saw in it the fulfillment of scriptural commands and the embodiment of Christ's main purpose for his Church. So it came to dominate the policy of the denominations—or, that is to say, the mission-minded did.

It was inevitable that such an expanding and aggressive movement should become a conspicuous example of the saying of a great missionary, that the Church had the treasures of God's grace in "earthen vessels." Its mistakes and failures sometimes hid its successes. They were the weaknesses of its human agents—i.e. of the churches. If the work was of God, he had known that it must be done by imperfect men and women and foreseen undoubtedly the defeats which would befall it.

Leaving aside this question and judging the outcome in pragmatic terms we note that the movement had to its credit a record of untold good. At great personal sacrifice those who bore the brunt of the work in out-of-the-way and unknown places, had made a beginning, at least, of preaching the Gospel to all nations. They had planted churches up and down the continents where exploding populations contended for ill-understood rights and needs, insuring that Christian love would have some small part, at least, in the mad surge of human selfishness. Whether these outposts of faith would survive or not, the swift events would soon tell. So long as they stood, the world would have some faint light and hope. All who had helped build them could rejoice for the fruits of their labors and feel that there still was something to live for.

The ecumenical movement had grown out of the missionary movement, and logically it had itself to be missionary. Whatever it did, it would look for returns in the missionary effect. Unity, as attained, would cause many, the expectation was, to believe the Gospel. Inter-Church Aid, study, Christian social action, work with men, women, and youth—all were evangelism through deed, supplying convincing support of the word. Missions and unity were coordinates and lost meaning in separation.

6. Inter-group Relations: Racial and Ethnic Tensions

Against the background of Christian hope, Section V at Evanston studied the sub-theme "Inter-Group Relations—The Church amid Racial and Ethnic Tensions" and in a report restated the ecumenical reaction to the massive problems in this area of world unrest. (See Appendix M.)

> Everywhere there is restlessness . . . due, in great part, to the hunger of millions . . . for status and recognition . . . and for a fuller share of the fruits of the earth. The impact of technically advanced civilization . . . has affected every country. . . . Now a new phase has been entered, with the struggle of disadvantaged peoples of many races to participate fully in

the opportunities and responsibilities of society. While the advance and emancipation of any people . . . are causes of rejoicing . . . impending events are so menacing and their approach so swift . . . that fear and anxiety afflict us all. . . .

Hatreds, jealousies and suspicions . . . are deepened. . . . In some situations men . . . accept race conflict as inevitable and lose hope of peaceful solution. . . .

What is the Christian hope in this disunity? It is Jesus Christ, who revealed God as Father and . . . died for all men, reconciling them to God and to each other by his cross. From every race and nation a new people of God is created, in which the power of the Spirit overcomes racial pride and fear. . . . So to us is given the gift of sharing in and working for the Kingdom even now. . . .

This is the calling of the Church with regard to race, to witness within itself to the kingship of Christ and the unity of his people, in him transcending all diversity. . . .

All churches and Christians are involved. . . . But it is in communities where segregation prevails that they face the plainest difficulties and the most challenging opportunities; for such segregation denies . . . equal rights and results in deep injuries to the human spirit, suffered by offender and victim alike. . . .

The great majority of . . . churches affiliated with the World Council of Churches have declared that physical separation within the Church on grounds of race is a denial of spiritual unity and of the brotherhood of man. Yet such separation persists . . . and we often seek to justify it on other grounds than race. . . .

The Church is called . . . to set aside such excuses and to declare God's will both in words and deeds. . . .

If Christian obedience leads to suffering, that is part of the price. . . . The whole pattern of racial discrimination is . . . an unutterable offence against God, to be endured no longer. . . .

The churches have a special duty toward those . . . who feel called to challenge . . . the conscience of society, and thus offend against custom and incur loneliness and suffering. . . .

As part of its task . . . it is the duty of the Church to protest against any law or arrangement that is unjust to any human being or which makes fellowship impossible, or would prevent the Christian from practising his vocation. Some of its members may feel bound to disobey such law. The Church does not contemplate lightly any breaking of the law, but it recognizes the duty of a Christian to do so when he feels that he has reached that point where the honor and glory of God commands him to obey God rather than man. . . The Church . . . cannot approve of any law which discriminates on grounds of race.

The Second Assembly had approved a recommendation that the Central Committee, in consultation with the International Missionary Council, make provision for an organization, "preferably a department," to assist "the constituent churches in their efforts to bring the Gospel to bear more effectively upon relations between racial and ethnic groups."

Money for implementing this action could not be got from budgetary sources; but in the early months of 1957 the National Council of the Churches of Christ in the United States released to the World Council

Dr. Oscar Lee to help with formulating a plan to be submitted to the Central Committee at its annual meeting later that year in New Haven.

The Fund for the Republic had agreed to bear the expenses of Dr. Lee's services, and this suggested to the Committee that special contributions might be obtained to finance the program his report would outline until the Third Assembly, or such time as the funds could be provided through the World Council budget. It was agreed to explore possibilities in that direction.

The Division of Ecumenical Action accepted responsibility for this step, as well as the development of other proposals of Dr. Lee and his associates. These included the appointment of a "consultant" to assist with integrating "the concerns of racial and ethnic relations . . . into every relevant aspect of the programs" of the World Council and "other ecumenical agencies" and the promotion of "a study of the biblical and theological bases of racial and ethnic relations" leading to the development of fresh approaches to the subject and the "production of material designed to stimulate further study by groups in the churches of each country."

The solicitation of extra-budget contributions failed to elicit an adequate response. However, a gift by an interested individual made possible in 1958 the appointment, "as an interim measure," of Rev. Daisuka Kitagawa, who had been working on the study of areas of rapid social change, to "produce a report on ways in which the experience of American churches in dealing with situations of racial prejudice, ethnic tension and inter-group conflict, [might] be suggestive to churches in other continents" facing the same problems, complementing Dr. Lee's work during the previous year.

In the area of study, the responsibility of the Division of Ecumenical Action was, in this case, shared by the Division of Studies. The joint decision was that no urgent need existed to organize "the proposed international and ecumenical inquiry on the biblical and theological bases of racial and ethnic relations," particularly in view of the extensive discussion in progress under the program on areas of rapid social change.

Meantime, the Committee on Program and Finance of the World Council came forward with the recommendation that provision be made through the operating budget for a secretariat on racial and ethnic relations after the Third Assembly, whatever might be done until then through *ad hoc* actions to raise funds and employ temporary workers.

The World Council had been criticized for not having included in the studies at Amsterdam a section on ethnic and racial relations. Now it drew criticism by its slowness in implementing the recommendation of Section V adopted at Evanston that a department and secretariat on work in this field be created. Six years had brought little beyond the promise to do something after New Delhi.

From the Division of Ecumenical Action came complaint that the Council ought not to authorize the establishment of departments without providing means to finance them.

The explanation of such frustrations was not far to seek. With the self-imposed task of building a responsible world society, the World Council found itself, in whatever it undertook, always in danger of being drawn into depths beyond its resources. At St. Andrews—its last meeting before going to New Delhi—the Central Committee, though unable to carry out the instructions from Evanston to set up a secretariat on racial and ethnic relations and with warning from the Working Committee on Church and Society that the study of "Christian Responsibility toward Areas of Rapid Social Change" faced the necessity of premature discontinuance because of lack of funds, had placed before it a new proposal for a World Council of Churches Social Development Program. This would involve, if adopted, several of the Council's divisions and departments, the Commission of the Churches on International Affairs, and the International Missionary Council and require over a four-year period at least a million dollars.

The report of the Department on Church and Society at St. Andrews illustrated the intense pressure of demands on the World Council.

> Our attention is immediately drawn to Africa where the winds of change are blowing at gale force. . . . The failure to understand in time the dynamic forces working underneath African society; the inadequacy of the traditional patterns and structures of the churches and missions to deal creatively with these . . . and the lack of a theology which will enable Christians to play their part in the political, economic and social struggle for realizing the African personality and social justice, require the ecumenical movement urgently to help the churches in study and action. . . . It is necessary to share with those involved in political life and administration, who want to see their own involvement in the light of the Gospel, and to make available to them the body of Christian insights which come out of recent Christian social thinking. . . .
>
> The ecumenical movement, if it is to act responsibly, cannot leave the churches, the national Christian councils and regional bodies in these areas without assistance in their struggle to awaken their members for Christian witness and action amidst the violent changes in society and the groping for new national and social goals. . . . Ecumenical study remains of vital importance. . . . The awakening to new responsibilities has just begun. . . .
>
> Urgent requests have come from various areas. The rapidity of change in Africa is such that opportunities now opening will soon be lost, if not met now. . . . But it will require additional finance for the work in Northern Rhodesia . . . the Middle East . . . West Africa . . . Mexico . . . the Caribbean, in addition to the continuation of the existing program. . . . Without this . . . the "rapid-social-change" study will have to be prematurely cut short.[29]

[29] De Vries in "The Report of the Working Committee on Church and Society," Minutes of the Central Committee, St. Andrews, 1960, p. 126.

Some members of the Central Committee feared that the World Council would be forced too deeply into the struggle of the peoples of underdeveloped countries for social emancipation. It seemed to them that the World Council had a more distinctive and vital mission, whatever came of these revolutionary movements, which only it could accomplish.

For example, there was the spiritual mission of keeping the emphasis on responsibility in the demand for rights. Aims in this struggle, however justified they might be, were tinged always with a degree of selfishness and were in that measure unchristian; for the Christian looked first on the things of others. Persons striving for what they considered to be justice were tempted often to descend to harshness and cruelty. It was forgotten by those desiring to help the deserving that the contending parties in social and political conflicts were of like passions, one no less sinful than the other. While the scales of justice might seem, in a particular instance, to tip in the direction of those fighting for their rights, and Christian judgment could only support their cause, whatever was done should be with the knowledge that success would probably only transfer from the vanquished to the victor the tyranny that brought on the warfare in the first place. Unless the grace of God came into play and hearts were changed, the battle would continue through alternating reversals of power, to the defeat eventually of all concerned. This, the sole cure of human strife, must be made clear, whether the warring factions would countenance it or not; and only the Church could bring it about.

Without condoning injustice or excusing those who oppressed others, the Church must help the afflicted to see and appreciate such good as they had received as members of an evil society. It was a fact that peoples of underdeveloped nations had benefited in numerous ways, as many of them freely admitted, from their relations with colonial powers. That they had the understanding and strength now to seek independence was evidence of this. However bitter the memory of their exploitation by others might be, they had cause to be grateful, and their gratitude would make them morally stronger for their struggle.

It must be understood, further, that the drive for emancipation could never be fully won. When a people was victorious over its enemies, it had still itself to conquer, or new—and possibly worse—tyrannies would rise to enslave it. Exultation over the passing of foreign rule should be tempered for the thoughtful by the realization that colonialism could return in worse forms. If won by revolutionary violence, liberty and independence would be harder to keep. If they came as an evolution under conditions of goodwill and patience, they would be enjoyed with greater assurance of their permanence.

Also, successful liberation of the peoples of underdeveloped countries depended on world peace, which, in turn, would be influenced more than they might realize by their own actions. With the bitter rivalry which existed between nations, armed conflict in even the smallest could lead to war involving all, with the devastation or destruction of all. Every nation, large or small, had the responsibility to conduct its affairs with the view of strengthening the supports of peace.

These were basically religious considerations bearing in the most practical way upon the conditions of human survival. If the churches had a mission, it was to labor to give them effect in the thinking of mankind.

This was not an easy task. The experience of the Founder of the Church made that clear. Revolution, as always, demanded partisanship of all. Only they would be acceptable who took sides. Those who weighed the right and wrong on both sides and refused to approve all contentions of the party which seemed the more deserving would in their attempt to be fair become suspect and exposed to cross fire. Jesus had compassion for the poor, but when he had to refuse their demands they fell away, abandoning him to their oppressors, who with their acquiescence, if not their help, crucified him.

The churches must devote themselves, in season and out of season, to inculcating these basic truths, and must practice them. The world was being turned upside down, but it would remain the same world, whoever might chance to land on top. No matter how splendid and strongly financed the programs of social amelioration, the sinfulness of the human heart was the constant threat of all they accomplished. There truly was no remission of sin without the shedding of blood—the blood of Christ, if you would, but also the blood of his followers.

This would be the case still when the budget of the World Council of Churches had been stretched to cover the cost of a secretariat on racial and ethnic relations. The problem would remain of convincing the nations, the underdeveloped as well as the economically and politically advanced, that responsibility came before rights, or there would be no civilization, no lasting freedom, no peace for anybody.

The churches could serve the cause of peace between the races better if they reconciled their views on biblical teachings in this area. It would be a gain if they recognized and admitted that the Bible had no clear and direct word here, as it had not on other social questions.

By selecting references from the priestly inspired portions of the Old Testament, one could make out a case against racial intermarriage. On the other hand, there were strong implications in the prophetical writings of the unity of all mankind. The story of Ruth, the Moabite girl who married into the family of Bethlehemites, had probably been intended to counteract the priestly notions.

If the Bible was to be invoked for textual guidance, it could be interpreted as supporting the brotherhood of men in virtue of their common creation by God the Father; but its stronger emphasis might be shown to be on the new birth through faith in Christ as the condition of divine sonship. Christians in the early centuries of the Church were called the third—or new—race and willingly accepted the implied differentiation on the scriptural ground that "as many as received him [Christ] to them gave he power to become children of God," and as many as were in Christ were "a new creation."

The dichotomy at this point in the interpretation of the Scriptures concerning brotherhood ran through ecumenical pronouncements. One encountered in the statements of the World Council of Churches many references to the universal brotherhood of man; but here and there—as in the Report of Section V of the Second Assembly—were found the more spiritual conception of the relationship: e.g. "This is an especial time of testing for the faith that we all live and have our truest being in God the Father, whose children we are in Christ and whose redemptive love enables us to treasure all men as brothers. . . . We need to repent of something far deeper than our disunity. . . . We need to repent of our separation from God from which this springs. . . . To us is given power to become the sons of God and to be everyone members of one another." Thus were jumbled together confusingly the idea that all men were brothers whom God created and the idea that they were true brothers whom he re-created through Jesus Christ.

The churches had an especially urgent responsibility to give intelligent leading in respect of civil obedience and disobedience.

Many Christians held the conviction that no slight encouragement ought to be given to the growing spirit of lawlessness. Defiance of unjust and discriminatory laws might have been justified once, when the wars likely to result could be isolated and kept a concern of the community or nation, but hardly in the modern world where the repercussions of local incidents were felt instantly everywhere and might precipitate universal conflict. In a society, indeed, in which the local had become universal, the scriptural injunction against resisting evil took on new dimensions of meaning. But, in its counsel to the Church, the World Council went beyond advising protest against "any law or arrangement that is unjust to any human being, or which would make Christian fellowship impossible, or would prevent the Christian from practising his vocation" and working for its repeal, and said:

> Some of its members may feel bound to disobey such law. The Church does not contemplate lightly any breaking of the law, but it recognizes the duty of a Christian to do so when he feels that he has reached that point where the honor and glory of God commands him to obey God rather than man.[30]

The danger implicit in this course was the natural proneness of men to identify the "honor and glory of God" with their own. God's greatest glory was his humility, and in this respect Christians were especially

[30] See Report of Section V, Appendix M.

committed to emulate him as they knew him through Jesus Christ, "who took upon himself the form of a servant . . . and became obedient unto death, even the death of the cross."

The Negro of a southern state in the United States, who in a televised interview said that he would rather rot in jail than be free in a segregated society, easily won sympathy; but there was no man, black or white, who could Christianly meet the discriminations of life in this world without humility. All that anyone could gain by other methods was as nothing compared with the rewards of doing justly, whatever the injustices suffered; loving mercy, though unmercifully treated; and walking humbly with God, if need be under the insults of the selfish and haughty.

This would be to counsel, not supine resignation under wrongs, but reliance upon the power of good returned for evil and obedience to laws so long as they were the law. Jesus would not die as a lawbreaker. Could the honor and glory of God demand that a Christian should?

Scarcely any part of the world could claim to be free of racial or ethnic tensions, though the countries in which overt strife resulting therefrom received the popular attention, to the exclusion of others where rival feelings might be even more acute. In those nations where resentment ran high against whites, different elements of the native populations were, in many instances, unable to live peaceably with one another. Examples were, among many, the Chinese and the indigenous peoples in Thailand and Indonesia; the Chinese, again, and the Indians in Malaya; the Singhalese and the Tamils in Ceylon; the Japanese and Koreans in Japan; the Karens and neighboring tribes in Burma; the Bengali and the Burmese in Burma; the Indians, again, and the natives in southeastern Africa; and the warring Congolese, who, according to Premier Joseph Ileo, were not actually "a people, but a collection of large ethnic groups."

The World Council of Churches moved during this period to intervene in the dangerous situation in the Union of South Africa under the national policy of *apartheid*.[31] Its approach was through the eight denominations of that nation which were its members—the Dutch Reformed Church of the Transvaal, the Nederduitse Gereformeerde Kerke of the Cape, the Nederduitsch Hervormde Kerk van Afrika, the Church of the Province of South Africa (Anglican), the Methodist Church, the Presbyterian Church, the Bantu Presbyterian Church, and the Congregational Union.

When the World Council was considering how it might with propriety and acceptance act on its own initiative, a way was opened by a public clash between officials of the Reformed and Anglican Churches in the wake of the riots in 1960 which led to the tragic Sharpeville and Langa incidents.

[31] Minutes of the Central Committee, St. Andrews, 1960, p. 70.

The Reformed Churches supported generally the *apartheid* policy of the government.[32] Their extensive Bantu and colored missions were organized apart, the members of these having practically no contact, except through the missionaries, with the white congregations. On the other hand, the English-speaking denominations opposed segregation, jointly affirming "that the Church planted by God in this country [was] multiracial and must remain so." The Anglican Church was most outspoken and forward in its espousal of desegregation. Its Johannesburg Bishop Ambrose Reeves was forced to leave South Africa and eventually to resign because of his criticism of the government's program. Archbishop Joost de Blank called for expulsion of the Dutch Reformed Church of South Africa by the World Council of Churches. This led to the suggestion from the contending sides, as well as from ecumenical sources outside the Union of South Africa, that Geneva send a commission, in the words of the Archbishop, "to investigate the underlying causes of the present outbreak and disturbances from the Christian standpoint."

The "consultation" took place at Cottesloe, Johannesburg, December 7-14, 1960, and was attended by seven representatives of the World Council of Churches—Doctors Fry, Visser 't Hooft, Bilheimer, and Niesel, Bishop De Mel, Sir Francis Ibiam, and Charles C. Parlin—drawn from the United States, West Germany, the Netherlands, Ceylon, and Nigeria, and ten delegates from each of the denominations in the Union of South Africa belonging to the World Council. Among the conferees were twenty-four non-whites.

The delegation of the World Council approached the meeting on the basis of Resolution I of Section V, adopted by the Evanston Assembly:[33]

> The Second Assembly of the World Council of Churches declares its conviction that any form of segregation based on race, color or ethnic origin is contrary to the Gospel, and . . . incompatible with the Christian doctrine of man and with the nature of the Church of Christ.
>
> The Assembly urges the churches within its membership to renounce all forms of segregation or discrimination, and to work for their abolition within their own life and within society.
>
> In doing so, the Assembly is painfully aware that, in the realities of the contemporary world, many churches find themselves confronted by historical, social and economic circumstances which make the immediate achievement of this objective extremely difficult. But, under God, the fellowship of the ecumenical movement is such as to offer to these churches the strength and encouragement to help them and individuals within them to overcome these difficulties with the courage given by faith, and with the desire to testify ever more faithfully to our Master.

"It is not a part of the nature of the World Council of Churches," the commissioners explained in their letter agreeing to a meeting, "to pronounce judgments upon churches or nations or people, nor to attempt

[32] The Ecumenical Review, Vol. IX, No. 1, October 1956, p. 64 ff.
[33] *Ibid.* Vol. XII, No. 4, p. 488.

to enforce convictions which have been crystallized in ecumenical debate. It is the function of the ecumenical movement to witness to such convictions, and . . . of the World Council of Churches to continue conversations concerning these with those who disagree with them."

The English-speaking churches of the Union of South Africa came to the conference, if in a less conciliatory spirit, in full agreement with the action of the Second Assembly cited by the Geneva deputation.

The attitude of the Dutch Reformed Churches had been set forth some time previously by Rev. C. B. Brink, a member of the Central Committee of the World Council and the moderator of the largest of the three South African Reformed Churches:

Apartheid, or segregation, or separate development, has been a feature of South African society for three hundred years. During all this time, the measure of separation between the races was determined more by social and economic conditions than by fixed and deliberate policy. *Apartheid* between races has become a way of life in this country.

In 1957, the Dutch Reformed Churches decided to organize separate parishes for their non-white members. This led to the establishment of autonomous churches for the Bantus (Negroes) and Coloreds (mixed-bloods) throughout the country.

In 1937, the synod issued a declaration of . . . the principles by which the Church sought to guide its members and to direct its . . . work. It reads:

"While the Church acknowledges the existence among the nations of the world of different color, cultural and language groups, it also acknowledges that God made of one blood all the nations of men . . . and that all souls for whom the Saviour shed his blood are equal in the eyes of God."

The Dutch Reformed Church has tried to apply this principle as consistently as possible, and there can be no reason, therefore, to assume that *apartheid* is understood or willfully applied as a policy of suppression or discrimination by the Church.

On the contrary, the synod has declared that, "since the Gospel arouses a desire in its converts to improve their conditions, it is the duty of the Church not to thwart such aspirations but to assist them by deed and advice and to direct them along the right course."

In its own work, the Church applied most of its resources to this end and established schools and training centers throughout the country. It was felt for a long time by the Church, however, that the system of subsidized education was open to abuse, and that it no longer could conform to the requirements of the rapidly developing Bantu society.

The Church argued that the state should assume responsibility for Bantu education as an integral part of its service for the non-white section of the population.

The Church has no objection against the Bantu Education Law on religious or educational grounds and considers this Law, if properly applied, a great step forward in the advancement of the non-white section of the population.

It should be remembered, however, that the position is not static and that further developments can be expected that could be used to achieve the ultimate aim of complete independence and self-determination for the non-white in all matters that affect his existence in the community.

The day before the consultation in Johannesburg, Prime Minister Hendrik F. Verwoerd had announced the government's policy with reference to the civil status of the Coloreds. He had made it clear that they were not to be integrated with the white population or admitted to membership in Parliament. The Ministry of Colored Affairs—presumably headed by a white—would, he said, take "an active part in a virile socio-economic development program," under which they would run their own urban councils and municipal bodies and have separate schools, hospitals, sports, and entertainment facilities. A development and investment corporation would be established for them under the administrative authority of the Colored Affairs Council. There would be annual discussions by the Prime Minister, the Minister for Colored Affairs, and the elected leaders of the colored community on matters of mutual interest, "on the same lines as Prime Ministers' conferences in the Commonwealth."

Similar arrangements would be made, he stated, for South Africa's Indian community.

The consultation concluded its sessions after seven days by issuing a "statement," which had been adopted "by at least eighty per cent of the participants."

In this document of some twenty-five hundred words they said, in part:[34]

We have met as delegates from the Member Churches in South Africa of the World Council of Churches, with representatives of the World Council itself, to seek under the guidance of the Holy Spirit to understand the complex problems of human relationships in this country, and to consult with one another on our common task and responsibility in the light of the Word of God. . . .

The general theme . . . has been the Christian attitude toward race relations. . . .

We are united in rejecting all unjust discrimination. . . .

Nevertheless, widely divergent convictions have been expressed on the basic issues of *apartheid*. They range, on the one hand, from the judgment that it is unacceptable in principle, contrary to the Christian calling and unworkable in practice, to the conviction, on the other hand, that a policy of differentiation can be defended, from the Christian point of view, that it provides the only realistic solution to the problems of race relations and is, therefore, in the best interests of the various population groups. . . . In the nature of the case, the agreements here recorded do not—and we do not pretend that they do—represent in full the convictions of the member churches.

The Church of Jesus Christ, by its nature and calling, is deeply concerned with the welfare of all people, both as individuals and as members of social groups. . . . In its social witness, the Church must take cognizance of all attitudes, forces, policies and laws which affect the life of a people; but the Church must proclaim that the final criterion of all social and political

[34] *The Ecumenical Review*, Vol. XIII, No. 2, Jan. 1961, p. 244 ff.

action is the principles of Scripture regarding the realization for all men of a life worthy of their God-given vocation. . . .

We recognize that all racial groups who permanently inhabit our country are part of our total population . . . [and] have an equal right to make their contribution towards the enrichment of . . . [its] life . . . and to share in the ensuing responsibilities, rewards and privileges. . . .

The Church has a duty to bear witness to the hope which is in Christianity both to white South Africans in their uncertainty and to non-white South Africans in their frustration. . . . The Church as the Body of Christ is a unity, and within this unity the natural diversity among men is . . . sanctified.

No one who believes in Jesus Christ may be excluded from any Church on the grounds of his color or race. The spiritual unity among all men who are in Christ must find visible expression in acts of common worship and witness, and in fellowship and consultation on matters of common concern. . . .

The whole Church must participate in the tremendous missionary task . . . to be done in South Africa. . . .

Our discussions have revealed that there is not sufficient consultation and communication between the various racial groups. . . .

There are no Scriptural grounds for the prohibition of mixed marriages. . . . The well-being of the community . . . requires, however, that due consideration . . . be given to certain factors which make such marriages inadvisable.

We call attention . . . to the disintegrating effects of migrant labor on African life. . . . It is imperative that the integration of the family be safeguarded. . . . The wages received by the vast majority of the non-white people oblige them to exist well below the generally accepted minimum standard for healthy living. . . . Opportunities must be provided for the inhabitants of Bantu areas to live in conformity with human dignity.

. . . The right to own land wherever he is domiciled, and to participate in the government of his country, is part of the dignity of the adult man, and for this reason a policy which permanently denies to non-white people the right of collaboration in the government . . . cannot be justified. . . . There can be no objection in principle to the direct representation of Colored people in Parliament. . . .

The Church has the duty and right to proclaim the Gospel to whomsoever it will, in whatever circumstances, and wherever possible, consistent with the general principles governing the right of public meetings in democratic countries. We, therefore, regard as unacceptable any special legislation which would limit the fulfillment of this task. . . .

Whenever an occasion arises that a Church feels bound to criticize another Church or Church leader, it should take the initiative in seeking prior consultation before making any public statement. . . .

Churches are requested to provide full information to other Churches of their procedures in approaching the Government. . . . In approaches to the Government, delegations, combined if possible, multi-racial where appropriate, should act on behalf of the Churches. . . .

Any body which may be formed for co-operation in the future is requested to give attention to the following: A constructive approach to separatist movements; the education of the Bantu; the training of non-white leaders for positions of responsibility in all spheres; African literacy and the provision of Christian literature; the concept of responsible Christian society in all areas in South Africa, including the Reserves; the impact of Islam on South Africa.

We give thanks to Almighty God for bringing us together. . . . We resolve to continue in this fellowship. . . . We acknowledge before God the feebleness of our often divided witness to our Lord Jesus Christ and our lack of compassion for one another. We . . . dedicate ourselves afresh to the ministry of reconciliation in Christ.

Definite constructive results of the meeting were the drawing more closely together of South African church leaders and the initiatory steps by them to form a cooperative organization to be known as the South Africa Conference of the World Council of Churches Member Churches.

Apologies and words of forgiveness by prominent clergymen who had criticized one another in the controversy over *apartheid* helped erase lingering ill feeling. The Anglican and Dutch Reformed Churches were brought together in such mutual concern as they had not felt since Archbishop Joost de Blank of Capetown threatened to resign from the World Council of Churches if the Reformed Churches did not revise their attitude on the racial question.

Officials of the World Council of Churches expressed the opinion that the consultation had marked a turning point in cooperation and social thinking by the churches in the Union of South Africa.

Noting that the multi-racial delegations had lived, eaten, and worked together, Dr. Visser 't Hooft said, at a press conference: "We have come back very happy. We had a consensus on the important points . . . of far-reaching importance. We feel that we went to South Africa at the right moment. All the factors led to certain points of crystallization. We believe the consultation helped this."

There was reason to doubt, however, that the outcome had been as favorable as it may have seemed to some members of the commission.

"We are united in rejecting all unjust discrimination," declared the statement issued by the consultation. For the members of the deputation and the delegates from the South Africa English-speaking churches this meant rejection of *apartheid*. In the ecumenical view, *apartheid* was "unjust discrimination," but not in the opinion of the Reformed Churches of the Union of South Africa. "We wish . . . to state quite clearly," declared the delegates of the Nederduitsch Hervormde Kerk van Afrika in a statement after the adjournment of the consultation, "that it is our conviction that separate development is the only *just* solution of our racial problem." Said the representatives of the Nederduitse Gereformeerde Kerke of the Cape and Transvaal in their memorandum: "We wish to confirm that . . . a policy of differentiation can be defended, from the Christian point of view, that it provides the only realistic solution to the problems of race relations and is, therefore, in the best interests of the various population groups. We do not consider the resolutions adopted by the consultation as in principle incompatible with the above statement."

Apartheid, in its—to them—true sense of differentiation, affording opportunity for development according to ethnic and cultural circumstances, was thus plainly regarded by the Dutch Reformed leaders as the nearest to just solution of the race question. It was the right way, they thought, because it only would save Christianity and civilization, and so, in the long run, work for the best interests of all races. Injustices would occur under it, of course, as in all systems. Individuals upon whom they fell must be willing to suffer them for the common good. Christians would willingly accept this cross.

It was the duty of the Church to resist the surge of underdeveloped peoples who demanded to be given the full advantages of life in Christian society without learning its disciplines. Neither fear nor expediency should move the Church to yield. It must obey its true mission, at whatever cost. The ecumenical policy invited and encouraged the admission of all peoples into the Church and Christian society, whatever their cultural background and condition, into the liberties of democratic equality, at any hazard to the costly treasures it had taken ages of toil and sacrifice to gain. The ideal of a responsible society upheld by the World Council of Churches could not be attained in this way, according to *Apartheid*. The irresponsibility of the underdeveloped should be met with truly responsible action, though it meant having to bear a cross. The Church should not, because it had made mistakes and had failed in many ways, be intimidated by those who chose to forget what they had received through its ministry and to destroy the "earthen vessel" in which the gifts of God were borne for generations to come. The menace in the rising of backward races would be met by the ecumenists from abroad through attempts at integration, which could only result in eventual engulfment for the West. *Apartheid* would take a stand against it at "the bounds" God had himself predetermined, "who made the world . . . and . . . all nations of men for to dwell on the face of the earth" (Acts xvii, 24ff.).

This was actually the semantics of the discussion at Cottesloe and of the "consensus" which was reached, and too optimistic interpretations of what had happened would only confuse the issues.

It had to be recognized also that there were in the denominations of the World Council outside the Union of South Africa many people who thought that "a policy of differentiation [could] be defended, from the Christian point of view, that it [provided] the only realistic solution to the problems of race relations, and [was], therefore, in the best interests of the various population groups." They would have agreed with the Dutch Christians of South Africa that the ecumenical policy, as interpreted by the World Council of Churches and advanced by its deputation to the consultation, was fraught with the gravest danger.

At the end of March, 1961, the Dutch Reformed Church of Africa (Hervormde Kerk van Afrika) announced its withdrawal from the World Council of Churches. By its constitution, only white persons could be admitted as members, and the Johannesburg conference had said: "No one who believes in Jesus Christ may be excluded from any church on the grounds of his color or race." At about the same time, the Dutch Reformed Church of Transvaal also voted to withdraw from the World Council, though expressing its purpose to "remain in correspondence with the Council"—whatever that meant.

Remarking on this turn of events, Dr. Visser 't Hooft said, on behalf of the World Council of Churches: "We regret deeply that the Transvaal Dutch Reformed Church has decided to leave our fellowship, but we do not regret that the consultation in Johannesburg has made a clear Christian witness about justice in race relations. And we will want to maintain the fullest possible fellowship with all those in South Africa in member churches and in other churches who are working for the realization of a truly ecumenical conception of the Church and for a constructive, peaceful and just solution of the race problem."

Racial and ethnic tensions as they involved Jews in particular received no extended formal attention from the World Council of Churches during the post-Evanston period. Section V of the Second Assembly had understood that the terms of reference under which its study was defined precluded this subject. It only reaffirmed that anti-Semitism was incompatible with Christian faith and recommended that study of ways of combating it "be pressed forward by the Central Committee, in conjunction with the International Missionary Council's Committee on the Christian Approach to the Jews."

On the deletion from the Advisory Commission's Report on the Main Theme of the paragraphs concerning the fulfillment of God's promise to the people of ancient Israel, the Assembly had instructed the Central Committee "to make suitable arrangements for further study and ecumenical conversation on the subject." The statement "The Hope of Israel," which was presented following the rejection by the Assembly of the part of the text of the Advisory Commission's Report just indicated, had borne the names of some of the foremost churchmen in the World Council—among them H. Berkhof, M. Boegner, A. Koechlin, P. Maury, T. F. Torrance, J. Sittler, O. S. Tomkins, J. Smemo, E. Schlink, H. d'Espine, J. Hromadka, and M. Niemöller—but the weight of their influence was not enough to move the Central Committee to vigorous action on the matter.

The Central Committee did, however, ask the Joint Committee of the World Council of Churches and the International Missionary Council to arrange, in cooperation with the latter body's Committee on the Christian Approach to the Jews, a "consultation on 'Christian Convictions and Attitudes in Relation to the Jewish People,'" and this was done.

The meeting was held at the Ecumenical Institute in September, 1956, and reported to the Executive Committee of the World Council the following February. The Executive Committee decided that the subject called for discussion by groups more fully representative of different theological views than it had been possible to convene at Bossey and passed the document with the findings to the Division of Studies for further consideration, with the request that it be published in *The Ecumenical Review,* "not as a statement of the World Council of Churches," but as "a basis for more wide-spread reading on the issues . . . central to the Christian Gospel and the Church's task."

At St. Andrews in 1960 Dr. H. Berkhof, who had signed the statement at Evanston on "The Hope of Israel," suggested to the Central Committee "the need to reach a clearer theological understanding of the Christian attitude toward the Jews," which he believed to be, he said, "the first and the last ecumenical question." He expressed the hope that preparations were being made for its presentation at New Delhi and asked what had been done since Evanston to set the promised special committee to work on it. Dr. Visser 't Hooft replied that few comments had been received from the churches on the consultation's report and that there was little reason at the moment for another meeting; and Dr. Goodall of the International Missionary Council added that the study begun at Bossey was still in process but was encountering stubborn issues on which agreement could not be reached without further expressions from the churches.

The study-conference at the Ecumenical Institute had approached "the problem of the Jew" through the Bible:[35]

> The promise of the Kingdom of Christ is offered to all men, to Jew as to Gentile. . . .
>
> The revelation of the living God is given through all Scripture, the Old Testament and the New. . . . We must use the Old Testament in worship, prayer and study, while seeing that the whole revelation of God finds its focus and fulfillment in Jesus Christ. . . .
>
> The Jews had a unique role in the purpose of God as bearers of his revelation. . . . As Christians we owe a special debt to the Jewish people, and still have much to learn from them. . . .
>
> Since Christ is Lord over all the world, when he shall reign at his second coming, the fulness of both Jew and Gentile will have been brought into his Kingdom. In the New Testament a "remnant" from the Jews accept Christ. A hardening has happened to other Jews, but God still holds out his promise for them, and their conversion is closely associated with the hope of the second coming. . . .
>
> Our hope for the Jews does not mean that we can calculate the time or define the nature of the coming of Christ in his Kingdom. . . . Of the fact of the hope for Jew and Gentile in Christ we are assured; as to the nature of its fulfillment we rightly keep an expectant mind, lest . . . we should be blinded by our . . . definitions, and so be unprepared when he comes to claim his own.
>
> For these reasons, we should maintain a certain caution in applying prophecies, whether from the Old Testament or the New . . . to contempo-

[35] *The Ecumenical Review,* Vol. IX, No. 3, April 1957, p. 303 ff.

rary events. . . . One thing, however, we proclaim with absolute assurance. Christ will come. Christ will reign. God has committed all things into his hands. His love embraces both Jew and Gentile. His Church must embrace both. . . .

As Christians, we affirm that the Jewish people will not find their true destiny until they turn and acknowledge Jesus Christ as Lord. . . .

At the same time, we acknowledge that the whole world is also guilty before God in its failure to acknowledge Christ as Lord; and, further, we acknowledge the sins of Christian people in their frequent failure to manifest the love and power of Christ to the people from whom he came. In addition to this, the Church has been guilty through the centuries in presenting a distorted picture of the Jews to the world, and this has been a major factor in anti-Semitism. . . .

We acknowledge that the Jewish people have . . . preserved truths of the revelation of God through the Old Testament. . . . In particular, Judaism has an abiding message for the Church in . . . the Law and the Prophets—that God is Lord over every realm of life. . . . Recognizing this . . . we must ask whether the centuries-long preservation of the Jews as an ethnic, as well as religious, group . . . is not intended by God to teach both us and them new lessons concerning the problems of race and nationality, which so gravely vex the world. . . .

Concerning [the] new situation of the Jews, there are diverse views within the Church, as . . . indeed . . . amongst the Jewish people themselves. Our uncertainty over . . Jewish nationalism reflects our failure throughout the world to solve the issues of nationalism. . . .

The setting up of the State of Israel, while it has relieved the sufferings of many Jews, has involved great suffering for many Arabs who have lost their land and . . . homes; and they also are a people under God's care. Moreover, while we understand the desire of many Jews to have a country of their own, we believe it is their calling to live as the people of God, and not to become merely a nation like others. . . .

The issue before the Jewish people has been expressed in the difference between *laos* and *ethnos;* and the working out of this distinction is significant also for other peoples. As *laos,* the Jewish people were called to be "the people of God"; *ethnos* stands for a secular national or racial pride. As *laos,* the prophets saw that they had a responsibility towards other nations; every secularized *ethnos* stands in revolt against God and in antagonism over against other nations.

The land which included Judea, Samaria and Galilee . . . is now divided by lines of demarcation . . far more a barrier to communication than normal frontiers between states. This prevents the Holy Land from being, as we should hope, a place of meeting and mutual understanding for people of various faiths. . . .

All nations stand under judgment for the present *impasse* in the Near East. While the Church, as such, is not called to pronounce particular solutions for this or . . . any political problem, the Church does call all its members to pray that a solution may be found, only as we recognize that Arab and Jewish people alike are under God's care, under his judgment, under his pity and mercy. . . .

It is clear that the Church has an abiding and imperative mission to proclaim Christ to the people from whom he came. . . .

All mission has the nature of dialogue, inasmuch as in the work of evangelism we must listen as well as speak, receive as well as give, learn as well as teach. . . .

We shall not single out the Jewish people for particular attention in evangelism, where that would only emphasize the separation which we seek to overcome. . . .

"The Christian Approach to the Jews" was one of the "concerns of the churches" to which a place had been given on the program of the Amsterdam Assembly. That it did not evoke a wider and continuing response may have been, in part, on account of the implication in its presentation that the evangelization of the Jews would become a responsibility of the World Council of Churches.

Evangelism in that connection bore connotations of a kind of method which most Jews, understandably, resented, and which embarrassed some of their Christian friends.

While the duty of proclaiming the Gospel to all peoples was admitted, most Christians, when it came to "approaching the Jews," could not see clearly what more might be done than manifesting toward them goodwill and a true spirit of neighborliness, and cooperating with them, if possible, in giving emphasis to the religious and moral principles common to Judaism and Christianity.

The whole question was complicated by variant interpretations of the Scriptures as they related to Jews. A majority of Christians in the ecumenical movement, perhaps, rejected—or felt uncertain about—the traditional view that Jews were the chosen people and had been given the right by divine promise to lay claim to Palestine as their own country, and that fulfillment of the Christian hope of the coming of Christ to earth again in a visible manner to consummate his rule was in God's plan linked with their resettlement there. The Jews themselves were known to be discarding or reconstruing the chosen-people concept, under the teaching of some of their ablest and most trusted teachers and leaders. Had it not been their greatest prophets who insisted that God's chosen were those people, of whatever race or nation, who themselves chose him for their portion? And as for locating the denouement of history in Palestine, with the gathering together of the Jews there and Christ's appearing in judgment, the revised canons of biblical exegetics compelled the substitution of an eschatological outlook more at home in the twentieth century and more intelligible and convincing to those, Jews and Gentiles alike, who would hold on to their faith in God and make a place for him in contemporary life.

The nationalization of Israel in Palestine deepened and intensified the tensions involving Jews and gave them new and frightening dimensions. The displacement and the dispossession in the process of nearly a million Arabs, who were the larger element of the population, aroused a passionate resentment which nothing that might be done in the way of atonement could ever, it appeared, mollify. This incredible injustice could have been perpetrated only in a time of such profound psychological trauma as had been inflicted upon mankind by the insanities and brutalities of World War II. First in the complex of causative circumstances had been the even more shocking injustices against Jews under Hitlerian influences, climaxed by the murder of some six millions of them. Zionists, who, despairing of the success of any effort that could be made to overcome anti-Semitism, determined to flee from it, could hardly be denied at the time whatever they demanded. A refuge—a place of their own—had to be given the Jews against extinction, and in the emotional and moral confusion that existed, the cost in suffering to others, even if they had no direct responsibility for what had happened, weighed little. The Church had been saying through the centuries that Palestine belonged to the Jews, that it was their Land of Promise. Let it now be given to them to possess. So was created a climate for political actions. The chosen people of God were returning to their ancestral homeland. The day of Christ's coming drew nigh. The kingdom of God was indeed at hand. Christian nations would pay their debt to the Jews and in some measure, at least, right the wrongs done them. Always alert to expediencies, the politicians rose up to decree it.

The problem thus created was so explosive that it could easily destroy anybody attempting to deal with it realistically. Perhaps the World Council of Churches was well advised in bypassing it and confining its concern to conferences on the plight of the Arab refugees and appeals on their behalf for material aid. It was, deeply, an instance of a wrong's having been done, no way of rectifying which could be found, and which all people of goodwill would try to keep, by whatever action was possible, from leading to worse calamities.

It could only be hoped that the lessons of these tragic events would not be lost upon synagogue or church. Both were under obligation to give more conscientious thought to the improvement of their relations, Jews by seeking to avoid what in their life long experience had shown to be provocative of anti-Semitism, Christians by applying the Scriptures more responsibly as they related to Jews, and both by cultivating the humility taught by the Old and New Testaments alike. Eventually there would be room in their hearts for love toward each other as children of the same God and heirs together of his spiritual promises—the one power that could check the destructive preoccupation with their own rights and ambitions and impart the grace to look each upon the things of the other with sympathy and generosity.

The election of most Jews to support the cause of Zionism with their money and to continue living wherever they would outside the Holy Land defined the battleground for the war against anti-Semitism. Like all ethnic tensions, it would remain a disease endemic in society and impossible to flee. It could be escaped only by conquering it. That would be no easy or quickly won fight. Its success would wait, not only on the growth of godly charity in the minds of both Jews and Christians, but, in the case of the latter, on understanding acceptance of changes in biblical interpretation long indicated by sound criticism, which would remove the whole subject of the Jew and his mission from the realm of the romantic into the revealing light of historical reality.

7. Toward a Responsible International Society

In 1955 the Commission of the Churches on International Affairs sent to the delegates to the United Nations a memorandum on "issues of concern to the churches." It pointed out that no fewer than thirty-two of the items printed in the United Nations Assembly's tenth anniversary provisional agenda were related to matters falling in that category, and cited pertinent ecumenical records and statements which would be found useful as explaining the position of the churches on them. This communication went to denominational leaders also in some seventy countries. A covering letter stated that prayers for the Assembly would be offered in many churches during the forthcoming sessions, and studies on questions listed for consideration by the Assembly would be undertaken. Further, the Commission's official representatives would be accessible to members of the Assembly at all times for consultation.

This action is mentioned here because of its characteristic nature. The Commission of the Churches on International Affairs approached its work largely through the United Nations and its various organizations, in which most of the major problems in the Commission's sphere eventually came to focus, and contacts could be made most naturally and effectively with those persons in each country competent to advise concerning them.[36]

The interests of the churches emphasized in the Commission's memorandum to the United Nations delegates included the settlement of international disagreements by negotiation or arbitration; the development of practical procedures for effecting political change peacefully; the launching of a program of progressive disarmament; the creation of a commission of scientists and technicians to define the requirements for trustworthy inspection of agreed-on armament reductions; the promotion of constitutional guarantees of basic human rights in all nations; the adoption of more comprehensive and efficient measures for the care and resettlement of refugees; recognition of the right of self-determination for peoples aspiring to nationhood and independence; and the broadening of the conditions of membership in the United Nations, to admit all nations.

[36] The Commission was registered officially with the United Nations Department of Public Information and had a consultative status with the Economic and Social Council in Category B. It was authorized by its constitution to seek "such contacts with other organs and specialized agencies as the administrative officers [might] determine necessary to accomplish its aims." Consideration was being given to its need of a representative at UNESCO headquarters in Paris.

To be added later were the conversion to peaceful uses and the control of atomic energy, and international cooperation on the problem of relieving the pressures of overpopulation.

From time to time the Commission issued statements on these and other subjects. Experience in the broad field of world affairs enabled it to advise other departments of the World Council seeking guidance in their work when it involved international implications—e.g., Inter-Church Aid and Service to Refugees and the inquiry on the Christian mission in areas of rapid social change.

The activities at the United Nations were, of course, "broader than the headquarters," leading, as they did inevitably, to meetings and work assignments for officers of the Commission in many parts of the world. During this period many new nations were emerging into independent statehood, and the unique opportunity to encourage their enactment of laws affirming and safeguarding human rights would not wait. Neither would the crises in the numerous revolutionary situations which dotted these turbulent years: Suez, Lebanon, Turkey, Hungary, Cyprus, Algeria, Morocco, Tunis, Iraq, Jordan, the Congo, Burma, Laos, Viet Nam, Indonesia, Ceylon, Tibet, South Africa, West Africa, East Africa, Haiti, Cuba, and still others. The churches had in every such event a stake and a responsibility. By its constitution the Commission served the World Council of Churches and the International Missionary Council wherever their far-flung commitments on behalf of the world Christian mission made them factors in the human struggle.

According to Drs. W. A. Visser 't Hooft and Charles W. Ranson:

> The existence of the Commission of the Churches on International Affairs has made a great difference in the ecumenical situation. Before 1946[37] the ecumenical bodies had in many ways been concerned with the issues of international relationships. And they had often expressed themselves vigorously on specific situations of conflict which endangered peace or created physical or mental suffering. But it was only through the creation of the Commission . . . that it became possible for the churches and missionary bodies to deal with these situations in a continuous manner and through men and women who had gained specific competence and experience . . . with the intricacies of international affairs.[38]

The "Statement on Disarmament and Peaceful Change" adopted by the Central Committee of the World Council of Churches at Davos-Platz in 1955 embodied substantially the thinking of the Commission of the Churches on International Affairs on the relation and solution of these two problems:

> The Commission . . . has consistently advanced the thesis that both moral and political factors must be taken into consideration, as well as the mathe-

[37] The Commission was founded in August, 1946.
[38] *The Ecumenical Review,* Vol. VIII, No. 4, July, 1956, p. 362.

matical and mechanical approach to the reduction of armaments. These factors apply to two indispensable and complementary processes:
(1) The process whereby all armaments will be progressively reduced under adequate international inspection and control; and
(2) The process of developing and securing international acceptance of methods for peaceful settlement and change to rectify existing injustices. . . .

Progress in "these complementary approaches" was dependent upon mutual confidence, and the Commission—and likewise the Central Committee—was "encouraged by the willingness of representatives of government to talk together." They urged that "such exchanges be continued."

Conversations, however, whether of diplomats or heads of governments, often did not lead to more confidence. According to Dr. Nolde, Director of the Commission, at St. Andrews five years later, "mutual trust" was less in evidence than at any time in recent years:[39]

True international community is wanting in today's world. The international situation, as reflected in the attitudes and acts of national leaders, is more dangerous . . . than at any time . . . perhaps since the end of the Korean War. . . . It is not fundamentally different from that which existed prior to the Berlin crisis and the exchange of visits by the heads of governments. . . . Relations between the major communist powers and the Western powers stand at a low ebb. . . . Improvement . . . will require greater readiness for conciliation by both sides than has recently been manifested. . . . In this tense atmosphere, the possibility of further deterioration or of miscalculation places mankind in a precarious position which can be ignored only at grave risk.

In a report to the Central Committee at Galyatetö in 1956, the Director had said:

Without minimising the importance of discussion on disarmaments held in various organs of the United Nations, it must be admitted that little, if any, progress has been made. . . . In face of seemingly insuperable difficulties . . . the churches should continue to press for a system of disarmament which will safeguard equally the security of all nations.

The efforts of four intervening years appeared now to have been of no avail.

Concerning nuclear energy, "the prospect of benefits which could come to mankind from its discovery" was dimmed by the "fear that its military use might lead to catastrophic destruction." The responsibility of all men was "to see to it that this power should be used solely for . . . constructive purposes."

"We, therefore, welcome the expressed desire of the United Nations General Assembly 'to promote energetically the use of atomic energy to . . . serve only the peaceful pursuits of mankind. . . .'"

[39] Minutes of the Central Committee, St. Andrews, 1960, p. 147 ff.

The resolution adopted supported the proposal to establish within the framework of the United Nations an International Atomic Energy Agency and commended the decision to convene the International Conference on Peaceful Uses of Atomic Energy "to study the development of atomic power and consider other technical areas—such as biology, medicine, radiation, protection and fundamental science—in which international co-operation might most effectively be accomplished."

Urged also was "an unwavering effort to devise and put into effect, under adequate inspection and control, a system for the elimination and prohibition of atomic, hydrogen and all other weapons of mass destruction, as well as the reduction of all armaments to a minimum."

The statement cautioned, at the same time, "against oversimplified formulas . . . advanced merely to secure propaganda advantage or superficial agreements," reliance on which "could subsequently expose an unprepared world to greater danger."

The two especially urgent tasks remained: (1) to devise a system of inspection and control; (2) to find a starting point for the reduction of armaments.

As for the first, "the establishment by the United Nations of an international commission of scientists and technicians to identify the essential requirements for an adequate system" was recommended, the members of the commission to be selected from a panel named by their governments but to serve in their individual capacity.

A successful disarmament plan, as previously stated, called for removal of "the occasion or purported justification for military action." So far as possible, "injustices should be prevented from arising, and, if they do occur, measures should be taken promptly to rectify them. . . . Every effort should be made to reach agreement on necessary changes by peaceful means—accurate analysis, negotiation, arbitration and the like. . . ."

The menace of nuclear energy seemed to grow with every year, and the Commission of the Churches on International Affairs appealed for a halting of the testing of atomic weapons. "The people of the world have been visited by a new fear," said its Executive Committee in a statement which was adopted by the Central Committee of the World Council at New Haven in 1957. "They are moved, indeed deeply alarmed, by current tests. . . . These to them appear to be a portent or shadow of world conflict."

But fear alone was no sufficient basis for the pursuit of moral ends, it was agreed. "We must point out that this world-wide concern . . . has deeper roots. Tests are taken to be a visible sign of preparation for atomic warfare. . . . The main concern must always be the prevention of war itself, for the evil of war is an offence to the spiritual nature of man. But since any war carries increasing danger of becoming an atomic war, which shocks the conscience of mankind with a peculiar repugnance, this task becomes all the more imperative."

Once again, the Commission, supported by the Central Committee, proposed steps for overcoming the menace of atomic war, among them the following:[40]

Stop by international agreement the testing of nuclear weapons.

Bring to a halt the production of nuclear weapons, under such controls as will most fully ensure compliance.

Develop measures which will reduce national armaments, nuclear and conventional, with provision for necessary safeguards as such measures are progressively taken.

Accelerate international co-operation in the development of atomic power for peaceful purposes, under proper safeguards.

Establish more effective mechanisms for peaceful settlement of international disputes and for peaceful change.

"It is important to stress all these objectives in their interrelationship," said the Commission. "Yet simultaneous progress toward all of them seems improbable, until there is a much greater degree of international confidence. Is it safe to advance toward one or more, without the others? Choices will have to be made, and they are hard choices. Any decision involves risks. But to make no decision may be even more dangerous."

The Commission thought that, for the sake of peace, there was a risk Christians, especially in countries projecting tests of nuclear weapons, were justified in advocating, in the hope of breaking through barriers of distrust. They could urge their governments to declare "their resolve to forego tests for a trial period, in the hope that others would do the same, a new confidence would be born and foundations laid for reliable agreements."

Recognizing the potential hazard to health in the fallout of nuclear explosions, the Commission had formed a Medical Consultative Group to keep it supplied with accurate data for its recommendations, from time to time, concerning this phase of the problem. It was expected that this body would be able to establish a working relationship with the United Nations World Health Organization.

During the period of voluntary moratorium on nuclear weapons testing by some of the nations, the Central Committee, at its meeting in Rhodes in the summer of 1959, urged these powers not to resume tests unilaterally, but to allow statesmen to achieve agreements, and so to keep the international situation from deteriorating. A treaty to cease all tests—atmospheric, space, and underground—should be sought, it said, not least for the fact that it would represent a beginning of specific controls, which might lead to measures of disarmament verified by interna-

[40] Minutes of the Central Committee, New Haven, 1957, p. 114.

tional inspection and control. At the least, it would help eliminate dreaded risks to health. Said the Central Committee and the Commission: "We affirm that no nation is justified in deciding on its own responsibility to conduct nuclear weapons tests when the people of other nations, who have not given their consent, may have to bear the consequences. . . . We call upon each nation contemplating tests to give full recognition to this moral responsibility, as well as to considerations of national defense and international security." [41]

The modern world had suddenly become a neighborhood but not in any recognizable sense a community. The nations had in common only the desire to profit by the development of nuclear energy for peaceful uses and the fear lest this new power might become their annihilation. These were emotions more likely to set them against one another than to draw them together. There was no general acceptance of moral principles as a basis of approach to peaceable relations—indeed, no agreement as to what constituted morality. The Commission of the Churches on International Affairs, working and hoping for a responsible society and seeing the progressive deterioration of international relations, could only turn its thoughts to what the churches might do through their social ministry to help create an ethos under the influence of which all peoples would come to see their rights qualified by their duty to one another, and so be drawn to act in concert, even at sacrifice, to secure the greatest good of all.

Sir Kenneth Grubb described to the Central Committee at Davos-Platz in 1955 "a long-range study on the Christian approach to an international ethos," which had been organized by the Commission of the Churches on International Affairs. "The first outline of the study to be undertaken" was not prepared, however, until the following year, after a consultation with the Executive Committee of the World Council at Galyatetö. In *The Ecumenical Review* (July, 1956) John Foster Dulles wrote hopefully:

> The determination of policy in relation to international problems and the appraisal of risks which are inevitably involved can be left neither to caprice nor expediency. International policies must, on the one hand, be dependably embraced by the people of a country, and, on the other hand, reflect through responsible consultation a decent respect for the opinions of mankind. It would seem that only principles which conform to moral law meet that specification. . . .
>
> In this connection, religious agencies such as the Commission of the Churches on International Affairs have a vital part to play. . . . Its current study of an international ethos will seek to identify the common foundation of moral principles upon which genuine world community must be based.
>
> I am confident that, if the religious resources throughout the world are

[41] *Ibid*. Rhodes, 1959, p. 43.

effectively utilized, the dynamic action which is an indispensable requisite for a creative peace will be assured.

The procedure to be followed, which gave some intimation of the difficulties likely to be encountered and of the time to be required, was explained at greater length by Sir Kenneth at Galyatetö in a paper on "The Churches and the Building of a Responsible International Society":

We must take into our purview the whole range of motives, of instincts, of ambitions and of backgrounds that make international life either possible or impossible. This is the significance of the studies which have recently been authorized under the general heading of "Toward an International Ethos."

In the first instance, it is necessary for Christians themselves to clear their minds about what they mean by such an approach. They must examine the reasons which in all ages have led men to prefer some measure of order to disorder, and peace with truth to the ravages of war. They must look carefully at the assumptions which have bound Christian nations together even through times of war, and have enabled them to live together afterwards. They must review the approaches made by the great jurists of the Christian tradition, not least in times of decline of popular faith, to the need for an international system of law. . . .

Christians . . . are . . a very small minority among the peoples of our crowded planet. Thus, there must come a stage when we must share our own formulations with men of other faiths and of none, with those who do not even admit the dignity of man and the inalienable demands of his being as an individual and person, an end in himself.

This may be difficult. Yet, there are many who reject the absolutism of the State as the sole monopolist of power, or the uncertain tyranny of a law which is the mere command of the sovereign and who are searching for a true moral ground and sanction. We may indeed find that the State is true to its real nature today to the extent to which it directs its energies to the recovery and maintenance of international law. Yet that this will involve the further abridgment of national sovereignty and the emphasis on interdependence, rather than independence, is an almost certain consequence.

It is along such lines . . . that one can foresee the development of the churches' thought and work for a responsible international society. Any more limited goal fails to match up to the real demands of an atomic age which has rendered national boundaries largely irrelevant. On the other hand, excited advocacy of world government now ignores some of the deepest of men's fears and cleavages which cannot be readily overcome. . . .

We must continue to work at successive concrete issues as they constantly arise. We must remember that principles can only make the substance of policy when they have been tested in action. Whether in the church or in the secular order, we have to work with existing institutions and transform them.

It was clear and understandable that those who had borne longest the burdens of the Commission in its work for better human relations thought that the evolution of an international ethos giving to the quest for peace the dynamic of a moral unity might perforce have to proceed at a pace dooming it to failure. The time required might prove longer than the patience of men. Talking about the achievement of a Christian ethos was too much like looking for the coming of the kingdom of God. "The reach should exceed the grasp," or heaven's inspiration would be lost to the human struggle; but the minds of practical leaders turned to immediate, more mundane things. Said Dr. O. Frederick Nolde at St. Andrews in 1960:[42]

> A positive approach to international problems requires that all leaders of governments accept essential rules of behavior in negotiation. An international ethos is a fundamental prerequisite, but, since no adequate ethos has yet been achieved, effort should be made to win acceptance of a limited number of elementary but basic rules of conduct.

This, the consensus was, "might help to bring more decency in international diplomacy and parlance," and so to create an atmosphere more favorable to successful discussion and negotiation. Learning to live with certain problems was, suggested Bishop Lilje, "an aspect of the Christian ethos."

Baron F. M. van Asbeck, President of the Commission since its foundation in 1946, resigned at Evanston. Sir Kenneth G. Grubb served as Chairman and Professor O. Frederick Nolde as Director during the succeeding period. Dr. Richard M. Fagley had, as Executive Secretary, responsibility particularly in matters relating to Christian interests in the areas of economic and social developments, including special studies in demography, and Dr. Elfan Rees continued his supervision of the Commission's activities on behalf of refugees when they involved intergovernmental collaboration. Rev. Dominique Micheli was assistant to the Director at the United Nations in New York. Professor Werner Kägi and Dr. J. Leimena served the Commission as vice-chairmen; and the treasurers in New York and London, respectively, were Rodman W. Parvin and W. Douglas Menzies. Rev. E. Philip Eastman was the London secretary.

As organ of both the World Council of Churches and the International Missionary Council, the Commission would have to readjust its structure upon the merging of these bodies. Accordingly, a suggested revision of its constitution was accepted by the Central Committee at St. Andrews for presentation at New Delhi with the resolution for effecting the proposed union. Under it the Commission would continue, without major changes of functions, as a "specialized agency of the World Council of Churches with a mandate to express the convictions of the . . . Council . . . and the churches in the realm of international affairs."

Because of its specific functions, the Commission would have a special status and be directly related to the General Secretariat. It would have "the power to act and speak within its field of work, subject to the provisions of the Regulations of the Commission . . . and provided

[42] Minutes of the Central Committee, St. Andrews, 1960, p. 147.

that when questions arise on which the governing bodies of the World Council of Churches have not specifically expressed themselves, it consults with the officers of the World Council of Churches."[43]

When the Commission speaks, it indicates clearly whether it speaks in its own name or in the name of the World Council of Churches, or on behalf of one or more of the member churches at their request.

In its . . . field of work, the Commission . . . serves the interests of all divisions of the World Council of Churches. In view of both the historical and functional relationships, it entertains special relations with the Division of World Mission and Evangelism. There is also a close link with the Division of Inter-Church Aid and Service to Refugees.

These relationships find their expression in cross-representation at the committee level, co-operation at the staff level, and financial support of the Commission . . . from the divisions concerned.

The Commission would have, as previously, its own budget and would administer it.

August 6, 1956, was the tenth birthday of the Commission. It had been organized on the first anniversary of the bombing of Hiroshima, "to prevent, if possible, any such thing ever happening again."

"If the world today is somewhat saner, a little more responsible, a bit more humane than the reeling, spiritually nauseated world of 1946," editorialized *The Christian Century* (August 8, 1956), "some of the credit should go to this small but highly specialized agency of the churches. Its largely unheralded ministry of reconciliation in the United Nations and in other places where the relations between nations are determined could give an effective answer to those who charge Protestant and Orthodox Christianity with being irrelevant to the fateful issues of our time."

The World Council of Churches took special note of the occasion by devoting *The Ecumenical Review* for July, 1956, to articles by distinguished churchmen on various aspects of the Christian responsibility for a peaceful and just international order.

"The best way to celebrate the tenth anniversary of the Commission. . . . ," wrote the General Secretary and Editor, Dr. W. A. Visser 't Hooft, and General Secretary Charles W. Ranson of the International Missionary Council in a joint introduction, "is certainly not to concentrate attention on the Commission itself, but rather to emphasize again the decisive importance of the concerns which brought it into being, and which it seeks to represent in relation to churches and governments." However, they thought "the fact that so many men and women in responsible positions in the international world had contributed articles showed that the Commission had come to play a significant role in world affairs."

[43] *Ibid.* St. Andrews, 1960. Revised C.C.I.A. Constitution, p. 162 ff.

Among those contributing were John Foster Dulles, Secretary of State of the United States, who had presided at the Cambridge Conference which organized the Commission; Dag Hammarskjöld, Secretary General of the United Nations; Ralph Bunche, Under-Secretary of the United Nations; Max Huber, former President of the Permanent Court of International Justice; Charles Malik, erstwhile Ambassador of Lebanon to the United States and presently Chairman of the United Nations Commission on Human Rights; Asuncion A. Perez, former Administrator of Social Welfare of the Philippine Republic; Philippe de Seynes, Under-Secretary for Economic and Social Affairs in the United Nations; Arnold J. Toynbee, ex-Director of Studies of the Royal Institute of International Affairs (London) and historian; Baron F. M. van Asbeck of Leyden University, President of the Commission of the Churches on International Affairs from its founding; G. J. van Heuven Goedhart, United Nations High Commissioner for Refugees; Kenneth Scott Latourette, Sterling Professor of Missions and Oriental History, Emeritus, Yale University; Luther A. Weigle, Dean Emeritus, Yale Divinity School, and Chairman of the World Council of Christian Education and Sunday School Associations; H. F. E. Whitlam, Representative of Australia on the United Nations Commission on Human Rights; David Owen, Executive Chairman of the Technical Assistance Board of the United Nations; R. A. Butler, Lord Privy Seal and Leader of the House of Commons, Great Britain; Eric Fletcher, Member of Parliament, Great Britain; Eugen Gerstenmeier, President of the German Bundestag; and Johannes Leimena, Member of the Indonesian Parliament and Chairman of Parkindo.

The titles of some of the papers suggested the breadth of the Commission's purview:

Ecumenical Resources in Solving International Problems
Social Problems and International Responsibility
New Relations in a New World
Religious Liberty: Recent Phases of the Problem
World Community in Historical Perspective
Peaceful Uses of Atomic Energy
Problems of Economic and Social Development in Asia
Christian Unity in Divided Europe
International Law and International Ethos
Christian Approach to International Affairs
Historical Background for Ecumenical Co-operation in International Affairs
World Health and World Community
Positive Christianity and Communism
The Student Christian Community and Peace
The Place of Smaller Countries in the Community of Nations
The Need for a Philosophy of the United Nations
International Law and International Institutions
Race Tensions: Is a New Approach Possible?

Christian Education and International Affairs
The South Pacific: Meeting Place of the Nations

Dr. Toynbee wrote of "The Role of the British Commonwealth:" "The crucial event in the history of the evolution of the British Commonwealth has been the grant, in 1947," he said, "of full dominion status including freedom to secede from the Commonwealth, to four Asian countries—India, Pakistan, Ceylon and Burma. . . . These four countries contain about one-sixth of the total population of the world. A revolutionary change in their status is . . . bound to affect, not only Asia and not only the Commonwealth, but the world . . . with consequences . . . irreversible."

The United Kingdom's action "made it certain that all subject peoples in Asia and Africa would win the same status in the near future. It has been won already by Indonesia, Viet Nam, Laos, Cambodia, Libya, Tunisia, Morocco, French West Africa, the Gold Coast, Nigeria, the Sudan. It can hardly be long delayed in Algeria and Cyprus. What is going to happen in Kenya, British Central Africa, and South Africa we do not know, but it would be surprising if a European minority were still dominant in any African country fifty years from now."

One lesson of what has happened in Asia and Africa, he said, is "that the timing of the granting of self-government is all-important."

A second lesson is "that a moderate delay . . . will be beneficial to the people . . . being emancipated, if the emancipating power . . . makes use of the time for training its former subjects to govern themselves."

Another lesson is "that it is impolitic and disagreeable, as well as immoral, to try to hold unwilling subjects by force."

The British Commonwealth's role is to establish and maintain friendship, on a footing of psychological as well as juridical equality, between peoples of Western and non-Western civilizations.

Compulsorily, if not voluntarily, the peoples of Western origin are going to take, once more, their normal position in the world—a position of equality with the rest of mankind, and not one of dominance. The existence of the British Commonwealth, as a fraternity in which Western and non-Western peoples can live together on equal footing, may help to bring about the world's return to normality peacefully, and not at the cost of a further series of tragedies and catastrophes.

Mr. Hammarskjöld repeated, in substance, his message to the Evanston Assembly:

For the Christian faith, "the cross is that place at the center of the world's history . . . where all men and all nations, without exception, stand revealed as enemies of God . . . and yet where all men stand revealed as beloved of God, precious in God's sight." (I quote from the Report on the Main Theme of the Evanston Assembly.) So understood, the Cross, although it is the unique fact on which the Christian churches base their hope, should not separate those of Christian faith from others, but should be instead that element in their lives which enables them to stretch out their hands to peoples of other creeds in the feeling of universal brotherhood which we hope one day to see reflected in a world of nations truly united.

The statement of Mr. Dulles revealed a sensitive understanding of human needs and desires the world over and the burden of statesmen to whom fall decisions which may mean their fulfillment or disappointment:

Positive measures to promote peace must be responsive to the basic needs and desires of people as they pursue their lives within their respective countries. . . . People want simple things . . . the opportunity to worship and serve God in accordance with the dictates of their conscience . . . to think in accordance with the dictates of their reason . . . to exchange views with others and to persuade or be persuaded by what appeals to their reason and . . . conscience. They want the right to live in their homes without fear . . . the opportunity to draw together in the intimacy of family life, of community life, and to establish worthy and honorable traditions, which they can pass on to their children and their children's children . . . to be able to work productively and creatively in . . . tasks of their own choosing, and to enjoy the fruits of their labors. They want government based on consent.

In relations between the peoples and nations of the world, peace must be founded upon independence, not domination; freedom, not servitude; diversity, not conformity.

Acceptance of these facts would create between nations a solid basis for fellowship, and enable the peoples of the world, as mutual friends and helpers, to pursue hopefully the destiny which they share in common. . . .

New powers at man's disposal have infinitely heightened [war's] destructive potentialities. . . . War, more than ever, involves compulsory enmity, outrages against the human personality, cruelty, vengefulness, and wanton distortions of truth. Today, throughout the world, there is a rising demand for protection against the misery, the agony of body and spirit, the massive destruction of life and property which modern man wreaks upon man.

While modern developments have made war more terrible, we should remember that they have made the consequences of retreat and surrender more terrible. Modern war could destroy much of the life on this planet. But it also may be possible that craven purchase of peace at the expense of principle can result in destroying much of the human spirit on this planet. Peace bought at this price could lead to a degradation of the human race and to subjecting human beings to a form of mental decay which obliterates the capacity for moral and intellectual judgment.

In many international situations, fundamental human values are threatened and good . . . relations are in jeopardy. Men thus frequently face a serious dilemma in choosing between action to preserve peace and action to defend values which will make peace worthwhile. The effort to resolve this dilemma calls for perception and courage in taking calculated risks.

There is a risk in seeking to convince a potential aggressor that his contemplated act . . . will not pay. But the failure to register such a clear warning . . . may be an inducement to those . . . bent upon aggression.

There is a risk in extensive economic assistance to countries whose governments are unstable or whose society does not conform to our own views.

But it is a betrayal of responsibility to withhold the help that is needed and merited, or to hem it in with such conditions as will make it unacceptable or repulsive.

There is a risk that a freer exchange of persons will be used for propaganda purposes, but if that risk is not taken, we shall seem to lack confidence in the strength of our own heritage and lose the opportunity for its effective impact. . . .

So, not only the basic faith of a people, but also enlightened self-interest combine to urge that moral principle be a guide, not merely to individual conduct, but also to the conduct of nations.

Writing of the Commission itself, Dr. Richard M. Fagley said:

The continuous process of consultation initiated at Cambridge in 1946 is one of the distinctive values in the current ecumenical approach to international affairs. The continuity of day-to-day work centering in the Commission . . . has cumulative benefits. The persistent pursuit of selected issues enables church representatives to acquire some technical competence on particular problems, and to gain sufficient background and contacts to help identify the time, place and form for relevant and effective Christian witness. Influence in intergovernmental bodies grows, as a reputation for responsible action accumulates.

Three-fourths of the Commissioners . . . are lay men or women. The emphasis on the lay expert reflects the desire for authentic information, a certain distrust of theories not related to hard facts of international life, and a concern for effective channels of communication to governments. . . .

The Commission's operations have been of modest proportions, limited both by small resources and by a cautious approach. Beginning with work on religious liberty and related rights, the scope of operations has been enlarged slowly, and step by step. Only a small fraction of the churches' concerns in international affairs are as yet reflected in the work. This selective and modest approach has values, in that in a new venture of this type it is important to build soundly. Also, the object is not a powerful ecclesiastical "lobby" but a procedure for presenting timely witness, the influence of which depends principally upon the merits of its insights. . . .

To act, even prudently, on the tangled problems of world economics and politics means to run risks of error and mischance. The Commission and its parent bodies have not yet had to face the test of adversities which such risks can impose. Then it will be seen how substantial is the base of this enterprise. The mandate of the Christian witness is that we be faithful and obedient, even in the jungle of international affairs. We must strive to act responsibly, knowing that ultimately the event is in the hands of God. . . .

Professor Latourette sketched the background of ecumenical cooperation in international affairs, which "would go back, at least, to the Truce of God and the Peace of God initiated in the ninth and tenth centuries and repeatedly given the endorsement of synods and councils of the Catholic Church—then the sole ecumenical body in Western Europe . . . and include the pioneer efforts by the Basque Dominican, Francisco de Vitoria, and the Dutch Protestant, Hugo Grotius, to formulate a body of law to govern the relations between the nation states which were emerging in the sixteenth and seventeenth centuries, and also the projects of Emeric Cruce, the Roman Catholic monk, and William Penn, the Quaker, for international organization to promote peace."

"A spate of peace societies begun by Christians under the stimulus of the Wars of Napoleon . . . flourished throughout the nineteenth century," toward the end of which "efforts to arouse the churches to prayer and common action for peace" resulted in the formation of the Christian Union for Promoting International Concord.

With the turn into the twentieth century was organized the Associated Councils of Churches in the British and German Empires for Fostering Friendly Relations between the Two Peoples (1910), the Federal Council of the Churches of Christ in America (1908), the Church Peace Union and the World Alliance for Promoting International Friendship through the Churches (1914).

During World War I the Neutral Church Conference, initiated by Nathan Söderblom, was added to the lengthening list of peace efforts. It was followed, after the Armistice, by the Universal Christian Conference on Life and Work, the Conference on Christian Politics, Economics and Citizenship (in Britain); the Conference on Church, Community and State (1937), the Department of International Justice and Goodwill of the Federal Council of the Churches of Christ in America, the Commission on a Just and Durable Peace (in the United States), the Commission of Churches for International Friendship and Social Responsibility (in Britain), and the World Council of Churches.

To some of the members of these commissions it seemed . . . obvious that as soon as the cessation of hostilities made it possible, the scope of their efforts should be broadened to enlist the collaboration of churches the world around.

Since, particularly in North America, where the Foreign Missions Conference had shared with the Federal Council of Churches in the Department of International Justice and Goodwill, the missionary interests had become deeply involved, it was through a group representing both the World Council of Churches and the International Missionary Council that the Commission of the Churches on International Affairs was inaugurated.

In receiving from the Commission at St. Andrews a paper on "Some Aspects of the Current International Situation," the Central Committee took note of a reference to the People's Republic of China, to the effect that any conventions relating to disarmament and the testing of nuclear weapons could be effective only if that nation were in a position to cooperate in their formulation and implementation, and requested the Commission "to continue the study and to help in the creation of conditions which [would] permit the six hundred fifty million people of China to share in the benefits and accept the responsibilities common to all members of the international community."

This action envisaged, of course, the eventual admission of the People's Republic of China to membership in the United Nations.

In the discussion, the recommendation of the Cleveland Study Conference[44] that Red China be recognized by the other nations and received into the United Nations was mentioned with approval, and Chairman Grubb of the Commission said that "the China-United Nations issue . . . was kept constantly on the agenda."

Explaining that there had not been "sufficient consensus" to permit a "representative statement," Director Nolde said the committee of reference had nevertheless concluded that the Central Committee could properly make a statement of principle, without presuming to attempt a solution of political aspects of the problem. To avoid misunderstanding of the "motivation and intent," he offered some observations, as follows:[45]

> The statement recognizes as artificial and dangerous a situation where six hundred fifty million people are isolated from the rest of the world. The danger increases, the longer the artificiality persists.
>
> No adequate treaty on disarmament or the cessation of nuclear weapons testing is possible, unless the government in effective power on the mainland of China is party thereto.
>
> The statement implies that other governments should have diplomatic dealings with the government in effective power, and does not imply that such dealings place upon that government a stamp of approval.
>
> The people of China should be in a position to share in the benefits and accept the responsibilities common to all members of the international community. Both benefits and responsibilities should be stressed as important.
>
> The situation in Thibet, the border dispute with India, the ideological conflict between Moscow and Peking about the desirability or inevitability of world war—these and other factors suggest the existence of conditions which militate against an immediate solution of the China problem.
>
> Nevertheless, if the Central Committee at this time urges action which would be helpful in the creation of conditions favorable to the responsible participation of China in the international community, it will not only underscore the goal to be sought, but will also voice a sense of urgency in encouraging measures to speed its achievement.

While the People's Republic of China had not expressed a desire, so far as anyone knew, to join the United Nations, it was quite in keeping with the policy of the World Council of Churches to encourage it to do so and to bespeak for it a friendly reception.

The state of mind which had been forming in the churches on this issue was of much significance, whether considered from the standpoint of those approving or of those opposing the World Council's position.

[44] Under the auspices of the National Council of the Churches of Christ in the United States of America (1958).

[45] Minutes of the Central Committee, St. Andrews, 1960, p. 86.

The World Council was inviting participation in its work by the churches of communist countries, on the conditions that it identified itself with no political philosophy and reserved the right to criticize any and all governments. The conflicts to which this mixing of ideologies had led accounted for the withdrawal of the Chinese churches from active cooperation with the World Council and they were likely to flare up at any time in the Central Committee.

After listening to the paper on "Some Aspects of the Current International Situation," members from behind the Iron Curtain spoke of the Christian Peace Conference of Prague in 1958 as a proper and effective way of supporting the World Council's efforts on behalf of conciliation and understanding, and expressed regret that more of the "member denominations" had not taken part in it. The limitations of the Prague Conferences because of communist influences had been such, in the opinion of the Commission of the Churches on International Affairs, that Sir Kenneth Grubb was moved to say, in reply to the supporters from Czechoslovakia, that it was necessary to promote the kind of Christian consultations—for example, Arnoldshain—that crossed the boundaries between blocs and nations and gave a broader perspective and a surer lead.

The movement of Christian minds toward the proposal of seeking communist collaboration had even more serious possible consequences for the United Nations; or so many friends of that body had come to think. It was already in the way of becoming, it seemed, an exhibit of the disastrous effects of the idea that peace would come of discussion. Yet, many idealists, whose trust was in conferences, consultations, conversations, colloquiums had not learned that by so much as talk increased were words discounted; that the actual problem was not communication, of which so much was heard, but the will of some nations, for whatever reason, not to understand.

The United Nations already had in its membership the Union of Soviet Socialist Republics and its satellite powers which disregarded at will the provisions of its charter. What could the addition of their ally, the People's Republic of China, do but profane further the temple dedicated to the honest search for the ways of peace? The need was a cleansing, a moratorium on talking, the banishment into moral isolation of those nations which deliberately and consistently violated their pledged word. Such concerns of forthrightness and courage should have taken precedence, it might have been expected, in the councils of the Church over fear of nuclear bombs. Was not death to be dreaded less than craven resignation to inner chaos and the consequent intellectual and moral deterioration?

The staff members and others associated with them gained through the activities of the Commission considerable experience in the ways of diplomacy and a degree of competence in international politics, all which could be of practical worth to the ecumenical movement.

However, opinion divided on what proper use might be made of these acquisitions. Some persons hoped that the knowledge and experience which had been gained might teach the World Council and its organizations to keep clear in the future of such complicated political problems as it and the Commission had more than once tackled. A good many friends of the ecumenical movement inclined to the view expressed by John Foster Dulles at the First Assembly (1948): that "the churches ought not to make authoritative pronouncements in respect to detailed action in political, economic and social fields." "Those who act in the political sphere," he had said, "must deal with the possible," and for this reason the churches "should exercise great caution in dealing with international political matters. . . . They should not seem to put the seal of God's approval upon that which, at best, may be expedient, but which cannot wholly reflect God's will."

On the other hand, it is quite certain that a majority of those exercising the authority of the World Council through its Central Committee and the Commission of the Churches on International Affairs had different thoughts. Many of them represented state churches, and some held seats in parliaments. They were accustomed to action by the clergy in politics. The late Bishop of Chichester, Dr. G. K. A. Bell, a foremost spokesman of the World Council and one of its best interpreters, illustrated the easy naturalness which characterized the appearance of churchmen of the establishments at ecumenical gatherings to discuss and move actions in respect of social, economic, and political matters. Many statements submitted—and, for the most part, drafted—by him could have been adaptations of speeches in the House of Lords.

In countries where disestablishment had taken place, governmental collaboration in various degrees and ways continued, under which the churches had a recognized stake, and generally some voice, in politics.

This was the case even in totalitarian nations, the governments exercising the authority, however, of telling the churches on what issues they should be heard and what they should and should not say.

For representatives from churches with such backgrounds, pronouncements and other actions by the World Council on social and political questions bore no suggestion of innovation or disconsonance.

Moreover, many liberal ecumenical leaders who came out of the Christian social-action movement in the so-called free churches had relaxed their position on the principle of state-church separation to the degree of accepting the necessity of the Church's making its voice heard and its influence felt in Socio-political matters affecting the everyday life of the people. This had to be, they decided, if religion was to have any real relevance. They were willing collaborators with their colleagues who from long tradition thought in terms of ecclesiastical procedures under an establishment or an authoritarian government. From their ranks, in fact, came some of the most vigorous leaders in the World Council's program of social action.

The Scriptures were interpreted as giving plausible support to this policy. While there was not complete agreement on what the Bible taught, there was a near consensus that Jesus had the answers to the world's problem and that Christian social action represented a substantially faithful application of his precepts and principles.

The theological rationalization could be said to have rested, in a very general way, on the doctrine of the lordship of Christ. On this point the reasoning was, broadly, that in virtue of his victory on the cross Christ was Lord of all life—individual and corporate. All power had been given to him. The Church, consisting of those who acknowledged his lordship in their own lives, was under mandate to declare him Lord and to work to make his authority actual in society, against his coming at the end of history to consummate his triumph. The Church had been sent to pursue its mission boldly and confidently. The program was a militant one borrowing spirit from the victorious kingdom which was already appearing with extensive manifestations and would yet come in fullness.

There were influences stronger than theology and the ever-present temptation to avoid inciting division and incurring criticism that acted to persuade many to accept the ecumenical social policy who had doubts about it. Finding themselves in a situation in which it was impossible to be certain of the will of God, and feeling themselves to be a minority, they decided to follow the judgment of the apparent majority, who acted with an air of confidence, and watch results for an eventual clearer revelation. The complexion of events grew from year to year more disturbing, until responsible statesmen talked freely of the possibility of self-annihilation by mankind. If the condition of the patient was so hopeless and all remedies had failed, there could hardly be justifiable objection to trying other measures in which many believed—or at least hoped. If they proved ineffective, the predicament would not be worse.

Remarked one delegate, after a certain meeting in which a proposal of action by an important ecumenical body in an international crisis had been debated and approved: "The decision was of no great matter really, whichever way it went. Only the instinct of self-preservation anyway can save men from destruction they are feverishly preparing for one another; and what we have said here or left unsaid, and the way we have voted, will weigh not at all in the balance, when dictators ponder their chance of killing each other without being killed, or some idiot plays with the impulse to set the world on fire by triggering a bomb."

There were friends of the ecumenical cause who viewed the actions of the World Council of Churches and its organizations with more appreciation of their potential instrumentality for help or hurt and were more uneasy when they found themselves at variance with them.

As for the Commission of the Churches on International Affairs, these hesitant members would, almost without exception perhaps, have praised the ability and sincerity of its officers and staff and recognized the good they had accomplished in numerous and difficult assignments taking them into many troubled parts of the earth. But, because of its structural nature, its rules and regulations, its policy and methods, and the probable over-all effects of its operations on the functioning of the organs of both governments and churches responsible in their respective ways for international peace, the Commission appeared to them, not only unlikely to fulfill the hopes placed in it, but in danger actually of becoming a hindrance to their realization.

Called "the Commission of the Churches," it could hardly be said to have been created by the churches; nor was it ever to develop any close bond with them. Structurally, it was a step further removed from them than were the International Missionary Council and the World Council of Churches, which sponsored and had a certain measure of authority over it. Yet it had "the power to speak and act within its field of work . . . provided that when questions [arose] on which the governing bodies of the World Council . . . [had] not specifically expressed themselves, it [consulted] with the officers of the . . . Council," and that "it [indicated] clearly whether it [spoke and acted] in its own name, or in the name of the World Council . . . , or on behalf of one or more of the member churches, at their request."

It was essentially a self-perpetuating body, having the right to nominate candidates for membership and to approve or disapprove names proposed through the two Councils or other ecumenical bodies designated by them.

Its function was avowedly political. "The question is sometimes raised whether . . . the churches and missionary bodies have now 'gone into politics,' " wrote Drs. Visser 't Hooft and Ranson in the anniversary number of *The Ecumenical Review* previously quoted:[46]

> The answer is that in a certain sense this is certainly the case. The ecumenical movement has always believed that the lordship of Christ embraces all the realms of life, and that the Church of Christ is called to serve as "watchman" giving warning to the nations. But that does not mean that the Commission . . . is "in politics" for political ends. On the contrary, its purpose is, according to its charter, to formulate the bearing of Christian conviction and Christian principles upon immediate issues. It does not represent any particular interest or power. It is not a "lobby" representing the interests of churches and missions affiliated in its parent-bodies. It seeks

[46] Vol. III, No. 4, July 1956, p. 362.

simply to throw the light of the common Christian convictions held by the membership of its parent-bodies upon the concrete problems of international life.[47]

In discharging its function in this respect the Commission was looked upon as sometimes giving added justification for Mr. Dulles' warning: "The churches should exercise great caution in dealing with international political matters. . . . They should not seem to put the seal of God's approval upon that which, at best, may be expedient, but which cannot wholly reflect God's will." Red China had not the moral qualifications for membership in the United Nations. The proposal that it be recognized by other nations and admitted to the United Nations rested on expediency. In no other way could there be, it was felt, control of nuclear weapons or disarmament. Many churchmen were apparently convinced that God would approve as moral the necessary actions to gain these ends.

The Commission worked with and through governmental and intergovernmental agencies, so far as it could, centering its efforts in the United Nations and its various organizations. If this was a legitimate strategy for the churches, it raised many practical questions. What would its effect be on the program of the United Nations, an international body consisting of representatives of many governments having close ties with non-Christian faiths and of others hostile to all religions? The Commission was uncomfortably aware of being regarded as a pro-Western agency and sought to establish a working relationship with the East Asia Christian Conference, partly to refute this criticism. With the churches working to win converts in Hindu, Buddhist, Muslim, and communist countries, and the World Council claiming the right, while extending its membership into these areas, to pass judgment on their governments and rulers, would not a Commission of the Churches on International Affairs, with even the most tenuous tangential relations, be a handicap to the United Nations? The frequent intimations that officials of the Commission at the United Nations headquarters had been able to act influentially on behalf of causes in which the churches were especially interested helped, some believed, neither the United Nations nor the churches. The Commission, by all reports, gave eloquent and effective support through its agents to the Declaration of Human Rights and to measures relating to religious liberty, not only in the United Nations itself, but in governmental councils where their local implementation was the issue; but some who rejoiced in the advancement of these humane aims thought that they could have been aided in other ways, to the advantage of both the churches and the United Nations.

Organized to advise the World Council of Churches and the Inter-

[47] The Commission spoke on such situations as those arising in Cyprus, Suez, and South Africa, which involved actions of governments.

national Missionary Council on international affairs, the Commission, with them, was frequently brought to face situations requiring quick action, in which decisions on the course to be taken became the responsibility of a few accessible officials. It could only have followed that what many regarded as unwise judgments were sometimes reached. During the post-Evanston period, grave crises developed in some nations—Hungary, Cyprus, South Africa, Egypt, for example. The statements put out by Geneva on these occasions, although welcomed by many who believed the churches should speak, met with widespread objection on the ground that they concerned, in most instances, internal matters with which the nations would consider it their prerogative to deal without outside interference. Some ecumenists looked upon "witnessing" in such circumstances as a duty of the churches, regardless of the effects, which could be left to God. But others thought that practical considerations urging the silencing of pronouncements often pointed to the overruling will of God.

In the membership of the Commission were a number of distinguished persons of international repute, whose presence gave it, supposedly, a certain authority and prestige. If this was an advantage, it had also its disadvantages. It tended to identify the decisions of the Commission with the judgments of influential members active in political affairs and thus to invest them in the public thought with partisan bias. There were withdrawals, it was reported privately, on this account. What commissioners with the ear of the world said could have disturbing repercussions in the controversial areas of international life where the Commission's work lay. An example was Arnold Toynbee's alleged comparison of the dispossession of Palestinian Arabs by the Jews with the crime against Jews in Europe under Hitler.

In the anniversary issue of *The Ecumenical Review* Drs. Visser 't Hooft and Ranson wrote:

> The Commission seeks simply to throw the light of the common Christian convictions held in the membership of its parent-bodies upon concrete problems of international life. This is more easily said than done. Many churches are only beginning to understand that they have a responsibility in this realm; others which are fully aware of that responsibility are often far apart in their basic theological and ethical presuppositions; even if a fundamental consensus in the realm of principle has been reached, there remains the delicate task of translating principle into concrete and relevant proposals for constructive actions. But there are also positive factors: the remarkable far-reaching agreements in ecumenical meetings such as the reports on international affairs received by the Assemblies and endorsed by so many churches; the help received from responsible statesmen and officers of international organizations; and especially, underlying all, a great desire on the part of Christians all over the world to manifest that the Church of Christ transcends the frontiers of nation and race and is entrusted with the ministry of reconciliation. . . .
>
> Through the Commission . . . the churches and missions have [not] done

what they ought to have done in the realm of international relations. Our divided world, in which there is so much conflict, so much injustice, so much suffering, reminds us constantly of our sins of commission and of omission, and of the disproportion between the witness which the churches render in fact and the spiritual and moral needs of the nations in an age when the very life of humanity depends on the finding of a new basis for international relationships. . . .

But we are grateful that we have in the Commission . . . an instrument through which the convictions which we hold in common about the peace, the justice, the power of reconciliation which are offered to men in Jesus Christ can become relevant to our international problems.

8. The Churches and the Problem of Overpopulation

The Commission of the Churches on International Affairs took the initiative in this area. "Convinced of the urgency of the problem of rapid population increase for the international order," its Executive Committee invited the Central Committee of the World Council of Churches, after the appearance of the Arnoldshain Conference's statement on this subject, to cooperate in a review of relevant data, preparatory to the formulation, if that should seem advisable, of an ecumenical policy.

The proposal was "received" by the Central Committee at Galyatetö in 1956. In acting on it, the World Council asked Dr. Norman Goodall, Executive Secretary of the International Missionary Council—that body having concurred in the Commission's suggestion—to convene a conference on "Responsible Parenthood and the Population Problem," and the General Secretary of the World Council requested the Commission to prepare, meanwhile, a paper on "Christian Concerns for Economic and Social Development," with special reference to the "growing disparity between richer and poorer nations," to which certain churches of Denmark thought the Council should give attention.

The study of this latter task, which fell to the Commission's Executive Secretary, Dr. Richard M. Fagley, brought into clearer light the close relation between the overpopulation problem, most acute in the underdeveloped countries, and the ecumenical relief and technical aid programs. "Indigenous and international efforts" toward providing help for these nations were, it found, "being swallowed up by the maintenance of growing populations," so that little was left for measures to promote economic advance.

The conference on "Responsible Parenthood and the Population Problem" was held at Mansfield College, Oxford, April 12–15, 1959, and its report was published in *The Ecumenical Review* for October of that year.

Coming from the study at Oxford, of which he had served as secretary, to the Rhodes sessions of the Central Committee, Dr. Fagley spoke particularly of "the neglected factor of rapid population increase in the less developed countries." The paper on "Christian Concerns for Economic and Social Development," presented the year before at Nyborg Strand, had proved "useful in contacts at the intergovernmental level," he said, and it was hoped that the churches would give it serious attention. He mentioned that the increase of world population in 1959 would reach "the fifty-million mark," three-fourths of it being concentrated in regions least prepared to cope with the attendant pressures. "The main factor" in this development, he explained, was "the success of international disease control which, wherever applied, reduced dramatically death rates and enlarged the number of live births." In poorer countries with young populations, this was setting off "an explosion." An anti-malaria campaign on the island of Mauritius, for example, had raised the birth rate from 1.0 percent to 3.3 percent, and this meant a doubling of the population in less than twenty years. Health programs were overdue, of course, but, unless matched with other ministries, they would only cause new disasters.

Dr. Fagley voiced the hope that the Mansfield College report, which had been sent to the churches, and replies that might be forthcoming from them would "provide the Central Committee at its next meeting with data necessary to serious consideration of this neglected problem." It was high time, he thought, that Christian responsibility for these conditions, "which threatened freedom, justice and peace itself," be faced.

The report on "The Witness of the Churches amidst Social Change in Asia" from the East Asia Christian Conference in Kuala Lumpur, Malaya, in May, 1959, mentioned among the problems faced in attempts to deal with overpopulation in Asian countries the unwillingness of "some churches in East Asia . . . to discuss these questions." Through political pressures the same religious attitude prevented countries looked to for material aid from helping crowded areas with measures of population control.

Part of the reason, for example, why legislative plans for foreign aid were meeting with increasingly stubborn opposition—as in the Congress of the United States—was that the startling rise in population in the underdeveloped countries tended to wipe out the gains made by the vast sums already voted. "Our five-year plans have no meaning, if our population grows at a rate one can never catch up with . . . ," confessed Prime Minister Nehru of India. Indian officials had informed the United States that the effect of the three billions it had previously given was "being nullified by the increase of population." President Ayub Khan of Pakistan, on a visit with the President of the United States in Washington, said, "If we continue to increase at the present rate, it will ultimately lead to a standard of living which will be little better than that of animals." But, for political reasons, Mr. Kennedy, like Mr. Eisenhower before him, could say only that the question of controlling or not controlling population was a decision each country had to make for itself.

The Population Reference Bureau estimated in 1961 that Latin American population would double in the next twenty-five years. Yet the President of the United States was saying, in effect, that this was none of the business of the United States. He had told the nations of Latin America that unless they controlled their economies and used the vast amounts of money promised them by the government of the United States to raise the standard of life for all their people, they could not expect to get further aid. How could they control their economies or raise their standards of living if they did not control their populations?

> Probably never in history has so obvious and significant a fact been so widely evaded or minimized by the governments of men [wrote James Reston in *The New York Times*, July 21, 1961]. World population is now increasing at a rate of fifty millions a year. In the United States alone it has gone up by over twenty-five millions since Eisenhower entered the White House and by approximately a million and a half since Kennedy succeeded him six months ago. . . . Across the world in China the population is rising at the rate of sixteen millions a year, which is one main reason for that communist regime's pressure against the nations of Southeast Asia. . . . In fact, it may be that the greatest menace to world peace and decent standards of life today is not atomic energy, but sexual energy.

At St. Andrews in 1960 the Central Committee, after discussing an address by Bishop Stephen Bayne, Jr., Anglican Executive Officer and Chairman of the Section on the Family of the Lambeth Conference, on "Population and Family Problems," and another by Professor Egbert de Vries, Director of the Institute for International Development at the Hague and Chairman of the Department on Church and Society of the World Council of Churches, on "Population Growth and Christian Responsibility," adopted the following statement:

> The family must always be a major concern of the Christian Church. Today, it is under the pressure of powerful forces of moral and social change.
>
> The Central Committee, considering this to be a matter of great importance, transmits to the member-churches the addresses of Bishop Stephen Bayne, Jr., and Professor Egbert de Vries on population growth and Christian responsibility, and calls attention to recent official church statements on this subject.
>
> The Central Committee invites the churches to examine the theological, moral and social issues in this world-wide problem, together with those encountered in ecumenical discussion, sharing their conclusions with the World Council of Churches.
>
> The Central Committee directs the Executive Committee to take appropriate steps to keep this concern before the churches.

This was regarded in some circles as "a weak resolution." In the debate, the Committee was reminded by certain of the members that many churches had already made pronouncements on population control and admonished that the position of the World Council should be kept at least abreast of them and the national councils—which also had spoken. The Central Committee evidently had no objection to being behind—if it was—in this instance.

The Committee was deeply divided. All were for responsible parenthood, of course, but they could not agree on what it meant. To some members, it included limiting the size of the family according to income and the indicated requirements in other respects for the greatest good of all the members, with the aid, if necessary, of modern techniques of birth control. Others could accept no curb on the number of children, except continence. Speaking for certain of the others, as well as for himself, Bishop John of San Francisco said he could find no biblical basis for family planning. His fellow churchman, Professor Georges Florovsky of Harvard Divinity School, thought contraception was attractive to young couples because of wrong moral standards. Marriage was a sacrament, he said, and the marital relation was for procreation and education of children. The main issue was not demographic or geographical, declared Archimandrite Timiadis, but moral. Competent theologians should explore further such matters as the stewardship of the body and the control of sexual desires, he suggested. Dr. Berkhof of Holland allowed that the course of nature could not be identified with the will of God, but love of God implied the acceptance by man of the idea of controlling nature. The element of discipline was seen in the command of the Creator: "Be fruitful . . . multiply . . . replenish . . . *subdue*."

Principal Chandran of India considered "study of the problem of extending Christian ideals to non-Christian . . . family patterns most vital for the churches of Asia," which was welcoming the possibility of population control through scientific means. It appeared necessary to take advantage of such methods, but there was danger in their indiscriminate use. The Church must stand for human dignity and high moral standards. It was here that the churches, especially where they were in a minority in a non-Christian environment, had a duty.

There being no consensus in sight, the Central Committee declared that "the family must always be a major concern of the Christian Church" and asked the denominations to read up on the general subject and share their conclusions with the World Council.

Whatever the critics thought, it could perhaps have done worse. Those looking for what would have been regarded as more advanced action might have tried defining for themselves what the churches (which were in the position of being responsible for having helped create the conditions accelerating population growth) could do. They could not undo what they had done, if they wished to. Nor could they be expected to repent of their good works and have done with their relief programs, close their hospitals, stop treatment of the sick, disband their schools: this would have been tantamount to renouncing Christianity, as they had understood it. Nor would they be likely to support a campaign for suicide for incurables or euthanasia for the aging, or for sterilization of the potent poor. They would have, without doubt, to continue with their humanitarian services, which would keep people of all sorts and conditions alive and progressively step up the population increase of the planet, already setting out "Standing Room Only" signs. Just about everything the churches could do would have the effect of boosting the earth's tenantry. Even family planning would. Responsible folk would adopt it, thereby only making more room for the irresponsible to propagate.

"Jesus Christ is Lord over All Life," the World Council of Churches was proclaiming. But who knew what he would do about the population explosion, if he came fully into his kingly power in the midst of these perplexing times? The answer was, of course, that nobody knew or could know.

Science would have to work at this problem with the light given it, and no one could foresee what measures would have to be resorted to in accommodating race increase to available space. And it was perhaps just as well that they could not be known in advance, for some of them probably would not be pleasant to contemplate.

Though they would have to leave the problem mostly to the scientists, the churches would not be without their work: that is to say, without the preaching of the Gospel. Whatever society had to do to limit the world's population would call for Christian interpretation. Men would have to be helped to find in the new conditions their peace in God. That had always been the Church's real work—to see the hand of God in the cosmic process and to help the lost know that his providence enfolded them when they passed through "the deep places of the earth."

This was what really mattered.

Christ walked by this way. There was no room for him—in the inn at Bethlehem, in Herod's kingdom, in Galilee, or Judea, or in the Holy City of his people—no room, until he had been lifted up by a cross above the milling throngs and lay at last in a grave beyond reach of their trampling feet. Yet he said, "The Father is with me. . . . I go to the Father. . . . Father, into thy hands I commend my spirit." He had spoken of life, and this was it—eternal fellowship with God. This life the Church existed to help all people possess in the midst of their brief days on earth and to enjoy forever. Life was not studying to add to our years or to build a kingdom which could have only the shape and duration of our mortality. In the midst of time, imperishable life was within men's grasp, and the endless kingdom, not of earth, was already come, with gates open to all who would enter. The Church had in all ages the mission of making real these unseen eternal things, of bringing to bear upon every moment of the present existence their reality and truth, validated by the experience of believing hearts in the long history of man, and so of lighting the way through darkness to God.

It could be that this would prove to be the Church's indispensable contribution at the impasse civilization was now fast approaching.

V

DEPARTMENTS AND PROGRAMS

1. Work for the Laity—Co-operation of Men and Women

The Departments on Work for the Laity and Co-operation of Men and Women in Church and Society—both in the Division of Ecumenical Action of the World Council of Churches—were in some ways an organizational overlap resulting from a complication of historical, sociological, psychological, and theological circumstances, quite defying concise and clear analysis.

Work for the laity had been a "concern" at Amsterdam to which the Assembly decided to give a departmental status. At the same time, the attempt was made to meet the desire for greater official recognition of women by authorizing the Central Committee to set up a commission for them (The Commission on Work for Women) which, with the reorganization of the World Council in 1954, became a department. It was at their own request that the membership of the commission, and later of the department, included also men.

It had not been easy to arrive at agreement on an acceptable program for women in the ecumenical movement. While the Department on Work for the Laity had been intended for both sexes, it stood, in the thoughts of the uninformed, for work by and for laymen. Women were unable to see that it offered them more opportunities than they already had to gain an equal role with men in the life of the churches.

On the other hand, they were not asking for a separate organization which they might call their own and run as they would. As they understood it, the ecumenical movement envisaged the wholeness of the Church and, to that end, the integration of the entire laity, including themselves. It was well, they said, to understand and make allowance for the complementary functions of men and women, but these could be realized, in their fullness, only through a true partnership.

Women thought that they were capable of leadership which they had not been given a chance to exercise, and which the Church required for the attainment of wholeness. They regarded it as unfortunate, from the standpoint of the Christian cause itself, that the official direction of the Church was in the hands, almost completely, of men, and particularly that there should be so few women in ecumenical organizations. They made bold to say that the World Council of Churches could strengthen and enrich its program by increasing the number of women on its staff and committees, where they would serve side by side with men in the same undertakings. The perpetuation of separateness through the creation of a commission or a department for women only would, in their opinion, confirm rather than challenge existing inequalities.

Moreover, it was not just in the Church that women were seeking what they considered their rightful place, but in society as well; and the Church had the duty to lead by example in opening the way for them.

So it was the women themselves who asked for a commission "on co-operation of men and women in Church and society." If they were going to overcome the inhibitions of tradition and win freedom to make their full contribution of service, they must have the help of men—help through real, thoroughgoing cooperation.

Church men, it appeared, often misunderstood the real motive of women in organizing themselves separately for the various kinds of religious services. The United States was looked upon as perhaps the most conspicuous example of what some critics called, with their eyes upon its women, "activity for activity's sake." Besides the large National Council of Church Women, there were in the United States some two thousand state and smaller-area councils for women. And all these operated alongside national and local denominational organizations for the same women. Laymen, and many of the clergy, smiled indulgently upon their wives and sisters, who were supposed to be never so happy as when they were busy with their own programs, in which they could speak and plan as they pleased. However, it is enlightening to read, in this connection, the definition of purpose adopted by the National Council of Church Women at its founding in 1941: "To unite church women . . . looking toward their integration into the total life and work of the Church." The women had turned to associations of their own because, more largely than realized, the Church had by its attitude forced them to this less desired alternative. What they wanted most was full cooperation in the life of the Church.

That this is the aim of the women in the World Council of Churches is clear from a statement of objectives by the Working Committee of the Department on Co-operation of Men and Women in Church and Society in 1955,[1] which the Central Committee of the World Council commended "to the member-churches for their study and comment," as follows, in part:

The basic concern of this Department . . . is the wholeness of the Church. . . . Wholeness can be achieved only when every part of the membership . . . is enabled to participate fully. . . . Effective participation in-

[1] *The Ecumenical Review,* Vol. VIII, No. 1, p. 72.

cludes working together with others who have different gifts. The special concern of this Department is the co-operation between men and women.

It is inherent in our faith that men and women are called and sent together to do God's will in the Church and in society. God created men and women and put them together under his blessing and his order. Christ came to save men and women and called them together to his discipleship. The Holy Spirit was given to men and women as members of the new community to witness together for the sake of Christ in the world.

This emphasis on "togetherness" implies recognition of the incompleteness of man and woman . . . in isolation from each other. For this reason, the co-operation of men and women is not a special doctrinal issue, nor yet a single feature of Church life or organization. Still less is it an emphasis on the interests or rights of a single group in the Church. It touches nearly all doctrinal and practical issues with which the Church is concerned.

For example, we cannot overlook the fact the Bible speaks of the very close connection between the nature of the Church and the mystery of the right relationship of the sexes (Ephesians v, 23).

Again, looking at the membership of the body of Christ, we have to face the fact that the new community contains men and women, both contributing their gifts to the common life. And any consideration of the nature of man must take into account the two-foldness of the sexes and their unity in diversity.

This gives the basis for putting the right emphasis on what we have to say on certain questions of modern society. If we are to avoid measuring social developments and changes all over the world merely by the presuppositions of Western or Eastern civilizations or of modern secular movements and doctrines, we must constantly criticize these pre-suppositions in the light of fresh and serious study of the Bible.

As we face the lack of co-operation, the deep misunderstandings, and the rivalry between men and women in some of our societies, and sometimes even in our churches, we are convicted under Christ of our disobedience and our failure to respond faithfully to the tasks to which we are called.

We may profitably ask ourselves: To what extent are some interpretations of the Scriptures among the causes of disorders in our churches and societies? (For example, the legalistic interpretations of the biblical conception of subordination perpetuated faulty patterns of relationship between men and women.) In the face of modern demands for equality of rights and opportunities, to what extent have our churches given teaching on true partnership based on the insights of the Bible? To what extent have our churches taken account of the new psychological, social, economic and political situations in the world and developed forms of ministry and service appropriate to the needs of these new situations? To what extent must the understanding of vocation, of mission, of service and of various forms of the Christian ministry be re-examined, so that our churches may demonstrate in their own life right relationships between men and women, and inspire and challenge the world to work toward such relationships?

In concrete situations of tensions between the order willed by God and the actual disorders of our churches and societies, this Department is called to remind the churches of their needs, and of the opportunities which lie before them for a true witness to the purposes underlying God's creation of the two sexes. For example, it has already been found that when men and women co-operate in ecumenical discussion, some of the well-known dangers of abstract and impersonal thinking can be avoided, and more vital encounters achieved between practical and devotional life and theological discussion. . . .

If the implications of the co-operation of men and women in all doctrinal and practical issues of the Church were generally recognized by the members of the churches and the departments of the World Council of Churches, there would be no further need for this Department.

For the good of the Church and the effectiveness of its witness in the world, it is necessary, for the present, to continue to emphasize this special concern.

The Department is trying to put the whole discussion of this issue on a new level and on the basis of theological thinking and sociological observations to stimulate the churches to re-discover the full meaning of co-operation between men and women in Church and society. . . .

The Department on Co-operation of Men and Women moved into its work after Evanston with the considerable momentum which had been gained under the leadership earlier of Miss Saroe Chakko and Dr. Kathleen Bliss, and, since 1953, of Mlle. Madeleine Barot, who succeeded to its executive secretaryship.

The time was favorable for considering the relation of men and women in the Church and in society. Interest in Dr. Bliss' book, *The Service and Status of Women in the Church,* had been widespread, as it had also in the study booklet, *The Man-Woman Relationship*. Inquiries for information, and requests for help from individuals and churches came in increasingly. Avenues into all the continents and most of the nations were thus opened. Women everywhere, particularly in the emerging new states, were eager to explore the bid to world fellowship, with its promise of greater usefulness and self-realization. The Department had not the staff or the means to respond to more than a comparatively small number of the appeals received.

The reports of the Department for the years from Evanston onward reflected the many-sidedness and remarkable extent of its program, and the vigor and capability, as well, of its Working Committee[2] and Secretaries.[3] There is mention, among many activities, of:

Journeyings to Canada, the United States, Mexico, Brazil, Argentina, Uruguay, Greece, Morocco, Algeria, Tunisia, Ghana, Nigeria, Madagascar, India, Pakistan, Burma, Malaya, Indonesia, France, Germany, Great Britain, Austria, and still other countries.

Conferences, consultations, interviews, and addresses in Herrenalb, Arnoldshain, New Haven, Geneva, Athens, Spittal, Salonika, Kuala Lumpur, Rangoon, Calcutta, Karachi, and many more places.

Work with the United Nations Commission on the Status of Women,

[2] Among the laymen on the Working Committee were Dean W. G. Muelder, Canon S. L. Greenslade, Dr. H. Thimme, Dean Sherman Johnson, President Nathan Pusey, and Dr. Mossie Wyker.

[3] Mlle. Barot and Miss Turnbull.

the Department of Adult Education for Women of the United Nations Educational, Scientific and Cultural Organization, the International Labor Organization and other secular agencies, in the interest of women.

Consultations with other world Christian societies: the World's Alliance of the Young Men's Christian Associations, the World Young Women's Christian Association, The World's Student Christian Federation, and others.

Promotion of surveys on marriage and part-time work for married women.

Cooperation in the Study of Rapid Social Change and other inquiries originated by the World Council of Churches through its Division of Studies and other divisions and departments.

A study of celibacy and monastic traditions in the different churches and their effects for both men and women.

Assistance to the East Asia Christian Conference in the establishment of a department on the cooperation of men and women.

The agreed assumption, upon the integration of the World Council of Churches and the International Missionary Council, of the latter organization's program on "Home and Family Life."

The appointment, in response to a request from the National Christian Council of Ghana and a recommendation of the All-Africa Church Conference at Abadan in 1958, of a team of trained women to work three years in Gabon, Togoland, Nigeria, Ghana, and possibly other African countries.

Collaboration with the Department on Work for the Laity in printing *Laity*.

Publication of a widely distributed brochure on "Men and Women in Church and Society" in German, French, and English.

The establishment of commissions on the cooperation of men and women in England, the United States, and Canada.

The development of theological, anthropological, and historical studies in relation to the position of women in society.

A growing world-wide consultative service through the Geneva office for the churches and other agencies concerned with the freedom and well-being of women and the family.

These are some of the features of the Department's program that catch the eye in a casual thumbing through the records.

The Working Committees of the Departments on Work for the Laity and Co-operation of Men and Women in Church and Society at Spittal in 1959 "discussed, once again, the question whether a merger . . . could be contemplated, in view of the fact that this is a suggestion which comes up regularly. . . . The reply continues to be firmly negative, the aims of the two departments being entirely different."

The World Council's Committee on Program and Finance recommended at St. Andrews in 1960 that, in the interest of better coordination and of economy, the Department on Co-operation of Men and Women in Church and Society be reduced to the status of a secretariat with one staff member.

Concerning this, the Working Committee of the Department said:

We have always held the view that this Department has a specific objective which should be achieved within a limited period of time. In the statement issued at Davos in 1955, we said: "If the implications of the co-operation of men and women in all doctrinal and practical issues of the Church were generally recognized by the member churches and the World Council of Churches, there would be no further need for this Department. For the good of the Church and the effectiveness of its witness . . . it is necessary, for the present, to continue to emphasize this special concern." Although considerable progress has been made in the past five years, we believe that the time has not yet come to discontinue the Department. . . .

The setting-up in 1948 of the Commission on the Life and Work of Women in the Church was both encouragement to those who had been concerned with this question and a stimulus to remarkable change. When the Commission was replaced, after six years, by a Department whose mandate was extended to cover the co-operation of men and women in Church and society, important new discussions were opened up. It could be a serious discouragement to many now at work in this field, and a disservice to the churches, if a change were made before the objectives of the Department had been more nearly achieved. Such a change might well be interpreted as indicating that the World Council of Churches had lost interest in the question of the service and status of women. It is still a fact that the member-churches and the World Council itself have not an adequate number of women in their delegations, their committees and their staff. . . .

We have been confirmed in our conviction as to the continuing need for a Department on the Co-operation of Men and Women by the fact that . . . the International Missionary Council has suggested that, in the event of a merger of the World Council of Churches and the International Missionary Council, its important work in home and family life should be administered by the . . . Department, re-named as the Department on the Co-operation of Men and Women in Church, Family and Society. We are willing to accept this added responsibility, since the co-operation of men and women in the home and family is already one of our basic concerns. But, obviously, such a development would be impossible without a full department of two staff members and a working committee set up so as to represent our existing interests and those of the former International Missionary Council.[4]

The Central Committee at St. Andrews, where the proposal to change the status of the Department and the reply had been made, voted that after the Third Assembly the work of cooperation of men and women in Church, family, and society be continued in a department with a staff of two secretaries, rather than through a secretariat with one secretary, as recommended by the Committee on Program and Finance, with the provision that "contributions . . . be secured through the Divisions of Inter-Church Aid and Service to Refugees and World Mission and

[4] Minutes and Reports of the Central Committee, St. Andrews, 1960, p. 143.

Evangelism and/or from other sources, including missionary boards and societies," to supplement the regular budgetary appropriation, which would probably be inadequate.

Whereupon, the Chairman of the Committee on Program and Finance, Dr. Blake, explained that the recommendation to change the Department on Co-operation of Men and Women in Church and Society to a secretariat had not been "motivated by any under-estimation of the importance of its work or of the faithfulness and competence of its working committee and staff-members," but by the opinion that the program should be related organizationally to the Department on the Laity. He suggested "that there would be real value in permeating the work of the Laity Department by the concerns of the Department on the Co-operation of Men and Women."

The Department on the Co-operation of Men and Women should have, it was agreed, a special relation to the Division of World Mission and Evangelism, by reason of the merging of the International Missionary Council with the World Council of Churches, as follows:

It should be renamed "The Department on Co-operation of Men and Women in Church, Family and Society," and to its functions should be added that of assisting "churches and Christian councils to discover and express the significance of the Christian faith in the realm of marriage and family life, particularly in the context of other religions and secularism."

The Division of Ecumenical Action should consult the officers of the Division of World Mission and Evangelism before submitting to the Central Committee names of persons for appointment to the Department's Working Committee.

The Division of World Mission and Evangelism should refer requests from national and regional councils for assistance in the field of home and family life to the Department, with such recommendations as it wished to make.

There should be "reciprocal consultation," whenever necessary, on requests for help received directly by the Department. Responsibility for formulating and carrying out work in this area, in the first instance, should rest with the Department.

The Division of World Mission and Evangelism should offer, and the Department welcome, assistance "in securing funds and personnel for work approved"; and, where appropriate, the Division should make available the part-time services of its own staff for these purposes. Should the Department be unable to undertake an approved project, the Division might assume responsibility for it, in consultation with the Department.

The Department on the Laity (changed in name from Department on Work for the Laity in 1955) had for an aim "to be a centre of information, study and stimulation on the role of the laity, both men and women, in the life and mission of the Church."

This definition of purpose could have been interpreted as comprehending broadly all that the World Council of Churches hoped to accomplish, as well, through the Department on Co-operation of Men and Women in Church, Family and Society. Both Departments believed that "the role of the laity" could be fully effective only on the condition of understanding cooperation by men and women. But their conceptions of what cooperation should mean were so divergent at many points that their Working Committees could say, after studying a proposal that they be merged, "The reply . . . continues to be firmly negative, *the aims of the two . . . being entirely different* (italics added).

There were reasons for thinking that working together implied for the Department on the Laity a relationship following closely the traditional pattern of the Church, with little broadening of the scope of women's participation. The Department on Co-operation of Men and Women in Church, Family and Society envisaged, as stated, their having the full support of men in reaching out for important positions of service and responsibility beyond the conventional bounds of their activity; and it was quite certain that most ecclesiastical authorities were not ready for cooperation on that scale.

The Department on the Laity brought its thinking to focus on the early ecumenical emphasis of giving "affirmation of the ministry of the laity." The Church had been commissioned to go into all the world with its witness but had seemed to have come to a standstill, if not to have suffered actual loss of ground, in its evangelistic conquests. The early leaders of the ecumenical movement thought that hope of recovery rested with the laity, who by reason of their dispersion in all walks of life were already the Church in the world and responsible for the Christian witness beyond its organizational reach. While not new, this was a stimulating idea, especially for many in a position to know how strongly the tide was running against the Church at this critical salient of its mission.

The problem, however, was to get beyond merely affirming the ministry of the laity. The response often left much to be desired, even when the service proposed was of the stereotyped kind performed in some official capacity within and for the local parish, under the direction and with the assistance of the clergy. Those in the pews might feel that this kind of ministry was not anything to be undertaken with great confidence. It carried demands in respect of character, reputation, and "spirituality" at which they might well hesitate. When it came to assenting to the affirmation that they were the Church in the world and commissioned to make their work, whatever its nature, their Christian vocation, the laity could hardly be expected to act without questionings.

Laymen at Evanston confessed their inability to understand the theological terminology in which most of the studies and reports were cast. It was obvious to them that if they took seriously the call to "a ministry of the laity" of the sort described they would need to be prepared to understand its theological implications. Could the language of scholarship be vernacularized, so that laymen and those to whom they spoke could understand it? Would the clergy, who generally met with only indifferent success in gaining a hearing, even with the members of their churches, be qualified to instruct those called to relay the Gospel in the streets? With deeper misgivings, the better-informed laymen were asking, with some of the clergy themselves, whether there must not be a thoroughgoing reconstruction of Christian theology before anyone, clergy or laity, could speak with intelligibility to the world. It seemed clear that the block in communication was the result more of the incomprehensibility of the Church to the masses than of their indifference.

Inevitably, the discussion at this point left some fearing that placing such great emphasis on "the ministry of the laity" might encourage anti-clericalism. Rev. H. R. Weber, Executive Secretary of the Department, spoke in regard to this in his report to the Central Committee at Nyborg Strand, Denmark, in 1958. It was the "main task" of the Department, he said, to show that each member of the Church had the duty "to participate fully in Christ's ministry in and to the world." Christian fathers and mothers, politicians and industrialists, farmers and technicians had, he asserted, " a specific, irreplaceable role to play in God's design," their ministry being not less holy or vital than that of ordained pastors and missionaries. But "this high doctrine of the ministry of the laity" by no means excluded, he insisted, but rather strengthened, that "of those set apart within God's people to become what some called now 'the other laity'; namely, ordained, full-time or part-time ministers and clergy."

However, the function and training of those thus set apart would have to be reconsidered, he believed, in view of the ministry of the whole people of God in the world. The peculiar situation of Christians who were "in the world but not of the world" demanded, he thought, "a continuing critical examination of the whole pattern of church-life, which often had the effect of diverting them from, rather than of preparing them for, the call to 'holy worldliness.' "

Referring to "the danger of 'schism' between the laity and the ordained ministry," Colonel Francis P. Miller, a member of the Department's Working Committee, stressed that the purpose was only to help the laity rediscover that they "really had a part in the ministry of the Church in the world." Bishop Fuglsang-Damgaard of Denmark and other members of the clergy expressed themselves as grateful to God for the revived interest of the laity.

The ecumenical ministry of the laity proposed a dedication to "a holy worldliness" of broader social dimensions than this term had in the common evangelical context. It called not only for Christian uprightness and charity and the utilization of contacts in the course of everyday pursuits for personal witness-bearing, but also—and more especially—for *involvement* in the total social process, so far as that would be possible, with the purpose of changing society according to the Christian pattern.

And from this standpoint, too, it was a mission requiring educational preparation. To briefing in the theology of their evangelistic calling would need to be added instruction in the social teachings of the Christian religion.

Both phases of training posed their peculiar practical problems. A common difficulty was the summoning for group study and discussion of laymen who, for the most part, would be unable or unwilling to leave their daily work or to bear personally the expense of the necessary travel. Area conferences met this condition only partially, leaving unchallenged, as they must, parochial views put forward as ecumenical.

Sociological indoctrination could proceed with comparatively few hindrances because the economic and political philosophies within the World Council of Churches followed, in their main lines, the principles of state socialism of one kind or another, which was prevalent in most of the countries with denominational representation in its membership. On the subject of theology there was much confusion; but the consensus was that the pattern of the welfare society, extended to international affairs, had sufficient sanction in the spirit of the Christian Gospel.

Laymen attending meetings in Geneva or in national and regional centers in other parts of the world, whether on their own initiative or at the solicitation of their church authorities, would probably be predisposed to the ecumenical politico-economic position, as would certainly the instructors and consultants engaged to conduct the discussion. The reported findings would consequently show a substantial unanimity in the conclusions reached.

Whether because of inability to find competent lay leadership or of a purpose to shape the thinking of the Department on the Laity in conformity with the World Council's policies, the Working Committee appeared to have been constituted with a view to keeping control in the hands of the clergy. The executive secretarial officers of the Department, who were appointed by the Central Committee, were ministers.[5]

During the post-Evanston period, here under review, the Department participated in many conferences and inquiries, which, whatever their intentions, seemed to produce few concrete results. A book on "The

[5] Rev. H. H. Walz, until 1954, when he became Vice-Chairman of the Working Committee of the Department on the Laity; Rev. H. R. Weber after 1954, Executive Secretary.

Laity in Historic Perspective" was projected. One study concerned stewardship, emphasizing that the dedication of a tenth embraced, besides the money tithe, a like share of time and talent—which the report announced as a new discovery or amplification of the well-understood principle.

> Special attention has been given so far (1958) to the so-called pioneering experiments at the frontier between the Church and the world. Lay training centres, certain experimental parishes, brotherhoods and bridge-heads [are] signs of renewal, because they attempt to renew church-life in the view of its mission. . . .
>
> What the Department on the Laity stands for is *the renewal of the total life and mission of the Church*. The Department will, therefore, continue to keep in contact with these prophetic signs of renewal, but at the same time work for a closer contact with parish life, men's, women's and youth movements, and other organs of the normal instituted churches.
>
> What is most needed today for the renewal to break through is a two-way conversation between the persons involved in the prophetic signs and the responsible leaders of the "normal" church-life.

This was characteristic of reports from the Department in these years. They bore few indications that a program of real interest to rank-and-file laymen was in the shaping. They lacked the sure sense of what had relevance and at the same time practicability. Wanting were a genuine understanding of human need, a clear perception of the spiritual quickening of which average people in an encounter with God are capable, a down-to-earth stance in the actual involvement in the social process, which gave inspiration and zest, it was noted, to the activities of the companion Department on Co-operation of Men and Women in Church, Family and Society. The theoretical and academic set off lengthy soliloquizing arriving at nowhere in particular. Questions of little or no practical import were blown into distorted importance: e.g., that of the ordained and unordained ministries.

> No re-consideration of the ministry of the laity is possible without sooner or later leading to a necessary re-consideration of the ministry of those set apart within the people of God. If the Church as a whole has not only a ministry but is a ministry for the world, and if every believer shares in this ministry, why then are certain believers set apart in a special way, and what is the function of their special ministry within the ministering community of the Church? If the Church has not only a mission but is a mission to the world, and if the laymen are the spear-head of this mission, why are there missionaries and evangelists especially set apart and sent out, and what is their role within the missionary Church?
>
> What are the fruits and dangers of professionalism in the special ministries of the Church, and what part of the Church's ministry can best be fulfilled by "non-professionals"? [6]

[6] Minutes of the Central Committee, 1958, pp. 106-7.

And so on and on. "These questions become urgent, not only in Europe and North America," the report says, "but also in Asia, Africa and Latin America." "Do they?" one could but ask. The idea that they did might only have suggested the need of the World Council of Churches for a department of the laity, run by the laity for the laity.

2. The Youth Department

"The main present concern" of the Youth Department in 1955, according to its Working Committee's report to the Central Committee at Davos-Platz, was "the problem of integrating young people into the life of their churches," which inquiries had shown to be "beyond the competence of any one church or country to solve." "Many millions . . . had completely lost touch with any church after confirmation," the Committee said. "They disappear with alarming speed [also] . . . from our lay youth movements."

The Department proposed inaugurating "a series of . . . consultations on local, national, regional and . . . international levels, for leaders of the churches . . . , youth councils and the Christian lay organizations (Young Men's Christian Association, Young Women's Christian Association, World's Student Christian Federation and the World Council of Christian Education and Sunday School Association), to examine together the issues, share experiences and experiments, gain new insights for action, and in this way contribute further to the renewal of the churches through the effective and adventurous commitment of their young people to the Lord of the Church. . . ."

The Central Committee of the World Council of Churches approved.

In the general spirit and purpose of this plan many actions relating to youth work were taken by the Department during the next six years, under the leadership of the Executive Secretary, Rev. Bengt-Thure Molander, and of Rev. Philip Potter, who in 1957 succeeded to this office.

Youth commissions were formed in many countries—Germany, Switzerland, Great Britain, Australia, Japan, Lebanon, Holland, a number of the nations of Latin America, Africa, and Asia—to arrange for the consultations, which were, on the whole, well attended. Young people everywhere, according to reports, responded eagerly to the ecumenical approach. In the United States, the Department's efforts proceeded in close coordination with the established youth departments of the denominations and the interchurch councils. Canadian churches associated themselves with the program.

It was decided to narrow the emphasis from international to continental or regional gatherings, with the view of bringing local interests and problems more to the fore. The presence usually of fraternal delegates and guest consultants from outside the designated territories of the conferences helped to maintain the world perspective.

Important youth meetings in New Zealand, Australasia, Europe, the United States, and Canada drew representatives of the churches from many other countries, including officials of the World Council of Churches and of other major interchurch bodies.

Members of the Department's staff attended the founding assembly of the East Asia Christian Conference at Kuala Lumpur and counseled that body on the organization of its youth work.

In 1956 a team of six youth leaders from Canada, France, Sweden, the United States, and India visited Mexico, Costa Rica, Colombia, Ecuador, Peru, Bolivia, Chile, Argentina, Uruguay, Paraguay, Brazil, Venezuela, and Cuba (from December, 1956, to February, 1957). They also participated in the Fourth Congress and Assembly of the Union of Latin American Evangelical Youth in Barranquilla. "The main purpose of the visitation was to interpret the ecumenical movement to Christian youth in Latin America, to share with them the concerns and experiences of Christian youth in other parts of the world, and to survey the needs of youth work in the area."

During this period various studies related to the problem of integrating young people with the churches were projected. Included for special attention were intercommunion and baptism and confirmation.

Work camps continued to thrive, increasing in number from eight in 1948 to fifty in 1960. It was estimated that during these twelve years from seven to eight thousand individuals were enrolled, at one time or another, in their programs. Fifty-three camps registering some twelve hundred young people from thirty-six countries were projected for 1961. Eventually transferred to the supervision of the Division on Inter-Church Aid and Service to Refugees, this program still depended largely for the recruitment of personnel on the Youth Department.

World youth projects also enjoyed a healthy growth. By 1961 thirty-odd had been set up in twenty-three countries. In addition, over one hundred young people had volunteered for work under the Division of Inter-Church Aid and Service to Refugees.

There were few nations, it would appear, that had not, in one way or another, come to know firsthand something of the burgeoning activities of the Youth Department during the years between Evanston and New Delhi.

The drift of Christian young people's thinking in this period was indicated by the subjects discussed at their gatherings. The fifteen hundred attending the New Zealand Conference at the end of 1956 had for their theme "Christ Unites," and those meeting in the Third Australian Conference of Christian Youth in 1959 considered "The Lordship of Christ over Australia and the Pacific."

The findings of the European Ecumenical Conference at Lausanne in 1960, which applied itself particularly to the main theme of the Third Assembly of the World Council of Churches—"Christ, the Light of the World"—gathered up the principal threads of thought young people of the churches were in these years trying to weave into a coherent pattern for their own intellectual and moral guidance.

Declared the more than sixteen hundred delegates:[7]

It weighs upon our conscience that we so easily allow ourselves to be led by other lights than the Light of Jesus Christ—by money and material goods, by false ideas of happiness and success, joy and fulfillment; we are so ignorant of the Scriptures and of the faith of the Church, that we are unpractised in prayer and sacrifice; the body of Christ is so tragically divided; here in Lausanne we have not been able to join together in Holy Communion; there are so many questions—ecclesiastical, political, and personal—on which we have not been able to agree; the differences of nation and ideology, of upbringing and ways of life, and the agonizing differences of language, exercise such sway over us, that we can find no convincing expression of our unity in Christ; above all, after so many years of the ecumenical movement, we are still unable and unprepared by our churches to enter into effective conversation with each other; in our blindness to the light of Jesus Christ and in our disunity we fail in so many ways in our duty to the world.

We know how great is the need suffered by people in the countries of Asia, Africa and Latin America, and even in many countries of our own continent. We know how much the European peoples are to blame for this need which exists in the non-European countries. We know how disastrous are the consequences of the splitting up of Europe and the world into power blocs and zones of national self-interest. We are shocked to discover how badly informed we are about all these things; and we know that this defective knowledge hampers our service to the world.

As "the light of the world," the members of the Youth Assembly felt themselves challenged by the need of the non-European peoples "to a movement of aid and reparation" and were agreed on:

the necessity of certain steps: that Europeans must proceed more resolutely on their way from domination over the world to service to the world . . . ; that in Europe selfish acquisitiveness must be increasingly replaced by the discipline of neighborly love, even if it means personal sacrifice and a lowering of our standards of living . . . ; that "the countries of rapid social change" cannot be helped by charity alone, but only by the dedicated action of people who will give their energy and years of their lives . . . ; that every responsible campaign to help [these countries] demands specialized knowledge . . . [and] this must determine the shaping of the program of our youth groups, our contributions to the life of the adult congregation, our work on publications and our personal study.

They agreed further:

[7] Statements and reports of the Lausanne Conference appear in the Central Committee Minutes, St. Andrews, 1960, pp. 135-140.

That mission is a concern of the whole Church and calls for united witness . .. ; that the principal bearers of mission today in the countries of Asia and Africa must be the churches of those areas themselves . . . ; that these churches, however, in order to bear witness, need the solidarity and support of the whole Christian world . . . down to the smallest local church . . . ; that the credibility of the witness of the Asian and African churches is intimately bound up with the example of those Europeans and Americans who go to the areas of rapid social change, not as missionaries or helpers, but as technicians, engineers, agriculturists, etc. . . . Whether these white people look upon themselves and behave as Christians or not, they appear in the non-Christian environment as representatives of the Christian faith.

Addressing themselves to the problems of political and economic division, the members of the Assembly found themselves agreed:

That, whatever our attitude to . . . co-existence, it is our task . . . to resist with all our might, in both East and West, the uncritical way of thinking in terms of friend and foe . . . ; that every responsible criticism of other social groups . . . , nations and . . . systems demands clear information and must be balanced by a capacity for self-criticism in the light of God's Word; that one of the most important contributions the Christian can make to the well-being of his group, his people and the international sphere of influence in which he lives is his . . . struggle against all forms of prejudice and resentment; that the service of reconciliation directly rooted in the work of Jesus Christ has nonetheless a clear political aspect . . . [and] must operate in terms of personal involvement in public life, where the Church acts as watchman; that the Church in this age of technology and automation has a special responsibility in the field of culture and education . . . : that Christ sets us free to adventure in the search for peace.

The Assembly resolved, moreover, that "the ecumenical movement [was] not a liberation from the bonds of the local church, but a calling to more conscious participation. . . ." We are agreed that we are, more than ever, committed to our local churches . . . but we belong to them now as people who know that . . . the whole Church is supposed to be there for the whole world in its need. We belong to our local churches henceforth as restless and impatient members called to critical participation."

The young people felt that their eyes had been "opened to the pain and guilt of disunity, not only between the denominations, but also within our own congregation." The "silence between the older and younger generations" must be replaced "by respect for each other's gifts and knowledge and a readiness to give and take," they said; and they believed it their special task to establish this relationship, "by asking questions of the older people and drawing them into conversation, and [by] listening to their answers."

Here at Lausanne we have discovered across the denominations our unity in Christ. We believe that we may also expect to make this discovery between the denominations in the areas where we live, and that we should bring it about. . . . Many of us believe that it is time to seek direct contact (through ecumenical Bible study, intercession, joint schemes of service and the formation of local youth councils) also with Roman Catholics. . . . We have learned in Lausanne that, in any case, it cannot be just a question of defending our own point of view, but also of seriously expecting our brethren in other denominations to have something to contribute in the way of knowledge of Christ and of the mystery of his Church.

It would be difficult to evaluate the success with which the Youth Department of the World Council met in its concentration upon "the integration of young people with the life and work of their churches" —the objective adopted, it will be recalled, following the Evanston Assembly. If, in its contacts with the youth of many lands and its study with them of the problem in its manifold phases, the Department came to New Delhi with only a clearer grasp of its declared task, the labor expended would not have been in vain.

"The silence between the generations" was broken by the elders, and their "readiness to give and take" demonstrated upon the receipt by the Central Committee of the findings from Lausanne. The young people had said "pointedly and provocatively":

It weighs upon our conscience that here in Lausanne we have not been able to join together in Holy Communion. . . . We are going home . . . profoundly disturbed by the guilt of division. We are going home as Christians who have experienced what it means not to be able to become one at the Lord's Table, and who do not want to shrug off this pain and no longer want to conceal this guilt from ourselves . . . who know ourselves to have been made responsible by God for seeing that our own denominations' uneasiness about disunity and the passionate longing for visible unity grows continually. We will not stop asking: What really keeps us apart from the others? Which of our objections, measured against the testimony of the Bible, are today no more than prejudice and non-theological traditions? How far are we kept apart only by our national loyalties and state church organizations? Are we really making any effort to clear away these differences? Have we seriously examined the possibility of a dynamic union, such as that established in the Church of South India? What about our intercession for one another and our co-operation on practical issues? Let us not forget also that Christ prayed for us to become one, that the world may believe.

We shall not cease to demand of our denominations, of the neighboring denominations, and of the World Council of Churches: Work seriously towards the establishment of an increasingly inclusive inter-communion: do not come to a standstill on this most urgent task. We hope and pray that before we come together again in an ecumenical youth conference progress will have been made on this point. . . . There is no unity at the expense of truth. But there is also no obedience to the truth which does not compel us to recover unity.

The Central Committee at St. Andrews resolved that the following statement should accompany the dispatch of the findings to the churches:

The Central Committee has received the findings of the Lausanne Youth Assembly, and rejoices in the seriousness and enthusiasm with which the young people gathered there and addressed themselves to the issues of church division and church unity. It expresses the hope that the churches will give careful attention to that part of the findings which deals with the question of communion services in ecumenical gatherings. It confirms that the present position of the World Council of Churches is laid down in the statement on this subject in the Report of the Lund Conference on Faith and Order. [See The Report of the Third World Conference on Faith and Order at Lund, Sweden, August 15-28, 1952, pp. 44-45.]

In the debate on the resolution, some members thought the Central Committee, though giving a "warm welcome to the Report in general, should avoid specific reference to intercommunion." Others commended the Youth Assembly for focusing attention on "the sacrament of the Lord's Supper, whatever judgment might be held with regard to the way this had been done."

Professor Georges Florovsky stated that it would be contrary to the basic discipline and doctrine of the Orthodox Churches even to discuss intercommunion. They would be bound to protest against any proposal of "open" Communion services at ecumenical gatherings.

Objections were voiced, on the other hand, to the suggestion that the World Council of Churches was bound by the Lund statement, and it was pointed out that other groups were dissatisfied with the practice of the World Council with regard to Communion. The opinion was expressed that there must be progress beyond Lund.

A certain bishop spoke of having given the Holy Communion to sick and dying prisoners of war without asking whether they had been baptized or what they believed, accommodating himself to what amounted to "an eschatological situation." Possibly, he said, the youth at Lausanne had experienced something of such a confrontation.[8] Some of the observers at Lausanne thought the Assembly "reflected the young people's dissatisfaction with the abnormality of the present predicament." This sense of "the abnormal" had been underlined by their having been brought together in ecumenical conferences. There was evident the strong feeling that "the ecumenical rules" of the churches had been outrun by events.

Others said confessional positions must be respected, while preserving an understanding relationship between the churches and their youth—so far as truth permitted. Ecumenical fellowship must have depth as well as breadth.

Alan Paton expressed the hope that the efforts of youth to provoke conversation between the generations on the subject of intercommunion might be successful.

In his report to the Central Committee at Rhodes in 1959, the General Secretary of the World Council spoke of the loss of "so many

[8] Statement by Bishop John of San Francisco in the Central Committee Minutes, 1960, p. 93.

men whose lives had been largely devoted to the creation and development of the ecumenical movement," and of the necessity of facing "the question whether that movement could live and grow without the inspired and prophetic leadership of these pioneers." He said:

> We remember especially how we had come to expect . . . that Bishop Bell would bring us at every meeting some new idea, some inspiration, some prophetic perspective which would add significance to our deliberations. . . . We remember equally how Bishop Berggrav could throw light on an inextricable situation by a remark which showed profound Christian wisdom. But the greatest thing about that first generation was that they expected great things from God and believed that God had something better in store for the churches than their present relationships, which are as yet semi-ecumenical and do not manifest the full unity which Christ wants his Church to have. And so we cannot help asking whether that sense of expectation and . . . of the inadequacy of our present relations lives as strongly in our generation. . . . At this point, much depends on the coming generation. And there is a definite reason for encouragement.

This particular reason was "the spontaneous initiative taken by the World's Student Christian Federation to hold next July a conference in Strasbourg wholly devoted to the theme: 'The Life and Mission of the Church.' "

"In the very thorough process of preparation for this conference," said Dr. Visser 't Hooft, "it has already become clear that this meeting will deal with the fundamental issues of the ecumenical movement."

> We rejoice [he added] in the fact that many World Council of Churches leaders will participate in that conference, and so seek to establish a close link with the generation which will have to carry the movement forward in coming decades. . . .
>
> Similarly, our own Youth Department will hold next year in Lausanne a European Youth Conference, which will be the first of several regional youth conferences, and which will also seek to give young people that "mountain-top vision" (as John R. Mott used to call it) of the comprehensive calling of the Church and its mission in and to the world, which is the ABC of a dynamic ecumenical movement.

The North American Youth Assembly on the campus of the University of Michigan in August, 1961, another of the series of regional conferences, brought together some two thousand delegates, including about two hundred from overseas, for a program built around the theme "Entrusted with the Message of Reconciliation" (II Corinthians v, 6). It developed these sub-themes "The World We Live In," "The Gospel We Live Under," and "The Mission of the Church." The Committee on Young People's Work of the Canadian Council of Churches and the United Christian Youth Movement of the National Council of the Churches of Christ in the United States shared the sponsorship of the event with the Youth Departments of the World Council of Churches and the World Council of Christian Education and Sunday School Association. Represented were the International Society of Christian Endeavor, Boy Scouts of America, Girl Scouts of the United States of America, Campfire Girls, the Y.M.C.A. and Y.W.C.A. organizations of the United States and Canada, and the Ministry to Armed Forces Personnel, along with fifteen national denominational youth bodies and a selected number of state Christian youth councils—through their leaders. Among the speakers were Dr. George Johnston, Principal of the United Theological College of McGill University, Montreal, Canada, and Rev. U Kyaw Than, Associate General Secretary of the East Asia Christian Conference. Dr. Robert Seaver of Union Theological Seminary in New York City directed the dramatic productions.

The evidence was unmistakable that whenever the young people were given opportunity to come to grips with the task of the Church in the context of the ecumenical movement their response was earnest and intelligent, allowing for the natural interference at times of immaturity and inexperience. The question was whether or not they could be prepared for leadership in the World Council of Churches while its work would benefit from their visions and enthusiasms.

One following with concern the fortunes of the Youth Department could but wonder why, like the Department on the Laity, it drew its staff and so many of its leaders from the ranks of the clergy. "Some of us are of the opinion," recorded the Lausanne findings, "that it is time the churches gave their young people more freedom in ecumenical endeavor, but we are not agreed on this point." Who was saying this? By the World Council categories, young people were those between approximately sixteen and thirty, with the active majority qualifying nearer the upper limit. If the churches were enabling their most capable young people to represent them in the ecumenical movement, the sense of frustration so plain in the report from the Lausanne Youth Assembly may have indicated a waste of talent they could ill afford.

3. The Ecumenical Institute

With the Evanston Assembly, the Ecumenical Institute began, in the words of its board's new Chairman, Mrs. Kathleen Bliss, "a second distinct period in its development."

Dr. Hendrik Kraemer, who had been Director of the Institute nine years, retired, and with him Mlle. Suzanne de Dietrich, his assistant. The appointment of a new staff became the first task. Dr. H. H. Wolf was called to succeed Dr. Kraemer, and Dr. Robert Paul to be Associate Director. Rev. Charles West joined the staff in 1956, and H. Makulu in 1960. Dr. Nick Nissiotis in 1958 accepted appointment to the vacancy caused by Dr. Paul's resignation.

In a reappraisal of the work of the World Council, the Second Assembly defined the aim of the Institute as being, "to serve the churches as a center of ecumenical study and teaching, worship and experience, where men and women may deepen their understanding of questions affecting the unity, renewal and witness of the Church."

These functions the Institute continued to discharge through the instrumentality of its many-sided program, which included the regular classes in ecumenical education, the Graduate School, occasional study groups led on request by members of the faculty in communities outside Switzerland, consultations for various delegations to Bossey—pastors, missionaries, social workers, nurses, industrialists, scientists, philosophers, lawyers, physicians, chaplains, and others—*ad hoc* conferences on special interests, speaking engagements of staff members abroad, worship services in the chapel, Bible study, and fellowship at the Institute.

As explained by the Board in its report at Davos-Platz:[9]

> The distinctive character of the Institute . . . derives from the fact that it is a continuing institution, where people live together in a fellowship, and in which the aspect of ecumenical education which derives from experience, rather than the acquisition of information, has a major place. This experience includes not only personal contact and intellectual exchange with people of other confessions and nationalities, but also the riches and tensions of ecumenical worship and an element of personal re-commitment and spiritual renewal.

Concerning the influence particularly of worship, the report said:

> Numbers of people already think with gratitude of the Institute as the place at which they experienced most deeply the pain of the division of the Church in its worship and the joy of entering into the richness of traditions other than their own. The deepening of worship there takes its place alongside the biblical revival and the rediscovery of the vocation of the laity, as a third aspect of the renewal of the Church which the Institute can serve. . . . The Board has discussed this matter with special attention, not only because of its intrinsic importance, but also because it affects every course or conference held at the Institute. . . . Worship at an ecumenical center should not be regarded as being primarily an education in comparative liturgiology. It is, in the first place, the worship of Almighty God, in which all who take part in the activities . . . , whether student or staff, can participate.

Demands on the Institute beyond its capacities necessitated "careful . . . choices between proposed projects," so that the limited resources would be made available where most needed. Each year there was the problem of maintaining a balance between (1) classes in ecumenical

[9] Minutes of the Central Committee, Davos-Platz, 1955, p. 109 ff.

training, and consultations on "work on the frontiers between the Church and the world"; (2) courses and conferences for those responsible for the normal institutional work of the churches, and meetings for representatives of the laity "pioneering for the churches in new fields"; and (3) projects organized by the Institute staff themselves, and those in which other departments of the World Council or outside bodies assisted.

Care was taken also to provide opportunity for personal contacts and reflection. It had been found that attendance at ecumenical meetings was "a most critical experience for many individuals," who ought not to be so overburdened with fixed assignments that they could not enjoy "the deeper fruits of ecumenical encounter."

The Graduate School of Ecumenical Studies,[10] in which the World Council was associated with the Faculty of Theology of the University of Geneva, offered the more advanced courses in ecumenics leading to licentiate and doctoral degrees in theology. From within a short time of its founding, well-qualified applicants for admission began to exceed the number that could be accepted. The School in 1956-57 enrolled thirty-four students from the United States, Great Britain, Germany, France, Holland, Denmark, Russia, New Zealand, Africa, Mexico, Turkey, Ceylon, Indonesia, Malaya, India, and Madagascar. In 1960-61 there were fifty registrants, who came from twenty-seven countries and eleven denominations. This was the eighth term of the School, and the study centered on the subject "The Christian Witness in the Post-Christian and Non-Christian Worlds."

"The Graduate School . . . gives us, more and more, the opportunity of developing a new type of academic study, which does not stop with mediating . . . knowledge of abstract problems," advised the Board of the Institute in its report to the Central Committee for 1956-57, "but tries to go as far as possible into the application of fundamental theological insights in an ecumenical perspective. We see that it is an essential task of [the] Institute to communicate these experiences to those who are concerned with . . . training in theological faculties and seminaries. . . . The aim is to avoid the danger that ecumenism will be limited to a special field which is just added to the normal theological curriculum."

This will be remembered by those acquainted with the history of the Institute as one of the objectives which Dr. Adolf Keller and other members of the staff presented in the early years to the theological seminaries of Europe and the United States.

While the program of the Institute was a crowded one, incorporating many and varied phases of the Christian mission, the enrollment in all classes and conferences from year to year consisted of but a few hundred persons, mostly from western Europe and the United States, where in

[10] The Board of Governors, a legal entity responsible to the World Council of Churches and the University of Geneva and jointly appointed by them, consisted of H. Alivisatos, J. Courvoisier, D. G. Moses, W. G. Muelder, L. Pope, R. Prenter, E. Schlink, O. S. Tomkins, W. A. Visser 't Hooft, H. Kraemer, C. K. Sansbury.

the one instance distances were not a serious problem, and in the other money to defray the expenses of travel could be provided for more applicants qualified and willing to attend. For those who might have come in greater numbers from other continents, the journey, with living during the stay in Geneva, would have run into prohibitive cost. Only meager means for aiding students under such conditions were available. Those needing the Institute most and needed by it most could not come.

The financial problem was in other respects also a serious one. Special reserves[11] on which the Institute had been able to draw for its own needs prior to Evanston had been reduced to less than fifty thousand dollars, and it was becoming dependent increasingly on appropriations from the current receipts of the World Council of Churches and the member denominations.[12]

Ecumenical budgets were almost uniformly of parochial dimensions, the total of those for all the World Council's departments being scarcely more than the amount raised by many local churches for their own expenses.

However, the growth of the World Council of Churches in all its divisions and departments showed again that a cause to which vast numbers of people respond in spirit may gather power compensating for any almost material lack.

The Ecumenical Institute, while praying for greater financial support, used the means it had cheerfully and with confidence, knowing that those who came to study in its classes or to take part in the consultations were returning home to share what they had received with and through their churches, and that in this way the ecumenical movement was increasing and reaching out into all the world. "So is the kingdom of God, as if a man should cast seed into the ground; and should sleep, and rise night and day, and the seed should spring and grow up, he knoweth not how. For the earth bringeth forth fruit of herself; first the blade, then the ear, after that the full corn in the ear." (Mark iv, 27.)

The Board's report for 1959-60 at St. Andrews mentioned that the year had begun with a consultation on prayer for unity. "It is significant," it observed, "that in church-life today, along with a deepened engagement in mission and service towards the world, there is a new and growing desire for a better understanding of what it means to be bound together in a community whose head is the living Christ." This drew "attention especially to the importance of intercessory prayer as a part of the life of the serving community," whether local or global. "It is our hope that through this consultation the prayer-life of Bossey will be strengthened, so that the Institute may be able to make in this respect also an impact on all those who come to conferences and courses, that they may better understand the promise and power which is given to

[11] From a gift by John D. Rockefeller, Jr.
[12] Some of the denominations made special gifts.

prayer, and . . . may spread these insights throughout their churches and local congregations."

Building operations occupied a large place in the Institute's program at the end of the Evanston-New Delhi period. Additional dormitory rooms were being constructed in the top story of Petit Bossey, and plans for the erection nearby of a new library with rooms for conference purposes were going forward.

4. The Department of Information

What the churches were doing to make their spiritual unity manifest in organizational relations and to translate it in terms of practical co-operation in Christian work was news with a wide appeal, and the World Council at the time of its founding authorized the establishment of "a publicity department."

There had been attempts under the earlier provisional program[13] to meet this need, but without much coordination or over-all direction.

The implementation of the action at Amsterdam had to be postponed. In fact, nothing was done about it during the interim between the First and Second Assemblies. Adequate funds were lacking, no budgetary provisions having been made for this purpose. And the realization that the movement should have a special kind of publicity requiring a staff with competent technical skill and the understanding of the Church and its life to interpret them accurately and acceptably, which would be difficult to find, also had something to do with the delay.

Not only was the World Council's program news to be reported for its potential contribution to the general enlightenment. The people of the churches, which were making it, were especially entitled to know what was being done and its meaning; and support for the developing work depended upon their being informed. The interactions between the churches and the world underlined the importance of doing everything possible to make the Council and its activities intelligible and engaging to the unchurched as well. This, again, called for expert handling of the modern means of communication by a staff thoroughly conversant with the motivations of Christian work. All these considerations brought up against the necessity of large expenditures of money, which tended to cool enthusiasm.

The World Council could not be regarded as, on the whole, publicity-minded. There were those church authorities who said the "work of the Lord" needed no publicizing. Given due time, results would advertise themselves. Some thought that they could cite scriptural grounds in support of this view. Members from the United States were most inclined

[13] The program under the Provisional Committee of the World Council of Churches, "in process of formation."

to disagree. In New York the American Committee for the World Council of Churches relied on a subcommittee on "interpretation and support" in raising its own considerable budget and promoting appeals for gifts to the general expense budget of the World Council. Its methods met with scant appreciation in some sectors of the ecumenical fellowship.

It was not until the Second Assembly that the World Council got around to setting up "a publicity department," which it named the "Department of Information." Rev. John Garrett of Australia accepted the bid to become its Executive Secretary. Alexandre de Weymarn was continued as editor of the *Ecumenical Press Service,* now brought under the new Department of Information. Theodore Pratt and John Taylor were asked to carry on with phases of publicity at which they had been engaged, and later Miss Betty Thompson became Secretary of Public Relations in the New York Office.

The Committee of the Department of Information, under the chairmanship of Charles P. Taft, a Protestant Episcopal layman of the United States, readily discovered more to be done than it had a staff or other means to undertake.

The management of the publications of the World Council had been transferred, for the most part, to the Department. This arrangement obtained for *The Ecumenical Review,* the *Ecumenical Press Service,* and the several bulletins issued by other departments and the divisions. Among the latter were *The Inter-Church Aid News-letter, The Bulletin* of the Division of Studies, the Youth Department's *News Sheet, Laity* of the Department of the Laity, and the *News-letter* of the Department of Evangelism. In addition to these, occasional reports and announcements were handled for most of the divisions and departments. A handbook on the World Council of Churches was published and its sale promoted to upwards of 100,000 copies. Printed matter for the New Delhi Assembly also became, in part, a responsibility of the Department.

Through the Department was developed the plan of offering all World Council publications at a joint subscription price.

The Department supplied the secular and church presses with news and feature stories, and church and non-religious agencies with occasional special articles, on request.

"Big" releases listed in the Department's report at Galyatetö for 1955-56 indicated the scope of the year's work: the Rockefeller financial grant to the Division of Studies; the riots in Istanbul, with their destruction of Orthodox churches, and the work of the Geneva Mission to Turkey; the closing of the Protestant Seminary in Madrid by the police; the statement of the General Secretary of the World Council on the deportation of Archbishop Makarios of Cyprus; the action also of the Commission of the Churches on International Affairs with reference to the Cyprus civil war; the meeting of the Central Committee of the World Council in Hungary—the first ecumenical gathering in communist territory; the semiannual session of the Executive Committee of the World Council in Australia; the Beirut Conference on the Problem of Arab Refugees. In addition, coverage had been given important conferences of the departments and commissions at Les Rasses, Arnoldshain, Herrenalb, and Bossey. With each year the list of events for which the publicity was handled by the Department grew.

In the area of visual aids, much labor went into the production of photographs, pictorial brochures, films and film-strips and projector slides.

Attempts to develop an adequate radio and television program came to a halt short of realization on account of its cost; likewise, the proposal to install teletype in the offices for collecting and disseminating ecumenical information, as well as for expediting the World Council's administrative business.

There were journeys by staff members of the Department to different parts of the world to gather original photographs and firsthand news of Christian work.

Exhibits describing the activities of the World Council of Churches statistically and graphically were assembled for use at church conventions; and the Department cooperated with other bodies in raising money to maintain a Protestant center at the Brussels World's Fair.

The barrier of language in ecumenical education was difficult to surmount. English, German, and French were spoken in meetings and employed in writings and translations. In a world body like the Council, reports reached great numbers of the members, if at all, through numerous additional languages. The peoples of vast areas, for example, spoke Spanish, and the demand was insistent that attention be given to the improvement of communication with them. The Department of Information had recognized the seriousness of this problem and taken first steps toward its solution. When it came to the printing of informational matter in many tongues, however, the expense quickly became prohibitive. The churches of certain South American countries had been able to assist in this connection with measures toward meeting their own need, and it was hoped that their experiment might have set a course others could and would follow.

The Department reported at Rhodes (1959) that, while its efforts had been received, on the whole, favorably, theologians, the church press, and the broadcasters of religious news "seemed not to have awakened quite to the immense changes in popular culture . . . because of increasing literacy and the electronic revolution." Many denominations were not taking their own publications seriously enough, it had found. "Technical standards for them were low, budgets pathetic, contact with non-Christians ineffectual or old-fashioned and calculated to repel." Full-time "information staffs" were given a low priority in budgeting by the denominations and the interdenominational councils. "Training and marshalling Christians for lay action within the radio and television industries were, in most cases, feeble and unrelated to the key role of the media in creating the tone of our new world-wide popular culture," the statement continued. "Many churches are spending money on other projects that spring from the modes of thinking and acting of yesterday. . . . Allocations of thought, time, initiative and money for creative work by true artists in radio and television production are one of the highest priorities for churches that wish to be in touch with the rising generation . . . [which] is going to be influenced in its deepest springs of imagination and action by the mass media."

All these aspects of the problem were seen urging swift decision.

"Popularization, the sense of being where the people are, is often disliked because of the expense involved and of the fear of getting 'dirty hands,' " the Department had found. "But the world of the mass media, which has come to stay, demands a presence. If this world . . . sometimes looks unredeemed, perhaps that is our fault." [14]

The Department of Information had formed some conclusions concerning its mission and position in the World Council of Churches:

> The range of discussion in the meetings of the . . . Department's committee indicates that every side of ecumenical work is now unavoidably committed to considering the implications of existing in a world of fast, full and accurate mass communications. The Department . . . is not an optional convenience for those of us who are reluctantly forced to resort to some measure of vulgarization. It exists within the Council and the ecumenical movement to help our whole community to accept a powerful means for speaking simply and effectively to other people everywhere. . . . Its task should be seen as central, not marginal. . . .
>
> The committee on future information policy at the Third Assembly will need to give full attention to this matter at New Delhi, so as to recommend the funds and technically competent people needed to satisfy the requirements of the new World Council as a whole.
>
> Ecumenical information should never become a lavish operation designed to justify and protect bureaucracy. Our unpretentious aim is to tell the truth simply, graphically, and as fast as our new mass communication systems demand; but this in itself calls for trained workers in adequate numbers, with the equipment and money the work requires. We need prayer, co-operation, imagination and hard work to ensure that through a flexible and modest unit, helping to tell the story and prepare the way for the Good News, the churches and the world can keep pace with God's on-going plans.

Did the Department of Information consider that the service needed of it by the churches and the world outside consisted of something more than the mere reporting of superficial facts about the World Council by the latest techniques?

Beneath the thin veil of these temporalities loomed questions of the greatest moment, on which multitudes in the churches and many others

[14] For statements of the Department of Information, see Minutes of the Central Committee, St. Andrews, 1960, pp. 56, 149-156.

besides craved light, waiting for an interpreter. They desired to know the *meaning* of the facts in relation to the deeper movements of life, and the distance the World Council had been able to negotiate on the way to its discovery. With a world perspective and the leadership of foremost churchmen of all communions, the Council had, they could only feel, a responsibility beyond the broadcasting of what relatively amounted often to trivia.

A major part of the Council's work consisted, for example, of relief—aid to refugees; flood, earthquake, and famine victims; the poor of the underdeveloped nations. Reports and pictures of its operations in this area easily "satisfied our new mass communication systems' demand." Could the Council not have spoken to the mounting concern over the results of this program in relation to the "population explosion"?

The merger of the International Missionary Council with the World Council of Churches was in the way of being effected. With the resurgence of nationalism throughout the world, many of the new nations were announcing that Christian missionaries were no longer wanted. Could these bodies, which had been conceived under missions and dedicated to missionary ends, not have spoken to the questions raised in the lay mind by the seeming retreat of the churches on this front?

And what could they have said about the need in missions—and the possibility—of a new approach to the ethnic religions?

The actions of the Commission of the Churches on International Affairs were featured information during this period, lending what seemed in some quarters to be further support to the charges that the World Council "played politics." Could the truth about the policy of the Council in this sphere have with reason gone unexplained—or inadequately explained—and the people of the churches and the unevangelized left to conclude whatever they might?

The top leaders of the World Council of Churches were in these years reiterating with growing insistence that the ecumenical movement had no abiding significance beyond serving to prepare the way for the reunion of Christians. Should they not have given to the people whatever reasons they saw for thinking that the Orthodox Churches could unite with the Protestant, or the Roman Catholic Church with either?

Ecumenical study reports and pronouncements had urged, more and more, the application of "welfare state" principles to international life. Ought the Council not have taken the pains to set forth explicitly what this meant, in its own thinking, in the way of envisaged social advances and in the sacrifices which would have to be made by average church members for their consummation?

The World Council had gathered into its meetings representatives from churches in many countries, including those under communist domination. Delegates from these totalitarian nations were essentially appointees of their governments. Some of them, it was known, had been chosen by the state against the will of their denominations. They had been seated by the Assembly of the World Council and certain of them elected to important offices and re-elected from year to year. The World Council had its reasons for this practice, which to it undoubtedly seemed tenable. Why should it have left anything undone to make these clear to the churches and the world?

Theological statements by the World Council—such as, for example, the one on Christian hope at Evanston—had left multitudes of Christians unsatisfied, if not more confused than they had been. Could it not have spoken more plainly and relevantly on the great verities of Christian faith?

Many of the scholars—perhaps a majority of them—who sat in the consultations of the Council had, it was known, abandoned the traditional approach to the interpretation of the Bible, though they might continue to use the terms and symbolisms of the ancient formulas. Had there not been a responsibility to translate the new valid techniques of Bible study into language intelligible to the laity, who in no area of their thinking were more in need of guidance?

These were a few of the questions which had called for answers. The frank discussion of them in the vernacular would have helped to bridge the distance between the World Council of Churches and its much-talked-of "grass-roots" constituency. Some of the issues were controversial and were involving the World Council in attack. It stood in need of understanding loyalty on the part of the people of the churches. If it could not arrive at a consensus on them, it owed those on whose support it must depend information concerning the measure of agreement which had been reached and the positions currently held. Only so could the pulpit and the pew grow with the Council and judge whether or not they were being led toward a fuller apprehension of God and his purpose.

It is not to be inferred that the World Council had not spoken concerning these matters. Most of them had forced their way into its deliberations and become subjects of special study. And the Council had published its findings on them, but mostly in learned treatises, which reached the eyes of few besides the scholars, and in minutes of meetings where they were reduced to sentences which, out of the context, were, to the uninitiated, often more confusing than enlightening.

A movement of the dimensions of the World Council did not lend itself to nutshell reporting. Worthwhile interpretation of it could not be capsuled. Under the circumstances, the Department of Information might not have been able to do more than "tell the truth simply, graphically, and as fast as our new communication systems demand," but the World Council would have been well advised to broaden the purview of its communications to make room for truly ecumenical education for the millions in its churches who remained uninformed and in the dark as to what it was doing and saying as their spiritual monitor about the pressing religious and moral issues of the day.

5. Concerning World Council Finances

The member denominations contributed toward the general expense budget of the World Council of Churches in 1954—the year of the Second Assembly—$314,720.32. The Assembly at Evanston requested an increase, beginning in 1955, to at least $420,000 a year. The Assembly had approved a work program under the new organization of the World Council calling for the expenditure eventually of approximately $446,500 annually. Even if the churches responded with contributions providing the amount indicated, some of the work would have to be deferred until still more funds became available. Some of the denominations made extra gifts, in response to the special appeal, and the receipts for 1955 came to $408,942.80. In 1956 they increased to $416,724, and in 1957 to $424,159.

The income was obviously still inadequate. In 1958 the Central Committee of the World Council approved a recommendation by the Finance Committee that the denominations be asked "to consider seriously" increasing their present giving 15 percent by 1960, and if possible also in 1959. If they found that they could not act on the matter by 1959, they might in 1960, the Committee suggested, make their gifts for the two years together. The general response to this proposal accounted for the larger returns during the second half of the Evanston-New Delhi septennium: in 1958, $460,500; in 1959, $506,286; in 1960, $550,000; and in 1961, $566,000.

Deficits in these years, comparatively small, were absorbed by the reserves. The Finance Committee, under the chairmanship of Eugene Carson Blake, supervised the budget watchfully, maintaining an essentially pay-as-you-go policy.

Twenty thousand dollars from the current receipts was transferred annually to the general reserve fund, which at the end of the Second Assembly had stood at $127,972—still an insufficient amount, it was agreed, for an organization with the commitments of the World Council.

Under certain conditions the Finance Committee and the Central Committee approved *ad hoc* solicitations in the interest of special projects not in the regular budget, and some of these efforts were successful. The Fund for the Republic underwrote the study on religious liberty. On the other hand, the endeavor to obtain financial support in this way for setting up a secretariat on racial and ethnic relations and maintaining it until the necessary funds could be provided through the treasury failed.

The general operating budget covered the expenses of the World Council's New York office. The United States Conference of Member Churches of the World Council had a special dispensation to raise money for its own needs, which in 1953 amounted to $70,000 but increased by 1960 to $83,100. Its principal function was to promote the raising of funds for the World Council, some 80 percent of which had to come from the United States.

It was estimated that financing the Third Assembly would require approximately $300,000. The member denominations were invited to contribute severally for this purpose sums, if possible, bearing to this amount the same proportion as their annual gifts sustained to the operating budget of the World Council.

Economy was definitely the order. An instance of this was the agreement of the denominations, at the request of the Finance and Central Committees, to pay the traveling expenses of their representatives who were elected to committees of the World Council. This practice extended to membership in the Central and Executive Committees, except in the case of a few churches without the means to comply.

The plans for establishing a retiring fund for employees of the World Council, which had been considered prior to the Evanston Assembly, were taken up anew and consummated during this period.

The Division of Inter-Church Aid and Service to Refugees was raising for its work at this time budgets ranging annually from around seven or eight hundred thousand dollars to over a million dollars, and the Finance Committee was jointly responsible with the Division for the handling of this money.[15] Approximately a million and a half dollars was received for Hungarian relief, following the revolt of 1956.

Building projects also claimed the attention of the Finance Committee. The reconstruction of the top floor of Petit Bossey, to provide more dormitory rooms for the Ecumenical Institute, and the erection of an additional building for library and assembly purposes were begun toward the end of the interim between Evanston and New Delhi. For the latter undertaking, between Fr. 400,000 and 500,000 would be needed, it was estimated. A special gift of DM 110,000 toward it had been received from Germany.

After the decision not to reconstruct and enlarge the headquarters of the World Council because of the unavailability of the needed adjoining land, it had been agreed to exchange the property in Route de Malagnou for a new site offered by the city of Geneva and erect new buildings. The cost of the proposed enlargement of the old facilities had been expected to run to about $750,000, and certain of the denominations

[15] The Finance Committee (of the Central Committee and the World Council) had authority over the departmental and divisional budgets, albeit certain departments and divisions were given the right of defined independent actions within this over-all management.

had promised gifts toward it amounting to some $300,000. With the expectation that those who had pledged would be willing to transfer their commitment to the new building program, the Central Committee asked Bishop Henry Knox Sherrill to form a group to raise the remainder, which, according to estimates, would be between two and two and a half million dollars. While it was anticipated that still other denominations would contribute, individuals and foundations would be solicited for the greater part of this amount. Early reports of the appeal encouraged the hope that the receipt of cash and pledges entirely covering it could be announced at New Delhi.

It was estimated that the operating budget of the World Council in 1962, the year after the Third Assembly, would rise to a figure, if the foreseen contingencies were met fully, necessitating a 47 percent increase in the already stepped-up giving of the member denominations.

The Committee on Program and Finance[16] had in 1958 submitted a memorandum listing "fifteen factors" which might help in determining the extra amount to be raised after New Delhi, as follows:

Assistance in the General Secretariat to free the General Secretary for the most important matters.
Strengthening the program and staff of Faith and Order.
A Race Relations Secretariat, as approved by the Evanston Assembly in 1954.
A Religious Liberty Secretariat, as approved at New Haven in 1957.
Employment of a fourth faculty member for the Ecumenical Institute.
Strengthening the Information Department in the use of languages other than English, and to handle radio, TV and audio-visual aids in its work.
Strengthening the Department of Finance and Administration, particularly in relation to administrative developments in the light of the expanding program.
Strengthening of the Commission of the Churches on International Affairs, especially for increased educational work and the coverage of meetings, and improved archives and documentation.
Increased expenditures for salaries which might be found necessary in the continued study of this question.
Adoption of the principle that all departments needed two executive secretaries to minister to a world-wide constituency.
Provision for implementing new projects which might be undertaken by the Third Assembly or before the Fourth Assembly (similar to Race Relations and Religious Liberty at and after Evanston).
Provision against inflation and the decline in the value of monies.
Possible expense on account of new regional developments.
More adequate library services.
Adequate provision in the annual general budget for the expenses of the Fourth Assembly.

[16] The Committee on Program and Finance had been appointed in 1956, to study the work program and the financial requirements of the World Council of Churches in their extensive interrelations. Members: E. C. Blake, Chairman, H. Krüger, F. P. Miller, E. A. Payne, K. Slack, Eugene Smith, S. van Randwijck. Staff consultants: W. A. Visser 't Hooft, R. S. Bilheimer, L. E. Cooke, Francis House, Frank Northam. See Minutes of the Central Committee, 1958, p. 20 for the memorandum.

To this list of probable needs, General Secretary Visser 't Hooft, in a paper on "The Scope of the World Council of Churches Program" prepared for the Central Committee's meeting at Nyborg Strand, Denmark, in 1958, added:

Study on Christian Education and Family Life.
Study on Rural Problems.
Study on Stewardship.
Study on Theological Education.
(Others mentioned by the General Secretary had been met or were included in the later summary of the Committee on Program and Finance given above.)

In his address at Nyborg Strand (1958), Dr. Visser 't Hooft commented on the causes of the constant pressures on the World Council of Churches to expand its work.

Decisions concerning the creation of new departments or the undertaking of additional activities were made, he said, by the Assemblies or the Central Committee; but it was important to identify "the sources of initiative."

The World Council had at its organization taken over several departments and functions, he explained, from the Faith and Order and Life and Work Movements. The Theological Secretariat of the former had been continued in the present Faith and Order Department. The Research Department (originally the Christian Social Institute) of Life and Work had become the Division of Studies and the Department of Church and Society in the World Council, and its Youth Commission the Youth Department. The Information Service of Life and Work had appeared under the new organization as the *Ecumenical Press Service,* and its Committee on Refugees had been merged with the Division of Inter-Church Aid.

The Amsterdam Assembly had adopted the program of activities developed by the Provisional Committee of the World Council of Churches in Process of Formation prior to 1948. The Central Committee in 1951 had initiated the study on the structure and functioning of the World Council, which led to the authorization by the Evanston Assembly in 1954 of the now existing divisions and departments. At the same time the Second Assembly had voted to establish, in addition, a Department on Inter-Group Relations. In 1957 the Central Committee had approved a resolution at New Haven to inaugurate a study on Religious Liberty.

The Assemblies and the Central Committees had not found it possible always to provide adequate funds for the programs they adopted, observed Dr. Visser 't Hooft. The Evanston Assembly recognized that the Division of Studies which had been created could not be fully implemented and had recommended that "additional resources and personnel be sought."

Proposals of new activities had come also from churches which were members of the World Council, he said. The origin of the Department on the Co-operation of Men and Women in Church and Society had been a request of the French Reformed Church to put this matter on the agenda of the First Assembly. The East Asia Secretariat had been created in response to representations from the Asian Churches.

The experience had been that divisions and departments of the World Council encountered in their work, from time to time, new needs seeming to require expansions in their programs.

"Functional groups" of councils of churches and voluntary organizations, wishing to form international contacts, had sometimes approached the World Council with the suggestion of liaison arrangements.

And so in various ways and from many sources the demands arose, and the World Council was confronted nearly all the time with more than it could undertake to meet.

The problem of expanding its work was always related, the General Secretary explained, to another question: "how we can finance our program, without giving up basic principles." The main funds must come from the member denominations, so that they shall remain truly in control; and all the churches must share the total financial burden on an equitable footing.

The size of the World Council's program depended also, Dr. Visser 't Hooft explained, on the available spiritual resources. If there were men and money for larger undertakings, it might be that the ecumenical movement had not developed in its inner spirit sufficiently to give substance to the work envisaged.

Growth had to be responsible. The amount of the budget and the number on the staff were not the only indexes of "ecumenical consciousness." The attitudes prevailing in the churches themselves and their behavior in relations with their neighbors were fully as important factors in the development of Christian unity. There was danger, he said, in a growth that was simply response to opportunity and incidental pressures, however justifiable in themselves. "Growth is responsible, only if it does not bring with it a straining of the spiritual, human and financial resources of the churches, to such an extent that it leads in fact to a weakening of the foundations. . . ."

That the World Council stood for the wholeness of the Church's life did not imply, he thought, that it must attempt "every conceivable or important ecumenical task." It seemed to him worth considering whether certain activities should not be undertaken on a temporary basis, with the intention of discontinuing them after due time and so liberating the means for other needs. Some tasks could best be left, he suggested, to the denominations themselves.

Criteria should be elaborated to enable "the governing bodies" to select the truly urgent causes among the many proposed. Some such considerations should be:

Whether the new activities were a necessary expression of the declared principles of the World Council.
Whether they represented concerns shared by a considerable number of member churches.
Whether enough of the churches would participate.
Whether the work could be undertaken equally well on a regional or national basis.
Whether the total program remained within the limits of the financial resources which could be secured without violation of the principles that the main funds must come from the denominations of the World Council and there must be a fair sharing of the burden by all.

When the World Council of Churches was organized, the member denominations in the United States voluntarily assumed the responsibility of raising approximately 80 percent of the budget. At the time of the Second Assembly, this relationship as to giving remained essentially unchanged. When the appeal to the denominations to make their goal in 1955 $420,000 went out from Evanston, the expectation was that about $310,000 would come from the United States and the balance of $110,000 from the rest of the churches.

This disparateness in giving could hardly be regarded as a healthy condition. It arose, of course, from the unevenness of economic circumstances in the nations after World War II, which was generally well enough understood. But this did not prevent altogether its hurtful effects. The Committee on Program and Finance submitted a memorandum in 1958, in which these were discussed:[17]

The difference between the financial contributions available . . . from American and non-American churches is apt to create some uneasiness, both within and without the ecumenical movement. . . . It may all too easily lead, in regard to the financial decisions which have to be taken, to a frustrating feeling of superfluity and irresponsibility among those churches whose contributions . . . , however generous in proportion to their . . . capacity, cannot by far match the North American churches' share in . . . size. Any decision . . . entailing financial consequences tends, therefore, to be looked upon by the non-American majority of churches as a proceeding . . . not basically their responsibility. . . . Moreover, the North American financial preponderance . . . is likely to be interpreted by outsiders as implying decisive United States influence in any ecumenical decision touching on international affairs.

There are good reasons for taking these considerations seriously. They should not, however, be too hastily or uncritically accepted. First of all, it should be noted that, with few exceptions, all member-churches contribute . . . and that small contributions from financially weak churches may rep-

[17] Minutes of the Central Committee, Nyborg Strand, 1958, p. 95 ff.

resent a larger percentage of their total income than large contributions from financially strong churches. But there is more to be said. We must challenge the tacit assumption, which is so often made, that in an ecumenical organization the influence wielded by any . . . church is, or should be, at least partly proportionate to its financial contribution. This assumption . . . is of an essentially worldly character.

The contribution . . . the World Council hopes to receive from its . . . churches [is] not primarily of a financial nature, and there are . . . burdens to be borne . . . which, not appearing in financial accounts, are none the less real. . . . The only valid authority in this fellowship . . . is that of Holy Scripture and of the Holy Spirit. The only valid influence is that of faith, understanding, obedience, witness and service. . . . No inequality in size, culture, history or financial strength of its . . . churches could ever justify an unequal influence of their representatives.

There is no evidence in the history of the ecumenical movement that the financially stronger members have acted upon the false worldly assumption. . . . There is every reason for other member-churches . . . so to exercise their full responsibilities that the invalidity of these considerations will be apparent.

But when all this has been said, there are good reasons for insisting that, whatever the difficulties, the financial contributions from the non-American churches should be not only maintained, but their relative size increased, even if—as some anticipate—outward circumstances exert pressure the other way. Just as it is unwise and unhealthy for individual churches to depend too much upon endowments or . . . a few generous individuals, so it is with a body like the World Council of Churches. The wider the constituency, the sounder the enterprise. . . . And further concentration of the financial resources . . . in one area . . . should be agreed to only with the greatest reluctance, and if all other means of spreading support fail. . . .

6. New Headquarters in Geneva

The buildings in Route de Malagnou, Geneva, had never been adequate headquarters for the World Council of Churches, and in 1955 the Central Committee approved steps to provide a more commodious meeting room, to enlarge the library, and to make overdue repairs on the offices. This plan had to be abandoned, however, when the offer of adjacent grounds was withdrawn. An appeal for a fund of $750,000 for its prosecution had been authorized and some subscriptions received. Under these circumstances, it was decided to undertake the building of new quarters on a site in Grand-Saconnex, which the city had indicated its willingness to exchange for the World Council's property.[18]

The understanding reached called for the erection of modern structures of functional design, architecturally styled to harmonize with the environment. Some two and a half million dollars would have to be raised, in addition to the gifts which had been made toward the original project of reconstruction and repairs in Route de Malagnou.

Bishop Henry Knox Sherrill consented to form an international com-

[18] Minutes of the Central Committee, Rhodes, 1959, p. 72.

mittee for a campaign to obtain the money needed, and in 1959 he was able to report that approximately one and a half million dollars had been subscribed. The greater part of this amount had been pledged by individuals and foundations. However, contributions and promises running to a substantial sum had come from fifty-nine churches in twenty-four countries. Concern was felt on account of the million dollars still to be secured, but the committee declared its purpose to carry the appeal forward vigorously and hopefully. It was agreed to end the drive on November 18, 1961, the date on which the Third Assembly would convene. The response during 1960 encouraged confidence that the goal would be attained by that time.

Dissatisfaction with the plans offered originally by the architect for the chapel delayed the building, which had been expected to begin in 1959, or 1960, at latest. Meeting at St. Andrews in August, 1960, the Central Committee moved that "the work should be started as soon as possible—probably in March of 1961—on the construction of all buildings, except the chapel; and that the position and approximate . . . volume of the chapel should be determined in the preparation of the final plans for the other buildings, but that new endeavors should be made to find an architectural form for the chapel which would meet with wider approval than the proposals so far received." Actually, ground-breaking ceremonies took place the last week of June, 1961.

By the terms of the trade with the city of Geneva, the World Council of Churches could occupy the old headquarters in Route de Malagnou until June 1, 1962, without paying rent.

According to the statement released by the World Council at the commencement of the building operation, plans for the chapel had been approved by the Executive Committee. They provided for "permanent seating for one hundred eighty persons, with a potential capacity for four hundred." The chapel would be of rectangular shape, two stories high, "and would be located on the ground floor as an integral part of the main block, which would house also the entrance hall, exhibit area and conference rooms. . . . Seats would face the altar from three sides. Above the entrance would be a stylized symbol of baptism indicating that all Christians are united in baptism."

The new headquarters, the announcement stated, would contain 250 offices housing, in addition to the staff of the World Council of Churches, the personnel of the Geneva staffs of the Lutheran World Federation, the World Presbyterian Alliance, the Brethren Service Commission, "and other World Council of Churches-related bodies."

A report that all but $300,000 of the two and a half million needed was "completely assured" added to the spirit of thankfulness which marked the launching of the construction program. It had already been made known that donors might, if they desired, designate their gifts as memorials to leaders of the ecumenical movement.

7. Regional Conferences

The appearance on each of four of the continents during the post-Evanston period of a regional conference of churches marked a new development in ecumenical strategy.

Although not integrated structurally with the World Council of Churches, these new bodies consisted of churches and councils of churches belonging, for the most part, to the World Council or interested in its program and seeking to make a maximum contribution of service to it by developing a closer fellowship with one another and acquiring a better knowledge of their own peculiar needs and resources.

The East Asia Christian Conference was the first to organize. The churches and councils it comprised had been served since the Bangkok Conference in 1949 by the Joint Secretariat for East Asia of the World Council of Churches and the International Missionary Council. Their leaders, meeting at Prapat, Sumatra, Indonesia, in March, 1957, agreed on plans for the new organization so generally acceptable that their official delegates to the inaugural assembly at Kuala Lumpur, Malaya, in May, 1959, could proceed forthwith and unanimously to a motion of adoption.

The resolution was presented by Bishop Enrique C. Sobrepena of the Philippines, who presided:[19]

> Believing that the purpose of God for the churches in East Asia is life together in the common obedience of him for the doing of his will in the world, the East Asia Conference of Churches is hereby constituted, its constitution being accepted as an organ of continuing co-operation among the churches and national Christian councils in East Asia within the frame-work of the wider ecumenical movement.

The Conference proved both the breadth of its program and its will to work by appointing committees on Inter-Church Aid for Mission and Service; International Affairs and Religious Liberty; the Life, Message and Unity of the Church; Lay Witness in the Church and Industrial Evangelism; Religion and Society; Co-operation of Men and Women in Home, Church and Society; and Youth Work.

The emphasis in the discussion of the assembly was on evangelism.

It was recognized that as minority groups in countries where non-Christian religions dominated cultural and social patterns many churches and councils would be tempted to be introversive communities with a defensive attitude. Dr. Daniel T. Niles, who had been General Secretary of the World Council of Churches and the International Missionary Council for East Asia since the resignation in 1956 of Dr. Rajah B.

[19] See *The Ecumenical Review,* Vol. XI, No. 4, July 1959, for statements and reports of the Kuala Lumpur Assembly.

Manikam, suggested that "ghetto-ism," rather than syncretism, which was generally feared, would be the great danger for Asian Christians. Speaking in the same vein, U Kyaw Than, the Associate General Secretary, said:

> The gift of fellowship in the East Asia Christian Conference cannot be for ourselves, but for those outside the churches in East Asia and in the world at large. Our desire for a regional organ cannot be for ourselves, but for manifesting Christ to the world. As a regional body having such a basis, it must never allow itself to become a bloc using pressure . . . to achieve its own sectional desires; nor must it allow itself to appear to a misunderstanding world as an inspired front declaring what our listeners understand not as the mighty works of God but of somebody else.

The Conference would not be, the understanding was, "a regional council of the World Council of Churches." At the same time, it would be served by the secretariat of the World Council. The prevailing mood of suspicion toward alien ideologies evidently seemed to make it necessary to be most explicit about the independence and autonomy of the newly created organ of the churches.

"Because of their colonial past, the Burmese have looked upon Christianity as presented by Western missionaries as another 'trick to enslave them,' " said Dr. Pe Maung Tin, Vice-Chancellor of Rangoon University. They felt, he added, that, having lost their country to the conquerors, they stood in danger of losing their culture to the missionaries. Yet, he told the Conference, Christianity had not been able "to dent the thought of the average Buddhist."

In any case, the meeting made plain the fact that the actual leadership must pass into native hands.

"As we heard from country after country," reported *The Ecumenical Review* of the Prapat consultation, and might with equal truth have said of the Kuala Lumpur Assembly, "of the needs and opportunities, of the obstacles and misunderstandings with which missions have to struggle, of the Western 'hosts' having become 'guests,' but at the same time of the 'hosts' depending still so largely in financial and other ways upon the 'guests,' of Asian churches becoming sending churches and helping one another in evangelism, of the unsolved problems of true indigenisation [sic], it became clear to all that the calling of the Asian churches can only be fulfilled, if they accept the main responsibility for the evangelistic tasks themselves and if they develop a common strategy."

> We must ask, however, what such a regional development means for the world movements [wrote Dr. Visser 't Hooft]. Regionalism can easily lead to bloc-formation and a certain isolationism, particularly in the world of our day, in which intercontinental tensions are becoming stronger every day.
>
> Is there a danger that this and similar regional developments may weaken the cohesion of the World Council? Those of us who had the privilege to participate . . . are able to reply . . . that there were no signs of separatist

tendencies. The regionalism . . . advocated was not directed against other parts of the world. . . . These churches and councils desire to co-operate because they feel a common responsibility for the evangelization of Asia. The whole content of the discussions was the evangelistic calling of the Church in Asia. It was felt . . . that calling could be fulfilled more adequately, if the churches of Asia learned to work together, to assist one another, to exchange fraternal workers. At the same time, it was made perfectly clear that the regional co-operation should in no way weaken the participation of the Asian churches and councils in the World Council of Churches and the International Missionary Council. And the plan to set up an enlarged secretariat will be related both to the committees of the Conference and to the world bodies. . .

This solution of the problems of regional relationships may well become a precedent which will have a bearing on developments in other parts of the world.[20]

There were no delegates from Western churches at Kuala Lumpur, but the International Missionary Council and the World Council of Churches had sent consultants and observers. The 180 persons attending came from Australia, Burma, Ceylon, Hong Kong, India, Indonesia, Japan, Korea, Malaya, New Zealand, Okinawa, Pakistan, the Philippines, Taiwan, and Thailand. Unofficial observers were present from Cameroun, Kenya, Nigeria, Canada, Germany, the United Kingdom, the Netherlands, and the United States.

There was a special significance in the invitation of the Asian churches to the churches of Australia and New Zealand to associate themselves with the Conference. This came of "the deep interest which had arisen in the churches in Australia and New Zealand for the Asian churches."

"From the standpoint of the ecumenical movement as a whole," declared Dr. Visser 't Hooft, "this is not merely a natural, but also a most desirable step. Ecumenism begins at home, and—although there are vast differences between Asia, on the one hand, and Australia and New Zealand, on the other—there is a sense in which that whole area is an *okios,* a geographical unit in which the people have common problems and . . . tasks."

The outlook of the Kuala Lumpur Assembly was indicated in a message "to the member churches and councils":[21]

There is much evidence of the work of the Holy Spirit in our churches. In areas of extreme difficulty and danger the Church is growing. New ways of evangelism are being pioneered. Most of the churches of Asia are now sending out missionaries to other lands, as well as receiving them, and helping one another with many kinds of service, as well as receiving manifold help from churches in other parts of the world. . . .

We rejoice that in most parts of East Asia there is religious freedom. We recognize, however, that there are large areas in which this freedom is severely curtailed. We affirm that the right of every adult to profess and to

[20] Minutes of the Central Committee, New Haven, 1957, p. 83.
[21] *The Ecumenical Review,* July 1959, p. 450 ff.

propagate his faith, and the right to change his religious affiliation is a God-given right. . . .

Our countries and peoples have changed beyond recognition in the past twenty-five years. The achievement of national freedom, the drive toward better standards of living, and the rebirth of the ancient religions combine to create a new revolutionary situation for the ordinary man. . . .

Christian people must go into every part of the life of our peoples, into politics . . . social and national service . . . the world of art and culture, to work in real partnership with those who are Christians, and to witness for Christ. Every Christian must recognize that his primary service to God is the daily work he does in the secular world. . . . We must give our minds to the task of understanding what God is doing . . . so that Christians engaged in these secular tasks may have guidance and help in the decisions they have to make, and . . . the churches may be ready, when necessary, to speak a prophetic word of warning or encouragement to those in authority and to the peoples. . . .

Each congregation must know that it is put into the world by the Lord as his representative, and that it must, therefore, be chiefly concerned, not with itself, but with the world—concerned to send its members out as witnesses, and to invite all men into the family of God. Its minister . . . should train every member for this ministry. . . . Its worship should be such that those around are drawn to the worship of the true God as their Father . . . its forms of organization . . . such that every member can be, and know himself to be, an active member of the Body of Christ. . . .

Our churches are in many cases small and weak, too dependent on the support of older churches, too much imprisoned in traditional forms. But the Holy Spirit is . . . able to open new paths and . . . create new things. . . .

The other regional conferences in mission areas were only in the process of organization as the Evanston-New Delhi period drew toward an end. Plans for one for Latin America had been projected at an assembly in Argentina during August, 1961, which was attended by invited representatives of the World Council of Churches and the International Missionary Council.

Observers from a number of African countries had attended the Kuala Lumpur Assembly by invitation. The Continuation Committee of the All-Africa Conference at Ibadan the year before had in hand the commission to work toward the development of an All-Africa Christian Conference. Peter Dagadu said at Kuala Lumpur that Christians in Africa had been deeply moved by the action of the East Asia Christian Conference, and that it was "a challenge to the churches of Africa."

The East Asia Assembly at Kuala Lumpur sent a special message to the churches in Africa:

We have learned . . . with deepest interest of your All-African Conference in Ibadan, and of the steps already taken towards the development of an All-African Council, and we assure you of our prayers for the growth of such an ecumenical fellowship, that in greater co-operation and unity your witness may abound throughout the continent.

The European Conference of Churches, although there had been an earlier meeting at Liselund, Denmark, had its formal beginning at Nyborg Strand, Denmark, in January, 1959, when a more inclusive convention brought together a number of churches, besides a majority of those in Europe which were members of the World Council of Churches.

This assembly proved of especial advantage as a meeting ground for Eastern and Western churches of Europe. It set up a continuation committee and chose Dr. H. H. Harms to be its secretary, a position he accepted while remaining Director of the Division of Studies.

The Conference convened at Nyborg Strand in October, 1960, for another meeting, which was attended by 120 delegates of Protestant, Anglican, and Orthodox churches and was the most representative ecumenical gathering of European churchmen ever held. The Russian Orthodox Church sent nine members, the British Council of Churches seven. Bishop Johann Wendland, Russian Orthodox Exarch for Central Europe, was added to the Executive Board, and Dr. Harms continued as secretary.

The conferees agreed that their churches desired more exchange and cooperation between the annual meetings of the Conference. A resolution repeating its earlier appeal to the nations "to liberate the world from the menace of atomic warfare" and to abolish all forms of force was adopted.

At Nyborg Strand in 1958 the General Secretary of the World Council of Churches discussed in his annual report to the Central Committee questions of policy raised by regional cooperative movements of churches and church councils "within the membership of the World Council." He said, among other things:[22]

> From the point of view of the World Council, [regional co-operation] is a most welcome development, for co-operation on a world scale becomes unreal, unless it is undergirded by co-operation on the level of regions or continents. The ecumenical movement needs the regions, and that not so much as channels for its various activities, but as centers of creative common thinking within a concrete situation. At the same time, the regional bodies can perform a number of tasks which would have to be performed by the World Council of Churches, if they did not exist.
>
> But the growth of these bodies means that we have to face new problems concerning the structure of the Council and the ecumenical movement as a whole. . . . What exactly is the responsibility of the World Council with regard to these bodies? What is their responsibility with regard to the World Council . . . ?
>
> It would seem that all concerned agree in rejecting the two possible extreme solutions.
>
> One is that the only role of regional bodies is . . . to carry out the policies of the world body. The other is that their only role is to represent the interests and concerns of the regions. . . .

[22] Minutes of the Central Committee, Nyborg Strand, 1958, p. 77 ff.

None of them wants to be separatist. This is indicated by the fact that in several cases the regional secretariats are in the hands of men who are members of the World Council staff. From the point of view of secular organizational thinking, this may seem like an impossible compromise. . . . But from the point of view of the Christian Church, this is our specific contribution to the problem of international collaboration. For do we not believe that we are all members one of another, and that, therefore, true Christian fellowship must . . . express itself in a combination of full-fledged solidarity and of recognition of the specific charisma of every member or group of members? It is likely that at times this dialectic between regional and world interests will cause trouble, and it is certain that those who are placed in the position that they are to represent the views of a region in world meetings and the concerns of the world body in regional meetings will have a difficult task; but I would express the hope that we will not give up the principle underlying it, for it is a Christian principle. . . .

During the first stage, we must be careful not to ask the regional bodies to give a disproportionate amount of time and energy to their task of acting as channels for world-wide programs. It is in the interest of the ecumenical movement itself that the regional bodies become strongly rooted in the life of the churches, so that they can bring the full spiritual contribution of these churches to the ecumenical movement as a whole.

8. New Members of the World Council, 1954–61

1954–55

The Dutch Reformed Church of the Cape Province.
The Bantu Presbyterian Church of South Africa.

1955–56

The Evangelical Church of the Augsburgian Confession in Silesia in the Czechoslovak Republic (Lutheran).
The National Baptist Convention of America.

1956–57

The Baptist Church of Hungary.
The Church of the Province of Central Africa (Anglican).
The Shindo Evangelico Aleman del Rio de la Plata.
The Armenian Church.

1957–58

The Evangelical Lutheran Church in the United States of America.
The Presbyterian Church of East Africa.
The Gereformeerde Church in Indonesia.
The Burma Baptist Convention.
The Presbyterian Church of Jamaica.
The Church of Latvia (Evangelical Lutheran).
The Ecumenical Council of the Churches of Poland.
The Ecumenical Council of Finland.

1958–59

L'Église Évangélique du Cameroun.
The Hungarian Reformed Church in America.
The Independent Church of the Philippines.

1959–60

The Ecumenical Council of the Churches of Austria.
The Ecumenical Council of the Churches of Czechoslovakia.
The National Council of Churches of Korea.

1960–61

L'Église Évangélique de Malagasy (Madagascar).
The London Missionary Society Synod in Malagasy (Madagascar).
The Syrian Orthodox Patriarchate of Antioch and All the East.
L'Église Évangélique du Togo.
The Sudanese Christian Church of West Java.
The Methodist Church of Ghana.
The Church of the Province of East Africa (Anglican).
The Presbyterian Church in the Republic of Korea.
The American Lutheran Church.[23]

The Nederduitsch Hervormde Kerk van Afrika resigned from membership in the World Council of Churches in 1960 because of its policy of *apartheid* (separate development of the white and dark peoples), which it held to be "the only just solution of our racial problem." The Dutch Reformed Church of Transvaal also resigned, though expressing its intention "to remain in correspondence with the World Council."

In 1961 the membership of the World Council stood at 174 after the indicated withdrawals and mergers.

9. Looking Toward the Third Assembly

Preparation for the Third Assembly was begun in the Central Committee at Evanston with the discussion of a critical appraisal of the Second Assembly, just ended, by a Sub-Committee on Assembly Procedure.

At Davos-Platz, the following year, the appointment of a committee from the Executive Committee on the Organization of the Third Assembly was authorized, with the provision that it should work in conference with a Committee on Rules of Debate and Procedure, also from the Executive Committee.

The Central Committee received the reports of these committees at Galyatetö in 1956 and considered them at length when it met in New Haven a year later. On the latter occasion, it accepted an invitation from the National Christian Council of Ceylon to hold the Third Assembly at the University of Ceylon in Peradeniya at a date toward the end of 1960.

[23] Formed by the merging of the American Lutheran Church, the Evangelical Lutheran Church, and the United Evangelical Lutheran Church, which had been independently members of the World Council of Churches.

The main theme, "Christ, the Light of the World," and the subsidiary themes, "Unity," "Witness," and "Service," had been chosen in 1958 at Nyborg Strand.

Meanwhile, it had become necessary to postpone the date of the Assembly a year, to give the Joint Committee responsible for the negotiations on the proposed merger of the International Missionary Council and the World Council of Churches time to complete its work. And the development in Ceylon of unstable political conditions had led to the abandonment of plans to go there for the Assembly and the acceptance of an invitation from the National Christian Council of India and the member churches of the World Council in that country to come to New Delhi.

This action was accompanied by an expression from the Central Committee of appreciation and regret to the churches of Ceylon.

Acting on behalf of the German churches, Bishop Otto Dibelius had invited the Assembly to Berlin; but New Delhi was chosen, partly in consideration of the fact that the previous Assemblies had been held in Europe and in North America, and it was logically the turn of another continent. Moreover, it seemed especially appropriate that the churches should have opportunity to gather for this historic occasion in the midst of Asia, their most extensive mission field, and this when the World Council and the International Missionary Council would, it was expected, be uniting.

An effort should be made, it was agreed, to enlist the churches generally in the preparatory study of the main theme. This was felt to be the more necessary for the fact that attendance would have to be limited to a figure much below that of Evanston, and the Third Assembly would in other ways also have fewer and less immediate contacts with many of the major member denominations of the World Council. Over 2,300 persons were enrolled in some capacity at Evanston, and a much larger number, many of whom traveled long distances, attended the public sessions. Available accommodations in New Delhi would make it necessary to restrict the official registration to approximately one thousand.

Some concern was expressed over the development of the main theme. "Christ, the Light of the World" was regarded by many as a concept lending itself to devotional study but hardly to theologizing. Who could be sure of what Jesus meant when he said, according to the Gospel of John, "I am the light of the world"? Was he claiming, for example, to be the one and only light of mankind, or the bearer to his generation of the light from God which many before him had seen and others after him would herald?

The traditional interpretation was reflected in a recommendation of the Executive Committee at Rhodes concerning titles for the studies by the sections at the Third Assembly, which proposed for the first: "Jesus Christ Is the One Light—the Unity of the Church."

However convinced many Christians might be that Jesus Christ was "the one light," the world had other lights it would be more than loath to abandon. Dr. Pe Maung Tin, Vice-Chancellor of Rangoon University, for example, told the East Asia Christian Conference at Kuala Lumpur that Christianity had not been able "to dent the thought of the average Buddhist." Would reaffirmation of faith in Jesus Christ as "the one light" not confirm still more trust in other lights and deepen in the minds of the uncommitted masses the distrust of all lights?

The declaration of Jesus to his disciples, "Ye are the light of the world," would be studied in connection with the Assembly theme, though it definitely should not be inscribed on banners or blared by loud-speakers. The first effect of possession of the true light would be humility. Jesus might have said, "Ye are the light of the world," but the harder his followers worked to measure up to his words, the less would they be inclined to speak of them, and the more to wonder that he should ever have uttered them.

The light from God would become incandescent in the humble spirit, seeing which, men would glorify God as its recognized source. "Let your light so shine before men, that they may see your good works and glorify your Father which is in heaven." Those who were going to New Delhi would do well to concentrate on good works, rather than on doctrine, whether in the deliberations of the Assembly or in private encounter with the people of Asia.

There would be at New Delhi the usual denominational and confessional observances of the Lord's Supper, certain of which would be open to all wishing to participate. The Church of India, Pakistan, Burma and Ceylon (Anglican) had informed the Central Committee, however, that it was prepared to be "the host church" to the Assembly at a service of Holy Communion on Sunday evening, November 26, "to which all delegates and other members would be invited."

The date of the Assembly would be November 18–December 5, 1961, and the place Vigyan Bhavan, the new public hall of India's capital city.

10. Post-Evanston Perspective: A Narrow Road

It is one of the greatest facts in the history of the ecumenical movement, that it has in general succeeded in maintaining relations of fellowship and confidence between churches and individuals separated by political divergencies or even by international conflicts and war. But owing to the depth of the gulf which has come to divide the world, this task of maintaining unity is increasingly hard to fulfill. Moreover, the fundamental spiritual independence which the World Council must maintain, if it is to be true to its mission, is constantly being challenged.

The Council has sought to make it clear that it believes in the lordship of Christ over all realms of life, that it must therefore speak out when great questions of principle are at stake, but that it cannot identify itself with any ideology or group of nations.

The great question in this respect will be whether the member churches are ready to stand by this policy and to help the Council in avoiding both irrelevance and partisanship. At this point much ecumenical education is still needed.

The road along which the Council must travel in the world of our time is a narrow road. It can only praise God for the foretaste of the unity of his people which he has given to it, and continue hopefully to serve the churches as they prepare to meet their Lord, who knows only one flock.[24]

The road ahead for the World Council of Churches is cause of concern to many. Others besides the General Secretary have foreseen that it can only be a narrow road. Some fear that it may turn out to be a dead end. The World Council may, they think, be attempting the impossible. At any rate, it is undertaking too much, they say. And certain of its policies and methods inspire misgivings.

Whether or not such feelings are justified cannot be determined at this early stage of modern ecumenical history. If the Council is truly an enterprise of God, its mistakes can be providentially overruled. "The vessel . . . was marred in the hand of the potter: so he made it again another vessel, as seemed good to the potter to make it" (Jeremiah xviii, 4). Much in the experience of the movement has seemed to support the conviction that it rose in the divine will and advanced with a power not of itself. But the future for men and their institutions, like the end of a tortuous trail into mountainous country, is hidden. Ecumenical journeying is not, moreover, by a well-worn path with footprints to guide the traveler. They who set out upon it must walk by faith.

"The World Council . . . believes in the lordship of Christ over all realms of life," its General Secretary says; and here, at the outset, is a most difficult problem.

All Christians accept, in principle, the lordship of Christ. But what, in practical terms, does his lordship mean? Ecumenical studies have reported that they found in the Bible no clear guidance when it came to determining his will in reference to modern social questions. Do the implications of his lordship not have to be left, in any given instance, to the judgment of the individual? He will, of course, have regard for the decisions of the Church, which represent a consensus arrived at through experience broader than his own. But he is certain to find the Church, or its spokesmen, divided in their opinion. He may see also that facts of which he has perhaps a better knowledge than the theologians have not received the consideration they deserved, or have in the larger consultation been bypassed altogether; and it will be impos-

[24] W. A. Visser 't Hooft in *A History of the Ecumenical Movement,* p. 723.

sible for him to accept with full assurance what has been said by or in the name of the Church to be the will of Christ.[25]

So the Church will not, for all its intentions, speak with one voice through the World Council "when great questions of principle are at stake." It should have spoken differently, some will say, and others that it ought not to have spoken at all.

All a religious body, whether a denomination or an association of many denominations, can do is seek the truth "in dependence . . . on the Holy Spirit, and in penitence and faith," and the Christian giving it his support can only hope that it will learn wisdom from its mistakes, which may be one means of divine enlightenment. He may follow at times with hesitation, and always with the certainty that in the end he must himself be judge of what the will of Christ is. Infallibility belongs only to Rome, and most persons casting their lot with the World Council of Churches could not acknowledge such a claim by any body.

Those who say the World Council undertakes the impossible have what looks—superficially at least—like corroboration of a factual nature. The Council gathers into its membership churches from many nations and commits them to work together to make Christ "Lord over all realms," exposing its unity to the widest differences concerning the principles which seem to be implicit in the doctrine of his lordship. It feels called to "speak out" on important social and political issues and at the same time to maintain "relations of fellowship and confidence between churches and individuals separated by . . . divergencies [in these matters] or even by international conflict and war." It will not "identify itself with any ideology or group of nations," it says. It will seek to be relevant in its pronouncements and actions, and not partisan. Surely, only the greatest faith could support the choice of such a policy.

By accepting the invitation to hold the meeting of the Central Committee in 1956 in Hungary, said Dr. Visser 't Hooft:[26]

> the World Council showed once again that it lives its own life in complete independence from any particular political or economic system or ideology. . . . Whenever we meet, we stand for certain great fundamental truths

[25] "With respect to public pronouncements, the Council regards it as an essential part of its responsibility to address its own constituent members as occasion may arise, on matters which require united attention in the realm of thought or action.

"Further, important issues may arise which radically affect the Church and society. While it is certainly undesirable that the Council should issue such pronouncements often, and on many subjects, there will certainly be a clear obligation for the Council to speak out when vital issues concerning all churches are at stake. But such statements will have no authority save that which they carry by their own truth and wisdom. They will not be binding on any church unless that church has confirmed them, and made them its own. But the Council will only issue such statements in the light of God's revelation in Jesus Christ, the Lord, and the living Head of the Church; and in dependence on the power of the Holy Spirit, and in penitence and faith." (Amsterdam Assembly, 1948.)

[26] Minutes of the Central Committee, Galyatetö, 1956, p. 72.

> concerning man as a creature of God and . . . his right and duty . . . to witness in full freedom to the lordship of Christ over all aspects of life. One of our main themes in these days [at Galyatetö] will be "The Churches and the Building of a Responsible International Order." In this concept of a responsible society, to which we are committed . . . we proclaim together that society has a responsibility for the well-being of its members, that every person in society has a right to participate as a responsible member . . . and that society is not an aim in itself, but is responsible to God. . . . We will surely seek to apply these convictions to the international life.

During the provisional stage the World Council incurred criticism by its pronouncements on economic and political questions; but in that early period its work in the field of Faith and Order and, toward the end, of wartime relief rather overshadowed its activities in the area of social action. Not until the Amsterdam Assembly was attention turned with deepening concern to this phase of the program, albeit the alleged political activity of the Council had been mentioned by the Russian Orthodox Church as one of the reasons for its sudden rejection, after earlier manifestations of interest, of the invitation to send representatives to the First Assembly. Complaints followed soon from various other quarters because of what were regarded as political involvements on the part of the Council. In the West these came from denominations not in the Council, and also from dissident groups of some which were.

Officials of the World Council rejected the charge that it "meddled in politics," contending that its actions consisted only of declaring Christian principles that should be applied to political as well as other problems, and that it acted "without partisan bias." Its observers at the United Nations kept the churches informed on matters before that body of special concern to them and interpreted to it their mind on pending issues. This or other like actions did not mean, its leaders said, that the World Council was "in politics" for political ends. It was not a "lobby" representing the interests of the churches and missions affiliated with the ecumenical movement. It sought only to throw the light of common Christian convictions upon the concrete problems of international life.[27]

This policy in the West, where liberty in such matters was generally upheld, resulted in both gain and loss of support for the World Council. Outside the free world the problem assumed a different shape. To totalitarian nations assertion of "the right of all people to freedom, independence and self-determination" amounted to attacking the government or at least to interfering in matters of policy belonging to the state. It was so regarded in Hungary, and likewise by the Union of South Africa when the World Council promoted there a conference of the churches on *apartheid,* the declared position of the government on race relations.

Another effect was embarrassment for Christians in the totalitarian

[27] *The Ecumenical Review,* July 1956, p. 362.

countries whose denominations were members of the World Council and shared the responsibility for its actions, whether approving them or not. It was in the situation thus created that T. C. Chao felt it necessary to withdraw from the Presidium following censure by the Central Committee of the People's Republic of China as aggressor in Korea in 1950, and the Chinese churches ceased to participate as members of the World Council.

When the Provisional Committee of the World Council of Churches, "in process of formation," had been urged to make a statement concerning the issues of World War II, William Temple had dissented:[28]

> If we speak corporately, we may find that we have erected fresh barriers to the reconstruction of the fellowship. Christians from one country can meet Christians from another country with which they have been fighting in an organization which has not corporately taken sides; it will be difficult, almost impossible, to do this in an organization which has officially condemned, directly or by implication, their own country. . . . I want us all to prophesy individually and to do this in contact with one another . . . so the message will be given ecumenically, though with a variety of emphases.

In its relations with churches in communist nations during the early postwar years, the World Council was unquestionably influenced by the belief that many of their people shared its own aversion to communism and would welcome support from Christians outside the Iron Curtain, and that encouragement ought to be given to the existing latent spirit of revolt. But not only had serious hope of the unseating of communist powers by revolution soon to be abandoned; there was evidence that the denominations, though there were possibly many persons in them who inwardly rebelled, were accepting the new status and accommodating themselves to it. Some of their spokesmen, indeed, went farther and declared their more than willing acceptance of the change from the old regimes.

The National Committee of the Protestant Churches in China, which was formed in 1950 under the auspices of the People's Republic "to insure support of Protestants for the Peiping government," in January, 1961, "pledged continued support to the communist powers." Approving this action were over three hundred delegates from all parts of mainland China to a conference in Shanghai, which had been called by the National Committee. Speakers declared that the Chinese Protestant churches had made "great progress during recent years in their patriotic, anti-imperialistic movement and had transformed themselves from an instrument of imperialistic aggression into churches administered by Chinese Protestants themselves." The conference adopted a resolution thanking the government for granting religious freedom and asserting that the Protestant churches were "determined to oppose imperialistic

[28] *A History of the Ecumenical Movement,* p. 710.

aggression, defend world peace and adhere to socialism." The National Committee claimed that it had helped other Protestant churches not belonging to it to survive and grow under the People's Republic.

Anglican Bishop K. H. Ting of Peking had in 1956 informed the Central Committee at Galyatetö, before which he appeared by invitation, that Chinese Christians did not regard the rise of the People's Republic as an act of God's wrath but of his love. He said they would not wish to end the new regime if they could. Christians in China did not pretend to agree with communists in their views on religion, he declared, but this did not prevent their recognizing the value of the good things the People's government was doing. They were humbled and gave thanks to God for their improved circumstances.

Professor Josef Hromadka had not made any secret of his full acceptance of the communist revolution in Czechoslovakia, because of the (in his view) beneficial social changes wrought by it for the people.

The churches of Russia, excepting perhaps those of the former Baltic states, had manifested no desire to be "liberated."

It was claimed that Christians in all communist nations might reject the party's materialistic philosophy, as many did, without incurring any penalty.

The churches were not chafing under state control so much, it was said, as might have been imagined, for the fact that offices on religious affairs were an established part of government of long standing in most countries. In reply to protests by the Lutheran primates of Scandinavia against Hungary's usurpation of authority over the Lutheran Church, Premier Janos Kadar remarked that it was not unknown for the governments of their own nations to take a hand in ecclesiastical matters. He reminded them, if not with perfect appositeness, that the sovereign of the United Kingdom of Great Britain was head of the Church of England and nominated its bishops for election by Parliament.

While conditions under communism were not ideal for the churches, some changes had worked, at least temporarily, to their immediate advantage. The restriction on the number of churches, with the attendant reduction of expenses and added provisions for subsidies from the state, had helped rather than hindered the work as a whole. At the same time, it was claimed that the revolution had brought a more abundant life in every way to the people. If this had resulted, in part, from killing off many citizens and expropriating their property, there were ways of rationalizing it to ease the more sensitive consciences.

Christians belonged to their motherlands and could see that it was their duty and best ultimately from the standpoint of their own interests to accommodate themselves to the new conditions, even if it involved difficult religious adjustments and painful sacrifices.

They were not unaware of the declared purpose of the Communist party to destroy the Christian religion, or of the studied and often ruthless methods it employed to accomplish this. But they believed that faith would survive and God would have the last word. Moreover, the world was changing, they reasoned, and there must be a general readaptation. What was false or anachronistic in communism would have inevitably to yield to new revelations. The conviction was widely held that the West would have to undergo the same sort of transformation, that it must embrace communistic principles and methodology, and that there would be eventually a social coalescence on a world scale which would close the now impassable rift between West and East.

It was Christian tradition that commitment to the lordship of Jesus Christ supplied in the first centuries the martyrs whose blood was "the seed of the Church." While martyrdom could easily occur under communist and other totalitarian tyrannies, the case was different from that of the early Christians. Commanded to worship Caesar, they chose to die rather than set any man above Christ. Under communism, worship of God was not proscribed. The dictator did not call himself God. He might, to all practical purposes, usurp the place of God, as Nikita Khrushchev apparently thought to do, when he declared on one occasion in the United Nations Assembly that he and his colleagues were not present by anybody's grace—not even God's, whom they had discarded. But, with the banishment of the idea of God altogether, deification could hardly follow. It was possible that communism had learned something the Caesars had not, namely, that not martyrdom but slow strangulation and forced compromise were the technique for killing Christianity and its churches.

It seemed possible that Christianity was definitely on the way out wherever communism held sway, and that it could be kept alive and conquering only by the action of Christians willing to resist unto death. Most observers, judging from developments under the ecumenical policy, did not look for any decisive stand against the paralyzing control of religion by its atheistic enemies. They saw no hope for a breaching from within of the Iron or the Bamboo Curtain. The future seemed to promise only continuing submission by the churches, with slow but destructive attrition.

Some looked for the situation to give birth providentially to new Christian values. Speaking at the Salonika Conference in 1959, Dr. Daniel T. Niles, who had observed communism at close hand in many lands, expressed concern over the tendency to evade "any prophetic interpretation of the Chinese upheaval."

"Sooner or later," he said, "we must begin a real conversation among the churches about what . . . God is doing in, for and with China."

It might be asked whether, under these circumstances, the World Council of Churches or other international Christian organizations—denominational, confessional, or other—had any legitimate mission to communist nations beyond the dispensing of charity as conditions arose from time to time calling for obedience to the apostolic injunction to do good unto all men as there was opportunity, especially to those of the household of faith. They might continue to welcome Christians of these countries to fellowship and membership, as at present, if the latter desired this at the cost of the disabilities it inflicted. But there was in this course the danger of compromising their own testimony and of laying themselves open further to the suspicion of "softness" toward communism.

Whenever they proclaimed "that society had a responsibility for the well-being of its members, that every person in society had a right to participate as a responsible member and that society was not an aim in itself, but was responsible to God," and undertook to apply these convictions to international life, they would not be tolerated by totalitarianism. The state would bid them be gone, and, if the example of China meant anything, Christians who had to continue to live in the state would feel relief at their departure.

It may, after all, be a mistake to say that the road ahead for the World Council of Churches is a narrow one. "Maintaining relations of fellowship and confidence between churches and individuals separated by political divergencies or even by international conflict and war," if at the cost of compromising the Gospel, may actually be taking unwittingly the "broad way."

Part Eight

ABOUT NEW DELHI

We are called to glorify God in the church. We are equally called to glorify him in the world. For however rebellious that world has become, it is destined to be the theatre of his glory. The light which we receive from him who is the light of the world is not to be put under a bushel, not even under the domes of cathedrals or the roofs of parish churches; it is to shine among our fellow-men. The manifold wisdom of God, manifold and therefore to be expressed by the gifts of grace received by all the members of the body together, is to be made known through the Church, in the principalities and powers which dominate the world. The world has a right to expect from our churches that they follow the pattern of the incarnation, enter deeply into the life of humanity, live in true solidarity with the whole human family, and especially with those who suffer in spirit or in body. . . . So we are called to glorify God together by helping the needy inside and outside the Christian fellowship, by struggling for a responsible society, by seeking to orient the process of rapid social change to constructive ends, by replacing racial discrimination by inter-racial co-operation, by seeking to create conditions of international justice and by resisting the vicious and infernal circle of nuclear re-armament and nuclear testing.

—Willem A. Visser 't Hooft
(at New Delhi)

INTRODUCTION

The Program At New Delhi

The Third Assembly of the World Council of Churches convened at New Delhi, India, on November 19, 1961. The program of the Assembly followed, in a general way, the pattern set by Amsterdam and Evanston.

Matters presented by or through the Central Committee constituted the greater part of the agenda. Significant among them were the proposed merger of the International Missionary Council and the World Council of Churches, with the structural changes it necessitated; revision of the Basis of the World Council of Churches; and admission of qualified new applicants to membership, including the Russian Orthodox Church. Further items on the program were recommendations by the Committee on Program and Finance relating to budgets and organizational readjustments; proposals of new undertakings submitted in the divisional and departmental reports; official statements by the Chairman of the Central Committee and the General Secretary of the World Council; findings of the committees of review on the work of the divisions and departments, including the Commission of the Churches on International Affairs; the Assembly's message to the churches; a special appeal to the governments of the world and their peoples to renounce war and work for peace; and the election of the new Presidium and Central Committee.

Interspersed with the business were study of the "main theme" of the Assembly, "Jesus Christ, the Light of the World," particularly as it pertained to Christian witness, service, and unity; disquisitions bearing especially on these sectional subtopics; daily Bible study; and worship.

A shamiana (Indian tent) hard by Vigyan Bhawan (House of Wisdom) accommodated meetings to which the visitors and the local public were invited, including the opening Assembly worship on Sunday, November 19; programs featuring addresses on timely ecumenical interests; and a celebration of Holy Communion under the auspices of the Church of India, Pakistan, Burma and Ceylon (Anglican) for all baptized members of the Assembly wishing to participate. The closing worship of the Assembly, also announced for the shamiana, had to be transferred, because of wintry cold, to Vigyan Bhawan, which proved of too limited capacity for all New Delhians who wanted to witness the final proceedings and hear Dr. Martin Niemöller, preacher of the sermon.

Prime Minister Jawaharlal Nehru spoke at a special session of the Assembly, and the Vice-President of India, Dr. Sarvepalli Radhakrishnan, received the members at a reception at Rashtrapati Bhawan (House of the Father of the Nation), the presidential mansion, substituting for Dr. Rajendra Prasad, the President, who because of illness was unable to welcome them in person.

Vigyan Bhawan had been built by the Indian government (1956-58) for meetings of the United Nations Educational, Scientific and Cultural Organization. It provided unsurpassed facilities for the complete accommodation of the Assembly and its numerous committees. An efficient communications system carried to the delegates at their desks in the main auditorium simultaneous translations in the official languages of the plenary proceedings, and through microphones connected with it they could address the Assembly from their respective positions. All necessary means were thus made available for registering whatever wisdom God might give the conferees for the churches in a time much beset by folly.

What an Assembly of the World Council of Churches did required more than translating if it was to be made intelligible; and for its interpretation—if that was the word—more wisdom was needed than anyone sitting through its deliberations was likely to feel he possessed, its discussions and actions involving so largely imponderables and futurities, which only time could appraise.

Though unable to see fully the significance of the days at New Delhi, the delegates had the sense of taking part in what might be adjudged eventually one of the great ecumenical councils of the Church of all time, if mankind survived long enough to assimilate its insights and rise to the challenge of its hopes.

As always, the Christian Gospel was proclaimed as "by dying men to dying men," whether history was to be only for the day or for endless tomorrows; and to none was it given to know how far its entreaty would reach or what its fruits would be. The Assembly could be only a pilgrimage of faith. "For they that say such things declare plainly that they seek . . . a better country." What more was ever any such assemblage—from Edinburgh onward?

One concerned to listen and to report what he heard and saw could only hope that his readers might remember that he spoke for himself alone, and this often out of blurring half-light and always with a hesitant pen.

I
CHRIST, COMITY, AND COMMUNION

1. The Main Theme

The choice of the main theme, "Jesus Christ, the Light of the World," many thought unfortunate. The emphasis of the announcement on the definite article of the text indicated the committee's intent. Christianity was to be proclaimed the true religion in a world of competing faiths. This could not have been described as psychologically a felicitous or practical approach to that world. If Christ was "the one true light," it would have been better, the opinion seemed to be, to let him shine without a declaration that could only be, as anyone who had talked with Hindus and Buddhists knew, an invitation to argument—a method winning few converts or friends to any cause.

Such an introduction could not avoid appearing to point to special virtue in those resorting to it, whatever their protestations to the contrary. It would be remembered that, according to one of the Gospels, Jesus told his disciples that they too were "the light of the world." The proclamation that they came bearing the only true light from God immediately put the members of the Assembly at a disadvantage nothing they might say or do would altogether overcome. Those who wrote the report of one of the study sections said, "We are not the light," and pointed from themselves to Christ. But if the light they talked about shone but dimly in them, as they confessed, was it all that they claimed for it, and could its promise of help interest those already committed to following other lights?

Bristling statements of religious assurance often belie the certitude they seem to imply and must be justified by the witness' life. The mood of the creeds becomes Christians more, "I believe" being the most anyone can say. Having weighed such knowledge as is available, one chooses, in the face of intellectual inconclusiveness, to believe. New Delhi needed to exemplify the spirit of humility implicit in this decision more than to reassert theological dogmatisms.

Those appointed to elucidate and elaborate the main theme for study in the churches in advance of the Assembly found in their hands a familiar devotional thought set forth in metaphorical language, which had been worked over until little more could be added. Others before them had searched the Scriptures and garnered all references to light, and about all the committee could do was arrange this biblical information within the framework of current ecumenical theology, a dull and thankless task at best.

The study guide prepared by them and issued and publicized by the Department of Information turned out to be a triumph in sales promotion. Over 600,000 printed copies were distributed. That the book should have been criticized for its alleged insipidity by some church leaders with greater frankness perhaps than grace could easily be understood. Even so, it had more substance to commend it than the general run of such documents, which were seldom permitted to go to press until revised and made acceptable promotionally.

The orientation by the Assembly study sections of the subjects "Witness," "Service," and "Unity" to the main theme was suggestive of the sometimes described homiletical practice of taking a text of Scripture and promptly leaving it.

The development of these so-called sub-themes revealed almost nothing new in the thinking of the churches—or, at least, of their representatives at New Delhi; the reports were largely recastings of previous ecumenical statements. This could be said without disparaging anyone's work or reputation. It might only have meant that the movement had been talking faster than it was growing intellectually or spiritually and so had really nothing to add on evangelism, service, and unity.

If this was a justifiable appraisal, it would have been reasonable to suggest changes in the programs of future Assemblies—and, more immediately, in ecumenical dialogue from New Delhi onward. While reiteration from meeting to meeting could be educational for new members who were being initiated into the World Council of Churches, was it necessary to continue subjecting veteran ecumenists to repetitious declarations of conclusions long since reached and accepted? The Lund Faith and Order Conference, nearly a decade earlier (1952), had decided it was not.

As it was—at New Delhi, and at Evanston and Amsterdam as well—the agendas were too full for convenience or deliberation, and at least some of the time allotted to study in the sections could have been used profitably for more important matters. There were always too few periods for reflection and conversation for the delegates. If possible, the over-all duration of the Assembly needed to be shortened, for its labors fell largely to denominational officials with responsibilities at home demanding attention. Study Reports produced in the Assembly were not altogether gain to the cause.

Documents, composed as they had perforce to be, could at best be little more than hodgepodges of ideas, not only confused and confusing, but sometimes self-contradictory. The need for an editorial secretary, discussed again at New Delhi, was apparent (see page 1079). But did what was said need to be published, much of it having already been said many times and better?

On the other hand, the reports of the Assembly committees, some eighteen of them, on the various departments and commissions of the World Council of Churches were, with their recommendations, generally of real merit. Ably chaired, as a rule, and representing cross sections of the Assembly, these committees nearly always had among their membership persons with some experience and even expertness in the phases of the work of the World Council under examination. The resulting statements were usually knowledgeable and authoritative, and the Assembly could turn to them for guidance in its deliberations. They clearly deserved all the space given to them, and more. There was, however, never time enough for correlating them fully, a fact definitely limiting their usefulness to the Assembly.

2. The Basis Revised

Prior to New Delhi, the Basis of membership in the World Council of Churches had been:

> The World Council of Churches is a fellowship of churches which accept our Lord Jesus Christ as God and Saviour.

The Central Committee recommended that it be revised to read:

> The World Council of Churches is a fellowship of churches which confess the Lord Jesus Christ as God and Saviour according to the Scriptures and therefore seek to fulfill together their common calling to the glory of the one God, Father, Son and Holy Spirit.

The motion to adopt carried, if not unanimously, "overwhelmingly," as the reports said.

The debate on the resolution had a certain interest because of the theological subtleties of the phrasings and the changes made in them. "Accept" in the original statement had been dropped for "confess," in keeping, the explanation was, with early usage in the Church. The older word may have seemed to carry a somewhat broader connotation than "accept," which to many implied explicit acknowledgment of the lordship of Christ by the Church and Christians individually. Ecumenical theology had been stressing "the lordship of Christ over all life" as ground for the social action program of the churches. He was

Lord, whether accepted or not; and "confess" was thought to convey better this claim concerning his universal dominion and sovereignty.

Substituting the definite article for the possessive pronoun in the phrase "our Lord Jesus Christ" could have followed from the same reasoning. Christ was "Lord of all," and not of Christians and churches only.

The confession of "the Lord Jesus Christ as God and Saviour" was "according to the Scriptures," the committee on revision said; and this apostolic expression was incorporated in the amended version of the Basis, in response to the churches which had asked that explicit recognition be given to biblical authority.

"According to the Scriptures" sounded to most members of the Assembly plain and unobjectionable enough. But not to all. "According to what Scriptures?" some asked, pointing out that biblical ascriptions to Christ were addressed to him as Lord, rather than as God. It would have been preferable, they said, to confess "Jesus Christ as Lord and Saviour." That would have avoided stressing his deity to the obscuration of his humanity.

These suggestions met with rejection. The theologians who had chosen the so-called Lausanne Basis in 1927 and insisted on its adoption later by the World Council of Churches as a condition of the Faith and Order Movement's joining maintained their stand. The argument was that "tampering with the key words" would throw open the doors to theological elaborations which could easily proliferate into creedal proportions, and it prevailed.

The adoption of the words "Lord Jesus Christ as God and Saviour," in the first place, and now their retention, while in the name of sound doctrine, could be regarded quite apart from that as a triumph of practical wisdom.[1]

Whether Jesus was God or not, a point not likely ever to be settled, belief in him as God had become inseparably part of the weft of Christian thought. Creeds, catechisms, homilies, hymns, prayers had fixed the image indelibly in the minds of believing multitudes, to whom he was the embodiment in human form of God, the everlasting Word from behind the impenetrable mystery of man's existence, bringer of salvation, divine teacher, and ever-present helper in the earthly struggle. Thus had the Incarnation become experientially the core of Christian faith, the essential unity of the churches, the thrust of the Christian confession. This, whether history or myth.[2] If myth, its inspiration and usefulness as a vehicle of revelation arose out of the religious endowment God had given to man when he created him "a little lower than

[1] The Lausanne Basis had been borrowed apparently from the International Conference of the Y.M.C.A. in Paris in 1854, though this has been questioned.

[2] "Myth" is used here in the sense of a literary form in which truth is conveyed.

the angels." It was a path on which trusting souls had immemorially found, and been found of, God, and on which the feet of multitudes in all continents and climes still walked as in "a bright and shining light." Insofar as they had helped out of their God-given nature to create the Christ of the Incarnation, if myth it was, he had a contemporaneousness for them. Investing him with every new spiritual insight, they saw him as always leading them into knowledge of the truth, a companion in the way; and they believed that the ultimate word was with him and he would never be surpassed.

Earnest Christians would indubitably go on believing, some in the history, some in the myth of the Incarnation. They could walk together if they understood that in either case they dealt with man's experience of God in history and abided by the principle of private interpretation, accepted by the World Council of Churches with reference to the Bible and the creeds.[3]

The Orthodox and some others had asked for mention in the revised Basis of the Holy Trinity, and this also was voted.

The churches in the World Council would in the future "seek to fulfill together their common calling to the glory of the one God, Father, Son and Holy Spirit."

Thus, the trinitarianism of the World Council of Churches would be made explicit. Those like the prominent churchman at New Delhi who wondered aloud what the Trinity meant and "whether Jesus believed in it" would be shut up to living with their confusion against a time when new revelations, if not dismissing the trinitarian dogma, might disclose to all its inspired significance.

3. The World Council and Church Unity

The renewed emphasis on unity, which had been building up since Evanston, reached something of a crescendo at New Delhi. Whatever the subject engaging the Assembly at any time, the feeling seemed to be that its meaning had to be assessed in terms of unity, the word being understood as signifying what earlier in the ecumenical movement had been called more often organic or visible, in differentiation from merely spiritual, unity. The churches were under mandate of Jesus Christ, New Delhi agreed, to make manifest and concrete their oneness in suitable organization, though none ventured to say exactly what shape the structural rearrangements to accomplish this end should take.

In its report at St. Andrews in 1960, however, the Commission on

[3] This paragraph should not be taken as expressing a policy or belief of the World Council of Churches. It reflects only the author's thought.

Faith and Order had made a beginning of supplying a tentative pattern:

The Commission on Faith and Order understands that the unity which is both God's will and his gift to his Church is one which brings all in each place who confess Christ Jesus as Lord into a fully committed fellowship with one another through one baptism into him, holding the one apostolic faith, preaching the one gospel, and breaking the one bread, and having a corporate life reaching out in witness and service to all, and which at the same time unites them with the whole Christian fellowship in all places and all ages in such wise that ministry and members are acknowledged by all, and that all can act and speak together as occasion requires for the tasks to which God calls the Church.

In presenting the Faith and Order report at St. Andrews, Professor Henri d'Espine had added the following comment:[4]

By its very nature, such a unity is visible, but it does not imply a single centralized ecclesiastical institution—which is very generally set aside as being undesirable. It is compatible with a large degree of institutional and liturgical diversity, but it is neither "federal" nor merely "spiritual."

While leaving many questions unanswered, the Commission on Faith and Order had at least opened the doors wide to discussion, and many entered, most of the speakers on the program of the Assembly, regardless of the assigned subjects, taking occasion to pay their respects to unity, if only in passing references.

With all the speaking concerning unity, nothing really new was suggested. Good things were said, but not many that were provocative. Nobody spoke against unity, though there were questionings in the corridors. Little was done about unity beyond discussing it.

Archbishop Arthur Michael Ramsey contributed some discerning comments on Christ's prayer in the seventeenth chapter of the Gospel according to John—"a prayer [for unity] which is everlasting," he said.[5]

Our Great High Priest is interceding. And for what does he pray? That his disciples may be one: that they may be sanctified in truth. Unity, holiness, truth: as the prayer is indivisible, so the fulfillment is indivisible too. It is useless to think that we can look for unity in Christ's name, unless we are looking no less for holiness in his obedience and for the realization of the truth which he revealed. . . .

It is for unity in truth and holiness that we work and pray. Let that always be made clear. A movement which concentrates on unity as an isolated concept can mislead the world and . . . us, as indeed would a movement which had the exclusive label of holiness or . . . of truth. . . .

It is when we get back to the depth and comprehensiveness of our Lord's prayer, that we see the depth and comprehensiveness of our quest for unity. . . . It includes the ascetical, as well as the intellectual and the diplomatic and ethical. It includes the negotiation of the union of churches, and of the bringing of churches into practical fellowship. It includes the

[4] Minutes of the Central Committee, St. Andrews, 1960, p. 112-117.
[5] *Ibid.*

task, within them all, of learning the truth in Christ, in scripture, in the fathers, in the liturgies, in contemporary scholarship, in self-criticism of systems and formulations—a task in which we have been finding ourselves, thank God, rather less like rivals and . . . more like fellow-learners. It includes the doing by all of us, and where possible together, of those things which belong to our understanding of Christian conscience, so that even now Christendom may be a reality with an impact and a voice. It includes the ministering to Christ in those who are homeless and hungry. It includes the inner consecration to Christ, in union with his Passion, whereby his holiness is wrought out in us. It includes the constant prayer of Christians everywhere, praying in which they humble themselves, praying *fiat voluntas.* All this, in depth and breadth, is what the movement to unity must be; and therefore the word "unity" does not suffice to describe it. "I believe in one Church"—we did not learn to say that. We learn to say, "I believe in one, holy, catholic, apostolic Church," and the notes of the Church are a symphony in depth telling of the depth of Christ's prayer and of . . . its . . . fulfillment. . . .

Just as the way of holiness cannot be hurried, and the way of truth cannot be hurried, so too there is concerning unity a divine patience. Guarding . . . against confusing divine patience with our human sloth, we know that there is a divine patience to be imitated in our patience with others, in our patience with ourselves, and in our patience with God's age-long patience. . . . Patience is needed between those who ask that intercommunion should be immediate and general and those who, with deep conviction and no less concern for unity, think otherwise. We need to remember the moving pleas . . . by Archbishop William Temple at Edinburgh for mutual respect of consciences on this matter.

With so many talking about unity, it should hardly have been surprising that some unwise things were said—and others of unclear meaning, inviting imaginings and misunderstandings.

The report of the study section on witness declared, for example, that without unity there could be "no faithful preaching of the gospel." There was objection to this, delegates protesting that it was tantamount to saying that there never had been, was not then, and would not be soon—with the slow movement of the churches in the direction of union—any faithful preaching. The statement was remanded to the drafting committee for revision, who substituted for it: "The question of the Church's unity is of vital importance, since the Bible teaches us that the gospel cannot be authoritatively proclaimed to the world by a disunited Church." The Assembly still could not be sure of what the section meant. To some, these muddy sentences seemed to envisage a union of all denominations under some authoritarian order, which, embracing "the whole Church," could define the Gospel, in the first place, and then see that the prescribed version of it was preached.

Anything approaching that idea was, of course, unacceptable to those denominations believing in the Spirit's direct calling and authority in preaching. They had heard of "the one and undivided Church" often in ecumenical conversations and speculated about what would happen to their cherished "liberty of prophesying" if union came to some such end. During the discussion on the faithful-and-authoritative-preaching passage, a foremost American free-church minister remarked, "We appear to be talking ourselves out of a job!"

It ought to be reiterated, in the interest of clarity, that the Assembly was not itself speaking in the speeches from the floor and the platform or in the study units' findings. These latter, after such revision as could be accomplished in hurried plenums, were approved only in substance —not adopted—"and commended to the churches for study and appropriate action"; and individuals, whether in the debates or by appointment on the program, spoke only for themselves.

However, in what was said under any of these circumstances might be reflected trends of thought influencing the policy of the World Council of Churches. For this reason, the public's habit of charging the World Council with whatever anybody in the Assembly took it upon himself to say was, in a degree, excusable. The Assembly was exposing the churches to ideas, some of which would eventually be incorporated in the policy and work of the World Council. Most of those speaking could move resolutions and vote.

Christian unity was suffering from overemphasis, as well as from wrong kinds of emphasis.

Prominent ecumenical leaders who asserted that their sole interest in the World Council of Churches was in making it a means of uniting the denominations were not a help to the cause. Often they belonged to the churches which seemed least able—or willing—to give up anything in their creeds or practices to make mergers possible.

Those who believed in the World Council of Churches as an agency of cooperation, whether or not it brought about union, agreed that some churches could undoubtedly unite and perhaps ought to do so. Denominations of the same or similar polity occupying overlapping or closely adjacent territories might in this way strengthen themselves for service. For others of different orders, union might be in specific instances advantageous if it could be effected without fragmenting dissent. Examples of churches which had united successfully under various conditions were to be seen in many countries: Canada, the United States, India, Japan, and elsewhere. But the magnification of unity until it eclipsed the values of cooperation many thought unwise, even hurtful to the whole ecumenical movement.

Hindered thus by its overzealous promoters, the cause of unity was unfortunate also in those of its advocates who were given to talking about "the scandal of disunity." These latter were at New Delhi and by their charges making themselves, it seemed to some of the Assembly members, something of a scandal to the churches. Whatever their purpose, they certainly were not persuasive exponents of unity. And they did little to strengthen the Christian program in the world, which would for some time to come have to depend upon the divided and scandalizing denominations.[6]

Abbé Paul Couturier concluded, it was said, that "the process of reestablishing unity among Christians was to be accomplished by an integration of Christian values," and while "looking ahead for unity" turned his attention "to the works of mercy of Orthodox St. Seraphim, St. Francis of Assisi and others who had attained in their own lives the union of churches and were citizens of the same Church, holy and universal, and at the height of their spiritual lives had gone beyond the walls which separate us, but—in the words of Father Platon of Kiev—do not reach up to heaven."[7]

The integration of Christian values was a slower process than many imagined, as the denominations in the World Council of Churches were discovering, and the rash language heard occasionally in the household of faith only advertised that looking ahead for unity called for patience some members of the family did not have. It was particularly to them that the Archbishop of Canterbury spoke: "We know that there is a divine patience to be imitated in our patience with others . . . with ourselves, and . . . with God's age-long patience. . . . Patience includes, above all, the will to expect that God's blessing upon our cherished plans may not in his wisdom be separated from his disciplining us in holiness and truth."

[6] Those calling disunity a scandal may have thought they were speaking with a degree of scripturalness, but this could hardly have been substantiated.

The Greek word *skandalon,* meaning "trap" or, more literally, the trigger or bait-stick of a trap, was rendered generally in English versions of the New Testament "offense" or "stumbling-block." The offense could be something put in the way of others, usually with sinful intent; or it might arise out of one's own inability to discern and understand the good in others, as in the case of the Pharisees who were offended at Jesus because they disagreed with his teaching.

The use of *skandalon* in these or other scriptural meanings to describe denominationalism was unjustifiable. However deplorable, the fragmentation of the Christian fellowship by disunity was not a result of wicked scheming by anybody to mislead or entrap others; and if denominational divisions had been a stumbling-block to some persons, as they themselves said, multitudes on the other hand had found their way into the kingdom of God through the ministry of sectarian churches. Characterizing denominationalism as scandalous (i.e., "giving offence to the conscience or moral feeling," according to Webster's *New International Dictionary*) could have the effect of confirming the decision of those who had rejected Christianity because of its dividedness and of weakening the confidence and loyalty of others who were denominational church members, and in the degree it did either—or both—it was itself scandalous.

Condemning as wrong a thing believed good by others was, of course, a familiar way of zealotry in debate. Actually, there was no evidence that denominational differences barred from the kingdom of God more persons than would find "the coming Great Church," if it ever materialized, an offense and a stumbling-block.

[7] *The Life and Work of Abbé Paul Couturier, Apostle of Unity,* by Maurice Villain, S.M. (1959), pp. 3-4. Translation by the sisters of the Holy Cross Convent. From the first French edition of *Témoignages,* published under the imprimatur of the Vicar General of Lyons, 1954.

Preoccupation with unity probably followed, in part, from the search for an explanation of the ineffectiveness of organized Christianity in the face of world crisis. The disunity of the churches offered itself as a near-at-hand answer, which certain key passages of Scripture, by the generally accepted interpretations, seemed to confirm.

Did not Jesus pray that his followers might be one, to the end that the world might believe? (John xvii, 20). Did this not mean that the acceptance by mankind of the Gospel waited upon the visible union of Christians? Many, of course, thought so. Nobody knew. There were grounds for reserving judgment. The exact sense of the prayer was not clear. The classical exegesis of the passage did not take into account all the relevant hermeneutical facts. And the same was true of other scriptural buttressings of the traditional belief.

The union of Christians might, indeed, be the will of God, whether or not there was explicit scriptural support for it. And their drawing together might well increase in many ways the success of their endeavors. But it must have been obvious that unity, however important, was not the full answer to the problem of the churches' sometimes ineffectual ministry.

At that last-night meeting with his disciples Jesus spoke of love, and his words were luminous and clear: "This is my commandment, that ye love one another." This sentence raised itself above the mists of the past, like the highest peak of the distant Himalayas in the evening shadows. Did it not speak the definitive word, mark beyond question the secret of strength and triumph in hours of deepening darkness?

If Christians loved one another, unity would follow. If it came without love, it would not be unity, but a mechanical thing having no conductivity for spiritual power. Love was the goal pointing down the divine way, because creative. "He that loveth is born of God." By love God would have entrance into the churches. The promise "I am with you alway" would come alive.

Reference was to love, not to its counterfeits in common circulation in and outside the churches. And it was love of Christians toward one another. The focus had to be kept steadily on that point. It had a way of wandering off to other loves which had their importance but often distracted attention from this primary commandment to love one another —as a letter by Lord Altrincham[8] in one of the New Delhi newspapers during the Assembly and apropos to its objective of Christian unity, which he considered theologically impossible, perhaps illustrated. "It is much easier to find a common ground for what a Christian ought to do," he wrote, "than for what a Christian ought to believe. There are many possible interpretations for Christ's reported statements on his relationship with God . . . the significance of the bread and wine and such

[8] In the *Indian Express,* New Delhi.

other theological subjects. But there could be no serious argument about what was meant in the parable of the good Samaritan."

Being a good Samaritan and ministering to others in need, whoever they might be, was indeed Christian love, but it could bypass the "new commandment." Christians might throw in their contributions together for relief programs around the earth, as in the World Council of Churches, and yet not love one another. Charity for those in need did not present the real test, but the fellowship of the churches in which Christians were gathered by their common confession of Jesus Christ. Of different nationalities and races, social and economic statuses, cultural inheritances, customs, habits, tastes, theologies, idiosyncracies—all in one respect or another quite unlovable persons—they must learn to love one another if the Church was to be different from other institutions and able to speak out of an experience of God commanding obedience.

All that love of Christians toward one another meant and how they could achieve it was the "main theme" all the time, whether voted by any committee of the World Council of Churches or not. To its study would have to be brought the highest intelligence and most steadfast application. Christians must will to love with irrevocableness and renew their resolution every day—morning, noon, and night. They would not be able to keep this commandment by emotional calisthenics. Rather, they must love in spite of their emotions, which had a way of finding immediate short-lived satisfactions in the imitations of love.

If Christians in the nearly two hundred denominations of the World Council of Churches—Old Catholic, Orthodox, Anglican, and Protestant —and the Roman Catholic Church learned to love one another, the problem of organizational unity would largely take care of itself. It was in the realm of Christian love that the miracle of manifest oneness, concerning which so much was being said, would have to happen. The World Council of Churches and the Second Vatican Ecumenical Council would need to keep in mind, when they turned to the Bible for guidance, that Christ's prayer that his disciples might be one was in the same context with his new commandment—that they love one another; and that the commandment interpreted the prayer.

4. The Nature of the World Council

The World Council of Churches had not been able, for all its discussion of the nature of the Church, to reach a consensus generally acceptable. The Commission on Faith and Order had labored some years with the subject without arriving at publishable conclusions. Nor had there been agreement about the relation of the churches and the Church. It was, therefore, not surprising that the nature of the World Council of Churches had eluded definition.

That the World Council was an organization of denominations (or churches) seemed to be a clear enough statement as a first step toward an answer. But what did it mean? What was an organization, in a religious or theological sense?

In a certain denomination in a simpler day, a standard popular definition of a church was: "An organized body of baptized believers." This implied more than it made explicit. The "organized body of baptized believers" was supposed to be Spirit filled, and so united by a common spiritual life. The members had been baptized "into Jesus Christ" and were in consequence assumed to have "the mind of Christ." Such characteristics invested a church with the nature more of an organism than of an organization. When it was formed, God had contributed something. Through his indwelling, the church had become, in a sense, his body.

There were ecumenical scholars who said that a council of churches, whatever its agreed purpose, could not rightly be treated as a mere organization. Guided by the Spirit of God and functioning under the recognized lordship of Jesus Christ, it had the same nature essentially as a church. Many looked upon the phenomenal growth and increasing unity of the World Council as proof of its churchlike dynamism.

The discussion on this point had arisen especially in connection with the control supposed to be exercised by the parent denominations over the World Council of Churches. The nature of the World Council being not unlike that of its creators and constituents, did not its insights and decisions have the same validity as theirs? Might these not, indeed, be even better informed and more authoritative in some matters than theirs, by reason of the World Council's broader experience and expert knowledge?

This issue had not been raised out of controversial motives. Rather, some of the most able and loyal leaders thought the World Council of Churches unnecessarily limited its usefulness by trying to avoid the appearance of usurping authority belonging to the denominations. Specifically, they thought the World Council ought to be free to promote the union of churches. By the accepted interpretation of the constitution and special regulatory resolutions, it had been restricted to merely providing opportunity for the denominations to become acquainted by working together and keeping them informed annually on the progress of attempted self-initiated church mergers around the world. This seemed to some ecumenists to be an area in which the World Council could, with full propriety, take a more prominent role.

Other calls for the World Council to expand its services had met with discouragement by the churches. The constitutional authority of the member denominations was fully recognized, but had they the moral right to veto responses by the World Council to the leading of the same Spirit who inspired them to found it, in the first place, and now was so manifestly operative in its life?

The ecumenical movement had been committed to the vigorous promotion of Christian social action. This had proved to be a highly controversial policy, and in local and national councils of churches, where oppositions were strongest, withdrawals of support had occurred. The World Council also had been affected. Many ecumenical officials carried responsibilities at all these levels, and their experience on the entire front persuaded some of them that the true nature of the councils of churches, whether local, national, or international, needed to be better understood, so that the spiritual authority of their leadership would be respected.

For still other reasons the nature of the World Council of Churches particularly was of continuing concern.

From its organization the World Council had been suspected of being—or of aiming to become—a kind of super-church. Many who accepted the denial of such intentions as in good faith nevertheless believed that, whatever its constitution said or its own thoughts about its aim were, the Council could not help developing into an entity with a life and individuality of its own. They questioned whether the denominations forming such a body could reasonably expect to be able to control it. The fears of those who took this view would, of course, only be strengthened by the new theology—or ecclesiology—of the nature of the World Council of Churches.

Statements at New Delhi concerning the World Council of Churches, its Central Committee, and certain of its divisions and departments could also only have increased further the anxiety of those who believed the Council was in danger of growing into a body of the nature of a super-church.

In its report to the Assembly, the Central Committee—which had been, by the constitution, the World Council of Churches during the interval between Evanston and New Delhi—stated that it had felt "called not only into the tide of events, but to be ahead of them."[9] Concerning this interpretation of function, the Policy Reference Committee, consisting of members mainly of the Central Committee, and headed by the Rt. Rev. Lakdasa de Mel, Bishop of Kurunagala, Ceylon, commented as follows:[10]

The Committee appreciates the statement that the World Council of Churches sees itself called not only into the tide of events but to be ahead of them, and recommends that this should be the continued aspiration of the Council. It feels that the Council should give its member-churches spiritual and practical guidance in a Christian approach to the actual questions and problems of our day, such as materialism, secularism, peace and war, social justice, et cetera. The World Council should certainly not wait to be pushed into critical situations, but should always take the lead and initiative

[9] *The New Delhi Report,* p. 144-45, 336.
[10] *Ibid.* See also Franklin Clark Fry's statement, p. 1081.

in asking, "What is the commandment of our Lord in this present time?" At the same time, the churches themselves should be encouraged to bring their requests in this regard before the World Council of Churches. While it is universally recognized that the Council is a Council of Churches, and can do only what its member-churches authorize it to do, we feel that the Council, as the ecumenical conscience of the churches, should be constantly vigilant for occasions where ecumenical action is particularly desirable, and where it may call upon its members to consider such action. . . . We feel the time has come when increasing emphasis should be placed upon action, and would like to see the work of the Division of Ecumenical Action still further developed and strengthened, particularly in relation to the task of the Council in keeping the whole people of God "ahead of events."

While acknowledging the authority of the denominations over the World Council of Churches, this statement, whether so intended or not, implied a moral perceptiveness on the part of the Council that they themselves did not possess.

The Council was referred to as "the ecumenical conscience of the churches." It would be always taking "the lead and initiative in asking, 'What is the commandment of our Lord in this present time?' " And "the churches themselves should be encouraged to bring their requests in this regard" before it for answers, as they would look to it also for "spiritual and practical guidance in a Christian approach to the actual questions and problems of our day, such as materialism, secularism, peace and war, social justice," and the rest.

Some members of the Assembly reading such utterances may have seen in them meanings not intended. However, that the World Council understood the responsibilities of the denominations in the world Christian mission better than the denominations themselves was a more or less unconscious assumption in ecumenical councils.

The emphasis on education stemmed partially from this. The churches were to be enlisted in study, using materials and outlines prepared by the World Council. Hope was expressed that the churches would participate critically and send in findings, so that conclusions embodying, so far as possible, the opinions of the congregations might be reached. But there was never a general response.

The World Council regarded its inability to draw the churches into this sort of dialogue as one of its most regrettable failures.

Said Dr. Visser 't Hooft at New Delhi:[11]

An important and difficult task . . . remains one which cannot be performed at the world level, but which has to be done in every local congregation. . . . For what is the use of deep convictions and imaginative plans about unity which rise at the level of world meetings, if our church-members are indifferent, lukewarm or even hostile with regard to unity? There is as yet an immense task to be performed by all of us together to prepare our churches spiritually for action toward unity.

[11] Dr. Visser 't Hooft was discussing at this point interesting the churches in unity, but what he described as the problem in that connection obtained in the whole World Council program.

With an outlook on the whole work of the World Council of Churches, Bishop de Mel's Policy Reference Committee said further in its statement, part of which has been quoted:

> The gravest problem facing the Council is that of familiarizing the general membership of our churches with the details and significance of its work. Many delegates to this Assembly are themselves hearing of much of this work for the first time; while the majority of our church membership is either totally ignorant thereof or is indifferent or . . . hostile towards it. . . . Every possible effort should be made to popularize the Council's activities by promoting distribution of its publications through national councils, as well as through member-churches.

In short, the Christian denominations had organized the World Council of Churches, which had developed a program their members knew little about. This work of the Council was a responsibility, ecumenical leaders thought, of the denominations, which ought to be interested enough to go to school to Geneva and learn about it. But it was next to impossible to get them to enroll.

The unresponsiveness of the member denominations was something of an enigma. It might have been explained, in part, by their own overcrowded programs; and this was a condition the expanding ecumenical movement itself had helped create, with its departments of Christian education, youth activities, work with men and women, international peace and other social action interests parallelling, more or less, at all levels those of the denominations. But those acquainted with the parish mind knew that there were more determinative factors in the problem, among them distrust on the part of many rank-and-file church members of policies and methods of the World Council of Churches, particularly in the areas of social Christianity. They rarely knew all the facts; but many of them had read or been told that the movement had fallen into the hands of "radicals" who were using it to promote "alien ideologies."

They were disturbed, moreover, by the Council's plans with reference to church union. Though believing in Christian co-operation, they listened to those who spoke of it in the name of the ecumenical movement as a prelude to union and were skeptical about the feasibility and desirability of that. They knew that their own church officials were their representatives in the World Council of Churches; but, though trusting them in their appointed work at home, they were not sure that these leaders could find their way in a venture of such international scope.

Urged to help with correcting the faults they thought they saw in the World Council, they could find no practicable way to remedy them. The average layman lacked training for such responsibilities, and the not too happy results in the case of a few willing churchmen who acted on the challenge to stop criticizing and lend a hand stood to discourage others. The natural and usual procedure of the denominations was, anyway, to choose for their delegates persons believing in the

World Council as it was, the movement being young and needing the unquestioning support of those not having to be converted to it. So, rightly or wrongly, many laymen decided to leave the Council and its interests to others who had no doubts about them and to devote themselves to Christian duties which they could undertake with assurance. They were generally respected and influential members of their churches and communities, and their feeling concerning the World Council—and the larger ecumenical movement—influenced others. Under the circumstances, the climate in the churches was often not favorable to dialogue with Geneva which, many church people imagined, sought adoption of its program more than advice about altering it.

Laymen thus characterized would be slow to accept the thesis that the World Council of Churches approached them with a spiritual authority equalling, or superseding, that of the Church. To them, the Council was an agent of the churches taking orders from them when it truly fulfilled its nature and function. That it had experienced phenomenal growth was certain; but that this indicated God's special approval did not, in their opinion, necessarily follow. Fortuitous reasons alone could have explained what had happened. Organized Christianity had not done too well. There was a feeling of frustration in the churches. It was a temptation for them to think that by getting together they could gain attention and work more effectively. New nations were emerging. The churches of these countries would join the World Council, as their governments were seeking admission to the United Nations, looking for status and financial aid. With reference to union there were many denominations and many minds. As stated, some wished only to co-operate; others thought uniting was the desired goal. Those denominations which regarded themselves as *the* Church saw in the World Council their opportunity. If union came, the others would join them. Perhaps God was working through the World Council, but to many average laymen this was not clear enough to be reduced to a theology.

So was the drift of the inquiry into the nature of the World Council of Churches in danger of discouraging, rather than encouraging, response from the pew.

Such matters as this had no place in the formal program at New Delhi, but they thrust themselves into discussions in committee meetings and study groups concerned with other subjects. They had a relevance to all the Assembly did. Unless it understood and reckoned with them, the Assembly would not find solutions to the problems it struggled with from session to session. The World Council of Churches had not the broad and solid basis in the understanding, acceptance, and loyalty of the people in the pews it ought to have had. Unless this was achieved, its future would be uncertain. It had to be more than an international confederation of denominations if it was to do its work. It must, as its leaders realized, win the people.

5. Communion at New Delhi

The Third Conference on Faith and Order at Lund, Sweden, in 1952 had agreed that opportunities for open Communion services should be provided at ecumenical gatherings by such of the denominations as might wish to assume the responsibility. In the spirit of this understanding, the Church of India, Pakistan, Burma and Ceylon (Anglican) invited all baptized members of the Assembly, whatever their church affiliation, to Holy Communion in the shamiana under its auspices.[12] The celebrant was the Rt. Rev. Frederick Willis of Delhi. Some thirty archbishops, bishops, metropolitans, and priests assisted. In the sermon, Bishop Lakdasa de Mel of Ceylon asked the communicants to try to "look at the world with the calm, compassionate eyes of Jesus Christ, whose cross was the answer to its suffering, pain and squalor."

The Liturgy of Saint James (Holy Qurbana), a rite which originated, according to tradition, with James, the brother of Jesus, was conducted by the Syrian Orthodox Church of Malabar (India). The historic "kiss of peace" was passed by the officiants to the congregation and by its members to one another. Those who went to the altar received the Holy Eucharist, bread and wine.

All "baptized communicant members" of the denominations of the World Council of Churches were invited to receive the sacraments also at a Lutheran service in the shamiana.

The invitation at the Orthodox Church's Divine Liturgy of Saint John Chrysostom, which ordinarily culminates in a sanctification of gifts and the Holy Eucharist, was also understood to be open to all baptized Christians.

While nobody belonging to any church in the World Council was forbidden to participate in any of them, these separate celebrations of Holy Communion drew attention, as always, to the disunity of Christians. With the exception of the Anglican service, they appeared to be attended by comparatively few delegates of the non-officiating churches. And it was reported that some members of the sponsoring denominations abstained from Communion at their own services because of their conviction that a true observance of the Lord's Supper could not be held under the circumstances.

There was comment at New Delhi and afterwards to the effect that, despite its concern for unity, the Assembly had not been able "to bring off the essential, visible and confirming evidence of its unity: a fully shared intercommunion at one table."[13]

[12] The Church of England had held a similar Communion service in 1937 in St. Mary's Church, Oxford, for members of the Life and Work Conference on Church, Community and State.

[13] As viewed by a reporter for *The Christian Century,* January 10, 1962, p. 46.

It would be considered, no doubt, quite unecumenical not to take this lament seriously. But at that risk, it might be asked what scriptural grounds there are for making intercommunion the supreme test of unity. Appealing to those he addressed to walk worthy of their Christian calling, "endeavoring to keep the unity of the Spirit," the author of the Epistle to the Ephesians iv, 3-5) spoke of "one Lord, one faith, one baptism," but made no reference to the Supper in this category of things he regarded as belonging to the oneness of the Body of Christ. The Communion could be interpreted as symbolical of many things, and the unity of Christians might be one of them; but seeing in it the essential and confirming evidence of their spiritual oneness would seem to be investing it with a significance no writer of the New Testament went so far as to suggest—unless exegetes are disposed to take what many scholars think are unwarrantable liberties with a few isolated scriptural passages of uncertain meaning, such as, for example, I Corinthians x, 16, 17.

Attempts to bring all the churches in the World Council together at the Lord's Table always run into the irreconcilable incompatibilities of sacramentalism and what may be called memorialism. Between a service of merely commemorative character, which any group of Christians may appoint, and one mediating divine grace through ministrants in historical succession to the first apostles, there are fundamental contradictions which are logically unresolvable.

The worst damage of the situation thus created is, after all, not its disclosure of disunity, but the pride it nurtures in otherwise kindly folk who, notwithstanding their natural desire to be brotherly, succumb to the sin of exclusiveness which is last to yield to the grace of God. This is not what they think they are doing, of course; in their eyes they are showing devotion to truth. The division that results, they assure themselves, is due to conscience, and this compensates for the pain of it and reduces penance, so often professed, to mere words. "Being of the true Church which gives validity to the Communion, we must not compromise our witness," they say. At the same time, those outside the circle they have drawn say, "We must be intelligent about the matter. We can only reject all these fanciful notions of superiority." In either case the attitude brought to the Table can hardly be the mind of Christ.

Believing that the efficacy of the Communion is in the spirit of the communicant, not in the church or the officiant, the memorialist may be able to join in the celebration, wherever and by whomever offered, seeking the spiritual enduement which, in his belief, is communicated directly to the soul of the true worshiper. In this conviction he can eat and drink, even as he can worship, with other Christians on any and all occasions, whatever the liturgy followed. If sacramentalists can partake only under the conditions prescribed by their church, he will try to respect their convictions, though they may seem quite incredible. Perhaps both, while communing together in this manner, can, without affront to the Lord of the Table, pray, "God be merciful to us miserable sinners!"

Under these circumstances it is not surprising that some Christians think the Lord's Supper ought to be kept out of the meeting of the World Council of Churches and off its study agenda.

6. Youth and Intercommunion

One hundred sixty young people gathered at New Delhi from many parts of the world for a pre-Assembly meeting in the Baptist Mission Compound, and 106 of them stayed to take part in the Assembly, several as delegates and the rest as stewards in one capacity or another.

For their own conference they had a threefold object: to give themselves "opportunity to reflect on the concerns of unity, witness and service," as these related to youth; to orient themselves on Asian church life and the significance of the Third Assembly; and to review the work of the Youth Department of the World Council of Churches and make recommendations concerning it. They met and heard from World Council and Asian church leaders, visited in homes and churches of Indian Christians, attended various programs which had been prepared especially for them, and gave part of their time to group study and discussion. Thirty-odd had helped with work-camp projects in Pakistan and Ceylon before coming to New Delhi. After the Assembly some formed teams and "travelled throughout India to acquaint the people in the remotest areas with the ecumenical movement."

A main focus of their conference and study sessions was intercommunion. Some of them had been at Lausanne in 1960 for the European Conference of Christian Youth, and all were familiar with its emphasis on this subject. Their section on unity in the pre-Assembly meeting drafted a statement on intercommunion which provoked considerable discussion. A basic point of their argument was that, having generally accepted one another's baptism, the denominations ought logically to do the same with Communion. They were not unmindful, however, of the obstacles in the way.

"We recognize," they said, "that, for some, full communion is a manifestation of unity in terms of ministries and the Church . . . and becomes possible only in consequence of our growing unity at these other points. . . . We believe the issue of intercommunion cannot be isolated from . . . worship, witness and service of the Church."

"There are avenues of ecumenical growth open to us," the statement continued, "even though we do not yet have full intercommunion. On the other hand, to share in these aspects of ecumenical life without being able to meet at the Lord's Table raises the question of intercommunion between local churches, as on the ecumenical level."

Referring to the 1960 Lausanne Conference, the young people at New

Delhi expressed concern that many churches of the World Council had not considered at "high levels" its challenge, as the Central Committee requested. "We are concerned," they said, "that some of our churches continue to charge us with disobedience when intercommunion is practised on ecumenical occasions, even according to the Lund rules." [14]

"We have to find that arrangement of communion services which, while respecting the discipline of the churches and individual consciences, give the fullest expression to the essential oneness of the Church of Christ which at such gatherings we confess," a consultation under the sponsorship of the World Council's Youth Department and the Faith and Order Commission in March, 1961, had agreed, after examining the findings of the Lausanne youth conference of 1960.

"We believe that the re-ordering of the Lund principles, together with the new steps recommended in the March consultation," the New Delhi statement concluded, "represents a significant move toward giving the Holy Communion service its proper place in ecumenical work and witness. We believe the March recommendations should be accepted by the Youth Department of the World Council of Churches and by the youth departments of national councils for youth assemblies. . . . The recommendations and the history behind them should be a major part of the preparation of all delegates attending youth assemblies."

With this outlook the pre-Assembly youth conference urged all young Christians to "act in the spirit of Lausanne in local and national ecumenical situations, defining that spirit as a sense of urgency balanced with loyalty to their respective denominations." The Commission on Faith and Order ought to accept the recommendations of the March consultation, it thought, "as the basis of a practice of intercommunion which represents the present stage of the ecumenical situation." The Commission should probably consider, it suggested further, whether "a new expression of the theology of communion is not necessary in view of the facts of the ecumenical situation."

The conference in its statement confessed:[15]

> Our fear is lest the churches under-estimate the demands the ecumenical movement is making upon them, lest they fail to appreciate the extent of the changes in outlook and structure that will become necessary as the ecumenical movement bears fruit. . . . For we believe that the ecumenical movement gives us the perspective to discern what is contradictory with the Christian faith within a culture and what is acceptable; what is essential in our expression of the faith and what is non-essential.

[14] The Lund (1952) decision was that there should be opportunity for open Communion services at ecumenical gatherings, if held on the invitation of churches sanctioning them.

[15] Mimeographed Report, distributed at New Delhi.

II

NOTABLE EVENTS

1. The Merger of the International Missionary Council with the World Council of Churches

Approval of the merger of the International Missionary Council and the World Council had been indicated in advance by the constituencies of both, and audible dissent at New Delhi was negligible.

Nevertheless, the action raised certain questions. Missions belonged to the churches and therefore to their World Council. Broadly conceived, they comprised all the churches did, whether separately or through their councils. This supporting logic seemed flawless. But was the venture practicable? Could the World Council manage the greatly enlarged load? Could the submersion of missionary interests by organization be avoided in union? Might the responsibilities of both bodies not be discharged more effectively as they had been working, separately but with studied coordination of their plans?

The union had not had the aim primarily of saving money, though economy and the elimination of overlapping of activities were certainly desirable, what with the rapid expansion of their programs. The union had been decided on because it seemed to be the right course. On this ground, the two bodies had acted in the belief that the problems created, although forbidding in some of their aspects, would not be impossible of solution. They trusted that the long-tested promise "As thy days, so shall thy strength be" had not expired. If the idea of unity was valid, two Christian organizations as completely complementary in their functions as the World Council of Churches and the International Missionary Council ought to act upon it and rely on obedience to bring the needed new accessions of spiritual power.

The Assembly approved the merger, it was realized, with the sense that the churches faced in their missionary work other problems more disquieting and more difficult even than these having to do mainly with considerations of the functional and practical.

Doors were being closed to missionaries. Traditional methods were losing their effect. The jealous new type of nationalism was allowing no room to religious divisiveness. The missions were under pressure to unite. Western parent churches had become an embarrassment. Their money could still be used, and on certain conditions their counsel welcomed, but they would have to withdraw from management.[1]

There was, moreover, no longer a unifying theological consensus about missions. Their scriptural warrant was undergoing re-examination. The World Council of Churches and the International Missionary Council had announced studies in the theology of missions, but they were slow-moving.

Under reconsideration also was the approach to non-Christian religions. The International Missionary Council had organized on the mission fields centers for research on this problem.

Even more than the main arguments advanced for merging, these circumstances tended to push missions steadily toward the focus of ecumenical concern and organization. Before New Delhi, it was seen that the time had come for closing ranks to meet what could be a struggle for survival. If in the approaching conflict ground could be held and new foundations laid, there would be hope for a fresh beginning with the Church's world mission when the passions of revolution had spent their force.

There would be years, it was certain, of continuing division, confusion, and consequent weakness in Christian ranks. Western non-Roman missionaries working in Africa, Asia, Latin America, and the Pacific area were, according to statistics, approximately equally divided between the churches affiliated with the World Council and those outside its membership.[2]

The division was theological, as well as organizational. In general, missionary-minded Protestants not in the International Missionary and World Councils called themselves "the evangelicals"—an historic name with connotations of theological soundness that, although having no longer a really definitive meaning, was appropriated by them to distinguish themselves from other Christians whom they as loosely styled "liberals."

[1] It was known during the Assembly that Ceylon, for example, was pressing its campaign to keep missionary activity at a minimum. Shortly afterwards, the government ruled that a new missionary coming to Ceylon would be eligible for a visa only if he replaced one who had left the island within the previous twelve months. In practice, this meant that no new missionary would be admitted until the predecessor had left. The government had already moved to take over all church schools. India likewise had tightened control of the missions.

[2] According to the Missionary Research Library (Vol. XI, No. 9), the "World-wide Protestant Foreign Missionary Force" was 42,250 in 1960. Of this number, 27,219 were "North American Protestant Missionaries." Something over 40 percent of these latter were regarded as belonging to "co-operative" or "ecumenical" missions. A much larger percentage of the other 15,031, who had gone from the United Kingdom, Belgium, Denmark, Finland, France, Germany, Iceland, the Netherlands, Norway, Sweden, Switzerland, Australia, New Zealand, South Africa, and "the Younger Churches" in other countries (35.6 percent of the total Protestant Missionary Force) were to be listed in the same category. These figures were the basis for the above estimate.

The so-called evangelicals had met with considerable success in missionary work. Their more or less traditional version of the biblical theology of missions still had a strong appeal, especially in the more isolated places. They were undiscouraged and persevering in the face of opposition. They had regard to the command of Christ to go, whether it was clear where they could go or not. They recruited their missionaries; and if all doors closed, the appointees returned home and pursued their calling there until such time as God, if it proved his will, made openings for them overseas. His was, after all, the responsibility. It was his work, his call, to which they had surrendered.

Evangelicals had not concerned themselves overmuch about the non-Christian religions. Were they not still the blind groping after God, whom they would not find until they acknowledged Jesus Christ as the only way and followed him? All faiths of this kind must be bypassed and their masses reached individually with the Gospel. It would be treason to try to form any kind of alliance with them. Despite their false teachings, some of their devotees had honest hearts and would receive the word of the kingdom unto fruit many-fold. This was the churches' mission—to scatter the seed.

The approach through social services had comparatively little appeal to the evangelicals. If they made use of such ministries, it was frankly with the purpose of winning those helped. And they did not send out missionaries to build the kingdom of God or any kind of welfare state. Their mission, as they conceived it, was to convert lost persons and help them live godly lives in a doomed society.

There was little possibility, therefore, of cooperation by the evangelicals and the ecumenical organizations. The latter could undoubtedly have collaborated under their inclusive policy, but the evangelicals would have looked upon such an arrangement as betrayal of their cause. They tended to identify "the faith once for all delivered" with their own peculiar theological interpretation of the Christian experience and so rejected the ecumenical principle of unity in diversity, being at times unable to achieve that kind of *modus operandi* even among themselves.[3]

The Christian churches thus could not present a firm front for the conflict before them—a sobering realization influencing every discussion and every action at New Delhi.

Among the member churches of the World Council acquiescing reluctantly in the merger were the Orthodox, which had bitter recollections of the proselytizing of their ranks by overzealous Protestant missionaries in the regions of southeastern Europe and the Middle East. The Orthodox Churches had, as well, their own particular conception of the nature of the Church's missionary calling and responsibility. The adoption at St. Andrews and New Delhi of the declaration of the World

[3] They were divided under scores of different and, for the most part, unrelated boards.

Council on proselytism, which had long been in preparation, eased their anxiety somewhat on that score. This and the realization that they needed to renew their own missionary program, which in their preoccupation with the problems of survival they had neglected, overcame their opposition in the end, even if not disposing of the anomaly for them of membership in an organization now comprising, in addition to the denominations originally constituting it, the major Protestant missions and their boards and councils.

Following the vote to approve, Dr. Henry Pitney Van Dusen, chairman of the committee which promoted the merger and worked out the structural adjustments to accommodate it constitutionally, led the Assembly in a service of thanksgiving. The Service had been prepared in advance, on instructions from the Central Committee at St. Andrews in August, 1960, after it had received the returns from the churches showing them favorable to recommending action at New Delhi.

For many, undoubtedly, the voicing of gratitude gave place, regardless of the printed words of the liturgy, to earnest prayer that the complex plan now adopted—which earlier had been considered logically, psychologically, ecclesiologically, and practically unfeasible—might succeed. Was it only imagination that to some who offered thanks the occasion resembled a wedding that, because of suspected incompatibilities of the principals, left the onlookers with a sense of uneasiness?

2. Admission of the Russian Orthodox Church

Advance reports of the application of the Russian Orthodox Church for membership in the World Council of Churches and a foregone assurance of the Assembly's approval robbed the balloting session of some of its potential drama. Still, the realization that the ready affirmative vote was marking for both the Church and the Council a fateful step, whether for good or ill, invested the occasion with quite enough emotion for one day's work.

The Russian Orthodox Church had been one of the denominations expected at Amsterdam in 1948 for the constitution of the World Council of Churches. Why it had decided suddenly not to come, whether because it was unsure of full accord with the purposes of the World Council or because some domestic political influence had barred the way, was unknown. Nor was it known now, thirteen years later, why the Russian Church was acting at New Delhi to end its isolation, whether because upon reassessing the Council's policy after more than a decade it had found the program sufficiently acceptable or because exterior obstacles to membership—if there were any—had been removed.

It was common belief that in coming to New Delhi the Russian Church could have acted only with the Soviet government's consent, despite the insistence by the Russian delegation that it enjoyed complete freedom in the management of its own affairs. Soviet Russia's definition of freedom was different from the West's.

What were the unknown factors at work? Why had the government relaxed its control to the extent of permitting alliance by the Church with an international ecclesiastical body—largely of Western origin—which had been free with its criticism of communism?

Denied information on this point, the members of the Assembly were left to conjecture. Some wondered whether the Soviet government thought to establish a "listening post" deep in the free world it sought to conquer, or perhaps an apparatus to counteract the uncomfortably effective agitation by the World Council of Churches for real democratic freedom. Did it plan, by striking from an inside position, to divide or destroy the World Council and to set up an Eastern counterpart under its own domination?

It was difficult to believe that the government of Russia had acted without political motives. The becoming behavior of the Russian delegation at New Delhi, however, made it equally difficult to believe that the Church was lending itself wittingly to any scheme of this sort, though there remained the possibility of its being "used" unsuspectingly.

The opinion in the Assembly appeared to be generally that the Russian Orthodox Church was moved mainly by its need of the wider fellowship and a desire, sincere enough, to promote Christian unity and world peace.

While the walls separating Christians did not reach up to heaven, as Platon of Kiev had said, they did destroy intercourse between churches vital to spiritual life and growth. The Russian Orthodox Church had suffered deeply during the long years of its imprisonment behind the Iron Curtain. The feeling was that it deserved the utmost encouragement as it reached out now to the world beyond, so long as the evidence supported belief in its sincerity.

In a memorandum to the denominations of the United States Charles C. Parlin, a lay member of the new Presidium elected at New Delhi, set forth the considerations which had influenced the Assembly to approve the application of the Russian Orthodox Church:[4]

> The World Council of Churches is a religious body, and applications for membership are judged on the basis of religious beliefs. . . . Relationships of a particular church to its government and the government's political or economic theories are not determinative. Member churches, in fact, have their headquarters in lands representing the widest range of political and economic form. Member churches in their relationship to their respective governments also vary widely—for example, in the United States there is no relationship, whereas in Great Britain and in Sweden there is a close relationship in the case of their established churches. . . .

[4] Mimeographed statement at New Delhi.

The Russian Church, in spite of unrelenting government opposition and at times intense pressure and persecution, has maintained Christian worship. . . . Persons who have seen their services are unanimous in agreeing that the churches are filled . . . and that their liturgy and music is moving and of deep spiritual significance. . . .

The Orthodox Churches, which hold themselves to be the mother churches of Christendom in direct descent from the earliest churches at Jerusalem and Antioch, came into being in a period of persecution by the Roman Empire. They survived centuries of persecution by dominant Islam powers. The Church in Russia lived under the heavy hand of the Czars and has since lived under the dominance of a communist state dedicated to atheism.

In our contacts with the Russian Church over a period of recent years none of their churchmen has questioned the form of his government's political structure or the economic theory which it has adopted. But on the issue of whether Russia is to be an atheist or a Christian nation there is a head-on collision between Church and State. On this issue no Russian churchman has given any indication that he is prepared to . . . compromise. On this issue, an historic struggle currently goes on within Russia.

The battle is: Are science and religion compatible or irreconcilable? The Russian state maintains, and teaches in its schools, that the two cannot be reconciled and that science is true and . . . our faith is based on fabrications and therefore false. . . . The Russian Church maintains and preaches that science and religion are compatible and that God has revealed himself to man through the Holy Scriptures and also through the ever-expanding books of science. . . .

The members of the World Council of Churches welcome into their fellowship the Russian Orthodox Church, and they pray God's blessing on the heroic struggle . . . to propagate the Gospel in their land and to restore their country to the status of a Christian state.

Most such statements left untouched—perhaps wisely—questions more disturbing than those they answered.

One question concerned the political involvements of the Russian Orthodox Church. Bishop Nikodim, who headed the Russian Orthodox delegation to New Delhi, had succeeded only recently to the office of his Church on governmental relations and foreign affairs, generally rated in importance as the next-to-the-top position in the hierarchy. His predecessor, Metropolitan Nikolai,[5] had been described in press reports as "a tireless purveyor of Soviet propaganda . . . once identified as a Soviet state security agent" and collaborator with the Soviet government in bloody persecutions of the churches of the Ukraine during the years when it was forcing unification in the nation under communism. The new young prelate, thirty-two years old, impressed those who met and talked with him in New Delhi as being both capable and Christian-minded. Would he introduce a better rule more in keeping with the moral teaching of the Church? Could he, if he wished to do so?

[5] For Nikolai's actions in relation to the World Council of Churches, see pp. 794 ff. At the time of the Third Assembly he was seriously ill in Moscow, and his death occurred the following January, at the age of sixty-nine.

Reports that a new generation in Russia was demanding greater liberty and a return to normal contacts with the world, accented by Nikodim's advancement, encouraged hope of a change for the better. But persistent rumors of current persecutions of Christians and pograms against the Jews in Russia were soon to be confirmed authoritatively.

The Russian Orthodox delegates at New Delhi served notice that their Church would not confine itself to the questions of Faith and Order, which were supposed to be their main interest, but would participate fully in the World Council's program of social action. What would be the effects of its activity in this tension-packed area?

When decisions of the World Council were unwelcome to the Soviet government, would the Russian Church not have to abstain? Even so, might it not be pressured to withdraw from membership, as the Chinese churches were after the World Council's charge in 1950 that Red China had committed aggression against Korea? Because of the possibility of developments of this kind, might not the presence of the Russian Orthodox Church in the World Council jeopardize, rather than further, the cause of world peace?

What, more specifically, would the World Council of Churches do about the Soviet-inspired Prague Peace Conferences, in which it had declined so far to cooperate? The Russian Orthodox Church had helped promote them and had professed not to understand the reason for the World Council's aloofness. Certain officers of the World Council attending them unofficially had criticized its non-cooperative attitude. From the Prague platform the West and the Council had been denounced. At the most recent Conference (1961), Bishop K. H. Ting of China had pushed aside the topic assigned to him and delivered an invective against the United States and its churches that by its violence astounded many who heard him. The occasion had made evident the existence of tensions which could easily disrupt the ties any denomination behind the Iron or Bamboo Curtain might form with the ecumenical movement. If this should happen in the case of the Russian Orthodox Church, would it not deepen the rift between the East and the West? Might it not possibly tear apart the World Council of Churches?

Part of the answer to such questions as these would have been, of course, that, whether inside or outside the World Council of Churches, the Russian Church posed a problem for the ecumenical movement. Its admission might be found to have created more difficulties than it resolved. However, detached from the World Council, it would have been more in danger of becoming part of the nucleus of a new global organization of churches gathering its constituency in the main from the East and putting an end to the hope of achieving the unity of the non-Roman elements of Christendom.

There was need to bear in mind that the Russian Orthodox Church had not knocked unbidden at the door of the World Council of Churches. It had been invited. "Invited" was hardly a strong enough word to describe what had happened. The Russian Church had been encouraged, cultivated, persuaded. Some of the most influential church leaders in the World Council believed that it had a potential contribution to make toward the unity of the Church Universal that was indispensable. And it would bring into the World Council many millions of Christians, not only from its own vast domains, but from other Orthodox Churches as well, which would be induced by its decision to join. This would help greatly to establish a better balance in the membership of the World Council of Churches as between East and West, and refute the repeated charge that the World Council was a Western organization bent mainly on furthering the interests of the West.

So, there had been reciprocating visits, and conferences and negotiations. The Russian Orthodox authorities had evidently been made to feel that the time had come when they could enter the World Council of Churches with reasonable assurance of being received with understanding, and in a manner helping them with their problems at home—or at least not complicating them.

Admittedly, the move would be fraught with perils for both Church and Council. But the Council was used to dangers, and undoubtedly the Church was. The Council had never sought to be a safety island in the world's swirling traffic. Significantly enough, its emblem was a ship. Its confidence was, so to speak, in a built-in buoyancy which would, it trusted, ride out any storm. At any rate, it prayed for courage at the helm to face the roughest weather. The Russian Church, which had known perhaps more adversity than any other in the World Council, must have responded deeply to this audacious spirit.

For the delegates of the Assembly, it was a time for the reflection that the World Council's program was not for the timid, nor for those so certain of their doctrinal correctness that they could believe God had put all his hopes for mankind in them alone. The venture on which the World Council had embarked was hazardous. It might prove impossible. Only faith could say "No" to fears. If the end turned out to be disaster, it would be failure on a grand design, worthy of men at their best and of God who in his wisdom challenged them with goals always within reach but forever exceeding the grasp.

3. Observers from Rome

Five Roman Catholic priests, the first officially appointed observers of their communion to attend a major meeting of the World Council of Churches, were regularly in their appointed seats at the sessions, accompanied generally by a number of fellow priests who sat in the section reserved for press representatives. Silent and unobtrusive, their diligence in attendance could have been matched by but few of the delegates. They were readily available for "tea-time chats," but not for comment on the proceedings of the Assembly.[6]

It was noted that they watched with close interest as the Assembly received into membership in the World Council of Churches the Russian Orthodox Church, revised the Basis of the World Council to include specific reference to the Holy Trinity, and approved the report of the committee on proselytism, which strongly disapproved of that practice by member denominations. It was understood that they would take back to the Vatican a detailed report of the Assembly's entire transactions.

Their presence at New Delhi was regarded by ecumenical leaders as one more important link in the lengthening chain of communication between the major divisions of Christendom—Roman Catholic, Eastern Orthodox, and Protestant. It was looked upon as another step on the steep and slippery road toward Christian reunion.

Chosen by the Vatican's Secretariat for Promoting Christian Unity, of which Augustin Cardinal Bea was Secretary, the deputation consisted of the Rev. Edward J. Duff of St. Louis, Missouri; the Rev. Joseph Edmaran, Head of the Jesuit Vice-Province of Kerala, India; the Rev. Ivan Extross, Chancellor of the Diocese of Allahabad in northern India; the Rev. M. J. le Guillou of the Istina Ecumenical Centre in Paris; and the Rev. Jan C. Groot of the Roman Catholic Seminary at Warmond, The Netherlands.

At the time of the New Delhi conference it had not been announced whether observers from the World Council of Churches—or from Orthodox and Protestant churches—would be invited to the Second Ecumenical Council of the Roman Catholic Church, to begin in Rome in October, 1962.[7] The Assembly nevertheless voted to send a fraternal message to the Vatican Council.

Objection by Archbishop Nikodim to the message caused something of a commotion. "We feel one way about Roman Catholicism," he said, "and another way about Vatican City, which is an organized state and not a religion." The fact that he had been put on the World Council's important policy committee gave his words, the Roman Catholic observers felt, more than usual force and authority, and they took umbrage at them. "Our presence here is more than just a contact." one of the observers was heard to say privately. "If the Russians can't understand that, we might as well . . . go home." However, they accepted the in-

[6] The Roman Catholic bishops of Switzerland asked their people to pray for the Assembly, that they and all whom they represented, would be inspired by the light and strength of the Holy Spirit. "If we pray . . . for one another," they said, "it is impossible that the Lord will not help us to understand one another better."

[7] Observers were subsequently invited and attended the sessions of the Vatican Council in 1962, 1963 and 1964.

cident, it was reported—after explanations by Assembly officials—with the allowances due it as a not uncommon example of frank debate under the rules of free speech.

4. East and West: Confrontation and Community

A condition of attaining Christian community, a much-talked-about ecumenical objective, is, it might be said, learning to speak the truth in love and to hear in love the truth so spoken.

New Delhi may have been a short step, at least, in that direction. The East (by which is meant here mainly those from the younger churches) spoke as it had never had opportunity to speak in interchurch assemblages; it may have raised its voice at times; it sometimes spoke impatiently. Still the West listened, often with indicated assent, sometimes with doubts and reservations, but always with restraint and with belief in the East's intention to speak the truth. Nothing happened to suggest that it was not, on the whole, a dialogue of Christian love.

Asking of Jesus what truth was, Pontius Pilate, as Francis Bacon wrote, "would not tarry for an answer." There was long waiting at Vigyan Bhawan for the answers to many questions which, for all that there was much speaking of what honest people believed truth, did not come. It was clear that there would have to be other Assemblies and more speaking of truth in love—and more listening in love.

The question was whether or not love would last. Could East and West go on speaking and listening to all the truth they would have to learn together if there was ever to be one world fellowship—if East and West were to meet in *koinonia?* [8]

The impatience of the East resembled at times that of a man who had just wakened, knowing that he must be up and doing but not reckoning that with greater deliberation he might make faster progress. The West counseled patience, maintaining the attitude of one resolved to listen, whatever happened. It spoke out of a larger ecumenical experience and knew better the weakness in impetuosity and the mastery in moderation.

The West heard from the East the verdict against missionary paternalism. It knew in advance what the judgment would be. The mission churches had come of age. The government must be shifted to their shoulders. For better or worse, the responsibility would be theirs. They would continue to look to the West for counsel, financial assistance, friendship, and a measure of collaboration. But the initiative and the decision would thenceforth rest with themselves.

The West heard reiterated the condemnation of everything that had been associated with colonialism. The East was saying, in short, "No

[8] The Greek word in the New Testament meaning Christian fellowship.

hard feelings intended, but you will have to fall in behind or go home."

The West heard, again, the charge that it had pushed its competitive denominational systems into the religious life of the mission countries, to their confusion and spiritual hurt. It was made to face the demand to take steps at once to help with repairing this damage. It was called from discussion of unity to action.

The West faced the presentment against it of prejudice and discrimination in race relations; of nationalism with its rivalries, which had brought mankind to the brink of annihilation; of secularism belying its professed belief in God; of the prostitution of science and its skills to self-enrichment, while two-thirds of mankind starved; of continuing designs to maintain economic control over the underdeveloped nations, old and new; of contentions between its major powers which made even its plans for aiding others hinge upon considerations of self-gain; and of rejection generally of the obligations of stewardship and the Christian injunction that the strong ought always to bear the burdens of the weak.

All these charges had been made before, of course, but it was important to those repeating them at New Delhi to be heard in an ecumenical gathering fully representative of the churches from which they came and affording a rostrum from which their voices carried to the ends of the earth.

The dictum of Edmund Burke that a whole nation could not be indicted was even more applicable to continents and hemispheres. And such sweeping criticism of one part of the world by another as the Third Assembly heard could be discounted and indulged as of the nature of a catharsis for those holding the floor.

More grace was needed to listen to it in silence when it lapsed into denunciation and became personal, as when Sir Francis A. Ibiam turned his attention to missionaries he had observed, describing them as "guardians of white supremacy" little given to "visiting the homes of African Christians, much less the homes of non-Christians." This was resented, even by some of his fellow Africans, and there was talk of rejecting the proposal, which had been made, that he be nominated for election to the Presidium. However, he was named in the slate and elected one of the six Presidents of the World Council of Churches, though with fewer votes than the other nominees received.[9]

Sir Francis' linking of white supremacy and the apparent social aloofness of some missionaries he had known may have pointed to an unfortunate misunderstanding rather common among indigenous Christians of mission countries. Those who go from Europe or North America to tropical or semitropical lands are always uncomfortably conscious of health hazards and diseases to which they have not the acquired or

[9] Sir Francis, converted from paganism and holding membership in a Presbyterian church, was governor of Eastern Nigeria, Africa. Having been detained at his capital, Lady Ibiam read his speech.

natural immunity of those who have lived there all their lives. This realization, rather than any feeling of superiority, may make them appear awkward at times or reluctant to accept the hospitality of the people. Stories of missionaries summoned to meet the tribal chieftain and eating whatever he set before them, even if it made them deathly ill, belong to the past. Here is an opportunity for the educated local people to lead others and to assist the newcomers in adjusting themselves to unfamiliar surroundings.

More than that, here is an opportunity to speak and to hear the truth in love—the condition of Christian community. Perfect frankness on the part of all would prevent misunderstanding and pave the way for mutual confidence and respect. There would have been better feeling in New Delhi, it ought to be said, if Christian frankness with respect to living accommodations had been practiced by all parties before and during the Assembly.

There were two sides to the East-West issue. If one of the principals had an indictment to present, the right course for the other certainly was to hear it. That it went largely unanswered may have been fortunate.

Outside Vigyan Bhawan also, the East spoke—in the streets and hotels, on the trains, airplanes, and ships, in the buses and taxis, in business offices and temples of religion, over radio and television and through the newspapers. It was New Delhi, and the voice was predominantly that of Hinduism, which was intent on driving home the point that Christian missions had no rightful place in India unless they were content to leave off their preachments and confine themselves to social services.

This Hindu East's view of Christians, whether of East or West, was perhaps best summed up in a phrase from a lecture delivered some years before at Oxford University by Dr. Radhakrishnan, who called them "very ordinary persons given to making most extraordinary claims." The East rejected the suggestion of Jesus Christ's uniqueness. A light? Yes. *The* light? No. Indians readily gave him a place among their prophets, linking his name with Gandhi's.

From India, Ceylon, Burma, and beyond, Buddhism spoke. Its hierarchs had just met in Kuala Lumpur in a world conference on unity and peace within their own councils, which adjourned in the midst of a factional quarrel, with—of course—no encomiums for the Christian Prince of Peace. In New Delhi "the seat of light" was the new Buddhist temple, according to a yellow-robed monk explaining the symbolism of its richly jeweled altar to Assembly members. It was the real House of Wisdom, he asserted. The light of Buddha would never pale or fail.

Declared a prominent political leader, "For Christianity as a light there is a large place in India and in all Asia—for its moral teachings, its works of charity, for Jesus as prophet and its saints. But for the church and 'churchianity' there is no room." The Assembly was a conclave of bishops and their lackeys, he thought. What could it expect to do to justify coming all the way to India?

According to a wealthy Brahmin, the West condemned itself by "tying strings to its aid." "When I pass five thousand or so to a friend in need, I bid him join with me in keeping it a confidence between ourselves," he said. "You remember the words attributed to your Christ—'When thou doest alms, let not thy left hand know what thy right hand doeth.'" He was honest enough to admit that well-to-do Indians like himself were not much given to charity, that Hinduism by its teaching discouraged giving aid to the destitute, because of its fear of prolonging their earthly probation.

An Indian government official believed in Christianity; but, although once a member of the Church and educated in a church college on scholarship aid, he had, as he said, "no use for churches."

Asked whether this attitude was characteristic of the Indian people, a college student, the son of a native Protestant pastor, replied, "Yes, of the educated." He added that the strength of Christianity in India was in the rural areas where the people were poor and their ministers often had less than a bare subsistence. "If you would get the true picture of the Christian religion in India," he said, "you should visit the villages."

Outside the Assembly, in New Delhi and in India, despite widespread resentment of Red China's invasion of Tibet, little hostility toward communism itself was apparent. Influential circles in India tended to accept the equation of many of the social goals of communism and Christianity by such teachers and writers as E. Stanley Jones, and there was little evidence that a determined movement to deliver the nation into communist hands would meet with wholehearted popular resistance. The supposed effort of Nikita Khrushchev "to do the things Christianity teaches and the Church doesn't do" elicited approval. His methods were excused as being necessary under the handicaps he faced. The end sought justified them. The policies of the United States were blamed for many of his actions. He resorted to nuclear weapons because the United States had, and was currently testing them in defiance of world opinion because the United States had. After all, the United States had been the first and only nation to attack another with nuclear bombs. "The people knew that Khrushchev in his way was trying to help them, while the Church only talked about the fine things God wanted done for them," it was said.

Mr. Nehru declared in a public statement during the Assembly that he was committed to democracy, in which he believed, but that he would not hesitate to use stronger measures than had been employed, if they became necessary, to enable India to reach her goal of economic self-sufficiency.

The Christian West met condemnation from some quarters of the Christian East outside Vigyan Bhawan.

The Archbishop of Bombay and Primate of the Indian National Church,[10] His Eminence Mar Athanasius Joel S. Williams, warned against the dangers of foreign missionaries and their Indian agents who controlled thousands of Christians by a discipline emanating from their respective countries.[11]

> Foreign missions and their native agents [he said] have unfortunately carved out in India a state within a state, where the will of the "Vicar of Christ" who is also the ruler of the Vatican state in Italy is supreme, where the ruling sovereign of England is the "Supreme Governor" of faith and British nationals exercise control over Indian Christians through their native mercenaries, employed to propagate the Anglican faith, and where thousands of Indian Christians are being controlled by a "discipline" which is finalized every fourth year in America. It is therefore necessary that such a state of affairs be brought to an end in the interest of the safety and security of our country. The Government and the people of India must realize the danger, especially at a time when our mother-land is surrounded by enemies in the north, east and west, and also in Goa, within the very heart of India. The control of alien powers over India, in the garb of religion, is in fact a slur upon the name of Christianity. India's own indigenous Church—the Indian National Church—is sufficient to safeguard the interest of Christians in India, and also to see to the propagation of the life and teaching of their Lord and Savior Jesus Christ without any proselytising activities.

The "ecumenical" West did not reply to the "ecumenical" East at New Delhi in Vigyan Bhawan, or to the non-Christian or the Christian East outside. It stood with the ecumenical East in affirming belief in Christ as the light of the world and the purpose to continue working to carry his truth to all men, while seeking new approaches and trying to correct manifest mistakes in its methods.

"We do not proclaim ourselves the light of the world, but Christ," the ecumenical West and the ecumenical East joined in confessing. "Him we would give every opportunity to illumine the way for all mankind. We want to get out of the way of his light, so that it may shine undimmed by human faults. We realize that he is only dimly reflected in what we try to do, that his light is often turned into darkness by the eclipse of our sins."

The Church would not give up its mission in the world because it was asked to. Its orders came from Christ. This was the answer of the church of the West, as it was of the ecumenical East. It spoke with confident testimony. It admitted its earthenness as the vessel of Christian truth. There had been many errors of judgment in missionary plans and their execution, unwarrantable and inexcusable divisiveness in denominational policies, evils in Western colonialism, all the sins of racism

[10] According to the most reliable information obtainable, the Indian National Church is of no great influence in the life of India. It obviously aims to exploit the nationalist interest.

[11] As reported in *The Indian Express.*

that had been categorized to its shame and of self-seeking nationalism. Stewardship of possessions and of power had been only partially accepted. In more ways than the East had named, the West stood condemned in its own conscience.

Rebuttal was not attempted. That would have to wait, if undertaken at all. The only convincing answer would be in the conscience of the East, when there had been time for sober reflection undisturbed by the crush of Westerners in the hotels and public places of India's capital city, whose manner at times had understandably made dispassionate thinking difficult.

Would India or any of the "mission lands," because there had been mistakes by the churches, give up the blessings they had enjoyed under Christian missions? Hardly anyone believed they would. Asia had drunk more deeply than it knew of the "living water." If the pitcher had been broken at the fountain, new means of getting at the life-giving spring would be contrived. Those who sat in darkness—in Asia, Africa, the islands of the Pacific—had seen a great light, and in the minds of many of them it would never be extinguished. It was a light like the sunrise of a new day, which would increase until all nations would see it and walk in it. This would surely be the long answer of the soul of the East.

In time also—if the world survived—the East would come to look at colonialism, now rejected by the West too, with clearer eyes and would see that it must not allow the vacuum created by the withdrawal of the older powers to be occupied by other nations bringing worse evils. The East would see the folly of continuing to make the West a whipping boy for its own failures and gather its forces for a maximum drive for renewal and recovery. In time the East would realize, too, that its wrath on account of class and caste in the Occidental state and church would better be turned upon these evils in its own society; that the secularism and chauvinism it condemned in others were faults to be cured in its own statesmen, lest its decisions, so vital to the peace of the world, be informed more by expedient and materialistic considerations than by democratic principles. The East knew well enough that peace was a result, not of absolutes held in perfect balance by natural laws, but of laborious human effort to establish a working harmony between nations of conflicting interests and wills.

Perhaps East and West would in time be able to learn together the inexorable condition of community in speaking and hearing the truth in love. Only so could the deep chasm between the hemispheres, geographical or racial, be bridged to support humankind in peaceful one-world traffic.

III

THE CHURCHES AND THE WORLD

1. Christian Witness

The first study section of the New Delhi Assembly developed in its report the function of the Church to witness for Jesus Christ—a work of the whole Church, clergy and laity. If laymen thought this beyond them, they were counseled to bear in mind that the reliance of the witness was not on "his own cleverness," but on God who was always present to bless honest and humble testimony.

Those putting together the document for the section, however, were, for the most part, professional religious leaders, and they proceeded to speak of preparation for witnessing, unintentionally shifting the emphasis from God's part to man's to an extent that could, some feared, discourage lay participation.

Laymen would require training in theology—enough to know the truth they would be trying to communicate. They must then be able to tell what they had learned in language the people understood. This could be done, the drafters suggested, without trying to "popularize the gospel."[1]

For the necessary theological instruction, the witness would look, in part, to his minister, whom, in turn, he would out of his own experience help to understand conditions in the world beyond the parish and to adapt his preaching and counseling to the needs of the larger community.

Witnesses, whether lay or clerical, should identify themselves with the condition of those to whom they spoke. To this end, they must "study the *milieu* in which the message would be proclaimed."[2]

> To get alongside our hearer, to sit where he sits, is the essential condition upon which alone we may claim the right to be heard. By such sympathetic identification, in which the love of Christ is reflected, the Christian witness shows that he is not proclaiming his own message or superior gifts, but the truth of Christ. . . .

[1] Some modern methods used in evangelistic campaigns to "popularize the gospel" were distasteful to many of the conferees.

[2] *The New Delhi Report,* p. 82 ff.

Witnesses must join in the struggle for social justice and make clear that the Church stood to help—to be in every sense an ally.

In order to qualify for such service, they should be trained also in the principles and practices of welfare work. Considerable knowledge of conditions in this area could be got through association with social workers and consultations with other like-minded lay volunteers coming from the various vocations and pooling their experiences. The Church would be prepared to place at their convenience the results of its continuing inquiries in this field, in cooperation with the ecumenical organizations. The Commission of the Churches on International Affairs, for example, would keep them informed through their churches and other channels on the issues of world Christian citizenship and on measures for promoting peace and helping the peoples of all lands in need.

> There are certain areas of life today where this kind of sympathetic identification is particularly needful and in which it is especially important that the witness should himself be first of all a listener.
>
> Among these . . . may be mentioned the spheres of youth, the worker and the intellectual. If they are to be won, we must share their concerns, sympathize with their aspirations and learn their language. Otherwise, they will translate our words into their own terms and . . . not understand what we are saying. . . .
>
> The resurgence of ancient faiths under the stimulus of nationalism is an example of the kind of challenge which demands from us . . . understanding, if we are to convince their adherents that in the Universal Christ is to be found the answer to the desire of all nations.
>
> Or again . . . the view of many intellectuals in our technological society that all religious language, including Christian language, is a using of words that have no meaning at all, is an expression of disillusionment which demands from us a patient study and a sincere attempt to understand its deep causes.
>
> Only if we enter the world of our hearers will they be able or willing to listen to us. Instead of dismissing men's negative reactions to our message, we should take upon ourselves the burden of their unbelief.

So were set forth some of the preparatory steps for witnessing effectively—that is to say, for making it possible for God to give power to witnessing. As stated at the beginning, witnessing was to be a matter, not mainly of the workers' "cleverness," but of the Spirit's direction and use of their ministry.

If the would-be lay witness felt that he could not take time from his occupation for the necessary preparation, he would need to be encouraged to think of the Christian calling to witness as his first responsibility and of his job as incidental to it. He was sent to be, with other laymen like himself, the Church in the world, and it was more important that he discharge this duty than that he succeed in material ways.

If the layman attained success in a profession or a business, he would have in his witnessing the handicap of "affluence in a world where others were hungry and naked."

There was no indication in the study that he might witness by attention to the demands of a successful business which provided work for others and the means of helping the disabled and poor.

The reasoning of Section I at this point would have to be criticized as actually narrowing the view of witnessing, though emphasizing theoretically that its arena was the whole of life.

The report's reference to what it called "affluence" as a handicap to witnessing betrayed the influence in the study of an erroneous notion too common in the churches, namely, that possession of more than the means for bare subsistence was a kind of treason to the poor. It might have been asked what hope the hungry and naked, spoken of in the report, had apart from the proceeds of successful business, which were the source of whatever benefits charity, whether of private foundations or the welfare state, had to bestow, of employment for those who would work and earn a livelihood, and of capital for the development of economically backward states and communities.

Also, it might have been asked why religious leaders would indulge and encourage, rather than attempt to correct, the idea that a disparity in respect of worldly goods divided people into classes between whom communication of the Gospel was impossible.

The report on witnessing went far to support the opinion of many members of the Assembly that such studies by delegates to ecclesiastical conventions were of little use practically to the average lay person, man or woman; that they should be discouraged and the large amount of time reserved for them—in the World Council of Churches particularly—given to more profitable activities.

In the Assembly there was not enough time, as previously noted, for the generally excellent committee reports on the work of the several divisions and departments of the World Council of Churches; for adequate debate on important matters of business; for ample free periods for conversation and relaxation; or for holding even a single unprogrammed session at which the delegates might have spoken to one another and the officers occupying the platform continuously during the nearly three weeks in New Delhi "as the Spirit gave them utterance." There was always complaint after such gatherings that they had been planned so tightly, so to speak, that God had no opportunity to break into them for a suggestion. But nobody ever did anything about it.

With reference to witnessing, it might have been profitable—if there had been time for an answer—to ask what qualifications were really essential, besides true Christian character in the members of the churches who live out their days bearing faithfully the burden of the world's work.

It appeared to be the view of the Eastern Orthodox Churches that the Church itself was the convincing witness as it treasured and gave exemplification of the Gospel through its liturgies and instructional congregational and pastoral ministry. Was there not here a fundamental concept which needed emphasizing, whatever else might be done to strengthen Christian witnessing?

Said the report itself, apparently expressing the Orthodox view: "In apostolic witness, coming to us in the Scriptures in the Spirit-indwelt Church, God gives us the foundation of all subsequent witness. In the sacraments of baptism and the Eucharist, God down the ages . . . has drawn near to men in Jesus Christ and borne witness to his own faithfulness. In the very existence of the Church, there is a constant witness —in silence, as it were—to the reality of God's dealing with men in Jesus Christ."

But the "witness in silence" and all else that the Church might do depended on the character of the Church—that is to say, of its ministering pastors and worshiping congregations—and not merely, nor chiefly, on its doctrines and creeds. The exposition of the Gospel through the corporate acts of the Church and the lives of its faithful members was a kind of ministry no new technique in communication would be needed to make intelligible and effective. In the words of the report of the Witness Section of *The New Delhi Report*:

> Christian witnesses must be prepared to be tested by the gospel they proclaim. . . . Our message will have to be embodied in our life. . . . The Church as manifested by the local congregation will exhibit or obscure the presence of Christ, and onlookers will judge by what they see. . . . Our message has not been truly proclaimed until it has been lived. . . . This . . . reflection throws us back upon the mystery that God can, and does, use us in . . . our inadequacy to make manifest the truth which our imperfect works conceal. It is Christ, not Christianity, which is to be proclaimed as the truth, as it is God's power, and not ours, which brings men to accept it.

2. The Problem of Government—Political and Ecclesiastical

As an international interchurch body, the World Council of Churches had in its membership denominations and interdenominational councils in nations under about every known type of government. The results of this comprehensiveness could be observed in its life.

Clergymen and laymen of the established churches, for example, brought to the World Council special experience and skill in the affairs of their governments which gave them understanding and influence in its social action program, particularly in the political sphere.

Though dying before the World Council of Churches was formally organized, Nathan Söderblom of Sweden and William Temple of England had, through their connection with the Life and Work Movement, led in setting its course in this respect.

Said Dr. Visser 't Hooft at New Delhi: "One of the main reasons why the World Council was created was, as both Nathan Söderblom and William Temple stated in the early [provisional] days, to give to the Church 'a more permanent and . . . effectual means of declaring . . . its judgment' [Temple at Edinburgh, 1937]. . . . It remains an important fact that the voice of the Church is heard at the world level where the great decisions affecting the future of humanity are taken."

Geoffrey Fisher, who had succeeded William Temple as Archbishop of Canterbury, presided at Amsterdam when the World Council of Churches was constituted and from that time until his retirement was an able interpreter in its deliberations of the mutual responsibilities of the state and the church.

The World Council enjoyed during these years the extraordinary service of George Kennedy Allen Bell, Bishop of Chichester, whose expert knowledge of statecraft could be seen especially in its pronouncements.

The Established Church laity had outstanding representation in Sir Kenneth Grubb of the staff of the Commission of the Churches on International Affairs and Dr. Kathleen Bliss of the Commission on work with women.

Complaints of "too much state church" were heard from time to time, but these were subdued generally—and often on the lips of the very persons voicing them—by the realization that those who spoke under the discipline of an establishment were usually saved from the embarrassing excesses of amateurs and extremists and rendered, on the whole, invaluable service to the cause. On occasion, it was the spokesmen of this group who opened the way for the World Council of Churches to act with more confidence and propriety than would otherwise have been possible, as, for example, when the Archbishop of Canterbury (Fisher) in a public statement in 1956 defined what the Church considered to be the duty of the British government in the Suez crisis.

Between Oxford and New Delhi—that is, from 1937 to 1961—there was a noticeable change in the attitude of many of the free churches to Christian social action. Lingering pietistic inhibitions to participation in activities relating to political affairs gave way to growing support of the Life and Work program in this area. This could be attributed, in a considerable degree, to the influence and leadership of established church men—Söderblom, Temple, Bell, Fisher, J. H. Oldham, Berggrav, and others in less conspicuous positions.

With the movement away from establishment on the Continent, the states generally had retained some legal connection with the churches through special governmental departments on religious affairs.

This arrangement satisfied religious-minded persons, so long as the Church was left free to conduct its own business. It was acceptable to statesmen also, who felt that complete divorcement of church and state would weaken the national unity, as some churchmen feared that such separation would expose the Church to factional strife and possible disunity.

The significance of this policy for the World Council of Churches was that it conditioned multitudes of its membership to partial control of the churches by the states, always a threat to religious freedom. It may have worked justly and to advantage in some instances, as in 1961 when the Church of Greece was unable to act unitedly on the case of its patriarch, charged with misconduct, and the state assumed responsibility. But in some nations totalitarian regimes took control of the churches for their own purposes, as in Poland, Hungary, Rumania, Czechoslovakia, and East Germany.

This meant that there were in the World Council of Churches many denominations limited in the exercise of their membership by the states. Some of these had to have permission from their governments, in the first place, to join the World Council; and whether they continued in the relationship or not depended on the same political will. They were not free agents. The states decided even whom they should have represent them in the World Council. Their own officials were, in effect, chosen by the government and were, to all practical purposes, accountable ultimately to the same authority.[3]

There were denominations from countries outside Europe in the World Council of Churches similarly answerable to their respective governments.

Whether the representatives of these state-controlled churches in the World Council believed in the political philosophies of their governments was, of course, generally indeterminable. Some of them undoubtedly did. With perhaps more of them it was a case of accommodating themselves to the ineluctable, whatever their private convictions. Their situation did not encourage frank speaking. Friendly inquiries would elicit from them such replies as:[4]

Our government is suited to present social conditions in our country.

Our nation is better off now than it was under the old regime.

The system we are living under now is, of course, not all we should like it to be, but then none would be.

A good government is one accommodating itself to the people's needs, rather than to some utopian ideal, and ours is meeting the situation we are in quite satisfactorily, all things considered.

[3] Delegates appointed by East German churches to New Delhi were denied passports. Six had been elected, along with three advisers and one guest. None of these could be present.

[4] These were opinions recorded at New Delhi.

The effects of the influence in the World Council of Churches of the totalitarian-state denominations showed up in the more or less unconscious adjustment of its program to their limitations. Without experiential knowledge of the meaning of democracy and human rights in the Western sense, they were skeptical of the value of these, and their distorted image of nations in which such principles had been followed most successfully made difficult their learning from them. Self-defensively, they were inclined to extol the superiority of their own position. They were better off under state control, they said, than they had been under the old order. With governmental subsidies, their churches could give undivided attention to spiritual things. Interdenominational rivalries were being eliminated, they declared, and cooperation was increasing. Authoritarianism afforded more real freedom than capitalistic democracy.

The World Council, whether consciously or not, was in a degree accommodating itself, as the New Delhi Assembly gave evidence, to this attitude. Reiterating that the Council stood for no particular ideology, the discussions turned to other matters—relief, race, unity, witness, peace. There were reports on principles of human rights, but no adequate interpretation of them and not enough discussion of their political implementation.

"The age of universal history" was bringing the World Council of Churches something quite unanticipated. It was a familiar truism that crowds tended to move on a lower moral level than their more perceptive members. Was this law operating in the ecumenical movement? Many ecumenists had looked forward to the day when a world Christian fellowship would give expression to the Gospel in its fullness. New Delhi could hardly have been said to justify this hope.[5]

Most of the denominations and their conciliar bodies belonging to the World Council of Churches were in nations under socialist governments of one pattern or another. Whether or not this had any direct influence

[5] There were differing views on whether or not New Delhi accommodated its statements on social issues to totalitarian limitations. Heinrich Stubbe, in an article in the *Neue Züricher Zeitung,* criticized the World Council of Churches for "meaningless compromises" because of consideration for the Russian Orthodox Church. Hans-Heinrich Brunner, replying to this charge, declared that the section on "Service" at New Delhi had examined with clarity, in the light of the Christian faith and with reference to the concrete social and political conditions of today, the importance of the open society, of human rights and the fundamental freedoms. He recalled that no attempt was made at Amsterdam or Evanston to "mobilize Christendom against communist totalitarianism" and took the position that if the Assembly at New Delhi did not "it was not due either to the dark machinations of any hirelings in the pay of Khrushchev nor to a fear-complex in face of such powers." The Assembly of the World Council was not "an ethical court of justice," he said. Its work was "not primarily to evaluate systems and ideologies, but to consider man with his problems and hopes, his gifts and responsibilities." The ecumenical fellowship had always regarded the totalitarian state, not as *sui generis* evil, but rather as one of the many forces menacing human rights and freedoms, he argued, and this attitude had been maintained at New Delhi. (*Ecumenical Press Service,* January 19, 1962, p. 6.)

on its actions, the "welfare state" or "responsible society" concept was incorporated in the World Council's social action program.

There was never a really clear and comprehensive definition of the nature of the responsible society as conceived by the World Council; but it would not have been far from the meaning to say that as a welfare state it would expect, among other things, to take care of everybody in need by distributing through charity and taxation what the successful and otherwise fortunate had, the office of the churches in the process being to continue nurturing the charitable spirit and to bless in the name of justice such compulsive measures beyond voluntary giving as might be found necessary.

This was an aim with instant appeal to the already overpopulated world demanding the fruits of material progress as a common right and believing, from the humblest poor to many of the most learned social theorists, that these were to be got in the desired amount by obtaining them from the minority who had succeeded in more or less monopolizing them, along with the means of acquiring them.

The immediate phenomenal acceptance of the World Council of Churches, as it recognized, was in large part due to its relief program. This was only as it should be, the leaders agreed, Christian witnessing being, as New Delhi reasserted, unrealistic and impossible apart from serving. Christian missioners must go bearing gifts, not to buy converts, but to express the concern of God and the Church in terms of the needs of the whole man.

Most ecumenical leaders knew that the meaning of the responsible society was not as simple as this. They understood that there were not goods enough in the world's storehouses to go around, and that taking from the few and giving to the many, by whatever process, would tend to reduce all to want and to dry up the sources of charity, as well as of taxes; that industry and thrift on the part of all members of society were elements of responsible citizenship so indispensable that an apostle had been moved to lay down the rule that they who would not work should not eat;[6] that responsibility in the receiving of charity was quite as obligatory as in the giving; that bearing one's own burden, so far as possible, was "the law of Christ" quite as definitely as bearing one another's burdens; and that the noble design of the welfare state, if there was not compliance with these elementary principles of morality, was not worth the paper on which it was drawn.

But the rating of all charitable organizations in the popular mind plummeted when consideration turned from what the people should get to what they ought to give. Like the rest, in the face of overwhelming need, the World Council of Churches talked first and almost entirely about the things which stimulated liberality and conditioned the minds

[6] II. Thessalonians iii, 10.

of those able to give for the inevitable legal expedients for supplementing their largess which must follow.

A search of the volumes of reports, resolutions, and dissertations from New Delhi for mention of the duties of those aided discovered only a hesitating sentence or two warning against expecting "too much material security" and suggesting that churches and nations seeking assistance ought to make long-range plans for attaining economic independence.

Declared the study report on "Service," characteristically: "Above all, the churches must not cease to champion the cause of making the riches of the developed countries available to those of poor resources" (p. 78).

With members from countries of varying types of government and churches of numerous new states knocking at its door, what guidance had the World Council of Churches for those confronted with the necessity of choosing a political system?

For reasons not obvious, the World Council was given to reminding its members that no political system could be equated with the kingdom of God. The question, after all, was not about finding a perfect government, it should have been unnecessary to say, but one promising conditions most favorable to the freedom, security, and development of its people. On this the Assembly had nothing definitive to say.

The Amsterdam Assembly in 1948 had compared capitalistic democracy and communistic collectivism and advised the churches to reject both and seek an alternative. The Evanston Assembly in 1954 had adopted some criteria of good government: protection of human rights; guarantee of freedom to express religious, moral, and political convictions; provision of channels by which the people could change incumbents in public office without recourse to violence; and respect for forms of association within society having their own foundations and principles independent of the state, such as the family, unions of various kinds, and churches.

The New Delhi Assembly reaffirmed the declaration at Evanston that government should be with the consent of the governed and the often repeated statement that "the Church cannot identify itself with any particular . . . political system." [7]

> However, both because of the opportunities afforded by political action for the improvement of conditions and because of many forms of evil and suffering which result from the misuse of political power, the Church should encourage the individual Christian to be active in the public life of his country.
>
> Recognition of the limitations under which Christians must live and work in many nations does not mean that one form of government is as good as another or that Christians can be indifferent to the nature of political institutions.

[7] *The New Delhi Report,* page 100 ff.

The Third Assembly thought "it was possible for a Christian to live . . . with integrity under any political system. . . . Mature Christians may grow in grace and in courage under oppressive governments." And Martin Niemöller volunteered the opinion that "the more oppressive a government was, the more conducive to Christian growth living under it might be, for the reason that, with the loss of worldly supports, Christians were driven to trust only in God."

> But under such governments [the Assembly was reminded] churches may be rigorously limited in their education of the younger generation, in their opportunity for public witness and in their pastoral service to the community. Love for . . . neighbor must move Christians to use whatever opportunities may exist to work for political institutions which encourage participation by all citizens, and which protect both the people's freedom of conscience and . . . freedom to express . . . convictions.[8]

There was tolerance enough in the Assembly toward totalitarianisms to give place in the study report on "Service" to the following advice:

> So many new nations have come into being and are in the early stages of establishing political institutions, that more account must be taken of the difficulties which such nations face. We live in a highly dynamic situation with many quite different national experiments. . . . Some of these systems are more authoritarian than those whose outlook has been molded by Western traditions of democracy would find acceptable. Yet the difficulty of maintaining order, of avoiding civil strife, of establishing governments strong enough to deal with the desperate need for economic development, may call for new forms of political life.

But not without this warning:

> No present difficulties justify Christians or churches in acquiescing in either old or new forms of tyranny. Where emergencies seem to call for temporary authoritarian regimes, let all who support them be warned that power corrupts, and that those who assume it will usually try to keep it. In recent times we have seen on a vast scale the use of methods of terror under many systems on the part of political authorities to preserve their power. There is no greater desecration of the human in men than to intimidate and torture them in order to force them to obey . . . against their consciences.

As will have been observed, the Assembly was not very articulate in what it said on government. Perhaps it spoke to itself, as well as to the churches, when it declared: "There is need of a much deeper understanding of the structural aspects of political life."

The World Council of Churches was conducting seminars and inquiries on many subjects, with the purpose of guiding the churches in their thinking. Why should it not have set up a study on "Comparative Political Government"?

Study of the influence of political backgrounds on the churches and,

[8] *Ibid.* p. 100-101.

through them, on their cooperative organizations brought up eventually the question of a proper workable government for the World Council.

The New Delhi Assembly was criticized as undemocratic in some of its procedures. There was complaint especially on account of the rules governing nominations. By notifying the chair, six or more delegates could propose a candidate from the floor. But they would have to indicate whom of those named by the Committee on Nominations the person they brought forward would, if elected, supplant. This requirement seemed to some to discourage nominations from the floor, because offering a substitute candidate would be construed by many as implying an invidiousness unbecoming in a religious body, though not so intended. The common way of handling such situations in most organizations was voting on all aspirants and seating the one—or ones, if there were more than a single office to be filled, as there were in the Presidium and the Central Committee of the World Council of Churches—receiving the greatest number of votes. By this plan, each person was in a sense running against all, and the contest would appear somewhat less personal.

However, in the World Council this method could easily have failed, in view of the nature of the positions to be filled. The distribution of official posts equitably among the denominations necessitated that nominations be made with reference to confessional and geographical representation, as well as "fair and adequate representation of the major interests of the World Council . . . and the personal qualifications of the individual for the task for which he is to be nominated," and these conditions were set forth in the Rules, which were printed in the Assembly Work Book for the information of the delegates. A random naming of persons from the floor could not have complied with this obviously fair requirement. It was stipulated, further, that before anyone was nominated for the Presidium or the Central Committee, it should be ascertained whether he would be acceptable to the denominational or other constituency he would represent, if elected.

It was recalled that at Evanston in 1954 there had been differences among the German delegates as to whether Dr. Otto Dibelius or Dr. Martin Niemöller should be nominated for election to the Presidium representing the Continental churches. Dibelius, who was later elected, was named by the Committee on Nominations, and Niemöller was proposed from the floor. At New Delhi the German delegation apparently agreed that the latter should succeed to the Presidium.

It seemed doubtful that many persons could be found among those in position to observe the business of the World Council at close range to question the essential democratic fairness of decisions on the whole.[9]

[9] As in other bodies, there may have been occasional instances of undemocratic action at the behest of aggressive individuals in the absence of objection from the floor, but such departure from the spirit and the letter of the rules was rare indeed. See Fry's reference to the democratic procedure of the Central Committee, p. 1084.

"Democracy" was a word of so many different connotations in usage, East and West, that one employing it needed to have regard for the results to be achieved as well as for the method of arriving at them. Especially was it important to remember that "pure democracy" was a misleading concept. Something approaching it could perhaps still be achieved in small town meetings and not-too-large local church congregations, where the people involved knew one another and had the same general background of community and customs. Beyond these limits, however, democracy could be practiced only through representation.

Democracy in the churches and their councils depended more on the spirit than on the rules. The ideas and values associated with the word, which derived from the New Testament, had to be preserved if the Church was to be kept true to its nature. First was the worth of the individual: "one of the least of these my brethren." Then came the exercise of authority by persuasion informed by spiritual insight and love, rather than by legal, financial, or other sanctions, and the idea of the Church as a family, in which there was neither Jew nor Greek, bond nor free, male nor female, and all had their places as members and kept at heart the interest of the whole—"All ye are brethren, and one is your Master." And finally, the Church was to be regarded as the *laos* (people) of God, with different gifts, functions, and responsibilities, but a unit —ministry and laity—in concern continuously for the work, welfare, and witness of the Church, by the principle "from each according to his ability, to each according to his need," interpreted in terms of time, strength, and endowments, and not only of money. These were the underlying concepts of democracy which had to be implemented in all Christian relations and kept watchfully and vigorously in force.[10]

It was always easy to see the failures of the "democratic process," whether in political or ecclesiastical government. Dr. Geoffrey Fisher was moved, following the constitution of the World Council of Churches at Amsterdam in 1948, to speak, as it appeared, extemporaneously concerning the erroneousness of the conception of democracy in the Church as popularly understood. Democracy meant the rule of the people, he said, but according to the New Testament and the nature of the Church the people were not to think of themselves as rulers of the Church. Democracy was for human institutions, he said. The Church was a divine society, with Christ its head and ruler. A more appropriate slogan for the members, he suggested, would be "demopractic," which denoted practicing what the Lord of the Church commanded.

Who would decide what the will of Christ was in the Church and in the World Council of Churches?

The apostle had been writing to all Christians, both pastors and the

[10] The author would gratefully acknowledge his indebtedness to the Rt. Rev. A. H. Legg for some of the thoughts and phrasings in this paragraph. See *The South India Churchman,* November, 1961, p. 5.

laity, when he said, "Let this mind be in you that was in Christ."[11] This implied competence on the part of the whole Church to help in arriving at the will of Christ. Upon every member of the body of Christ, therefore, was laid the responsibility of seeking to discern the mind of Christ in all things, in the spirit of his own promise, "He that willeth to do his will shall know . . . the truth."

There would be decisions, particularly in administrative matters, which the Church and its councils would leave to trusted leaders to take for them. Others would be taken by the larger congregations. In both instances the results would at times be such as to raise doubt that Christ had anything to do with them. Government, political or ecclesiastical, was not an exact science, as knowing the mind of Christ was not. Avoidance of fatal miscarriages of his will in the life of the Church and of the World Council depended on the diligent cultivation by all his people of the mind of Christ through study of the Scriptures, prayer, and fellowship.

Here was a responsibility that comprehended and stood above all others. Christians should devote themselves earnestly to it in their several churches and denominations—and in the World Council of Churches, where differences of religious background, social customs, language, cultures, nationality, political persuasions, race, and economic status made it tremendously difficult but not impossible of measurable attainment.

3. Resolution on Angola

By a margin of two votes, 179 to 177, the Assembly adopted a resolution on Portugal's policy in Angola, as follows:[12]

The Third Assembly of the World Council of Churches in session in New Delhi, cognizant of the situation in Angola, desires to appeal to the Government of Portugal, in the name of humanity and all that the Christian conscience cherishes, to bring to an end promptly and without delay the continuing tragedy in that land. We are deeply grieved at the acts of repression by Portuguese authorities over groups and peoples in Angola, and at the wide-spread violence in the land. We are further grieved that a nation with a great Christian tradition should have so departed from the pursuit of human values, that it stands accused at the bar of world opinion.

Believing that the fate of Angola is of international import, the Assembly urges Portugal to take immediate steps, so that the legitimate rights and political aspirations of the indigenous African people of Angola may be met expeditiously.

The Assembly draws the attention of member churches to the large number of refugees from Angola and urges them to treat the work of relief and

[11] Philippians ii, 5.

[12] *The New Delhi Report,* p. 39, 284-89.

rehabilitation among these . . . as of urgent priority, and to step up and extend relief measures already undertaken.

The Assembly notes with sorrow that many Christian missionaries in Angola have been subjected to great difficulties in their legitimate work of ministry to a people in great distress. The Assembly urges Portugal to restore to missionary bodies working in Angola such facilities as would enable them to continue their vocation in freedom. . . .

Aside from the serious matter with which it dealt, this action was noteworthy as bringing into rare focus questions raised from time to time by the World Council's social action program, which in the abstract may have been thought to be more fully accepted than it actually was.

The role of the World Council in relation to public affairs had sometimes been described as that of "a watchman on the wall." It was to alert the churches to social and political developments on which they should be informed and able to speak, while the Council itself might issue pronouncements and initiate such other steps as were indicated. The Angolan revolt had been regarded as falling within this definition, and prior to the New Delhi Assembly, officers of the World Council and the Commission of the Churches on International Affairs had sent the Portuguese government sharp notes expressing concern over the severity of the measures which had been taken by the authorities of the colony in quelling disorder. Many natives had been reported killed. The membership of at least one Protestant mission had, by reports, been nearly wiped out and their buildings destroyed. The Assembly was slated to approve the sending of these earlier communications, but had not received them on the floor when the new resolution on the Angolan situation was brought forward.

This motion, as indicated by the final vote, aroused immediate and strong objections, among them the following:

An undetermined number of delegates opposed on principle the World Council of Churches' interfering with the internal political affairs of any nation.

The Assembly had not itself investigated—and was in no position to do so—what had actually happened in Angola and was, therefore, not able to voice a fair or responsible opinion.

Angola was only one of a number of international trouble spots, and it ought not to be singled out for attention. The Ulbricht regime was building "the wall" through Berlin and shooting East Germans who dared to cross it. If resolutions were in order, it was asked from the floor, why was there none about that?

It would be unfair to censure a small nation such as Portugal, which had no representative in the Assembly who could offer a defense or an explanation.

If passed, the resolution against Portugal would set a dangerous precedent.

The action now proposed was unnecessary, in view of the notes already forwarded to Portugal by the Executive Committee of the World Council of Churches and the Chairman and Director of the Commission of the Churches on International Affairs.

India and Portugal being at the time at odds over the status of Goa, which belonged to the latter, courtesy and prudence demanded that nothing be done which might be construed as intended to put either country at a disadvantage in public opinion.[13]

The debate was significant as revealing important trends of thinking in the World Council of Churches. Apropos to the opposition's criticism of the World Council of Churches for "meddling" in the internal affairs of nations, Chairman Nathan Pusey of the Committee on the Commission of the Churches on International Affairs—through which the resolution had been sent to the floor—expressed hope that the Assembly would not be influenced to vote in the negative for that reason. He declared it his own strong conviction that the churches had not only a right but a duty to speak against injustice wherever it existed. This was necessary, he said, to the vitality of the churches themselves and was a service which they owed to society.

In somewhat the same vein, others insisted that action on social questions was an essential part of confessing "the lordship of Jesus Christ over all life." Still others said that the churches and their conciliar bodies ought to be ready at all times to meet the challenge in human oppression to prophetic condemnation.[14] The near evenness of the decision softened defeat for the opposing half of the Assembly and largely negated the moral effect of the balloting victory. Because of the closeness of the vote on the resolution, Dr. Franklin Clark Fry suggested that the whole matter be referred to the Foreign Affairs Committee; but at a later session it was agreed, after further debate, to ask the Central Committee, in consultation with the officers of the Commission of the Churches on International Affairs, to decide what should be done. The recommendation by the Central Committee called for the Assembly's associating itself with the statements on Angola by the Executive Committee of the World Council of Churches and the officers of the Commission of the Churches on International Affairs and the writing of a letter to Sr. Dr. Franco Nogueira, the Portuguese Foreign Minister, explaining the indecisive action of the Assembly and expressing again the World Council's "pain and sorrow at the reports from Angola."

The letter, which was written by Sir Kenneth Grubb and Dr. O. F. Nolde, stated that the resolution had not gained the support of a

[13] At the time, India had begun mobilization for an attack against Goa.

[14] The discussion on the Angola resolution—on the floor of the Assembly and in the corridors—revealed a perhaps growing impatience with so-called "prophetic" actions. The greatest prophets could make mistakes, as the Old Testament witnissed. The would-be Amos or Jeremiah could easily be a menace in a modern trigger-happy society.

decisive majority "solely because the Assembly was reluctant to take an isolated action against a single nation." The message went on:[15]

> We are far from holding that Portugal alone has made mistakes in Africa; she is by no means the only nation to have found herself in a difficult position. In other African territories and elsewhere, there have been serious uprisings and disturbances of public order and grave loss of life. The Committees of the World Council of Churches and this Commission have considered it their duty from time to time to draw attention to some of these and to deplore actions done or words uttered, in the heat of controversy.
> We believe that a policy of steady and speedy growth towards a representative and autonomous government of Angola by Angolans is the only path to peace with justice, and we trust that an assurance to this effect may soon be given to satisfy the peaceful evolution of the aspirations of the people of Angola.

This letter, which went to the Foreign Minister of Portugal about two weeks after the Assembly adjourned, exemplified the extraordinary methods sometimes employed by the World Council of Churches to gain ends which to the officers seemed desirable and right. A resolution had been presented and approved, but in a manner discounting the intended effect, which was to censure Portugal for her policy in Angola. On the face of the returns, nearly half of the delegates were against this. Why? There were a number of reasons, as explained above. One was, as noted, the feeling that it would be invidious to act against Portugal alone when other nations were known to be guilty of even worse offenses. But who was really in position to say that the resolution "did not gain the support of a decisive majority *solely* because the Assembly was reluctant to take an isolated action against a single nation?"

Because of this misstatement and the rather tactless offer to Portugal of "the services of the World Council of Churches in the cause of reconciliation and reconstruction" hard upon the gratuitous advice "that a policy of steady and speedy growth towards representative and autonomous government of Angola by Angolans" was "the only path to peace and justice," it is doubtful that the letter, had it come before the Assembly for approval, would have fared much better than the resolution. The handling of the matter, from first to last, went far to support the contention of those who doubted that the World Council of Churches had the right or competence to act in such situations.

4. Communists at New Delhi?

As has been noted, there were persons in the Assembly who came from countries behind the Iron Curtain. It did not follow that they were members of Communist parties or believed in the philosophy of com-

[15] Ecumenical Press Service, January, 1962.

munism. That they had been able to obtain passports showed that they were not in overt conflict with their political authorities, that their churches had achieved with their governments an acceptable *modus vivendi*.

The World Council of Churches imposed no political condition of membership. Christian denominations joined by affirming their acceptance of the Basis, which was a statement of faith in "the Lord Jesus Christ as God and Saviour." As its name implied, the World Council was an international body, denominations and church councils in a majority of the more than one hundred nations belonging to it.

The World Council identified itself with no political ideologies, but reserved the right to criticize any and all.

Representatives of all denominations which were members of the Council were eligible for election to office. None of the six Presidents chosen at New Delhi was from a communist country; but five members of the Assembly from Russia, two each from Rumania and Hungary, and one from Czechoslovakia were among those elected to the Central Committee. And two of these were appointed to the Executive Committee: Dr. Josef Hromadka of Czechoslovakia and Bishop Nikodim of Russia.[16]

Nobody holding the communist doctrine of atheism could legitimately qualify for membership in the World Council of Churches. But one not an atheist could believe in the socioeconomic principles of communism; and certain delegates at New Delhi from behind the Iron Curtain expressed the opinion that their respective nations were more prosperous under the present regimes than they had been under the old. Some thought their citizens enjoyed quite as much freedom as the people of Western countries. Political restrictions on the exercise of religion they could accept without the protests which would have greeted these in the Western democracies, because they had always lived under the authority of governmental offices on church-and-state relationships.[17]

The position of the World Council of Churches with reference to communism was not unlike that of the Christian denominations in its membership, nearly all of which had missionary programs of international scope and belonged to world confessional bodies embracing churches in both communist and non-communist countries. The Lambeth Conference of Anglican Bishops, the Friends' World Committee for Consultation, the Baptist World Alliance, the World Lutheran Federation, the Alliance of Reformed Churches (Presbyterian), the World Convention of the Churches of Christ, the World Methodist Council, the International Association for Liberal Christianity and Religious Freedom, the International Congregational Council, the Old Catholic Union.

[16] Dr. Hromadka had been a member of Central and Executive Committees since Amsterdam.

[17] See pp. 1048-49.

Most of these organizations comprised churches of their orders in many nations, regardless of existing types of political rule. Likewise the major national councils of churches, e.g., the National Council of the Churches of Christ in the U.S.A., participated in missionary and other services extending into communist-controlled countries.

None of these bodies, denominational or conciliar, in admitting to membership churches from behind the Iron or Bamboo Curtains, endorsed communist principles or practices. They were seeking to establish a world Christian fellowship and to make Christianity a bond of international unity and peace.

That there were dangers in this policy was fully recognized.[18] The World Council and the denominations and other conciliar bodies would be exposed to the suspicion of "softness" toward communism. They would seem to many to be treating too lightly the abridgment or abrogation by totalitarian governments of the so-called human rights, including religious liberty, which had become identified with the Christian faith in the Western democracies. They might appear to be getting themselves organizationally into a position in which the false teachings, indignities, and oppressions of totalitarian collectivisms would have to be accepted in silence in the interest of harmony. Under such circumstances, how could compromising the truth be avoided?

There was definitely this side of the matter, and those viewing it so were within their rights, so long as the good faith of trusted leaders of

[18] The August, 1962, *Religious News Service* published an interview with Bishop Otto Dibelius, who declared, "Many German churchmen are disturbed over the silence concerning Soviet policies which has emanated from the World Council of Churches since the decision was reached last November (at New Delhi) to receive the Russian Orthodox Church into the world body." Events tended to show, he said, that by receiving the Russian Church the World Council might be committing itself to compromising its Christian witness in world affairs. A "nefarious but successful" technique of dictators was to silence critics in the free world by threats to hostages, and the Russian churchmen are hostages, he asserted. "If a Christian stand is taken in this ecumenical body on issues of evident international justice," he said, "the Russian churchmen will be called on the carpet when they return home and asked why they did not counter this anti-communism. So to avoid embarrassing and endangering their Russian delegates, the World Council seems to be heading in the direction of silencing its Christian witness where conscience should take a stand." The Bishop cited the report on world affairs at the Paris meeting of the Central Committee of the World Council, which had just been held, in which, he pointed out, Dr. O. Frederick Nolde, Chairman of the Commission of the Churches on International Affairs, reviewed numerous world problems unrelated to the communist world conspiracy and "then, at the end, as a kind of appendix . . . did mention the Soviet threat to Berlin, expressing the hope that negotiation might ease the situation." Actually, Dr. Dibelius added, "the threat of Berlin is a major issue before the world today. Whether or not World War III breaks out may depend on a just solution of the Berlin harassment. Great issues of historical morality are at stake here. To pass over these issues because of expediency drives blood to our faces. . . . Powerful influences in the Central Committee are increasingly concerned. Not only the true Christian effectiveness of the World Council's witness but the cause of peace in our time hangs on the courageous facing of social immorality, whether in the West or the East."

the churches who differed from them was admitted and respected. The other side also had support in reason in the belief of many who were praying and working just as earnestly for the defeat of communism. These latter saw no practicable way of dividing Christians on the basis of their political faith. They thought that drawing a line of separation between the denominations of communist and non-communist nations, even if it were possible and theologically justifiable, would be fraught with graver dangers than the present inclusive policy posed. It would be deepening the rift between East and West and lessening, if not destroying, the opportunity for a mediatorial mission by the World Council of Churches in their conflict. They believed Christian truth would win, if given opportunity. If it meant risking compromise, the danger would be greater, they thought, for the Marxist-Leninist philosophy. In any case, the sooner the test was made the better.

Attempts to find guidance for these perplexities in the New Testament seemed likely to lead to conclusions no less difficult to resolve.

It had become a habit with certain ecumenical groups to emphasize that since the Christian faith originated under totalitarianism there was no cause to think the Church would be less able now to cope with its materialistic, secularistic, and militaristic environment, which was certainly not more menacing than that of the Roman Empire in the first century.

However, there was an important difference between the Church's conceptions of its mission in the first and the twentieth centuries. This difference was the present-day policy of social action. Take the idea of building a responsible society out of the modern ecumenical Church, and there would be left substantially the church of totalitarian ancient Rome and modern Moscow. In the earlier milieu it had possessed a dynamism that, according to one report, turned the world upside down, and now under communism it was bringing to the people, or so they themselves declared, a new sense of God and a rebirth of spirituality. As a result the people were banishing desire for freedom on the other side of the wall to interest themselves in more mundane concerns—contentions of governments, racial antagonisms, class conflicts, and group wranglings—those very concerns which engaged the churches of the West.

The World Council of Churches' main problem, as it extended its fellowship to Christians behind the communist front, was the social action program. There were prospects that the Council would be pressured to accommodate itself for the sake of harmony to the innocuous habit of talking of peace and other desirable social goals but doing little else about them.[19]

For this reason it was that a chilling anxiety swept over the New Delhi Assembly at thought of the possible influence of Orthodoxy in the World

[19] See note, No. 5, p. 1050. Also *The New Delhi Report,* p. 64 ff.

Council of Churches. Could anyone imagine the Russian Orthodox hierarchs teaming up with the social action experts at Geneva to protest to Nikita Khrushchev on account of the Berlin Wall or anything else? A legend of St. Paul's heading a delegation of Christians to admonish Nero on the burning of Rome would not have been more fanciful.

5. The Problem of Growing Populations

It was probable that in years not distant the Assembly would be reviewed with incredulity for the little concern it had, according to the records of its proceedings, about the problem of overpopulation. Social scientists were describing this as perhaps the most menacing dilemma confronted by mankind, rivaling, if not overshadowing, the threat of nuclear war. The Assembly, when it came to this matter, seemed to be bound by the paralysis affecting most of the nations and their rulers.

The Central Committee had in 1958 heard demographic specialists on the subject and, after discussion, referred it under the head of family planning to the churches, with a request that they "read up" on it and report their conclusions. There evidently had not been, after three years, sufficient response to command a place for it in the main Assembly program. The nearest it got was the shamiana, where Dr. Richard M. Fagley, Executive Director of the Commission of the Churches on International Affairs, presented a paper on "The Population Problem and Christian Responsibility" at a meeting for visitors at the Assembly, which was open to the public and attended by representatives of certain local social organizations of women who had been specially invited.

The Commission of the Churches on International Affairs had included in its printed report to the Assembly (in the section concerning the economic and educational development of backward nations) a statement which it had published previously, as follows:[20]

> In this context, special emphasis is laid on the need to control the growth of population. . . . It is an error to think that such control is needed for only densely populated countries. The immediate necessity is to bring population pressures and economic growth into a more balanced relationship. It is known that even in countries where the national income has increased markedly within the last decade, the benefits of such increase have been largely off-set by mounting population pressures. As standards of health improve, mortality rates decrease dramatically, and unless birth rates are brought into balance, many countries that have obtained political independence will find the prospects for genuine economic independence remote.
>
> While some developing countries have taken steps to promote responsible family-planning, more energetic and comprehensive steps are needed. . . .

[20] *The New Delhi Report,* p. 267.

It could be expected that the Roman Catholic Church and certain of the churches which were members of the World Council would resist such "steps" as the report thought necessary.

The Roman Catholic Church was the dominant Christian influence in many parts of the mission countries. It would discourage requests by the less-developed nations for technical knowledge of procedures for birth control, and also the granting of such help by the governments in a position and willing to respond. At least, that had been its attitude.

Some of the non-Christian religions were not favorable to joining in any action to limit the populations. And there was the inertia of the people themselves to be overcome, even if they were not unwilling to cooperate.

Dr. Fagley asserted at the shamiana meeting that "none of the major religions and no branch of Christianity" insisted "on unlimited procreation." If this was a fact, it seemed that all the faiths ought to study the problem together, with a view to determining what, if anything, they might be able to do jointly about it.

This could be perhaps one of the social areas in which spokesmen for the Vatican thought the Roman Catholic Church and the denominations of the World Council of Churches might find that they would be able to collaborate.

6. Resolution on Anti-Semitism

Evidencing the continuing ecumenical concern for the welfare of the Jews, the Assembly passed a resolution on anti-Semitism, as follows:[21]

> The Third Assembly recalls the following words which were addressed to the churches by the First Assembly of the World Council of Churches in 1948: "We call upon all the churches we represent to denounce anti-Semitism, no matter what its origin, as absolutely irreconcilable with the profession and practice of the Christian faith. Anti-Semitism is sin against God and man. Only as we give convincing evidence to our Jewish neighbors that we seek for them the common rights and dignities which God wills for his children can we come to such a meeting with them as would make it possible to share with them the best which God has given us in Christ."
>
> The Assembly renews this plea in view of the fact that situations continue to exist in which Jews are subject to discrimination and even persecution. The Assembly urges its member churches to do all in their power to resist every form of anti-Semitism. In Christian teaching the historic events which led to the crucifixion should not be so presented as to fasten upon the Jewish people of today responsibilities which belong to our corporate humanity and not to one race or community. Jews were the first to accept Jesus and Jews are not the only ones who do not yet recognize him.

The World Jewish Congress took note of this action "with great satisfaction." In a letter to Dr. Willem A. Visser 't Hooft, Dr. Nahum

[21] *The New Delhi Report,* p. 148.

Goldman wrote, on behalf of the Congress: "I want . . . to express to you and the World Council of Churches our appreciation of your having passed this resolution, which will, I am sure, be of the utmost importance in our common goal of fighting racial discrimination generally and anti-Semitism especially. The World Council of Churches has set an example to many other groups by taking this action."

7. Statement on Race and Ethnic Relations

The Third Assembly also welcomed the establishment of a new secretariat to handle problems in the important field of race and ethnic relations. In this connection it adopted the following resolution:[22]

The Third Assembly of the World Council of Churches meeting in New Delhi, having considered the serious and far-reaching implications of racial and ethnic tensions for the mission of the Church in the world, in the light of Christian unity, witness and service;

(1) calls attention of the member churches to the mounting racial and ethnic tensions which accompany rapid social change and the struggle for social justice in many areas;

(2) notes with gratitude: (a) the witness of the churches and their members in difficult situations, struggling to uphold the unity of the Christian fellowship transcending racial and ethnic divisions; (b) the courage and sacrifice of individuals and groups, both Christian and non-Christian, who, in spite of forces urging to violence, are giving leadership in the struggle for human rights in a spirit of forgiveness and non-violence; (c) those churches which, though divided by different approaches to the question of race relations, are willing to meet with each other within the unity of the Christian faith, to talk to each other and to discover together the will of God for their common witness to Christ in society;

(3) welcomes the establishment of the World Council of Churches' Secretariat on Race and Ethnic Relations and urges the member churches to give support to developing the program of the Secretariat;

(4) reminds all the churches of the declaration on inter-group relations by the Evanston Assembly that "any form of segregation based on race, color or ethnic origin is contrary to the Gospel, and is incompatible with the Christian doctrine of man and with the nature of the Church of Christ," and urges them to act more resolutely than they have heretofore "to renounce all forms of segregation or discrimination and to work for their abolition within their own life and within society."

The Assembly commends all those involved to the prayers and moral support of all the churches and Christians within the fellowship of the World Council.

8. Declaration on Religious Liberty

A declaration on religious freedom was issued by the Assembly, as follows:[23]

[22] *Ibid.* pp. 187-88.
[23] *Ibid.* pp. 159-161.

1. Mankind is threatened by many forces which curtail or deny freedom. There is accordingly urgent need to re-invigorate efforts to ensure that every person has opportunity for the responsible exercise of religious freedom.

2. Christians see religious liberty as a consequence of God's creative work, of his redemption of man in Christ and his calling of men into his service. God's redemptive dealing with men is not coercive. Accordingly, human attempts by legal enactment or by pressure of social custom to coerce or to eliminate faith are violations of the fundamental ways of God with men. The freedom which God has given in Christ implies a free response to God's love, and the responsibility to serve fellow-men at the point of deepest need.

3. Holding a distinctive Christian basis for religious liberty, we regard this right as fundamental for men everywhere.

4. We re-affirm the Declaration of Religious Liberty adopted by the World Council of Churches and the International Missionary Council in August-September 1948, and hold to its provisions. We recognize the Universal Declaration of Human Rights, proclaimed by the United Nations in December 1948, as an important instrument in promoting respect for and observance of human rights and fundamental freedoms.

5. Although freedoms of every kind are inter-related, religious liberty may be considered as a distinctive human right, which all men may exercise, no matter what their faith. The article on religious freedom in the Universal Declaration is an acceptable standard, always provided that it be given a comprehensive interpretation.

"Everyone has the right to freedom of thought, conscience and religion; this right includes freedom to change his religion or belief, and freedom, either alone or in community with others and in public or private, to manifest his religion or belief in teaching, practice, worship and observance."

6. The recognition of the inherent dignity and of the equal and inalienable rights of all members of the human family requires that the general standard here declared should be given explicit expression in every aspect of society. Without seeking to be inclusive, we illustrate as follows:

7. Freedom of thought, conscience and belief, even considered as inner freedom, requires freedom of access to reliable information.

8. Freedom to manifest one's religion or belief, in public or in private and alone or in community with others, is essential to the expression of inner freedom.

a. It includes freedom to worship according to one's chosen form, in public or in private.

b. It includes freedom to teach, whether by formal or informal instruction as well as preaching with a view to propagating one's faith and persuading others to accept it.

c. It includes freedom to practise religion or belief, whether by performance of acts of mercy or by the expression in word or deed of the implications of beliefs in social, economic and political matters, both domestic and international.

d. It includes freedom of observance by following religious customs or by participating in religious rites in the family or in public meeting.

9. Religious freedom includes freedom to change one's religion or belief without consequent social, economic and political disabilities. Implicit in this right is the right freely to maintain one's belief or disbelief without external coercion or disability.

10. The exercise or religious liberty involves other human rights. The Uni-

versal Declaration proclaims among others, the right to freedom of peaceful assembly and association; the right to freedom of opinion and expression, including freedom to seek, receive and impart information and ideas through any media and regardless of frontiers; the prior right of parents to choose the kind of education that shall be given to their children; freedom to participate in choosing the desired form of government and in freely electing officials; freedom from the retroactive application of penal law; and freedom to leave and to return to one's country and to seek asylum elsewhere.

11. The freedom with which Christ has set us free calls forth responsibility for the rights of others. The civil freedom which we claim in the name of Christ must be freely available for all men to exercise responsibly. It is the corresponding obligation of governments and of society to ensure the exercise of these civil rights without discrimination. It is for the churches in their own life and witness recognizing their own past failures in this regard to play their responsible role in promoting the realization of religious liberty for all men.

9. The Christian Conception of Man in World Crisis

Those who compiled the findings of the study section of the Assembly on "Service" wrote, "The Christian is not afraid of change." This sentence must have caused more than one of the members to ask whether they were Christians. For who in the days at New Delhi did not tremble as he watched the world he had known disappearing? Could it have been that the drafting committee of Section II had not? It might well be that with change some evil things which made life hard for many people would, as they said, be swept away. But what would be the fate of much-cherished things which had been attained at untold sacrifice? Would they outride the tides of destruction? Other civilizations had perished and their good become as a root in dry ground.

The transformation of life by science and invention had been so rapid that only a sudden conversion of mankind seemed sufficient to take up the moral lag exposing the nations to self-annihilation. It was difficult to read history without concluding that there was, as older theologians said, "a general providence" shaping the destiny of humankind, and that in such swift and deep-moving changes as the modern world was undergoing evolution must at times lapse temporarily into revolution; but it was equally clear that if the movement of man was to continue upward and eventually out upon a higher plane religion would be a determinant in the process. And though he might not be overmuch concerned about what happened to himself, the Christian could hardly help sharing the common anxiety, lest in the kind of society he saw evolving Christianity could not survive to be this needful dynamic force.

Would the Christian concept of the value of man find a place in the new order? It had had little enough in the old. But that little had made a difference so great that no thoughtful person could contemplate without fear—with all due respect to the authors of the Section II report on

"Service"—the possibility of its erasure from the human mind. Lives still were cheap and exposed to unspeakable abuses, as a walk through the streets of New Delhi or any other modern city would reveal. The cruelty of men to their kind passed belief. The days of Rome with its slavery, corruption, degradation of womanhood, child murder, sadistic brutalities seemed far removed, but the evils which besmirched its vaunted glory existed still, some of them a thousand-fold more devastating. But they now were challenged to a warfare unto the death by those who fought in the strength and hope of righteousness, who believed in the infinite worth of all men because they believed in God who loved all and willed that none should perish, and called all to brotherhood through Jesus Christ.

Would this belief in man survive?

With eyes ahead, the Assembly exhorted, "Remember that God is alive and working in the world!" But God worked effectually and fully in the conservation of human values when there were men of faith to work with him. "My Father worketh, and I work," Jesus had said. And he had looked out upon his age and asked, "When the Son of Man cometh, will he find faith on earth?" Would he? That was the question troubling some at New Delhi, the question making them afraid.

The report on "Service"—give it due credit—stated the case at this crucial point: " 'Can the Christian Church be the nucleus around which will crystallize the culture of tomorrow?' is a question about the present response of man's faith, not . . . about the ability of God."

Faith was, indeed, the crucial issue. And the concern was what the World Council of Churches and its numerous constituent denominations and conciliar bodies could do, if anything, to help mankind to faith in the time of surging revolutions and wars and of their aftermath of wrack and desolation.

Faith would not come, it was certain, by exhortation. The solemn affirmations of New Delhi failed to evoke the ready and grateful response on which they once could have counted. Why? They sounded anachronous. They were the Church still proclaiming its convictions as knowledge, and they had little appeal in the sixth decade of the twentieth century, for whose multitudes traditional props of faith had crumbled. This late day might respect religious convictions when it saw them being wrought into life and could listen with interest to explanations by those holding them of how they had come by them. But it could no longer accept the Church's traditional interpretation of history with its theological deductions. If Christian doctrines were true, evidence more intelligible and convincing to the modern mind, East and West, would need to be brought forward.

The Assembly had thoughts of the peril to the Christian belief in man's worth in the mounting talk about the problem of overpopulation, the imminence of nuclear war, the possible—or probable—sudden extermination of hundreds of millions of people, and the certain slower death, war or no war, of even greater numbers from diseases bred by hunger and exposure. It spoke of the menace of these dread conditions to the minds and spirits of men and said something would have to be done; but the only thing it could think of, beyond adding the weight of its own anxieties to the world's burden, was to appeal to the churches for more millions for relief and call on the nations "to turn back from the road towards war into the paths of peace."

To the youth of the world passing under the lowering international storm clouds into what might prove the longest and most turbulent night mankind had known, the Assembly appeared not to have any adequate word.

Perhaps the generation responsible for the Assembly felt that it was about to go with its youth to a common fate, in which together they would discover whether the light which had brought them to New Delhi would survive the blinding flashes of bombs and mark the way beyond. Companions now in the days of foreboding, they would look forward beyond the impending ordeal to comradeship in what they hoped would be a brighter tomorrow.

By the Christian code, they who set the highest value upon human lives cared least for their own. The seal of this code bore the cross of Christ, who had come to minister as a servant and to give his life. Its spiritual paradox had early been exemplified by those men who welcomed death to be his first disciples for a few fleeting days and by their successors, the first Christian missionaries, who "hazarded their lives for the gospel." The greatest of these spoke for all when, describing his own attitude, he said, "Neither count I my life dear unto myself, so that I might finish my course." (Paul in Acts xx, 24).

The sum of this code was love. So wrote the veteran Paul to his young recruit, Timothy, with whom he had walked together through the "gross darkness" of the pagan world of the first century: "Now the end of the commandment is love out of a pure heart, and of a good conscience, and of faith unfeigned" (I Timothy i, 5). When understood in "its length and breadth, its height and depth"—in all its exacting but rewarding disciplines—love was the Christian life.

This divine law would not change with man's circumstances. With the control by science of disease and aging, populations would soar, within the lifetime of some of those at New Delhi,[24] to astronomical proportions; the scarcity of food would be increasingly a problem; opportunity for education and employment would be closed to growing numbers of young people the world over; and it would become more and more

[24] The names most frequently on the lips of the delegates at New Delhi were, among many, Sittler, Noth, Takenaka, Devanandan, Potter, Nissiotis, de Vries, Niles, Zulu, Nikodim. The average age of these was forty-eight years and eight months. (*The Christian Century,* January 10, 1962, p. 50.)

evident that the room and attention the elderly required were needed for the young who had not yet had a chance to live. And under such conditions the temptation for life to develop into an every-man-for-himself struggle would grow even more irresistible than it had been. But, far from suspending the law of love, these changes—and others which could not be imagined—would only make clearer its absoluteness.

Only love could save mankind from universal panic in these circumstances. And it alone had the intelligence—and the motivation—to redirect the forces now poised for a suicidal duel into the building of a global social order with promise of a more peaceful day and a more abundant life.

Had the World Council of Churches the wisdom, and could it find the time in its preoccupation with the warrings of nations, races, classes, and groups over social status and material advantage, to teach the people this truth?

Here was a root subject for "grass-root" study, if there ever was one. And it would evoke a surer response than some of the topics sent down to the churches. The people would recognize that it spoke to their need. They would be getting in due time the appeal to join in the long inquiry on "The Finality of Christ in the Age of Universal History," voted at New Delhi for the interim between the Third and Fourth Assemblies, and they would find that if Christ had any finality in a world where all was transitory it was the love he exemplified and enjoined. It was an everlasting love, and from it neither death nor life could separate those in whose hearts it dwelt. It had not the property of decay inherent in all else. Would the World Council and its churches speak to the people of this love when other lights for them were dimming and cherished blessings of their pilgrimage failing?

Let it not be taken for granted that love, because much talked about, was understood. The counterfeits of love with their weak sentimentalisms had well-nigh insulated the minds even of Christians against its stern but benign disciplines. If there was one subject concerning which all men needed to know the truth, it was the true nature of the love of Christ and of the love he evoked in human hearts.

Not that this love would guarantee anyone an easy victory over the world. The fact that its insigne was a cross disproved this. Rather would its guerdon be "many a sorrow, many a labor, many a tear."[13] But there would be salvation in its sanity and in its strength in the soul.

In a time of overwhelming tribulation, this code would command and steady the mind, for it faced upon two worlds—the seen and the unseen, the temporal and the eternal. This had been always the confession and witness of those surrendering to its authority. "We look not at the things which are seen, but at the things which are not seen: for the things which

[25] Quoted from a Russian Orthodox hymn: "Art thou weary, art thou languid?" —translation by J. M. Neale (1862).

are seen are temporal; but the things which are not seen are eternal." What men called life was a probation—a chance to qualify for "life that was life indeed." The temporal could gain the eternal or forfeit it. These alternatives were the only actual success and failure. The meaning of existence stood revealed in them.

10. The Finality of Christ in the Age of Universal History

The announcement that during the forthcoming interval between Assemblies the churches would be organized to study "The Finality of Christ in the Age of Universal History" continued the World Council's habit of choosing its themes for their apologetic potential. Whatever the intention, it was likely that this one would be used for little more than confirming the churches in the traditional orthodox interpretation of Christ's unique nature and authority.[26]

With the great volume of readily available matter on this subject, little research or new thought would be necessary, and the time could be given over to mobilizing the churches for another effort rivaling, if not surpassing, the successful promotional accomplishment with the main theme of the Third Assembly, "Jesus Christ, the Light of the World."

It appeared that, notwithstanding the disappointing quality of the study materials for that undertaking, a habit of response had been formed which could be relied on to carry another program, more pretentious and deliberate, to record-breaking participation by the churches.

If the Assembly, in adopting the proposed theme and the time suggested for its study, intended to do more, this was not evident from the presentation or the motion. And there was not much chance that the project as it proceeded would develop a direction and purpose of its own and turn into ways apart from those contemplated. The time was not yet for unbridled action in such ventures by ecumenically docile churches, more inclined to stay in the familiar theological ranges carefully fenced and tended by the managers, than to follow scholars who might be interested in new fields beckoning to exploration.

There were well-learned scriptural precepts about "keeping to the old paths." The faith "was once delivered to the saints." Jesus Christ was "the same yesterday, and today, and forever."

Some ecumenists had not learned that it was because Christ remained ever constant that the Church, moving into new scenes and circum-

[26] "What was generally recognized has now been officially conceded, and the Central Committee now has before it . . . the task of removing the ambiguity which the Third Assembly permitted to settle like a fog around its central theme, 'Jesus Christ, the Light of the World.' The churches of the World Council will be encouraged to know that the Central Committee will now seek to affirm and to proclaim 'the finality of Jesus Christ in the age of universal history.' " (*The Christian Century,* May 9, 1962, p. 594.)

stances, had always to be readjusting its sight of him and reflecting the reckoning in its teaching. Nor could they all see that it was the *faith* which was delivered once to the saints, and not their own theological explanation of the experience.[27]

[27] For the report of the Committee on "The Finality of Christ in the Age of Universal History," refer to *The New Delhi Report,* p. 164 ff.

IV

THE COUNCIL AND THE CHURCHES

1. Finance and Structure

The World Council's universe was an expanding one. Organizational adjustments and extensions were the order—and therefore growing budgets.

In 1949 the budget had been $265,770. It had increased by 1961 to approximately $530,000. The Assembly at New Delhi, on a recommendation of the Committee on Program and Finance, voted to ask the denominations to raise $774,200 for the work in 1962—about 47 percent more than they had given in 1961.

In addition, in 1962 the Council would spend more than a million dollars through the Division of Inter-Church Aid and Service to Refugees and $201,150 through the Commission and the Division of World Mission and Evangelism (continuing the program of the International Missionary Council, now merged with the World Council of Churches). These sums would be raised separately from the so-called general budget of $774,200.

The general—or administrative—budget, though so much larger than it had been, was still inadequate. In it were provisions for assistants to the General Secretary in Geneva and the Associate Secretary in New York, and for implementing the new secretariats on race relations and religious liberty. Several other divisions and departments were greatly in need of more funds, for which it did not provide.

Most of the money to meet these demands would have to be given by western European and North American churches. Little help could be expected from the approximately seventy millions of Christians who were entering the World Council from behind the Iron Curtain. It was understood that the Russian Orthodox Church, the largest of the twenty-three admitted, had "no lack of money, interest or willingness to give," but that Moscow was not likely to consent to its remitting funds to Geneva or elsewhere. (Russian Orthodox delegates to New Delhi were reported to have said, probably with tongues in their cheeks, that their Church gilded the domes of its cathedrals to use up its surplus of gold.) The Church had made a pledge to the new headquarters building of the World Council, however, and promised to supply in payment needed materials of various kinds.

For the construction of the projected official seat of the Council in Geneva $2,700,000 had been sought, and by the adjournment at New Delhi about $2,500,000 had been received or pledged. Substantial contributions had been made by the Lutheran World Federation and the World Presbyterian Alliance, which would occupy offices in the building, a 250-room structure.[1]

The new site comprised eight and one-half acres in Geneva near the Palais des Nations (European center of the United Nations) and the international headquarters of other religious and social organizations. The building would consist of a central block with two floors and radiating wings of three, four, and five stories. Of special interest would be the library and the chapel. The World Council would expect to move from 17 Route Malagnou by the summer of 1963.[2]

That the World Council was largely dependent on churches of the West for pledges to underwrite its budgets and its building in Geneva was unfortunate for many reasons, one of which was the impression it gave of Western control. The saying that who paid the fiddler called the tune would inevitably express the thoughts of many minds, especially if the facts were not fully understood or there was distrust or hostility toward the movement. The truth was that no area had ever made any attempt on the basis of its financial support to influence the actions of the World Council of Churches in any way whatsoever. And the giving of large amounts, as in the case of North American churches, had been willing and with full understanding that no special credit or advantage was claimed or desired for what had been done.

The greatest harm resulting from this situation was in the ingratitude manifested at times, particularly in the attitude toward those giving, as it was assumed, out of an abundance at little or no sacrifice. Worse still in its effect was the occasional criticism of peoples as materialistic because they happened to have greater wealth than some, although they gave of what they had liberally toward the relief of others through the World Council's budgets, as well as in other ways. The hurt of this was mainly in the minds of those helped, whose charges seemed often to reflect the materialistic spirit they condemned in others. Stewardship was a duty to be performed without reference to praise or blame, and those practicing it faithfully had their reward. But, because human nature was what it was, giving would have been a happier experience for all concerned, could there have been assurance that it had awakened in those it sought to bless an appreciative response.

These matters could be spoken of only reluctantly. It was easier to

[1] It was found later, however, that a rise in construction costs made necessary leaving a wing of the building unfinished or raising nearly a half-million dollars more.

[2] The move was postponed until mid-year, 1964.

forget them. But if Christian community was to have a chance of realization in the world, those helping to bring it to pass—or trying to—would have to learn to speak the truth in love about many things, and this was one of them.

2. The Laity in the World Council

Article V of the Constitution of the World Council of Churches provided that "The members of the Assembly shall be both clerical and lay persons—men and women. In order to secure that approximately one-third of the Assembly shall consist of lay persons, the Central Committee, in allocating to the member churches their places in the Assembly, shall strongly urge each church, if possible, to observe this provision."

It would be quite impossible to apply this proportional principle in the appointment of delegates unless the denominations acted jointly in an over-all way, which probably would not be acceptable to either the churches or the World Council.

If five or six hundred delegates were to be apportioned among some two hundred denominations, members of the World Council, taking into account their numerical sizes as the Constitution instructed, not more than one could be allotted to many—perhaps a majority—of them. Rarely would a denomination sending only one representative consider it appropriate or desirable to pass over its clerical top officials and designate a member of the laity; nor would the World Council be likely to feel that it ought to do so. A denomination, to discharge its full duty as a member, must have acting in its behalf those with authority in its own councils, who, almost without exception, were clergy; and the business of the World Council required such representation if its decisions were to be accorded the necessary support by the churches. In the light of these considerations—and there were others—it was clear that only the larger communions could comply with the request that their delegations consist of the indicated proportional number of clergymen and laymen.

Candor compelled recognition of the fact that the ordained ministers regarded it not only as their prerogative but as their duty to—in the vernacular—"run the churches." In the hierarchical bodies they were completely supported in this attitude. In the other churches, even those of strictest congregational polity, the people and the pastors were not in actual practice as averse as might be supposed to this view of their comparative responsibility.[3]

[3] Implicit in the idea of the ministry of the laity is the demand for pastors capable of bringing the body of believers to an effective level of Christian participation in the world. This is the positive accent of Richard Niebuhr's phrase "pastoral director." It is stated convincingly by Masao Takanaka of Japan when

As a matter of fact, few laymen were situated, because of the demands of other normal interests, to give the time for a service that would satisfy themselves or the Council. And it was confusing, under such circumstances, to say that their first duty was to the kingdom of God, as though what they were doing in large and important ways in the professions or in business was not their Christian calling and completely essential to the Church of God and its ministries in the world.

The clergy—many of them anyway—had a great deal to say about enlisting laymen in the churches and the ecumenical movement. What they had in mind actually and properly was educating them for service in the ranks, under their own leadership, as, for example, in evangelism.

Charles C. Parlin, one of two laymen elected to the Presidium of the World Council of Churches at New Delhi, apparently sensed this. Writing in *The Ecumenical Review* after the Assembly (July, 1962), he said:

> Throughout the Assembly, an important place was given to the so-called "lay question." It appeared not only in the "laymen" program part of the Assembly, but it reappeared in practically every one of the sections and committees and commissions. On many sides, and particularly among the clergy, enthusiasm was expressed that the "lay question" had been given such a large place throughout the Assembly. The Assembly Committee declared that it was "thankful for the place given to this subject in the program, deliberations and reports of the New Delhi Assembly."
>
> If I can summarize the proceedings, it would be that the emphasis was not on lay representation in the voting councils of the churches or in the Assemblies of the Councils of Churches. The emphasis was on the fact that the laity was in a unique position to carry the message of the gospel into the secular world. The terms "where each stands in his own place" and "in his own special situation" were phrases that appear again and again through the reports of the committees, commissions and sections. The basic concept was that wherever a church is concerned with evangelism or with mission or with witness or with service, the place where it starts is with the individual.
>
> "The need is not for further proclamation of the Gospel on a larger or smaller scale, to people who have never listened to it," a speaker from Great Britain, incidentally a lay-woman, said. "The task is rather to educate and re-educate those who have listened in the past to good, bad and indifferent preaching and teaching. The challenge to the Church is to interpret in the situation in which the people are that which they have already heard, or mis-heard, or failed to hear."
>
> Perhaps the clergy can reach these people; certainly the lay people can. Because it is the laymen who associate with these people . . . in their daily work and in social contacts throughout the work days of the week.

The following approximate information may be gleaned from statistical surveys:

---

he speaks of the need for a "new style" of Christian living in the East. This style of living—the fruit of the Spirit—will involve a "wrestling presence" of Christians in the world, precisely where people work and play and live. (*Tomorrow,* published by the Ministers and Missionaries Benefit Board, American Baptist Convention, September, 1962, p. 13.)

Laymen constituted 20 percent of the 365 delegates at the First Assembly of the World Council of Churches at Amsterdam in 1948, 27 percent of the 502 at the Second Assembly in Evanston in 1954, and 18 percent of the 577 at the Third Assembly in New Delhi in 1961.

The Central Committee elected at New Delhi consisted of 100 members—106 including the Presidium. Seventeen of these—16 percent—were laymen. Five of the lay group were women.

The new Presidium, with its membership of two archbishops, two clergymen, and two laymen, was the only body in the World Council of Churches achieving the constitutional objective of a one-third lay representation.

Women had not been accorded by the churches anything like the proportionate number of delegate seats the Constitution called for. Among the twelve appointees of the American Baptist Convention, for example, there was only one woman who was not professionally employed by the denomination or some other religious body. The Disciples of Christ in the United States sent one. The four from the Methodist Church in the United States were staff members. Generally other denominational delegations came no nearer to compliance with the provisions relating to the appointment of "lay persons, men and women."

Salvation Army Commander Norman S. Marshall proposed a motion commending those churches which already ordained women and urging others to relax their restrictions against this policy. It was duly seconded but only briefly debated, having been withdrawn by the mover, after conference with the General Secretary, because of opposition voiced by representatives of the Anglican and Orthodox Churches. Members of the Assembly saw this as meaning that the status of women at least in the decisions of the World Council of Churches would probably remain for years to come much as it had been.

3. Report of the Committee on Faith and Order

The Committee on Faith and Order at New Delhi concurred with the request of the Commission on Faith and Order that the latter be given the status of a division in the World Council of Churches. It agreed with those members of the Commission who thought that there should be "a radical revision of theological language" as a step toward "popularizing" Faith and Order studies in the churches. It offered no thoughts on the revision of theology itself. Mention was made of the aim to give special attention to the theology of Eastern Orthodoxy, with the view of helping the World Council to become more familiar with the subject.

The growing friendliness of the Church of Rome was noted with appreciation, and likewise the increasing interest of the confessional groups in the World Council's program.

Observance of the Week of Prayer for Christian Unity in many countries was, the Committee thought, cause for satisfaction and hopefulness.

The Committee offered "the following suggestions to the staff for appropriate action:"[4]

A. 1. In Australia and New Zealand, because the conditions are similar (e.g., rapid mobility in population and specific moves toward church unions), the issues to be studied should be similar to those obtaining in North America and Great Britain. These studies should make full use of material from previous Australasian conferences and should have the greatest possible relevance for those churches that are seeking a way to union.

2. In Europe, including Great Britain, the studies should be such as to invite the churches to grapple with the problems caused by "the rapid drift towards the various forms of materialistic secularism and sophisticated nihilism." They face the same need for a radical revision of theological language, and will find a unity in their efforts to adapt traditional ways of speaking about Christ. The central Christian doctrines have become increasingly unintelligible to the contemporary European mind, and their re-formulation has become an urgent and inescapable task. This may require the formation of a special commission on theological discourse, which should seek a common, modern conceptual structure, and so help in the diagnosis of those divisions which are due primarily to varying modes of expression. The committee further requests the Working Committee to establish a study of the theological, biblical and ecclesiological issues involved in the ordination of women.

3. In North America, the studies should include an analysis of the general problem of theological discourse, giving attention to the varying and powerful facts in contemporary urban and scientific civilization which make the very intention and substance of Christian affirmations difficult to apprehend. The studies should also be designed to help congregations to understand discussions about baptism, eucharist and ministry, and especially to help congregations to understand the reasons for the positions and policies of those in other traditions.

4. In Asia, the studies assigned to *ad hoc* regional groups should include four items: (1) The growing influence and participation of the laity in the life of the churches, and the impossibility of full-time paid ministries in many areas. (2) The divisive forces which undermine the unity of the congregation, e.g., language, race, culture and caste. (3) The process of indigenization [sic] which presents both opportunity and danger to the churches, and effects changes in the relationship of Asian churches to parent denominations. (4) The situation of united churches in Asia which experience a tension between a movement to further union with other Asian churches and a tendency towards increasing self-consciousness, integration and institutionalism.

5. In Africa, attention should be given to the need for a united Christian witness in face of the missionary successes of Islam; to the disentangling of loyalty to race and culture from loyalty to the Church; to the relationships between the historical churches and the newly emerging sects; and to the need to sanctify both African and European cultures and to bring them both within the one Church.

6. In Latin America, there is great need for Faith and Order consultations in specific areas.

[4] *The New Delhi Report,* pp. 171-75.

7. In the Near East, study needs to be concerned with the lack of vital contact between Orthodox churches and between Orthodox and Evangelical churches; with the battle to reach the secularized educated intellectual; and with the world of Islam.

B. The committee recommends to the Central Committee that it ask the Division of Studies to establish at an early date a special program of study on the whole problem of theological discourse, including the problem of hermeneutics. . . .

C. The committee makes the following recommendation:

> There are two tasks to be done: to popularize Faith and Order discussions, so that congregations may share in them intelligently, and to achieve wider distribution for all Faith and Order literature. . . . The committee recommends that the resources and personnel be made available for more extensive translation and wider dissemination of Faith and Order studies. The appointment of an editorial secretary to the World Council of Churches might serve all the departments in this vital task.

D. The committee has been gratified to learn of the enlarged secretariat and greater significance already accorded to the Faith and Order Commission in the World Council of Churches. Yet it has also expressed the strong conviction that the present position of the Commission and Secretariat of Faith and Order within the Division of Studies is neither satisfactory to the Commission on Faith and Order nor appropriate to the specific nature of its purpose and task. The committee therefore wishes to inform the Assembly that it is requesting the Central Committee to take action at an early date to give the Commission and Secretariat of Faith and Order the status of a Division within the World Council of Churches as part of its proposed review of the organization of the World Council of Churches.

E. The committee has noted with gratitude the ecumenical interests of the world confessional bodies, and their co-operation with the World Council of Churches. The committee hopes that the collaboration will continue and increase, both between the confessional bodies themselves and between them and the World Council of Churches, particularly to avoid duplication of effort and undue pressure upon the churches' resources of persons and time. The committee draws the attention of the Working Committee of Faith and Order to the discussion in the section on Unity of the opportunities and the difficulties present in the relationships between the confessional bodies and the World Council of Churches.

F. The committee welcomes the consideration by the section on Unity of the statement adopted at St. Andrews in 1960 and the commendation of it, in a slightly revised form, and with a commentary, for study and appropriate action by the member churches. The committee suggests that the Faith and Order Commission keep the responses of the churches under careful review and report them from time to time to the Central Committee. The committee further recommends that special attention should be given to the implications of the Toronto, St. Andrews and . . . New Delhi statements for the theological self-understanding of the World Council of Churches, and suggests that this study should be accompanied by a thorough research into the nature and function of councils throughout the history of the Church. Further, the committee requests the Faith and Order Commission to convene a consultation on the significance of seeking unity without uniformity.

G. The committee wishes to remind the Assembly that the work of the Commission and Secretariat on Faith and Order depends upon a lively intercommunication between these on the one hand, and the regional, national and local Faith and Order committees on the other. The committee therefore urges the member churches of the World Council to establish and strengthen Faith and Order work at local, national and regional levels, and asks the Secretariat to supply to all Faith and Order committees such information and help as may be desired.

H. The committee requests the Commission on Faith and Order to establish a program of joint study of theological problems by Orthodox and non-Orthodox theologians, and to encourage local, national and regional as well as member churches to initiate similar work wherever possible.

I. The committee, conscious of the fact that many Protestant churches and groups do not share in ecumenical conversations, requests the Faith and Order Commission to seek relationships with these bodies in the interests of Christian truth and unity. The committee recognizes the great diversity of national and regional situations, and urges member churches to take whatever local initiative seems possible.

J. The committee notes with appreciation the recent growth of conversations, notably those arising out of biblical studies, between theologians of the Roman Catholic Church and those of other communions. It welcomes the many new contacts with Roman Catholics in an atmosphere of mutual good will, and in particular, the establishment by the Vatican of the secretariat for promoting Christian unity. The committee requests the Faith and Order Commission to make special provision for conversations with Roman Catholics, and asks member churches and local councils to take whatever initiative seems possible.

K. The committee requests the Faith and Order Commission to seek the best means of discussing with Roman Catholic theologians the fundamental theological issues at stake between non-Roman churches and the Roman Catholic Church, and to consider their implications for policies and practices (e.g., mixed marriages).

L. The committee notes with deep satisfaction that the observance of the Week of Prayer for Christian Unity has steadily increased in many parts of the world, and commends its further observance to member churches as a focus of ecumenical prayer and witness. . . .

4. The Central Committee, the Assembly, and the World Council

From the statement by Chairman Franklin Clark Fry at New Delhi concerning it, the Central Committee's program appeared to have developed into an expression on a large scale of the type of religious activism supposedly particularly characteristic of American churches and long frowned upon in ecumenical circles.

Referring to the Assembly handbook, *Evanston to New Delhi,* which summarized the activities of the divisions, departments, commissions, and special committees of the World Council of Churches, Dr. Fry said:[5]

Anyone who presumes to report for the Central Committee . . . is undertaking a formidable task. The dimensions are big, no matter how one

[5] *The New Delhi Report,* pp. 334-342.

measures them. As the responsible organ of the World Council between Assemblies, the Committee's duties are exceedingly broad . . . , ranging over the whole gamut of our common life and activities. . . . The tempo for the World Council . . . has been intense. The winds of history . . . have blown . . . with gale force. . . . The acceleration of events, without and within . . . , has been relentless. . . . The World Council has never experienced a really calm day. . . . God called it simultaneously into life and to strenuous action. . . . The tumult of these hectic days has conscripted, compelled *common* efforts of Christians through the ecumenical movement. . . . It has not been optional. . . . Neither the World Council nor the separate churches could ignore that demand or insulate themselves against it, without going far toward vitiating the very reason why God brought them into being. . . .

Actually, our Council . . . sees itself called not only into the tide of events but to be ahead of them—and there is where it has earnestly striven to be. The Christian community, acting together, needs to feel an obligation nowadays to be the path-finder. . . . We need to guide or at least to contribute to guiding. . . .

In that spirit the World Council since 1954 has not only been panting to keep up with life; it has pioneered in a far-sweeping series of inquiries as to how Christians in widely differing environments can help their nations to cope with rapid social change. It has commendably been in the van, through the Commission of the Churches on International Affairs and by the Central Committee's own actions, in dealing with emergent issues affecting war and peace by a living enunciation of principle while decisions are still in the balance and by skillful liaison in the places where they are being made. The World Council has striven for a consensus in the face of the population explosion; it has interested itself constructively in the emerging status of women; it has been alert in advance to the need for constitutional safeguards of religious liberty in nations, new and old. . . .

Even with that, the list is only partial. . . .

Not included were the immense and gushing programs of Inter-Church Aid and Service to Refugees; the ever-widening work of the Commission on Faith and Order; the world-encircling ministry of the International Missionary Council, now brought within the World Council's new Division of World Mission and Evangelism; the several other divisions and their dozen departments, all burgeoning with activities.

This phenomenal development, General Secretary Visser 't Hooft had explained in his report in the Assembly handbook, had not been "due to a deliberate policy for enlarging the scope and activity of the Council."[6]

Many in the responsible committees and staff of the Council would have preferred a more gradual development of the movement. . . . Decisions about the pace . . . , however, cannot be taken *in vacuo*. They have to be taken in the light of the opportunities to be accepted and the needs to be met. If there is a danger of forcing the pace, there is also a danger—perhaps a greater one—of refusing to carry out duties which, though not of our choosing, are presented to us.

[6] *Evanston to New Delhi,* p. 983 ff. See also *Assembly Handbook.*

Said Dr. Visser 't Hooft, further:

> Interest in all that pertains to church unity is widespread. The scope of ecumenical conversation has widened. . . . The churches have become . . . aware of the great resources of the ecumenical movement . . . and are looking increasingly to the World Council . . . to make [these] available to them. . . . Almost all the churches, both large and small, have become eager to share, as well as to receive, and they look to the Council as the main instrument for such spiritual exchange.

Chairman Fry also described the reasons for the extraordinary expansion as inherent in the nature of the World Council of Churches. The growth had been logical, he said, not a haphazardly mechanical adding of project to project.

The Council's actions had "not been characterized by discontinuity. . . . It had not worked in spasms. . . . It had become more deeply confirmed than ever in the personality which it . . . had from the beginning."

Here he interposed: "This ought not to be interpreted to mean that your Council and those . . . at its helm since Evanston have been lacking in ingenuity and creativity. New applications of . . . tested principles can be numbered in the scores, with adaptations . . . all along the line, as there ought to be in any organism as vividly alive as ours is."

"No symptoms are to be found that there has been stagnation," he added; "anything but that! Nor, even less, has there been any settling down, subsiding into institutional rigidity."

However it had happened, the impression was given that the Central Committee had on its shoulders a massive task.

In what he said about avoiding "institutional rigidity," the Chairman may have been speaking for the special benefit of an element who had made known their fears that the World Council of Churches under the growing and complicated organization was in danger of ceasing to be a movement and becoming an institution. The point had been raised that the policy of the World Council had been concerned too much with problems of structure and maintenance, and not enough with the pioneering spirit which earlier had been such an important factor. Most of the complainants had belonged to the vanguard of earlier years and worked alongside the founders. The Chairman, who had arrived more recently, had shown signs of impatience with their veiws. What the "present policy of the Central Committee really meant," he insisted, was "that the wisdom of the builders of the Council had been vindicated by the test of the thronging events of these years." "The grand design with which they—and, we devoutly believe, the Holy Spirit—endowed it has been proved sound," he declared.

From this point Dr. Fry took the Assembly on a tour, so to speak, of the internal functioning of the Central Committee. "A very human element, whether we like it or not, is involved in all our judgments," he said, "and, for the sake of a true perspective, you deserve to have that pictured clearly too."

There were three aspects of the Committee's method to which he gave attention:[7]

> Perhaps the most distinctive single feature is that in every meeting . . . there is a conscious balance. A study or thought component is introduced to match the action component. . . . The Committee keeps scholarship and reflection based on research in something like equipoise with the oversight that it has to give to the Council's far-flung and accelerating program. . . . One and all have been resolved that our meetings must never be allowed to deteriorate . . . into mere management. . . . Theory and actuality, thought and action are not rigid antitheses, not by any means, in the World Council of Churches. Each is a large ingredient of the other. . . . Ideas stream into functional activities, and the tide flows back. . . .

The Chairman turned next to the fiscal business of the Committee.

> A special paragraph should be included about finances. . . . The basic fact is this: from the standpoint of its cost, the Council is far, very far from being the behemoth . . . it is sometimes pictured. . . . The truth, seen in fair perspective, really is the exact opposite; the Council is a notably frugal operation, so much so that numerous parts of its program suffer from both acute and chronic fiscal anaemia. Year by year, it requires little less than a *tour de force* to balance the slender resources . . . the member churches are able to make available to the Council with even the ecumenical imperatives, let alone the massive opportunities of our day. Every rupee, franc, crown, pound that is given sacrificially . . . is carefully husbanded and cautiously disbursed; it receives the diligent attention of some of the Council's most capable leaders.[8] The marvel is that so little . . . has been made to go so far. The spending, no less than the giving, exhibits stewardship of a high order.

The Chairman desired to dispel, if he could, one misconception:

> The World Council does not exist primarily to receive from the churches; it exists to do for them and to give to them. The whole predisposition . . . is to search for avenues through which it can enrich, not drain, the churches; to find ways to become an instrument which . . . will be increasingly valuable and effective, but always wholly in their hands. . . .

This observation led directly to the procedure within the Committee, and on this he said:

> It has seen itself as the voice—a kind of miniature parliament—of the churches; it has been a representative democracy in which every individual

[7] *The New Delhi Report,* p. 342 ff.

[8] Dr. Eugene Carson Blake, Stated Clerk of the United Presbyterian Church, U.S.A., was Chairman of the Committee on Program and Finance.

is honored and his contribution is welcomed and cultivated. . . . Nobody has ever been slighted or rebuffed. No matter how earnestly we have been seeking consensus on any issue; if the authentic voice of even a single church is raised in the minority, it has been respected and listened to. . . . Churches are esteemed in the World Council, not only for their numbers or financial power or depth of history, but equally for the height of their potential, and often even in proportion to the problems that confront and sometimes threaten to overwhelm them. It is the kind of spiritual mathematics that only Christians would employ . . . very foreign to the world. . . . Instinct in it is the feeling of the family of God. . . .

If the question is ever asked, "Are the churches in control?" the answer is an emphatic "Yes." Nobody who has ever seen the Central Committee in action would have the slightest doubt about it. . . .

The World Council not only disavowed becoming a super-church at its beginning . . . its total development . . . has been the most convincing refutation of the . . . notion.

Actually, the World Council is not even an "outside force," except to the degree . . . a church—or churches—keep it outside. If there is any failure of contact, the fault usually goes back to the structures the churches have created or failed to create within themselves to keep in touch with the Council and give their guidance to it. . . . The World Council and the Central Committee as its organ solicit your communications and your counsel, earnestly await them, never shrug them off, attentively hear when you speak.

The chairmanship of the Central Committee was the most important non-staff office in the World Council of Churches.[9] Dr. Fry's address was delivered with an air of confidence. He believed—it was evident from his manner—that he and the Committee had managed the work of the World Council during the seven years of their incumbency fairly and well. His allusions to the all but overwhelming events through which they had brought it betrayed no suggestion of anxiety or hesitation. He —and, by implication, his colleagues—had played a role not unlike that of "the children of Issachar" (I Chronicles xii, 32) in a critical period of Old Testament history, "which were men that had understanding of the times, to know what Israel ought to do." Before leaving New Delhi for home, the Committee elected him for another term.

The deeper, less self-revealing mood of the Assembly at large would perhaps have found a scriptural parallel in the lament of a prophet of the Old Testament who thought he heard God saying, "My people perish for lack of knowledge" (Hosea iv, 6).

New Delhi was situated in the midst of a continent with masses of perishing, and the international travel lanes reaching it skirted or lay through many other such areas. What the members of the Assembly had seen en route, the scene India spread before them upon arrival, the news reports which from day to day allowed no surcease from the international tumult conspired to turn the approach of Advent for probably most of them into a time of somberness. Many were a long way from

[9] Membership in the Presidium was a more or less honorary office.

home, and some were discovering at first hand depths of the world's lostness of which until then they had only read. All had no doubt a more acute sense than ever of the darkness into which the inextinguishable Light first shone.

Though human knowledge and its application in the physical sphere had increased phenomenally, until nearly all peoples were beneficiaries, to some extent, of its aids to better health and living, there had not been a corresponding advance in the social and political sciences. The nations still were making hardly noticeable progress toward achieving relations insuring peace and a cooperative employment of its fruits in the common service. Rather, they appeared to be drawing day by day nearer to war and a possible nuclear holocaust. Whether the World Council of Churches could do anything to save them was an open question. It could only have been asked whether God's priests in the twentieth century would, for all their busyness and buoyant confidence, prove abler to help his people to a saving knowledge than those of whom the prophet Hosea despaired in his day, when there were—it seemed to him—"no fidelity, no kindness, no knowledge of God in the land, nothing but perjury, lying, and murder, stealing, debauchery, burglary—bloodshed on bloodshed!" (Hosea iv, 1, 2; Moffatt's translation).

The answer may have depended on what saving the people was conceived to mean—on which also there would not have been agreement.

Certainly, the churches, however capable and faithful their hierarchies, had never been—and never would be—sufficient for such conquests as the prophets proposed, which early had the objective of a kingdom of God with Israel its seat and all peoples "flowing unto Zion" and in later ages the equally utopian vision of a globe-embracing state of justice and peace under the kingship of Jesus Christ. Salvation of that kind clearly was not to be. It was a subject on which prophetism in any dispensation could wax poetic and to which hopeful multitudes would thrill. Linked with the principles of morality and religion, which were preached as conditions of its materialization, the idea was not without value as a stimulus to righteousness, and in times of tribulation a support for the despairing; but it could only lead in the end to disappointment. The world would break in pieces again and again and re-collect itself, and the looked-for kingdom would not come. After each recurring convulsion, the earth would be still the same planet of strife and killings, of ravishment and desolation, of dimming longings and unrewarded patience.

How could it be expected that tiny Israel would become a dominant political power or that a world kingdom of mercy and truth would rise, by any providence, out of such a place as this earth? Either hope was unrealistic, if not irresponsible. The prophets would blame the failure of their dreams on the people's sins; and there would be in ancient Israel or modern world society no lack of wickedness, whether among Jews or

Gentiles. But that would not be the actual reason why fulfillment tarried. The kingdoms so romantically envisaged simply were not God's will or plan. The fact was that the earth with its commingling good and evil was the only environment in which the sons of men could attain to the moral stature of sons of God. What sort of persons would they develop —or deteriorate—into in a society from which all antagonisms and injustices had been banished? Surely not into citizens of the kind of kingdom God would establish, indeed had already established—the kingdom of the Spirit which thrust itself into human existence, with gates always open to all who would enter and commence to live in the power of God now.

If saving the people meant helping them to see and to enter this heavenly kingdom, in which the souls of men were reborn in the fusion of the temporal and the eternal, the Assembly had a responsibility to assess the success of the World Council of Churches with this essential mission. The Council and its Central Committee had said repeatedly that evangelism was the ultimate ecumenical objective, and this call to all peoples to the soul's true homeland certainly was of the essence of evangelism.

The World Council of Churches understood salvation to be concerned with the whole person, the body as well as the spirit. Its manifold activities had to justify themselves in terms of this concept.

This was the case with such programs as those of relief and social action. Though not of the world, Christians were in the world, as Christ had been and prayed they might be, bringing into its troubled life the redemptive ministry of his kingdom, which stopped short of no necessary service.

That the World Council always saw clearly the problems this situation raised for its evangelistic mission was doubtful. At any rate, it could not be said that these had been fully and frankly defined and made the subject of continuing study.

The immediacy and urgency of physical needs tended to make them obsessive with the aided and monopolizing for the ministering. Bodies often got fed while souls famished. The bestowal of charity was not conditional on evidence of religious interest or response; but until the Gospel had been given, the Church's work remained unfinished. Without spiritual rebirth, even material needs could not be fully met—the crucial fact Christ himself faced when he found the multitude following him because he had fed them, and dismissed them with the word about "bread from heaven," for which they had no time or appetite.

Making political action a component of evangelism met with even more and greater difficulties. If the World Council believed itself qualified to take a hand in the conflicts between nations, races, classes, and other contending groups, it risked in that kind of venture forfeiting whatever opportunity it had to gain a hearing for the Gospel on the part of the opposition certainly, and eventually even of those supported, whose decisions and tactics could not be allowed to go uncriticized when unchristian, as they would certainly be at times.

In no controversy would right or wrong be confined to one side. All contestants would look for partisan backing and be in no mood to hear the Gospel bidding them manifest humility; think on "the things of others" and not their own; give them asking for their coats their cloaks also, and go two miles with those demanding their help for a mile; love their enemies and do good to them at whose hands they had received evil; and pray for those despitefully using them.

Only when the Church spoke to all would the Gospel stand any chance of being listened to. Without its moral therapeutic, no adjudication of differences could amount to more than temporary accommodation, which governments, courts, and other mediatorial institutions were generally more competent to negotiate than the Church.

It must have been the realization of this that prompted Christ's refusal to act as referee in the case of brothers at odds over an estate. His reply was "Who made me a judge or divider over you?"

In social action, as in relief, help given was not conditional on religious response. The Church acted in the name of justice, whether the plaintiff was Christian or pagan. As in relief, it was observable in social action that services rendered seldom persuaded the benefited to give God the glory or a pledge of self-commitment. If their triumph had been won on the issue of justice, they were less aware than before of their sins, and so of their need to be saved.

The World Council of Churches knew well enough, at least theologically, that the Gospel was more than justice; that, in respect of justice, all men stood condemned before God; that, even if winning over one another, they faced together wars and strivings in which, without the Gospel, all would perish, body and soul. What would it profit them, if they gained equal status in politics, race, economics, but inflicted on one another losses triggering destruction for all?

The Gospel still was "Seek ye first the kingdom of God and his righteousness, and all these things shall be added unto you." (Luke XII, 14).

At a meeting during the Assembly at New Delhi one speaker remarked—not necessarily reflecting the mind of anyone but himself, yet significantly, in the light of a strong drift of thought in modern times—that one quoting this declaration of Christ seriously today would immediately lose his audience. It was suggested, in rebuttal, that there were worse losses even a preacher might suffer than this! If he proclaimed the Gospel, he would give the Spirit of truth a chance to convict those disposed to walk out on him, and them an opportunity to repent and be converted, and so to find their way into the eternal kingdom of new and abundant life—which was or ought to have been the object of his speaking.

The first problem in evangelism was keeping the Gospel from becoming only incidental. It demanded serious attention by all sons of Issachar and of the understanding in other tribes as well.

5. Members of the Central and Executive Committees After New Delhi

A shift of the confessional and geographical centers of the World Council of Churches was seen in the membership of the Central Committee and its Executive Committee chosen at New Delhi.

The Eastern Orthodox Churches, with seventeen representatives—five from the Holy Orthodox Church of Russia—were the largest group. Members from Africa increased from one to nine. Asian and Latin American representations were upped from one to thirteen and one to three, respectively. Very slight reductions were observable in the number of members from the continents of Europe and North America. All told, approximately 80 percent of the 100 members of the Central Committee were newly elected at New Delhi.[10]

The tabulation confessionally stood as follows:

Eastern Orthodox	17
Lutherans	16
Reformed	15
Anglicans	12
Methodist	11
United Churches	10
Baptists	5
Congregationalists	4
Syrian Orthodox	2
Coptic Churches	1
Ethiopian Church	1
Disciples of Christ	1
Old Catholic Church	1
Mar Thoma Syrian Church	1
Philippine Independent Church	1
Moravian Church	1
Salvation Army	1

Dr. Franklin Clark Fry of the United Lutheran Church of the United States of America and Dr. Ernest A. Payne, Baptist from the United Kingdom, were re-elected Chairman and Vice-Chairman, respectively, of the Central Committee. They, with the six Presidents of the World

[10] For the complete roster of the Central Committee, including those elected in 1961, see Appendix B.

Council *ex officio,* and the following members of the Central Committee would constitute the Executive Committee:

Dr. Eugene Carson Blake, United Presbyterian Church, U.S.A.
Dr. Kathleen Bliss, Anglican, Great Britain.
Dr. Josef L. Hromadka, Reformed Church, Czechoslovakia.
Archbishop Gunnar A. E. Hultgren, Church of Sweden.
Dr. Christian G. Baëta, Presbyterian Church, Ghana.
Bishop Sante U. Barbieri, Methodist Church, Argentina.
Dr. Alford Carleton, United Church of Christ, U.S.A.
Dr. Russell Chandran, Church of South India.
Dr. Ivy Chou, Methodist Church, Sarawak.
Bishop Hanns Lilje, Evangelical Church of Germany (Lutheran).
Mr. J. Irwin Miller, International Convention of Christian Churches (Disciples of Christ), U.S.A.
Archbishop Nikodim, Holy Orthodox Church of Russia.
Metropolitan Iakovos of North and South America, Greek Orthodox
Archbishop Frank Woods, Church of England, Melbourne, Australia.

Other officers elected by the Third Assembly were as follows:

Honorary President:

Dr. J. H. Oldham, United Kingdom.

The Presidium:

The Most Rev. Arthur Michael Ramsey, Archbishop of Canterbury, Church of England, United Kingdom.
Sir Francis A. Ibiam, Presbyterian Church of Nigeria, Enugu, Nigeria.
The Most Rev. Iakovos, Archbishop of North and South America, Ecumenical Patriarchate of Constantinople, New York, U.S.A.
Dr. David G. Moses, United Church of Northern India and Pakistan, Nagpur, India.
The Rev. Martin Niemöller, Evangelical Church in Germany (United), Wiesbaden, Germany.
Mr. Charles C. Parlin, the Methodist Church, New York, U.S.A.

6. New Churches Added to the World Council

Twenty-three denominations had qualified for membership in the World Council of Churches since the meeting of the Central Committee in St. Andrews, and they were admitted at New Delhi, raising the total number of members to 198.

Of these, four were Orthodox—Russian, Rumanian, Bulgarian, and Polish. Other parts of the world represented in the new group were Pakistan, New Caledonia, Trinidad, New Hebrides, Samoa, and the United States.

It was pointed out that there had not been previously any applications for membership from churches in the islands of the Pacific.

The churches received consisted of five Presbyterian, three Lutheran, three Evangelical, two Congregationalist, two Pentecostal, one United, one Moravian, one Baptist, and one Anglican, besides the four Orthodox. Their constituencies totaled approximately fifty millions, the Russian Orthodox Church comprising more than twenty-five millions, with thirty thousand priests and twenty thousand parishes inside the Union of Soviet Socialist Republics. Eleven of the new members were located in Africa: two each in South Africa, Cameroun, and Tanganyika, and one each in Rhodesia, Uganda, Gabon, Nigeria, and the Congo. The number of members from that continent, at Evanston thirteen, now stood at thirty.

All applicants had expressed agreement with the Basis of the World Council of Churches. Admission was by written ballot, each member denomination, regardless of the number of its communicants, having one vote. It was announced that each applicant had received more than the two-thirds majority required. In fact, with about 150 churches represented in the Assembly, there were few negative votes and still fewer abstentions. The final tabulation showed that eight ballots had been cast against each of the Pentecostal churches, and three against the Russian Orthodox Church. The number favorable to these churches were, respectively, 138 and 142.

The new churches received were, in the order of their applications:

The United Church of Central Africa in Rhodesia.
Iglesia Pentecostal de Chile.
Moravian Church in the Western Cape Province.
Église Évangélique en Nouvelle-Calédonie et aux Îles Loyauté.
Union des Églises Baptistes du Cameroun.
Orthodox Church of Russia.
United Presbyterian Church of Pakistan.
Church of the Province of Uganda and Ruanda-Urundi (Anglican).
Presbyterian Church in the Cameroons.
Presbyterian Church in Trinidad.
Finnish Evangelical Lutheran Church of America, Suomi Synod.
Mision Iglesia Pentecostal (Chile).
Bulgarian Orthodox Church.
Église Évangélique du Gabon.
Bantu Congregational Church in South Africa.
Presbyterian Church of Nigeria.
Rumanian Orthodox Church.
Evangelical (Lutheran) Church of North-Western Tanganyika.
Église Évangélique Manianga Matadi (Congo).
Presbyterian Church of the New Hebrides.
Usambara-Digo Lutheran Church (Tanganyika).
Orthodox Church of Poland.
Congregational Christian Church in Samoa.

The accession to membership of so many additional churches, with the statement by Assembly officials that inquiries indicated the intentions of others to apply,[10] emphasized the phenomenal growth of the World Council of Churches.

What had been the reasons for such a general desire on the part of Christian denominations in all the continents to associate themselves with the World Council? Without attempting to set down all of them, the following were obvious.

Many Christians, whatever their confessional ties, enjoyed the ecumenical fellowship. Realizing that they shared in common the fundamental experiences of faith, they were interested in learning how others understood and gave expression to them.

Foreign missionaries had early experimented with interconfessional conferences for prayer and discussion, and their meetings increased in popularity and attendance because they were profitable. The representatives of the communions participating in them had not thought that they were laying foundations for the ecumenical movement which eventually grew out of them. They had been doing only what they liked and believed helpful.

Whatever their opinion of the World Council of Churches, those attending its assemblies were likely to find the educational value of its programs worth traveling far to share. And personal contacts were equally rewarding.

The churches had decided, moreover, that the work they would do must be undertaken cooperatively, so far as possible, without obligations beyond their own willingness to contract. In the World Council of Churches they themselves determined what they would and would not do in decisions democratically taken. What they derived from the World Council and what they were able to contribute through it—which were the two sides of the compact—they thought worth the cost to them in effort and money. The Assembly in New Delhi was the third. The World Council had been in existence thirteen years, not counting the provisional decade between Utrecht and Amsterdam, and the judgment with regard to its usefulness had not changed. Time had confirmed it in many ways unforeseen.

Nearly all Christians believed that unity was in the nature of the Gospel. They had different ideas about the meaning and the implementation of this unity but welcomed opportunity for conversation with one another about such questions, so long as it involved no commitment beyond their own choosing.

Probably no member denomination of the World Council of Churches

[10] Soon after the New Delhi Assembly, seven additional churches applied for membership, approved by the Central Committee at its Paris meeting in August, 1962: the Evangelical Lutheran Church of Estonia, the Armenian Apostolate Church, the Evangelical Lutheran Church of Latvia, the Georgian Orthodox Church, the Union of Evangelical Christians (Baptists) of Russia, the American Apostolic Catholicate of Cilicia, and the Evangelical Lutheran Church in South Africa—South-East Region. Their total membership was approximately seven million.

found its organization and policy altogether acceptable; but there was also almost surely none that did not believe itself able to belong and make its contribution, without compromising its own convictions. In such exchange there was an important kind of unity making possible the search through prayer, study, and fellowship for still fuller agreement.

Messages to the members of the Assembly from their families and constituencies—and also from persons outside the churches—appeared, according to reports, to be alike in their expression of hopefulness that the denominations might be of decisive help through their conference in arresting the accelerating movement of the nations toward war. Other actions having proved unavailing, the world seemed to feel it had recourse only to prayer, which had been neglected until it faced stark disaster. This concern for peace had from the beginning been an impelling reason with the churches themselves for throwing their support to the World Council.

Paradoxically, criticism and hostility had furthered the progress of the World Council. Some Christians, influenced by them, had remained aloof; but others, keenly cognizant of the weaknesses of the churches themselves and not looking for a perfect cooperative instrument, had been led to give the movement a fair trial. Controversy quickened interest. Even opponents could not deny that the World Council had its good features, which, some feared, only made it more seductively dangerous. But Gamaliel-minded persons advised withholding final judgment as an alternative to risking opposing what God might be found eventually to approve. At any rate, they said, it was plain that some of the works of the World Council of Churches were so greatly needed that, if it were to go out of business, an agency like it would have to be set up to take them over.

A movement of such impressive aims and accomplishments was either of God or a colossal blunder. In either case it could not be ignored.

7. The Message of the Assembly to the Churches

The Third Assembly of the World Council of Churches meeting in New Delhi addresses this letter to the member churches and their congregations. We rejoice and thank God that we experience here a fellowship as deep as before and now wider. New member churches coming in considerable numbers and strength both from the ancient Orthodox tradition of Eastern Christendom and from Africa, Asia, Latin America and other parts of the world visibly demonstrate that Christianity now has a home in every part of the world. In this fellowship we are able to speak and act freely, for we are all partakers together with Christ. Together we have sought to understand our common calling to witness, service and unity.

We are deeply grateful for the prayers of countless people and for the study of our theme "Jesus Christ, the Light of the World" by which many of you have shared in our work. Now we return to our churches to do, with you, the things that have been shown to us here.

All over the world new possibilities of life, freedom and prosperity are being actively, even passionately, pursued. In some lands there is disillusionment with the benefits that a technically expert society can produce; and over all there hangs the shadow of vast destruction through war. Nevertheless mankind is not paralyzed by these threats. The momentum of change is not reduced. We Christians share men's eager quest for life, for freedom from poverty, oppression and disease. God is at work in the opening possibilities for mankind in our day. He is at work even when the powers of evil rebel against him and call down his judgment. We do not know what ways God will lead us; but our trust is in Jesus Christ who is now and always our eternal life.

When we speak to men as Christians we must speak the truth of our faith: that there is only one way to the Father, namely Jesus Christ his Son. On that one way we are bound to meet our brother. We meet our brother Christian. We meet also our brother man; and before we speak to him of Christ, Christ has already sought him.

Christ is the way and therefore we have to walk together witnessing to him and serving all men. This is his commandment. There is no greater service to men than to tell them of the living Christ and no more effective witness than a life offered in service. The indifference or hostility of men may check our own speaking, but God is not silenced. He speaks through the worship and the sufferings of his Church. Her prayers and patience are, by his gracious acceptance of them, made part of the witness he bears to Christ.

We need to think out together in concrete terms the forms of Christian service for today and together act upon them. In no field has Christian cooperation been more massive and effective than in service to people in every kind of distress. There is no more urgent task for Christians than to work together for community within nations and for peace with justice and freedom among them, so that the causes of much contemporary misery may be rooted out. We have to take our stand against injustice caused to any race, or to any man on account of his race. We have to learn to make a Christian contribution to the service of men through secular agencies. Christian love requires not only the sharing of worldly goods but costly personal service. All over the world young people are giving an example in their spontaneous offering of themselves.

We must together seek the fulness of Christian unity. We need for this purpose every member of the Christian family, of Eastern and Western traditions, ancient churches and younger churches, men and women, young and old, of every race and every nation. Our brethren in Christ are given to us, not chosen by us. In some things our convictions do not yet permit us to act together, but we have made progress in giving content to the unity we seek. Let us therefore find out the things which in each place we can do together now; and faithfully do them, praying and working always for that fuller unity which Christ wills for his Church.

This letter is written from the World Council of Churches' Assembly. But the real letter written to the world today does not consist of words. We Christian people, wherever we are, are a letter from Christ to his world "written not with ink but with the Spirit of the living God, not on tablets of stone but on tablets of human hearts." The message is that God in Christ has reconciled the world to himself. Let us speak it and live it with joy and confidence, for it is the God who said, "Let light shine out of darkness" who has shone in our hearts "to give the light of the knowledge of the glory of God in the face of Jesus Christ."

First Sunday in Advent 1961

Part Nine

RETROSPECT AND PROSPECT

RETROSPECT AND PROSPECT

Whatever its providential character, the World Council of Churches might be described as a natural phenomenon of the age, the complex of circumstances surrounding and giving shape to its beginnings and its growth being clearly discernible in general outline.[1]

From this point of view, it would have been seen as a result, in part, of the slow softening of dogma under the influence of scientific thought, which, to a degree greater than most of the faithful realized or would admit, left hardly any article of belief as it had been and made necessary a reorientation of all religions and their institutions.

A ready example of this was the new understanding of the origin and nature of the Old and New Testament Scriptures and of the principles of their interpretation, for which modern research in the field of historical criticism was to be credited.

Although the Bible remained the "Word of God," it was that in a different sense. Sectarian readings of it slowly lost their authority. Many doctrinal distinctions and denominational demarcations, whatever the occasion for the continued emphasis on them, ceased to be supported by supposedly scriptural sanctions once stoutly maintained. Gradually the spirit triumphed over the letter, and the experience of God through faith and love, however explained theologically, was recognized as the deepest common bond between believers.

From this inner well of shared spiritual being in the eternal life of God in the soul flowed new revelations of truth, as in the luminous earlier days of the Church. Without dismissing ancient insights, these were unmistakably of the Word and equally disclosures of the will of God.

Whether the churches should keep on in their separate ways or join fortunes became more a practical than a theological question, when looked at levelly, albeit the age which had thrust it upon them would perhaps pass away before the guardians of "the faith once for all delivered" would learn to accommodate themselves and their immemorial systems to the inexorable.

The World Council of Churches would, from this standpoint, be fur-

[1] Regard is had here to theological categories. Actually, no valid differentiation can be made between the natural and the providential, the one being comprehended in the other.

ther characterized as a development of the times in its identification of the social meaning of Christianity with the philosophy of equalitarianism as expressed in current collectivisms.

The favor with which it met, in this respect, was attributable partly to its multifarious works of charity in the wake of two world wars, but even more to its espousal of such sociopolitical causes as the welfare state, the abolition of colonialism, independence and autonomy for emerging new nations, racial integration, and the international sharing of wealth under governmental compulsion. It stood for economic and political justice as conceived by many religious liberals of the first half of the century, rallying the churches in support of the struggle of the multitudes of the world's poor for improvement of their condition.

While proclaiming that it acted thus obediently to the lordship of Jesus Christ, it acknowledged as a further motive fear of the menace of massive antisocial movements which were bent upon seizing their opportunity in human misery.

Its policy and program were thus so shaped in response to the pressures of the world about it that it brought down upon itself criticism by churchmen who, like Karl Barth,[2] believed it was the Christian imperative for the Church to start with God, rather than with man.

From this earthward perspective the World Council of Churches would have been explained with special reference also to its concern for world peace. With mankind sundered by competing ideologies and war an ever-present threat, international conciliation presented the most pressing problem. Delayed in its organization by World War II, the World Council, in its provisional status, had in 1946 joined with the International Missionary Council in setting up the Commission of the Churches on International Affairs, the extensive activities of which, in cooperation with departments of the United Nations and other bodies, secular and religious, in the months before the First Assembly and during the post-Amsterdam period, have been reported in other chapters. Approval of this program had been instant. Men hoped that reconciliation of the nations, which had eluded the best efforts of warriors and statesmen, scientists and philosophers, philanthropists and reformers, publicists and educators, might be brought nearer by the churches, with so many of them the world around working and praying together to accomplish it.

Again, there was objection that the World Council's approach to its mission from below eclipsed its feebler attempts to discern the leading from above. Pre-occupied with the mundane, it seemed to its critics at times to confuse the meanings of things belonging in the separate categories of sociology and theology. Discussions of peace which failed to

[2] Barth said of the main theme of the Amsterdam Assembly, "Man's Disorder and God's Design," that he would have reversed it, making it read "God's Design and Man's Disorder," starting from above rather than from below, where little could be done and that with doubtful results.

keep the distinctions clear between peace in the relation of man with God and peace in the political meaning afforded, they thought, an example of this.[3]

Viewed thus in light of the events of the time, the World Council of Churches took on definite aspects of inevitability. Many who, for various reasons, were disinclined to approve it nevertheless agreed that if it had not existed some organization like it would have had to be devised to do the socially useful work that was such a large part of its agenda.

From this position could have been distinguished clearly the two problems to which the Council, with its constituent churches, must give priority if it was not to disappoint the hope in the Christian religion kindled by its social objectives.

The first of these problems was theological. It arose from the failure of the churches to come to terms with knowledge in its expanding dimensions.

Reference has been made to the advances of science as factors in the opening of ways for closer rapprochement between the churches in the ecumenical movement. But theology had made scarcely more than a beginning of the reinterpretation and readjustment necessary because of the progress of learning and the resultant changes in the life of man.

Liberal theology stood more or less discredited as, in the opinion of many, too superficial and negative. Fundamentalism was sounding a call for retreat to the old comforts of traditionalism. In language which to the uninitiated seemed rather to smack of double-talk, neo-orthodoxy summoned the churches to its haven behind biblical bulwarks which looked secure to many but actually were already giving under the pressure of surging modernism.

The Christian faith had no authentic gospel[4] and could have none until recast in the intellectual matrix of the age which had swept away old miracles with new; and this, if it could be done at all, would have to be, there was reason to think, the work of liberalism.[5]

But liberal theology would have first to be emancipated from the fear of full obedience to "the heavenly vision." And the hard conditions which had brought the progress of theological reorientation to a halt in the first place could not be expected to disappear or to change much—

[3] See Statement by Franklin Clark Fry, p. 578.

[4] "One of the things we share together as Christians is a common incomprehensibility to the mass of mankind. In the whole modern world, the language, the thought, the tradition of Christianity are increasingly meaningless to millions of our contemporaries." (Dr. Oliver S. Tomkins, Secretary of the Commission on Faith and Order, at Lund, 1952.)

"The Church must find a language for modern men." (Høgsbro, reporting on religious conditions in Denmark at the First Assembly of the World Council of Churches.)

[5] True liberalism holds that all knowledge by which religion can be affected necessarily affirms the fundamental truths of Christianity, which, however, must be restated theologically in the languages of successive stages of civilization.

the resistance of traditionalism, the domination of religious education by institutionalism, the reluctance of the teachers to admit that they had sometimes confused conviction with knowledge under demands for "evidence of things not seen" when there was none, the lack of intellectual and spiritual capacity in the case of multitudes of Christians for the reconstruction of beliefs—these and still others as intractable. On the other hand, the urgency of the need for its accomplishment would not cease or diminish.

There was not, however, any general awareness of these circumstances in the churches, which made the problem posed by them more serious. The churches of the West did not connect the failures of theology with their loss of influence at home or their waning power in non-Christian lands. But it was in Central Europe, where modern scholarship had done its first and best work and the churches had generally rejected its results, that the estrangement of the masses from Christianity had been greatest. There, in the orbit of Protestantism, dictators could defy the churches successfully and, by employing the findings of critical study out of the context of a valid experiential faith, break down the confidence and loyalty of their members. In the domains of Orthodoxy the people were even more completely at the mercy of these profane men. The scriptural words "My people are destroyed for lack of knowledge" were never more truly descriptive in any period of history than in these years of moral collapse in the midst of Eurasia. And in the United Kingdom and North America the state of Christianity was far from reassuring, while in Oriental and other mission countries outside the conventional bounds of Christendom the survival of the work of Western churches grew steadily more uncertain.

It was a time for prayer in the churches for their theologians, who stood in need especially of fresh accessions of courage, as well as of insight. Those who knew the crucial importance of their mission in such a time could only have hoped that they might be allowed greater latitude in reporting what they saw; and that, whether given more liberty to speak or not, they might remember their duty as interpreters of an ever-expanding experience of God to declare the whole truth—or the whole, at least, of what was revealed to them—even if it meant they must, in the words of James Russell Lowell:

> . . . share her wretched crust
> Till the multitude make virtue
> Of the faith they had denied.

The other problem faced by the World Council and the churches was sociological; but, if examined deeply, it also would have been found to be theological.[6]

[6] "With regard to the . . . question whether the growth of the World Council is a harmonious growth, it seems to me that the main issue is whether theology

There was need in the Council especially for guidance in developing a soundly Christian social program and in building under it an ideological foundation with real relevance to the swiftly changing situation; and the necessary help for this task would have to come, if at all, largely from theology.

But when the ecumenical theologians could be got to give their attention to these problems, it usually was more to justify already accepted social action theories and practices than to define the modifications of these that might have been indicated by new revelations. Their efforts at Evanston showed how they followed, rather than led, the policy makers, their sometimes awkward and artificial scripturalizing of the Council's social pronouncements and actions leaving many who attended the Assembly more convinced than they had been that little effective leadership for critical study and reinterpretation could be expected of them.

With disconcerting success, communism was meantime driving ahead in its anti-religion crusade. Its philosophy was essentially a negative one and should not logically have made the headway it apparently had against Christianity. With men natively desiring more to believe in God than not to believe, the Christian faith should have been able to hold the ground against dialectical atheism, even though the latter was linked with the lure of a spurious kind of justice, which promised to provide for the material wants of its supporters by expropriating what others possessed. The strength of communism seemed to be not only that it appealed to the covetousness in men, as the popular supposition was, but that it preached an intelligible and apparently relevant, if false, doctrine, whereas the formulas of religion, with their archaic terminologies

---

and policy, reflection and action are in step or out of step in our life. There are those who feel that the World Council is already too much concerned with theology. Personally, I fear that our real weakness is the opposite. We have our important theological commissions of Faith and Order; we have the biblical study on the Lordship of Christ, and these fulfill an important function. But we give little, if any, time to the serious study of the theological problems arising in the life of the World Council itself. Now it is increasingly clear that many of our structural and organizational problems are essentially theological. The relation of the World Council to the missionary movement, the relation between interchurch aid . . . and the evangelistic and missionary task . . . or the task of the Church in areas of rapid social change, or the vocation of the laity, or the co-operation of men and women, or the question of our Basis, or the whole problem of the ecclesiological implications of the existence of the World Council, or a host of other seemingly practical issues, cannot be clarified if we do not arrive at a clear theology concerning the nature and mission of the Church. Who is to produce this theology which is to serve as a basis of our . . . work? It is unfortunately a fact that there is no one in the full-time service of the World Council who can give a major part of his time to theological study. . . . So in this matter we have been largely dependent on voluntary help from the theologians in the different churches. Few of them have yet discovered the importance of these questions. . . . Is the Council . . . already too much taken for granted by its own member churches, especially its theologians? We must hope that before long the theological faculties will give us the help we need in order to get firm ground under our feet. . . ." (Report of Dr. Willem A. Visser 't Hooft, General Secretary, to the Central Committee. Minutes of the Committee, 1956, p. 71).

and symbolisms, had become meaningless, so that the intellectual capacity to grasp the Christian assurance of God had all but perished. Many who once had believed could no longer give a reason for their faith that satisfied themselves or anybody else. It may be recalled that a Study Department publication of 1949 made this observation: "The rise of historical and scientific criticism has wrought a revolution in the concept of the authority of the Bible, and of the relationship between Scripture and tradition. Even those who maintain in words the traditional positions very rarely maintain them completely in their own deepest thinking." [7]

The failure had been theological. The people had not been taught, in language they understood, how they could go on believing in the Gospel of Jesus Christ in the strange new universe into which theoretical and applied science had suddenly precipitated their generation. If their bodies were hungry, so, in many cases, were their minds.

The source of the trouble lay, of course, back of Amsterdam. Denominations without an adequate theology could only have created a World Council of Churches with the same deficiency. All they could do theologically with the new organization was set it harmonizing their variant creeds, which, if ever reconciled, would still have to be rewritten.

That the World Council of Churches should have fallen into what many thought serious error in the development of its social action policy could not have surprised anyone with a knowledge of the circumstances under which it originated and was obliged to function. What would have been more natural than that it should adopt the economic and political theories of the majority of its dominant leaders, most of whom were committed to socialist egalitarianism as, in their belief, the social ideal nearest to the Christian?

From these premises it could only follow that the Council and its member churches would be forced to recognize a degree of validity in the doctrine of materialistic determinism and to intensify their efforts to "make Christianity work" (in its social application, that is) as a condition of successful evangelization. On this one point there appeared to be substantial unanimity in the Council—that, in order to carry forward their program of world evangelism, the churches would have to demonstrate that they were concerned and able to work effectually for the economic improvement of life for those to whom they offered the Christian Gospel. The injunction of Jesus, "Seek ye first the kingdom of God and his righteousness," and its sequent promise, "and all these things shall be added unto you," would have to be rephrased to read, in effect, "Seek the kingdom of God and all these things together," from which rendering it could be but a short step to the conclusion of the

[7] Refer to footnote on page 595. *The Bible and the Church's Message,* an ecumenical inquiry, published by the Study Department of the World Council of Churches, 1949, p. 6.

Christian African political leader, turned communist, that "to seek all these things is to seek the kingdom."

In his report to the Second Assembly, the Director of the Commission of the Churches on International Affairs spoke of the need to build a theological foundation under the proliferating program of that organization.[8] Although undoubtedly not so intended, this seemed to imply that the theologians could be called upon, whenever required, to search the Scriptures for authority for whatever course the World Council and its departments had thought they found by experience necessary to the socialization of the Gospel.

Aside from helping as they might in this area, the theologians would continue under the Commission on Faith and Order their examination of the minutiae of creedal disagreements which supposedly kept the denominations apart.

Few voices were raised in the Assembly to emphasize the urgency of a thoroughgoing theological reorientation, which would help remove from the churches the impediment of their shared "incomprehensibility to the mass of mankind." The question was whether continuing unconcern at this point would not leave the World Council of Churches without promise of competent spiritual guidance for its social action program, or a successful implementation of its evangelistic mission.[9]

[8] Dr. O. Frederick Nolde, as quoted in Part Six, Section IV, *8*.

[9] As suggested above, theological reconstruction was a responsibility belonging to the denominations which composed the World Council; but recognition of the need of it from the standpoint of the practical problems of their cooperative mission should have encouraged any disposition they might have had to address themselves seriously to it.

APPENDIXES

APPENDIX A

Original Constitution of the World Council of Churches

Adopted at Amsterdam, August 30th, 1948

I. Basis

The World Council of Churches is a fellowship of Churches which accepts our Lord Jesus Christ as God and Saviour. It is constituted for the discharge of the functions set out below.

II. Membership

Those Churches shall be eligible for membership in the World Council of Churches which express their agreement with the basis upon which the Council is founded and satisfy such criteria as the Assembly or the Central Committee may prescribe.

Election to membership shall be by a two-thirds vote of the member Churches represented at the Assembly, each member Church having one vote. Any application for membership between meetings of the Assembly may be considered by the Central Committee; if the application is supported by a two-thirds majority of the members of the Committee present and voting, this action shall be communicated to the Churches that are members of the World Council of Churches and unless objection is received from more than one-third of the member Churches within six months the applicant shall be declared elected.

III. Functions

The functions of the World Council shall be:

(i) To carry on the work of the world movements for Faith and Order and for Life and Work.

(ii) To facilitate common action by the Churches.

(iii) To promote cooperation in study.

(iv) To promote the growth of ecumenical consciousness in the members of all Churches.

(v) To establish relations with denominational federations of world-wide scope and with other ecumenical movements.

(vi) To call world conferences on specific subjects as occasion may require, such conferences being empowered to publish their own findings.

(vii) To support the Churches in their task of evangelism.

IV. AUTHORITY

The World Council shall offer counsel and provide opportunity of united action in matters of common interest.

It may take action on behalf of constituent Churches in such matters as one or more of them may commit to it.

It shall have authority to call regional and world conferences on specific subjects as occasion may require.

The World Council shall not legislate for the Churches; nor shall it act for them in any manner except as indicated above or as may hereafter be specified by the constituent Churches.

V. ORGANIZATION

The World Council shall discharge its functions through the following bodies:

(i) An assembly which shall be the principal authority in the Council, and shall ordinarily meet every five years. The Assembly shall be composed of official representatives of the Churches or groups of Churches adhering to it and directly appointed by them. Their term of office shall begin in the year before the Assembly meets, and they shall serve until their successors are appointed. It shall consist of members whose number shall be determined by each Assembly for the subsequent Assembly, subject to the right of the Assembly to empower the Central Committee, if it thinks fit, to increase or to diminish the said number by not more than twenty per cent. The number shall be finally determined not less than two years before the meeting of the Assembly to which it refers and shall be apportioned as is provided hereafter.

Seats in the Assembly shall be allocated to the member Churches by the Central Committee, due regard being given to such factors as numerical size, adequate confessional representation and adequate geographical distribution. Suggestions for readjustment in the allocation of seats may be made to the Central Committee by member Churches or by groups of member Churches, confessional, regional or national, and these readjustments shall become effective if approved by the Central Committee after consultation with the Churches concerned.

The Assembly shall have power to appoint officers of the World Council and of the Assembly at its discretion.

The members of the Assembly shall be both clerical and lay persons —men and women. In order to secure that approximately one-third of the Assembly shall consist of lay persons, the Central Committee, in allocating to the member Churches their places in the Assembly, shall strongly urge each Church, if possible, to observe this provision.

(ii) A Central Committee which shall be a Committee of the Assembly and which shall consist of the President or Presidents of the World Council, together with not more than ninety members chosen by the Assembly from among persons whom the Churches have appointed as members of the Assembly. They shall serve until the next Assembly, unless the Assembly otherwise determines. Membership in the Central Committee shall be distributed among the member Churches by the Assembly, due regard being given to such factors as numerical size, adequate confessional representation and adequate geographical distribution. Any vacancy occurring in the membership of the Central Committee between meetings of the Assembly shall be filled by the Central Committee upon nomination of the Church or Churches concerned.

VI. Appointment of Commissions

The World Council shall discharge part of its functions by the appointment of Commissions. These shall be established under the authority of the Assembly, whether they be actually nominated by the Assembly or by the Central Committee acting under its instructions. The Commissions shall, between meetings of the Assembly, report annually to the Central Committee which shall exercise general supervision over them. The Commissions may add to their membership clerical and lay persons approved for the purpose by the Central Committee.

In particular, the Assembly shall make provision by means of appropriate Commissions for carrying on the activities of Faith and Order and of Life and Work.

There shall be a Faith and Order Commission which shall conform to the requirements of the Second World Conference on Faith and Order, held in Edinburgh in 1937, as follows:

(i) That the World Council's Commission on Faith and Order shall, in the first instance, be the Continuation Committee appointed by this Conference.

(ii) In any further appointments made by the Council to membership of the Commission on Faith and Order, the persons appointed shall always be members of the Churches which fall within the terms of the Faith and Order invitation addressed to "all Christian bodies throughout the world which accept our Lord Jesus Christ as God and Saviour."

(iii) The work of the Commission on Faith and Order shall be carried on under the general care of a Theological Secretariat appointed by the Commission, in consultation with the Council and acting in close co-operation with other secretariats of the Council. The Council shall make adequate financial provision for the work of the Commission after consultation with the Commission.

(iv) In matters of common interest to all the Churches and pertaining to Faith and Order, the Council shall always proceed in accordance with the basis on which this Conference on Faith and Order was called and is being conducted.

(v) The World Council shall consist of official representatives of the Churches participating.

(vi) Any Council formed before the first meeting of the Central Assembly shall be called Provisional, and the Assembly, representing all the Churches, shall have complete freedom to determine the constitution of the Central Council.

VII. Other Ecumenical Christian Organizations

(i) Such World Confessional Associations and such Ecumenical Organizations as may be designated by the Central Committee may be invited to send representatives to the sessions of the Assembly and of the Central Committee in a consultative capacity, in such numbers as the Central Committee shall determine.

(ii) Such constituent bodies of the International Missionary Council and such nation-wide councils of Churches as may be designated by the Central Committee may be invited to send representatives to the sessions of the Assembly and of the Central Committee in a consultative capacity, in such numbers as the Central Committee shall determine.

VIII. Amendments

The Constitution may be amended by a two-third majority vote of the Assembly, provided that the proposed amendment shall have been reviewed by the Central Committee, and notice of it sent to the constituent Churches not less than six months before the meeting of the Assembly. The Central Committee itself, as well as the individual Churches, shall have the right to propose such amendment.

IX. Rules and Regulations

The Assembly or the Central Committee may make and amend Rules and Regulations concerning the conduct of the Council's business, of its Committees and Departments, and generally all matters within the discharge of its task.

APPENDIX B

The Central Committee of the World Council of Churches

Elected at Amsterdam, 1948; Evanston, 1954; New Delhi, 1961

The years given after members' names indicate the dates of their election. As will be noted, some served more than one term. The list does not include substitutes or those appointed to fill vacancies.

Mr. Shiro Abe, *United Church of Christ,* Japan. 1961
Dr. Josue Cardoso d'Affonseca, *Methodist Church,* Brazil. 1948
Professor H. Aharonian, *Armenian Evangelical Church,* Lebanon. 1954
Bishop Alexis, *Russian Orthodox Church,* U.S.S.R. 1961
Professor Hamilcar Alivisatos, *Church of Greece,* Greece. 1948, 1954, 1961
Bishop S. F. Allison, *Church of England,* U.K. 1961
Rev. J. A. Do Amaral, *Methodist Church,* Brazil. 1954
Dr. Nicolaidis Ambrosios, *Orthodox Church,* Greece. 1948
Archbishop Athenagoras of Thyateira, *Patriarchate of Constantinople,* Turkey. 1954
Bishop Athenagoras, *Patriarchate of Constantinople,* Canada. 1961
Dr. A. S. Atiya, *Coptic Church,* Egypt. 1954
Dr. M. E. Aubrey, *Baptist Union,* U.K. 1948

Rev. Christian G. Baëta, *Presbyterian Church,* Ghana. 1961
Rev. James Baird, *Presbyterian Church,* New Zealand. 1948
Dr. James Chamberlain Baker, *Methodist Church,* U.S.A. 1948
Rev. Eric W. Baker, *Methodist Church,* U.K. 1954, 1961
Bishop Sante Uberto Barbieri, *Methodist Church,* Argentina. 1961
Bishop Tibor Bartha, *Reformed Church,* Hungary. 1961
Rev. Norman J. Baugher, *Church of Brethren,* U.S.A. 1961
Archbishop Leonard J. Beecher, *Anglican Church,* East Africa. 1961
Dr. G. K. A. Bell, *Church of England,* U.K. 1948, 1954
Mrs. F. O. Bennett, *Presbyterian Church,* New Zealand. 1954
Bishop Eivind Josef Berggrav, *Church of Norway,* Norway. 1948
Dr. S. F. H. J. Berkelbach van der Sprenkel, *Dutch Reformed Church,* Netherlands. 1948
Professor Hendrikus Berkhof, *Dutch Reformed Church,* Netherlands. 1954, 1961

Dr. Petru O. Bersell, *Evangelical Lutheran Church,* U.S.A. 1948, 1954
Rev. Hermann F. Binder, *Ausburgian Evangelical Church,* Rumania. 1961
Dr. Klaus von Bismarck, *Evangelical Church,* Germany. 1961
Dr. Eugene Carson Blake, *United Presbyterian Church,* U.S.A. 1954, 1961
Dr. Kathleen M. Bliss, *Church of England,* U.K. 1954, 1961
Rev. Vitaly Borovoy, *Russian Orthodox Church,* U.S.S.R. 1961
Rev. J. R. Boyd, *Presbyterian Church,* Ireland. 1954
Professor P. Bratsiotis, *Orthodox Church, Greece.* 1954
Rev. Gerhard Brennecke, *Evangelical Church,* Germany. 1961
Dr. Yngve Torgny Brilioth, *Church of Sweden,* Sweden. 1948, 1954
Dr. C. B. Brink, *Dutch Reformed Church,* South Africa. 1954
Mrs. Frank G. Brooks, *Methodist Church,* U.S.A. 1954
Rt. Hon. Ernest Brown, *Baptist Union,* U.K. 1948
Dr. George W. Buckner, Jr., *Disciples of Christ,* U.S.A. 1948, 1954
Bishop B. B. Burnett, *Anglican Church,* South Africa. 1961

Rev. Alfred Carleton, *United Church of Christ,* U.S.A. 1961
Bishop Jan Chabada, *Lutheran Church,* Czechoslovakia. 1954
Rev. J. Russell Chandran, *Church of South India,* India. 1961
Rt. Hon. Francis D. Charteris, *Church of Scotland,* U.K. 1961
Professor Pierre Chazel, *Reformed Church,* France. 1948
Dr. W. Y. Chen, *Anglican Church,* China. 1948
Dr. Ivy Chou, *Methodist Church,* U.S.A. 1961
Dr. James H. Cockburn, *Church of Scotland,* U.K. 1948
Rev. Norman H. F. Cocks, *Congregational Union,* Australia. 1961
Dr. Leslie E. Cooke, *Congregatioanl Church,* U.K. 1948
Archimandrite James Coucouzis, *Orthodox Church,* Turkey. 1954
Professor G. A. Coulson, *Methodist Church,* U.K. 1961
Commissioner Alfred G. Cunningham, *Salvation Army,* U.K. 1948

Rev. Peter K. Dagadu, *Methodist Church,* West Africa. 1954
Dr. Edwin T. Dahlberg, *American Baptist Convention,* U.S.A. 1948
Rev. G. P. David, *Lutheran Church,* India. 1954
Rev. Leonard Dia y Granada, *United Evangelical Church,* Philippines. 1954
Dr. K. F. O. Dibelius, *Evangelical Church,* Germany. 1948
Dr. Angus Dun, *Protestant Episcopal Church,* U.S.A. 1948, 1954

Dr. A. Eeg-Olofsson, *Mission Covenant Church,* Sweden. 1954
Rev. Frank Engel, *Presbyterian Church,* Australia. 1961
Bishop Francis G. Ensley, *Methodist Church,* U.S.A. 1961
Professor Henri C. W. d'Espine, *Protestant Church Federation,* Switzerland. 1954, 1961

Dr. Geoffrey Francis Fisher, *Church of England,* U.K. 1954
Dr. Robert N. Flew, *Methodist Church,* U.K. 1948
Dr. Georges Florovsky, *Orthodox Church in North America,* U.S.A. 1948, 1954
Dr. Franklin Clark Fry, *United Lutheran Church,* U.S.A. 1948, 1954, 1961
Dr. H. Fuglsang-Damgaard, *Church of Denmark,* Denmark. 1948, 1954
Rev. Austin A. Fulton, *Presbyterian Church,* Ireland. 1961

Bishop Macario V. Ga, *Independent Church,* Philippines. 1961
Dr. Gustav Bernh Gerdener, *Dutch Reformed Church,* South Africa. 1948
Frederick William Gilpin, Esq., *Church of England,* U.K. 1948
Dr. William Goebel, *Evangelical and Reformed Church,* U.S.A. 1948

Canon S. L. Greenslade, *Church of England,* U.K. 1954
Kenneth G. Grubb, Esq., *Church of England,* U.K. 1948

Rev. Hans H. Harms, *Evangelical Lutheran Church,* Germany. 1961
Mrs. Lillian E. Harrington, *Presbyterian Church, U.S.,* U.S.A. 1948
Mr. B. J. Hartwell, *Congregational-Christian Church,* U.S.A. 1954
Bishop Ignatius Hazim, *Orthodox Patriarchate of Antioch,* Lebanon. 1961
Professor V. Herntrich, *Lutheran Church,* Germany. 1954
Dr. Robert A. Hilts, *Anglican Church,* Canada. 1948
Dr. Ivan Lee Holt, *Methodist Church,* U.S.A. 1948
Dr. Douglas Horton, *Congregational-Christian Church,* U.S.A. 1948
Dr. Josef L. Hromadka, *Evangelical Church of Czech Brethren,* Czechoslovakia. 1948, 1954, 1961
Archbishop Gunnar A. E. Hultgren, *Church of Sweden,* Sweden. 1961

Archbishop Iakovos, *Ecumenical Patriarchate (Orthodox),* U.S.A. 1961
Rev. Ioann (Wendland), *Russian Orthodox Church,* Berlin. 1961
Professor Basil Ioannidis, *Church of Greece,* Greece. 1954, 1961

Dr. Joseph H. Jackson, *National Baptist Convention,* U.S.A. 1954, 1961
Bishop Jacobus, *Ecumenical Patriarchate (Philadelphia),* Turkey. 1954
Bishop Petrus J. Jans, *Old Catholic Church,* Netherlands. 1961
Mrs. Ernest Jarvis, *Church of Scotland,* U.K. 1954
G. Vedanayagam Job, Esq., *Presbyterian Church,* India. 1948
Bishop John, *Orthodox Church of North America,* U.S.A. 1954, 1961
Dr. Mar Thoma Juhanon, *Mar Thoma Syrian Church,* India. 1948
Dr. W. W. Judd, *Anglican Church,* Canada. 1954
Archbishop Justin (Moisesco), *Orthodox Church,* Rumania. 1961

Bishop Zolton Kaldy, *Evangelical Lutheran Church,* Hungary. 1961
Dr. Enkichi Kan, *Anglican Church,* Japan. 1954
Miss Frances H. Kapitzky, *United Church of Christ,* U.S.A. 1961
Dr. Alphons Koechlin, *Protestant Federation,* Switzerland. 1948
Archimandrite Parthenios Koinidis, *Orthodox Church,* Egypt. 1954
Archbishop Chrysostomos Konstantinidis, *Ecumenical Patriarchate,* Turkey. 1961
Professor Jerome Kotsonis, *Orthodox Church,* Greece. 1954, 1961
Rev. Jean Kotto, *Evangelical Church,* Cameroun. 1961
Rev. Michio Kozaki, *Church of Christ,* Japan. 1948, 1954
S'Aye Mya Kyaw, *Burma Baptist Union,* Burma. 1961

Rev. Hilmer J. Lazarus, *Evangelical Lutheran Church,* India. 1948
Principal Robert B. Lew, *Methodist Church,* Australia. 1954
Mr. Kenneth T. Li, *Church of Christ,* China. 1948
Bishop Arthur Lichtenberger, *Protestant Episcopal Church,* U.S.A. 1961
Bishop J. E. R. Lilje, *Evangelical Lutheran Church,* Germany. 1948, 1954, 1961
Mrs. Margit Lindstrom, *Church of Sweden,* Sweden. 1954
Dr. Ralph W. Lloyd, *United Presbyterian Church,* U.S.A. 1954
Rev. Ernest E. Long, *United Church,* Canada. 1961
Rev. E. Luka, *Coptic Church,* Egypt. 1948
Mr. Thomas C. Luke, *Anglican Church,* Sierra Leone. 1948

Dr. John A. Mackay, *Presbyterian Church,* U.S.A. 1948
Rev. Ezekiel E. Mahabane, *Methodist Church,* South Africa. 1961

Fr. Makary el Souriany, *Coptic Church,* Egypt. 1961
Dr. Charles Malik, *Orthodox Church,* Lebanon. 1954
Bishop Rajah Manikam, *Evangelical Lutheran Church,* India. 1961
Rev. John Marsh, *Congregational Union,* U.K. 1961
Bishop William C. Martin, *Methodist Church,* U.S.A. 1954
Rev. C. Mataheru, *Reformed Church,* Indonesia. 1954
Professor C. P. Mathew, *Mar Thoma Syrian Church,* India. 1961
Bishop James K. Mathews, *Methodist Church,* U.S.A. 1961
Dr. Pierre Maury, *Reformed Church,* France. 1954
Bishop G. J. F. May, *Augsburgian Evangelical Church,* Austria. 1948, 1954
Dr. Benjamin E. Mays, *National Baptist Convention,* U.S.A. 1948
Rev. Paul Mbende, *Baptist Union,* Cameroun. 1961
Dr. Hans O. Meiser, *Evangelical Church,* Germany. 1948
Bishop H. L. de Mel, *Church of India, Pakistan, Burma, and Ceylon,* Ceylon, 1954
Archbishop Meliton, *Ecumenical Patriarchate,* Turkey. 1961
Rev. James A. Millard, *United Presbyterian Church,* U.S.A. 1961
Mr. Francis P. Miller, *Presbyterian Church U.S.,* U.S.A. 1954
Mr. J. Irwin Miller, *Disciples of Christ,* U.S.A. 1961
Mr. Valentin G. Montes, *United Church of Christ,* Philippines. 1961
Dr. J. Earl Moreland, *Methodist Church,* U.S.A. 1948
Archbishop H. W. K. Mowll, *Anglican,* Australia. 1954
Bishop Reuben H. Mueller, *United Brethren Church,* U.S.A. 1961

Dr. Reuben E. Nelson, *American Baptist Convention,* U.S.A. 1954
Bishop Lesslie Newbigin, *Church of South India,* India. 1954
Dr. Algie I. Newlin, *Society of Friends,* U.S.A. 1948
Bishop D. W. Nichols, *Methodist Church,* U.S.A. 1954
Principal C. M. Nicholson, *United Church,* Canada. 1954
Dr. Martin Niemöller, *Evangelical Church,* Germany. 1948, 1954
Dr. Wilhelm Niesel, *Evangelical Reformed Church,* Germany. 1948, 1954, 1961
Archbishop Nikodim of Rostov, *Russian Orthodox Church,* U.S.S.R. 1961
Dr. Aimo T. Nikolainen, *Evangelican Lutheran Church,* Finland. 1954, 1961
Bishop Gottfried Noth, *Evangelical Lutheran Church,* Germany. 1954, 1961
Dr. Anders T. S. Nygren, *Church of Sweden,* Sweden. 1948

Dr. Rudolf Obermüller, *Evangelical German Synod,* Argentina. 1961
Bishop L. Ordass, *Lutheran Church,* Hungary. 1948
Bishop G. Bromley Oxnam, *Methodist Church,* U.S.A. 1954

Bishop Panteleimon, *Church of Greece,* Greece. 1948, 1954, 1961
Dr. Laszlo Pap, *Reformed Church,* Hungary. 1948, 1954
Mr. Charles C. Parlin, *Methodist Church,* U.S.A. 1954
Bishop C. Parthenios-Aris, *Orthodox Church,* Libya. 1961
Dr. Rajaiah D. Paul, *Church of South India,* India. 1954
Rev. Ernest A. Payne, *Baptist Union,* U.K. 1954, 1961
Professor Penayotides, *Orthodox Church,* Turkey. 1948
Rev. Korah Philipos, *Orthodox Syrian Church,* India. 1954, 1961
Rev. T. C. Poincenot, *Lutheran Church,* France. 1948, 1954
Dr. Liston Pope, *Congregational-Christian Church,* U.S.A. 1954
Rev. Basuki Probowinoto, *Christian Church of Mid-Java,* Indonesia. 1961
Dr. William Barrow Pugh, *Presbyterian Church U.S.A.,* U.S.A. 1948
Dr. Nathan M. Pusey, *Protestant Episcopal Church,* U.S.A. 1954, 1961

Rev. Titus Rasendrahasina, *London Missionary Society Synod,* Malagasy. 1961
Bishop Chandu Ray, *Church of India, Pakistan, Burma and Ceylon,* Pakistan. 1961
Bishop Richard A. Reeves, *Church of England,* U.K. 1948, 1954
Rev. Heinrich G. Renkewitz, *Moravian Church,* Germany. 1948
Dr. Andreas Rinkel, *Old Catholic Church,* Holland. 1948, 1954
Dr. Harold Roberts, *Methodist Church,* U.K. 1954
Dr. Alexander Rotti, *Protestant Church of Timor,* Indonesia. 1948
Dr. Fedor Ruppeldt, *Augsburgian Evangelical Church,* Czechoslovakia. 1948
Rev. C. D. Ryan, *Congregational Union,* Australia. 1954

Bishop John W. Sadiq, *Church of India, Pakistan, Burma and Ceylon,* India. 1961
Dr. Ilmari J. Salomines, *Evangelical Lutheran Church,* Finland. 1948
Rev. R. David Say, *Church of England,* U.K. 1961
Rev. Fredrik A. Schiotz, *American Lutheran Church,* U.S.A. 1961
Rev. Ernesto T. Schlieper, *Evangelical Lutheran Church,* Brazil. 1961
Dr. Henry F. Schuh, *American Lutheran Church,* U.S.A. 1954
Dr. Herbert G. Secomb, *Methodist Church,* Australia. 1948
Mr. Alexander Shishkin, *Russian Orthodox Church,* U.S.S.R. 1961
Bishop Roy H. Short, *Methodist Church,* U.S.A. 1961
Rev. Tunggul Sihombing, *Protestant Batak Church,* Indonesia. 1961
Rev. Kunnumpurath M. Simon, *Syrian Orthodox Patriarchate,* U.S.A. 1961
Commissioner W. G. Simpson, *Salvation Army.* U.K. 1954
Dr. Gordon A. Sisco, *United Church,* Canada. 1948
Rev. K. Sitompul, *Lutheran Church,* Indonesia. 1954
Dr. Samuel A. J. Sköld, *Mission Covenant Church,* Sweden. 1948
Bishop Johannes Smemo, *Church of Norway,* Norway. 1954
Bishop B. Julian Smith, *Christian Methodist Episcopal Church,* U.S.A. 1961
Rev. John C. Smith, *United Presbyterian Church,* U.S.A. 1961
Bishop E. C. Sobrepena, *United Church,* Philippines. 1954
Dr. Ralh W. Sockman, *Methodist Church,* U.S.A. 1948
Dr. John S. Stamm, *Evangelical Union Brethren,* U.S.A. 1948
Rev. F. G. A. Stenström, *Mission Covenant Church,* Sweden, 1961
Bishop Kaare Stoylen, *Church of Norway,* Norway. 1961
Bishop Bengt Sundkler, *Evangelical Church,* Tanganyika. 1961
Dr. Anna Canada Swain, *American Baptist Convention,* U.S.A. 1948, 1954
Dr. Jan Szerdua, *Augsburgian Evangelical Church,* Poland. 1948

Mr. Charles P. Taft, *Protestant Episcopal Church,* U.S.A. 1948
Dr. Murray Taylor, *Church of Scotland,* U.K. 1948
Dr. Reinhold von Thadden-Trieglaff, *Kirchentag,* Germany. 1948, 1954
Dr. Andrew Thakur Das, *United Church of North India and Pakistan,* India. 1954
Dr. Alexis Theodosios, *Orthodox Syrian Church,* India. 1948
Bishop Abuna Theophilos, *Orthodox Church,* Ethiopia. 1948, 1954, 1961
Mrs. Sadie M. Tillman, *Methodist Church,* U.S.A. 1961
Professor William S. Tindal, *Church of Scotland,* U.K. 1954, 1961
Bishop Andrew Y. Y. Tsu, *Anglican Church,* China. 1948
Dr. Edwin H. Tuller, *American Baptist Convention,* U.S.A. 1961

Rev. Evelyn C. Urwin, *Methodist Church,* U.K. 1948

Bishop Lajos Vetoe, *Lutheran Church,* Hungary. 1954

Dr. James E. Wagner, *Evangelical and Reformed Church,* U.S.A. 1954
Bishop W. J. Walls, *African Methodist Episcopal Zion Church,* U.S.A. 1948
Bishop Alwyn K. Warren, *Anglican Church,* New Zealand. 1954, 1961
Bishop I. S. Watkins, *Church of England,* U.K. 1954
Bishop Willy Westergaard-Madsen,*Church of Denmark,* Denmark. 1961
Rev. Charles Westphal, *Reformed Church,* France. 1961
Dr. Roy D. Whitehorn, *Presbyterian Church,* U.K. 1948
Archbishop Frank Woods, *Anglican Church,* Australia. 1961
Commissioner R. W. J. Woods, *Salvation Army,* U.K. 1961
Archbishop William L. Wright, *Anglican Church,* Canada. 1961
Mrs. B. R. Wyllie, *Methodist Church,* Australasia. 1961

Dr. M. R. Zigler, *United Brethren Church,* U.S.A. 1954

APPENDIX C

Constitution of the Commission on Faith and Order

Adopted at Amsterdam, 1948

Title

1. The Commission shall be called the Commission on Faith and Order of the World Council of Churches.

Meanings

2. In this Constitution:

The Commission means the above-named Commission on Faith and Order of the World Council of Churches.

The Working Committee means the Working Committee of the Commission on Faith and Order.

The Council means the above-named World Council of Churches.

The Assembly means the Assembly of the World Council.

The Central Committee means the Central Committee of the World Council.

Functions

3. The functions of the Commission are:

(i) To proclaim the essential oneness of the Church of Christ and to keep prominently before the World Council and the Churches the obligation to manifest that unity and its urgency for the work of evangelism.

(ii) To study questions of faith, order and worship with the relevant social, cultural, political, racial and other factors in their bearing on the unity of the Church.

(iii) To study the theological implications of the existence of the ecumenical movement.

(iv) To study matters in the present relationship of the Churches to one another which cause difficulties and need theological clarification.

(v) To provide information concerning actual steps taken by the Churches towards re-union.

4. All activities of the Commission shall be in accordance with the four principles of the Faith and Order Movement, viz.:

(i) Its main work is to draw Churches out of isolation into conference, in which none is to be asked to be disloyal to or to compromise its convictions, but to seek to explain them to others while seeking to understand their point of view. Irreconcilable differences are to be recorded as honestly as agreements.

(ii) Its conferences are to be conferences of delegates officially appointed by the Churches to represent them.

(iii) The invitation to take part in these conferences is addressed to all Christian Churches throughout the world which accept our Lord Jesus Christ as God and Saviour.

(iv) Only Churches themselves are competent to take actual steps towards re-union by entering into negotiations with one another. The work of the Movement is not to formulate schemes and tell the Churches what they ought to do, but to act as the handmaid of the Churches in the preparatory work of clearing away misunderstandings, discussing obstacles to re-union, and issuing reports which are submitted to the Churches for their consideration.

ORGANIZATION

5. (i) World Conferences on Faith and Order are to be held when main subjects are ready for submission to the Churches, and when, on recommendation of the Commission on Faith and Order, the Central Committee so decides.

(ii) The Commission on Faith and Order shall consist of eighty-five members appointed by the Assembly of the World Council, with power to nominate additional members up to the number of fifteen for appointment by the Central Committee, all these to hold office until the next Assembly (subject however to any revision advised by a World Conference on Faith and Order as hereinafter provided). At each Assembly the list of membership shall be revised in the light of recommendations made by the Commission. When a World Conference is held, it shall advise the Central Committee on any necessary revision of the membership of the Commission between that Conference and the next Assembly. In making appointments care shall be taken to secure the adequate geographical and confessional representation of Churches.

The Commission may include members of Churches which accept our Lord Jesus Christ as God and Saviour but are not members of the World Council.

Vacancies shall be filled by the Central Committee on the recommendation of the Commission.

Before appointments are made, steps shall be taken to ensure that the appointments proposed are acceptable to the Churches concerned.

(iii) The Commission shall normally meet every three years but may be called together at any time when major theological commission reports need to be reviewed by a larger body than the Working Committee.

(iv) The Commission shall nominate from its own members, for appointment by the Central Committee, a Working Committee of not more than twenty-two members with power to nominate not more than three additional members. The Working Committee shall normally meet annually and shall be responsible (a) for administration, (b) for directing study work and other activities of Faith and Order and (c) for co-operation with other agencies of the World Council.

Vacancies in the Working Committee shall be filled by the Working Committee itself from the membership of the Commission and submitted to the Central Committee for appointment.

(v) There shall be various theological commissions set up by the Commission or Working Committee. Theological commissions may include as members or consultants persons who are not members of the Commission.

MEETINGS OF THE COMMISSION

6. The Chairman of the Commission, or in his absence the Vice-Chairman, shall preside at meetings of the Commission. In the absence of these officers, the meeting shall elect its own Chairman. One-sixth of the total membership shall constitute a quorum.

7. The notices of the meetings shall be issued by the Secretary.

8. Members of the Commission can name substitutes to represent them at meetings at which they are unable to be present themselves.

9. On questions of Faith and Order the Commission shall not adopt any resolutions, but shall confine itself to recording for the information of the Churches such agreements and disagreements as are discovered.

10. Questions of procedure and the conduct of the business of the Commission shall be decided by a majority vote of those present and voting.

11. The Working Committee may, either at a meeting of the Commission or previously, determine the rules of procedure and of debate for the meeting.

12. Persons not being members of the Commission may be invited by the Chairman or the Secretary to be present and speak, but they cannot vote.

CHAIRMAN

13. The Chairman shall be elected by a majority of votes at a duly convened meeting of the Commission, on the nomination of the Working Committee.

14. The Chairman shall hold office for three years from the date of appointment, but shall be eligible for re-election.

15. In the event of the office of Chairman falling vacant by reason of resignation, incapacity or death, the Vice-Chairman shall act as Chairman of the Commission until such time as a meeting of the Commission can be called.

VICE-CHAIRMAN

16. A Vice-Chairman shall be elected by the Commission on the nomination of the Working Committee, shall hold office for three years, and shall be eligible for re-election.

THE SECRETARIAT

17. There shall be at least one Secretary who shall be a member of the staff of the Council employed for the work of the Commission on a full-time basis.

18. The Secretary or Secretaries shall be nominated by the Commission to the Central Committee.

19. It shall be the special responsibility of the Secretary to maintain full consultation and co-operation with the General Secretariat and with the other Departments of the Council, and particularly with the Study Department.

20. The salaries or honoraria to be paid to the Secretary or Secretaries shall be determined by the Working Committee and the officers of the Council in consultation.

The Working Committee

21. The Commission shall appoint the Chairman of the Working Committee.

22. Members of the Working Committee shall hold office until the next meeting of the Commission, when the list of membership shall be revised.

23. The Working Committee shall have power to act on behalf of the Commission in all matters where action is required before a meeting of the Commission can be convened.

24. The Working Committee shall meet at such times and places as the Chairman and the Secretary shall decide to be required for the performance of its duty.

25. The quorum for a meeting of the Working Committee shall be seven members present, of whom at least three must be elected members.

26. If at any time when it is inconvenient to convene a meeting the Chairman and Secretary shall decide that there is business needing an immediate decision by the Working Committee, it shall be permissible for them to obtain by post the opinions of its members and the majority opinion thus ascertained shall be treated as equivalent to the decision of a duly convened meeting.

The Department

27. The Chairman, the Vice-Chairman, Secretaries, Chairman of the Working Committee and the Chairmen of the Theological Commissions shall together be known as the Council's Faith and Order Department.

28. The Department shall be responsible for continuously carrying on the work of the Commission between meetings of the Commission and the Working Committee, both by (i) promoting the studies of the Theological Commissions and (ii) following all developments in the matter of the union of Churches and keeping all the Churches informed of these developments. It shall maintain full consultation and co-operation with the Study Department of the Council.

29. The Secretary shall be the only officer of the Commission employed by the Council on a full-time basis; the other members of the Department shall be persons giving part-time service to the Commission whilst being also actively engaged in the service of their own Churches.

The Theological Commissions

30. The work of the Theological Commissions shall be to prepare reports which may serve as the basis for discussion in the Commission, at the Assemblies of the World Council, or at Conferences on Faith and Order, on the subjects referred to them under paragraph 5 (v) above.

31. Each Theological Commission shall be composed of a Chairman, Vice-Chairman and Secretary with other members chosen for their special competence in the particular field of study and representing as wide a variety as possible of ecclesiastical traditions. The Chairman, Vice-Chairman and Secretary shall be appointed by the Commission, and they shall then select and appoint the other members in consultation with the Secretary.

The Budget

32. The Commission's financial year shall run from 1st January to 31st December.

33. An annual budget of expenditure shall be drawn up by the Secretary in consultation with the Finance Committee of the Council; it shall be submitted to the Working Committee for its approval and when so approved shall be submitted to the Council for final adoption. Copies shall then be sent to all members of the Commission.

34. The budget shall specify the amount to be allocated for the expenses of each Theological Commission, and each Theological Commission shall be responsible for deciding its manner of using its allocation within the limit prescribed in the budget.

Revision

35. Any amendment to this Consitution must be approved by the Assembly or Central Committee of the Council, but no amendment shall be valid which contravenes the provisions of paragraph 4 above or of this paragraph.

APPENDIX D

Notes of a Study on the Place of Women in the Ecumenical Movement

Oxford and Bossey, 1952-54

A

There is a deep conviction everywhere that if the message of the Church is to find a hearing . . . the Church must bear witness in its own life to the transforming power of Christ. This will mean a radical renewal of many aspects of Church life. One of the most significant factors in this renewal is the quality of men-women relationships.

Christ's teaching about the human personality and his attitude to woman have been as leaven deeply affecting the prevailing conceptions of the position of women and the relation of the sexes in family life and outside, though he never violently broke down the social customs. This liberating effect with regard to women has been repeated whenever the Gospel of Christ was brought to new lands; striking evidences of this are to be seen in the history of modern missions. Everywhere we find, however, that when the preaching of the Gospel loses its freshness and tends to be overshadowed by emphasis on the Law and when organized church-patterns are inclined to become static, this liberalizing power can no longer exercise dynamic force and old and new restraints regarding women emerge. In our day this leads to great tensions, emphasized by the anomalous position of the Church compared to that in the secular world.

The problem must be faced in its fundamental aspect: the full recognition of the equal value of joint responsibility of the two-fold human being: man-woman as members of the Church of Christ. The urgency of facing this fundamental problem cannot be over-stated, because only then can the questions arising around it, such as the place of women's organizations, women's participation in church government and at other policy-making levels, or even the complex questions of ordination of women, be solved.

Following this understanding of man-woman relationships, some issues that are of greatest significance for the renewal of the Church can be tackled, such as the strengthening of the sense of fellowship in church life. If anywhere, it is here that the Church must bear witness to Christ, the hope of the world for the millions that are in danger of breaking down with the strain of solitude and are in deep despair because of the lack of a sense of meaning in life and of true companionship. Modern man and woman can only find this in a community where there are no discriminations on grounds of sex, but the value of their fellowship is recognized. This is not only of significance for those for whom the message of the Church is new, but for the large group of those who are becoming more and more alienated from the Church to which they still nominally belong.

Another important issue is the full sharing of women in responsibility for the life of the Church. The power of women through all ages has been considerable, but it has nearly always been restricted to influence exercised indirectly, while not sharing direct responsibility. Unfortunately, this situation is preferred by many women, who need to learn to accept full responsibility and to take criticism. The bearing of responsibility being of the very essence of true human existence, the Church should not withhold this from woman in any realm, but open up opportunities for women to grow in responsible living and encourage them to enter into their heritage as full-grown partners with men in being children of God, equal in His sight and jointly called in His service.

A third issue concerns the family. A new conception as to the man-woman relationship, this very foundation of all human relations, cannot but radically affect the family, the living cell of society and the Church.

If Christ is the Hope of life, a new experience of his transforming power can never merely mean the defence of old values, but must contain the eager expectation of new richness. As a true partnership of man and woman, spiritually and intellectually, as well as physically and emotionally in dedicated freedom of both personalities is achieved, a renewal of family life on a higher level will undoubtedly ensue.

This will be of great significance for the Church in as far as the family is saved from considering itself as an end in itself, but is made more and more conscious of being the unit by the means of which its members are called to bring their joint contribution to the life and fellowship of the Church, witnessing to unity and wholeness, which are essential characteristics of the Church. It may be that this unity will be one of the means through which the Church of Christ will be led to a deeper knowledge of spiritual truth, which it cannot understand while abiding in divisions (I Corinthians iii, 1-4).

B

The call of God to the Christian is that he should live the whole of his life under God's commandment and by His grace. If men and women are called of God to obey Him in the whole life, then they have to examine what it means to be obedient in their own particular daily work.

Our purpose in this memorandum is to examine this general statement as it particularly affects women. . . .

There seems to us a certain confusion in Christian teaching about the calling of women. In much of church teaching there is the implicit assumption that the proper calling of a woman is to marriage. . . . By this is meant both the married state and the functions of occupations which are thought of as going with it—the service of husband, the care of a home and the upbringing and education of children. Thus the state of marriage and the occupations dependent on it are to a certain extent confused.

Marriage is a state to which God may call many women, and the churches rightly stress the supreme importance of marriage to the family, Church and society. But it seems to us that often the very urgency of the Church's teaching carries with it by implication the suggestion that the single state is a second-best, or incomplete, condition, to be made the best of in default of marriage. Such a view, even if it is only implied, is not only unjust: it is unscriptural and contrary to many of the traditions of the Church. In the

New Testament marriage and the single state are equally commended by St. Paul as pleasing to the Lord.

The Church brought into the world an entirely new attitude to marriage. It is not a biological and social necessity hallowed by religion, but a choice. It is a choice because there is an alternative choice in the single life which God approves and blesses equally with marriage. The presence in the Church of this alternative choice enters profoundly into the Christian conception of marriage. The recovery of a constructive emphasis on the Christian idea of the vocation of the single life—for men as well as for women—is necessary in Christian teaching today, the more so because popularisations of certain biological and psychological insights tend to create the impression that men are not complete human persons without sexual experience, nor women without child-bearing.

Marriage, at least in the West, is commonly followed by the making of a home by the married couple, and the woman then embarks upon her major occupations which will fill most of her time for most of her life—caring for a husband, keeping house and nurturing children.

The separate household following on each marriage with one woman as wife, another as housekeeper, is a bourgeois phenomenon, very largely the result of social and economic conditions. In the West it is often supposed that a new home following on every marriage is natural, right and necessary. In the East and Africa, where patriarchal or extended family systems prevail, a new marriage does not necessarily create a new home, nor does a wife immediately become a house-wife, nor are children brought up solely by their parents. The small family unit of the West has been in a particular culture and epoch the means whereby certain Christian insights on marriage and family have been given living form. Here man and wife can develop a mutuality of loving service, each fulfilling the other: here also Christ's teaching when he set a child in the midst can be fulfilled. But it is not the only possible form of family living or wifely occupation. . . .

The occupation of homemaking and housekeeping is not only a derivative from marriage. Homes are made in modern society by single women living alone (less rarely by single men)—by friends or sisters, by mothers and daughters. The personal satisfactions which homemaking offers should be recognized by the Church and society as legitimate hopes for the unmarried woman. . . . Society often refuses to grant her any claims on behalf of her home—her chances of getting a home in a municipal housing estate or block of flats are very slender, though her presence there might be of great benefit.

That "a home of one's own" is the ideal makes the married woman without a home conscious that she belongs to the dispossessed. In Christian propaganda "marriage and the home" are spoken of in one breath as though they belonged together. Though they may . . . ideally, they do not warrant the association in a vast and growing number of cases. A young married woman often goes to work since there is not room for two housewives in her mother's or her mother-in-law's home. Modern society, when this ideal of a home of one's own is frustrated, offers no alternative recourse. . . .

The occupation of the woman in the home . . . is . . . comparable with other occupations: a man who is a widower or bachelor may hire a woman to perform these functions . . . buying, cooking, and serving food, keeping the house clean, seeing that clothes and furnishings are washed and kept in repair, keeping the house supplied with the necessities of living. The wife usually performs such tasks, with or without help. What opportunities for Christian witness does such an occupation offer, and what temptations?

The work is largely under the woman's control, she can create a routine and make out of her work an orderly context for her own and others' lives. In the course of her work she enters into numbers of personal relationships with neighbors, tradespeople, et al. . . . House-wives are the buyers in the community: their spending power and . . . potential influence in industry and commerce are enormous, but seldom realized. . . . [They] are the great supporters of and workers for our churches. . . . The house-wife can nearly always manage to give time, whether in service or by turning her time into produce. . . . It would not be too sweeping to say that thousands of local churches keep afloat financially . . . because the occupation of house-wife provides . . . the possibility of turning time and materials to creative use. . . .

[Temptations include] individualism, shutting out other claims . . . love of possessions . . . competitiveness . . . appearance . . . social and political irresponsibility. . . .

We would strongly emphasize the need for a specific act of witness on the part of Christian house-wives . . . to a simpler mode of life, with more emphasis on worship . . . service to the community, personal friendship, the cultivation of the mind through reading and of the imagination through the arts. . . .

The work of women in society [is] in urgent need of objective study based on facts, with Christian insights. . . .

Over an area containing at least five-sixths of the world's population . . . women are engaged in primary production in fields, gardens and markets, and their work is not terminated by marriage. . . . Ecumenical conversations ought to help Westerners to see the question of women's work in a vaster perspective. . . . While they cherish the possibility of deep personal relationships between husband and wife, parents and children, which the separate family home provides, they should perhaps realize that the Western pattern is not the only good life and that other patterns may be also made a vehicle of Christian living.

The work of women has been one of the main agencies to transform certain areas of society in recent years. Education and medicine could hardly have developed as they have without . . . women teachers and nurses. The social services . . . draw largely on the service of women. Teaching, medicine and social work . . . supplement the home; and to the weak, unfortunate or feckless family they may mean restoration, or at least the rescue of the children. All this is, or can be, a profoundly Christian labor.

But women have also been swept into industry and commerce. . . . Labour [there] has . . . raised the standard of living of the poorest. . . .

It is necessary . . . to look . . . at the personal aspects of women's work. Some . . . find deep . . . satisfaction in work: many like it not for the work itself, but for the companionship that goes with it. The vast majority . . . work . . . from economic necessity. . . . Most are employed in occupations offering little scope for advancement. . . . The average wage of all women . . . does not reach the average of unskilled male labour. Several women's occupations . . . are purely auxiliary and . . . make possible . . . certain male occupations. . . . There could scarcely be business directors and managers . . . if there were not stenographers, filing clerks and telephone operators, the overwhelming majority of whom are women. . . . Young women look on work, with rare exceptions, as a stop-gap . . .

till marriage comes. . . . The woman who does not marry or who returns to work as a widow reaps a bitter harvest from this indifference (of the young woman waiting for marriage and not participating in collective action which looks to improving the workers' lot). . . . Women's work is often characterized by amateurishness. . . . There seems to be also a large element of strain in a woman's attitude to her work, partly induced by the fact that in some professions she has to be far better than a man to be thought as good. . . . She is often surrounded by a certain amount of suspicion and jealousy. But part of the difficulty at least lies in the lack of a full acceptance of work as a God-given task. . . .

Since it is in doubt during her early years whether a woman will work all her life or marry, she ought . . . to be educated to . . . fulfill either vocation. . . .

We should like to see emphasized in church teaching . . . that both man and woman are called to the task not only of replenishing the earth but of subduing it and making it plentiful. Woman's task . . . is not merely indirect through man, it is also direct. . . .

God intended men and women to live in relationship with each other, not only in marriage of one man to one woman, but in the social task of humanity. This can never be achieved by segregating the sexes. . . .

Good work depends on good relationships. Relations between the sexes bring both difficulties and enrichment. While for the married woman life is mainly centered in one relationship . . . the single woman works with many men in a comradeship of work. Too many men are oblivious to any demand of God in relationships at work with women, and blind to the richness that can come to their work from women's particular insights. Christians, both men and women, have a calling to witness to the reality of comradeship in work and genuine friendship. . . .*

* The foregoing notes are extracted from a mimeographed Study Report issued at the Evanston Assembly, 1954.

APPENDIX E

Letters Exchanged by Indian Young Communists and the World Youth Conference at Kottayam, 1952-1953

. . . We extend to you a very hearty welcome. We welcome this conference of World Christian Youth in the hope that your deliberations will help the Christian youth of this land to face the innumerable problems confronting them. It is our hope that you will not only discuss the problems confronting Christian youth but also declare in unequivocal and concrete terms your attitude to these problems:

First, there is the problem of war and peace. The [Conference] study pamphlet on the problem of war and peace states, "To allege that the conflict can permanently be resolved in history is to assume a millennium by God's intervention, something theology may hope for, but which the layman's understanding can scarcely permit him to expect. At best, the lay Christian may expect a gradual evolution to a point where his intelligence requires structures to restrain aggression, and cultivate the confidence which will make it less frequent and finally unlikely." Accepting this approach to the problem of war, it follows that the Christian has the difficult duty to help the preservation of the structures that are created to restrain aggression and to promote better understanding between the peoples of the world. It is to further this cause of opposing war and defending peace, of preserving structures like the United Nations Organization meant to restrain aggression that the World Peace Movement has been carrying on a ceaseless campaign. We hope your Conference will consider the following declaration of the Asian Peace Conference which met at Peking:

"The peoples of the Asian and Pacific regions firmly adhere to a common aim, namely: to oppose war and defend peace.

"We re-affirm our conviction that countries with different social systems and ways of life can co-exist in peace and mutually beneficial co-operation.

"We realize keenly that peace cannot be awaited, it must be won. In order to win lasting peace, we must unite and wage tireless struggles.

"The peace of this area and the world demands:

"Immediate peace in Korea on a just and reasonable basis, an end to wars in Viet Nam, Malaya and other regions, and the withdrawal of all foreign troops from these regions.

"A halt to the revival of Japanese militarism; conclusion of a genuine peace treaty between Japan and the countries concerned; an establishment of an independent, democratic, free and peaceful Japan.

"Opposition to the intervention in the internal affairs of one country by another and encroachment on the sovereignty of one country by another.

"Defense and achievement of national independence.

"Opposition to blockade and embargo. Promotion of economic co-operation and cultural exchange between the countries on the basis of equality and mutual benefit.

"Prohibition of incitement to war, opposition to racial discrimination and protection of women's rights and promotion of child welfare.

"Speedy conclusion of a Five Power Peace Pact, arms reduction and a ban on the use of atomic, bacteriological and chemical weapons and other weapons of mass murder."

If the cultural achievements of long centuries are not to be wiped out, if life is not to become a bestial struggle for existence, if the life of man is to retain any elements of humanity, the orgy of bloodshed in Korea, Viet-Nam, Malaya and other countries must be stopped. The grim prospects of a World War imperils the life of every man, woman and child. It is our earnest wish that you will declare support to the struggle waged by persons of goodwill all over the world to dispel dark clouds of war and clear man's horizon for the dawn of universal friendship and lasting peace.

Second, there is the problem of national independence. As the sponsors of your Conference rightly admit, "Asia is today no longer the changeless East, symbol of all that is ancient and static. It has today the power to play a decisive role in world affairs and can throw its weight on the side of peace or catastrophe. The struggle for peace is inextricably bound with the Asian people's struggle for national independence. In many countries of Asia the struggle to win national liberation and to preserve national independence is being subjected to foreign intervention. National sovereignty and territorial integrity are being violated by the acquisition of military bases and the imposition of military alliances. The national wealth of many lands is being plundered and their economic resources diverted to serve plans for aggressive foreign wars. In countries that are being compelled to join the arms drive high prices and inflation have adversely affected the people's living standards. Heroic struggles for national liberation are being waged in Malaya, Viet Nam and a number of other countries. Even in countries like India which claim to have achieved independence the economy is still strangled by foreign interests with the result that a large majority of the people are driven into unemployment and poverty. In addition to the already existing foreign interests there is the new American infiltration into India and other Asian countries under the cover of "aid programmes."

Mighty liberation movements are growing in almost all countries of Asia for national liberation and against foreign intervention. It is unfortunate that blind anti-communism has landed some Christians in the camp of the oppressors. We are unable to see how differences with communists on the basis of basic Marxian philosophy will make a Christian take the fatal decision of betraying the national liberation movement of his country. It is our hope that as Christians concerned for economic and social justice in the modern world you will declare support to these growing national liberation movements. Further, the stories of barbaric repression including wholesale murders, wiping out of villages, starving freedom fighters to death, that are coming out of Malaya, Kenya and the colonial countries are a challenge to the Christian conscience and we expect you to come out in open condemnation of the reign of terror that is unleashed by the imperialists.

[To this letter of the communist leaders the Conference Committee replied as follows:]

We thank you for your letter and are grateful for the friendly interest you show in the success of this Conference and for helping us to confront some of the vital issues which face the world and ourselves as young Christians. We are glad you share our hopes about the Conference.

I. We share with you the most urgent concern for peace. The programme of the Conference includes five commissions. The theme of one of these is "Jesus Christ and the Search for Personal Freedom and Social Justice," and of another "Christ in a World of Tensions." Both of these commissions cover a large field and take into consideration the factors you mention, together with others.

With regard to peace, there is not a single person here who does not abhor the tendencies towards war which appear in our world. The prospect of a conflict in which weapons of mass destruction might be used appals us and we will do everything in our power to reduce international tensions and to contribute towards a just solution of international problems. For this purpose at this Conference we must understand more deeply what are the causes of conflicts, what is at stake in them, and what action we can take.

In this connection, we have to ask a question about the sponsors of the World Peace Movement whose Peking resolutions you quote. The Indian peace plan, sponsored by a country taking an independent stand in international affairs and accepted at United Nations Organization by representatives of fifty-four nations, we believe, would have led to "immediate peace in Korea on a just and reasonable basis." Why, then, did the sponsors of the Peace Movement not openly press the governments of China, the United Soviet States of Russia and the few countries voting against the plan to accept it? Does not the doubt arise whether the Peace Movement desires above all a peace taking account of the interests of all parties concerned? And does not the further doubt arise that the Peace Movement is not simply a peace movement but is also involved as an instrument in a struggle of power politics?

II. You have rightly raised the question of movements for national and social liberation and for the preservation of such freedoms where they have been gained. As young people, this note strikes a very sympathetic chord in us. We realize that millions in different parts of the world until now submerged have been "awakened to a new sense of dignity and historical mission" (Bangkok statement), and are sure that they should not be betrayed. It is the duty of us all, from whatever country we come, to understand and assist the fulfillment of the legitimate human hopes in this revolutionary urge.

But here we must face a further question. Is not the possibility of the betrayal of these hopes more complex than your letter suggests? They may be betrayed by colonialism and economic pressure from outside. May they not also be betrayed from within by people who do not recognize the dignity of the human person? or by people who act as if states and societies were ends in themselves and as if there were no higher law over them, in which human dignity and social justice are grounded? Such action has already led to new oppressions of the human person in totalitarian collectivisms.

And does not the struggle between great powers form a context within which men strive for national and social liberation? If so, we cannot isolate entirely any particular national situation from its international setting and from the possibility that the big powers may use for their own purposes the hopes and fears of peoples in Asia and elsewhere. These points, concerning the inherent claims of the dignity of the human person as the basis of any proper social order and concerning the international struggle for power affecting every national situation, are so fundamental that it is a surprise to find no mention of them in your letter.

A further question arises about true national freedom and independence. In a world where there can be no power vacuum, national freedom can be genuine only within a framework of interdependence. In the present international situation an attempt to work out true independence, understood in this way, is always in danger of breaking down into new forms of domination. This is true wherever weaker nations are associated with stronger, on any side of the power struggle. Therefore, we are anxious to support such organs as the United Nations Organization which seek to hold international relations within a structure of law. In this connection we ask ourselves: Is it not the duty of nations having large resources to assist others with less towards a greater fulness of life? And are there not methods of doing this without exploitation and loss of national dignity? (Note: Incidentally, we note your report of Dr. J. C. Kumarappa's opinion about the effects on India of United States aid to national community projects. Is it not worth mentioning that this issue is at least debatable and that Pandit Nehru, second to none in his work for national independence, has made a very different judgment?)

III. In all these matters we have to consider the role of the Church. The Church, of course, while never making itself into a political party, must speak and act without fear and in terms of God's judgment, mercy and love. This means that the Church is always responsible for bringing all parties in political life to face the authority of God. In certain circumstances parties strive about the means towards ends upon which they agree. This is a technical choice on which the Church is not competent to judge. In other circumstances there is no such agreement. Party strife is not only about the means to agreed ends, but also about those very ends. Then the Church is bound to judge against any party whose understanding of human life in society conflicts radically with that given in the Christian revelation. Certainly the Church must be ready to learn at all times from those whom she finds herself compelled to oppose, but can she keep silent if any party through its practice or its ideology threatens human dignity as she understands it?

It seems that on this matter your letter is not clear, for on the one hand you recommend us to give precise answers and clearly to take sides, and on the other you criticise the action of some of the bishops in Travancore at the last election. We do not know enough of the facts of the situation to which you refer in Travancore, but might it not be that the bishops were constrained to speak in order to clarify the true purposes of society? In any case, we acknowledge that the Church throughout the world has often defended vested interests and failed to speak out clearly in defense of the oppressed and the victims of injustice. Yet we strongly believe that there are signs that the Church is awakening to her true task through repentance and a new response to the claims of her Lord, to whom belongs sovereignty over the whole world. We hope that this Conference will make its contribution towards this renewal.

We thank you for your greetings and hope that what we have said here may be useful in your own further thought about these issues.*

* The foregoing exchange of letters appeared in *The Ecumenical Press,* a mimeographed bulletin circulated among the churches.

APPENDIX F

Constitution of the Committee of the Youth Department

Adopted at Evanston, 1954

1. Powers of the Committee

The Youth Department Committee will have the power to initiate and administer policy and program. This committee will be responsible to the Central Committee of the World Council of Churches.

2. Membership of the Committee

The voting members of the Youth Department Committee will be not more than thirty-five in number. They shall be elected by the Assembly of the World Council or its appropriate organ.

3. Principles of Nomination

In order that the structure of the Youth Department Committee may correspond as nearly as possible to the structure of the World Council as a whole, in the process of selecting the members of the Committee due regard shall be given to those factors which govern the allocation of places in the Assembly of the World Council, namely, numerical size, adequate confessional representation and adequate geographical distribution.

4. Methods of Nomination and Appointment or Election

a. Committee Members

(i) The member churches of the World Council, either singly or at their option in confessional or regional groups, will submit nominations for the membership of the Youth Department Committee. Nominations may include Youth executives as well as young people taking a leading part in Christian youth activities.

(ii) The Youth Department Committee may add to this list of nominations other names submitted by national and/or regional Christian councils which are constituent bodies of the International Missionary Council, especially from those churches which are members of these Councils even though they are not members of the World Council.

(iii) In case any important geographical area would be still left unrepresented, the Youth Department Committee may add further nominations.

(iv) The out-going Youth Department Committee, after reviewing the full list of nominations thus compiled, shall make its recommendations to the electing body, taking into full consideration the principles set out in Section 3 above.

b. Representatives of the World Christian Youth Organizations: Appointed by Their Respective Organizations
c. Experts: Invited by the Youth Department Committee
d. Staff: Appointed by the World Council after Consultation with the Youth Department Committee
e. The General Secretary of the World Council (ex officio)

5. Composition of Committee

At the time of election of the Committee, at least one-third of its voting members must be under the age of twenty-seven, and at least another third must be under the age of thirty-two. The Committee will also take particular account of the need to secure adequate representation of (a) the two sexes, and (b) laymen, and of the need for continuity in the membership of the Committee.

6. Term of Service

(i) The Youth Department Committee will serve normally for three years, and in no case for more than five years.

(ii) Members of the out-going Committee will be eligible for re-election, subject only to the rule concerning age distribution on the Committee given in Section 5 above.

7. Officers of the Committee

The Youth Department Committee will nominate its own officers for appointment by the appropriate organ of the World Council.

8. Meetings of the Committee

(i) The Committee shall meet normally at least once a year, and the meetings should be held as far as possible in different continents in turn. Time and place of meeting should be so arranged that the Committee can meet in connection with world gatherings of Christian Youth.

(ii) Where any member of the Committee is unable to attend, an alternate approved by the Committee may take his place, provided that in no case is the Committee responsible for the traveling expenses of the alternate.

(iii) There shall be an Administrative Committee that will meet from time to time, composed of the staff and officers of the Youth Department, together with as many as the Youth Department Committee shall elect.

(iv) The Administrative Committee will fill all vacancies on the Youth Department Committee, with the consent of the World Council Central Committee.

9. Consultation with Regional Conferences

(i) The Youth Department Committee will take advantage of such occasions as (a) representative regional conferences, or (b) World Conferences of Christian Youth, to consult with such larger and internationally more representative groups regarding all important points of policy, nominations for the membership of the Committee, etc.

(ii) The Church Youth delegations to the World Conferences of Christian Youth should be so selected and prepared to be able, if it is practicable, to serve as an "Assembly of Church Youth" which could consult with the Youth Department Committee and advise on the development of the Department's work.

10. Amendments to the Constitution

Subject to the final approval of the appropriate authority of the World Council, this constitution may be amended by decision of the Committee.

APPENDIX G

Regulations Governing the Commission of the Churches on International Affairs*

Adopted at Evanston, 1954

1. Name

The Commission shall be called Commission of the Churches on International Affairs, Commission des Églises pour les Affaires Internationales, Kommission der Kirchen für Internationale Angelegenheiten.

2. Parent Bodies

The Commission is jointly constituted by and is the joint agent of the World Council of Churches and the International Missionary Council.

3. Aims

The general responsibility of the Commission is to serve the churches and councils which are members of the World Council of Churches and the International Missionary Council as a source of stimulus and knowledge in their approach to international problems, as a medium of common counsel and action, and as their organ in formulating the Christian mind on world issues, and in bringing that mind effectively to bear upon such issues. More particularly, it shall be the aim of the Commission:

I. To call the attention of churches to problems especially claimant upon the Christian conscience at any particular time and to suggest ways in which Christians may act effectively upon these problems, in their respective countries and internationally.

* Note: This is a lengthy instrument, but its inclusion is deemed necessary because of the light it throws upon an important sphere of the activity of the World Council of Churches. The Commission of the Churches on International Affairs enters the wider field of political issues, in the name of the Councils (World and International Missionary), where its actions are exposed to criticism, so much so that its establishment was regarded by some of the churches with serious misgivings. A knowledge of how it is constituted, of what it may and may not do, and of the procedures prescribed for its work is certainly essential to a true appraisal of the World Council of Churches. (See the section on the Commission of the Churches on International Affairs in the account of the Second Assembly for discussion of questions which are raised about this phase of ecumenical organization and activity.)

II. To discover and declare Christian principles with direct relevance to the inter-relations of nations, and to formulate the bearing of these principles upon immediate issues.

III. To encourage in each country and area and in each church represented in the parent bodies the formation of organisms through which the consciences of Christians may be stirred and educated as to their responsibilities in the world of nations.

IV. To gather and appraise materials on the relationships of the churches to public affairs, including the work of various churches and church councils in these fields and to make this material available to the churches represented in the parent bodies.

V. To study selected problems of international justice and world order, including economic and social questions, and to make the results of such study widely known among all the churches.

VI. To assign specific responsibilities and studies to committees or special groups, and to claim for them the assistance of persons especially expert in the problems under consideration.

VII. To organize conferences of church leaders of different nations.

VIII. To represent the parent bodies in relations with international bodies such as the United Nations and related agencies.

In particular, the Commission should maintain such contacts with these bodies as will assist in:

(a) the progressive development and codification of international law and the progressive development of supranational institutions;

(b) the encouragement of respect for and observance of human rights and fundamental freedoms; special attention being given to the problem of religious liberty;

(c) the international regulation of armaments;

(d) the furtherance of international economic co-operation;

(e) acceptance by all nations of the obligation to promote to the utmost the well-being of dependent peoples, including their advance toward self-government and the development of their free political institutions;

(f) the promotion of international social, cultural, educational and humanitarian enterprises.

IX. To concert from time to time with other organizations holding similar objectives in the advancement of particular ends.

4. Membership

The Commission shall consist of a number of Commissioners to be determined from time to time by the parent bodies, including among them the President, Vice-Presidents if appointed, Chairman, Director, Treasurer of the Commission, the General Secretary of the International Missionary Council, the General Secretary of the World Council of Churches, and one representative each, nominated by such ecumenical agencies as are named by the parent bodies.

5. Commissioners

On the nomination of the Executive Committee, Commissioners shall be appointed by the parent bodies for a period of three years with due regard to area representation and that of ecumenical organizations, as the parent bodies shall from time to time determine.

For the purpose of appointing any Commissioner, the Chairman shall consult with the Director and such general inter-church councils or representative church committees as the parent bodies may recommend as appropriate, and in the light of such consultation he shall determine what area or areas or what ecumenical organization the Commissioner is to represent, and shall select a person competent to represent the area or areas concerned, and shall, if the person so selected is acceptable to both parent bodies, and willing to serve, proceed to recommend him to the Executive Committee for nomination.

The duties of a Commissioner shall be:

(a) To correspond with the officers of the Commission, drawing their attention to matters which, in his view, should occupy their attention and advising them of the relevant data.

(b) To co-operate with the recognized local inter-church councils, or church agencies and committees in educating public opinion or in making representations to authorities on matters in the international sphere of concern to the Christian conscience.

(c) To attend or to be represented by an alternate at duly convened meetings of the Commission.

6. Representatives

Such world confessional associations and ecumenical organizations as may be determined by the officers of the Commission shall be invited to send one representative each to meetings of the Commission and to enlarged meetings of the Executive Committee, in a consultative capacity, provided that the Executive Committee may always meet in a session of its own members.

7. Meetings of the Commission

The Commission shall meet as often as the Executive Committee shall convene it.

8. Officers

The officers of the Commission shall be President, Vice-Presidents if appointed, Chairman, Director, Treasurer, and such other officers as may be deemed necessary, to be elected by the Commission subject to the approval of the parent bodies. It shall be the duty of the Chairman and the Director, as administrative officers, to carry on the work of the Commission in accordance with its aims and subject to the direction of the Executive Committee.

9. Executive Committee

(a) The Executive Committee shall consist of the officers, acting ex officio, together with the General Secretary of each of the parent bodies and not more than ten members of the Commission in addition. In the absence of either of the General Secretaries he may be represented by an alternate, with the right to vote.

Provided that the allocation of seats on the Executive Committee may be varied by a majority of votes at any meeting of the Commission, but so that the parent bodies shall always be entitled to a minimum of one seat each.

(b) Members of the Executive Committee shall be elected by the Commission and shall hold office for a period of three years from the date of their appointment, but shall be eligible for re-election.

(c) In the event of a vacancy occurring through death or resignation, the Executive Chairman may appoint a member to fill the vacant seat until the next meeting of the Commission. At such meeting the person appointed shall retire, but shall be eligible for re-appointment.

(d) The Executive Committee at a full meeting may approve an announcement proposed to be made on behalf of the Commission on any matter within its Aims, provided such an announcement is indorsed by a majority of those present, and that the majority includes the representatives of the parent bodies.

(e) The Executive Committee shall hold a full meeting at least once a year at a place and time to be determined by the Chairman in consultation with the President. A minimum notice of one month shall be given of meetings, except in cases of emergency.

(f) Any five members of the Executive Committee, of whom at least one shall be a representative of one or other of the parent bodies, may require a meeting to be convened for any purpose within the Aims of the Commission and the Chairman shall forthwith convene a meeting with due notice of the purpose of it.

(g) The members of the Executive Committee may name alternates to attend full meetings of the Committee, provided at least a fortnight's notice of the intention to do so and the name of the alternate is given to the Chairman and the Chairman approves. Such alternates are entitled to vote.

(h) The quorum for full meetings of the Executive Committee shall be one-quarter of its members.

10. The Budget

(a) The Commission's financial year shall run from 1st January to 31st December.

(b) The Commission may:

(i) Request and receive grants-in-aid from either or both of the parent bodies.

(ii) Request and receive with the knowledge and consent of the parent bodies, subscriptions and donations from corporate bodies and foundations, and individuals.

(iii) Request and receive legacies, provided that no conditions are attached which are incompatible with its Aims.

(c) The Commission shall operate on the basis of a single budget. Its expenditures shall be kept within the total guarantees of pledged support. The accounts of the Commission shall be audited annually.

11. Contact with the Churches

A. *National or Regional "Committees"*

1. In the formation of national or regional "committees" as required by Aim III, the procedure shall be as follows:

(a) Enquiry shall be made of the parent bodies whether there is a collective church council of a church body recognized as generally representative by one of the parent bodies.

(b) It shall be ascertained by the officers of the Commission whether such a council or body possesses or is ready to establish a department or committee dealing with international affairs, and if so the Commission shall recognize that department or committee as a national or regional committee as implied by Aim I, provided that it is ready to accept the responsibility therein implied.

(c) Provided no action is possible under (b) above, the officers of the Commission may, in consultation with collective church councils or, in the absence of such collective church councils, with local church leaders, (1) designate a correspondent and (2) proceed to encourage the formation of national or regional committees.

2. The duties of a National or Regional Committee are:

(a) To promote the Aims of the Commission of the Churches on International Affairs in its own territory.

(b) To interest local churches in the significance of the work of the Commission of the Churches on International Affairs and the importance of a Christian approach to international affairs.

(c) To draw the attention of national governments or other national entities to representations purporting to advance a Christian view on any problem within its Aims, including any problem in the field of Human Rights. The Commission shall communicate on such matters with the National or Regional Committee.

(d) The National or Regional Committee shall decide by whom and on behalf of what local organization a representation shall be made.

Provided that, if a representation be made in the name of a national or regional committee of the Commission, it shall confine itself to the immediate question under consideration, and the Commission be not committed to the endorsement of any general principles, except in so far as it has previously authorized them.

B. *Circulating Materials*

In circulating materials to Commissioners, national or regional committees, and other church bodies as prescribed in Aim IV of the Charter, the officers shall proceed as follows:

(a) They may circulate material direct or through any office of the Commission to Commissioners, and to the Secretary and/or Chairman of a National or Regional Committee or a correspondent.

(b) They may act similarly in regard to the members of a local committee subject to the permission of its Chairman.

(c) They may act similarly in regard to the constituent members of the parent bodies or their duly appointed representatives. By arrangement with world confessional bodies, circulation may proceed through their offices.

(d) In circulating materials to other individuals or organizations in any country, they will normally proceed in consultation with the Chairman of the national or regional committee, or, if such does not exist, with the Chairman of any church council or committee regarded by one or the other of the parent bodies as generally representative and responsible.

Provided that in any country where the Commission maintains its own office, the officer in charge may require that the distribution of all materials be handled through him.

(e) Where correspondence with individuals is directed to important matters, the Chairman of the National or Regional Committee will normally be informed.

12. Contacts with International Political Bodies

General Principles of Contact

In making or recommending an approach to governments or intergovernmental authorities, the Commission's procedure shall be as follows:

(a) As described in Aim VIII, the Commission may directly negotiate in its own name and that of the parent bodies with the United Nations and other international bodies subject to the provisions of (2) and (3) below.

(b) If and when the Commission desires that the attention of national governments or other national entities be drawn to representations purporting to advance a Christian view on any problem within its Aims, including any problem in the field of Human Rights, the Commission shall remit the matter simultaneously to the Commissioners and to the national or regional committees of the country or countries concerned.

(c) The affiliated committees shall have full discretion in determining whether such representation is desirable, what it shall include, and how it shall be made. They shall assume full responsibility for their action and, unless otherwise specifically authorized, shall in no case make their representation in the name of the Commission of the Churches on International Affairs. In instances where national or regional committees decide against representation to their government, action by the Commission of the Churches on International Affairs is not debarred, but will be undertaken only on issues of extreme urgency. In this event it is understood that in turn the national or regional committees will not be in any sense responsible.

(d) A local commission, committee or department on international affairs upon proposing or taking action, may invite the support of the Commission of the Churches on International Affairs. When the officers of the Commission . . . consider the action to be both representative and justified by its importance, they may support it by such measures as they deem appropriate.

Representations to the United Nations

In making representation in its own name as prescribed in Aim VIII, the Commission may

(a) Utilize any general principles on Human Rights, Religious Liberty, or other subjects covered in its Aims, which have been agreed at a meeting of the Commission, or agreed by correspondence, which included the members of the Commission and Executive Committee.

(b) Appropriate for its use in its own name any general principles on these subjects agreed at representative ecumenical conferences called by either or both of the parent bodies.

Christian Principles and Their Use

In defining Christian principles and in using them for representation as prescribed in Aim VIII, or for public statements, as prescribed in Aim II, the following procedures may be employed:

(a) A statement by the Commission may be made by it when meeting, or on its behalf by the Chairman or Director, following postal communication wherein a substantial and representative agreement has been expressed.

(b) A statement may be made by or on behalf of the Executive Committee, which has been authorized by it at a meeting, or agreed by postal communication wherein a substantial and representative agreement has been expressed.

(c) A statement may be made by the Chairman or the Director in his capacity as such and on his own behalf, provided that it is in agreement with the Commission's policy as provided in its Aims and after consultation with at least one of the officers of each of the parent bodies.

(d) A national or regional committee or Commissioner may not make a statement in the name of the Commission or of any of its officers or committees unless specific authorization has been given.

(e) The Commission may in addition prepare and recommend to the parent bodies statements for their consideration, separately or together, at an assembly, conference or committee called by either or both of them.

Procedures of Contact

In accordance with the arrangements provided by the United Nations and its Specialized Agencies, the administrative officers of the Commission are empowered to seek and to maintain on behalf of the Commission the following contacts:

1. Official registration with the United Nations Department of Public Information.
2. Consultative status with the Economic and Social Council with the understanding that the Commission's status in Category B shall be continued until, in the judgment of the administrative officers, it seems advantageous to seek a status in Category A.
3. Such contacts with other organs and specialized agencies as the administrative officers may determine necessary to accomplish the Commission's Aims.

13. CONTACTS WITH OTHER ORGANIZATIONS PROMOTING WORLD PEACE AND ORDER

As a general principle, the Commission shall not establish organic relations with other organizations but, where deemed advisable, may co-operate with other bodies in such ways as will permit the exchange of information and promote action by the Commission in accomplishing its aims.

14. THESE RULES MAY BE AMENDED BY THE EXECUTIVE COMMITTEE OF THE COMMISSION, SUBJECT TO THE APPROVAL OF THE EXECUTIVE COMMITTEE OF THE WORLD COUNCIL OF CHURCHES AND THE COMMITTEE OF THE INTERNATIONAL MISSIONARY COUNCIL.

APPENDIX H

Report of the Advisory Commission on the Main Theme

Evanston, 1954

I. Christ Our Hope

A. A Hope Both Sure and Steadfast

God summons the Church of Jesus Christ today to speak plainly about hope. Jesus Christ is our hope. In all humility and boldness we are bound to tell the good news of the hope given to us in Him.

The hope of which we speak is something different from what men usually mean when they speak of hope. In common speech "hope" means a strong desire for something which may be possible but is not certain. What is spoken of here is something that we wait for expectantly and yet patiently, because we know that it can never disappoint us.

We have this confidence because our hope is based upon what we know of God, and because we know of Him through what He has done. Our hope is not the projection of our desires upon an unknown future, but the product in us of God's acts in history, and above all of His act in raising Jesus Christ from the dead. That mighty event is faith's assurance that Christ has overcome the world and all the powers of evil, sin, and death; it is the beginning of a new life in the power of the Spirit; it is the guarantee of God's promise that in His good time His victory will be manifest to all, His Kingdom come in glory, and He Himself be known everywhere as King. It therefore begets a living hope, an ardent longing for that glorious consummation, and an eager expectation of its coming.

Our hope comes to us from God and rests in God. The Lord of heaven and earth is the Righteous One who has said, "Ye shall be holy for I am holy," the Judge who will by no means leave evil unchecked and unpunished. Therefore we dare not speak of hope in God except we speak at the same time of judgment and repentance. He who was raised from the dead is He who died for our sins. Therefore what we say is said under the sign of the Cross. The Cross is that place at the centre of the world's history where the Lord of history has finally exposed the sin of the world and taken that sin upon Himself, the place where all men and all nations without exception stand revealed as enemies of God, lovers not of truth but of the lie, children not of light but of darkness, and yet where all men stand revealed as beloved of God, precious in God's sight, children for whom the Son of God was content to die. It is the crucified Lord who is the hope of the world.

Therefore the hope of which we speak, so far from being a mere extension or re-affirmation of our desires, begins at the place where we and all our desires are brought to naught. When we stand at that place where the Son of God died for our sins, all our human desires are judged by Him. We are stripped naked of all our claims and pretensions and clothed afresh with His mercy. We are dead and made alive again. In the words of the Apostle, we are begotten again to a living hope. This, the act of God Himself, is the beginning of our hope. The Creator and Lord of all has come forth in wrath and loving-kindness to shut up every false way, and to bring us face to face with Himself, the living Lord. He, by His own act, has put us in the place where we must hope and can hope only in Him.

We live at a time when very many are without hope. Many have lost the hopes they had for earthly progress. Many cling with the strength of fanaticism to hopes which their own sober reason cannot justify. Multitudes ask themselves, "What is coming to the world? What is in front of us? What may we look forward to?" The answer to those questions has been given to us in the Gospel. To those who ask "What is coming to the world?" we answer "His Kingdom is coming." To those who ask "What is in front of us?" we answer "It is He, the King, who confronts us." To those who ask "What may we look forward to?" we answer that we face not a trackless waste of unfilled time with an end that none can dare to predict; we face our living Lord, our Judge and Saviour, He who was dead and is alive for evermore, He who has come and is coming and will reign for ever and ever. It may be that we face tribulation; indeed we must certainly face it if we would be partakers with Him. But we know His word, His kingly word: "Be of good cheer; *I have overcome the world*."

B. The Promises of God

The good news of hope which we proclaim comes to us through the Holy Scriptures. It is the gift of God Himself and rests upon His deeds in the world and His promises for mankind. In the Old Testament God reveals Himself as the Creator and Lord of all men and all things, who places His creation under the obligation of obedience and gives to it the hope of fulfillment. He promises seed-time and harvest as long as the earth remains, and gives men visions of a day when the disorders of life shall be done away, and righteousness, truth, and peace shall prevail.

God's revelation of His faithfulness to His promises was given in His dealings with Israel. Throughout her long history this people learned to know the mighty hand of God in acts of deliverance and of judgment, and to cherish the hope for a Kingdom in which God's will should be done. This indestructible and life-giving hope is what gives unity to the whole history of Israel and makes it the story of a single pilgrimage. Though that people continually exchanged her God-given hopes for others that depended upon her own strength and wisdom, in every generation God's faithfulness produced men of faith, who in hope believed against hope, and recalled a wayward people to their appointed way. God's promise in the Old Testament is that He will Himself establish His Kingdom and that men shall come to know Him as God.

The story is told by many men gripped by God's promise and possessed by His Spirit. They declare the doings and promises of God as concretely as possible, although these exceed the capacities of human language, whether historical prose or poetic imagery. God has used and uses their testimony to recall His people to the promise of the reign of righteousness, truth, and peace. Their testimony has often been distorted, both by those literalists who have mistaken symbol for fact, and by those philosophers who tried to treat facts as mere symbols of timeless truth. Yet through His servants in the Old Testament, as in the New, God continues to address His word of promise to all men.

The promise that God would Himself establish His Kingdom focused the hope of Israel upon the coming of the Messiah. As God refined Israel's hope in the crucible of failure and disappointment, it became hope for a Deliverer who should release them not only from their external foes but also from their bondage to sin and death. He who was to come would bear their iniquities and carry their sorrows. By His stripes they would be healed.

The New Testament announces that the promised Deliverer has come. The powers of the coming Kingdom are already at work in the world in Jesus Christ, and in the Holy Spirit poured out upon His people. God in Jesus Christ has entered into the tangled web of earthly history and met and mastered evil in all its forms. By His life, death, and resurrection He became for us both sin's Victim and at the same time sin's Victor. We cannot fathom all that He there did for us, but we know that He bore the judgment that was against us all, freed us from sin and death, and reconciled the world to Himself. His coming fulfilled the hope of earlier times—and transformed it. He brought to men a new birth into a new life, a new community, and a new hope. The new life is born in forgiveness; it finds both its pattern and its power in Jesus Christ, whose obedient love has freed men from the guilt and power of sin and from the fear of death, to serve their fellow-men. The new community is the Church, of which He is the source, the head and the vitalizing power. The new hope is still hope in God, the maker and ruler of all things, but it is hope at once fulfilled and expectant. What we possess in Christ is the most glorious life of which we know anything, for it is fellowship with Him who is our Saviour and our Lord. And yet this fellowship in the Spirit is but the foretaste, the earnest, of the inheritance laid up for us. Christ is not only our righteousness and our peace; He is also present in us as the hope of glory.

C. The Kingdom That Now Is

We must now speak both of what we have in Christ and of what we hope for, of what is given and of what is promised. And first of what is given. In the ministry of Jesus Christ we see the gracious power of the Kingdom already at work among men, and in His teaching, especially in the parables, we read His own interpretation of that working. The same Spirit who was in Jesus Christ was, after His exaltation and ascension, poured out upon His people. In Him a new humanity begins. As we die daily with Christ, we are exalted with Him to receive His life-giving Spirit and to participate in the glory of His Kingdom. To us as new men all things become new. We see individual and social experience in a new perspective. The whole course of history is transfigured. We see the victorious Lord continuing His ministry of intercession and carrying on His warfare against every ruler of darkness. As we walk by the Spirit, we participate in His warfare, and participate also in His victory. In Christ and His community we are already sons of God and heirs of glory.

Although even now we live in the New Age, its reality and power are not yet fully revealed. "The earth," indeed, "is the Lord's, and the fulness thereof." It is His creation, and His work is good. Moreover God so loves His world that He gave His only Son for man's salvation. His providence governs it, and His Spirit lives and works in the midst of it, overcoming evil with good in countless ways, and bringing to fruit beyond human expectation or contrivance the deeds of devoted men and women. But neither the world of nature nor the world of men is as yet what God would have it be. Both are still enmeshed in the disorder of the unredeemed age and await their liberation. The ignorant and the wilful wrong-doing of many generations of men has distorted God's work and subjected human life itself to grievous corruption. Every man is born into a social order deeply pervaded by the accumulated results of individual and corporate aggression, deceit, and irresponsible self-seeking. And every man so born and reared adds his own share of distortions and corrupting falsehoods and starts new trains of suspicion, cruelty, and hatred. Evil, deeply ingrained and powerfully operating in all creation, often quite beyond our understanding or control, bedevils the whole course of earthly history.

Because this is so, neither the Church nor individual Christians can expect to escape suffering and at times even catastrophe. For the Church must live now in the world that crucified her Lord. Sometimes the suffering of Christian believers or congregations results from their own ignorance or unfaithfulness. Christians are not exempt from divine judgment; indeed they are more directly exposed to it than others. It is only as believers know themselves to stand under the judgment of God that they can know His mercy and yield themselves as instruments to His gracious purposes. Sometimes, on the other hand, their suffering results from their faithfulness in facing the powers of evil, in bearing the assault of slanderers, oppressors or persecutors, or in identifying themselves with Christ by carrying upon their hearts the burden of the world's sin and sorrow. But those who accept such judgment and such suffering without bitterness or despair are made sharers in the sufferings of their Lord, and sharers also in the power of His resurrection. They therefore receive strength to endure in faith towards God, in love towards all men, and in hope of Christ's final victory.

The trials which again and again come upon the Church are reminders that in this present age the Church dare not try to settle down in earthly peace and prosperity. They are "signs of the times" that should keep every Christian and every congregation alert, knowing that the Church on earth is, even when danger seems remote, a pilgrim people forbidden by its divine calling to be at peace with the powers of evil, or to forget that in the living Body of Christ, when one member suffers, all the members suffer together. Moreover such trials, when they lead the Church to lay fresh hold on the hope set before it, provide a special witness whereby the world may see the power of the living Lord who in weakness makes us strong and in the midst of darkness enables us to hold fast our hope in Him. Not only so, they also disclose unmistakably the tangled, precarious nature of earthly existence itself—not least when its technical achievements and political powers have reached imposing heights. If the Church is to find complete fulfilment, and if earthly existence is to be saved from meaninglessness, we must look not only to the course of earthly history itself, but beyond it. Our hope must be anchored in God who comes to us in Jesus Christ; it must look at once to what He has done, and to what He is doing now, and to what He will do for His people and His world, in completion of His saving work.

D. Having and Hoping

The fact that our hope is thus anchored in a Kingdom that both has come and is coming gives to the life of every believer a double orientation. He both has eternal life and hopes for it. He has the first fruits, and therefore he longs for the full harvest. The Messiah, who though rich became poor, has given him surpassing riches. Yet he has this treasure in an earthen vessel. The flesh wars against the Spirit and the Spirit against the flesh. He remains part of this fallen world, involved in its corruption and mortality. His life is therefore a warfare, even though he is guarded by Christ's peace.

In this situation the believer faces a double temptation. On the one hand he is tempted to despair of this world and to fix his whole attention on that which is to come. He may forget that God keeps him in this world precisely as a minister of its reconciliation to Himself. He may be so daunted by the apparently unconquered power of evil that he loses all faith in the possibility that God who created and sustains the world can also make His power known in it. In his longing for the heavenly city with all its blessedness he may pass by his fellow-man, fallen among thieves, and leave him by the roadside.

On the other hand the believer is tempted in the opposite way. Because he has been brought out of darkness into light and made a sharer here and now in Christ's risen power, he may forget that what is given here is still only a foretaste. He may so confine his attention to the possibilities of this present world as to forget that the whole world lies under judgment. He may confuse man's achievements with God's Kingdom and so lose the only true standard of judgment upon human deeds. He may forget the true dimensions of man's existence as a child of God created and redeemed for eternal life, and by seeking the end of human life within earthly history make man the mere instrument of an earthly plan, and so dehumanise him.

We are guarded from these temptations not only by the logic of faith but also by our common fellowship in the Lord. Listening to His Word we are brought again and again to the point of decision, whether to accept both His No and His Yes. Sharing the Church's mission to the world, we experience both the distance and the nearness of the Kingdom. Week after week the routines and emergencies of the common life remind us of our wealth and our poverty. A true index of our having and hoping is given to us in the sacrament which under various names—Lord's Supper, Holy Communion, Eucharist, Mass—is common to the whole Church. Here Christ's people, united in an act of faith and adoration, call to mind at once His coming of old in great humility and His coming at the end in power and glory, and both are made present to them in communion with their living Lord, who comes to them in the breaking of the bread.

E. The Kingdom That Is to Come

The Kingdom that is now real moves with God's power and faithfulness towards its full realisation in the manifestation of God's glory throughout all creation. The King reigns; therefore He will reign until He has put all enemies under His feet. What we hope for is the fullness of what we already possess in Him; what we possess has its meaning only in the hope for His coming.

What Is Its Character? In the new age that now is, God has disclosed to eyes of faith what is the character of the age that is to come. We must here speak of matters which, in the nature of things, defy direct expression in explicit speech, matters for which the language of inspired imagination employed in the Scriptures is alone adequate, for these are things that can be discerned and communicated only by the Spirit. The pure in heart shall see God as He is and know Him as they are known by Him. Those who are now sons of God will receive the fullness of their inheritance as joint heirs with Christ. There will be a new heaven and a new earth. We shall all be changed. The dead will be raised incorruptible, receiving a body of heavenly glory. The agony of the created world will be recognised as the travail of childbirth. Blind eyes will see, deaf ears will hear, the lame will leap for joy, the captive will be freed. The knowledge of God will cover the earth. The Holy City will appear, made ready as a bride adorned for her husband. The choir which no man can number will sing Hallelujahs to the praise of the Eternal. God's people will enter into the sabbath rest, and all created things will be reconciled in the perfect communion of God with His people. It is in such visions as these that the Spirit enables us to point to the splendour of the salvation that is ready to be revealed in the last days. It is towards this salvation that God guides us in hope. This hope is not seen, or it would not be hope; but it is promised to us as suffering, sinning, dying, and believing men. Therefore we wait for it with patience.

What Is Its Range? In His Kingdom that has already come God has unveiled the unlimited range of His love. In Christ He has already broken down the barriers betwen races, nations, cultures, classes, and sexes: how much more will the coming Kingdom demonstrate the breadth of His redemption! Christ came not to the righteous but to sinners, to the lost, the least, the last; how much more will His return demonstrate the triumph of His descent into the abyss. In His death He suffered for His enemies in loving forgiveness and thus overcame every enmity; how much more at His coming will His sovereignty be disclosed even to all who crucify Him. "As in Adam all die, so in Christ, shall all be made alive." Because our hope is *in* Christ, He commands us to hope *for* all those whom He loves. Because His love is shed abroad in our hearts, we are empowered to hope all things for all His brothers. And we hope also for our own participation in the endless life of His Kingdom. Of that participation we possess a sure token in His power to make our bodies the temple of His Spirit and to raise us from our daily dying. This power, however, prevents us from hoping for our own glorification apart from the fullness of glory that shall come to the whole body of Christ; for all who participate in the dying and rising of Christ are being knit together into a single body "until we all attain . . . to mature manhood, to the measure of the stature of the fullness of Christ." We long, therefore, for this perfecting of the Body of Christ. But not only so, the love of Christ prevents us from being content with any hope for a glorified Church which leaves the destiny of the world to the powers of evil. Solidarity with Him requires and produces solidarity through Him with the world in its transiency, futility, sin, and death. For God has promised the reconciliation of the whole creation, and we therefore hope for nothing less than the renewal of all things. This hope, however, never allows us to think of cosmic transformation apart from God's care for the falling sparrow and the hundredth sheep. Christ our hope thus embodies in Himself the destiny of individuals, of the Church, of earthly communities, and of all creation. So great is this hope in Christ that we are impelled both to press forward eagerly to its fulfilment and also to listen with full soberness to His command: "Strive to enter by the narrow door, for many I tell you, will seek to enter and will not be able."

What Is the Time of Its Coming? What has God revealed to His Church concerning the time of consummation? He has bidden the Church to live with loins girt and lamps burning, like servants waiting for their master's return, and to serve faithfully day after day, like a steward undismayed by his lord's delay. Our hope therefore bears the marks of patience and eagerness, of confidence and urgency, of waiting and hurrying. God has not disclosed to us just when His Kingdom will come in glory. In fact when we attempt to calculate the nearness or the distance of His Kingdom we confuse that hope of which Jesus Himself provides the clear pattern. His whole concern was the fulfilment of God's purpose rather than the satisfaction of man's curiosity. He met his impatient disciples with the command "Take heed, watch; for you do not know when the time will come." Our obedience is one measure of our hope. It is for the Church to stand vigilantly with its Lord, discerning the signs of the time and proclaiming that now is the time of judgment, now is the day of salvation.

He who is both the beginning and the end, in whom all is to be consummated, is the One who meets us now and every day and invites us to commit everything to Him. We do not know what are the limits of human achievement, of our own personal history, or of the history of the race. We do not know what possibilities are in store for us or what time is before us. We do know, however, that there is a limit, for we must all die. If we do not know Christ, death is the only limit we know. And in that situation men try to find grounds for hope either in merely individual survival or in social progress. The one offers to individuals the promise of fulfilment but denies it to history as a whole; the other offers meaning to human history but denies the significance of the human person. Those who take death seriously but have not met Christ are shut up to these two alternative ways by which human wishing seeks to cross the chasm of death. But in Christ something utterly different is offered. He who has died for us and is alive for us confronts us with a totally new reality, a new limit, a new boundary to our existence. It is He who meets us; it is He with whom we have to do in every situation. It is He who is our life. He who is life for every man. We can commit ourselves and all our deeds into His hands with complete confidence, knowing that death and destruction have been robbed of their power; that even if our works fail and are buried in the rubble of human history, and though our bodies fall into the ground and die, nothing is lost, because He is able to keep that which we commit to Him against the Day.

What Is Its Relation to This World? On Calvary God's Kingdom and the kingdoms of this world met. Whoever has lived through Good Friday and Easter Day has the key to final judgment and eternal life. To him has been demonstrated the fragility of this world in comparison with the immense stability of that world which Christ brought within human reach. At the Cross God condemned the world which turns from Him and hates Him. In the coming Day this condemnation will be revealed in all its terrible finality. At the same Cross God accepted the world and disclosed how much He loves it. In the coming Day this loving acceptance will be revealed in all its unsearchable riches. Confidence in this terrible and glorious consummation of all things in Christ means neither that the history of this world will be swept aside as irrelevant, nor that our efforts will be finally crowned with success. The long history of this world which God created and sustains from day to day, and for the sake of which He sent His Son, is not rendered meaningless by the coming of His Kingdom. Nor, on the other hand, is His Kingdom simply the final outcome of this world's history. There is no straight line from the labours of men to the Kingdom of God. He rejects that history of which man fancies himself to be the centre, creator, and lord; He accepts that history whose beginning, middle, and end He Himself fixes and determines.

Thus at the boundary of all life stands One who is both Judge and Saviour. Because we know Him as Judge, we shall beware of confusing any achievement of ours with His holy and blessed Kingdom; because we know Him as Saviour, who died for the world, we shall beware of that selfish concern for our own salvation which would cause us to neglect our worldly tasks and leave the world to perdition. The operation of God's judgment and mercy in the Crucified is far from self-evident. But we know that in the age that is to come, what is now hidden from our senses will be openly revealed. The Church sees now through a glass darkly; she will then see face to face. But what she sees now she is bound to proclaim.

II. Christ and His People

A. The Pilgrim People of God

We have spoken of Christ our hope. We must now go on to speak of that People which He has called into being to be the bearer of hope, the sign and witness of God's mighty acts, the means of His working, and the field wherein His glory is to be revealed. Our hope is grounded in one great Event, comprising the incarnation, ministry, death, and resurrection of Jesus Christ. In this Event the purpose of God for mankind, foreshadowed in His dealings with Israel and declared by the prophets, found fulfilment, and His Kingdom was inaugurated on earth, to be consummated hereafter.

This tremendous Event occurred within a brief epoch which soon passed, leaving the broad scenery of history ostensibly unchanged. One concrete result alone was to be discerned: the Christian Church. It appeared as a small, obscure community, unwelcomed and almost unnoticed by the great world. It knew itself to be a colony of the heavenly fatherland planted in an alien territory, and looked forward to an end lying beyond this earth and a day when the fullness of what God had done in Christ would be finally disclosed. It also knew itself to bear responsibility for the world for which Christ died, a responsibility that drove it to action and to suffering.

This Church still exists. It is a historical society living among other societies in the world, and yet not of the world. It is constantly tempted to settle down among secular societies, content with the achievement, influence, and reputation which a well-ordered and enlightened secular society might enjoy. But to do so is to deny both its origin and its end, and in fact it is seldom permitted to do so for long. It is of its very nature that its members should know themselves to be strangers and pilgrims on the earth, pressing on towards the moment at which the Lord who died and rose again will confront them in His power and glory.

The Church lives in this world by the proclamation of the Gospel, by worship and sacraments, and by its fellowship in the Holy Spirit. In proclaiming the Gospel it is permitted to engage in God's own work of bringing His purpose to fulfilment. In worship and sacraments it participates in the life of the heavenly fatherland. In the fellowship of the Spirit it receives divine powers of growth, renewal, and enlightenment to which we cannot place a limit.

The Church thus becomes, in the first place, witness and evidence of that which God has done, and the sign of that which He is doing and will yet do. By this alone the world is apprised of the historical Event and its more-than-historical significance and issues.

Second, the Church is also the means through which God is carrying His purpose to effect. It is the Body whose members are members of Christ, united with Him and at His disposal. Its life therefore is both the extension of His earthly ministry and also a participation in His present and continuing work as risen Lord and Saviour.

Third, the Church is designed to be the field where the glory of God, once manifested in Jesus Christ to those who had eyes to see, will be revealed to the whole created universe, which meanwhile waits for the manifestation of the sons of God. The Glory of God is already reflected in the Church's proclamation of the Gospel, in its worship and in its fellowship in the Holy

Spirit, but the reflection is partial and imperfect, and the Church waits upon Him through whom alone it is changed from glory to glory.

This Church, as a historical body, is made up of frail, ignorant, and sinful men. Its foundation members were discredited deserters from their Master's cause. They became pillars in the temple of God only because, having stood under the judgment of God when the sun was darkened, they found forgiveness in the light of Easter Day. They could proclaim God's judgment and forgiveness to the world because they knew themselves the objects of both. The Church is still able to declare judgment and forgiveness to the world only because, and in so far as, its members have stood and stand under the judgment of God in penitence and have accepted His forgiveness. In doing so, they are exposed to the full impact of His grace, which has won its victories in the world, and is still winning them, through human beings who in themselves have neither strength nor merit.

The Church fails of its calling when its members suppose themselves to have already attained that which awaits them only at the end of the way; when, blind to their faults and proud of their virtue and insight as Christians, they despise their fellow-men and speak self-righteously to the world; when they seek glory of men and refuse the reproach of the Cross.

And yet, even when the Church fails to be itself, when its members fall short of their calling, nevertheless God is God, and He cannot deny Himself. In spite of assaults from without and flaws within, the Church stands upon the Rock and the gates of hell do not prevail against it. By God's ordinance and through His power it remains witness, instrument, and field of action for Him while history lasts, and will stand before Him at the end to be made perfect through His final judgment and final forgiveness.

B. The Mission of the Church

It is thus of the very nature of the Church that it has a mission to the whole world. That mission is our participation in the work of God which takes place between the coming of Jesus Christ to inaugurate God's Kingdom on earth, and His coming again in glory to bring that Kingdom to its consummation. "I have other sheep that are not of this fold; I must bring them also, and they will heed my voice." This is His word to us; this is the work in which He is engaged and in which we are engaged with Him. For He whose coming we expect is also He who is already present. Our work until His coming again is but the result of our share in the work which He is doing all the time and everywhere. The Church's mission is thus the most important thing that is happening in history.

And yet because the mission of the Church points beyond history to the close of the age, it has this significance too, that it is itself among the signs that the end of history has begun. The hope of our calling is set towards the hope of His coming. It is written, "This Gospel of the Kingdom will be preached throughout the whole world as a testimony to all nations; and then the end will come." In giving His commission to the Church, Christ has given also this promise: "Lo, I am with you always, to the close of the age."

Thus, moreover, are the true nature and dimensions of the Church's missionary work determined, for they are determined by Him whose work it is. It is a work which embraces the whole world, limited by no racial, social, national, historical, or political considerations. Jesus Christ is King over all the world. He died for all; and the world-wide proclamation of the Gospel is the direct consequence of His world-wide sway and all-embracing love.

We evangelise, but it is He who is the Evangelist, the Messiah who is come and who is gathering the nations.

It is for this reason that we, who now have the earnest of our inheritance and the foretaste of salvation, yet have to wait for it. The same Lord is Lord of all—believer and unbeliever alike. He is rich in mercy towards all who call upon Him. "But how are men to call upon Him in whom they have not believed? And how are they to believe in Him of whom they have never heard? And how are they to hear without a preacher? And how can men preach unless they are sent?" The consummation awaits our obedience to His word "Go ye." In very truth we cannot know the fulness of God's salvation until all for whom it is intended share it with us. We without them cannot be made whole.

When the Lord's Apostles asked Him whether the Kingdom would not come at once, He answered, "Ye shall be My witnesses to the ends of the earth." To our cry "Lord, how long?" He answers, "Go ye and preach the Gospel to all nations." That is our summons to share Christ's compassion for all mankind; only as we obey it can we live as those who share His hope for all men. Indeed, when we contemplate the millions who have not yet known His love or heard His name, do we not stand rebuked for our slackness and callousness? We are among those who call Him "Lord" and do not the things which He commands. Not only does Christ say to the Church "Go," but through the non-believer He is also saying to the Church "Come." And the Church that fails to obey this doubly voiced command does not merely fail in one function; it denies its own *nature*.

How necessary it is, then, that the Church's obedience to the Gospel should also involve a determination on the part of the Church in every country to take this Gospel to other lands. There are frontiers which the Gospel must cross within each land, areas of life which must be brought into subjection to the mind of Christ. But it is of special significance when the Gospel crosses geographical frontiers, for it is when a Church takes the Gospel to another people and another land that it bears its witness to the fact that the new age has dawned for all the world.

The urgency of the Church's mission derives from the fact that its mission is the result of participation in the work of God. We can avoid the task of preaching the Gospel only by refusing to allow the Gospel to take possession of our lives. When we do allow it so to take possession, we are swept into the current of God's redemptive activity, and find it hard to keep pace with Him. It is because we have failed so largely to let the Gospel take possession of us that we have failed also so greatly to fulfil our evangelistic task. There is no other way of believing in the Gospel than by witnessing to it. If we really took our stand upon it we should be compelled by that very situation to be urgent in staking Christ's claim for all men and for all of life. If we but truly believed that Christ had already claimed the Hindus, the Buddhists, the Muslims, the Jews, the Communists, and the great pagan masses of our time for Himself, we should no longer skirt around these groups as hesitantly as we often do. Our evangelism is not to be determined by the likelihood of immediate response. It is to be determined by the nature of the Gospel itself.

And yet in spite of our every failure we must affirm what the Church is and what it is meant to do, and thankfully acknowledge that God is faithful even when we are faithless. To all men the Church offers welcome to their Father's home, where they are treated as persons, children of God known to God by name and precious in His sight. In the Church they come into living membership of Christ's body, receiving forgiveness of their sins, partaking in the healing processes of the Spirit, and engaged in the Church's mission to the world. In the Spirit, also, they have the pledge and instalment of their common heritage: of the worship of God and of work in His service, of the communion of saints, of the power of the resurrection, and of the life everlasting.

All this means that the function of the Church is, in the last analysis, to be both the instrument of God's purpose in history and also the first realisation of the life of His Kingdom on earth. It invites all men to share in its life, both as realisation and as instrument. It bids them enter in and possess their inheritance. It also testifies to the nature of the end towards which its hope is set. That end is not an unrelated intervention on the part of God, for which the only possible preparation would be an attempt to escape from the wrath to come; it is the promised climax of what God has done and still continues to do, and the true preparation for it lies in faithful living by these deeds of God.

C. The Unity of the Church

As the instrument and first fruits of God's Kingdom on earth, the Church is in its essential nature one. Where the one Christ is at work, where the apostolic witness to Him is truly set forth in word and sacrament, there is the one Church. We all come from Him, we all go towards Him, and He is among us. This threefold bond is stronger than all discord among Christians, for it is wrought by Christ Himself.

This we must affirm in face of all contradiction. The unity of the Church is so concealed by our many divisions that to affirm it must often appear little better than mockery. But the Church knows of a certainty that at the end of its pilgrimage its unity in Christ will be complete and manifested. Our unity in Christ belongs to the ultimate structure of reality. This is the goal to which all history and all creation move. In pressing forward towards this goal we are one. Let us not forget that when we stand before our Lord at the end we shall stand before our Judge—the Judge of His Church as well as of the world. His judgment will bring about a separation that goes much deeper than all our present divisions and cuts across them all.

Yet even in our present condition He has not left us without tokens of our unity. In our separateness we have attested the operation of the one Christ across all boundaries that divide us. We have heard the voice of the Good Shepherd in the testimony of communions other than our own. We have experienced the power of the Name of Christ in their prayers. We have acknowledged the love of Christ to which they have borne witness in word and deed. In the fellowship of the ecumenical movement we have come together in a way which forbids us, in spite of all stresses, to break away from one another. Thus we have been led to see that the reality of Christ is more comprehensive than the limitations of our confessional traditions, and have confessed in faith our oneness in Christ.

All this we thankfully accept as a token of our Lord's grace to His Church. And yet we are divided. Our true unity remains concealed. There are divisions between the separate communions in which Christians are grouped. There are also divisions within each communion, sometimes no less sharp than those which divide one communion from another. At no point is this scandal of division more grievous in its consequences than in the Church's endeavour to proclaim the one hope of the Kingdom to all nations. All work of evangelisation, however great its history and glorious its results, remains crippled by the divided state of the Church.

This is no mere matter of missionary tactics. Our sense of urgency in the task of overcoming our divisions is something more than a desire to combine in facing hostile forces or unsolved social and political problems. The mission of the Church aims at gathering all men into unity. The disunity of the Church contradicts that purpose.

We are not at one concerning the form which the corporate unity of the Church should take. Our discussions have not yet led us to a common conviction as to a way which we can take all together towards that end. We trust our common Lord to continue to guide us towards that fullness of unity which is His Will for His people. In this situation it is the indispensable condition of receiving further light that each Church should actually take whatever may be clearly indicated as the next step.

To discern what that next step is each Church should face such questions as the following: What are the implications of the discovery which we have made that when we seek to understand together how the whole Church depends for its life on its Lord Jesus Christ we are at once aware of a greater and deeper unity than we have known before? Where Churches have already discovered a large measure of agreement in doctrine, are they justified in remaining separate? In what new ways can we seek to live and to act together in all matters in which no deep differences of conviction are involved? Have we become sufficiently clear-sighted in detecting the purely worldly factors which play their part in our divisions?

D. The Renewal of the Church

The Church is God's new creation, united to Christ as the body to the head, filled and quickened by His Spirit, God's holy temple. And yet in this pilgrimage through earthly history there are Christians who are individually and corporately guilty of narrowness of mind, imprisoned in sectarianism, parochialism, or nationalism, and indifferent to the claims of the Church's world-wide mission. Sometimes the Church pitches too low the demands it makes for self-sacrifice and devotion. It often tolerates among its members low standards of faith and knowledge and a worship of Almighty God which is utterly unworthy. Christian believers often reflect the timidities and vacillations and even the despair of worldly men.

The Church knows that it is a society not of the perfect but of those who are in constant need of God's grace and mercy. The life of the Church in the world is a spiritual battle, continuing in Christ's power His warfare against the principalities and powers of evil. Humility and constant self-examination are a necessary part of the climate of the Church's life. An attitude of penitence belongs to the nature of the historical Church; it invites worshippers day by day to make corporate confession of sin. The old Adam needs to die again and again.

Anything that we speak, we can speak only in penitence. Nevertheless we possess a sure and certain hope even for the Church. God has promised and He is faithful. He has promised the presence and power of the Holy Spirit, ever guiding, ever renewing, ever enabling the Church to perform the task to which it is sent. The Church goes on its way ever looking to the heavenly city, knowing that it shares in the life of that city even here and now.

In spite of our unholiness, we know that the Church of God is holy, for it is God's action and not our penitence which sanctifies and renews it. He has sent it, has called it to be His instrument. Though Word and Sacraments may be ministered by unworthy men, they do not fail of their effect. By their means, God acts from moment to moment and from generation to generation, re-creating the Church ever anew by the Spirit who indwells it, renewing its faithfulness, its purity, its self-sacrifice, its courage.

History shows many examples of such renewal, amounting almost to a resurrection of dry bones. And in our time we still find authentic signs of renewal. Amidst persecution and loss of material resources or civil liberty, there are many instances—East and West—in which the community of believers has triumphed and is triumphing by the power of God. These victories lead us to thanksgiving; they lead us also to deeper penitence for ourselves, and to more earnest waiting upon God's quickening Spirit.

E. The Church Triumphant

In Christ, the Church's Lord and Saviour, God has triumphed. In the very defeat of the Cross the Son of God, who made Himself our brother, won the fight. He won it for us. Even in judgment His grace triumphed. He who was crucified for us, for us also rose from the dead. It follows that we His people both share and shall share His victory. But first of all we must let Him win the victory over ourselves. That victory is won when in our sinfulness we are rebuked, consoled, and sanctified by the Holy Spirit. That is the triumph of grace, which gives faith the victory over all the powers of sin and death.

The Church which thus lets itself be conquered by its Lord has part also in His conquest of this world. It is permitted even to help God to win the victory. Where His word is preached and heard, where consciences are first rebuked and then consoled, where the proud are humbled and the despairing lifted up, where the parched ground of dead hearts is changed by the quickening Spirit into a garden yielding fruit to the glory of God, there the Church celebrates the triumph of its Lord; there by faith it triumphs with Him. Where deeds of charity are done, where evil is overcome with good, there the love of God wins the victory over us, in us, and through us. When the Church prays, "Hallowed be thy name; thy Kingdom come; thy will be done," it is taking part, by the grace of God, in God's own triumph.

But here we face a dangerous temptation—the temptation to identify the victory of God with the worldly success of the Church, or to seek a triumph after the manner of the world by worldly means. To do this would be to betray our crucified Lord, to deny Him before the world.

The Church's true privilege and duty is, on the contrary, to humble itself in deep thankfulness because, feeble as it is in itself, exposed to constant attacks from without and always under the shadow of rejection, persecution and shame, it is nevertheless given a part in God's victory of the Cross. In this present age the Church fights its battle of faith, hope, and charity amidst sufferings. Yet in these very sufferings the Church possesses a token of the glory of its crucified Lord. Through thick darkness it marches towards a future that is the Lord's, who as Judge and Saviour will manifest His victory incontrovertibly before the whole world.

The Church's visible structure passes away with this age, but as the chosen people of God it will enter into the glory of the Kingdom of God that is to come. Here at last the true meaning and purpose of its mission will be realized, for all kindreds of mankind will be brought in. Here at last the Church will know fully what it is to be one in Christ.

We must all die, one generation after another. But Christ died—and is risen again. Christ's own people are still members of His living Body. They are with Him. Within the communion of saints they remain united with one another. In the resurrection they will be manifested, each and all, in a new mode of being. They will know God, for they will see Him.

In the fellowship of those who are made perfect they will know and love one another. All of them, even those who died immature or undeveloped, the despised, the failures, the defeated, will, in the communion of saints, draw upon the inexhaustible treasure of life which is God's gift to them all in Christ.

Beyond all defeat and persecution, beyond their own sin and guilt, beyond death and hell, the people of Jesus Christ will raise the hymn of triumph, and the new heaven and earth will join the strain. Their worship will have no more need of a temple, for their Lord and Saviour will Himself be a temple for them, as His glory will be their light. The great Supper of the Lamb will be the marriage feast for the Church triumphant, for He will make His triumph theirs. His own will reign with Him. Their highest blessedness will be that God is God; and He will be all in all.

III. Christ and the World

A. The Christian Hope and the Meaning of History

The centre of world history is the earthly life, the cross and the resurrection of Jesus Christ. In Him God entered history decisively, to judge and to forgive. In Him are revealed the present plight of man, and the end towards which the world is moving. The full character and significance of historical events are known only to God. But in that life and death and resurrection He discloses to men that divine purpose over-arches the whole of the world's history, both the time before Christ and the time that comes after.

God is creator of the world, and all time is within His eternal purpose. Christians reject those philosophies, ancient or modern, that regard history and time as illusory or meaningless. History is being made at every moment by the acts of God and of men; and Christians look to the consummation of God's purpose, in which the full significance of history will be finally disclosed. They know the relative and transitory nature of earthly affairs. Nevertheless they know also that history is within the providence of God. Man's strength and wisdom are small, and he is beset by all manner of irrational powers. But the Christian knows that man and all the powers of this world are under the sovereignty of their Maker whose wisdom and power are infinite.

God not only has created the world and is sustaining it, He moves and acts within it as the ever-living God. There is a divine ordering of history, active and purposeful, however difficult it may be to discern it in particular events. At the same time, the Bible teaches the moral responsibility of man for affirming good or evil. God has established with men a covenant, a living relationship of commandment and promise by which they are called to live as responsible men and women in faithful obedience to His purpose. The commandment is that men should love God and their neighbours. The promise is the gift of abundant life as children of God for those who hear and follow the divine call.

In the actual course of history, men's responses are distorted by sin, and the results of sin. Not only are men ignorant, weak, and vulnerable, but by self-seeking and rebellion they break the covenant that gives meaning and direction to their lives. In both individual and corporate action preferring falsehood instead of truth, exploitation instead of justice, cruelty instead of mercy, they try to set at naught the divine commandment and to achieve an abundant life on their own terms. Not only particular sins but deep-seated and pervasive sinfulness, corrupting the life of mankind and the will of every man, deface God's world. Between God and the enemies of His righteousness, within the life of every person and every group, a continuing struggle goes on as long as there is human life on earth. The struggle is against evil; not against men, but on their behalf, even when they wilfully commit themselves to the enemy. And only God who knows the hearts of men can see exactly where the line of battle lies.

History is full of wreckage that results not only from man's ignorance and weakness, but from man's misuse of the strength and knowledge that God has given him. Upon all such rebellion God's judgment is sure. The wages of sin is death, for individuals and societies. God is not vindictive, but He is inexorably the living God of truth and right. Men and nations violate the demands of His holy will to their own disaster. But God's patience endures. He is faithful even to unfaithful men. Though they break the covenant, He has maintained it and reaffirmed it—reaffirmed it once for all in Jesus Christ.

Because God is the Lord of history, Christians must reject all doctrines of automatic progress or of fated decline. Man's hope is not in any process or achievement of history. It is in God. There can be no identification of any human act or institution with God and His righteousness. Yet we have been given the assurance that God's grace works in and through and all about us, that He grants us the gift of sharing in His Kingdom even now, and that continually repentant and continually forgiven, we can go forward in hope towards the consummation of all things in Christ. That will be both the judgment and the transformation of history, and also its redemption and fulfilment. The light of that final victory even now shines into our darkness.

B. The Christian Hope and the Hopes of Our Time

Mankind today is uncertain of its future. Most men are confused. Many are anxious. Some are despairing. But it would be a great mistake to suppose that most men are without hope. On the contrary, many hopes of many kinds—some newly born, some revived, some not yet clearly recognised or defined—claim the allegiance of millions. In seeking to declare its hope in Christ, the Church must understand and take account of these other hopes of our time.

In one respect or another, each of these hopes is reaching after truth which the Christian Gospel affirms. Some borrow directly from Christian tradition or deviate from it. All profess to satisfy human longings which Christians have too often neglected, and in that sense the very existence of these other hopes is a judgment upon us. But each of them also in some way distorts the true perspective disclosed to Christian faith, and offers men deceptive grounds for hope, misleading ways to follow, and delusive visions of fulfilment. All these and their followers stand with us under the judgment of God in Jesus Christ, and to each of them we must speak as clearly and fairly as we can the word of Christian hope.

It is plain that we cannot here examine, or even name, all the rival hopes of our time. We have chosen to speak of some that enlist the devotion of many of our fellows, and that seem to us representative though far from all-inclusive. Nationalism, reviving Fascism, devotion to one or another sort of economic and technological order as the way of salvation, nostalgic efforts to recapture the supposed glories of a bygone era, faith in power politics and military force—these and other delusive hopes might have been examined, and must be faced in the spirit of Jesus Christ wherever they appear. Meanwhile, we turn here to speak of four representative hopes of our time.

(i) *Democratic Humanism.* Until very recently, it was widely assumed that the spread of democracy guaranteed a progressively secure, just, and peaceable ordering of life for mankind. Even those movements which today stand in sharpest antagonism to "western democracy" claim for themselves the true democratic faith, and promise to bring in a "People's Democracy." Though chastened by wars and economic crises, confidence in democracy, however conceived, remains for millions the one sure hope for the cure of man's ills. Nor is this confidence confined to those who deny or ignore the Christian faith. Many Christians wrongly identify the democratic hope with the Christian hope for society. For them, democracy is Christianity expressed in social and political structures.

Historically, indeed, the relation of Christian faith to democratic humanism is very close. Modern democracy came to birth and has had its fullest development among peoples steeped in a Christian tradition. In its basic convictions and concerns, democracy is a child, or step-child, of Christian belief and Christian compassion. To Christian teaching it owes, in large part, its recognition of the worth of every person, of the fundamental equality of all men as human beings, of their interdependence, and of their mutual obligation one to another. To the same source it owes its understanding of men's lust for and misuse of power, of the peril of placing unchecked power in the hands of a few, and of the obligation of governments to safeguard each man against injustice, tyranny, and exploitation, and to seek the welfare not of a privileged few, but of all.

But modern democratic humanism has multiple origins. To a variety of sources other than Christian—among them classical humanism, the Renaissance, the Enlightenment, Romanticism, and modern scientific and cultural humanism—it owes other ingredients that vitiate its understanding of man. From these other sources have come faith in the capacity of education or technology to solve all human problems, belief in inevitable progress, and above all, disregard or denial of God's sovereignty over the world, and failure to recognise the imperfect, precarious, and transient character of all human achievements. According to democratic humanism, man is master of his own destiny and can achieve a perfect society. Men should rely wholly on their own powers to realise the good life for themselves and their communities, and their hopes need not reach beyond the improvement of their earthly existence. These beliefs are illusions. In holding them, democratic humanism even when still professedly Christian has become largely a Christian heresy.

The illusions of democratic humanists include also a confusion of ideals and facts. They hold the ideals of equality, freedom, and justice, and assume far too easily that in societies committed to the democratic way of life none of these ideals is denied in fact. But inequality, discrimination, injustice, reliance on naked power, exploitation, and aggression are not absent from democracies; and only man-centred self-righteousness can believe that they are.

Especially because of the historic connections of Christian conviction and democracy, Christians who dwell in democratic societies have the responsibility to bring to bear Christian judgment upon their societies, and to purge them of false assumptions and unjustified hopes. They must affirm men's indebtedness to God for the good earth and their own lives; men's obligation to hold all human possessions and accomplishments as stewards of God, in the service of His purpose for His children; men's dependence upon God for wisdom to do right and forgiveness for wrongdoing. They may share the hope that the institutions of society will be ordered more fully to protect and minister to the needs of all men; but they must know and declare that only in utter reliance upon God and obedience to Him can legitimate earthly hopes be truly discerned and rightly held. And they must insist that all human achievements, like all human persons, must suffer death and final judgment. Men's only sure hope is in the power, justice, and mercy of God in Christ Jesus.

(ii) *Scientific Humanism*. The hope of the scientific humanist is centred in the confidence that man, through the resources of science, technology, and education, can not only mitigate and perhaps remove hunger, poverty, disease, and ignorance, but also create a social order that will satisfy man's deepest needs and resolve his basic conflicts.

The scientific humanist, as we call him, is not necessarily himself a scientist. He is one who sees in science, applied to human affairs, the hope for mankind. He accepts the scientific method as the surest road to truth and most highly values truth of the kind that science gives. He believes that the most clamant needs of men today are needs that science alone can satisfy.

The ground of the scientific humanist's hopes lies in man's past achievement. Man has subdued nature; he has immensely developed his own mental powers; he has created in civilised society a specifically human world in the midst of nature. Civilisation is the sheet-anchor of the scientific humanist's hope. If it disappears, all hope disappears with it. But if it continues to grow, it can provide satisfaction for all legitimate human needs.

The hopes of the scientific humanist sometimes take an extravagant form, but they are more usually characterized by sobriety and hard work. The Christian can welcome a sober humanist as colleague in many common tasks, and thank God for his human compassion and disinterested service. But the scientific humanist by his very centering of all hopes on man must reject the Christian faith as an enemy. Man, he says, ought to carry the destiny of the world, Atlas-like, on his own back, but the Christian keeps man in leading-strings to God. He accuses the Christian, moreover, of thinking too highly of the virtues of suffering to be in earnest about abolishing it. He regards the Christian's doctrine of sin as a morbid influence, of psychopathic origin. Above all, he says that the Christian does not really care about the survival of civilization, because his hopes are not in this world.

The Christian must accept such criticism as far as it is valid. But he must fearlessly insist that man's hope is in God and not in himself. The hope that man can shoulder the burden of the world is an illusion that leads men through anxiety to despair. Its root is the deadly sin of pride, that will not admit man's dependence upon God, and that may involve him in all the evils of a quest for unbridled power. The Christian's joy in believing that God reigns is, for a consistent scientific humanist, impossible.

Of the Christian's impulsion to relieve and prevent suffering we speak elsewhere. When the scientific humanist sees suffering only as something to be abolished, he does not face the fact that to be human is to suffer, and that Christ has brought joyous hope out of suffering to thousands of people to whom scientific humanism can speak only of stoical endurance.

The Christian doctrine of sin, far from being an antiquated or neurotic theory, describes precisely the situation in which every man stands, the humanist along with all the rest. Out of good intentions evil as well as good arises, to thwart personal endeavours, and to plunge men into tyrannies and wars, civil chaos and social despair. The Christian hope gives strength to men who face this human situation in all its tragic depths. None of man's achievements can be the true ground of hope. But the Christian knows that the sin and evil which frustrate the humanist and blight his hopes are met and mastered by God's abounding grace. With his hope in God, the Christian can labour joyfully for men.

(iii) *Marxism.* Marxism is at once a philosophy of history, a practical programme, and, for many of its adherents, a powerful secular religion alive with hope. Its simplest appeal is to the disinherited multitudes everywhere, who need food, clothes, shelter, and enough security and freedom for decent living. They are the true proletariat, the chosen people of Marxist theory. But Marxism speaks also to more prosperous workers who feel cramped and dehumanized in their work, to warm-hearted friends of the downtrodden, to men and women ambitious to lead or hungry for comradeship, and to highly trained scientists, soldiers, patriots, and statesmen impatient for a new day. To all these men and women in many lands, Marxism offers an exciting word of hope.

First of all, Marxism is a philosophy of history, closely relating theory and action. It finds in conflict both the driving force of progress and the source of evil to be overcome. It teaches that man has no fixed nature, but is continually being made and remade in history, which in turn by social action he helps to make. God and divine sovereignty are denied. History and human existence alike begin when, in his struggle with Nature, man produces the means for his own existence and so differentiates himself from the other animals. Communism (and this is its great strength) addresses itself to the worker, and declares that it is through work that man achieves his humanity and fashions history. The most humble of workers thus has an essential role to play.

But if history is the cradle of humanity, it is also a struggle in which occurs *alienation* of men from one another and of each from himself. For the objects that man produces by his labour, and the parts of Nature that come under his control, are unequally divided between stronger and weaker, and so a class struggle begins. Since economic activities and relations are fundamental in society, the hostility between those who possess and those who are dispossessed poisons all human relationships for both classes. Happiness, justice, and love are no longer possible; and man in the class struggle is no longer truly man. Not individuals merely, but history itself is thus corrupted.

The conflict and the crises it engenders become most acute in capitalist society, and deepen as time goes on. But in that very agony arises a great hope. For the end of the age is at hand: a final cataclysm of revolution, in which the oppressive society will collapse, and the oppressed will be set free. The proletariat, the workers deprived of property, country, and family life, taught and led by a disciplined Communist party and united across national frontiers, can bring the revolution at the opportune moment, and so fulfil a messianic task for all mankind.

The fulfilment of history in the resulting classless society is above all a *reconciliation.* No longer separated by the products of their own work or by private exploitation, men will finally be able to meet one another freely and become real neighbours, as truly social men. The free association of producers will provide for all men the goods they need. Nature itself will cease to be man's enemy. There will be no more social classes, no class struggle, and therefore no coercive government, nor any cause for violence. All the wealth that mankind has amassed through the years will be gathered together, and made available for all.

It goes without saying that the demand for economic and social justice is one that all Christians must affirm, without vindictiveness or partisanship, but without compromise. Moreover, the Church and every Christian must acknowledge their full share of guilt for ineffectual preaching and practice of equity that has helped to open the way for Communist attacks. There is need also to recognise the powerful attraction of the confident Marxist reading of history, and the promise that the end of conflict and alienation is near. The Christian understanding of history and its fulfilment have not often been presented in our time with nearly so much persuasiveness and force.

On the other hand, the means employed by Communist leaders to seize and to hold power in the name of the proletariat, and the explicit teaching that any means required to break the power of class enemies are justified, have repelled many who have been drawn towards Communism by its demand for justice and its promise of peace. In practice, moreover, the Communist doctrine of the dictatorship of the proletariat has led in most cases to totalitarian dictatorship, in which the freedom of man is in fact denied.

But the Christian must press on to point out the illusions by which the Marxist creed itself is vitiated. First, the denial of God and the rejection of His sovereignty over all human history opens the way to the idolising of the party or the economic system. Second, the Marxist belief in the capacity of proletarian man to lead human history to its consummation, to be the Messiah of the new age, is belied by the facts of human nature as we know it. Third, the belief that mere stripping away of economic disabilities can abolish the strife and self-seeking that have marked all human history finds no support in actual Marxist behavior. The Christian doctrine of man's nature and destiny stands on more realistic ground.

(iv) *National and Religious Renaissance*. In many countries today, especially in Asia and Africa, whole peoples are in the midst of a revolution that is at once social, political, and religious. This vast upheaval has gathered momentum rapidly during the past decade. The Second World War, while it brought untold suffering to many, has opened up a new world to them, and history, once a wearisome repetition of unvarying events, has become for them suddenly alive.

Dwellers in towns and cities, and especially their leaders, had long known the benefits of applied science and political independence. But inhabitants of remote jungles were introduced to some of these benefits for the first time by the armies fighting in their territories. Moreover, the swiftness with which Western dominion was broken in many countries after the war brought to subject peoples everywhere a new sense of power and national self-consciousness, while those who, as in India, had fought for their independence mainly by non-violent methods found in the outcome a new confidence in their moral and spiritual resources.

At the same time, the religious and cultural patterns of their living show the impacts of the Christian Gospel, and of communism and humanism in various forms. In many lands it was through the Christian Church that men first came to see the possibilities of a new and better life. Both Christianity and its rivals have helped to quicken a new awareness of human dignity and of man's responsibility for his fellows. They have helped also to evoke a vigorous counter-assertion of the ancient religions as adequate to meet the problems of our perplexed generation.

The result of all this is a strong and growing nationalism, together with a revival of each people's concern for its own cultural and religious heritage. There is a new confidence among the adherents of Buddhism, Hinduism, and

Islam that their several religions hold the answer to the ills of the world. Buddhists today are planning a great world-wide missionary campaign. Neo-Hinduism is never weary of preaching that by virtue of its readiness to recognise truth wherever found, it alone can sum up the best in all traditions. Islam is recovering its missionary zeal, and offering membership in a world-wide brotherhood that transcends race and nationality. African peoples are seeking to revive their indigenous faiths to meet contemporary need.

We rejoice with the peoples of Asia and Africa in the new release of power which they have found, and share their anxiety to use it for the fullest benefit of their own homelands and the good of the whole world. It is good that there should be serious concern here and now for human values—for social justice, for better living conditions, for the preservation of cultural heritages—especially where these things have suffered long neglect. It is good that the cultural awakening in Asia has created a temper of purposeful activity, which seeks to cope with present demands and to shake off the lethargy bred of an age-long tendency to fatalism.

If it be urged, with some justice, that such activity is incompatible with the genius of world-denying religions like Hinduism and Buddhism, it must be remembered that these faiths grant a relative and provisional value to concern for personal worth, social justice, and human community. They regard the events of history with tentative optimism, even though history as such is denied any ultimate validity. This underlying pessimism, in turn, is negated by a transcendent optimism that sees the resolution of all conflicts, fears, and frustrations, and even of all hopes, in ultimate Reality which is beyond all change, activity, and purpose.

Islam, widespread in both Asia and Africa, gives a more positive place to human activity. It is the only one of the great world religions which had its origin within the boundaries of Christendom, and it bears clear traces of this origin, in creed and cult, in characteristic modes of expression, and even in its vehement rejection of the Cross as a blasphemous scandal. Its holy scripture, professing to be God's final revelation, opens with the praise of Allah as Lord of the worlds and King of the Day of Judgment. In the last days a Messiah, the rightly-guided Mahdi, will come in God's time to reform the world according to Muslim ideals. These are set forth in the Sacred Law (Shariat), that professes to be rooted in the revelation given to the Prophet, and that demands scrupulous obedience from the people of God.

But the real force which today is sweeping through the world of Islam is not the expectation of the Day of Judgment and the coming of the Rightly-Guided, but the power of rising nationalism. In this form, at once political, cultural, and religious, Islam is asserting again its confidence that it can heal the ills of mankind. Yet there runs underneath this self-assertion a deep feeling of frustration and bewilderment. The pattern of the ideal Muslim society is believed to be laid down in the unalterable Sacred Law, yet its actual life has to be carried on in the world of today. Modern Islam lives in a state of permanent religious crisis, of tension between the guardians of the old and the various groups of modern, forward-looking Muslims. The peoples of Islam, suspended between violent self-assertion and paralysing frustration, are in deep need of understanding from the side of the Western world.

In this whole situation the Church is called upon to engage far more seriously in its missionary task. This must include a real effort to understand the faith and hope by which so many millions in Asia and Africa are seeking to shape their national and personal lives. We must indeed warn them to remember that wherever absolute claims are made for nations or cultures, disaster follows. But at the same time we cannot stand by unmoved while our brethren of other faiths struggle to achieve social righteousness and the common good of their peoples. The Church needs to be warned against clouding its witness and neglecting its present duty by a disproportionate emphasis on other-worldly hopes. The preaching of the Gospel in Asia and Africa must be related to the immediate tasks in which we are bidden to do the will of God whose Kingdom is at work in the world now.

(v) *The Hope of the Hopeless.* We have spoken of some of the various hopes in which men in our time are seeking refuge. But what of those who, finding no such refuge, are without hope of any kind?

There are those whose experience of life has been so bitter that nothing of value or interest seems left to them. Dogged by disappointment, frustrated in all their dreams, or crushed by injustice and by man's inhumanity to man, it seems to them that they are the victims of a blind fate, or even that things have somehow been arranged by a malicious practical joker set only on their damage and destruction. As they regard the future, they are confronted at best with a bleak and dreary prospect, at worst with a prospect of suffering and misery hardly to be borne. To such embittered souls the whole business of politics and all nostrums for social amelioration appear only as moves in a futile game invented to distract their minds from the profound tragedy of life. When we remember the dreadful sufferings of the vast number of refugees and displaced persons in different parts of the world, we cannot wonder that many of them should fall victim to this kind of hopelessness.

There are others to whom life has not been so unkind but who, having for a time supported their spirits by one or other variety of anthropocentric hope, have now fallen into disillusionment. Their god has failed them, and they are left desolate. It is difficult to exaggerate the extent to which Western man, during the last century and a half, as he lost hold of his traditional Christian faith, has fastened upon some alternative dogma, progressionist or utopian, which enabled him to face the future with confident expectation; and it is difficult also to exaggerate the tenacity with which over a long period these dogmas continued to be held. But in our own time, partly under the pressure of disastrous events, but partly also through a more open-eyed examination of their own presuppositions, a growing number of our contemporaries are abandoning these hopes, even though they have nothing to put in their place. There is here an honesty of thought which can only be respected, but it issues in a situation which should at once evoke our deepest sympathy and cause us the profoundest alarm. However clearly we ourselves may see the illusoriness of such humanistic hopes, we should recognise the responsibility we take upon ourselves when we undertake the negative task of their destruction, lest the last state should be worse than the first.

In certain quarters a still further stage has been reached. There are those among us who, having rigorously purged their minds and their philosophies of every variety of temporising and ill-grounded optimism, of every illusion of progress, of every utopian expectation, of every shoddy or shadowy idealism, and having accordingly faced without blinkers the desperateness of the human situation in a godless world, have found a new courage coming to them from the very clarity and depth of their despair. Such are the atheistic "existentialists" who in some countries are now given so wide a hearing and many of whom write with great ability and with real literary grace. They are atheists, but atheists of a new kind. They no longer flout the issues with which Christian faith is concerned, but take them most seriously. They do not rejoice in the non-existence of God, but regard it as placing us in a situation of the most terrible solemnity. Each of us is completely alone, surrounded only by meaninglessness, so that if his life is to have any meaning or any value, he must create such meaning and value for himself, not forgetting that death swiftly puts an end to all. There is here a certain positive attitude to life, a certain courage, though it can hardly be called a hope, that arises and can arise only out of utter negation, out of the very death of hope. Here we have what is the most honest of all forms of anthropocentrism, and perhaps the only consistent form of it. In its open-eyed realisation of the desperate plight of those who are without God in the world, it repeats what is a central Christian affirmation; while its talk of a courage that can emerge only out of the darkness of the complete renunciation of hope seems to echo, even if only in a perverted form, the Christian teaching that only through the darkness of the Cross, with its cry of dereliction, can hope ever be reborn.

For all who, in any of these ways, are without hope in the world, our only message of hope is that there is One who understands them better than they understand themselves. Jesus Christ has plumbed the depths of human existence as no one else. He passed through the darkest night of the human soul, through utter loneliness and dereliction, before rising victorious over death and hell. In speaking this message to them, we must speak as those who have continued to crucify Him, for we share responsibility for the present hopelessness of so many of our fellow-men for whom Christ died. God give us grace and wisdom to speak the word of hope and to manifest it in acts of love in such a way that they may understand.

We have surveyed, all too briefly, some of the non-Christian hopes of our time on which the eyes of many men are fixed. We discern in their midst the presence of our exalted Lord, who in His earthly ministry moved among outcasts, refugees, political agitators and zealots, sophisticated intellectuals, simple workmen and soldiers, all of them with their thwarted hopes and unfulfilled aspirations. He accepted rejection, suffering, and death at the hands of those He came to save, and on His Cross prayed for them. As the exalted Lord He bids His Church, as today it confronts on every side men whose hopes are mocked or starved or fastened upon false gods, to walk the road He trod, for only as it goes the way of the Cross can the Church offer in word and deed a sure and steadfast hope.

C. The Christian Hope and Our Earthly Tasks

We must speak now of the present tasks to which God calls us, and of the hope we have in seeking to carry them out. Here as everywhere Christ is our hope. In Him, the crucified and risen Lord, God delivers us from the power of sin, quickens us into new life, and sets us free to serve Him, without fear, illusion, or idolatry, here and now.

For this world, disfigured and distorted as it is, is still God's world. It is His creation, in which He is at work, and which He sustains in being until the day when the glory of His new creation will fully appear. He is at once the creator and the redeemer. He preserves both those who serve Him and those who refuse Him service. He makes the sun to shine on the evil and the good. He is good to all, and His tender mercies are over all His works. We are forbidden therefore to treat this world as of small account, to turn away from it, to go by on the other side. On the contrary, all who are God's children must find joy in doing their Father's will in the world. God's will has been revealed to us in Christ. In His obedience until death He has manifested that will in action. In Him we have a foretaste of the Kingdom wherein His will is to be consummated. We are to do that will here and now, so far as in us lies. If the only-begotten Son came not to be served, but to serve, those who have been made His brethren are bound to do likewise.

The direction of our service is given in the all-embracing commandment: "Thou shalt love the Lord thy God with all thy heart, and with all thy soul, and with all thy strength, and with all thy mind; and thy neighbour as thyself." What, concretely, does love to God and our neighbour require of us? Most simply it requires us to recognise that in every human being Christ Himself comes to claim our service. God who has called us into the fellowship of His Son, has called us to serve Him in serving men.

Further, His calling lays upon us the obligation to do heartily that share of the world's work which is assigned to us in the place where we now are. Our daily work, indeed, provides the normal context for the many humble and obscure deeds of service which He will own at the last day as deeds done to Himself. We are often tempted to evade the demands of our immediate neighbourhood, giving all our attention to large plans concerning distant goals. But His solemn word about neglecting the daily needs of His humblest brethren we dare not ignore. Moreover, love to God and our neighbour must find regular expression in the faithful doing of that work which occupies the main part of our waking life. The busy scene where thousands of laymen are engaged in their ordinary business is a much-forgotten meeting place between the living Christ, His Church, and the world.

In the third place, our calling lays upon us responsibilities for seeking a better social and political life. Our own day has furnished another terrible demonstration of the suffering that follows the breakdown of stable social order. The misery of vast multitudes of hungry, homeless, and hopeless people is not only a challenge to Christian compassion and brotherly love; it is a reminder to every Christian that he is responsible before God for his due share of political and social action to secure for all men justice, freedom, and peace. For God who in His loving-kindness preserves this world which He has redeemed, sustaining in life even those who rebel against Him, wills that there shall be order, justice, and freedom among men. He has taught us to seek earthly justice, freedom, and peace, and to set our faces against injustice, oppression, and tyranny as evils which He abhors. Obedience to His will requires of us much more than the proclaiming of general ethical principles. It requires us to enter fully into the duties of the common life, understand to the best of our ability the economic, political, and social problems of our time, participate actively in the effort to solve them. We are to seek in all ways the just ordering of society, to promote wise legislation, and to share in responsible planning for the future. And we are to act in no light-hearted or half-hearted spirit, but counting the cost and being ready to pay it.

Obedience to God's will must lead the believer deep into the heart of all the world's sorrow, pain, and conflict. There is no man who does not meet us with Christ's claim for loving service, and no part of human life in which God's will is not to be done. It is God's will that men should have *life*, and have it abundantly. We cannot pray, "Thy will be done," unless we are at the same time willing to go to the help of those who are denied the necessities for human life. The cry of half the world's people for bread enough to sustain life in their bodies must be heard by the Christian as the cry of Christ. He who spoke the parables of Dives and Lazarus and of the Last Judgment will surely not leave us without condemnation if we are content to eat sumptuously while millions are in want. To all who are hungry, without decent clothing or housing, or bearing intolerable burdens in their personal or family lives, we are called to be neighbours. And the fulfilment of that duty will include every kind of responsible action, including political action, that is required to meet their needs. Moreover, while thinking of the physical needs of life, we must not forget the deep longing of men and women the world over for simple human love. Our restless, depersonalised society, with its nervous preoccupation with excitement and movement, does not favour the growth of lasting personal relationships in marriage, friendship, or community. We must show in our lives as Christians the splendour of human love when it is touched by the love of Christ, and do all that is in our power to provide for others the conditions in which human love may flourish.

It is God's will that men should know and love the *truth.* We cannot remain silent while men's minds are being drugged with lies. In our day seekers after truth are often compelled to sacrifice integrity to party orthodoxy, and the means of mass communication have become tools for producing social conformity. We must be ready to speak the truth at whatever cost, and where scepticism and relativism have robbed men of their ultimate convictions, we must lead them to know Him who is Himself the truth, and who requires us to seek and love the truth in every realm of life.

It is God's will that men should be *free,* to know and to serve Him. We cannot remain aloof when man's freedom is threatened. We cannot ourselves enjoy in any kind of self-complacency that inward freedom with which faith endows us, but must step in wherever the freedom of man is denied. We must stand for freedom of belief and conscience and for the right of all to witness openly to the truth of God. We must set ourselves against every political and economic oppression, and against the inhuman terror by which men seek to compel their fellows to submit to arbitrary laws and dictates, and to the service of false gods.

It is God's will that "*justice* roll down like waters and righteousness like a mighty stream." We must be ever alert to seek a greater measure of justice in social and political relationships, and to do battle against every unjust discrimination against class or race, and every denial of human rights, whether political or economic. We do not hold with those who think that they themselves can bring about a perfect social order, if necessary by the employment of terror and the silencing of the individual conscience. But neither do we hold with those who are content to be mere onlookers in the face of the miseries of prisoners, refugees, the dispossessed, the displaced, and the exploited, as if nothing could be done to better their lot.

It is God's will that *peace* should prevail among men. We cannot pray, "Thy will be done," while in the present world situation we do nothing, dare nothing, and sacrifice nothing for the sake of peace. We cannot abandon ourselves to the prospect of a third world war as an ineluctable fate, or regard the present competition in armaments with an easy conscience. Here we are not concerned with rival world views and abstract principles, but with fellow-men, who hunger for peace yet live under the threat of a war that would cast them into utter chaos.

Both the Church in its corporate acts and public words, and every single Christian in his deeds and words, are thus required to affirm Christ's Lordship over every part of human life. What that affirmation will involve in the spheres of international politics and race relations, in the development of a responsible society, and in the daily work of Christian laymen, is discussed in other Assembly papers.

Acting in society, the Christian is frequently confronted by the problem of compromise. Group responsibility and group decision are common and necessary features of modern life which often give rise to acute conflicts between corporate loyalty and individual conscience. Further, many situations in real life offer no possibility of doing what is wholly good. A Christian may well find himself compelled by the facts to stand for a lesser against a greater injustice. In extreme situations a Christian may have to take the decision to resign from public responsibilities, or to withhold obedience from civil authority and to challenge its acts at the risk of freedom and even of life. The Church must stand with all its members in prayer, in understanding, in Christian fellowship, and in action. Only if it does so, wisely and patiently, can the Church clearly recognise compromise that is sinful, and rebuke those who fall into it; or support and confirm decisions by its members to withdraw from public office, or to oppose civil authority in the name of Christ.

To such tasks as these God calls us, to act in the power of His Spirit. It is God the Holy Spirit who Himself brings forth in us the good works which are His own fruit, and guides our feet in facing the new tasks of every age. Though the Spirit is one, His gifts are many, distributed in rich variety to the members of Christ's body for their various services to one another and to the world. The nature of the tasks to be performed and of the gifts required varies from age to age and from place to place. The Church in the twentieth century is called to duties different from those which God laid upon the Church in the first century. Today our churches face situations and tasks of immense variety, some old and familiar, some new and profoundly perplexing. Yet in the face of all these the Christian may act humbly but confidently, assured that the Holy Spirit will furnish the gifts and power needed for faithful service in the world to those who are willing to ask the Father for His help, to hear His call, and to submit to His will.

In times of trial it is good to remember what God has in fact wrought in and through the Church in the nineteen centuries of its pilgrimage. The very existence of this people of God in the world, growing from age to age as new peoples are drawn into its fellowship, bears witness to God's power and faithfulness. In spite of all man's sin, the light of God shines upon and through His people in the darkness and perplexity of the world's life.

The life of service lived in Christ is therefore a life of unquenchable hope. We know that God's will must at last prevail, that His Kingdom will fully come. That is a certainty which no earthly failure or disaster can take away. Moreover, we know that what we do here and now for His sake in faith and hope is not in vain. It is not possible for us to know exactly how God will use our work, or what degree of visible success He will grant us in any particular project. The Christian is no more sure of success than his secular neighbour. But he is secure against despair, for he knows that what he commits into God's hands is safe.

At the same time, our actions and expectations will have a certain modesty. We shall not confuse our programmes with God's Kingdom. We cannot know in advance whether we shall achieve a stable and just social order for mankind in any way that we now have in view. The peace and the justice that we seek among men are still not God's perfect peace and God's holy righteousness. Even as we act in the honest intention to do God's will, we must still pray, "God be merciful to me a sinner."

Nevertheless, because God has not abandoned this world, because He rules and overrules its tangled history, and because we have been given a share in the power of His Spirit, we can with confidence hope and expect that what is built upon the foundations which He has laid will stand. We can hope for and expect miracles of help in answer to the prayers we make in our extremity of need. We can hope for and expect the success of concrete plans for the good of our fellow-men. We have no right to set limits to what God may be pleased to do within this present age. Indeed, such hopeful and expectant action for the doing of God's will in the world, in the face of apparently overwhelming odds, is an essential part of our full witness to the present reign of God. All our action will be but humble, grateful, and obedient acknowledgment that God has redeemed the world, and that in it we are called to participate in His ministry of reconciliation. We can therefore live and work as those who know that God reigns, undaunted by all the arrogant pretensions of evil, ready to face situations that seem hopeless and yet to act in them as men whose hope is indestructible.

IV. The Sum of the Matter

That then is what we have to say, in this present hour, and as delegates of the Christian churches here represented, in witness to the great truth that Jesus Christ is the hope of the world. It is a human witness to a thing that is itself divine. We are well aware of the poverty and obscurity of our expression of it. Only in part can this defect of our witness be ascribed to the divergencies of thought and understanding which still divide us. Nor can it be ascribed only to the finitude of human knowledge which must condition all our speaking. Rather do we know and confess that all we who venture to address the world, and the Church in the world, are not only fallible men but also sinful men, hard and dull of heart. The mystery of Christian hope deserves altogether more adequate expression than we have been able to give it. We must therefore be ready to place this message of ours under the sign of God's merciful judgment. Among the earthly hopes of which we have spoken we must place also this one—that it may be given to those who come after us, in saying again the selfsame thing, to say it differently, more clearly and more truly. And beyond that we await the eternal light which will at last illumine the darkness that besets even the best thoughts and words of sinful men.

Yet this does not stay us from being profoundly thankful to God for the measure of knowledge which, without any merit of our own, enables and emboldens us to say so much in common and with one voice. Nor does it at all qualify the earnestness with which we enjoin all whom it may concern to consider well what we have here undertaken to say, in good conscience and according to the best we knew, in testimony to Jesus Christ as the sole hope, the whole hope, the sure and certain hope of the world. We pray God that He may permit our word—once again quite apart from and contrary to any deserts of our own—to be of service to His own holy and righteous Word through the power of His Holy Spirit.

To whom do we say what we say here? We say it in the first place simply to the *world* whose hope—whether it be a Christian or a non-Christian, a believing or an unbelieving world—Jesus Christ is. The world in which we and all other Christians live is the world that God has loved from all eternity in Jesus Christ. To this world God has spoken through Him. In Him God has taken upon Himself the world's sin, its guilt, its darkness and its death, that from all these the world might be delivered. In His resurrection God has made manifest to all who believe on Him the world's salvation and its true life. As judge of the world He will appear as God's final revelation to every ear and every eye and as the final goal of all God's ways. To testify to the world concerning the world's hope is the meaning of the Church's existence in every age and every clime, and it is the purpose of all we have said. He that hath ears to hear let him hear! Let him hear not our word as such, but the Word of God which has impelled us to speak—the Word of God which is identical with the Work of Christ which was, and now is, and is still to be. He is not our Lord only but the Lord of all mankind. He is not our future only but the future of all mankind. There exists no man who is not called to find his brother in Him and his Father through Him. There exists no man who is not guilty before Him, beholden and answerable to Him. What is here said is said in solidarity with every man, for every man, and to every man; yet not in our own name, but in the Name of Him who as the world's Saviour is at the same time the Saviour of every man.

But for this very reason what we have said has been addressed also to *ourselves* and to the Christian congregations throughout the whole world whom we here represent. We proclaim no dogma. Even to the churches we speak as men to men. Yet with brotherly earnestness we speak to them as follows: Through what we have tried to say in this message you and we are confronted by the magnitude of the gift and task which have been entrusted to Christ's Church—by the dignity and responsibility of its mission as bearer of and witness to the only full and certain hope in the midst of a world darkened by so much false hope and also by so much hopelessness. You and we should know that it is not death which is the goal of mankind and its history, but the revelation of the Name, the Kingdom, and the Purpose of the holy and merciful God, that is to say, eternal life. And the meaning and dignity of our Christian existence is just to spread abroad this good news. But, because we look first at our Lord and only then at our own thoughts and words and works, this assignment of ours is at the same time our deep humiliation and a powerful challenge to embrace with far greater faithfulness than heretofore the hope that has been granted to the world and to ourselves. If we Christians, or if our Christian congregations, do not so live in the joy of this hope that others will thereby be brought to share our joy, who else is there who can do this? What are we doing with that which has been entrusted to us?

Here is a question which we desire in this message to engrave upon the conscience of Christ's Church and of ourselves as members of it. Is the Church the authentic witness of its Lord and Head, and so of the whole world's Hope, as it is called to be? Is it the pilgrim people who have here no continuing city but seek one to come, and who reckon not the sufferings of the present time as worthy to be compared to the glory that shall be revealed? Is it the company of watchmen who, because they have seen light in the east, know that the new day has already broken, and are sounding the trumpets to announce it to all their fellows? Is it the fellowship of those who now in this very time are able to recognize the coming King in His hungry, thirsty, naked, sick, captive, and refugee brethren, and are accordingly willing and ready in His Name to give them food and drink and clothing, to visit them and company with them? Is it a confessing rather than a denying Church? It does not lie with us who in this message to our Christian congregations address the whole world, to answer this question for them; but we may and must say to them that this is most certainly the question which is directed to them through our message. And further we must say that they have not understood our message aright unless and until they have understood our question (as we would wish to understand it for ourselves) as an occasion for repentance, for conversion and for faith, and a challenge to a new beginning. And further still, we must say that their and our proper answer to this question can consist only in the prayer that God the Father, the Son and the Holy Ghost may have mercy upon the Church in all lands, making it through

His Word to be the Church of hope and thus His Tabernacle among men. And finally, we must say that wherever a Christian congregation answers this question and lives in and through this prayer, the Church of hope is already present and at work—the people of God who, in order that we might proclaim His mighty acts, has called us out of darkness into His marvellous light.

APPENDIX I

Report of Section I: Faith and Order—Our Oneness in Christ and Our Disunity as Churches

Evanston, 1954

Introduction

We speak as those who have met together in the World Council of Churches and have known for a fact that we have been given a "oneness in Christ," in spite of our "disunity as churches."

This oneness is no mere unity of sentiment. We become aware of it because it is given to us by God as the Holy Spirit reveals to us what Christ has done for us. In this report we have tried to make clearer what we believe about this given unity, in the prayer that if we, and the churches from which we come, strive earnestly to lay hold upon the meaning of that which is already given, the Spirit of God will open our eyes to still deeper understanding, and our hearts to still fuller enjoyment of the unity which is ours in Christ. To that end:

First, we speak together with one mind, and in accordance with the witness of the New Testament, of the oneness of the Church, as grounded in the whole work of Christ, as growth into the fulness of Christ and as partially realized even in our present divided state.

Secondly, we speak of our disunity as churches as partaking of that disobedience over which Christ has won His victory, granting us even in our disunity some foretaste of our ultimate unity in Him.

Thirdly, we speak of some of the consequences for us, in the obedience of faith, as we meet together in His saving Name to beg Him to fulfil His unifying work in us.

I. Our Oneness in Christ

A. Christ's Unifying Work

The New Testament conceives of the unity of the Church not as sociological but as having its essential reality in Christ Himself and in His indissoluble unity with His people (Acts 9:4 ff.; I Cor. 12:12; Jn. 15:1 f.). Hence we must still ask Paul's question about division in the Church: "Is Christ divided?" (I Cor. 1:13), and assert with the Apostle the indestructible unity that belongs to the Church in Christ. Christ is the *one* Lord who represents and gathers to Himself the *many* of redeemed humanity, and it is therefore He alone who makes the many to be one in the Church (I Cor. 12:12; Eph. 1:10, 22; cf. Jn. 14:20; 17:4 f; I Cor. 6:16 f.).

The New Testament speaks in many ways of the relationship of Christ and His people to describe their unity in Him. The Church is many members in one body (I Cor. 12:12); the several members are subject to the one Lord as Head of the body (Eph. 1:22; 4:15; 5:23; Col. 1:18; 2:19); the Church is His bride, to be united to Him, the bridegroom (Mk. 2:19; Rev. 19:7; cf. Mt. 22:2 ff.; 25:10 f.; Lk. 12:36; Eph. 1:22 ff.); the faithful are His People (I Pet. 2:9 f.; Col. 3:12; Rom. 11:2, 11 f., 32); He is the new temple in whom true worship is offered (Jn. 2:19 ff.; cf. 4:21 ff.) or the one building of which the believers constitute living stones (I Pet. 2:5; Eph. 2:20; cf. I Cor. 3:9); He is the vine of which we are the branches (Jn. 15:1 ff.); or the shepherd whose flock we are (Jn. 10:1 ff.).

The New Testament thinks of the one life of the Church as deriving from the whole Person and work of Jesus Christ as Savior and Lord. The Church's unity is grounded in His taking of our nature upon Him; in His own words and works by which the power and life of His kingdom were manifested; in His calling of men into the fellowship of His kingdom, and in the appointing of the Twelve to share in His messianic ministry and work; in His passion and death, where sin was finally conquered and the power of divisiveness defeated; in His resurrection, where He manifested the new man unto whom we all grow (Eph. 4:11 ff.), in whom all human divisions are done away (Gal. 3:28); in His ascension and heavenly reign, by which all history is brought under His authority; in His outpouring of the Holy Spirit on the whole Church at Pentecost, which gives to each subsequent baptismal rite its deepest significance; and in His promise to come again as the triumphant and glorious king. Through the indwelling Spirit, the Comforter, who leads the Church into all truth, the unity of the Church even now is a foretaste of the fulness that is to be because it already is; therefore, the Church can work tirelessly and wait patiently and expectantly for the day when God shall sum up all things in Christ.

B. The Oneness of the Church in its Earthly Pilgrimage

From the beginning the Church has been given an indissoluble unity in Christ, by reason of His self-identification with His people. But the Church has never realized the fulness of that unity. From the beginning discord has marred the manifested unity of Christ's people (Lk. 22:24 ff.; Mk. 10:35 ff.). Thus we may speak of the oneness of the Church in its earthly pilgrimage as a growth from its unity as given to its unity as fully manifested (Eph. 4:3, 13). In this way we may think of the Church as we are able to think of the individual believer, who may be said at one and the same time to be both a justified man and a sinner (*simul justus et peccator*). In each Christian there is both the "new man" who has been created and yet must be put on daily (II Cor. 5:17) and also the "old man" who has been crucified with Christ and yet must be daily mortified (Col. 3:1-5). So the Church is already one in Christ, by virtue of His identification of Himself with it (Jn. 14:20; 15:1-5), and must become one in Christ, so as to manifest its true unity (Eph. 4:11-16) in the mortification of its divisions.

Christ of His love and grace has given His Church such gifts as it needs for its growth from unity to unity. The gifts are severally and together none other than Christ Himself, but each has its place and its function in the life of the Church as it strives to give obedience to its Lord. Christ has given His Spirit, which is the bond of peace and love, and the guide to all truth. He has given apostles, prophets, evangelists, pastors and teachers, that the unity of the body may be continually built up. He has given the Scriptures, the preaching of the Word, Baptism and Eucharist by which the Church proclaims the forgiveness of sins and by which, in the power of the Holy Spirit, faith is quickened and nourished. He has given the Church the gift and power of prayer, by which the Church can plead both for its own unity and for the reconciliation of men to God and to one another. He has given it faith and hope and love, that in its own life a new and divine unity shall be manifest in deeds, and that its service to the world shall be both a manifestation of unity and a summons to it.

The New Testament, therefore, testifies to us that the Church shares in the life both of this world and of that which is to come. Indeed the Church's life is encompassed by a "great cloud of witnesses" (Heb. 12:2)—and the Church must never forget that its citizenship is really there, in the heavenly places (Eph. 2:6). Its responsibilities must be discharged in this present world, but it must never become conformed to the world.

Thus the fellowship (*koinonia*) that the members of the Church have is not simply human fellowship; it is fellowship with the Father and with His Son Jesus Christ through the Holy Spirit and fellowship with the saints, in the Church triumphant. In all the Church's life there is being manifested not simply the activity of mortal men, but the life of the whole Church, militant on earth, triumphant in heaven, as it has its unity in the one Lord of the Church, who is its life.

But all this cannot be asserted without understanding that the unity given to the Church in Christ, and gifts given to the Church to help and enable it to manifest its given unity, are not for the sake of the Church as an historical society, but for the sake of the world. The Church has its being and its unity in the "Son of Man, who came not to be ministered unto, but to minister and to give his life a ransom for many." The being and unity of the Church belong to Christ and therefore to His mission, to His enduring the Cross for the joy that was set before Him. Christ wrought "one new man" for us all by His death, and it is by entering into His passion for the redemption of a sinful and divided world that the Church finds its unity in its crucified and risen Lord.

C. The Oneness of the Church Partially Realized

Jesus Christ has given to His Church the gift of Himself and thereby the means of corporate life. These gifts were given not solely to the Church of New Testament days, nor are they reserved for the Church in some ideal state which ought to exist but unhappily does not. We acknowledge these gifts as being in a real sense present possessions.

It would be ungrateful to a merciful God if we did not speak now of those gifts which assure us that the undivided Christ is present amongst us, pouring His life into us all, in spite of our divisions.

We all wait upon one Father, through the one Holy Spirit, praying that we may be ready to hear and obey when He takes of the things of Christ and shows them to us. We all read the Holy Scriptures and proclaim the Gospel from them in the faith that the Word speaking through them draws us to Himself and into the apostolic faith. We all receive His gift of Baptism whereby, in faith, we are engrafted in Him even while we have not yet allowed it fully to unite us with each other. We all hear His command to "do this" and His word "This is my body . . . this is my blood" in the Sacrament of the Eucharist, even whilst our celebration of the Lord's supper is not yet at one Table. We all receive a ministry of the Word and Sacraments, even whilst our ministries are not yet recognized by all and not understood in the same sense. We all are called to be imitators of Christ and to follow Him in moral obedience as we confess Him before men even though we are still unprofitable servants.

As we have come to know each other better in the World Council of Churches, we have come to appreciate the immense range of common practice and intention which we share. The *fact* of our common (though diverse) use of these gifts is a powerful evidence of our unity in Christ and a powerful aid to reminding us that unity lies in His work and not in our own achievements. We have also discovered that the old confessional divisions are being crisscrossed by new lines of agreement and disagreement.

We give thanks to Our Father for these evidences that our unity in Christ is a present reality, both in the World Council of Churches and in relation to other Christians whose fellowship we do not yet as fully enjoy. But the very fact that, in every case, our benefit from these mercies is marred by our separation from each other, compels us now to examine seriously how it is that our disunity as Churches contradicts our unity in Christ.

II. Our Disunity as Churches

Only in the light of the oneness of the Church in Christ can we understand the difference between diversity and division in the Church, and their relation to sin. There is diversity which is not sinful but good because it reflects both the diversities of gifts of the Spirit in the one Body and diversities of creation by the one Creator. But when diversity disrupts the manifest unity of the Body, then it changes its quality and becomes sinful division. It is sinful because it obscures from men the sufficiency of Christ's atonement, inasmuch as the Gospel of reconciliation is denied in the very lives of those who proclaim it.

Divisions in the Church have been caused and are perpetuated, to a large degree, by sincere concern for the Gospel. Some believed that others were departing from the God-given structure and faith of the Church by unwarrantable claims and unfounded doctrines. So came the schism between East and West. Some believed that God had called them to such reformation of the faith and order of the Church as would restore it to its primitive purity. They found their work could not be completed within the framework of Roman Catholicism; thus came the separate Churches of the Reformation. Some believed that the faith must indeed be reformed but within the framework of ancient and historic episcopacy. So the Anglican and Old Catholic communions became separated both from Rome and from many of the Reformed Churches. Some believed that the established churches of their day would not give free course to the Word of salvation. So the older Free Churches and the Methodist connexion felt themselves forced to adopt independent church orders. Similar acts of conscientious obedience to the will of God have likewise resulted, even if unintended, in breaches of Christian fellowship in doctrine, sacraments and order. God in His mercy has used such decisions to save souls, to build up communities who worship Him and to preserve or recover aspects of His truth. All this we can and must say. But He has also given to us today a fresh awareness of the sin which characterizes the divided state which we have inherited. We shall never, in this life, escape from our sinfulness, but we can repent of sin when it is revealed to us. Even when we have done that which we thought it right to do, we must remember that we are culpably implicated in sin not wholly of our own making and cannot dissociate ourselves from the sin of division. Confession of oneness with Christ carries with it confession of solidarity with our brethren in sin.

We ask each other whether we do not sin when we deny the sole lordship of Christ over the Church by claiming the vineyard for our own, by possessing our "church" for ourselves, by regarding our theology, order, history, nationality, etc., as our own "valued treasures," thus involving ourselves more and more in the separation of sin. The point at which we are unable to renounce the things which divide us, because we believe that obedience to God Himself compels us to stand fast—this is the point at which we come together to ask for mercy and light. So what we believe to be our "faithfulness" must bring us together at the foot of the Cross. The Cross tells us that where the dividing power of sin was most manifest, there God has gained the victory. By the same Cross He is able to make all things to work together for good—even our divisions. By planting the Cross of Christ in the midst of our divisions we believe He will overrule all their sin and make them serve His purpose of unity.

Concretely, this means that when churches, in their actual historical situations, reach a point of readiness and a time of decision, then their witnessing may require obedience unto death. They may then have to be prepared to offer up some of their accustomed, inherited forms of life in uniting with other churches without complete certainty as to all that will emerge from the step of faith. Otherwise, acts of apparent re-union might be merely acts of calculated self-aggrandisement and a betrayal of the true calling of the Church. But when churches have been ready in this sense "to die with Christ," they have found that He who raised Jesus from the dead is faithful and powerful still.

It is certain that the perfect unity of the Church will not be totally achieved until God sums up all things in Christ. But the New Testament affirms that this unity is already being realized within the present historical order. By the power of His Resurrection, Christ has granted this grace to His Church even now, and the signs of His work are discernible to him who has eyes to see. In the upheavals of the present hour, Jesus Christ is gathering His people in a true community of faith and obedience without respect for existing divisions.

We must not assume that the divisions which now separate Christians from one another correspond to those which Christ brings about in times of tribulation. Still less can we think that they will coincide with the separation finally to be made by the Son of Man. In this eschatological perspective all our human divisions are provisional.

III. The Action of Faith

Christ has made us one by breaking down walls of partition. We are nevertheless disunited as churches. How are we to act in the obedience of faith and hope in our one Lord?

At least we all ought to be united in thinking of our divisions with repentance: not the repentance we may expect of others, but that which *we* undertake ourselves—cost what it may—even when others are unwilling to follow. True repentance is the acknowledgment before God that we have sinned so as to be caught in the net of inexplicable evil and rendered unable to heal our divisions by ourselves. But we cannot in sincerity and truth repent of our various understandings of God's will for His Church, unless the Spirit Himself reveals that our understandings have been in error. Penitence cannot be hypocrisy. Neither can it truly be expressed without desire for forgiveness and amendment of life.

All of us as members of churches believe that we have been entrusted by God with certain elements of the one Church of Christ which we cannot forfeit. But at least we in the World Council of Churches are committed to a fellowship in which we are ready to bring our convictions under scrutiny in the presence of our fellow-Christians and in the presence of the living Christ. In common we seek to know the judgment of the Word of God upon these convictions as to any error which may be involved in them.

Together we suggest the following ways in which, being both united and divided, we all must seek to be obedient:

(i) In thanking God joyfully for the actual oneness He has given us in the World Council of Churches, we must try to understand the theological implications of this ecumenical fact and to implement it in the concrete relations of neighbor churches. With the Lund Conference on Faith and Order, we ask the churches "whether they should not act together in all matters except those in which deep differences of conviction compel them to act separately." We do not minimize the deep differences separating some churches. Nor do we ignore the numerous attempts to unite churches and the achievements of such reunion. In the World Council of Churches we still "intend to stay together." But beyond that, as the Holy Spirit may guide us, we intend to unite. The World Council of Churches is not . . . a Super-Church.* Hence we do not ask the World Council of Churches to initiate plans for union, but to keep providing occasions for honest encounter between divided Christians.

(ii) We must all listen together in the midst of our disunity to our one Lord speaking to us through Holy Scripture. This is a hard thing to do. We still struggle to comprehend the meaning and authority of Holy Scripture. Yet whenever we are prepared to undertake together the study of the Word of God and are resolved to be obedient to what we are told, we are on the way toward realizing the oneness of the Church in Christ in the actual state of our dividedness on earth. In this connection we need also to study together the significance of Christian Tradition and our various traditions, as reflected in liturgy, preaching and teaching.

(iii) We must consider frankly the influence of social and cultural differences upon the matters of faith and order which cause divisions, and also perceive how the events and developments of current history make disunity a most urgent question.

(iv) We must speak the truth in love with one another and practise that love towards those with whom we disagree (Eph. 4:15, 25). Sometimes this involves us in judgments which fellow-Christians cannot recognize as being made in love. At other times, we are so conscious of both the sin and the cultural conditioning with which all our judgments are infected that we are tempted to be more tolerant than truth allows.

(v) We must learn afresh the implications of the one Baptism for our sharing in the one Eucharist. For some, but not for all, it follows that the churches can only be conformed to the dying and rising again in Christ, which both Sacraments set forth, if they renounce their eucharistic separateness. We must explore the deeper meaning of these two sacramental gifts of the Lord to His Church as they are rooted in His own redeeming work.†

(vi) We must seek to acknowledge beyond the bounds of our own church each ministry that preaches the Gospel of reconciliation as a means whereby Christ performs His saving deeds. Especially need we to discover the meaning of the ministry of the laity for Christian unity.

(vii) We must bear witness together to the Gospel of Him who has al-

* See *The Church, the Churches and the World Council of Churches,* W.C.C. Central Committee, Toronto, 1950.

† Cf. Lund Report, Chapter V.

ready overcome our sins and divisions and who graciously uses sinners as His servants. Our divided witness is a necessarily defective witness, and indeed a scandal in the face of the non-Christian world. We have scarcely begun to work out the essential connection between "mission" and "unity." Our Lord's own prayer (John 17:21 f.) must become our own, not only on our lips but in our lives.

(viii) The measure of our concern for unity is the degree to which we pray for it. We cannot expect God to give us unity unless we prepare ourselves to receive His gift by costly and purifying prayer. To pray *together* is to be drawn together. We urge, wherever possible, the observance of the Week of Prayer for Christian Unity, January 18-25 (or some other period suited to local conditions) as a public testimony to prayer as the road to unity.

We cannot discern all that will be disclosed to us when we look to Him who is the Head of the Body and affirm our oneness in Him. We know that we shall be changed, but wherein we shall be changed we cannot know until, in the act of faith and self-denial, we are given to discern, through crucifixion and resurrection, the lineaments of the one true Body of Christ which our sinful dividedness obscures from ourselves and from the world. Rejoicing in the grace which has been bestowed upon us in His various gifts even in our sin and separateness, we here set our hope on our one Lord Jesus Christ, who comes to take control over our divided and broken estate and to heal it by His grace and power. At Amsterdam we said that we intend to stay together. He has kept us together. He has shown Himself again as our Hope. Emboldened by this Hope, we dedicate ourselves to God anew, that He may enable us to grow together.

APPENDIX J

Report of Section II: Evangelism—The Mission of the Church to Those Outside Her Life

Evanston, 1954

I. The Evangelizing Church

Jesus Christ is the gospel we proclaim. He is also Himself the Evangelist. He is the Apostle of God (Heb. 3:1) sent to the world to redeem it. As the Father sent Him so He sends us. He calls us and we must obey. He sends us and we must go.

We were hopeless about life and our place in it; He has given us hope and filled our life with meaning. We were hopeless in our sin, unable to do the right; Christ has given us hope. We were hopeless in our suffering and distress; we have seen our affliction turned into blessing by His grace and used for the furtherance of His glory. We were hopeless about the final outcome of the human story, in distress about the futility of our own efforts; Christ has given us hope. We were hopeless in face of death, trembling between the fear of annihilation and the fear of future punishment, but Christ having overcome the sharpness of death has opened to us the gates of the Kingdom.

Who are the "we" who have hope not only for themselves but for all the world? The people of God, the Church of Christ on earth. For the Church is the community which is able to say this "we" in truth. Indeed, called from heaven and answering on earth, set by God as the sign and sharer of the life and work of Jesus Christ, the Church's very existence is a miracle of grace. To evangelize is to participate in His life and in His ministry to the world.

This ministry is the ministry of the risen and ascended Christ: Christ as He is today. It is the ministry of God become man, by which God's Kingdom is come among men. It is the ministry of Christ's life on earth by which God is revealed as the Father. It is the ministry of His death on the Cross by which the sin of the world is taken away. It is the ministry of His resurrection by which the powers of death and evil have been decisively defeated. It is the ministry of the heavenly Intercessor who does not will that any should perish. It is the ministry of the coming Christ by whose mercy and judgment the world is governed even now.

In and by this ministry the Church lives in the power of the Holy Spirit whose work enables and confirms its testimony. He changes the lives of sinful men and they, forgiven and restored to their true heritage as God's children, are being gathered together against the day of Christ's return in power. They are called by Him to be witnesses of His gospel. We have, alas, to confess with shame that we have all too often failed our Lord by the feebleness of our testimony and the slackness of our zeal. Nevertheless, where the gospel has found true lodgment in men's hearts, they have been inspired with compassionate desire to share it with their fellows. The love of Christ constrains them through their understanding of His death for all men. It impels them, in loving gratitude to Him to whom alone they owe their salvation to share with others the unspeakable benefits they have themselves received, so that all may enter into the joy of the Lord.

Therefore, whether it meet success or failure, closed doors or open doors, the Church in its work of evangelism is delivered from bondage to visible results. The gospel is preached because the Lord is risen and the age of the Messiah begun and "He must reign until He has put all enemies under his feet." Meanwhile we await the full disclosure of His kingly glory. Nevertheless He has not left His people at any time without some sign that He is at work victoriously, nor are such signs lacking in the time in which we now live. Thus is the Church enabled to find its joy in simple obedience to the divine call.

II. The Evangelistic Dimension

The people of God are in this world as the Church, and they are never alone with their Lord in isolation from the world. It is the *world* which He came to save. Without the gospel the world is without sense, but without the world the gospel is without reality. Evangelism is no specialized or separable or periodic activity, but is rather a dimension of the total activity of the Church. Everything the Church does is of evangelizing significance. Through all the aspects of its life the Church participates in Christ's mission to the world, both partaking of the gospel and seeking to communicate it. Evangelism is the place where the Church discovers itself in its true depth and outreach.

But this witness of the Church to its Lord is weakened by our faithlessness —not least by our divisions. Therefore will the Church deal with these divisions with holy impatience and passionately strive for unity. Unity is destroyed where there are confessional antagonisms, nor will unity of faith and life among Christians be achieved except as churches increasingly work together to bring the gospel to the whole world. Also, wherever Christians find themselves separated by caste, class, racial, or other barriers, they will boldly cross them, manifesting Christ's solidarity with the whole of mankind. In a divided world they will fulfill Christ's ministry of peace, manifesting in their own life the new mankind which has begun in Jesus Christ. Wherever they encounter social injustice, they will do battle for its redress, bearing witness to the restoration of humanity in Christ.

These truths, however, have frequently remained platitudes to which we have paid lip service, while we ourselves rest in self-satisfaction and sloth.

What then are the concerns of evangelism? One is surely so to proclaim the gospel that it will transform the groupings and patterns of society in which men and women are involved, to the end that human institutions and structures may more nearly conform to the divine intention, and respect the limiting prerogative of God. We who think ourselves converted to the Christian gospel, and who have indeed entered into many of its blessings, should beware lest whole areas of our thought and outlook remain unregenerate, so that it is after all not the whole gospel to which we have been converted. No man is fully regenerate until he has brought every thought into captivity to the obedience of Christ.

Still another aspect of evangelism is the attempt to bring people into the full life of the Church as expressed in a local congregation; for an isolated Christian, if such were possible, would be in a tragic state.

But underlying these concerns of evangelism is the bringing of persons to Christ as Savior and Lord that they may share in His eternal life. Here is the heart of the matter. There must be personal encounter with Christ. It is not enough to present Him merely as an example to follow. The gospel proclaims a living Christ. Just as to remain with Him is the mark of Christian experience, so to bring men to meet Him is the purpose of all evangelism. For on his relationship to God in Christ depends the eternal destiny of every man.

III. Communicating the Gospel

We must remember that evangelism is God's work in which we are His agents. It is not our work, and therefore we must wait upon Him in prayer and in meditation upon His holy Word, that we may learn what He would have us do and so be able to say, "It seemed good to the Holy Spirit and to us." Through His guidance we must seek lines of effective communication with those outside the Church's life and be prepared to face the demands which the proclamation of the gospel makes upon us.

We must recognize that the first requisite for communicating the gospel is to be possessed by the transforming power of Jesus Christ. As we witness to it, so do we also live by it. If it stops with us, it begins to fade in us. The second requisite is that we must love our neighbor as he is, even as Christ has loved us. He must feel that we understand him and that he can trust us. By some form of acceptance and helpfulness he must come to feel that we truly care for him.

The Church which God uses to communicate the gospel is a fellowship, a *koinonia,* drawn and held together by the love of Christ through the power of the Holy Spirit and by the need and desire of its members to share this experience with each other and to draw those outside into that *koinonia.* The evangelizing Church will offer this gift in its preaching and teaching; in its acts of worship and administration of its sacraments; through the individual and group witness of its members; by leading its people to base their life upon God's Word used in personal and family devotions; by fostering small fellowships; and by works of social service.

Although no strategy of communication is itself a guarantee of success, communication with those outside the life of the Church makes the following demands:

First, there must be encounter with the world. The Church must break out of its isolation and introversion, meeting the individual where he is with the compassion and comprehension of Christ. While this initial demand applies to all evangelism, it is particularly relevant to workers and intellectuals, many of whom are conspicuously outside the life of the Church. No social group lies outside the orbit of the compassion of Christ.

Secondly, there must follow the speaking of a word which is intimately related to the problems of the individual in his world. We must let every man know that he is of inestimable worth in the sight of God. There are times of personal crisis when the relevant word can only be the good news of the loving compassion of God in Jesus Christ. In addressing the worker, the word must be related to his social condition and aspirations; and the word can not be spoken to the intellectual unless we make it clear that in the Church's message there is a cogent and coherent view of life.

Thirdly, too often our words have been impotent because they have not been embodied in works of service, compassion and identification. It is not enough for the Church to speak out of its security. Following our incarnate and crucified Lord we must live in such identification with man, with his sin, his hopes and fears, his misery and needs, that we become his brother and can witness from his place and condition to God's love for him. Those outside the Church make little distinction between faith and works.

Fourthly, in order to possess the power to evangelize, the Church must nourish its life on the Bible. To recover for current thought the great biblical concepts is one of the pressing needs of evangelism. In the communication of the gospel the Bible occupies a unique and central place. The Bible speaks to all, provides a common language for the Church, transcending our divisions. The translation and distribution of the Holy Scriptures is an inescapable task of the evangelizing Church.

IV. Exploring Frontiers

A. Renewal of the Inner Life

The first area of evangelism is our own inner life. When Jesus gave us the solemn and joyous commission to be His witnesses, He commanded us to wait for the power of the Holy Spirit. This does not mean that we should delay our mission until we become perfect. As we seek to communicate our faith to others, we are inwardly renewed and forced back upon the resources of the Spirit. This is equally true of the congregation in its corporate witness.

B. The Witnessing Laity

The laity stand at the very outposts of the Kingdom of God. They are the missionaries of Christ in every secular sphere. Theirs is the task to carry the message of the Church into every area of life, to be informed and courageous witnesses to the will of our Lord in the world. To this end they will need training and guidance. Such training involves instruction in the content of the Christian faith and in the significance of that faith for obedience and witness in the different contexts of lay life. This kind of training will require the services both of ministers and of experienced laymen.

C. Christian Education

One of the most important areas of evangelism is that of childhood and youth. Every new generation requires the fresh presentation of the gospel. Among the most important methods of Christian nurture are Sunday schools, youth programs, Bible fellowships, discussion groups and, most of all, Christian training in the home.

D. Chaplaincies

New forms of specialized ministries are appearing. Because they are more fluid and indigenous, they enable the Church to penetrate structures and groups partially or wholly outside its life. In them the ecumenical approach of the churches working together can achieve what the various denominations acting separately can never bring to pass. Among such chaplaincies are those to hospitals, prisons, the armed forces, industry, the universities, and schools.

E. Parish Experiments

Traditionally the Church's congregational life has been based on the family and on the geographical area. Where this is breaking down, it is urgent that the Church come to life in small neighborhoods, e.g., in "street or house churches" where neighbors, church and non-church, gather to think and pray, with the help of the minister, about their work and leisure, and thence enter the Church's continuing life. Such fellowships often cut across denominational boundaries.

But in many parts of the world today the determining context of a person's life is not where he lives but where he works. The companionship of those with whom he works largely determines the framework of his beliefs and attitudes. What has been and is still true of village life in Asia or Africa, where decisions are decisions of the group, is now true in many social environments in the West also. It has become imperative, therefore, that the gospel be addressed to the group as well as to the individual. Where this has been done successfully, the result has been the emergence of a Christian community whose locus is the factory, the mine, the office, the waterfront, the university. When a Christian community emerges and when this community seeks to express its life and faith in worship and witness, its members form to all intents and purposes a Christian congregation.

Such developments raise questions about the adequacy of traditional forms of parish life, and about the cooperation of the churches, since the groups are often interdenominational. They also raise questions about the role of the minister and about the way in which he should identify himself with the group which he seeks to lead to faith in Jesus Christ.

We would urge the churches to give serious thought to these questions; for they point to a challenge which the new form of society in our technical age makes to the present social structure of parish life.

F. Media of Mass Communication

Literature and the arts play an increasing part in the shaping of men's outlook; but we also face today the overwhelming impact of the cinema, radio and television, as well as the greater perfection of posters, newspapers, and magazines. The result is that the convictions and decisions of individuals in many countries are reached under the pressure of a common mental climate which these media of mass communication tend to create. Hence the Christian Church must use these same media: for it is essential that Christianity, the questions it asks and the answers it offers, should permeate the general consciousness, if the ground is to be prepared for individual decision for Jesus Christ. In many countries the churches can make full use of these opportunities only if they are prepared to work together.

There are dangers in the use of these media. When the gospel is secularized, vulgarized, or diluted into an easy alternative to facing the demand of God for a personal response, it does much harm. The main means by which the Holy Spirit brings men out of passive looking and listening into personal commitment to Christ in His Church is personal meeting with a living Christian. Yet religious broadcasts and films, and Christian messages in the daily press, and in tracts, can do much to preserve channels of communication for the gospel.

Religious material for broadcasting should be of the best quality and should by no means be confined to services of worship. In our day, Christians in many parts of the world have numerous opportunities for following up religious broadcasts in casual conversation and discussion, since such broadcasts reach great numbers who are not committed members of any church.

G. A Trained Ministry

Because of its importance in the life of the Church, serious thought should be given to a more realistic training of the ministry, including provision for the service of theological students in industry and agriculture, and the addition of social studies and field work to the curriculum.

V. Non-Christian Faiths

The renascence of non-Christian religions and the spread of new ideologies necessitate a new approach in our evangelizing task. In many countries, especially in Asia and parts of Africa, these religious revivals are reinforced by nationalism and often present themselves as effective bases for social reform. It is not so much the truth of these systems of thought and feeling which makes appeal, but rather the present determination to interpret and change oppressive conditions of life. Therefore they confront us not only as reformulated creeds but also as foundations for universal hope. Such hope is based on man's persistent desire to be master of his own destiny. The gospel hope, on the contrary, does not rest upon what man can do for himself but on God's promise, in judgment and mercy finally to fulfill His purposes.

The Christian knows and believes that in Jesus Christ God has given to man the full and only-sufficient revelation of Himself. "There is none other name given under heaven by which we must be saved." The Christian will proclaim the gospel as God's judgment upon all human quests and questionings. But in his approach to men of other faiths he will humbly acknowledge that God has "not left himself without witness." Wherever he finds light he will not try to quench it but bear witness to Jesus Christ, the true light—"the light which lighteth every man."

The ambassador of Christ is primarily concerned not with the faith that a man professes, though he should understand it with sympathetic insight, but with him as he really is, a sinner like himself and one for whom Christ died. This means that the first step in evangelism must always be not that of controversy but of identification and alongsidedness.

In our task of evangelism among the adherents of non-Christian religions we must proclaim the whole truth of the Christian gospel. But we must always bear in mind that there are human elements in our witness to it which stand under the judgment of God. The gospel is greater than any particular human testimony to it. It is also the ultimate standard of God's judgment on every aspect of our response to His light and truth. There is always the danger, in the case of both the Christian and the non-Christian, of limiting the gospel to his own understanding of it. In our missionary effort we must always measure our conformity to the gracious will of God by the gospel, assured that, as we pray, the Holy Spirit will lead us into all truth. Also, only as we are willing to put our life and witness under the constant judgment of our Lord, and have been enriched by the fruits of evangelism, can we guard against this danger and bear witness to the gospel in ever-increasing measure.

The proclamation of the gospel and every argument to commend it must be accompanied by the demonstration of its transforming power. The gospel is not the emergence of a new ideal in man, but the entrance of a new power from God into the world. It must, therefore, be proclaimed in the context of power in action. The seeds of the Kingdom are not words and arguments but the children of the Kingdom themselves, scattered and sown in the field of the world.

Finally, since the gospel is the lifting up of the cross of Jesus Christ as the sole hope of mankind, He asks His witnesses to walk the way of the cross, in complete self-sacrifice and faithfulness unto death.

VI. Come, Lord Jesus

The Church partaking through the Holy Spirit in the life of its Head is assured of the fulfillment of His work. The messenger of the unlimited grace of Christ looks towards the consummation of the Kingdom in which His redeeming love shall have achieved its full intention. How thoughtlessly they speak who say, "Where is the promise of His coming? For ever since the fathers fell asleep, all things have continued as they were from the beginning of all creation." To them the answer has been given, "The Lord is not slack concerning his promise, as some men count slackness, but is long-suffering to us-ward, not willing that any should perish, but that all should come to repentance." The time of expectation is the time of evangelism, even as the time of evangelism is the time of expectation. For He who comes as our Judge is also our Redeemer.

The tragedy of the world is that it knows no judge, no lord of history. To the Church it is given to know that man is not condemned to an endless succession of meaningless nights and days, to never completed toil, to uncomforted mourning or ever-disillusioned hoping. It possesses, or rather is possessed by, the hope of a glorious fulfillment.

In this hope we are saved and by it we live, considering "the sufferings of this present not worthy to be compared with the glory which shall be revealed in us." The time of evangelism will not last forever; it will be succeeded by the time of the Kingdom fulfilled. The good news will not remain forever a promise made: it will become a promise kept. The gospel will not be the knowledge of the privileged few: it will be revealed to all. Seeing in a glass darkly will not be our ultimate vision of God: we will know even as we are known until we say, "We are complete in Him."

Therefore are Christians under constraint to declare this hope to the world until the consummation of the Kingdom and the coming of the King.

APPENDIX K

Report of Section III: Social Problems—The Responsible Society in a World Perspective

Evanston, 1954

Introduction

Christian social responsibility is grounded in the mighty acts of God, who is revealed in Jesus Christ our Lord. He has created the world, and all time is embraced within His eternal purpose. He moves and acts within history as the ever-living God. The center of world history is the earthly life, the cross and the resurrection of Jesus Christ. As has been affirmed in the Report on the Main Theme, in Him God entered history decisively, to judge and to forgive. In Him are revealed the present plight of man, and the end toward which the world is moving.

He has established with men a living relationship of promise and commandment in which they are called to live in faithful obedience to His purpose. The promise is the gift of abundant life as children of God for those who hear and follow the divine call. The commandment is that men should love God and their neighbors. In the call to responsible social action, the promise and the commandment of the righteous and loving God require us to recognize that in every human being Christ Himself comes to claim our service. Responding to God's love in Christ, and being aware of His final judgment, Christians will act responsibly. The call to social righteousness is sustained by the sure hope that the victory is with God, Who in Christ has vanquished the powers of evil and in His own day will make this victory fully manifest in Christ.

Man and all the powers of this world are under the sovereignty of their Maker who calls men in families, societies, nations, and all human groups to responsibility under Him. From Christ men receive the direction for their service, the obligation to share heartily in the world's work and daily tasks, and the responsibility to seek a better social and political life. Our hope in Christ enables us to know that there are limitations set upon every human ideal and achievement, so that we never make an idol out of any social cause, institution, or system. Moreover, because our hope is in Christ, we are saved from frustration where our efforts to influence public opinion or social action are seemingly in vain and we are saved from despair when all human hopes collapse.

The churches have come to realize more fully that they have a duty to society as part of their mission in the world. The scope of this mission is defined in the inclusive reports of this Assembly, but its relation to the responsible society is the assignment of this report.

Our hope in Christ does not offer technical answers or specific solutions which statesmen and experts have not found. But in the context of Christian faith we gain new insights into our dilemmas and ways to overcome them. In all the specific tasks with which this report deals we attempt to give expression to that hope.

I. The Meaning of the Responsible Society

The first assembly of the World Council of Churches at Amsterdam coined the term "The Responsible Society." It was stated that the responsible society is a society "where freedom is the freedom of men who acknowledge responsibility to justice and public order and where those who hold political authority or economic power are responsible for its exercise to God and to the people whose welfare is affected by it."

"Responsible society" is not an alternative social or political system, but a criterion by which we judge all existing social orders and at the same time a standard to guide us in the specific choices we have to make. Christians are called to live responsibly, to live in response to God's act of redemption in Christ, in any society, even within the most unfavorable social structures.

This report will deal mainly with large-scale institutions. But the realization of a responsible society must be achieved in small groups as well as in large. Human living acquires meaning and depth only in relations with other persons, and since an individual can have direct and close contact only with a limited number of people the art of social living has to be learned in small groups.

The most fundamental of these is the family. For this reason the churches must give strong warning against the widespread disruption of family life. The family itself needs to be protected; for this the witness of the Christian family is all-important. More attention should be given to the conditions which cause the forcible separation of families and every effort should be made to reunite those who have been separated. For right development into responsible adulthood, children need security and love, and the discipline which family life preeminently secures. Disintegration here is closely related to disintegration in the larger groupings of society. In predominantly non-Christian countries, the building of a Christian family life implies in some cases a rupture with old non-Christian family systems. The specifically Christian attitude toward the family should be clarified within different cultural circumstances in order to strengthen the community life of Christians in its most elemental form.

But the family is not the only group in which man can practice the art of living as "little men in big societies." There is often in modern life a family egotism which hinders social responsibility rather than furthering it. We are called to serve in other communities also. People cooperating in the same work or in the same factory should form nuclei of human relationships in a technical world; for young people teamwork and cooperation with friends sometimes provides the best opportunities for learning the art of living together; where in some parts of the world the village community or tribal group still offers a protection for human relations, they should be preserved and adapted to modern circumstances.

The Christian congregation itself should be a visible center of community and a base for local social responsibility. Its worship should be discernibly relevant to the total life of the society in which it is set. It must break down those barriers within its own life which deny fellowship so that it may begin to show in its action a solution to the real problems troubling the local community. It should also be concerned with the possibilities of renewing personal life through the corporate life of small groups. And it must, equally with the family, beware of egotism that prevents its sharing in the wider life of the church or of the community as a whole.

A. The Structure and Function of the State

The Oxford Conference on Church, Community and State in 1937 gave the following definition of the function of the state with regard to justice: "Since we believe in the Holy God as the source of justice, we do not consider the state as the ultimate source of law, but rather its guarantor. It is not the lord but the servant of justice. There can be for the Christian no ultimate authority but very God."

True justice is dynamic and its forms must vary to meet changing needs. Those who seek it should be made sensitive by love to discover such needs where they have been neglected. Justice involves the continuous effort to overcome those economic disadvantages which are a grievous human burden and which are incompatible with equal opportunity for people to develop their capacities. Justice requires the development of political institutions which are humane as they touch the lives of people, which provide protection by law against the arbitrary use of power, and which encourage responsible participation by all citizens.

In recent years the Churches have had to give fresh thought to the nature and functions of the state. No one form of government has a universal claim on Christians, but any political system must include some elements without which it tends to become an oppressive tyranny. For these, Christians should work by active participation in political affairs. In some situations where it may at present seem impossible to work directly for them, the Christian has chiefly the obligation to do what he can to defend other persons against particular acts of cruelty and injustice.

Christians should work for the embodiment of the Responsible Society in political institutions by emphasizing the following:

(1) Every person should be protected against arbitrary arrest or other interference with elementary human rights.

(2) Every person should have the right to express his religious, moral, and political convictions. This is especially important for those who belong to minorities.

(3) Channels of political action must be developed by which the people can without recourse to violence change their governments.

(4) Forms of association within society which have their own foundations and principles should be respected, and not controlled in their inner life by the state. Churches, families, and universities are dissimilar examples of this non-political type of association.

The Oxford statement applies in the following way to the function of the state with regard to social justice in economic life. While the state is sometimes the enemy of freedom, under many circumstances the state is the only instrument which can make freedom possible for large sectors of the population. The state is not the source of social justice, but it must be its guardian, ready if necessary to accept responsibility to counteract depression or inflation and to relieve the impact of unemployment, industrial injury, low wages, and unfavorable working conditions, sickness and old age. But in doing so the state remains the servant, not the lord, of social justice. Therefore we must warn against the danger that the union of political and economic power may result in an all-controlling state. In contradistinction to actions of the state it is the task of the non-governmental sectors in economic life to be the guardians of responsible private action in society. But within the private sector, both employers and employees in all their varied organizations in their turn are the servant, and not the lord, of freedom and welfare. When necessary in the public interest, the state must intervene to prevent any centre of economic or social power which represents partial interest from becoming stronger than itself, for the state alone has the power and the authority under God to act as trustee for society as a whole.

At all stages of political development and in the face of all the problems noted here, a Christian community must act as a conscience for the nation and ceaselessly remind all who hold power of God's purpose for the nation and of God's judgment upon their use of power.

B. Problems of Economic Life

New Trends. One of the most important features of the modern world is the way in which society has increasingly taken the control of economic affairs out of the sphere of "automatic responses." Full employment policies, the spread of state action in economic life, and the growing economic power of organized groups of employers, employees, farmers, and professional people have brought great changes in the highly industrialized countries.

The need for inter-governmental cooperation in economic affairs accompanies the increase in domestic state action. In some areas, such as Europe, social reconstruction and supranational integration go hand in hand and challenge many old political and economic ideas. At the same time, the priority given to full employment policies in many countries strengthens tendencies towards economic self-sufficiency and can threaten international economic cooperation.

The new emphasis on state initiative and international organization in the development of economic life has been accompanied by a fresh recognition of the importance of relative freedom in enterprise and of the regulating role of the price system. Many socialists have come to appreciate the importance of the private sector of the economy and the necessity for the energetic, enterprising and expert business man as well as being aware of the dangers of centralized government.

New Problems. These developments suggest that disputes about "capitalism" and "socialism" disguise the more important issues in the field of economic and social policy. Each word is applied to many different social forms and economic systems. It is not the case that we have merely a choice between two easily distinguishable types of economic organization. Private enterprise takes many shapes in different countries at different stages and in different parts of one economy and is profoundly affected by the forms of government regulation. The operations of the state in business also take various forms, such as post offices run by government departments, supply of electric power or gas by local authorities, and national or state public corporations. In all types of economy there is to be found a variety of forms; there is no one pattern that is universally valid. There are also various types of cooperative organization. In some countries the "welfare state" or the "mixed economy" suggests a new pattern of economic life; others may be regarded as "capitalist," but the capitalism of today is very different from the capitalism of even twenty or thirty years ago. The concrete issues in all countries concern the newly-evolving forms of economic organization, and the relative roles of the state, organized groups and private enterprises.

The Church's Role. The Church is concerned with economic life, because of God's concern for human beings who work to produce goods and services, who use them, and for whom business exists. The Church cannot uncritically support any particular form of organization as it exists in any particular country, but should be especially concerned with the following moral implications of economic life:

(1) State action in recent years has taken many new forms. The state must do those things for the economy that private industry cannot do properly, such as planning for urban development, stimulating industrial expansion and soil conservation, some types of large-scale industrial and agricultural research, and guidance of the distribution of industry. But state action needs to be decentralized, limited, and adaptable. The Christian should be ready to welcome fruitful new experiments, whether in the field of state action, private business or cooperative endeavor.

(2) Efficient production is important as well as fair distribution. Much Christian social thought in the past has tended to ignore the former and stress primarily the latter. Laziness and waste are sins before God no less than selfishness and greed.

(3) The churches have been properly critical of monopolistic practices, and of the effects of many irresponsible business practices on people and society generally. But they also need to understand and lay stress on the valuable contribution which the skilled executive has to make to society, irrespective of the form of ownership or organization. At its best the business system has provided incentives for the responsible initiative and hard work which produce economic progress, and has embodied the wisdom of decentralized decisions and widely distributed power. These are virtues needed in any system.

(4) The churches must never fail to recognize that the worker should have a status in society which accords with his responsibilities and his human dignity. Much has been done in recent years, but Christians are too ready to forget how much needs to be done, even in countries where social security and re-distribution of income and power have gone far.

(5) One of the most important economic roles is that played by the world's farmers. In some countries they have met urgent needs by extraordinary advances in productivity. For the feeding of increasing populations with a better diet, radical changes in farming methods will have to be carried through in many other countries, but always with due regard to the human consequences. The churches should recognize the justice of the farmers' demand for a reasonable measure of security of income; but even as they advance their legitimate demands for justice, farmers must resist the temptations to exhaust the soil, to exploit those who work for them, or to take unfair advantage of the consumers.

There are a number of places where our Christian concern for society makes us uneasy about the existing situation or where there is a demand for positive action.

(1) We can never forget the warnings in the Bible about the dangers to the rich man. In our day these warnings must be applied to the temptations facing everyone in a rich society. The tendencies to create unlimited wants, to overemphasize material values and to appeal to motives of social pride, envy and lust, stimulated by irresponsible salesmanship and advertising, are dangerous and need curbing.

(2) Not only increased production but a stronger regard for equity in the distribution of wealth and income is also required. At the same time such factors as the place of incentive and the desire to avoid regimentation necessi-

tate a measure of inequality in modern economic life. But every society should recognize the extent to which great contrasts between rich and poor destroy fellowship and undercut the political institutions of a responsible society.

(3) The churches have a duty to promote adequate assistance on the national and international level for children, the sick, the old, the refugees, and other economically weak groups, by means of church organizations, voluntary societies, and local or national governments. It is the duty of the Christian to work for improved national or local welfare legislation and for the provision of adequate medical care. It may also be his duty to fight against any tendency for the state to monopolize social welfare activity.

(4) Serious problems arise from the great importance of organized groups, such as trade unions and associations of employers, farmers, or professional people. Christians can bear witness that these groups must be responsible to the whole of society, that their leadership must be responsible to their members, and that the members must participate responsibly in the organization.

We welcome the role of responsible trade unions in fighting exploitation and promoting a humane environment for workers, and also the growing cooperation between labor and management to increase the material resources available for human welfare.

(5) Christians have a duty to bring to the attention of their governments that national policies have effects on the lives and welfare of peoples in other countries. National economic and political stability, justice, freedom and peace are dependent upon world economic and political stability. National and international policies are far more closely interrelated than ever before. Excessive barriers to trade can create economic crises elsewhere. The greater the economic power, the larger is the responsibility in this field. The richer countries particularly must remember that one test of their policies is their effect on the underdeveloped areas of the world.

II. The Church In Relation to Communist–Non-Communist Tension

The conflict between communists and non-communists affects the political and economic life of nearly every nation in the world, and creates divisions even within the Church regarding the right attitude toward communism. Only as Christians work for social justice and political freedom for all, and rise above both fear and resentment, will they be fully able to meet the challenge of this conflict. It is our concern for the brother for whom Christ died that should impel us to fulfill our obligations in the face of this conflict. In this way Christians living in different parts of our divided world may contribute to the creation of the necessary conditions for different systems to live side by side. This concern of Christians does not alter the mission of the churches to bear witness in the face of all atheistic and self-righteous ideologies.

The churches at Oxford and Amsterdam indicated the various points of conflict between the Christian faith and Marxist ideology and totalitarian practice.* We wish to reaffirm this statement about these basic conflicts, as

* At Amsterdam the churches referred to the following points of conflict: (1) "The communist promise of what amounts to a complete redemption of man in history; (2) the belief that a particular class by virtue of its role as the bearer of a new order is free from the sins and ambiguities that Christians believe characteristic of all human existence; (3) the materialistic and deterministic teachings, however they may be qualified, that are incompatible with belief in God and with the Christian view of man as a person, made in God's image and responsible to Him;

well as to stress that the growth of communism is a judgment upon our modern societies generally for past or present indifference to social injustice, in which the Church is also involved.

In one form or another the conflict about communism has important consequences for the political and economic life of nearly every nation. In some regions of the world, especially in Asia, Africa, and Latin America, communism has strong appeal. Here poverty, misery, the newly-aroused aspirations for freedom and security, doubts as to the effectiveness of democracy, and the tendency of those in power to brand all reforms as communistic, combine to make the promises of communism attractive in spite of the totalitarianism which accompanies it. For many there seems to be no alternative which will bring essential social change quickly enough. There are Christians who think that they can cooperate with the communist movement in their countries because they see it as the way to a new order of material abundance and greater justice. We must ask: "Can communism be an effective instrument for these limited purposes or must we give warning that, where such social and economic methods are introduced, the total communist scheme will come to dominate the minds of men as well as their institutions?"

Christians must consider carefully the serious effects the conflict with communism is already producing: for example, the tendencies in democratic societies to lower their standards of civil liberties, and sometimes to strengthen reactionary forces in countries abroad. Preoccupation with the real dangers of subversion in many situations has led to a less widely recognized and more subtle danger to society from those who identify as subversive any unpopular opinions or associations. Enemies of essential human freedom appear on both the political right and the political left and Christians have a duty to strengthen the forces of freedom which fight on both fronts. Yet we must not forget the love due to the neighbor who stands for an ideology which we reject.

There is a particular danger that nations will over-emphasize the military aspect in their defense against communism and fail to see the need for reforms in political, social, and economic institutions as an important part of their response to its challenge. These nations can have greater influence on the course of the present world conflict if they show their ability to deal justly with the legitimate aspirations of the dependent peoples, to cope successfully and creatively with their own social problems, and to remain self-critical.

It will be the task of the churches to point to the dangers inherent in the present situation: on the one hand the temptation to succumb to anti-communist hysteria and the danger of a self-righteous assurance concerning the political and social systems of the West; on the other hand the temptation to accept the false promises of communism and to overlook its threat to any responsible society.

Christians in communist and non-communist countries are called to hold each other in special brotherly concern and prayer across all barriers. Those of us in non-communist lands affirm our unity with these churches in the ecumenical fellowship and the bond of the Spirit, and our confidence in their loyalty to Christ. We rejoice with them in the Christian witness which they make in these new circumstances and seek to understand and affirm our fellowship with them in their temptations and in their Christian hope, for

---

(4) the ruthless methods of communists in dealing with their opponents; (5) the demand of the party on its members for an exclusive and unqualified loyalty which belongs only to God, and the coercive policies of communist dictatorship in controlling every aspect of life."

this witness and these temptations are relevant also to our social responsibility. Therefore we are presented with a number of questions which challenge Christians in communist as well as in non-communist countries in different ways. All Christians must wrestle with the following questions which are urgent in a special way in communist lands.

1. What are the ways and what is the content of Christian witness in the face of atheistic ideologies?

2. What is the social significance of the existence of the Church as an inclusive worshipping and evangelistic community? How can the life of the congregation in all its forms, including its pastoral and social work, affect society? How does the Church's teaching ministry relate to state education under a communist regime?

3. What reforms are necessary in the life and structure of the Church? What are the values and dangers of agreements between Church and State?

4. At what points can the Church and Christians cooperate with governments in their plans for social reconstruction? What are the limits of this cooperation? How does Christian social responsibility avoid both surrender to communism and the temptations of a negative resistance?

5. What new forms of prophetic ministry are required? How far are public statements by the Church on social questions effective?

6. What Christian witness can church members bear in their daily work? What is the place of suffering in Christian social witness?

7. What, if any, is the Church's responsibility for standards of truth in all fields? For pre-communist social and cultural traditions? What is the relation between a Christian demand and a communist for repentance for past social injustices?

The following questions are especially urgent for Christians in non-communist countries:

1. What are the special temptations of the church in a traditional "Christian society"?

2. Does secularism in the non-communist world differ from the materialism in the communist world?

3. What is the content of Christian witness toward the large mass of secularized people? How far is this secularization due to the class nature of the Church and the accommodation of its life and message to bourgeois interests and values? What reforms in the life of the Church are necessary to meet these challenges?

4. How far are the churches in non-communist lands genuinely prophetic in their relation to society and the state?

5. What is the responsibility of the churches in non-communist lands for the cultivation of traditions of freedom and community over against the growing pressure toward social conformity?

III. Problems in the Economically Underdeveloped Regions

Society in Asia, Africa, and some parts of Latin America today is characterized by the urge to national self-determination in political and economic matters. There is a growing shift of social, economic and political authority from those persons and institutions who by inheritance or tradition possessed it, to those who exercise it because of the function they perform. The peoples of these countries have awakened to a new sense of fundamental human rights and justice and they are in revolt against enslaving political, economic, religious, and social conditions. There is also the pressure to achieve changes rapidly. All of the processes of social development—increasing productivity, raising standards of living, democratization, and the rest—which have taken centuries in the West, demand in these areas to be completed together and within decades. The temptation is to use irresponsible methods of collectivism, whether of the right or of the left, in the desire for rapid results. In such circumstances the Church has the duty to point the way to responsible society and herself to follow it.

The Ecumenical Study Conference. Lucknow. India. in December. 1952 presented a number of specific points which can be faced and tackled only as world problems and should be the concern of all the churches.

(1) *Development of Political Institutions.* Political institutions must be developed which are strong enough to accomplish the needed social and economic changes while extending and promoting fundamental human rights and freedom. It is necessary to redefine democratic political, economic, and social values and objectives in the new context of Asian life and in the light of a more realistic understanding of human nature than can be provided by utopian concepts.

(2) *Land Reform and Rural Development.* Absentee landlordism and other unjust forms of land tenure and privilege, not least where the churches themselves are guilty of such practices, must be abolished. At the same time, positive measures should make possible new systems of productive land use and community life. In the rural areas bold programs of agriculture, rural industry, social education, cooperatives and the provision of rural credit and professional services are urgently needed. The rural community development program in India recognizes agriculture as a way of life as well as an occupation. The churches can give concrete assistance in this development everywhere.

(3) *Industrial Development.* In order to raise standards of living underdeveloped countries properly insist upon developing industry. Ways should be found of obtaining capital within the country without endangering standards of consumption; technical assistance and foreign capital should be provided without doing violence to social objectives; the role of the state and public and private enterprise in industry need to be examined in the light of local circumstances; forms of industry which can be integrated in suitable ways with village community life need to be found. In countries where industries are being developed rapidly, e.g., Brazil, India, Japan, Mexico, and South Africa, special care should be given to protect new industrial laborers and their families from the dehumanizing factors which often accompany such industrialization.

(4) *Population.* Many underdeveloped countries, especially in Asia, are very densely populated in relation to their resources. Redistribution of population nationally and internationally, family planning and birth control are burning questions. The profound ethical, political and social issues which they raise need to be courageously examined and guidance should be given by the churches.

(5) *Independence and the Responsibilities of Interdependence.* A number of the underdeveloped countries have attained national freedom and full sovereignty after a colonial period. There are difficulties in adaptation to an international situation where national sovereignty in political and economic affairs, especially for weaker nations, is necessarily limited by the facts of interdependence. At the same time they need capital from the outside for development and industrialization. The flow of capital from former colonial powers having dried up, they find it difficult to mobilize the necessary capital, since private investors hesitate to enter the scene without specific guarantees, and public funds without political strings attached are hard to procure. Unless the responsibilities of interdependence are clearly defined and ac-

cepted by all concerned, this impasse could easily lead to bitterness and a sense of frustration.

The churches must be especially concerned with the way in which the present world struggle with its hot and cold wars militates against progress in the social reconstruction of the underdeveloped countries. It is significant for Christians on all continents that the Ecumenical Study Conference at Lucknow gave the following illustration concerning this:

"When American foreign policy is determined primarily by the criterion of anti-Communism it generally strengthens conservative and reactionary political groups in the East Asian scene and tends to weaken the forces of healthy social reform. This line is bound to be self-defeating because in the final analysis social and spiritual health is the best answer to Communism."

Underlying all the problems of the underdeveloped countries is the need for extension of opportunities for education. Special attention should be given to the training of experts in public administration and technology. The churches have a direct responsibility towards education, especially in the rural areas and with regard to women.

Conclusion

In all these fields the real dangers are complacency, lack of imagination, and the dull sense of hopelessness that settles upon those of little faith. World economic and social interdependence involves a new dimension in the task of creating a responsible society, which men will have to face realizing that statistics are only inadequate indications of desperate human need. Upon Christians rests a special responsibility to see the challenge, to press their governments to take the issue seriously, and themselves to act sacrificially.

Because Jesus Christ is Lord in earth and heaven, the call to responsible social action which God addresses to His Church does not present us with an impossible task. We are not called upon to shoulder the burden of this world, but to seek justice, freedom and peace to the best of our ability in the social order. The Church knows that in obedience and prayer our efforts will bear fruit. For God has called us unto liberty to serve one another by love. "Faithful is he that calleth you, who also will do it."

APPENDIX L

Report of Section IV: International Affairs—Christians in the Struggle for World Community

Evanston, 1954

Introduction

The Assembly of the World Council of Churches proclaims the Christian hope in an hour of grave international crisis. Social and political systems are in conflict. Opposing ideologies compete for the minds and souls of men. Rival power blocs imperil the peace of nations large and small. An arms race of unprecedented dimensions casts its ominous shadow over the face of the earth. Natural and human resources, intended by God for the enrichment of society, are diverted to purposes alien to His holy will. Science is conscripted. Hydrogen weapons carry the threat of mass destruction on a scale hitherto unknown.

Nations arbitrarily divided by war and the aftermath of war press for the restoration of their unity, as free and sovereign peoples. Millions of God's children are in revolt against economic deprivation, political bondage and social inequality. Other millions of God's children, uprooted from the land of their fathers, seek refuge from the storms by which they are beset. Curtains of disunity and divisiveness create situations of tension around the globe. Nations and peoples whose primary desire is to dwell in peace, live in fear lest they will be destroyed by the conflict of power.

This troubled world, disfigured and distorted as it is, is still God's world. He rules and overrules its tangled history. In praying, "Thy will be done on earth as it is in heaven," we commit ourselves to seek earthly justice, freedom and peace for all men. Here as everywhere Christ is our hope. Our confidence lies not in our own reason or strength, but in the power that comes from God. Impelled by this faith, all our actions will be but humble, grateful, and obedient acknowledgment that He has redeemed the world. The fruit of our efforts rests in His hands. We can therefore live and work as those who know that God reigns, undaunted by all the arrogant pretensions of evil, ready to face situations that seem hopeless and yet to act in them as men whose hope is indestructible.

With this situation before us, and our hope in Christ within us, we commend to the 170 millions of our fellow-Christians, in the 163 member-churches of the World Council of Churches, the following concerns on which the common judgment of Christians should be exercised, with a view to our corporate and individual action in world affairs.

I. The Desire for Peace and the Fear of War

Deeply and persistently man longs for peace. He no longer finds any glamour in war; he has tasted the fruit of its insanity and found it bitter and poisonous. His ideals are mocked, his liberty curtailed, his possessions destroyed and his future undermined by total war even as its high-sounding goals have eluded his grasp. He is sick of it, and wants to be at peace!

Christians everywhere are committed to world peace as a goal. However, for them "peace" means far more than mere "absence of war"; it is characterized positively by freedom, justice, truth and love. For such peace the Church must labor and pray.

Christians must also face the fact that such a peace will not be easily or quickly attained. We live in a world in which from generation to generation ignorance of God and rebellion against Him have resulted in greed and an insatiable lust for power. War and its evils are the consequences. Basically the problem is a spiritual one, and economic and political measures alone will not solve it. Men's hearts must be changed. This is always the supreme evangelistic challenge to the Church, although we must confess that our response has been tragically casual and feeble.

The development of nuclear weapons makes this an age of fear. True peace cannot rest on fear. It is vain to think that the hydrogen bomb or its development has guaranteed peace because men will be afraid to go to war, nor can fear provide an effective restraint against the temptation to use such a decisive weapon either in hope of total victory or in the desperation of total defeat.

The thought of all-out nuclear warfare is indeed horrifying. Such warfare introduces a new moral challenge. It has served to quicken public concern, and has intensified awareness of the urgency of finding means of prevention. War's consequences can no longer seem remote to any individual; all mankind is vulnerable to a disaster from which there may be no escape.

The foremost responsibility of the Christian Church in this situation is undoubtedly to bring the transforming power of Jesus Christ to bear upon the hearts of men. Christians must pray more fervently for peace, repent more earnestly of their individual and collective failures to further world order, and strive more urgently to establish world contacts for reconciliation, fellowship and love.

Lofty objectives so often invented to justify war cannot conceal the truth that its violence and destruction are inherently evil. Therefore, Christians, in their respective countries, must not lend themselves to, but expose, this deceit.

It is not enough for the churches to proclaim that war is evil. They must study afresh the Christian approaches to peace, taking into account both Christian pacifism as a mode of witness and the conviction of Christians that in certain circumstances military action is justifiable. Whatever views Christians hold in respect to these approaches, they must seek out, analyze, and help to remove the psychological and social, the political and economic causes of war. Without forsaking their conviction that all weapons of war are evil, the churches should press for restraints on their use. Christians in all lands must plead with their governments to be patient and persistent in their search for means to limit weapons and advance disarmament.

But this is not enough. An international order of truth and peace would require:

1. Under effective international inspection and control and in such a way that no state would have cause to fear that its security was endangered, the elimination and prohibition of atomic, hydrogen and all other weapons of mass destruction, as well as the reduction of all armaments to a minimum.
2. The development and acceptance of methods for peaceful change to rectify existing injustices.

However, it must be recognized that on the basis of current suspicions and distrust the nations at the moment have reached a stalemate on the issue of control of atomic and nuclear weapons, either through international inspection or by mere resolution. What constructive steps can be proposed in this impasse?

We first of all call upon the nations to pledge that they will refrain from the threat or the use of hydrogen, atomic and all other weapons of mass destruction as well as any other means of force against the territorial integrity or political independence of any state.

If this pledge should be broken, the charter of the United Nations provides for collective action and, pending such international action, recognizes the right of national self-defense. We believe that any measures to deter or combat aggression should conform to the requirements of the United Nations Charter and Christians should urge that both the United Nations and their own governments limit military action strictly to the necessities of international security.

Yet even this is not enough. The churches must condemn the deliberate mass destruction of civilians in open cities by whatever means and for whatever purpose. The churches should press through the Commission of the Churches on International Affairs and other channels for the automatic stationing of U.N. Peace Commission teams in areas of tension to identify any aggression if it takes place. Christians must continue to press for social, political and economic measures to prevent war. Among these should be the giving of strong moral support for the positive use of atomic power for the benefit of mankind.

We must also see that experimental tests of hydrogen bombs have raised issues of human rights, caused suffering, and imposed an additional strain on human relations between nations. Among safeguards against the aggravation of these international tensions is the insistence that nations carry on tests only within their respective territories or, if elsewhere, only by international clearance and agreement.

Above all, Christians must witness to a dynamic hope in God, in whose hands lie the destinies of nations, and in this confidence be untiring in their efforts to create and maintain an international climate favorable for reconciliation and goodwill. The specific problems and tasks will vary in each country according to circumstances. Civil authorities may be hostile to the Church or even avowed enemies of Christ. We know that the power of the Holy Spirit does work effectively through the witness of faithful and obedient and suffering Christians, and the purposes of God will not be denied but will be fulfilled in His time.

II. Living Together in a Divided World

The Assembly believes that an international order conformed to the will of God and established in His peace can be achieved only through the reconciliation which Christ makes possible. Only thus will those transformed attitudes and standards, agreements and practices which alone will insure lasting peace become possible. Because of their belief in this Gospel of reconciliation and their experience of its power, Christians can never accept, as the only kind of existence open to nations, a state of perpetual tension leading to "inevitable" war. On the contrary, it is the Christian conviction that war is not inevitable, because God wills peace.

From this it follows that the first responsibility of Christians is to live and work for the reconciliation of men to God and, therefore, as individuals and nations, to one another. Endeavors to secure that nations shall live together in peace on any basis less fundamental than this are always precarious; at any moment they may prove to be but frail expedients in a world which has not yet become subject to the power of the Cross.

Nevertheless, the preservation even of these "frail expedients," in a world where Christ's reign is not yet acknowledged, is morally imperative as a minimum condition of international order. Today there is urgent need for this moral imperative to be recognized and acknowledged. The clash of national interests, social systems and ideologies tends to dominate every phase of international life. Hostile propaganda, border incidents and a suicidal competition in arms more deadly than any hitherto used, characterize a situation which is unfit to be described as peace. Over all there moves the specter of total war. Only as these current tensions are reduced and controlled will time be secured for bringing to bear the deeper and more creative influences of reconciliation.

A current political definition of such endeavors is "co-existence." We avoid the use of this term because of its unhappy historical significance and some of its current political implications. "Co-existence" as conceived by Christians cannot imply any willingness to disguise from themselves or others the vast difference which lies between the search for an international order based on belief in Christ and His reconciling work, and the pursuit of aims which repudiate the Christian revelation. There can be no abandonment of the right to assert this fundamental difference and the faith on which it rests.

We stand against submission to, engulfment by, or appeasement of totalitarian tyranny and aggression. We also stand against the exploitation of any people by economic monopoly or political imperialism. In the world community we must stand for the freedom of all people to know the truth which makes men free and for the basic civil liberties of all people to struggle for a higher freedom.

Christians claim the right to propagate their faith, by proclamation and persuasion, by example and suffering, just as they uphold the same right for others. Nevertheless, conflicts of conviction about the origin and destiny of man have long existed within societies essentially peaceful and Christians must continue to condemn totalitarianism as false in doctrine and dangerous in practice. They will be no less firm in continuing to oppose atheistic materialism. Yet however deep the conflict may be it is not necessarily an insuperable bar to living together in a divided world. The same may be said of methods of political and economic organization, whether they be democratic or dictatorial.

Such living together does, however, require that certain minimum conditions be met on both sides:

1. A conviction that it is possible for nations and peoples to live together, at least for a considerable period of years.
2. A willingness not to use force as an instrument of policy beyond the existing frontiers. This would not mean the recognition and freezing of present injustices and the unnatural divisions of nations, but it would mean renouncing coercion as a means of securing or redressing them.

3. A vigorous effort to end social and other injustices which might lead to civil, and hence international, war.
4. A scrupulous respect for the pledged word.
5. A continuing effort to reach agreement on outstanding issues, such as the peace treaties and disarmament, which are essential to a broader stabilization and pacification of relations.
6. Readiness to submit all unresolved questions of conflict to an impartial international organization and to carry out its decisions.

These are minimum requirements. This limited form of living together can only be a transitional stage or a point of departure. It must move, through untiring endeavor, beyond these minimum requirements into an order of genuine cooperation. The first move into such an order must surely be in the direction of peaceful competition with growing cooperation. This order will be facilitated and reinforced through the free exchange of persons, culture, information and goods; through common undertakings for relief and human welfare and through the growth of the United Nations as an instrument for peaceful change. Christians must go still further. They must promote the reconciliation of the nations; they must work for the establishment of justice based on a rule of law, so that a responsible society, grounded in truth, may be possible.

For the Christian the ecumenical fellowship of the churches is evidence of progress towards this goal, and of God's use of the Christian Church as one of the foundation stones of world order. Further, by its supra-national character the Church also provides the point of meeting where the search for the truth as it is in Christ in its bearing on all the problems of human society may be pursued in faith and hope as well as in love's creative power.

III. What Nations Owe to One Another

The world community has become interdependent. The status of hitherto dependent people has undergone radical change, resulting in entirely new relationships between them and the rest of the world. The older types of colonialism and imperialism are surely dying out, but new forms of imperialism call for vigilance.

Nationalism in many countries has been a creative force and has enabled people to win and preserve their freedom; but it displays a tendency to become an end in itself. The self-sufficient attitude of nationalism is an obstacle to international cooperation.

The exploitation of one people by another, in any form, is evil and unjustifiable. Those countries which administer non-self-governing territories have a special obligation so to promote the educational, economic, social, and political advancement of dependent peoples, that they may be enabled to play their full part in the international community.

We welcome the development of international responsibility in place of old colonialism, and the principle of international study and review, exemplified by the United Nations Trusteeship System. While this System is open to abuse, the progress made by Trust Territories under it testifies to its value. Administering authorities should consider placing their non-self-governing territories not yet ready for self-government or independence under the Trusteeship System.

The legitimate right of the self-determination of peoples must be recognized. Specific assurance of independence or self-government should be given and administering authorities should take reasonable risks in speeding progress toward this goal.

In the new context of our age relations between peoples hitherto "subject" and "ruling" should be one of partnership and cooperation. Countries enjoying new political freedom urgently need economic and technical help. The response of more developed countries through expanded international programs of technical assistance is one of the brightest pages of recent history; but the effort thus far has been small in comparison with the needs of the less developed countries and the resources of those more developed. A progressively sustained effort will for a long time be required and involves mutual responsibilities and benefits which challenge all who cooperate in such endeavors.

Many of the politically new nations are old nations with centuries of culture and civilization behind them. In this partnership of sharing they have their own distinctive contribution to make. But for this partnership to be fruitful there is required in nations "young" or "old" a readiness always to learn from one another.

IV. The United Nations and World Community

Despite the critical post-war tensions which have divided the international community, the United Nations has made significant contributions to order and justice. Its recurrent meetings have provided opportunities for continuing diplomatic contacts and for peaceful settlement. Major international problems have been brought before the forum of world public opinion in the U.N. General Assembly. An historic Universal Declaration of Human Rights has provided an international standard. In the Expanded Technical Assistance Program the U.N. and Specialized Agencies have served as a center for harmonizing the actions of states for human welfare.

Yet the weaknesses of the United Nations, which reflect the divisions within the international community, are also clear. Little or no progress has been made towards world disarmament or the creation of an international police force. On many other questions effective action has been frustrated by the deadlocks of the cold war. Too often issues have been viewed solely on the basis of narrow self-interest, rather than on the basis of merit. While the United Nations stands and grows, the international crisis deepens.

The brief history of the United Nations has been one of growth and development and if it is to live it must continue to grow. The United Nations can become comprehensive in its membership. The world organization can grow through more loyal and responsible use of the Charter provisions by the members. At many points Charter commitments are neglected or by-passed through unilateral action. Again, the U.N. can grow through the evolution of powers inherent in the Charter or delegated to it by common consent.

A further method by which the United Nations can develop is through revision of the Charter. While the common moral convictions essential for major improvement of the Charter are not now apparent, it is important that a dynamic concept of the world organization be kept alive and that the U.N. structure be subjected to periodic review. After taking into due consideration the experience and accomplishments of the U.N. and the U.N.'s growth and development under the present Charter, a review conference should try to determine the organic and structural requirements of the U.N. for carrying out programs dealing with universal enforceable disarmament, human rights, greatly expanded technical assistance, and more rapid development of self-government in colonial areas. On the basis of its study, if a review conference finds Charter changes to be advisable and necessary, the appropriate Charter amendments can then be recommended for ratification by the nations.

A related issue is the continued development of regional organizations for collective self-defense and the pursuit of common interests. The Council of Europe and the Organization of American States provide the major examples. In all such regional arrangements, including those existing arrangements which have not been formally announced, there are potential benefits and potential dangers.

Regional groupings, notably those for economic and cultural cooperation, are a natural reflection of the cultural, economic and historical ties which link the nations of a given area in a regional community. They also reflect in part the failure of the nations to organize a sure global security through the U.N. Despite the potential danger to international peace and security seen in regional associations, they have a valid place in a cooperative world order, provided:

1. They are clearly defensive in character and military actions are subject to collective decision;
2. They are subordinate to and reinforce the aims of the Charter of the United Nations;
3. They serve the genuine mutual interests and needs of the peoples of the region.

Regional associations which meet these requirements can strengthen the world organization by reducing threats to the peace and by lessening the number of international questions thrust before the world forum. Christians have an obligation to measure regional groupings by the interests of the world community.

One of the fundamental principles of international community in the U.N. Charter is that of the "sovereign" equality of states, great and small. This principle is again and again in danger of being disregarded by the Great Powers, not merely through efforts to dominate, but also through efforts to impose a type of organization on the community of nations. Christians therefore, should stand firmly for the respect and protection of the essential rights of smaller nations.

V. The Protection of Human Rights

A call for the protection of human rights is all the more insistent in this age when, in various parts of the world, totalitarianism—based on ideologies sometimes atheistic and sometimes under the guise of religion—oppresses the freedom of men and of institutions and denies those God-given rights which are His will for all men. A system of justice which defends the rights and dignity of the human person is fundamental. Denials of religious freedom and other rights, against which the churches have repeatedly raised voices of protest, are signs of the moral sickness of the world. The struggle for the essential freedoms of man as defended in the Universal Declaration of Human Rights is the struggle for peace. The World Council of Churches' current study and support of the right of conscientious objection, as authorized by the Central Committee in 1951, is a necessary step in the direction of national and international action for its protection. Meanwhile, as far as possible, the churches should plead for just judgment and humane treatment of those who know themselves called to this personal witness for peace.

The proclamation of international standards in the Declaration of Human Rights, and efforts to provide international safeguards through Covenants on Human Rights with effective implementation reflect an awakening international conscience.

The importance of attempts to secure international legal safeguards for human rights is not diminished by the obstacles. The fundamental concern of the churches, however, is to promote mutually recognized rights in the ethos and practices of society. International covenants offer a valuable means to this end, but there are limits to what can be achieved through such means. International law is more often the fruit than the source of community. To build a strong defense of human rights requires vigorous, broad and persistent educational efforts. Christian education can make an important contribution here.

The love of God for man lays upon the Christian conscience a special measure of responsibility for the care of those who are the victims of world disorder. By governmental action and by international cooperation, as well as by the direct effort of the churches, measures should be taken for the relief of refugees, migrants, still unrepatriated prisoners, civil and military, and similar groups of suffering and oppressed men and women, whatever their origin, race or religion. More important still than their relief is a just and permanent solution to their problem.

VI. Towards an International Ethos

Underlying the more obvious barriers to a genuine world community is the lack of a common foundation of moral principles. At the root of the most stubborn conflicts is the failure of governments and peoples to treasure any common set of guiding principles. Attempted settlements involving differing ideologies are essentially unstable and tend to produce new frictions, not only because of political differences but also because of underlying differences as to moral values.

The world of nations desperately needs an international ethos to provide a sound groundwork for the development of international law and institutions. This requires not only attempts to find wider areas of common moral understanding, but also efforts to bring the guiding principles of international life into greater harmony with God's will. Christians should urge statesmen to devote more attention to this fundamental task. In order to do this with authority Christians must be clear on their own understanding of the essential principles. This can be done only by sustained study. Tentatively, we advance the following considerations:

1. All power carries responsibility and all nations are trustees of power which should be used for the common good.
2. All nations are subject to moral law, and should strive to abide by the accepted principles of international law to develop this law and to enforce it through common actions.
3. All nations should honor their pledged word and international agreements into which they have entered.
4. No nation in an international dispute has the right to be sole judge in its own cause or to resort to war to advance its policies, but should seek to settle disputes by direct negotiations or by submitting them to conciliation, arbitration, or judicial settlement.
5. All nations have a moral obligation to ensure universal security and to this end should support measures designed to deny victory to a declared aggressor.
6. All nations should recognize and safeguard the inherent dignity, worth, and essential rights of the human person, without distinction as to race, sex, language, or religion.
7. Each nation should recognize the rights of every other nation, which

observes such standards, to live by and proclaim its own political and social beliefs, provided that it does not seek by coercion, threat, infiltration or deception to impose these on other nations.

8. All nations should recognize an obligation to share their scientific and technical skills with peoples in less developed regions, and to help the victims of disaster in other lands.
9. All nations should strive to develop cordial relations with their neighbors, encourage friendly cultural and commercial dealings, and join in creative international efforts for human welfare.

The churches must, therefore, see in the international sphere a field of obedience to Jesus Christ. They cannot agree that it falls outside the range of His sovereignty or the scope of the moral law. Their first duty is to fulfill their calling to manifest the Kingdom of God among men. Their fellowship must be a bond of union among all, a bond both more patient and more resistant than any other. The Church must seek to be the kind of community which God wishes the world to become. By virtue of its calling it must act as a redemptive suffering fellowship in the form and manner of its Lord Jesus Christ. Within it differences of sex, class, nation, color, or race are to become a source of mutual enrichment, and not of rivalry or antagonism. Its members must rise above the limitations of nationalism to a truly ecumenical outlook. It must carry into the turmoil of international relations the real possibility of the reconciliation of all races, nationalities and classes in the love of Christ. It must witness to the creative power of forgiveness and spiritual renewal.

All these things the churches must do as an essential part of their evangelistic task. But they can never be content with words. Through the life, service, and sacrifice of their members, they must make their contribution to justice and peace, to the improvement of human conditions, and to the care of the needy and of the refugee. They must serve humbly the needs of the less developed peoples. In persecution and oppression they can still witness to the spiritual freedom which their members enjoy, and which no human authority can take away. Thus they will testify, both by deed and word, to the hope which Jesus Christ has brought to the world.

VII. The Churches and Specific International Tensions

Because this statement has painted a tempestuous scene with a broad brush it must not be assumed that the churches are indifferent to particular international tensions. The reverse is the truth. The churches' work is likely to be effective only when they direct themselves to the causes of friction and to friction itself as, when, and where they arise.

Even to agree on a limited list of places of friction would be almost impossible. They are very numerous and those that seem trivial to some loom up as vital to others. And these questions are often so complex and in the course of long negotiation vary their character so considerably that it would be difficult for the Assembly to speak confidently and unanimously about them. Further, agreed pronouncement by the Assembly on particular issues would almost certainly have to be in broad and general terms. But international conflicts, large and small, do not yield to broad generalizations.

It is for this among other reasons that the churches and bodies in the World Council of Churches and the International Missionary Council have established the Commission of the Churches on International Affairs to give heed to these issues. It is therefore important that councils, federations, and groups of churches should develop and make full use of their own Committees or Commissions on International Affairs. In this way they may express the mind of the churches on international relations, increase their influence in the search for positive solutions, and seek to build up an enlightened and effective Christian public opinion on international affairs.

[Four resolutions adopted by the Assembly and submitted at the same time as the Section IV report, appear in the text, Part VI, Chapter 3.

APPENDIX M

Report of Section V: Inter-Group Relations—The Church Amid Racial and Ethnic Tensions

Evanston, 1954

I. The State of the World

Everywhere there is restlessness in the world. This is due in great part to the hunger of millions of people for status and recognition, for a meaning for both life and work, and for a fuller share of the fruits of the earth.

The impact of technically advanced civilization on all parts of the world has affected every country, for good or ill. Now a new phase has been entered, with the struggle of disadvantaged peoples of many races to participate fully in the opportunities and responsibilities of society.

While the advance and emancipation of any people, and the removal of any deprivation under which men, women and children have suffered, are causes of rejoicing for any Christian, impending events are so massive and their approach so swift and the new weapons of war so terrible, that fear and anxiety afflict us all.

The hatreds, jealousies and suspicions with which the world has always been afflicted are deepened by racial prejudices and fears, rooted in the sinful human heart and entrenched in law and custom. In some situations men come to accept race conflict as inevitable and lose hope of peaceful solution.

II. The Hope of the World

Yet it is the nature of men to seek always for some new ground of hope. Some believe that the solution of the world's racial problems lies in the economic and political re-ordering of society; others that it lies in the pursuit and use of knowledge; others that man must rid himself of dependence on some Greater Being, and look only to himself; others that their safety lies in the power of their race or class or nation.

Disadvantaged people have their especial and individual hopes, that by education, the achievement of the franchise, and a higher standard of living, they will find the security which they seek, and that justice which is the right of every human being.

It is our Christian belief that our Lord is concerned for all just hopes of men but in Himself He offers the hope that transcends them all. The Bible teaches us that God is the Sovereign Creator of all men, and by Him they are sustained and have their being. When He made the world, He saw that it was good. But man by his sin—by his disobedience and pride and the lifting of his arm against his brother—has filled it with division and distrust.

What is the Christian hope in this disunity? It is Jesus Christ, who revealed God as Father and who died for all men, reconciling them to God and to each other by His Cross. From every race and nation a new people of God is created, in which the power of the Spirit overcomes racial pride and fear. So far from being without hope or purpose, God's people now as new creatures are co-workers with Him, and are filled with joy and assured His final victory.

So to us is given the gift of sharing in and working for the Kingdom even now. Assured that the final victory is Christ's, we can work actively, continually repentant and continually forgiven, for that reconciliation which we believe to be God's will.

III. The Calling of the Church

This is the calling of the Church with regard to race, to witness within itself to the Kingship of Christ and the unity of His people, in Him transcending all diversity. Jesus Christ in His Incarnation and redemptive action restores this unity which from the beginning was God's design.

Their calling requires Christians to witness to the Kingship of Christ and the unity of all mankind, and to strive through social and political action to secure justice, freedom, and peace for all, as a foretaste of that Kingdom into which the faithful shall be gathered.

All churches and Christians are involved, whether they recognize it or not, in the racial and ethnic tensions of the world. But it is in communities where segregation prevails that they face the plainest difficulties and the most challenging opportunities; for such segregation denies to those who are segregated their just and equal rights and results in deep injuries to the human spirit, suffered by offender and victim alike.

The great majority of Christian churches affiliated with the World Council have declared that physical separation within the Church on grounds of race is a denial of spiritual unity, and of the brotherhood of man. Yet such separations persist within these very churches, and we often seek to justify them on other grounds than race, because in our own hearts we know that separation solely on the grounds of race is abhorrent in the eyes of God.

We seek to justify such exclusion on the ground of difference of culture, or on the ground that a residential pattern of segregation necessitates it, or on the ground that the time is not yet ripe. We even say that we are willing to abandon all separations, but must retain them because so many others are unwilling to abandon them. We often make use of the unregenerateness of the world to excuse our own.

The Church is called upon, therefore, to set aside such excuses and to declare God's will both in words and deeds. "Be not conformed to this world, but be ye transformed by the renewing of your mind, that ye may prove what is that good, and acceptable, and perfect, will of God." We believe it to be the will of God that such proof in word and deed now be given.

IV. Repentance and Obedience

Many churches and many Christians have striven to be obedient to God's will in matters of race; for every such obedience we give our thanks, both for God's power and His servants' faithfulness. Increasingly racial and ethnic barriers are breached in the life of the churches. But it is the most obedient who would best understand the need of all churches and Christians for deep repentance that they are so largely conformed to the world's compromises. This same world watches any denial of human brotherhood, and is not deceived. This is an especial time of testing for the faith that we all live and have our truest being in God and Father, whose children we are in Christ and whose redemptive love enables us to treasure all men as brothers.

But we need to repent of something far deeper than our disunity and our offences. We need to repent of our separation from God, from which these spring, and of our feeble grasp of the truth of the Gospel. To us is given power to become the sons of God and to be every one members one of another.

True repentance is followed by a new assurance of God's power and a new obedience, and this new assurance fills Church and man with hope. Our faith is renewed that love is indeed God's power: churches and nations and men may rebel against it but never can prevail.

Therefore the problems of race, difficult as they are, insoluble as they sometimes appear to be, provide for Christians an opportunity for obedience, and for a deeper understanding that bond and free, Jew and Gentile, Greek and barbarian, people of every land and continent, are all one in Christ.

If Christian obedience leads to suffering, that is part of the price. For the Lord of all was in Gethsemane in an agony, and His sweat was as it were great drops of blood falling down to the ground; but He endured the Cross, despising the shame, for the joy that was set before Him.

When we are given Christian insight the whole pattern of racial discrimination is seen as an unutterable offense against God, to be endured no longer, so that the very stones cry out. In such moments we understand more fully the meaning of the Gospel, and the duty of both Church and Christian.

V. The Task of the Churches*

Racial and ethnic fears, hates, and prejudices are more than social problems with whose existence we must reckon; they are sins against God and His commandments that the Gospel alone can cure. To the Church has been committed the preaching of the Gospel; to proclaim "the healing of the nations" through Christ is verily her task. The Gospel has a power of its own, which manifests itself despite the shortcomings of the churches.

It is, however, only when the churches come to Christ in penitence and obedience, and receive from Him His cleansing, that they receive from Him authority to proclaim His will with the voice of prophecy. Never should they cease to search themselves and to declare and repent their disobedience, especially in those multi-racial countries where they proclaim the noblest principles, yet are in their own practice largely conformed to the principles of this world. Equally is it the duty of those few churches which have given segregation the status of a principle, to search themselves continually whether their theology is not the child of fear, and meanwhile to test every application of segregation by the standard of Christian love.

The churches have this twofold duty, to obey and to proclaim the word of judgment, to repent and to call to repentance. It is their task to challenge the conscience of society; if there is no tension between the church and society, then either the society is regenerate or the church is conformed. Yet it also has a duty to create and to keep open every possible line of com-

* This section of our report is both complementary and supplementary to Chapter IV of the Ecumenical Survey on Intergroup Relations. In considering the task of the churches, we would begin by calling attention to Section C in that chapter, in which there is set out an illustrative list of specific activities in which churches may engage.

munication between people, between political opponents, between people of differing views, cultures, races, languages, between the conservative and the venturesome.

The churches have a special duty toward those of their members who feel called to challenge actively the conscience of society, and who thus offend against custom, and incur loneliness and suffering. It is a great duty of the Church to offer its love and fellowship, and even its admonition in the light of the Gospel, to all who strive to be obedient whatever the world's opinion. It is chastening to remember how often both churches and parents have been estranged from their children who tried in obedience to do what they were taught.

The duty of the Church is not accomplished when it has given its support to its more adventurous sons and daughters. It also has a duty to alert all its members to the nature and scope of their responsibilities, to help them to carry out their duties, and to stand by them when they do. So would the frequent loneliness of Christian action be tempered, the unity of Christian fellowship affirmed, and its members made to feel not helpless, but confident in the face of great events. It is hard to overestimate the importance of this comforting and strengthening role of the Church.

As part of its task of challenging the conscience of society, it is the duty of the church to protest against any law or arrangement that is unjust to any human being or which would make Christian fellowship impossible, or would prevent the Christian from practicing his vocation. Some of its members may feel bound to disobey such law. The Church does not contemplate lightly any breaking of the law, but it recognizes the duty of a Christian to do so when he feels that he has reached that point where the honor and glory of God command him to obey God rather than man. In so doing, the Church must point out the possible consequences of such action and the consequent necessity for spiritual discipline according to the Gospel.

The Church of Christ cannot approve of any law which discriminates on grounds of race, which restricts the opportunity of any person to acquire education to prepare himself for his vocation, to procure or to practice employment in his vocation, or in any other way curtails his exercise of the full rights and responsibilities of citizenship and of sharing in the responsibilities and duties of government. While it can find in the Bible no clear justification or condemnation of intermarriage but only a discussion of the duties of the faithful in marriage with partners of other religions, it cannot approve any law against racial or ethnic intermarriage, for Christian marriage involves primarily a union of two individuals before God which goes beyond the jurisdiction of the state or of culture.

A minister of the Church should advise young people, when preparing them for the grave responsibilities of intermarriage, both of the potential richness of such marriages and of the painful consequences in some situations, which consequences are often caused by the hardness of men's hearts and by cultural differences. There is no evidence that the children of such marriages are inherently inferior, and any treatment of them as such should be condemned.

The Churches are not alone in their concern for the welfare of society and the need for resolving the tensions within it betwen racial and ethnic groups. Many international agencies are at work in this field and in nearly every country there are governmental, civic, and private bodies that are devotedly using their resources—often including expert knowledge—in the solution of these problems. It is impossible to generalize on the nature and scope of the churches' cooperation with these agencies. Amongst them there are those which accuse the churches and their members of being preachers of love, but lukewarm in their passion for justice, slow in action, and afraid of public opinion and unpleasant consequences. The courage of some of these bodies, and the success of some of their experiments, often put the churches to shame. On the other hand some churches feel that cooperation with these bodies is impossible because of their political or other views. Where such cooperation seems impossible, despite a common aim, the churches should take action of their own. Every congregation should concern itself with action in this field of racial and ethnic tensions in society, seeking continually opportunities to make its contribution.

What good grounds for hope there are in the ecumenical movement that give to our divided churches an opportunity to speak with more certain voice on the problems of the world, and to exercise greater influence in its affairs! In a world in which national and international problems are complicated by the facts of race and color, there are great grounds of hope in the existence of Christians of every nation whose supreme loyalty is to Christ their Lord. A great duty lies upon us all to reject utterly any claims of racialism or nationalism that are incompatible with our faith, to extend fellowship to those at whose hands we may have suffered, and to forget hurts of the past. Out of such love and generosity, new hope can be born.

And what hope there is in the existence of so many Christians amongst peoples whose whole way of life was changed by the expansion of western civilization into their countries! In the very situations in which some of the greatest tensions exist, they will help their fellow-Christians, in humble obedience to God, to form a right judgment upon problems in which judgment has hitherto been so confused.

We are concerned here with our hopes for the peace and unity of all mankind, but what greater hope there would be if only our Christian unity were achieved, a unity transcending the ethnic and racial differences of all believers! This is our urgent and immediate task; when it is accomplished how great the further contribution that we might make.

Has any greater challenge ever been presented to the Church? If not, then no greater opportunity has ever been offered it. And this opportunity is, simply, to be the creative instrument of our God of love in a restless and changing world and the faithful servant of our Lord who is its hope.

Resolutions

Adopted by the Assembly in the general tenor of the report of Section V, as follows:

I

The Second Assembly of the World Council of Churches declares its conviction that any form of segregation based on race, color or ethnic origin is contrary to the Gospel, and is incompatible with the Christian doctrine of man and with the nature of the Church of Christ. The Assembly urges the churches within its membership to renounce all forms of segregation or discrimination and to work for their abolition within their own life and within society.

In doing so the Assembly is painfully aware that, in the realities of the contemporary world, many churches find themselves confronted by historical, political, social, and economic circumstances which may make the immediate achievement of this objective extremely difficult. But under God the fellowship of the ecumenical movement is such as to offer to these churches the strength and encouragement to help them and individuals within them to overcome these difficulties with the courage given by faith, and with the desire to testify ever more faithfully to our Master.

From its very beginning the ecumenical movement by its very nature has been committed to a form of fellowship in which there is no segregation or discrimination. The Assembly of the World Council of Churches rejoices in this fact and confirms this practice as the established policy of the Council.

II

This Second Assembly of the World Council of Churches recognizes that one of the major problems of social justice in situations involving racial and ethnic tensions is that of securing for all the opportunities for the free exercise of responsible citizenship and for effective participation by way of franchise in both local and central government activity. It commends this matter to the attention of all Christian people for such action as, under God, they may be led to take in order to secure the solution of this problem.

III

While the questions of the Christian approach to the Jews and of anti-semitism present certain problems in the realm of racial and ethnic tensions, this Section was, by its terms of reference, precluded from giving attention to them. It nevertheless reaffirms that anti-semitic prejudice is incompatible with Christian faith, and it recommends to the Central Committee that the study of anti-semitism be pressed forward in conjunction with the International Committee on the Christian Approach to the Jews.

IV

The Second Assembly recommends to the Central Committee that, in consultation with the International Missionary Council, it make structural provision for an organization, preferably a department, giving assistance to the constituent churches in their efforts to bring the Gospel to bear more effectively upon relations between racial and ethnic groups. Such organization should provide leadership and assistance not only in (a) continuing study of the problems of inter-group relations, especially of racial and ethnic tensions; (b) exchanging information on the matter of racial and ethnic groups and on the positions and work of the churches; and (c) producing and distributing reports and educational materials to increase concern and understanding with regard to these matters in the constituency of the Council; but should also be the means whereby the various contributions of the rich cultural heritages of the groups within the Council's constituency may strengthen the life and witness of all the churches and of this Council as a whole.

APPENDIX N

Report of Section VI: The Laity—The Christian in His Vocation

Evanston, 1954

I. The Ministry of the Laity

The title of this report is here taken to signify Christian vocation in the sphere of daily work. The Assembly of the World Council of Churches at Amsterdam in 1948 declared: "Only by the witness of a spiritually intelligent and active laity can the Church meet the modern world in its actual perplexities and life situations. Since one of the hard facts of the present time is that millions of people think of the Church as floating above the modern world and entirely out of touch with it, the importance of this simple pronouncement cannot easily be overestimated." Since 1948 much has been done by the churches and by pioneering groups within them to rediscover the role of the laity as the Church's representatives in the world. In different lands an awakening sense of the responsibility of the laity is attested by such developments as "Kirchentag," Evangelical Academies, the Christian Frontier, the "Christian and His Daily Work" movement, the concern for Christion Stewardship, Aktines, Zoe, and many similar enterprises.

Clergy and laity belong together in the Church; if the Church is to perform her mission in the world, they need each other. The growing emphasis in many parts of the world upon the function of the laity since the Amsterdam Assembly is not to be understood as an attempt to secure for the laity some larger place or recognition in the Church, nor yet as merely a means to supplement an overburdened und understaffed ordained ministry. It springs from the rediscovery of the true nature of the Church as the People of God. The word "laity" must not be understood in a merely negative way as meaning those church members who are not clergy. Though not yet fully articulated, a more positive understanding of the ministry of the laity is gaining acceptance. The phrase "the ministry of the laity" expresses the privilege of the whole Church to share in Christ's ministry to the world. We must understand anew the implications of the fact that we are all baptized, that, as Christ came to minister, so must all Christians become ministers of his saving purpose according to the particular gift of the Spirit which each has received, as messengers of the hope revealed in Christ. Therefore in daily living and work the laity are not mere fragments of the Church who are scattered about in the world and who come together again for worship, instruction and specifically Christian fellowship on Sundays. They are the Church's representatives, no matter where they are. It is the laity who draw together work and worship; it is they who bridge the gulf between the Church and the world, and it is they who manifest in word and action the Lordship of Christ over that world which claims so much of their time and energy and labor. This, and not some new order or organization, is the ministry of the laity. They are called to it because they belong to the Church, although many do not yet know that they are thus called.

But no attempt is here made to find an unexceptionable definition of the term "laity." "Layman" and "laity" are used to indicate those members of the Church, both men and women, who earn their livelihood in a secular job and who therefore spend most of their waking hours in a "worldly" occupation (not excluding housewives). This is what distinguishes them in a sociological sense from the clergy and from full-time church-workers. Accordingly, the theme of *work* is prominent in this discussion, not because it is the only aspect of life in this world, but because it is a very important one and one which has not received from the churches the attention it deserves, although some important attempts to redress this situation have been made. God calls the whole Church to a life of faith, obedience, service and worship; this is the meaning of Christian vocation in the teaching of the New Testament. Every Christian has a vocation in this biblical sense. In modern usage, however, the term is frequently employed to mean "occupation" or "profession"; and, though we cannot prevent this secular use of a great biblical word, we shall here use "vocation" in the Christian meaning of God's call which comes to each member of his household, the Church. The principal object of this discussion is, therefore, to make clear the true meaning of Christian vocation in all the occupations or professions in which Christian lay-folk engage.

II. The Present Situation: Christian Faith and Daily Work

Today many people are asking whether Christianity has any relevance to their daily work. They feel that there is a gulf between the Church and its worship and their workday lives. Both Christians and non-Christians are aware of this gulf and are concerned with it. It would appear that in comparison with the Church's effort to teach the application of the Gospel to the life of the family and to personal relations, the effort to apply the Gospel to the world of work has been relatively slight. The following reasons may be mentioned as accounting for the gulf that seems to exist between the faith and worship of many lay people and the work which they do during the week:

(a) The old local community in which men used to work and spend their leisure, make their homes and offer their worship, has in many places disappeared as a result of industrialization. Many do little more than sleep in their "parish," while they spend their working hours, and often their leisure also, in another environment. It is small wonder that the clergy have little contact with their parishioners at work and know little of the conditions, stresses and fellowship of the working group. Many people no longer worship with their work-fellows but with a quite different group. Unless the Church is embodied in the laity who know Christ as the hope of the world, the parish has little chance of coming into direct contact with the world of work.

(b) In lands which were once "Christendom," the Church through its clergy controlled great areas of human life, which today stand altogether outside the Church's realm. The old order cannot, and many Christians would say should not, be restored; nevertheless, the resultant separation of Church and world has made it difficult for many people to see the relation between the two. Because they do not understand their ministry as laity, they are often misled into narrowly religious ways or else are carried into an unconscious acceptance of secular viewpoints. There are often no visible distinctions between the Christian's hopes and purposes and his work and those of unbelievers.

(c) The gulf is widened when current evaluation of different kinds of work are accepted by Christians. Thus academic or highly skilled work is over-valued, despite the fact that from a Christian standpoint the most menial work possesses a high dignity; and this still happens even in a day in which society itself is in many lands overthrowing this outdated scale of values. In some parts of the world Christians who have received a higher education when they cannot find the kind of work which they expect, will refuse other forms of work out of a defective sense of the true dignity of work. On this subject the Church should have much to teach to its own members.

(d) Though it is right to stress the importance of work as God's ordinance for human life, it happens in some places that an idol is made out of work. Work is not the whole of life, and when men make it their chief object in living, they are prevented from coming into right relationships with God and with their fellow-men.

(e) Certain inherited false views of work are still in some places effective in dividing the Church from the working world. There is a tendency in some sections of Church life to be interested in man only as a soul to be saved without regard to his physical, mental, and social welfare. Work is accordingly viewed only as a field for evangelism, a sphere of opportunity for personal witness. While, of course, the Christian layman will miss no suitable occasion for bearing his testimony to the truth, he will regard his job as itself a matter in which he may directly serve his Lord. He will bear witness not only with his lips but by the quality of his workmanship; he will do his work as "unto his Master in heaven." A right understanding of the doctrine of Creation will remind him that God has given to man an awesome capacity to change the face of nature by his work; the wonderful achievements of man in his work must neither be ignored nor regarded as manifestations of his sinful pride.

III. The Christian Understanding of Work

This gulf between the Church and the life of the world can be bridged by those who have a Christian view of work. Certain aspects of work may be distinguished. In real life they overlap, and there is an element of each in all work.

(a) In one aspect work is the necessary ordering of daily life so that human needs may be fulfilled and as such work begins every morning in farm, factory, and home. Such work can under good conditions become a source of profound satisfaction, but it has often become a drudgery which has led to futility and despair. In either case, and perhaps especially in the latter, Christians will find strength in the confident hope that this world will be consummated in the Kingdom of Christ. Obedience to the divine ordinance of work, doing one's work not as men-pleasers but as unto our Master in heaven, is a deliverance from the frustration of men's efforts; it bears the assurance that all honest toil derives meaning from this final consummation. Earthly success will not be the highest standard by which Christians judge their daily work. While they will want to insist that work receives a decent and just recompense, adequate for the worker and his dependents, Christians yet know that, whatever may be its reward in this life, their labor is not in vain in the Lord.

(b) Furthermore, all honest work is service rendered to society. Even amongst those who are not Christians, this truth is often recognized and is a source of gratification. When it is ignored and men think only of their rights and not of the service which they may render to the community, they violate their own nature; increased production or higher rewards become ends in themselves. When this happens the very rewards of work, greater wealth and increased leisure, are wasted in selfish enjoyments which bring no benefit to society at large. The relevance of the Christian teaching about service to one's neighbor is obvious here. Every human being, worthy or unworthy, becomes one's neighbor and the Christian rejoices that in his work he may thus, however feebly, reflect the goodness of God, who causes his sun to shine and his rain to fall on the just and the unjust alike.

(c) Implanted in all men is a desire to create new forms of being and of value, and it is in the work of the very few that this power of creation is seen at the highest level. These are the individuals who transform the face of nature, change men's view of the world, and create new forms of value—the great philosophers, scientists, artists, poets, craftsmen, and so on. If we speak of the work of such men as creative, we must do so with the utmost circumspection, since it is all too easy for men in their pride to say to themselves, "ye shall be as gods." The biblical writers use the word "create" only of God, never of men, and they shrink from speaking of man's work as creative. This kind of work becomes demonic in its mighty achievements as soon as men trust in their own power to re-create the world by means of their scientific and technical skill. Yet, properly understood, man's spontaneous joy in the creative element in work is a sign of that freedom for which creation longs and of the truth that man shall subdue the earth and have dominion over it. That his freedom and dominion are achieved only in Christ and his "new creation" is the profound biblical truth to which all human "creative" aspiration points, even though men often do not know this.

God is not only the Creator of the world, he is also its Redeemer. The Church of Christ is the sphere of God's redemptive work, the new creation which is destined to renew the old. Every member of the Church, and therefore every layman, is called by God to witness to the reality of this new creation, that is, to the redemptive work of Christ, in all his work and words and life; this is the meaning of Christian vocation in secular affairs. Every situation in daily life provides an opportunity to respond to this call of God. In this way the Church through the laity becomes the leaven in the lump, the constant sign at the center of the world's affairs of the divine mercy and admonition.

Of course, serious conflicts will arise as Christians seek to relate their divine vocation to their daily work. Duties towards dependents, fellow-workers, and society frequently conflict with one another. Work that is socially harmful or which thwarts the worker's sense of craftsmanship is an offence to the awakened conscience, as is also work that is relentless drudgery. The use of machinery has abolished much (though not all) backbreaking toil in industrialized areas. But it has as yet hardly affected vast agricultural communities in other parts of the world, where Christians also have to learn to serve God in their work, even while that work is still largely drudgery. Moreover, the use of machinery has created problems as well as solved them.

There is special need for Christian consideration of some of the new problems in a highly organized industrial society. For example, in such societies today the making of decisions passes into the hands of the few at the top of the organization, unless strenuous attempts are made to devolve control. Furthermore, many important decisions are not personal decisions based on personal responsibility, but group decisions based on group responsibilities. Both the company director and the trade unionist act as members of a group. The individual Christian will make his voice heard, and a group decision is reached on a basis of compromise. He is not of course always or necessarily at variance with the group. The difficulty arises from the fact that the churches are still working only with an ethic of individual responsibility and have not yet thought out the ethics of group responsibility.

Another matter to which the attention of Christians should be directed is the way in which work brings men into new forms of association with their fellows. The working group often becomes a real community in which effective bonds of loyalty, fellow-feeling and mutual interest are engendered. Hence it happens that a working community in this sense may become opposed to the wider community around it as it seeks to promote its own ends; or perhaps it may be exploited by the state in its effort to subordinate the individual and to reduce man to the status of a worker and nothing more. Here again it is necessary that the traditional concern of Christian ethics with personal morality should be widened so that the insights of Christian faith may be brought to bear upon this important problem of group behavior. The working community must be seen to be neither an end in itself nor a means to the ends of the state, and its true status and character must be defined in the light of the Christian understanding of man.

Because work is a divine ordinance for human life, there is an obligation upon society to provide all its members with opportunity to work. Unemployment is not only a problem for economists but for all Christian people; the Christian view of the nature of work lays upon the laity the duty of promoting measures which will ensure the opportunity of all those who wish to work to secure employment. Similarly, the Christian will sometimes judge in the light of his Christian understanding that the structure of his occupation should be changed. His divine calling may enable him to transcend the framework of secular society, but if he is to transform it he must associate with his fellows in a united struggle to improve working conditions. Labor unions, farmers' groups, professional associations and the like can be organs through which a Christian layman may serve God's purpose as truly as he serves it in what is conventionally recognized as "church work." The Christian should work within such groups, or in the political party which he deems to be the most useful in combatting social ills, and in this effort he is sustained by his hope in Christ. While he accepts at its full weight the fact of sin in all human ideals and achievements, he will not give way to apathy because of his Christian hope; nor will he share the despair of those who have not this hope but are conscious of their insignificance in face of the vast processes which they seem powerless to change or bend to righteous ends. The Christian will hold firmly to the fact of Christ as the hope of the world, and he will therefore view the resources of nature not as so much raw material to be used entirely as man wills, but as God's gifts to be used responsibly in the light of this Christian hope concerning the end for which all things were made.

Thus, all human life and work are transformed by hope in Christ. All work honestly done, whether undertaken for the sake of earning a livelihood, or for the sake of the community, or out of spontaneous joy in creative effort, has genuine value and meaning in the purpose of God. Regarded solely from the standpoint of this world, the work which men do is of transient worth; even man's most enduring achievements must one day pass away. But regarded from the standpoint of hope in the coming Kingdom of Christ, every act of obedience to God's law possesses abiding significance and worth.

IV. The Ministry of the Laity: How Can It Become Effective?

The time has come to make the ministry of the laity explicit, visible and active in the world. The real battles of the faith today are being fought in factories, shops, offices, and farms, in political parties and government agencies, in countless homes, in the press, radio and television, in the relationship of nations. Very often it is said that the Church should "go into these spheres"; but the fact is, that the Church *is* already in these spheres in the persons of its laity.

So far, although in varying degrees, our churches have failed to give their members the support they need to make them effective representatives of the Church in their working life. Millions of men who know they belong in the world and speak its language and who are also faithful church members are still looking for the Church that will stand beside them as they work. Only if our churches succeed in being with their laity in the struggles of our present world will the laity in their turn become genuine representatives of the Church in areas of modern life to which otherwise the Church has no access. An immense opportunity is open to the churches in the world through their laity not to be seized for ecclesiastical domination but for Christian witness. But this opportunity for witness can only be seized if there is a change of emphasis and of prevailing atmosphere in many churches.

(1) Churches can become preoccupied with their own internal organization programs and activities to such an extent or in such a manner that they fail to grasp the importance of Christian witness in and through secular organs of society, and to encourage their members to participate fully in them. The Christian who, for example, throws himself into the social and political struggle should be actively encouraged and considered a gain, not a loss, to the Church.

(2) There is need to change the atmosphere which strikes the newcomer so forcibly in many churches, the atmosphere of an old-fashioned, middle-class culture, now radically changed in society but surviving in the Church. A tendency to choose the lay leadership of a congregation from among white-collar workers often prevents others, especially young industrial workers, from feeling at home in the Church.

(3) It is often thought in the Church that the clergy are the only ones who are obliged to walk worthily of their Christian calling wherever they may be. From the laity a lower standard is tolerated or even expected. The clergy have their appointed function in the Church, the ministry of Word and Sacraments. God calls men to this ministry, and every Christian needs to ask whether it is to this ministry or to the ministry of the laity that God's call comes. But on clergy and laity alike God lays the demand for total commitment to Him. The ministry of the laity should mean nothing less than this total commitment of all man's time, deeds and possessions.

Many people are conscious that they are ill equipped for their task of ministry. The following suggestions are put forward with a view to equipping them for their task.

(1) In churches with many recent converts, basic Christian teaching in

the faith, in prayer, worship and Bible reading is the first task, proceeding step by step with Christian witness and obedience in the home and daily work. Even in long-established congregations it cannot be taken for granted that such basic instruction is unnecessary. An active and organized laity could be a menace if it were not well instructed in the essentials of Christian faith and life.

(2) Among the laity there will be those who by reason of their devotion and gifts hold positions of responsibility and influence amongst the rank and file of church members. It is of especial importance that they should be able to bring the truths of Christian doctrine to bear upon the lay experience of life and work in the world. Theology is not for clergy only; it must be accessible to lay people in a form which they recognize as relevant and essential to their proper task.

(3) The clergy need a better acquaintance with present-day working society, both by study and experience, in order that they may help their laity and follow them with their prayers. Some theological seminaries have already made notable progress in this respect.

(4) The home should become a place where children grow up to regard work and occupation as a sphere of Christian vocation. In it children can learn to recognize God's voice and obey Him when He calls. Parents need to learn in the Church Christian attitudes toward work and vocation, and teach them to their children in place of the prevailing worldly standards of "getting on" or "keeping up with the Joneses." Christian youth organizations should reinforce this teaching by helping young people to choose their occupations in the light of Christian teaching about vocation.

(5) Any emphasis on the ministry of the laity means not only training but a special kind of pastoral care. Laymen and women should be encouraged to use the pastoral gifts that many of them possess. Mutual care of members by each other as well as by the clergy is needed in the Church. Christians have many natural opportunities for the pastoral care of neighbors, workmates and others.

(6) Christians from the same or related occupations should have some opportunity to meet occasionally. In fellowship with Christians in similar work they can study and discuss common concerns, including problems of the structure of their occupation, in the light of Christian faith. This practice is spreading to many parts of the world, taking different forms. In many instances the single parish is not large enough to draw people together in a specialized way and a regional and ecumenical basis serves the purpose better. There is room for more experiment and for a wide interchange of experience between the many associations, groups and cells of laity, residential colleges, and "Evangelical Academies." These, along with other specific activities such as lay retreats, conferences and consultations, are rapidly growing in number and scope.

The Church is sent into the world as a ministering community, not only in the sense that the parts serve each other, but that all serve the world. Here we see the relevance of the main theme of the Assembly to the subject under discussion. Christ died for the whole world and a deep conviction that this was so would make the Church the bearer of hope to the world. The Church would become outward-going both in evangelism and in daily service through work.

Our world is characterized by unprecedented technical, organizational and scientific achievements and at the same time by disillusionments, cynicism and fear of final self-destruction. The Church must not become an escape for those who do not dare to look such a world in the face. The Church cannot offer men security in this world, but because she preaches the Cross and Resurrection of Jesus Christ, she brings hope to men. It is for this reason that Christians can never abandon the world.

APPENDIX O

The Report on the Structure and Functioning of the World Council of Churches

Evanston, 1954

Preamble

This report sets out the proposals which the Central Committee wishes to submit to the Assembly regarding the structure and functioning of the World Council of Churches in the period following the Second Assembly.

A. Origin of Proposals

In its report to the First Assembly at Amsterdam in 1948, the Committee of the Assembly on Programme and Administration recommended that the detailed plans for the organization of the World Council of Churches should be approved in principle and referred to the Central Committee for further consideration. In making this recommendation, the Committee recognized that experience was needed before clear judgments could be reached regarding the organization of the World Council and that the first period must in many respects be regarded as experimental. The Central Committee at its meeting at Rolle, Switzerland, in August 1951, therefore decided to set in motion a detailed study of the experience of the first few years with a view to preparing for submission to the Second Assembly detailed and carefully considered proposals for the structure and functioning of the World Council of Churches in the period following that Assembly. The Central Committee appointed a Committee on Structure and Functioning "to evaluate the structure and review the procedures of the World Council and to report to the Central Committee, with a view to the preparation of a full report of the Central Committee to the Second Assembly." The following were appointed to the Committee:

Dr. Leslie E. Cooke, Chairman
Dr. Alphons Koechlin
Dr. Carl Lundquist
Dr. Philippe Maury
The Rev. R. David Say

The Central Committee also nominated as advisers to the Committee:

The Rt. Hon. Ernest Brown
Dr. Samuel McCrea Cavert

Dr. W. J. Gallagher
Sir Kenneth Grubb
Bishop H. Høgsbro
Bishop H. Lilje
Bishop S. K. Mondol
Principal T. M. Taylor

The Committee on Structure and Functioning held two further meetings of three days, and two days, duration respectively and then reported again to the Executive Committee at its meeting in Bossey in August 1953. It then held one further two-day meeting at which its report was prepared for final presentation to the Executive Committee meeting at Frankfurt (Germany) in February 1954. The Executive Committee approved the report and agreed that it should be circulated to all who should receive Assembly documents.

B. Status of This Report

The status of this report at the time of its circulation is thus that it has the approval of the Executive Committee and that an earlier one, not differing greatly from the present report, was considered and approved by the Central Committee. The report in its present form will receive final consideration by the Central Committee at its meeting immediately prior to the Assembly and the Central Committee will decide at that meeting with what comments it wishes to present the report to the Assembly.

C. Scope of Report

An attempt has been made to cover the whole field of activity of the World Council of Churches while observing the following principles:

(a) That no recommendations may be made which involve changes in the constitution but that changes in the rules may be recommended where necessary;
(b) That the provisions laid down at Amsterdam concerning the organization are not binding, since their report is intended for presentation at the Second Assembly;
(c) That as far as possible, proposed changes in organization should be made within the present budgetary limitations.

The report is presented in four parts:

Part 1. General Report divided into the following sections:
- I. The Structure of the Governing Bodies
- II. Communication with the Member Churches
- III. The External Relationships of the World Council of Churches
- IV. Divisional and Departmental Structure
- V. Committees and Commissions
- VI. Nomination Procedure for Officers and Members of Committees
- VII. Financial Provisions
- VIII. Office Organization and Administration

Part 2. Proposed Statements of Aims and Functions of the Proposed Divisions and Departments.

Part 3. Proposed Revisions of the Rules of the World Council of Churches (partly consequent on the proposals in Part 1 of the report and partly independent thereof).

Part 4. Conclusion.

PART 1. GENERAL REPORT

I. The Structure of the Governing Bodies

A. The Assembly

Since there has been only one Assembly of the World Council of Churches and that of a unique character, it is felt that there is insufficient experience and evidence to warrant any proposals for major change in the form and constitution of the Assembly. The Central Committee at Toronto decided to increase the number of delegates and not to repeat the Amsterdam provision for the presence in the Assembly of an alternate to each delegate. The Committee recalls to the attention of the Second Assembly that a decision should be taken by that body as to the date of the Third Assembly and that the constitution provides that the Assembly "shall ordinarily meet every five years."

B. Presidium

The Presidium has, in the opinion of the Committee, proved a valuable part of the organization of the World Council of Churches. The Committee submits the four following recommendations concerning provisions to be added to the rules regarding the constitution of the Presidium, and suggests that the nomination of its members be subject to the provisions outlined in Section VI of this report on Nomination Procedure:

(1) That a maximum of six be fixed for the number of Presidents;
(2) That a President shall be ineligible for immediate re-election when his term of office ends;
(3) That the term of office of a President shall end at the adjournment of the next Assembly following his or her election;
(4) That the President or Presidents shall be entitled to attend the Assembly with full right of speech even if not appointed as delegates by their churches.

C. Central Committee

It is the Central Committee which acts on behalf of the Assembly and which, between meetings of the Assembly, is the authoritative body of the World Council of Churches. It therefore seems important that the status and responsibility of the Central Committee should be preserved and enhanced. Close attention has therefore been given to the procedure of the Central Committee, the duration of its meetings and its sub-committee structure.

It is felt that the practice of considering one or more main issues of the ecumenical movement at each meeting—e.g., "The Calling of the Church to Mission and Unity" and "The Role of the World Council of Churches in Time of Tension" at the Rolle meeting—has proved to be of real value.

Clearly there are two sub-committees of the Central Committee which must be regarded as permanent features of every Central Committee meeting—the Finance Committee and the Nominations Committee.

On the other hand, it is considered that there has been inadequate consideration of the Executive Committee's Report and that undue time has been taken in receiving oral reports from departments. It is further considered that the Central Committee will act more effectively if matters of policy arising either from reports or in the course of the Central Committee's discussions are referred to a Reference Committee or Committees. Such Committees would report to a plenary session of the Central Committee.

The following recommendations are therefore submitted:

1. That the report of the Executive Committee to the Central Committee

covering the work done by the Executive Committee since the previous Central Committee meeting, shall be given greater importance in the agenda of the Central Committee; that the report of the General Secretary be, however, retained and cover the activities of the Council and a general review of the most important developments in the church situation throughout the world;

2. That divisional reports to the Central Committee be in future circulated in writing and be in the hands of the Central Committee members at least one month before each meeting;

3. That a motion for the reception of each report shall be included in the agenda of the Central Committee thus providing an opportunity for questions to be raised on the written reports or on any other matters concerning the work of the division in question;

4. That it shall not be the rule in future that every division or department shall report orally to each meeting of the Central Committee but the Central Committee may call for an oral report from any division or department if it sees fit to do so;

5. That the Central Committee shall normally meet for eight days from a Tuesday night to a Wednesday night;

6. That the Central Committee shall have the following sub-committees:

(a) Finance Committee (a standing committee);

(b) Nominations Committee (newly appointed at each meeting);

(c) Reference Committee or Committees (appointed as needed at each meeting) to advise the Central Committee on any other question arising which calls for special consideration or action by the Central Committee;

7. That the practice of taking one or more main issues for consideration at each Central Committee meeting has proved highly creative and profitable and [shall] be continued;

8. That it should be recommended to the Assembly that the Central Committee should be kept in existence until its report has been received and discharge has been given;

9. In the event that the Chairman and/or Vice-Chairman of the Central Committee shall not be appointed as delegates to the Assembly by their churches, they shall be entitled to attend the Assembly as consultants.

It is further recommended that recommendations 6, 8, and 9 above shall be incorporated into the Rules of the World Council of Churches (see Part 3 of this report*).

D. Executive Committee of the Central Committee

The mandate of the Executive Committee was not clearly defined at Amsterdam. Experience has shown that the Executive Committee has had to carry a considerable amount of responsibility, and on one occasion at least has found it necessary to issue a statement in the form of a letter to the churches concerning public affairs. The pattern of procedure in the Executive Committee has been similar to that in the Central Committee, which has meant a considerable amount of duplication.

The fact that hitherto the Chairman of the Executive Committee has also been Chairman of the Central Committee has meant that the Executive Committee report has been given from the Chair of the Central Committee. This represents a situation which could limit the freedom of discussion in the Central Committee.

* This part of the report (the Rules of the World Council of Churches) appears in its amended form as Appendix 12 of *The Evanston Report,* pp. 312 ff.

Experience has shown that there has been clear advantage in having as members of the Executive Committee persons closely connected with the work of certain divisions of departments, since from their own knowledge they have been able to focus the attention of the Committee on salient matters concerning those divisions or departments. Other reports have suffered in the Executive Committee from lack of personal contact on the part of members of the Executive Committee with the activities covered by the reports.

It has become apparent that while a meeting of the Executive Committee before the Central Committee is imperative, there would be advantages in an arrangement whereby the Executive should meet for a short time after the Central Committee so that the implementing of Central Committee decisions should not be left entirely in the hands of the staff of the World Council without opportunity of further consultations and advices.

In light of these considerations it is recommended:

1. That the present provision of the Rules that "the Chairman of the Central Committee shall be also the Chairman of the Executive Committee" (Rule V. 1[c])* be left unchanged, but that during the reports to the Central Committee of the Executive Committee and of the General Secretary, the Chair shall be taken by a member of the Presidium;

2. That the functions of the Executive Committee at present defined as follows: "The Executive Committee shall carry out the decisions of the Central Committee. It shall meet ordinarily twice a year" (Rule V, 2) shall be redefined in the following terms:

> The Executive Committee is a committee of the Central Committee appointed by it and responsible to it. The Executive Committee shall, between meetings of the Central Committee, carry out the decisions of the Central Committee and implement the policy laid down by it. It shall meet ordinarily twice a year. The Executive Committee shall have no authority to make decisions on policy except that in circumstances of special urgency it can take provisional decisions. It may only issue public statements under the provisions laid down in Rule IX, 4. It shall have power to appoint heads of departments provisionally, but such appointments shall be subject to confirmation by the Central Committee. It shall supervise the operation of the budget and have power to impose limitations on expenditure if necessary.

3. That certain members of the Executive Committee shall be given assignments of interest in specific fields of World Council work, without any particular executive or administrative responsibility for that work;

4. That the Executive Committee shall meet normally twice a year. It shall meet for two days before each meeting of the Central Committee and may also hold a one-day meeting after the Central Committee, if considered necessary on any occasion.

5. That there should be no power for the appointment of substitutes for members of the Executive Committee unable to attend meetings and that this shall be explicitly stated in the Rules. The Executive Committee might, however, wish use to be made of the power granted to the officers "to invite others to attend a meeting of the Executive Committee for consultation, always having in mind the need of preserving a due balance of the confessions and of the geographical areas" (Rule V, 1 [d]).

It is not thought desirable to recommend that a quorum should be fixed in

* References are to the official Report of the Amsterdam Assembly, 1949, pp. 202-213.

the Rules for the meetings of the Executive Committee; it is felt that flexibility is needed on this point. It is, however, recommended that it should be understood that at the request of any member, the number of members present when any particular decision is taken shall be recorded in the minutes.

As to the relative claims of continuity and change in the membership of the Executive Committee, it is considered that neither complete continuity nor complete change is desirable and that no limitation of the Central Committee's choice should be imposed.

II. Communication with the Member Churches

A. Direct Communication

The problem of communication has arisen in several ways; the response of the churches to communications from the Secretariat of the World Council of Churches is disappointing; the variety of documents issued from Geneva is sometimes bewildering; and the relative authority of each document not clearly defined. No communication with the churches is more effective than the personal visitation by World Council staff, especially by the General Secretary, and the proposed arrangements for divisional and departmental structure are designed to make such visitation possible in greater measure than in the past.

As regards written communications, it is recommended:

1. That it be re-affirmed that the World Council must maintain direct communications with the member churches, their committees and boards;

2. That where a member church agrees:

(a) Communications relating to important policy questions shall be sent to the chief executive of a church;

(b) World Council divisions and departments shall communicate directly with the offices and departments of a church responsible for the corresponding fields of work;

3. That documents should bear a clear indication of their authority; e.g., reports of conferences should bear a clear indication that their conclusions are not World Council conclusions.

B. Relations with National Councils

Rulings governing the relations of the World Council of Churches with national councils were adopted by the Central Committee at its first meeting immediately following the Amsterdam Assembly. Developments over the subsequent period have demonstrated the significance of national councils in relation to the World Council of Churches and it is considered desirable that appropriate provisions should now be introduced into the Rules. The revised Rules which are suggested below have been discussed and approved by the Joint Committee of the International Missionary Council and the World Council of Churches.

It is therefore recommended:

(i) That the present clause under Rule X be left unaltered but be given the sub-heading: "1. International Missionary Council";

(ii) That there be added to Rule X a new clause reading:

2. National Councils

(a) The World Council, recognizing that national councils of churches or national Christian councils have been established in a number of countries for purposes of fellowship and co-operation with one another and for the promotion and support of ecumenical activities and other common interests within their own area, shall invite selected national councils to enter into working relationships as associated councils.

(b) The purpose of such working relationships shall be to help national councils in their work and to encourage them to help the World Council of Churches in the promotion of ecumenical activities in the area concerned and in the furthering of the plans and policies which the Central Committee has laid down for the various divisions and departments of the Council.

(c) These councils shall be regularly designated to receive invitations to send a fraternal delegate to the Assembly and a consultant to the Central Committee (in accordance with Section VII, ii of the Constitution).

(d) Opportunity shall be provided at the time of any meeting of the Assembly or Central Committee for the representatives of national councils to meet together for mutual consultation.

(e) While the World Council retains the right to deal with its member churches directly, no action shall be taken by it which would disturb any already existing fellowships or ecumenical organization within a nation or region.

(f) Any member church which prefers to have direct relationships with the World Council in any field of work can have such direct relationships.

(g) The following criteria, among others, shall be applied by the Central Committee in selecting national councils for these working relationships:

(i) that the national council accept the Basis of the World Council of Churches or express its willingness to co-operate on that Basis;

(ii) that there be prior consultation with the member churches of the World Council in the area concerned;

(iii) that there be prior consultation with the International Missionary Council in the case of national councils which are members of that body;

(iv) that the membership of the national council consist wholly or to a large extent of churches which hold membership in the World Council of Churches;

(v) that the national council have an interest in the work of the World Council of Churches and be willing to work for that Council;

(vi) that the national council give evidence of stability and have a staff with time to devote to the World Council of Churches.

(h) In the case of countries where national missionary councils exist, whether integrated in or associated with national councils of churches or independently, the Central Committee may invite such a national missionary council to send a fraternal delegate to the Assembly and a consultant to the Central Committee.

C. World Confessional Associations

It may be noted with satisfaction that almost all world confessional associations have gone on record as wishing to support the ecumenical movement, and it is suggested that the General Secretary shall arrange for informal consultations from time to time, with three or four representatives from each association, to discuss the implementation of that desire and other common problems. There is provision in the Constitution (paragraph VII) for the representation at sessions of the Assembly and of the Central Committee of such world confessional associations as may be designated by the Central Committee, but the status of such representatives is not fully defined and it is therefore recommended that there be added to Rule X a further new clause reading:

3. World Confessional Associations

Such world confessional associations as may be designated by the Central Committee shall be invited to send fraternal delegates to the Assembly, and consultants to the Central Committee.

III. The External Relationships of the World Council of Churches

A. International Missionary Council

The Amsterdam Assembly agreed that the words "in association with the International Missionary Council" should be a part of the general description of the World Council of Churches and also approved the continuation of a Joint Committee with the International Missionary Council to which all questions with regard to collaboration between the two bodies should be referred. Fruitful progress has been made over the first six years in giving substance to this "association." At the time of the Amsterdam Assembly, the International Missionary Council and the World Council of Churches had created a joint organ in the Commission of the Churches on International Affairs and were considering the possibility of establishing a joint office in East Asia. In the period since Amsterdam, a Joint Secretary for East Asia has been appointed and the World Council Department of Inter-Church Aid and Service to Refugees has been given responsibility for the co-ordination on behalf of the two bodies of emergency inter-church aid and relief outside Europe. The Joint Committee is further recommending that there should be one Division of Studies which should serve both the International Missionary Council and the World Council of Churches and should include three World Council Departments for Faith and Order, Church and Society and Evangelism, and one International Missionary Council Department of Missionary Studies, and also that steps should be taken to ensure closer ties in public relations and information. It is further recommended that the Joint Committee, which has increasingly become an effective instrument for dealing with matters of common concern, should be strengthened in its membership and provided with a full-time secretary so that it may be still better equipped to develop further the association between the International Missionary Council and the World Council of Churches. The relationships between the two bodies are set out more fully in the report of the Joint Committee on pages 322-327 [of *The Evanston Report*].

B. United Bible Societies

There have been close and cordial relationships with this body since its inception. At present there is a member of the United Bible Societies staff working at the World Council of Churches headquarters in close co-operation with the Secretariat of Evangelism. In view of the vital importance of the promotion of Bible distribution and Bible reading for the life of the churches and for the ecumenical movement, it is recommended that these relationships should be developed and encouraged.

C. Other Designated Ecumenical Organizations

At present the Central Committee has fraternal representatives from the World's Committee of the Young Men's Christian Associations, the World's Young Women's Christian Association, the World's Student Christian Federation and the World Council of Christian Education and Sunday School Association. All these bodies are members, along with the World Council of Churches, of the World Christian Youth Commission, which carries out an important piece of co-ordination in the field of youth work. Further relations between the Youth Departments of the World Council of Christian

Education and the World Council of Churches are particularly close and cordial; indeed the two Departments share the majority of their committee members and hold their committee meetings at the same time.

Relationships with these four organizations are not confined to the youth field and it is therefore recommended that regular discussions between the general secretaries and *ad hoc* consultations on specific questions of common interest should be encouraged.

IV. Divisional and Departmental Structure

When considering the departmental structure of the World Council of Churches, it must be remembered that the World Council is an organism rather than an organization. The present structure of the World Council is the result of a series of responses made to a series of stimuli. As a new need has become manifest the Council has sought to meet it by developing a new piece of organization. Co-ordination and integration have been achieved at the personal level rather than by strategic planning. One result of this is that the World Council has developed too many departments whose secretaries live in constant tension between field and office work while at the same time they seek to meet the demands made upon them to effect cross-representation between the departments. An immense burden rests upon the General Secretary and the organization inevitably suffers during his necessary absences from Geneva.

There would appear to be no single integrating principle under which the existing departmental organization is subsumed and there is a serious lack of liaison between the departments and the Central Committee. The suggested changes in structure are designed in the belief that if they are adopted the whole position will be improved.

The main changes involved in the proposals set out below are a strengthening of the General Secretariat and the creation of two new divisions bringing together departments which have certain common functions to perform.

It is recommended that there shall be four Associate General Secretaries, three of whom will be responsible for a division and the fourth for the Commission of the Churches on International Affairs. One Associate General Secretary will be the Deputy General Secretary who will act for the General Secretary in his absence. In addition to their special responsibilities, the Associate General Secretaries shall share with the General Secretary responsibility for the life of the World Council of Churches as a whole. The General Secretary and the Associate Secretaries, together with the Directors of Finance and Administration and of Information, will provide at the center of the organization a central secretarial group capable of discussing the whole work of the Council and co-ordinating its activities. The Executive Secretary of the New York office and the East Asia Secretary will, when available, sit with this secretarial group.

The centralizing of the Secretariat in Geneva, which to some, at first sight, may seem undesirable, will make possible greater personal contact of the chief executives of the World Council and the constituency. Personal visits to the churches by the chief executives of the World Council are of the greatest value and importance. The adoption of the present proposals will make possible a representation by them to the churches not only of those details which are their personal responsibility but of the total concerns of the World Council of Churches. Those contacts will be made with less interruption of the work of the central offices and with less anxiety for the executives themselves who at present, when they are abroad, know that essential tasks in Geneva are being generally neglected.

The principle underlying the proposed divisional and departmental structure is *that the Principle of Integration must be Unity of Function.*

There can of course be no complete and absolute differentiation between the proposed divisions nor would such differentiation be desirable. On the other hand, there is need for definition of the areas of operation and at the same time provision must be made for the fullest possible co-ordination.

In the light of these considerations the Committee believes that the organization of the World Council of Churches should be reconstructed upon a divisional basis, each division being constituted so as to bring together departments which have certain common functions to perform.

A division will, therefore, be the organ for putting into effect a particular part of the policy of the World Council. It will be an entity in the World Council organization having freedom to initiate policy and take action in its own field, although it will do so in relation to the other divisions and subject to the Assembly and Central Committee, whose total policy it is the responsibility of the General Secretariat to administer and direct.

The division, besides operating as an entity in itself, will work through departments to which will belong the responsibility for study and action in certain specified fields. The grouping of the departments and divisions will make possible strategic planning of departmental work and integration of departmental activities. The departments will also have freedom to initiate projects, prepare programmes and take action in their own fields, subject to the general policy of the division itself.

It is proposed that each division shall have a divisional committee and shall operate under the supervision of an Associate General Secretary. Each department will have a working committee and a director or executive secretary.

It is also proposed that the committee membership shall be such as to establish a direct relationship between the divisional and departmental committees and the Central Committee.

The departments will therefore be integral parts of the divisions in which they have their place, and thus will have the benefit of co-operation and planning. The division and its Associate General Secretary will serve the departments in keeping them in close touch with the policy of the World Council and the General Secretariat. While the report to the Central Committee on a departments work will normally form a part of the division's report, the departments will, if occasion arises, have opportunity to present particular concerns direct to the Central Committee.

The divisions may, with the sanction of the Central Committee, create new departments to meet needs, or effect rearrangements within the existing departmental structure.

This arrangement will call for recognition by the departmental committees and by the departmental secretaries themselves, that the departmental secretaries are not only members of the World Council staff to whom departmental responsibilities have been entrusted, but that they are also members of a divisional team under the immediate leadership of the Associate General Secretary and that the divisional committees may assign tasks to them in the working of the divisions as a whole, in addition to those which belong to them as departmental secretaries.

The Committee is of the opinion that an organization such as this, which provides for both a unified committee and secretarial relationship is most likely to effect that integration of the organization of the World Council which is the immediate need.

It is therefore recommended:

A. That there shall be three divisions:

(i) The Division of Studies

This Division shall co-ordinate all work of a study nature. Within the Division there will be departments for Faith and Order, Church and Society and Evangelism, each with at least one full-time secretary. Provision has also been made in the committee structure for a close liaison between this Division and the Ecumenical Institute, especially with regard to study conferences. The decisions made by the World Conference on Faith and Order at Lund took account of a number of recommendations made by the Committee on Structure and Functioning and have made possible the integration of the work of Faith and Order into the structure of the World Council. The Joint Committee of the International Missionary Council and the World Council of Churches, at its meeting in January 1954, agreed to recommend that the Division of Studies of the World Council should also be the Division of Studies of the International Missionary Council and should include a Department of Missionary Studies, of which the Research Secretary of the International Missionary Council should be Executive Secretary. This recommendation was approved by the Executive Committee of the World Council at its meeting in February 1954 and will go forward to the meetings of the Ad Interim Committee of the International Missionary Council and the Central Committee of the World Council which will be held shortly before the Second Assembly (see Report of Joint Committee).

(ii) The Division of Ecumenical Action

This Division shall be concerned with helping the churches to make their membership in the World Council a practical, living reality. It shall include the Ecumenical Institute, including the Graduate School of Ecumenical Studies, the Youth Department, the Department on Co-operation of Men and Women in Church and Society and the Department on Work for the Laity. Through the work of these Departments, and through other means which may from time to time be chosen, the Division will aim at building up ecumenical consciousness and understanding. It shall not be primarily concerned with making known the activities of the World Council, but with promoting activities within the churches which are ecumenical in character. The Ecumenical Institute is included in this Division because it is an essential experimental ground for ecumenism, where new groupings and new methods of approach are being tried out. At the same time the Ecumenical Institute shall have a special relationship to the Division of Studies since it is preeminently a place where ecumenical study and action are being fruitfully related for the benefit of the World Council as a whole as well as for the member churches.

(iii) The Division of Inter-Church Aid and Service to Refugees

This Division, which already exists within the present structure, helps the churches to fulfill their obligations to help one another and also to give help to groups in special need, such as the millions of refugees in the world today. It shall be responsible for all work of the World Council in the field of inter-church aid and service to refugees, including the new responsibility for emergency interchurch aid and relief, in the name of both the International Missionary Council and the World Council of Churches, in countries outside Europe. It will collaborate with the Commission of the Churches on International Affairs in public representations on behalf of refugees and other suffering groups.

B. That there shall be a commission appointed jointly by the World Council and the International Missionary Council:

The Commission of the Churches on International Affairs

This Commission already exists and no change in its structure or relationship to the World Council is proposed. (The Executive Committee of the Commission of the Churches on International Affairs, meeting at Willingen in July 1952 considered this question and decided that no major change of structure was needed.)

C. That there shall be two departments both directly responsible to the General Secretary:

(i) The Department of Finance and Administration

This Department shall be responsible for providing for all of the divisions and departments of the World Council all financial, accounting and general services. It has a clear responsibility to relieve the General Secretary, as far as possible, of administrative work. It shall be headed by a director and shall have an adequate staff of departmental secretaries.

(ii) The Department of Information

This Department shall be responsible for making known the activities of the World Council through the church and secular press and other media and for press offices at the time of meetings. It shall also serve the churches by providing them with news about the life of their sister churches. It shall be responsible for the co-ordination of all publications issued by the World Council. Since its task is to interpret the work of the World Council, the Director of this Department should be a man with a knowledge of the ecumenical movement and the churches, who will be able to give leadership to the Department. He must be supported by an adequate staff of departmental secretaries. With safeguards to insure that publicity, especially promotional publicity concerning inter-church aid and refugee work should not be hampered, the information service of the Department of Inter-Church Aid shall be included in the Information Department, under the control of the Director. The Joint Committee of the International Missionary Council and the World Council of Churches, at its meeting in January 1954, welcomed a suggestion that the International Missionary Council should use the facilities of the new Department of Information and this suggestion, which was approved by the Executive Committee of the World Council in February 1954, will go forward to the meetings of the Ad Interim Committee of the International Missionary Council which will be held shortly before the Second Assembly (see Report of the Joint Committee).

D. That there shall be regional representation of the World Council in two areas:

(i) The New York Office

An office was established in New York because of the large group of member churches in the United States of America—at a long distance from Geneva—with which relations have to be maintained, and because of the importance of New York as a point of contact with extensive missionary and ecumenical interests.

The New York office is under the general supervision of the Central Committee and directly responsible to the General Secretary. It is proposed that its staff include the following, subject to review from time to time by the Central Committee:

1. Executive Secretary in the United States of America, appointed by the Central Committee.

The Executive Secretary shall:

(a) Have oversight of all of the activities of the New York office;

(b) Maintain continuous liaison with the General Secretary in Geneva on all matters of policy and interpret World Council policies to the American people;

(c) Serve the three Divisions—Inter-Church Aid, Studies (including Faith and Order), Ecumenical Action—and the Departments of Information and of Finance and Administration in their relations with the Churches in the United States;

(d) Co-operate with the office and staff of the Commission of the Churches on International Affairs in New York;

(e) Be a member of the staff executive group of the Council and meet with the General Secretary and Associate General Secretaries whenever practicable;

(f) Render such service as may be required to the United States Conference for the World Council of Churches.

2. Associate (or Assistant) Executive Secretary—as may be found desirable—appointed by the Executive Committee.

The Associate (or Assistant) Executive Secretary shall:

(a) Assist the Executive Secretary in discharging the general duties of the New York Office;

(b) Carry special responsibility for such phases of the programme as the General Secretary and the Executive Secretary in the United States of America may assign.

3. Secretary of the Youth Department.

This Secretary shall be a part of the regular staff of the Youth Department and be under its direction in all matters of programme and policy, and under the administrative supervision of the Executive Secretary in the United States of America.

Other members of the New York Office staff, if deemed necessary by the Executive Committee (for example, for service in finance and publicity) may be appointed by the General Secretary and the Executive Secretary in the United States of America.

4. Secretariat for East Asia.

This Secretariat, which serves both the World Council and the International Missionary Council, was set up following the Bangkok Conference at which it was requested that the East Asia Secretary should be an Asian Christian and should have "official membership and status in the secretariat of the International Missionary Council and the World Council of Churches and that his budget should be included jointly in the several secretarial budgets of the International Missionary Council and the World Council of Churches." It was further suggested at that conference that he should "give his full time to visiting churches and Christian councils in East Asia, helping the churches to share more fully their thought and experience, with a view to strengthening the churches in their evangelistic task in East Asia, and establishing closer contact than at present exists between the East Asian churches and councils and the world-wide movement of the Church." Experience over the last few years has fully justified the existence of this Secretariat. It is therefore recommended that there should be a Secretary for East Asia who should be a full staff member of the World Council of Churches and should when available sit in with the General Secretariat.

It should be noted here that it is not recommended that a World Council of Churches office should be maintained in London. The British Council of Churches, which has had a working relationship with the World Council of Churches since its inauguration, is willing to accept responsibility for the financial and administrative work at present done by the London office, and it is felt that there is now no justification for the maintenance of the World Council of Churches office there.

V. Committees and Commissions

The following recommendations regarding divisional and departmental committees are in the main an application to committee procedure of the proposals in Section IV of this report on divisional and departmental structure. It is recommended that with the exception of recommendation (2 c), they should be incorporated in the rules of the World Council of Churches.

It is recommended that:

1. There shall be a small committee for each division whose responsibility shall be to carry out the aim of the division. It shall be responsible for the preparation and presentation to the Central Committee of the reports on the division's work.

2. Divisional committees shall be appointed by the Central Committee as follows:

(a) For the Division of Studies and the Division of Ecumenical Action, the committees shall consist of three persons who are not members of any departmental working committee within the division, plus the chairman and one other member of each departmental working committee within the division. One of the two representatives of each departmental working committee must be a member of the Central Committee. For the purpose of co-ordination, the Division of Studies should be represented by one or two members on the Committee of the Division of Ecumenical Action and vice versa.

(b) For the Division of Inter-Church Aid, the committee shall consist of seven members, at least two of whom shall be members of the Central Committee.

(c) The exceptional position of the Commission of the Churches on International Affairs was recognized and no change is suggested in respect of its committee structure, but it is recommended that at least two members of the Executive Committee of the Commission of the Churches on International Affairs shall be drawn from the membership of the Central Committee.

Departmental secretaries shall normally be present at the meetings of divisional committees.

3. There shall be working committees for each department appointed by the Central Committee and responsible for the preparation of departmental programmes for submission to the divisional committees and for the execution of the programmes. The chairmen of departmental working committees shall be *ex officio* members of the appropriate divisional committees. Departmental working committees shall have power to call in *ad hoc* consultants as needed on particular problems. In the case of the Ecumenical Institute, its Board shall be regarded as the working committee. Normally a working committee shall consist of fifteen members at least one of whom shall be a member of the Central Committee. In the interest of closest possible coordination of the Department on Evangelism and the Department of Missionary Studies, the working committee of these Departments shall meet together from time to time.

Some departments have constitutions which have been approved by the Central Committee. In some measure those constitutions are superseded by the statements of aims and functions set out in Part 2 of this report; in certain cases they also provide for committees with titles different from those proposed in this report. The Constitution of Faith and Order adopted by the Lund Conference in August 1952 was drafted after consultation with the Committee on Structure and Functioning and no change in the status of the Faith and Order Commission is suggested. The Commission of the Churches on International Affairs is in a special position as a semi-autonomous body created by and with a constitution approved by the International Missionary Council and the World Council of Churches and there appears to be no occasion to revise its constitution. It is further suggested that the Youth Committee and the Annual Consultation of the Deparment of Inter-Church Aid and Service to Refugees, provided for in the constitutions of those two Departments, shall continue to exist, in addition to the departmental or divisional committees. It is recommended that all departments, other than Faith and Order and the Commission of the Churches on International Affairs, which have constitutions shall be directed to redraft them under the title of "Departmental Bye-laws," incorporating the statement of aims and functions as adopted by the Assembly and adopting the terminology of the Structure and Functioning Report as adopted by the Assembly, and shall submit the revised departmental bye-laws to an early meeting of the Central Committee after the Assembly.

VI. Nomination Procedure for Officers and Members of Committees

In an international body made up of churches of various nations and confessions, the task of securing fair and adequate representation is of paramount importance. The present nomination procedure has been reviewed, taking into account previous decisions. There would appear to be need for a tightening up of procedure and a clear definition of responsibility.

The following recommendations are therefore submitted:

1. That no change be made in the present provision in the Rules concerning the Nominations Committee of the Assembly, namely:

(1) At an early session of the Assembly, the Assembly shall appoint a Nominations Committee, on which there shall be appropriate confessional and geographical representation of the membership of the Assembly.

(2) The Nominations Committee in consultation with the officers of the World Council and the Executive Committee shall draft proposals concerning (a) the President or Presidents of the World Council of Churches and (b) a list of persons proposed for membership on the Central Committee.

(3) The President or Presidents shall be *ex officio* members of the Central Committee and of the Executive Committee.

(4) The Nominations Committee shall present its proposals to the Assembly for its acceptance and revision.

(5) It shall be open to any six members of the Assembly acting together to put forward in writing other proposals.

(6) Election shall be by ballot unless the Assembly shall otherwise determine.

2. That the rule regarding the Nominations Committee of the Central Committee, reading as follows:

(2 b) For this purpose it shall appoint a Nominations Committee of not more than four persons, who shall bring before the Central Commit-

tee one or more names for each office. Any member of the Central Committee may make alternative proposals,

should be revised to read:

The Central Committee shall appoint a Nominations Committee which shall:

(a) Nominate individuals to the Central Committee for the offices of Chairman and Vice-Chairman or Vice-Chairmen of the Central Committee.
(b) Nominate individuals for election as President, if between Assemblies need arises for such appointments, under the power conferred on the Central Committee by the Constitution and Rules.
(c) Nominate the members of the Executive Committee and divisional committees and departmental working committees.

3. That the following new paragraph should be added to the Rules:

In making nominations, the Nominations Committee of the Assembly and the Central Committee shall have regard to the following principles:

(a) The personal qualifications of the individual for the task for which he is to be nominated;
(b) Fair and adequate confessional representation;
(c) Fair and adequate geographical representation;

and shall satisfy itself as to the general acceptability of the nominations to the churches to which the nominees belong. In applying the principles (b) and (c) above to the nomination of members of the divisional committees and the departmental working committees, the Nominations Committee shall consider the representative character of the combined membership of all such committees.

VII. Financial Provisions

Under the proposed new structure, each division will have an expenditure budget sub-divided into sections covering:

(a) The expenses of its Associate General Secretary and any other central staff and other divisionals expenses;
(b) The expenses of each department within the division.

On the basis of proposals made by divisional committees, the General Secretariat, assisted by the Department of Finance and Administration, will prepare for submission to the Finance Committee of the Central Committee, a consolidated budget for the operations of the World Council of Churches as a whole.

The divisional committee will have power to vary the allocations of the total budget as between the various headings within the budget at its discretion, provided that the authorized total be not exceeded and the policy of the division be thereby advanced.

VIII. Office Organization and Administration

After consideration, it was concluded that an enquiry into the internal office organization could not profitably be undertaken until after the establishing of a revised structure by the Evanston Assembly.

PART 2. PROPOSED STATEMENTS OF AIMS AND FUNCTIONS OF THE PROPOSED DIVISIONS AND DEPARTMENTS

The Central Committee submits to the Assembly the following draft statements of the aims and functions of each of the divisions and departments proposed in Part 1, Section IV of this report. It will be recalled that in Part 1, Section V it is recommended that these statements should be incorporated in departmental bye-laws, which should be submitted for approval to an early meeting of the Central Committee after the Assembly and that such departmental bye-laws should supersede the constitutions which are at present in force for certain World Council departments, but not the constitutions of the Faith and Order Commission nor of the Commission of the Churches on International Affairs.

I. Division of Studies

The aim of the Division shall be to serve the churches by promoting ecumenical studies on the fundamental issues of their faith and life, so that they may increasingly think together, advance in unity, render common witness and take common action in the social and international field.

The functions of the Division shall be:

(i) to work out the policy and determine the programme of studies concerning questions which are of critical importance for the life of the churches and of the ecumenical movement as a whole;
(ii) to be responsible for and to plan studies in preparation for the Assemblies and other major meetings of the World Council;
(iii) to co-ordinate and to help to plan studies which are required by the work of other divisions;
(iv) to serve as a clearing house for studies undertaken in and by the churches;
(v) to provide background information on trends of thought and life about which the churches need to be informed;
(vi) to co-ordinate the studies undertaken by the Departments on Faith and Order, Church and Society, and Evangelism;
(vii) to advise the churches about actions resulting from the studies.

Note. The Joint Committee of the International Missionary Council and the World Council of Churches, at its meeting in January 1954, agreed to recommend that the Division of Studies of the World Council should also be the Division of Studies of the International Missionary Council and that the International Missionary Council should adopt, with appropriate modifications arising from the difference in constituent membership, the above statement of the Aims and Functions of the Division.

A. Department on Faith and Order

The aim of the Department shall be to draw the churches out of isolation into conference about questions of faith and order.

The functions of the Department are stated as follows in paragraph 3 of the Constitution of the Faith and Order Commission:

(i) to proclaim the essential oneness of the Church of Christ and to keep prominently before the World Council and the churches the obligation to manifest that unity and its urgency for the work of evangelism;
(ii) to study questions of faith, order and worship with the relevant social, cultural, political, racial and other factors in their bearing on the unity of the Church;
(iii) to study the theological implications of the existence of the ecumenical movement;
(iv) to study matters in the present relationships of the churches to one another which cause difficulties and need theological clarification;
(v) to provide information concerning actual steps taken by the churches towards re-union.

B. Department of Church and Society

The aim of the Department shall be to serve the churches by the study of problems arising out of their mission in and to society.

The functions of the Department shall be:

(i) to select for recommendation to the Division the crucial problems of society about which the churches should declare their common mind and take action including (in consultation with the Commission of the Churches on International Affairs) such basic problems of international life and inter-racial relations as require long-range study;

(ii) to study in the light of the Christian faith, and together with competent persons from different churches and walks of life, relevant problems in this field;

(iii) to disseminate the results of such studies;

(iv) to keep the churches informed about important developments in society;

(v) to acquaint the churches with the action taken by other churches in this field;

(vi) to assist other divisions or departments in relating their activities to society.

C. Department on Evangelism

The aim of the Department shall be to serve the churches by promoting ecumenical study and consultation on the evangelistic calling and task of the churches.

The functions of the Department shall be:

(i) to keep prominently before the World Council, all its divisions and departments and its member churches, the importance of the Church's evangelistic and missionary obligation and its call to unity;

(ii) as and when requested, to help churches in activities of common witness and evangelism;

(iii) to undertake studies concerning the methods and content of the evangelistic approach of the Church towards those outside its life;

(iv) to collect and circulate to the churches information on effective approaches to evangelism.

D. Department of Missionary Studies

The aim of the Department shall be the furtherance of the world mission of the Church. To this end it shall seek to initiate and co-ordinate studies and enquiries regarding the missionary task of the churches.

The functions of the Department shall be:

(i) to study the emergence and growth of "younger churches" and the relationship of the work of the missionary societies to such churches;

(ii) through such studies to help churches and missionary societies in the formulation of mission policy;

(iii) to undertake, within the resources available to it, such special studies as may be requested by the member councils of the International Missionary Council;

(iv) to promote and co-ordinate studies of the missionary task of the Church;

(v) through publication of the results of special studies and by other means available, to provide churches and missions with information regarding developments of special importance in the field of missionary thinking.

II. Division of Ecumenical Action

The aim of the Division shall be to serve the churches by promoting the growth of ecumenical consciousness amongst their members, by relating ecumenical knowledge and experience to the whole life of the churches and by working for the renewal of the churches through active ecumenical encounter.

The functions of the Division shall be:

(i) to work out policies and methods which will enable the World Council to achieve these aims, and in particular to help in ensuring the participation of local congregations in the life of the ecumenical movement;

(ii) to co-ordinate the plans of the Ecumenical Institute, the Youth Department, the Department on Work for the Laity, and the Department on Co-operation of Men and Women in Church and Society;

(iii) to guide the four Departments in the carrying out of their activities so as best to achieve the aims of the Division;

(iv) to help the churches to relate ecumenical thinking to Christian education in all its aspects;

(v) to foster co-operation between the World Council and other organizations in so far as this will further the aims of the Division;

(vi) to serve as a clearing-house for experiments and new methods of ecumenical education and consultation.

A. Ecumenical Institute

The aim of the Ecumenical Institute shall be to serve the churches as a centre of ecumenical study and teaching, worship and experience, where men and women may deepen their understanding of questions affecting the unity, renewal and witness of the Church.

The functions of the Ecumenical Institute shall be:

(i) to hold educational courses for a wide variety of individuals and groups within the churches with a view to the development of ecumenical consciousness at every level;

(ii) to arrange for consultations of representatives of the same professions or occupations with a view to studying the fundamental assumptions of a given profession and the Christian witness of individuals within it, and in co-operation with the Department on Work for the Laity, to help in coordinating work done in this realm by national groups;

(iii) to arrange study conferences of lay experts and theologians on problems which call for pioneering in thought and action on the part of the churches or of the ecumenical movement as a whole;

(iv) to provide through the Graduate School of Ecumenical Studies a thorough grounding in the history, objectives, and problems of the ecumenical movement for senior students, pastors and members of theological teaching staffs and to help them to undertake specialized studies on ecumenical subjects;

(v) to co-operate with the Department on Work for the Laity, the Department on Co-operation of Men and Women in Church and Society, and the Youth Department, so that all work in this field may be integrated;

(vi) to co-operate with the Division of Studies in those activities of the Institute which are relevant to the work of that Division.

B. Youth Department

The aim of the Youth Department is, within the general policy of the Division of Ecumenical Action, to keep before the churches their responsibility for the evangelization of young people and their growth in Christian faith, to keep before the young people their responsibility to play their part in the ecumenical movement and especially in the World Council of Churches, to create ecumenical fellowship among Christian young people and to strengthen the youth work of the churches in all parts of the world.

The functions of the Department are:

(i) to enable the youth of all churches to meet, to learn about one another, and so to share their faith in Christ in relation to the whole of life;
(ii) to encourage young people to participate fully and responsibly in the life and witness of their own churches and of the World Council of Churches;
(iii) to interpret the aims and work of the World Council of Churches and the ecumenical movement to youth leaders and young people;
(iv) to offer young people the means of expressing active ecumenical concern through spiritual and material aid; for churches and national councils wishing to establish or develop youth work; in emergency situations affecting young people; by sponsoring international inter-confessional service projects and encouraging national initiative in setting up such projects;
(v) to encourage the participation of young people themselves in the formulation of policy and the direction of activity in youth work at the local, national, regional and world levels;
(vi) to provide opportunities for the churches to examine together the needs of youth and to advise each other about policy, programme and activities leading to Christian commitment and growth of young people in Christian faith and life;
(vii) to provide opportunities for fellowship and exchange of experience among church youth leaders;
(viii) to co-operate with world Christian youth organizations in ecumenical activities of common concern.

C. Department on Co-operation of Men and Women in Church and Society

The aim of the Department shall be to help the churches to work towards such co-operation between men and women as may enable them both to make their full contribution to church and society.

The functions of the Department shall be:

(i) to promote among men and women, through the Division of Studies, and directly, the study of questions affecting the relationship, the co-operation, and the common service of men and women in the churches and in society;
(ii) to help women to make their contribution to the total life of the churches and at the same time to encourage the churches to accept the contribution of women to a fuller extent and in more varied ways;
(iii) to foster an ecumenical outlook in women's organizations in the various churches and countries, to promote co-operation among them and to secure their participation in the ecumenical movement as a whole;
(iv) to advise and co-operate with the Ecumenical Institute, the Department on Work for the Laity, the Youth Department, and any other ecumenical body on the work of the Division of Ecumenical Action;
(v) to keep actively in touch with other divisions of the World Council of Churches and with other bodies whose work may have a bearing on the work of the Department.

D. Department on Work for the Laity

The aim of the Department on Work for the Laity shall be to keep before the churches their responsibility for helping the laity to serve their churches and to witness before the world, to strengthen work for the laity in the churches, to promote fellowship between church-related organizations of laity throughout the world, to foster ecumenical understanding among the laity.

The functions of the Department shall be:

(i) to assemble and disseminate information about developments in the work for the laity in different countries;

(ii) to consult with national institutes and organizations for the laity on topics requiring study, and to arrange for the ecumenical consideration of these topics;
(iii) to provide a news bulletin, surveys, bibliographies and particular studies as may be required;
(iv) to arrange for regional conferences of the laity;
(v) to arrange for the visitation of laity in different countries by persons able to advise on the development of work for the laity and to stimulate new experiments;
(vi) to co-operate with the Ecumenical Institute, the Department on Co-operation of Men and Women in Church and Society, the Youth Department and the Division of Studies in all matters concerning the work of this Department.

III. Division of Inter-Church Aid and Service to Refugees

The aim of the Division shall be to further, on an ecumenical basis, the renewal of the churches through practical help which churches may render one another, through the relief of human need, and through services to refugees.

The functions of the Division shall be:
(i) to provide, on the basis of mutual study and consultation, a total strategy of Inter-Church Aid and Service to Refugees in which the initiative and programmes of all churches and national committees can be related to one another, and thus give maximum usefulness;
(ii) to secure and disseminate information about the needs of the churches and of refugees, and also about the gifts and services which may be made available to meet these needs;
(iii) to find contributions to meet requests;
(iv) to suggest projects and spheres of need which might be neglected and should receive attention;
(v) to operate, at the request of the churches, such services as may best be carried out co-operatively, e.g. for refugees;
(vi) to receive and administer such gifts, whether earmarked or unearmarked, which churches and other bodies place at its disposal;
(vii) to co-operate with the International Missionary Council on terms mutually agreed, and to report to its officers and governing committees on all matters concerned with Emergency Inter-Church Aid and Relief in countries outside Europe.

IV. Department of Information

The aim of the Department shall be to make the policies of the World Council of Churches known and understood, to provide and disseminate news of its activities, and to inform the churches about each other's life.

The functions of the Department of Information, under the supervision of the General Secretary, shall be:
(i) to carry out the information policy of the World Council;
(ii) to issue general publicity material about the World Council of Churches and to supervise departmental publicity;
(iii) to represent the World Council in relation to the church press and the general press and to issue all press releases in the name of the World Council of Churches and its divisions;
(iv) to provide such information and articles as will help the churches to be well informed about the life of other churches and about the ecumenical movement as a whole;

(v) to prepare publicity material for those divisions or departments which require the services of the Department for this purpose;
(vi) to work out a general policy concerning the regular publications of the World Council of Churches, to co-ordinate such publications, and to give guidance to those who are responsible for their preparation and presentation;
(vii) to co-operate with other agencies in the fields of radio, television and film, and to help to ensure the intelligent use of these media by the churches.

V. Department of Finance and Administration

The aim of the Department shall be to provide the World Council and its divisions and departments with financial, accounting and general services needed, and to assist the General Secretary in certain specified fields of administrative responsibility.

The functions of the Department shall be:
(i) to maintain the books of account, to supervise expenditure in relation to budgets and approved levels of expenditure and to prepare all financial reports and the annual accounts;
(ii) in consultation with the General Secretariat and the divisions and departments, to prepare draft budgets and to collect the contributions of member churches to the General Budget;
(iii) to make all payments and operate all bank, postal cheque and cash accounts, both in relation to the General Budget and to the Division of Inter-Church Aid and Service to Refugees, and to supervise all salary and pension payments, keep salary records and administer the salary scales for office staff;
(iv) to operate the following general services at Geneva headquarters: mail, telephone, telegrams, insurance, cyclostyle, maintenance, heating and lighting of buildings, provision of office furniture and supplies and the purchase and transportation of all supplies needed;
(v) to undertake specific responsibilities at the request of the General Secretary, particularly in connection with the organization and administration of Assemblies and meetings;
(vi) to administer the properties of the World Council of Churches.

PART 4. CONCLUSIONS *

The Central Committee believes that if the recommendations made in this report are adopted, the structure and functioning of the World Council of Churches will be improved and strengthened. It will be observed that one objective has been to provide for an increased involvement of the representatives of the churches, not only in responsibility for the World Council of Churches but in its actions and life. On the other hand, the proposals regarding the General Secretariat and divisional and departmental structure should enable increased personal communication and visitation of the member churches by the executives of the World Council.

The recommendations involve a revision of the structure but increased staff is needed only at the following two points. The creation of a Department of Information was envisaged by the first Assembly but was not found possible in the first period; the proposals in this report represented merely drawing together into one department of activities which have been carried on in the first period and the appointment of a director to co-ordinate and direct the

* Part 3 of the Report on Structure and Functioning contained the Rules and Constitution of the W.C.C. with suggested amendments. The Constitution and its amendments will be found elsewhere in the Appendixes.

work. The report also suggests the creation of a Department on Work for the Laity to continue within the framework of the General Budget the important work which for the past few years has been carried on under the Service Programme of the Department of Inter-Church Aid.

It must be recognized that the World Council of Churches is still young and for that reason an endeavor has been made to retain flexibility so as to permit the Central Committee and the Executive Committee to act in response to changing situations. It should also be noted that the decisions which may be taken by the Assembly on the basis of the recommendations made in this report, cannot become fully effective until 1955. In the judgment of the Central Committee, the proposals in this report should not be regarded as final and there may well be need for a further review of the structure and functioning of the World Council to be undertaken by the Third Assembly in the light of further experience.

APPENDIX P

Constitution of the Commission on and Division of World Mission and Evangelism

New Delhi, 1961

THE COMMISSION ON WORLD MISSION AND EVANGELISM

1. There shall be a Commission on World Mission and Evangelism constituted in accordance with the Constitution of the World Council of Churches (Sec. VI, (3)).

2. AIM

Its aim shall be to further the proclamation to the whole world of the Gospel of Jesus Christ, to the end that all men may believe in him and be saved.

3. FUNCTIONS

The functions of the Commission shall be:

(i) to keep before the churches their calling and privilege to engage in constant prayer for the missionary and evangelistic work of the Church;

(ii) to remind the churches of the range and character of the unfinished evangelistic task and to deepen their sense of missionary obligation;

(iii) to stimulate thought and study on the Biblical and theological bases and meaning of the Church's missionary task and on questions directly related to the spread of the Gospel in the world;

(iv) to foster among churches and among councils and other Christian bodies more effective co-operation and united action for world evangelization;

(v) to deepen evangelistic and missionary concern in the whole life and work of the World Council of Churches;

(vi) to assist in securing and safeguarding freedom of conscience and religion as formulated in declarations of the World Council of Churches on religious liberty;

(vii) to co-operate with other units of the World Council of Churches;

(viii) to take such further action in fulfilment of the declared aim of the Commission as is not otherwise provided for within the World Council of Churches.

4. Authority

The Commission shall have no mandatory authority over any of the councils related to it, whether in affiliated or consultative relationship, in accordance with the principles enunciated in the Constitution of the World Council of Churches.

5. Operations

(i) The Commission shall ordinarily meet once every five years. Special meetings may be convened at the call of the Divisional Committee with the approval of the Central Committee.

(ii) The Commission shall formulate the general lines of policy and programme to be followed by the Division of World Mission and Evangelism, for submission to the Central Committee for its approval. The Division shall be responsible for the execution of this policy and programme.

(iii) The Commission shall keep its related councils fully informed and consult them regularly on matters of policy and programme. It shall send its reports and recommendations to the councils.

(iv) The Commission shall report regularly to the Assembly and the Central Committee.

(v) The Commission shall develop appropriate organs for fulfilling its functions in the area of evangelism, including the provision of staff for this purpose.

(vi) (a) The Commission may sponsor—or, with the approval of the Assembly or Central Committee, co-operate with other bodies in sponsoring—agencies for specialized activities.

(b) In each case of a sponsored agency, the constitution and the appointment of the principal executive officer shall be subject to the approval of the Commission. Each sponsored agency shall report to the Commission from time to time on its acts and programme.

(c) The World Council shall not be responsible for the financing of sponsored agencies except as it may in advance explicitly accept such responsibility.

6. Affiliation and Membership

(i) All member councils of the International Missionary Council at the time of integration will be regarded as affiliated to the Commission.

(ii) Thereafter national or regional Christian councils and national or regional missionary organizations which accept the aim of the Commission may become councils affiliated with the Commission, on the approval of a regularly constituted meeting of the Commission by a two-thirds majority of those present and voting. Any application for affiliation between meetings of the Commission may be considered by the Divisional Committee; if the application is supported by a two-thirds majority of the members of the Committee present and voting, this action shall be communicated to the councils affiliated to the Commission, and unless objection is received from more than one-third of these councils within six months the council shall be declared affiliated. The following criteria shall determine eligibility for affiliation:

(a) The council shall express its acceptance of the aim of the

Commission on World Mission and Evangelism and desire to co-operate in the functions of the Commission as defined in the Constitution.

(b) The council shall satisfy such other criteria as may be determined by the Commission. In considering applications for affiliation, the Commission on World Mission and Evangelism will take into account the size and stability of the council concerned and the relevance of its programme to the aim and functions of the Commission.

(c) There shall be consultation with the member churches of the World Council of Churches in the area concerned, and with the Committee on National Council Relationships.

(iii) A council which performs functions in several fields of activity may be represented in the Commission on World Mission and Evangelism through its appropriate unit(s) or division(s).

(iv) National or regional Christian councils and national or regional missionary organizations which are not affiliated to the Commission may become councils in consultation with the Commission. If any member council of the International Missionary Council informs the International Missionary Council before integration that it cannot accept affiliation, it shall automatically become a council in consultation with the Commission under this rule. Thereafter, councils in consultation shall be councils which are not yet eligible to become affiliated councils or which do not desire affiliation, but which

(a) accept the aim of the Commission and desire a consultative relationship with it; and

(b) are accepted by the Commission as eligible for such a relationship. Councils in consultation shall be entitled to send consultants to meetings of the Commission; they shall be entitled to speak but not to vote.

(v) In accordance with a schedule which shall be prepared before each regular meeting of the Commission by the Divisional Committee and approved by the Central Committee, the Commission shall consist of members appointed by the affiliated councils and of members appointed by the Central Committee. The members appointed by Central Committee shall include persons representative of the field of evangelism. Their number shall not exceed one half of the number of places allotted to affiliated councils.

(vi) In addition to the consultants representing councils in consultation, the Divisional Committee may provide for the attendance at meetings of the Commission of persons with special competence in the field of missions as advisors. They shall be entitled to speak but not to vote.

(vii) Each sponsored agency may appoint a representative to attend the meetings of the Commission and of the Divisional Committee. They shall be entitled to speak but not to vote.

(viii) The Divisional Committee may also invite observers to meetings of the Commission from councils and other missionary agencies which are not related to the Commission. Observers shall be entitled to speak but not to vote.

(ix) The members of the Commission shall serve until appointments have been made for the next meeting of the Commission or until their successors are appointed.

(x) An affiliated council may withdraw from the Commission, but must give at least one year's written notice to the next regularly constituted meeting of the Commission or of the Divisional Committee; withdrawal shall become effective at the close of that meeting.

7. OFFICERS AND SECRETARIAT

(i) At each regular meeting the Commission shall appoint a Chairman and one or more Vice-Chairmen whose term of office shall extend from the beginning of that meeting to the beginning of the next regular meeting. The nomination of the Chairman and Vice-Chairmen shall be made by the Divisional Committee prior to the meeting of the Commission.

(ii) The same Secretariat shall serve both the Commission and the Division.

(iii) The Commission may appoint an Honorary Treasurer or Treasurers.

8. FINANCE

(i) The Commission in consultation with its affiliated and other supporting councils shall prepare a budget for submission to the Central Committee for its approval.

(ii) The Commission shall be responsible for the raising and expenditure of funds in accordance with the approved budget.

(iii) The funds formerly vested in the International Missionary Council for general or specific purposes, together with such additional funds as may from time to time be entrusted to the Commission for the discharge of its functions, shall be vested in the World Council of Churches. Such funds shall be used solely for the purposes of the Commission and, if designated, in accordance with the wishes of the donor or testator. These funds shall be administered by the Commission, subject to the approval of the Central Committee.

(iv) The Commission shall provide for the cost of its staff and offices, of the meetings of the Commission and the Division and its committees, of all operations authorized by the Commission and of all services provided for the Commission by the World Council of Churches.

(v) In their financial operations the Commission and Division shall follow the procedures prescribed in the By-Laws.

9. QUORUM

One-third of the members of the Commission shall constitute a quorum at any given session, provided that those present at the session come from at least three continents and represent at least one-third of the affiliated councils.

10. BY-LAWS

The Commission may make, amend and repeal By-Laws for the conduct of the business of the Commission.

11. REVISION

The Constitution of the Commission and of the Division may be amended, subject to the approval of the Central Committee, by a two-thirds majority of the Commission, provided the proposed amendment shall have been reviewed by the Divisional Committee and notice of it sent to the affiliated councils not less than six months before the meeting of the Commission. The Divisional Committee as well as the affiliated councils shall have the right to propose amendments.

THE DIVISION OF WORLD MISSION AND EVANGELISM

1. The Division of World Mission and Evangelism shall consist of the Divisional Committee and staff.

2. Function

The Division of World Mission and Evangelism shall be responsible for carrying out the aim and functions of the Commission on World Mission and Evangelism and shall act for it between its meetings save in such matters as the Commission may have reserved to its own authority.

3. Activities

The activities of the Division shall include:

(i) aiding the churches in their missionary and evangelistic task and where requested by churches or councils acting on their behalf;

(ii) maintaining relationships of mutual helpfulness with councils affiliated to and in consultation with the Commission and with member churches of the World Council of Churches concerning the work of the Commission and Division;

(iii) fostering relationships with other councils;

(iv) publishing such literature as may be called for in the furtherance of the aim and functions of the Commission;

(v) convening such conferences as may be required;

(vi) responsibility for any departments which may be created within the Division and guiding their work;

(vii) co-operating with the other divisions of the World Council to carry out the purposes and functions of the Commission and of the World Council effectively;

(viii) responsibility for the raising and administration of the funds of the Commission in accordance with clause 8 (ii) of the Constitution of the Commission.

4. The Divisional Committee

(i) There shall be a Divisional Committee responsible for the general conduct of the work of the Division, which shall report to the Assembly and to the Central Committee as well as to the Commission. It shall also report to its related councils.

(ii) The Committee shall consist of not less than twenty or more than twenty-five members appointed annually by the Central Committee on the nomination of the Commission or, in the absence of a meeting of the Commission, of the Divisional Committee. The Chairman and one member of each departmental committee within the Division shall be included in the membership of the Committee. At least two members shall be drawn from the membership of the Central Committee. Two members of the divisional committee shall be appointed after consultation with the officers of the Division of Inter-Church Aid, Refugee and World Service. The membership of the Committee shall be as representative as possible, geographically and confessionally, and of men and women. The Chairman and Vice-Chairman of the Commission shall be *ex officio* members of the Divisional Committee.

(iii) The Divisional Committee shall ordinarily meet once a year. Special meeting may be called on the authority of the officers.

(iv) The Committee shall prepare, through such procedures as the Commission may determine, an annual budget, which shall be submitted in advance of the beginning of each year to the Finance Committee of the Central Committee, which shall forward it to the Central Committee with any comments it may wish to make. The Committee shall submit financial reports to each meeting of the Finance Committee of the Central Committee.

(v) The Divisional Committee shall nominate its Chairman for appointment by the Central Committee.

(vi) The Director of the Division shall be nominated by the Divisional Committee in consultation with the staffing committee of the Executive Committee and shall be appointed by the Central Committee as an Associate General Secretary of the World Council and Director of the Division. The Divisional Committee shall determine, subject to the approval of the Central Committee, the number of the staff of the Commission and the Division. The Secretaries shall be appointed according to the Rules of the World Council, on the nomination of the Divisional Committee.

(vii) The Divisional Committee shall determine the principal duties of the staff of the Commission and the Division.

(viii) One half of the membership of the Divisional Committee shall constitute a quorum at any ordinary meeting, provided that those present come from at least three continents and five affiliated councils.

APPENDIX Q

The Constitution and Rules of the World Council of Churches

As Amended, New Delhi, 1961

I. Basis

The World Council of Churches is a fellowship of churches which confess the Lord Jesus Christ as God and Saviour according to the Scriptures and therefore seek to fulfill together their common calling to the glory of the one God, Father, Son, and Holy Spirit.

It is constituted for the functions set out below.

II. Membership

Those churches shall be eligible for membership in the World Council of Churches which express their agreement with the Basis upon which the Council is founded and satisfy such criteria as the Assembly or the Central Committee may prescribe. Election to membership shall be by a two-thirds vote of the member churches represented at the Assembly, each member church having one vote. Any application for membership between meetings of the Assembly may be considered by the Central Committee; if the application is supported by a two-thirds majority of the members of the Committee present and voting, this action shall be communicated to the churches that are members of the World Council of Churches, and unless objection is received from more than one-third of the member churches within six months the applicant shall be declared elected.

III. Functions

The functions of the World Council shall be:

(i) To carry on the work of the world movements for Faith and Order and for Life and Work and of the International Missionary Council.

(ii) To facilitate common action by the churches.

(iii) To promote co-operation in study.

(iv) To promote the growth of ecumenical and missionary consciousness in the members of all churches.

(v) To support the churches in their world-wide missionary and evangelistic task.

(vi) To establish and maintain relations with national and regional councils, world confessional bodies and other ecumenical organizations.

(vii) To call world conferences on specific subjects as occasion may require, such conferences being empowered to publish their own findings.

IV. Authority

The World Council shall offer counsel and provide opportunity of united action in matters of common interest.

It may take action on behalf of constituent churches in such matters as one or more of them may commit to it.

It shall have authority to call regional and world conferences on specific subjects as occasion may require.

The World Council shall not legislate for the churches; nor shall it act for them in any manner except as indicated above or as may hereafter be specified by the constituent churches.

V. Organization

The World Council shall discharge its functions through the following bodies:

(i) An Assembly which shall be the principal authority in the Council, and shall ordinarily meet every five years. The Assembly shall be composed of official representatives of the churches or groups of churches adhering to it and directly appointed by them. Their term of office shall begin in the year before the Assembly meets, and they shall serve until their successors are appointed. It shall consist of members whose number shall be determined by each Assembly for the subsequent Assembly, subject to the right of the Assembly to empower the Central Committee, if it thinks fit, to increase or diminish the said number by not more than twenty per cent. The number shall be finally determined not less than two years before the meeting of the Assembly to which it refers and shall be apportioned as is provided hereafter.

Seats in the Assembly shall be allocated to the member churches by the Central Committee, due regard being given to such factors as numerical size, adequate confessional representation and adequate geographical distribution. Suggestions for readjustment in the allocation of seats may be made to the Central Committee by member churches, or by groups of member churches, confessional, regional or national, and these readjustments shall become effective if approved by the Central Committee after consultation with the churches concerned.

The Assembly shall have power to appoint officers of the World Council and of the Assembly at its discretion.

The members of the Assembly shall be both clerical and lay persons—men and women. In order to secure that approximately one-third of the Assembly shall consist of lay persons, the Central Committee, in allocating to the member churches their places in the Assembly, shall strongly urge each church, if possible, to observe this provision.

(ii) A Central Committee which shall be a Committee of the Assembly and which shall consist of the President or Presidents of the World Council, together with not more than (one hundred) members chosen by the Assembly from among persons whom the churches have appointed as members of the Assembly. They shall serve until the next Assembly, unless the Assembly otherwise determines. Membership in the Central Committee shall be distributed among the member churches by the Assembly, due regard being given to such factors as numerical size, adequate confessional representation, adequate geographical distribution and the adequate representation of the major interests of the World Council.

Any vacancy occurring in the membership of the Central Committee between meetings of the Assembly shall be filled by the Central Committee upon the nomination of the church or churches concerned.

The Central Committee shall have the following powers:

(a) it shall, between meetings of the Assembly, carry out the Assembly's instructions and exercise its functions, except that of amending the Constitution, or modifying the allocation of its own members;

(b) it shall be the finance committee of the Assembly, formulating its budget and securing its financial support;

(c) it shall name and elect its own officers from among its members and appoint its own secretarial staff;

(d) the Central Committee shall meet normally once every calendar year, and shall have power to appoint its own Executive Committee.

Quorum. No business, except what is required for carrying forward the current activities of the Council, shall be transacted in either the Assembly or the Central Committee unless one-half of the total membership is present.

VI. Appointment of Commissions

(1) The World Council shall discharge part of its functions by the appointment of Commissions. These shall be established under the authority of the Assembly in accordance with the Rules of the World Council and the constitutions of the respective Commissions. The Commissions shall, between meetings of the Assembly, report annually to the Central Committee which shall exercise general supervision over them. The Commissions may add to their membership clerical and lay persons approved for the purpose by the Central Committee. The Commissions shall discharge their functions in accordance with constitutions approved by the Central Committee.

In particular, the Assembly shall make provision by means of appropriate Commissions for carrying on the activities of Faith and Order, Life and Work and the International Missionary Council.

(2) There shall be a Faith and Order Commission of which the following shall be the functions:

(i) to proclaim the essential oneness of the Church of Christ and to keep prominently before the World Council and the churches the obligation to manifest that unity and its urgency for world mission and evangelism;

(ii) to study questions of faith, order and worship with the relevant social, cultural, political, racial, and other factors in their bearing on the unity of the churches;

(iii) to study the theological implications of the existence of the ecumenical movement;

(iv) to study matters in the present relationships of the churches to one another which cause difficulties and need theological clarification;

(v) to provide information concerning actual steps taken by the churches towards reunion.

The Commission shall discharge these functions in accordance with a constitution approved by the Central Committee.

In invitations to World Conferences on Faith and Order, it shall be specified that such conferences are to be composed of official delegates of churches which confess Jesus Christ as God and Saviour.

(3) There shall be a Commission on World Mission and Evangelism.

Its aim shall be to further the proclamation to the whole world of the Gospel of Jesus Christ, to the end that all men may believe in him and be saved.

The functions of the Commission shall be:

(i) to keep before the churches their calling and privilege to engage in constant prayer for the missionary and evangelistic work of the Church;

(ii) to remind the churches of the range and character of the unfinished evangelistic task and to deepen their sense of missionary obligation;

(iii) to stimulate thought and study on the Biblical and theological basis and meaning of the Church's missionary task and on questions directly related to the spread of the Gospel in the world;

(iv) to foster among churches and among councils and other Christian bodies more effective co-operation and united action for world evangelization;

(v) to deepen evangelistic and missionary concern in the whole life and work of the World Council of Churches;

(vi) to assist in securing and safeguarding freedom of conscience and religion as formulated in declarations of the World Council of Churches on religious liberty;

(vii) to co-operate with other units of the World Council of Churches;

(viii) to take such further action in fulfilment of the declared aim of the Commission as is not otherwise provided for within the World Council of Churches.

VII. Other Ecumenical Christian Organizations

(1) Such world confessional associations and such ecumenical organizations as may be designated by the Central Committee may be invited to send representatives to the sessions of the Assembly and of the Central Committee in a consultative capacity, in such numbers as the Central Committee shall determine.

(2) Such national councils of churches, other Christian councils and missionary councils as may be designated by the Central Committee may be invited to send non-voting representatives to the Assembly and to the Central Committee, in such numbers as the Central Committee shall determine.

VIII. Amendments

The Constitution may be amended by a two-thirds majority vote of the Assembly, provided that the proposed amendment shall have been reviewed by the Central Committee, and notice of it sent to the constituent churches not less than six months before the meeting of the Assembly. The Central Committee itself, as well as the individual churches, shall have the right to propose such amendment.

IX. Rules and Regulations

The Assembly or the Central Committee may make and amend Rules and Regulations concerning the conduct of the Council's business, of its Committees and Departments, and generally all matters within the discharge of its task.

RULES OF THE WORLD COUNCIL OF CHURCHES

The World Council of Churches shall be governed by the following Rules which are to be interpreted in the light of its Constitution:

I. Membership of the Council

Members of the Council are those churches which have agreed together to constitute the World Council of Churches and those churches which are admitted to membership in accordance with the following rules:

(1) Churches which desire to become members of the World Council of Churches shall apply to the General Secretary in writing. Under the word churches are included such denominations as are composed of local autonomous churches.

(2) The General Secretary shall submit such applications to the Central Committee (see Article II of the Constitution) together with such information as will be sufficient to enable the Assembly or the Central Committee to make a decision on the application.

(3) The following criteria, among others, shall be applied, in addition to the primary requirement of the Constitution that churches eligible for consideration for membership shall be those "which express their agreement with the Basis upon which the Council is formed."

(a) *Autonomy.* A church which is to be admitted must give evidence of autonomy. An autonomous church is one which, while recognizing the essential interdependence of the churches, particularly those of the same confession, is responsible to no other church for the conduct of its own life, including training, ordination and maintenance of its ministry, the enlisting, development and activity of the lay forces, the propagation of the Christian message, the determination of relationship with other churches and the use of funds at its disposal from whatever source.

(b) *Stability.* A church should not be admitted unless it has given sufficient evidence of stability in life and organization to become recognized as a church by its sister churches, and should have an established programme of Christian nurture and evangelism.

(c) *Size.* The question of size must also be taken into consideration.

(d) *Relationship with Other Churches.* Regard must also be given to the relationship of the church to other churches.

(4) Before churches which are recognized as full members of one of the confessional or denominational world alliances with which the Council cooperates are admitted, the advice of these world alliances shall be sought.

(5) Where a church is a member of a council associated with the World Council of Churches or affiliated to the Commission on World Mission and Evangelism, there shall be consultation with the council concerned.

(6) A church which desires to resign its membership in the Council can do so at any time. A church which has once resigned but desires again to join the Council, must again apply for membership.

II. The Assembly

(1) *Officers and Business Committee*

(a) At the first business session of the Assembly the Executive Committee shall present its proposals for the chairmanship of the Assembly and for the membership of the Business Committee of the Assembly.

(b) Additional names may also be proposed at the first or second business session by any group of six members of the Assembly. Such proposals must be made in writing.

(c) Election shall be by ballot unless the Assembly shall otherwise determine.

(2) *Composition of the Assembly*

(a) *Members.* Full membership of the Assembly is confined to delegates appointed by the constituent churches to represent them. In appointing their delegates churches are urged not only to bear in mind the need for lay representation mentioned in paragraph V (i) of the Constitution but also to give due regard to the major interests of the Council.

(b) *Alternates.* The Central Committee shall make regulation for the appointment of alternates and for their duties and functions if and when appointed.

(c) *Advisers.* The Executive Committee is authorized to invite persons who have a special contribution to make to the deliberations of the Assembly or who have participated in the activities of the World Council. Such advisers will be appointed after consultation with the churches to which they belong. They shall be entitled to speak on the invitation of the Chairman but not to vote.

(d) *Fraternal Delegates.* The Executive Committee is authorized to invite fraternal delegates from organizations with which the World Council of Churches entertains relationship. They shall be entitled to speak on the invitation of the Chairman but not to vote.

(e) *Observers.* The Executive Committee is authorized to invite a limited number of observers from churches which have not joined the World Council of Churches and/or from councils in consultation with the Commission on World Mission and Evangelism. Observers will not be entitled to speak or to vote.

(f) *Youth Delegates.* The Executive Committee is authorized to invite youth delegates who will be entitled to attend the full sessions. They shall be entitled to speak on the invitation of the Chairman but not to vote.

(3) *Agenda.*

The Agenda of the Assembly shall be determined by the Executive Committee and presented by it for approval to the first business session of the Assembly. Any member may move to have included in the Agenda such items of business as he may have previously notified to the Executive Committee.

III. Presidium

(1) The maximum number of Presidents shall be six.

(2) A President who has been elected by the Assembly shall be ineligible for immediate re-election when his term of office ends.

(3) The term of office of a President shall end at the adjournment of the next Assembly following his or her appointment.

(4) The President or Presidents shall be entitled to attend the Assembly with full right of speech even if they are not appointed as delegates by their churches.

(5) The President or Presidents shall be *ex officio* members of the Central Committee and of the Executive Committee.

IV. Nominations Committee of the Assembly

(1) At an early session of the Assembly, the Assembly shall appoint a Nominations Committee, on which there there shall be appropriate confessional and geographical representation of the membership of the Assembly and representation of the major interests of the World Council.

(2) The Nominations Committee in consultation with the officers of the World Council and the Executive Committee shall draft proposals concerning (a) the President or Presidents of the World Council of Churches, and (b) a list of persons proposed for membership of the Central Committee.

(3) The Nominations Committee shall present its nominations to the vote of the Assembly for its acceptance or revision. In making nominations, the Nominations Committee shall have regard to the following principles:

(a) the personal qualifications of the individual for the task for which he is to be nominated;
(b) fair and adequate confessional representation;
(c) fair and adequate geographical representation;
(d) fair and adequate representation of the major interests of the World Council.

The Nominations Committee shall endeavour to secure adequate representation of lay persons—both men and women—so far as the composition of the Assembly makes this possible. It shall also satisfy itself as to the general acceptability of the nominations to the churches to which the nominees belong.

(4) It shall be open to any six members of the Assembly acting together to put forward in writing other nominations.

(5) Election shall be by a ballot unless the Assembly shall otherwise determine.

V. Central Committee

(1) *Membership*

(a) The Central Committee shall consist of the President or Presidents of the World Council together with not more than one hundred members elected by the Assembly (see Constitution, paragraph V (ii)).
(b) Any member church, not already represented, which desires to be represented directly on the Central Committee, shall have the right to send one representative to the meetings of the Central Committee, provided it does so at its own expense. Such a representative shall be entitled to speak but not to vote.
(c) If a regularly elected member of the Central Committee is unable to come to the meeting, the church to which the absent member belongs shall have the right to send a substitute, provided that the substitute is ordinarily resident in the country where his church has its headquarters. Such a substitute shall be entitled to speak and to vote.
(d) Chairmen and vice-chairmen of divisional and departmental

committees and commissions who are not members of the Central Committee have the right to attend Central Committee sessions as advisers without vote.

(e) Advisers for the Central Committee may be appointed by the Executive Committee after consultation with the churches of which they are members. They shall be entitled to speak but not to vote.

(f) Members of the staff of the World Council appointed by the Central Committee as specified under Rule IX, 1, shall have the right to attend the sessions of the Central Committee unless on any occasion the Central Committee shall otherwise determine. When they do so attend, it shall be as advisers and without the right to vote.

(g) The newly appointed Central Committee shall be convened by the General Secretary during or immediately after the meeting of the Assembly.

(2) *Officers*

(a) The Central Committee shall elect its own Chairman and Vice-Chairman or Vice-Chairmen to serve for such periods as it shall determine. They shall be entitled to attend the Assembly as advisers, should they not be reappointed as delegates by their churches.

(b) The Central Committee shall appoint a Nominations Committee which shall:

(i) nominate individuals to the Central Committee for the offices of Chairman and Vice-Chairman or Vice-Chairmen of the Central Committee;

(ii) nominate individuals for election as President, if between Assemblies need arises for such appointments, under the power conferred on the Central Committee by the Constitution and Rules;

(iii) nominate members of the Executive Committee of the Central Committee;

(iv) nominate members of the divisional committees and departmental working committees.

In making nominations, the Nominations Committee of the Central Committee shall have regard to the principles set out in Rule IV, 3, and in applying principles (b), (c) and (d) to the nomination of members of the divisional committees and the departmental working committees, shall consider the representative character of the combined membership of all such committees. Any member of the Central Committee may make alternative proposals.

(c) Election shall be by ballot unless the Committee shall otherwise determine.

(d) The General Secretary of the World Council of Churches shall be *ex officio* secretary of the Central Committee and the Chairman of the Finance Committee of the World Council of Churches shall be *ex officio* its treasurer.

(3) *Meetings*

(a) The Central Committee shall meet ordinarily not less than once every year. An extraordinary session of the Central Committee shall be called, whenever one-third or more of the members request a meeting to be called or when in the opinion of the Executive Committee that is desirable.

(b) A quorum of the Central Committee shall be fifty voting members. The General Secretariat shall take all possible steps to ensure that there be adequate representation from each of the main confessions and from the main geographical areas of the membership of the World Council of Churches and of the major interests of the World Council.

(c) The Central Committee shall have power to determine its own place of meeting and to fix the date and place for the meetings of the Assembly.

(4) *Functions*

The Central Committee shall have the following duties:

(a) It shall, between meetings of the Assembly, carry out the general policy laid down by the Assembly and take such actions as shall be necessary to carry out the decisions of the Assembly. It shall have authority to make decisions and take action in all matters where decision or action is required before the Assembly can meet again, provided that it shall not make any decision or take any action inconsistent with the policies laid down by the Assembly.

It shall have the following sub-committees:

(i) Finance Sub-Committee (a standing committee);

(ii) Nominations Committee (newly appointed at each meeting);

(iii) Committee on National Council Relationships (a standing committee);

(iv) Reference Committee or Committees (appointed as needed at each meeting) to advise the Central Committee on any other questions arising which call for special consideration or action by the Central Committee.

(b) It shall vote the Annual Budget of the Council.

(c) It shall deal with matters referred to it by member churches.

(d) It shall consider applications for membership received between meetings of the Assembly.

(e) It shall have the responsibility of setting up such divisions and departments and regional offices or representations as may be necessary to carry out the policy laid down by the Assembly. It shall appoint divisional and departmental committees and their chairmen and vice-chairmen. It shall determine the general policy to be followed in the work of the divisions and departments of the World Council.

(f) It shall report to the Assembly on the actions it has taken during its period of office, and shall not be discharged until its report has been received.

VI. Executive Committee

(1) *Appointment*

(a) An Executive Committee shall be elected by the Central Committee at its first meeting after its appointment by the Assembly, and shall hold office until the next meeting of the Central Committee. Its elected members shall be eligible for re- election.

(b) The Executive Committee shall consist of the President or

Presidents of the World Council *ex officio* and the Chairman and Vice-Chairman of the Central Committee *ex officio* and of fourteen other members of the Central Committee. Substitutes shall not be permitted to attend in place of elected members.

(c) The Chairman of the Central Committee shall also be the Chairman of the Executive Committee.

(d) The officers shall have the power to invite others to attend a meeting of the Executive Committee for consultation, always having in mind the need of preserving a due balance of the confessions and of the geographical areas and of the major interests of the World Council.

(e) The General Secretary of the World Council of Churches shall be *ex officio* the secretary of the Executive Committee.

(2) *Functions*

The Executive Committee is a committee of the Central Committee appointed by it and responsible to it. The Executive Committee shall, between meetings of the Central Committee, carry out the decisions of the Central Committee and implement the policy laid down by it. The Executive Committee shall have no authority to make decisions on policy except that in circumstances of special urgency it can take provisional decisions. It may only issue public statements under the circumstance laid down in Rule X, 4. It shall have power to appoint Associate General Secretaries and heads of departments provisionally, but such appointments shall be subject to confirmation by the Central Committee. It shall supervise the operation of the budget and have power to impose limitations on expenditure if necessary.

VII. DIVISIONAL, DEPARTMENTAL AND OTHER STANDING COMMITTEES

(1) There shall be a small committee for each division whose responsibility shall be to carry out the aim of the division. It shall be responsible for the preparation and presentation to the Central Committee of the reports of the division's work.

It shall propose to the Central Committee the names of persons to fill the offices of secretary or secretaries to the division and, on the basis of proposals from the departmental working committees, of secretary or secretaries in the departments within the division.

(2) Divisional committees shall be appointed by the Central Committee as follows:

(a) For the Division of Studies and the Division of Ecumenical Action, the Committee shall consist of up to five persons who are not members of any departmental working committee within the division, plus the chairman and one other member of each departmental working committee within the division. One of the two representatives of each departmental working committee must be a member of the Central Committee.

(b) For the Division of Inter-Church Aid, Refugee and World Service, the committee shall consist of not more than seventeen members, two of whom shall be members of the Central Committee. Two members of the divisional committee shall be appointed after consultation with the officers of the Division of World Mission and Evangelism.

(c) For the Division of World Mission and Evangelism the Committee shall consist of not less than twenty or more than twenty-five members appointed annually by the Central Committee on the nomination of the Commission or, in the absence of a meeting of the Commission, of the Divisional Committee. The Chairman and one member of each departmental committee within the Division shall be included in the membership of the Committee. At least two members shall be drawn from the membership of the Central Committee. Two members of the divisional committee shall be appointed after consultation with the officers of the Division of Inter-Church Aid, Refugee and World Service. The membership of the committee shall be as representative as possible geographically and confessionally and of men and women.

Departmental secretaries shall normally be present at the meetings of divisional committees.

(3) There shall be a working committee for each department appointed by the Central Committee and responsible for the preparation of the departmental programme for submission to the divisional committee and for the execution of the programme. It shall propose to the divisional committee the names of persons to fill the offices of secretary or secretaries in the department. The chairmen of departmental working committees shall be *ex officio* members of the appropriate divisional committees. Departmental working committees shall have power to call in *ad hoc* advisers as needed on particular problems. In the case of the Ecumenical Institute its Board shall be regarded as the working committee. Normally a working committee shall consist of fifteen members, at least one of whom shall be a member of the Central Committee.

(4) There shall be a committee on National Council Relationships which shall consist of not more than fifteen members, including persons actively engaged in the work of each of the four Divisions and persons from related councils.

The aim of the Committee shall be: to give continuous attention to the development of relationships of mutual helpfulness between the World Council of Churches and national councils of churches and other Christian councils.

The functions of the Committee shall be:

(i) to develop patterns of relationship and co-operation whereby the World Council of Churches and national councils of churches and other Christian councils can strengthen each other and best serve the needs of their constituencies;

(ii) to assist such councils in utilizing the resources of the World Council of Churches and to assist divisions of the World Council to relate their programmes to the needs of such councils;

(iii) to keep before all the divisions and departments of the World Council and its member churches the significance of such councils in the fulfilment of the purposes of the ecumenical movement;

(iv) to recommend to the Central Committee ways in which such councils can participate most effectively in the life of the World Council;

(v) to advise the Central Committee regarding recognition of councils as 'associated councils' of the World Council of Churches and to consult with the Commission on World Mission and Evangelism regarding recognition of councils as 'affiliated councils' of that Commission or 'councils in consultation' with that Commission;

(vi) to provide opportunities for fellowship and exchange of experience among the officers and staffs of national and regional councils and the World Council of Churches, and in particular to arrange for consultations of representatives of associated councils as provided in Rule XI, (4);

(vii) to provide advisory staff service to national and regional councils when requested.

VIII. Financial Provisions

(1) The draft annual general budget of the World Council of Churches shall be prepared for presentation to the Finance Committee of the Central Committee by the General Secretariat assisted by the Department of Finance and Administration, on the basis of proposals made by the divisional committees.

(2) In the case of commissions, divisions and other units of the World Council of Churches which may be authorized to raise and administer separate budgets, the responsible commission, division or unit shall prepare annual budgets for submission in advance of the beginning of each year to the Finance Committee of the Central Committee of the World Council, which shall forward any such budgets to the Central Committee with any comments which it may wish to make. The responsible commission, division or unit shall further submit financial reports to each meeting of the Finance Committee of the Central Committee of the World Council of Churches.

(3) The Finance Committee of the Central Committee shall have the following duties:

(a) to present annually to the Central Committee an account of income and expenditure for the previous twelve months, and a balance sheet in respect of operations of all departments of the World Council of Churches;

(b) to present annually to the Central Committee in advance of the commencement of each year, budgets covering the operation of all the departments of the World Council of Churches;

(c) to consider and make recommendations to the Central Committee on all financial questions concerning the affairs of the World Council of Churches, such as:

approval of budgets or increases in budgets;
approval and granting of discharge for the accounts in respect of completed periods;
accounting procedures;
investment policy;
principles governing scales of salaries and pensions and travel expenses and other such expenses;
basis of calculation of contributions of new member churches;
methods of raising funds;
appointment of auditors, who shall be appointed annually by the Central Committee and shall be eligible for re-election.

The Committee shall have power to consider all matters concerning the World Council of Churches in so far as they bear upon its financial position.

(4) The items of the budget of a division may be subsequently varied by the divisional committee at its discretion provided the authorized total be not exceeded, and the policy of the division be thereby advanced.

IX. Staff of the World Council of Churches

(1) The General Secretary, the Associate General Secretaries, and the Heads of Departments shall be appointed by the Central Committee.

(2) The normal terms of appointment for an Associate General Secretary

shall be five years and for a Head of Department three years. Unless some other period is stated in the resolution making the appointment, the term of office of members of the staff of the World Council shall be from the date of the appointment until three months after the end of the next meeting of the Central Committee. All appointments made for a term exceeding one year shall be reviewed one year before expiring.

(3) Retirement shall be at 65 for men and 63 for women or not later than the end of the year in which a staff member reaches the age of 68 for men and 66 for women.

(4) If the position of General Secretary becomes vacant, the Executive Committee shall appoint an acting General Secretary.

(5) The General Secretariat (i.e. General Secretary and Associate General Secretaries) is responsible for carrying out the decisions of the Assembly, the Central Committee and the Executive Committee.

(6) The General Secretariat shall be responsible for the conduct of the business of the Council, for relations with member churches and other ecumenical bodies, for the preparation and administration of the meetings of the Assembly, of the Central Committee and of the Executive Committee, for the general supervision and co-ordination of the activities and publications of the commissions and departments of the Council, for the interpretation of the work of the Council to the churches and the public and for the carrying on of activities not otherwise assigned.

(7) The General Secretariat shall have the right to attend the meetings of departmental committees and other meetings called under the auspices of the Council.

X. Public Statements

(1) In the performance of its functions, the Council through its Assembly or through its Central Committee may publish statements upon any situation or issue with which the Council or its constituent churches may be confronted.

(2) While such statements may have great significance and influence as the expression of the judgment or concern of so widely representative a Christian body, yet their authority will consist only in the weight which they carry by their own truth and wisdom and the publishing of such statements shall not be held to imply that the World Council as such has, or can have, any constitutional authority over the constituent churches or right to speak for them.

(3) The Executive Committee or any commission of the Council may recommend statements to the Assembly or to the Central Committee for its consideration and action.

(4) No committee or commission of the Council other than the Central Committee shall publish any statement until it has been approved by the Assembly, except that in circumstances of immediate urgency statements may be published by any commission of the Council on matters within its own field of concern and action, if approved by the Chairman of the Central Committee and the General Secretary, and in these cases the committee or commission shall make it clear that the World Council of Churches is not committed by any statement set forth in this manner.

(5) In cases of exceptional emergency, statements may be issued by the Chairman of the Central Committee on his own authority after consultation with the Vice-Chairman of the Central Committee and the General Secretary provided that such statements are not contrary to the established policy of the Council.

(6) Nothing in these regulations shall contravene the special provisions of the Constitution regarding the Commission on Faith and Order and the Commission on World Mission and Evangelism.

XI. Relationships with National and Regional Councils

(1) The World Council, recognizing that national councils of churches or national Christian councils have been established in a number of countries for purposes of fellowship and co-operation with one another and for the promotion and support of ecumenical activities and other common interests within their own area, shall invite selected national councils to enter into working relationships as associated councils.

(2) The purpose of such working relationships shall be to help national councils in their work and to encourage them to help the World Council of Churches in the promotion of ecumenical activities in the area concerned and in the furthering of the plans and policies which the Central Committee has laid down for the various divisions and departments of the Council.

(3) These councils shall receive invitations to send a fraternal delegate to the Assembly and may, at the discretion of the Central Committee, receive an invitation to send a representative to the Central Committee; such representatives shall have the right to speak but not to vote.

(4) Opportunity shall be provided at the time of any meeting of the Assembly or Central Committee for the representatives of national councils to meet together for mutual consultation.

(5) While the World Council retains the right to deal with its member churches directly, no action shall be taken by it which would disturb any already existing fellowship or ecumenical organization within a nation or region.

(6) Any member church which prefers to have direct relationships with the World Council in any field of work can have such direct relationships.

(7) The following criteria, among others, shall be applied by the Central Committee in selecting national councils for these working relationships:

(i) that the national council accept the Basis of the World Council of Churches or express its willingness to co-operate on that Basis;

(ii) that there be prior consultation with member churches of the World Council in the area concerned;

(iii) that there be prior consultation with the Committee on National Council Relationships;

(iv) that the membership of the national council consist wholly or to a large extent of churches which hold membership in the World Council of Churches;

(v) that the national council have an interest in the work of the World Council of Churches and be willing to work for that Council;

(vi) that the national council give evidence of stability and have a staff with time to devote to World Council concerns.

(8) The Central Committee may, in consultation with the Committee on National Council Relationships, invite councils affiliated to the Commission on World Mission and Evangelism to send a representative to meetings of the Assembly and Central Committee with the right to speak but not to vote, to a number not exceeding ten in the Assembly and five in the Central Committee.

XII. World Confessional Bodies

Such world confessional bodies as may be designated by the Central Committee shall be invited to send fraternal delegates to the Assembly, and advisers to the Central Committee.

XIII. Legal Provisions

(1) The duration of the Council is unlimited.

(2) The legal headquarters of the Council shall be at Geneva. Regional offices may be organized in different parts of the world by decision of the Central Committee.

(3) The World Council of Churches is legally represented by its Executive Committee or by such persons as may be empowered by the Executive Committee to represent it.

(4) The World Council shall be legally bound by the joint signatures of two of the following persons: the President or Presidents, the Chairman and Vice-Chairman or Vice-Chairmen of the Central Committee, and the General Secretary. Any two of the above-named persons shall have power to authorize other persons, chosen by them, to act jointly or singly on behalf of the World Council of Churches in fields circumscribed in the power of attorney.

(5) The Council shall obtain the means necessary for the pursuance of its work from the contributions of its member churches and from donations or bequests.

(6) The Council shall not pursue commercial aims but it shall have the right to act as an agency of inter-church aid and to publish literature in connection with its aims. It is not entitled to distribute any surplus income by way of profit or bonus among its members.

(7) Members of the governing bodies of the Council or of the Assembly shall have no personal liability with regard to the obligations or commitments of the Council. The commitments entered upon by the Council are guaranteed solely by its own assets.

XIV. Rules of Debate During Sessions of the Assembly and the Central Committee

1. *Categories of Session*

The Assembly shall sit either in general session, in business session or in deliberative session.

2. *Presiding Officers*

(a) The Chairman of the Assembly in general session shall be one of the presidents or the Chairman of the Central Committee, as appointed by the Executive Committee.

(b) The Chairman of the Assembly in business session shall be the Chairman or Vice-Chairman of the Central Committee, or some other member of the Central Committee appointed by the Executive Committee or by the Business Committee of the Assembly.

(c) The Chairman of the Assembly in deliberative session shall be a member of the Presidium, an Officer of the Central Committee or a delegate appointed by the Executive Committee or the Business Committee of the Assembly.

3. *Responsibilities of the Chairman*

The responsibilities of the Chairman shall be to announce the opening, suspension and adjournment of the meeting; his first action shall be to announce clearly that the Assembly is in general session, or in business session, or in deliberative session; he shall ensure the observance of the applicable Rules of Debate; he shall grant the right to speak and declare the debate closed; he shall put questions to the vote and announce the result of the voting. He shall not make a motion himself. His decision is final in all matters except as to the result of voting. If the Chairman's decision as to the result of voting is challenged, a vote shall immediately be taken on the motion: 'that the Chairman's decision be reconsidered'; and reconsideration shall be permitted, if a majority of the members present and voting vote in favour of this motion.

4. *General Sessions*

When the Assembly is in general session (for ceremonial occasions, public acts of witness, formal addresses, etc.) the only business that shall be in order, except with consent, is that which is proposed by the Chairman or Secretary of the Executive or Business Committee.

5. *Business Sessions*

The Assembly shall sit in business session when any of the following types of business are on the agenda: adoption of agenda presented by the Business Committee, nominations, elections, proposals with reference to the structure, organization, budget, or programme of the World Council of Churches, or any other business requiring action by the Assembly, except as provided in paragraphs 4 and 6 of this Rule.

The Special Rules of Debate for the Assembly in business session:

(a) If any member desires to propose a motion not on the agenda, he shall be permitted to have his motion read. A vote shall be immediately taken as to whether or not his motion shall be included in the agenda.

(b) All motions and amendments must be proposed and seconded, handed to the Chairman in writing, and read before a vote is taken. The Chairman has the power to rule an amendment out of order as being substantially a negative of the motion.

(c) Any motion or amendment may be withdrawn by leave of the Assembly.

(d) All speeches must be addressed to the Chair.

(e) No member shall speak more than once on the same motion or amendment, except that the mover shall have the right to reply.

(f) When an amendment has been proposed and seconded the Chairman shall allow discussion on the amendment only. An amendment to an amendment is in order, but an amendment to an amendment to an amendment shall be out of order. Discussion and voting shall be in reverse order of the motions made. When the Assembly has voted to approve or disapprove the amendments which have been proposed and seconded, and the original motion is before the Assembly (amended or not as the case may be), additional amendments are in order except those which are judged by the Chair to be substantially the same as proposals already discussed and decided. A motion to refer a resolution back to the responsible committee with or without pending amendments, is always in order. Debate on such a motion shall be limited to three minutes by the maker of the motion, and three minutes by a representative of the committee making the original proposal, and comments by the chairman and Secretary as to the feasibility of handling the matter later in the agenda.

(g) During the discussion, speeches shall be limited to five minutes. A bell shall be rung one minute before a speaker's time is up. A second bell shall be rung one minute later and the speaker shall then sit down, unless the Chairman proposes and receives consent that an additional minute or minutes be allowed the speaker. If translation (other than simultaneous) is required, sufficient additional time shall be allowed by the Chairman.

(h) Those voting with the minority may have their names recorded. Those who abstain from voting may, if they wish, have the fact and number of abstentions recorded.

(i) Those who desire to speak for or against a main proposal before the Assembly must hand to the Secretary, as early as possible, cards with their names, the capacity in which they are attending the Assembly, their church connection, and whether they desire to support or oppose the motion. Those who wish to propose amendments shall follow the same rule, adding on the card precise information as to the part of the resolution they desire to amend. Those who wish to amend an amendment or to discuss an amendment already proposed shall stand in their places for recognition by the Chairman. The mover of an amendment and a representative of the committee reporting shall be allowed additional final statements in this order before the vote on each amendment is taken.

(k) A motion to close the debate in order to proceed immediately to vote on the pending amendments and on the main question shall be in order when admitted by the Chairman. The Secretary shall be asked to report to the Assembly the names of delegates still desiring to be heard and the names of delegates whose proposed amendments have not been heard, after which the Chairman shall ask the Assembly, 'shall the Assembly now conclude the matter before it?' The Chairman shall put the question to the Assembly, without debate, when it has been moved and seconded or when he judges that the Assembly desires to conclude the matter before it. If two-thirds of the delegates present and voting agree, the vote or votes shall be taken without further debate.

(m) Any member may submit a point of order or procedure to the Chairman, and may, if necessary, interrupt a speaker for the purpose.

(n) Voting shall be by show of hands or by standing unless otherwise decided by vote of the Assembly. The Chairman shall read the motion immediately before any vote is taken. He shall first ask those in favour of the motion to vote, and then those opposed. The Chairman may, if he thinks fit, appoint members or staff to act as tellers, and he shall do so in case of doubt as to the result of the vote. A majority of those voting shall determine the decision except as may be otherwise provided in these rules. When the Assembly is equally divided, the motion shall be regarded as defeated.

If a motion for a vote by written ballot is proposed and seconded, the Chairman shall put this motion to the vote without further debate. A simple majority of those present and voting shall decide the issue.

(o) The three official languages are English, French and German. A speech made in any one of these languages shall, if desired, be translated into the other two. It shall be the duty of the Secretary to make arrangements for such translation. A member may speak in a language other than English, French or German on condition that he arrange for the translation of his speech into one of the three official languages. If the Chairman shall judge that injustice has been done to a member by the strict application of these Rules of Debate due to the business having been done too quickly for comprehension in a language other than that of the member, the Chairman may suspend the strict application of the rules to allow reconsideration, motions, amendments, or speeches that would otherwise be out of order.

6. *Deliberative Sessions*

The Assembly shall sit in deliberative session when resolutions or reports are before it which are of such a theological or general policy nature that in the judgment of the Executive Committee or the Business Committee they ought not to be amended in so large a body as an Assembly. A body reporting shall indicate to the Business Committee its preference regarding procedures. The reports of sections shall be debated in deliberative session.

The Special Rules of Debate for the Assembly in deliberative session are the same as those for the Assembly in business session, except that provisions 5 (a), (b), (f), (g), and (h) shall not apply, and that the following additional rules shall be in effect:

(a) The only recommendation that shall be in order from committees or sections reporting is that the Assembly approve the substance of the document, and commend it to the churches for study and appropriate action.

(b) The only motions from the floor that are in order are: (i) to refer back to the committee with instructions to consider whether a new or different emphasis or emphases shall be included by the committee in their report, or (ii) to instruct the committee to provide for an open hearing or an additional open hearing on the report before bringing it again to the Assembly.

(c) Those who desire to speak on the resolution or report before the Assembly must hand to the Secretary, as early as possible, cards with their names, the capacity in which they are attending the Assembly and their Church connection, and whether they desire to speak to the report as a whole or to a particular section or sections thereof.

(d) Those who desire to propose either of the motions allowed in Rule (b) above must add this information on their card when sent forward, or else their motion shall be out of order. The Chairman, in introducing them, shall indicate that a motion is to be moved.

(e) Speeches shall ordinarily be limited to ten minutes. The bell shall be rung at the end of eight minutes and again two minutes later and the speaker shall then sit down unless the Chairman proposes and receives consent that an additional minute or minutes be allowed. When the number of those desiring to speak is large, the Chairman may ask the Assembly to agree to a shorter time. When translation (other than simultaneous) is required, sufficient additional time shall be allowed by the Chairman.

(f) Rule 5(k) shall be followed so far as it applies to close the debate.

(g) Those voting with the minority may have their names recorded. Those who abstain from voting, may, if they wish, have the fact and number of abstentions recorded.

7. *The Central Committee*

The Central Committee shall ordinarily sit in business session and these rules shall be followed except that Rules 5 (g) (length of speeches) and (j) (handing in name cards) shall only apply when it is so decided by the Central Committee itself. If on recommendation of the Executive Committee the Central Committee shall agree to sit in a general or deliberative session, the rules for these sessions shall be the same as the rules for the Assembly in general session or deliberative session, except that Rules 6 (c), (d), (e), and (f) shall not apply.

XV. Amendments

Amendments to these Rules may be moved at any meeting of the Assembly or at any meeting of the Central Committee by any member and may be adopted by a two-thirds majority of those present and voting, except that no alteration in Rules I, V, and XV shall come into effect until it has been confirmed by the Assembly. Notice of a proposal to make any such amendment shall be given in writing at least twenty-four hours before the meeting of the Assembly or Central Committee at which it is to be moved.

BIBLIOGRAPHY

NOTE: The following list comprises most of the important works consulted by the author, but is not offered as a professional or complete bibliography of the subject.

ADDISON, J. T. *The Episcopal Church in the United States, 1789-1931.* New York, 1931.

AINSLEE, PETER. *The Message of the Disciples for the Union of the Church.* New York, 1913.

ALLEN, ROLAND. *Jerusalem: A Critical Review of "The World Mission of Christianity."* London, 1928.

ALLEN, W. O. B. AND MCCLURE, EDWARD. *Two Hundred Years: The History of the Society for Promoting Christian Knowledge, 1698-1898.* London, 1898.

American Congress of Churches. Proceedings, 1885 and 1886. Hartford, Conn., 1885, 1886.

AMMUNDSEN, VALDEMAR. *In Memoriam: Bishop Valdemar Ammundsen, 1875-1936.* Geneva, 1937.

ANDRAE, TOR. *Nathan Söderblom.* Uppsala, 1932.

ANDREWS, THEODORE. *The Polish National Catholic Church in America.* London, 1953.

ANSHELM, CARL. *Peter Fjellstedt.* Stockholm, 1930.

ANSHEN, RUTH NANDA, ed. *Science and Man—A Symposium.* New York, 1942.

ANSTADT, P. *Life and Times of Rev. S. S. Schmucker, D.D.* York, Penna., 1896.

APPEL, THEODORE. *Life and Work of J. W. Nevin.* Philadelphia, 1889.

ARANGADEN, A. T. *Church Union in South India.* Mangalore, 1947.

ARNOLD, THOMAS. *Principles of Church Reform.* London, 1833.

ATKINS, G. G. *Religion in Our Times.* New York, 1932.

AUBREY, E. E. *Living the Christian Faith.* New York, 1932.

AXENFELD, KARL. *Germany's Battle for the Freedom of the Christian Missions.* Berlin-Stieglitz, 1919.

AYRES, ANNE. *Life and Work of W. A. Muhlenberg.* New York, 1880.

BAILLIE, DONALD M. AND MARSH, JOHN. *Intercommunion: Report of the Theological Commission, W.C.C.* Geneva, 1954.

BAILLIE, JOHN. *The Belief in Progress.* New York, 1951.

———, ed. *Revelation: A Symposium.* London, 1937.

BAINTON, ROLAND H. *Here I Stand: A Life of Martin Luther.* Nashville, 1950.

———. *The Reformation in the Sixteenth Century.* Boston, 1952.

Baptist World Alliance, Official Report, 1960. Nashville, 1960.

BARCLAY, W. C. *The World Mission of the Christian Religion*. Nashville, 1934.
BARNES, ROSWELL P. *A Church Imperative*. New York, 1941.
BARTH, KARL. *The Word of God and the Word of Man*. Tr. by D. R. Horton. New York, 1957.
BATE, H. N., ed. *Can the Churches Unite?—Report of the First World Conference on Faith and Order, Lausanne, 1927*. London, 1927.
BATES, SEARLE M. *Data on the Distribution of the Missionary Enterprise*. New York, 1943.
———. *Religious Liberty: An Inquiry*. New York, 1945.
BATTEN, J. M. *John Dury: Advocate of Christian Reunion*. Chicago, 1944.
BATTY, J. D. *The Australian Proposal for Intercommunion*. London, 1948.
BAUM, GREGORY. *That They May Be One*. Westminster, Md., 1958.
BELL, G. K. A. *Christianity and World Order*. London, 1954.
———. *Documents on Christian Unity*. Three Series, 1924-48. London, 1924, 1930, 1948.
———. *The Kingship of Christ*. London, 1954.
———. *The Stockholm Conference: Official Report of the Universal Christian Conference on Life and Work*. London, 1926.
———. *Thomas Randall Davidson, Archbishop*. London, 1952.
BENNETT, JOHN C. *Christianity and Communism*. New York, 1949.
———. *The Christian Answer to the Challenge of Communism*. Study Dept., W.C.C. Geneva, 1950.
———, ed. *Liberal Theology: Essays in Honor of Eugene W. Lyman*. New York, 1942.
The Bible and the Churches' Message to the World Today. Study Dept., W.C.C. Geneva, 1949.
BILHEIMER, R. S. *The Quest for Christian Unity*. New York, 1952.
BIRKBECK, W. J. *Life and Letters:* Ed. by his wife. London, 1921.
———. *Russia and the English Church*. London, 1895.
BIXLER, JULIUS SEELYE. *Religion for Free Minds*. New York, 1939.
BLISS, KATHLEEN. *The Service and Status of Women in the Church*, London, 1952.
BOEGNER, MARC. *Fallot: La vie et la pensée*. 2 vols. Paris, 1914, 1926.
———. *Le problème de l'unité chrétienne*. Paris, 1946.
BOEHME, KURT. *Die Weltkonferenz in Amsterdam*. Hamburg, 1948.
BOLSHAKOFF, SERGE. *The Doctrine of the Unity of the Church in the Works of Khomyakov and Moehler*. London, 1946.
———. *Russian Nonconformity*. Philadelphia, 1950.
BRANDRETH, HENRY R. T. *Ecumenical Ideals of the Oxford Movement*. London, 1947.
———. *Unity and Reunion. A Bibliography*. London, 1948.
BRASH, ALAN A. *Amsterdam, 1948*. Christchurch, N.Z., 1948.
BRENT, CHARLES H. *Understanding*. New York, 1928.
BRIGGS, C. A. *Church Unity*. New York, 1909.
BROWN, ARTHUR JUDSON. *One Hundred Years: A History of the Foreign Missionary Work of the Presbyterian Church, U.S.A*. New York, 1937.
BROWN, WILLIAM ADAMS. *Church and State in Contemporary America*. New York, 1936.
———. *The New Order in the Church*. Nashville, 1943.
———. *A Teacher and His Times: An Autobiography*. New York, 1940.
———. *Toward a United Church*. Ed. by S. M. Cavert. New York, 1946.
BRUNNER, EMIL. *The Divine Human Encounter*. Philadelphia, 1943.

———. *Revelation and Reason.* Philadelphia, 1946.

BULGAKOV, S. *The Orthodox Church.* London, 1935.

BUTTERFIELD, KENYON L. *The Christian Mission in Rural India.* New York, 1930.

———. *The Rural Mission of the Church in Eastern Asia.* New York, 1931.

CAIRNS, DAVID. *A Gospel Without Myth? Bultmann's Challenge to the Preacher.* London, 1960.

CAMPBELL, ALEXANDER. *Christianity Restored.* Bethany, Va., 1835.

———. *Memoirs.* Cincinnati, 1872.

———. *Life of Thomas Campbell.* Cincinnati, 1861.

CANTON, W. *History of the British and Foreign Bible Society.* 5 vols. London, 1904.

CAREY, EUSTACE. *Memoir of William Carey.* Hartford, 1837.

CAREY, S. PEARCE. *William Carey.* New York, 1923.

CARPENTER, EDWARD. *Thomas Tenison, His Life and Times.* London, 1948.

CAVERT, S. M., ed. *The Church Faces the World.* I.M.C. studies. New York, 1939.

——— AND VAN DUSEN, H. P. *The Church Through Half a Century.* New York, 1936.

Chinese Christian Council: Proceedings of the Continuation Committee. Shanghai and New York, 1907-29.

CHIRGWIN, A. M. *The Churches Co-operate.* London, 1944.

Christians and Jews: Report of the Conference on the Christian Approach to to Jews, Atlantic City, 1931. New York, 1931.

———. *Report of the Budapest and Warsaw Conferences, 1927.* London, 1927.

The Christian College in India: Report of the Commission on Christian Higher Education in India. London and Oxford, 1931.

Christian Education in Japan: Study by a Commission on Christian Education in Japan. New York, 1932.

The Christian Hope and the Task of the Church: Six Surveys on the Main Theme at the Evanston Assembly. New York, 1954.

Christian Literature in Moslem Lands. New York, 1923.

Christian Work in Latin America: Report of the Panama Congress of 1916 and Seven Subsequent Regional Conferences. New York, 1917.

Christus Victor: Report of the Amsterdam Youth Conference, 1939. Geneva, 1939.

The Church, the Churches, and the World Council of Churches. W.C.C., Geneva, 1950.

Church, Community and State Series: Messages and Decisions of the Oxford Conference, 1937. 8 vols. London, 1937.

The Churches and the International Crisis. Geneva, 1939.

CLARK, J. ELMER. *Small Sects in America.* New York, 1950.

COHEN, ARTHUR, et al. *Religion and the Free Society.* New York, 1958.

COLE, STEWART G. *The History of Fundamentalism.* New York, 1931.

COMENIUS, JOHN AMOS. *An Exhortation of the Churches of Bohemia to the Church of England.* London, 1661.

———. *The Labyrinth of the World.* Chicago, 1942.

Commission of the Churches on International Affairs. Report of the Conference at Cambridge, England, 1946. New York, 1946.

———. *Report, 1949-50.* New York and London, 1950.

COMPLAND, R. *William Wilberforce.* Oxford, 1926.

Coxe, A. C., ed. *The Anti-Nicene Fathers.* 9 vols. New York, 1925.
Craig, C. T. *The One Church in the Light of the New Testament.* London, 1952.
Cunningham, Merriman, ed. *Christianity and Communism.* Dallas, 1958.

Davies, Horton. *The English Free Churches.* London, 1952.
Davis, J. Merle. *The Economic and Social Environment of the Younger Churches.* London, 1939.
———. *Modern Industry and the African.* London, 1933.
———. *New Building on Old Foundations.* New York, 1945.
———. *The Preparation of Missionaries for Work in the Post-War Era.* New York, 1944.
Dawson, Christopher. *The Judgment of the Nations.* New York, 1942.
De Bude, E. *Lives of the Elder and the Younger Turretini.* Lausanne, 1871, 1880.
Deissmann, Adolf. *Die Stockholmer Weltkirchenkonferenz.* Berlin, 1926.
———. *Una Sancta. Zum Geleit in das ökumenische Jahr 1937.* Gütersloh, 1936.
Devasahayam, D. M., and Sudarisanam, A. M. *Rethinking Christianity in India.* Madras, 1938.
De Vries, Egbert. *Man in Rapid Social Change.* London, 1961.
Diffendorfer, Ralph E. *Christian Literature in the Mission World.* New York, 1946.
Dodd, C. H. *History and the Gospel.* New York, 1938.
Doggett, L. L. *History of the Y.M.C.A.* New York, 1896.
Döllinger, Ignaz. *The Reunion of the Churches.* London, 1872.
Douglass, H. Paul. *A Decade of Objective Progress in Church Unity, 1927-36.* New York, 1937.
———. *Unity Movements in the United States.* New York, 1934.
Dowding, W. C. *The Life and Correspondence of George Calixtus.* Oxford and London, 1963.
Drummond, A. L. *German Protestantism Since Luther.* London, 1951.
Dun, Angus. *Prospecting for a United Church.* New York, 1948.
Du Pin, L. E. *Bibliothèque Universelle des Auteurs Ecclésiastiques.* 58 vols. (Complete history of the theological literature of the Church). Paris, 1686-1704.
Dwight, H. O. *Centennial History of the American Bible Society.* New York, 1916.

Eastman, Max. *Reflections on the Failure of Socialism.* New York, 1955.
Ecumenical Youth Assembly, Lausanne, 1960, Report. Geneva, 1960.
Eddy, Sherwood. *Pathfinders of the World Missionary Crusade.* Nashville, 1945.
Edwards, Jonathan. *Works.* Volume III. New York, 1943.
Ehrenstrom, Nils. *Christian Faith and the Modern State.* Chicago, 1937.
Evanston Report: Second Assembly of the World Council of Churches. ed. by W. A. Visser 't Hooft. New York, 1954.
Evanston to New Delhi, 1954-61. Report of the Central Committee at the Third Assembly of the W.C.C. Geneva, 1961.
Ewing, J. W. *The Goodly Fellowship: The World's Evangelical Alliance.* London, 1946.

Fahs, Charles H. and Davis, Helen. *Conspectus of Co-operative Missionary Enterprises.* New York, 1935.

FAIRWEATHER, E. R. AND HARDY, E. R. *The Voice of the Church: The Ecumenical Council in Rome.* Greenwich, Conn., 1962.

Faith and Order Pamphlets. Number 1, April, 1911, through Number 52. New York, 1911-27.

FARMER, H. H. *Revelation and Religion.* New York, 1954.

FENN, ERIC. *That They Go Forward: An Impression of the Oxford Conference.* London, 1938.

The First Six Years, 1948-54. Report of the Central Committee at the Second Assembly of the W.C.C. New York, 1954.

FISHER, G. P. *A History of the Christian Church.* New York, 1914.

———. *The Reformation.* New York, 1899.

FLEW, R. NEWTON, ed. *The Nature of the Church: Report of the Theological Commission of the W.C.C.* London, 1952.

FLOROVSKY, GEORGES. *The Ways of Russian Theology.* Paris, 1956.

FOSDICK, H. E. *Great Voices of the Reformation.* New York, 1952.

GAIRDNER, W. H. T. *Edinburgh, 1910: An Account and Interpretation.* Edinburgh and London, 1910.

GERMANOS STRENOPOULOS. *Kyrillos Loukaris, 1572-1638.* London, 1951.

———, ed. *Report of the World Council of Churches, Amsterdam.* Athens, 1949.

GIBSON, B. D., ed. *The Place of Women in the Church on the Mission Field.* London and New York, 1927.

GIFFORD, W. A. *The Story of Faith.* New York, 1946.

GLASSTONE, S. *Effects of Nuclear Weapons.* Washington, D.C., 1957.

GOODALL, NORMAN, ed. *Missions Under the Cross: Addresses and Statement at Willingen.* London, 1953.

Guiding Principles for the Interpretation of the Bible. Oxford, 1950.

GULICK, SIDNEY L. *The Winning of the Far East.* New York, 1923.

——— AND MACFARLAND, C. S. *The Church and International Relations.* New York, 1915.

——— AND MACFARLAND, C. S. *Report of the Commission on Peace and Arbitration.* New York, 1917.

HALIFAX, LORD. *The Conversations at Malines.* Original Documents. Paris, 1930.

———. *Leo XIII and Anglican Orders.* London, 1912.

HARDY, E. R. *Orthodox Statements on Anglican Orders.* New York, 1926.

HARKNESS, GEORGIA. *Understanding the Christian Faith.* Nashville, 1947.

HASTINGS, JAMES. *Dictionaries: Christ and the Gospels,* 1917; *Bible,* 1919; *Apostolic Church,* 1919. New York.

HAYEK, FRIEDRICH. *The Road to Serfdom.* Chicago, 1944.

HAYMAN, ERIC, et al. *Ways of Worship: Report of the Theological Commission, W.C.C.* London, 1952.

HEADLAM, A. C. *Grace: A Study for the Second Faith and Order Conference, Edinburgh.* London, 1938.

HEARD, GERALD AND OPITZ, E. A. *The Kingdom Without God.* Los Angeles, 1956.

HEDLEY, GEORGE. *The Christian Heritage in America.* New York, 1946.

HENRY, CARL F. H., ed. *Revelation and the Bible.* Grand Rapids, 1958.

HERKLOTS, H. G. G. AND LEIPER, H. S. *Pilgrimage to Amsterdam.* New York and London, 1949.

HERMAN, STEWART. *The Rebirth of the German Church.* London and New York, 1946.

HOCKING, WILLIAM E. *The Church and the World Mind.* The Drake Lectures. St. Louis, 1944.

———. *Living Religions and a World Faith.* New York, 1940.

———. *Rethinking Missions: A Layman's Inquiry . . .* New York, 1932.

HODGE, J. Z. *Bishop Azariah of Dornakal.* Madras, 1946.

HODGSON, LEONARD, ed. *Convictions: Responses of the Churches to Lausanne, 1927.* London, 1934.

———. *The Ecumenical Movement.* Sewanee, Tenn., 1951.

———. *The Second World Conference on Faith and Order, Edinburgh.* London, 1938.

HOFFMAN, JEAN G. B. *Nathan Söderblom, prophète de l'oecuménisme.* Geneva, 1948.

HOGG, WILLIAM RICHEY. *Ecumenical Foundations: A History of the International Missionary Council and Its 19th Century Background.* New York, 1952.

———. *Sixty-five Years in the Seminaries: The Interseminary Movement.* New York, 1945.

HOPKINS, C. H. *The Y.M.C.A. in America.* New York, 1951.

HORDERN, WILLIAM. *A Layman's Guide to Protestant Theology.* New York, 1955.

HORTON, DOUGLAS. *Congregationalism: A Study of Church Polity.* London, 1952.

HORTON, R. F. *The Reunion of English Christendom.* London, 1905.

HORTON, W. M. *Contemporary English Theology.* New York, 1936.

———. *Christian Theology, An Ecumenical Approach.* New York, 1955.

———. *Toward a Reborn Church.* New York, 1949.

HUME, R. E. *The World's Living Religions.* New York, 1939.

HUMPHREYS, J. D., ed. *Correspondence and Diary of Philip Doddridge.* London, 1830.

HUNTINGTON, W. R. *The Christian Idea: An Essay on Unity.* New York, 1870.

———. *A National Church.* Bedell Lectures, 1897. New York, 1898.

HUTCHINSON, JOHN A. *The Christian Faith and Social Action.* New York, 1953.

———. *We Are Not Divided: A Critical Study of the Federal Council of Churches, U.S.A.* New York, 1941

HUTTON, W. H. *The English Church from the Accession of Charles I to the Death of Anne.* London, 1903.

INGE, W. R. *The End of an Age.* New York, 1949.

———. *Lay Thoughts of a Dean.* Garden City, N.Y., 1926.

———. *Outspoken Essays.* London, 1920.

International Missionary Council. Minutes and Reports: Crans, 1921; The Ad-Interim Committee, 1921; Lake Mohonk, 1921; Whitby, 1947; Willingen, 1952; Accra, 1958-59.

———. *Quarterly Notes:* Bulletin to 1924. New York.

———. *Fundamental Questions of Policy.* London, 1925.

———. *Jerusalem Meeting, 1928.* 8 vols. New York and London, 1928.

———. *Report of the Church History Deputation to the Orient, 1931.* London, 1932.

———. *Madras Conference, 1938.* 7 vols. Oxford, 1939.

———. *The World Mission of the Church: Findings and Recommendations of the I.M.C., Madras, 1938.* New York, 1939.

———. *General Report for the Years 1939-45: Continental Missions in War-time.* New York, 1946.
———. *The Witness of a Revolutionary Church: Statements at Whitby.* New York, 1947.
———. *Tomorrow Is Here: The Mission of the World Church as Seen from the Meeting at Whitby.* New York, 1948.
———. *Joint Committee (IMC and WCC) on East Asia, Minutes of the Meeting at Manila, P.I.*, 1948.
Interseminary Series: 5 vols. I. *"The Challenge of Our Culture,"* II. *"The Church and Organized Movements,"* III. *"The Gospel, the Church and the World,"* IV. *"Toward World-Wide Christianity,"* V. *"What Must the Church Do?"* New York, 1954.
IREMONGER, F. A. *William Temple, His Life and Letters.* London, 1948.

JABLONSKI, DANIEL E. *Vorstellung der Einigkeit und des Untershiedes im Glaubennbeides evangelischen. . . .* Berlin, 1697.
JESSOP, T. E., et al. *The Christian Understanding of Man.* Chicago, 1938.
JOHNSTON, JAMES. *Centenary Conference of Protestant Missions of the World, 1888.* 2 vols. London, 1888.
JONES, T. J. *Education in Africa.* New York and London, 1925.
JURJI, EDWARD J., ed. *The Great Religions of the Modern World.* Princeton, N.J., 1946.

KARLSTRÖM, N. *Archbishop Nathan Söderblom.* Stockholm, 1931.
KATZ, P. *Nathan Söderblom: Prophet of Christian Unity.* London, 1931.
KELLER, ADOLF. *Church and State on the European Continent.* London, 1936.
———. *Five Minutes to Twelve: An Interpretation of the Oxford Conference.* Nashville, 1938.
———. *Karl Barth and Christian Unity.* New York, 1933.
——— AND STEWART, GEORGE. *Protestant Europe: Its Crisis.* London, 1927.
KELSO, L. O., AND ADLER, M. J. *The Capitalistic Manifesto.* New York, 1958.
KENNEDY, JAMES W. *Venture of Faith.* New York, 1948.
KENNEDY, WILLIAM S. *The Plan of Union.* (Presbyterians and Congregationalists.) Hudson, Ohio, 1856.
KEPLER, THOMAS S. *Contemporary Thinking About Jesus.* Nashville, 1944.
KIDD, BENJAMIN. *Social Evolution.* New York, 1894.
KILPATRICK, JAMES J. *The Southern Case for School Segregation.* New York, 1962.
KINGSLEY, CHARLES. *Memoirs and Letters.* Ed. by his wife. 2 vols. London, 1877.
KRAEMER, H. *The Christian Message in a Non-Christian World.* London and New York, 1938.
KÜNG, HANS. *The Council: Reform and Reunion.* Rome, 1962.

Lambeth Conference, Bishops' Encyclicals, Resolutions and Reports. London, 1930.
LATOURETTE, KENNETH SCOTT. *The Christian Message for the World Today.* New York, 1934.
———. *The Christian Outlook.* New York, 1948.
———. *A History of Christian Missions in China.* New York, 1929.
———. *A History of the Expansion of Christianity.* 7 vols. New York, 1937-45.

———. *Missions Tomorrow*. New York, 1936.
———. *The Twentieth Century Outside Europe*. New York, 1962.
——— WITH HOGG, W. R. *Tomorrow Is Here*. London, 1948.
——— WITH HOGG, W. R. *World Christian Community in Action*. New York, 1949.
LAUD, WILLIAM. *Works*. 7 vols. Oxford, 1847-60.
LEE, F. G., ed. *Sermons on the Reunion of Christendom*. By Members of the Roman Catholic, Oriental and Anglican Communions. London, 1865.
LEIBNIZ, G. W. *Philosophical Writings*. New York, 1954.
LEIPER, H. S. *Christianity Today*. New York, 1947.
———. *World Chaos or World Christianity*. Chicago and New York, 1937.
LERNER, MAX. *America as a Civilization*. New York, 1957.
LEWIS, W. H. *Church Union and the Episcopal Church*. New York, 1855.
LIDDON, H. P. *Life of E. B. Pusey*. London, 1893-97.
LITZMANN, HANS. *The Beginnings of the Christian Church*. New York, 1937.
———. *The Foundations of the Church Universal*. New York, 1938.
LLOYD, ROGER. *The Church of England in the Twentieth Century*. London, 1946.
LOCKHART, J. G. *Archbishop Cosmo Gordon Lang*. London, 1949.
London Secretaries' Association, Minutes. 10 vols. London, 1819-1946.
Lordship of Christ over the World and the Church. W.C.C. Division of Studies. Geneva, 1961.
LOVETT, RICHARD. *The History of the London Missionary Society, 1795-1895*. 2 vols. London, 1899.
LUNN, SIR HENRY S. *Chapters of My Life, with Special Reference to Reunion*. London, 1918.
LUPTON, J. H. *Archbishop Wake and the Prospect of Union Between the Gallican and Anglican Churches*. London, 1896.

MACFARLAND, C. S. *Across the Years*. New York, 1936.
———. *Christian Unity in the Making: First Twenty-Five Years of the Federal Council of Churches, 1905-30*. New York, 1948.
———. *Church Unity in Practice and Prophecy*. New York, 1933.
———. *International Christian Movements*. New York, 1921.
———. *Pioneers for Peace through Religion: The Church Peace Union, 1919-45*. New York, 1946.
———. *Steps Toward the World Council: Origins . . . in the Universal Christian Council for Life and Work*. New York, 1948.
MACLENNAN, KENNETH. *Twenty Years of Missionary Co-operation*. London, 1927.
MACQUARRIE, JOHN. *The Scope of Demythologizing*. New York, 1961.
MACY, PAUL G. *An Ecumenical Bibliography*. New York, 1946.
Man's Disorder and God's Design. Four study syllabuses for the First Assembly of the W.C.C., Amsterdam, including: 1. *"The Universal Church in God's Design,"* 2. *"The Church's Witness to God's Design,"* 3. *"The Church and the Disorder of Society,"* 4. *"The Church and the International Disorder."* New York, 1949.
MARTIN, HUGH. *Edinburgh, 1937: The Second World Conference on Faith and Order*. London, 1937.
MARTINDALE, C. C. *The Faith of the Roman Church*. London, n.d.
MASCALL, E. D., ed. *Anglo-Russian Symposium on the Church*. London, 1934.
MASSIE, J. W. *The Evangelical Alliance—Its Origin and Development*. London, 1847.

MATHEWS, SHAILER. *The Church and the Changing Order*. New York, 1913.
MATTHEWS, BASIL. *Roads to the City of God. Outlook from Jerusalem*. London, 1928.
———. *John R. Mott: World Citizen*. New York, 1934.
MAURICE, FREDERICK DENISON. *The Kingdom of Christ*. London, 1838.
MCCOWAN, C. C. *The Genesis of the Social Gospel*. New York, 1929.
MCGIFFERT, A. C., JR. *Jonathan Edwards*. New York, 1932.
———. *A History of Christian Thought*. Vols. I and II. New York, 1932.
MCGLOTHLIN, W. J. *The Course of Christian History*. New York, 1918.
MCKINNON, J. *Luther*. 4 vols. London, 1925-30.
MCNEILL, J. T. *Unitive Protestantism*. New York, 1930.
MESSENGER, E. C. *Rome and Reunion*. London, 1934.
MINEAR, PAUL S. *Christian Hope and the Second Coming*. Philadelphia, 1953.
———. *The Nature of the Unity We Seek: Official Report of the Oberlin Conference on Faith and Order, 1958*. St. Louis, 1958.
Missionary Conferences, Reports:
——— Africa: *United Conference, British East Africa, at Kikuyu, 1918*. Nairobi, 1918.
——— China: *General Conference, Protestant Missions, at Shanghai, 1890*. Shanghai, 1890.
——— China: *Centenary Conference, 1907*. New York, 1907.
——— *Ecumenical Conference of 1900*. New York, 1900.
——— *General Conference at London, 1878*. London, 1879.
——— India: *Bengal Protestant Missionaries at Calcutta, 1855*. Calcutta, 1855.
——— India: *South India Conference at Ootacamund, 1858*. Madras, 1858.
——— India: *Punjab Conference at Lahore, 1862*. Dodina, 1863.
——— India: *General Conference at Allahabad, 1872-73*. Madras, 1873.
——— India: *South India and Ceylon at Madras, 1879*. Madras, 1880.
——— India: *Second Decennial Conference at Calcutta, 1882-83*. Calcutta, 1883.
——— India: *Third Decennial Conference at Bombay*, 1892-93. Bombay, 1893.
——— India: *Conference at Madras, 1900*. Madras, 1900.
——— India: *Fourth Decennial Conference at Madras, 1902*. Madras, 1903.
——— Japan: *Protestant Missions Convention at Yokahama, 1872*. Yokahama, 1872.
——— Japan: *General Conference at Tokyo, 1900*. Tokyo, 1901.
——— *Liverpool Missionary Conference, 1860*. London, 1860.
——— *North America: Foreign Mission Conference at New York, 1893*. New York, 1893.
——— South Africa: *First General Conference at Johannesburg, 1904*. Johannesburg, 1905.
——— South Africa: *Second General Conference at Johannesburg, 1906*. Johannesburg, 1907.
——— South Africa: *Third General Conference at Bloemfontein, 1909*. Capetown, 1909.
——— South Africa: *Fourth General Conference at Capetown, 1912*. Capetown, 1912.
——— *Union Missionary Convention, New York, 1854*. London, 1854.
Missionary Record of the United Church of Scotland. Edinburgh, 1901.
MODE, PETER G. *The Frontier Spirit in American Christianity*. New York, 1923.

MOEHLMAN, C. H. *The Catholic-Protestant Mind*. New York, 1929.
MOFFATT, JAMES. *The First Five Centuries of the Church*. Nashville, 1938.
MÖHLER, J. A. *Unity in the Church, or the Principle of Catholicism*. Mainz, 1925.
MOODY, JOHN. *John Henry Newman*. New York, 1945.
MOODY, WILLIAM R. *The Life of Dwight L. Moody*. New York, 1900.
MORRISON, C. C. *The Unfinished Reformation*. New York, 1953.
MOSHEIM, J. L. *An Ecclesiastical History*. London, n.d.
MOSS, C. B. *The Old Catholic Movement: Its Origin and History*. London, 1848.
MOTT, JOHN R. *Addresses and Papers*. 6 vols. New York, 1947.
———. *The Decisive Hour of Christian Missions*. New York, 1910.
———. *The Evangelization of the World in This Generation*. New York, 1901.
———. *The World's Student Christian Federation*. New York, 1920.
MUHLENBERG, H. M. *Journals*. Philadelphia, 1945.
MUNBY, D. L. *God and the Rich Society*. London, 1961.
———. *Moral Problems in Economic Life Today*. Study Dept. W.C.C. Geneva, 1950.

NASH, ARNOLD S. *Protestant Thought in the Twentieth Century*. New York, 1951.
NEALE, JOHN MASON. *A History of the Eastern Church*. 4 vols. London, 1847-50.
NEILL, STEPHEN C. *The Lambeth Conference, 1867-1948*. London, 1948.
———. *A Survey of the Training of the Ministry in Africa*. London, 1950.
———. *Toward Church Union, 1937-52*. London, 1952.
NELSON, HORATIO. *Home Reunion*. London, 1905.
NEWBIGIN, J. E. L. *A Faith for This One World?* New York, 1962.
———. *The Household of God*. New York, 1953.
———. *The Reunion of the Church*. London, 1948.
New Delhi Report: Proceedings of the Third Assembly of the World Council of Churches. New York, 1962.
NEWMAN, JOHN HENRY. *Parochial and Plain Sermons*. Oxford, 1885.
NICHOLS, J. H. *Democracy and the Churches*. Philadelphia, 1951.
———. *Evanston: An Interpretation*. New York, 1954.
———. *Primer for Protestants*. New York, 1947.
NIEBUHR, H. R. *The Social Sources of Denominationalism*. New York, 1929.
NIEBUHR, R. *Moral Man and Immoral Society*. New York, 1932.
NIEMAN, FRASER, ed. *Essays, Letters and Reviews by Matthew Arnold*. Cambridge, Mass., 1960.
NIXON, JUSTIN WROE. *Responsible Christianity*. New York, 1950.
NOEL, BAPTIST. *The Unity of the Church*. London, 1836.
NORTHCUTT, CECIL. *Christian World Mission*. London, 1952.
NORTHROP, F. S. C. *The Meeting of East and West*. New York, 1946.
———. *Ideological Differences and World Order*. New Haven, 1949.

OLDHAM, H. W. *The Student Christian Movement of Great Britain and Ireland*. London, 1899.
OLDHAM, JOSEPH H. *The Christian Message in the Modern World*. London, 1932.
———. *Church, Community and State: A World Issue*. London, 1935.
———. *The Churches Survey Their Task*. Vol. VIII and Summary of The Church, Community and State Series. London, 1937.

———. *An International Missionary Organization.* London, 1920.
———. *The Meaning of Work in Modern Society.* Study Dept. W.C.C. Geneva, 1949.
———. *The Oxford Conference: Official Report.* Chicago, 1937.
———. *The World and the Gospel.* London, 1916.
Old Catholic Congress: Minutes, Munich, 1871. London, 1872.
ORCHARD, R. K. *Report and Messages of the Meeting of the International Missionary Council in Ghana.* New York, 1958.
OUTLER, ALBERT C. *The Christian Tradition: The Unity We Seek.* New York, 1957.
OVERBECK, J. J. *Catholic Orthodoxy and Anglo-Catholicism.* London, 1866.
OVERTON, J. H. AND RELTON, F. *The English Church from George I to the End of the 18th Century.* London, 1906.
OWEN, JOHN. *The History and Origin of the British and Foreign Bible Society.* London, 1816.
OXNAM, G. BROMLEY. *On This Rock.* New York, 1951.

PALMER, WILLIAM. *Dissertations on the "Orthodox" Communion . . .* London, 1853.
———. *Harmony of Anglican Doctrine with Doctrine of the Catholic Church of the East . . .* Aberdeen, 1846.
———. *Notes on a Visit to the Russian Church, 1840-41*, ed. by J. H. Newman. London, 1844.
Pan-Anglican Congress, Proceedings. 7 vols. London, 1908.
PAPADOPOULOS, C. *The Validity of Anglican Ordinations.* Tr. by J. O. Douglas. London, 1931.
PARKER, J. L. *Interpretative Statistical Survey of the World Mission of the Christian Church.* New York, 1938.
PASCOE, G. F. *Two Hundred Years of the Society for the Propagation of the Gospel, 1701-1900.* 2 vols. London, 1901.
PATTEN, JOHN A. *These Remarkable Men: Evangelicals Associated with the Bible Society.* London, 1945.
PHILARET, V. M. D. *Exposition of the Differences Between the Eastern and Western Churches.* London, 1833.
———. *Select Sermons.* London, 1873.
PHILLIPPS DE LISLE, AMBROSE. *The Future of Christendom.* London, 1857.
PICKERING, W. S. F. *Anglican-Methodist Relations—International Factors.* London, 1961.
PIDGEON, G. C. *United Church of Canada.* Toronto, 1950.
Protestant Episcopal Church, Journal of the General Convention, 1886. Chicago, 1886.
PROTHERO, R. E. *Life and Letters of Dean Stanley.* London, 1909.
PUSEY, E. B. *The Church of England a Portion of Christ's One Holy Catholic Church . . . an Eirenicon.* London, 1865.
———. *Is Healthful Reunion Impossible? Eirenicon, Part III.* London, 1870.
———. *Letter to J. H. Newman on Love Due the Ever-Blessed Theotokos . . . Eirenicon, Part II.* London, 1869.

RANSON, C. W. *The Christian Minister in India.* London, 1945.
———, ed. *Renewal and Advance: Outlook from Whitby.* London, 1948.
RAUSCHENBUSCH, WALTER. *Christianity and the Social Crisis.* New York, 1907.
———. *Christianizing the Social Order.* New York, 1912.
RAWLINSON, A. E. J. *The Church of South India.* London, 1951.

RAWLINSON, F. et al. *National Christian Conference at Shanghai, 1922.* Shanghai, 1922.

RICE, ANNA V. *A History of the World's Y.W.C.A.* New York, 1947.

RICHARD, J. W. *Philip Melanchton.* New York, 1898.

RILEY, ATHELSTAN, ed. *Birkbeck and the Russian Church.* London, 1917.

RICHARDSON, ALAN. *The Biblical Doctrine of Work.* Study Dept. W.C.C. Geneva, 1950.

RITSON, J. H. *Christian Literature in the Mission Field:* Survey Under the World Missionary Conference, 1910. Edinburgh, 1910.

———. *The World Is Our Parish.* London, 1939.

ROBERTSON, E. H. *Lund, 1952.* London, 1952.

ROBINSON, WILLIAM. *The Biblical Doctrine of the Church.* St. Louis, 1948.

ROERICH, E. *Samuel Gobat, His Life and Work—from His Journals.* Pref. by Lord Shaftesbury. London, 1884.

Roman Catholic Papal Encyclicals—Bearing on Unity.

Ad Petri Cathedram, 1959. John XXIII

Aeterna Dei Sapientia, 1961. John XXIII

Ecclesia Catholica, 1949. Pius XII

Humani Generis, 1950. Pius XII

Mortalium Animos, 1928. Pius XI

Mystici Corporis Christi, 1943. Pius XII

Orientalis Ecclesiae, 1944. Pius XII

Satis Cognitum, 1895. Leo XIII

ROUSE, RUTH. *John R. Mott, An Appreciation.* Geneva, 1930.

———. *The World's Student Christian Federation.* London, 1948.

——— AND NEILL, S. C. *A History of the Ecumenical Movement.* Philadelphia, 1954.

RUSHBROOKE, J. H. *The Baptist Movement in Europe.* London, 1923.

RUSSELL, BERTRAND. *New Hopes for a Changing World.* New York, 1951.

SANFORD, ELIAS B. *Origin and History of the Federal Council of Churches.* Hartford, 1916.

SATWELL, W. *Evangelical and Catholic Unity.* London, 1682.

SCHAFF, DAVID S. *Life of Philip Schaff.* New York, 1897.

SCHAFF, PHILIP. *The Creeds of Christendom.* 3 vols. New York, 1919.

———. *History of the General Conference of the Evangelical Alliance . . .* 1873. With S. Irenaeus. New York, 1874.

———, ed. *The Schaff-Herzog Encyclopedia of Religious Knowledge.* 13 vols. New York, 1911.

SCHLEIERMACHER, F. D. E. *Kurze Darstellung des Theologischen Studiums.* Berlin, 1811.

———. *Life.* Tr. by Rowan. 2 vols. London, 1860.

SCHMUCKER, SAMUEL. *A Fraternal Appeal to the American Churches . . .* New York, 1839.

———. *The True Unity of Christ's Church . . . A Renewed Appeal.* New York, 1870.

SECKER, THOMAS. *Works.* 6 vols. London, 1811.

SENAND, AUGUSTE. *Christian Unity, a Bibliography.* Geneva, 1937.

SHAW, P. E. *American Contacts with the Eastern Churches, 1820-1870.* Hartford, 1930.

———. *Early Tractarians and the Eastern Church.* London, 1930.

SHEDD, C. P. *Two Centuries of Student Christian Movements.* New York, 1934.

———. *History of the World's Alliance of Y.M.C.A.'s.* New York, 1956.

SIEGMUND-SCHULTZE, F. *Die Weltkirchenkonferenz von Lausanne.* Berlin-Steglitz, 1927.
———, ed. *Friendly Relations Between Great Britain and Germany . . .* Berlin, 1910.
SINCLAIR, MARGARET. *William Paton.* London, 1949.
SKYDSGAARD, K. E. *The Roman Catholic Church and the Ecumenical Movement.* London, 1948.
———, ed. *The Papal Council and the Gospel.* Minneapolis, 1961.
SLACK, K. *The Ecumenical Movement.* London, 1960.
SLOSSER, GAIUS J. *Christian Unity: Its History and Challenge in All Communions.* London and New York, 1929.
SMITH, GEORGE. *The Life of Alexander Duff.* 2 vols. New York, 1879.
———. *The Life of Henry Drummond.* New York, 1898.
———. *William Carey.* London, 1884.
Society for the Propagation of the Gospel, Proceedings. London, 1908.
SÖDERBLOM, ANNA S. *Nathan Söderblom, Sommarminnen.* Stockholm, 1941.
SÖDERBLOM, NATHAN. *In Memoriam.* Stockholm, 1931.
———. *The Living God.* Introduction by Yngve Brilioth. Oxford, 1933.
SOPER, EDMUND D. *Lausanne: The Will to Understand.* Garden City, N.Y., 1928.
South India, Scheme for Church Union. Madras, 1943.
SPEER, ROBERT E. *"Re-Thinking Missions" Examined.* New York, 1933.
———, et al. *South America—Official Report of the Congress of Church Work, Montevideo, Uruguay, 1925.* New York, 1925.
SPERRY, W. L. *Religion in America.* New York, 1946.
STANLEY, A. P. *Life and Letters of Dr. Arnold.* London, 1891.
STAUFER, MILTON T., ed. *Christian Students and World Problems.* New York, 1924.
STEWART, GEORGE. *The Church.* New York, 1938.
STEWART, JAMES H. *Memoirs, 1776-1854.* By his son. London, 1857.
STOCK, EUGENE. *The History of the Church Missionary Society.* 3 vols. London, 1899——.
STONE, BARTON W. *Biography Written by Himself.* Cincinnati, 1847.
STOUGHTON, JOHN. *A History of Religion in England.* 8 vols. London, 1901.
———. *Life of John Stoughton. By his daughter.* London, 1898.
STRACHEY, JOHN. *Contemporary Capitalism.* New York, 1956.
STRATON, H. H. *Baptists: Their Message and Mission.* Philadelphia, 1941.
STRONG, ESTHER B. *The Church at the Heart of the World Christian Community.* New York, n.d.
———, WITH A. L. WARNSHUIS. *Directory of Foreign Missions.* New York, 1933.
STRONG, JOSIAH. *Our Country: Its Possible Future and Present Crisis.* New York, 1885.
SUGRUE, THOMAS. *A Catholic Speaks His Mind on America's Religious Conflict.* New York, 1952.
SWEET, W. W. *Religion on the American Frontier, 1783-1840.* Chicago, 1946.
———. *Religion in Colonial America.* New York, 1942.
———. *Religion in the Development of American Culture.* New York, 1952.
———. *Revivalism in America: Its Origin, Growth and Decline.* New York, 1945.
———. *Story of Religion in America.* New York, 1939.
SYKES, NORMAN. *Church and State in England in the Eighteenth Century.* Cambridge, 1934.

———. *The Church of England and Non-Episcopal Churches in the Sixteenth and Seventeenth Centuries . . .* London, 1948.
———. *Daniel Ernest Jablonski and the Church of England.* London, 1950.

TATLOW, TISSINGTON. *The Story of the SCM of Great Britain and Ireland.* London, 1933.
TAYLOR, JEREMY. *Works.* 10 vols. London, 1847-52.
TAYLOR, T. M. *The Scope and Initiative of the Modern State.* Study Dept. W.C.C. Geneva, 1950.
TEMPLE, WILLIAM. *Christianity and the Social Order.* London, 1942.
———. *Nature, Man and God.* London, 1953.
———. *The Preacher's Theme To-day.* London, 1936.
Ten Formative Years: The World Council of Churches, 1938-48. Geneva, 1948.
THOMAS, G. F., ed. *The Vitality of the Christian Tradition.* New York, 1944.
THOMPSON, H. P. *Into All Lands: A History of the Society for the Propagation of the Gospel, 1701-1950.* London, 1951.
THOMPSON, R. E. *A History of the Presbyterian Churches in the United States.* New York, 1895.
TIFFANY, C. C. *A History of the Protestant Episcopal Church in the United States.* New York, n.d.
TILLICH, PAUL. *Biblical Religion and the Search for Ultimate Reality.* Chicago, 1952.
TOMKINS, O. S. *The Church and the Purpose of God.* London, 1950.
———. *The Third World Conference on Faith and Order, Lund.* London, 1953.
———. *The Wholeness of the Church.* London, 1949.
TORBET, R. G. *A History of Baptists.* Philadelphia, 1950.
TOWNSEND, W. J. *The Story of Methodist Union.* London, n.d.
TOYNBEE, ARNOLD. *An Historian's Approach to Religion.* London, 1950.
———. *Christianity Among the Religions of the World.* New York, 1957.
TRACY, JOSEPH. *History of the American Board of Commissioners for Foreign Missions.* New York, 1842.
TULGA, C. E. *The Case Against Modernism in Foreign Missions.* Chicago, 1950.
TURNER, F. P. AND SANDERS, F. K., eds. *Addresses of the Washington Foreign Mission Convention, 1925.* New York, 1925.
TURRETINI, JEAN ALPHONSE. *Oratio de Componendis Protestantium Disodiio.* Geneva, 1719.

Universal Christian Council for Life and Work. Minutes of the Continuation Committee: Winchester, 1927; Chexbres, 1930; Geneva, 1932; Novi Sad, 1933; Fano, 1934; Paris, 1934.
United Church of Christ in the United States: The Basis of Union. New York, 1947.
URE, RUTH. *The Highway of Print.* World-Wide Study of the Production and Distribution of Christian Literature. New York, 1946.

VAIL, THOMAS N. *The Comprehensive Church: or Christian Unity and Ecclesiastical Union in the Protestant Episcopal Church.* Hartford, 1841.
VAN DER LINDE, H. *Rome en de Una Sancta.* Bibliography. Nijkerk, 1947.
VAN DUSEN, H. P. *For the Healing of the Nations.* New York, 1940.
VAN KIRK, W. W. *Religion Renounces War.* Chicago, 1934.
VEDDER, H. C. *A Short History of Baptist Missions.* Philadelphia, 1927.

VILLAIN, MAURICE. *The Life and Work of Abbe Paul Couturier, Apostle of Unity*. 1959.

VISCHER, LUKAS. *Survey of Church Union Negotiations, 1959-61*. New York, 1961.

VISSER 'T HOOFT, W. A. *Anglo-Catholicism and Orthodoxy: A Protestant View*. London, 1933.

———, ed. *The First Assembly of the World Council of Churches*. New York, 1949.

———, WITH J. H. OLDHAM. *The Church and Its Function in Society*. Vol. I of the Church, Community and State Series. Chicago, 1937.

WARD, HARRY F. *Our Economic Morality and the Ethic of Jesus*. New York, 1929.

———. *The Social Creed of the Churches*. New York, 1914.

WARNECK, GUSTAV. *Outline of a History of Protestant Missions*. Edinburgh, 1901.

WARNSHUIS, A. L., ed. *The Christian Message for the World Today*. New York, 1934.

———. WITH ESTHER SHING. *Partners in the Expanding Church*. New York, 1935.

WARR, CHARLES L. *The Presbyterian Tradition*. London, 1933.

WATTS, ALAN W. *This is IT and Other Essays on Zen and Spiritual Experience*. New York, 1958.

WEDEL, THEODORE O. *The Coming Great Church*. New York, 1945.

WEIGEL, GUSTAVE. *Catholic Theology in Dialogue*. New York, 1961.

WESTCOTT, ARTHUR. *Life and Letters of Brooke Foss Westcott*. 2 vols. London, 1903.

WHERRY, E. M. et al. *Islam and Missions*. New York, 1911.

———. *Papers on the Training of Missionaries for Moslems*. Madras, 1911.

WHITE, C. L. *A Century of Faith*. Philadelphia, 1932.

WHITGIFT, JOHN. *Works*. 3 vols. Cambridge, 1851.

WHITNEY, W. T. *The Doctrine of Grace*. London, 1932.

WICHERN, J. H. *Leben und Werken*. 2 vols. Hamburg, 1882.

WIEMAN, HENRY AND HORTON, W. M. *The Growth of Religion*. Chicago, 1938.

WILLIAMS, G. M. *The Church of Sweden and the Anglican Church*. Milwaukee, 1911.

WILLIAMS, G. *The Orthodox Church of the East in the Eighteenth Century*. London, 1868.

WILLIS, J. J. *The Kikuyu Conference: A Study in Christian Unity*. London, 1914.

WISEMAN, STEPHEN. *Letter on Catholic Unity*. London, 1847.

WIX, SAMUEL. *Reflections Concerning a Council of the Church of England and the Church of Rome . . .* London, 1818.

WOOD, H. G., ed. *Handbook, Conference on Christian Politics, Economics and Citizenship at Birmingham, 1924*. London, 1924.

WORDSWORTH, CHARLES. *Public Appeals on Behalf of Christian Unity*. Edinburgh, 1886.

WORDSWORTH, JOHN. *The National Church of Sweden*. London, 1911.

World Alliance for Promoting International Friendship Through the Churches: Annual Minutes and Reports. London and New York, 1914-1946.

———. *Handbooks*. London and New York, 1916-1938.

———. *Report of the Constance Conference*. London and New York, 1914.

———. *Report of the Ninth International Conference, Chamby, Switz., 1935*. London and New York, 1935.
World Council of Churches. Amsterdam, 1948—Report of the First Assembly. 5 vols. Geneva, 1948.
———. *Assembly Handbooks:* Amsterdam, 1948; Evanston, 1954; New Delhi, 1961.
———. *Central Committee, Minutes and Reports of Annual Meetings*. 14 vols. Geneva, 1949-62.
———. *Provisional Committee, Minutes of the Meetings at Geneva, 1946; Buck Hill Falls, Pa., 1947*. Geneva 1946 and 1947.
World Missionary Conference, Edinburgh, 1910: Minutes of the Preparatory Meeting. London, 1910.
———. *Conference Minutes and Reports*. 9 vols. Edinburgh, 1910.
———. *Daily Conference Paper*. Edinburgh, 1910.
———. *Findings of the Continuation Committee*. London, 1912-1913.
———. *Monthly News Letter*. Edinburgh, Oct. 1909-May, 1910.
———. *Official Handbook*. London, 1910.

ZABRISKIE, ALEXANDER C. *Bishop Brent, Crusader for Christian Unity*. Philadelphia, 1948.
ZANDER, L. A. *Vision and Action*. London, 1952.
ZERNOV, NICHOLAS. *The Church of the Eastern Christians*. London, 1942.
———. *The Ecumenical Church and Russian Orthodoxy*. London, 1952.
———. *The Reintegration of the Church*. London, 1952.
ZWEMER, S. M. et al. *The Mohammedan World of Today . . . Missionary Conference, Cairo, 1906*. New York, 1906.

PERIODICALS

American Lutheran Survey. Columbia, S.C., 1914-18.
At-one-ment. Annual for Seminarians on Christian Unity. Friars of the Atonement, Washington, D.C.
Christendom. Chicago, 1935-38; New York, 1939-48.
The Christian Advocate. Methodist. Chicago, 1826—.
The Christian Century. Chicago, 1884—.
The Christian East. Quarterly organ of the Anglican and Eastern Churches. London, 1920—.
Christianity and Crisis. New York, 1940—.
Christianity Today. Washington, D.C., 1950—.
The Christian Union Quarterly. Baltimore, 1911-34.
Le Christianisme Social. Paris, 1887—.
Christian Work. New York, 1866-1926.
The Constructive Quarterly. New York, 1913-28.
The Congregational Quarterly. London, 1923—.
Cross Currents. Nyack, N.Y., 1961-62.
The East and the West. Quarterly issued by the SPCK. London, 1903-27.
The Eastern Churches Quarterly. Roman Catholic. London, 1936—.
Ecumenical Courier. Bi-monthly issued by the W.C.C. New York, 1949—.
Ecumenical Press Service. Geneva, 1933—.
The Ecumenical Review. Quarterly issued by the W.C.C. New York and Geneva, 1948—.
The Ecumenist. Bi-monthly of the Paulist Fathers. New York.
Die Eiche. Quarterly. Gotha, Germany, 1913-34.
Eine Heilige Kirche. Munich, 1919—.

Evangelical Christendom. London, 1847—.
Evangelisches Missions. New Series. Basel, 1957—.
Faith and Order Trends. Quarterly of the National Council of Churches. New York, 1914—.
Friends of Reunion Bulletin. London, 1933—.
Frontier. Quarterly incorporating *The Christian News-Letter* and *World Dominion*. London, 1957—.
Goodwill. A Review of International Christian Friendship, succeeding *The Peacemaker*. London, 1915-38.
The Hibbert Journal. Oxford, 1902—.
Indian Journal of Theology. Quarterly. Serampore, 1951—.
Internationale Kirchliche Zeitschrift. Quarterly. Berne, 1910—.
International Review of Missions. London, 1912—.
International Quarterly Review of the Social Activities of the Churches. Trilingual. Gottingen, 1928-31.
Irenikon. Bi-monthly of the Benedictines of Amay. Chevotoque, Belgium, 1926—.
Japan Christian Quarterly. Federation of Christian Missions. Tokyo, 1926-41.
The Living Church. Weekly. Episcopal. Milwaukee, 1878—.
Lunds Missions-Tiding. Lund, 1844-1919.
National Christian Council Review. Mysore, 1924—.
Oekumenische Einheit. Munich and Basel, 1948—.
Oekumenisches Jahrbuch. Zurich, 1934-35; Leipzig, 1936—.
1936—.
Religion in Life. Methodist. Nashville, 1932—.
La Revue Anglo-Romaine. Paris, 1895-96.
The Review of the Churches. Monthly. London, 1891-95; 1924-30.
Unitas. Bimonthly. Garrison, New York, 1946.
The Watchman-Examiner. Baptist. New York, 1819—.

INDEX

NOTE: Certain church and ecumenical organizations have been abbreviated herein, as follows: C.C.C.S—Conference on Church, Community and State; C.C.I.A.—Commission of the Churches on International Affairs; C.O.P.E.C. —Conference on Christian Politics, Economics and Citizenship; F. and O.—Faith and Order Movement; L. and W.—Life and Work Movement; W.C.C.—World Council of Churches; Y.M.C.A. —Young Men's Christian Association; Y.W.C.A.—Young Women's Christian Association.